RESEARCH HANDBOOK ON HUMAN RIGHTS AND POVERTY

RESEARCH HANDBOOKS IN HUMAN RIGHTS

Elgar Research Handbooks are original reference works designed to provide a broad overview of research in a given field whilst at the same time creating a forum for more challenging, critical examination of complex and often under-explored issues within that field.

Chapters by international teams of contributors are specially commissioned by editors who carefully balance breadth and depth. Often widely cited, individual chapters present expert scholarly analysis and offer a vital reference point for advanced research. Taken as a whole they achieve a wide-ranging picture of the state-of-the-art.

This highly original series offers a unique appraisal of the state-of-the-art of research and thinking in human rights law. Each volume, edited by a prominent expert, either covers a specific aspect of human rights law or looks at how human rights impacts upon, or intersects with, other areas of law. Combining positivist approaches to international and human rights law, with more critical approaches, the volumes also draw, where appropriate, on research from adjacent disciplines. Addressing current and sometimes controversial legal issues, as well as affording a clear substantive analysis of the law, these *Research Handbooks* are designed to inform as well as to contribute to current debates.

Equally useful as reference tools or introductions to specific topics or issues, the *Research Handbooks* will be used by academic researchers, post-graduate students, practicing lawyers and lawyers in policy circles.

Titles in the series include:

Research Handbook on Human Rights and Humanitarian Law
Edited by Robert Kolb and Gloria Gaggioli

Research Handbook on Human Rights and the Environment
Edited by Anna Grear and Louis J. Kotzé

Research Handbook on Human Rights and Digital Technology
Global Politics, Law and International Relations
Edited by Ben Wagner, Matthias C. Kettemann and Kilian Vieth

Research Handbook on Labour, Business and Human Rights Law
Edited by Janice R. Bellace and Beryl ter Haar

Research Handbook on Human Rights and Business
Edited by Surya Deva and David Birchall

Research Handbook on Economic, Social and Cultural Rights as Human Rights
Edited by Jackie Dugard, Bruce Porter, Daniela Ikawa and Lilian Chenwi

Research Handbook on Torture
Legal and Medical Perspectives on Prohibition and Prevention
Edited by Sir Malcolm D. Evans and Jens Modvig

Research Handbook on Human Rights and Poverty
Edited by Martha F. Davis, Morten Kjaerum and Amanda Lyons

Research Handbook on Human Rights and Poverty

Edited by

Martha F. Davis

University Distinguished Professor, Northeastern University School of Law, USA

Morten Kjaerum

Adjunct Professor, University of Aalborg, Denmark and Director of the Raoul Wallenberg Institute of Human Rights and Humanitarian Law, Lund, Sweden

Amanda Lyons

Executive Director and Lecturer in Law, Human Rights Center, University of Minnesota Law School, USA

RESEARCH HANDBOOKS IN HUMAN RIGHTS

EE Edward **Elgar**
PUBLISHING

Cheltenham, UK • Northampton, MA, USA

Cover image: LSE Library on Unsplash

Published by
Edward Elgar Publishing Limited
The Lypiatts
15 Lansdown Road
Cheltenham
Glos GL50 2JA
UK

Edward Elgar Publishing, Inc.
William Pratt House
9 Dewey Court
Northampton
Massachusetts 01060
USA

Paperback edition 2023

A catalogue record for this book
is available from the British Library

Library of Congress Control Number: 2020952358

This book is available electronically in the **Elgar**online
Law subject collection
http://dx.doi.org/10.4337/9781788977517

MIX
Paper | Supporting
responsible forestry
FSC
www.fsc.org   FSC® C013604

ISBN 978 1 78897 750 0 (cased)
ISBN 978 1 78897 751 7 (eBook)
ISBN 978 1 0353 1211 5 (paperback)

Printed and bound by CPI Group (UK) Ltd, Croydon, CR0 4YY

To Alison, Carl and Janet, with love and gratitude (MFD)
To Ernesto, Karlo and Hektor with the hope that you will experience a world
with much less inequality and poverty (MK)
To Áine, a relentless champion for justice, a generous mentor, a dear friend
(AL)

Contents

List of contributors x
Opening note xviii
Foreword xix
Acknowledgements xxiv
Introduction to the Research Handbook on Human Rights and Poverty xxv

PART I DEFINITIONS, MEASUREMENTS AND STANDARDS

1 A human rights-based approach to measuring poverty 2
Olivier De Schutter

2 From stigma to rights: uncovering the hidden dimension of poverty 21
Magdalena Sepúlveda Carmona

3 Current perspectives on global poverty: rights, capabilities and social exclusion 37
Ayşe Buğra

4 Is economic inequality a violation of human rights? 53
Gillian MacNaughton

5 Poverty and political rights: an exercise of recovery from oblivion 69
Karolina Miriam Januszewski and Manfred Nowak

6 Human rights and poverty reduction: what are the linkages? 88
Hans-Otto Sano

PART II CROSS-CURRENTS

A. POVERTY, HUMAN RIGHTS AND IDENTITY

7 Breaking the link between poverty and disability: re-purposing human
rights in the 21st century 106
Gerard Quinn

8 Poverty, older persons and human rights 125
Andrew Byrnes

9 Child impoverishment and the human rights of children 141
Wouter Vandenhole

10 Capping motherhood 156
Meghan Campbell

11   The price that is paid: violence and discrimination based on sexual
      orientation and gender identity and poverty   171
      Victor Madrigal-Borloz

12   Assessing racialized poverty: the case of Romani people in the European Union 192
      Margareta Matache and Simona Barbu

13   Rights, racism and poverty: failures of the global commitment to leave
      no one behind   211
      Gay McDougall

B.   POVERTY AND HUMAN RIGHTS, INTERSECTING
            WITH GEOGRAPHY AND PLACE

14   Immigration, poverty and human rights   230
      Tally Kritzman-Amir

15   Human rights and a-legality: destitution of persons seeking asylum in the EU   247
      Eleni Karageorgiou

16   Seeing human rights *like* a city: the prospects and perils of the 'urban turn'   264
      Natalia Ángel-Cabo and Luisa Sotomayor

17   Local authorities, poverty and the implementation of human rights norms   279
      Moritz Baumgärtel

18   Addressing poverty at its base: the housing and land rights approach   295
      Miloon Kothari

19   The land rights-poverty nexus   309
      Alfred Lahai Gbabai Brownell Sr.

20   Indigenous Peoples' land rights: a culturally sensitive strategy for
      poverty eradication and sustainable development   323
      Alejandro Fuentes

C.   POVERTY, HUMAN RIGHTS AND PARTICIPATION

21   Human rights, poverty and mobilizations   338
      Domingo A. Lovera-Parmo

22   Advancing human rights through legal empowerment of the disadvantaged   354
      Lisa Hilbink and Valentina Salas

PART III   MECHANISMS AND POLICIES

23   A human rights critique of contemporary social policy paradigms: new
      behaviourism, social investment and new universalism   370
      Volkan Yilmaz

24 The human right to housing in the age of financialization   385
    Leilani Farha and Kaitlin Schwan

25 The right to health for people living in poverty: a human rights perspective 401
    Mette Hartlev

26 Human rights and abortion access for people living in poverty:
    implications for the United States and globally   416
    Risa E. Kaufman and Diana Kasdan

27 What is wrong with the privatization of education as anti-poverty policy
    from a human rights perspective?   432
    Antonio Barboza-Vergara and Esteban Hoyos-Ceballos

28 Poverty, labour law and human rights: a necessary connection   446
    Lee Swepston and Constance Thomas

29 Minimum wage, poverty reduction and human rights in Cambodia: a case study 462
    Sophal Chea

30 Fair taxes to end poverty   474
    Åsa Gunnarsson

PART IV   STRUCTURAL BARRIERS

31 Climate change, human rights and poverty: intersections and challenges   489
    Sumudu Atapattu

32 Corruption as a human rights violation   506
    Khulekani Moyo

33 Conflict, poverty and human rights violations   521
    Zafer Kizilkaya

34 Human rights, technology and poverty   535
    Linnet Taylor and Hellen Mukiri-Smith

35 Beyond the state: holding international institutions and private entities
    accountable for poverty alleviation   550
    Lucy Williams

Index   566

Contributors

Philip Alston is the John Norton Pomeroy Professor at New York University School of Law. From 2014 to 2020 he was United Nations Special Rapporteur on extreme poverty and human rights. Prior to that he was Special Rapporteur on extrajudicial executions (2004–10) and Chairperson of the UN Committee on Economic, Social and Cultural Rights (1991–98).

Natalia Ángel-Cabo is a Professor of Law at Universidad de los Andes (Bogotá, Colombia) and Chief editor of Latin American Law Review. Professor Ángel-Cabo has been Deputy Justice of the Colombian Constitutional Court, founder and former director of the Action Program for Equality and Social Inclusion – PAIIS, and consultant in various human rights projects. In 2017 she was nominated as a candidate for Magistrate of the Colombian Constitutional Court and currently serves the Court as Associate Justice.

Sumudu Atapattu, LLM, PhD (Cambridge), Attorney-at-Law (Sri Lanka) is the Director of Research Centers and International Programs at the University of Wisconsin Law School and the Executive Director of the Human Rights Program. She serves as the Lead Counsel for Human Rights at the Centre for International Sustainable Development Law and is affiliated faculty at the Raoul Wallenberg Institute of Human Rights and Humanitarian Law, Sweden. She has published extensively on environmental rights, climate change and human rights, and sustainable development.

Antonio Barboza-Vergara holds a Masters in Political Science from Universidad de Antioquia, a Masters and a PhD in Law from Universidad Pompeu Fabra (Barcelona, Spain). He is an Assistant Professor of Constitutional Law at Universidad EAFIT School of Law in Medellin, Colombia. His areas of research include judicial review and social and economic rights, theories of justice and public health.

Simona Barbu is a human rights activist and researcher who has specialized in working with Roma communities in Romania, as well as across Europe. She has experience with academic ethnographic research, holding an MA in Anthropology of Education and Globalization (Aarhus University, Denmark) and from working as a research assistant at the University of Copenhagen. She works to defend and realize Roma rights, by contributing to reports and articles for organizations such as the RomArchive or Central European University (the Roma Civil Monitor project).

Moritz Baumgärtel is an assistant professor at the School of Law of Utrecht University and University College Roosevelt. He is also the senior researcher at the NWO research project 'Cities of Refuge' and a fellow of the Netherlands Institute of Human Rights. Baumgärtel's research concerns the human rights of vulnerable migrants such as refugees, asylum seekers and undocumented migrants. He is the author of *Demanding Rights: Europe's Supranational Courts and the Dilemma of Migrant Vulnerability* (Cambridge University Press, 2019).

Alfred Lahai Gbabai Brownell Sr. is Associate Research Professor and Distinguished Scholar in Residence at the Program on Human Rights and the Global Economy, Northeastern University School of Law, the Inaugural IIE-SRF Beau Biden Scholar, Tom and Andi Bernstein Human Rights Fellow and a Visiting Research Scholar at the Yale University Law School and the 2019 Goldman Environmental Prize Winner for Africa.

Ayşe Buğra received her PhD in Economics from McGill University. She is currently an Emeritus Professor at Bogazici University and an affiliate of the Bogazici University Research Center Social Policy Forum, which she co-founded in 2004. She has taught and published in the areas of development studies, social policy, state-business relations and the socio-economic history of modern Turkey. She is currently working on the political context of economic and social policy and different dimensions of inequality.

Andrew Byrnes is Professor of International Law and Human Rights, Faculty of Law, University of New South Wales, Sydney, Australia, a research associate of the Australian Human Rights Institute and the UNSW Ageing Futures Institute. He was inaugural legal adviser to the Australian Parliamentary Joint Committee on Human Rights, has acted as adviser to the Asia Pacific Forum of National Human Rights Institutions and GANHRI and as a consultant to the UN OIHCHR and the UN Department of Economic and Social Affairs on the human rights of older persons.

Meghan Campbell is an Associate Professor at the University of Birmingham and Deputy Director of the Oxford Human Rights Hub. Her monograph, *Women, Poverty, Equality: The Role of CEDAW* (Hart 2018) was shortlisted for the Socio-Legal Scholars Association-Early Career Research Prize. She is the executive producer of the OxHRH documentary series *Shaping the Future* which explores the role of human rights and the Sustainable Development Goals in achieving women and girls' sexual and reproductive health rights.

Esteban Hoyos-Ceballos holds an LLM and a JSD from Cornell Law School. He is an Associate Professor of Constitutional Law at Universidad EAFIT School of Law in Medellin, Colombia. His areas of research include judicial review and social and economic rights, clinical legal education and public interest law.

Sophal Chea currently serves as a Team Leader – Assessment and Stakeholders Engagement for ILO/BFC. He is an LLD student for the Doctor of Law Programme at Pannasastra University of Cambodia. He has contributed to a number of articles including Labour Rights and Trade Union, Labour Rights in Cambodia, and Practical Challenges for Maternity Protection in the Cambodian Garment Industry. The viewpoints expressed in this chapter are of the author, which are not necessarily those of the ILO/BFC.

Martha F. Davis is University Distinguished Professor of Law at Northeastern University in Boston, Massachusetts, where she is a faculty co-director of the Program on Human Rights and the Global Economy. Davis's publications include *Human Rights Advocacy in the United States* (co-author) and *Global Urban Justice: The Rise of Human Rights Cities* (co-editor). She is co-editor of the Human Rights at Home Law Profs Blog and an affiliated scholar of the Raoul Wallenberg Institute of Human Rights and Humanitarian Law.

Olivier De Schutter is professor at UCLouvain and SciencesPo and the United Nations Special Rapporteur on extreme poverty and human rights. He was formerly the UN Special Rapporteur on the right to food (2008–14) and a member of the Committee on Economic, Social and Cultural Rights (2015–20).

Leilani Farha is the former United Nations Special Rapporteur on the right to housing and Global Director of The Shift, an international movement to secure the right to housing. She has helped develop global human rights standards on the right to housing, including through her reports on homelessness, the financialization of housing, and informal settlements. She has worked to advance the right to housing around the world, including in Egypt, India, Indonesia, Nigeria, Philippines, Portugal, South Korea, Spain, and Sweden.

Alejandro Fuentes is a Senior Researcher at the Raoul Wallenberg Institute of Human Rights and Humanitarian Law (Sweden). He received his PhD (in International Law) and LLM (in Comparative and European Legal Studies) from Trento University (Italy), and Law degree from the University of Córdoba (Argentina). He is a regular lecturer at the Master's Programme in International Human Rights Law at the Faculty of Law, Lund University (Sweden), where he directs a course on human rights and cultural diversity.

Åsa Gunnarsson serves as professor of tax law and jurisprudence at Umeå University. She has coordinated the Horizon2020 project *Revisioning the 'Fiscal EU': Fair, Sustainable, and Coordinated Tax and Social Policies* (FairTax). She has written extensively on tax policy and the law, tax fairness, the tax/benefit interface, gender equality and taxation, social citizenship and gender equality law. Her approach to legal scholarship is cross-disciplinary, comparative and socio-legal.

Mette Hartlev is Professor of Health Law, PhD, LLD at the Faculty of Law, University of Copenhagen, Denmark. Her research is focused on patients' rights, health and human rights, health disparities, public health law and regulatory and ethical strategies to ensure a non-discriminatory implementation and application of new technologies (such as PM and big data) in the health care services. She has extensive experience in interdisciplinary and international research and is a co-editor of the European Journal of Health Law.

Lisa Hilbink (PhD, UC-San Diego) is Associate Professor of Political Science and a member of the Human Rights Faculty at the University of Minnesota, Twin Cities. Her research addresses a wide range of issues related to the changing role of law and courts in polities around the world, with a particular focus on Latin America and Iberia. Her ongoing work focuses on the origins of public perceptions of judicial institutions and their consequences for access to justice in the Americas.

Karolina Miriam Januszewski is currently working as political advisor on foreign affairs, human rights and migration for The Greens at the Austrian Parliament. She is a Lecturer in general international, humanitarian and human rights law at the Vienna Master of Arts in Human Rights. Her research focus and publications address political theory and human rights, questions of governance, state agency and the role of non-state actors in international human rights law.

Eleni Karageorgiou is the Ragnar Söderberg Postdoctoral Fellow at Lund University, Faculty of Law and a research affiliate at the Raoul Wallenberg Institute of Human Rights and Humanitarian Law. Previously visiting at the Danish Institute for Human Rights and the Refugee Studies Centre at University of Oxford, Karageorgiou's work on international refugee law and European migration law and policy has been published in the Oxford Handbook of International Refugee Law and the Nordic Journal of International Law.

Diana Kasdan is the director of US Judicial Strategy at the Center for Reproductive Rights, where she leads the Center's work with scholars, advocates and the broader legal community to articulate and advance the constitutional doctrines, principles, and values that protect reproductive rights as human rights in the United States. Previously she was Senior Counsel and Director of Foundation Relations at the Brennan Center for Justice and Senior Attorney with the American Civil Liberties Union, Reproductive Freedom Project.

Risa E. Kaufman is the director of US Human Rights at the Center for Reproductive Rights, where she leads the Center's efforts to integrate international human rights norms and strategies to advance reproductive rights as human rights in the United States. Previously, she was Executive Director of the Columbia Law School Human Rights Institute. She is a lecturer-in-law at Columbia Law School, where she teaches US human rights advocacy, and a co-founding board member of A Better Balance.

Zafer Kizilkaya holds a PhD in Political Science at Free University of Brussels (VUB). His research interests are in the field of Ethics in International Relations, Non-state armed groups and Middle Eastern studies. He is currently teaching Conflict Resolution at Vesalius College. He also has previous professional experience at NATO, covering the conflicts in Iraq and Syria and preparing regular reports on the political, economic and security developments in the Middle East.

Morten Kjærum is Director of the Raoul Wallenberg Institute of Human Rights and Humanitarian Law, Lund, Sweden and Adjunct Professor at Aalborg University, Aalborg, Denmark. He was the first director of the European Union Agency for Fundamental Rights, and Executive Director at the Danish Institute for Human Rights. He was member of the UN Committee on Elimination of Racial Discrimination from 2002–08. He is Chair of The Board of the European Council on Refugees and Exiles (ECRE) and Chairs the Board of Trustees for the UN Voluntary Fund for Technical Cooperation in the field of Human Rights appointed by the UN Secretary General. He is a frequent author on human rights issues.

Miloon Kothari is an independent expert on human rights and social policy based in New Delhi, India. He is President of UPR Info. He was the first Special Rapporteur on adequate housing with the UN Human Rights Council (2000–08). As Special Rapporteur he led the creation of the UN Basic Principles and Guidelines on Development-based Evictions and Displacement. From 2013–14 he was appointed Dr. Martin Luther King Visiting Scholar at MIT. In 2017 he received an honorary Doctor of Laws from Simon Fraser University.

Tally Kritzman-Amir is a Visiting Assistant Professor of Law in Boston University School of Law, a Visiting Associate Professor at Harvard University Department of Sociology, an Honorary Research Associate at the Hadassah Brandeis Institute and a Senior Lecturer at the College of Law and Business, Israel. She holds an LL.B and a PhD from Tel Aviv University School of Law.

Domingo A. Lovera-Parmo is the Associate Professor of Law at Universidad Diego Portales (Chile). He holds a PhD from Osgoode Hall Law School (2016) and LLM from Columbia University (2007, Human Rights Fellow – Harlan Fiske Stone Scholar). His research focuses on the right to protest and constitutional law, social rights and constitutional rights of children and adolescents. He teaches constitutional law at Universidad Diego Portales, where he is also a researcher for the Public Law Program.

Amanda Lyons, JD, is the Executive Director at the Human Rights Center at the University of Minnesota Law School, where she teaches on Poverty and Human Rights. Her research and advocacy work has focused on human rights and development, the human right to water and gender justice. Prior to joining the University she worked with human rights organizations in Brazil, Colombia, and the United States.

Gillian MacNaughton, JD, MPA, DPhil, is Associate Professor of Human Rights in the School for Global Inclusion and Social Development at the University of Massachusetts Boston. She works on economic and social rights and their relationship to equality rights, as well as human rights-based approaches to social justice. Her research has been funded by the World Health Organization and the Law and Society Association, and she has consulted for WHO, UNDP, UNICEF and the UN Special Rapporteur on the Right to Health.

Víctor Madrigal-Borloz (Costa Rica) is the UN Independent Expert on protection against violence and discrimination based on sexual orientation and gender identity and a senior visiting researcher at Harvard Law School's Human Rights Program. He is the former Rapporteur on Reprisals for the UN Subcommittee on the Prevention of Torture. He previously led human rights work at the International Rehabilitation Council for Torture Victims, the Inter-American Commission and Court of Human Rights, and the Danish Institute for Human Rights.

Margareta (Magda) Matache is a justice activist and scholar, director of the FXB Center for Health and Human Rights' Roma Program, and a Harvard instructor. In 2017, with Jacqueline Bhabha and Andrzej Mirga, she co-edited *Realizing Roma Rights*, a volume investigating anti-Roma racism in Europe. With Jacqueline Bhabha and Caroline Elkins, Matache co-edited *Time for Reparations*, a volume exploring the issue of reparations across a broad range of historical and geographic contexts.

Gay McDougall is Adjunct Professor at Fordham School of Law. She served for eight years on the UN Committee on the Elimination of Racial Discrimination and six years as UN Special Rapporteur on minorities. She received a JD from Yale Law School and an LLM from the London School of Economics and Political Science and has Honorary Degrees from nine universities. She has taught at Georgetown University School of Law and Oxford University's Masters of International Human Rights Law Program.

Khulekani Moyo is a Lecturer at the School of Law, University of the Witwatersrand. Khulekani received his doctoral degree in Public Law from Stellenbosch University, his LLM in Public International Law from the University of Oslo, and his LLB (Hons) from the University of Zimbabwe. Khulekani's research interests include general international law, human rights law, business and human rights, constitutional law and regional integration law.

Hellen Mukiri-Smith is a barrister, and development and human rights specialist. She is currently a PhD Researcher on an ERC funded Global Data Justice project at Tilburg Law School, Tilburg University. She is researching governance, regulation and the impact of financial services technologies and biometric technologies in Kenya. She has an LLB from the University of Northampton, an LLM in Commercial and Corporate Law from King's College London and an MSc in Development Studies from the London School of Economics.

Manfred Nowak is Professor of Human Rights at Vienna University, Secretary General of the Global Campus of Human Rights (a network of 100 universities, based in Venice) and Independent UN Expert leading the Global Study on Children Deprived of Liberty. His past UN expert functions related to enforced disappearances, torture (Special Rapporteur on torture) and a human rights-based approach to poverty reduction strategies. He held professorships at various universities and is author of more than 600 academic articles and books.

Gerard Quinn is the UN Special Rapporteur on the rights of persons with disabilities. He was the founding director of the Centre for Disability Law & Policy at the National University of Ireland and now holds the Wallenberg Chair at the Raoul Wallenberg Institute and a research chair at the University of Leeds. He has authored studies for the UN OHCHR and the European Commission on disability and was a drafter of the UN disability convention. A graduate of Harvard Law School, he holds three lifetime awards for his international disability law work.

Valentina Salas is a PhD Candidate in Political Science at the University of Minnesota, Twin Cities. She holds a Master of Arts degree in Political Science from the Universidad Católica in Chile. Her research interests are access to justice, legal mobilization and rights consciousness in Latin America. She has previously worked as a researcher for the United Nations Development Programme in Chile, where she conducted policy research on the quality of democracy in Chile.

Hans-Otto Sano is Research Director at the Danish Institute for Human Rights. He has worked at the Institute for more than 20 years. He joined the World Bank for 2010–13. Earlier, Dr. Sano worked in Denmark and Sweden and conducted research in several African countries. His expertise is in human rights and development; he has written extensively on human rights indicators, human rights-based approaches, research methodology, social accountability and poverty.

Kaitlin Schwan is Director of Research at The Shift, an international movement to secure the right to housing. She is a Senior Researcher at the Canadian Observatory on Homelessness. She teaches social policy at the University of Toronto's Faculty of Social Work, where she is appointed Assistant Professor, Status Only. Her research focuses on homelessness prevention, particularly for women and youth. She uses research to build bridges between evidence, advocacy, policy and lived expertise in order to advance housing justice.

Magdalena Sepúlveda Carmona is the Executive Director of the Global Initiative for Economic, Social and Cultural Rights. She is a member of the Independent Commission for the Reform of International Corporate Taxation (ICRICT) and the High-Level Panel on International Financial Accountability, Transparency and Integrity for Achieving the 2030 Agenda. From 2008–14 she was the United Nations Special Rapporteur on Extreme Poverty and Human Rights. From 2013–17 she was a member of the High-Level Panel of Experts on Food Security and Nutrition.

Luisa Sotomayor is an Assistant Professor and the Coordinator of the Graduate Programs in Planning in the Faculty of Environmental and Urban Change at York University in Toronto, Canada. Her research and teaching interests are focused on the various dimensions of urban inequality and their connections to urban and regional planning practice, particularly in the Latin American context.

Lee Swepston is a Visiting Professor at the Raoul Wallenberg Institute and School of Law of the University of Lund (Sweden). He teaches a course in the Lund Masters Programme on international human rights and labour. He was an official of the International Labour Organisation (ILO) for 34 years and was Senior Advisor on Human Rights. He has written extensively on human rights and international labour law, child labour, forced labour, freedom of association, discrimination and Indigenous and Tribal Peoples.

Linnet Taylor is an Associate Professor at the Tilburg Institute for Law, Technology, and Society (TILT). Her research focuses on digital data, representation and democracy, with particular attention to transnational governance issues. She leads the ERC Global Data Justice project, which aims to develop a conceptual framework for the ethical and beneficial governance of data technologies on the global level. The research is based on insights from technology users, providers and activists around the world.

Constance Thomas, JD, is a Visiting Professor at the Lund University School of Law and Raoul Wallenberg Institute Human Rights Masters Programme in Sweden. She previously worked at the International Labour Office (ILO) as the Director of the Fundamental Principles and Rights at Work Department and the Director of the International Programme to Eliminate Child Labour (IPEC), among other roles. Her research and writing focus has been on international labour standards, non-discrimination and equality, and child labour.

Wouter Vandenhole is a human rights and law-and-development scholar. He holds the human rights chair at the Law Faculty of the University of Antwerp and is a member of the Law and Development Research Group. Between 2007 and 2018 he also held the UNICEF Chair in Children's Rights. His research interests include children's rights, economic, social and cultural rights, and the relationship between human rights law and development.

Lucy Williams is a law professor at Northeastern University, faculty director of its Center for Public Interest Advocacy and Collaboration and co-director of its Program on Human Rights and the Global Economy. Her activism and scholarship have focused on domestic and global inequality. She founded and has coordinated for 15 years the International Social and Economic Rights Project, a group of academics, judges and activists primarily from the Global South working to encourage transformative thinking about social and economic rights.

Volkan Yilmaz is an Associate Professor of Social Policy and the Director of the Social Policy Forum Research Centre at Bogazici University. Yilmaz completed his PhD in Politics at the University of Leeds after receiving his bachelor degrees in Political Science and Sociology from Bogazici University. Yilmaz's research has been published in the Journal of Social Policy, Disasters, and Gender Work & Organization. Yilmaz's expertise lies in social policy, healthcare policy, humanitarian assistance, welfare politics, human rights and discrimination.

Opening note

Most of my public life has been committed to confronting poverty and inequalities, the discriminations from which they arise and the deprivations they bring about.

Inequalities undermine universal rights, social progress and economic and political stability. For those living in poverty, basic rights are often out of reach.

It is clear to me that reducing inequalities and ending poverty is the path to achieving universal human rights for all.

The COVID-19 pandemic has exposed systemic failures to uphold human rights. Its uneven incidence and impact unmasked deep, diverse and pervasive inequalities in every society in every corner of the globe. Sadly, but not surprisingly, the most vulnerable to the pandemic have been those already at risk, including people living in poverty.

Now we are assessing not whether, but how much, the pandemic will set back our efforts to achieve the Sustainable Development Goals by 2030. We are faced with the prospect that the pandemic will drive tens of millions of people into extreme poverty, undoing a decade or more of development gains. It's a stark and striking example of how depriving people of their social and economic rights kills and of the real need to prioritize economic, social and cultural rights of all those in a precarious state.

The safety and prosperity of all is dependent on how we address the needs of everyone, including the less fortunate. Leaving no one behind is not only a moral imperative, it is a practical one. We cannot afford to leave millions without access to water, without adequate housing or in poverty. It is simply not acceptable to move back to the way things were. It is our duty to build back better.

That means adopting strong, transformative measures to heighten the powerful protections that human rights-based policies can provide – by promoting public health, trust and greater social and economic resilience.

It means forging a new economy that is environmentally sustainable and equitable, fair and inclusive.

It means leadership grounded in clarity, evidence and principle to protect the most vulnerable members of society. And it means the full respect of all rights, political, economic, civil, social and cultural.

In sum, building back better requires the unequivocal recognition that poverty is a violation of human dignity and an assault of fundamental human rights.

This is an issue of urgent concern to my Office and myself. By providing a human rights perspective to diverse and intersecting challenges related to poverty, this book and its authors bring an inestimable contribution to the discussion.

Michelle Bachelet, United Nations High Commissioner for Human Rights

Foreword

This volume brings together many of the leading thinkers and advocates who are exploring what international human rights law has to offer to efforts to eradicate extreme poverty and to ensure that the least well-off in society are not deprived of many of their human rights, solely or largely because they lack resources. Despite how insightful and encouraging these analyses are, the exceptionally uncertain times in which we live make it difficult to predict where the debate over poverty and human rights is really heading. There are strong reasons for pessimism. The COVID-19 pandemic has not just set back pre-existing efforts to tackle poverty but is likely to push hundreds of millions of additional people into poverty over the years ahead. Dramatic protests worldwide focused on police brutality have helped to demonstrate the depth of racial and ethnic inequality in many, if not most, societies, as well as expose the far higher rates of poverty among such groups. And the inexorable march of global warming threatens to be especially devastating for people living in poverty, thereby generating a 'climate apartheid' scenario in which the well-off will be shielded and the poor devastated.

But there are also grounds for optimism, including the fact that a time of crisis is also a time of opportunity. The dire threats posed by COVID-19, entrenched racism and global warming might all be seen to revolve in one way or another around the world's continuing failure to adequately tackle poverty and rapidly growing inequality. That realization might in turn actually provoke the sort of reflection and action needed to bring about the adoption of truly transformative changes in economic and social policy. In a major study of historical efforts to tackle extreme inequality in centuries past, Walter Scheidel observed that concerted and effective efforts to do so have only ever occurred subsequent to one or other of four violent ruptures.[1] The 'Four Horsemen of Leveling' that he identified are mass mobilization warfare, transformative revolution, state failure and lethal pandemics.[2] The last of these – a lethal pandemic – is clearly upon us, and the penultimate horseman – state failure – will loom increasingly large as the existential threat represented by global warming becomes ever more unavoidable.

While there has been increasing recognition of the need for a dramatic response to these cumulative challenges within the United Nations context, the organization's basic strategy is, in my view, flawed in some crucial respects. Before looking at those flaws, however, it is appropriate to note some of the principal recent policy statements. The Secretary-General, António Guterres, in delivering the Nelson Mandela Annual Lecture in July 2020, decried the terrible rise in inequality, the dramatic increase in poverty and the continuing challenges resulting from colonialism and patriarchy.[3] He rolled out the rhetorical big guns by calling not just for a 'New Social Contract', as so many international organizations have done in recent

---

[1]   Walter Scheidel, *The Great Leveler: Violence and the History of Inequality from the Stone Age to the Twenty-First Century* (Princeton University Press 2017).

[2]   ibid 6.

[3]   United Nations Secretary General, 'Secretary-General's Nelson Mandela Lecture: "Tackling the Inequality Pandemic: A New Social Contract for a New Era"' (18 July 2020) <www.un.org/sg/en/content/sg/statement/2020-07-18/secretary-generals-nelson-mandela-lecture-%E2%80%9Ctackling-the-inequality-pandemic-new-social-contract-for-new-era%E2%80%9D-delivered> accessed 28 July 2020.

years, but also for a 'New Global Deal'.[4] For the time being at least, he does not seem to have formally endorsed the detailed program put forward by the UN Conference on Trade and Development for a 'Global Green New Deal'.[5]

UN Member States have collectively followed the Secretary-General's lead in recognizing the scale of the current crisis. A prominent example is the Declaration on the Commemoration of the Seventy-Fifth Anniversary of the United Nations adopted by the Heads of State and Government in September 2020. Like most such statements, it was the product of lengthy negotiations designed to ensure that every symbolically important box was ticked, even if little was added in terms of meaningful commitments. It mentions the word 'poverty' three times, but on each occasion it does so as part of a laundry list of woes. Thus, for example, the governments proclaimed that '[w]e will address the root causes of inequalities, including violence, human rights abuses, corruption, marginalization, discrimination in all its forms, poverty and exclusion, as well as lack of education and employment. It is our responsibility'.[6]

But when it comes to the means by which these goals will be achieved, the default setting returns to the solutions locked-in in 2015. In his Mandela Lecture, the Secretary-General declares that the 2030 Agenda for Sustainable Development (laying out the Sustainable Development Goals (SDGs)), the Addis Ababa Action Agenda on financing for development and the Paris Agreement on climate change together show the way forward. In his view, these policies 'address precisely the failures that are being exposed and exploited by the pandemic'.[7] The Secretary-General consistently asserts that the Paris Agreement and the SDGs 'provide the blueprint and the tools for a better recovery'.[8]

In the Seventy-Fifth Anniversary Declaration, governments also take refuge in the SDGs:

> We will leave no one behind. … We are determined to implement the 2030 Agenda in full and on time. There is no alternative. The peoples have to be at the center of all our efforts. Particular attention must be given to people in vulnerable situations.[9]

Yet the available evidence clearly indicates that the SDG targets will not be met in many key areas, including poverty elimination, the reduction of inequality, the meeting of climate change targets and the elimination of gender inequality.[10] To take the latter by way of example, at pre-COVID-19 economic growth rates, closing the gender gap in economic opportunity was

---

[4]   In 2019 the World Bank called for a global New Deal at the international level, supplemented by a 'new social contract' at the national level. World Bank Group, 'World Development Report 2019: The Changing Nature of Work' (2019) 125–27.

[5]   United Nations Conference on Trade and Development (UNCTAD), 'Trade and Development Report 2019: Financing A Global Green New Deal' UN Doc UNCTAD/TDR/2019.

[6]   United Nations, 'Declaration on the Commemoration of the Seventy-Fifth Anniversary of the United Nations' (21 September 2020) <www.un.org/pga/74/wp-content/uploads/sites/99/2020/06/200625-UN75-highlight.pdf> accessed 28 July 2020.

[7]   Mandela Lecture (n 3).

[8]   António Guterres, 'A Time to Save the Sick and Rescue the Planet' *The New York Times* (28 April 2020) <www.nytimes.com/2020/04/28/opinion/coronavirus-climate-antonio-guterres.html> accessed 28 July 2020.

[9]   Declaration (n 6).

[10]   Philip Alston, 'The Parlous State of Poverty Eradication, Report of the Special Rapporteur on Extreme Poverty and Human Rights' (2 July 2020) UN Doc A/HRC/44/40.

projected to take another 257 years.[11] It is not clear why it should be assumed that the constant reaffirmation of a failing Agenda will miraculously turn existing trends around.

But the biggest flaw in UN anti-poverty efforts is the organization's insistent reliance on the World Bank's international poverty line as its basic benchmark. Utilizing this minimalist indicator enables the UN and others to put an unwarranted triumphalist spin on poverty eradication achievements in recent decades. Thus, in his Mandela Lecture, Guterres celebrated the fact that '[m]ore than a billion people have moved out of extreme poverty' in recent years.[12]

But such a claim raises many questions, including where the figure comes from, what it tells us about real progress achieved and the conclusions that it suggests about the effectiveness of poverty eradication efforts to date. These questions are of vital importance for the analyses contained in this volume because the starting point for any endeavor to eradicate poverty must be a realistic assessment of how bad or how good the current situation is. There is no doubt that huge progress has been made in improving the quality of life for billions of people, especially over the past two centuries. Few would disagree with Angus Deaton that '[l]ife is better now than at almost any time in history. More people are richer and fewer people live in dire poverty'.[13] But it is a large step from this well-grounded observation to the conclusion that 'extreme poverty is being eradicated'.[14] Yet all too often in recent years the balanced picture provided by Deaton and others has been translated into a deeply problematic triumphalism that plays down the significance of various factors including the miserable conditions in which billions of people continue to live, the extent to which governments at all levels have so consistently failed to take eminently feasible steps that could have led to vastly better outcomes, the growing global dominance of an ideology that justifies marginalizing concern for the plight of the poor and the calamitous looming impact on the poor of global warming.

Instead, world leaders including the Secretary-General, economists and pundits have enthusiastically proclaimed progress against poverty to be 'one of the greatest human achievements of our time',[15] for which humankind should not be shy to take credit. The Chief Economics Commentator for *The Financial Times* echoed many in proclaiming that 'the decline [in poverty] … to less than 10 per cent, is a huge achievement'.[16] Others have paid tribute to the role of economic growth and capitalism in lifting a billion people 'out of dire poverty into something approaching a decent standard of living'.[17]

---

[11] United Nations Development Programme (UNDP), 'Tackling Social Norms: A Game Changer for Gender Inequalities' (2020) 1.

[12] Mandela Lecture (n 3).

[13] Angus Deaton, *The Great Escape: Health, Wealth, and the Origins of Inequality* (Princeton University Press 2013) 1.

[14] Steven Pinker, *Enlightenment Now* (Viking 2018) 116.

[15] World Bank Group President Jim Yong Kim, quoted in World Bank, 'Decline of Global Extreme Poverty Continues but Has Slowed' (19 September 2018) <www.worldbank.org/en/news/press-release/2018/09/19/decline-of-global-extreme-poverty-continues-but-has-slowed-world-bank> accessed 28 July 2020.

[16] Martin Wolf, 'The Case for Sane Globalism Remains Strong' *The Financial Times* (16 July 2019) <www.ft.com/content/ade39e66-a6dc-11e9-b6ee-3cdf3174eb89> accessed 28 July 2020.

[17] Abhijit Banerjee and Esther Duflo, 'How Poverty Ends' *Foreign Affairs* (January/February 2020) <www.foreignaffairs.com/articles/2019-12-03/how-poverty-ends> accessed 28 July 2020; see also Paul Krugman in 'Poverty in America' *Bigger Than Five* (25 December 2019) <www.trtworld.com/video/bigger-than-five/poverty-in-america/5e031e03b53db8001717e81a> accessed 28 July 2020.

Almost all of these commentaries were based upon the data generated by the World Bank's $1.90 a day international poverty line (IPL), which showed that poverty had fallen from 1.895 billion to 736 million between 1990 and 2015, and thus from about 36 to 10 percent of the world's population.[18] Whatever the merits of the IPL, the reality is that it reflects a standard of miserable subsistence rather than an even minimally adequate standard of living. This in turn facilitates greatly exaggerated claims about the impending eradication of extreme poverty and downplays the parlous state of impoverishment in which billions of people continue to subsist.

Using a more defensible line generates a radically different understanding of progress against poverty. Even under the Bank's line, the figures are terrible: 700 million people living under $1.90 a day is abhorrent. Using more realistic measures, the extent of global poverty is vastly higher and the trends discouraging. Rather than one billion people lifted out of poverty and a global decline from 36 percent to 10 per cent, many lines show only a modest decline in rate and a nearly stagnant headcount. The number living under a $5.50 line held almost steady between 1990 and 2015, declining from 3.5 to 3.4 billion, while the rate dropped from 67 percent to 46 percent.[19] Using Martin Ravallion's weakly relative line, the number in poverty declined slightly from 2.55 billion to 2.3 billion between 1990 and 2013, falling from 48 to 32 percent.[20] Under the Bank's societal poverty line, the headcount declined from 2.35 billion to 2.1 billion between 1990 and 2015, and the rate declined from 44.5 percent to 28.5 per-cent.[21] Today, the leading global non-monetary measure of deprivation, the Multidimensional Poverty Index, covering 101 developing countries, yields a poverty rate of 23 percent.[22]

The stark reality is that the world is not even close to ending poverty. While SDG 1 calls for a rate of zero under the IPL by 2030, the World Bank does not foresee an end to poverty even under that line. Assuming that every country grows as it did between 2005 and 2015 (doubt-ful), the Bank projects a poverty rate of 6 percent in 2030.[23] Under a $5.04 line, projections show 28 percent of the world, or 2.35 billion people, in poverty in 2030.[24] These projections will deteriorate immensely as COVID-19 continues to ravage economies and public health and as global warming accelerates.

Several challenges emerge from this more sober and evidence-based assessment of the current state of world poverty. First, there is little cause to be in the least bit satisfied with the progress made over the past forty years or more, given the immense wealth that has been generated during that period. The fact that some two billion people still live in poverty, based on any reasonable conception of an adequate standard of living, means that the economic and social policies being promoted by mainstream neoliberal orthodoxy have failed vast numbers

---

[18]   World Bank, 'Poverty and Shared Prosperity 2018: Piecing Together the Poverty Puzzle' (2018) 2.
[19]   ibid 83.
[20]   Martin Ravallion, 'On Measuring Global Poverty' (2019) National Bureau of Economic Research (NBER) Working Paper No. 26211 22–23.
[21]   Espen Beer Prydz and Dean Jolliffe, 'Societal Poverty: A Global Measure of Relative Poverty' (11 September 2019) <https://datatopics.worldbank.org/world-development-indicators/stories/societal-poverty-a-global-measure-of-relative-poverty.html>; The World Bank, 'Poverty and Shared Prosperity' (2018) 77.
[22]   UNDP, 'Human Development Report 2019' (2019) 68 <http://hdr.undp.org/sites/default/files/hdr2019.pdf> accessed 28 July 2020.
[23]   Poverty and Shared Prosperity (n 18) 24.
[24]   Sanjay G. Reddy, 'Global Absolute Poverty: The Beginning of the End?' (10 February 2020) <https://papers.ssrn.com/sol3/papers.cfm?abstract_id=3537705> 17–18.

of people, while creating immense wealth for a few and hugely exacerbating inequality. Second, redistribution needs to be at the top of the list of policy priorities and genuine steps need to be taken to reduce inequality and ensure social protection floors for all. Third, the Sustainable Development Goals, as currently formulated and pursued do not provide the sort of roadmap, blueprint, or whatever other evasive metaphor might be used, that will be needed to eradicate extreme poverty or significantly reduce inequality.

In the years ahead, the existential threat posed by climate change will further overshadow the prospect of achieving many of the goals reflected in the SDGs. The basic acknowledgement of global warming in Agenda 2030 is entirely inadequate and is not effectively integrated into the overall agenda. When we add in the radically changed economic situation that has emerged as a result of the COVID-19 pandemic, it is clear that nothing short of truly transformative solutions will work to eliminate poverty in the decades ahead. The chapters in this volume should be assessed against that reality.

Philip Alston

Acknowledgements

A volume of this size and complexity can only come together through the work of many people over a long period of time. The editors are grateful to Anna Maria Annino, Kelly Gibson, Jenni Oprosko and Kristin Trapp for their excellent research and technical assistance. Jennifer True and Craig Eastland provided important assistance with production and citations, respectively.

Martha Davis thanks Dean James Hackney and the Northeastern University School of Law for supporting her work on this project.

Morten Kjaerum thanks Lena Olsson, Head of Library and other colleagues at the Raoul Wallenberg Institute for all their support with this project.

Amanda Lyons would like to thank Barb Frey, Steve Meili, Fionnuala Ní Aoláin and Chris Roberts at the University of Minnesota for their support.

We are grateful for the opportunity to present earlier chapters and the concept for this volume at the Law and Society Association Annual Meeting in Washington D.C. in May 2019, in which 12 of the authors were able to meet and advance this collective project.

We also thank the more than 30 anonymous reviewers who assisted with expert, thorough, constructive peer reviews of the chapters, often with short deadlines. Their insights were invaluable for both the chapter authors and the editors.

Introduction to the *Research Handbook on Human Rights and Poverty*

Poverty is both pervasive and predictable across the globe. It exacerbates the impact of catastrophes from hurricanes to pandemics and heightens human-caused challenges such as economic downturns and discrimination. Poor people are likely to experience more hardship and distress than others on a daily basis. These everyday stresses are dramatically increased, and made more visible, when nations, regions, neighborhoods, families or individuals face unanticipated calamities or confront structural inequalities.

Yet despite its ubiquity, myths about the nature of poverty persist. These include the notion that poverty is a matter of individual choice or a product of culture, and the idea that poverty is an inevitable and tolerable outcome of generalized economic progress.

Examining poverty through a human rights lens directly challenges these myths and contributes new insights. A human rights perspective on poverty raises important questions regarding the role of governmental entities – particularly nation States and international institutions – in perpetuating poverty by failing to meet their obligations to prevent and alleviate it and to respect, protect and fulfil human rights. At the same time, the human rights perspective, which brings together civil, political, economic, social and cultural rights, illuminates the myriad ways in which this failure affects the opportunities of both individuals and groups to live with dignity, autonomy and meaning. Human rights-based approaches also have the potential to identify new sites and strategies for interventions that address root causes, empower rights-holders and hold duty bearers accountable.

The premise of this volume is that there is more research to be done to explore these aspects of the human rights lens, while also challenging some of the assumptions underlying modern human rights concepts. Why, for example, should human rights obligations be limited to public actors and not encompass all key power holders? And why should explorations of poverty stop short of examining political inequality, or overlook the spatial aspects of deprivation? The chapters that make up this volume outline the status quo of poverty and human rights and raise probing questions about that status quo. They also respond to important critiques of the human rights project and point toward future research to further hone our understandings of the issues, a necessary step toward crafting more effective responses.

In this introductory essay, we first identify common groundings that serve as through-lines for the chapters in this volume. We then introduce the themes of the book as expressed in the chapters themselves.

I. POVERTY BASICS

A. What Is Poverty?

It is no surprise that a phenomenon as complex and varied as poverty has no single accepted definition. Below, we review several approaches as background for the chapters that follow.

Some of these chapters explore definitional questions in greater detail; others assume a common understanding of poverty or rely on everyday, specific examples as a basis for contextualizing the discussion without seeking to define the term. Regardless, a brief survey of the range of definitions is a useful starting point before reading further.

Many governments and institutions focus on income as a sole or primary poverty measure, though this approach is increasingly subject to criticism. Some national poverty lines – including the European Union's (EU) standards – define the poverty threshold as households with disposable income below the 60 percent median income level.[1] Similarly, the United States (US) has an established poverty line based on bright line indicators of household income and assets relative to expected consumption levels.[2] The World Bank pegs extreme poverty at $1.90/day, though it also recognizes that inequality is an important component of assessing poverty levels.[3] The understanding of poverty as a multidimensional phenomenon is central to the design of the Sustainable Development Goals (SDGs), yet they also define extreme poverty in economic terms, as people living on less than $1.90 a day.[4]

More nuanced poverty definitions eschew strict financial calculations and define poverty in relation to social deprivation, including inequality. For example, the 2001 statement of the Committee on Economic, Social and Cultural Rights (CESCR) defines poverty as 'a human condition characterized by the sustained or chronic deprivation of the resources, capabilities, choices, security and power necessary for the enjoyment of an adequate standard of living and other civil, cultural, economic, political and social rights'.[5] This definition reflects the influence of scholars such as Amartya Sen and Martha Nussbaum who identify 'capabilities' as a key component of the experience of poverty.[6]

Comparing poverty across geographies and borders is particularly complex but necessary in a globalized world. The Oxford Poverty and Human Development Initiative (OPHI) has developed a Multidimensional Poverty Index (MPI) to measure non-monetary comparative poverty over time.[7] Using three dimensions (health, education and standard of living) and ten indicators (for example, the indicators for health are nutrition and child mortality), the MPI

---

[1]   Zsolt Darvas, 'Why is it so Hard to Reach the EU's "Poverty" Target?' (Bruegel, 2017) 2 <http://aei.pitt.edu/83767/1/PC-01-2017-1.pdf> accessed 22 July 2020.

[2]   United States Census Bureau, 'How the Census Bureau Measures Poverty' (27 August 2019) <www.census.gov/topics/income-poverty/poverty/guidance/poverty-measures.html> accessed 22 July 2020.

[3]   Roy Katayama and Divyanshi Wadhwa, 'Half of the World's Poor Live in Just 5 Countries' (World Bank Blogs, 2019) <https://blogs.worldbank.org/opendata/half-world-s-poor-live-just-5-countries> accessed 22 July 2020.

[4]   United Nations (UN), 'Goal 1: End Poverty in all its Forms Everywhere' <www.un.org/sustainabledevelopment/poverty/> accessed 22 July 2020.

[5]   United Nations Committee on Economic, Social and Cultural Rights (CESCR), 'Substantive Issues Arising in the Implementation of the International Covenant on Economic, Social and Cultural Rights: Poverty and the International Covenant on Economic, Social and Cultural Rights' (10 May 2001) UN Doc E/C.12/2001/10, para. 8.

[6]   Amartya Sen, 'Human Rights and Capabilities' (2005) 6(2) Journal of Human Development 151, 155; Martha Nussbaum, 'Poverty and Human Functionings: Capabilities as Fundamental Entitlements' in David B. Grusky and Ravi Kanbur (eds), *Poverty and Inequality* (Stanford University Press 2007) 47–75, 53.

[7]   Oxford Poverty & Human Development Initiative, 'Global Multidimensional Poverty Index' <https://ophi.org.uk/multidimensional-poverty-index/> accessed 24 July 2020.

is designed to illuminate who is poor, why they are poor, and the intensity of their poverty.[8] Note that this approach is intended to complement income-based poverty measures rather than supplant them.

In sum, poverty measures in use today may be objective or subjective, absolute or contextual. While purely economic measures can facilitate governmental analyses and comparisons, these measures are incomplete. Poverty is most fully described and defined when human experiences, including human rights impacts, are taken into account.

B. Human Rights Institutions and Poverty

Many of the chapters in this volume either build on, or challenge, the work done by human rights institutions to articulate the connections between human rights and poverty. In this section, we briefly describe the backdrop of that institutional work.

As early as 1944, the International Labour Organization affirmed that 'poverty anywhere constitutes a danger to prosperity everywhere', and explicitly linked the 'war against want' to social justice goals.[9] Four years later, the Universal Declaration of Human Rights (UDHR) articulated the 'freedom from fear and want' in its preamble and affirmed the fundamental right to an adequate standard of living.[10]

Building on the UDHR, the International Covenant on Economic, Social and Cultural Rights (ICESCR) reinforced in Article 11 'the right of everyone to an adequate standard of living for himself and his family, including adequate food, clothing and housing, and to the continuous improvement of living conditions' as well as the 'fundamental right of everyone to be free from hunger'.[11] The CESCR has made clear its position that poverty, by its own definition, constitutes a denial of human rights. For example, in its General Comment 19 discussing Article 9 of the ICESCR, the Committee stated that '[s]ocial security, through its redistributive character, plays an important role in poverty reduction and alleviation', thereby enabling individuals to enjoy their rights under the Covenant.[12]

The UN's work rests on the three pillars of development, peace and human rights; the struggle to end poverty has gradually made these three dimensions more interrelated and interconnected. The 1992 Rio Declaration on Environment and Development recognized that eradicating poverty is an indispensable requirement for sustainable development.[13] In 1995, Chapter 2 of the Programme of Action of the Copenhagen Summit on Social Development

---

[8]   Oxford Poverty & Human Development Initiative & UN Development Program, Charting Pathways Out of Multidimensional Poverty: Achieving the SDGs (2020) 4–5 <https://ophi.org.uk/wp-content/uploads/G-MPI_Report_2020_Charting_Pathways.pdf> accessed 29 July 2020.
[9]   International Labour Organization (ILO) Constitution, 'Annex: Declaration of Philadelphia' (10 May 1944) <www.ilo.org/legacy/english/inwork/cb-policy-guide/declarationofPhiladelphia1944.pdf> accessed 24 July 2020.
[10]   Universal Declaration of Human Rights (adopted 10 December 1948 UNGA Res 217 A(III) (UDHR) art 25.
[11]   International Covenant on Economic, Social and Cultural Rights (adopted 16 December 1966, adopted into force 3 January 1976) UNGA Res 2200A (XXI) (ICESCR) art 11.
[12]   CESCR, 'General Comment No. 19: The Right to Social Security (Art. 9 of the Covenant)' (4 February 2008) UN Doc E/C.12/GC/19.
[13]   Rio Declaration On Environment and Development (12 August 1992) UNGA A/Conf.151/26 vol 1.

was devoted to poverty eradication.[14] The UN's Millennium Development Goals, in effect from 2000–15, identified eradication of extreme poverty and hunger as the first of eight goals.

Building on these precedents, the SDGs – in effect from 2015 to 2030 – include the target of eradicating extreme poverty for all people everywhere and reducing at least by half the proportion of men, women and children of all ages living in poverty in all its dimensions according to national definitions.[15] The SDGs acknowledge that the 'tyranny of poverty' is a multidimensional phenomenon occurring in developed and developing countries, and its eradication is the 'greatest global challenge and an indispensable requirement for sustainable development'.[16] Notably, the SDGs incorporate human rights norms more fully than any of the UN's previous development initiatives, a fact that has been reiterated on numerous occasions since their adoption.[17]

The successive UN Special Rapporteurs on Extreme Poverty and Human Rights have spoken directly to the issue of poverty as a human rights violation. For example, former Special Rapporteur Magdalena Sepúlveda Carmona developed the Guiding Principles on Poverty and Human Rights. These Principles, endorsed by the UN Human Rights Council in 2012, explicitly identify poverty as 'an urgent human rights concern', that is 'both a cause and a consequence of human rights violations'.[18]

Despite global attention, extreme poverty worldwide has decreased at a glacial pace in recent years.[19] Moreover, progress at the global and even national levels often hides intractable, entrenched poverty among vulnerable groups.

Philip Alston, the Special Rapporteur on Extreme Poverty from 2014 to 2020 and author of the Foreword to this volume, has pointedly observed that poverty is a 'political choice'.[20] This choice will be tested when the international community and states devise their policies for building back following the COVID-19 crisis, which has the dangerous potential to increase extreme poverty and thereby reverse the slow but positive trends of recent decades.

II.   OVERVIEW OF THE BOOK

The chapters in this volume break new ground both by critically examining historic approaches to poverty and human rights and proposing new perspectives to move beyond the impasses that mark the current moment. The diverse group of contributing authors hail from six continents

---

[14] Copenhagen Declaration on Social Development (14 March 1995) UNGA A/Conf.166/9.

[15] SDG 1.

[16] UN, 'Transforming our World: the 2030 Agenda for Sustainable Development' <https://sustainabledevelopment.un.org/post2015/transformingourworld> accessed 26 July 2020.

[17] UN, 'Human Rights and the 2030 Agenda for Sustainable Development' <www.ohchr.org/EN/Issues/SDGS/Pages/The2030Agenda.aspx> accessed 26 July 2020.

[18] United Nations Human Rights Office of the High Commissioner (OHCHR), 'Guiding Principles on Extreme Poverty and Human Rights' (27 September 2012) <www.ohchr.org/Documents/Publications/OHCHR_ExtremePovertyandHumanRights_EN.pdf> accessed 27 July 2020.

[19] World Bank, 'Decline of Global Extreme Poverty Continues but has Slowed: World Bank' (19 September 2018) <www.worldbank.org/en/news/press-release/2018/09/19/decline-of-global-extreme-poverty-continues-but-has-slowed-world-bank> accessed 27 July 2020.

[20] See for examples OHCHR, 'Statement on Visit to the United Kingdom, by Philip Alston, United Nations Special Rapporteur on Extreme Poverty and Human Rights' (16 November 2018) <www.ohchr.org/en/NewsEvents/Pages/DisplayNews.aspx?NewsID=23881&LangID=E> accessed 27 July 2020.

and draw their expertise from their roles as current or former UN special procedure mandate holders, treaty body experts, scholars, advocates and activists.

There are many cross-cutting themes in these 35 chapters and many ways that these rich writings might have been meaningfully grouped. In the end, we chose to divide the chapters between four broad Parts: I. Definitions, Measurements and Standards; II. Cross-currents – Identity, Place and Participation; III. Mechanisms and Policies; and IV. Structural Barriers. Here, we provide an overview of the Parts and chapters that we hope will introduce the range of topics while also inviting readers to make new connections between the Parts and chapters that will be of value to continued research in this field.

PART I: DEFINITIONS, MEASUREMENTS AND STANDARDS

This Part takes as a starting place the belief that shared definitions of poverty and common understandings of how to measure it are essential to crafting, implementing and assessing responses to poverty.

In the opening chapter in this Part, Olivier De Schutter, the current UN Special Rapporteur on Extreme Poverty, proposes an understanding of poverty that goes beyond income-based measures and even multidimensional approaches focused on entitlements. He proposes a more intentional focus on the processes of social exclusion that create and perpetuate poverty. Following on De Schutter's contribution, Magdalena Sepúlveda Carmona, who served in the Special Rapporteur role from 2008 to 2014, traces the growing adoption of a more complex understanding of poverty, particularly in the SDGs, and calls for greater attention to stigma and shame as a mechanism by which the social exclusion of the poor is effectuated. Taking a step back to provide a theoretical grounding for this definitional discussion, Ayşe Buğra examines three distinct perspectives in the study of poverty: capabilities, rights and social exclusion. Applying these, she considers differences and similarities in researching and addressing poverty in the Global North and South as well as the responsibilities of national governments, wealthy countries, and international organizations.

The next two chapters, the first by Gillian MacNaughton and the second by Karolina Januszewski and Manfred Nowak, challenge the content of the human rights related to poverty by bringing rights traditionally identified as 'civil and political' into the debate. MacNaughton argues that economic inequality is itself a human rights violation that exists independently of specific poverty measures, but which also fills out an understanding of poverty itself. Drawing on feminist critiques, Nowak and Januszewski assert that discussions of poverty, by focusing on social and economic aspects of the issue and never decoupling 'civil and political', have tragically relegated political rights into 'oblivion'. They argue that the connection between poverty and political rights must be recovered and restored.

Finally, Hans-Otto Sano raises important questions about the practical implications of introducing a human rights perspective into poverty reduction initiatives in sub-Saharan Africa. He concludes that human rights-based efforts have played a positive role locally, but human rights thinking has not influenced poverty-reduction policies and national poverty trends significantly.

PART II: CROSS-CURRENTS

Poverty and human rights intersect with disability, age, sex, sexual orientation and gender identity/expression, ethnicity, race and other forms of oppression and bases of discrimination. Likewise, dynamics of power and human rights shift over geographic and spatial landscapes, complicated by the movement of peoples across borders and the variability of legal regimes. In each instance, these intersections raise critical issues regarding the political participation of those most affected. These cross-currents are the subject of Part II, addressed in three sections: A. Poverty, Human Rights and Identity; B. Poverty and Human Rights: Intersection with Geography and Place; and C. Poverty and Participation.

A.   Poverty, Human Rights and Identity

In the opening chapter of this section, Gerard Quinn, current UN Special Rapporteur on the rights of persons with disabilities, interrogates the disability-poverty connection and argues that a positive human rights agenda, informed by the principle of 'inclusive equality', can challenge the exclusions of disabled people in both the private and public spheres. Quinn acknowledges that the viability of this positive vision owes much to the 'key breakthrough' represented by the Convention on the Rights of People with Disabilities. Introducing the topic of older persons, poverty and human rights, Andrew Byrnes postulates that a new convention on the rights of older persons might herald a similar breakthrough. The COVID-19 crisis has raised awareness of the many human rights challenges facing subgroups of older individuals, and this momentum might be reinforced by the international attention that a new convention would bring. At the other end of the age spectrum, a treaty addressing children already exists. However, Wouter Vandenhole identifies several significant research questions raised by children's continued impoverishment, a phenomenon that is not inevitable, he avers, but results from policy decisions that deepen global child poverty. He proposes a novel children's rights-based approach to poverty.

The next grouping of chapters addresses intersections of poverty and human rights with sex, sexual orientation and gender identity, and race. Meghan Campbell leads off this section with a deep analysis of gender stereotypes, parenting and poverty traps. Analyzing several social benefits cases from the United Kingdom, she finds hope that a human rights-based approach to poverty grounded in equality rights might counteract policies that exacerbate women's poverty. Victor Madrigal-Borloz, the UN Independent Expert on Sexual Orientation and Gender Identity (SOGI), draws on his country missions to survey the state of SOGI, poverty and human rights. His observations drive home the day to day impacts of social exclusion, specifically naming '[t]he price that is paid by LGBT persons who live openly' in diminished human dignity and economic well-being. The case of Romani people in Europe is laid out in the chapter by Margareta Matache and Simona Barbu, who argue that an array of justice-based approaches should be adopted to address the multidimensional challenges of Roma poverty. Gay McDougall's chapter closing this section addresses disproportionate poverty of African descendants in the American hemisphere as a manifestation of racism. A former member of the UN Committee on the Elimination of All Forms of Racial Discrimination (CERD), McDougall extensively analyzes the Committee's findings over time and distills a set of recommendations for States that are serious about addressing and redressing racism and poverty.

B.   Poverty and Human Rights: Intersecting with Geography and Place

The first two chapters of this section address the situation of people on the move, crossing borders and encountering legal regimes that take poverty into account in both negative and positive ways. Tally Kritzman-Amir specifically notes this tension, observing that human rights law has much to offer to people in need of asylum and non-refoulement, yet destination countries have not always implemented these human rights norms and may even actively contribute to the impoverishment of people in furtherance of anti-refugee and anti-immigrant agendas. Examining European asylum law, Eleni Karageorgiou observes that the very structure of asylum law may discourage the movement of poor people, with the tacit approval of potential destination countries.

Urban poverty and human rights are central to the next two chapters. Natalia Ángel-Cabo and Luisa Sotomayor critique the urban turn in human rights law, ultimately concluding that there is a role for human rights perspectives to contribute to addressing urban poverty but it is no panacea and is less robust than some proponents have suggested. A more hopeful view of the role of local authorities in addressing poverty and implementing human rights is offered by Moritz Baumgärtel, who lays out a series of examples to support his argument that local governments have become central actors in the realization of human rights norms, with potential to do even more.

Miloon Kothari, the UN Special Rapporteur on the Right to Adequate Housing from 2000 to 2008 and an architect by training, argues that the causes of poverty, and potential responses, can be more fully understood through a combination of a human rights and spatial justice approach that examines the role of location in income disparities and persistent poverty. Land rights are the focus of Alfred Brownell, a scholar activist, who draws on his work in West Africa to offer a detailed examination of how land rights are manipulated to make poverty and displacement a pre-determined outcome among Indigenous Peoples in the region. Responding to such concerns for indigenous rights, Alejandro Fuentes mines the jurisprudence of the Inter-American Court of Human Rights to argue that recognition of Indigenous Peoples' right to collective property over their traditional lands and natural resources is an indispensable and promising strategy for poverty reduction that takes into consideration the affected populations' own cultural distinctiveness.

C.   Poverty, Human Rights and Participation

Participation of those most affected in the development of policy responses is integral to human rights approaches and is a key concern for designing poverty eradication strategies that guarantee human rights in both processes and outcomes. The final two chapters in this Part address participation issues in depth. Resonating with earlier chapters stressing the connection between poverty and political rights, Domingo Lovera-Parmo argues that social protests are protected forms of participating in political affairs – and may be the only type of participation open to poor people who are otherwise marginalized from influencing decisions. Lisa Hilbink and Valentina Salas likewise look at how people living in poverty are often excluded from formal institutions of justice and accountability and argue that advancing human rights requires 'going beyond institutional reforms and taking an approach anchored in legal empowerment' – an approach that reinforces dignity while at the same time requiring a new conception of how justice is achieved.

PART III: MECHANISMS AND POLICIES

In this Part, we turn to discussions of policy approaches to poverty and human rights. Though much of this Part is grounded in specific substantive policies and policy approaches, the Part begins with a more theoretical contribution from Volkan Yilmaz. Taking theory seriously, Yilmaz asks 'How can a human rights perspective push the study of ideas and paradigms in social policy toward a better understanding of their human rights implications?' To explore this question and others, Yilmaz offers a critical and contextual analysis of three dominant global paradigms in contemporary social policy literature: new behaviorism, social investment and new universalism.

The human right to housing is the focus of the contribution by Leilani Farha, UN Special Rapporteur on the Right to Housing from 2012 to 2020, and her colleague Kaitlin Schwan. Drawing on their work with the UN mandate, the authors survey the extensive data on financialization of housing and its aggravating impact on poverty. They argue that a 'seismic shift' is needed 'that reclaims the value of housing as home, not as equity'. Mette Hartlev, in turn, explores poverty and the human right to health. Hartlev exposes the ways in which poverty, human rights and health are mutually influencing and then turns to vexing questions on the horizon posed by algorithms and other interfaces between health care, poverty and technology. One specific aspect of women's healthcare has attracted controversy worldwide: abortion. Risa Kaufman and Diana Kasdan examine the issue from the perspective of both poverty and human rights, spelling out implications of this perspective for global and domestic jurisprudence as well as organizing and mobilization.

Privatization is an issue that cuts across social institutions, from prisons to water providers, with many human rights scholars and advocates expressing skepticism about the marketization of services traditionally provided by government. Antonio Barboza-Vergara and Esteban Hoyos-Ceballos, however, ask 'What is wrong with privatization of education' as an anti-poverty policy from a human rights perspective? Grounded in the realities of public education systems that often fail low-income individuals, the authors propose a concrete research agenda designed to give this issue a more complete airing.

Workers' rights are the subject of the next two contributions. Lee Swepston and Constance Thomas explore the human rights perspective on labor standards, arguing that the legal framework that protects workers from exploitation is a bulwark against poverty. Sophal Chea offers a case study from Cambodia testing the impacts of that nation's minimum wage policy on the human rights of workers.

While it is seldom denominated as such, tax policy is among the most widespread means of effectuating social priorities and addressing poverty. Åsa Gunnarsson's chapter provides a cogent analysis of possible rationales for moving away from taxation solely to support income generation and instead, designing tax policy to promote social justice. Human rights-based tax policies can be an important tool in the effort to end extreme poverty.

PART IV: STRUCTURAL BARRIERS

Externalities and structural flaws in governance mechanisms can have significant implications for both poverty and human rights. Similarly, a narrow focus on government action, inherent in formal human rights frames, fails to address the role of private actors in poverty creation and alleviation. The chapters in this Part examine a selection of meta-issues that can exacerbate poverty and human rights violations while also serving as a barrier to implementation of human rights-informed measures to address poverty.

Sumudu Atapattu leads off this section, chronicling the growing recognition of the linkages between climate change, human rights and poverty. Atapattu notes that climate change will undermine both the enjoyment of rights and the efforts to eradicate poverty, and she suggests that a human rights approach to climate change can improve outcomes on both accounts.

Corruption is another significant impediment to the realization of human rights, with particular impacts on poverty. Khulekani Moyo spells out these often-hidden impacts in detail, evaluates the effectiveness of human rights institutions' responses to corruption and asserts that corruption itself constitutes a human rights violation.

In his contribution, Zafer Kizilkaya sheds light on the ways that conflict heightens poverty and exacerbates human rights violations. This area has been under-researched, in part because of the difficulties of collecting data in conflict zones. Kizilkaya concludes by emphasizing the importance of developing conflict resolution approaches informed by human rights and poverty reduction.

Technological changes have significant implications for poverty and human rights. Potential interfaces include data gathering and service delivery, an issue previously raised by Mette Hartlev in the context of health care. Authors Linnet Taylor and Hellen Mukiri-Smith argue that new technologies in these spaces are not neutral tools and must be utilized with due attention to the power and information asymmetries that they reproduce.

Finally, Lucy Williams reminds readers that poverty is created and sustained by private as well as public actors – a point emphasized in earlier chapters by Farha and Schwan (housing) and Brownell (land grabbing). Williams offers a detailed analysis of several recent cases expanding potential liability of international development banks and multinational corporations for human rights violations, arguing that advocates should be consciously developing theories to support claims against these entities as well as governments.

As these 35 chapters, Preface and Foreword document, decades of committed and innovative scholarship and activism have generated a wealth of insights into the crucial linkages between human rights and poverty. The rights-based lenses presented here allow researchers, policymakers and advocates to enrich their understanding of the lived experiences of poverty, the root causes, and the potential for transformation. Our hope with this diverse collection of expert analyses and recommendations is to inspire and orient future research that is committed to understanding and advancing the conditions for all people to live free and equal in dignity and rights.

Martha F. Davis
Morten Kjaerum
Amanda Lyons
Editors

PART I

DEFINITIONS, MEASUREMENTS
AND STANDARDS

1. A human rights-based approach to measuring poverty

Olivier De Schutter

A human rights-based approach to poverty is one that goes beyond an identification of unfulfilled needs to address deprivation: it seeks to identify the causes of poverty redefined as the result of a process of exclusion and discrimination. As such, it redefines poverty not simply in static terms, as a condition facing the most disadvantaged segment of the population, but also in dynamic terms as the outcome of societal choices that should be challenged. A human rights-based approach to poverty thus presents a strong relationship to the 'social exclusion' understanding of poverty. This understanding contrasts with an approach focused on incomes, in which an individual is deemed poor if his or her income is insufficient to meet the cost of a basket of food and non-food items essential to be an active participant in society,[1] and it also contrasts with a multidimensional approach focused on entitlements. Both of these approaches see poverty as a condition facing a group of the population rather than as the outcome of certain policy choices.[2]

Until the mid-1990s, poverty had been defined in purely monetary terms – as a lack of income. It is now seen, instead, as a multidimensional phenomenon, associated with multiple violations of human rights resulting from the lack of entitlement to a number of goods and services that are essential for the enjoyment of rights.[3] The Programme of Action adopted at the 1995 World Summit for Social Development states that:

> Poverty has various manifestations, including lack of income and productive resources sufficient to ensure sustainable livelihoods; hunger and malnutrition; ill health; limited or lack of access to education and other basic services; increased morbidity and mortality from illness; homelessness and inadequate housing; unsafe environments; and social discrimination and exclusion. It is also characterized by a lack of participation in decision-making and in civil, social and cultural life.[4]

---

[1] Martin Ravallion, 'Poverty Lines in Theory and Practice' Living Standards Measurement Study (LSMA) Working Paper 133 <http://documents1.worldbank.org/curated/en/916871468766156239/pdf/multi-page.pdf> accessed 30 June 2020.

[2] C Gore, 'Introduction: Markets, Citizenship, and Social Exclusion', in C Rodgers, C Gore and JB Figueiredo (eds), *Social Exclusion: Rhetoric Reality Responses* (Geneva: International Labour Organisation, 1995) 1–2; AM Fischer, *Poverty as Ideology. Rescuing Social Justice from Global Development Agendas* (London: Zed Books, 2018) ch 5.

[3] On the notion of the multidimensional understanding of poverty and its value, see in particular Sabina Alkire and others, *Multidimensional Poverty Measurement and Analysis* (Oxford: OUP 2015); A Atkinson, *Monitoring Global Poverty. Report of the Commission on Global Poverty* (World Bank 2017).

[4] United Nations World Summit for Social Development, 'Programme of Action of the World Summit for Social Development' UN Doc A/Conf.166/9 (14 March 1995) ch 2 art 19.

In a statement adopted in 2001, the Committee on Economic, Social and Cultural Rights (CESR) defined poverty as 'a human condition characterized by sustained or chronic deprivation of the resources, capabilities, choices, security and power necessary for the enjoyment of an adequate standard of living and other civil, cultural, economic, political and social rights'.[5]

These definitions of poverty frame it as both a cause and a consequence of violations of human rights – whether civil, cultural, economic, political or social rights.[6] People in poverty not only face numerous obstacles in accessing rights and entitlements (including education, housing, nutritious food, healthcare and work, but also political participation); they also are caught in a vicious cycle in which those deprivations themselves make it more difficult for them to escape poverty. It is this vicious cycle, with its dynamic dimension, that relates poverty to a process of social exclusion. Persons experiencing extreme poverty in particular 'live in a vicious cycle of powerlessness, stigmatization, discrimination, exclusion and material deprivation, which all mutually reinforce one another'.[7]

This is well expressed in the 2005 Principles and Guidelines for a Human Rights Approach to Poverty Reduction Strategies, which describe poverty not only as multidimensional (linked to a range of deprivations) but also as a process in which the various deprivations are 'mutually reinforcing', and associated with 'stigma, discrimination, insecurity and social exclusion'.[8] These Principles and Guidelines conclude that any effective anti-poverty strategy should be defined as a strategy aimed at improving the protection of the human rights of people living in poverty: 'The commitment to ensure respect for human rights will act as a force against all these forms of deprivation'.[9] This is the only way to break the vicious cycle between poverty and the lack of enjoyment of human rights, thus 'connecting the powerless with the empowering potential of human rights'.[10]

In the context of a human rights-based approach to poverty reduction, poverty should therefore be defined as a process of exclusion that leads to various forms of deprivation that are mutually reinforcing and not only trap individuals into poverty but also lead to an intergenerational transmission of poverty.[11] The lack of income (monetary poverty) matters of course, but

---

[5] UN Committee on Economic, Social and Cultural Rights (CESCR) 'Substantive Issues Arising in the Implementation of the International Covenant on Economic, Social and Cultural Rights: Poverty and the International Covenant on Economic, Social and Cultural Rights' (10 May 2001) UN Doc E/C.12/2001/10 para 8.

[6] Although the emphasis has generally been on economic, social and cultural rights in the discussion of poverty-reduction policies, the poor also face systematic violations of their civil and political rights, including as a result of police brutality, of excessive subjection to pretrial detention, or denial of voting rights. See UN General Assembly (UNGA), 'Extreme Poverty and Human Rights, Note by the Secretary-General' (4 October 2017) UN Doc A/72/502.

[7] Office of the UN High Commissioner for Human Rights (OHCHR), 'Guiding Principles on Extreme Poverty and Human Rights' (27 September 2012) <www.ohchr.org/Documents/Publications/OHCHR_ExtremePovertyandHumanRights_EN.pdf> accessed 30 June 2020.

[8] OHCHR, 'Principles and Guidelines for a Human Rights Approach to Poverty Reduction Strategies' (2005) UN Doc. HR/Pub/06/12 para 15.

[9] ibid. For a detailed description of the relationship between poverty and human rights, see OHCHR, 'Human Rights and Poverty Reduction: A Conceptual Framework' (2004) UN Doc HR/Pub/04/01.

[10] CESCR (n 5) para 6.

[11] On the inter-generational transmission of poverty, see Anna Cristina d'Addio, 'Intergenerational Transmission of Disadvantage: Mobility or Immobility Across Generations? A Review of the Evidence across OECD Countries' (2007) OECD Social, Employment and Migration Working Paper 52; O Causa and A Johansson, 'Intergenerational Social Mobility in OECD Countries' 'OECD Journal: Economic

so does the lack of access to the goods or services essential to the enjoyment of human rights and which would otherwise allow individuals to escape poverty: housing, education, health-care, food, work and social security. Ideally, indicators should be developed to track, for each of these, availability (in relation to needs), accessibility (including economic accessibility, physical accessibility, and non-discrimination), and adequacy, in order to identify deprivations that require the most urgent action.

Section I provides further clarifications as to the components of a human rights-based approach to poverty reduction: it considers respectively the principle of accountability, the principle of equality and non-discrimination and the principle of participation, explaining how taking into account these principles can significantly improve the legitimacy and effectiveness of poverty-reduction strategies. Section II then focuses on the role of human rights in guiding poverty measurement, which should not be seen simply as a means to quantify existing levels of poverty in a country but also as a tool to ensure accountability and one which requires not only assessing how many people are poor, but also who the poor are. Section III offers a brief conclusion.

I.   THE ROLE OF HUMAN RIGHTS PRINCIPLES IN SHAPING POVERTY-REDUCTION STRATEGIES

The Guiding Principles on extreme poverty and human rights (Guiding Principles), which the Human Rights Council endorsed on 27 September 2012 in resolution 21/11, are the most authoritative guidance on how human rights should be taken into account in the fight against poverty. They provide that States should adopt a human rights-based poverty reduction strategy 'that actively engages individuals and groups, especially those living in poverty, in its design and implementation'.[12] Three human rights principles play a key role in the design and implementation of poverty-reduction strategies thus conceived.

A.   Accountability

A human rights-based poverty reduction strategy sees the adoption of such a strategy not as voluntary for the State but as a legal obligation imposed under its human rights commitments and for which the State must be held accountable. It follows that the strategy should provide beneficiaries with rights that they may claim: once rights are introduced into the context of policymaking

> the rationale of poverty reduction no longer derives merely from the fact that the people living in poverty have needs but also from the fact that they have rights—entitlements that give rise to legal obligations on the part of others. Thus, the human rights perspective adds legitimacy to the demand for making poverty reduction the primary goal of policymaking.[13]

Studies' (2010) <https://read.oecd-ilibrary.org/economics/oecd-journal-economic-studies/volume-2010/issue-1_eco_studies-v2010-1-en#page1> accessed 2 June 2020; Chronic Poverty Research Centre (CPRC), 'Asset Inheritance and IGT of Poverty' <www.chronicpoverty.org/publications/keyword/Asset+inheritance+and+IGT+of+poverty+series> accessed 2 June 2020.

12   Guiding Principles (n 7) para 50.
13   OHCHR (n 8) para 19.

It also follows that the implementation of the strategy should be monitored by independent mechanisms, such as national human rights institutions, courts, parliamentary committees and regional and international human rights mechanisms.[14] For such monitoring to be effective, the strategy should include appropriate indicators (both quantitative and qualitative), benchmarks and timetables (both sufficiently ambitious and realistic), ensuring that progress shall be achieved in accordance with a specific timeline.[15] It should also include a participatory dimension in order to ensure that the poor themselves are involved in monitoring adequate implementation.[16]

Human rights-based indicators are distinct from macro-economic or development indicators that simply register socio-economic facts. Human rights-based indicators include those that refer to: State commitments or the legal, institutional and policy frameworks that the State establishes (structural indicators); State efforts to ensure that the commitments are effectively implemented, i.e., translated into the adoption of concrete measures and policies (process indicators); and finally, the results achieved (outcome indicators).[17] These three categories of indicators are interdependent and mutually supportive: the structural indicators ensure that the beneficiaries of measures adopted by the State shall have access to remedies (judicial and non-judicial) and that the State's performance shall be adequately monitored, in particular, by independent bodies (including national human rights institutions). The process indicators ensure that States shall effectively deliver on their promises, in particular by making the required budgetary investments. Finally, the outcome indicators, which present the closest resemblance to development indicators, serve to ensure the policies actually make a difference – that they are having an impact – so that misguided or ineffective policies can be revised and improved.

B.   Equality and Non-Discrimination

It is noteworthy that Article 2(2) of the International Covenant on Economic, Social and Cultural Rights (CESCR) mentions 'social origin' and 'property' among the prohibited grounds of discrimination, alongside, inter alia, race, colour, sex, language or religion. Indeed, the CESCR insists that such grounds should be included in the anti-discrimination framework adopted by the States parties to the Covenant.[18] In its General Comment No. 20 on non-discrimination, the Committee reiterated that

> Individuals and groups of individuals must not be arbitrarily treated on account of belonging to a certain economic or social group or strata within society. A person's social and economic situation when living in poverty or being homeless may result in pervasive discrimination, stigmatization and

---

[14]   Guiding Principles (n 7) paras 103, 107.
[15]   ibid 104.
[16]   ibid 107.
[17]   UN International Human Rights Instruments (HRI), 'Report on Indicators for Promoting and Monitoring the Implementation of Human Rights' (6 June 2008) UN Doc HRI/MC/2008/3 (introducing this framework).
[18]   CESCR, 'Concluding Observations on the Sixth Periodic Report of Canada' (23 March 2016) UN Doc E/C.12/CAN/CO/6 para 17 (referring to 'social condition' as a prohibited ground of discrimination).

negative stereotyping which can lead to the refusal of, or unequal access to, the same quality of education and health care as others, as well as the denial of or unequal access to public places.[19]

1.   The requirement of equality and non-discrimination in combating poverty

Protecting the poor against discrimination on the basis of their social condition is key to removing the structural determinants of poverty, because poverty and discrimination are mutually reinforcing: 'Discrimination may cause poverty, just as poverty may cause discrimination'.[20] As regards the homeless for instance, the Special Rapporteur on the right to adequate housing noted that discrimination 'is both a cause and a consequence of homelessness': not only may discrimination result in exclusion and increase the likelihood of a person becoming homeless, but in addition, once homeless, one may experience additional discrimination as a result.[21] The explicit protection from discrimination on grounds of social condition has symbolic value, sending a clear message to policy-makers that people may not be treated less favourably because they are poor. It also has institutional consequences by allowing Equality Bodies (independent institutions tasked with preventing and addressing discrimination and promoting equality) to contribute more effectively to the fight against poverty, alongside the contributions other human rights mechanisms can make.

In practice however, the requirement to protect people from discrimination on grounds of social status is, at best, highly uneven.[22] Relying on such a ground of discrimination raises specific challenges, both because the meaning of the socio-economic status ground is poorly understood[23] and because, in the large majority of cases, discrimination on grounds of social condition (or socio-economic status) is combined with discrimination on other grounds (particularly sex, race or ethnic origin, disability or age), requiring specific methodologies to be developed to address appropriately multiple discriminations.[24]

The potential role of the prohibition of discrimination on grounds of 'social condition' could be maximized by relying on an expanded notion of the concept of 'social origin' which appears in article 2(2) of the International Covenant on Economic, Social and Cultural Rights.

---

[19]   CESCR, 'General Comment No. 20: Non-discrimination in Economic, Social and Cultural Rights' (2 July 2009) UN Doc E/C.12/GC/20 para 35.

[20]   CESCR (n 5) para 11.

[21]   UNGA, 'Report of the Special Rapporteur on Adequate Housing as a Component of the Right to an Adequate Standard of Living and on the Right to Non-discrimination in this Context' (30 December 2015) UN Doc A/HRC/31/54 para 39.

[22]   Margaret Thornton, 'Social Status: the last bastion of discrimination' (2018) 1(3) ADLR 1–26.

[23]   Guidance may be found in the interpretation provided to the prohibition of discrimination based on the term 'social condition', which appears in art 10 of the Charter of Human Rights and Freedoms of the Canadian Province of Québec: 'The definition of "social condition" contains an objective component. A person's standing in society is often determined by his or her occupation, income or education level, or family background. It also has a subjective component, associated with the perceptions that are drawn from these various objective points of reference. A plaintiff need not prove that all of these factors influenced the decision to exclude. It will, however, be necessary to show that as a result of one or more of these factors, the plaintiff can be regarded as part of a socially identifiable group and that it is in this context that the discrimination occurred' Comm. des droits de la personn v. Gauthier (1993) 19 C.H.R.R. D/312 [English summary].

[24]   See Equinet (European Network of Equality Bodies), 'Addressing Poverty and Discrimination: Two Sides of the One Coin' (December 2010) <www.archive.equineteurope.org/IMG/pdf/poverty _opinion_2010_english.pdf> accessed 2 July 2020.

The CESCR understands this expression to refer to the 'social and economic situation when living in poverty or being homeless'.[25] As noted by Angelo Capuano, however, this definition may be unnecessarily restrictive and thus potentially irrelevant in many contexts where discriminatory treatment is based. First, the 'social status' of a person 'is reflected more by prestige and esteem rather than merely property status, wealth or economic status'.[26] Moreover, 'the criteria which the CESCR seems to use to give content to the concept of "social status" – property status, caste, and economic and social status such as homelessness and poverty – are not likely to be bases upon which an employer will commonly have the opportunity to discriminate'.[27] Instead, he suggests, discrimination most frequently occurs on the basis of family relationships, of the schools the person has attended, or of childhood circumstances: these are instances of 'ascribed status', rather than 'achieved status', and it is these instances in particular that one should be devoting more attention to.[28]

2. The three roles of equality and non-discrimination in combating poverty
The first implication of the prohibition of discrimination on grounds of social condition or property is that (to borrow from the classic definition of discrimination in human rights law) any distinction, exclusion, restriction or preference or other differential treatment that is based on such grounds and which has the purpose or effect of impairing the enjoyment or exercise of human rights should be prohibited as a form of unlawful discrimination. The reference in Article 2, paragraph 2 of the International Covenant on Economic, Social and Cultural Rights to 'property' (in French: 'fortune') implies that the poor cannot be treated adversely simply because they are poor: in principle, their underprivileged socio-economic situation cannot be allowed to result in a reduced ability to enjoy human rights.

There is an additional and more interesting implication of the prohibition of discrimination on grounds of social origin or property. Human rights law prohibits any action or omission that disproportionately affects members of a particular group, in the absence of a reasonable and objective justification, thus constituting de facto discrimination.[29] Thus, regulatory or policy measures that are neutral on their face may be considered discriminatory if they do not take into account the disparate impacts they may have on certain groups of the population, defined for instance on the basis of 'property' or income levels. It is this idea that is at the heart of a 'positive duty' to consider the impacts on poverty in law- and policy-making, as imposed for instance in Scotland since April 2018 as part of the Equality Act 2010: this duty, referred to as the 'Fairer Scotland Duty', imposes on a number of public bodies in Scotland the duty to 'actively consider ("pay due regard" to) how they can reduce inequalities of outcome caused by socio-economic disadvantage when making strategic decisions'.[30] In practice, this means that decisions such as where to locate a school or a hospital or how to develop a neighborhood

---

[25] CESCR (n 19) para 35.
[26] Angelo Capuano, 'The Meaning of "Social Origin" in International Human Rights Treaties: A Critique of the CESCR's Approach to "Social Origin" Discrimination in the ICESCR and its (Ir) relevance to National Contexts such as Australia' (2017) 41 NZJ Empl. Relations 105.
[27] ibid 106.
[28] ibid 109–10.
[29] HRC, 'CCPR General Comment No. 18: Non-discrimination' (10 November 1989); CESCR (n 19) para 8.
[30] Scottish Government, 'The Fairer Scotland Duty Interim Guidance for Public Bodies' (March 2018), <www.gov.scot/binaries/content/documents/govscot/publications/advice-and-guidance/2018/03/

should be made with the involvement of the local community and aim at reducing, rather than increasing, the exclusionary impacts of lack of income – thus contributing to a more inclusive, less divided society.[31]

Human rights impact assessments serve to alert policy-makers to the impacts on human rights of the poor of the policies they design and implement.[32] They are distinct from other types of assessments, including social impact assessments or sustainability impact assessments. The specificity of human rights impact assessments is that they examine the intended and unintended impacts of policy measures on the ability of the States parties to these agreements to respect, protect and fulfil the human rights of people living in poverty. They therefore should be based explicitly on the normative content of human rights, as clarified by the judicial and non-judicial bodies that are tasked with monitoring compliance with human rights obligations. References in impact assessments to development goals or to poverty are therefore not a substitute for a reference to the normative components of human rights. Human rights impact assessments also require reliance on disaggregated data to measure impacts;[33] the impacts should be measured through diverse methodologies, including methodologies based on the participation of the poor, using both quantitative and qualitative indicators.

The requirement of non-discrimination against the poor is especially important where States face an economic or financial crisis and adopt fiscal consolidation (so-called 'austerity') programmes in order to reassure their creditors as to the health of their public budgets. In a letter to States parties in 2012, the Chairperson of the CESCR emphasized that fiscal consolidation policies 'must not be discriminatory and must comprise all possible measures, including tax measures, to support social transfers to mitigate inequalities that can grow in times of crisis and to ensure that the rights of the disadvantaged and marginalized individuals and groups are not disproportionately affected'.[34] The duty to ensure austerity programmes shall not negatively impact people in poverty is also emphasized in the Guiding Principles on Extreme Poverty and Human Rights.[35] The Guiding principles on human rights impact assessments of economic reforms presented in 2018 by the Independent Expert on foreign debt and human rights provide further guidance as to how the such human rights impacts should be conducted.[36]

---

fairer-scotland-duty-interim-guidance-public-bodies/documents/00533417-pdf/00533417-pdf/govscot%3Adocument/00533417.pdf> accessed 2 July 2020.

[31]   One telling example is the relocation of the Monklands University Hospital in North Lanarkshire. After plans were announced for the University Hospital to move, concerns were expressed during consultations that low-income families in the vicinity of the existing hospital might not be able to travel to the new location to seek treatment. A compromise was struck, providing for some primary health care services to remain in Monklands. (Personal communication with Diana Skelton, ATD Fourth World, April 2020).

[32]   Such a tool is under development within the Belgian Service to Combat Poverty, Insecurity and Social Exclusion: see for details (in Dutch): <www.armoedebestrijding.be/themaarmoedetoets.htm> accessed 6 December 2020.

[33]   Guiding Principles (n 7) para 52.

[34]   See also the Statement adopted by the CESCR, 'Public Debt, Austerity Measures and the International Covenant on Economic, Social and Cultural Rights' (22 July 2016) UN Doc E/C.12/2016/1 para 2.

[35]   Guiding Principles (n 7) para 54.

[36]   UNGA, 'Guiding Principles on Human Rights Impact Assessments of Economic Reforms' (19 December 2018) UN Doc A/HRC/40/57.

The third implication is that the equality requirement goes beyond this negative duty: in cases of entrenched discrimination, States may be under an obligation to adopt special measures to attenuate or suppress conditions that perpetuate discrimination. In human rights law, such measures are legitimate to the extent that they represent reasonable, objective and proportionate means to redress de facto discrimination and are discontinued when substantive equality has been sustainably achieved.[37] Courts have sometimes been suspicious of differential treatment that benefits certain underprivileged groups defined by their ethnicity or gender. This reflects adherence to a formal understanding of equality, resulting in a restrictive reading of non-discrimination law as forbidding the 'sin' of discrimination, rather than as a tool to remedy injustices that have their source in society-wide mechanisms of exclusion.[38] However, since socio-economic condition is not a suspect ground, courts have been far more open to affirmative action measures taken to improve the situation of those who are economically deprived. In fact, such measures are at the very heart of the construction of welfare states, the main purpose of which is to provide support to those who are excluded by the mechanisms of the market.[39]

States therefore should dedicate greater resources to improve the condition of groups who face systemic discrimination.[40] They should move up the causality chain and also tackle the underlying causes of social exclusion. Indeed, once it is recognized that 'a great deal of poverty originates from discriminatory practices—both overt and covert', it follows that poverty reduction strategies shall only be fully effective if they also address 'the socio-cultural and political-legal institutions which sustain the structures of discrimination'.[41] The fight against inequalities, based in particular on social condition, should concern not only the sphere of economic, social and cultural rights, but also the sphere of civil and political rights, since political influence and socio-economic inequalities are mutually reinforcing.[42]

The prohibition of discrimination on grounds of social condition or property therefore has three implications: (1) a negative duty not to disadvantage on those grounds, (2) a positive duty to avoid de facto discrimination, and finally (3) a positive duty to prioritize people who are facing systemic disadvantage, in particular as a result of poverty. These duties can only be effectively discharged if the impacts on people living in poverty are adequately measured, which requires the disaggregation of general development indicators, inter alia, by income.

---

[37] CESCR (n 19) para 9.
[38] Kathleen M Sullivan, 'Sins of Discrimination: Last Term's Affirmative Action Cases' (1986) 100 Harv. L. Rev. 78.
[39] This should be nuanced, since not all welfare states seek to achieve equality: some models only aim at protecting individuals from extreme deprivation, without setting wealth redistribution as an objective in its own right. See Gosta Esping-Andersen, *The Three Worlds of Welfare Capitalism* (Princeton, NJ: Princeton University Press, 1990).
[40] CESCR (n 19) para 39.
[41] Principles and Guidelines (n 8) para 21.
[42] HRC, 'Report of the Special Rapporteur on Extreme Poverty and Human Rights' (27 May 2015) UN Doc A/HRC/29/31 para 21; United Nations Research Institute for Social Development, 'Combating Poverty and Inequality: Structural Change, Social Policy and Politics' <www.unrisd.org/unrisd/website/document.nsf/(httpAuxPages)/92B1D5057F43149CC125779600434441?OpenDocument&panel=additional> accessed 2 July 2020; UNGA (n 21) para 21.

C.   Participation

Ensuring the participation of the poor in the design of poverty-reduction strategies is key to both their legitimacy and their effectiveness. As noted by the CESCR:

> a policy or programme that is formulated without the active and informed participation of those affected is most unlikely to be effective. Although free and fair elections are a crucial component of the right to participate, they are not enough to ensure that those living in poverty enjoy the right to participate in key decisions affecting their lives.[43]

The Guiding Principles on extreme poverty and human rights provide that:

> States must ensure the active, free, informed and meaningful participation of persons living in poverty at all stages of the design, implementation, monitoring and evaluation of decisions and policies affecting them. This requires capacity-building and human rights education for persons living in poverty, and the establishment of specific mechanisms and institutional arrangements, at various levels of decision-making, to overcome the obstacles that such persons face in terms of effective participation. Particular care should be taken to fully include the poorest and most socially excluded persons.[44]

Low levels of education, lack of self-confidence, poor access to information, the difficulty to organize collectively, time poverty, and lack of trust in the officials or institutions organizing the consultation are all important obstacles that poor people face in exercising their right to take part in the conduct of public affairs. Yet, ensuring such effective participation is the only way to break the vicious cycle in which poor people are underrepresented in decision-making and therefore the policies do not prioritize removing the obstacles they face, resulting in further economic marginalization and, thus, in their political disempowerment.

The Guiding Principles on extreme poverty and human rights also note that anti-poverty strategies and plans of action

> should be devised and periodically reviewed through a transparent, inclusive, participatory and gender-sensitive process. The process by which the strategy and plan of action are devised, and their content, should pay particular attention to vulnerable or marginalized groups. States should define and publicize opportunities for participation and information about proposed policy measures should be disseminated widely and in an accessible manner.[45]

Such participation is certainly not a substitute for ensuring that the poor are protected from discrimination in the exercise of civil and political rights (such as freedom of assembly, freedom of association, freedom of expression and the right to vote), which ensure accountability and allow participation in the polity in general. But it is key to understand the real obstacles the poor face and to identify the solutions that are best suited to their circumstances.

The best recent example of the role of participation in improving our understanding of poverty is the Hidden Dimensions of Poverty research project, co-led by ATD Fourth World and Oxford University, involving 1,091 participants across six countries (including 665 adults and children in poverty), both from the North (France, the United Kingdom and the United

---

[43]   CESCR (n 5) para 12.
[44]   Guiding Principles (n 7) para 38.
[45]   ibid para 104.

States) and from the South (Bangladesh, Bolivia and Tanzania).[46] The report was based on a 'Merging of Knowledge' methodology (*Croisement des savoirs et des pratiques*), defined as a process in which academics, practitioners (activists, social workers) and people in poverty first build knowledge independently in peer meetings and then merge these various sources of knowledge in order to develop new insights into poverty. The process recognizes and values the specific understanding gained from the experience of poverty and exposes each participant to the knowledge and experience of others 'in order to build knowledge that is more complete and greater than the sum of its parts'.[47] The process led to the identification of six 'hidden dimensions' of poverty. These dimensions are called 'hidden' because they go beyond the more classic forms of deprivation referred to both in the money-metric and in the multidimensional approaches to poverty. The first three dimensions relate to what the research describes as the core experience of poverty, a mix of anguish and agency. These are (1) 'suffering in body, mind and heart' ('experiencing intense physical, mental and emotional suffering accompanied by a sense of powerlessness to do anything about it'), (2) 'disempowerment' (defined as 'lack of control and dependency on others resulting from severely constrained choices'), and (3) 'struggle and resistance' (the 'ongoing struggle to survive, which includes resisting and counteracting the effects of the many forms of suffering brought by privations, abuse, and lack of recognition').

The three other dimensions are relational: (4) social maltreatment ('people in poverty are negatively perceived and treated badly by other individuals and informal groups', 'behaviour towards people in poverty is characterized by prejudicial negative judgements, stigma and blame'), (5) institutional maltreatment ('the failure of national and international institutions, through their actions or inaction, to respond appropriately and respectfully to the needs and circumstances of people in poverty, and thereby to ignore, humiliate and harm them'), and (6) unrecognized contributions ('The knowledge and skills of people living in poverty are rarely seen, acknowledged or valued. Often, individually and collectively, people experiencing poverty are wrongly presumed to be incompetent'). These are 'relational' because they result from how people who are not living in poverty affect the lives of people in poverty, either by ignorance or by prejudice. This links these hidden dimensions of poverty with a definition of poverty based on 'social exclusion': underlying both is the idea that poverty does not have its source in the failings of the person living in poverty but rather in the inadequate design of institutions or policies that continue to tolerate the intergenerational transmission of poverty, ignore qualifications acquired by practice rather than formally recognized in diplomas, or undervalue the innovations from people in poverty, particularly the solidarity mechanisms they establish to cope with deprivation.

The Hidden Dimensions of Poverty research illustrates how participation is important not only for the design and implementation of poverty reduction strategies but also to guide the methodological choices concerning data collection and poverty measurement. Indeed, as noted

---

[46]   R Bray and others, *The Hidden Dimensions of Poverty* (Montreuil: Fourth World Publications, 2019).

[47]   Fourth World-University Research Group, *The Merging of Knowledge: People in Poverty and Academics Thinking Together* (University Press of America, 10 August 2007); *Guidelines for the Merging of Knowledge and Practices when Working with People Living in Situations of Poverty and Social Exclusion* <www.4thworldmovement.org/wp-content/uploads/2013/05/Guidelines_for_the _Merging_of_Knowledge_and_Practices.pdf> 5, accessed 6 December 2020.

by the Special Rapporteur on the right to adequate housing, those concerned 'are best placed to ensure that methods of measurement are accurate and inclusive and at the same time sensitive to their circumstances'.[48] In order to ensure such participation is effective, human rights mechanisms, including national human rights institutions, should cooperate with national statistical offices, to ensure that the methodologies adopted in a country to measure poverty are adequately informed by the experiences of the poor.[49] It is to this question of measuring poverty that we now turn.

II.   THE HUMAN RIGHTS-BASED APPROACH TO MEASURING POVERTY

There are three reasons why an adequate measurement of poverty is essential to the effectiveness of poverty reduction strategies.[50] First, measuring poverty allows the issue of poverty to remain visible and to be kept on the top of the political agenda by more informed voters. Second, disaggregated data provides a guide to action and allows poverty-reduction measures to be better targeted. Regulations or policies that might result in worsening inequalities or exclusion can only be identified and improved if poverty is properly measured. Finally, poverty measurement and monitoring serve to assess the outcomes of poverty reduction strategies and interventions, thereby allowing opportunities to improve the effectiveness of poverty-reduction strategies as well as our understanding about the various mechanisms that perpetuate poverty.

However, apart from references to independent monitoring and to the use of disaggregated data,[51] as well as to the need to define the attributes of poverty through participatory processes,[52] the consensus documents are less explicit about how poverty is to be measured. Four key principles should be kept in mind in the design of poverty measurement tools.

A.   Measure Not Only the Number of the Poor, but Who the Poor Are

The Principles and Guidelines emphasize that 'the objective of the exercise should not merely be to come up with a number, such as the percentage of poor people in the population, but to ascertain who these people are and how poor they are' and to identify, within the poor, those who are 'especially deprived and marginalized'.[53] This is another reason why the disaggregation of data related to poverty and social exclusion matters in a human rights perspective: in addition to identifying potential instances of discrimination, as discussed above in Section I, it allows for identifying who is poor, taking into account characteristics such as sex, age, ethnic origin, nationality, disability, or place of residence in particular. This allows more targeted action to be taken towards the groups affected and serves to identify which interventions

---

[48]   UNGA (n 21) para 73.

[49]   OHCHR, 'Everyone Counts: Ensuring a Response of Official Statistics to Sustainable Development Goals Consistent with Human Rights' (8 May 2015) UN Doc. ECE/CES/2015/35 para 7 (c).

[50]   UN Economic Commission for Europe, 'Guide on Poverty Measurement' (2017) UN Doc ECE/CES/STAT/2017/4 para 20.

[51]   Guiding Principles (n 7) para 105.

[52]   Principles and Guidelines (n 8) para 33.

[53]   ibid paras 35–36.

shall be the most effective. It is also a first condition towards understanding the structural determinants of poverty, i.e., the processes of social exclusion that lead to people becoming and remaining poor.

Identifying who the poor are also allows for distinguishing between transient and chronic poverty.[54] Indeed, it is only by asking who the poor are that statistical offices and other actors can assess whether the poor in year one are the same as the poor in year zero or in year two. This is important information to guide policies, since transient and chronic poverty call for very different poverty-reduction approaches, and since only longitudinal data allow for understanding the exclusionary processes leading to poverty.[55]

B.   Design Specific Methodologies to Identify the 'Missing Poor'

Measuring certain dimensions of poverty may pose specific challenges, particularly where the groups concerned are difficult to include in surveys covering a sample of the general population.[56] This is the case in particular for institutionalized people (in elderly care homes, children's homes, and mental health institutions), for undocumented migrants or for homeless people, as well as for street children.[57] For some groups, such as street children or irregular migrants, 'being identified by government authorities may be threatening',[58] and this may impede proper data collection. Other factors may also play a role. Data on homelessness, for instance, is scarce in most countries not only because governments may prefer not to be held accountable but also because of the sheer difficulty of collecting such data.

Yet, without accurate measurement of poverty across all groups, an accountability gap emerges and the effectiveness of poverty reduction strategies is significantly reduced. The invisibility of certain groups of the population living in poverty or at risk of poverty may lead underdeveloped policies that are ad hoc, temporary or short-term, rather than fully addressing the challenge.

Some good practices are worth noting. Starting in 2011, the Italian statistical office Istat teamed with the Ministry of Education and Social Policy, the Italian Federation of Associations for the Homeless (fio.PSD), and the charity Caritas, to develop an understanding of how many people were homeless in Italy and who they were.[59] After the shelters and canteens serving homeless people were identified in 158 municipalities, interviews were conducted during a one-month period, individual diaries were kept to reduce the risk of double counting people using multiple services during the month. In total, 50,724 homeless people were estimated to have used at least one of the services during the November-December 2014 period, representing a small increase over 2011 results. Researchers also found a larger proportion had been homeless for at least three months (83 per cent) and for more than two years (41 per cent) compared to 2011. The survey suggested that the vast majority of the homeless were men (85.7 per cent), foreigners (58.2 per cent), and living alone (76.5 per cent).

---

[54]   Michael Hoy, Brennan Scott Thompson, Buhong Zheng, 'Empirical Issues in Lifetime Poverty Measurement' (2012) 10(2) J Econ. Inequality 163–89.

[55]   United Nations Economic Commission for Europe (n 50) para 81.

[56]   Roger Tourangeau and others (eds), *Hard-to-Survey Populations* (Cambridge: CUP, 2014).

[57]   United Nations Economic Commission for Europe (n 50) paras 428–32.

[58]   Committee on the Rights of the Child (CRC), 'General Comment No. 21 (2017) on Children in Street Situations' (21 June 2017) UN Doc CRC/C/GC/21 para 72.

[59]   United Nations Economic Commission for Europe (n 50) 30–31.

An important limitation of this approach is that the study relied on night shelters and canteens. The method was deemed more feasible than conducting surveys in public spaces (parks) where the homeless may also be found, however it gives a biased picture of the reality of homelessness, since some homeless people, especially families and women, may not visit shelters nor eat at canteens, relying instead on the solidarity of neighbors or extended family.[60]

Various proposals have been made to overcome such limitations.[61] In order to increase the rate of response from the poorest households, the questionnaires should be simplified, and the option should be offered to answer only certain questions. In addition, the interviewers should be better trained to support the interviewees in answering complex questions such as those related to income levels. The more experienced interviewers should identify good practices that could improve response rates, for instance in the way the initial contact is made or in the kind of support provided to the persons surveyed. As regards specifically the 'missing poor' – people living in institutions, caravan dwellers or homeless people, or undocumented migrants – surveys complementary to household surveys should be conducted at regular intervals, in close collaboration with the social services. In Belgium, the methodology was tested to reach homeless people and undocumented migrants (particularly difficult to reach due to both to language barriers and to their fear of contacts with public authorities). As noted by the research team, 'the fact that this has worked in two target groups that are very hard to reach suggests that it should also work with other target groups, provided the required resources and preparation are envisaged for this'.[62]

Fear of seeking out social services may be one particularly disturbing reason why poor households are underrepresented in general surveys. Indeed, in addition to the examples above, poor families may be reluctant to engage in such surveys because of the precariousness of their living conditions. This may be especially the case where social services may threaten to remove children from their families due to poor living conditions. A vicious cycle may emerge: because a family fears that the social services will recommend removing the children from the household, it may seek to evade contacts with such services, and with administrative agents in general, including with surveyors. This may be one major reason why poor households are underrepresented in general surveys, albeit one that is generally overlooked. It may be seen as the reverse of the 'service statistics paradox', according to which the poor that are supported by social services (for instance, homeless people that are accommodated in shelters, as opposed to those living on the streets) tend to be overrepresented in statistics, leading to another distortion in the data guiding poverty reduction strategies.[63]

---

[60]   As noted by the Special Rapporteur on adequate housing: 'Homelessness among single men living on the streets or using emergency shelters is more easily measured. It is more difficult to measure homelessness among women, children and young people living temporarily with family or friends, or among those most marginalized and precariously housed within informal settlements, who may be altogether left out of census or data collection' (UNGA (n 21), at para. 70).

[61]   Ingrid Schockaert and others, 'Poverty Between the Cracks. Complements and Corrections to EU-SILC for Hidden Groups of Poor People' (May 2012) Belgian Federal Science Policy Office (BELSPO).

[62]   ibid 6.

[63]   G Tipple and S Speak, *The Hidden Millions: Homelessness in Developing Countries* (London: Routledge, 2009).

C.   Combine Quantitative Data with Qualitative Data

While quantitative data about all groups facing poverty are of course important both for purposes of accountability and to ensure poverty reduction strategies work effectively, numbers alone may not suffice. Such quantitative estimates should be complemented by qualitative assessments of poverty, as experienced by people living in poverty. This was the intuition at the heart of the 'Voices of the Poor' project launched in the late 1990s.[64] It is also a lesson that emerges within the UN human rights system. Thus, in her 2015 report on homelessness, the Special Rapporteur on the right to adequate housing relied on conclusions of the Institute of Global Homelessness[65] to underline 'the critical importance of qualitative evidence, including, for example, oral testimony, photographs or videos. A human rights-based measurement of homelessness should focus on prevention and on addressing underlying causes, and qualitative information capturing actual experiences often reveals more about how to prevent or solve it than numbers alone'.[66] The Office of the High Commissioner for Human Rights makes a similar point: 'For the smallest groups or those invisible in official statistics, new partnerships and use of innovative technology and statistical techniques, including mapping, targeted surveys, small area estimation may be required'. [67]

The experience of people living in poverty cannot be adequately reflected solely in statistical data. Such data should be complemented by other means to convey information to provide different framings and narratives both to policy-makers and to the broader public, in order to improve the salience of poverty in public discourse and to broaden political imagination.[68]

There are two major advantages to this. First, if achieved through the participation of the poor – allowing for the emergence of a plurality of narratives – it can support the poor in becoming more reflective about their predicament. This contributes to empowerment and capacity-building, especially in circumstances where, as described by the World Development Report 2015, poverty ends up generating its own taxes due to the obstacles that poor people face in imagining different futures for themselves and to the cognitive limitations poverty entails.[69] Poverty, this report notes, 'is not simply a shortfall of money. The constant, day-to-day hard choices associated with poverty in effect tax an individual's bandwidth, or mental resources. This cognitive tax, in turn, can lead to economic decisions that perpetuate poverty'.[70] This is because poverty leads one to focus on the present (the satisfaction of immediate needs) to the detriment of the future (planning in the longer term); because the poor may find it difficult to aspire to another future, and thus to 'take advantage of the opportunities that

---

[64]   D Narayan and others, *Can Anyone Hear Us? Voices from 47 Countries* (Oxford: OUP, 1999); D Narayan and others, *Voices of the Poor. Crying out for Change* (Oxford: OUP, 2000).

[65]   V Busch-Geertsema and others, 'A Global Framework for Understanding and Measuring Homelessness' (July 2016) 55 Habitat International 124.

[66]   UNGA (n 21) para 72.

[67]   OHCHR (n 49) para 7 (a).

[68]   On the importance of such framing, see George Lakoff, *The Political Mind. A Cognitive Scientist's Guide to your Brain and its Politics* (Penguin Books: New York, 2008); World Bank, 'World Development Report 2015: Mind, Society and Behaviour' (2015) <www.worldbank.org/en/publication/wdr2015> accessed 2 July 2020.

[69]   ibid ch 4; J Haushofer and E Fehr, 'On the Psychology of Poverty' (23 May 2014) 344 Science 862–67.

[70]   ibid 81 (based on S Mullainathan and E Shafir, *Scarcity: Why Having Too Little Means So Much* (New York: Times Books, 2013).

do present themselves';[71] and because, finally, 'the environments of people living in poverty make additional cognitive demands', especially in poor countries where infrastructures are weak or non-existent.[72] Mapping poverty by taking into account the voices of the poor can help to gradually overcome these obstacles, since the alternative narratives that emerge should make it easier for them to reflect about their predicament and permit policymakers to adopt a more realistic view of poverty and of the traps, including the cognitive traps, into which the poor may fall. The participation of the poor, the design of a plurality of methodologies to measure poverty, and capacity-building are mutually reinforcing and, combined, can form a virtuous cycle.

The second contribution of a qualitative approach to poverty based on the experience of people living in poverty is that such an approach is much more appropriate to identifying the relational dimensions of poverty, i.e., the constraints that have their source in agency/social relations, often trapping people in poverty.[73] Understood as a process of social exclusion, poverty can only be adequately described based on the dynamic of how poverty is caused and perpetuated, as experienced by the people affected. By adopting what anthropologists call an 'emic' perspective, as opposed to the 'etic' perspective of the external observer, additional issues are identified such as disempowerment by local elites and traditional authorities, shame leading the destitute to cut themselves off from social relationships that could provide a way out of poverty, or the weight of cultural norms related to gender, to loyalty towards one's family members or to gestures of solidarity towards the community.

There is therefore a link, real although indirect, between the methodologies used to capture poverty on the one hand, from the most expert-driven, quantitative and 'objective', to the most participatory, qualitative and 'subjective', and the definition of poverty on the other hand, from the most money-centric to the most attentive to the process of social exclusion. Table 1.1 seeks to capture this relationship. It is based on typologies of poverty measurement tools developed by Andrew Martin Fischer,[74] on the 'Merging of Knowledge' methodology developed by ATD Fourth World[75] and on the contrast between quantitative and qualitative approaches to poverty drawn by Jones and Tvedten in their study of poverty in Mozambique.[76] The table aims to ask the question of how we should understand the complementary ways in which poverty is defined and assessed. Jones and Tvedten take the view that:

> while quantitative and qualitative approaches overlap somewhat in their recognition of the material aspect to poverty, their understandings of what poverty is and the mechanisms that produce it are distinct. Consequently, a forced marriage of qualitative and quantitative approaches into an integrated

---

[71]   ibid. Arjun Appadurai has most explicitly put forward the argument that strengthening the 'capacity to aspire' can be an essential tool in the fight against poverty. He conceived of the 'capacity to aspire' as 'a cultural capacity', which could be an ally in development, since 'the poor could find the resources required to contest and alter the conditions of their own poverty'; A Appadurai, 'The Capacity to Aspire: Culture and the Terms of Recognition', in V Rao and M Walton (eds), *Culture and Public Action* (Stanford: Stanford University Press, 2004) 59–84.

[72]   ibid.

[73]   S Jones and I Tvedten, 'What Does it Mean to be Poor? Investigating the Quantitative-Qualitative Divide in Mozambique' (2019) 117 World Development 158.

[74]   Fischer (n 2).

[75]   Bray et al (n 46).

[76]   Jones and Tvedten (n 73).

Table 1.1　　*Relationship between definition of poverty and methodologies for measurement*

		Etic		Emic
		Academic experts	**Practitioners**	**People in poverty**
Static	Money-metric	Income-based measures of poverty relying on a price assessment of basic needs		
	Multidimensional	Entitlements-based approaches based on a multidimensional understanding on poverty		
Dynamic	Social exclusion			Participatory methodologies such as the reconstruction of the chain of events that led to a situation of poverty (histograms), the mapping of power relationships within the community, and wealth ranking (perception within the community of different categories of 'wealthy' and 'poor' people)

analysis, risks losing the inherent diversity of perspectives and types of knowledge that comes from different ways of seeing poverty.[77]

In contrast, the 'Merging of Knowledge' approach pioneered by ATD Fourth World is prem-ised on the idea not only that the knowledge of experts, of practitioners and of people with an experience of poverty are complementary and bring different insights to the understanding of poverty, but that they can be brought together to provide a new form of knowledge, the result of the 'merger' – of what Jones and Tvedten call 'forced marriage'. Are these approaches conflicting? Perhaps not, if we consider that the knowledge of each category of actors, and the associated methodology, has a distinct function to fulfil, but that a separate and perhaps richer understanding can emerge from trying to combine them. Improvements in quantitative indicators measuring poverty could be related, for instance, with processes of empowerment (can empowerment explain improvements in the material conditions of the poorest segments of the population?), or quantitative data showing the increase in inequalities despite overall economic growth and improvement of material conditions could be a powerful tool to create awareness of the inequitable nature of growth (should growth not be better shared?): in such processes, the fusion of knowledges and the combination of methodologies is the source of new insights in the process of poverty creation, with a strong potential for empowerment.

D.　　Measure Not Only Theoretical Access to Rights, but also the Non-take-up of Rights

The phenomenon of the non-take-up of rights (whether in the form of benefits or of services) should be given specific treatment in poverty measurement, in order to understand better why

---

[77]　ibid 164.

potential beneficiaries of support schemes do not claim their rights and what can be done about this.[78] Specific indicators should be designed that focus not only on the effective enjoyment of the right (social security, housing, education, healthcare, food) or only on the legal entitlements provided, but on the gap between the two.

Why is it that certain people do not claim what they have a right to, or do not rely on certain services that are in principle available to them?[79] This may be because of a lack of information about their rights; because of the bureaucratic hurdles (especially as compared to the level and unpredictability of the benefits);[80] because they need an urgent solution and cannot afford to wait; because of a lack of trust in the relevant authorities;[81] because of the so-called 'welfare stigma', especially where the scheme is based on fine targeting; because they consider that they will not be able to prove the lack of income; because they believe they will not be able to comply with conditionalities attached to the benefit; or finally, because of a vicious cycle in which the lack of access to a certain right (such as housing) leads to a denial of other rights (such as education).[82]

Which lessons can be drawn from the non-take-up of rights in designing poverty measurement tools? As explored above, a human rights-based approach to poverty reduction should combine the use of structural, process and outcome indicators, assessing the legal/regulatory and institutional framework, the efforts of public authorities (including budgetary commitments), and the results achieved. In principle, this combination should identify gaps between accessibility in theory of certain benefits, as measured by structural and process indicators, and their enjoyment in fact, as measured by outcome indicators. That information alone, however, will be insufficient to identify the solutions that can help overcome the gap. As noted above, it is only by complementing statistical data with narratives from the poor themselves that the reasons for non-take-up can be identified and public policies be made more effective.

III.   CONCLUSION

Poverty-reduction efforts will only be as effective as the poverty measurement tools on which we rely. Precise measurement is essential to track progress and improve accountability, to

---

[78]   See Odenore, 'Welcome to the Observatory on Non-Take Up (NTU) of Social Rights and Public Services' at <https://odenore.msh-alpes.fr/en/content/welcome-observatory-non-take-ntu-social-rights -and-public-services> accessed 2 July 2020; Antoine Math, 'Non-Recourse in France: A Real Problem, A Limited Interest' (1996) Research and Forecast; W Van Oorschot, 'Failing Selectivity: On the Extent and Causes of Non-take up of Social Security Benefits' in HJ Andress (ed), *Empirical Poverty Research in Comparative Perspective* (Aldershot: Ashgate, 1998) 101–32.

[79]   Natascha Van Mechelen and Michiel Van Der Heyden, 'The Fight Against Non-Take Up: An Inventory of Policy Measures and Reflection in the Light of Literature Scientific and Experiments of Politics in the UK and Sweden' (October 2017) Policy Brief No. 1/2017; W Van Oorschot, *Take it or Leave it: a Study of Non-take-up of Social Security Benefits* (Tilburg: Tilburg University Press, 1994); F De Boe and others, *Poverty and Ineffectiveness of Rights. Non-take-up of Rights* (Brussels: Die Keure / La Charte, 2017).

[80]   Philippe Warin, 'What is the Non Take-up of Social Benefits?' (Books and Ideas 9 June 2014).

[81]   UNGA, 'Report of the Special Rapporteur on the Human Rights of Migrants' (3 April 2014) UN Doc A/HRC/26/35 para 103.

[82]   A Catrice-Lorey, 'Inequalities in Access to Social Protection Systems and Cultural Poverty' (1976) 30(4) French J of Social Affairs 127–37.

ensure that the question of tackling poverty remains high on the political agenda, and to ensure that efforts are adequately focused on the causes of poverty, rather than simply on the symptoms. A human rights-based approach to poverty measurement also requires recognizing that human rights violations and material deprivation are interlinked and seeing poverty as a multidimensional phenomenon that cannot be reduced to income poverty but instead is a set of deprivations in access to health, education and housing, and worsened by political disempowerment. But the human rights-based approach to poverty measurement goes beyond that: it calls for using a range of methodologies in combination, including participatory methodologies, which are best suited to highlight power relationships and the causal links that lead to poverty and its reproduction.

This chapter emphasizes three major benefits of approaching poverty reduction as a human rights issue. First, using the human rights lens emphasizes that the reduction of poverty, which is both the cause and consequence of human rights violations, is not a matter of choice for the State, but a duty, grounded in human rights. Therefore, accountability mechanisms should be built into the poverty reduction strategy, including independent monitoring of progress.

Second, a human rights-based approach to poverty reduction should include a component related to equality and non-discrimination. This requires not only an explicit protection from discrimination on grounds of social (or social and economic) condition but also the disaggregation of data concerning access to the basic goods and services that correspond to the full enjoyment of human rights (housing, education, healthcare, food, work and social security) by income, gender, age, race, ethnicity, nationality, migratory status, disability, educational background, geographic location and other characteristics relevant in national context. If such disaggregated data reveal disparities in outcomes, targeted policies should be adopted to close the gaps.

Third, the design and implementation of poverty reduction strategies, and the methodological choices concerning data collection and poverty measurement, should be informed by the participation of the poor. This can be time-consuming and demanding, but it is the only way to ensure that the strategies and measurements are sufficiently inclusive and well informed by the experience of those living in poverty or at risk of poverty or social exclusion. Indeed, poverty as social exclusion cannot be adequately understood otherwise.

This leads to several specific recommendations for the measurement of poverty. Such measurement should allow for arriving not at a single figure (such as the percentage of the population at risk of poverty or the absolute number of people facing severe material deprivation), but also at an improved understanding of the causes of poverty in accordance with the multidimensional nature of poverty. It should also allow, by an adequate disaggregation of data, for identifying who the poor are, and for unpacking the processes through which poverty is caused and perpetuated. In measuring poverty, particular care should be taken not to ignore the 'missing poor', i.e., the groups that tend to be invisible in statistics, for instance because they are not covered by household surveys or because they avoid contacts with social services. This requires the use of a plurality of methodologies to collect data about poverty, going beyond the classic reliance on household surveys.

Numbers alone may not suffice to convey the actual experiences of the poor – the circumstances in which they live, the obstacles they encounter, and the solutions they imagine for themselves. Statistical data should be complemented by other sources of information about poverty, providing other framings and narratives, ideally coming from the poor themselves. Finally, because it is not unusual for the poor not to take up the financial benefits they could claim, or not to use the services accessible to them, even when such services are free or affordable, it is essential that poverty measurement efforts focus on the non-take-up of rights. The phenomenon should be given specific treatment in poverty measurement, in order to understand better why potential beneficiaries of support schemes do not claim their rights and what can be done about this. In the setting of political priorities and in designing public programmes, only what is counted matters: we should ensure that, in the future, the poor count more.

2. From stigma to rights: uncovering the hidden dimension of poverty

Magdalena Sepúlveda Carmona

The 2030 Agenda for Sustainable Development reflects a worldwide consensus towards recognizing multidimensional poverty. It seeks to reduce poverty in 'all its forms and dimensions'.[1] The Sustainable Development Goal (SDG) target 1.2, for example, commits to 'by 2030, reduce at least by half the proportion of men, women and children of all ages living in poverty in all its dimensions according to national definitions'.[2] This reflects the emerging consensus that multidimensional measures of poverty should complement monetary ones.

Increasingly the definitions and measurements of poverty have gone beyond the lack of income and have incorporated social or relational dimensions.[3] The Multidimensional Poverty Index (MPI)[4] developed at Oxford University and the United Nations Development Program (UNDP)'s Human Development Report Office is already used by many countries to measure progress towards SDG 1.

Over the years human rights monitoring bodies have also defined poverty from a multidimensional perspective.[5] In 2001 the Committee on Economic, Social and Cultural Rights (CESCR) stated that poverty was 'a human condition characterized by the sustained or chronic deprivation of the resources, capabilities, choices, security and power necessary for the enjoyment of an adequate standard of living and other civil, cultural, economic, political and social rights'.[6] Extreme poverty, in turn, has been defined as 'the combination of income poverty, human development poverty and social exclusion'.[7] Thus, United Nations (UN) human rights monitoring bodies have stressed that poverty is not solely an economic issue but rather a multidimensional phenomenon that encompasses a lack of both income and the basic capabilities to live in dignity.

---

[1] UNGA, 'Transforming Our World: The 2030 Agenda for Sustainable Development' (21 October 2015) UN Doc A/RES/70/1, para 2.

[2] ibid para 1.2.

[3] See chapter one by Olivier De Schutter in this book.

[4] Sabina Alkire and Maria Emma Santos, 'Acute Multidimensional Poverty: A New Index for Developing Countries' (2010) Oxford Poverty and Human Development Initiative (OPHI) Working Paper 38 <www.ophi.org.uk/wp-content/uploads/OPHI-wp38_with_note.pdf> accessed 29 June 2020.

[5] For example, the 2005 Principles and Guidelines for A Human Rights Approach to Poverty Reduction Strategies developed by the Office of the United Nations High Commissioner for Human Rights underline the multidimensional nature of poverty (UN Doc HR/PUB/06/12).

[6] Committee on Economic, Social and Cultural Rights (CESCR), 'Substantive Issues Arising in the Implementation of the International Covenant on Economic, Social, and Cultural Rights: Poverty and the International Covenant on Economic, Social, and Cultural Rights' (10 May 2001) UN Doc E/C.12/2001/10, para 8.

[7] Human Rights Council, 'Promotion and Protection of all Human Rights, Civil, Political, Economic, Social and Cultural Rights, Including the Right to Development' (28 February 2008) UN Doc A/HRC/7/15, para 13.

Respect for the inherent dignity of all is at the very foundation of human rights. Thus, a key dimension of poverty that should not be neglected is the feeling of shame that those experiencing poverty feel due to the stigma or negative prejudices. The UN Guiding Principles on Extreme Poverty and Human Rights,[8] drafted by the UN Special Rapporteur on extreme poverty and human rights, adopted by consensus by the Human Rights Council[9] and endorsed by the General Assembly[10] state:

> Persons living in poverty have a right to be protected from the negative stigma attached to conditions of poverty. States must prohibit public authorities, whether national or local, from stigmatizing or discriminating against persons living in poverty and must take all appropriate measures to modify sociocultural patterns with a view to eliminating prejudices and stereotypes.[11]

Even though the notions of stigma – and the shame it produces – have been defined as a critical dimension of poverty in human rights documents for a long time,[12] human rights monitoring bodies, practitioners and academics fail to systematically assess whether public policies comply with the obligation to avoid stigmatization of those living in poverty. This is a major gap considering that dignity and respect are at the core of a human rights approach.

This chapter first reviews how stigma and shame are neglected dimensions of poverty. Then it seeks to show how negative prejudices or stereotypes against people living in poverty are entrenched in those who are better off in society and who often influence public policies. By using the example of social assistance programs (non-contributory social protection programs) in developed countries (i.e. welfare programs) and in low- and middle-income countries (i.e. conditional cash transfers programs), the chapter seeks to show that when social policies are designed or delivered in a way that is perceived as stigmatizing by recipients, they may seriously infringe the human rights of recipients instead of upholding their dignity and rights.

The chapter concludes that applying a rights-based approach to define the dimensions of poverty requires moving beyond income to emphasize the experience of those living in poverty. Treating people living in poverty as 'rights-holders' and upholding their dignity would require that policy makers, human rights practitioners and monitoring bodies at the national and international levels give further attention to issues of stigma and shame and more regularly assess whether social policies respect the inherent dignity of those experiencing poverty. This can only be achieved if those living in poverty can participate in determining the various dimensions of poverty and in the design, implementation and evaluation of social policies.

---

[8]   Human Rights Council (HRC), 'Final Draft of the Guiding Principles on Extreme Poverty and Human Rights, Submitted by the Special Rapporteur on Extreme Poverty and Human Rights, Magdalena Sepúlveda Carmona' (18 July 2012) UN Doc A/HRC/21/39.

[9]   HRC Res 21/11: Guiding Principles on Extreme Poverty and Human Rights (18 October 2012) UN Doc A/HRC/Res/21/11.

[10]   ibid.

[11]   Guiding Principles on Extreme Poverty and Human Rights (n 8) para 21.

[12]   Principles and Guidelines for A Human Rights Approach to Poverty Reduction Strategies (n 5) para 15.

I. STIGMA AND SHAME, THE NEGLECTED KEY SOCIAL DIMENSIONS OF POVERTY

The ways in which poverty is defined and measured are not irrelevant. Among other things, measures of poverty are key to inform national public policies aimed at reducing poverty. Effective public policies and interventions require a clear understanding of who is living in poverty and of what they are deprived. From a human rights perspective, poverty definitions and the methodology chosen to measure it should comprehensively encompass all dimensions of poverty, including the experiences of those living in poverty that might impact their sense of dignity and autonomy.

Applying a rights-based approach to define the dimensions of poverty requires moving beyond income to emphasize the experiences, dignity, autonomy and social inclusion of those living in poverty. It also requires considering some procedural aspects, such as the participation of those living in poverty in determining the various dimensions of it. Without a lived experience of poverty, policymakers might fail in understanding the various dimensions of poverty. While some measurements such as the MPI have incorporated some forms of participation by people living in poverty,[13] from a human rights perspective, the participation of those living in poverty is not only desirable but a right.[14]

A critical dimension of poverty that is often neglected is the stigma and feeling of shame experienced by those living in poverty.[15] While some scholars, notably Amartya Sen, have argued that shame lies at the 'absolutist core' of poverty,[16] this dimension is often invisible to policymakers, practitioners and human rights monitoring bodies. This is a major gap and a critical obstacle to ensuring that poverty reduction measures respect the dignity and rights of those living in poverty.

Increasingly studies have shown that people living in poverty, in all parts of the world, often prioritize the emotional consequences of poverty even more than material concerns.[17] Recent participatory studies about poverty in developed and developing countries have shown that feelings of shame and humiliation are central in accounts of those living in poverty.[18] Shame has been defined as an effect or emotion that occurs in response to social rejection or perceived loss of social attractiveness. It is an assault to one's self-esteem and sense of social connection and power.[19]

---

[13]   Carolina Moreno, 'Defining MPI Dimensions through Participation: The Case of El Salvador: OPHI Briefing 49' (*OPHI*, June 2017) <www.ophi.org.uk/wp-content/uploads/B49_El_Salvador_vs2_online.pdf> accessed 29 June 2020.

[14]   See, HRC, 'Report of the Special Rapporteur on Extreme Poverty and Human Rights, Magdalena Sepúlveda Carmona' (11 March 2013) UN Doc A/HRC/23/36.

[15]   Robert Walker, *The Shame of Poverty* (OUP 2014).

[16]   Amartya Sen, 'Poor, Relatively Speaking' (1983) 35 Oxford Economic Papers 153, 159.

[17]   Walker (n 15). See also 'My World Survey' (*UNDP*) <https://myworld2030.org/> accessed 30 June 2020.

[18]   Xavier Godinot and Robert Walker, 'Poverty in All its Forms: Determining the Dimensions of Poverty Through Merging Knowledge' in Valentin Beck, Henning Hahn and Robert Lepenies (eds), *Dimensions of Poverty: Measurement Epistemic Injustices, Activism* (Springer 2020).

[19]   Jessica Van Vliet, 'Shame and Resilience in Adulthood: A Grounded Theory Study' (2008) 55 Journal of Counseling Psychology 233.

A unique participatory research project undertaken by ATD Fourth World and Oxford University[20] in conjunction with people with direct experience of poverty in six countries (Bangladesh, Bolivia, France, Tanzania, the United Kingdom and the United States) found that the experience of 'disempowerment' and 'suffering in body, mind and heart' are among the 'core dimensions' of poverty. Furthermore, 'institutional maltreatment', 'social maltreatment' and 'unrecognized contributions' are among the 'relation dynamics' of poverty. All these dimensions, which are critically important for those living in poverty, are also essential to understand their lack of enjoyment of rights and are closely linked to the lack of take-up of social protection programs.

A 'rights-based' approach to poverty should encompass these social dimensions of poverty. It should go beyond the lack of material resources to include the social and power relationships involved, embracing the way in which people in poverty are treated.[21] While these social dimensions of poverty are often imperceptible for those who are better off in society, they are a major impediment to the enjoyment of rights by those living in poverty. Stigma and shame deny their dignity and autonomy and may be major barriers to effectively tackling poverty. They reduce the social capital of those living in poverty and limit their agency. They are often associated with negative coping behaviours, including turning away from responsibilities; self-oriented distress; anger and aggression; and psychological problems such as depression.[22] Moreover, they are compounded by practical impediments such as the lack of money to pay for transportation to reach a work opportunity or a public service, lack of childcare support or not speaking the official language. All of these interrelated and mutually reinforcing deprivations prevent people living in poverty from realizing their rights.

II.   DIGNITY AND RIGHTS AT RISK

Prejudices and stigma against people living in poverty are so entrenched among those who are better off in society that they often find their way into government policy, intentionally or not. When this occurs, such policies fail to recognize that those living in poverty should enjoy their rights and freedoms in an equal manner with the rest of the population and overlook all the obstacles that they face in seeking to achieve better standards of living.

Some of the deep-seated stigma and stereotypes portray persons living in poverty as lazy, irresponsible, indifferent to their children's health and education, dishonest and undeserving, and can even paint them as criminals. Poverty is considered a personal failing, the result of 'not taking responsibility' for one's own life. Those living in poverty are considered as the authors of their own misfortune, who can remedy their situation by simply 'trying harder' or 'working harder'.

Robert Walker refers to three types of stigma: the social stigma, described as the 'process entailing attitudes, thoughts and actions on the part of the majority group, and the perception

---

[20]   Rachel Bray and others (eds), *The Hidden Dimensions of Poverty* (Fourth World Publications 2019).

[21]   Walker (n 15).

[22]   Keetie Roelen, 'Shame, Poverty and Social Protection' (2017) Institute of Development Studies (IDS) Working Paper No 489 <https://opendocs.ids.ac.uk/opendocs/bitstream/handle/20.500.12413/12998/Wp489_Online.pdf?sequence=174> accessed 30 June 2020.

and responses to these by the people stigmatized'; the institutional stigma, 'evidenced in the framing, structure and or delivery of benefits', which can be an intentional or inadvertent element of policy; and the personal stigma, understood as 'a person's own feeling that claiming benefits is shameful'.[23] All three types of stigma are an affront to our sense of dignity and at odds with the protection of human rights.

By their demeaning and degrading nature, prejudices against people living in poverty go directly against the idea of dignity that human rights norms seek to protect. When such prejudices inform public policymaking, the resulting policies fail to tackle the systemic factors that prevent those experiencing poverty from overcoming their situation.

A key public policy area that is often informed by negative narratives around poverty is social protection. This section will address how the negative stereotypes against people experiencing poverty are at the core of arguments that seek to restrict or deny the enjoyment of the right to social protection, leading to the violations of other rights.

A.   The Right to Social Protection

The right to social security or social protection[24] was one of the few economic, social and cultural rights included in the Universal Declaration of Human Rights (UDHR).[25] Subsequently it has been included in various UN human rights treaties,[26] regional human rights treaties[27] and conventions adopted within the framework of the International Labour Organization (ILO),[28] as well as being adopted at the domestic level in many constitutions and national laws.[29]

---

[23]   Walker (n 15) 54–58.

[24]   Following the position of United Nations human rights treaty bodies and ILO, this article uses the terms 'right to social protection' and 'right to social security' interchangeably. See, for example CESCR, General Comment No 19: The Right to Social Security (Art. 9) (4 February 2008) UN Doc E/C.12/GC/19 2008, para 4; International Labour Organization (ILO), *World Social Protection Report 2017-2019: Universal Social Protection to Achieve the Sustainable Development Goals* (ILO 2017) <www.ilo.org/wcmsp5/groups/public/---dgreports/---dcomm/---publ/documents/publication/wcms _604882.pdf> accessed 30 June 2020.

[25]   Universal Declaration of Human Rights (adopted 10 December 1948) UNGA Res 271 A(III) (UDHR).

[26]   For example, Articles 9 and 10 in the International Covenant on Economic, Social and Cultural Rights (1966) (ICESCR); Article 5(e)(iv) in the International Convention on the Elimination of All Forms of Racial Discrimination (1979); Article 11(1)(e) in the Convention on the Elimination of All Forms of Discrimination against Women (1979); Article 26 in the Convention on the Rights of the Child (1989); Article 27 in the International Convention on the Protection of the Rights of All Migrant Workers and Members of Their Families (1990); and Article 28 in the Convention on the Rights of Persons with Disabilities (CRPD) (2006).

[27]   For example, the Additional Protocol to the American Convention on Human Rights in the Area of Economic, Social and Cultural Rights (1999) (Article 9), the European Social Charter (1996) (Article 12) and the African Charter on Human and Peoples' Rights (Articles 4, 5, 6, 15; 16; 18(1), (2) and (4)) (1981).

[28]   For example, Convention 102 (1952), Convention 118 (1962), Convention 157 (1982), Convention 168 (1988) and Convention 183 (2000).

[29]   For a detailed analysis of the constitutional provisions from around the world containing the right to social security, see ILO, 'The Right to Social Security in the Constitutions of the World: Broadening the moral and legal space for social justice'. ILO Global Study, 2016 available at www.ilo.org/wcmsp5/ groups/public/---ed_norm/---normes/documents/publication/wcms_518153.pdf accessed 7 December 2020. For a focus on Europe, see Lola Tonini Alabsio, 'The Protection of the Right to Social Security

According to ILO, 'social protection, or social security, is a human right and is defined as the set of policies and programmes designed to reduce and prevent poverty and vulnerability throughout the life cycle'.[30] Social protection systems include contributory schemes (social insurance) and non-contributory benefits, financed mainly through taxes (social assistance).

From a rights perspective all people, by virtue of their humanity, are deserving of and entitled to the enjoyment of the right to social protection. Human rights law imposes obligations not only to implement social protection systems but also to establish standards for designing and evaluating such systems.[31]

Thus, social assistance benefits – the non-contributory component of social protection systems – are not a handout or a luxury but rather a right that belongs to everyone. Social assistance benefits often respond to a criterion of need and their benefits are designed to provide regular and predictable support to vulnerable and disadvantaged people. Social assistance benefits are provided in developed as well as in developing countries. These benefits include, for example, unemployment, single parents and disability benefits, but also conditional cash transfers, social pensions, food and in-kind transfers, and school feeding programs.[32]

Social assistance programs can potentially enhance dignity and reduce stigma of the beneficiaries.[33] However, when social protection policies are based on prejudices, several rights are under threat, including the right to social security; the prohibition of non-discrimination; right to privacy and family life; and the best interests of the child. Moreover, such policies undermine the agency and autonomy of those living in poverty and overlook the obstacles they face to achieving more fulfilling lives. This is the case when instead of being considered 'rights-holders', those who receive social assistance benefits are portrayed by some policy makers and the media as 'dependent', in comparison with those who are 'self-sufficient' and 'productive', who are the 'hard-working' and 'good people'.[34]

Derogatory terms against recipients of social assistance programs are common in developed and developing countries. It is not uncommon to hear that those who receive social benefits 'fail to take responsibility', are 'addicted', 'illegitimate', 'unambitious' and 'likely to deceive the system'.[35] In the case of women, they are also often called 'sexually promiscuous', espe-

---

in European Constitutions' (Online edn, *ILO*, 2012) <www.ilo.org/wcmsp5/groups/public/---ed_norm/---normes/documents/publication/wcms_191459.pdf> accessed 30 June 2020.

[30]   ILO, *World Social Protection Report 2017-2019* (n 24).

[31]   It is not the intention of this chapter to explain the human-rights based framework for social protection systems, which is well established elsewhere in detail. Instead see Magdalena Sepúlveda and Carly Nyst, 'The Human Rights Approach to Social Protection' (*Ministry of Foreign Affairs of Finland*, 2012). See also the Human Rights and Social Protection electronic platform available at http://socialprotection-humanrights.org/ (last accessed April 2020).

[32]   World Bank Group, *The State of Social Safety Nets 2018* (The World Bank 2018) <https://openknowledge.worldbank.org/bitstream/handle/10986/29115/9781464812545.pdf?sequence=5&isAllowed=y> accessed 30 June 2020.

[33]   Francesca Bastagli and others, 'Cash Transfers: What does the Evidence Say?: A Rigorous Review of Programme Impact and of the Role of Design and Implementation Features' (*Overseas Development Institute*, 2016) <www.odi.org/sites/odi.org.uk/files/resource-documents/10749.pdf> accessed 30 June 2020.

[34]   Robert Walker and Elaine Chase, 'Adding to the Shame of Poverty: The Public, Politicians and the Media' (2014) 148 Poverty: Journal of the Child Poverty Action Group 9.

[35]   See, for example, Frederick Mills, 'The Ideology of Welfare Reform: Deconstructing Stigma' (1996) 41 Social Work 391; Mary O'Hara, *The Shame Game: Overturning the Toxic Poverty Narrative* (Policy Press 2020).

cially if they are single mothers.[36] These negative prejudices have an enormous influence on policy debates. They are often used by those advocating for restrictive social assistance policies.[37]

The use of expressions such as 'handout', 'benefit scrounger', 'skiver' and 'welfare dependent' – contrasted with 'hard-working responsible citizens' – became common among politicians advocating for austerity measures after the global financial crisis in 2008. These negative narratives might have exacerbated the devastating impact of the crisis on human rights[38] and increased inequality.[39]

In 2012 the then Chancellor of the Exchequer of the United Kingdom argued that cutting welfare benefits was about 'being fair to the person who leaves home every morning to go out to work and sees their neighbour still asleep, living a life on benefits'.[40] Under this rhetoric, the conservative-liberal government undertook severe cuts to social security and public services.[41] In 2017 President Donald Trump, speaking about welfare reforms in very similar terms, noted that people on welfare 'do not work at all', 'and have no intention to work' and make more money than people who 'live next door working three jobs'.[42] Similar negative stereotypes are also common in countries where the majority of the population live in poverty and a considerable percentage of the population are on social assistance programs. For example, in 2019 the President of Mexico, Andrés Manuel Lopez Obrador, compared those receiving benefits with pets that one must feed for them not to die[43] and suggested that those receiving social assistance are not making an adequate use of the benefits received.[44]

The media often exacerbates the problem of false generalizations and the idea that recipients would not make good use of funds by negatively influencing public perception about such programs. A study in the United Kingdom, for example, has shown the considerable increase in the number of newspaper articles related to welfare fraud and alleged abuses in 2010 when the government was promoting the welfare cuts.[45] In the last decade, these stigmatizing narratives have been utilized in policy debates to promote budgetary cuts to social protection programs

---

[36] Mills (n 35).

[37] ibid.

[38] See, e.g., Aoife Nolan, *Economic and Social Rights after the Global Financial Crisis* (CUP 2014).

[39] See, e.g., Tracy Shildrick, *Poverty Propaganda: Exploring the Myths* (Policy Press 2018).

[40] 'British Attitudes to Welfare have Undergone a Quiet Revolution' [13 July 2019] The Economist 29 (quoting the then chancellor George Osborne in 2012).

[41] Edwin Lane, 'Q&A: Government Spending Review' (*BBC*, 18 October 2010) <www.bbc.co.uk/news/business-10810962> accessed 30 June 2020.

[42] Ian Scwartz, 'Trump: Some Welfare Recipients Make More Than Person Working Their "Ass Off"' (*Real Clear Politics*, 29 November 2017) <www.realclearpolitics.com/video/2017/11/29/trump_some_welfare_recipients_make_more_money_than_person_working_their_ass_off.html> accessed 30 June 2020.

[43] See AMLO Compares Caring for People in Poverty with Caring for Animals (Animal Politico, 29 March 2019) <www.animalpolitico.com/2019/03/amlo-compara-atencion-pobreza-animales/> accessed 30 June 2020.

[44] 'AMLO Urges Program Beneficiaries "Not Play Dumb" and Use Money Well' (Aristegui Noticias, 13 December 2019) <https://aristeguinoticias.com/1312/mexico/insta-amlo-a-beneficiarios-de-programas-a-no-hacerse-patos-y-usar-bien-el-dinero-video/> accessed 30 June 2020.

[45] The study included national and selected regional titles in the United Kingdom. 'British Attitudes to Welfare Have Undergone a Quiet Revolution' [13 July 2019] The Economist. See also O'Hara (n 35).

and the establishment of restrictive and punitive design features under the rubric of 'austerity measures', which have been expanded around the world.[46]

In low- and middle-income countries, although social protection is increasingly grounded on a widely shared understanding that poverty is multidimensional and persistent in time and across generations, the idea of reaching only the 'deserving poor' continues to underpin many social assistance programs. This is evident, for example, in the widespread expansion of conditional cash transfers programs (CCTs) as the main social protection program in developing countries. According to data from 2016, 129.8 million people in Latin America and the Caribbean receive conditional cash transfers. In terms of population percentage, this equals to 20.2 per cent of the regional population.[47]

CCTs are monetary benefits for lower-income households that require beneficiaries to meet specific behavioral requirements called conditionalities or co-responsibilities, such as school attendance, immunizations and health checks. The consequences for noncompliance with the conditionalities vary. It goes from the suspension of benefits (in most cases) to specific support interventions to help families fulfill the conditionalities.[48]

Proponents of conditionalities argue that they are necessary to influence the behavior and attitudes of the recipients in order to improve health and education outcomes.[49] This argument is based upon the assumption that in the absence of conditionalities beneficiaries would not make the same investment in human capital. This argument is not only paternalistic but demeaning. It assumes that recipients are irrational or incapable of making rational choices to improve their livelihood. Evidence suggests that it is possible that the same improvements in health and education could be achieved without imposing conditionalities.[50]

Conditionalities deprive the poorest of the freedom to make decisions about their own welfare and that of their family, and the autonomy to determine their own lives. Moreover, conditionalities may also infringe the principle of equality and non-discrimination. They entail behavioral control over the poorest segments of the population that is not imposed on other social and economic sectors that also benefit from public policies. For example, in many countries high-income families are eligible for tax exemptions just because they have children. This tax credit which is, strictly speaking, a kind of transfer, comes with no conditions at all. In contrast, CCTs which are targeted to poor families with children, impose conditions and

---

[46]   Isabel Ortiz and others, 'The Decade of Adjustment: A Review of Austerity Trends 2010-2020 in 187 Countries' (2015) Extension of Social Security (ESS) Working Paper No 53 <www.ilo.org/wcmsp5/groups/public/---ed_protect/---soc_sec/documents/publication/wcms_431730.pdf> accessed 30 June 2020.

[47]   Simone Cecchini and Bernardo Atuesta, *Conditional Cash Transfer Programmes in Latin America and the Caribbean: Coverage and Investment Trends* (The Economic Commission for Latin America and the Caribbean (ECLAC) 2017) <https://repositorio.cepal.org/bitstream/handle/11362/42109/1/S1700429_en.pdf> accessed 30 June 2020.

[48]   Pablo Ibarrarán and others (eds), *How Conditional Cash Transfers Work: Good Practices after 20 Years of Implementation* (Inter-American Development Bank 2017) <https://publications.iadb.org/publications/english/document/How-Conditional-Cash-Transfers-Work.pdf> accessed 30 June 2020.

[49]   Ariel Fiszbein and others, *Conditional Cash Transfers: Reducing Present and Future Poverty* (The World Bank 2009) 10–11 <http://documents1.worldbank.org/curated/en/914561468314712643/pdf/476030PUB0Cond101Official0Use0Only1.pdf> accessed 30 June 2020.

[50]   Joseph Hanlon, Armando Barrientos and David Hulme, *Just Give Money to the Poor: The Development Revolution from the Global South*, United States (Kumarian Press 2010).

causes them to be stigmatized.[51] Another argument in favor of conditionalities is that they may ensure the support of taxpayers who would not see them as 'pure handouts' but tied to beneficiaries' 'positive behaviors'.[52] However, this argument can hardly be considered an objective and reasonable justification for differential treatment under international human rights law (see section B).

Stigmatization and prejudices also underpin claims that cash transfers will induce higher spending on tempting goods such as alcohol or tobacco, create dependency (reduce participation in productive activities) and increase fertility. While these claims are still very common in policy debates, there is strong evidence refuting these stigmatizing stereotypes.[53]

Programs based on prejudices and stigmatization not only threaten the enjoyment of rights but are also often ineffective and counterproductive. For example, studies suggest that stigma associated with social protection programs and perceptions of unfriendly social protection staff (e.g. 'institutional stigma' by social workers, teachers and healthcare providers) can be deterrents to seeking registration or taking up the transfer.[54] As a result, the effectiveness of the program in reaching the most vulnerable will decrease, and it will generate social exclusion.[55] A study in South Africa found that a substantial number of South African Social Security Agency (SASSA) staff were of the view that teen mothers seek pregnancy just to get the Child Support Grant (CSG). The prevalence of this attitude was found to be a common 'push factor' prompting several teenagers, as well as young women, not to apply for the CSG for their infants.[56] Sometimes programs inadvertently stigmatize their beneficiaries, particularly where they require them to admit publicly their poverty (e.g. through proxy means testing[57]) or a health condition (e.g. HIV/AIDS or disability) to qualify for support. For instance, evidence

---

[51] Simone Cecchini and others (eds), *Towards Universal Social Protection: Latin American Pathways and Policy Tools* (ECLAC 2015) <https://repositorio.cepal.org/bitstream/handle/11362/39484/1/S1500752_en.pdf> accessed 30 June 2020.

[52] Fiszbein and others (n 49).

[53] Sudhanshu Handa and others, 'Myth-Busting? Confronting Six Common Perceptions about Unconditional Cash Transfers as a Poverty Reduction Strategy in Africa' (2018) 33 The World Bank Research Observer 259.

[54] Jessica Stephens and Samantha Artiga, 'Key Lessons from Medicaid and CHIP for Outreach and Enrollment Under the Affordable Care Act' (The Kaiser Commission on Medicaid and the Uninsured, June 2013) 7 <http://files.kff.org/attachment/key-lessons-from-medicaid-and-chip-for-outreach-and-enrollment-under-the-affordable-care-act-issue-brief> accessed 30 June 2020.

[55] Quentin Wodon (ed), *Improving the Targeting of Social Programs in Ghana* (The World Bank 2012) <http://documents1.worldbank.org/curated/en/851201468030342038/pdf/764840PUB0EPI001300PUB0DATE09022012.pdf> accessed 30 June 2020.

[56] 'Preventing Exclusion from the Child Support Grant: A Study of Exclusion Errors in Accessing CSG Benefits' (*South African Social Security Agency (SASSA) and UNICEF*, 2013) 56 <www.unicef.org/southafrica/sites/unicef.org.southafrica/files/2019-07/ZAF-preventing-exclusion-from-the-child-support-grant-2013.pdf> accessed 30 June 2020.

[57] In the determination of indirect means (proxy means test), a series of variables are used as a welfare indicator: for example, income, consumption, income generation capacity, the quality of life index, and the vulnerability index. This estimate is calculated using variables statistically associated with the level of welfare. Typically, it includes demographic variables (e.g., household size), socio-economic variables (e.g., adult education level, asset holding and housing characteristics) and geographic variables (e.g., place of residence). The proxy generates a score that allows households to be sorted by estimated level of welfare. Together with the proxy formula, an eligibility threshold is determined for each program. Ibarrarán and others (n 48) 15–20.

shows that a program might create stigma simply by characterizing beneficiaries as being from the poorest households or living with HIV/AIDs or a disability.[58]

To comply with human rights norms and standards, social protection programs must uphold the dignity of those entitled to them and must avoid exposing recipients to any form of personal, social or institutional shame or stigmatization.[59] This limits the policy options in designing such programs. For example, in a school feeding program, the range of options go from those that stigmatize children (e.g. a program targeted to the 'poorest' children that directly or indirectly exposes them to other students or school staff) to those that do not generate stigmatization (e.g. providing the benefit to all children in the school). From a rights perspective, the former option must be excluded. Nonetheless, there are several other design options that might be in line with human rights, for example using pre-paid cards, so the children receiving free meals cannot be distinguished from those who are purchasing their meals, neither by other students nor by school staff.

As discussed below, when social protection programs are based on prejudices or include design or implementation features that stigmatize the beneficiaries, additional rights – beyond the right to social protection – might also be violated. As a result, those living in poverty end up more disempowered, vulnerable to other abuses and pushed into negative coping mechanisms. For example, evidence shows that some design features of the Universal Credit system in the United Kingdom, such as the mandatory wait of five weeks for receiving the initial payment, have pushed families into debt and into the hands of the exploitative loan industry which charge exorbitant interest rates.[60] Some beneficiaries have been driven to negative coping mechanisms such as survival sex.[61]

B.   The Right to Equality and the Prohibition of Discrimination

When social protection measures are based on prejudices, there are also infringements on the right to equality and the prohibition of discrimination. As noted by the CESCR:

---

[58]   Bernd Schubert and others, 'The Impact of Social Cash Transfers on Children Affected by HIV and AIDS: Evidence from Zambia, Malawi and South Africa' (*UNICEF*, 2007) <https://bettercarenetwork .org/sites/default/files/The%20Impact%20of%20Social%20Cash%20Transfers%20on%20Children %20Affected%20by%20HIV-AIDS.pdf> accessed 30 June 2020; Natalia Winder and Jenn Yablonski, *Integrated Social Protection Systems: Enhancing equity for children* (*UNICEF*, March 2012) 29 <https:// socialprotection.org/sites/default/files/UNICEF_SPSFramework.pdf> accessed 30 June 2020.

[59]   See e.g., CESCR, 'Concluding Observations on the Third Periodic Report of Japan, Adopted by the Committee at its Fiftieth Session' (10 June 2013) E/C.12/JPN/CO/3.

[60]   Mandy Cheetham, Suzanne Moffatt and Michelle Addison, '"It's Hitting People That can Least Afford it the Hardest": The Impact of the Roll out of Universal Credit in Two North East England Localities: A Qualitative Study' (*Fuse* and *Gateshead Council*, November 2018) <www .gateshead.govuk/media/10665/The-impact-of-the-roll-out-of-Universal-Credit-in-two-North-East -England-localities-a-qualitative-study-November-2018/pdf/Universal_Credit_Report_2018pdf.pdf?m= 636778831081630000> accessed 30 June 2020.

[61]   See e.g., the oral evidence presented to the Work and Pensions Committee of the House of Commons on 10 October 2018 on Benefit Cap, HC 1477 available at: http://data.parliament.uk/ writtenevidence/committeeevidence.svc/evidencedocument/work-and-pensions-committee/benefit-cap/ oral/91648.html (accessed September 2019). See also Marilyn Howard, 'Universal Credit and Financial Abuse: Exploring the Links' (*Women's Budget Group*, June 2018) <https://wbg.org.uk/wp-content/ uploads/2018/09/FINAL-full-report-financial-abuse-and-uc.pdf> accessed 30 June 2020.

Discrimination constitutes any distinction, exclusion, restriction or preference or other differential treatment that is directly or indirectly based on the prohibited grounds of discrimination and which has the intention or effect of nullifying or impairing the recognition, enjoyment or exercise, on an equal footing, of Covenant rights. Discrimination also includes incitement to discriminate and harassment.[62]

It is well-established in international law that, in addition to the prohibited grounds of discrimination expressly mentioned in international human rights treaties, i.e. race, colour, sex, language, religion, political or other opinion, national or social origin, property, or birth, the inclusion of 'other status' indicates that the list is not exhaustive and other grounds may be incorporated in this category. The CESCR has expressly noted that discriminating against those who live in poverty or are homeless implies a discrimination based on 'economic and social situation', which is a ground implicitly prohibited under Article 2 of the International Covenant on Economic, Social and Cultural Rights (ICESCR).[63] As noted, stigmatization and negative stereotyping can lead to the refusal of, or unequal access to, the enjoyment of certain rights such as education and health. [64]

The principle of equality does not mean that all persons should be treated equally and that all distinctions in treatment constitute discrimination.[65] There may be situations in which different treatment is justified. Under international law, a distinction, exclusion, restriction or preference is compatible with the principle of equality when (1) it has an objective and reasonable justification, (2) it pursues a legitimate aim under human rights law and (3) there is a reasonable relationship of proportionality between the means employed and the aim sought to realize.[66]

Differential treatment that complies with the criteria mentioned above is not discriminatory and does not infringe on the principle of equality and non-discrimination. Nonetheless, these criteria significantly limit the discretion of States in designing and implementing social protection programs. Regional human rights courts have expressly assessed stigma and negative stereotypes under the prohibition of discrimination, however not with the regularity that they should.

In assessing whether there is a violation of the prohibition of discrimination (if the difference in treatment was not objectively and reasonably justified), the European Court of Human Rights (ECHR) has noted that when people have suffered from widespread stigma and ostracism, States have a narrow margin of appreciation in choosing measures that subject those vul-

---

[62]   CESCR, General comment No. 20: Non-discrimination in Economic, Social and Cultural Rights (Art. 2, para 2, of the International Covenant on Economic, Social and Cultural Rights) (2 July 2009) UN Doc E/C.12/GC/20, para 7.

[63]   ibid para 35.

[64]   ibid.

[65]   For more information on the prohibition of discrimination in human rights law, see Sandra Fredman, *Discrimination Law* (2nd edn, OUP 2011).

[66]   These requirements have been developed by some of the major human rights' supervisory bodies. See, e.g. *Marckx v Belgium* App No 6833/74 (ECtHR, 13 June 1979) para 33; *Proposed Amendments to the Naturalization Provisions of the Constitution of Costa Rica*, Advisory Opinion OC-4/84, Inter-American Court of Human Rights Series A No 4 (19 January 1984) para 57; HRC, 'General Comment No. 18: Non-discrimination' (10 November 1989) UN Doc HRI/GEN/1/Rev9, para 13; CESCR, General Comment No. 20 (n 62) para 32.

nerable groups to differential treatment.[67] While the Court has focused on people living with HIV,[68] Roma, homosexuals and persons with mental disabilities,[69] the same reasoning would apply to the prejudices and social exclusion suffered by those living in poverty. Moreover, in several cases due to intersectional discrimination, people from the groups mentioned above might also be discriminated against for being poor (i.e. based on their economic situation). According to the ECHR, in the case of violation of rights, authorities must take all possible steps to ascertain whether a discriminatory attitude might have played a role.[70] Similarly, the Inter-American Court on Human Rights (I/A Court HR) has ruled that the failure to adopt positive measures to address the vulnerability caused by poverty, marginalization or economic circumstances amounts to discrimination.[71]

In addition to the prohibition of discrimination, several human rights treaties include specific provisions compelling States parties to adopt immediate and effective measures to combat stereotypes and prejudices. This is the case with the Convention on the Elimination of All Forms of Discrimination Against Women (Art. 5) and the Convention on the Rights of Persons with Disabilities (Art. 8). Both provisions are particularly important regarding intersectional discrimination when poverty converges with gender and disability. Increasingly, UN treaty bodies have addressed the stigma against those living in poverty under the prohibition of discrimination and the general provisions to combat stereotypes.[72] The treaty monitoring body that most regularly assesses issues of stigma is the Committee on the Rights of the Child (CRC). The CRC has expressed particular concern regarding the stigmatization of children with disabilities, children living with or affected by HIV/AIDS, street children, pregnant teenagers and adolescent mothers.[73]

However, this type of assessment is still not common in the work of UN treaty monitoring bodies, and there is much room for improvement in their analysis. For a more comprehensive assessment of the impact of stigma and stereotypes in the enjoyment of rights of those experiencing poverty, human rights monitoring bodies should deepen their understanding of poverty[74] and more consistently use a multidimensional understanding of poverty that

---

[67]   *Kiyutin v Russia* App No 2700/10 (ECtHR, 10 March 2011) para 64.

[68]   The prohibition of stigma against those living with HIV/AIDS has also been widely addressed by the United Nations and human rights monitoring bodies.

[69]   See e.g., *Kiyutin* (n 67) para 48; *Alajos Kiss v Hungary* App No 38832/06 (ECtHR, 20 May 2010) para 42.

[70]   See e.g., *B.S. v Spain* App No 47159/08 (ECtHR, 24 July 2012).

[71]   *Trabajadores de la Hacienda Verde v Brazil*, Judgement, Inter-American Court of Human Rights Series C No 318 (20 October 2016) paras 337–341.

[72]   See, e.g., CESCR, 'Concluding Observations on the Initial Report of Pakistan' (adopted 23 June 2017); UN Doc E/C.12/PAK/CO/1; CESCR, 'Concluding Observations on the Second Periodic Report of Lebanon' (adopted 7 October 2016); E/C.12/LBN/CO/2; and CESCR, 'Concluding Observations on the Initial Report of Uganda' (adopted 19 June 2015); E/C.12/UGA/CO/1.

[73]   See, e.g., Committee on the Rights of Child (CRC), 'Concluding Observations on the Combined Second and Third Periodic Reports of Saint Vincent and the Grenadines' (13 March 2017); UN Doc CRC/C/VCT/CO/2-3; CRC, 'Concluding Observations on the Fourth Periodic Report of Georgia' (9 March 2017); UN Doc CRC/C/GEO/CO/4; CRC, 'Concluding Observations on the Combined Second to Fourth Periodic Reports of Samoa' (12 July 2016); UN Doc CRC/C/WSM/CO/2-4; and CRC, 'Concluding Observations on the Combined Third to Fifth Periodic Reports of Kenya' (21 March 2016); UN Doc CRC/C/KEN/CO/3-5.

[74]   As it has been argued, understanding the complex and cross-cutting intersectional nature of poverty would enable the use of discrimination law not only by addressing poverty as a ground of

addresses stigma and stereotypes and aims to bring about structural change and tackle power imbalances.

C.   The Right to Privacy and Family Life

Other rights that are often violated by social assistance policies that are based on stereotypes and prejudices are the right to privacy and family life. Detractors of social protection programs claim that such programs would be a disincentive to work, that the beneficiaries would misuse money by purchasing alcohol or other superfluous things, or that they would try to deceive the system. Often their conclusion is that the only way this can be prevented or minimized is by putting in place excessive requirements and conditions on access to services and benefits as well as severe sanctions for non-compliance. Such measures include behavioral conditions on applicants (e.g. being required to actively seek work to receive unemployment benefit) and establishing complex systems of collecting information and intrusive checking of beneficiaries (e.g. searching their homes for evidence of fraudulent activity). Such measures often gain political traction as they are implemented alongside rhetoric that suggests they will ensure that only the 'deserving poor' receive support. However, these claims are not based on evidence but on unsupported prejudices.[75]

Sometimes those entitled to welfare benefits are subject to intensive examinations and investigations against supposedly fraudulent activity. This is particularly the case for those receiving lone parent benefits (the majority of which are mothers). Due to the entrenched stereotype of single mothers receiving benefits as sexually promiscuous, it is not uncommon that the system allows for intrusive, unannounced visits from social workers searching their homes for evidence of a 'man in the house' as sole evidence of fraud. In addition to violating the right to privacy and family life, these measures seek to control women's sexuality and impose presumed ideas of 'proper motherhood'.[76] Intrusive measures and welfare conditionalities have pushed some beneficiaries into negative behaviours, ranging from disengagement from the social security system to survival crime.[77]

These excessive and intrusive requirements undermine beneficiaries' independence, seriously interfere in their right to privacy and family life (e.g. Articles 16 CRC and 17 ICCPR), make them vulnerable to abuse and harassment and weaken community solidarity. These measures go against the dignity of the beneficiaries, as they punish, humiliate and undermine the autonomy of recipients of social assistance, exacerbating the challenges they face in overcoming their situation.[78]

---

discrimination but making discrimination law substantively relate to the disadvantages and inequalities. Shreya Atrey, 'The Intersectional Case of Poverty in Discrimination Law' (2018) 18 HRL Rev 411.

[75]   Handa and others (n 53).

[76]   Mills (n 35); Nancy Fraser, 'Women, Welfare and the Politics of Need Interpretation' (1987) 2 Hypatia 103.

[77]   'Final Findings Report: Welfare Conditionality Project 2013-2018' (*Welfare Conditionality*, June 2018) <www.welfareconditionality.ac.uk/wp-content/uploads/2018/06/40475_Welfare-Conditionality_Report_complete-v3.pdf> accessed 30 June 2020.

[78]   Emma Blower and Vijay K Nagaraj, *Modes and Patterns of Social Control: Implications for Human Rights Policy* (International Council of Human Rights Policy (ICHRP) 2010) <https://reliefweb.int/sites/reliefweb.int/files/resources/ECF99A000DD6839249257817000BBC5C-Full_Report.pdf> accessed 30 June 2020.

D.   The Best Interests of the Child

The principle of the best interests of the child is a paramount principle under the Convention on the Rights of the Child (CRC). The principle is also applied by regional human rights monitoring bodies, such as the I/A Court HR and the ECHR.[79]

According to the Committee on the Rights of the Child, the best interests of the child should be respected not only in judicial and administrative decisions, but also in all stages of the adoption of laws, policies, strategies, programs, plans, budgets, legislative and budgetary initiatives, and guidelines concerning children in general or as a specific group.[80] This includes upholding the child's best interests in designing, implementing and evaluating social protection programs.[81]

Sometimes, with the aim of reaching the 'deserving' poor, design features of social assistance programs may ignore the best interest principle. This is the case when parents or guardians are pushed into negative coping mechanisms. For example, forcing single mothers to seek employment when they have no access to childcare or delays in payments that create unnecessary stress can have negative impacts on their parenting. Parents' financial and psychological distress can negatively affect family relationships and parenting behaviors, increasing the risks of violence against children.[82]

Children can also be placed in potentially stigmatizing positions, in particular when social protection interventions are not sensitive to their specific vulnerabilities such as HIV/AIDS status, disability or ethnicity. One example is cash transfer programs that are targeted to AIDS-affected households. Although well-intentioned, this targeting is problematic due to issues related to stigma.[83] The stigmatization caused by targeted and conditional programs is one of the critical human rights arguments in favour of universal programs.

III.   THE CHALLENGES OF MOVING FROM 'UNDESERVING POOR' TO 'RIGHTS HOLDERS'

States have the discretion to formulate the public policies that are most appropriate for their circumstances. However, their discretion is limited by their human rights obligations. While it might be easier to gather political support for programs that are perceived to be effective in reaching those who 'deserve them' – and easier to portray such programs as resource-efficient

---

[79]   See, for example, *Juridical Condition and Human Rights of the Child*, Advisory Opinion OC-17/2002, Inter-American Court of Human Rights Series A No 17 (28 August 2002) para 65. At the European level, see e.g. cases Johansen v Norway App No 24/1995/530/616 (ECtHR, 7 August 1996); S.C. v The United Kingdom App No 60958/00 (ECtHR, 15 June 2004); C v Finland App No 18249/02 (ECtHR, 9 May 2006). The African Charter on the Rights and Welfare of the Child includes the principle in Article 4.

[80]   CRC, 'General Comment No. 14 on the Right of the Child to Have His or Her Best Interests Taken as a Primary Consideration (Art. 3, Para. 1)' (29 May 2013) UN Doc CRC/C/GC/14.

[81]   Sharon Detrick, *A Commentary on the United Nations Convention on the Rights of the Child* (Martinus Nijhoff Publishers 1999) 92.

[82]   Alexander Butchart and Susan Hillis, *INSPIRE: Seven Strategies for Ending Violence Against Children* (World Health Organization 2016) <www.who.int/publications/i/item/inspire-seven-strategies -for-ending-violence-against-children> accessed 30 June 2020.

[83]   Winder and Yablonski (n 58) 29.

– States have assumed a variety of legally binding obligations under which the respect of the dignity and rights of all recipients of social protection must be the main concern. Under such obligations, choices around policy options for social protection should not be based on negative stereotypes about those living in poverty or paternalistic considerations but rather on an understanding of beneficiaries as 'rights-holders'. The respect of their dignity, autonomy and full enjoyment of rights must prevail over any other political consideration.

Respect for dignity is an essential element of a rights-based approach. This means that any policy, design feature or de facto implementation of a social protection program with the potential for inducing shame due to their stigmatizing nature or explicit shaming must be avoided. Policies that reinforce a sense of dignity and freedom to make one's own choices and promote rights should be reinforced.

To this end, it is essential for both policymakers and human rights advocates to have a better understanding of the dignity-policy linkages. Policymakers as well as human rights practitioners and monitoring bodies should gain a better understanding of the interactions between shame, poverty and policy, and of the pathways through which policy can reduce shame or instill a sense of dignity.[84] They should also be able to assess whether the design and implementation of social protection programs are compatible with human rights norms and standards. Thus, at the domestic level, human rights advocates as well as national human rights monitoring bodies (e.g. national human rights institutions, parliamentary committees, or judges) should have the capacities and resources to hold policymakers accountable for policies that might violate human rights.

However, several challenges must be overcome. First, members of various communities of practice tend to work in silos. It would not be possible to address the complexities of poverty and inequality without working in an interdisciplinary manner, including development practitioners, economists, human rights lawyers, sociologists and anthropologists. Second, given the asymmetry of power between the beneficiaries of social assistance programs and policymakers who design, implement and monitor them, participation by those living in poverty is essential to ensure that their dignity and autonomy are respected. To this end, it is essential that social assistance programs incorporate mechanisms for ensuring meaningful and effective participation by those groups they are trying to benefit. There is a need to challenge technocratic styles of policymaking and more actively engage social movements, associations and NGOs legitimately representing those living in poverty as well as the direct participation by those living in poverty.

Participation is not only a right of those entitled to social protection, but their inclusion is also a way by which they can exert their agency and voice to shape the outcomes of social assistance programs instead of leaving program developers to 'guess' their needs based upon externally defined indicators.[85] Without their voices, the experience of disempowerment, discrimination and social exclusion of recipients will be overlooked, depriving authorities of the information needed to improve the design and implementation of programs.

---

[84]   Roelen (n 22).
[85]   Stephen Devereux and others, 'Evaluating Outside the Box: An Alternative Framework for Analysing Social Protection Programmes' (2013) IDS Working Paper No. 431 <https://onlinelibrary .wiley.com/doi/pdf/10.1111/j.2040-0209.2013.00431.x> accessed 30 June 2020.

IV.   CONCLUSIONS

Traditional poverty indicators are considered by many to be simplistic and unreliable. Effective and meaningful responses require finding consensus on the definition and measurement of poverty. Effective public policies and interventions require a clear understanding of who those living in poverty are and of what they are deprived.

The 2030 Agenda for Sustainable Development calls for the reduction of multidimensional poverty.[86] It also recognizes that a rights-based approach should underpin all poverty reduction efforts.[87] This multidimensional approach to poverty implies moving to measurements beyond income and deprivation to include dimensions which are important for those living in poverty. As argued here, this would require including the disempowerment caused by the infringement on their sense of dignity.

Policymakers should ensure that their policies do not stigmatize those living in poverty. Similarly, human rights practitioners should not neglect the feelings of shame and of humiliation that those experiencing poverty feel. Studies have shown that often individuals in poverty prioritize the emotional consequences of poverty even over material concerns. Ignoring issues such as stigma – and the shame it produces – would be ignoring the protection of the dignity of those living in poverty, which is the *raison d'etre* of human rights.

Human rights monitoring bodies have recognized the multidimensional aspect of poverty, at least when poverty has been defined by various bodies. However, they fail to regularly assess all aspects of poverty when monitoring compliance with human rights obligations. When monitoring compliance with human rights norms, human rights bodies should regularly assess whether actions or omissions from States infringe on the dignity and autonomy of those experiencing poverty. They should also better use the standards related to equality and non-discrimination, privacy and family life, and the principle of best interests of the child to determine whether those living in poverty are treated on an equal basis with those who are better off in society.

Finally, multidimensional poverty measures should reflect the experiences of those living in poverty. This will not be possible if people living in poverty do not have the opportunity to express their views and to actively and meaningfully participate in decision-making policies that affect their lives. The voices of those living in poverty must be included in the design, implementation, and evaluation of public policies. Their experiences of poverty must be sought to improve the understanding of multidimensional poverty. Social dimensions of poverty such as stigma and shame must be considered among its multidimensional components.

We have a collective responsibility for ensuring that stigmatizing messages around poverty do not influence public policies or infringe the rights, dignity and autonomy of those living in poverty. Despite progress made in recent years, interdisciplinary research on stigma and shame is still needed to advance understanding of poverty and how to fight it, respecting the rights of those experiencing poverty. This is an agenda that needs to be pushed forward by a range of actors but particularly by those who work on human rights.

---

[86]   Transforming our World (n 1).
[87]   ibid paras 18–20.

3.   Current perspectives on global poverty: rights, capabilities and social exclusion

Ayşe Buğra

The acute poverty that currently affects large groups of people in the countries of the Global South appears as a particularly disturbing problem since it co-exists with impressive developments in technological progress and wealth accumulation at a global level. In this context, debates on poverty include philosophical inquiries into moral norms and human rights as well as socioeconomic analyses of the problem.

The link between poverty and human rights, which was clearly articulated in the Universal Declaration of Human Rights, could not be said to have strong influence on the policy environment of the early post-Second World War period. The factors that explain the absence of this link in the framing of the dominant policy approaches of the period were of a different nature in developed and developing countries. In developed countries of the North, the idea of social rights was central to the emerging welfare state institutions and policies, but poverty was hardly a serious policy concern. In the South, the problem of poverty *within* nations was largely dominated by the debates on the poverty *of* nations, and there was not much interest in rights-based social policy ideas in the growing field of development studies. It was in the later decades of the post-Second World War period that poverty was recognized as an important social and political problem addressed by new methods of measurement, analysis and policy.

The human rights perspective is one of the dominant perspectives on poverty in the current social science literature. In this chapter, the human rights perspective is discussed in its relationship with 'capability' and 'social exclusion' perspectives to examine the similarities and differences in how each approach addresses salient questions in the poverty debate. The discussion does not engage with the debates around the legal framework of human rights and its core principles; rather it focuses on the arguments on poverty found in moral philosophy, political theory and the social sciences with reference to their implications for comparative poverty research as well as domestic and international policy efforts.

While the chapter insists on the problem of poverty in the Global South, it also discusses the evolution of the academic and policy concern for poverty in the Global North to investigate the applicability of the similar terms and frameworks of analysis in both contexts. Such an investigation must of course consider the difference between economic organizations, employment relations and political regimes in these different country contexts. However, the socio-economic changes brought along by the late twentieth century globalization have affected all countries, and the new forms of poverty that have emerged everywhere constitute a relevant subject of analysis across rich and poor countries. Poverty as a global phenomenon is now discussed in its different dimensions beyond the problem of extreme poverty, whereby the language of social rights acquires a novel relevance for policy analysis also in the countries of the Global South. This chapter addresses these developments in the context of the discussion on the theoretical grounding and policy relevance of the three perspectives on poverty: human rights, capabilities and social exclusion.

The first section of this chapter presents a discussion of the historical background to contemporary poverty analysis and policy. The second section examines the human rights perspective together with the capability approach and discusses the language of rights in relation to the language of capabilities and needs. In the third section, the social exclusion perspective is presented with its potential to integrate the moral framing of human rights into the policy-oriented approaches insisting on social citizenship rights as a response to world poverty. The conclusion draws attentions to the ongoing dialogue among different approaches to poverty in different country contexts and suggests that this dialogue provides important insights to future research agendas with the potential to contribute to the advent of a rights-based international policy environment.

I.   HISTORICAL BACKGROUND OF CONTEMPORARY POVERTY DEBATES

In Europe, concern with poverty as a problem that calls for policy action has a centuries-long history. Geremek writes that 'the first European attempts at statistical analysis were concerned primarily with estimating the number of poor', citing the works of Florentine chroniclers of urban life as an early example.[1] The origins of social policy can be traced back to sixteenth-century Europe, where both the scale and form of poverty associated with the emergence of early capitalism rendered traditional mechanisms of religious charity inadequate, and the lay authorities of rapidly growing European cities were required to introduce public policies of assistance to the poor. Juan Luis Vives's treatise on *Assistance to the Poor (De Subventione Pauperium)*, which was written in this context, could well be seen as a text in social policy.[2] The treatise was intended to contribute to social reform initiatives in European cities, and although some of its arguments were not of a nature to receive a positive response from the Catholic Church, it enjoyed widespread popularity and was influential in the policy circles in several countries.[3]

The policy environment, which was shaped by the rise of a new consciousness of poverty as a social problem in early modern Europe, could be described with reference to the attempts 'to regulate poverty' in a way that would reconcile the economic interests in having a growing supply of labour force with the social uneasiness caused by the sight of human deprivation and the fear of crime and disease associated with the proximity of poor people.[4] However, the sixteenth-century arguments insisting on the political responsibilities to assist the poor brought along a new approach to poverty – beyond the sentiments of benevolence and charity – which might also be said to anticipate the emergence of the language of rights in the approaches to poverty.

After the Second World War, the link between poverty and human rights was clearly articulated in the Universal Declaration of Human Rights (UDHR), the foundational document of

---

[1]   Bronisław Geremek, *Poverty: A History* (Blackwell 1997) 118– 9.

[2]   Juan Luis Vives, *On Assistance to the Poor* (University of Toronto Press in association with the Renaissance Society of America 1999).

[3]   ibid; See also Geremek (n 1) 184–205.

[4]   See, for example, Frances Fox-Piven and Richard A Cloward, *Regulating the Poor: The Functions of Public Welfare* (Vintage Books 1993).

the global human rights regime, and strengthened in the International Covenant on Economic, Social and Cultural Rights (ICESCR). Article 25 of the UDHR touched upon many different aspects of poverty as a multidimensional problem while also making a statement about the content of social rights.[5] Social rights also constituted a central concept around which the emerging welfare state policies and institutions were being shaped. In a seminal contribution to the theoretical foundations of the welfare state, T.H. Marshall extensively discussed how social rights had come to complement civil and political rights in the twentieth century.[6] However, poverty was hardly addressed in the policy environment in developed capitalist countries at that time.

In these countries, the question of social rights was addressed mainly in relation to social security provision and access to social services for the population at large. The long historical legacy of policies targeting the poor were not considered to be relevant for the framing of a rights-based approach. The priority assigned to full employment with the conviction that it was a both necessary and attainable objective, formed an important basis for welfare state policies.[7] Unemployment was emphasized as the crucial policy problem, and the question of social rights was addressed mainly in relation to social inequality. It was not until the 1970s that the limitations of the welfare state to make social rights a reality for all members of the society began to be discussed. The awareness of the need to combat persistent poverty also appeared as one of the priorities of the European Commission in the 1970s. Between 1975 and 1980 several reports on poverty were prepared in the context of the first European anti-poverty program. Other anti-poverty programs followed; by the 1990s the social exclusion perspective became central to poverty analysis and policy in Europe.[8]

In the countries of the South, too, many of the terms and concerns of the contemporary poverty debate were not present in the early post-Second World War era. In the 1950s and 1960s, it was underdevelopment and development of nations, rather than individual poverty as a social and human problem that dominated intense debates at the international level. Development economics was a new and inspiring sub-field of economics contributing to a widely shared optimism about the possibility of the poor countries catching up with the rich ones through structural and institutional changes guided by right policies and supported by international organizations.

The origin of the contemporary poverty debate in the South can be traced back to the loss of this optimism and the widespread disillusionment about international development performance in the early post-war decades.[9] In the beginning of the 1970s when the reality of persistent poverty in developing countries could hardly be overlooked, the existing theories and policies of development came under critical scrutiny from different directions. There

---

[5] Universal Declaration of Human Rights (adopted 10 December 1948 UNGA Res 217(A)(III) (UDHR) art 25).

[6] Thomas Humphrey Marshall, 'Citizenship and Social Class' in Thomas Humphrey Marshall, *Class, Citizenship, and Social Development: Essays by T. H. Marshall* (1st edn, Doubleday Anchor Books 1965) 71–134.

[7] William Beveridge, *Full Employment in a Free Society* (George Allen and Unwin 1944) 11–23.

[8] Bernd Schulte, 'A European Definition of Poverty: The Fight against Poverty and Social Exclusion in the Member States of the European Union' in Peter Townsend and David Gordon (eds), *World Poverty: New Policies to Defeat and Old Enemy* (The Policy Press 2002) 147–70; Martin Evans, 'Behind the Rhetoric' (1998) 29(1) IDS Bulletin 42.

[9] Gerald Meier, *Leading Issues in Economic Development* (Oxford University Press 1976) 1–11.

were, first, critical assessments of the context of international relations, which were seen as perpetuating and enhancing the underdevelopment of nations. There were intense discussions calling for a 'New International Economic Order' (NIEO), in which the structures of economic and decision-making power would be reshaped by considering the grievances and claims of developing nations. The independent Brandt Commission Report *North-South: A Programme for Survival* was a prominent contribution to the international reform initiatives addressing the inequalities between nations.[10] Critical views on the suggested reforms included those that emphasized the role of the dominant economic interests of the rich nations in keeping other countries in a state of underdevelopment and poverty.[11]

Theories and policies of development also came under attack from mainstream economics. In his Nobel Prize lecture of 1979 entitled *The Economics of Being Poor*, Theodore Schultz explicitly targeted development economics by dismissing the claims of the sub-discipline to introduce a methodologically different approach to problems specific to underdeveloped countries. Rejecting the idea that standard economic theory is inadequate for understanding low-income countries and following a line of analysis developed by human capital theory in economics, Schultz called for research projects directed at understanding and improving the potential for 'efficient entrepreneurship' of poor people and developing their 'human capital' with investments in health and education.[12]

Human capital theory was not the only channel to approach health and education as important issues to consider in poverty analysis and policy. Around the time of Schultz's Nobel Prize lecture, the idea of 'human development' became central to a new policy agenda that reflected the awareness that beyond the statistics on income or consumption, indicators on health and education were also significant for the assessment of poverty. The 1980 World Development Report (WDR) of the World Bank was entitled *Poverty and Human Development*. In 1990 UNDP began to publish the annual Human Development Reports (HDR), which use the Human Development Index (HDI). In contrast to rankings based only on Gross National Income per capita, the HDI also considered health and education outcomes. Since then, the HDRs were expanded with the introduction of different indicators, such as the Human Poverty Index in 1997 and the Multi-dimensional Poverty Index in 2010, which constitute valuable sources of information for comparative poverty research.

The human development approach has been important in generating new avenues of research beyond the existing theories of development and underdevelopment. Central to this new research orientation is Amartya Sen's seminal contribution to the analysis of poverty. Sen's work in this area originated in the context of the world food crisis of the mid-1970s, which had an important role in the growing concern with poverty with its association with natural, economic or political crisis situations.[13]

---

[10]   Willy Brandt, *North-South, A Programme for Survival: The Report of the Independent Commission on International Development Issues under the Chairmanship of Will Brandt* (Pan 1980).

[11]   Theresa Hayter, *The Creation of World Poverty* (Pluto Press 1982).

[12]   Theodore Schultz, 'The Economics of Being Poor' (1980) 88(4) Journal of Political Economy 639.

[13]   Some approaches to the food crisis of the mid-1970s have drawn attention to the relationship between food supply and population growth. But the debates about the dynamics of international relations as the main cause of the problem at hand were also important. Susan George for example, insisted on agribusiness interests in rich countries as the main determinant of food scarcity and starvation in poor countries: Susan George, *How the Other Half Dies: The Real Reasons for World Hunger* (Penguin Books 1976).

Sen's *Poverty and Famines* was prepared for the World Employment Programme (launched by the International Labour Organization), and it was published as a book in 1981.[14] By examining particularly devastating famine cases, Sen shifted the emphasis from food supply to the opportunities of access to food as the crucial factor behind mass starvation. He insisted that one has to look at *entitlement relations*, which define the opportunities of access to commodities in general, and to food during a crisis situation in particular, in order to understand starvation (or poverty more generally). He observed that the decline in 'exchange entitlements', which was the precipitating factor in the famines he analysed, did not occur in functioning democracies. He thus posited a relationship between famines and democracy.

Sen defined entitlements as the set of alternative commodity bundles that a person can command in a society using the totality of rights and opportunities that he or she faces. Some of his critiques insisted that this definition is descriptive rather than normative; it does not extend to the ethical connotations of the term entitlement and does not, therefore, incorporate a statement on the right to food or other basic items.[15] Nevertheless, Sen's idea of entitlements would later lead to the development of the capability approach, which has certain parallels with the human rights perspective, as will be discussed in the following section.

II. CAPABILITIES, RIGHTS AND NEEDS

A. Poverty as Capability Deprivation

The importance of *Poverty and Famines* in giving direction to the analysis of poverty cannot be overstated. The criticisms directed at the fundamental assertions and the methodological bases of the entitlement approach constitute a growing literature in the decades following the publication of Sen's study. The idea that famines do not occur in functioning democracies has been the subject of ongoing empirical questioning. Other criticisms include those that insist on the importance of war and violence, which Sen did not consider in his emphasis of the natural and economic factors in food shortage.[16]

Conflict prevention would later appear as a central issue to be considered in the attempts to alleviate the immediate impact of food crises, as well as to combat poverty in general. In this regard, Frances Stewart wrote that at the end of the 1990s 'eight of the ten countries with the worst Human Development Index (HDI), and similarly eight of ten countries with the lowest gross national product (GNP) per capita, have had major civil wars in the recent past'.[17] As she was drawing attention to the importance of conflict prevention, Stewart also pointed at 'horizontal inequalities' among different political, economic and social groups, which provide the basis for inter-group animosity; she therefore suggested a methodological orientation where groups, rather than individuals or households, would become the unit of analysis.[18]

---

[14] Amartya Sen, *Poverty and Famines: An Essay on Entitlements* (Clarendon Press 1981).

[15] Stephen Devereux, 'Sen's Entitlement Approach: Critiques and Counter-critiques' (2001) 29(3) Oxford Development Studies 245.

[16] ibid.

[17] Frances Stewart, 'Crisis Prevention: Targeting Horizontal Inequalities' (2000) 28(3) Oxford Development Studies 245.

[18] ibid.

Against the background of Sen's early work on famines where the emphasis was on the absence of opportunities rather than the availability of resources, the concept of capabilities has emerged as the determining factor behind starvation and suffering. The same emphasis informs the definition of poverty as 'capability deprivation'. This means the absence of freedom to avoid hunger, ill health, illiteracy, but also other limitations such as political repression or various forms of discrimination that prevent people from pursuing their valued ends of life. The idea of capability refers to the opportunity to achieve valuable combinations of human *functionings* – what a person is able to do and to be. Capabilities are substantive freedoms to avoid deprivations that any reasonable person would seek to avoid. In Sen's words: 'Many of the terrible deprivations in the world have arisen from a lack of freedom to escape destitution. Even though indolence and inactivity had been classic themes in the old literature on poverty, people have starved and suffered because of a lack of alternative possibilities'.[19]

The capability perspective was particularly important in situating poverty in development studies as a problem of central significance that could be rigorously analysed in a policy relevant approach. In *Development as Freedom* Sen presents the expansion of substantive freedoms as the objective of development and discusses freedoms that have an instrumental value to attain this goal. These instrumental freedoms include political freedoms, economic resources (owned, obtained by exchange or by access to credit), social opportunities (i.e. access to education or health services), protective security (i.e. unemployment insurance or income support mechanisms), and transparency guarantees (openness and trust in institutions or policies). As such, they define a broad area where both the underlying causes of and remedies for capability deprivation can be depicted.[20]

An important aspect of the capability approach is Sen's distinction between means or resources, and actual opportunities. The distinction emerges from a series of factors, including characteristics of the environment (natural hazards, epidemic diseases or high crime rates) and physical or mental differences between people (related to disability or sickness for example). The capability approach also allows for the consideration of intra-household allocation of resources among different family members with particular reference to the disadvantaged position of women. Sen highlights the gender dimension of capability deprivation in a striking fashion in an article drawing attention to the discrepancy between the normally expected and actual statistics of male and female populations.[21] Comparing the female/male sex ratios in developed countries (around 1.5 or 1.6) with those in South and West Asian countries and China (as low as 0.94), he found a considerable number (about a 100 million) of 'missing women'. He explained the excessive female mortality as resulting from the unequal allocation of food and care favouring boys.[22] The question of missing women continues to be a prominent issue in the literature on gender discrimination and disadvantage.[23]

---

[19]   Amartya Sen, 'Human Rights and Capabilities' (2005) 6(2) Journal of Human Development 151, 155. See also Amartya Sen, *Commodities and Capabilities* (North Holland 1985).

[20]   Amartya Sen, *Development as Freedom* (Alfred A. Knopf 1999).

[21]   Amartya Sen, 'More Than 100 Million Women are Missing' (20 December 1990) The New York Review of Books.

[22]   ibid.

[23]   Elisabeth J Croll, 'Amartya Sen's 100 Million Missing Women' (2001) 29(3) Oxford Development Studies 225; see also Martin Ravallion, *The Economics of Poverty* (Oxford University Press 2016) 370–71.

The capability approach has been very influential in carrying the analysis of poverty beyond concerns about income and consumption. By highlighting the importance of domestic political factors, national institutions and policies in the occurrence and prevention of deprivation in a given society, it has played an important role in shifting the emphasis from the poverty of nations to poverty within nations, and provided a basis for comparative, policy-oriented research on the subject.

B.   Poverty as a Violation of Human Rights

Approaches to poverty as a violation of human rights came later to the agenda of the United Nations (UN). The mandate on extreme poverty was first established by the UN Commission on Human Rights and was taken over by the Human Rights Council in 2006. At the same time there were also expressions of frustration about the delay with which the widespread academic interest in the question of poverty in the social sciences reached the legal studies and philosophy.[24] Philosophical inquiries into human rights to basic necessities of life, Alan Gewirth's work in particular, have been particularly important in giving direction to later work in the area. Thomas Pogge's *World Poverty and Human Rights* also constitutes an important early contribution to the subject in political theory.[25] In 2002 UNESCO launched a project on poverty including a series of workshops. A collection of articles published on the basis of the first cycle of these workshops was edited by Pogge and was dedicated to Alan Gewirth.[26]

Gewirth had passed away before the publication of the book, but the edited collection includes an article by him. The article is developed around the idea that the poor have a moral right to be assisted in achieving the basic necessities of life and this moral right imposes correlative duties: 'not imperfect duties of charity, humanity or solidarity, but perfect, stringent, and in principle enforceable duties of justice'.[27]

In Gewirth's approach, it is the concept of 'human action' that underlies and justifies the invocation of rights. He presents the actions that are prescribed in moralities as having two necessary conditions: (1) the voluntary behaviour of the persons that have autonomy and (2) purposiveness or intentionality. He calls these conditions freedom and well-being, which every agent must regard as necessary goods for himself, since without them 'he would not be able to act either at all or with general success in achieving his purposes'.[28] All agents must therefore hold that they have rights to freedom and well-being to be accepted by others, and consequently, accept that others also have these rights. Severe economic deprivation, like political oppression, is inimical to the fulfilment of the necessary conditions of human action and the development of the abilities of agency. It therefore presents a violation of human rights.

This formulation presents the basic tenets of the human rights perspective on poverty. This perspective is based on the view that rights are pre-political rather than the outcomes of insti-

---

[24]   Octavio L. M. Ferraz, 'Poverty and Human Rights' (2008) 28(3) O.J.L.S. 585.
[25]   Alan Gewirth, *Community of Rights* (Chicago University Press 1996); Thomas Pogge, *World Poverty and Human Rights: Cosmopolitan Responsibilities and Reforms* (Polity Press 2002).
[26]   Thomas Pogge (ed), *Freedom from Poverty as a Human Right* (Oxford University Press 2007).
[27]   Alan Gewirth, 'Duties to Fulfil the Human Rights of the Poor' in Pogge (n 26) 219–36, 219.
[28]   ibid 222.

tutional arrangements. As Gewirth puts it: 'right is a moral concept before it is a legal one'.[29] As such, rights are universal and entail duties unbounded by national boundaries toward all persons everywhere whose capacity for moral agency is at risk because their freedom and well-being is undermined by their lack of the means of subsistence.

Contributions from the human rights perspective have used striking statistics on human deprivation to draw attention to the seriousness of the problem. For example, Pogge writes that 'Roughly one-third of all human deaths, 18 million annually or 50,000 each day, are due to poverty-related causes, preventable through better nutrition, safe drinking water and sewage systems, cheap rehydration packs, vaccines, antibiotics, and other medicines . . . Despite undisputed great importance of such basic necessities for human life, there is no agreement on whether human beings have a *right*, or *human right*, to such necessities'.[30]

C.   Human Rights Perspective and Policy Related Questions

Theoretically-based justification of poverty as a human rights problem, along with statistical grounding of the seriousness of the problem, has the potential to play an important role in raising consciousness and generating concern about global poverty. However, the transition from the framing of poverty around ethical necessity and moral responsibility to a frame focused on policy design and implementation is not very straightforward. Anti-poverty policies need to address a series of questions pertaining to the identification of rights, the duties entailed by rights, the bearers of these duties, and the manner in which what is necessary for the fulfilment of human rights is provided to right holders.[31]

In her answer to the question 'what are human rights rights to?', Nussbaum appeals to the concept of capabilities and attempts to provide an overreaching list of capabilities to bring precision to the content of human rights.[32] Sen, however, thought that such a list, prepared once-for-all, for all societies, without public debate, would be highly problematic. First, it would be difficult to prepare an exact list of capabilities and to determine the relative weights to be assigned to the items on the list without the specification of the social and economic context of their use, which would vary in different societies and is likely to change in time. Second, the preparation of such a list would necessarily preclude continued social discussion on its specific content; public reasoning would have no place in this process. Sen's insistence on public reasoning does not stem from a concern for the inter-cultural differences on the subject of freedoms and rights; rather it reflects a belief in the importance of dialogue and intellectual interaction within countries and across borders, which would affect people's ideas and claims. It is precisely this type of dynamic development of people's claims that would be arrested by an expert-prepared list of fundamental capabilities as a basis for giving content

---

[29]   ibid 219–36, 221; See also Martha Nussbaum, 'Poverty and Human Functionings: Capabilities as Fundamental Entitlements' in David B Grusky and Ravi Kanbur (eds), *Poverty and Inequality* (Stanford University Press 2007) 47–75, 53.

[30]   Thomas Pogge, 'Severe Poverty as a Human Rights Violation' in Pogge (n 26) 11–54, 12–13.

[31]   For a discussion of the difficulties that emerge in relation to these questions, see Arjun Sengupta, 'Poverty Eradication and Human Rights' in Pogge (n 26) 323–44.

[32]   Nussbaum (n 29); In an analytically less rigorous fashion, the UN reports sometimes use the language of rights along with the language of capabilities: United Nations Human Rights Council, *Guiding Principles on Extreme Poverty and Human Rights* (Office of the United Nations High Commissioner for Human Rights 2012).

and precision to human rights. With these concerns in mind, Sen was reluctant to see 'freedom from poverty as a human right', although he accepted that in certain ways, the capability approach has a close affinity with human rights perspective.[33]

In relation to the question 'who are the bearers of correlative duties?', the human rights approach examines the role of human decisions that contribute to the persistence of severe poverty. These decisions are made by national governments as well as other political actors who contribute to the shaping of the global economic order. In this regard, Pogge distinguishes between 'acts' that actually contribute to the violation of the human rights of the poor and 'omissions' that have to do with the failure to take action to mitigate poverty where this could be done without incurring significant costs. While acts are directly associated with the negative duties of not actively causing deprivation rather than with the positive duties to mitigate poverty, Pogge insists that an exact line is difficult to draw between acts and omissions, and thus between negative and positive duties.[34]

It could be argued that the duties entailed by rights claims fall upon not only national and international political decision makers, but also on the affluent members of rich countries who could play a role in alleviating poverty at a low cost to them.[35] However, these duties would be easier to specify and more plausible if, rather than individual responsibilities, the role of the institutional order and the duties of governments were addressed. Pogge, for example, accepts that awareness of the dimensions of the problem among affluent individuals could help to mobilize concerted action to combat poverty. However, he affirms that the rules governing economic transactions are the most important causal determinant of the incidence and depth of poverty: 'Morally successful rules are so much easier to sustain than morally successful conduct'.[36]

By questioning the extent to which morally successful rules could be effectively set by national governments, the human rights perspective draws attention to the limitations of 'internalist' approaches – where the duty of poverty mitigation is expected to be carried out solely, or primarily, by national governments. Even where democratic governments aim to respond to the rights claims of their citizens, their ability to eradicate the obstacles to the fulfilment of human rights could be limited by prevailing international power relations as well as the availability of resources.[37]

Pogge, who insists on the role of international institutions in generating and enhancing global poverty, tends to follow a distinctly externalist position. He argues that the causal factors behind the contemporary scope and depth of extreme poverty stem from injustices that could be traced back to the legacy of colonialism and significantly involve the institutional framework of global economic transactions. The negative responsibility of changing this global institutional order that causes poverty and harms the poor should be assumed by the governments of rich countries and by international organizations. These actors also have

---

[33]   Amartya Sen, 'Human Rights and Capabilities' (2005) 6(2) *Journal of Human Development.*
[34]   Pogge (n 30).
[35]   Elizabeth Ashword, 'The Duties Imposed by the Human Right to Basic Necessities' in Pogge (n 26) 183–218.
[36]   Pogge (n 30) 11–54, 26.
[37]   Gewirth (n 27); Pogge (n 26).

positive responsibilities to contribute to the fulfilment of the human rights for millions of individuals living in extreme poverty.[38]

The human rights approach highlights how extreme poverty cripples the agency of poor people and limits the effective use of civil and political rights. As Pogge puts it: 'The very poor people are typically unable to defend their civil and other legal rights effectively. They may be illiterate due to lack of schooling or preoccupied with their family's survival. Or they may be compelled by social dependency to put up with illegal treatment'.[39] This argument, which starts by accepting the limits of poor people's agency, could be criticized for incorporating a tendency to regard the poor as passive victims and for suggesting that little input is expected from them regarding what basic necessities of life should be made available for the fulfilment of their human rights.

D.   Needs and Rights

The criticisms directed at poverty experts for their presentation of the poor as passive victims have an old history. Chambers, for example, insists on how the standardized views of the professionals differ from the reality of poor people's lives as experienced and understood by them. He highlights the importance of participatory field research to enable the poor to analyse and articulate the nature of their deprivations and claims.[40] Some of the responses to the idea of 'basic needs' also take issue with the patronizing tendency inherent in the attempts to identify poor people's needs without allowing them to have a voice in the process.[41]

The basic needs approach has appeared in the development literature especially through the contributions of Paul Streeten.[42] Streeten has insisted on policies targeting the most basic means of subsistence rather than introducing the question of rights to policy attempts to eradicate severe poverty in the countries of the Global South, which would impose unrealistically rigid demands and utopian expectations on the policy process. However, since the idea of basic necessities becomes central to the human rights perspective in the extension of theoretical justification to the realm of policy, the language of rights begins to be used in ways similar to the language of needs. The patronizing tendency criticized in the basic needs approach therefore acquires some validity also for the human rights perspective on poverty.

However, there are also arguments about the advantages of discussing rights and needs together in policy-oriented analyses of poverty. Frances Stewart, for example, has argued that discussing basic needs together with rights has the advantage of conferring a legal status to the former and enhancing political commitment to their satisfaction.[43] In a recent article, Gough

---

[38]   Pogge (n 30).

[39]   Thomas Pogge, 'Introduction' in Pogge (n 26) 1–10, 3.

[40]   Robert Chambers, 'Poverty and Livelihoods: Whose Reality Counts?' (1995) 7(1) Environment and Organization 173.

[41]   Ravallion (n 23) 119–20; Derrill D Watson, 'Poverty and Basic Needs' in David M Kaplan and P Thompson (eds), *Encyclopedia of Food and Agricultural Ethics* (Living Edition, Springer 2014).

[42]   Paul Streeten, 'The Distinctive Features of a Basic Needs Approach to Development' (1977) 19 (3) International Development Review 8; Paul Streeten, Shahid J Burki, Mahbub Ul-Haq, Norman Hicks and Frances Stewart, *First Thing First: Meeting Basic Needs in Developing Countries* (Oxford University Press 1981).

[43]   Frances Stewart, 'Basic Needs Strategies, Human Rights, and the Rights to Development' (1989) 11(3) Hum. Rts. Q. 347.

follows a different approach and presents an argument for social rights by drawing on a theory of universal basic needs which must be met in order for people to avoid harm, to participate in society, and to reflect critically on the conditions in which they find themselves.[44]

In his discussion of the identification of 'intermediate needs', which are need-satisfiers in a given social setting, Gough proposes a dual strategy which would incorporate citizen involvement and decentralized practices as well as the contribution of professional expert knowledge on generic need-satisfiers and ways of dealing with the constraints on their provision in specific social contexts. In Gough's approach, this strategy forms part of a general understanding of collective responsibilities entailed by the existence of core human needs and calls for a renewal of social citizenship. He argues that social rights provided a fundamental moral argument for the collective obligation to meet the basic needs of citizens in western welfare states and, in spite of the criticisms directed at the welfare state, the moral dialectic in the ascription of rights and obligation has an enduring relevance for the present. The idea of social citizenship might need to be re-imagined in light of the currently pressing problems of refugees and immigrants and extended beyond the nationals of given countries, but it remains a strong moral anchor to poverty analysis and policy.

III.　HUMAN RIGHTS, SOCIAL RIGHTS, AND THE SOCIAL EXCLUSION PERSPECTIVE: DEBATES ON INSTITUTIONS AND RESOURCES TO COMBAT POVERTY IN THE CONTEMPORARY GLOBAL ECONOMY

The references to the UDHR's statements on economic and social rights have an important place in the discussions of poverty as a violation of human rights. Questions emerge, however, about the extent to which the language of human rights now used in the literature is in conformity with the framing of social rights in the context of welfare state theories and policies. Through the emergence and development of the welfare state, nation states appeared as the main bearers of the correlative duties entailed by social rights, and unemployment and inequality were the major concerns addressed in terms of class relations.[45] The debate on social rights was, first and foremost, a political debate concerned with the politics of class and citizenship.

The difference between this particular approach to social rights and the moral framing of human rights in the discussions on extreme poverty is highlighted by Samuel Moyn, one of the harshest critics of the human rights movement, who uses such terms as 'antipolitics' and 'moral utopia' to describe the movement.[46] Moyn argues that in the post-Second World War era of national welfare, social rights were integral to human rights and were linked to egalitarian ideals. This, according to Moyn, contrasts with the post-cold war environment, when the

---

[44]　Ian Gough, 'Universal Basic Services: A Theoretical and Moral Framework' (June 2019) Pol.Q. <https://doi.org/10.1111/1467-923X.12706> accessed 12 June 2020; On theoretical foundations and ethics of needs, see Len Doyal and Ian Gough, *A Theory of Human Need* (Palgrave Macmillan 1991); Sarah Clark Miller, *The Ethics of Need: Agency, Dignity and Obligation* (Routledge 2012).

[45]　Marshall (n 6) 71–134; Walter Korpi, 'The Power Resources Model' in Christopher Pierson and Francis Castles (eds), *The Welfare State Reader* (Polity 2006) 76–87.

[46]　Samuel Moyn, *The Last Utopia: Human Rights in History* (Belknap Press 2012).

human rights movement prioritized 'sufficiency' over equality and the politics of equality was replaced by a new version of humanitarian concern for the global poor.[47]

While it is true that the human rights perspective is marked by the emphasis on extreme poverty, Moyn's point about the lack of a concern for international inequality is not justified. It is also not true to say that the language of human rights is always used without any concern for the question of domestic inequalities. Townsend and Gordon, for example, explore national as well as international responsibilities in an attempt to construct an anti-poverty policy strategy that recognizes the close relationship between the fulfilment of human rights and the fundamental right to social security. They argue that to combat poverty national governments should face the challenge of extending social security benefits to the population at large, a challenge which relates to the current problems of widespread informality and insecurity in employment relations. They also highlight the importance of government action to check the inequality of market outcomes and insist on redistributive policies that involve both taxation and public spending on universal benefits rather than targeted and means-tested transfers.[48] This introduces the point that not only the availability of basic necessities but also the manner in which they are made available to right holders must be considered in the discussion of the relationship between rights and poverty.[49] In this policy-oriented approach, the language of human rights continues to be used, but the approach also draws on the social exclusion perspective. It is also true that in some studies social exclusion is conceptualized as the lack of enforceable rights.[50]

The establishment of the ESRC Centre for Analysis of Social Exclusion at the London School of Economics has been important in generating a series of policy-oriented academic studies on social exclusion.[51] However, even in this European context, approaches to poverty as social exclusion differ in diagnosis of the problem and policy design.[52] In her analysis of the theoretical foundations of the concept of social exclusion, Hilary Silver defines three paradigms (solidarity, specialization and monopoly) to distinguish between the republican, liberal and social democrat approaches to the causes of poverty and the nature of social policy measures to be adopted for social inclusion.[53]

Notwithstanding these differences, the term social exclusion has dominated the European social policy arena since the 1990s. The term was originally introduced in reference to men-

---

[47]   Samuel Moyn, *Not Enough: Human Rights in an Unequal World* (Belknap Press 2018).

[48]   Peter Townsend, 'Poverty, Social Exclusion and Social Polarisation: The Need to Construct an International Welfare State' in Townsend and Gordon (n 8) 3–24; Peter Townsend and David Gordon, 'Conclusion: Constructing an Anti-poverty Strategy' in Townsend and Gordon (n 8) 413–31.

[49]   Arjun Sengupta, 'Poverty Eradication and Human Rights' in Pogge (n 26) 323–44, 336 ('A society of slaves having all these basic necessities will not be reckoned as enjoying human rights, not just because they lack the right to liberty but because those necessities are not provided in a rights-based manner.').

[50]   Tania Burchardt, Julian Le Grand, and David Piachaud, 'Introduction' in John Hills, Julian Le Grand and David Piachoud, *Understanding Social Exclusion* (Oxford University Press 2002) 1–12.

[51]   Anthony B Atkinson and John Hills (eds), 'Exclusion, Employment and Opportunity' (1998) LSE STICERD Research Paper No CASE004 <https://ssrn.com/abstract=1158895> accessed 12 June 2020 and Hills, Le Grand and Piachoud (n 50).

[52]   Martin Evans, 'Behind the Rhetoric: The Institutional Basis of Social Exclusion and Poverty' (1998) 29(1) IDS Bulletin 42.

[53]   Hilary Silver, 'Social Exclusion and Social Solidarity: Three Paradigms' (1994) 133(5–6) Int'l Lab.Rev. 531.

tally and physically handicapped, marginal and a-social persons.[54] It was in the context of the new challenges faced by the Keynesian welfare state that the term was adopted in the analysis of social disadvantage in European countries. The rise of neo-liberalism, as well as a series of transformations in the economic organization and the family structure, was instrumental in bringing about a widespread questioning of the underlying assumptions of welfare state policies. The questions raised had to do with the limits of welfare provision by the nation state in globalizing economies, the possibility of maintaining full employment in post-industrial societies with flexible employment relations, and changing gender relations that challenged the assumption of stable families with male breadwinners and female care providers. Social security systems have come under pressure with the newly significant reality of persistent unemployment, a-typical, precarious forms of employment, and the changing structure of the family. In this context, European anti-poverty programs have begun to define the poor as 'persons whose resources (material, cultural and social) are so limited as to exclude them from the minimum acceptable way of life in the member states in which they live'.[55]

The concern with inequality is reflected in the way the concept of social exclusion is used in the analysis of relative poverty with reference to people whose incomes are below a certain percentage of the median income of their country, for example by taking 40, 50 or 60 per cent of the median income as the relative poverty threshold. Not only people who are in relative income poverty, but those excluded from the labour market or regular employment, consumption or social security are also considered in this policy analysis.[56] Those excluded could be individuals, but also communities or neighbourhoods, occupational groups or groups such as women or ethnic minorities. Hence, policies aiming at the mitigation of income disparities at the national level are to be implemented along with policies targeting specific groups facing the threat of social exclusion.

While the social exclusion perspective has originated and is now widely used in Europe, the interest in this perspective has also extended to research and policy in development studies, especially with the studies initiated by the ILO.[57] Approaching poverty through the lens of social exclusion could foster dialogue between researchers in the North and the South and contribute mutual learning and understanding of the shared problems that emerge through global dynamics, as well as the differences associated with different levels of development and social contexts.[58]

Attempts to build such a bridge between poverty analysis and research in the North and the South seem meaningful in the current context of the global economy, where the changing

---

[54] René Lenoir, *Les Exclus* (Seuil 1974).

[55] Bernd Schulte, 'A European Definition of Poverty: The Fight against Poverty and Social Exclusion in the Member States of the European Union' in Townsend and Gordon (n 48).

[56] Atkinson and Hills (n 51). The exclusionary dynamics brought along by flexible employment relations in post-industrial societies and the questions of employment and class are highlighted by Byrne: David Byrne, *Social Exclusion* (Oxford University Press 1997).

[57] Charles Gore and Jose B Figueiredo (eds), *Social Exclusion and Anti-Poverty Policy: A Debate* (ILO 1997); See also Ajit Bhalla and Frederic Lapeyre, 'Social Exclusion: Towards an Analytical and Operational Framework' (1997) 28 Development and Change 413. More recently, the IDS Bulletin, a journal published by the Institute of Development Studies at the University of Sussex, had a special issue where many of the articles were on social exclusion: October 2017 48(1A) IDS Bulletin.

[58] Richard Longhurst, 'Introduction: Universal Development-Research and Practice' (October 2017) 48(1A) IDS Bulletin.

nature of human deprivation requires thinking beyond the old approaches to mass poverty in the South. To the extent that social policy has relevance for the development of new approaches to new problems, insights offered by the social exclusion perspective could be important for policy formulation and implementation.

In his Nobel Prize Lecture, Theodore Schultz said:

> Most of the people in the world are poor, so if we knew the economics of being poor, we would know much of the economics that matters. Most of the world's poor people earn their living from agriculture, so if we knew the economics of agriculture, we would know much of the economics of being poor.[59]

Today, it seems much more difficult to make such a categorical statement with confidence. While the rural population employed in agriculture is still important in the South, since the last decades of the twentieth century rural-urban migration has gained impetus and cities have grown as sites of extreme forms of urban deprivation.[60] In his statistical overview of the current dimensions of poverty and inequality, Martin Ravallion also observes that poverty is becoming more urban over time, and since the poor are urbanizing faster than the population as a whole, the pace of urban poverty reduction is lower than the average.[61]

Statistics on relative poverty also reveal the changing form of poverty in the South. Falling numbers of absolutely poor people in the world coincide with rising numbers of relatively poor. What is striking is that the incidence of relative poverty is higher in developing countries than in high-income ones. In Ravallion's words:

> While very few people living in rich countries are poor by the standards of the world's poor countries, when one adopts a concept of poverty that tries to allow for social exclusion and relative deprivation consistently with the structure of national poverty lines one also finds that relative poverty – as well as absolute poverty – is overwhelmingly found in the developing world.[62]

The reality of the increasing numbers of urban poor along with the rising importance of relative poverty in the Global South now make it more important to think about social policies that address the problems of employment and social security, as well as effective redistributive measures dealing with the inequality within nations. It is in this light that the relevance of the social exclusion perspective for poverty analysis and policy in the Global South should be assessed, albeit with due attention to the importance of international collaboration.

Townsend, for example, calls for an international welfare state by arguing for the development of national welfare states along with the establishment of an internationalized legal framework to protect human living standards. Steps in this direction would require scientific consensus to operationally define and measure international forms of poverty and social exclusion.[63] Furthermore, Townsend argues that statements about human rights need to be extended to the close monitoring of trends in access to rights and the contribution of key policies to those trends. The roles of major transnational corporations and international financial institutions

---

[59]   Schultz (n 12) 639.
[60]   See especially Mike Davis, *Planet of Slums* (Verso 2006).
[61]   Ravallion (n 23) 338.
[62]   ibid 350.
[63]   Townsend (n 48) 3–24.

such as the World Bank and the IMF should be assessed and redefined in conformity with the objective of more universally and securely establishing human rights and democratic values. Prioritizing redistribution in action programs and strengthening 'collective principles of public service, planning and social insurance' are significant elements of Townsend's proposals for international collaboration in the eradication of poverty as a violation of human rights and the prevention of social exclusion in legal and institutional policy frameworks.[64]

Whether poor nations have the financial resources necessary to provide universal social security benefits to their citizens remains a valid question. Nevertheless, one could also ask whether the share of public social spending in developing countries, which is currently much lower than in advanced countries, could not be increased even in a limited way by reconsidering development priorities. Still, international collaboration in the effort to combat poverty also extends to the contribution to overcome of financial resource constraints in the countries of the Global South. Proposals in this area include the introduction of a financial transaction tax, similar to Tobin's proposal in the 1970s to penalize short term speculative capital movements, or a Global Resources Dividend discussed by Pogge.[65] In spite of its widely discussed problems, official development assistance remains on the agenda of anti-poverty debate. For example, an aid target of one per cent of the GDP of advanced countries, an important element in the discussions on the New Economic Order in the 1970s, was revived by Atkinson with specific reference to the role the EU could play in the combat against poverty in the South.[66]

As Gordon writes: 'Ending poverty is largely a matter of political will. It is not a matter of lack of money or scientific knowledge on how to eradicate poverty'.[67] Dismantling the obstacles set by the limits of political will and administrative capacity in developing countries requires the involvement of international actors. This does not mean, however, that national policy efforts do not have an important place in policy-oriented poverty analysis.

IV.   CONCLUSION

The human rights perspective on poverty is characterized by the moral framing of poverty as a violation of human rights and by the emphasis on the present global economic order as a causal factor contributing to widespread poverty and harm the poor. Presenting a theoretically-based justification of poverty as a human rights problem and drawing attention to the duties entailed by the human rights of the poor, this perspective contributes to the development of an enhanced awareness and a stronger sense of responsibility among powerful decision makers and affluent individuals in developed countries. However, several questions emerge in relation to the contribution this perspective could make to comparative analysis of poverty and policy design in the current global environment.

Since the economic and social dislocations engendered by the dynamics of the late twentieth-century globalization now affect all countries in spite of their different levels of

---

[64]   Peter Townsend, 'Human Rights, Transnational Corporations and the World Bank' in Townsend and Gordon (n 48) 351–76.

[65]   ibid 368–69; Pogge (n 27) 196–215.

[66]   Tony Atkinson, '1% of €10,000 Billion' in Townsend and Gordon (n 48) 401–12.

[67]   David Gordon, 'The International Measurement of Poverty and Anti-poverty Measures' in Townsend (n 49) 53–80, 73.

development and institutional differences, new forms of poverty with similar causal determinants and manifestations emerge in both the Global South and in the Global North. The rise of urban poverty associated with unemployment and precarious employment, along with the increasingly significant relative poverty in the Global South, make comparative research in countries at different levels of development more relevant. The problem of poverty within nations, which until now had been overshadowed by the concern with the poverty of nations, has now acquired novel significance and has introduced social policy intervention as a new dimension in development studies. Consequently, the emphasis on social rights, which has been central to the emergence and development of the welfare state in developed countries, comes to provide a moral argument for the collective obligation to combat poverty through policy action. At this point, it becomes necessary to question the extent to which the language of human rights now used in the literature is in conformity with the framing of social rights in social policy formation and implementation. What needs to be further explored is the possibility of aligning the discussion of poverty as a human rights violation with the introduction of social rights in the international policy environment by considering the responsibilities to be assumed by domestic and international actors.

The challenges faced by attempts to combat poverty are both domestic and international; they involve both resource constraints and limitations of institutional capacity and political will. The development of a rights-based response to these challenges could significantly benefit from the contributions of all three perspectives on poverty discussed in this chapter. The perception of poverty as social exclusion would be an important element in the analysis of politics and institutions of social policy. Notwithstanding the difference between the language of rights and capabilities, the uniquely significant contribution of the capability perspective to the understanding of poverty as a multi-dimensional problem would continue to form the background to policy-oriented analyses of poverty.

There is a considerable overlap between the language of rights, capabilities and social exclusion. In fact, there is an ongoing dialogue among the three perspectives, which coincides with a parallel dialogue between poverty research in the countries of the Global North and the Global South. This interaction among different approaches to poverty has the potential to open fruitful avenues to policy-oriented research on one of the most pressing problems of our global order.

4. Is economic inequality a violation of human rights?

Gillian MacNaughton

In the early 2000s, leaders in the human rights movement, including then UN High Commissioner for Human Rights Louise Arbour and Amnesty International Secretary General Irene Khan, declared that poverty was the most pressing human rights challenge of the time.[1] In 2001, the Committee on Economic, Social and Cultural Rights issued a *Statement on Poverty and the International Covenant on Economic, Social and Cultural Rights*, in 2006 the Office of the High Commissioner for Human Rights issued *Principles and Guidelines for a Human Rights Approach to Poverty Reduction Strategies*, and from 2007 to 2010 UNESCO published a four volume compilation on human rights and poverty in its Philosopher's Library Series.[2] The focus of the human rights community on poverty during the first decade of the new millennium reflected the focus in the larger international community as it was enshrined in the Millennium Development Goals in 2001–2015 as MDG 1, which aimed to eradicate extreme poverty.[3]

Poverty remains a central concern of the international human rights community and in the Sustainable Development Goals (SDGs) adopted in 2015, which begin with SDG 1: "End poverty in all its forms everywhere."[4] At the same time, however, human rights scholars and practitioners, among others, have begun to also address the challenges of extreme economic inequalities.[5] This turn follows several publications by economists and others, alerting us to the dangers of extreme economic inequality, including growing economic and political insta-

---

[1]   Office of the High Commissioner for Human Rights (OHCHR) "Principles and Guidelines to a Human Rights Approach to Poverty Reduction Strategies" (2006) UN Doc HR/PUV/06/12, iii; Irene Khan, *The Unheard Truth: Poverty and Human Rights* (W.W. Norton & Company 2009) 20.

[2]   Committee on Economic, Social and Cultural Rights "Substantive Issues Arising in the Implementation of the International Covenant on Economic, Social and Cultural Rights: Poverty and the International Covenant on Economic, Social and Cultural Rights" (10 May 2001) UN Doc E/C.12/2001/10; Thomas Pogge (ed), *Freedom from Poverty as a Human Right: Who Owes What to the Very Poor?* vol 1 (UNESCO and OUP 2007); Thomas Pogge (ed), *Freedom from Poverty as a Human Right: Theory and Politics*, vol 2 (UNESCO 2010); Bard A. Andreassen, Stephen P. Marks and Arjun Sungupta (eds), *Freedom from Poverty as a Human Right: Economic Perspectives*, vol 3 (UNESCO 2009); Geraldine Van Bueren (ed), *Freedom from Poverty as a Human Right: Fulfilling Law's Duty to the Poor*, vol 4 (UNESCO 2010).

[3]   Report of the Secretary General, "Road map towards the implementation of the United Nations Millennium Declaration" (6 September 2001) UN Doc A/56/326, Annex, 56.

[4]   UNGA, "Transforming Our World: The 2030 Agenda for Sustainable Development" (21 October 2015) UN Doc A/RES/70/1, 14.

[5]   For example Philip Alston, "Report of the Special Rapporteur on extreme poverty and human rights," UN Doc A/HRC/29/31 (27 May 2015); Center for Economic and Social Rights (CESR), "From Disparity to Dignity: Tackling Economic Inequality Through the Sustainable Development Goals, Human Rights Policy Brief" (2016), http://cesr.org/sites/default/files/disparity_to_dignity_SDG10.pdf, accessed 25 January 2019.

bility and slower economic growth.[6] Concern among human rights scholars and practitioners about extreme economic inequality follows on the heels of these publications and is also related to three other recent developments.

First, unlike the 1990s when most poor people in the world lived in poor countries, in the new millennium, most poor people live in middle-income countries.[7] Middle-income countries also have the highest levels of economic inequality. These developments raise the question whether reducing domestic economic inequality is the most important step to reducing global poverty, rather than, or in addition to, richer countries providing international aid to poorer countries. Today, evidence suggests that most poverty in the world (75 percent) – particularly extreme poverty – could be eliminated via new domestic taxation and redistribution of national resources.[8] Thus, eliminating poverty has become increasingly a domestic issue, rather than a global issue. This makes poverty particularly amenable to human rights challenges, which generally hold the national government accountable for realizing human rights, including the right to an adequate standard of living. Further, the issue of poverty elimination is now clearly linked to reducing domestic economic inequalities.

Second, there is growing evidence that economic inequality – even in the absence of absolute poverty – negatively impacts societies. Hundreds of studies on wealthy countries (OECD countries, as well as studies across US states and Canadian provinces) have concluded that in more unequal societies, there are (1) higher rates of homicides; (2) more discrimination against women, ethnic minorities, and other marginalized groups; (3) lower participation in elections; (4) shorter life expectancy; and (5) higher rates of imprisonment, among other adverse outcomes.[9] These adverse indicators implicate the international human rights to life, personal security, nondiscrimination, health, and government by the will of the people.[10] Thus addressing economic inequality is important from a human rights perspective – even in the absence of poverty – because it appears to adversely impact the enjoyment of many human rights.

Third, the recent global attention to extreme economic inequalities is reflected in the Sustainable Development Goals, in which SDG 10 aims to reduce inequalities within and between countries.[11] Thus, there is now great motivation among countries and the UN system to address economic inequalities, funding is more readily available to study economic inequality, and greater information is available to the public about measures of economic inequality, the impact of economic inequality, and the change in economic inequality over time. The

---

[6]   See for example, Joseph E. Stiglitz, *The Price of Inequality: How Today's Divided Society Endangers Our Future* (W.W. Norton & Company 2012); Thomas Piketty, *Capital in the Twenty-First Century* (Belknap Press 2014); Anthony B. Atkinson, *Inequality: What Can Be Done?* (Harvard University Press 2015).

[7]   Andy Sumner, "Global Poverty and the New Bottom Billion: What If Three-Quarters of the World's Poor Live in Middle-Income Countries?" (2010) Institute of Development Studies, Brighton, IDS Working Paper 349.

[8]   Chris Hoy and Andy Sumner, "Global Poverty and Inequality: Is there a New Capacity for Redistribution in Developing Countries?" (2016) 7(1) JGD 117–57.

[9]   Richard Wilkinson and Kate Pickett, *The Spirit Level: Why More Equal Societies Almost Always Do Better* (Allen Lane 2009) 19. But see Andrew Leigh, Christopher Jenks, and Timothy M. Smeeding "Health and Economic Inequality" in Brian Nolan, Wiemar Salverda, and Timothy M. Smeeding (eds), *The Oxford Handbook of Economic Inequality* (OUP 2011).

[10]   Universal Declaration of Human Rights (adopted 10 December 1948) UNGA Res 217 A(III) (UDHR) arts 2, 3, 21 and 25.

[11]   UNGA (n 4).

increased attention, motivation, funding, and shared information can also help to provide the energy and evidence necessary to sustain human rights claims that gross economic inequalities are direct violations of human rights – and not just indirectly impacting on human rights.

Despite these converging developments that have led the global community to focus on economic inequalities, and the human urgency of the gross economic inequalities in the world today, human rights scholars and practitioners have struggled to find a basis in international human rights law for addressing them. In 2015, Philip Alston, then UN Special Rapporteur on Extreme Poverty and Human Rights declared: "At present, there is no explicitly stated right to equality, as such, under international human rights law."[12] Although there are numerous provisions in international human rights law on equality and nondiscrimination, and these rights are repeatedly invoked as core principles in human rights, human rights scholars and practitioners generally address only status-based discrimination (also known as horizontal inequalities). With few exceptions, they ignore economic inequalities (also known as vertical inequalities).[13] Accordingly, Alston has called upon human rights scholars and practitioners to move beyond the limits of nondiscrimination:

> [F]or all the attention given to affirmative obligations to eliminate discrimination, much of the work of the treaty bodies seems unduly confined to a focus on specific violations of non-discrimination. Linked to this is a reluctance to develop notions of distributive equality, which has been much debated in the literature, and would give an important added dimension to the effort to combat extreme inequality.[14]

This struggle to find a right to economic (and related social) equality in international human rights law is puzzling as the Universal Declaration of Human Rights (UDHR) and core international human rights treaties refer frequently to terms such as "equal in rights," and "equal protection." To address this puzzle, this chapter examines the equality and nondiscrimination provisions in the International Bill of Human Rights and how they have been interpreted to date. It then explains why the narrow interpretation – that equality and nondiscrimination both mean status-based nondiscrimination – must be wrong. Given this conclusion, this chapter considers what the right to equality, distinct from status-based nondiscrimination, might mean. Drawing on rules for interpretation of international law, as well as US constitutional law – the source of the language "equal protection" – this chapter concludes that the right to equality in international human rights law must encompass the right to economic (and related social)

---

[12]   Alston (n 5) [54].

[13]   Exceptions include Gillian MacNaughton, "Beyond a Minimum Threshold: The Right to Social Equality" in Lanse Minkler (ed), *The State of Economic and Social Human Rights: A Global Overview* (CUP 2013) 271–304; Doutje Lettinga and Lars van Troost (eds), *Can Human Rights Bring Social Justice? Twelve Essays* (Amnesty International Netherlands, 2015); Gaby Oré Aguilar and Ignacio Saiz, "Introducing the Debate on Economic Inequality: Can Human Rights Make a Difference?" (*OpenDemocracy*, 27 October 2015) <www.opendemocracy.net/en/openglobalrights -openpage/introducing-debate-on-economic-inequality-can-human-ri/> (and subsequent blogs in this debate) accessed 22 June 2020; Radhika Balakrishnan, James Heintz, and Diane Elson, *Rethinking Economic Policy for Social Justice* (Routledge, Abingdon 2016); Samuel Moyn, *Not Enough: Human Rights in an Unequal World* (Belknap Press, 2018); Philip Alston and Nikki Reisch (eds), *Tax, Inequality and Human Rights* (OUP, 2019); Daniel Brinks, Julia Dehm and Karen Engle, "Introduction: Human Rights and Economic Inequality" (2020) 10(3) Humanity 363 (and subsequent articles in this issue).

[14]   Alston (n 5) [55].

equality, not just the right to civil and political equality. Finally, this chapter considers what conditions of economic (and related social) inequality would amount to violations of human rights.

I.   THE STATE OF ECONOMIC INEQUALITY IN THE WORLD

The economic inequalities that have raised alarms over the past decade include inequalities of income and wealth, as well as the associated social inequalities in, for example, education, health, housing, and social protection. Numerous reports in recent years have pointed to stark disparities in income around the globe. The *Global Inequality Report 2018*, for example, indicates that in 2016, the share of national income that went to the top 10 percent of earners (top 10 percent income share) was 37 percent in Europe, 41 percent in China, 46 percent in Russia, 47 percent in the US and Canada, about 55 percent in Sub-Saharan Africa, Brazil, and India, and 61 percent in the Middle East.[15]

Since 1980, income inequality has increased in almost all countries, except in the Middle East, Sub-Saharan Africa, and Brazil, where income inequality has remained fairly stable at extremely high levels. In Europe, income inequality has grown moderately, while in North America, China, India, and Russia, inequality has increased rapidly.[16] For example, income inequality in Western Europe and the United States was fairly similar in 1980, but today the two regions have vastly different inequality situations. While the top 1 percent share of income has increased from 10 percent to 12 percent in Western Europe, it increased from 10 percent to 20 percent in the US.[17] Simultaneously, the bottom 50 percent share of income declined only slightly in Western Europe (23.5 percent to 22 percent) while it declined considerably in the United States (20.5 percent to 13 percent).[18] These different rates of increase in income inequality across countries and regions suggest that institutions and policies may impact inequality.[19]

In dollars, the average pay of CEOs in the 350 largest companies in the United States in 2018 was US$ 17.2 million in contrast to the average pay of workers in these companies of US$ 62,000.[20] This is a ratio of 278 to 1. In 1969, this ratio was 20 to 1 and in 1989, it was 58 to 1. From 1978 to 2018, CEO pay grew by almost 1000 percent, in contrast to worker compensation, which grew by 11.9 percent.[21] In sum, inequalities in income in the United States have been growing for over 40 years. They are now alarming and continue to grow. The same is true globally. Since 1980, "the top 1% richest individuals in the world captured twice as much growth as the bottom 50% individuals," thereby increasing income inequality globally, while there has been little to no income growth for individuals with incomes between the bottom 50

---

[15] World Inequality Lab, "World Inequality Report 2018" <https://wir2018.wid.world/files/download/wir2018-full-report-english.pdf>, accessed 27 January 2019, 9.

[16] ibid.

[17] ibid 10.

[18] ibid 12.

[19] ibid.

[20] Lawrence Mishel and Julia Wolfe, "CEO Compensation has Grown 940% Since 1978; Typical Worker Compensation has Risen Only 12% During That Time" (*Economic Policy Institute*, 14 August 2019) <www.epi.org/publication/ceo-compensation-2018/>, accessed 19 September 2019.

[21] ibid.

percent and the top percent.[22] Meanwhile, tax rates for top earners have been reduced by about half over a similar period.[23]

Wealth inequality is even greater than income inequality, as people with higher incomes do not need to expend as much of their income to survive and therefore are able to save more of that income. These savings accumulate and then can be passed on to the next generation. The *Global Wealth Report 2018* indicates that the richest 1 percent of adults owns almost 50 percent of global wealth, the richest 10 percent of adults owns 85 percent of global wealth, and the poorest half of all adults owns less than 1 percent of global wealth.[24] In mid-2018, there were 42.2 million millionaires in the world, which was 2.3 million more millionaires than the year before.[25] The United States added 878,000 millionaires, France, Germany, and the United Kingdom, about 200,000 each, China 186,000, and Japan 94,000.[26] These 42.2 million millionaires own 45 percent of global wealth. In contrast, 3.2 billion adults have wealth of less than US\$ 10,000, which amounts to just 1.9 percent of global wealth.[27] In the ten years since the 2008 financial crisis, the number of billionaires in the world rose from 1,125 to 2,208.[28] Meanwhile, almost half the world's population lives on less than \$5.50 per day.[29]

Many social inequalities correlate to these economic inequalities. For example, in low-income countries, children in the poorest 20 percent of households are more than twice as likely to be stunted (substantially below average height or length) compared to those from the wealthiest 20 percent of households.[30] Further, children in the poorest 20 percent of households are four times as likely to be out of school than those in the wealthiest 20 percent of households.[31] On average, the under-five mortality rate for children in the poorest quintile of households is almost double that of children in the wealthiest quintile of households.[32] The level of correct knowledge about HIV among women and men age 15–24 is about double in wealthy households (35 percent women, 48 percent men) than in the poorest households (17 percent women, 25 percent men).[33] In short, economic inequality equates with social inequality.

Economic inequalities are undesirable because they have numerous negative impacts on the well-being of individuals and society. As the World Bank acknowledges, global poverty cannot be eliminated by 2030 at the current rate of economic growth.[34] Reaching this

[22] World Inequality Lab (n 15) 11.
[23] Oxfam, "Public Good or Private Wealth" (2019) <https://oxfamilibrary.openrepository.com/bitstream/handle/10546/620599/bp-public-good-or-private-wealth-210119-en.pdf>, accessed 27 January 2019, 13.
[24] Credit Suisse Research Institute, "Global Wealth Report 2018" <www.credit-suisse.com/media/assets/private-banking/docs/uk/global-wealth-report-2018.pdf>, accessed 27 January 2019, 9.
[25] ibid 10.
[26] ibid.
[27] ibid 20.
[28] Oxfam (n 23) 76 n 22.
[29] ibid 12.
[30] United Nations, "The Millennium Development Goals Report 2015" <www.un.org/millenniumgoals/2015_MDG_Report/pdf/MDG%202015%20rev%20(July%201).pdf>, accessed 15 September 2019, 8.
[31] ibid 8.
[32] ibid 34.
[33] ibid 45.
[34] The World Bank, *Poverty and Shared Prosperity 2016: Taking on Inequality* (International Bank for Reconstruction and Development / The World Bank, 2016) 7.

goal – SDG 1 – will require some redistribution.[35] Thus, the Bank advocates that "efforts to foster growth need to be complemented by equity-enhancing policies and interventions."[36] Redistribution can help to eliminate poverty by transferring resources from wealthy people to those living in poverty. Further, reducing economic inequalities leads to greater growth for longer durations,[37] while extreme inequalities tend to slow growth and may also cause economic volatility and instability.[38] Thus, SDG 1 (end poverty in all its forms everywhere) and SDG 10 (reduce inequality within and among countries) are closely intertwined.

Economic inequality also impacts social cohesion and political stability.[39] Extreme inequalities result in social stratification and residential segregation, which undermine trust and thereby contribute to social instability.[40] The rich tend to insulate themselves from gross inequalities in society, ignore the negative impacts on other segments of the population, and lobby politicians to increase their share of wealth.[41] These tendencies result in lower investments in education, health care, and social protection, weakening social trust and increasing the risk of social, political, and economic instability.[42] Additionally, greater economic inequalities reinforce other disparities and result in lower levels of political participation by ethnic minorities, women, Indigenous people, youth, and other disadvantaged social groups.[43] High levels of economic inequalities are also associated with elite capture of the media and less media freedom – especially in democracies.[44]

Further, economic inequality is bad for individual and society health and well-being. It is not surprising that "[r]icher people tend, on average, to be healthier and happier than poorer people in the same society."[45] In *The Spirit Level*, Richard Wilkinson and Kate Pickett also show that high-income countries with greater economic inequality have worse health and greater social problems. They document dozens of studies that show that more unequal countries have: (1) higher rates of infant mortality, (2) lower life expectancy, (3) higher rates of mental illness, (4) higher rates of drug and alcohol addiction, (5) greater rates of obesity, (6) higher rates of teenage births, and (7) lower levels of educational performance by children, among other negative social outcomes.[46] It is not the wealthier countries, but the more equal countries, that are healthier and have fewer social problems.

---

[35]   ibid 30.

[36]   ibid 2–3.

[37]   ibid 30. In the context of global climate change and environmental degradation, however, the present rates of consumption in wealthy countries are not sustainable, and alternatives to growth, including redistribution, must be considered.

[38]   UN Department of Economic and Social Affairs (UN DESA), "Inequality Matters: Report on the World Social Situation 2013" (2013) UN Doc ST/ESA/345 64.

[39]   ibid 70.

[40]   ibid.

[41]   ibid.

[42]   ibid 71.

[43]   ibid 72.

[44]   ibid.

[45]   Wilkinson and Pickett (n 9) 13; see also Commission on the Social Determinant of Health, "Closing the Gap in a Generation: Health Equity Through Action on the Social Determinants of Health" (*World Health Organization*, 2008) <www.who.int/social_determinants/final_report/csdh_finalreport _2008.pdf> accessed 10 December 2020, 31.

[46]   Wilkinson and Pickett (n 9) 19.

Aside from these instrumental reasons to support greater economic equality, equality is also intrinsically valuable. People enjoy feeling equal to those in their communities and the larger society, and feeling unequal simply does not feel good. Indeed, research indicates that people in more equal societies are happier and have greater life satisfaction.[47] Plainly, economic inequality negatively impacts a wide range of human rights, including the rights to health, education, social protection, nondiscrimination, personal security, and participation in democracy, as well as human dignity and happiness. But is economic inequality *per se* a violation of human rights?

II. EQUALITY RIGHTS BEYOND STATUS-BASED NON-DISCRIMINATION

Human rights scholars and practitioners do not agree on whether economic inequality is a violation of human rights. At one end of the spectrum are those who think human rights – by focusing largely on civil and political rights – have been complicit with neoliberalism over the past forty years and thus have contributed to growing economic inequalities.[48] A closely related view is that human rights, while not complicit with neoliberalism, have been powerless to stop growing economic inequalities.[49] For example, Samuel Moyn contends that human rights do not call for any level of distributive equality, rather they demand only sufficiency – a minimum level of economic and social rights. Thus, he maintains that human rights have an accommodating relationship with both market fundamentalism and unequal outcomes.[50]

In contrast, most human rights scholars and practitioners who have addressed these issues recognize that extreme economic inequalities make it difficult to realize human rights, and that greater economic equality than exists today is instrumentally important to realizing human rights for all.[51] From this perspective, Radhika Balakrishnan, James Heintz, and Diane Elson maintain that "there is an implicit obligation within the human rights framework for states to consider the impact of inequality on the realization of rights and, where inequality impedes the realization of rights, to take steps to move towards a more just distribution of income."[52] Similarly, Philip Alston has stated, "It must be accepted that extreme inequality and respect for human rights are incompatible."[53] He contends that it would be an important step forward to formally recognize that there are limits to the level of inequality that can be reconciled with realizing human rights for all.[54] Additionally, Magdalena Sepúlveda Carmona, formerly UN Special Rapporteur on Extreme Poverty and Human Rights, has called for reduction in

---

[47] Shigehiro Oishi, Selin Kesibir and Ed Diener, "Income Inequality and Happiness" (2011) 22(9) Psychological Science 1095, 1095–100; Shigehiro Oishi and Selin Kesebir, "Income Inequality Explains Why Economic Growth Does Not Always Translate to an Increase in Happiness" (2015) 26(10) Psychological Science 1630, 1630–38.

[48] Samuel Moyn, "A Powerless Companion: Human Rights in the Age of Neoliberalism" (2014) 77 Law and Contemporary Problems 147, 147.

[49] ibid.

[50] Moyn (n 13) 10.

[51] See for example Alston (n 5) 21, 26–27, 29; Balakrishnan, Heintz, and Elson (n 13) 39–40.

[52] Balakrishnan, Heintz, and Elson (n 13) 48.

[53] Alston (n 5) 48.

[54] ibid.

economic inequalities via taxes, and in particular personal income taxation, in order to reduce poverty and realize economic and social rights.[55] And some human rights practitioners argue that human rights have a role to play in reducing economic inequalities indirectly via State obligations for nondiscrimination, maximum available resources, and international cooperation and assistance.[56]

Some scholars and practitioners think that human rights must address economic inequality more directly. For example, Sakiko Fukuda-Parr urges: "What is needed now is a more coherent articulation of human rights norms and inequality as injustice, which is currently underdeveloped, if not entirely absent."[57] In a similar vein, Philip Alston has called for "revitalizing the equality norm" in international human rights law to encompass inequalities beyond status-based nondiscrimination to include distributive equality.[58] And Moyn has challenged human rights advocates "to extricate themselves from their neoliberal companionship ... to restore the dream of equality to its importance in both theory and practice."[59]

An inquiry into the potential of human rights to address economic inequality directly – rather than through nondiscrimination, maximum available resources, and other indirect means – begins by examining the equality provisions in the International Bill of Human Rights. The Universal Declaration of Human Rights (UDHR) includes three relevant provisions. Article 1 states in part: "All human beings are born free and equal in dignity and rights." This provision, at the beginning of the UDHR, suggests that freedom and equality of rights – along with dignity – are the cornerstones of human rights. The following sentence in article 1 declares that human beings "are endowed with reason and conscience and should act toward one another in a spirit of brotherhood." This sentence indicates that "brotherhood," or "solidarity" in more inclusive language, is the third cornerstone of human rights.

Second, article 2 of the UDHR states: "Everyone is entitled to all the rights and freedoms set forward in this Declaration, without distinction of any kind, such as race, colour, sex, language, religion, political or other opinion, national or social origin, property, birth or other status." This provision – the "nondiscrimination" provision – appears in almost the same form in article 2 of the International Covenant on Economic, Social and Cultural Rights (ICESCR) and article 2 of the International Covenant on Civil and Political Rights (ICCPR).[60] These nondiscrimination provisions focus on eliminating status-based discrimination, which is a well-developed area of international human rights law.

Third, article 7 of the UDHR states: "All are equal before the law and are entitled without any discrimination to equal protection of the law. All are entitled to equal protection against

---

[55]   Magdalena Sepúlveda Carmona, "Report of the Special Rapporteur on extreme poverty and human rights" (22 May 2014) UN Doc A/HRC/26/28 [46].

[56]   See for example CESR (n 5).

[57]   Sakiko Fukuda-Parr, "It's About Values: Human Rights Norms and Tolerance for Inequality" (*OpenDemocracy*, 22 December 2015) <www.opendemocracy.net/en/openglobalrights-openpage/it-s -about-values-human-rights-norms-and-tolerance-for-inequalit/>, accessed 22 June 2020.

[58]   Alston (n 5) 18.

[59]   Moyn (n 13) 11.

[60]   International Covenant on Civil and Political Rights (adopted 16 December 1966, entered into force 23 March 1976) 999 UNTS 171 (ICCPR) art 2(1); International Covenant on Economic, Social and Cultural Rights (adopted 16 December 1966, entered into force 3 January 1976) 993 UNTS 3 (ICESCR) art 2(2).

any discrimination in violation of this Declaration and against any incitement to such discrimination."

This UDHR article contains four equality rights: (1) equality before the law, (2) equal protection of the law, (3) equal protection against discrimination in violation of the UDHR, and (4) equal protection against incitement to such discrimination. Similarly, ICCPR article 26 recognizes four equality rights: (1) equality before the law, (2) equal protection of the law, (3) the prohibition against discrimination, and (4) equal and effective protection against discrimination on the grounds listed in article 2 of the ICCPR. In addition, there are numerous provisions in the UDHR, ICCPR, and ICESCR that address equality with respect to specific rights, such as ICCPR article 23(4) on equal rights in marriage and ICESCR article 7(a)(1) on equal pay for equal work.

In 1989, the Human Rights Committee (HRC), which is charged with supervising State party implementation of the ICCPR, issued General Comment 18 on equality and nondiscrimination.[61] Although the Committee recognized the myriad equality and nondiscrimination provisions in the ICCPR in articles 2, 3, and 26, as well as those related to specific rights (such as equality before the courts and equality in marriage), it failed to explain the difference between these rights. Indeed, paragraphs 1 to 5 of the General Comment list all the equality and nondiscrimination provisions, and paragraphs 6 to 11 and 13 define discrimination and explain the State party obligations necessary to eliminate it. Paragraph 12 alone highlights a difference between article 2 and article 26. It states that article 2 is limited to protection against discrimination in the exercise of the rights in the ICCPR. In contrast, article 26 is "an autonomous right."[62] This means that article 26 applies "in any field regulated and protected by public authorities"; it is not limited to those rights in the ICCPR.[63] Article 26 is "concerned with the obligations imposed on State parties in regard to their legislation and the application thereof."[64] This difference between article 2 and article 26 is important, as it means that the article 26 equality and nondiscrimination provisions apply to all the areas covered by the ICESCR as the government is obligated to act in these areas.

However, the Committee fails to explain the difference between the various provisions in article 26. On the contrary, the Committee essentially merges all the equality provisions (equal before the law, equal protection, equal and effective protection) with the nondiscrimination provision, referring to them as "a basic and general principle relating to the protection of human rights," as though there is no difference at all between them.[65] To the Committee, equality and nondiscrimination both mean status-based nondiscrimination. This interpretation seems "unduly confined" and also substantially limits the uses of the right to equality in international human rights law.[66] Although widely accepted among human rights scholars, this narrow interpretation flies in the face of logic as well as rules of treaty interpretation.

In general, a treaty must be interpreted to align with the intentions of the drafters.[67] Besides the text of the treaty itself, the relevant rules of interpretation to determine the intention of

---

[61] UN Human Rights Committee (HRC), "General Comment 18: Non-discrimination" Thirty-seventh Session (10 November 1989).
[62] ibid 12.
[63] ibid.
[64] ibid.
[65] ibid 1.
[66] Alston (n 5) 55.
[67] *Costa Rica v Nicaragua* [2009] ICJ Rep 213, 237.

the parties are those (1) in the treaty itself and (2) in the Vienna Convention on the Law of Treaties articles 31–33.[68] Thus, to begin, article 5(1) of the ICCPR indicates that the Covenant may not be interpreted to destroy or limit the rights and freedoms in the Covenant. In other words, "Covenant rights may not be interpreted in such a way as to destroy another right."[69] Nonetheless, the current interpretation of equality and nondiscrimination in the ICCPR, and in international human rights more generally, conflates all provisions in ICCPR articles 2 and 26 to mean status-based nondiscrimination, thus eliminating the equality provisions.[70] This cannot be correct, as this interpretation makes superfluous several equality provisions and thereby destroys them, contrary to ICCPR article 5(1). Considering UDHR articles 1, 2, and 7, as well as the ICCPR articles 2 and 26, the multiple equality provisions must mean more than status-based nondiscrimination.[71] This raises the question: what do these equality provisions mean?

III.   THE RIGHT TO EQUAL PROTECTION OF ECONOMIC AND SOCIAL RIGHTS

The phrases "equal before the law" in the UDHR, and "equal before the courts" in the ICCPR, derive from the Declaration of the Rights of Man (1789), during the French Revolution.[72] They mean that the law must be applied to everyone in the same manner; further, no one is above the law. These provisions do not give rise to entitlements to substantive equality, but rather are directed at *enforcement* of the law.[73] Thus, they apply to actions of law enforcement officers, administrative officials, and judges enforcing the law, and not to the legislature.[74] In contrast, "equal protection of the law" derives from the 14th Amendment to the United States Constitution adopted in 1868 following the Civil War. According to Manfred Nowak, "equal protection of the law," now adopted into many national constitutions, has gradually transformed into "a substantive principle binding on the Legislature."[75] He contends that the logical interpretation of the equal protection provision is that it guarantees "protection of the law" to all.[76]

From this perspective, "equal protection" demands more than "equal before the law" as it requires the law to be created in a manner that will guarantee that the law protects everyone equally. Indeed, scholars have suggested that the equal protection provision can more readily

---

[68]   Daniel Moeckli, "Interpretation of the ICESCR: Between Morality and State Consent" in Daniel Moeckli, Helen Keller, and Corina Heri (eds), *The Human Rights Covenants at 50: Their Past, Present, and Future* (OUP 2018) 51–52; Vienna Convention on the Law of Treaties, 1155 UNTS 331 (adopted 23 May 1969, entered into force 27 January 1980).

[69]   Moeckli (n 68) 52.

[70]   See also *Andrews v. Law Society of British Columbia* [1989] 1 SCR 143 [72] (opinion of Justice La Forest that the four provisions on equality and nondiscrimination in Canadian Charter could "reasonably be argued" to be excessive to cover only nondiscrimination).

[71]   Gillian MacNaughton, "Equality Rights Beyond Neoliberal Constraints" in Gillian MacNaughton and Diane F. Frey (eds), *Economic and Social Rights in a Neoliberal World* (CUP 2018) 103–23, 112.

[72]   UDHR (n 10), art 7; ICCPR (n 60), art 14; Manfred Nowak, UN Covenant on Civil and Political Rights: CCPR Commentary (N.P. Engle, Kehl Germany 1993) 459.

[73]   Nowak (n 72) 466.

[74]   ibid.

[75]   ibid 459.

[76]   ibid 468.

be interpreted to encompass positive obligations upon the government than the nondiscrimination provisions.[77] While Nowak and other scholars distinguish "equal before the law" from "equal protection of the law," admittedly, the case law does not clearly do so.[78] Nonetheless, there is adequate jurisprudence and scholarship upon which the HRC could distinguish these rights, particularly given that the ICCPR includes both provisions and that ICCPR article 5 demands that the interpretation of each of these rights should not destroy or limit the other.

As the right to equal protection of the law derives from the US Constitution, to aid in its interpretation, it may be useful to examine how the US Supreme Court has construed this provision. While the HRC is under no obligation to follow the US Supreme Court, the Court's jurisprudence may provide a path for the HRC to re-interpret "equal protection" in a manner that would not conflate it with status-based discrimination and thereby violate ICCPR article 5. The US Supreme Court has employed a higher level of scrutiny when examining allegations of status-based discrimination in a manner that parallels, although not precisely, nondiscrimination in international human rights law.[79] Additionally, the Court has recognized another type of equality right – that is not status-based – under the equal protection provision. The Court's precedent holds that infringements on rights-based equality may also violate the right to equal protection of the law even in the absence of discrimination based on a protected status.

Rights-based equal protection is based on the importance of the right infringed, rather than on the identity of the group disadvantaged. One example is the well-accepted principle of one-person-one-vote, which means that individuals are entitled to one vote of equal weight to the votes of each of the other individuals voting. This rights-based equality associated with the right to vote is recognized by the US Supreme Court under the equal protection clause of the US Constitution in *Reynolds v. Sims*.[80] In that case the Court held that the equal protection clause requires substantially equal legislative representation for all citizens regardless of where they live.[81] This rights-based equality is also recognized by the HRC under article 25(b) in General Comment 25, which states: "The principle of one person, one vote must apply, and within the framework of each State's electoral system, the vote of one elector should equal the vote of another."[82] In both US constitutional law and international human rights law, the status of the individual whose right is diluted by apportionment is irrelevant. It is the importance of the right that is central to the inquiry.

The US Supreme Court has recognized a number of fundamental rights under the US Constitution that trigger the equal protection clause, including for example, the right to travel (invalidating a one-year residency requirement to vote in particular state),[83] the right to marry (invalidating same-sex marriage ban),[84] and the right to privacy (invalidating statute that

---

[77]   Lord Lester of Herne Hill QC and Sarah Joseph, "Obligations of Non-Discrimination" in David Harris and Sarah Joseph (eds), *The International Covenant on Civil and Political Rights and the United Kingdom* (Clarendon Press, Oxford 1995) 569.

[78]   Nowak (n 72) 467.

[79]   See for example *Brown v. Board of Education*, 347 US 483 (1954).

[80]   *Reynolds v. Sims*, 377 US 533 (1963).

[81]   ibid 568.

[82]   Human Rights Committee, 'General Comment 25' (27 August 1996) UN Doc CCPR/C/21/Rev.1/Add.7 [21].

[83]   *Dunn v. Blumstein*, 405 US 393 (1972).

[84]   *Obergefell v. Hodges*, 135 S Ct 2584 (2015).

allowed only married persons to access contraception).[85] On the other hand, the Court has held that education is not a fundamental right under the US Constitution, and therefore, it does not require states to provide equal educational opportunities to children across districts.[86] It has also held that welfare benefits and housing are not fundamental rights that would trigger strict scrutiny under the equal protection clause.[87]

Contrary to the US Constitution, however, the International Bill of Human Rights recognizes education, housing, and welfare benefits as fundamental human rights.[88] Thus, rights-based equality should extend to these fundamental rights as well. In international human rights law, just as the human right to vote implies a vote of equal weight, the human rights to education, housing, and welfare benefits, among other economic and social rights, must trigger equal protection concerns. In other words, the equal protection provision in ICCPR article 26 must require equality – of some kind that is complementary to but different from status-based nondiscrimination – with respect to all the rights in the ICESCR.[89]

As the equal protection provision in international human rights law must encompass entitlements that differ from status-based nondiscrimination and from equality before the law, it is incumbent upon the HRC to consider further its meaning.[90] Consistent with the Vienna Convention on the Law of Treaties, in interpreting the ICCPR, the HRC should consider the context of the equal protection provision, including the preamble to the ICCPR, and any instrument made in connection with the ICCPR and accepted by the parties as related to the ICCPR.[91] Specifically, the preamble to the ICCPR acknowledges that civil and political rights can only be achieved in conditions where everyone may also enjoy economic, social, and cultural rights, and the UN General Assembly adopted the ICESCR in conjunction with the ICCPR. Thus, the ICCPR article 26 equal protection provision must be interpreted in light of this broader context of the two indivisible, interrelated, and interdependent Covenants.

Construing the equal protection provision to require rights-based equality with respect to all human rights (as a complement to status-based nondiscrimination) is a legitimate means to distinguish the equality and nondiscrimination provisions in ICCPR articles 2 and 26 and move beyond the narrow interpretation of equality in international human rights law as encompassing only status-based nondiscrimination. This is the interpretation of equal protection in the US Constitution that the US Supreme Court has endorsed, and this Constitution is the source of the equal protection provision in ICCPR article 26. Once the nondiscrimination and equality provisions in the ICCPR are distinguished, and particularly if equal protection is construed to require equality with respect to fundamental rights (rights-based equality) as the US Supreme Court has construed the US provision on equal protection, it raises the question: does equal

---

[85]   *Eisenstadt v. Baird*, 405 U.S. 379 (1965).

[86]   *San Antonio Independent School District v. Rodriguez*, 411 US 1 (1973).

[87]   *Dandridge v. Williams*, 397 US 471 (1970) (welfare benefits); *Lindsey v. Normet*, 405 US 56 (1972).

[88]   ICESCR (n 60) arts 9, 11, 13.

[89]   See Rory O'Connell, "From Equality Before the Law to Equal Benefit of the Law: Social and Economic Rights in the Irish Constitution" in Oran Doyle and Eoin Carolan (eds), *The Irish Constitution: Governance and Values* (Thomas Round Hall, 2008) 335 (drawing on US Supreme Court precedent to argue that rights-based equality should be recognized under the Irish Constitution and extended to social rights).

[90]   MacNaughton (n 71) 116.

[91]   Vienna Convention (n 68) art 31(2).

protection, specifically rights-based equality, require some degree of equality with respect to economic and social rights?

IV.   ECONOMIC AND SOCIAL INEQUALITY AS A VIOLATION OF HUMAN RIGHTS

Just as equal protection of the right to vote requires each vote to be of substantially equal weight, the equal protection provision in the ICCPR (and the similar provision in the UDHR) must require some level of equality with respect to economic and social rights – not just with respect to civil and political rights. The right to equality with respect to civil and political rights is well accepted and is an essential part of each right. The right to vote is largely meaningless if it is not to a vote of equal weight, and the right to be recognized as a person before the law implies recognition as a person of equal dignity and rights. In the context of the International Bill of Human Rights, this rights-based equality must extend to the rights in the ICESCR. What is the meaning of the right to equal protection with respect to economic and social rights? And what level of economic or social inequality rises to the level of a violation of equal protection?

Three brief illustrations demonstrate that rights-based equality could play an important role in international human rights actions to address gross economic and social inequalities. First, consider the right to free and compulsory primary education.[92] What does the right to equal protection with respect to free and compulsory education require? At minimum, it must require that the government ensure the same number of years of schooling across the country. It seems quite obvious that the government cannot provide three years of free primary education in one district and twelve years in another. Beyond such basics, the right to equal protection would require that the government ensure that schools are funded in a manner such that the per-child expenditure is substantially equal across the country, unless there is a justifiable reason for higher expenditure for specific children, such as those with learning disabilities. This equal expenditure requirement has indeed been adopted by many courts that have recognized education as a fundamental human right and therefore have required the government to provide for equal educational opportunities – and thus substantially equal funding – for all.[93]

Second, consider the right to health care.[94] The World Health Organization (WHO) has recognized that direct fees at the point of service – when a patient must pay the health care provider directly in order to receive services – is the main barrier to achieving universal health care.[95] WHO therefore recommends that governments establish a system of health insurance, so that people pay in advance into a pool and then do not have to pay the health care provider directly at the time that services are needed.[96] "In general, the bigger the pool, the better able it is to cope with financial risks."[97] Some countries have, however, instituted tiers of public

---

[92]   ICESCR (n 60) art 13(2)(a).
[93]   See *Serrano v. Priest*, 557 P2d 929 (Cal 1976); *Edgewood Independent School District v. Kirby*, 777 SW2d 391 (Texas 1989); *Brigham v. State of Vermont*, 692 A2d 384 (Vt 1997).
[94]   ICESCR (n 60) art 12(2)(d).
[95]   World Health Organization (WHO), *The World Health Report: Health Systems Financing – The Path to Universal Coverage* (World Health Organization 2010) vi, 5.
[96]   ibid 6.
[97]   ibid.

health care insurance, also called segmented health care systems, so that people in different social groups do not have equal health insurance or equal health care. For example, in some countries, people who are formally employed have one scheme of health care insurance, while those who are self-employed, informally employed, or unemployed have another.[98] In another country, people are offered platinum, gold, silver, and bronze schemes of health insurance in the private sector at differing rates, and therefore, wealthier people are more likely to have better coverage than poorer people, who need it more.[99] To the extent that the government establishes or regulates tiered or segmented systems of health insurance coverage, it would appear to violate equal protection of the right to health care.

Third, consider the right to fair wages and equal remuneration for work of equal value.[100] The fact that the average salary for CEOs in the top 350 companies is US$ 17.2 million and the average pay of workers in these companies is US$ 62,000[101] should be adequate to show a violation of the right to equal protection with respect to the right to fair and equal wages. These incomes are, on their face, not fair, and the difference in incomes is far beyond any standard that could ensure that all people are equal in dignity and rights. Some jurisdictions have recognized that such gross wage and compensation inequalities are intolerable and are searching for solutions.[102] The City of Portland, USA, passed an ordinance that requires businesses to pay a surtax if the ratio of CEO to median worker compensation is equal to or greater than 100:1.[103] The City of San Francisco, USA, is considering passing a similar law.[104] While these laws do not (yet) approach anything near equal protection of the law with respect to fair wages, they are beginning to address the issue of extreme wage inequalities. Governments can take many other measures to reduce inequality in wages, including increasing protections for labor unions, requiring "just cause" to terminate employment, and providing a national job guarantee of decent work.[105] These and other laws, policies, and programs should be required to guarantee equal protection of the right to decent work and fair remuneration.

Beyond equal funding for educational opportunities, equal health care insurance, and some reasonable limit on the inequality of wages, the right to equal protection must limit gross inequalities in wealth that negatively impact on civil and political rights, giving elites the power to make the decisions that affect all our lives. The right to equality with respect to economic and social rights – the right to economic and social equality – does not require exact equality

---

[98]   Julio Frenk, "Universal Health Coverage in Latin America 4 – Leading the Way Towards Universal Health Coverage: A Call to Action" (2015) 385 The Lancet 1352–58, 1354.

[99]   Adam Gaffney and Danny McCormick, "America: Equity and Equality in Health 2 – The Affordable Care Act: Implications for Health-Care Equity" (2017) 389 The Lancet 1442.

[100]   ICESCR (n 60) art 7(a)(i).

[101]   Mishel and Wolfe (n 20).

[102]   See for example City of Portland Ordinance No. 188129, "Surtax to Business License Tax if Ratio of Compensation of a Company's Chief Executive Officer to Median Worker is Equal to or Greater than 100:1" (7 December 2016) <https://efiles.portlandoregon.gov/Record/10464332/>, accessed 20 September 2019.

[103]   ibid.

[104]   Sarah Anderson, "Will San Francisco Be the Second City to Tax Extreme CEO-Worker Pay Gaps?" (*Inequality.org*, 11 July 2019) <https://inequality.org/great-divide/san-francisco-ceo-tax/>, accessed 20 September 2019.

[105]   National Economic and Social Rights Initiative and others, "A New Social Contract for Workers" (*NESRI.org*, 13 September 2019) <www.nesri.org/news/2019/09/a-new-social-contract-for-workers-see -report>, accessed 20 September 2019.

in income or wealth – just as the one-person-one-vote rule does not require the exact same number of voters for each representative in government. Yet, at some point, economic and social inequalities become so severe that they must implicate the right to equal protection.

V.   CONCLUSION

Is economic inequality a violation of human rights? Or could it be? Rights-based equality under the equal protection provision in ICCPR article 26 is one avenue that might prove fruitful for pursuing direct claims for economic and social equality. Interpreting the equal protection provision in ICCPR article 26 to extend beyond nondiscrimination is not a stretch. Rather, it follows logically from the dictate in ICCPR article 5(1) not to interpret any right to destroy another right because merging the concepts of nondiscrimination and equality has eliminated the right to equality. A broader interpretation of equal protection also follows from the precedent of the US Supreme Court interpreting the equal protection clause of the US Constitution, from which the ICCPR equal protection provision was derived, to protect rights-based equality that is not status-based nondiscrimination. Although the US Supreme Court has not extended the equal protection clause to economic and social rights, that is because the US Constitution does not include economic and social rights. In contrast, the International Bill of Human Rights includes economic and social rights, and the equal protection clause in ICCPR article 26 should apply to these rights as well.

Several scholars – including Philip Alston, Sakiko Fukuda-Parr, and Samuel Moyn – have called for human rights scholars and practitioners to develop a robust concept of equality in international human rights that goes beyond nondiscrimination (horizontal inequalities) and addresses directly economic inequalities (vertical inequalities). Yet, to date, very little work has been done on this urgent project. To conceptualize a comprehensive and coherent equality norm in human rights, there are several important areas for future research. At the international level, they include: (1) unpacking and distinguishing the multiple equality provisions in UDHR article 7 and ICCPR article 26; (2) considering the implications of equal protection in ICCPR article 26 in relationship to the full array of human rights, including those in the ICESCR; and (3) examining in full detail the implied equality component of each economic and social right in the UDHR and the ICESCR.[106] At the domestic level, reflecting their obligations under the UDHR and the ICCPR, over forty national constitutions include an equal protection provision. Research is also needed to determine the jurisdictions with the most potential for developing a robust and comprehensive equality norm, and to develop the arguments for courts in those jurisdictions to do so as a starting point for building the precedent for equal protection of economic and social rights.

Beyond conceptualization of a robust equality norm in international and domestic law, there is a need for research on economic inequalities and human rights on the ground. As economic and social inequalities have soared over the past forty years, at first glance Moyn's contention that human rights are powerless companions to neoliberalism appears correct. On the other hand, numerous advocates for economic and human rights have disagreed basing their claims largely on anecdotal evidence of campaigns, social movements, advocacy, and results in spe-

---

[106] Gillian MacNaughton, "Vertical Inequalities: Are the SDGs and Human Rights Up to the Challenge?" (2017) 21/8 IJHR 1050, 1065.

cific locales. More research is needed to collect evidence from around the world on whether human rights are or could be effective in countering economic and social inequalities. There is already a growing body of empirical research on whether litigation on economic and social rights makes societies more or less economically and socially equal.[107] But what about other human rights efforts? Do human rights-based campaigns, social movements, policymaking, and impact assessments reduce economic inequalities and contribute to the realization of human rights? Further, what evidence is there of economic inequalities impacting negatively on human rights? While there is much evidence that economic inequality in a society correlates to poor social outcomes, the causal connections continue to be rigorously debated.[108] Research is also necessary to link these poor social outcomes explicitly to specific human rights obligations of the State parties.

Research on the development of the equality norm and on the impact of human rights on economic inequalities and vice versa calls for research by scholars from multiple disciplinary and interdisciplinary fields drawing on evidence from around the world. From these diverse places and perspectives, more research is needed on a broad range of issues from measurement to the history of equality in human rights. What are appropriate measures of economic inequality for human rights bodies to use and promote for state reporting? What is the relationship of poverty and economic inequality, especially in view of the move to measure poverty in relative rather than absolute terms in recent years? What is the history of the equality provisions in the various human rights instruments adopted to date? How do economic inequalities and human rights manifest in comparative contexts within a global region and between global regions? What policies promote both economic equality and human rights? How do global inequalities impact domestic inequalities and vice versa? Taking into consideration the capacity of the planet, what role does redistribution, within and between countries, play in ensuring realization of economic and social rights for all? From a human rights perspective, what are the (dis) advantages of addressing economic inequalities via minimum and maximum wages, basic income, or taxation?

Now that the human rights community has opened the door to consider economic inequalities as human rights issues, just as it decided two decades ago to consider poverty a human rights issue, an enormous research agenda is before us. Ultimately, the question is what is a human rights approach to economic inequalities?

---

[107]   See for example Varun Gauri and Daniel M Brinks (eds), *Courting Social Justice: Judicial Enforcement of Social and Economic Rights in the Developing World* (Cambridge University Press 2008); Alicia Ely Yamin and Siri Gloppen, *Litigating Health Rights: Can Courts Bring More Justice to Health?* (Harvard University Press 2011).

[108]   Compare Wilkinson and Pickett (n 9) with Leigh, Jenks, and Smeeding (n 9).

5. Poverty and political rights: an exercise of recovery from oblivion

Karolina Miriam Januszewski and Manfred Nowak

In recent years, there has been quite an upsurge in literature on poverty, inequality and human rights. Apart from sweeping claims for participation, empowerment and inclusion of the poor to be found in scholarship and practice, there also seems to be a general awareness of the interdependence of the social, economic and political dimensions of a good life. The Universal Declaration of Human Rights (UDHR) of 1948 embraces the indivisibility and interdependence of civil, political, economic, social and cultural rights, a commitment that has been reiterated many times since, most famously in the 1993 Vienna Declaration and Programme of Action.

Likewise in the 1990s, this understanding entered the development world. Amartya Sen's seminal work emphasized the importance of political rights not only for the fulfillment of needs but for their formulation.[1] Similarly, the World Bank in its path-breaking study *Voices of the Poor* recognized that people living in poverty feel unheard and silenced, defenseless against the power of the state and the elite.[2]

Despite those fundamental insights, the attention of the human rights community has been rather selective. On the one hand, as Samuel Moyn recently reminded us, human rights politics has reduced the larger, egalitarian vision of human rights underpinning the UDHR to basic provision and protection from state abuse.[3] On the other hand, in his function as Special Rapporteur on Extreme Poverty, Philip Alston has observed a systematic neglect of the civil and political rights of the poor by mainstream human rights actors.[4]

In this contribution, we will engage with these critical observations of 'oblivion', by approaching the issue of poverty and political rights from a relational perspective. The starting point is the understanding that poverty is an undisputable, horrific fact of modernity, a multidimensional state of un-freedom and political, social and economic exclusion. However, as much as poverty is a fact, this fact is neither natural nor inevitable. On the contrary, poverty is a political choice, human-made, and created by political, socio-economic processes, which simultaneously generate law and are generated and regulated by it.[5]

---

[1]   Amartya Sen, *Poverty and Famines: An Essay on Entitlement and Deprivation* (Clarendon Press 1981); Amartya Sen, *Development as Freedom* (OUP 1999); Amartya Sen, 'Human Rights and Economic Achievements', in Joanne R Bauer and Daniel A Bell (eds) *The East Asian Challenge for Human Rights* (CUP 1999) 88–102.

[2]   Deepa Narayan and others, *Voices of the Poor: Can Anyone Hear Us?* (vol 1, OUP for the World Bank 2000) (hereinafter '*Voices of the Poor*') 83.

[3]   Samuel Moyn, *Not Enough: Human Rights in an Unequal World* (Harvard University Press 2018).

[4]   Philip Alston, 'Report of the Special Rapporteur on Extreme Poverty and Human Rights' (4 October 2017) UN Doc A/72/502.

[5]   Ronald Dworkin, *Sovereign Virtue: The Theory and Practice of Equality* (Harvard University Press 2000) 1; Jason Beckett, 'Creating Poverty' in Anne Orford and Florian Hoffmann (eds), *The Oxford Handbook on the Theory of International Law* (OUP 2016) 985–1010.

Introducing a relational approach, which builds strongly on the insights from feminist theory, to our analysis of poverty and political rights might help to critically assess the potentials and limits of political rights (and human rights in general) with respect to poverty.[6] Feminist critique has been vehemently resisting the dominant dichotomy of autonomy and dependence, marginalizing care work and (re-)productive labor of women, often resulting in gendered poverty. Deconstructing this myth of the independent, self-sufficient individual – in sharp contrast to the actual position of us humans as interdependent social beings in an inter-subjective network of relations – might help to resist the triumphant rhetoric of individual, anti-statist human rights, and eventually shape a more integrated thinking about poverty and rights.

Such a relational approach is not particularly new, yet its insights tend to be forgotten in mainstream political, legal and economic thought. On that note, the purpose of this contribution is rather modest. We first and foremost want to recover and tentatively discuss the complexities of political rights and poverty, which have fallen into oblivion in academia and practice.

Political rights seem to offer a particularly good hook to introduce this relational approach to poverty and human rights. The intellectual history of political rights has the potential to complexify, enrich and disturb the common understanding of human rights and human nature. Looking at poverty through the lens of political rights, and not as is usually done through the prism of socio-economic rights, allows us to discuss certain aspects that usually get ignored far too readily, and which thus remain understudied within the human rights community. These instances of oblivion are (1) the fact of human interdependence; (2) the collective dimension of political rights; (3) the egalitarian potential of political rights; and (4) class awareness and the political rights of the poor. We will address each of these moments of oblivion in turn, starting with the fact of human interdependence.

I.   RECOVERING FROM OBLIVION STEP I: FROM DENIAL OF (INTER)DEPENDENCE TO RELATIONAL AUTONOMY

Before turning to the understudied aspects of political rights, let us first discuss a closely related oblivious attitude within the human rights community – how we as scholars and practitioners are engaged in the construction of the 'human' as the universal subject of rights.[7] This 'human' of human rights is not a pre-social, natural given but instead has been shaped and re-shaped by our understandings of the connection between the individual and the collective.

Human rights doctrine conceives of human beings as a particular kind of political and legal subject: free and equal rights-bearing individuals who have come together in the social

---

[6]   Our approach in this chapter draws particularly from Jennifer Nedelsky, *Law's Relations: A Relational Theory of Self, Autonomy, and Law* (OUP 2011); see also Catriona Mackenzie and Natalie Stoljar (eds), *Relational Autonomy: Feminist Perspectives on Autonomy, Agency and the Social Self* (OUP 2000).

[7]   Mainstream human rights scholarship rarely engages with this constitutive role of human rights; notable exceptions: Anna Grear, "Framing the project" of International Human Rights Law: Reflections on the Dysfunctional "Family" of the Universal Declaration', in Conor Gearty and Costas Douzinas (eds) *The Cambridge Companion to Human Rights Law* (CUP 2013) 17–35; Jack Donnelly, *Universal Human Rights: In Theory and Practice* (3rd edn, Cornell University Press 2013).

contract. These individuals are essentially built on an idea of the white, European, rational, property-owning, self-sufficient and self-realizing man of Western philosophy. He became the norm to represent all humanity, not only in legal, political or economic thought but in human science in general.

Other disciplines such as psychology, sociology, anthropology, philosophy or neuroscience, while still to some extent operating on this gender bias, have turned towards more relational accounts of autonomy. The parent-child relationship central in developmental psychology is arguably the most obvious of such relationships of dependence and connection. We are neither born into the world in full isolation nor with pre-developed, independent tastes, desires and needs; they are – to a considerable amount at least – socially acquired.

Language offers another excellent example. The acquisition of language is only possible through interaction with others. The very function of language is to communicate with others. Language thus evolves in social relations, and we – our individual selves – evolve through language, in conversation with others.[8]

Given this fundamental role of social relations for human life, it is astounding that a deeper appreciation of human nature has not found its way into human rights theory. This is particularly remarkable as law is a social technique of ordering, constituting and regulating relations among individuals.[9] Denying the obvious fact of the interconnectedness of human beings will not serve autonomy well.

Interestingly, early liberal thought had a comparably realistic perception of human nature. Jeremy Bentham for example held that:

> All men are born free? All men remain free? No, not a single man: not a single man that ever was, or is, or will be. All men, on the contrary, are born in subjection, and the most absolute subjection – the subjection of a helpless child to the parents on whom he depends every moment for his existence. In this subjection every man is born – in this subjection he continues for years – for a great number of years – and the existence of the individual and of the species depend on his doing so.[10]

The understanding that the individual is part of a larger social fabric is thus the very reason why we have law(s): *ubi societas, ibi ius*. However, through the liberal prism, law's main function is understood as 'mediating conflict, not … mutual self-creation'.[11] It was in particular during the nineteenth century that *laissez-faire* liberalism started to develop a certain anti-social self-understanding, denying human (inter-)dependence as an inherent feature of human life and crucial source of autonomy. This is particularly reflected in the notorious Lockean image of the (hu)man who goes off on his own following his own free will, into unoccupied territory to acquire property through his own labor. Autonomy as independence from others, the community and the state is thus the ideal to which to aspire.[12]

Based on this vision of 'negative freedom', laissez-faire liberalism sees law and rights as the instrument to limit the government as strictly as possible, to protect the private sphere and the

---

8   Charles Taylor, *The Language Animal: The Full Shape of the Human Linguistic Capacity* (Harvard University Press 2016).
9   cf Hans Kelsen, 'The Law as a Specific Social Technique' (1941) 9 U Chi L Rev 75.
10   Jeremy Bentham, 'Anarchical Fallacies' reproduced in Steven G Medema and Warren J Samuels (eds), *The History of Economic Thought: A Reader* (Routledge 2003) 188–92.
11   Nedelsky (n 6) 249; cf Donnelly (n 7) 30–31.
12   cf Pierre Rosanvallon, *The Society of Equals* (Harvard University Press 2013) 68.

free marketplace. Accordingly, the state is not first and foremost the guardian and guarantor of its population's well-being but their primary and constant threat.[13] That the state can be both, guardian and violator does not fit easily in this dangerously one-sided perception of liberalism. Similarly, pursuant to this understanding of freedom, human beings simply cannot be 'both uniquely individual and essentially social creatures'.[14]

This pathology of liberalism is also reflected in the fact that dependency on others, such as the dependence on assistance, is usually seen as a threat to autonomy, as a consequence of personal failings and as something to be overcome. By turning the self-realizing man into the telos of human life, we stigmatize and marginalize those most commonly associated with dependence and care, such as women, people of color, the working class and the poor.[15] While devaluing dependency, we carelessly overestimate the capacity of individuals to take care of themselves. This, in turn, affects how we theorize liberty, equality, democracy or poverty. The ideas of the independent individual and the menacing state govern our political choices, and thus, charges of creating dependency are often brought forward as an argument to justify the retrenchment of welfare programs.[16]

Given these implications, feminist theorists argue that we should shift our focus away from the individual to the structuring of relationships that foster autonomy. Autonomy, so the argument goes, 'is made possible by constructive relationships – including intimate, cultural, institutional, national, global and ecological forms of relationship – all of which interact'.[17]

Recognizing the embeddedness of human beings does not mean that relations are determinant or inherently benign. Relationships can be destructive, and it is the role of politics, law and rights to balance out these damaging effects. Moreover, relational autonomy does not entail the supremacy of the collective nor the loss of individuality. Acknowledging the relational nature of autonomy, 'simply' shifts our focus from the individual to the relations within which the individual finds herself and to how those relations are structured, by whom, and whether they are constructive or not.[18] This also requires that we understand values and human rights in a relational way. The core values of liberty, equality and solidarity underlying human rights are themselves relations, and democracy is a way of participating in their structuring and thus a way of making society.[19]

Focusing on the relations among individuals, between individuals and collectives (above all the state), and among states, might also lead to a deeper understanding of the 'political' in which human rights guarantee that individuals can participate. It allows for thinking beyond the individual and her rights to take part in the conduct of public affairs (to vote, to be elected, to speak freely, to assemble peacefully, etc.), opening space for questions of the role of political empowerment, governance or state agency in human rights protection. Eventually,

---

[13]   Manfred Nowak and Karolina Januszewski, 'Non-State Actors and Human Rights' in Math Noortmann, August Reinisch and Cedric Ryngaert (eds), *Non-State Actors in International Law* (Hart Publishing 2015) 113–62.

[14]   Nedelsky (n 6) 249.

[15]   See, e.g., Mackenzie and Stoljar (n 6). On the stigmatization of the worker, see, e.g., Rosanvallon (n 12) 88–92.

[16]   On the problematic concept of 'welfare dependency' and its racialization, see, e.g., Ruth Lister, *Poverty* (Polity Press 2004) 64.

[17]   Nedelsky (n 6) 119.

[18]   ibid 30–34.

[19]   ibid 41; see also Rosanvallon (n 12) 255ff.

such a relational approach might also encourage us to (re-)gain some 'class awareness' and conceive of bolder visions of distributional equality and welfare, beyond narrow anti-poverty measures of basic provision.

To assess rights in relation to others is not unknown in human rights doctrine. The UDHR embraces a particularly communitarian spirit, stressing the fact that individuality is realized through sociality.[20] This fundamental embeddedness of human beings entails an understanding of the mutuality of human rights, including 'duties to the community in which alone the free and full development of his personality is possible'.[21]

Although this communitarian consensus of the UDHR started to fade with the escalation of the ideological rifts during the Cold War, human rights law is nonetheless susceptible to questions of human relationality. Human rights require a constant balancing of competing values. Relative rights allow for proportionate limitations, if such restrictions are necessary in a democratic society to protect the rights of others. Moreover, it is generally acknowledged that human rights entail positive obligations to protect and fulfil, which at least indirectly pose obligations on private actors. Hence, rights structure relations not only between the citizen and the state but also among individuals.

Despite this 'reflexivity' of human rights law, our disciplinary imagination still tends to stick to the ideal of the self-realizing human of modernity and liberalism. This is exactly where political rights and their rich history offer the possibility to challenge the prevailing narrative in political and legal thought.

II. RECOVERING FROM OBLIVION STEP II: POLITICAL RIGHTS

Civil and political rights are usually mentioned in the same breath. It has become almost a reflex to pair 'civil and political rights' as a liberal, 'Western concept' of Enlightenment, and to contrast them with the 'socialist concept' of 'economic, social and cultural rights'. As 'classic human rights' of the 'first generation', civil and political rights were solemnly proclaimed in the revolutionary bills of rights of the late eighteenth century, further developed in national constitutions during the nineteenth century, and famously 'internationalized' in the twentieth century through the International Covenant on Civil and Political Rights (ICCPR). Economic, social and cultural rights, in turn, are most commonly said to belong to the 'second generation', born out of the proletarian struggles in the late 19th century and beginning of the 20th century. That is also when they were incrementally enshrined on the domestic level as well as in separate international treaties.[22]

While the first-generation rights, according to the conventional story, were originally conceived as negative rights protecting the private sphere of the individual against undue state intrusion, second-generation rights were designed as positive programmatic rights, requiring

---

[20]   Johannes Morsink, *The Universal Declaration of Human Rights: Origins, Drafting, and Intent* (University of Pennsylvania Press 1999) 242–48.
[21]   Universal Declaration of Human Rights (adopted 10 December 1948) UNGA Res 217 A(III) (UDHR) art 29.
[22]   This generational approach to human rights was proposed by Karel Vasak in 'A 30 Year Struggle' [November 1977] UNESCO Courier 29.

the state to actively pursue their realization. More a state function than an individual right, traditional theories of human rights would conclude that economic, social and cultural rights are not justiciable, while classic liberal human rights are; that is their very essence.[23]

This common pairing of civil and political rights into one category is telling and misleading at the same time. It is misleading as it does not capture the rich history, nature and character of political rights and thus has contributed to the instances of oblivion we address in this chapter.[24] As a first step, we consequently suggest decoupling political from civil rights to gain a better understanding of the plurality of values and ideas of freedom underpinning political rights.

The conceptual consolidation of civil and political rights, passed down from one generation of lawyers to the next, is not only deceptive but also telling. Over time, and particularly during the nineteenth century, when political rights were institutionalized nationally as individual rights, the dominant liberal logic of civil rights was extended to them.[25] This 'civilizing' process was embedded in a general shift in political thought. Liberalism became the dominant philosophical paradigm with its own logic and politics, domesticating rival ideas (such as republican egalitarianism) by accommodating them in a de-radicalized form within the liberal paradigm.[26] This de-politicization eventually stripped political rights of their radical emancipatory and redistributive potential to challenge the status quo. Their collective and egalitarian dimensions were reduced to a positivist, one-dimensional understanding of rights as negative liberties of the independent individual against the state.[27]

This impoverished account of political rights continues to govern the disciplinary imagination of us lawyers. In particular, we seem to have difficulties appreciating national constitutions and international human rights treaties as intricate amalgams of different competing and potentially contradictory conceptions of freedom. Focusing on political rights, sketching out their historical and conceptual complexity might, however, show us a way out of the cognitive grip. The 'political' of 'political rights' points to a nuanced understanding of freedom and autonomy, one which is realized in community with others.

As products of revolutions against domination and inequality, of collective struggles for recognition and redistribution, human rights can per se be understood as political rights. Social movements run like a common thread through the history of human rights.[28] Today, rights continue to be a powerful rhetorical tool for intervening in and shaping politics.

---

[23]   cf, e.g., Manfred Nowak, *Introduction to the International Human Rights Regime* (Martinus Nijhoff Publishers 2003).

[24]   Similar criticism of over-simplification has been formulated regarding the analytical myopia of dividing rights into generations or into negative and positive rights respectively. See, e.g., Patrick Macklem, 'Human Rights in International Law: Three Generations or One?' (2015) 3 Lon Rev Int Law 61.

[25]   For the periodization of civil, political and social rights see famously Thomas H Marshall and Tom Bottomore (eds), *Citizenship and Social Class* (Pluto Press 1992).

[26]   cf Michael J Thompson, 'The Demise of the Radical Critique of Economic Inequality in Western Political Thought' in Christian Olaf Christiansen and Steven L B Jensen (eds), *Histories of Global Inequality: New Perspectives* (Palgrave Macmillan 2019).

[27]   cf Manfred Nowak, *Politische Grundrechte* (Springer Verlag 1988) (hereinafter '*Politische Grundrechte*') 4.

[28]   Nowak and Januszewski (n 13) 135; Paul Gordon Lauren, *The Evolution of International Human Rights: Visions Seen* (3rd edn, University of Pennsylvania Press 2011).

And then, there are specific rights that are usually assembled under the category of political rights. These are the rights to vote or be elected, to hold public offices, to associate, to assemble peacefully and to speak freely.[29] It is this group of rights that is often only treated as a side note to so-called classic civil rights.

A.   The Collective Dimension of Political Rights

Political rights have a much stronger collective dimension to offer than is usually recognized. They are not about individuals leading monologues or simply casting a vote once in a while but about engaging with others, privately or in public. They are about deliberation and joining forces to champion political causes. They are thus characteristically exercised and can only be enjoyed in community or through collective action. They give space for participation within the *polis*, to be part of the recognized *demos* of a democracy, to access political process, to amplify (individual) voices and to effectively renegotiate society, time and again. They are rights of participation and membership in a community, of 'active citizenship', and of representation and inclusion in the institutionalized democratic decision-making processes.[30]

Moreover, political rights allow challenges to those formal institutions through informal, extra-parliamentarian action. They are individual freedoms, and as such protect the individual against interference by other individuals and the collective. They are there to protect individual autonomy and self-determination in the bigger process of collective decision-making. Yet political rights are not simply about keeping the state or others away, but about entering into active relations of engagement with them. They demand access to the state and its decision-making processes. They are about challenging the status quo, and thus demand responsiveness of the political processes. They constitute individual rights, yet at the same time they have a crucial ordering function telling us how a society should organize itself.[31]

The material history of voting offers some impressive insights into the collective nature of political rights. Originally, voting meant participating in lengthy gatherings of people, the electoral colleges of collective deliberation.[32] As Pierre Rosanvallon reminds us, those assemblies of individuals were 'the very symbol of popular sovereignty'.[33] In addition, festivals were held to 'allow participants to experience a truly public space'.[34] Voting was a loud and social event, not the short, silent, solitary, individualistic ritual at the ballot box we have today.[35] Still, even this solitary exercise has its collective dimension. Judith Shklar captured this collective aspect of voting quite aptly when she stressed: 'I know how illusory would be the belief that my vote determined anything; but nevertheless when I go to the polls, I have a satisfaction in the sense that we are all engaged in a common venture'.[36]

---

[29]   See, e.g., *Politische Grundrechte* (n 27) 10–12; Manfred Nowak, *U.N. Covenant on Civil and Political Rights: CCPR Commentary* (2nd edn, NP Engel Publishers 2005) (hereinafter '*CCPR Commentary*') 563ff; Morsink (n 20) 233–34.

[30]   *CCPR Commentary* (n 29) 576ff; *Politische Grundrechte* (n 27).

[31]   cf *Politische Grundrechte* (n 27) 152ff.

[32]   Rosanvallon (n 12) 38.

[33]   ibid 38.

[34]   ibid 42.

[35]   ibid 39.

[36]   ibid 41.

All this implies that political rights are not simply rights of the individual to be left alone in their 'castle of independence'. On the contrary, political rights can be understood as the very 'locus of interdependence', recognizing that 'the human embeddedness in communities is not only an important feature of the human predicament, but also a significant aspect of human flourishing'.[37]

Therefore, political rights are based on an idea of freedom of the individual through sociality. At their center is the human as *zoon politikon*, social, relational creature or as species-being ('Gattungswesen'), an expression famously coined by Karl Marx. Political rights thus offer a space where different conceptions of human nature, freedom and justice meet and interact. Aristotelian interdependence of classical antiquity encounters Kantian independence of modernity. A republican understanding of positive freedom through participation in community, requiring access to political processes (*liberté-participation*), encounters the liberal notion of negative freedom from arbitrary interference by others and the state (*liberté-autonomie*).[38]

Political participation guarantees self-determination through co-determination. These aspects – the constitution of a community, the membership therein, and the allocation of individual rights to members of the community – clearly came together in the American and French Revolutions.[39]

Conceptually, there is an essential but often overlooked difference between political rights, on the one hand, and socio-economic rights and civil rights. While the latter are directed at the individual as a private 'I', the former category is an invitation to engage with others. Yet, socio-economic rights, or more precisely material resources and the command over them, are needed to realize both the private retreat from the public space of mutual, intersubjective obligations as well as to follow the invitation issued by political rights to actively engage in common will-formation and influence democratic legislation.

Today, many international human rights treaties explicitly recognize political rights. Given their particular character, however, it was far from clear during the drafting processes of the European Convention on Human Rights and the two UN human rights covenants that political rights would be included. The question that has proven to be most divisive was whether the right to political participation should be understood as a programmatic principle, obligation or function of the state to guarantee popular participation, or as a subjective, directly applicable and thus justiciable individual right. In particular, Western states stressed the essentially aspirational nature of the right to universal suffrage as a democratic ideal, an unfinished and potentially unfinishable project.[40]

In contemporary human rights theory, this double nature of rights, encompassing both a directly applicable, justiciable individual right and a further reaching aspirational, programmatic component is partly reflected in the idea of the tripartite state obligations to respect, protect and fulfil.

---

[37]   These two expressions, 'castle of independence' and 'locus of interdependence', are borrowed from Hanoch Dagan, *Property: Values and Institutions* (OUP 2011), XIV.

[38]   cf Philippe Braud who spoke of the two faces of freedom, '*les deux visages de la liberté*' in Philippe Braud, *La Notion de Liberté Publique en droit Français* (Librairie Générale de droit et de Jurisprudence 1968) 11ff; see also *Politische Grundrechte* (n 27) 30 (referring to Benjamin Constant (1767–1830) who drew a distinction between collective-participatory freedoms of antiquity and the individual freedom of modernity).

[39]   Rosanvallon (n 12) 37, 41.

[40]   *Politische Grundrechte* (n 27) 155ff; *CCPR Commentary* (n 29) 590ff.

The doctrinal differences regarding the legal nature of political rights also point to another important aspect: the pivotal role of courts in human rights protection. Courts are usually understood as the main institution in charge of enforcing rights. Human rights are only considered 'real', i.e. legal/juridical, rights if they are justiciable. While 'classic negative civil rights' were in general always seen as justiciable rights, both political and economic, social and cultural rights were, due to their 'nature' (their positive and aspirational dimension), seen as state functions or principles rather than individual rights.

The role of courts and unelected judges in protecting human rights furthermore points to the inherent tensions and complexity of liberal democracies and thus poses difficult questions of democratic legitimacy. How can courts be both democratically responsive and 'loyal' to the law? Moreover, democratic rights of participation remind us that not only state institutions (the judiciary, the legislature and the executive) enforce, interpret and define human rights. Ordinary citizens can and should be key agents in giving meaning to rights; an aspect, which also points towards the egalitarian potential of political rights.

B.   The Egalitarian Potential of Political Rights

The idea(l) of equality is without a doubt fundamental to human rights doctrine. Famously, the UDHR exclaims in its first article that '[a]ll human beings are born free and equal in dignity and rights'.

Political rights have a particularly deep connection to this highly complex and essentially contested fundamental concept of legal theory and political philosophy. This strong nexus between political rights and equality is reflected in the relevant treaty provisions. Article 21 of the UDHR explicitly provides for the rights to equal access to public services and universal and equal suffrage. Similarly, Article 25 of the ICCPR, directly preceding the right to equality and non-discrimination postulated in Article 26, makes three explicit references to equality.

The interdependence between political rights and equality is not particularly surprising. Republicanism, popular sovereignty and democracy are the normative ideals underpinning political rights. From antiquity until today, these ideals have been carrying a specific egalitarianism, which could be described as each person's interests shall matter equally. They 'individualize' a collective and 'equalize' individuals with the aim to turn a community (as restricted it might be) into a 'society of equals'.[41] It is this normative underpinning, this promise of equality, which gives political rights their specific content and aim.

In its simplest, and probably most famous and least controversial form, political equality boils down to 'one person, one vote'. This principle relies on a radical yet purely formal and arithmetical understanding of equality.[42] Differences and privileges are abstracted away, humans are 'reduced to a number', namely one, and then these numbers are counted together to reach an ultimate decision. However, as sketched out above, political participation is not limited to ultimate decision-making. Political rights are about participation, representation and authorship, having the political power to influence the public debate, and experiencing the state as responsive to individual and collective concerns. Formal equality alone is not able to capture these dynamic and relational dimensions of political participation.

---

[41]   Rosanvallon (n 12).
[42]   *CCPR Commentary* (n 29) 581.

The calls for political equality at the heart of the American and French revolutions clearly went beyond a minimalistic conception of status equality. These struggles for popular sovereignty were struggles against actual subordination, slavery and serfdom, feudalism, monarchy and the privileges of the nobility and the clergy.[43] The revolutionaries were not simply concerned with formally ending the concentration of political power in the hands of a few. The very logic of feudalism, its hierarchical structuring into different estates, was ultimately grounded in an unequal distribution of (inherited) wealth. Questions of wealth distribution were thus part of the general fight against domination and for autonomy as self-governance.[44]

This (neo-)republican understanding of freedom – freedom as non-domination – figures centrally in past and contemporary struggles for political equality. Freedom from domination, although also defined in the negative, differs from the dominant liberal understandings of freedom of non-interference. Freedom as 'non-domination' might actually require state intervention to counter-balance power asymmetries and guarantee autonomy.[45]

What the revolutionaries of the eighteenth and nineteenth century brought about in reality was, as we know, not universal suffrage. Democratic participation remained a privilege restricted to a fairly small group of white and propertied men. The greater part of the population was left out of the equation. Only fierce and persistent struggles for recognition have been able to incrementally open up this exclusive club of active citizenship. Today, even though established democracies are from a historical perspective the most inclusive, and human rights catalogues guarantee political participation on paper, political freedom continues to be distributed unevenly.

But returning to a point made earlier: Those suffrage movements usually encompassed radical demands of redistribution. The right to vote not only allows marginalized groups to potentially win elections but to eventually legislate redistributive policies and to regulate the future allocation of power. That is why suffrage movements usually encountered forceful resistance from those whose privileges they wanted to undo, irrespective of whether the privileged few feared expropriation and redistribution from the middle classes, industrial workers or potential new elites.[46] Even the rather progressive liberal thinker John Stuart Mill famously proposed in his *Considerations on Representative Government* the introduction of a plural voting system to curtail the irrational power of the uneducated masses.[47]

Karl Marx, coming from the opposite side, was also well aware of this radical egalitarian potential of democracy and political rights. In his view, the demands of the working class could only be realized in a 'red republic'. The political rights of citizens (*droits du citoyen*)

---

[43]   Rosanvallon (n 12) 251ff; Lauren (n 28) 61–65; *CCPR Commentary* (n 29) 576ff; Jospeh Fishkin and William E Forbath, 'The Anti-Oligarchy Constitution' (2014) 94 B U L Rev 671–98 (aiming to recover the egalitarian potential of the US Constitution).

[44]   Rosanvallon (n 12) 295; Axel Honneth, *The Struggle for Recognition: The Moral Grammar of Social Conflicts* (Polity Press 1995); Axel Honneth and Nancy Fraser, *Redistribution or Recognition? A Political-Philosophical Exchange* (Verso 2003).

[45]   Philip Pettit, *Republicanism: A Theory of Freedom and Government* (OUP 2010).

[46]   Ruth Berins Collier, *Paths Toward Democracy: The Working Class and Elites in Western Europe and South America* (CUP 1999); Carles Boix, *Democracy and Redistribution* (CUP 2003); Daron Acemoglu and James A Robinson, *Economic Origins of Dictatorship and Democracy* (CUP 2006); Sirianne Dahlum, Carl Henrik Knutsen and Tore Wig, 'Who Revolts? Empirically Revisiting the Social Origins of Democracy' (2019) 81 The Journal of Politics 1494–99.

[47]   John Stuart Mill, *Considerations on Representative Government* (London 1861).

such as the freedom of expression, press or association were instrumental to reach this goal. In his essay *On the Jewish Question*, Marx criticized the 1789 French Declaration for potentially undermining this egalitarian potential by coupling political rights with civil rights of 'the egoistic man' (*droits de l'homme*).[48]

As political equality thus cannot be reduced to the concept of formal equality of civil rights, some scholars consider the independent right to equality and non-discrimination, as enshrined in Article 7 UDHR and Article 26 ICCPR, to belong to the category of political rights.[49] A close reading of Article 26 ICCPR and its drafting history reveals how controversial the meaning of equality was and still is. It also shows how this provision aims to capture these complexities by referring to four different idea(l)s of equality and non-discrimination, which, although explicitly mentioned in the treaty text – tend to be forgotten.[50]

The right to equality before the law goes back to the Aristotelian maxim that likes should be treated alike to prevent arbitrariness and guarantee consistency as well as procedural fairness. Laws shall be formulated in general and abstract terms, and courts and administrative agencies are required to apply these laws in an equal manner, i.e. non-arbitrary and non-discriminatory. The right to equality before the law does not, however, protect against discriminatory laws. As long as the law is formulated in a general and abstract manner, it may be even as deeply unjust and discriminatory as the former Apartheid legislation in South Africa. Thus, such a purely formal, abstract conception of equality can in fact perpetuate existing patterns of disadvantage.

The prohibition of discrimination is directed against the state, which is required to eliminate all discriminatory aspects in its legal order (such as the Apartheid laws), whereas the protection against discrimination demands from the state positive legislative, administrative and political measures to eliminate, as far as possible, discrimination by private actors, such as the exclusion of people of color from private hotels and restaurants.[51]

With regard to the last of the four aspects of equality enshrined in Article 26 ICCPR, the right to the equal protection of the law, we enter highly contested terrain. It aims to go beyond the formal, abstract right to equality before the law and introduces a notion of substantive equality, closely linked to the socialist concept of applying equality to the political, economic and social spheres of life.[52]

Yet, within human rights scholarship and practice, these different notions of equality and non-discrimination are typically conflated into one: The terms 'equality' and 'discrimination' are regularly used interchangeably and understood as describing the positive and negative side of the same principle. As a consequence, this multi-faceted right to equality has been reduced to a 'simple' right to non-discrimination.

---

[48] Karl Marx, *On the Jewsish Question* (*Zur Judenfrage*) (Paris 1844).

[49] *Politische Grundrechte* (n 27) 198–99.

[50] cf Torkel Opsahl, 'Equality in Human Rights Law, with Particular Reference to Article 26 of the International Covenant on Civil and Political Rights' in Manfred Nowak, Dorothea Steurer and Hannes Tretter (eds), *Fortschritt im Bewusstsein der Grund- Und Menschenrechte (Progress in the Spirit of Human Rights): Festschrift Felix Ermacora* (Engel Publishers 1988) 51; *CCPR Commentary* (n 29) 598ff.

[51] ibid.

[52] Usually, substantive equality is discussed under two different variants: equality of opportunity and equality of outcome. On the socialist concept of applying equality to the political, economic and social spheres of life, see Friedrich Engels, *Herrn Eugen Dühring's Umwälzung der Wissenschaft* (Verlag von JHW Dietz 1894).

Discrimination as a consequence of poverty is definitely a serious and neglected issue. However, antidiscrimination law might not be able to address the main challenge we face with regard to poverty. Our task is not to recognize and respect the differences between the rich and the poor. On the contrary, the challenge is to address the asymmetric power relations at the core of poverty. Poverty is a multidimensional state of un-freedom, of political, social and economic exclusion. Thus, the question arises whether the right to the equal protection of the law can be understood so as to redress distributive inequalities. Or to put it differently: Can we conceive the right to equality in a multidimensional manner as we started to do with poverty?[53] The history of political rights sketched out above seems to support a positive answer.

III.   RECOVERING FROM OBLIVION STEP III: CLASS AWARENESS AND THE POLITICAL RIGHTS OF THE POOR

Although the poor have experienced serious disadvantages throughout history and socio-economic, redistributive struggles were at the heart of democratization, there seems to be a considerable lack of 'class awareness' within the human rights community.

What do we mean by 'class awareness' in this context? We will use the term loosely here, not really referring to the idea of self-identification with a class in the Marxist sense of class consciousness. Rather we want to point to the fact that 'the poor' as a separate vulnerable, historically disadvantaged group and protected category of persons within human rights law seems to have been largely forgotten. This oblivion, the tendency of human rights lawyers to eschew any reference to the socio-economic status or class of rights-holders is in many ways remarkable.

Above all, this silence is astounding because the concept of 'class', as Morsink reminds us, was present during the drafting process of the UDHR and specifically its equality and antidiscrimination clauses. Although 'class' was eventually not explicitly listed as a prohibited ground of discrimination, the drafters extensively discussed discrimination based on socio-economic status and struggled to find the right phrase to capture the different historical and current practices of subordination on the basis of (inherited) legal, social and economic differences. Most of the delegates, including those from France and Great Britain, were willing to accept the term 'class'. The British delegate explicitly mentioned that '[t]he government of the United Kingdom … was working on just such a classless society'.[54] The Indian delegate suggested the insertion of 'caste', which was rejected by the other drafters as too specific. In the end, the phrase 'social origin, property, birth, or other status' was adopted, with the understanding that this passage would encompass the multiple historic, as well as newer forms and nuances of socio-economic subordination ranging from estates, serfdom, property and wealth to caste or class.

---

[53]   cf Sandra Fredman, 'Substantive Equality Revisited' (2016) 14 ICON 712; Gillian MacNaughton, 'Equality Rights Beyond Neoliberal Constraints' in Gillian MacNaughton and Diane F Frey (eds), *Economic and Social Rights in a Neoliberal World* (CUP 2019) 103–24; Manfred Nowak, *Menschenrechte: Eine Antwort auf die wachsende ökonomische Ungleichheit* (Edition Konturen 2015) 95–97.

[54]   Morsink (n 20) 114–15.

Thus, the UDHR proclaims that 'distinction of any kind, such as race, colour, sex, language, religion, political or other opinion, national or social origin, property, birth or other status' in the enjoyment of the rights set forth in the document are illegitimate.[55] The different translations of the UDHR do still hint at the difficulty of properly capturing those various nuances, cultural particularities and linguistic differences regarding socio-economic practices of subordination. The French version, for example, speaks of '*fortune*' (wealth) instead of property; the Spanish official translation uses '*posición económica*', the economic position or status of a person. Despite these difficulties in finding the proper, all-encompassing phrase, the drafters were well aware of the radical character of this provision. It clearly reflected the 'far-reaching egalitarianism' of the time.[56]

While the *travaux préparatoires* of the ICCPR suggest that the formulation of the independent right to equality enshrined in Article 26 of the Covenant was in general the result of lengthy and highly controversial deliberations, those controversies were related to the independent nature of the right and its two aspects – 'equality before the law' and 'equal protection of the law' rather than the list of prohibited grounds of discrimination. The ICCPR's list corresponds one-to-one to the one in the Universal Declaration, including the phrase 'social origin, property, birth or other status'. Similarly, the European Convention on Human Rights of 1950 prohibits discrimination based on 'social origin, ... property, birth or other status'.[57] Again, these criteria did not seem particularly controversial.

Most of the prohibited grounds of discrimination such as race, sex, nationality, political opinion, language or religion are familiar to any human rights activist. They are well discussed in human rights scholarship and practice and have been progressively developed in an extensive body of case law. Moreover, a growing consciousness of discriminatory practices has facilitated the addition of 'new' criteria including gender, sexual orientation, age and disability. The grounds of 'social origin', 'property' and 'birth' have however, several decades after their adoption, fallen into oblivion. As Philip Alston in his position as UN Special Rapporteur on extreme poverty and human rights reminded us, these criteria remain completely unelaborated and understudied by all relevant human rights actors.[58] Human rights commentaries, textbooks, case law and other international documents are rather silent on this matter.

This does not mean that poverty flies under the human rights radar. On the contrary, there actually is a rich body of literature on poverty, economic inequality and human rights. However, poverty and economic inequality are usually dealt with as a matter of (economic) development and poor people's rights are primarily addressed through the lens of economic, social and cultural rights and sweeping demands for social participation. Although poverty is understood as both a cause and a consequence of discrimination, it is not studied as a protected category itself. Practices of subordination, discrimination, marginalization and stigmatization of people affected from poverty, are studied as part of other forms of discrimination, for instance discrimination based on gender, sexual orientation, disability, age, race or religion.

The lack of 'class awareness' within the human rights community is also astounding for another reason: 'Class' – together with 'race' and 'gender' – is not only present in popular

---

[55] UDHR, art 2.

[56] Morsink (n 20) 114; see also Moyn (n 3) particularly at 41–88; Donnelly (n 7) 235–53.

[57] Convention for the Protection of Human Rights and Fundamental Freedoms (European Convention on Human Rights, as amended) (ECHR) art 14.

[58] Alston (n 4).

discourse but constitutes one of the most common analytical categories in social sciences.[59] As a theoretical frame, class is not only used by Marxist scholars but also by those, for example, relying on Weber or Bourdieu.[60]

Amartya Sen has also stressed 'class' as an important category for understanding inequality, while acknowledging the concept of intersectionality:

> Class does not act alone in creating and reinforcing inequality, and yet no other source of inequality is fully independent of class … Gender is certainly an additional contributor to societal inequality, but it does not act independently of class. Class is neither the only concern, nor an adequate proxy for other forms of inequality, and yet we do need class analysis to see the working and reach of other forms of inequality and differentiation.[61]

As used today in social sciences 'class' is, as Chimni explains, 'a complex unity which encompasses the gender and race divides. The latter categories are thus neither simply subsumed under the category of class nor are mere additions to it. These are interpenetrating and overlapping categories which intersect in multiple ways'.[62]

Sen and Chimni make an important point about the complexity of discrimination and equality. The concept of intersectionality has arguably been developed to at least in part address this complexity. Intersectionality highlights the fact that a given individual or group might suffer from several different, intersecting modes of discrimination.[63] Does the plurality of identities and relations as well as the concept of intersectionality make the category of 'class' irrelevant? No, on the contrary, the concept of intersectionality should remind us that class is (still) relevant. How can we understand the interaction and intersection of different modes of discrimination if we leave out a crucial one?

Just like race or gender, the concept of class renders certain (groups of) people visible and allows for the identification of converging experiences, interests and needs. This visibility and voice in turn might lay the groundwork for pooling political power in collective actions to craft policies responsive to these common preferences. And just like race or gender, class refers to more than identity or status. At its core, the concept is about entrenched inequalities, power structures and dynamics. Using the prism of 'class', in addition to other lenses such as gender and race, might help to better locate individuals and collectives within this complex web of relations and interdependence in which we live. This idea is also reflected in the concept of multidimensionality of poverty, and we are suggesting that this multidimensional and multi-relational thinking should also be extended to the right to equality.

Given the instances of oblivion we have already discussed in this chapter, it is, at least at first glance, not surprising that the Special Rapporteur on Extreme Poverty concluded in

---

[59]   Lynn S Chancer and Beverly X Watkins, *Gender, Race and Class: An Overview* (Wiley-Blackwell 2006); Shirley Jackson, *Routledge International Handbook of Race, Class and Gender* (Routledge 2015); David Grusky and Szonja Szelenyi, *The Inequality Reader: Contemporary and Foundational Readings in Race, Class, and Gender* (2nd edn, Routledge 2018).

[60]   cf Erik Olin Wright, *Approaches to Class Analysis* (CUP 2005).

[61]   Amartya Sen, *The Argumentative Indian: Writings on Indian History, Culture and Identity* (Penguin Books 2006) 207–08.

[62]   BS Chimni, 'Prolegomena to a Class Approach to International Law' (2010) 21 EJIL 2010 57, 63.

[63]   Kimberle Crenshaw developed the concept of 'intersectionality' in her 1989 paper 'Demarginalizing the Intersection of Race and Sex: A Black Feminist Critique of Antidiscrimination Doctrine, Feminist Theory and Antiracist Politics' (1989) 1 University of Chicago Legal Forum 139–167.

his 2017 report that the political rights of the poor have been 'completely ignored, explicitly excluded from the analysis [of all relevant human rights actors] or mentioned only in passing'.[64] Considering the extensive body of non-legal scholarship on how poverty and economic inequality affect individual political participation and democracy at large, and vice versa, the neglect within the human rights community is perplexing and calls for closer examination.[65]

During the 1990s and at the beginning of the new millennium, there actually was a growing awareness on the close nexus between poverty and political participation within the international community.[66] Decades of unsuccessful international development and poverty reduction efforts had forced the experts at work in the international institutions to listen to the concerns of those living in poverty. In the extensive surveys which followed this realization, poor people drew a complex, multidimensional picture of poverty, proving quite clearly how inadequate the traditional economic approaches to development were. Probably the most famous research conducted throughout the 1990s in this respect was the one by the World Bank, which used participatory poverty assessment methods and eventually resulted in the publication of the mind-opening three volume study series *Voices of the Poor*.[67]

The study makes clear that although poverty has an undeniable economic component as poor people lack the command over their material resources, poverty is not simply reducible to a country's GDP or a person's low income. Poverty does not result from the lack of one thing, but from many interlocking factors such as lack of command over economic resources, education, inadequate living standards, poor health, precarious working conditions, disempowerment, lack of political voice or the threat of violence. Although these factors and their impact vary depending on the person's status and location, poverty can be described as a state of un-freedom, of political, social and economic exclusion experienced by poor people in their daily lives.

As a result of these studies, new measures of development and poverty, such as Amartya Sen's seminal capability approach, were developed to capture the intricate realities of those living in poverty. Sen's capability approach is based on his paradigm-shifting re-conceptualization of development as freedom. Not only does Sen adopt a multidimensional notion of poverty but as a staunch supporter of democracy he highlights the important role that democratic institutions and political rights such as freedom of expression or the right to vote play

---

[64]   Alston (n 4) para 1.

[65]   See e.g. Collier (n 46); Boix (n 46); Pablo Beramendi and Christopher Anderson, *Democracy, Inequality, and Representation in Comparative Perspective* (Russell Sage Foundation 2008); Anirudh Krishna (ed), *Poverty, Participation, and Democracy: A Global Perspective* (CUP 2008); Larry M Bartles, *Unequal Democracy: The Political Economy of the New Gilded Age* (Princeton University Press 2010); Ben W Ansell and David J Samuels, *Inequality and Democratization: An Elite-Competition Approach* (CUP 2014); Russell J Dalton, *The Participation Gap: Social Status and Political Inequality* (OUP 2017).

[66]   cf Susan Marks' critical and insightful observations regarding this triumphant rhetoric of liberal democracy during that period which she calls 'liberal millenarianism', Susan Marks, 'The End of History? Reflections on Some International Legal Theses' (1997) 8 EJIL 449. However, those calls for democracy and political participation also went beyond 'flat versions of political participation' demanding a deepening democracy. See, e.g., Archon Fung and Erik Olin Wright (eds), *Deepening Democracy: Institutional Innovations in Empowered Participatory Governance* (Verso 2003).

[67]   *Voices of the Poor* (n 2).

to prevent famines and reduce poverty.[68] For Sen, political rights are crucial in three ways. First, as we are social beings political and social participation has intrinsic value for our life and well-being. Second, democracy has an important instrumental value. It amplifies people's political voice, gives them the opportunity to draw attention to general needs and to demand appropriate public action. This makes governments responsive and accountable to ordinary citizens. Third, political rights and democracy are not only crucial for the fulfillment of needs but for their very formulation.[69] Democracy and political rights thus also have a constitutive value as they give citizens not only the opportunity to express their opinions but also to exchange opinions and gather information in order to form values, needs and priorities. A fourth value or aspect of political rights should be mentioned in this context: political rights give people the hope that they can improve their lives or the situation of their children.[70]

Sen's preoccupation with the role of democracy and political rights in poverty-reduction measures resonates with one of the clearest and most persistent themes documented in the World Bank study: the (perceived) powerlessness of those living in poverty. Impoverished people feel unheard and silenced, humiliated and hopeless, and defenseless against the power of an unresponsive state and a potentially corrupt elite.[71] As *Voices of the Poor* observes:

> The poor want desperately to have their voices heard, to make decisions, and not to always receive the law handed down from above. They are tired of being asked to participate in government projects with low or no returns … [T]he right to participate[] must be enshrined in law.[72]

Within the human rights community, the common view that poverty is a human rights issue emerged in the 1986 Declaration on the Right to Development.[73] In its Article 2 the Declaration held that the right to development is a right of peoples and individuals to 'constant improvement of the well-being of the entire population … on their basis of their active, free and meaningful participation in development and in the fair distribution of benefits resulting therefrom'.

In 1990 the UN Commission on Human Rights requested that its Sub-Commission consider the link between poverty and human rights.[74] The appointment of a special rapporteur on extreme poverty and human rights as well as respective reports on the issue followed. In 1993 the World Conference of Human Rights in its *Vienna Declaration and Programme of Action* stated that '[t]he existence of widespread extreme poverty inhibits the full and effective enjoyment of human rights; its immediate alleviation and eventual elimination must remain a high

---

[68]   See above all Sen's *Development as Freedom* (n 1); see also Martha Nussbaum's work, e.g., *Creating Capabilities: The Human Development Approach* (Harvard University Press 2011).

[69]   Amartya Sen, 'Democracy as a Universal Value' (1999) 10 Journal of Democracy 3.

[70]   cf Adam Przeworski, 'The Poor and the Viability of Democracy' in Krishna (n 65) 125, 146.

[71]   *Voices of the Poor* (n 2).

[72]   Deepa Narayan and others, *Voices of the Poor: Crying Out for Change* (vol 2, OUP for the World Bank 2000) 281–82.

[73]   'Declaration on the Right to Development' (4 December 1986) UN Doc A/RES/41/128; see also, e.g., Philip Alston, 'Making Space for New Human Rights: The Case of the Right to Development' (1988) 1 Harvard Human Rights Yearbook 3, 20; Stephen Marks, 'The Human Right to Development: Between Rhetoric and Reality' (2004) 17 Harvard Human Rights Journal 137, 149.

[74]   See UN Commission on Human Rights, 'Human Rights and Extreme Poverty' (23 February 1990) UN Doc E/CN.4/RES/1990/15.

priority for the international community'.[75] It further affirmed that 'it is essential for States to foster participation by the poorest people in the decision-making process by the community in which they live, the promotion of human rights and efforts to combat extreme poverty'.[76]

The 2002 Draft Guidelines for a Human Rights Approach to Poverty Reduction Strategies and their Conceptual Framework built upon the recognition of the complex, multidimensional nature of poverty, on the notion of the indivisibility of human rights and on the corresponding need to develop a comprehensive, integrated and people-centered approach.[77] 'While the common theme underlying poor people's experiences is one of powerlessness, human rights empower individuals and communities by granting them entitlements that give rise to legal obligations on others'.[78] What makes the Draft Guidelines and the Conceptual Framework particularly remarkable – especially in retrospect – is that both documents highlight the importance to the poor of the right to political participation.[79]

In 2008, the UN adopted a human-rights approach to the Millennium Development Goals (MDGs), which were silent on human rights in general and on the role political participation plays for the enjoyment of economic, social and cultural rights in particular.[80] While the Millennium Declaration still made reference to democracy, human rights and good governance, governments eschewed human rights language with regard to the MDGs to avoid legal enforceability, responsibility and accountability.[81] The goals, although covering aspects of economic, social and cultural rights, were meant to be understood as aspirational political pledges not enforceable rights. The OHCHR's human rights approach to the MDGs tried to bring rights back to the development agenda. It *inter alia* emphasized 'participation, as a key principle and right, is a fundamental element to achieve economic, social and cultural rights, as well as the right to development'.[82] Similarly, the 2012 UN Guidelines on Extreme Poverty and Human Rights acknowledge the centrality of political participation, empowerment, transparency and accountability for any poverty reduction strategy.[83] It is this understanding of a close, inextricable relationship between poverty, equality and political rights that got lost in more recent debates within the human rights and development communities.

---

[75] 'Vienna Declaration and Programme of Action' (12 July 1993) UN Doc A/CONF.157/23, para 14 and para 25.

[76] ibid para 25.

[77] Paul Hunt, Manfred Nowak and Siddiq Osmani, 'Draft Guidelines: A Human Rights Approach to Poverty Reduction Strategies' (OHCHR 2004) <www.refworld.org/pdfid/3f8298544.pdf> accessed 10 December 2020; Paul Hunt, Manfred Nowak and Siddiq Osmani, 'Human Rights and Poverty Reduction: Conceptual Framework' (2004) UN Doc HR/PUB/04/1.

[78] 'Human Rights and Poverty Reduction' (n 77) 14.

[79] See Guideline 5 of the 'Draft Guidelines' (n 77) as well as 'Human Rights and Poverty Reduction' (n 77) 11–12, 18–20.

[80] OHCHR, 'Claiming the Millennium Development Goals: A Human Rights Approach' (2008) UN Doc HR/PUB/08/3.

[81] See § V of the 'United Nations Millennium Declaration' (18 September 2000) UN Doc A/RES/55/2, paras 24, 25.

[82] OHCHR, 'Claiming the Millennium Development Goals' (n 80) 11; see also the UNDP, *Human Development Report 2010: The Real Wealth of Nations: Pathways to Human Development* (Palgrave Macmillan 2010) 66ff (dealing extensively with issues of democracy, political rights and empowerment).

[83] The final draft of the Guiding Principles on Extreme Poverty and Human Rights were presented by the Special Rapporteur on extreme poverty and human rights, Magdalena Sepúlveda Carmona, UN Doc A/HRC/21/39 (18 July 2012); the guidelines were subsequently adopted by consensus by the Human Rights Council, UN Doc A/HRC/RES/21/11 (18 October 2012).

Most human rights scholars and advocates utilize the growing interest in poverty and economic inequality to renew the attention for economic, social and cultural rights and explore their redistributive potential. In a 2015 report, Philip Alston proposed an 'agenda for the future for tackling inequality' where he argues for living up to the idea of indivisibility of human rights by giving economic, social and cultural rights prominence and priority equal to that of civil and political rights to ensure social protection floors, to implement fiscal policies to reduce inequality, to put questions of resources and redistribution back into the human rights equation, and to revitalize the right to equality. In this report – as a notable exception to the rule of oblivion – Alston also discusses how economic and political inequality are intertwined, with the effect that not all citizens are equally able to exercise their rights to political participation. He argues that states need to make sure that all citizens can effectively make use of their democratic rights.[84]

The Sustainable Development Goals (SDGs) adopted in 2015 illustrate particularly well how the political rights of the poor have been chronically neglected by both the development and the human rights community. Only one goal, number 16, which seeks to 'promote peaceful and inclusive societies for sustainable development, provide access to justice for all and build effective, accountable and inclusive institutions at all levels', is understood to cover all relevant dimensions of civil and political rights.[85] References to political participation or democracy are missing.

IV.   CONCLUSION

This chapter was an exercise of recovery from oblivion. Engaging with the persistent phenomenon of poverty through the largely neglected category of political rights allowed us to confront certain dominant habits of legal and political thought that we, human rights scholars and practitioners, operate within and which we tend to uncritically retell in commentaries, textbooks, jurisprudence and reports.

This exercise of recovery thus gave us the opportunity to enrich the story of human rights and introduce a relational approach to our understanding of poverty, inequality, autonomy and rights. First, by engaging with the collective dimension and egalitarian potential of political rights, we implicitly also recovered the third value on which the French Declaration was famously premised, solidarity. Adopting a relational approach to human rights and autonomy that embraces the value of solidarity allows us to move away from the automatic priority of the individual to society to a more complex understanding appreciating the constitutive relationships of (inter-)dependence, care and vulnerability in which we find ourselves.

Second, retelling the story of human rights through political rights also encourages a move away from the dominant idea of human rights as negative rights, guaranteeing freedom from state interference. The (hi)story of political rights and political equality paints a far richer

---

[84]   HRC, 'Report of the Special Rapporteur on Extreme Poverty and Human Rights, Philip Alston' (27 May 2015) UN Doc A/HRC/29/31; see also Alston (n 4).

[85]   However, OHCHR understands the SDGs, 'although … not framed explicitly in the language of human rights', as 'strongly grounded in international human rights standards'. Transforming Our World: Human Rights in the 2030 Agenda for Sustainable Development (*OHCHR*, 2015) <www.ohchr.org/Documents/Issues/MDGs/Post2015/HRAndPost2015.pdf> accessed 9 July 2020.

picture, one of the different faces of freedom, where the notions of non-domination, participation and co-determination play an important role.

Third, political rights point to a deeper understanding of equality, one that goes beyond formal status equality, puts class awareness back on the table, and asks us to understand equality in relational and substantive terms. The story of political rights reminds us to not automatically reduce the multifaceted right to equality and non-discrimination to a question of discrimination. There clearly is space to revitalize the redistributive dimension of the right to (political) equality and thus equally address political recognition, social inclusion and wealth distribution.

Lastly, engaging with poverty through political rights reminds us of the crucial relationship between poverty, inequality and political participation. Poverty affects the political rights of the poor in a particular way. Yet, rights of political participation play a crucial role in challenging the status quo. They have the potential to bring about change and give political voice and hope. Re-engaging with political rights is also a call to think about ways to deepen and strengthen democracy. Why?

Because '[p]ower is the protagonist of this story: the power of the few; the powerlessness of many; and collective power of the people to demand change'.[86]

---

[86]   Pedro Conceição, *Human Development Report 2019. Beyond Income, Beyond Averages, Beyond Today: Inequalities in Human Development in the 21st Century* (UNDP 2019) iii <http://hdr.undp.org/sites/default/files/hdr2019.pdf> accessed 9 July 2020.

6. Human rights and poverty reduction: what are the linkages?

Hans-Otto Sano

An important feature of present global economic trends is the decline in poverty. In accordance with overall trends, poverty is also declining in many African countries, albeit more so in urban than in rural areas.

In this chapter I address the intersections between human rights and poverty reduction, examining relevant economic and human rights literature and poverty trends in sub-Saharan Africa. Specific questions analysed are:

- In the context of poverty reduction, what is the effect on the poverty rate when rights-relevant, non-economic metrics are taken into account?
- According to the available evidence, how do trends of inequality and poverty reduction interact?
- Are human rights-based approaches effective in reducing poverty in sub-Saharan Africa, and at what levels – local or national?
- How does the human-rights discourse affect poverty policies and discourse?

According to the literature, declines in poverty are conventionally related to economic growth, increases in agricultural productivity and the growing importance of the service sector.[1] Generally, human rights do not figure in economists' interpretations of these changes. This could mean that human rights play an insignificant role, but it may also reflect a lack of attention on the part of economists and human-rights scholars. In fact, the inclusion of human-rights thinking may prompt a broader understanding of poverty, how it is measured and how it is understood.

Human-rights studies have recently taken a substantial interest in how processes of inequality undermine human rights. This has occurred in response to the documentation of extreme accumulation among the wealthiest, among whom one per cent account for 48 per cent of the global wealth. However, Samuel Moyn's critique that human rights law and politics have turned a blind eye to galloping inequality has also provoked debate, articles and studies on inequality.[2]

---

[1] Xinshen Diao, Peter Hazell and James Thurlow, 'The Role of Agriculture in African Development' (2010) 38 World Development 1375; Francisco G Ferreira, Philippe G Leite, Martin Ravallion, 'Poverty Reduction without Economic Growth?: Explaining Brazil's Poverty Dynamics, 1985–2004' (2010) 93 Journal of Development Economics 20.

[2] See Samuel Moyn, *Human Rights in an Unequal World* (HUP 2018); Radhika Balakrishnan and James Heintz, 'How Inequality Threatens all Human Rights' (*Open Global Rights*, 2015) (including references to Philip Alston as well as Samuel Moyn) <www.openglobalrights.org/how-inequality-threatens -all-humans-rights/> accessed 12 June 2020.

While the concern with inequality and its threat to human rights is justified from the point of view of dignity, non-discrimination and social policies, for the most part the focus on inequality has not been accompanied by a renewed strong interest in poverty among human rights scholars. This means that human rights scholars have been slow in addressing one of the most important trends of the last few decades: the fact that poverty is declining, but not in equal patterns everywhere. I examine these linkages in more detail in section III.

In 2000 Mary Robinson, then UN High Commissioner for Human Rights, described poverty as the 'worst human rights problem in the world today'.[3] Since then poverty has received limited international attention as a significant human rights challenge.[4] The lack of priority given to poverty during the last decade – and even before – resulted in the international human rights discourse having a diffuse agenda with respect to poverty. While human rights scholars and activists consider poverty important as it pertains to discriminatory practices, the subject tends to be overridden by discussions of vulnerability, and most recently by inequality. Knowledge about who exactly is 'poor' is inconclusive, and analytical work on changes in poverty tends to be missing. The lack of attention in this field has resulted in little evidence being accumulated on human rights and poverty reduction.

More recently, human rights-based approaches have been applied as a UN-recommended framework guiding the implementation of human rights in development.[5] Generally, scholars, activists and donors have been inspired by the approach. Local and international human rights NGOs have combined a human rights-based approach with a focus on vulnerability and non-discrimination, as well as participation, inclusion and accountability. However, the experiences of applying these conceptual entry points are not always well documented and questions remain as to their implications, impact and sustainability.[6]

---

[3]   Mary Robinson, 'Health, Human Rights and Development' in *OCED Forum 2004: Health of Nations* (OCED Publishing 2004) <https://books.google.com/books?id=N16wDwAAQBAJ&lpg=PA21&ots=V_AJAGMOCa&dq=Mary%20Robinson%20%22Health%2C%20Human%20Rights%20and%20Development%22&pg=PA21#v=onepage&q=Mary%20Robinson%20%22Health,%20Human%20Rights%20and%20Development%22&f=false > accessed 12 June 2020. See also Polly Vizard, *Poverty and Human Rights: Sen's 'Capability Perspective' Explored* (OUP 2006).

[4]   See HRC, 'Report of the Special Rapporteur on Extreme Poverty and Human Rights' (22 March 2017) A/HRC/35/26, [5] ('For its part, the human rights community has had all too little to offer in response to the profound challenges associated with deep economic insecurity. The human rights to an adequate standard of living, to work and to social security have been very low on the list of priorities of the major human rights groups and of the principal international and regional human rights organizations, with the exception of the International Labour Organization (ILO)').

[5]   'The Human Rights Based Approach to Development Cooperation Towards a Common Understanding Among Agencies' (*United Nations Sustainable Development Group*, September 2003) <https://unsdg.un.org/resources/human-rights-based-approach-development-cooperation-towards-common-understanding-among-un> accessed 12 June 2020.

[6]   See, for instance, Hans Peter Schmitz, 'A Human Rights-Based Approach (HRBA) in Practice: Evaluating NGO Development Efforts' (2012) 44 Polity 523, 540. Also Jeidoh Duni and others, 'Exploring a Political Approach to Rights-Based Development in North West Cameroon: From Rights and Marginality to Citizenship and Justice' in Sam Hickey and Diana Mitlin (eds), *Rights-Based Approaches to Development: Exploring the Potential and Pitfalls* (Kumarian Press 2009); Morten Broberg and Hans-Otto Sano, 'Strengths and Weaknesses in a Human Rights-Based Approach to International Development' (2017) 22 The International Journal of Human Rights 664; Maija Mustaniemi-Laakso and Hans-Otto Sano (eds), *Human Rights-Based Change, The Institutionalisation of Economic and Social Rights* (Taylor and Francis 2018).

In section I of this chapter, I examine the trends of poverty in African countries south of the Sahara, while section II discusses if, how and where human rights are linked to poverty reduction, including alternative explanations outside the human-rights domain for the decrease in poverty. Section III addresses the broader question of how human rights are affecting the discourse on poverty. Finally, section IV offers some conclusions.

I.   THE TRENDS OF POVERTY REDUCTION IN AFRICA SOUTH OF THE SAHARA

Hiding behind the current global data on poverty reporting are different concepts and indicators. Global extreme poverty is measured by the World Bank poverty line of USD 1.90 per day in 2011 purchasing parity prices (either expenditure or incomes). This is called the International Poverty Line (IPL). Using the IPL score on extreme poverty, 10 per cent of the world's population was estimated to be extremely poor by 2015, whereas the comparative figure for 1990 was 60 per cent.

The monetary IPL figure is complemented in some measurements by non-monetary figures on access to education, healthcare and basic infrastructure (drinking water, sanitation and electricity). The expanded multi-dimensional poverty score captures a broader and a more accurate definition of essential deprivation, which is related to human rights and important for understanding inclusive growth. This index is defined as the societal poverty line (SPL) by the World Bank.[7] For the countries in sub-Saharan Africa for which data are available, adding all multidimensional deprivations to the monetary one would mean that the poverty rate increased from 44.9 per cent to 64.3 per cent in 2013. In other words, the inclusion of multidimensional poverty implies a substantially higher level of poverty.[8]

The definition of extreme poverty is also what defines absolute poverty, understood as what is required to meet the most basic human needs. Relative poverty measures poverty in relation to general living standards. The poverty line in lower middle-income countries, for instance, is estimated at USD 3.20 per person per day (2011 PPP) and not at USD 1.90 per day.[9]

The Oxford Poverty and Human Development Initiative (OPHI) operates exclusively with non-monetary measures. The index of the OPHI is based on 10 indicators relating to health, education and living standards.[10] The OPHI disaggregates their data into non-poor (deprived in less than 20 per cent of the weighted indicators), vulnerable to poverty (deprived in 20–33 per cent of the weighted indicators), poor (deprived in 34–49 per cent of the weighted indicators) and severely poor (deprived in 50 per cent or more of the weighted indicators). The category 'vulnerable to poverty' underscores the important fact that groups are moving in and out of poverty. In contrast the category chronically poor sometimes used in the literature emphasizes

---

[7]   World Bank, *Poverty and Shared Prosperity 2018: Piecing Together the Poverty Puzzle* (World Bank 2018).

[8]   ibid 5.

[9]   ibid 7.

[10]   See 'Global Multidimension Poverty Index' (*Oxford Poverty & Human Development Initiative (OPHI)*) <https://ophi.org.uk/multidimensional-poverty-index/> accessed 12 June 2020. This index measures poverty based on non-monetary basic needs related indicators: health, education and living standards measurement. See also 'Global Multidimensional Poverty Index: Country Briefings' (*OPHI*) <https://ophi.org.uk/multidimensional-poverty-index/mpi-country-briefings/> accessed 12 June 2020.

groups whose poverty is so deep that they remain poor over longer periods of time irrespective of positive economic change.

Observing the trends in poverty in sub-Saharan Africa, where comparable measures over time are available, four important trends stand out:

- For sub-Saharan Africa as a whole, the World Bank estimates a decline of the proportion of the total population living in extreme poverty from 57 per cent in 1990 to 41 per cent by 2015. These data are based on the IPL poverty line (USD 1.90 per day).[11]
- Poverty is at a lower level in Eastern and Southern Africa compared to, in particular, the French-speaking part of West Africa. Burkina Faso, for instance, had an estimated poverty share of nearly 90 per cent in 2003, and the share had only improved to 82 per cent by 2015. In contrast, poverty rates fell in Eastern and Southern Africa from an average of 58 per cent in 2008–10 to an average of 50 per cent by 2014–16 for six countries.[12]
- Data from both the World Bank and the OPHI indicate that the total number of poor people has increased in Africa south of the Sahara. Population growth has eclipsed the general decrease in poverty.
- A fourth characteristic is that multidimensional poverty has fallen more in urban areas compared to rural ones. In Tanzania, for example, urban poverty fell from a rate of 34.8 per cent to 27.7 per cent between 2010 and 2015–16, while the rural share of poverty remained unaltered.[13]

These are broad trends confirmed irrespective of measurement methods. However, the fact that substantial differences occur between the extreme measurement of poverty and the multidimensional method underscores that poverty has not fallen as much as the data on extreme poverty would imply. Comparative OPHI data from 1990 are not available; hence, it is difficult to estimate poverty reduction over longer stretches in time according to the multidimensional measure. The OPHI estimates for most sub-Saharan African countries that poverty is at a higher rate compared to the IPL estimate on extreme poverty. For Ethiopia, while the IPL extreme poverty rate was estimated at 27.3 per cent, the OPHI headcount score was estimated at 83 per cent for 2016. If the OPHI measurement is restricted to only the severely poor, the figure still reaches 61.5 per cent, nearly three times higher than the USD 1.90 measurement.[14] Bringing in methods of measurement that relate to social-rights deprivations moderates the

---

[11] Kathleen Beegle and Luc Christiansen (eds), *Accelerating Poverty Reduction in Africa* (World Bank 2019) 3. See also 'Regional Aggregation Using 2011 PPP and $1.9/day Poverty Line' (*The World Bank*) <http://iresearch.worldbank.org/PovcalNet/povDuplicateWB.aspx> accessed 12 June 2020.

[12] See n 10.

[13] See Hans-Otto Sano, 'How Can a Human Rights-Based Approach Contribute to Poverty Reduction? The Relevance of Human Rights to Sustainable Goal 1', in Markus Kaltenborn, Markus Krajewski and Heike Kuhn (eds), *Sustainable Development Goals and Human Rights* (Springer Open 2020) 18.

[14] During 2007, there were only seven countries in sub-Saharan Africa whose poverty estimates, according to the international extreme poverty line, were at a level corresponding to the OPHI multi-dimensional measures; the remaining 20 countries for which data were available at the time indicated poverty levels significantly above the IPL. For Niger, while the IPL indicated 42 per cent, the OPHI data reached 92 per cent. See, for example, 'Global MPI Country Briefing 2019: Niger (Sub-Saharan Africa)' (*OPHI*, July 2019) <https://ophi.org.uk/wp-content/uploads/CB_NER_2019.pdf> accessed 12 June 2020; 'Global MPI Country Briefing 2019: Ethiopia (Sub-Saharan Africa)' (*OPHI*, July 2019) <https://ophi.org.uk/wp-content/uploads/CB_ETH_2019.pdf> accessed 12 June 2020.

perceived decrease in poverty and instead reveals an increase in the poverty rate in most sub-Saharan African countries.

Recent World Bank reports associate a slow reduction of poverty with fragility,[15] for instance in certain West African states, i.e. conflict-torn states with weak legitimacy and capacity of the governing structures. This is an important factor in explaining the levels of poverty. However, it cannot explain intra-state differences between rural and urban areas. Inequalities of incomes and of opportunities, namely the lower social mobility in rural areas, are important in explaining intra-state differences in rural and urban patterns of poverty. Modest growth in agricultural productivity may account for the important differences between rural and urban areas as further discussed below.

II.   HUMAN RIGHTS, INEQUALITY AND POVERTY REDUCTION

How do poverty reduction and trends of inequality interact? In addition, what role do human rights empowerment and human rights-based efforts play in inducing the decline of observable poverty in sub-Saharan Africa? The nexus between inequality and poverty is often simplified or glossed over in human rights discussions and often from a normative point of departure. In this chapter, an effort is made to draw on empirical evidence in order to bring in some of the complexity of the interaction of poverty and inequality. An attempt is also made to integrate local empirical evidence in the analysis on human rights-based approaches. It should be noted, however, that the data on Gini coefficients in sub-Saharan Africa are not the best and that data sources were not updated during the most recent decade. Also, studies on the implementation of human rights-based approaches are missing in the African context.[16]

A.   Reflecting on Poverty, Inequality and Human Rights Linkages

Much of the scientific knowledge about poverty reduction has been elaborated among development scholars, especially economists in universities, at the World Bank, in the UN, and at the regional development banks.[17]

---

[15]   Kathleen Beegle and others, *Poverty in a Rising Africa* (World Bank 2016) 16 <http://documents.worldbank.org/curated/en/949241467996692059/pdf/103948-PUB-POVERTY-AFRICA-Box394870B-PUBLIC.pdf> accessed 12 June 2020; Beegle and Christiansen (n 11) 199.

[16]   See *Human Development Report 2019: Beyond Income, Beyond Averages, Beyond Today: Inequalities in Human Development in the 21st Century* (United Nations Development Program (UNDP) 2016) 116–18 <http://hdr.undp.org/sites/default/files/hdr2019.pdf> accessed 12 June 2020; Abebe Shimeles and Tiguene Nabassaga, 'Why is Inequality High in Africa?' (2018) 27 Journal of African Economies 108, 108–10. For reflections on missing studies on human rights-based approaches, see Paul J Nelson and Ellen Dorsey, 'Who Practices Rights-Based Development? A Progress Report on Work at the Nexus of Human Rights and Development' (2018) 104 World Development 97.

[17]   Shaohua Chen and Martin Ravallion, 'The developing world is poorer than we thought, but no less successful in the fight against poverty' (2008) 125 The Quarterly Journal of Economics 1577; Francisco HG Ferreira, *Distributions in motion: economic growth, inequality, and poverty dynamics* (2010) World Bank Policy Research Working Paper No 5424 <https://papers.ssrn.com/sol3/papers.cfm?abstract_id=1678354> accessed 12 June 2020; John Page and Abebe Shimeles, 'Aid, employment and poverty reduction in Africa' (2015) 27 African Development Review 17; John C Anyanwu and Joanna C Anyanwu,

In the World Bank Handbook on Poverty and Inequality,[18] Haughton and Khandker classify anti-poverty activities into three groups:

- Fostering opportunity, through well-functioning markets and investments in infrastructure and education;
- Facilitating empowerment, including the involvement of people in decision-making – which in turn requires government accountability, strong media, local organizational capacity and mechanisms for participation in making decisions;
- Addressing income security, which tackles the problem of vulnerability, through for example insurance programmes, disaster-relief procedures and solid public-health infrastructure.

The linkage between inequality and poverty is still a point of debate in the economic literature of interest in a human rights context. In its African coverage, similar to most other sources, the recent UN Human Development Report[19] emphasizes income and consumption inequality, while the broader perspectives on inequality of opportunity (unequal access to services, for instance) is not discussed. On average in Southern Africa, it appears that inequality increased, as measured by the share of income going to the upper 10 per cent and to the bottom 40 per cent, but fell in East, West, and North Africa during the late 1990s and 2000s. The general trend of a decline in inequality since the late 1990s can be explained by a reduction of inequality in two of the most populous countries, Ethiopia and Kenya. The growth of incomes of the top 10 per cent of the income scale in Southern Africa region can be explained by the very skewed development in South Africa.[20]

How exactly do trends in inequality relate to poverty reduction? The more recent macro-economic research with a broader focus than Africa makes it clear that poverty reduction is not correlated with inequality on average; however, the data also indicate that in countries with rising inequality, the growth effect on poverty reduction was dampened or reversed. In addition, while economic growth generally contributes to poverty reduction even if there is no change in inequality, the poverty-reducing power is less in countries that are initially more unequal.[21] The prevalence of inequality is therefore conditioning the opportunities for poverty reduction and hampering progress. For Africa as a whole, inequality measured by the Gini coefficient peaked during the early 1990s but fell from the late 1990s to 2011. Yet despite the fall in inequality, it remained at a fairly high level on average (around index score

---

'The Key Drivers of Poverty in Sub-Saharan Africa and What Can Be Done About it to Achieve the Poverty Sustainable Development Goal' (2017) 5 Asian Journal of Economic Modelling 297.

[18]   Jonathan Haughton and Shahidur R Khandker, *Handbook on Poverty and Inequality* (World Bank 2009) 161 <http://documents.worldbank.org/curated/en/488081468157174849/pdf/483380PUB0Pove1 01OFFICIAL0USE0ONLY1.pdf> accessed 12 June 2020.

[19]   See for instance Christian Olaf Christiansen and Steven LB Jensen, *Histories of Global Inequality New Perspectives* (Springer 2019). The most recent Human Development Report (2019) is thematically focused on inequality. *Human Development Report 2019* (n 16).

[20]   See *Human Development Report 2019* (n 16) 116–18.

[21]   Ferreira (n 17); Roy Van der Weide and Branko Milanovic, *Inequality is Bad for Growth of the Poor (But Not for that of the Rich)* (2014) 32 The World Bank Economic Review 507. The latter study focuses on states in the US between 1960 and 2010. The authors conclude that high levels of inequality reduce the income growth of the poor and, if anything, help the growth of the rich.

40).[22] Poverty rates fell during the 2000s even though inequalities were fairly high.[23] In other words, the dynamic processes leading to a fall in poverty rates overruled the potential negative influence of inequality on poverty, but given the prevailing economic knowledge, a more impressive decline in poverty numbers could have been expected.

Where do human rights fit into this broad economic knowledge of poverty reduction and the three entry points of poverty-reduction activities outlined by Haughton and Khandkher? A strong point is the one of empowerment. Participatory measures, freedom of speech and measures such as civil-society mobilization that contribute to accountability will be important in reducing poverty. However, service provision and social-rights fulfilment (health, education, and water and sanitation rights), and the focus on vulnerable groups subject to discriminatory behaviour are also important human rights-based instruments in poverty reduction.[24]

A fourth factor in addition to those identified by Haughton and Khandker is that rights-holders themselves are endeavouring to improve their livelihood, for example through efforts to gain access to markets, to enhance labour or land productivities or to combine economic activities in new ways. Such efforts of economic and livelihood self-empowerment tend to be underestimated, as is the case in the World Bank Handbook which seem premised on outside actors implementing all of the activities.[25]

Focusing on potential linkages between human rights work and poverty, but without examining in empirical detail how human rights have actually contributed to poverty reduction, the Joseph Rowntree Foundation in the UK issued a report on Poverty, Inequality and Human Rights in 2009.[26]

Based on a review of international experience, the report reflected salient linkages and lessons learned outside the United Kingdom. It is based on a limited method of holding four regional seminars and interviewing 28 key informants active in using human rights in anti-poverty work internationally or at the country level. Despite the limits of the method – insufficient literature review and knowledge of the work of local civil-society organizations,

---

[22]   Shimeles and Nabassaga (n 16) 111.

[23]   Beegle and others (n 15) 14.

[24]   See the following two working papers elaborated as part of a research program on human rights and economic growth at the Danish Institute for Human Rights: Sigrid Alexandra Koob, Stinne Skriver Jørgensen, and Hans-Otto Sano, 'Human Rights and Economic Growth: An Econometric Analysis of Freedom and Participation Rights' (2017) Matters of Concern Human Rights Research Papers No 2017/1 <www.humanrights.dk/sites/humanrights.dk/files/media/dokumenter/udgivelser/research/matters_of _concern_series/final_human_rights_and_economic_growth_-_an_econometric_analysis.pdf> accessed 12 June 2020; Sigrid Alexandra Koob, Stinne Skriver Jørgensen, and Hans-Otto Sano, 'Human Rights and Economic Growth: An Econometric Analysis of the Rights to Education and Health' Matters of Concern Human Rights Research Papers No 2018/4 <www.humanrights.dk/sites/humanrights.dk/files/ media/dokumenter/udgivelser/research/matters_of_concern_series/wp_hr_economic_growth_2018 .pdf> accessed 12 June 2020.

[25]   A study on livelihood change in semi-arid Tanzania documented how affluent and also poorer farmers managed to exploit market access and complement maize farming on relatively poor lands with upland tomato cultivation that could be sold and transported to Dar es Salaam via truck haulers travelling from the Southern Regions to the capital. Torben Birch-Thomsen, Pia Frederiksen and Hans-Otto Sano, 'A Livelihood Perspective on Natural Resource Management and Environmental Change in Semiarid Tanzania' (2001) 77 Economic Geography 41.

[26]   Alice Donald and Elizabeth Mottershaw, *Poverty, Inequality and Human Rights: Do Human Rights Make a Difference?* (Joseph Rowntree Foundation 2009) <www.jrf.org.uk/report/poverty -inequality-and-human-rights> accessed 12 June 2020.

along with an overreliance on international NGOs – the report provides observations worth dwelling upon, not least with respect to the legal field.

The report emphasized the need to translate human rights so that they resonate with particular audiences. Human rights values of dignity, respect and fairness seemed to command the widest assent. A strategic approach linking human rights to anti-poverty work would stress four dimensions of human rights relevance:

- *Using human rights as a tool.* According to the report, governments only episodically use human rights as an anti-poverty tool. Efforts of donors and governments to work according to a human rights-based approach are not unimportant in the poverty context. Furthermore, the report shows how human rights are used as a tool of community mobilization relating to, for example, social rights in housing and health.[27]
- *Raising political accountability* of duty-bearers by monitoring and measuring human rights. This also relates to the use of the human-rights monitoring systems but also to the use of value-neutral tools, such as budget analysis, in order to pursue human-rights goals. The Rowntree report points to the creation of new data as a result of monitoring that can be used by civil society in auditing state and duty-bearer accountability. It provides one example from South Africa where the Alliance for Children's Entitlement to Social Security used human rights arguments to persuade the government to increase the budget allocation for child support.[28]
- *Legal accountability*, or using legal processes to realize rights and combat poverty. The social-rights jurisprudence in some cases produces tangible results. The report mentions examples in South Africa, India and Nigeria, but also relevant is the systematic work and assessment of Gauri, Brinks and Young.[29]
- *Using human rights to define broader agendas* of poverty. The report points to the ability of the rights language to facilitate alliances between disparate communities. While some communities in Ireland and Wales found human rights to be jarring with their perceptions of solutions-oriented approaches, other groups in the south saw the rights agenda as a powerful tool to increase confidence and a sense of entitlement.[30] Thus, the rights-based approach, according to the UK report, was an agenda against injustices and the feckless but also one of the fight for economic resources.

In summary, human rights can be used to frame advocacy on poverty, for example with a focus on social rights or discriminatory policies, while at the same time prompting leaders in governments or among donors to take actions in line with their human rights obligations. The latter may be realized through legal measures. Two common learning points stand out as important with respect to these various entry points of empowerment and accountability: (1) documen-

---

[27] At a general level without specific examples, Rukooko argues that the human rights conventions complement each other to offer a synergetic effect against poverty. In particular, economic and social rights are seen to be important given state and multinational companies' social impact. A Byaruhanga Rukooko, 'Poverty and Human Rights in Africa: Historical Dynamics and the Case for Economic Social and Cultural Rights' (2010) 14 The International Journal of Human Rights 13.

[28] Donald and Mottershaw (n 26) 24.

[29] Varun Gauri and Daniel M Brinks (eds), *Courting Social Justice: Judicial Enforcement of Social and Economic Rights in the Developing World* (CUP 2008); Katharine G Young, *Constituting economic and social rights* (Oxford University Press on Demand 2012).

[30] Donald and Mottershaw (n 26) 5–7, 39–40.

tation on the various policies and instruments in use is scarce and (2) the need to translate human rights to particular audiences seems vital. In the section below, a more detailed review of poverty and human rights-based approaches is undertaken in order to elaborate on potential effective linkages between human rights and poverty reduction. This is an angle where local experiences rather than national ones are in focus.

B.   The Local Experience of Human Rights-based Efforts

Poverty in sub-Saharan Africa may be discussed from an angle of human-rights violations, such as uprooting from ancestral lands, violence against vulnerable groups, exploitation and lack of state accountability towards social rights. The discussion below relates to these issues in some measure. However, poverty may also be discussed from an angle of empowerment: the efforts of individual and groups to raise their voices, to work collectively for social justice or to improve livelihoods and institutional access in daily struggles to cope with adverse economic plights. These processes of struggle, participation, empowerment and advocacy are often what is meant when human rights-based approaches are debated. However, positive examples tend to be rare in sub-Saharan Africa, and they are mostly taking place at very local levels. Therefore, the majority of human rights-based approaches are implemented at local levels.

Localization is used in recent research on human rights realization in developing countries to describe the 'travel, translation and transformation of human rights across scales'.[31] While Destrooper and Engle Merry's perspective centres around the meaning and understanding of human rights, Hafner-Burton uses the concept of 'localization' in addressing the consolidation of human rights locally through local community actors and NGOs. She sees such actors as crucial in creating stronger legitimacy around human rights.[32] According to Koen de Feyter,[33] it is at the local level that human rights can act as a line of defence against injustice.

Local human rights change is therefore highly relevant from different perspectives – not least because local change is often forgotten or remains unknown. Unfortunately, it is mostly in evaluation studies from donors and NGOs that the poverty impact of local change is addressed. During recent years, it is difficult to find substantive studies from human rights scholars who address the poverty impact of human rights-based approaches. In a recent article, Destrooper examined the gaps between the rhetoric and reality of the Human Rights-Based Approach (HRBA) in a water and sanitation project in the Democratic Republic of Congo.[34] She studied 12 indicators in her assessment of implementation strength. These indicators were inspired by the UN Common Understanding of the Human Rights-Based Approach and based

---

[31]   Tine Destrooper and Sally Engle Merry, *Human Rights Transformation in Practice* (University of Pennsylvania Press 2018).

[32]   Emilie M Hafner-Burton, *Making Human Rights a Reality* (Princeton University Press 2013).

[33]   Koen De Feyter and others, *The Local Relevance of Human Rights* (Cambridge University Press 2011).

[34]   Tine Destrooper, 'Linking Discourse and Practice: the Human Rights-Based Approach to Development in the Village Assaini Program in the Kongo Central' (2016) 38 Hum Rts Q 787. She examined 12 indicators of implementation inspired by the UN Common Understanding of the Human Rights-Based Approach and based on other UN documents. None of the indicators related specifically to poverty, but indicators on equality, inclusivity, participation, empowerment and forwarding of human rights claims could have a poverty dimension.

on UNICEF documents. None of the indicators related specifically to poverty, although the indicators of equality, non-discrimination, inclusivity, participation, empowerment and for-warding of human rights claims could have a poverty dimension. Destrooper's study revealed the considerable gap between rhetoric and reality and also that poverty indicators were not in focus in this particular rights-based project administered by an UN organization.

In a recent article examining the progress of pursuing human rights-based efforts in devel-opment, Paul J. Nelson and Ellen Dorsey summarize the achievements so far:

- The rhetoric of the development sector on implementing HRBA appears to have surpassed the practical work – a conclusion that confirms the one advanced by Destrooper regarding the UNICEF water and sanitation project discussed above.[35]
- The Millennium Development Goals tended to sideline rights-based work among most development donors. The authors do not provide much documentation on this. Though they recognize that the Sustainable Development Goals (SDGs) have inspired human rights organizations, the linkages between human rights, poverty and the SDGs are uncertain.
- The right to free, prior and informed consent has advanced the position of marginalized groups vis-à-vis extractive industries and other incursions.
- Smaller, more flexible organizations have been the vanguard of development work, but questions remain as to whether their achievements are durable. In contrast, donors have not achieved much.
- Finally, too little is known on the impact of HRBA on poverty.[36]

While Joel Oestreich's study of the UN in India demonstrates the modest achievements of rights-based UN programming in India,[37] Nelson and Dorsey do not seem to have a compre-hensive overview of the actual achievements of bilateral donors. Sano and Anyidoho's study from Ghana indicates significant differences in access to sanitation services and in malnutri-tion between poor and non-poor households in two districts of the Volta region in Ghana; the district supported under a right-to-services programme fared considerably better with respect to malnutrition and to access to sanitation, from which the poorer households also benefitted.[38] Obviously, the sustainability of such achievements can be questioned, but it remains important to underline that using rights-based thinking contributed to achievements over a short period of time.

---

[35] See also on the rhetorical dimension Koen De Feyter and Richard Lumbika Nlandu, 'Skimming The Surface' in Paul Gready and Wouter Vandenhole (eds), *Human Rights and Development in the new Millennium: Towards a Theory of Change* (Routledge 2013) 213–30.

[36] Nelson and Dorsey (n 16).

[37] Joel E Oestreich, *Development and Human Rights: rhetoric and reality in India* (Oxford University Press 2017).

[38] Thus, the rights-based support of the government of Ghana and Danida was instrumental in achieving positive impact among the poor in the district supported, while the contiguous district in the same region was exhibiting less persuasive indicators among the poor households, and, generally with respect to sanitation and malnutrition. However, it should also be taken into account that the government of Ghana and Danida had selected the better-performing district for the project. See Hans-Otto Sano and Nana Akua Anyidoho, 'The Right to Services and Poverty: A Case Study from the Volta Region in Ghana' (2017) Matters of Concern Human Rights Research Papers No 2016/3 <www.humanrights.dk/publications/right-services-poverty> accessed 12 June 2020. See also Broberg and Sano (n 6).

Among the international NGOs, DanChurchAid reports (following an evaluation study) that success has been achieved in enhancing the capacity of rights-holders to engage with duty-bearers, including at the community level. As a result of HRBA work, processes of democratization and improved practices of solidarity were among the success stories. Processes of empowerment were individual rather than institutional despite efforts of local organizations to reach the national level. Reduced discriminatory practices were also documented in African contexts but results in terms of redistribution of resources were not evident.[39]

An evaluation of the water and sanitation programme supported by German development cooperation (GIZ) also underlined the positive impact among poorer households in Kenya resulting from a focus on those who were underserved with a fast-track and up-scale access to services. The human rights-based approach promoted a comprehensive pro-poor orientation in the sector. An evaluation estimated that more than 50 per cent of a population sample in the programme area had seen an improvement in living standards.[40]

The examples available from the African context are fairly few. Questions can be raised about their sustainability and studies are rarely as precise concerning the impact on the poor as the German study. Of the few examples mentioned here, the positive change relates to service impact and to legal and non-legal mobilization in connection with advocacy efforts. Some of the examples emphasize decentralization initiatives[41] and efforts to bring about institutional change among duty-bearers. The latter also points to new institutional practices and to norm change with respect to gender. At this level of norm change, the impact of human rights-based efforts would extend beyond the local level.[42]

With the limited evidence available, it is difficult to confidently claim that the specific impact of human rights-based efforts has had a strong positive impact on poverty reduction in the African context. The human rights projects at local levels cannot explain the general reduction in poverty. The various cases of local human rights-based change indicate processes of better service access, community solidarity, democratization and possibly even norm change in society in general. But if human rights cannot provide a general explanation for the reduction in poverty, how can it be explained?

C.   Economic and Livelihood Empowerment

In the rural areas in sub-Saharan Africa, poverty tends to be inherited from generation to generation; the prevalence of poverty is determined by inherited lands and capital, health,

---

[39]   DCA actalliance, 'Documenting the Effects of HRBA in Development. Synthesis Reports' (Critical Rights & Gender Consult 2017). Laure-Hélène Piron and Hans-Otto Sano, *Lessons Learned on the Danish Human Rights-Based Approach* (Ministry of Foreign Affairs of Denmark 2016) <www .humanrights.dk/sites/humanrights.dk/files/media/researchpublications/downloads/evaluation_study _november_2016_published.pdf> accessed 12 June 2020.

[40]   See Federal Ministry for Economic Cooperation and Development (BMZ), 'Promising Practices: On the Human Rights-Based Approach in German Development Cooperation: Water and Sanitation: Ensuring Access for the Urban Poor in Kenya' (*Deutsche Gesellschaft für Internationale Zusammenarbeit (GIZ)*, 2013) <www.institut-fuer-menschenrechte.de/uploads/tx_commerce/promising_practices_water _and_sanitation_in_kenya.pdf> accessed 12 June 2020.

[41]   Duni and others (n 6) 49; Broberg and Sano (n 6).

[42]   Susanna D Wing, 'Human Rights-Based Approaches to Development: Justice and Legal Fiction in Africa' (2012) 44 Polity 504, 518.

educational status, gender relations, locality and unequal access to opportunities.[43] Within these broad parameters, research from the International Food Policy Research Institute (IFPRI) points to how rural peasants have managed to intensify production patterns and access to markets. A process of economic empowerment has taken place in parts of sub-Saharan Africa.[44]

A major factor in reduction of poverty is therefore the growth in agricultural productivity. Total agricultural factor productivities have grown especially in areas of Eastern and Southern Africa and in the humid parts of West Africa. The scarcity of land has forced farmers to intensify production, particularly in the 2000s. Total factor productivities (land and labour) have increased. The gains achieved have not been very remarkable compared to, for example, North Africa, but they have nevertheless surpassed achievements seen during previous decades. Due to the high numbers of poor people in the rural areas, this progress on the agricultural intensification frontier has contributed significantly to the fall in poverty since the turn of the millennium.

The improved rural living standards have spurred additional demand and exchange between rural and urban areas. This – in addition to higher educational levels and stronger urban markets – has been an important factor in poverty reduction.

The gains in productivity cannot, it seems, be attributed to the state duty-bearer efforts. While African states planned to allocate at least 10 per cent of their national budget for agriculture under the Maputo Declaration of 2003 under the Comprehensive Africa Agriculture Development Programme (CAADP), state support reached only 3.1 per cent on average for sub-Saharan Africa between 2001 and 2010.[45] The growth in productivity can mainly be attributed to struggles of peasants themselves to cope with the fact that new lands for cultivation were no longer available.

D.   The Non-Monetary Perspective of Poverty Reduction

Purportedly inspired by Amartya Sen's capability approach and OPHI, the World Bank Africa report[46] recognizes that well-being is difficult to price, not just because measurement is difficult but also because well-being is valuable in ways that cannot be monetized. Human rights are carefully not mentioned in the World Bank report, but it covers ground that makes the lack of reference to a substantial body of literature on human rights and non-discrimination remarkable and not in accordance with good scientific practice.

The 2016 World Bank Africa report assesses progress in non-monetary dimensions of poverty: education, health and freedom from violence. In addition, it addresses non-monetary aspects of inequality. While significant achievements were recorded in educational gender gaps, adult literacy and primary enrolment between the mid-1990s and 2012, levels of edu-

---

[43]   Andrew Dabalen and others, *Do African Children Have an Equal Chance? A Human Opportunity Report for Sub-Saharan Africa* (World Bank 2015) <http://documents.worldbank.org/curated/en/785981468191648289/pdf/Do-African-children-have-an-equal-chance-A-human-opportunity-report-for-sub-saharan-Africa.pdf> accessed 12 June 2020.

[44]   Samuel Benin (ed), *Agricultural Productivity in Africa: Trends, Patterns and Determinants* (International Food Policy Research Institute (IFPRI) 2016) 335–46 <http://ebrary.ifpri.org/utils/getfile/collection/p15738coll2/id/130468/filename/130679.pdf> accessed 12 June 2020.

[45]   ibid 11, 12.

[46]   Beegle and others (n 15) 83.

cational deprivation nevertheless remain high in sub-Saharan Africa. With respect to health rights, life expectancy at birth rose by 6.2 years during the same period and the prevalence of chronic malnutrition fell 6 percentage points to 38.6 per cent. Twelve of 16 countries experienced statistically significant improvements in immunization, while seven out of 16 countries improved with respect to stunting. While full immunization rates improved between 1998 and 2008, they still only covered about 60 per cent of the population during 2008. Generally, Francophone countries in sub-Saharan Africa performed less impressively compared to the Anglophone countries in terms of health indicators.[47]

A significant trait in the lack of enjoyment of freedom in sub-Saharan Africa is insecurity and domestic violence. As documented earlier by Narayan (2000) poverty is multidimensional and is associated with powerlessness, hopelessness and violence. She described how households were crumbling under the weight of poverty:

> While many households remain intact, many others disintegrate as men, unable to adapt to their 'failure' to earn adequate incomes under harsh economic circumstances, have difficulty accepting that women are becoming the main breadwinners and that this necessitates a redistribution of power within the household. ... Clearly, this is not necessarily empowering for women. Despite having assumed new roles, women continue to face discrimination in the labor market and gender inequity in the home. ... [E]mpowerment or income-earning does not necessarily lead to social empowerment or gender equity within households.[48]

The persistence of a high level of domestic violence in Africa indicates that the patterns of gender stereotypes and discrimination are still prevalent. The incidence of domestic violence is 50 per cent higher compared to the rest of the Global South. The Africa Barometer data from 2016–18 indicate that insecurity is pervasive. Among the respondents almost 50 per cent indicated that they fear political intimidation or violence, and 39 per cent indicated that they or a family member have felt unsafe at least once walking in the neighbourhood during the past year.[49]

Has inequality of access to social services changed over time within and among sub-Saharan African countries? The Human Opportunity Index (HOI) measures to what degree social opportunities (education, health, water, sanitation and electricity) are evenly distributed within countries. Between 1998 and 2008, HOI has increased in 20 African countries investigated, meaning services became more evenly distributed. While improvements have concerned general coverage (the upscaling of service provision and access), for a number of countries like Mali, Ethiopia, Mozambique, Nigeria and Senegal, the expansion has favoured underserved groups with respect to services such as education, water, immunization, nutrition and electricity. However, these modifications of patterns of inequality have been limited to five out of 20 countries. Access to the most basic services in sub-Saharan African countries is not universal. Wealth, location and the educational status of the household head continue to play

---

[47]   During the period 1996–2012 the adult literacy rate rose by four percentage points, the gender gap shrank considerably in adult literacy, and the primary enrolment increased dramatically. However, more than two adults out of five cannot read and write, and the quality of teaching is generally poor. See ibid 107–09, 147.

[48]   Deepa Narayan, *Voices of the poor: Can anyone hear us?* (World Bank 2000) <http://documents .worldbank.org/curated/en/131441468779067441/pdf/multi0page.pdf> accessed 12 June 2020.

[49]   See 'The Online Data Analysis Tool: 2016/2018' (*Afrobarometer*) <https://afrobarometer.org/ online-data-analysis/analyse-online> accessed 12 June 2020.

an important role in defining inequalities. Whether a child finishes primary school is primarily determined by the wealth of the household, and whether a one-year child is fully immunized is influenced by the educational status of the head of household.[50]

Related to the role of location in influencing within-country inequality is the lack of social mobility. The locality of birth and the occupation of parents are instrumental in defining social mobility. In the African context, being born in a rural and remote region into a family of farmers is an aspect of unequal opportunity that has a direct bearing on poverty. The likelihood that sons will stay in farming if born to a farmer is more than 70 per cent in countries such as Ghana, Rwanda and Uganda.[51]

The non-monetary poverty and rights-related variables qualify additionally the complexity of prevailing poverty and human rights in the sub-Saharan countries.

III. AFFECTING THE DISCOURSE ON POVERTY

In order to understand how human rights affect poverty reduction, it is relevant to reflect on how human rights influence the international discourse on poverty.

The 2016 World Bank African poverty study recognized that many aspects of well-being cannot be properly priced or monetarily valued, such as the ability to read and write, longevity, good health, security, political freedoms, social acceptance, status and the ability to move about and connect. The irreducibility of these aspects of well-being are acknowledged in the Human Development Index and the Multidimensional Poverty Index in their focus on achievements in education, longevity, health and living standards.[52]

The World Bank study expands this scope to include freedom from violence and freedom to decide (a proxy for the notion of self-determination).[53] This broader concept of poverty used by the World Bank is inspired by the Human Development Reports (and Amartya Sen), along with human rights language.

Rights-talk matters in these discussions on poverty and in the focus and data analyses on violence and decision-making powers. These decision-making powers include 'political freedom and participation but also social norms and the freedom to decide about routine matters in life, including within the household. Constraints can be based on gender, religion, ethnicity, sexual orientation, or other reasons'.[54] The influence of human rights in these formulations is obvious, which suggests that human rights have influenced the concept of poverty and its potential indicators.

However, this discursive impact – the travel of ideas as highlighted in Destrooper and Engle Merry[55] – is also discernible on the ground. The travel from the bottom up, which is often the

---

[50]   See Dabalen and others (n 43) 10–13. The information on the contribution of each circumstance (wealth, educational status, location, age and gender) to the inequality of opportunity derives from an analysis of the top 10 unequal countries among the 20 analysed.
[51]   See Beegle and others (n 15) 135.
[52]   ibid 11.
[53]   ibid 11.
[54]   ibid 102.
[55]   Wouter Vandenhole, 'Human rights-based approaches to development: the local, travel and transformation' in Tine Destrooper and Sally Engle Merry (eds), *Human Rights Transformation in Practice* (University of Pennsylvania Press 2018).

local perspective of human rights-based change, implies that human rights are seen as struggles and not as preconceived legal rules, according to Vandenhole.[56]

Local struggles are informed by human-rights principles of participation, non-discrimination and equality, and accountability of duty-bearers, but also broader concerns of access to information, control of resources, land inheritance, and norms relating to gender, marriage, domestic violence and security of girls.

Contextual factors that influence gender gaps and poverty involve all of these issues. Human rights standards, principles and broader developmental concerns are part of activities that are often specified when effective gender equality processes are analysed. However, it is scarcely possible to identify a single human rights-based approach to gender transformation; similarly, it is not possible to define a core developmental approach to changing gender relations that excludes human rights-based influence.[57]

Human-rights talk has therefore had an important impact in influencing the discourse on poverty and the practices of poverty reduction.

IV.   CONCLUSIONS

Measured from a human-rights point of view, poverty has not declined to the degree claimed in conventional measurements of extreme poverty in sub-Saharan Africa. Poverty has decreased, particularly in Eastern and Southern Africa, and especially in urban areas, but if social-service provision and access deprivations are taken into account, as seen in the OPHI, then the fall is less than claimed using the IPL measure. The discrepancy between the USD 1.90 per day conventional IPL measurement of extreme poverty and the data from the OPHI measurement of poverty is wide for the majority of countries in sub-Saharan Africa, for instance, conflicting estimates of poverty prevalence to the tune of more than 50 percentage points for Ethiopia.

An important trait is that irrespective of measurement method, the absolute number of poor people in sub-Saharan Africa has increased while poverty rates have fallen. Population growth on average has surpassed average poverty declines. Rural poverty (irrespective of measurement method) still remains high, and in many countries is above 50 per cent. Urban poverty thus remains substantially lower than the national averages.

The decline in poverty rates cannot be attributed to human rights-based efforts despite the fact that there are local positive experiences in reducing discriminatory patterns, in social mobilization, improved service access and advocacy. Neither can the decline in poverty be attributed to enhanced government efforts in rural areas despite ambitions of increased public investments in these areas. Such investments have not been realized in most countries. Rather the decline in poverty can be explained by the efforts of the rights-holders themselves to enhance land and labour productivity or to find new markets. The higher incomes in rural areas have implied more demand for rural and urban production and positive processes of economic growth. In countries where these processes have been slow, in some cases due to domestic conflicts, migratory patterns have been high, as seen in parts of West Africa.

---

[56]   ibid 81.
[57]   See the World Bank Group, *Ethiopia Gender Diagnostic Report: Priorities for Promoting Equity* (World Bank 2019) part III <http://documents.worldbank.org/curated/en/300021552881249070/pdf/Ethiopia-Gender-Diagnostic-Report-Priorities-for-Promoting-Equity.pdf> accessed 12 June 2020.

The data on inequality trends, whether measured by Gini coefficients or by inequality of opportunities, are still incomplete and lack updates. However, the available evidence indicates that high levels of inequality hamper poverty-reduction processes despite the fact that poverty is not correlated with inequality on average. The trends in sub-Saharan Africa based on the available evidence is that inequality has increased in Southern Africa but decreased in East and West Africa. For the countries where inequality of opportunity has been measured, the data also point to moderate improvements in terms of equal access. In spite of this, location, gender and the social position of parents are still important in determining social status.

Human rights-based efforts have played a positive role locally, but human rights thinking has not influenced poverty-reduction policies and national poverty trends significantly. Some scholars argue that poverty-reduction policies were channelled via the MDGs, and more recently the SDGs, rather than through human rights. Thus, human rights have not been used as a strong, explicit tool of poverty reduction.

Yet human-rights concepts and discourse have influenced the conception of poverty, often in tandem with general human development work. Non-monetary indicators have been added to the conventional income- and consumption-based measurements. The human rights awareness and the struggles to fight discrimination have meant achievements in women's access to education and in less national discrimination in social access. Domestic violence and insecurity remain high in sub-Saharan Africa. Along with a better formulated and more explicit human rights agenda on poverty reduction, equality, domestic violence, social mobility and empowerment are obvious areas for future intervention in human rights-based programming.

PART II

CROSS-CURRENTS

A.   Poverty, Human Rights and Identity

7. Breaking the link between poverty and disability: re-purposing human rights in the 21st century

Gerard Quinn

The extremely high prevalence of poverty amongst persons with disabilities is well known.[1] The Equality and Human Rights Commission in the UK recently stated that half of all households in poverty in the UK either have a disabled adult or a disabled child.[2] Given that persons with disabilities number close to one billion worldwide (mostly in the developing south) this is not a minor issue.[3]

Indeed, poverty and disability seem almost synonymous. Having a physical or psychosocial disability can lead to poverty. Of course, it is not so much the disability, as such, that leads to poverty. This usually happens due to a range of related negative social arrangements and policies that compound what is otherwise a natural part of the human condition. And being in poverty for other reasons can lead to both physical and psychosocial disabilities – destroying the body, mind and soul. This is described as a bi-directional relationship.[4] Given the primacy of market forces for the provision of even essential goods and services in modern societies, any lack of consumer power can easily lead to a downward spiral in health status. Escaping poverty – particularly intergenerational poverty – for persons with disabilities seems especially difficult.

Employment – the normal route for generating the means necessary for a good life – is exceptionally difficult for many people with disabilities across the world. Relative economic inactivity (and indeed in-work poverty) means reduced or no pension entitlement, which complicates life in old age. Even if the employment market were more inclusive, persons with disabilities might lack marketable skills due to non-inclusive educational systems. And it is not just persons with disabilities themselves who are locked into poverty. The ripple effect of poverty also affects many family members who provide care, and especially women, who

---

[1] See Michal Palmer, 'Poverty and Disability: a Conceptual Review' (2011) 21-4 Journal of Disability Policy Studies 210; Adam Tinson and others, 'Disability and Poverty: Why Disability Must be at the Centre of Poverty Reduction' (*New Policy Institute*, 2016) <www.npi.org.uk/files/3414/7087/2429/Disability_and_poverty_MAIN_REPORT_FINAL.pdf>.

[2] Equality and Human Rights Commission, 'Is Britain Fairer?: The State of Equality and Human Rights 2018' (*Equality and Human Rights Commission*, 2018) 38, 46, 52. See also Legatum Institute, 'Measuring Poverty in the UK Full Debate' (*Youtube*, 23 January 2019) <www.youtube.com/watch?v=WGIHuyLMHcA> (speech of Baroness Philippa Stroud to the House of Lords).

[3] This figure is from the World Bank webpage on Disability and Inclusion: www.worldbank.org/en/topic/disability.

[4] See Mónica Pinilla-Roncancio, 'Disability and Poverty: Two Related Conditions – A Review of the Literature' (2015) 63 Rev. Fac. Med. 113.

often find themselves without pension entitlements in old age.[5] Many social systems – whether in the Global South or in the Global North – depend on family carers (which usually means women) as a default.[6] The result is that women often end up being the tangible victims of this intersectional impact. This 'feminization of poverty' is an almost automatic effect of traditional policy approaches to disability.[7]

With economic systems relatively unreceptive to persons with disabilities, social protection programmes are hardly ever sufficient, and many poverty alleviation measures carry with them perverse poverty traps.[8] Very few social protection systems take adequate account of the extra costs of disability – costs often incurred because of other policy failings, such as the need for taxis *in lieu* of accessible public transport. Age-based benefits fail to keep track of the life course, and these failings at key inflection points can be extremely damaging.[9] Cash or in-kind benefits often taper away rapidly as persons earn an income, and this badly affects persons with disabilities who then find they do not earn enough to afford the ongoing costs of disability. International development assistance programmes are often based on assumed need instead of on the voices of persons with disabilities. There is a near-fatalism in much of the literature that seems to despair at any sustainable solution.

Until quite recently, several decades of international and regional human rights law and policy seem to have made little or no difference. Why not? Can human rights play a constructive role – and not just a rhetorical role – in breaking the umbilical bond that seems to link disability with poverty? I argue it can. But it has to more directly challenge deeply embedded cultural assumptions about disability and especially the invisibility of persons with disabilities in both the economic and social spheres. It has to interrogate why employment markets are so resistant to including workers with disabilities and then take the next steps to nudge them open. Human rights should have something tangible to say about how markets are structured and not just seek to ameliorate them after the fact when they fail to deliver.

Part I of this chapter sketches the many links between poverty and disability. These links were laid bare in graphic form in the 2018 UN Department of Economic and Social Affairs (UN DESA) Flagship Report on Disability and Development.[10]

Part II of this chapter unravels why traditional human rights-based approaches have not generally led to practical results. Put another way, it explores why traditional human rights

---

[5]   See literature from the Women's Institute for a Secure Retirement (WISER) available at: www .wiserwomen.org/index.php?id=38&page=National_Resource_Center_on_Women_and_Retirement _Planning. See also, 'Informal Care, Poverty and Social Exclusion' (Eurocarers, 2017) <https:// eurocarers.org/publications/informal-care-poverty-and-social-exclusion/>.

[6]   COFACE (Families Europe) is particularly active in the debate about the rights of carers in the disability context. To learn more about COFACE, visit their website at: www.coface-eu.org.

[7]   For an overview of the literature see Carolina Johansson Wennerholm, 'The "Feminisation of Poverty": The use of a Concept' (*SIDA*, 2002) <www.sida.se/contentassets/cfd458d3a45e41348afd0fe 45f1bed5c/13336.pdf>.

[8]   See Gerard Quinn, 'How Redistributive Cash Systems in Europe Create Poverty Traps for Persons with Disabilities, (*DISCIT*, 2013) <https://blogg.hioa.no/discit/files/2016/02/DISCIT-D8_1-How -Redistributive-Cash-Transfer-Systems-in-Europe-create-Poverty-Traps-for-Persons-with-Disabilities .pdf>.

[9]   See generally, Mark Priestly (ed), *Disability: A Life Course Approach* (Polity Press 2003).

[10]   UN DESA, 'Flagship Report on Disability and Development: Realizing the Sustainable Development Goals by, for and with Persons with Disabilities' (*United Nations*, 2018) <https://social.un .org/publications/UN-Flagship-Report-Disability-Final.pdf>.

doctrine did not forcefully and directly challenge systemic exclusion in economic systems and the inadequacy of social protection programmes. I argue that human rights doctrine from about 1948 to 1990 internalized 'mental reservations' prevalent in culture about persons with disabilities. Their discounted humanity had implications for the application of an equality doctrine that too easily accepted segregationist and exclusionary laws and policies.

Part III of this chapter constructs – or re-constructs – a much more positive agenda for human rights in the 21st century for breaking the bond between poverty and disability. It builds on some of the core philosophical underpinnings of the UN Convention on the Rights of Persons with Disabilities (UN CRPD), adopted in 2007. The doctrinal innovations of that treaty are rightly celebrated.[11] But it is the underlying philosophical premises of the Convention that deserve attention, including specifically its emphasis on the equal worth and personhood of persons with disabilities and the principle of 'inclusive equality' in challenging all manner of exclusion, whether in the private or public spheres. The philosophical shifts marked by the UN CRPD are both congruent with, and help seal the chemistry between, human rights and the UN Sustainable Development Goals (SDGs).[12] The SDGs are bound by and must be implemented in line with existing human rights treaties.[13] In this sense, the extensive filigree of human rights treaties form an anchorage point in understanding and implementing the SDGs. Especially in the case of disability, the SDGs also serve to ratchet upwards our expectations of human rights.

In conclusion I point to a new research agenda – one that focuses on a new kind of social market that embraces human difference including disability and re-conceptualizes social protection as underpinning and not undermining social inclusion and belonging.[14] This agenda should build more explicitly on the complementarity between human rights and the SDGs.

I.   THE LINKS BETWEEN POVERTY AND DISABILITY

The literature on the link between poverty and disability is voluminous, but here I focus on the key finding of the pioneering UN DESA Flagship Report of 2018 on Disability and Development.[15]

The Flagship Report confirms that persons with disabilities are more likely than others to live in poverty. Research conducted for the Report revealed that in some countries the poverty rate for persons with disabilities was 22 per cent higher than for others.[16] For example, while the poverty rate for the general population in the US was estimated at 11 per cent, it shot up to 29 per cent for persons with disabilities. In the Republic of Korea the equivalent figures were 13 per cent and 35 per cent. Data in the Report also reveals that the percentage of households with disabilities that were in poverty was on average higher compared to households without

---

[11]   See Ilias Bantekas, Michael Ashley Stein, and Dimitris Anastasiou (eds), *The UN Convention on the Rights of Persons with Disabilities: A Commentary* (Oxford University Press 2018).

[12]   UNGA, 'Transforming Our World: The 2030 Agenda for Sustainable Development' (21 October 2015) UN Doc A/RES/70/1.

[13]   ibid para 10 ('on shared principles and commitments').

[14]   A promising resource is the forthcoming book, Kelley Johnson and Jan Walmsley, *Belonging and Social Inclusion for Persons with Intellectual Disabilities* (Routledge, forthcoming 2021).

[15]   UN DESA (n 10).

[16]   ibid 34.

someone with a disability. Particular attention was drawn in the Report to the situation of women and girls with disabilities living in poverty.[17]

The Report assessed that the extra costs for disability could be 30 to 40 per cent extra for a moderate disability and 40 to 70 per cent extra for a severe disability.[18] This places a huge strain on family income – bearing in mind that most social protection programmes do not factor in these unavoidable extra costs. Access to credit for persons with disabilities – either through commercial bank loans or micro-credit – was also found generally wanting.[19]

Strikingly, the percentage of persons with disabilities without easy access to food in the countries analysed reached at least 30 per cent. That included children with disabilities going to school hungry.[20] Due mainly to the lack of inclusive educational systems, children with disabilities are often excluded from educational systems or their needs are inadequately addressed. They are therefore likely to exit the system with lower qualifications than their peers, lower literacy rates, and less marketable skills.[21] This means that no matter how inclusive the economic system, persons with disabilities are excluded without a genuinely inclusive educational system.[22]

According to the Flagship Report, the percentages of persons with disabilities who needed access to social welfare services but who did not get it (either because it was unavailable or they did not qualify) are staggering. This accounted for 90 per cent of persons with disabilities in Zambia and 75 per cent in Zimbabwe.[23] The Report concludes its analysis by saying that 'available data show that the proportion of persons with disabilities living under the national or international poverty line is higher, and in some countries double, than that of persons without disabilities'.[24]

Later in 2018, the UN Development Programme (UNDP) published a follow-through document intended to guide UNDP programming entitled: Disability Inclusive Development in UNDP – Guidance and Entry Points. It strongly reinforces the analysis in the DESA Flagship Report: the 'available date' strongly supports the existence of a link between disability and poverty.[25]

In the Global South, this stems largely from the lack of formal economic opportunities and sometimes the complete absence of a social protection system.[26] In the Global North this stems largely from economic systems that are not inclusive of the difference of disability and from

[17] ibid Ch II(E) ('Achieving gender equality and empowering all women and girls with disabilities'), 97–117.

[18] ibid 37.

[19] ibid 38.

[20] ibid 34–42.

[21] ibid ch II(D) ('ensuring inclusive and equitable quality education for all persons with disabilities' – Goal 4), 73–96.

[22] See generally Gauthier de Beco, Shivaun Quinlivan, and Janet E Lord, *The Right to Inclusive Education in International Human Rights Law* (Cambridge University Press 2019).

[23] UN DESA, 'Disability and Development Report: Realizing the Sustainable Development Goals by, for and with Persons with Disabilities' (*United Nations*, 2018) 42.

[24] ibid 25.

[25] 'Disability Inclusive Development in UNDP: Guidance and Entry Points' (*United Nations Development Programme*, 3 December 2018) <www.undp.org/content/undp/en/home/librarypage/democratic-governance/human_rights/disability-inclusive-development-in-undp.html>.

[26] See Shaun Grech and Karen Soldatic (eds), *Disability in the Global South: The Critical Handbook* (Springer 2016).

social protection systems that merely 'compensate' people for their absence rather than plot a course for inclusion and active citizenship.

II.   THE LIMITED POTENCY OF HUMAN RIGHTS IN BREAKING CYCLES OF POVERTY FOR PERSONS WITH DISABILITIES THUS FAR

A.   Legacy of Invisibility and Passive Welfare

Professor Conor Gearty has labelled the disability rights movement as a 'visibility project'.[27] By this is meant that the core issue had to do with the discounting of the humanity of persons with disabilities. The dominant image of disability in culture and public policy was one of passive dependency.[28] This was so much so, that the very personhood (and autonomy) of the person was denied.[29] This invisibility led to laws and policies that 'naturally' excluded the person.[30]

The physical exclusion reinforced deep-seated cultural assumptions. The person was framed as a 'problem' to be cared for or managed. The primary means for providing care was through the family (but largely unsupported).[31] In so far as care was publicly provided, it was done in separate, segregated silos (special schools, sheltered workshops, and passive welfare programmes). The resulting barriers were conceptualized as natural and inevitable, and indeed a 'fault' of the person. Failure to accommodate the difference of disability was seen as 'natural' and not framed as a conscious (or at least implicit) policy choice.

War and conflicts initiated the modern period of disability policy. Ever since the American Civil War,[32] and certainly since the First World War,[33] there began a clear policy focus on disability particularly in developed countries. Protean ideas at that time about the welfare state were gradually stretched to embrace the 'care' of persons with disabilities. Pensions for the blind were among the first to be established in the fledgling welfare states of Europe.

---

[27]   The phrase was first used by Professor Conor Gearty (London School of Economics) in public pronouncements in the late 1990s (email from Conor Gearty to author, 13 September 2019).

[28]   See Sarah F Rose, *No Right to be Idle: The Invention of Disability, 1840s–1930s* (University of North Carolina Press 2017).

[29]   The literature on autonomy (legal capacity) and disability is voluminous. A good ready reckoner is Kristin Booth Glen, 'Introducing a "New" Human Right: Learning from Others, Bringing Legal Capacity Home' (2018) 49[3] Columbia Human Rights Law Review 1.

[30]   This even led to laws proscribing people with disabilities being seen in public. See Susan M Schweik, *The Ugly Laws: Disability in Public* (NYU Press 2009). On the phenomenon of social exclusion in the context of disability, see Sarah Appleton-Dyer and Adrian Field, 'Understanding the Factors that Contribute to the Social Exclusion of Disabled People' (*Synergia* and *New Zealand Office for Disability Issues*, 2014) <www.odi.govt.nz/assets/Guidance-and-Resources-files/Understanding-the-factors-that-contribute-to-the-exclusion-of-disabled-people-November-2014.pdf>.

[31]   See Arie Rimmerman, *Family Policy and Disability* (Cambridge University Press 2015).

[32]   See Larry M Logue and Peter Blanck, *Race, Ethnicity and Disability: Veterans and Benefits in Post-Civil War America* (Cambridge University Press 2010).

[33]   See, e.g., Peter Verstraete, Martina Salvante and Julie Anderson, 'Commemorating the Disabled Soldier: 1914–1940' (2015) 6[1] First World War Studies 1.

Special legislative provisions were made for returning disabled veterans, especially after the Second World War.[34] The early emphasis was on rehabilitation and vocational training – on fixing the person to fit the system.[35] Most of the measures were framed as 'compensation' for a disability. You were at fault for your own exclusion; the terms of entry and participation into the lifeworld were left uninterrogated. No structural reform of the market or social protection systems was contemplated.[36]

Since welfare tended to be framed as the re-distribution of wealth after economic forces had run their course, it was natural to see these 'compensatory' measures as the primary policy responses to disability. In a sense, this narrow welfare approach purchased the absence of the other almost as a form of state-funded apartheid. As the quantum of resources dedicated to it grew steadily larger it became harder to challenge the myriad exclusions that gave rise to the need for 'compensation' in the first place. This set in train a vicious circle whereby disability groups naturally pressed for more and more resources, unwittingly reinforcing assumptions about indigence and dependency that had kept them apart in the first place. It did not help that large industries grew up around the service sector – industries with reasons of their own to continue the status quo.

B.   The Limited Impact of Human Rights (1948–1990s)

The advent of human rights from the late 1940s until the 1990s did not alter the policy default (non-inclusive labour markets and inadequate social protection systems) in any fundamental way. In fact, the formative period of the international human rights regime in the 1940s and 1950s coincided with the height of rehabilitation, compensation and separate treatment as the primary policy response to disability. Far from challenging these responses, the initial period of human rights internalised and accepted them.

For example, one interesting – though perhaps unintended – effect of the Universal Declaration of Human Rights (UDHR) was that it implicitly devalued those with cognitive impairments. Article 1 of the Declaration seems to suggest that, because humankind is 'endowed with reason', they have rights and responsibilities towards one another. What of those endowed with less reason? Is rationality really an essential criterion of personhood? Doubtless Article 1 was not specifically aimed at persons with cognitive impairments. But it did subtly reinforce cultural assumptions that cognitive disability somehow damaged the equal humanity of persons with impairments.

Article 25 of the UDHR goes on to specifically mention disability but only in the context of a right to (social) security 'in the event of disability'. Disability is specifically referenced only as a contingent source of the need for welfare. That is to say, the appropriate response to disability is a redistribution of wealth to maintain people in some dignity. Of course, there was/is nothing inherently wrong with the idea of a floor of material provision, but it was not accompanied by any more positive strategy of social inclusion. This was hardly propitious.

---

[34]   See generally, David A Gerber (ed), *Disabled Veterans in History* (University of Michigan Press 2012).
[35]   See, e.g., Theresia Degener, 'Disability in a Human Rights Context' (2016) 5 Laws 35.
[36]   A useful compendium of policy documents from the League of Nations and UN Specialised Agencies is Maria Rita Saulle, *The Disabled Persons and the International Organizations* (International Documentation Ent. 1981).

Even more tellingly, the various equality and non-discrimination clauses of the UN human rights covenants (in particular the ICCPR and ICESCR) did not explicitly mention disability as a prohibited ground of discrimination.[37] Thus, rampant unequal treatment of persons with disabilities, whether in the economy, in poverty alleviation programmes, or more generally, was not flagged as problematic. This left undisturbed many deep-seated cultural assumptions about disability and the inevitability or 'naturalness' of exclusion that followed.[38]

This was innocuous enough since such tracts could be later interpreted broadly to include the ground of disability by analogy. But even when stretched to encompass disability, the theory of equality used in the UN human rights system until the late 1990s tended to both problematize persons with disabilities and justify (maybe even require) segregated treatment.[39] To be sure, the problematization came from outside the law – from the prevailing culture of invisibility (and medicalization). Traditional equality analysis tended to simply internalize this problematization. In particular, traditional or formalistic conceptions of equality are 'normatively empty' in that they focus only on the relativities of treatment – of one group versus another with respect to a social good like education.[40] If a 'material difference' between the groups came to light (or was 'seen') then the difference in treatment might be justified or even understood as required. Persons with disabilities were victims of this hollow conception of equality. A classic case in point was *DH v Czech Republic* where, as late as 2007, the European Court of Human Rights (Second Section) stated that the exclusion of children with disabilities from mainstream school was purely a matter of discretional policy for the contracting parties and not a question of law – much less one that demanded justification under the ECHR.[41]

Human rights thinking on equality has evolved considerably.[42] But the juridical conception of equality that too easily accepts the economic and social exclusion of persons with disabilities still tends to predominate in State practice and in domestic courts.[43] For example, institutional living arrangements are said to be necessary because some persons with disabilities simply do not have the capacity to live in the community – thus problematizing the person again. It seems the invidious doctrine of 'separate but equal' on the ground of race has an afterlife on the ground of disability.[44]

[37]   International Covenant on Civil and Political Rights (adopted 16 December 1966, entered into force 23 March 1976) 999 UNTS 171 (ICCPR) art 26; International Covenant on Economic, Social and Cultural Rights (adopted 16 December 1966, entered into force 3 January 1976) 993 UNTS 3 (ICESCR) art 2(2).

[38]   See Emily Julia Kakoullis and Kelley Johnson (eds), *Recognising Human Rights in Different Cultural Contexts: The United Nations Convention on the Rights of Persons with Disabilities* (Palgrave Macmillan 2020).

[39]   On the different approaches see Oddný Mjöll Arnardóttir, 'A Future of Multidimensional Disadvantage Equality' in Oddný Mjöll Arnardóttir and Gerard Quinn (eds), *The UN Convention on the Rights of Persons with Disabilities: European and Scandinavian Perspectives* (Brill 2009).

[40]   See generally Peter Westen, *Speaking of Equality: An Analysis of the Rhetorical Force of "Equality" in Moral and Legal Discourse* (Princeton University Press 1990).

[41]   *DH and Others v Czech Republic* App no 57325/00 (ECtHR, Second Section, 7 February 2006) para 47.

[42]   See Arnardóttir (n 39).

[43]   See Lisa Waddington and Anna Lawson (eds), *The UN Convention on the Rights of Persons with Disabilities in Practice: A Comparative Analysis of the Role of Courts* (Oxford University Press 2018).

[44]   See Ruth Colker, *When is Separate Unequal?: A Disability Perspective*, (Cambridge University Press 2008).

Neither of the two UN human rights Covenants specifically mentioned disability in their substantive provisions. Article 16 of the International Covenant on Civil and Political Rights (ICCPR) did give everybody the right to recognition before the law. But that did not stop decades of highly restrictive legal incapacity laws affecting persons with disabilities around the world.[45] Article 9 of the ICCPR (right to liberty) did not specifically mention disability. Yet it was interpreted to mean that extremely wide civil commitment laws that stripped persons with mental illness of their liberty were acceptable. It was the gross abuse of such laws by the Soviets that prompted the first wave of mental health law reforms in the 1970s – not second thoughts about what Article 9 demanded in the context of disability.[46]

It is telling that the very first General Comment on disability under any UN human rights treaty came about as late as 1994 under the ICESCR.[47] Although far ahead of its time in terms of content (for example, its insistence in paragraph 11 that market forces should be shaped and regulated to ensure inclusion), the mere fact that it was adopted under the ICESCR meant that most people continued to see the issue simply as one of re-distributive welfare. This was perverse given the actual content of the General Comment, which was excellent. In terms of messaging, it probably would have been preferable if the first General Comment on disability had been issued under the ICCPR.[48]

Indeed, the original Article 15 of the Council of Europe's European Social Charter (the original Turin Charter of 1961) explicitly embraced disability mainly as an issue of rehabilitation and welfare. This changed dramatically in the 1990s with a Revised Social Charter and a new Article 15 that embraced inclusion, independence and community living in contrast to invisibility and segregation.[49] This has led to some very positive caselaw under the Charter demanding equal treatment and social inclusion. However, throughout its formative period, this otherwise enlightened instrument adopted quite a limited view of disability – and even lacked a free-standing and substantive provision proscribing discrimination.[50]

In sum, the impression given or reflected by the early human rights corpus was that disability was a tragedy of the person, something to be fixed or regularized and, in extremis, something to be managed or cared for. Disability – and the various exclusions to which it gave rise – was not conceptualized as an issue of justice or rights demanding justification. As we entered the 1990s, disability did not really figure into international human rights law.[51] Disability, where mentioned, was only an occasion for compensatory justice in a narrow

---

[45]   The best exposition of this field is by Amita Dhanda, 'Legal Capacity in the Disability Rights Convention: Stranglehold of the Past or Lodestar for the Future?' (2007) 34 Syracuse J. Int'l. L. & Com. 429.

[46]   See Sidney Bloch, 'Psychiatry as Ideology in the USSR' (1978) 4 Journal of Medical Ethics 126.

[47]   UN Committee on Economic, Social and Cultural Rights (CESCR), 'General Comment No. 5: Persons with Disabilities' (1994) UN Doc E/1995/22.

[48]   An influential 1992 report by Leandro Despouy recommended that the Committee on Economic, Social and Cultural Rights should take a lead on disability issues: Leandro Despouy, *Human Rights and Disabled Persons*, (*United Nations*, 1993) para 284.

[49]   The European Social Charter, its Additional and Amending Protocols, are available at www.coe .int/en/web/european-social-charter.

[50]   See Gerard Quinn, 'The European Social Charter and EU Anti-Discrimination Law in the Field of Disability: Two Gravitation Fields with One Common Purpose' in Gráinne de Búrca and Bruno de Witte (eds), *Social Rights in Europe* (Oxford University Press 2006).

[51]   An early and influential break was made in Theresia Degener and Yolan Koster-Dreese, *Human Rights & Disabled Persons: Essays and Relevant Human Rights Instruments* (Nijhoff 1995).

sense. In this way, the norms both reflected broader cultural assumptions about disability and cemented them into place.

Yet, I think there is another reason why the early human rights corpus was slow to see the treatment of persons with disabilities as an issue of justice and not just welfare policy and why the link between poverty and disability just did not count. This had to do less with the internalization of external cultural values into the headline norms and more to do with the intrinsic grain of human rights in the formative period from 1948 until the late 1990s. As a result, human rights could be seen as part of the problem until relatively recently. This is what concerns me here.

C.   Human Rights as Part of the Problem

Let us assume that the cultural overhang of devaluing people with disabilities and accepting their exclusion did not exist. Was there anything else holding the human rights firmament back in its formative period? I think there was. In this section I am interested in what was excluded by traditional human rights in the formative period (1948–1990).

All humans live multidimensional lives, interweaving between the private, the social, the economic, the political and the cultural spheres. This fact of life just happens to be much more visible for persons with disabilities. It is hard to separate one from the other and a lot is lost if one tries to do so. Yet that is exactly what human rights did – in its formative period – because of its historical fixation on the public/private divide.

The main problem facing the world in the late 1940s was not economic exclusion or social justice. The edifice the founders built had a different addressee and agenda.[52] Their main preoccupation was on how to prevent a slide back into the totalitarianism that had ruptured world peace in the 1930s. One victim of this crabbed narrative was our collective imagination of both the economy and society.

In a way, the welfare state, at least in market-driven polities, evolved as a response to the inevitable failures of the market – to offset chronic, episodic or cyclical unemployment and to cater for those not expected to be active in the market, like older people or those with chronic illnesses or disabilities. Most of the relevant tracts read like provision for contingencies that arise through an inability to generate enough means through market participation. The main legal issues, even in international law, were largely technocratic. Was the contingency correctly expressed (e.g., unemployment due to accident)? Were the criteria of eligibility sufficiently tailored to reach only those in genuine need? Was the process for making determinations of eligibility (e.g., assessments of the existence and severity of disability) sufficiently clear and fair? Broader policy purposes seemed wholly absent.

Only much later did the idea that the welfare state (and social rights) have a role to play in avoiding social and economic exclusion and in providing the means for a life of active citizenship.[53] A clean break in the Council of Europe was made as late as 2004 when the European Committee for Social Rights pronounced in its Decision in *International Association Autism Europe v France* that: '[T]he underlying vision of Article 15 [of the Revised European Social

---

[52]   An insightful account of the period is John P Humphrey, *Human Rights and the United Nations: A Great Adventure* (Transnational Pub Inc 1984).

[53]   A good resource is the series of papers published by the DISCIT project (making persons with disabilities full citizens) available at: https://blogg.hioa.no/discit/publications/.

Charter] is one of equal citizenship for persons with disabilities and, fittingly, the primary rights are those of "independence, social integration and participation in the life of the community"'.[54]

So, the main concern in the formative period of human rights became social protection in a passive sense – not economic activation, not re-structuring the market to be responsive to human difference, not a general theory of belonging to challenge walls of exclusion, and not a theory of equal citizenship.

One by-product of this reliance on economic and social rights as the primary human rights focus of disability was that it left the justice claims of persons with disabilities exposed to the vagaries of the 'lesser' obligation of 'progressive achievement' that applied to economic and social rights.[55] There is nothing inherently wrong or evil in this doctrine, but something subtle and damaging tended to happen when it came to the application to disability. When a group has been historically excluded or deemed to have less 'use value' in market mechanisms, it becomes easier to justify longer than usual delays in rolling forward spending programmes. The sub-text is that other, more productive, citizens have priority.

Indeed, when periodic financial retrenchments are deemed necessary on account of the general economic situation, it is usually persons with disabilities and others like them who get hit first and hardest and take longer to recover.[56]

The initial focus of the human rights corpus on preserving human dignity and autonomy especially against more authoritarian or totalitarian regimes was wholly justified. But what was lost was a sense of the importance of human rights in sculpting economic markets and informing social protection. That changed radically in the 21st century.

III.   RE-PURPOSING HUMAN RIGHTS IN THE 21ST CENTURY

Two instruments offer a way forward and serve to refresh our policy imagination.

The first has to do with the complete normative reset exemplified at the international level by the UN CRPD, which was adopted in 2007. This reset puts human rights back to where they should have been at the formative period of the 1940s.

The CRPD did not happen in a vacuum. Arguably the key moment sparking world-wide change happened with the enactment of the Americans with Disabilities Act (ADA) in 1990 which built on a strong and growing corpus of American disability law since the 1970s.[57] Although a complicated piece of legislation, the key message of the ADA was as simple as it was powerful: Persons with disabilities matter as persons and unjust economic and social arrangements have to be reversed in the name of their inherent right to equality and right to

---

[54]   *Autism-Europe v France*, Complaint no 13/2002 (European Committee of Social Rights, 8 March 2004) < http://hudoc.esc.coe.int/eng/?i=cc-13-2002-Assessment-en >.

[55]   The concept of 'progressive achievement' is embedded in ICESCR Article 2.1. Article 4.2 of the UN CRPD reiterates the concept when it comes to economic, social and cultural rights contained in that convention.

[56]   See particularly UN Human Rights Council, 'Visit to the United Kingdom of Great Britain and Northern Ireland: Report of the Special Rapporteur on Extreme Poverty and Human Rights' (23 April 2019) UN Doc A/HRC/41/39/Add.1, paras 76–77 <https://undocs.org/en/A/HRC/41/39/Add.1>.

[57]   See the ADA homepage, www.ada.gov/index.html.

belong.[58] It was only a matter of time before international standards absorbed this conceptual breakthrough and stretched it beyond civil rights to encompass social rights too.

The second has to do with the UN SDGs and especially the interaction of the SDGs with human rights. This is important since the challenges in breaking the link between disability and poverty are cultural and structural – a task for which the SDGs are admirably suited. Rather than see the SDGs as just mechanically pegged back to human rights and dependent on them, the SDGs breathe new life into human rights and powerfully reinforce the CRPD.

A.　The UN CRPD – A Complete Normative Reset

At one level, there should never have been a need for a dedicated thematic treaty on the right of persons with disabilities. If all human rights were genuinely universal, then the existing treaties should have been enough to enable persons with disabilities to directly challenge walls of exclusion. But persons with disabilities were not 'seen' as direct beneficiaries of these rights.[59]

When thematic treaties are drafted it is usually because the application of the general rights to a particular group (persons with disabilities in this instance) needs to be amplified or clarified (something not possible in general treaties). This requires an accurate assessment of the status of the group (i.e., the obstacles to be dissolved) as well as an intelligent tailoring of State obligations. In this sense the mechanical task of the CRPD was no different than other thematic treaties. However, there are several distinguishing features of the CRPD that bear emphasizing.

First of all, the underlying invisibility of persons with disabilities as persons had to be reversed. This normative invisibility was the true cause of negative policies that willingly accepted and even advanced exclusion and passive dependence. The rights that became emblematic of the paradigm shift of the Convention had to do with personhood, principally Article 12 on autonomy and legal capacity and Article 19 on the right to live in the community. That this focus on human agency was deemed necessary speaks volumes about the resistance of 'universal' norms to accommodate disability up to that point.

Secondly, the Convention leaves narrow or juridical conceptions of equality very far behind. The whole Convention is animated by the philosophy of 'inclusive equality' – the subject of General Comment 6 of the CRPD Committee in 2018:[60]

> Inclusive equality is a new model of equality developed throughout the Convention. It embraces a substantive model of equality and extends and elaborates on the content of equality in: (a) a fair redistributive dimension to address socioeconomic disadvantages; (b) a recognition dimension to combat stigma, stereotyping, prejudice and violence and to recognize the dignity of human beings and their intersectionality; (c) a participative dimension to reaffirm the social nature of people as members of social groups and the full recognition of humanity through inclusion in society; and (d) an accom-

---

[58]　On the transnational impact of the ADAs, see Gerard Quinn and Eilionoir Flynn, 'Transatlantic Borrowings: The Past and Future of European Non-Discrimination Law and Policy on the Ground of Disability' (2012) 60 American Journal of Comparative Law 23.

[59]　See Gerard Quinn and Theresia Degener, 'Human Rights and Disability: The Current Use and Future Potential of United Nations Human Rights Instruments in the Context of Disability' (2002) UN Doc HR/PUB/02/1.

[60]　UN CRPD, 'General Comment No. 6 on Equality and Non-Discrimination (26 April 2018) UN Doc CRPD/C/GC/6 <www.ohchr.org/EN/HRBodies/CRPD/Pages/GC.aspx>.

modating dimension to make space for difference as a matter of human dignity. The Convention is based on inclusive equality.

Rather than confine the equality tool (as in the past) to simply measuring bare relativities of treatment, it is now directly connected to economic and social justice which is, in turn, animated by a philosophy of inclusion. This linkage of equality with inclusion is novel and long overdue.[61] It seriously questions established exclusionary practices and habits. It leaves no room for them to be rationalized as being 'in the best interests' or simply for the 'welfare' of the individuals concerned.

Third, the Convention puts forward a very holistic conception of inclusion and participation.[62] The whole point was to re-centre persons with disabilities in their own lives and to break down barriers to inclusion in the mainstream. If traditional human rights treaties conceptualize the person as a disembodied individual then the CRPD accentuates the 'social self' – a person who becomes a person through free social interaction in the broader lifeworld.[63] Equalizing the terms of entry and participation in the lifeworld isn't just about access and employment; it is about the very scaffolding of personhood.

Fourth, economic, social and cultural rights assume a different role in the Convention. They are not there simply to provide a cushion of material provision after all else has failed. They are there to underpin human freedom and especially the right to belong and be included.[64] A prime example is Article 24 on the right to inclusive education. Almost every right in the convention is composed of a creative blending of civil and political rights alongside supporting economic and social rights. This was arguably the original intent behind the UN Bill of Rights.

These factors combined (personhood, inclusion, inclusive equality and a new role of economic and social rights) have powerful implications for the right to social protection in the context of disability. Take the right to social security under Article 28 CRPD ('Adequate Standard of Living and Social Protection'). It covers all of what might be expected, including non-discrimination, special attention to additional costs, access to housing and retirement benefits. What is especially interesting is the link drawn by the UN CRPD Committee under Article 28 to the theory of social inclusion. As the UN Special Rapporteur on the rights of persons with disabilities put it in her landmark 2015 study on social protection, the ultimate goal of Article 28 is the achievement of 'social inclusion and social citizenship'.[65] Indeed, the recent 2019 International Labour Organization (ILO) Recommendation No 202 on Social

---

[61] General Comment 6 was inspired by works of Professor Sandra Fredman. Her group's (Oxford, Human Rights Hub) submission to the CRPD Committee on General Comment 6 is available at: www .ohchr.org/EN/HRBodies/CRPD/Pages/WSPersonsDisabilitiesEqualityResponsability.aspx.

[62] An eloquent exposition on inclusion and the CRPD was written by the former chair of the drafting committee, Ambassador Don MacKay, 'The United Nations Convention on the Rights of Persons with Disabilities' (2007) 34 Syracuse Journal of International Law and Commerce 323, 329.

[63] See Anna Grear, '"Framing the Project" of International Human Rights Law: Reflections on the Dysfunctional "family" of the Universal Declaration' in Conor Gearty and Costas Douzinas (eds), *The Cambridge Companion to Human Rights Law* (Cambridge University Press 2012).

[64] The forthcoming book by Kelley Johnson and Jan Walmsley, *Belonging and Social Inclusion for Persons with Intellectual Disabilities* (Taylor & Francis forthcoming 2021) promises to reset the field.

[65] UNGA, 'Rights of Persons with Disabilities: Report of the Special Rapporteur on the Rights of Persons with Disabilities' (7 August 2015) UN doc A/70/297, para 5 <www.un.org/en/ga/search/view _doc.asp?symbol=A/70/297>.

Protection Floors ties the idea of minimum floors on provision to a policy of social inclusion (Principle 3.e). So even passive maintenance becomes part of a larger inclusion agenda.

Fifth, and related to the above, the CRPD does not avoid the private sphere. This is where most people spend most of their time – interacting with others including with non-natural persons like corporations. If this sphere is not fundamentally restructured, then no amount of public law will transform lives. Article 27 on Employment is no exception. In the past, especially in the Global North, employment options for persons with disabilities, in as much as there were any, did not include the open market. The options were generally employment in the public sphere (usually driven by a quota system)[66] or 'economic activity' (it is hard to call it 'employment' in the traditional sense) in a segregated social sphere (usually termed 'sheltered employment').

Usually, with respect to 'sheltered employment', there were legal exemptions from minimum wage laws since the presumption was that productivity levels would not warrant the full application of those laws.[67] Trade unions took little interest in the fate of the workers.[68] So, they held unequal bargaining power in setting terms and conditions. Competition law (especially rules against 'state aid') and public procurement law tended to be relaxed to enable these 'social enterprises' to compete on preferential terms for public contracts. Very few skills were in fact developed and the graduation rate outwards and onto the open market was generally negligible.

On the plus side, and in the absence of genuine inclusionary policies elsewhere, many people with disabilities made genuine friends in these 'social enterprise' environments and often found it hard to separate from them. Parents groups are often at the fore in advocating for their retention. But this was and is nearly always due to the absence of a sustainable alternative. As long as these enclaves existed and thrived there was little need felt to examine how the open market could be supported to better include workers with disabilities.

Article 27 CRPD adds new perspectives beyond public employment and sheltered workshops. It does genuflect to the tradition of encouraging States to become model employers of persons with disabilities.[69] However, I would argue that not all traditional tools of positive action in the form of quotas will pass muster under Article 27. Quotas that reserve low-level menial jobs for persons with certain disabilities (e.g., telephonists' jobs for blind persons) will arguably no longer satisfy the prohibition on non-discrimination[70] since they are based on gross stereotypes.

Article 27 says nothing directly about 'sheltered workshops'. Indeed, there was a proposal by Israel during the drafting of the Convention to both acknowledge their existence and to regularise them. This was rejected. The intellectual structure of Article 27, taken as a whole, seems to militate against 'sheltered workshops'. For example, the opening narrative of Article 27 is cast in terms of a right to 'gain a living by work freely chosen or accepted in a labour market and work environment that is open, inclusive and accessible to persons with disabili-

---

[66]   See, e.g., UK Disabled Persons (Employment) Act 1944 (introducing a quota system in the public sector).

[67]   See Charlotte May-Simera, 'Reconsidering Sheltered Workshops in Light of the United Nations Convention on the Rights of Persons with Disabilities (2006)' (2018) 7 Laws 6.

[68]   But see now, 'Trade Union Action on Decent Work for Persons with Disabilities: A Global Overview' (*International Labour Organization*, 2017).

[69]   CRPD, art 27.1.g.

[70]   CRPD, art 5, 27.1.

ties'. This hardly describes 'sheltered workshops'. Further, several parts of Article 27 refer to access to vocational training and guidance (normally a prerequisite to enter the open market),[71] promoting the employment of persons with disabilities in the private market with appropriate policies and measures 'which may include affirmative action programmes, incentives and other measures'[72] and promoting 'self-employment, entrepreneurship [and] the development of cooperatives' which usually assumes private market activity.[73]

Two immediate questions arise: (1) is there an immediate obligation to close down sheltered workshops? and (2) what exactly is the vision of employment in the open labour market in Article 27? The UN CRPD Committee has continually noted in its various Concluding Observations its concern about the promotion of sheltered workshops.[74] It has also called attention to the slow rate of movement from sheltered workshops into the open labour market.[75] It can certainly be argued that the logic of non-discrimination (and its positive analogue of placement 'in the most integrated setting possible') points strongly towards closure. This is the view of the US Department of Justice under US anti-discrimination law.[76] Sheltered workshops probably need to be phased out as intentional efforts are put in to ensuring that any alternative is effective and sustainable ('progressive achievement' in action). The worst outcome would be the immediate closure of such workshops with no viable alternative.

What then of the vision of the open and inclusive labour market under Article 27? Much of Article 27 deals with shaping the open labour market. A lot of space is given to the States to support and provide incentives on the demand side of employers. This could amount to tax incentives, capital grants, on-site training, job coaching, supported employment, advice on reasonable accommodation, etc. On the supply side a lot of space is given to vocational guidance and training, job skills programmes, job search programmes, in-job supports etc. It might be argued this is a tall order and fundamentally reshapes the market. However, if half the ingenuity (and resources) that was given to policy measures in the past to support sheltered employment was given towards supporting inclusion in the open labour market, this would immeasurably improve the current situation. This creative reshaping of the market amounts to an inclusion agenda in the economy – serving both social purposes and economic efficiency. To a certain extent, it also depends on changing corporate culture to be more attuned to the value of diversity – not just in the workforce but in the customer base.[77]

Resources are already out there to assist. The US Job Accommodation Network (JAN)[78] provides details in the US context and the European Union of Supported Employment (EUSE)

---

[71] CRPD, art 27.1.d.

[72] CRPD, art 27.1.h.

[73] CRPD, art 27.1.f.

[74] See UN Committee on the Rights of Persons with Disabilities, 'Concluding Observations on the Initial Report of Poland' (29 October 2018) UN Doc CRPD/C/POL/CO/1, para 47.b.

[75] See UN Committee on the Rights of Persons with Disabilities, 'Concluding Observations on the Report of Bulgaria' (22 October 2019) UN Doc CRPD/C/BGR/CO/1, para 57.

[76] For example, in a proposed settlement with the state of Oregon (2015) the US Department of Justice proposed allowing the state seven years to complete its transition away from sheltered employment towards supported employment. Visit: www.justice.gov/opa/pr/justice-department-reaches -proposed-ada-settlement-agreement-oregons-developmental.

[77] See Lisa Schur, Douglas Kruse and Peter Blanck, *People with Disabilities: Sidelined or Mainstreamed?*, (Cambridge University Press 2013) ch 3(e) ('Corporate Culture').

[78] US Job Accommodation Network, https://askjan.org.

has a useful Toolkit on the concept of supported employment.[79] The Toolkit stresses active collaboration, tailored responses, flexible working arrangements, and job reassignment where possible and needed. In 2016 the ILO produced its own guide.[80] Whatever else States say, they cannot say that they have no guidance.

To a certain extent, this new focus on sculpting the market for inclusion fits with emerging ideas about the future of work, which looks very different to the 40-hour week of the past. Capitalizing on the new flexibility emerging in the field of work, the 2019 ILO Centenary Declaration on the Future of Work specifically calls on the ILO to direct its efforts, inter alia, to ensure 'equal opportunities and treatment in the world of work for persons with disabilities'. Interestingly, the 2017 McKinsey report on the future of work indicates that new employment is likely to come from a gradual process of 'marketization' of work that was previously done either unpaid or underpaid.[81]

Last, and arguably most importantly, the UN CRPD centres persons with disabilities in their own lives.[82] Article 4.3 essentially creates a new legal obligation on States to actively consult with persons with disabilities and their representative organizations in the development and implementation of policies affecting them. This stands in stark contrast to the past where policy was made *about* persons with disabilities and not *with* them. In practical terms, this means that persons with disabilities and their representative organizations must be at the table when new economic policies are being formulated or when anti-poverty measures are being refined.[83]

This right of co-production now extends beyond 'normal' times to include situations of risk, including humanitarian crises (floods, pandemics) or armed conflicts (CRPD Article 11). It also extends to international development programmes seeking to alleviate poverty. CRPD Article 32 insists that such programmes should be 'inclusive of and accessible to persons with disabilities'. This is already reshaping development priorities away from simple resource transfers towards measures aimed at enhancing the capacity of civil society to engage constructively with governments as effective co-producers of change.[84]

The concept of co-production is now deeply embedded in the 2019 UNDIS (UN Disability Inclusion Strategy) which sets out goals and an evaluation framework for UN agencies on disa-

---

[79]   The European Union of Supported Employment Toolkit (2010) is available here: www.euse.org/content/supported-employment-toolkit/EUSE-Toolkit-2010.pdf.

[80]   Promoting Diversity and Inclusion Through Workplace Adjustments: A Practical Guide (2016) is available here: www.ilo.org/wcmsp5/groups/public/---ed_norm/---declaration/documents/publication/wcms_536630.pdf.

[81]   'Jobs Lost, Jobs Gained: Workforce Transitions in a Time of Automation' (*McKinsey & Company*, December 2017) 62 <www.mckinsey.com/~/media/McKinsey/Featured%20Insights/Future%20of%20Organizations/What%20the%20future%20of%20work%20will%20mean%20for%20jobs%20skills%20and%20wages/MGI-Jobs-Lost-Jobs-Gained-Report-December-6-2017.ashx>.

[82]   CRPD, art 12.

[83]   See generally Alexandre Cote, 'The Unsteady Path: Towards Meaningful Participation of Organisations of Persons with Disabilities in the Implementation of the CRPD and SDGS' (*Bridging the Gap*, 2020) <https://bridgingthegap-project.eu/wp-content/uploads/The-unsteady-path.-A-pilot-study-by-BtG.pdf>.

[84]   See IDDC's homepage, www.iddcconsortium.net/about/;: the GLAD Network: https://gladnetwork.net.

bility inclusion.[85] Persons with disabilities are described as 'agents of change and beneficiaries of the outcomes of the work of the United Nations'.[86] One of the main indicators for evaluation covers 'consultation [by the UN Agencies] of persons with disabilities' (Indicator 5).

In sum, the CRPD has transformed the field. In place of an overly rigid divide between the public and private spheres it paints a more complex picture of the human condition and the policy responses that are needed. It is grounded on a rich and broad theory of equality. It fuses thinking about civil and political rights with economic and social rights. It places the voices of persons with disabilities at the heart of policy-making. It considerably refreshes the corpus of human rights and arguably restores it to the original vision in 1948.

B.   The SDGs – Refreshing Human Rights

What then do the SDGs add? The 2030 Agenda for Sustainable Development, which includes the UN SDGs, is remarkable. Disability groups were at the fore during the drafting of the SDGs, adopted in 2015.[87] This shows in the content of the SDGs.

For one thing, all countries are bound by the SDGs. In a sense, all countries are conceptualized as developing countries. This stands in stark context with the UN Millennium Development Goals (MDGs) which only applied to the Global South. The Preamble contains important overarching principles, including People, Planet, Prosperity, Peace and Partnership. It starts with People, commencing with a faith in human potential regardless of difference. The Declaration states that the SDGs represent a 'people-centred' set of goals. Under Peace it commits to 'foster peaceful, just and inclusive societies'. And under Partnership it focuses in particular on the 'poorest and most vulnerable'. Paragraph 4 of the Declaration repeats the pledge to treat the 'furthest behind first' (which undoubtedly covers disability) and to leave no one behind.

The Declaration emphasizes that the Goals see the economic, social and environmental spheres not as separate spheres, as in the past, but as fundamentally interconnected. Until recently, human rights doctrine tended to see these as separate and hermetically sealed spheres.

Unlike the MDGs, which completely failed to reference disability, disability is now explicitly embraced in many of the SDGs. Even where not mentioned explicitly, disability is covered throughout since it is included within the category of the 'vulnerable'.

The SDGs themselves pivot on a sense of the primacy of people, meeting basic human needs (food, water, health care, sanitation), an overarching goal of inclusion and equality, and a concern for sustainability, especially with respect to environmental factors. This amounts to a very different image of the market and indeed a different image of social protection. With

---

[85]   UNDIS, www.un.org/development/desa/disabilities/wp-content/uploads/sites/15/2019/03/UNDIS _20-March-2019_for-HLCM.P.pdf.

[86]   ibid 6.

[87]   A High-Level Meeting on Disability & Development was convened by the UN in 2013 to consider how best to include disability in the instrument to succeed the Millennium Development Goals. It concluded by encouraging governments 'to seize every opportunity to include disability as a cross-cutting issue on the global development debate'. UN Commission for Social Development 'Commission for Social Development Approves Five Draft Resolutions by Consensus as Fifty-first Session Concludes' (*United Nations*, 15 February 2013) <www.un.org/press/en/2013/soc4806.doc.htm>. For an account of the input of the International Disability Alliance to the drafting of the SDGs see www.internation aldisabilityalliance.org/Sustainable-Development-Advocacy.

respect to the market, the SDGs force attention onto the need to ensure inclusion as a way to sustain markets and to temper the unbridled pursuit for ever higher levels of productivity as well as consumption (Goals 8 and 12).

Disability is specifically referenced in Goals 4 (Education), 8 (Employment), 10 (Equality), 11 (Transport) and 16 (Peace and Inclusive Societies). It is noteworthy that Goal 4 is styled 'inclusive and equitable education'. This maps onto the inclusive agenda of Article 24 of the CRPD. Goal 10, on 'reduc[ing] inequality within and among countries', speaks directly to promoting the 'social, economic, and political inclusion of all'. Goal 11 deals with inclusive cities. Goal 11.2 deals with transport and specifically includes accessibility as a key goal. This is a prerequisite for inclusion into all spheres including the economic one.

The uber-theme of social inclusion permeates the economic sphere as well as Goals 10 (Inclusion and Equality), 11 (inclusive cities) and 16 (inclusive and peaceful societies). It is in this light that Goal 1 (ending poverty for all) should be read. It specifically requires the extension of social protection systems in all countries to cover the 'vulnerable'. Like ILO Recommendation 202 on social protection floors, this should be animated by the social inclusion philosophy.

The truly remarkable thing about the SDGs is the re-shaping of categories that had become ossified in traditional policy thinking. We have tended to think of the State, the market and the social sphere as mutually exclusive. The SDGs forces us to think of them as an ecosystem – each with implications for the other and each dependent on the other. Take the economic sphere. Traditionally, we were primarily concerned with the structural integrity of markets and left externalities to fall by the wayside or be socialized by the State. Now the SDGs require us to think about sustainable production in the market as well as sustainable consumption. In other words, it blurs the line separating the social from the purely economic (if there ever truly was one). This brings a new agenda – how to achieve equity in the marketplace, which should no longer be judged simply in accordance with classical notions of efficiency. This comes close to valorizing a conception of the social market, a market harnessed not just to produce wealth and to do so efficiently, but also to meet other social goals. It follows that a newer kind of disability agenda based on active citizenship and co-production results.[88]

The fundamental harmony between the CRPD and the SDGs has not gone unnoticed.

What is remarkable is the degree to which the Concluding Observations and Recommendations of the CRPD Committee now explicitly encompass the SDGs. The CRPD Committee now routinely reinforces its conclusions with reference to analogous provisions in the SDGs. For example, in its May 2019 round, the Committee explicitly linked its recommendations under Article 27 (work and employment) with SDG Goal 8 (sustainable and inclusive economic growth) in its Concluding Observations with respect to Spain, Norway, Poland and Nigeria.[89] Likewise, the Committee explicitly linked many of its recent Concluding Observations (Spain, Poland, Nigeria) under Article 28 (Adequate Standard of Living) with SDG 10.2 (reduce inequality) and 1.3 (end poverty).[90]

---

[88]   On social market theory and practice see the Institute for New Economic Thinking (INET): www.ineteconomics.org.

[89]   The relevant Concluding Observations are available here: UN Treaty Body Database, https://tbinternet.ohchr.org/_layouts/15/treatybodyexternal/TBSearch.aspx?Lang=en&TreatyID=4&DocTypeID=5.

[90]   ibid.

In a tangible way, the SDGs powerfully reinforce the normative innovations of the CRPD. The celebrated emphasis in the SDGs on treating first the 'furthest behind' and leaving no one behind cuts through embedded assumptions about the naturalness of social and economic exclusion.[91] The SDGs re-conceptualize the economic sphere – and endorse a new approach to economics that is much more receptive to social ends.[92] And by insisting on inclusion and equality as overarching goals the SDGs endorse a new kind of social state – one that does not passively maintain people at the margins but facilitates their empowerment.

IV. CONCLUSIONS: MAKING IT WORK – TOWARDS A NEW RESEARCH AGENDA

What conclusions can be drawn from the above? What kinds of knowledge gaps exist, and what would amount to a useful research agenda?

First of all, the core cultural challenge remains the same: reversing the invisibility of persons with disabilities, especially in the framing and implementation of anti-poverty public policy programmes. Co-production is no longer optional; it is mandatory. Research is needed to track the process of the co-production of anti-poverty policy between civil society and governments (including partnerships with research entities) and to explore the critical success factors needed to make it work. This applies both to the domestic policy process and to formulation, implementation and monitoring of development assistance programmes.

Second, disability brings vividly to life the much vaunted (but seldom analysed or understood) interdependence thesis between civil and political rights with economic social and cultural rights. Disability is an ideal site to explore the many connectors between both sets of rights.

Third, the achievement of social ends through market mechanisms requires more in-depth exploration. Human rights are just as relevant to the shaping of the economic marketplace (especially employment) as they are to dealing with market failure. The image of the social market implicit in human rights and the SDGs needs further exploration. It too has limits which need to be explored and articulated. But it is the future, especially when one considers work in the 21st century.

Fourth, it is clear that traditional social protection systems need to be refreshed. There will always need to be a balance struck between maintaining people in some level of material comfort and ensuring they are enabled to assume active lives in the community. Making sure that social protection policies can perform both functions is the test of the future. Research is needed to show how this can be done.

Fifth, the 'feminization of poverty', especially as it affects caretakers, requires much more in-depth analysis. Caretakers have a right to social support to enable them to live their own lives. The default in nearly all cultures – whether in the Global South or North – of relying on families, needs to be much more closely interrogated. At a very minimum, this calls for more substantive family supports. The enormous economic disadvantages that accrue – particularly to mothers – needs to be tracked along with meaningful strategies to counteract it.

---

[91] UNGA (n 12) para 4.
[92] On the project of reimagining the economy see the Institute for New Economic Thinking, available at: www.ineteconomics.org.

If the innovations sparked in the disability field by the CRPD and the SDGs can be made to work well, this might signal a welcome return to the original vision of the Bill of Rights in the 1940s and help point the way forward for other groups.

8. Poverty, older persons and human rights

Andrew Byrnes

Identifying the extent and causes of the poverty that older persons experience is a complex exercise. Quite apart from the range of definitions of poverty employed by national governments and international organizations, obtaining comprehensive and fine-grained data is challenging, and the patterns of poverty are multifaceted and vary from region to region as well as within regions. Particular subgroups of the older population experience greater poverty than the general older population, while poverty rates relative to other population groups are sometimes higher, though often lower.

The bottom line is that there are significant numbers of older persons who experience poverty according to the different measures employed – and often they live in societies in which other groups also experience significant levels of poverty. The implications of this in general policy terms and in human rights terms are that some of the causes of poverty for different groups may be the same and need to be addressed by common measures. Yet at the same time there are specific circumstances that lead to poverty among older persons that need to be addressed by particular strategies and the focused deployment of human rights standards.

The alleviation of poverty has been a central concern of international human rights law for many decades, as well as a driving objective of various development frameworks over the same period, with the 2030 Agenda for Sustainable Development being the latest. Poverty has been a major concern of the international community and international institutions more broadly, including the World Bank, regional development banks and the United Nations (UN), though the place of explicit human rights frameworks in the activities of some of those bodies has been inconsistent and at times contested. Despite some early efforts, the focus on older persons generally and their human rights in particular at the international level has been more recent, and there is still no universal human rights treaty dedicated to the human rights of older persons, including their right to be free from poverty.[1]

This chapter first outlines the major demographic trends in the world that have led or are leading to ageing populations in all parts of the world. It then addresses the issue of who 'older persons' are for the purposes of this discussion. Third, it outlines some of the relevant measures of poverty and then fourth, describes the patterns of poverty that exist among older populations. Fifth, the chapter turns to the relevant international human rights standards relevant to the avoidance and alleviation of poverty among older people. Finally, I turn to issues of how the international human rights normative framework and its implementation might be strengthened, in particular through the elaboration of a new convention on the human rights of older persons, and how this could contribute to alleviating poverty among older persons.

---

[1]   See generally Annie Herro and Andrew Byrnes, 'Framing Contests Over the Human Rights of Older Persons' (2020) 38 Australian Yearbook of International Law 263–84.

I.   WORLD POPULATION TRENDS AND AGEING POPULATIONS

The changing demographics of the world's population have already led to significant increases in both the number and proportion of older persons in nearly all countries, and we will see even larger numbers and proportions of older persons in most nations in the coming decades.[2] In 2019 there were 703 million persons aged 65 or over in the world; this number is expected to grow to 1.5 billion people by 2050, with the largest number of older persons living in Eastern and Southeast Asia, followed by Europe and North America.[3]

While all regions of the world have seen or will see their population ageing, the growth has been greatest in Eastern and Southeast Asia and Latin America and the Caribbean. Eastern and Southeast Asia is projected to have the largest increase in numbers of persons over 65 between 2019 and 2050 (from 261 million to 573 million). The rate of growth is expected to be greatest in Northern Africa and Western Asia, followed by sub-Saharan Africa. Australia and New Zealand and Europe and North America will have relatively small increases in numbers of older persons – the populations in those regions are already significantly older than in other regions.

Life expectancy from birth and from age 65 has also been increasing and is set to grow further, meaning that more persons will live longer and well beyond 65 (17 more years globally in 2015–2020 and a projected 19 more years by 2045–2050, with higher figures in some regions).[4] Women tend to live longer than men in every region, and as a result, in 2019 the gender difference in life expectancy at 65 was globally 2.7 years; this ranged from 0.6 years in Oceania to 3.4 years in Eastern and Southeastern Asia.[5] Life expectancy at birth in 2019 was projected to be 74.7 for women and 69.9 for men, ranging from a difference of 3.0 years in Oceania to 6.5 years in Latin America and the Caribbean.[6]

The increase in life expectancy seen in most parts of the world means that many more people are living longer and generally in better health than two generations ago. However, on average it also means more years spent living with disability or illness in the later years of life. Decreasing fertility also means that in many parts of the world the ratio of older to younger persons is increasing, giving rise to concerns about increasing old age dependency ratios[7] and about the sustainability of national budgets, particularly in the areas of social security and health.[8] Although too often the approaches to assessing the economic impact of an ageing

---

[2]   UNDESA, 'World Population Ageing 2019: Highlights' (2019) UN Doc ST/ESA/SER.A/430.

[3]   ibid. at 5.

[4]   ibid. at 7.

[5]   ibid. at 9.

[6]   ibid. at 9.

[7]   ibid. at 11–20.

[8]   For example, Wang Feng and Alfonso Sousa-Poza, 'The Economics of Ageing and Health' (2018) The Journal of the Economics of Ageing 192. But see David Bloom and Uwe Sunde, 'Feature Interview with Dr. John Beard' (2018) The Journal of the Economics of Ageing 11, quoting *Beard*: 'A classic example is the persistence of outdated concepts such as the dependency ratio. Concepts like this are values driven, rather than based on evidence, and their continued use reinforces ageist stereotypes and leads to poor decision making. Economists must do better. A key problem is the common failure to consider older populations' diversity; another is failing to account for older people's various contributions (for example, through taxes, volunteering, caregiving, consumption, etc.)'.

population are simplistic and portrayed in alarmist terms ('the grey tsunami' is one frequently used metaphor),[9] the changes pose important policy and social challenges.

Increased life expectancy and larger numbers of older people give rise to concerns about the material and social deprivation that many older people do or will experience in older age. This deprivation may be a continuation of lives that have been lived in poverty, where people bring with them into older age the cumulative impacts of lifelong disadvantage, or it may be the result of adverse changes to the financial and social wellbeing of older persons that result from a full or partial exit from remunerated work or from a change in the nature of the work that they undertake.

At the same time, older persons, or some of them, are not the only group whose members are living in poverty. Children, persons with disabilities, women, Indigenous People and other groups (and those who have a number of these characteristics or statuses) also experience poverty in differing degrees in many countries. Older persons who belong to a number of these groups suffer multiple or intersectional disadvantage. There are many poor subgroups in our communities and there are some communities in which some or many older persons may be better off – or at least experience lower levels of poverty – than do other groups in their communities. These patterns of deprivation vary from society to society.

II.   'OLDER PERSONS'

The category of 'older persons' and the concept of 'older age' are not self-evident: their meaning and significance may vary from society to society and also depend on the purpose for which one is seeking to define them. Older age is the result not only of the natural process of biological ageing but a social construct that in many respects depends on how societies view the ageing process and those who are in the later stages of their lives.

Defining older persons simply by reference to a chronological age as an objective indicator of a particular status for all purposes can be both inaccurate and misleading, though it has some uses and is helpful for drawing clear lines when it comes to the allocation of social benefits such as pensions. Many countries set the age at which a person becomes entitled to a state-supported pension as the relevant age of being an 'older person', though increasing longevity and the broader budgetary need to keep more people in the paid labour force at ages beyond the historical retirement age has led to the lifting of standard retirement ages in many countries.

While the UN generally uses the age of 60 for defining the group of older persons, it has also accepted that this may be inappropriately high in certain circumstances and especially in some developing countries.[10] For example, it has been suggested that persons aged 50 and older may be appropriately classified as older persons in some African countries. In Australia the average life expectancy of Indigenous Australians is significantly less than those of non-Indigenous

---

[9]   David Bloom and Uwe Sunde, 'Feature Interview with Dr. John Beard' (2018) The Journal of the Economics of Ageing 11.

[10]   World Health Organization, 'Proposed working definition of an older person in Africa for the MDS Project' (2002) <www.who.int/healthinfo/survey/ageingdefnolder/en/> accessed 9 March 2020.

Australians.[11] This fact is recognized in the eligibility of Indigenous Australians to access the aged care system from the age of 50, whereas for non-Indigenous members of the community the age of eligibility for those services is set at 65.[12] On the other hand, superannuation benefits may not be accessible, and many Indigenous Australians die without being able to access their contributory superannuation savings, which are designed to help support an adequate standard of living in older age.

Simply setting a chronological age so that persons above that age are 'older persons' also has its limitations, given increasing longevity and the fact that many people are living into their eighties and nineties and beyond, especially in developed countries. The situation of someone in the age cohort 65–74 may be quite different from many in cohorts 75–84 and 85 and above. The category of the 'older old' is sometimes used to designated older cohorts within the older population, though that is not fixed either, with sometimes 75 or 80 being set as the threshold and at other times 85. Very often statistics combine all those aged 65 and above into one undifferentiated category, though the average range of experiences may vary widely between and within different cohorts of the 65+ population.

For the purposes of most calculations of poverty by bodies such as the World Bank and the UN Development Programme (UNDP), the threshold of 65 is used, with the assumption being that the 20–64 age bracket is when people will be deriving income from participation in the labour market and that after 65, they will not be. This is plainly an oversimplification that does not capture the realities of many peoples' lives, especially given the significant numbers of persons aged 65 and above who are engaged in the paid labour force or who work in the informal economy, and accordingly one needs to examine more closely the different experiences of specific groups within these cohorts.

III.   DEFINING AND MEASURING POVERTY

The concept of poverty that is used when inquiring whether particular sections of the population are poor is critical to the identification of those experiencing poverty and the interventions that may be necessary to alleviate or eliminate it.[13] There are many different measures of poverty used in international and national statistics. They fall into three broad categories:[14]

---

[11]   In 2015–2017 the life expectancy at birth for Indigenous males was 71.6 years and for Indigenous females 75.6, compared with 80.2 for non-Indigenous males and 83.4 non-Indigenous females, a gap of 8.6 and 7.8 years respectively: see Australian Government, 'Closing the Gap' (2020) <https://ctgreport .niaa.gov.au/sites/default/files/pdf/closing-the-gap-report-2020.pdf> accessed 29 June 2020.

[12]   Royal Commission into Aged Care Quality and Safety, 'Aged Care in Australia: A Shocking Tale of Neglect' (2019) <https://agedcare.royalcommission.gov.au/news/Pages/media-releases/interim -report-released-31-october-2019.aspx> accessed 29 June 2020; Australian Government Productivity Commission, 'Report on Government Services 2020' (2020) <www.pc.gov.au/research/ongoing/report -on-government-services/2020/community-services/aged-care-services> accessed 9 March 2020.

[13]   See Crystal Kwan and Christine Walsh, 'Old Age Poverty: A Scoping Review of the Literature' (2018) 4(1) Cogent Social Sciences <https://doi.org/10.1080/23311886.2018.1478479> accessed 2 July 2020.

[14]   ibid.

(a)   Income- (or expenditure-) related that identify a level of income representing a minimum requirement for an adequate standard of living[15] – examples are the OECD poverty level based on a percentage of the median household income in a particular country[16] or the World Bank's extreme poverty income level of USD1.90 per day.[17]

(b)   A measure that takes into account other specific features, including capabilities or measures of social exclusion – an example is the UNDP Multidimensional Poverty Index.[18]

(c)   Measures that are based on a subjective assessment of people as to the forms of material deprivation and associated social exclusion that they consider amount to poverty.[19]

The first two types are those that have the most currency in international debates about poverty and ways to alleviate or eliminate it. None of the measures are unproblematic, and all have to be used with an eye to their limitations. However, it generally seems that the type of measures that fall into category (b) generally show 50 per cent higher levels of poverty than measures that are solely income- or expenditure-based.[20]

For many years the World Bank has also used the concept of extreme poverty, defined by reference to an average of the poverty rate in some of the world's poorest countries, expressed as a US dollar value per day. This measure of extreme poverty – now USD1.90 per day – is a monetary measure, and the numbers of those living in extreme poverty have fallen over the last few decades, though there have been uneven falls across regions. Sub-Saharan Africa and South Asia are the major regions in which poverty reduction has been slower than in other regions.[21] There has been a fall from two billion people in 1990 living in extreme poverty (37.1 per cent of the world's population) to 900 million in 2012 (12.7 per cent of the global population). But the gains have not been so impressive in relation to the World Bank's two higher income lines of USD3.20 and USD5.50 per day. Nor do the reports on the reduction of extreme poverty appear to provide disaggregated data for older populations.

---

[15]   Development Initiatives 'Definitions and measures of poverty' (2016) 1 <devinit.org/wp-content/uploads/2016/07/Definitions-and-measures-of-poverty.pdf> accessed 1 July 2020.

[16]   The OECD uses a relative income poverty measure according to which the poverty threshold is set at 50 per cent of the median household income in the total population in a given country at a given time. It also measures poverty depth, which 'measures how much the average income of the poor is below the relative poverty threshold, in percent of this threshold': see 'Pensions at a Glance 2019: OECD and G20 Indicators' (2019) 186 <https://doi.org/10.1787/b6d3dcfc-en> accessed 2 July 2020.

[17]   A related approach is to use assets or wealth as an indicator of old age poverty: see Crystal Kwan and Christine Walsh, 'Old Age Poverty: A Scoping Review of the Literature' (2018) 4(1) Cogent Social Sciences <https://doi.org/10.1080/23311886.2018.1478479> accessed 1 July 2020.

[18]   UNDP, 'Beyond Income, Beyond Averages, Beyond Today: Inequalities in Human Development in the 21st Century' <http://hdr.undp.org/sites/default/files/hdr2019.pdf> accessed 29 June 2020; World Bank Group, 'Piecing Together the Poverty Puzzle' (2018) Poverty and Shared Prosperity *xi*.

[19]   Rosette Kabuye and Norman Mukasa, 'Older People's Conceptualisation of Poverty and their Experiences of Government Programmes in Uganda' (2017) 29(3) Development in Practice 349; UNFPA, 'Ageing in the Twenty-First Century: A Celebration and A Challenge' (2012).

[20]   Six hundred million people still live in extreme income poverty but this number rises to 1.3 billion when measured according to the Multidimensional Poverty Index, see UNDP, 'Beyond Income, Beyond Averages, Beyond Today: Inequalities in Human Development in the 21st Century' <http://hdr.undp.org/sites/default/files/hdr2019.pdf> accessed 29 June 2020; World Bank Group, 'Piecing Together the Poverty Puzzle – Poverty and Shared Prosperity 2018' (2018) *xi* at 87.

[21]   World Bank Group, 'Piecing Together the Poverty Puzzle – Poverty and Shared Prosperity 2018' (2018) *xi*.

The World Bank's extreme poverty measures (the international poverty line or IPL) has been criticised by many commentators – some of that criticism accepted by the Bank[22] – for its conceptual limitations and flaws and its setting of an excessively low benchmark. A prominent example is the trenchant analysis by the former UN Special Rapporteur on human rights and extreme poverty, Philip Alston in his final thematic report in 2020.[23] Alston argues that the IPL 'is designed to reflect a staggeringly low standard of living well below any reasonable conception of a life with dignity'[24] and suggests that it promotes the impression that one can '"escape" from poverty without an income anywhere near that required to achieve an adequate standard of living, including access to healthcare and education' and that the standard 'is a world away from the one set by human rights law and embodied in the UN Charter'.[25] He notes that a number of alternative measures would require two to four times the amount set by the IPL.[26]

He notes that reliance on the IPL underpins the claims of significant reductions in extreme poverty and that it is nearing eradication.[27] He argues that more accurate measures show that there has been only a small decline in the number of people living in poverty in the past thirty years.[28] Furthermore, he argues that the SDGs are 'inadequately framed, failing, and in need of revitalization' if they are to go any significant way to eliminating poverty, a need made only more urgent by the COVID-19 pandemic that will push many hundreds more people into poverty. COVID-19 has been a 'pandemic of poverty'[29] and the 'public health community's mantra for coping encapsulates the systemic neglect of those living in poverty'.[30] Alston does not draw attention specifically to older persons, but the general arguments he makes are applicable to many older persons. His call for the collection of better data also has relevance for older persons, given the limited data that is available.[31]

IV.   THE POVERTY THAT OLDER PERSONS EXPERIENCE

One of the challenges faced in relation to the poverty of older persons is the limited comprehensive data available; there is a lack of 'an international harmonized database of poverty rates disaggregated by age' and evidence that is available is 'limited to selected country or regional studies'.[32] In many cases this is the result of inadequate disaggregation of data by age.[33] Nevertheless, in most countries the risk of poverty increases as people get older, and it also increases as people move from the 'younger old' to the 'older old' cohort, with the latter

---

[22]   UNHRC, 'The Parlous State of Poverty, Report of the Special Rapporteur on Extreme Poverty and Human Rights' (2 July 2020), A/HRC/44/40, paras 22–26.

[23]   ibid. especially at paras 7–21.

[24]   ibid. at para 12.

[25]   ibid. at para 12.

[26]   ibid. at para 13.

[27]   ibid. at para 3.

[28]   ibid. at para 3.

[29]   ibid. at para 34.

[30]   ibid. at para 34.

[31]   ibid. at para 81.

[32]   See Crystal Kwan and Christine Walsh, 'Old Age Poverty: A Scoping Review of the Literature' (2018) 4(1) Cogent Social Sciences <https://doi.org/10.1080/23311886.2018.1478479> accessed 1 July 2020.

[33]   UNFPA, 'Ageing in the Twenty-First Century: A Celebration and A Challenge' (2012) at 42.

being the fastest growing cohort.[34] It may also be more difficult for older persons to get out of poverty: older age 'brings with it a reduced capacity for work, which increases the likelihood of older people becoming and remaining poor'.[35]

A.   Patterns

Older people are not homogeneous and their experiences and material and social well-being vary significantly within and between nations. Analysis of the poverty that older persons experience needs to take into account this diversity. In some instances, persons experience poverty as they enter older age as part of the continuum of poverty and deprivation with which they have lived with earlier in their lives and which has provided them with little opportunity to acquire material and other assets to support a decent standard of living in older age. For others the transition to older age may bring poverty through a decline in access to material and other forms of social support – for example, by giving up or reducing the amount of paid work that they do and without the income being replaced by state or other income – and new demands on their financial resources. On the other hand, in some societies, for some, including the 'working poor', reaching older age may mean that their situation actually improves, if there are adequate support payments from the State or other sources for those who have left the paid labour force.

In OECD countries, which are made up of developed economies, 13.5 per cent of individuals over 65 live in relative income poverty, with the average income of the poor 23.5 per cent below the poverty line. The poverty rate for the population as a whole in OECD countries is 11.8 per cent, so the rate is slightly higher for the 65-and-over population.[36] But these averages within the OECD developed country grouping disguise quite significant variations. In fifteen OECD countries older people are more likely to be income-poor than the total general population, 22 per cent compared to 14 per cent. However, in twenty other OECD countries older people are likely to experience poverty at a lower rate than the population overall (up to six per cent lower in some cases).[37] According to the OECD, poverty has shifted in recent decades from older people to those aged 18 to 25.[38]

1.   Poverty over the life course: Disadvantage at earlier stages of life can accumulate and increase the likelihood that a person will end up living in poverty in older age.[39] The adop-

---

[34]   ibid.

[35]   ibid. at 41.

[36]   ibid.

[37]   A similarly diverse range is seen in G20 countries beyond OECD countries. UNFPA, 'Ageing in the Twenty-First Century: A Celebration and A Challenge' (2012).

[38]   ibid.

[39]   'Poverty in older age is more often chronic, since the lack of economic opportunities and security during earlier life accumulates into vulnerability in old age'. UNDP, 'Sustaining Human Progress: Reducing Vulnerabilities and Building Resilience' (2014) <http://hdr.undp.org/sites/default/files/hdr14 -report-en-1.pdf> accessed 29 June 2020. See also UNDP, 'Human Development for Everyone' (2016) <http://hdr.undp.org/sites/default/files/2016_human_development_report.pdf> accessed 29 June 2020; UNDP, 'Beyond Income, Beyond Averages, Beyond Today: Inequalities in Human Development in the 21st Century' <http://hdr.undp.org/sites/default/files/hdr2019.pdf> accessed 29 June 2020; Vadim Kufenko, Klaus Prettner and Alfonso Sousa-Poza, 'The Economics of Ageing and Inequality: Introduction to the Special Issue' (2019) The Journal of the Economics of Ageing 14, <https://doi

tion of a life course approach that is based on the recognition that 'all stages of a person's life are … intricately intertwined with each other' and with the lives of others will help to design policies of intervention at critical stages in people's lives that will have a significant influence on the quality of their lives in older age.[40]

2. Gender: Gender, or at least being a woman, is also a risk factor for poverty in older age.[41] In most cases this reflects the results of discrimination against women over the course of their lives,[42] in particular resulting from their greater load of caring and related work that is unremunerated (and often not recognized in national accounts), the discontinuities in their workforce participation, the link of many contributory social insurance and pension systems to participation in the formal paid labour force (excluding work in the informal economy where many women in developing countries work) meaning that women's pensions are lower than men's,[43] and the fact that women live longer and are thus more likely than men to exhaust whatever resources they have been able to accumulate for their later years. Women who are widowed, divorced or who live with disability are at risk in all countries,[44] as are women who live in rural areas. Women's care burdens contribute to their poverty.[45]

Older persons living in rural areas are more likely to experience poverty than those living in non-rural areas; those who own their own homes are also likely to be better off than those who do not. Older members of disadvantaged racial or ethnic minorities are also more likely to experience poverty than members of other groups and there is often multiple disadvantages in these groups that contribute to deeper levels of poverty among some members of those groups. For example, in the US women of colour have higher rates of poverty than white women and 'for each demographic of women aged 65 and older, they experience rates of poverty that are consistently higher than those of their male counterparts'.[46]

.org/10.1016/j.jeoa.2019.100195> accessed 2 July 2020; Hal Kendig and James Nazroo, 'Life Course Influences on Inequalities in Later Life: Comparative Perspectives' (2016) 9 Journal of Population Ageing 1 <https://link.springer.com/journal/12062/9/1> accessed 2 July 2020.

40   As to the rationale and benefits of the life course approach, articulated in the context of health, see WHO, 'Minsk Declaration' (2020); WHO, 'The Life Course Approach: From Theory to Practice, Case Stories from Two Small Countries in Europe' (2018) 1.

41   'Pensions at a Glance 2019: OECD and G20 Indicators' (2019) <https://doi.org/10.1787/b6d3dcfc-en> accessed 2 July 2020; Crystal Kwan and Christine Walsh, 'Old Age Poverty: A Scoping Review of the Literature' (2018) 4(1) Cogent Social Sciences <https://doi.org/10.1080/23311886.2018.1478479> accessed 1 July 2020.

42   UNDP, 'Human Development for Everyone' (2016) <http://hdr.undp.org/sites/default/files/2016_human_development_report.pdf> accessed 29 June 2020 at 71–74 and Figures 2.8 and 2.9.

43   In 2015 in the European Union, women's pensions were on average 25 per cent lower than men's: 'Pensions at a Glance 2019: OECD and G20 Indicators' (2019) <https://doi.org/10.1787/b6d3dcfc-en> accessed 2 July 2020.

44   Women who were caring for grandchildren and children orphaned by AIDs were also more at risk: UNFPA, 'Ageing in the Twenty-First Century: A Celebration and A Challenge' (2012).

45   Magdalena Sepúlveda Carmona and Kate Donald, 'What Does Care Have to Do with Human Rights? Analysing the Impact on Women's Rights and Gender Equality' (2014) 22 Gender & Development 441 ('Heavy and intense burdens of unpaid care work entrench and exacerbate poverty …').

46   Shriver Center, 'Older Women and Poverty' Womanview (2016) <www.ncdsv.org/SSNCPL_Woman-View-Older-Women-and-Poverty_3-30-2016.pdf> accessed 2 July 2020.

3. Older persons with disability: While age is not to be equated with disability, the incidence of impairments and resulting disability does increase with age, and many older persons live with disability.[47] Equally, many older persons do not. But those who do may also benefit from guarantees in instruments such as the Convention on the Rights of Persons with Disabilities. The UN Human Rights Council's Special Rapporteur on the rights of persons with disabilities has noted that 'older persons with disabilities are at significant risk of living in poverty'.[48]

B.   Means of Alleviating or Avoiding Poverty for Older Persons

There are a number of factors that reduce the risk that older persons will spend their lives in poverty. One factor is the continuing participation of older persons in the workforce, where such work provides the sole source of income or supplements contributory or non-contributory pension income or other forms of social support. Many older persons continue working for longer than they might wish because of the unavailability or inadequacy of pensions. Increasing participation of older persons in the labour market is a means whereby older persons can seek to avoid poverty by generating income to live on which may also supplement income from other sources.

The participation of older persons in the paid labour force is increasing[49] and is motivated in many cases by the need to earn a sufficient income to enjoy a decent standard of living. The ILO has reported that both the share of 'older persons' – those aged 65 and above ('seniors') and those aged 55 and above ('near-seniors') in the working age population and in the labour force has increased over the last few decades and will continue to do so,[50] though these trends vary regionally.[51] The labour force participation of 'seniors' (65+) and 'near seniors' (55–64) has continued to increase as the total labour force participation has declined. Many of those in both groups continue working even though they may have reached traditional retirement age due to the unavailability or inadequacy of pension schemes or other resources on which they can draw if they are not engaged in paid work.

---

[47]   For the need to 'bridge' knowledge, policy research and practice in relation to disability and ageing, see Jerome E Bickenbach et al, 'The Toronto Declaration on Bridging Knowledge, Policy and Practice in Aging and Disability' (2012) 12 Int J Integr Care 1.

[48]   UNGA, 'Rights of Persons with Disabilities' (17 July 2019) A/74/186.

[49]   For example, in OECD countries the employment rate among individuals aged 55–64 has increased from 43.9 per cent in 2000 to 61.5 per cent in 2018. However, the OECD does not give figures for the 65 plus cohort. See 'Pensions at a Glance 2019: OECD and G20 Indicators' (2019) <https://doi .org/10.1787/b6d3dcfc-en> accessed 2 July 2020.

[50]   'What About Seniors? A Quick Analysis of the Situation of Older Persons in the Labour Market' (2018) ILOSTAT 1 <https://ilo.org/wcmsp5/groups/public/---dgreports/---stat/documents/publication/ wcms_629567.pdf> accessed 2 July 2020.

[51]   For example, 7 per cent of those over 65 in Europe and Central Asia participated in the labour force in 2015, while 39 per cent of the same group in Africa did so, see 'What About Seniors? A Quick Analysis of the Situation of Older Persons in the Labour Market' (2018) ILOSTAT 1 <https://ilo.org/ wcmsp5/groups/public/---dgreports/---stat/documents/publication/wcms_629567.pdf> accessed 2 July 2020.

However, ILO figures also suggest that those over 65 suffer higher levels of underemployment than other sectors of the population[52] and, although this group suffers from a lower unemployment rate than the overall population, this may be due to their not pursuing work when they have experienced difficulties in finding work.[53] Older workers are also overrepresented among the long-term unemployed.[54] The reasons for these difficulties may vary, including lack of relevant skills, the lack of suitable jobs, inflexible working arrangements or discrimination against older workers.[55]

The availability of contributory or non-contributory pensions and other forms of social support are a critical factor in whether older persons face poverty in older age:[56] older persons' 'access to social protection is crucial to ensure that they can leave the labour force at a desirable age with guaranteed decent living conditions'.[57] For those who are not participating in the paid labour market and who reach the age of eligibility for a pension, they may actually be better off individually because of those pension payments than they were when they were not in paid employment.

For example, the relative income poverty rate of those aged 65 or over in Australia dropped from 32.4 per cent in 2003 to 23 per cent in 2014. The three main reasons for this were an increase in labour force participation for those aged 65 and over from 6.9 per cent to 12.5 per cent; a larger rate of increase in state-funded pensions compared to allowances (such as unemployment benefits) for 'working age' people; and the increased availability of private pensions resulting in large part from the introduction of compulsory superannuation (a contributory pension scheme) in the early 1990s.[58]

As noted above, there can be considerable differences in people's experience of poverty as they move from their 60s into their 70s and 80s. The OECD has noted that average poverty rates in OECD countries increase as people move from the 'younger old' cohort (66–75) to the 'older old' cohort (75 and over), with average poverty rates of 11.6 per cent and 16.2 per cent respectively.[59] Once again this involves variations between countries with differences of up to 20 per cent, at least partly due to rates of indexation of pensions that are lower than the rate of wages growth and possibly also the increasing proportion of women at older ages and the fact that their lesser assets for retirement may not last into the later stages of their lives. On the other hand, there is a handful of OECD countries where those over 75 do better than those in the younger age cohort.

The discussion above shows that poverty among older persons is a variegated phenomenon. The identification of the full extent and nature of that poverty is made difficult by the lack

---

[52]   ibid. at 6–7.

[53]   ibid. at 8.

[54]   ibid. at 8–9.

[55]   ibid.

[56]   UNFPA, 'Ageing in the Twenty-First Century: A Celebration and A Challenge' (2012).

[57]   'What About Seniors? A Quick Analysis of the Situation of Older Persons in the Labour Market' (2018) ILOSTAT 1 <https://ilo.org/wcmsp5/groups/public/---dgreports/---stat/documents/publication/wcms_629567.pdf> accessed 2 July 2020.

[58]   Guyonne Kalb, 'Older People Now Less Likely to Fall into Poverty' (*The Conversation*, 12 December 2017) <http://theconversation.com/older-people-now-less-likely-to-fall-into-poverty-88634> accessed 2 July 2020.

[59]   'Pensions at a Glance 2019: OECD and G20 Indicators' (2019) <https://doi.org/10.1787/b6d3dcfc-en> accessed 2 July 2020.

of comprehensive standard statistics in all countries. Nonetheless, we do know that many older persons live in poverty – sometimes at a higher rate than that of the general population, sometimes at a lower rate, but in most countries there are significant numbers of older people living in poverty. The depth of that poverty varies and the rates increase when one goes beyond solely income- or expenditure-based measures of poverty. Specific groups of older people are more likely to live in poverty, or to be more vulnerable to it, than others; some of these factors are common to many societies, others may be specific to particular societies. Older women (including those who are widowed or divorced), older persons with disabilities, older persons living in rural areas, older persons living alone or in older-person only households (or ones with children), members of racial minorities, and older Indigenous Persons frequently experience higher levels of poverty than their counterparts, and multiple disadvantage exacerbates the likelihood that they will live in poverty.

Poverty in older age is also affected by what happens to people earlier in their lives, with disadvantage and deprivation at earlier stages of people's lives carried into older age and increasing the risk of poverty. Women often carry the disadvantages that arise from discrimination, stereotypes and caring roles that limit their opportunities to save for older age. The caring and other roles that they perform in older age can limit further their opportunities. Others who are poor and have limited opportunities in earlier life are also likely to face poverty in older age, to suffer from worse health and to die earlier than those who have enjoyed a higher standard of living in earlier years. The opportunities that older persons may have to earn income to alleviate their poverty may be limited – mandatory retirement laws and policies may force them out of the work force or into less well paid employment and force them into poverty, and ageism and discrimination in the labour market can make it difficult for many to get paid employment at all. The major way in which the poverty of older persons can be alleviated appears to be by ensuring that there is an adequate pension for older persons, whether a universal pension for all, or a means-tested pension that ensures that those who do not have sufficient private resources have the means to enjoy a decent standard of living.

Poverty in older age is thus part of broader social problems but comes with very specific features of its own. Therefore, general anti-poverty measures as well as specifically targeted measures are required to address its various manifestations.

V.   POVERTY AND THE HUMAN RIGHTS OF OLDER PERSONS

This section considers the role of human rights in relation to these patterns of poverty among older persons and whether the international human rights system offers adequate normative standards and strategies to address this phenomenon. It also discusses steps that might assist in bringing greater attention to addressing poverty experienced by older persons.

At the most general level, poverty is often said to itself be a violation of human rights, as well as involving violations of specific rights and giving rise to the inability to exercise others.[60] At an international level, there have been different approaches taken to alleviating poverty, often contested but often not explicitly taking into account human rights goals or standards, and in some cases leading in effect to violations of rights and the generation of

---

[60]   Stephen P Marks, 'Poverty' in Daniel Moeckli, Sangeeta Shah, Sandesh Sivakumaran and David Harris, *International Human Rights Law* (3rd ed, Oxford University Press, 2017) 597–618.

poverty at the national level (for example, the structural adjustment policies of international financial institutions during the 1990s). International development frameworks such as the Millennium Development Goals (MDGs) had limited success in explicitly framing their goals and actions in terms of human rights, though the achievement of some of their goals in many cases led to improvements in the enjoyment of human rights.

As a result of hard-fought advocacy, the 2030 Agenda for Sustainable Development (SDGs) incorporates human rights approaches to a greater extent than earlier frameworks such as the MDGs, though there are still many limitations. In particular, older age and the human rights of older persons are barely mentioned in the SDGs, their targets and indicators.[61] SDG 1 – 'to end poverty in all its forms everywhere' – and many of the other goals have a potential application to the situation of older persons among the many other sections of populations, even if only implicitly, either as members of subgroups such as women or as 'vulnerable persons'. However, this limited inclusion appears to have brought little visibility to how particular groups of older persons are faring.[62] The challenge is to ensure that those implicit promises become explicit and are implemented in practice.

Neither the Universal Declaration of Human Rights (UDHR) nor the principal UN human rights treaties contain an express right to be free from poverty. Nonetheless, Article 25 of the UDHR, along with other articles, effectively guarantees such a right with its proclamation that:

> Everyone has the right to a standard of living adequate for the health and well-being of himself and of his family, including food, clothing, housing and medical care and necessary social services, and the right to security in the event of unemployment, sickness, disability, widowhood, old age or other lack of livelihood in circumstances beyond his control.[63]

The guarantee of the right to social security in Article 22 and the right to work in Article 23 are also important dimensions of the right to be free from poverty and to enjoy an adequate standard of living. A principal focus of international human rights has been to ensure minimum standards for everyone in society rather than focusing on the elimination of inequalities within and between states.[64]

Article 2 affirms that these rights are to be enjoyed 'without distinction of any kind, such as race, colour, sex, language, religion, political or other opinion, national or social origin, property, birth or other status'. Age is not mentioned as a specific ground and does not appear to

---

[61]   UNHRC, 'Report of the Independent Expert on the Human Rights of Older Persons' (10 July 2018) A/HRC/39/50.

[62]   For example, the annual reports of the United Nations Secretary-General on progress in implementation of the SDGs from 2016 to 2019 make few references to older persons, with the extent of retirement pension coverage the main issue referred to, see 'Sustainable Development Goal 1: End Poverty in All its Forms' (*Sustainable Development Goals Knowledge Platform*, n.d.) <https://sustainabledevelopment.un.org/sdg1> accessed 2 July 2020.

[63]   Art. 25, UDHR.

[64]   For a criticism of the human rights system, see Samuel Moyn, *Not Enough: Human Rights in an Unequal World* (Harvard University Press, 2018). For responses, see Rhoda E Howard-Hassmann, '*Not Enough: Human Rights in an Unequal World* by Samuel Moyn (review)' (2019) 41 Human Rights Quarterly 515; Gráinne de Búrca, '*Not Enough: Human Rights in an Unequal World* by Samuel Moyn (review)' (2019) 16 International Journal of Constitutional Law 1347; Ioannis Kampourakis, '*Not Enough: Human Rights in an Unequal World* by Samuel Moyn (review)' (2020) 83(1) Modern Law Review 229.

have been a concern of the drafters,[65] though it is now accepted that it falls within the category of 'other status' in this and other international lists of prohibited bases of discrimination.

As with the UDHR, the principal UN human rights treaties, as well as the regional human rights treaties, guarantee the right to be free from poverty through the operation of a number of different rights, in particular the right to an adequate standard of living – the enjoyment of which is facilitated by rights such as the right to social security, the right to work, as well as most other rights (including civil and political rights). Older persons, just like all other individuals, are entitled to the enjoyment of these guarantees.

The right to non-discrimination in the enjoyment of those rights is also guaranteed, though generally without specific reference to age.[66] Both the Committee on Economic, Social and Cultural Rights (CESCR)[67] and the Human Rights Committee (HRC)[68] have stated that older age falls within the category of 'other status' in the non-discrimination articles in the International Covenant on Economic, Social and Cultural Rights (ICESCR) and the International Covenant on Civil and Political Rights (ICCPR), which replicate the wording of Article 2 of the UDHR.[69]

The right to an adequate standard of living may be viewed as the overarching right and should be viewed as guaranteeing not just the material conditions of existence necessary to lead a decent life (including the rights to food, housing and health), but also a broad notion of living conditions and capabilities that enable a person to participate in the community.[70] In the last decade or so the notion of a right to social protection which embraces both the right to social security and the right to an adequate standard of living has become a prominent organizing concept,[71] driven in significant part by the efforts of the International Labour Organization

---

[65]   See Johannes Morsink, *The Universal Declaration of Human Rights: Origins, Drafting, and Intent* (University of Pennsylvania Press, 1999) 113–16.

[66]   The exception is the International Convention on the Rights of All Migrant Workers and Members of Their Families, Article 1(1). At the regional level, the Revised European Social Charter (1996) provides protection of the rights of 'the elderly' (in particular Article 23, which guarantees the right to social protection), while the Charter of Fundamental Rights the European Union (2000) contains an express guarantee of non-discrimination on the grounds of age (Article 21) and also guarantees the rights of 'the elderly to lead a life of dignity and independence and to participate in social and cultural life' (Article 25). Broad protection of older persons' rights, including economic and social rights, are contained in the Inter-American Convention on Protecting the Human Rights of Older Persons 2015, while the Protocol to the African Charter on Human and Peoples' Rights on the Rights of Older Persons in Africa 2016 (not yet in force) also contains protections.

[67]   CESCR, 'General Comment 6: the Economic, Social and Cultural Rights of Older Persons', 8 December 1995, E/1996/22; CESCR, 'General Comment 20: Non-discrimination in Economic, Social and Cultural Rights', 2 July 2009, E/C.12/GC/20.

[68]   William A Schabas, *UN International Covenant on Civil and Political Rights: Nowak's CCPR Commentary* (3rd rev ed, N.P. Engel Publisher, 2019) 778–79.

[69]   UNGA, 'International Covenant on Economic, Social and Cultural Rights' (adopted 16 December 1966, entry into force 3 January 1976) Article 2(2); UNGA, 'International Covenant on Civil and Political Rights' (adopted 19 December 1966, entry into force 23 March 1976) Articles 2(1) and 26.

[70]   '[E]veryone should be able, without shame and without unreasonable obstacles, to be a full participant in ordinary, everyday interaction with other people. In other words, everyone should be able to enjoy their basic needs under conditions of dignity'. see Asbjørn Eide, 'Adequate Standard of Living' in Daniel Moeckli, Sangeeta Shah, Sandesh Sivakumaran and David Harris, *International Human Rights Law* (3rd ed, Oxford University Press, 2017), 186, 187.

[71]   The right to social protection includes 'the set of policies and programmes designed to reduce and prevent poverty and vulnerability across the life cycle'. ILO, 'World Social Protection Report 2017–2019: Universal Social Protection to Achieve the Sustainable Development Goals', 1.

(ILO) to reinvigorate these forms of protection and to introduce and popularize the concept of 'social protection floors'.[72]

The right to social security has an obvious direct and important application to older persons, given that one of the long-established branches of the right is 'old-age benefits', though other branches such as unemployment benefits, employment injury benefits, sickness benefits, disability benefits and survivors' benefits may also be relevant to older persons.

The ILO has been the major international source of detailed obligation and guidance in relation to the right to social security and social protection. Its Social Security (Minimum Standards) Convention, 1952 (No 102), the Old-Age, Invalidity and Survivors' Benefits Convention, 1967 (No 128) and its accompanying Recommendation No 131, and the Social Protection Floors Recommendation, 2012 (No 202), are the principal ILO instruments dealing with this subject.[73]

The CESCR has also played a significant role in developing understanding about the nature of the obligations of States in relation to ensuring the right to social security and the right to an adequate standard of living. It adopted a General Comment on the right to social security 2008,[74] which largely followed the framework of the ILO norms and standards.[75]

The discussion earlier in this chapter has shown that implementing the right to an adequate standard of living and social protection by older persons has been an important way of alleviating poverty, but that there are still significant gaps in the design and implementation of some of the schemes designed to ensure that these rights do achieve this goal within particular social or policy contexts.

For example, where states rely on contributory social insurance or pension schemes to provide social security or social support to older persons, there are a number of human rights concerns. These schemes tend to discriminate against women because of their links to employment in the formal economy – women's patterns of workforce participation due to family and care responsibilities mean that they often do not have the chance to contribute as much or for as long as men, something exacerbated by gender pay gaps, and their work in the informal economy in many countries means that they may have no contributions at all.[76] Even in the formal economy, they may be subject to discriminatory retirement ages when compared to men, with earlier departure from the workforce meaning that they may not have the opportunity make up some of the lost ground in contributions.[77]

---

[72]   See the discussion in UNHRC, 'Report of the Special Rapporteur on Extreme Poverty and Human Rights, Philip Alston' (11 August 2014) A/69/297.

[73]   They provide 'an international reference framework setting out the range and levels of social security benefits that are necessary and adequate for ensuring income maintenance and income security, as well as access to health care in old age'. ILO, 'World Social Protection Report 2017–2019: Universal Social Protection to Achieve the Sustainable Development Goals' 1 at 77.

[74]   CESCR, 'General Comment No 19: The Right to Social Security (Art 9)' (4 February 2008) E/C.12/GC/19.

[75]   ibid. at para 15.

[76]   For example, the Committee on the Elimination of Discrimination against Women found the failure to take into account time spent caring for a daughter with disabilities in the calculation of a social pension amounted to indirect discrimination against women and a violation of the Convention on the Elimination of All Forms of Discrimination against Women, see CERD, *Ciobanu v Moldova* (initially submitted 3 May 2016, views adopted 4 November 2019) CEDAW/C/74/D/104/2016.

[77]   CESCR, 'General Comment No 19: The Right to Social Security (Art 9)' (4 February 2008) E/C.12/GC/19 at para 32.

The importance of non-contributory pension schemes as a means to ensure that older persons can enjoy a decent standard of living has been emphasized as a matter of economic policy and human rights.[78] The ILO reports that major progress has been made on this front and that by 2017 nearly 68 per cent of the working age population were covered under existing laws regulating contributory or non-contributory pension schemes,[79] and 68 per cent of people above retirement age actually received a pension.[80] However, even where persons receive pensions, the sums paid are often not adequate to support a decent standard of living.[81]

For those who wish to engage in paid work to support themselves beyond statutory retirement ages or to supplement an inadequate pension, there are a number of difficulties. Mandatory retirement ages are still widely accepted as justifiable in certain circumstances under existing human rights standards, though often they are indiscriminately imposed.[82] Older workers may be forced to retire from their existing jobs and look for other forms of work. This can be hard to find because of labour markets conditions, including discrimination against older workers.

A further impediment to continuing paid employment of older workers is the lack of access to lifelong learning and education opportunities. International guarantees of the right to education focus primarily on earlier stages of life. None of the UN treaties other than the Convention on the Rights of Persons with Disabilities expressly refer to lifelong learning, and there are many barriers to access by older workers who wish to undertake training later in their working life.[83] While not limited to women, older women may be especially disadvantaged in relation to such opportunities as a result of assumptions about their roles and the significant load of caring and other domestic work that they bear.[84]

VI.   THE FUTURE: WHAT MEASURES ARE NEEDED TO ADDRESS POVERTY AMONG OLDER PERSONS?

The impact of COVID-19 has been to exacerbate existing inqualities and poverty and this will affect older persons, especially older persons who are particularly exposed because of the impact of intersectional discrimination and exclusion, as it will persons from other groups. The extent to which poverty has thus far been eliminated may have been overstated; at any rate there is an enormous amount yet to be done to ensure a decent standard of living for everyone.

---

[78]   Crystal Kwan and Christine Walsh, 'Old Age Poverty: A Scoping Review of the Literature' (2018) 4(1) Cogent Social Sciences <https://doi.org/10.1080/23311886.2018.1478479> accessed 1 July 2020.

[79]   The coverage of women is slightly lower, see ILO, 'World Social Protection Report 2017–2019: Universal Social Protection to Achieve the Sustainable Development Goals' 1 at 78.

[80]   ibid. at 79.

[81]   'Social Protection for Older Persons: Key Policy Trends and Statistics' International Labour Office Social Protection Department (2014).

[82]   A Byrnes, I Doron, N Georgantzi, W Mitchell and B Sleap, 'The Right of Older Persons to Work and to Access the Labour Market' (2019) UNGA Open-Ended Working Group on Ageing <https://ssrn.com/abstract=3504975> accessed 2 July 2020.

[83]   UNHRC, 'Report of the Independent Expert on the Human Rights of Older Persons, Rosa Kornfeld-Matte' (4 August 2015) A/HRC/30/43.

[84]   CEDAW, 'General Recommendation No. 27 on Older Women and Protection of Their Human Rights' (16 December 2010) CEDAW/C/GC/27. More generally, see CESCR, 'General Comment No 13: the Right to Education (Art. 13)' (8 December 1999) E/C.12/1999/10.

The discussion above has shown that there is a significant body of international human rights law in the form of both binding and non-binding standards that address many of the types of poverty that older persons face and that provide a reasonably workable framework for taking steps to prevent it. Much of that body of standards was first formulated at a time when people lived for much shorter periods after formal retirement than they do today and, to the extent that it relied on non-contributory pensions and other forms of state transfers, was premised on assumptions about the ability of the state to afford to support such systems, which have been challenged by the increases in the numbers and proportion of older persons in populations worldwide.

Nevertheless, there are a number of measures that need to be taken to give better effect to existing human rights standards to prevent and alleviate the poverty of older persons, using both existing frameworks and possible new frameworks, in particular a proposed new UN convention on the rights of older persons.

The measures that need to be taken include better data collection and disaggregation according to age and other characteristics (including different cohorts of older persons), and removing legal and attitudinal barriers to older persons continuing in paid employment when they reach traditional retirement age (including a reconsideration of whether mandatory retirement ages are ever justified and, if so, when).

A major component of eliminating the poverty of older persons is the expansion of non-contributory pension systems to ensure that all have sufficient income and capabilities to live a decent and fulfilling life in older age as a member of their communities. These might involve a combination of contributory or non-contributory arrangements or a universal basic pension, but it should at a minimum provide support for those who do not have sufficient assets to enjoy an adequate standard of living.

It is also important that attention be given to subgroups of the older population that may be particularly susceptible to poverty in specific communities. In this context the position of women generally and also subgroups such as women with disabilities, women who are living alone, and women in rural areas need to be taken into account in designing legal and policy interventions intended to eliminate poverty. Furthermore, in relation to women, as in other areas, it is important to ensure the enjoyment of equality at all stages of life in order to enhance the well-being of women once they reach older age, as well as supporting them at that stage of their lives.

Finally, there is much to be said for the elaboration of a new convention on the rights of older persons that would assist in addressing the poverty of older persons through the inclusion of a special and detailed right to social protection. A new instrument of this sort would add focus, provide momentum and spell out in greater detail the steps that need to be taken in order to eliminate the poverty that older persons face and more broadly the fuller enjoyment of their human rights.

The upshot is that any attempt to eliminate poverty in the lives of older persons and to ensure in practice the enjoyment of the right to an adequate standard of living, rights to health, and social protections, among other rights, need to be more ambitious and to form part of a broader conceptual and political challenges to existing frameworks, institutions and policies.

9. Child impoverishment and the human rights of children

Wouter Vandenhole

This chapter deals with poverty and the human rights of a particular group: children. If one accepts that children are fully-fledged human beings, no particular need may seem to arise to dedicate a specific chapter to them. However, poor children are often seen as deserving particular attention, for they cannot be blamed for their poverty (while adults can, the reasoning goes). They are also considered to be differently affected by poverty. Further, we have a specific set of human rights norms for children, as reflected in the 1989 UN Convention on the Rights of the Child. Taken together, these elements justify separate treatment in this book.

This chapter will pursue two main lines of inquiry: how to link conceptually poverty and children's rights, and what challenges a children's rights approach to impoverishment faces. The first section discusses child poverty. The next sections look into the framing of child impoverishment as a children's rights issue through three different lenses: (1) a right to protection against poverty, (2) a right to distributive equality and (3) a children's rights-based approach to poverty. The chapter then looks into seven challenges a children's rights approach to impoverishment faces.

I. COMBATING CHILD POVERTY: WHAT DO WE KNOW?

As of November 2019, 13.1 per cent of children in the 36 countries of the Organisation for Economic Co-operation and Development (OECD) lived in relative income poverty.[1] Globally, out of 767 million people living in extreme poverty in 2013, 385 million were children, a 2016 joint World Bank Group-UNICEF study revealed.[2]

The latter study also showed that children are more than twice as likely to live in extreme poverty (below $1.90 a day per person). In 2013 almost 20 per cent of children in developing countries were living in households in extreme poverty, compared to about 9 per cent of adults. In other words, children are disproportionately affected, and the youngest children are the worst off.[3] In many OECD countries too, children are slightly more likely to live in income poverty, and the relative poverty rates for children are higher than for the general population.

---

[1] Organisation for Economic Co-operation and Development (OECD), 'OECD Family Database' <www.oecd.org/els/family/database.htm#child_outcomes> accessed 24 June 2020 (explaining the child relative income poverty rate is defined as the percentage of children with an equivalized household disposable income (that is, income after taxes and transfers adjusted for household size) below the poverty threshold of 50 per cent of the median disposable income in each country).

[2] UNICEF, 'Ending Extreme Poverty: A Focus on Children' (2016) 2 <www.unicef.org/publications/files/Ending_Extreme_Poverty_A_Focus_on_Children_Oct_2016.pdf> accessed 24 June 2020.

[3] ibid; World Bank Group, 'Piecing Together the Poverty Puzzle' (2018) 129 <https://openknowledge.worldbank.org/bitstream/handle/10986/30418/9781464813306.pdf> accessed 24 June 2020 (providing more recent confirmation of the data).

Between 2006 and 2016 the prevalence of child relative poverty increased in about half of the OECD countries with available data. The poverty rate in single parent households is three times higher than in households with two or more adults. Likewise, poverty rates are much higher in jobless households: almost 64 per cent of persons living in jobless households with children live in relative income poverty, compared to only about 9 per cent of persons in working households with children.[4] A study of child poverty in Africa projects that 304 million sub-Saharan children will be living in extreme poverty in 2030, thereby accounting for 55 per cent of world poverty (compared with 43 per cent in 2018).[5]

The COVID-19 pandemic that hit the world in late 2019 is most likely to reinforce these trends. As the OECD points out, 'COVID-19 may present serious challenges for inclusive growth as the poorest children are likely to be hardest hit and their … life chances severely limited'.[6]

GDP is not decisive in determining the extent of child poverty: there is no strong relationship between per capita GDP and overall child well-being. UNICEF's Office of Research 2013 league table of child well-being ranked 29 developed countries according to the well-being of their children for five dimensions (material well-being, health and safety, education, behaviour and risks, and housing and environment). Portugal, for example, ranked higher than the United States, whereas per capita GDP in 2010 was USD 21,382 in Portugal, and USD 46,616 in the United States. The bottom four places in the table were occupied by three of the poorest countries in the survey, Latvia, Lithuania, and Romania, but also by the United States, one of the richest.[7] This means that arguments that child poverty is based on lack of resources cannot be accepted at face value.

In sum, child poverty deserves separate attention but not as a fact of life or a given. Poverty is human-made. (Child) poverty is the result of policy measures, or their absence, and may therefore be more appropriately referred to as child impoverishment or immiseration.[8] Just as child poverty is made through policies, it can also be addressed through the same: it is particularly susceptible to governments' policies. Two types of strategies may be adopted: benefits (and taxation) strategies, or work strategies. In the former, the emphasis is on welfare policies taken by the government, in the latter on labour activation policies. However, employment of parents does not suffice to lift families out of poverty.[9]

---

[4] OECD (n 1).

[5] Kevin Watkins and Maria Quattri, 'Child Poverty in Africa: An SDG Emergency in the Making' (2019) Overseas Development Institute (ODI) Briefing Paper <www.odi.org/sites/odi.org.uk/files/resource-documents/12863.pdf> accessed 24 June 2020.

[6] OECD, 'Combatting COVID-19's Effect on Children' (4 May 2020) 2 <https://read.oecd-ilibrary.org/view/?ref=132_132643-m91j2scsyh&title=Combatting-COVID-19-s-effect-on-children> accessed 24 June 2020.

[7] UNICEF Office of Research, 'Child Well-being in Rich Countries: A Comparative Overview' (2013) <www.unicef-irc.org/publications/pdf/rc11_eng.pdf> accessed 24 June 2020.

[8] John Linarelli, Margot Salomon and Muthucumaraswamy Sornarajah, *The Misery of International Law: Confrontations with Injustice in the Global Economy* (OUP 2018).

[9] Peter Whiteford and Willem Adema, 'Combating Child Poverty in OECD Countries: Is Work the Answer?' (2006) 8 E.J.S.S. 235, 241.

A.   A Child and Children's Rights-Specific Approach to Impoverishment[10]

In general human rights instruments and documents it is acknowledged that children are differently affected by poverty.[11] They tend to be mentioned as victims[12] and as a group that is particularly vulnerable to extreme poverty.[13] Normatively, in order to justify prioritizing children living in poverty, the need to ensure the best interests of the child and the irreversible harm to children's right to survival and development is mobilized,[14] together with more instrumental considerations that child poverty is a root cause of poverty in adulthood.[15] The Guiding Principles on Extreme Poverty and Human Rights call for 'immediate action to combat childhood poverty'[16] and identify three sets of obligations incumbent on states, which coincide with the popular tripartite typology in children's rights of provision, protection and participation.[17] First, states must ensure that 'all children have equal access to basic services', and that '[a]t a minimum, children are entitled to a package of basic social services that includes high-quality health care, adequate food, housing, safe drinking water and sanitation and primary education.'[18] Second, states must strengthen child protection strategies and programmes in order to protect children in poverty against exploitation, neglect and abuse.[19] And finally, children must have a voice in decision-making that affects them.[20]

Capturing child impoverishment legally in terms of children's rights is far more challenging. Poverty is not explicitly mentioned in the Convention on the Rights of the Child (CRC) nor is a right to protection against poverty or a right to be free from poverty. Proxies such as well-being and development feature in the CRC. In Van Bueren's view, children's economic and social rights are a 'concrete set of responses to specific facets of child poverty'.[21] Nevertheless, the relationship between the human rights of children and poverty remains conceptually vague. Therefore, I outline three approaches that more explicitly link poverty and children's rights under an obligations approach:[22] (1) a right to protection against poverty, (2) a right to distributive equality, and (3) a rights-based approach to poverty.

---

[10]   This and the following sections draw on W Vandenhole, 'Child Poverty and Children's Rights: An Uneasy Fit' (2013) 22 Mich.St.Int'l.L.Rev. 609.

[11]   United Nations General Assembly (UNGA), 'Report of the Independent Expert on the Question of Human Rights and Extreme Poverty' (13 August 2008) UN Doc A/63/274 para 38.

[12]   United Nations Human Rights Office of the High Commissioner (OHCHR), 'Principles and Guidelines for a Human Rights Approach to Poverty Reduction Strategies' (2006) HR/PUB/06/12 paras 109 and 127.

[13]   UNGA, 'Final Draft of the Guiding Principles on Extreme Poverty and Human Rights, Submitted by the Special Rapporteur on Extreme Poverty and Human Rights, Magdalena Sepúlveda Carmona' (18 July 2012) UN Doc A/HRC/21/39 para 8.

[14]   ibid para 96.

[15]   ibid para 32.

[16]   ibid.

[17]   W Vandenhole, G Erdem Türkelli and S Lembrechts, *Children's Rights. A Commentary on the Convention on the Rights of the Child and its Protocols* (Edward Elgar Publishing 2019) 7, 7–8.

[18]   UNGA (n 13) para 33.

[19]   ibid para 34.

[20]   ibid para 35.

[21]   G Van Bueren, 'Combating Child Poverty – Human Rights Approaches' (1999) 21 Hum.Rts.Q. 680, 681.

[22]   A R Chapman, 'A "Violations Approach" for Monitoring the International Covenant on Economic, Social and Cultural Rights' (1996) 18 Hum.Rts.Q. 23.

1.   A right to protection against poverty

The most direct way of linking children's rights and poverty is by coining a right to be free from poverty or a right to protection against poverty, as has been done in the Revised European Social Charter, a Council of Europe treaty. Article 30 of that Charter reads:

> With a view to ensuring the effective exercise of the right to protection against poverty and social exclusion, the Parties undertake:
> a.   to take measures within the framework of an overall and co-ordinated approach to promote the effective access of persons who live or risk living in a situation of social exclusion or poverty, as well as their families, to, in particular, employment, housing, training, education, culture and social and medical assistance;
> b.   to review these measures with a view to their adaptation if necessary.[23]

In essence, states commit themselves to a comprehensive and coordinated approach to the alleviation of poverty and social exclusion. In the view of the monitoring body, the European Committee of Social Rights (ECSR), the obligation to adopt an overall and coordinated approach requires the elaboration of 'an analytical framework, a set of priorities', 'measures to prevent and remove obstacles to accessing fundamental social rights', and inclusive or participative monitoring mechanisms.[24] An increase in the resources deployed is required as long as poverty and social exclusion persist. Where necessary, measures should 'specifically target the most vulnerable groups',[25] such as children.

Until 2015, the UN Committee on the Rights of the Child (CRC Committee) adopted this approach quite often; typically, it recommended that states elaborate a child poverty strategy and establish a coherent framework identifying priority action against social exclusion of children, 'including specific and measurable objectives, clear indicators, a time frame and sufficient and material support'.[26]

2.   A right to distributive equality

Drawing on recent debates about the equality norm, not only as a minimum floor of protection against indigence but also as a ceiling on extreme inequality, as well as on the literature on intersectionality, a second option to link children's rights and poverty consists of coining a right of children to distributive equality.

There is a growing awareness of human rights law's silence on extreme inequality and on distributive equality. Some have argued that human rights law and the principle of equality do

---

[23]   For further analysis, see A Nolan, *Protecting the Child from Poverty: the Role of Rights in the Council of Europe* (Council of Europe 2019).

[24]   *International Movement ATD Fourth World v France* App no 33/2006 (ECSR, 5 December 2007) para 164.

[25]   ibid para 166.

[26]   Committee on the Rights of the Child (CRC), 'Concluding Observations on the Combined Third to Fifth Periodic Reports of Uruguay' (5 March 2015) UN Doc CRC/C/URY/CO/3-5 para 56.

speak to power relations and the concomitant structural injustice,[27] while others believe that a ceiling on inequality is beyond human rights law.[28]

Minimum-threshold approaches have been criticized for not really being concerned with the level of societal equality. They rather seek to identify the poor and to ensure that they move beyond the poverty line, without really addressing multidimensional poverty.[29]

Therefore, a more ambitious approach than one relying on minimum core obligations may be needed to put redistributive equality at the centre, that is, one that seeks to bring about transformative equality.[30] Transformative equality focuses on structural causes of injustice: it pursues 'a total reconstitution of the power relations in society with the consequence that human development is maximized and material imbalances are redressed'.[31] Transformative equality is concerned with 'lasting change in the power and choices [people] have over their own lives'[32] and the 'underlying structural connections and the relations of power that produce situations of inequality and discrimination'.[33] MacNaughton argues that a right to social equality must be recognized. This could be done inter alia by sophisticating the analysis on the grounds of social origin and property and by inferring a right to equality from substantive economic and social rights. The importance of de facto equality, and of the grounds of social origin and status as prohibited grounds of discrimination in particular, has been echoed elsewhere in literature.[34] Parameters to assess the redistributive character of the principle of equality may include the extent to which it provides universal access to quality public goods, attributes a particular role to education and health and prioritizes universalism over targeted measures.[35]

The CRC Committee has addressed the question of child poverty occasionally under the general principle of non-discrimination, and it has also paid some attention to power and choice, but certainly not as a conscious effort to frame child impoverishment as a matter of distributive equality. Likewise, it has hinted at mechanisms of impoverishment, in particular by drawing attention to the impact of intellectual property rights on the affordability of med-

---

[27] Philip Alston, 'Extreme Inequality as the Antithesis of Human Rights' (openDemocracy 2015) 2–3 <www.opendemocracy.net/en/openglobalrights-openpage/extreme-inequality-as-antithesis -of-human-rights/> accessed 24 June 2020; cf G de Búrca, 'Not Enough: Human Rights in an Unequal World' (2018) 16 ICON 1347.

[28] Samuel Moyn, 'Human Rights and the Age of Inequality' (openDemocracy 2015) <www .opendemocracy.net/en/openglobalrights-openpage/human-rights-and-age-of-inequality/> accessed 24 June 2020.

[29] G MacNaughton, 'Beyond a Minimum Threshold: The Right to Social Equality' in L Minkler (ed), *The State of Economic and Social Human Rights: A Global Overview* (CUP 2013) 271, 284.

[30] D Barrett, 'Tackling Economic Inequality with the Right to Non-Discrimination' (openDemocracy 2016) 2–3 <www.opendemocracy.net/en/openglobalrights-openpage/tackling-economic-inequality-with -right-to-non-discrimination/> accessed 24 June 2020.

[31] C Albertyn and B Goldblatt, 'Facing the Challenge of Transformation: Difficulties in the Development of an Indigenous Jurisprudence of Equality' (1998) 14 SAJHR 248, 272.

[32] A Cornwall and A-M Rivas, 'From "Gender Equality" and "Women's Empowerment" to Global Justice: Reclaiming a Transformative Agenda for Gender and Development' (2015) 36(2) TWQ 396, 397.

[33] ibid.

[34] Van Bueren (n 21) 689–90.

[35] MacNaughton (n 29) 271.

icines for the poor[36] and drawn attention to persistent inequalities and inequitable distribution of available resources as root causes of poverty.[37] In the allocation of available resources, it has emphasized that there needs to be 'a special focus on eradicating poverty and reducing inequalities',[38] inter alia through child benefits or cash transfers.[39] More generally, it has recommended measures to address 'the structural causes of poverty and income inequalities to reduce pressure on and strengthen precarious families', including 'tax and expenditure policies that reduce economic inequalities; expanding fair-wage employment and other opportunities for income generation' and the introduction of pro-poor policies.[40]

3.   A rights-based approach to poverty

A third approach to children's rights and poverty consists of adopting a children's rights-based approach to poverty. The underlying idea is that child poverty cannot be addressed adequately through one or more separate rights, so that an integrated and holistic approach is needed.[41] Such a holistic analysis through the prism of children's rights is then coined 'a children's rights-based approach' (CRBA), which can be regarded as a child-specific version of a human rights-based approach (HRBA). There is no single approach or understanding but rather a multiplicity of human rights-based approaches to poverty. HRBAs typically approach poverty from a global perspective, whereby both domestic and global issues are taken into account. HRBAs focus not only on the end result or outcome (the full realization of human rights) but also on the overall process. Human rights principles central to HRBAs can be summarized in the acronym PANEN, i.e. participation, accountability, non-discrimination, empowerment, and normativity. These human rights principles are, for example, reflected in the UN Committee on Economic, Social and Cultural Rights' (CESCR) approach to poverty.[42]

The CRC Committee has linked measures to address child poverty with a holistic approach in which all rights, and in particular all socio-economic rights, are at stake. It has also emphasized rather strongly and consistently the participation dimension, as the next section shows.

4.   The approach taken by the Committee on the Rights of the Child

As indicated above, each of these three framings can be found in the CRC Committee's approach to poverty. The Committee has not yet adopted a general comment on child poverty, but it has paid quite some attention to poverty in its general comment on children living in

---

[36]   CRC, 'General Comment No. 15 (2013) on the Right of the Child to the Enjoyment of the Highest Attainable Standard of Health (art. 24)' (17 April 2013) UN Doc CRC/C/GC/15 para 82.

[37]   CRC, 'Concluding Observations on the Combined Third to Sixth Periodic Reports of the Lao People's Democratic Republic' (1 November 2018) UN Doc CRC/C/LAO/GC/3-6 para 37(b); CRC, 'Concluding Observations on the Combined Third to Fifth Periodic Reports of the Democratic Republic of the Congo' (28 February 2017) UN Doc CRC/C/COD/CO/3-5 para 38.

[38]   CRC, 'Concluding Observations: France' (22 June 2009) UN CRC/C/FRA/CO/4 para 19.

[39]   CRC, 'General Comment No. 21 (2017) on Children in Street Situations' (21 June 2017) UN Doc CRC/C/GC/20 para 51.

[40]   ibid para 51; cf CRC, 'Concluding Observations on the Fifth Periodic Report of Mongolia' (12 July 2017) UN Doc CRC/C/MNG/CO/5 para 37(a).

[41]   Van Bueren (n 21) 684.

[42]   Committee on Economic, Social and Cultural Rights (CESCR), 'Statement on Poverty and the International Covenant on Economic, Social and Cultural Rights' (10 May 2001) UN Doc E/C.12/2001/10 paras 5 and 11; Vandenhole (n 10).

street situations.[43] The CRC Committee considers poor children to belong to the group of children with heightened vulnerabilities.[44] There is recognition of both the particular vulnerability to poverty and deprivation of some groups of children – such as young children, indigenous children, children from foreign background and children living in single-parent households or in families with three or more children[45] – and of the particular risks to all children that result from poverty and social exclusion.[46] The Committee has also acknowledged that poverty is a structural determinant of child disease.[47]

A screening of concluding observations for the 2010–2019 period shows that the CRC Committee has become over time more concrete and specific in its recommendations on child poverty. Initially, it recommended in fairly general wording that states provide support and guarantee all children an adequate standard of living.[48] Since late 2011 it has given more detailed guidance, including the requirement to design specific policies, poverty reduction strategies and national plans to address child poverty,[49] to earmark specific budget lines for children[50] and strategic budget lines for vulnerable children,[51] and to hold targeted consulta-

---

[43]   CRC (n 39).

[44]   CRC, 'General Comment No 7: Implementing Child Rights in Early Childhood' (20 September 2006) UN Doc CRC/C/GC/7/Rev.1 para 24; CRC, 'General comment No 17 (2013) on the Right of the Child to Rest, Leisure, Play, Recreational Activities, Cultural Life and the Arts (art. 31)' (17 April 2013) UN Doc CRC/C/GC/17 para 3; CRC 'General Comment No 19 (2016) on Public Budgeting for the Realization of Children's Rights (art. 4)' (20 July 2016) UN Doc CRC/C/GC/19 para 3.

[45]   CRC Committee, 'General Comment No 11: Indigenous Children and their Rights under the Convention' (12 February 2009) UN Doc CRC/C/GC/11, paras 34 and 70; CRC Committee (note 43) paras 2(f) and 36; CRC Committee, 'Concluding Observations on the Fifth Periodic Report of Denmark' (26 October 2017) UN Doc CRC/DNK/CO/5 para 35(a).

[46]   CRC (n 4) para 8; CRC 'General Comment No. 13: The Right of the Child to Freedom from all Forms of Violence' (18 April 2011) UN Doc CRC/C/GC/13, para 72. Poverty has more recently been identified as a 'family risk factor' for violence against children, see CRC 'General Comment No. 13'; CRC No 17 (n 44) paras 35 and 49 (discussing the negative impacts on the right to rest, leisure, play, recreational activities, cultural life and the arts for children living in poverty; vulnerabilities and risks owing to climate change); CRC 'Concluding Observations on the Combined Third to Fifth Periodic Reports of the Dominican Republic' (6 March 2015) UN Doc CRC/C/DOM/CO/3-5 para 25 (explaining the lack of birth registration); CRC 'Concluding Observations on the Combined Third to Fifth Periodic Reports of the United Republic of Tanzania' UN Doc CRC/C/TZA/CO/3-5, para 71(c) (discussing sale, trafficking, abduction).

[47]   CRC (n 36) para 5; CEDAW and CRC 'Joint General Recommendation/General Comment No. 31 of the Committee on the Elimination of Discrimination against Women and No. 18 of the Committee on the Rights of the Child on Harmful Practices' (14 November 2014) UN Doc CEDAW/C/GC/31 and CRC/C/GC/18 para 60 (depicting the increased vulnerability of girls living in poverty to gender-based violence). Also during adolescence, see CRC 'General Comment No. 20 (2016) on the Implementation of the Rights of the Child During Adolescence' (5 December 2016) UN Doc CRC/C/GC/20 para 66.

[48]   CRC, 'Concluding Observations: Denmark' (4 February 2011) UN Doc CRC/C/DNK/CO/4 para 5.

[49]   CRC, 'Concluding Observations: Spain' (29 September 2010) UN Doc CRC/C/ESP/CO/3-4 para 53; CRC, 'Concluding Observations: Greece' (13 August 2012) UN Doc CRC/C/GRC/CO/2-3 para 59; CRC, 'Concluding Observations on the Combined Third and Fourth Periodic Report of Canada' (6 December 2012) UN Doc CRC/C/CAN/CO/3-4 para 68.

[50]   CRC, 'Concluding Observations on the Second Periodic Report of Andorra' (3 December 2012) UN Doc CRC/C/AND/CO/2 para 16.

[51]   CRC, 'Concluding Observations: Belgium' (18 June 2010) UN Doc CRC/C/BEL/CO/3-4 para 20.

tions with families and children in order to strengthen child poverty alleviation strategies.[52] The CRC Committee has called on states to ensure social protection benefits to all children through child benefits,[53] through income support to families in poverty,[54] and through comprehensive responses including parents' participation in the labour market.[55] States must ensure that social protection measures cover the real cost of a decent standard of living for children.[56] These income-related policies are seen as a preventive strategy for child labour.[57] Moreover, the Committee has urged states to adopt inclusive measures to protect the more poverty-prone groups[58] and to ensure equitable access to basic services such as adequate nutrition, housing, water and sanitation and electricity services, as well as to social and health services and education,[59] including through avoiding hidden or excessive costs for education, which disproportionately affect families living in poverty.[60] In response to the particular vulnerability of young children to and resulting from poverty, 'proper prevention and intervention strategies during early childhood' are recommended.[61] Exceptionally, the Committee has insisted on time-bound and measurable indicators as part of a poverty strategy for children.[62]

The Committee does not rely exclusively on income measures; social, cultural, geographic and other such structural determinants of poverty reduction must be considered, too.[63] Sometimes the Committee clearly goes beyond material assistance and urges State parties 'to render appropriate assistance to parents and legal guardians in the performance of their child-rearing responsibilities, in particular for families in crisis situations due to poverty, absence of adequate housing or separation'.[64] Nevertheless it continues to address child poverty most explicitly under the headings of 'allocation of resources' and/or 'standard of

---

[52]   CRC, 'Concluding observations on the Combined Fourth and Fifth Periodic Reports of Japan' (5 March 2019) UN Doc CRC/C/JPN/CO/4-5 para 38(b).
[53]   CRC, 'Concluding Observations on the Consolidated Second to Fourth Periodic Reports of Bosnia and Herzegovina' (29 November 2012) UN Doc CRC/C/BIH/CO/2-4 para 61.
[54]   CRC, 'Concluding Observations: Italy' (31 October 2011) UN Doc CRC/C/ITA/CO/3-4 para 58(d).
[55]   CRC, 'Concluding Observations on the Combined Fifth and Sixth Periodic Reports of Italy' (28 February 2019) UN Doc CRC/C/ITA/CO/5-6 para 30.
[56]   CRC, 'Concluding Observations on the Combined Third and Fourth Periodic Reports of the Marshall Islands' (27 February 2018) UN Doc CRC/C/MHL/CO/3-4 para 35(b).
[57]   CRC, 'Concluding Observations on the Combined Third to Fifth Periodic Reports of Tajikistan' (29 September 2017) UN Doc CRC/C/TJKL/CO/3-5 para 37.
[58]   CRC, 'Concluding Observations on the Combined Fifth and Sixth Periodic Reports of Portugal' (9 December 2019) UN Doc CRC/C/PRT/CO/5-6 para 39(b).
[59]   CRC, 'Concluding Observations on the Consolidated Second to Fourth Periodic Reports of Albania' (7 December 2012) UN Doc CRC/C/ALB/CO/2-4 para 67; CRC, 'Concluding Observations on the Combined Fifth and Sixth Periodic Reports of Portugal' (9 December 2019) UN Doc CRC/C/PRT/CO/5-5 para 39(c).
[60]   CRC, 'Concluding Observations on the Combined Third to Fifth Periodic Reports of Cameroon' (6 July 2017) UN Doc CRC/C/CMR/CO/3-5 paras 38(c) and 39(d).
[61]   CRC (n 44) para 50.
[62]   CRC, 'Concluding Observations on the Combined Fifth and Sixth Periodic Reports of Belgium' (28 February 2019) UN Doc CRC/C/BEL/CO/5-6 para 37(a).
[63]   CRC (n 54) para 58.
[64]   CRC (n 38) para 60; cf CRC, 'Concluding Observations on the Fifth Periodic Report of Pakistan' (11 July 2016) UN Doc CRC/C/PAK/CO/5 para 42.

living', which apply to material aspects only.[65] Since mid-2016 the Committee draws explicitly on target 1.3 of the Sustainable Development Goals to strengthen its recommendations.

B.   Seven Challenges for a Children's Rights Approach to Impoverishment

After having analysed the way in which the CRC Committee approaches poverty through a children's rights lens, I will now look into challenges that a children's rights approach to impoverishment faces in order to pursue a real welfare agenda.[66] For each of the challenges, I offer a short problem statement. The first two concern questions of legal qualification. The next three raise important considerations for intervention strategies. The final two speak explicitly to questions of global poverty.

1.   Can child poverty be considered a violation of children's rights?
Without a doubt, child poverty is an affront to human dignity, and it affects the enjoyment of each and every right. To mention just a few: poverty is not in children's best interests (art. 3 CRC). Discrimination and exclusion are often at the origin of poverty (art. 2 CRC).[67] Whenever child poverty is life-threatening, it is also affecting children's right to life, survival and development (art. 6 CRC).[68] Child poverty may be considered a form of violence (art. 19), and it is certainly not in line with children's right to a standard of living adequate for their physical, mental, spiritual, moral and social development (art. 27 CRC). By extension, at least all socio-economic rights (see arts. 24, 26, 28 CRC) are implicated: poverty is one of the structural determinants of mental and physical health,[69] but arguably also of the right to social security, education, and so on.

Legally however, child poverty can only be qualified as a children's rights violation to the extent that acts or omissions can be attributed to a state. Moreover, whereas economic, social and cultural rights (ESC rights) may 'create a legitimate claim for children to benefit from an equal share in the state's resources',[70] to establish a violation of ESC rights is not easy, given the weak general obligation of progressive realization. This is particularly problematic for children, since postponing realisation of their rights may impose unique harms on children.[71] Article 4 CRC limits the general obligation for the realization of ESC rights to 'the maximum extent of … available resources and, where needed, within the framework of international

---

[65]   CRC (n 38) paras 78–79.
[66]   J Grugel, 'Children's Rights and Children's Welfare after the Convention on the Rights of the Child' (2013) 13 Progress in Development Studies 19.
[67]   CRC (n 38) para 78.
[68]   The CRC Committee has explicitly linked absolute poverty with the right to life and survival. CRC (n 39) para 30; CRC, 'Concluding Observations on the Combined Third to Fifth Periodic Reports of Senegal' (7 March 2016) UN Doc CRC/C/SEN/CO/3-5 para 28(b).
[69]   CRC (n 36) para 5; UN Committee on the Protection of the Rights of All Migrant Workers and Members of Their Families and CRC Committee, 'Joint General Comment No. 4 (2017) of the Committee on the Protection of the Rights of All Migrant Workers and Members of Their Families and No. 23 (2017) of the Committee on the Rights of the Child on State Obligations Regarding the Human Rights of Children in the Context of International Migration in Countries of Origin, Transit, Destination and Return' (16 November 2017) UN Doc CRC/C/GC/23 para 54.
[70]   Van Bueren (n 21) 680–81.
[71]   I am grateful to M Davis for pointing this out.

cooperation'.[72] Child poverty may hence be justifiable with reference to the limited availability of resources. However, as the CESCR has clarified, this dependence on resource availability does not grant states a blank cheque; they must begin immediately to take steps in order to realize ESC rights as expeditiously as possible. In addition, they have to make maximum use of available resources.[73] States also need to adopt a strategy and plan of action to realize these rights. More fundamentally even, as argued above, very often the question of resources boils down to questions of distribution rather than availability or inability. In sum, the general obligation of progressive realisation does not preclude the finding of a violation.

2.   Austerity measures and poor children

Austerity measures are often an exacerbating factor of child poverty:[74] more children live in poverty in times of austerity, and those who lived already in poverty are pushed even further in more extreme forms of poverty due to austerity measures. The CRC Committee has therefore recommended that States conduct a comprehensive impact assessment, to devise more effective strategies to address adverse impacts, and to ensure that the rights of children from disadvantaged communities are not further adversely affected by austerity measures.[75] Indirectly, it has introduced a budgetary minimum floor by asking States to '[d]efine strategic budgetary lines for children in disadvantaged or vulnerable situations that may require affirmative social protection measures, especially children in situations of poverty … and [to] make sure that those budgetary lines are protected even in situations of economic crisis, natural disasters or other emergencies'.[76]

Technically, austerity measures – as retrogressive measures – require careful justification by the state and may not affect the minimum core of children's rights nor disproportionally hit poor children.[77] In Van Bueren's reading intention, a significant number of children being hit, and deprivation of essential goods are key factors in assessing the permissibility of retrogressive measures.[78] Given the legal justifiability of austerity measures that affect children – albeit only in circumscribed circumstances – the question remains whether the current children's rights analysis of austerity measures offers sufficient protection to children in poverty.

3.   Fragmentation of rights versus the need for a comprehensive approach to child impoverishment

In Van Bueren's view, '[t]he CRC provides an ideology for state intervention'.[79] That may be an overstatement, and the use of the word 'ideology' may be unfortunate. Nonetheless, it

---

[72]   P Cantwell, 'The Origins, Development and Significance of the United Nations Convention on the Rights of the Child' in S Detrick (ed), *The United Nations Convention on the Rights of the Child: A Guide to the 'Travaux Preparatoires'* (Martinus Nijhoff, 1992) 27; P Alston, 'The Best Interests Principle: Towards a Reconciliation of Culture and Human Rights' (1994) 8 Int'l J.L. & Fam. 1, 7.

[73]   S Skogly, 'The Requirement of Using the "Maximum of Available Resources" for Human Rights Realisation: A Question of Quality as Well as Quantity?' (2012) 12 Hum. Rts. L. Rev. 393.

[74]   Nolan (n 23) 17.

[75]   CRC (n 56) paras 7–8(a).

[76]   CRC (n 51) para 16(b).

[77]   CRC (n 42); CRC, 'Concluding Observations on the Combined Fifth and Sixth Periodic Reports of Argentina' (1 October 2018) UN Doc CRC/CARG/CO/5-6 para 36(e).

[78]   Van Bueren (n 21) 693.

[79]   ibid 692.

is true that the CRC requires a state to take a holistic approach to child poverty. A holistic approach may be 'daunting to genuinely resource-stretched governments'.[80] Beyond implementation challenges, a holistic approach is inherently difficult due to the individualistic approach that children's rights law tends to take.[81] The individualistic bias of children's rights law, in combination with the lack of a comprehensive right that tackles poverty, may lead to a fragmented approach. Moreover, root causes and structural causes may remain unaddressed, because monitoring bodies like the CRC Committee tend to look at child poverty through the adverse effects on the realization of specific rights or the vulnerability of specific groups of children. Above we have nonetheless seen how the CRC Committee tries not to overlook structural causes of poverty.

This raises the broader question of whether it makes sense to single out *child* poverty. Given the specific damage to and vulnerability of children living in poverty, as well as the long-term effects,[82] it does make eminent sense to address child poverty in its own right. Just like gender dimensions, age dimensions may tend to be ignored when taking the family as unit of analysis and intervention. However, child poverty cannot be addressed appropriately if the poverty of the family or community the child lives in is not also taken into account.[83] A comprehensive approach in which child poverty is addressed both separately and contextualized is therefore preferable.[84]

4.   Pitching children's rights against parents

The primary responsibility to keep children out of poverty lies with the parents, albeit within their abilities and financial capacities (article 27.2 CRC). This parental responsibility is mirrored in an obligation of the state to ensure that parents fulfil their obligations towards their child (obligation to protect).[85] This attribution of primary responsibility to the parents builds on the Convention's 'conception of the ideal type of setting for the upbringing of the child: a family with the will and the capability to care for the child during its many years, starting with the pregnancy and from birth to full maturity at the age of eighteen'.[86] However, parents' capacity to live up to this ideal is strongly dependent on their resources, material and non-material. If, despite their efforts, parents are unable to ensure proper conditions for the development of the child, the state has a subsidiary obligation to assist (article 27.3 CRC). This obligation may imply 'systematically supporting parents and families which are among the most important "available resources" for children'.[87] But it may be and often is a thin line

---

[80]   ibid 703.

[81]   W Vandenhole, 'The Limits of Human Rights Law in Human Development' in E Claes and others (eds), *Facing the Limits of the Law* (Springer 2009) 355.

[82]   Council of Europe, Declaration on the Occasion of the International Day for the Eradication of Poverty: Acting Together to Eradicate Extreme Poverty in Europe (17 October 2012) <www.assembly .coe.int/CommitteeDocs/2012/17102012_declaration_en.pdf> accessed 24 June 2020.

[83]   Eurochild, 'Child poverty – Family Poverty: Are they One and the Same? A Rights-Based Approach to Fighting Child Poverty' (2011) 1 <www.eurochild.org/fileadmin/public/05_Library/ Thematic_priorities/02_Child_Poverty/Eurochild/Position_paper_ch_pov_vs_family_pov_designed _FINAL.pdf > accessed 24 June 2020.

[84]   Van Bueren (n 21) 682.

[85]   A Eide, *Article 27: the Right to an Adequate Standard of Living* (Martinus Nijhoff 2006) 3, 2.

[86]   ibid.

[87]   CRC, 'Day of General Discussion on "Resources for the Rights of the Child – Responsibility of States"' (21 September 2007) para 25 <www.ohchr.org/EN/HRBodies/CRC/Pages/DiscussionDays .aspx> accessed 24 June 2020.

between supporting parents in their homes or 'supporting' them by placing their children into care. Children from families suffering extreme poverty and deprivation tend to be placed in institutional care instead of offering these families at risk better services and benefits.

However, neither the CRC nor the CRC Committee favour such an instrumentalization of children's rights. One of the reasons for allocating primary responsibility to the parents for an adequate standard of living (and for upbringing and development more generally, see art. 18 CRC) was precisely to protect parents against excessive state intervention.[88] Moreover, separation from parents is only permissible in the child's best interests, as set forth in article 9. It is accepted that the family usually provides the best setting for a child's development.[89] The CRC Committee has repeatedly and consistently argued that 'financial and material poverty, or conditions directly and uniquely imputable to such poverty', can never be the sole justification for the removal of a child from parental care, but should rather be seen as 'a signal for the need to provide appropriate support to the family'.[90] It has also clarified that out-of-home placements can only be used as measures of last resort, must be based on the need and best interests of the child and must be subject to adequate safeguards.[91] Likewise, it is established case-law of the European Court of Human Rights that children can only be removed from their family as a measure of last resort and for the shortest possible period. The Court has held explicitly that financial difficulties alone cannot justify placement of children, as these can be overcome by financial and social assistance.[92]

5.   Images of the poor child: children as deserving poor that need to be protected and/or empowered?

A further challenge for a children's rights approach to child poverty is not to reinforce a one-sided image of the poor child. Rights of poor children strike a sympathetic chord. The broadly shared assumption that children are in a very vulnerable situation makes them the prototype of 'deserving poor', who deserve to be assisted and protected. This image of the poor child may come at the price of associating children's rights mainly with vulnerability and protection, and much less with agency and participation.

A children's rights-based approach to poverty is believed to have empowering potential, in particular because of the shift from charity to rights, with the concomitant principles of participation, accountability, non-discrimination, empowerment and normativity.[93] The theoretical advantages of a children's rights-based approach do not materialize automatically or necessarily into practice. In fact, it may be very hard to prove empirically if or when the theoretical advantages of a children's rights-based approach do materialize, and very few attempts to do that have been undertaken so far.

---

[88]   Detrick (n 72) 459.

[89]   CRC (n 44) para 15.

[90]   CRC, 'General Comment No 14 on the Right of the Child to have his or her Best Interests Taken as a Primary Consideration (art. 3, para. 1)' (29 May 2013) UN Doc CRC/C/GC/14 para 62; cf Sepúlveda (n 13) para 72(b) and (c).

[91]   CRC, 'Concluding Observations on the Combined Fifth and Sixth Periodic Reports of Norway' (4 July 2018) UN Doc CRC/C/NOR/CO/5-6 para 21(a)(i).

[92]   *Soares De Melo v Portugal* App no 72850/14 (ECHR, 16 February 2016).

[93]   W Vandenhole, 'A Children's Rights-Based Approach to Sustainable Development from a Law and Development Perspective' in C Fenton-Glynn (ed), *Children's Rights and Sustainable Development* (CUP 2016) 12, 20.

There are several reasons for the gap between theoretical potential and realities. First, in a children's rights-based approach the state's responsibility with regard to poverty is a subsidiary one. Moreover, that subsidiary responsibility is centred on material conditions and access to social services (see art. 27 CRC). One may wonder whether that focus on material conditions corresponds to current understandings of the multidimensional nature of poverty. Second, it is not clear whether and to what extent the underlying assumption in children's rights law of the autonomy of the individual involves a risk of individuating and decontextualizing poverty. Also, with regard to empowerment, the inherent limitations of child participation have been pointed out, at least if the existence of (unequal) power relations and their impact is ignored.[94] Children's rights may presuppose rather than 'create' empowered, participating children. We may therefore place too much responsibility on those who may not have the power to change their circumstances.[95]

In other words, child poverty may impinge on children's ability not only to resist power but also to change power relations and the concomitant social exclusion.[96] In children's rights literature, it has been acknowledged that '[child] participation takes place within a framework of power dynamics' and that 'participatory approaches place a burden on children to reflect upon their situations and propose solutions for what are essentially problems caused by politics and economics'.[97] Hence the need for a broad understanding 'of how rights can, and do, function'.[98] In such a broad understanding, children 'are situated in webs of relationships'[99] rather than autonomous and separated individuals.

6.   Humanitarianism: saving the foreign poor child through international adoption

Somewhat similar to national approaches to lift children out of poverty by removing them from their family, intercountry adoptions too have been portrayed as a way to save foreign children from poverty. This form of humanitarianism is under attack. From a children's rights perspective, is international adoption an appropriate child poverty measure?

Article 21 CRC is dedicated to adoption. Allowing for intercountry adoption is certainly not a children's rights obligation. But intercountry adoption is also not prohibited under children's rights law. Nonetheless, it is beyond doubt that intercountry adoption is subsidiary to other forms of in-country appropriate care. Likewise, the best interests of the child necessitate a restrictive approach to intercountry adoption. The best interests of the child, although a notion that is open to multiple interpretations, emphasizes the need to keep the familiar environment of the child[100] and to preserve the cultural and religious identity. Added to this is the clear rejection, mentioned above, of economic or monetary poverty reasons to

---

[94]   J Hart, 'Children's Participation and International Development: Attending to the Political' (2008) 16 Int'l J. Child. Rts. 407.

[95]   R Hinton, 'Children's Participation and Good Governance: Limitations of the Theoretical Literature' (2008) 16 Int'l J. Child. R. 285, 287.

[96]   W Vandenhole, 'A Children's Rights Perspective on Poverty' in W Vandenhole and others (eds), *Why Care? Children's Rights and Child Poverty* (Intersentia 2010) 29–30.

[97]   V Morrow and K Pells, 'Integrating Children's Human Rights and Child Poverty Debates: Examples from Young Lives in Ethiopia and India' (2012) 46 Sociology 906, 916.

[98]   ibid 915.

[99]   ibid.

[100]   *Pini and others v Romania* App No 78028/01 (ECHR 24 June 2004) para 153.

remove a child from its family and familiar environment. Moreover, the best interests of the child must be the paramount consideration (and not just a primary consideration, as article 3 CRC requires) in cases of adoption (article 21 CRC) so that no balancing with other rights or interests is allowed.[101]

There is an increasing concern with intercountry adoption as a form of misguided human-itarianism: whatever the genuine motivations behind it to lift children out of poverty, there is not so much need for 'orphan rescue',[102] as for tackling directly the root causes of poverty.[103] Intercountry adoption does not tackle these root causes and may even contribute to sustain them.[104] Compounded with charges of neo-colonialism,[105] with child-laundering practices[106] including orphan production, child abduction and trafficking,[107] with marketization of alter-native care for children (the 'orphan industrial complex'),[108] and with the 'commodification' of children,[109] the arguments against intercountry adoption as a way of saving children from poverty on a global scale tend to be taken more and more seriously, and policies on intercoun-try adoption in countries of destination have become stricter and stricter.

7.   Global poverty, domestic obligations?

A conceptual (and political) challenge for children's rights in addressing child poverty at a global level is that the children's rights normative framework, with the CRC as the main point of reference, focuses mainly on the obligations of territorial states ('domestic obliga-tions'), while child poverty is a global issue. Rather than to resort to selective and misguided humanitarianism (see above), it may be more appropriate to strengthen notions of global obligations of cooperation and assistance.[110]

The CRC Committee has clarified that states have an obligation to cooperate for the real-ization of children's rights.[111] This means inter alia that states 'should collaborate with other states' efforts to mobilize the maximum available resources for children's rights'.[112] States that are unable to implement the CRC and its Protocols are obliged to seek international cooperation

---

[101]   For a more extensive analyses and further references, see Vandenhole (n 17) 229.

[102]   K E Cheney and K Smith Rotabi, 'Addicted to Orphans: How the Global Orphan Industrial Complex Jeopardizes Local Child Protection Systems' in C Harker and others (eds), *Conflict, Violence and Peace. Geographies of Children and Young People,* vol 11 (Springer 2017) 89.

[103]   D M Smolin, 'Intercountry Adoption and Poverty: A Human Rights Analysis' (2007) 36 Cap.U.L.Rev. 413.

[104]   Cheney (n 102) 93 and 96, 100–01.

[105]   J Martin, 'The Good, the Bad & the Ugly – a New Way of Looking at the Intercountry Adoption Debate' (2006) 13 U.C.Davis J.Int'l L& Pol'y 173, 174.

[106]   Smolin (n 103).

[107]   Cheney (n 102) 91–96.

[108]   ibid 93; S Vité and H Boéchat, *Article 21: Adoption* (Martinus Nijhoff 2008), 2 and 13.

[109]   K E Cheney, 'Conflicting Protectionist and Participation Models of Children's Rights: Their Consequences for Uganda's Orphans and Vulnerable Children' in A Twum-Danso Imoh and N Ansell (eds), *Children's Lives in an Era of Children's Rights: The Progress of the Convention on the Rights of the Child in Africa* (Routledge 2014) 251, 251–52.

[110]   W Vandenhole, 'Economic, Social and Cultural Rights in the CRC: Is There a Legal Obligation to Cooperate Internationally for Development?' (2009) 17 Int'l J. Children's Rts. 23.

[111]   CRC, 'General Comment No 5: General Measures of Implementation of the Convention on the Rights of the Child' (27 November 2003) UN Doc CRC/GC/5 paras 7 and 60.

[112]   CRC General Comment No 19 (n 44).

and to demonstrate they have made every possible effort in this regard.[113] States with resources are under an obligation to provide international cooperation 'with the aim of facilitating the implementation of children's rights in the recipient state'.[114] Moreover, the Optional Protocol on the Sale of Children, Child Prostitution and Pornography clearly identifies a shared responsibility for tackling the root causes of child exploitation, including child trafficking and the obligation of states 'in a position to do so' to provide financial, technical and other assistance (Articles 10(3) and (4) OPSC).[115] In light of the often blurred lines between child trafficking and intercountry adoption, the argument can be extended to intercountry adoption.

II.   GENERAL CONCLUSION

There are good reasons for dedicating specific attention to child impoverishment: poor children are often seen as deserving poor, they are also considered to be differently affected by poverty, and there is a specific set of human rights norms for children. On the other hand, it is rather unhelpful to focus exclusively on child poverty: poverty of children is in theory and in practice intimately connected to the impoverishment of adults (and in particular their parents). Even worse is the way in which a child poverty approach may lead to disempowerment of their parents, in particular in instances of placement into care or intercountry adoption due to material poverty. Child impoverishment can also not be properly understood within the confines of a particular state: it is a global issue that necessitates global responses and a rethinking of state obligations of international assistance and cooperation for the realization of children's rights.

Three common framings of a children's rights approach to child poverty can be found in the work of the CRC Committee: the right to protection against poverty; the right to distributive equality; and a children's rights-based approach to poverty. Still, children's rights law (just like human rights law) has no strong and unequivocal approach to poverty. It struggles to qualify child poverty as a violation of children's rights, even in times of austerity, and in adopting a comprehensive approach. Also, the image of poor children as deserving poor runs the risk of overemphasizing protection and fulfilment dimensions and overlooking participation dimensions. In sum, there is a range of challenges that future research needs to address in order to turn children's rights law into a robust driver of change in the fight against child impoverishment.

---

[113]   ibid paras 35–36.
[114]   ibid para 35.
[115]   Vandenhole (n 110).

10. Capping motherhood

Meghan Campbell

Traditional gender stereotypes interact with material deprivation to trap women into poverty.[1] Throughout their lives women disproportionately experience poverty. Due to a complex web of interlocking factors, becoming a mother can trigger or exacerbate poverty. Pregnancy increases the risk that a woman will be forced out of her job.[2] The 'motherhood penalty', the wage gap between mothers and fathers, is well-known and documented.[3] Women's disproportionate amount of unpaid childcare work in the home can limit their career opportunities.[4] Cuts in public services, reductions in social benefits and the lack of affordable childcare can channel women towards low-paid, precarious and poorly regulated employment.[5] Gender, parenting and poverty are inextricably connected with other intersecting identities including marital or migration status, disability, race or religion.[6]

The human rights framework with its strong commitment to women's equality holds great potential to accurately capture, and remediate, the relationship between gender, poverty and parenting. This chapter explores the untapped potential of equality law in tackling women's poverty. For nearly a decade, the UK has been at the forefront of neo-liberal approaches to poverty. It 'has been achieving radical social re-engineering [through] a dramatic restructuring' of the social safety net.[7] This re-engineering has had devastating consequences increasing both the prevalence and severity of poverty and 'perpetuat[ing] rather than tackl[ing] the gendered aspects of poverty.'[8]

Women have been turning to the courts for accountability and redress. This chapter examines three judgments on social-benefits schemes. These three cases are put under the analytical

---

[1] Meghan Campbell, *Women, Poverty, Equality: The Role of CEDAW* (Hart 2018) ch 1.

[2] The Department for Business, Innovation and Skills and the Equality and Human Rights Commission (UK), 'Pregnancy and Maternity-Related Discrimination and Disadvantage: Experience of Mothers' (2016) 58. <https://assets.publishing.service.gov.uk/government/uploads/system/uploads/attachment_data/file/509501/BIS-16- 146-pregnancy-and-maternity-related-discrimination-and-disadvantage-experiences-of-mothers.pdf> accessed 10 September 2019.

[3] Damian Grimshaw and Jill Rubery, 'The Motherhood Pay Gap: A Review of the Issues, Theory and International Evidence' (International Labour Organization Conditions of Work and Employment Series No 57, 2015) <www.ilo.org/wcmsp5/groups/public/@dgreports/@dcomm/@publ/documents/publication/wcms_348041.pdf> accessed 1 June 2020.

[4] UN Women, 'Progress of the World's Women 2015–2016: Transforming Economies, Realizing Rights' (2015) 83 <http://progress.unwomen.org/en/2015/pdf/UNW_progressreport.pdf> accessed 1 June 2020.

[5] UNGA 'Report of the Independent Expert on the Effects of Foreign Debt and Other Related International Financial Obligations of States on the Full Enjoyment of all Human Rights, Particularly Economic, Social and Cultural Rights' (2018) UN Doc A/73/179.

[6] Women's Budget Group, 'The Female Face of Poverty' (2018) <http://wbg.org.uk/wp- content/uploads/2018/08/FINAL-Female-Face-of-Poverty.pdf> accessed 3 June 2020.

[7] UN Special Rapporteur on Extreme Poverty and Human Rights, 'Visit to the United Kingdom of Great Britain and Northern Ireland' (2019) UN Doc A/HRC/41/39/Add.1.

[8] ibid [15].

microscope as they directly engage with social-benefits law, poverty and motherhood. In all three cases the claimants proved the law was discriminatory, but in each case the court found the discrimination was justified. In analyzing the interaction between gender, poverty and parenting (and why these claims failed) this chapter offers an alternative and richer human rights-based approach to poverty, grounded in the right to equality, that can be useful to all states, especially liberal-democratic states similar to the UK.

Section I defines women's poverty to illustrate the synergies between protected status identities and material deprivation. Section II examines equality and anti-discrimination law as a framework for redressing women's poverty. Section III evaluates three cases on gender, parenting and social benefits from the UK to understand how these arguments are being applied in practice. This reveals worrying trends that echo in other jurisdictions.[9] The courts continue to misunderstand the right to equality. They lapse into a thin, formalistic model of equality and focus myopically on the economic aspects of women's poverty. This ignores the role of discriminatory gender norms, and unequal gendered structures and institutions. Applying a lens of transformative equality to the three cases unearths the inextricable links between gender, poverty, parenting and human rights.[10] This chapter concludes by providing recommendations for future research on women's poverty.

I.   THE FACE OF POVERTY

Given the depth and grievous effects of poverty, it is somewhat surprising that there is no universally accepted definition. Historically, poverty has been 'defined as insufficient income to buy a minimum basket of goods and services.'[11] In the UK, the 'headline measure' of poverty is if an individual lives 'in a household with income below 60% of median household income'.[12] It is widely recognized that income-based definitions, common in many countries, are limited.[13] At the international level, there are new proposals on the meaning of poverty. This section canvasses these proposals to derive a definition of women's poverty. This lays the foundation for arguing that women's poverty is a matter of gender equality.

Goal 1 of the Sustainable Development Goals promises to eliminate poverty in all of its forms.[14] It recognizes that poverty is multi-dimensional. One dimension is the emotional experience of living in poverty. People in poverty report feeling powerlessness, exhaustion, exclusion, rejection, isolation, loneliness, insecurity, vulnerability, invisibility, worry, fear,

---

[9]   Gwen Brodsky and Shelagh Day, 'Beyond Social and Economic Rights: Substantive Equality Speaks to Poverty' (2002) 14 C.J.W.L. 185.

[10]   Sandra Fredman, 'Substantive Equality Revisited' (2016) 14(3) ICON 712.

[11]   UN Committee on Economic, Social and Cultural Rights (CESCR), 'Substantive Issues Arising in the Implementation of the International Covenant on Economic, Social and Cultural Rights: Poverty and the International Covenant on Economic, Social and Cultural Rights' (2001) E/C.12/2001/10 [7].

[12]   Brigid Francis-Devine, Lorna Booth and Fergal McGuinness, *Poverty in the UK: Statistics* (HC 2019, No 7096) 7.

[13]   Sylvia Chant, 'Gendered Poverty Across Space and Time' in Sylvia Chant (ed), *The International Handbook of Gender and Poverty* (Edward Elgar 2010).

[14]   'Sustainable Development Goals' <https://sustainabledevelopment.un.org/?menu=1300> accessed 3 June 2020.

stigma, humiliation and shame.[15] Poverty is not exclusively a condition of material want. An individual's sense of self is connected to their recognition within a community, and poverty has deep social impacts that further marginalize those living in poverty. The Guiding Principles on Extreme Poverty and Human Rights by the UN Special Rapporteur on extreme poverty and human rights recognize that 'Persons experiencing extreme poverty live in a vicious cycle of powerlessness, stigmatization … exclusion and material deprivation, which all mutually reinforce one another'.[16] Another prominent re-definition of poverty, used by The UN Development Programme and the UN Committee on Economic, Social and Cultural Rights, draws on the capability theory of Sen and Nussbaum.[17] These definitions of poverty seek to reflect on 'human capabilities and on the choices or freedom of poor people.'[18] Poverty is 'the absence or inadequate realization of certain basic freedoms, such as the freedoms to avoid hunger, disease, illiteracy and so on.'[19]

A person is poor, under this account, when their capabilities and functionings are impaired. These organizations measure poverty on a variety of dimensions needed to create a meaningful life including life expectancy, education, nutrition, sanitation, housing, assets, electricity and drinking water.[20]

Yet these new internationally prominent definitions of poverty still fail to address the causes of poverty. To fully understand poverty, it is imperative that its definition reflects 'the experiences of poverty *and* trace its causes'.[21] There is no single explanation for poverty, however some causes are more persistent and underappreciated. The relationship between gender and poverty is strong, even though poverty is a serious and pressing problem that affects both men and women. Gendered social norms and cultural attitudes that are based on the inferiority of women and the superiority of men contribute to women's poverty. These gendered norms are directly encoded into discriminatory laws that 'actively create and maintain poverty for women, limiting or obstructing their access to economic resources.'[22]

Gender stereotypes can also subtly pervade structures and institutions, which 'generates and reinforces women's poverty'.[23] Many factors combine to explain women's poverty: the gendered division of labor in both formal and informal employment, the lack of legal regulation of the informal labor market, the concentration of women in low-paying jobs, the gendered precarity of employment, the low valuation of work traditionally assigned to women, unequal pay

---

[15]   Deepa Narayan and others, *Voices of the Poor: Crying Out for Change* (OUP 2000) 31.

[16]   UN Special Rapporteur on Extreme Poverty and Human Rights, 'Guiding Principles on Extreme Poverty and Human Rights' (2012) UN Doc A/HRC/21/39 [4].

[17]   Martha Nussbaum, *Women and Human Development: The Capabilities Approach* (CUP 2000); Amartya Sen, *Development as Freedom* (OUP 2001).

[18]   United Nations Development Fund for Women (UNIFEM), 'Progress of the World's Women 2005: Women, Work and Poverty' (2005) 15 <www.unwomen.org/-/media/headquarters/media/publications/unifem/poww2005_eng.pdf?la=en&vs=1016> accessed 3 June 2020.

[19]   Office of the High Commission for Human Rights, 'Human Rights and Poverty Reduction: A Conceptual Framework' (2004) HR/PUB/04/01 [9].

[20]   UNDP and OPHI, 'Global Multidimensional Poverty Index 2019: Illuminating Inequalities' (2019) 2 <https://ophi.org.uk/wp-content/uploads/G-MPI_Report_2019_PDF.pdf> accessed 3 June 2020.

[21]   Campbell, *Women, Poverty, Equality* (n 1) 11.

[22]   Sandra Fredman, 'Women and Poverty: A Human Rights Approach' (2016) 24(4) A.J.I.C.L. 494.

[23]   ibid.

for work of equal value, gender power imbalances in the home, the disproportionate amount of unpaid childcare and elder care work women perform, and the more limited access women often have to education, bank loans, sexual and reproductive health services and land.[24] The sad reality is that women are often poor because they are women. Thus, it is necessary to build on prior definitions of poverty to incorporate the role of patriarchal power relationships between men and women. For this chapter, women's poverty is defined as material deprivation and limited access to economic resources (redistribution harms) that are derived from negative gendered socio-cultural attitudes (recognition harms).[25]

II.   WOMEN'S POVERTY AND THE RIGHT TO EQUALITY[26]

Discrimination in education, the labor market, caring responsibilities and social benefits trap women in poverty. The role of law in tackling poverty is in its relative infancy. The mainstream human rights-based approach is through socio-economic rights. A more effective method to tackle women's poverty might be through an equality or anti-discrimination framework. This argument is attractive as many national human rights instruments do not include socio-economic rights but there is almost universal protection for the right to equality and non-discrimination.[27] Focusing here on equality and anti-discrimination should not be read as denigrating efforts to strengthen the protection of socio-economic rights in national human rights instruments. Greater appreciation on the role of equality can positively feed into the realization of socio-economic rights. Applying an equality lens can ensure that efforts to implement the minimum core and progressively realize socio-economic rights do not cement inequality or power hierarchies.[28] This section explores how different models of equality can take account of the synergy between redistributive and recognition harms that underpin women's poverty.

A.   Formal Equality

Formal equality is the strict application of treating likes alike and treating differences differently. It requires consistent treatment, prohibits arbitrary distinctions, and aims to treat everyone on the basis of her merits.[29] Formal equality can address the blatant wrongs of women's poverty such as exclusion of certain types of work, informal work, or workers on zero-hour contracts from statutory maternity pay.

Formal equality has many limitations. First, it offers no moral framework for identifying similarities and differences. As Westen observes, equality 'contains no standards for distinguishing' 'good' reasons from 'bad' reasons.[30] For centuries women were seen as different from men. This supposed difference was used to justify depriving women

---

[24]   Brodsky and Day (n 9); Caroline Sweetman, *Gender, Development and Poverty* (Oxfam 2002).
[25]   Campbell, *Women, Poverty, Equality* (n 1) 13–14.
[26]   ibid ch 4.
[27]   *SC and others v Secretary of State for Work and Pensions and others* [2019] EWCA Civ 615 [29].
[28]   Meghan Campbell, 'Monitoring Women's Socio-Economic Equality Under the ICESCR' (2018) 30 C.J.W.L. 82.
[29]   Sandra Fredman, *Discrimination Law* (2nd edn, Clarendon 2011) 8.
[30]   Peter Westen, 'The Empty Idea of Equality' (1982) 95 Harv.L.Rev. 537, 575.

of property, rights over their own children, and even their own bodies.[31] Second, formal equality only requires that two similarly situated individuals being compared be treated consistently. Formal equality is indifferent to whether the individuals are treated equally badly or equally well. If the gender wage gap is narrowed due to a decrease or stagnation in men's wages rather than an increase in women's wages, formal equality is satisfied.[32] Third, formal equality requires a comparator. In the battle for pregnancy rights, the lack of a male comparator meant that maternity benefits were characterized as violating formal equality.[33] Similarly, it has been difficult to achieve equal pay in female dominated sectors without a male comparator.[34] Moreover, formal equality comparisons require conformity to the male norm.[35] This in turn devalues difference and does little to address the misrecognition harms associated with women's poverty. In practice, formal equality is a limited tool to break cycles of economic deprivation and social marginalization.

B.   Substantive Equality

Substantive equality seeks to transcend these problems and infuses equality with a normative underpinning.[36] It recognizes that men and women for historical, biological, social and cultural reasons are not the same and different treatment may be required to achieve equality.[37] Substantive equality is a contested term with various meanings proposed. This chapter zones in on transformative equality as it requires fundamental structural change that can tackle systems that perpetuate women's poverty.

There are overlapping conceptions of transformative equality. This chapter evaluates Fredman's four-dimensional model as it synthesizes and builds upon competing definitions and is being used by influential human rights actors – UN Women and the UN Committee on the Rights of Persons with Disabilities – to set international best practices.[38] Fredman argues that transformative equality pursues four overlapping aims: (1) to break the cycle of disadvantage; (2) to promote respect for dignity and worth; (3) to accommodate difference by achieving structural change; and (4) to promote political and social inclusion.[39] Looking at each dimension in turn, breaking the cycle of disadvantage recognizes that individuals and groups have suffered because of their personal characteristics. Targeted measures are required, such as covering 100 percent of childcare costs for women on social benefits.

Second, the inclusion of recognition harms addresses harassment, prejudice, stereotypes, stigmas, negative cultural attitudes, indignity and humiliation.[40] Social benefits that replicate

---

[31]   Fredman, *Discrimination Law* (n 29).

[32]   Jill Rubery and Aristea Koukiadaki, 'Institutional Interactions in Gender Pay Equity: A Call for Inclusive, Equal and Transparent Labour Markets' (2018) U of OxHRH J 115.

[33]   *Bliss v Canada (Attorney General)* (1979) 1 SCR 183 (Canadian Supreme Court); Robert Wintemute, 'When is Pregnancy Discrimination Indirect Sex Discrimination' (1998) 27(9) ILJ 23.

[34]   *Dumfries and Galloway Council v North* [2009] ICR 1363 (EAT).

[35]   Catherine MacKinnon, *Feminism Unmodified* (HUP 1987) 34.

[36]   *Minority Schools in Albania* (Advisory Opinion) [1935] PCIJ Series A/B No 64.

[37]   UN Committee for the Elimination of All Forms of Discrimination against Women, 'General Recommendation No 25: Temporary Special Measures' (2004) CEDAW/C/GC/28 [8].

[38]   Progress of the World's Women (n 4); UN Committee on Convention on the Rights of Persons With Disabilities, 'General Comment No 6: Equality and Non-discrimination' (2018) CRPD/C/GC/6.

[39]   Fredman, *Discrimination Law* (n 29) 25.

[40]   ibid 29.

a male breadwinner model by depositing payments into one household account operate to deny women access to financial resources and perpetuate relationships of powerlessness within and beyond the household unit.[41] Third, rather than requiring individual conformity, the structural dimension requires institutions to change. Equality demands reforms to formal labor markets to account for women's disproportionate role in childcare and encourage male employees to be active parents. Fourth, the participation element requires the meaningful inclusion of women in all public, private, political and social decision-making processes, including the design of benefit schemes.

C.   Non-Discrimination

Direct discrimination is explicit differential treatment that perpetuates gender disadvantage.[42] Invisible institutional structures often perpetuate disadvantage. In response, the law has developed the concept of indirect discrimination: when an apparently neutral rule disproportionately disadvantages a protected group.[43] Women are disproportionately employed as part-time workers, and legislation that does not protect these workers from unfair dismissal is indirectly discriminatory against women.[44]

Discrimination law has had a substantial impact in addressing status-based recognition harms. Direct discrimination prohibits less favourable treatment on the basis of a protected characteristic.[45] This ensures that individual merit is properly recognized. Removing prohibitions against women doing night work dispels stereotypes that women are weak. This is also true in cases of indirect discrimination. Requiring the seemingly neutral physical fitness qualifications for fire-fighters to take account of women's different physiology ensures they are not excluded for failing to meet a male norm.[46] This strengthens the recognition of women as physically strong, capable and courageous.

However, an anti-discrimination approach is not a complete solution to all the recognition harms associated with gender. Like formal equality, direct discrimination only requires removing the distinction and ensuring consistency of treatment.[47] It does not challenge the gender-based structures and institutions which perpetuate and contribute to redistribution and recognition harms that women in poverty experience. Removing the direct prohibitions against women entering the formal labor market has not resulted in re-valuing the work traditionally assigned to women nor has it addressed gender job segregation that concentrates women in low-status and low-paid jobs.[48] Removing direct prohibitions and reconceptualizing fitness

---

[41]   Work and Pensions Committee, '*Universal Credit and Domestic Abuse*' (2018) Sixteenth Special Report of Session 2017–19.

[42]   CEDAW, 'General Recommendation No 21: Equality in Marriage and Family Relations' (1994) CEDAW/C/GC/21.

[43]   *Griggs v Duke Power* 401 US 424 (1971) (US Supreme Court).

[44]   *R v Secretary of State for Employment ex p Equal Opportunities Commission* [1994] UKHL 2.

[45]   Denise Reaume, 'Discrimination and Dignity' (2003) Louisiana L.R. 1, 35–40.

[46]   *British Columbia (Public Service Employees Relations Commission) v BCGSEU* [1999] 3 SCR 3 (Canadian Supreme Court).

[47]   Fredman, *Discrimination Law* (n 29) 168.

[48]   Vincent Ferrao, 'Paid Work' in *Women in Canada: A Gender-Based Statistical Report* (Minister of Industry 2010); Kamala Sankaran and Roopa Madhav, 'Gender Equality and Social Dialogue in India' (2011) ILO Working Paper 1/2011 <www.ilo.org/wcmsp5/groups/public/---dgreports/---gender/documents/publication/wcms_150428.pdf> accessed 3 June 2020.

standards removes some but not all barriers preventing women from becoming fire-fighters. It does not address the structure of the working day, the lack of formal childcare outside regular working hours, and 'the underlying division of power within the family which leaves women with the primary responsibility for childcare'.[49]

Discrimination law has not had a significant impact on redistribution harms. Although women's ability to work at night, become fire-fighters, inherit land and property, and access credit in their own name break cycles of exploitation and positively impact a woman's access to economic resources, the real challenge arises when resources are required to remedy the wrongs of discrimination.[50] Women are often foreclosed from taking high paid positions because of their childcare responsibilities, yet discrimination law cannot mandate the creation of childcare facilities.[51]

III.   CAPS ON MOTHERHOOD

As currently conceived and applied, anti-discrimination law has not fully tackled the multiple dimensions of women's poverty. The right to equality, particularly the right to transformative equality, still holds untapped promise in redressing women's poverty. However, challenges remain. Perhaps the greatest is 'the plasticity of equality [which] means that it [is] always be open to different interpretations by the executive ... legislature and ... courts ...'.[52] Encouragingly, authoritative actors on the international plane are currently championing an evolutionary interpretation of equality and anti-discrimination to account for women's poverty.[53] To illustrate, this section investigates three judgments on social benefits and motherhood in the UK. These cases are complex and touch upon a wealth of issues. This chapter focuses solely on how the courts interpret the right to equality and anti-discrimination.

In all three judgments, the courts fail to appreciate the nuances of women's poverty. The courts fail to capture the synergy between redistribution and recognition harms. They do acknowledge that the benefit schemes push the claimants into economic deprivation, but they fail to see the relationship between gender, poverty, parenting, and discrimination. These cases show a marked inattention to the web of stereotypes against women, poverty and parenting and how those stereotypes are translated into the law. This leaves the court blind to the much richer potential of the right to substantive and transformative equality and non-discrimination.

This section analyses the thin approach to equality in the three cases and then applies Fredman's transformative model of equality to illustrate a broader approach to women's poverty. Although this model has not been officially adopted by the UK, it has been influential and accepted in international human rights law. Moreover, it is a helpful tool to organize and assess all aspects of the three claims against the backdrop of the UK's national and interna-

---

[49]   Fredman, *Discrimination Law* (n 29) 183.

[50]   Sandra Fredman, 'Redistribution and Recognition: Reconciling Inequalities' (2007) 23(3) South African JHR 214, 221.

[51]   ibid.

[52]   Catherine Albertyn, 'Contested Substantive Equality in the South African Constitution: Beyond Social Inclusion Towards Systemic Justice' (2018) 34 South African JHR 441.

[53]   Campbell, *Women, Poverty, Equality* (n 1) ch 5; CESCR, 'General Comment No 20: Non-discrimination in Economic, Social and Cultural Rights' (2009) E/C.12/GC/20.

tional commitments to end discrimination. Transformative equality provides a promising basis for future equality-based litigation.

A.   The Sword of Formal Equality

These three UK cases involve claims that various aspects of the social-benefits scheme violate the Human Rights Act 1998 (HRA) which domesticates the European Convention on Human Rights (ECHR). The claimants argued the application of various aspects of the social-benefits scheme ran afoul of the obligation not to discriminate in the enjoyment of the rights protected in the HRA/ECHR.[54] In all three cases, the claimants were single mothers with children who received social benefits. Several high-profile civil-society groups supported the litigation and acted as intervenors. Specifically, the claimants asserted that the benefits were indirectly discriminatory on the basis of sex in two of the cases and on the basis of single parenthood in the third, although in the UK 92 percent of single parents are women so this identity ground is almost inherently a proxy for gender.[55]

Indirect discrimination under the HRA/ECHR is a 'difference in treatment [that] may take the form of disproportionately prejudicial effects of a general policy or measure which, though couched in neutral terms, discriminates against a group'.[56] Benefits law may not be discriminatory on its face, but in application may have a disproportionate negative impact on protected groups, such as women. The focus is on the impact of the law. Indirect discrimination can be justified if the law proportionately pursues a legitimate aim.[57] The government defended the design of social benefits as necessary to achieve fairness between working and non-working households; to create incentives to undertake waged work; and to reduce public spending in the 'interests of the economic well-being of the country'.[58]

In assessing whether there has been discrimination under the HRA/ECHR, the UK courts apply what is, in essence, a formal model of equality. Lord Wilson explains that the fundamental principle of non-discrimination is 'that like cases should be treated alike [and] that different cases should be treated differently'.[59] This is a restatement of the Aristotelian formulation of equality. The analytical focus is on determining when sameness or difference is warranted. However, the courts have no rubric for identifying salient features that determine similarities or differences. The key sameness-difference the courts latch onto is material or economic inequality. The role of gender in women's poverty is minimalized and ignored. The analysis below evaluates the courts' reasoning, observing the focus on formal income equality and then argues it is this narrow focus that explains the failure to find the benefits scheme incompatible with human rights law.

First, in *SG and others v Secretary of State for Work and Pensions*, the claimants argue that the social-benefits caps indirectly discriminate against women because it affects more women (60 percent) than men (3 percent).[60] There is a nod to intersectionality, as the UK Supreme

---

[54]   Human Rights Act 1998 s 14.
[55]   ibid.
[56]   *DH and Others v The Czech Republic* (2007) App No 57325/00.
[57]   *Burden v the United Kingdom* (2008) App No 13378/05.
[58]   *SG and others v Secretary of State for Work and Pensions* [2015] UKSC 16 [4]; *SC* (n 27) [123]; *DA and DS v Secretary of State for Work and Pensions* [2019] UKSC 21 [7].
[59]   *DA* (n 58) [40].
[60]   *SG* (n 58) [26].

Court acknowledges that single mothers particularly bear the brunt of the cap.[61] The differential treatment that the cap imposes on women is exclusively framed in terms of reduction in income. Lady Hale in dissent explains that the prejudicial effect of the cap 'is obvious and stark [as] it breaks the link between benefit and need'.[62] Under the cap single mothers will be forced to live below the 'median after tax earnings of working households'[63] and will struggle to 'adequately house, feed, clothe and warm themselves and their children'.[64] There is little sustained engagement with gender beyond noting that women will mathematically suffer greater income poverty from the cap. A majority of the Court concludes that any disproportionate negative impact is justified, although Lady Hale and Lord Kerr dissenting conclude that depriving mothers and children of the necessities of life could not justify the government's objectives.

In *SC and CB v Secretary of State for Work and Pensions*, the claimants are challenging the availability of the child tax credit.[65] This is a means-test benefit that tapers off at a certain income level and is designed to meet the subsistence needs of children. Claimants who have a third child after 6 April 2017 will not receive the credit for that child or any additional children (two-child limit) unless the third child is the result of sexual violence. The Court of Appeal acknowledges that women are more likely to be single parents who rely on the child tax benefit and that the limitation has a different and more severe effect on women's financial circumstances than men's.[66] The Court holds that any prejudicial effects, without detailing what these were, are not 'too high a price to pay'.[67] It also does not question whether it is fair that women in poverty with children bear these prejudicial effects and costs. The indirectly discriminatory effects of the two-child limit are justified.

Third, single parents can escape the benefit cap if they undertake 16 hours of work a week ('working tax credit'). This is slightly less hours of work than required for those in a couple. In *DA and DS v Secretary of State for Work and Pensions*, the claimants argue the cap and work conditions to escape the cap are discriminatory against single parents with young children. Notably, again, the role of gender is invisibilized as the claim is analysed on the basis of single parents, despite an acknowledgment by the Court that single parents are overwhelming women.[68] A majority of the UK Supreme Court finds that although the cap and the conditionality create economic hardships, single parents are not different from any other persons subject to the cap.[69] The claimants and all persons bound by the cap equally experience economic hardships and there are no relevant differences to justify treating single parents differently. This is a levelling down rationale. Formal equality is satisfied even if everyone is equally worse-off. Again, Lady Hale and Lord Kerr dissent, concluding the caps and working conditions are discriminatory.

These three cases demonstrate that the courts in the UK are attentive to the links between social-benefits law and income inequality. However, using a thin model of equality with

---

[61]   ibid.
[62]   ibid [180].
[63]   ibid [19].
[64]   ibid [180].
[65]   *SC* (n 27) .
[66]   ibid [80].
[67]   ibid [130].
[68]   *DA* (n 58) [22(d)].
[69]   ibid [88], [119].

strong echoes of formal equality that focuses only on the material aspect of women's poverty, is problematic. Without a richer concept of equality, the judgments cannot identify or engage with the unequal structures and institutions that shape the lives of women in poverty, nor can they interrogate the discriminatory gender stereotypes that underpin the laws on social benefits. The next subsection maps out how transformative equality can more fully engage with the discrimination in the law of social benefits.

B.   Transforming Equality-Based Poverty Claims

Exclusively analysing these claims on the basis of material disadvantage prevents the courts from fully conceptualizing women's poverty as a form of discrimination and inequality. Brodsky and Day observe that 'for women, poverty enlarges every dimension of women's inequality, not just the economic dimension'.[70] Applying the four-dimensional transformative equality model provides a disciplined framework for interrogating the sameness-difference matrix and demonstrates the richness available in equality-based approaches to women's poverty.

1.   The disadvantage dimension

The first dimension is 'expressly asymmetric'.[71] It recognizes that due to historical, political, economic and cultural forces, disadvantage clusters on specific groups: women, people of colour, sexual minorities, or disabled persons. Equality is not blind to this antecedent disadvantage. Women in the UK are more likely to be poor than men.[72] An intersectional analysis reveals that almost half of single-parent households live in poverty and women make up the majority of single parents.[73] Single mothers are more prevalent in low-skilled employment in comparison with mothers in a relationship and they struggle to cover the costs of childcare.[74] In *SG* and *DA*, the UK Supreme Court strips out gender from the claim, which ignores the pre-existing disadvantaged role of women and mothers in society. The courts repeatedly refer to the Parliamentary debates and impact assessments that use gender-neutral language to refer to single parents. Although *DA* was argued on the grounds of being a single parent, rather than on gender, the Court does not adopt an approach that is sensitive to the intersectional context. No analytical weight is given to the fact that 92 percent of single parents are women and thus the impact of the benefit cap and working conditions are deeply gendered. The disadvantage dimension takes full account of women's disproportionate shouldering of care work, the economic and political discounting of caring labor and the discrimination embedded in the labor market when assessing the impact of the benefit cap and working conditions.[75] The court's inattention to the gendered reality is consistent with a long history of gender-neutral

---

[70]   Brodsky and Day (n 9) 220.
[71]   Fredman, 'Substantive Equality Revisited' (n 10) 728.
[72]   Women's Budget Group, 'Female Face' (n 6).
[73]   ibid; *DA* (n 58) [22(d)].
[74]   Women's Budget Group, 'Female Face' (n 6).
[75]   Mimi Abramovitz, 'Women Social Reproduction and the Neo-Liberal Assault on the US Welfare State' in Shelley Gavigan and Dorothy Chunn (eds), *The Legal Tender of Gender: Welfare, Law and the Regulation of Women's Poverty* (Bloomsbury 2010).

social-benefit policies that mask the impact on women and hide discourses on women, poverty and sexuality.[76] In contrast, transformative equality places women at the centre of the analysis.

The great insight from the disadvantage dimension is that equality does not aim for consistent treatment as in *DA* (everyone is equally worse-off under the cap) but recognizes that targeted measures are needed to end cycles of disadvantage. The right to equality seeks to redress and ameliorate this disadvantage rather than ignore and compound it. The UK courts do not acknowledge the need for social-benefits laws that are tailored to lived experiences and adopt an almost fatalistic attitude to women's poverty. In *SG*, the court held that 'since women head most of the households at which those aims are directed', the harsher economic impact on women than men 'appears … inevitable'.[77] Treating women in poverty with children as identical to other groups runs afoul of transformative equality. The disadvantage dimension demands that social-benefits laws and policies are tailored to different lived experiences of mothers in poverty.

2.   Recognition dimension

The recognition dimension seeks to valorize identity. Levelling down, accepting that all are equally burdened by the benefit cap, is impermissible under this dimension of transformative equality. This dimension also roots out prejudicial attitudes that are translated into law. In *SG*, *SC*, and *DA* the narrow focus on the 'dollars and cents' of social benefits erases the role of stereotypes in legal responses to women's poverty. These are two predominant stereotypes interwoven into benefit schemes that the courts fail to uncover and challenge.

a.   *Poverty is a personal moral failing*

The benefit cap, two-child limit, and working tax credit all characterize poverty as an individualized problem. Repeatedly the government's explanation for the two-child limit is to encourage women 'to reflect carefully on their readiness to support an additional child …'.[78] If the law allowed women in poverty to claim benefits for more than two children, this 'removes the need for families supported by benefits to consider whether they can afford to support additional children'.[79] This reflects beliefs that women are individually responsible for being in poverty because they do not make 'good' economic decisions. Similarly, the justification for the benefit cap in *SG* reflects the fact that 'Working people on low incomes had to cope with difficult circumstances, and they had to live within their means'.[80] Even though the cap disproportionately burdens single mothers, the government refers to 'families' or 'working people'. Again, there is a refusal to explicitly acknowledge the gendered impact. However, gender stereotypes animate these laws. They are premised on beliefs that women in poverty are financially incompetent and remain poor because of a private moral failing or character flaw. Rather than root out these stereotypes, the courts uncritically accept them. Conceptualizing poverty as a moral failing means that social benefits become a legitimate tool to 'responsibilize' women

---

[76]   Ruth Cain, 'Responsibilising Recovery: Lone and Low-Paid Parents, Universal Credit and the Gendered Contradictions of UK Welfare Reform' (2016) 11 British Politics 488.

[77]   *SG* (n 58) [76].

[78]   *SC* (n 27) [23].

[79]   ibid [17].

[80]   *SG* (n 58) [35].

through negative incentives and punishments.[81] This approach also ignores the deep structural roots of women's poverty.

The benefit caps and two-child limits rest on the idea that single mothers are lazy benefit scroungers. The government claims that it is unfair that single parents, most of whom are women, 'should be able to have as many children as they choose … without limit' and 'be subsidized … out of public expenditure'.[82] Framing the two-child limit in terms of fairness characterizes women in poverty as benefit-suckers who live an extravagant lifestyle on public resources. Under this scheme 'having more children when … on benefits is a form of welfare decadence'.[83] In a similar vein, the benefit cap threatens single mothers with living 'well below the poverty line' as a mechanism to channel them into paid employment.[84] Women in poverty are caricatured as being so indolent that only the threat of extreme poverty can force them into work.[85] These limitations and conditions are degrading, hostile towards women in poverty, and again further myths that women's poverty is the result of poor moral character.[86] Women in poverty with children 'want to work … [t]hey want to contribute to their society and communities [and] support their families'[87]; they are not seeking a 'free-ride' on social benefits. The Court of Appeal and Supreme Court, even the dissenting judgments, accept these prejudicial attitudes. They consistently hold that it is legitimate for social benefits to incentivize women to support themselves and their children through waged work by forcing them into poverty without questioning the recognition harms entwined in these conditionalities.[88]

b.   Controlling women's sexuality

The benefit schemes challenged in these three cases, especially the two-child limit, rely on myths about women's sexuality. One stubborn stereotype is that women in poverty are sexually promiscuous and are having too many children. One Member of Parliament asked how it would be fair to condemn the third or fourth child to a life of poverty because of a 'reckless mother who cannot keep her legs crossed'.[89] This is a graphic and highly prejudicial image of women in poverty and paints them as sexually promiscuous and immoral. Under this view, this deviant sexuality must be stopped through negative financial incentives. From an intersectional perspective, this approach is also problematic as family size can have a deeply cultural value for different communities.[90] Larger families are more common among individuals from black and minority ethnic backgrounds (BAME), and BAME women continue to struggle

---

[81]   Cain (n 76).

[82]   *SC* (n 27) [139].

[83]   Charlotte O'Brien, '"Done Because We Are Too Menny" The Two-Child Rule Promotes Poverty, Invokes a Narrative of Welfare Decadence and Abandons Children's Rights' (2018) 26(4) Int'l J.Children's Rts. 700, 706.

[84]   *DA* (n 58) [33].

[85]   Peter Dwyer and Sharon Wright, 'Universal Credit, Ubiquitous Conditionality and its Implications for Social Citizenship' (2014) 22(1) Journal of Poverty and Social Justice 27.

[86]   Martha Jackman, 'One Step Forward and Two Steps Back: Poverty, the *Charter* and the Legacy of *Gosselin*'(2019) 39 NJCL 85.

[87]   UN Special Rapporteur on extreme poverty and human rights (n 16) [8].

[88]   *SG* (n 58) [65], [190]; *SC* (n 27) [123]–[124]; *DA* (n 58) [7(c)].

[89]   *SC* (n 27) [154].

[90]   UN Women, 'Progress of the World's Women 2019–2020: Families in a Changing World' (2019) 56–60, 90–99 <www.unwomen.org/-/media/headquarters/attachments/sections/library/publications/2019/progress-of-the- worlds-women-2019-2020-en.pdf?la=en&vs=3512> accessed 3 June 2020.

against poverty and exclusion from the labor market.[91] Characterizing women in poverty as promiscuous is insensitive and demeaning to the positive cultural value placed on different family sizes. The child tax benefit draw 'clear lines between welfare receipt, poor people, large families, and moral degeneracy'.[92] This has both gendered and racial dimensions.

The role of the child tax credit in controlling women's sexuality is evidenced by its exceptions. If a woman can prove that the third child is the result of sexual violence, she is entitled to claim the credit (the rape clause).[93] The law is categorizing women as deserving or undeserving of support from the state based on consent to sex. Only women who are victims of sexual violence are deemed worthy of receiving child benefits for all of their children. This falls back on tropes of deserving/undeserving poor; women's level of worth is connected to their sexuality. The limitation stigmatizes the sexuality and reproductive choices of women in poverty. The Court of Appeal tacitly endorses these harmful stereotypes.[94] Applying the recognition dimension of transformative equality reveals that the two-child limit is based on fears of sexual promiscuity of women who live in poverty.

3.   Structural dimension

The structural dimension of transformative equality requires that 'existing social structures must be changed to accommodate difference rather than requiring [women] to conform to the dominant [male] norm'.[95] The design of social benefits must respect women's different life patterns and choices and the constraints on women's choices.

On multiple levels, the architecture of the UK benefit schemes echoes existing economic and social structural gender inequalities. To escape the benefits cap, single mothers must undertake 16 hours of work per week. The government argues in both *SG* and *DA* that the law does account for women's different life patterns and choices, as single mothers are required to work eight hours less a week than a couple to escape the punishing benefits cap.[96] This is at best a partial acknowledgement of how the male breadwinner model operates to disadvantage women. Single mothers must still obtain 16 hours of waged work per week and pay and arrange for 16 hours of childcare a week. This does not go far enough to disentangle male working patterns from criteria to access social benefits. Single mothers are at the heart of an interconnected web of caring and dependent relationships.[97] To escape the benefit cap, they must fight the logistical battle of finding paid work in a labor force that accommodates their sole responsibility for managing childcare arrangements. Lady Hale, in dissent, explains that to escape the cap, single mothers must deliver and collect children from childcare, make special arrangements for school holidays, respond to child illness and accidents, and find accommodating part-time work to escape the cap.[98] The working tax credit relies upon a model of an autonomous individual divorced from caring relationships. The design of social benefits

---

[91]   Women's Budget Group, 'Female Face' (n 6).
[92]   O'Brien (n 83) 706.
[93]   Child Tax Credit (Amendment) Regulations 2017/387.
[94]   *SC* (n 27) [143]–[144].
[95]   Fredman, *Discrimination Law* (n 29) 30.
[96]   *SG* (n 58) [19], [26]; *DA* (n 58) [27], [30].
[97]   *SG* (n 58) [264].
[98]   ibid [182].

must fully account for and value women's role in care work.[99] A truly transformative model would seek to valorize care, especially traditionally invisibilized and unpaid care work. Social benefits would be at a sufficient level that women could afford to take care of their children without having to seek waged work.

Furthermore, the conditionalities in *DA* do not acknowledge the gendered barriers to accessing the labor market and the structural constraints on women. Many women with children who are not in the workforce want to be employed, but accessing high quality jobs and affordable childcare are insurmountable obstacles.[100] Lord Kerr in dissent in *DA* points out that 'one can only incentivize parents to obtain work if that is a viable option.'[101] A recent Parliamentary Committee report powerfully illuminates that low wages, rocketing housing and childcare costs make it mathematically impossible for women in poverty with children to work in the paid labour force.[102] Only Lady Hale, in dissent in *DA*, observes that childcare is 'in short supply and very expensive' and it can be incredibly difficult for single mothers to find 'suitable work which will fit in with her child care arrangements ...'.[103] Escaping the income poverty imposed by the benefit cap can be a practical impossibility for many single mothers. An equal social-benefits system would not set women up to fail.

4. Participation dimension

This final dimension seeks to promote political and social inclusion and requires that women be included in all public, private, political, legal, economic and social decision-making processes. The single mothers in *SG* and *DA* lack voice. The majority judgments that justified the benefit caps did not even name the claimants and make no reference to their lives when assessing the differential treatment the cap imposes on women. They are literally erased from the legal analysis. In *SG*, it is not until paragraph 169, in Lady Hale's dissent, that there is any explanation of the claimants' personal circumstances. Both SG and NS are survivors of domestic violence. SG lives in London close to a religious school that her children attend and is embroiled in child custody proceedings. NS is a single mother of three children under 15 years old, she 'was allowed very little freedom by her husband and speaks very little English', and has not been able to work outside of the home.[104] A transformative-equality framework would explicitly acknowledge and give weight to the lived experience of claimants.

Lastly, the participation dimension recognizes that 'given that past discrimination ... [has] blocked the avenues for political participation ... equality laws are needed both to compensate for this absence of political voice and to open up the channels for greater participation ...'.[105] The Supreme Court and Court of Appeal give significant weight to the numerous debates in the House of Commons and House of Lords, government White Papers, reports from the Treasury, and Impact Assessments. The degree of high-level political scrutiny is used by the

---

[99] Kate Andersen, 'Universal Credit, Gender and Unpaid Childcare: Mothers' Accounts of the New Welfare Conditionality Regime' (2019) Critical Soc. Pol'y 1.

[100] Work and Pensions Committee, 'Universal Credit: Childcare' (2018) Twenty-Second Report of Session 2017-19 citing Department for Education, 'Childcare and Early Years Survey of Parents in England' (2017) SFR 73/2017, 15–16.

[101] *DA* (n 58) [190].

[102] Work and Pensions Committee. 'Universal Credit: Childcare' (n 100).

[103] *DA* (n 58) [144]–[145].

[104] *SG* (n 58) [174]–[177].

[105] Fredman, 'Substantive Equality Revisited' (n 10) 732.

court to justify judicial deference in economic and social policy.[106] However, the voice of women most affected by the changes is absent and excluded from the elite political participation. The government's Equality Impact Assessment on the benefit cap, which is only 14 pages long, refers to 'many people' suggesting that there should be a benefit cap. Nowhere in the assessment is the voice of women in poverty empowered or given weight in the executive decision-making process.[107] Transformative equality requires the government to meaningfully consult not only with the politically and socially privileged, but also with single mothers who are going to be affected by the laws.

IV.   CONCLUSION

Women's poverty is an interlocking web of material deprivation, negative stereotypes and oppressive structures. This web is tightened for mothers in poverty. The insight that women's poverty is greater than material deprivation opens up the potential of using rights to equality and non-discrimination to tackle women's poverty. Redressing gender stereotypes and transforming oppressive institutions and structures is at the core of the commitment to eliminate discrimination and achieve equality. The thin vision of equality applied by the UK courts in a series of social-benefit claims ignores these elements of women's poverty.

Transformative equality provides an alternative framework for addressing women's poverty. Future equality-based poverty litigation must emphasize the role of gender discrimination and the synergy between status and economic inequality. Canadian, South African, and Indian equality jurisprudence have recognized a richer concept of substantive equality.[108] Fredman's theory has been influential in shaping best practices and it could be equally as influential in domestic discourse in the UK. While there have been strong theoretical arguments laying the foundation for the court adjudicating the relationship between human rights and poverty,[109] greater research is needed to translate these abstract theories into practicably applicable doctrines. Women, poverty, parenting and equality are rich fields of study that stretch across disciplinary silos, and the litigation cited here repeatedly drew on social science evidence on the impacts of the benefits scheme. The UK Supreme Court, however, was sceptical of its role in using what it describes as 'conflicting factual and statistical evidence'.[110] More research is needed to understand how to translate the findings from social science into persuasive legal arguments. This is needed to establish a clear connection between equality in social sciences and equality in law. A greater appreciation of the multiple dimensions of women's poverty and the right to equality can mark out a stronger role for law all over the world in adjudicating economic and social law and policy cases.

---

[106]   *SG* (n 58) [96],.; *SC* (n 27) [158]; *DA* (n 58) , [95], [120].

[107]   Department for Work and Pensions 'Benefit Cap: Equality Impact Assessment' (2012) 8 <https:// assets.publishing.service.gov.uk/government/uploads/system/uploads/attachment_data/file/220153/eia-benefit-cap-wr2011.pdf> accessed 4 October 2019.

[108]   *Quebec (Attorney-General) Alliance du personnel professionnel et technique de la sante et des services sociaux* (2018) 1 SCR 464; *Harksen v Lane* [1997] ZACC 12; *Navtej Singh Johar & Ors v Union of India* (2018) 14961/2016.

[109]   Sandra Fredman, *Comparative Human Rights* (OUP 2018) ch 4.

[110]   *DA* (n 58) [123].

11. The price that is paid: violence and discrimination based on sexual orientation and gender identity and poverty

Victor Madrigal-Borloz[1]

Discrimination and violence based on sexual orientation and gender identity (SOGI) exist in different forms across most cultures. Within this context social status and, particularly, the experience of poverty, are indeed powerful determinants and amplifiers for discrimination, which in turn fuels violence and an environment of exclusion from opportunity in all facets of life, facilitated in a wide variety of public and private settings by family members, friends, church and community members, police officers, landlords and co-workers. These dynamics are further compounded by multiple, intersecting and equally determinant identities that every person reunites in one body.

This chapter examines the marginalization and social exclusion based on sexual orientation and gender identity and its connected impact on violence and discrimination, with particular focus on the sectors of health, education, employment and economic opportunities, housing, adequate standards of living, and violence. I begin by providing a meta-analysis of previously conducted scientific data collection efforts, noting the shortcomings of the evidence available. I proceed to propose several theoretical explanations for the linkages between stigma and poverty. Finally, I conclude with my thoughts on how States ought to take legislative, administrative or judicial action.

I. POVERTY IN LGBT AND GENDER DIVERSE PERSONS, COMMUNITIES AND POPULATIONS

Concepts of sexual orientation and gender identity vary greatly across the world – and a significant proportion of sexually and gender diverse persons do not identify with the political identities originally linked to social movements in the Global North, described by the acronym LGBT. This acronym will nonetheless be used in this chapter as an inevitably imperfect device to refer to all persons affected by violence and discrimination based on SOGI.

---

[1]   This chapter is an output of the research process conducted for the preparation of the author's 2019 Annual Report to the United Nations General Assembly in his capacity as UN Independent Expert on Protection from Violence and Discrimination based on Sexual Orientation and Gender Identity (United Nations A/74/181). All references to 'Submission' relate to documents presented in the call for inputs which have been published and are available at https://ohchr.org/EN/Issues/SexualOrientationGender/Pages/SubmissionsSocioCulturalEconomicInclusion.aspx. The author thanks Catherine de Preux De Baets and Alice Ochsenbein, Officers at the Office of the United Nations High Commissioner for Human Rights, and Matthew Keating, Research Assistant at the Harvard Law School's Human Rights Program for their valuable contributions.

In addition, it must be noted that scientific research on rates of poverty among LGBT persons is relatively new and, with very few exceptions, relies almost exclusively on data from persons living in the Global North. As a norm, information relating to poverty from most regions of the world does not include information disaggregated by SOGI, including data on demographic, economic, social and cultural characteristics, literacy rates, unemployment rates, homelessness and other key indicators. In fact, as a result of barriers created by criminalization, pathologization, demonization and other institutional drivers for stigmatization, there are generally no accurate estimates on the world population affected by discrimination based on SOGI.[2]

Only a handful of countries have systematically integrated SOGI into their data collection and analysis relating to socio-economic status[3] and in the vast majority of nations this function is carried out, with significantly varying degrees of amplitude, aptitude and depth, by academia, civil society and, in the specific areas of their competence, by regional and international organizations. Where information exists, it suggests that sexual orientation and gender identity is indeed a determinant and a predictor of poverty; for example, in October of 2019 the Williams Institute observed that in the United States, the odds of poverty are 42 per cent higher for LGBT people than for cisgender straight people.[4] Furthermore, very significant variances exist between members of the acronym. After disaggregation, the odds that a trans person lives in poverty are nearly double their cisgender, straight counterparts.[5]

While these findings cannot be automatically extrapolated to other latitudes, the evidence available globally strongly suggests that persons who are – or are perceived to be – transgressing what is seen to be the desirable norm in terms of sexual orientation or gender identity experience much higher poverty rates. The UN Special Rapporteur on Poverty made similar observations on the connection between SOGI and one's vulnerability to extreme poverty in his visits to Ghana,[6] China,[7] Chile,[8] Moldova[9] and Mongolia,[10] among others.

At the same time, the knowledge base on the relation between socioeconomic status and SOGI must be built on the awareness that not all LGBT people experience exclusion in the same way, and exclusion and marginalization are compounded by intersecting identities such

---

[2]   United Nations General Assembly (UNGA), 'Data Collection and Management as a Means to Create Heightened Awareness of Violence and Discrimination Based on Sexual Orientation and Gender Identity' (14 May 2019) UN Doc A/HRC/41/45 para 12.

[3]   UNGA, 'Extreme Poverty and Human Rights' (4 October 2017) UN Doc A/72/502 para 6.

[4]   MV Lee Badgett, Soon Kyu Choi and Bianca DM Wilson, 'LGBT Poverty in the United States. A Study of Differences Between Sexual Orientation and Gender Identity Groups' (2019 Williams Institute of the UCLA School of Law) 24. The Williams Institute uses a poverty variable based on the US federal poverty thresholds provided by the US Census Bureau. Using number of adults and children in the household, and household income, respondents are categorized as either experiencing poverty or not.

[5]   ibid.

[6]   UNGA, 'Report of the Special Rapporteur on Extreme Poverty and Human Rights on his Mission to Ghana' (10 October 2018) UN Doc A/HRC/38/33/Add.2 para 39.

[7]   UNGA, 'Report of the Special Rapporteur on Extreme Poverty and Human Rights on his Mission to China' (28 March 2017) UN Doc A/HRC/35/26/Add.2 para 39.

[8]   UNGA, 'Report of the Special Rapporteur on Extreme Poverty and Human Rights on his Mission to Chile' UN Doc A/HRC/32/31/Add.1 para 43.

[9]   UNGA, 'Report of the Special Rapporteur on Extreme Poverty and Human Rights, Magdalena Sepúlveda Carmona' UN Doc A/HRC/26/28/Add.2 para 67.

[10]   ibid para 61.

as ethnicity/race, indigenous or minority status, colour, socioeconomic status and/or caste, language, religion or belief, political opinion, national origin, marital and/or maternal status, age, urban/rural location, health status, disability and property ownership. The Williams Institute found, for example, that 30.8 per cent of black LGBT persons live in poverty compared to 15.4 per cent of white LGBT persons, and that 26.1 per cent of LGBT persons in rural areas live in poverty, while this rate is 21 per cent when they live in large cities.[11]

This complexity of the patterns has been described as follows:

> On one hand, cisgender gay and bisexual men have higher levels of education and fewer children, both of which protect them from poverty. On the other hand, they are less likely to be partnered, to be employed, or to be in good health, which tend to increase their risk of poverty. Cisgender lesbian and bisexual women are protected by having higher levels of employment than cisgender straight women but are at risk because of less education (for bisexual women), poorer health, and lower partnership rates. This complexity requires a more sophisticated statistical method to make detailed comparisons.[12]

If not a comprehensive picture, identities nonetheless represent a point of entry, a prism for the analysis of the texture of human experiences that capture some factors based on SOGI. For example, the pay gap between men and women, which continues to be a source of pervasive inequality all over the world, impacts lesbo-parental families doubly, and where data exists, it is documented that lesbian and bisexual women experience disproportionate discrimination in education.[13] Similarly, an examination from the point of departure of youth reveals particular concern in relation to homelessness, and in some places it is reported that LGBT youth account for as much as 40 per cent of the homeless population in their age group.[14] A cycle is then created, with LGBT youth disproportionately represented in foster care, begging and sex work, and more likely to be turned away from shelters.

II.   LAW, POLICY AND ACCESS TO JUSTICE

As of 2020, more than 70 countries in the world still criminalize same-sex relations or diverse gender identities, 11 of which maintain the penalty of death. A staggering two billion persons live in these contexts. This State-sponsored form of discrimination and violence, amply proven to be contrary to international human rights law, creates a context in which it is materially impossible to gather data on the connection between SOGI and poverty and has obvious implications for both legitimacy and the ability to implement public policies and access to justice that address social exclusion.

Other legislation and administrative policies, which on paper may appear neutral in intention, may have disproportionate and discriminatory impacts on LGBT persons. The UN High Commissioner on Human Rights noted that this is often the case with public decency legislation, which may be weaponized against persons who 'cross-dress' by breaking from societal norms surrounding gender presentation. Laws banning nuisance, loitering and vagrancy are

---

[11]   Badgett (n 4) 25.
[12]   ibid 25.
[13]   ILGA World, Submission (n 1) n 4.
[14]   Canadian HIV/AIDS Legal Network, Submission (n 1) 3.

often used as a basis to arrest and detain trans women or prosecute already impoverished and stigmatized LGBT sex workers. Even seemingly well-tested administrative requirements may have discriminatory impact: in the wake of the COVID-19 pandemic for example, several States in Latin America implemented gender-based curfews, which not only disproportionately impacted women because of social preconceptions around work but effectively impeded trans women and gender non-binary persons from circulating if their official identification documents did not correspond with their appearance. Gender quarantine laws then significantly restricted trans and gender non-binary persons' right to leave the house, affecting their ability to get food, access health facilities and procure basic goods.

Even in decriminalized environments, the law may permit discrimination against LGBT persons relying on the premise that sexual and gender diversity are immoral, contrary to the common good of society and, in the extreme, an institutionally-classified medical pathology. Law, religion and medicine have historically been used to enforce that notion, resulting in a variety of normative constructions that over time have reinforced negative preconceptions and stereotypes about LGBT persons.[15] As a result, LGBT persons are often excluded from formal sector relationships in a situation that I have described as one of absolute rupture between the State as duty bearer and the LGBT person as a rights holder. For example, all evidence available consistently suggests that a majority of trans women dedicate themselves to sex work – as a rule unrecognized as labour by the State and therefore operating outside all social and labour guarantees. In the absence of a safety net available to all under the jurisdiction of the State (universal health coverage, for example) these vulnerabilities are exacerbated.

Full respect for the human rights of LGBT persons also extends to full participation in public life through the overlapping spheres of family, community, education, workplace, health and cultural life. Yet research reveals consistent challenges in this regard. For example, the International Lesbian, Gay, Trans, Bisexual and Intersex Association (ILGA) reported that only 27 per cent of UN Member States have enacted broad protections against discrimination on the basis of SOGI, and only 38 per cent have legislation in the field of employment.[16] Similarly, only 14 per cent of UN Member States recognize same-sex unions (through marriage or civil union). As a result, same-sex or gender diverse family units are denied health insurance, tax, retirement and other social benefits. Lack of relationship recognition impacts individuals negatively on eligibility for pension entitlements and social security survivorship, which could – to give one example – leave them unable to pay their rent or mortgage, leading to eviction. LGBT persons might not be able to legally leave property to a surviving partner or remain in public housing following a partner's death.[17]

---

[15]   UNGA, 'Report of the Special Rapporteur on the Human Right to Safe Drinking Water and Sanitation, Catarina de Albuquerque' (2 July 2012) UN Doc A/HRC/21/42 para 65.
[16]   The International Lesbian, Gay, Bisexual, Trans and Intersex Association (ILGA) 'Maps – Sexual Orientation Laws' <https://ilga.org/maps-sexual-orientation-laws> accessed 4 July 2020.
[17]   ibid.

III.   SYSTEMS OF EXCLUSION OF LGBT PERSONS FROM SOCIO-ECONOMIC OPPORTUNITY

The analysis of discrimination and violence highlights four sectors – education, employment, housing and health – as key in the construction of experiences of discrimination leading to, perpetuating or resulting from poverty for LGBT persons.

A.   Education

As noted by the UN Committee on Economic, Social and Cultural Rights (CESCR), 'education is the primary vehicle by which economically and socially marginalized adults and children can lift themselves out of poverty and obtain the means to participate fully in their communities'.[18] In contradiction with this desideratum, LGBT pupils face abuse in education settings, including bullying, isolation, name-calling, intimidation (including death threats), physical violence and sexual assault in a manner disproportionate to the general population.[19] The abuse takes place in changing rooms, classes, toilets, playgrounds and other social areas, and on the way to and from school. Frequently, it happens online, extending feelings of isolation and discrimination beyond school hours,[20] and it fuels discussions that are evidently fuelled by stigma, such as those surrounding access to toilets in line with students' gender identity. As a result, students who are – or are perceived to be – lesbian, gay, bisexual, trans or gender diverse are more likely to feel unsafe, avoid extracurricular activities, miss classes, skip school altogether, and eventually drop out. They also achieve lower academic results.[21] This, in turn, promotes exclusion from socio economic opportunities, as suggested by research completed in 2016 by the International Labour Organisation (ILO) in Argentina, Costa Rica, France, India, Indonesia, Montenegro and South Africa.[22] These multiple causal mechanisms can compound to create a cycle of poverty for LGBT persons that begins as early as primary school.

The impact of these conditions and cycle is empirically reflected in data on educational attainment of the LGBT population. For example, lesbian and bisexual women are more

---

[18]   Committee on Economic, Social and Cultural Rights (CESCR), 'Implementation of the International Covenant on Economic, Social and Cultural Rights' UN Doc (8 December 1999) E/C.12/1999/10.

[19]   United Nations Educational, Scientific and Cultural Organization (UNESCO), 'Good Policy and Practice in HIV and Health Education: Booklet 8 – Education Sector Responses to Homophobic Bullying' (31 December 2012); Paulo Sérgio Pinheiro, 'World Report on Violence against Children' (Geneva, United Nations, 2006); Inter-American Commission on Human Rights (IACHR), 'Violence against Lesbian, Gay, Bisexual, Trans and Intersex Persons in the Americas' (2015) OAS/Ser.L/V/II.rev.1, Doc. 36; UN Committee on the Rights of the Child (CRC), 'General Comment No. 20 (2016) on the Implementation of the Rights of the Child during Adolescence' UN Doc CRC/C/GC/20 para 33.

[20]   UNESCO, 'Out in the Open: Education Sector Responses to Violence Based on Sexual Orientation or Gender Identity/Expression,' 2016 <www.right-to-education.org/sites/right-to-education.org/files/resource-attachments/UNESCO_out_in_the_open_2016_En.pdf> accessed 5 July 2020.

[21]   UNESCO 2012 (n 19); UNESCO 2016 (n 20); IACHR 2015 (n 19).

[22]   International Labour Organization (ILO), 'Gender identity and sexual orientation: promoting rights, diversity and equality in the world of work – results of the ILO's PRIDE project' (16 May 2016) Briefing Note <www.ilo.org/gender/Informationresources/Publications/WCMS_481575/lang--en/index.htm.> accessed 5 July 2020.

likely not to graduate from high school, and trans women are more likely not to graduate from primary school.[23]

Official policy has great influence in determining these outcomes. In certain contexts, it is lawful for schools to discriminate against pupils and teachers on the basis of 'doctrines, tenets, beliefs or teachings of a religion or creed'.[24] In January 2016, referring to LGBT students, the president of the Jamaica Association for Guidance Counsellors in Education stated that 'counsellors who are of the Christian faith ... will not ... look at [LGBT] students at all'.[25] Appropriate training and sensitization on diversity are unfortunately far more often the exception and not the rule; school systems are rarely equipped to provide efficient and effective responses to harassment of LGBT and gender non-conforming pupils. In its resolution on protecting children from bullying, the UN General Assembly has encouraged Member States to 'take all appropriate measures to prevent and protect children, including in school, from any form of violence ... by promptly responding to such acts, and to provide appropriate support to children affected by and involved in bullying'.[26]

Inclusion should not be limited to the faculty or staff of educational institutions. Educational materials and curricula should promote inclusion of persons of diverse sexual orientations and gender identities and expressions. The UN Special Rapporteur on the promotion and protection of the right to freedom of opinion and expression has expressed concern at bans of discussion of LGBT issues at school, as well as bans of wearing symbols of support for LGBT rights.[27] As the UN Independent Expert on SOGI I have addressed the issue in several communications, including allegations concerning regressive measures in the education curriculum in the province of Ontario in Canada[28] and allegations concerning the drafting of a discriminatory and stigmatizing by-law that prohibits the distribution of information on lesbian, gay, bisexual and transsexual people to children in Kazakhstan.[29]

Conversely, the meaningful inclusion of LGBT people in education can have a broad, positive impact. Comprehensive anti-bullying or anti-harassment policies make significant positive contributions. Similarly, UNESCO has highlighted research suggesting that curricula featuring SOGI positively impacts the attitudes and beliefs of students and teachers and makes the former feel safer at school.[30] Other measures, such as creating Gender and Sexuality alliances and other LGBT-inclusive after-school clubs are also connected to lower incidences of bullying.[31]

---

[23]   Badgett (n 4) 2.

[24]   Australian National Human Rights Commission, Submission (n 1) 3.

[25]   Canadian HIV/AIDS Legal Network, Submission (n 1) 4.

[26]   UNGA, 'Resolution Adopted by the General Assembly on 18 December 2014' (3 February 2015) UN Doc A/RES/69/158.

[27]   UNGA, 'Promotion and Protection of the Right to Freedom of Opinion and Expression' (21 August 2014) UN Doc A/69/335.

[28]   UN IE SOGI, 'Individual Communication OL CAN 4/2018' (19 December 2018) <https://spcommreports.ohchr.org/TMResultsBase/DownLoadPublicCommunicationFile?gId=24216> accessed 5 July 2020.

[29]   UN IE SOGI, 'Individual Communication OL KAZ 5/2018' (7 November 2018) <https://spcommreports.ohchr.org/TMResultsBase/DownLoadPublicCommunicationFile?gId=24175> accessed 5 July 2020.

[30]   UNESCO 2016 (n 20).

[31]   CHOICE, Submission (n 1) 6.

Furthermore, the UNESCO International Guidelines on Sexuality Education note the benefits of providing young people with age-appropriate, culturally sensitive and comprehensive sexuality education that provide scientifically accurate, realistic, non-judgmental information,[32] and avoid the secondary effects of socio-economic exclusion through substance abuse, mistrust of health services and self-medication.

Addressing LGBT issues in vocational trainings and ongoing professional education is equally important. LGBT-sensitive medical school curricula and trainings for health care professionals and administrative staff covering issues such as sexual and reproductive health and rights, suicide prevention, HIV/AIDS and trauma counselling, will help ensure the provision of accessible, available and acceptable LGBT-sensitive services.

B.   Employment

Exclusion is strongly linked to fewer opportunities and less access to work, resulting in disproportionate impact of poverty.

Discrimination based on SOGI occurs in all regions and throughout all steps of the employment cycle from hiring to advancement to training to compensation to termination. According to the ILO, LGBT workers face issues including verbal and physical abuse and discriminatory policies and practices. In most States, national laws do not provide adequate protection from employment-related discrimination on the grounds of sexual orientation and gender identity.[33] In the absence of such laws and particularly in contexts in which employment-at-will is the norm, employers may be able to fire or refuse to hire or promote people simply because they are, or are thought to be, homosexual or transgender.[34] The manner in which human resources collects information on employees can also result in outing LGBT people or in further discrimination. This can include information required on partner and family status and forms or communications that do not integrate a gender neutral and inclusive approach.

This can also translate to discriminatory workplace benefits and policies or policies that do not meaningfully include the diversity of employees, especially in regards to employee benefits like health insurance, pension contributions, and parental leave when compared to cisgender and heterosexual co-workers.[35] In *X. v. Colombia*, the UN Human Rights Committee found that the State party violated rights protected under the International Covenant on Civil and Political Rights by failing to extend pension benefits to an unmarried same-sex partner when such benefits were granted to unmarried heterosexual couples.[36] The same can be said when the barriers result from the absence of legal recognition of gender identity: trans persons

---

[32]   UNESCO, 'International Technical Guidance on Sexuality Education: an Evidence-Informed Approach' (2018).

[33]   International Lesbian, Gay, Bisexual, Trans and Intersex Association (ILGA): Lucas Ramon Mendos, 'State-Sponsored Homophobia 2019: Global Legislation Overview Update' (March 2019) 21.

[34]   UNGA, 'Discriminatory Laws and Practices and Acts of Violence Against Individuals Based on Their Sexual Orientation and Gender Identity' (17 November 2011) UN Doc A/HRC/19/41.

[35]   ILO, 'A Study on Discrimination at Work on the Basis of Sexual Orientation and Gender Identity in Thailand' (2015) Working Paper No 3; ILO 'A Study on Discrimination at Work on the Basis of Sexual Orientation and Gender Identity in South Africa' (2016) Working Paper No 4; see also Asia Pacific Alliance for Sexual and Reproductive Health and Rights, Submission (n 1) 3.

[36]   UN International Covenant on Civil and Political Rights (ICCPR), 'Discrimination in Granting Pension Transfer in the Case of Homosexual Couples' UN Doc CCPR/C/89/D/1361/2005) para 7.

who do not have identification documents reflecting their gender and those whose gender expression is the least conforming to gender norms face the highest rates of bullying and exclusion in seeking employment and in the workplace.[37]

In many cases, the perception of homosexuality or transgender identity puts people at increased risk of violence and harassment from supervisors, co-workers or clients.

Globally, LGBT people are consistently subject to labour market penalties. Social marginalization in the workplace, negative reporting to management and prevailing cultures of harassment and discrimination form severe barriers to promotion for LGBT workers,[38] and LGBT workers widely report being unfairly denied training and job advancement opportunities, as well as promotions. Even within the same employment level, studies suggest that gay males earn significantly less than their heterosexual counterparts. For example, a recent study in the United States revealed that, when compared to their heterosexual peers, gay males earn on average 11.7 per cent lower wages – with the wages of bisexual males being, on average, 12.4 per cent lower.[39] Additionally, lesbian women suffer compounding gender-based discrimination resulting in even more significant pay gaps.[40]

For trans workers, the absence of legal recognition of their gender identity can pose a significant barrier to their effective access to work, with qualified candidates often being filtered out at the application or interview stages.[41] Trans workers face high levels of sexual and verbal harassment and report being fired when they start transitioning during employment, or after their transition.[42] Trans women are particularly marginalized in accessing employment, leading to increased representation in the informal economy, and it is generally accepted that a significant number of trans women are forced to engage in sex work as their only recourse to an income.[43] Overrepresentation in sex work in regions in which sex work is criminalized increases health risks – as possession of condoms can be used as evidence – and conflicts with the law.[44]

---

[37]   OHCHR, 'Mandate of the United Nations Independent Expert on Violence and Discrimination Based on Sexual Orientation and Gender Identity, Country Visit to Georgia – 25 September to 5 October 2018' (5 October 2018) <www.ohchr.org/en/NewsEvents/Pages/DisplayNews.aspx?NewsID=23682& LangID=E> accessed 5 July 2020; ILO, 'Pride (PRIDE) at Work: A Study on Discrimination at Work Based on Sexual Orientation and Gender Identity in Costa Rica' (28 June 2016) ILO Working Paper <www.ilo.org/sanjose/publicaciones/WCMS_495184/lang--es/index.htm> accessed 5 July 2020; United Kingdom, Submission (n 1) 2.

[38]   ILO, 'A Study on Discrimination at Work on the Basis of Sexual Orientation and Gender Identity in Indonesia,' ILO Working Paper <www.ilo.org/gender/Informationresources/Publications/ WCMS_481580/lang--en/index.htm> accessed 5 July 2020; ILO, 'Pride (PRIDE) at Work: A Study on Discrimination at Work on the Grounds of Sexual Orientation and Gender Identity in Argentina' (14 May 2015) GED Working Document No. 2/2015 <www.ilo.org/gender/Informationresources/Publications/ WCMS_368648/lang--es/index.htm> accessed 5 July 2020; ILO Costa Rica (n 37).

[39]   CHOICE, Submission (n 1) 8.

[40]   ILO South Africa (n 35).

[41]   CESCR, 'Concluding Observations on the Fifth Periodic Report of Costa Rica' (21 October 2016) UN Doc E/C.12/CRI/CO/5 para 20.

[42]   ILO Argentina (n 38); ILO Costa Rica (n 37).

[43]   IE SOGI (n 37); UNGA (n 8) para 44; International Commission of Jurists, 'Living with Dignity: Sexual Orientation and Gender Identity-Based Human Rights Violations in Housing, Work, and Public Spaces in India' (June 2019) <www.icj.org/wp-content/uploads/2019/06/India-Living-with-dignity -Publications-Reports-thematic-report-2019-ENG.pdf> accessed 5 July 2020.

[44]   Asia Pacific Alliance for Sexual and Reproductive Health and Rights, Submission (n 1) 3.

Stereotyping and the promotion of outdated and patriarchal gender norms can inhibit the enjoyment of the right to work of LGBT and gender diverse people who are forced to wear gendered workplace attire or who are prohibited from using toilets and locker rooms in line with their gender identity.[45]

LGBT workers often have little recourse to redress workplace harassment and discrimination. Sexual orientation, gender identity and gender expression may not be explicitly protected grounds of discrimination under national laws or workplace policies.[46] A recent survey showed that out of 68 per cent LGBT people who reported being sexually harassed at work, two thirds did not report it to their employer.[47] Where protections do exist workers might not know about them or might fear negative repercussions should they use them.

Of those LGBT workers who did report workplace harassment, the majority were not satisfied with the results, and investigations were hindered by impossible burdens of proof for discrimination or by co-workers unwilling or afraid to speak out and support LGBT workers.[48]

The lack of effective response mechanisms for workplace harassment and discrimination on the grounds of sexual orientation and gender identity leads to a culture of impunity with few LGBT people seeking justice. All of these factors also lead LGBT persons to exclude themselves from a wide range and economic opportunities out of fear of harassment and violence, seeking employment only in environments in which their identity(ies) are accepted.[49]

In all cases, the resulting pay gaps translate to smaller contributions to pension schemes and therefore increased poverty in retirement.[50] The double impact of sexual orientation and the gender wage gap means that older cis women in same-sex couples are twice as likely to be poor than older cis straight couples (for couples aged 65 and over, 6 per cent of female same-sex couples live in poverty, compared to 3.5 per cent of straight cis couples).[51]

C.   Housing

The CESCR has clarified the positive obligations of States to prevent and address homelessness. These include an obligation to assess the extent of homelessness and inadequate housing and to prioritize those who are disadvantaged.[52]

---

[45]   UN Human Rights Committee (HRC), 'Report of the Special Rapporteur on the Human Right to Safe Drinking Water and Sanitation' (27 July 2016) UN Doc A/HRC/33/49 para 2.

[46]   CESCR, 'Consideration of Reports Submitted by States Parties Under Articles 16 and 17 of the Covenant' (30 May 2012) UN Doc E/C.12/PER/CO/2-4; ICCPR, 'Concluding Observations on the Second Periodic Report of Cambodia' (27 April 2015) UN Doc CCPR/C/KHM/CO/2 para 9.

[47]   Trades Union Congress (TUC), 'Sexual Harassment of LGBT People in the Workplace' (April 2019) <www.tuc.org.uk/sites/default/files/LGBT_Sexual_Harassment_Report_0.pdf> accessed 5 July 2020.

[48]   ILO South Africa (n 35); ILO Thailand (n 35); ILO Costa Rica (n 37).

[49]   ILO Costa Rica (n 37); ILO Indonesia (n 38).

[50]   Association BaBe, Submission (n 1) 2.

[51]   Movement Advancement Project and Center for American Progress, 'Paying an Unfair Price: The Financial Penalty for Being LGBT in America' (2014) <www.lgbtmap.org/unfair-price> accessed 5 July 2020.

[52]   CESCR, 'CESCR General Comment No. 4: The Right to Adequate Housing (Art. 11(1) of the Covenant)' (13 December 1991) UN Doc E/1992/23 para 8, 13.

LGBT persons have been found to be disproportionately affected by inadequate housing and homelessness,[53] often lacking security of tenure and suffering forced evictions or abusive rental conditions,[54] and unfair treatment by public and private landlords, estate agencies and credit providers.[55] LGBT individuals and same-sex couples may be denied leases and mortgages, evicted from their homes, harassed by neighbours and forced out of their homes.[56] In Jamaica, for example, reports have been made of setting homes on fire in attacks motivated by a desire to force persons out of their community,[57] while a 2012 survey in Sri Lanka revealed that 24 per cent of LGBT respondents had been unable to rent housing or had been forced to change their domicile as a result of their sexual orientation or gender identity. Likewise, 2016 situational testing in Slovenia showed discriminatory treatment of same-sex couples in 9.7 per cent of the surveyed cases.[58]

LGBT and gender non-conforming youth rejected by family or forced to leave situations of domestic violence and abuse are also over-represented among the homeless.[59] This and other exclusionary processes provoke a disproportionate representation of LGBT people, as well as their dependents and children, within the homeless population. In the very few countries where the correlation of data is possible, it suggests that LGBT persons are represented in homeless populations at a rate that is twice as high as their presence in the general population.[60]

In most countries there are no shelters specifically for LGBT persons,[61] and it is reported that those belonging to that group are more likely to be turned away from shelters serving the general population[62] or to conceal their sexuality or gender identity when accessing services.[63] Minors forced to leave their family homes because of their sexual orientation or gender identity are often not eligible for State benefits, which are received by their parents and designed to support families, leaving them with insufficient means to secure safe housing and exposing them at particular risks.[64] LGBT children and youth in shelter programmes risk finding themselves on the street once they reach the age of 18.

---

[53]   UNGA, 'The Right to Adequate Housing' (7 August 2014) UN Doc A/69/274 para 12; UNGA, 'Report of the Special Rapporteur on Adequate Housing as a Component of the Right to an Adequate Standard of Living, and on the Right to Non-discrimination in this Context' (30 December 2015) UN Doc A/HRC/31/54 para 39, 87; HRC, 'Report to the Special Rapporteur on Adequate Housing as a Component of the Right to an Adequate Standard of Living, and on the Right to Non-discrimination in the Context on her Mission to Serbia and Kosovo' (26 February 2016) UN Doc A/HRC/31/54/Add.2 para 52; UNGA (n 7) para 43.

[54]   PROMSEX, Submission (n 1) 8.

[55]   CESCR, 'General Comment No. 20' (2 July 2009) UN Doc E/C.12/GC/20 para 11.

[56]   UNGA, 'Discrimination and Violence Against Individuals Based on Their Sexual Orientation and Gender Identity' (4 May 2015) UN Doc A/HRC/29/23 para 59.

[57]   Canadian HIV/AIDS Legal Network, Submission (n 1) 3; Eastern European Coalition for LGBT+ Equality, Submission (n 1) 2.

[58]   ILGA World, Submission (n 1), n 10.

[59]   UNGA, 'Adequate Housing as a Component of the Right to an Adequate Standard of Living' (4 August 2015) UN Doc A/70/270 para 49.

[60]   New Zealand Human Rights Commission, Submission (n 1) 2.

[61]   Daniella Solano Morales, Submission (n 1) 3; Right Here, Right Now (Nepal), Submission (n 1) 5; XY Spectrum, Submission (n 1) 2.

[62]   UNGA, 2015 (n 53) para 44.

[63]   Australia, Submission (n 1) 2.

[64]   UNICEF, 'Current Issues' <www.unicef.org/media/files/Joint_LGBTI_Statement_ENG.pdf> accessed 5 July 2020.

Homelessness can result in further exclusion, criminalization and stigma; without a fixed address it can be difficult or impossible to gain access to employment, get a bank account, receive mail and register with health providers. Some legal systems have resorted to criminalization by declaring that living permanently on the street is illegal,[65] which exacerbates the possible conflict of homeless LGBT persons with the law. Homeless individuals are more likely to need to use public toilets and sanitation facilities. With facilities offering insufficient privacy, those who appear gender non-conforming are at increased risk of facing harassment and violence when trying to attend to their most basic human needs.

D.   Health

These economic and social realities have an adverse effect on the physical and mental health of LGBT people, while many face further abuse in accessing health care: lesbian and trans workers face exceptionally high rates of bullying and harassment, which can affect their physical and mental health, and LGBT children suffer depression, anxiety, fear, stress, loss of confidence, low self-esteem, withdrawal, social isolation, loneliness, guilt, sleep disturbance, alcohol and drug abuse, homelessness, self-harm, and suicidal tendencies that are higher than the rest of the population.[66] In addition, criminalization, discrimination, lack of dedicated, LGBT-sensitive and non-discriminatory services, and insufficient health insurance coverage may contribute to LGBT people avoiding health services altogether, leading to serious health disparities and increasing risks associated with self-medication and clandestine or black market treatments. These factors relate directly to Sustainable Development Goal (SDG) 3, concerning good health and well-being and the targets of which include 'access to quality essential health-care services'.

The pathologization[67] of LGBT people, stemming from health policies in vigour in a vast majority of the countries in the globe, shape attitudes and practices of health-care institutions and personnel, perpetuating stigma and remaining at the root of forced treatments such as so-called 'conversion therapies'[68] and institutionalization.

The right to health confers entitlements including to a system of health protection that ensures equality of opportunity for every person to enjoy the highest attainable level of health. LGBT people face barriers that render health services unavailable, inaccessible or unacceptable. Quality health facilities, goods and services must be available and accessible for all, especially the most vulnerable or marginalized sections of the population, without discrimination.

Criminal and discriminatory laws and policies, as well as the practices and attitudes of health care providers adversely affect the access and quality of health services provided to LGBT people. This includes laws criminalizing consensual same sex relations between adults,

---

[65]   Transvanilla, Submission (n 1) 5.

[66]   UNESCO 2012 (n 19); UNESCO 2016 (n 19); IACHR 2015 (n 19); UNGA, General Comment No. 20 (n 19) para 33; CRC, 'General Comment No. 21 (2017) on Children in Street Situations' (21 June 2017) UN Doc CRC/C/GC/21.

[67]   The process through which LGBT persons are automatically treated as if they were sick or disordered; see HRC, 'Report of the Special Rapporteur on the Right of Everyone to the Enjoyment of the Highest Attainable Standard of Physical and Mental Health' (28 March 2017) UN Doc A/HRC/35/21 paras 48 and 58.

[68]   New Zealand Human Rights Commission, Submission (n 1) 6.

forms of gender identity and gender expression, and sex work, as well as medical classifications that pathologize people as 'ill' or 'disordered' on the basis of their sexual orientation or gender identity. In addition, programmes related to sexual and reproductive health that were receiving global health assistance from the United States have been affected by the so-called global gag rule, which has in turn negatively impacted on the access to health services by LGBT populations.[69]

The negation of the existence of LGBT people has the disastrous result that the specific needs of this population are ignored and national health policies and strategies fail to address the health disparities, which include: poor outcomes in mental health based on minority stress; a disproportionate burden of HIV among gay and bisexual men and other men who have sex with men and trans women; sexual and reproductive health concerns, including access to reproductive cancer prevention; and prevalent alcohol and substance abuse as a coping mechanism. Research has confirmed strong links between access to treatment, such as hormones and surgeries, and better health outcomes for trans and gender diverse persons.[70]

Discrimination by health workers can manifest in refusals to make clinic appointments, refusals to treat LGBT people, or treatment with gross disrespect, violation of medical privacy, shaming and public disparagement.[71] In Argentina, a country with a vigorous legal framework of protection for trans persons, it is reported that five out of ten trans persons surveyed had stopped attending their health centres because they felt discriminated against.[72] A recent survey conducted in the United Kingdom shows that two in five trans respondents had a negative experience when accessing health services in the year preceding the survey due to their gender identity.[73] The negative and discriminatory attitudes of health care providers can deter individuals from seeking services[74] and can make LGBT people reluctant to share personal and medical information, jeopardizing their overall health and access to health services and undermining broader public health.

The treatment of same sex attraction and trans identities as pathologies that can be 'cured' contributes to the practice of involuntary institutionalisation and so-called 'conversion therapies' – often imposed on people without their consent. Conversion therapies have been found to be unethical, unscientific and ineffective and, in some instances, are tantamount to torture – leading to successful legal challenges and bans in several countries.[75] Such practices are deeply harmful and may cause severe pain and suffering and lead to depression, anxiety and suicidal ideation.[76]

Multiple international and regional human rights mechanisms have noted that medical classifications that label LGBT people as ill or disordered on the basis of their sexual orientation or gender identity/expression, are one of the root causes of the violence, discrimination and

---

[69]   HRC, 'Visit to Mozambique' (17 May 2019) UN Doc A/HRC/41/45/Add.2 para 61.

[70]   Australian National Human Rights Commission, Submission (n 1) 4.

[71]   World Health Organization (WHO), 'Sexual Health, Human Rights and the Law' (June 2015) <www.who.int/reproductivehealth/publications/sexual_health/sexual-health-human-rights-law/en/> 23.

[72]   National Defender of the People in Argentina, Submission (n 1) 2.

[73]   United Kingdom, Submission (n 1) 2.

[74]   WHO, 'Resolution CD52.R6' (30 September–4 October 2013) <www.paho.org/hq/dmdocuments/2013/CD52-R6-e.pdf> accessed 5 July 2020.

[75]   UNGA (n 55) para 50.

[76]   UNGA, 'Report of the Independent Expert on Protection Against Violence and Discrimination Based on Sexual Orientation and Gender Identity' (11 May 2018) UN Doc A/HRC/38/43 fn 46.

stigma that they face.[77] In addition, pathologization has had a deep impact on public policy, legislation and jurisprudence, penetrating all realms of State action in all regions of the world and permeating the collective conscience.[78] Pathologization allows for the easy vilification of LGBT persons and a justification for State-sponsored silencing, detention and overall negation of diverse identities.

While homosexuality was removed from the International Classification of Diseases (ICD) in 1990, some countries continue to classify homosexuality as an illness. In almost all countries trans people are treated as ill or disordered based on international and regional classification systems such as the ICD and the American Psychological Association's Diagnostic and Statistical Manual of Mental Disorders (DSM). The ICD has only recently moved trans identities from its chapter on mental disorders to the chapter on sexual health, recognizing the need to reassess the classification while maintaining provisions to facilitate health insurance coverage of gender affirming care, which is nearly impossible to attain without a medical diagnosis. Following this decision, the Independent Expert and the Special Rapporteur on the right to health called on States to review their medical classifications and adopt strong proactive measures, including education and sensitization campaigns to eliminate the social stigma associated with gender diversity.[79]

Private and public insurers often do not offer, or may specifically exclude, coverage for medical procedures for gender transition, and there are substantial variations in which services are covered and under what conditions.[80] Even in environments that are generally resourced adequately, the asymmetries in the situation of trans persons is painfully obvious: the New Zealand Human Rights Commission reports that national waiting lists to access publicly funded surgical procedures are in excess of 50 years for both trans masculine and trans feminine persons.[81] International and regional human rights bodies have specifically addressed access to, and reimbursement for, gender-affirming treatments.[82]

Such treatments, where available, are often prohibitively expensive. In the absence of public health provisions, trans people are forced into unsafe alternative measures to change their bodies to match their gender identity. In many countries, this includes the unregulated use of hormones and the dangerous practice of injecting silicon or industrial oil by non-medical providers.[83]

For some trans persons, surgery is an important aspect for their transition, while for others, such interventions are not necessary for them to feel comfortable or aligned with their gender identity (or lack thereof). For the former, acquiring physical sex characteristics congruent

---

[77]   UNGA, 'Protection Against Violence and Discrimination Based on Sexual Orientation and Gender Identity' (12 July 2018) UN Doc A/73/152; Council of Europe Commissioner for Human Rights, 'Human Rights and Intersex People' Issue Paper <https://wcd.coe.int/ViewDoc.jsp?p=&Ref=CommDH/IssuePaper(2015)1&Language=lanEnglish&direct=true> accessed 5 July 2020.

[78]   UNGA ibid para 14.

[79]   OHCHR, 'UN Experts Hail Move to "Depathologise" Trans Identities' (29 May 2019) <www.ohchr.org/en/NewsEvents/Pages/DisplayNews.aspx?NewsID=24663&LangID=E> accessed 5 July 2020.

[80]   WHO (n 71).

[81]   New Zealand Human Rights Commission, Submission (n 1) 2.

[82]   UNGA (n 34).

[83]   United Nations Development Programme (UNDP), 'Discussion Paper on Transgender Health & Human Rights' (4 December 2015) <www.undp.org/content/undp/en/home/librarypage/hiv-aids/discussion-paper-on-transgender-health---human-rights.html> accessed 5 July 2020.

with experienced gender identity improves health, wellbeing and quality of life, including better self-esteem and improved physical, mental, emotional and social functioning, and some have shown improvement in sexual function and satisfaction. Conversely, not being able to live according to one's self-identified gender is likely to be a source of distress, exacerbating other forms of ill health.[84] However, such treatment should never be forced or a prerequisite to access legal recognition, and not all trans people desire to modify their bodies through surgeries, hormones or other measures.

The pathologization of trans people through the concept that they require psychiatric or psychological assessment and must undergo full sex reassignment through surgery and hormones in order to live in their self-identified gender leads to systematized violations of trans persons' right to privacy, bodily integrity and freedom from inhuman and degrading treatment. In order for their identity to be legally recognized, trans people face abusive requirements as prerequisites for change of name, legal sex or gender, which seriously hampers their trust in medical institutions. Those include forced, coerced or otherwise involuntary sterilization, surgeries and hormonal therapies; undergoing medical diagnosis, psychological appraisals or other medical or psychosocial procedures or treatment; and forced divorce for those who are married.[85]

Such practices run contrary to international human rights standards.[86] States should ensure trans persons' right to recognition before the law, including of their gender identity, without requirements that violate their fundamental rights and freedoms. All treatment must be based on full, free, informed consent.

Research shows that the search for health services for lesbian women compared with heterosexual women results in a lower frequency of preventive and routine tests, such as preventive examination against cervical and breast cancer. The lack of LGBT health education in the school curricula further adversely impacts the health of lesbians and recent studies reveal that lesbians have negative experiences in gynaecological clinics, encountering inappropriate reactions and rejections from professionals.[87]

Lesbians, bisexual women and other gender non-conforming women are often discriminated against and misdiagnosed by medical providers, which deters them from seeking health services or carrying through with treatment. This is particularly related to sub-standard care for their sexual and reproductive health needs, including access to reproductive cancer prevention. In some contexts, they are subjected to coercive, inhumane and degrading practices such as 'corrective' or punitive rape and face challenges accessing post rape psycho/social and health care.

A lack of official relationship recognition can exclude significant individuals from family treatment or decision-making roles. The CESCR has called on States to ensure that individuals in same-sex unions are entitled to equal enjoyment of their economic, social and

---

[84]   WHO (n 71).

[85]   UNGA (n 77).

[86]   OHCHR and others, 'Eliminating Forced, Coercive and Otherwise Involuntary Sterilization: an Interagency Statement' (May 2014) <www.who.int/reproductivehealth/publications/gender_rights/eliminating-forced-sterilization/en/> accessed 5 July 2020.

[87]   Grayce Alencar and others, 'Access to Health Services by Lesbian, Gay, Bisexual, and Transgender Persons: Systematic Literature Review' (December 2016) 16(1):2 BMC International Health and Human Rights   <www.researchgate.net/publication/290479604_Access_to_health_services_by_lesbian_gay_bisexual_and_transgender_persons_systematic_literature_review> accessed 5 July 2020.

cultural rights,[88] which includes the consultation with, and inclusion of, same-sex partners in health-related decision-making or recognition by health insurance companies.

Even where laws and policies do not explicitly discriminate, and even where anti-discrimination provisions exist, health workers often lack basic information or training about specific health needs and concerns, and appropriate medical and counselling practices. Internationally very few medical curricula, health standards and professional training programmes have incorporated a comprehensive approach to LGBT health care. Health care providers may have an inadequate understanding of specific health needs and hold inappropriate assumptions about causes of health conditions faced by people of diverse sexualities and genders.

LGBT-sensitive health care institutions and personnel are scarce, and people often have to travel long distances to find clinics that can provide appropriate and comprehensive care.

IV.   THE DYNAMICS OF INCLUSION

Certain premises underlie successful measures of social inclusion. First and foremost, it must be acknowledged that, by their very existence and like every human being, lesbian, gay, bisexual, trans or gender diverse persons make a significant contribution to the social fabric. Second is the conviction that fulfilment of the aspirations of these persons, which derive from orientations and identities that are inherent to them, are not only a value deserving of support but the key to enriching their contributions to society. *Contrario sensu*, being compelled to conceal one's true identity and the connected desires and aspirations holds no redeeming social value and must therefore not be encouraged by any societal norm.

Across the world, State and non-State entities are designing and implementing creative strategies and frameworks to promote social inclusion of LGBT people. This is a complex task that must take into account the multidimensional and intersectional nature of discrimination and violence.

A.   Decriminalization

Social inclusion requires dismantling and reforming the legal and policy frameworks that support criminal persecution on the basis of sexual orientation and gender identity using the authority of the State. A similar situation occurs with legislation that has the intent or the consequence to criminalize trans or gender diverse persons, such as laws penalizing cross-dressing or establishing certain forms of gender expression as transgressive to morality.[89]

Repealing or amending laws that directly or indirectly criminalize or otherwise discriminate against persons on the basis of SOGI can have an immediate impact on the lived realities of LGBT people, including on their right to liberty and security, on their mental and physical health, and in terms of changing societal norms and perceptions.

Concomitantly, States have the obligation to adopt legislation and other relevant measures to redress systemic socio-economic marginalization and fulfil the State's duty 'to provide access to gender recognition in a manner consistent with the rights to freedom from discrim-

---

[88]   CESCR, 'Concluding Observations on the Fifth Periodic Report of Italy' (28 October 2015) UN Doc E/C.12/ITA/CO/5 para 17.

[89]   UNGA (n 77) para 26.

ination, equal protection of the law, privacy, identity and freedom of expression',[90] as failure to do so is at the root of denial of the right to health; discrimination, exclusion and bullying in education contexts;[91] discrimination in employment;[92] housing and access to social security. This includes affordable, accessible and simple legal gender recognition laws that do not impose abusive requirements, and measures to recognize relationships between people of the same sex/gender.

B.   Anti-discrimination Legislation

SOGI-inclusive anti-discrimination provisions are key to achieving parity in a number of contexts, from education, to housing, to employment, to medical care, to political expression. International human rights standards contain guarantees of equal access to the law and equal protection before the law without discrimination of any kind, as well as equal access to remedy for violations of rights. Most countries have constitutions and legislation that prohibit discrimination on broad grounds, many include specific protections on the basis of sex/gender,[93] and a handful extend explicit protections on grounds of sexual orientation and gender identity.[94] The Constitution of Fiji for example, protects against discrimination on the grounds of sexual orientation, gender identity and gender expression. The constitutions of Bolivia, Cuba and Malta include provisions on sexual orientation and gender identity, and those of South Africa and Ecuador protect on grounds of sexual orientation.

The explicit inclusion of SOGI as grounds for protection in anti-discrimination laws, including those on employment,[95] housing and social security, is an important step in setting a clear standard from which sectors can operate. For example, in Botswana, the Employment Amendment Act explicitly prohibits discrimination in the workplace on the basis of, inter alia, sexual orientation;[96] Georgia's anti-discrimination law explicitly prohibits discrimination on grounds of sexual orientation, gender identity and expression,[97] and Fiji's employment law prohibits discrimination based on sexual orientation in respect of recruitment, training, promotion, terms and conditions of employment, termination of employment or other matters arising out of the employment relationship.[98]

A number of countries, mostly across Western and Eastern Europe, have passed non-discrimination laws barring housing discrimination on the basis of sexual orientation. A handful of States, including Hungary and the UK, also protect against housing discrimination on the basis of gender identity. Modest but steadfast progress has been made at the

---

[90] ibid para 21.

[91] UNESCO 2016 (n 20).

[92] CESCR (n 41) para 20.

[93] Indonesian National Commission on Violence against Women, Submission (n 1) 1.

[94] Eastern European Coalition for LGBT+ Equality, Submission (n 1) 22; Australia, Submission (n 1) 3; Malta, Submission (n 1) 4; Advocate of the principle of Equality in Slovenia, Submission (n 1) 4.

[95] ILGA (n 33).

[96] International Commission of Jurists (ICJ), 'Botswana SOGI Legislation Country Report (2013)' <www.icj.org/sogi-legislative-database/botswana-sogi-legislation-country-report-2013/> accessed 6 July 2020.

[97] UNGA, 'Visit to Georgia' (15 May 2019) UN Doc A/HRC/41/45/Add.1 para 13.

[98] Pacific Islands Legal Information Institute, 'Employment Relations Promulgation 2007' <www .paclii.org/fj/promu/promu_dec/erp2007381/> accessed 6 July 2020.

local level in some States, or at the level of administrative guidelines. In the Philippines, an anti-discrimination ordinance in Quezon City prohibits discrimination based on sexual orientation, gender identity and gender expression in access to accommodation, while in Indonesia police regulations prescribe the obligation not to discriminate on the basis of a series of grounds that include sexual orientation.[99] In Slovenia the Municipality of Ljubljana developed an LGBT friendly certificate to be awarded on a regular basis to public and private institutions that undergo awareness-raising activities in order to provide for inclusive environments.[100]

Legislative measures of inclusion work best as part of a comprehensive State policy to address discrimination and violence. In this vein, Uruguay has enacted important norms to recognize the rights of same-sex couples and LGBT families, as well as legal recognition of gender identity.[101] The Mexican Social Security Institute issued an interpretation of article 84, paragraphs III and IV of the Social Security Law, to extend the benefits in case of illness and maternity insurance to the spouse of the insured pensioner, regardless of whether it is a marriage between persons of the same sex.[102] In Sweden, LGBT persons and same-sex couples are entitled to the same social protection and benefits as anybody else.[103]

Recognition of the particularities of LGBT peoples' needs, including in relationship recognition, must be extended to social security protections, benefits and pensions. However, it is essential that social security and protection measures do not treat LGBT people as a homogenous group, but rather consider the intersecting barriers they might face, including inter alia grounds of race, age, social status, place of origin and migration status. For example, shelters or programmes working with LGBT people must take into account how these persons, groups and populations are made vulnerable on intersecting grounds.

C.   Political Participation

LGBT people should feel encouraged and empowered to safely participate in government processes. This will not only enrich general perspectives but will permit the State to better identify, understand and remedy the ways in which sexual orientation and gender identity affect socio-economic marginalization in specific national, regional, cultural or social contexts. By engaging with a diverse spectrum of LGBT people representing different age groups, occupations, migrant status and livelihoods, policy makers can develop an intersectional understanding of how LGBT people are differently trapped in cycles of discrimination, pathologization, criminalization and poverty. Inclusion measures should be guided to the extent possible by a nuanced understanding of how LGBT people face marginalization on the basis of sexual orientation and/or gender identity and are affected as a result of intersecting factors. For

---

[99]   Indonesian National Commission on Violence against Women, Submission (n 1) 1.

[100]   Advocate of the principle of Equality in Slovenia, Submission (n 1) 15.

[101]   Law 18246 (2007), which recognizes same-sex couples; the modification of provisions referring to adoption, protecting and equalizing the rights of sons and daughters of LGBT families by allowing joint adoption by cohabiting couples through Law 18.590 (2009) Childhood and Adolescence Code; Law 18.620 (2009) on the Right to Gender Identity and the Change of Name and Sex in Identifying Documents, which allows trans persons to obtain a document consistent with their gender identity; Law 19.076 (2013) on Equal Marriage, which recognizes the right of same-sex couples to enter into marriage on equal terms with heterosexual couples.

[102]   Mexico, Submission (n 1) 4.

[103]   Sweden, Submission (n 1) 2.

instance, to inform its LGBTI+ National Youth Strategy 2018, Ireland consulted almost 4000 young people from across the country through an online survey and several consultations.[104]

Studies concerning political participation of LGBT persons have identified six types of measures that can be taken to promote better participation in government and access to public service: (1) strengthening the rights-based approach of electoral legislation; (2) implementing mechanisms to monitor the respect of rights; (3) adopting measures to eliminate prejudice from political organizations and the media; (4) promoting awareness of the human rights of LGBT persons by public officers; (5) investing in research and data concerning LGBT persons; and (6) promoting inclusion by explicitly including LGBT persons in the statutes and policies of political parties.

In this and all areas of social life, the safe and secure gathering and analysis of knowledge and data on the lived realities of LGBT people provides key guidance in identifying where legal and policy measures are necessary. Empowered, active and diverse LGBT individuals and groups are invaluable contributors in the process of identifying priorities and curating effective responses that can reach the most marginalized.

As a matter of due diligence, States should also work to ensure safe and enabling environments for civil society and human rights defenders, and meaningful consultation with civil society and community groups should be a starting point for any and all measures undertaken. It is likely that community groups will have provided social and economic support to LGBT people in need. Some may have undertaken some form of documentation, and many will have an informed understanding of the core concerns at hand. For example, in developing legislation impacting LGBT people in Malta, the government established an Advisory Council on LGBT Affairs, an independent consultative body comprised of local LGBT civil society representatives. The Council was tasked with drafting and reviewing legislation impacting LGBT people, allowing those most affected to directly influence policy development.[105] Similarly, Ecuador has taken measures to ensure thorough inclusion of LGBT civil society in the development and implementation of its Comprehensive Public Policy for LGBTI People 2014–2017, including through meetings in different regions of the country.[106]

LGBT representation need not be limited to community organizations. Comprehensive social and political inclusion should see the participation of, among others, LGBT health professionals, teachers, government representatives, members of parliament, police officers and union representatives. For example, the United Kingdom's Department for Education has established regional Equality and Diversity hubs that include and fund projects supporting and encouraging the visibility of LGBT teachers in the workplace and in the wider community,[107] and the New Zealand Council of Trade Unions has established an Out@Work network, which is an LGBT union for members.[108]

This level of participation can be reflected also in community service performed by LGBT persons, a field of action that allows those who so choose to contribute actively to the society.

---

[104]   Ireland, Submission (n 1) 2.
[105]   Malta, Submission (n 1) 3.
[106]   Ecuador, Submission (n 1) 1.
[107]   UK, Submission (n 1) 4.
[108]   New Zealand Council of Trade Unions, 'Out at Work Council' <www.union.org.nz/outatwork/> accessed 6 July 2020.

The National Human Rights Commission of India cites the recruitment of trans persons as civic police volunteers to manage traffic in Delhi as good practice in this connection.[109]

D.   Public Policy

The importance of effective public policy is evident in all sectors, including education. A main feature of successful education policy is its holistic nature; for example, the organization CHOICE calls for a 'sexual health framework that bridges relationship education, sex education, and dating violence' as an effective approach to improve sexual health among LGBT youth.[110] The Netherlands adopted a comprehensive national policy approach in the field of education consisting of an anti-discrimination law, action plan, inclusive national curricula, transgender recognition, data collection on bullying, support systems, information and guidelines, and partnerships with non-governmental organizations.[111] Malta adopted measures to tackle discrimination in education settings, including a policy on inclusive education, a policy to address bullying which is inclusive of homophobic and transphobic bullying, the development of a teacher training module, training to the National Student Support Service professionals on LGBT issues in education, and the introduction of inclusive books.[112]

The work of national leaders in adopting effective anti-discrimination measures is key. A number of States have adopted strategies and action plans to tackle discrimination and promote equality for LGBT persons.[113] In Australia, the government-funded Black Rainbow program supports health care settings in becoming more culturally responsive to the Indigenous LGBT community. As part of Australia's Reconnect program, specialist services are provided for LGBT young people and their families who are homeless or at risk of homelessness.[114]

Affirmative measures have a place. In the province of Buenos Aires in Argentina, the legislature passed Law 14.783, establishing a quota for trans persons in workspaces,[115] and in Uruguay the State conducted a pilot program on reintegration of trans people into secondary education, including by covering the cost of materials and travel.[116]

Similarly, programmes working with older persons should be equipped to support older LGBT individuals who have likely faced a lifetime of exclusion and marginalization at both social and economic levels and who may have little to no family support and low income. For example, Australia has launched the Aged Care Diversity Framework aimed at embodying diversity in the design and delivery of aged care services and has developed an action plan to target the particular barriers and challenges faced by older LGBT people.[117]

States have a leadership role to play in influencing cultural shifts, changing negative perceptions, bias and misconceptions around sexual and gender diversity, and dismantling rigid and patriarchal gender norms. While repealing discriminatory laws and adopting inclusive

---

[109] National Human Rights Commission of India, Submission (n 1) 1.
[110] CHOICE, Submission (n 1) 2.
[111] The Netherlands, Submission (n 1) 1.
[112] Malta, Submission (n 1) 2.
[113] Bosnia and Herzegovina, Submission (n 1) 8; Ireland, Submission (n 1) 1; Malta, Submission (n 1) 1.
[114] Australia, Submission (n 1) 5.
[115] Federal Public Defender of Argentina, Submission (n 1) 2.
[116] Uruguay, Submission (n 1) 20.
[117] Australia, Submission (n 1) 7.

legislation and policy are welcome steps, undertaking public awareness and sensitization campaigns can cement the likelihood of enthusiastic implementation. For example, between 2015 and 2017 the Slovenian Ministry of Labour, Family, Social Affairs and Equal Opportunities, together with the NGO Legebitra and the Faculty of Arts at the University of Ljubljana, implemented the project DARE ('Dare to Care About Equality') aimed at improving social attitudes towards LGBT persons, disseminating information on equality and non-discrimination, and developing monitoring mechanisms on non-discrimination and equality-promotion policies.

V.   CONCLUSION: THE PRICE THAT IS PAID BY LGBT PERSONS WHO LIVE OPENLY – SOCIO-ECONOMIC EXCLUSION

To advance the elimination of poverty, lesbian, gay, bisexual, trans and gender diverse persons must have full access to their human rights and be protected from violence and discrimination. Where data exists, the evidence suggests that marginalization is part of a vicious cycle that gives rise to other problems; when access to economic, social and cultural rights is hampered, a serious negative impact on individuals, their families and communities can be observed, resulting in cycles of poverty and exclusion, limiting access to assets that are essential to social mobility and shared prosperity and creating further vulnerability to discrimination and other forms of violence.

The individual dimensions of exclusion compound themselves in exclusion of communities and peoples and ultimately will undermine social progress.

The atmosphere that excludes people from the sociocultural environment inevitably exacerbates violence and discrimination, as it creates an inequality of opportunity and thus detrimentally limits one's ability to both contribute to and access the benefits of sustainable development.

Poverty, homelessness and food insecurity are higher among LGBT individuals than in the wider community, a situation that bears direct relation with SDGs 1, 8, 10 and 11, the targets of which include equal rights to economic resources and access to basic services, and which demand from States the creation of sound policy frameworks based on gender-sensitive development strategies.

The criminalization of sexual and gender diversity and the pathologization and demonization of orientations and identities seen as transgressive of desirable norms – arbitrarily established – shape perceptions, reactions, practices and policies in all sectors of society. It creates obstacles in access to the health sector, exclusion from quality education as a result of harassment, violent abuse and desertion rates, limitations to adequate housing, and significant barriers to employment. This, in turn, deepens exclusion from economic opportunities.

Legislative, administrative and judicial responses are required from State actors to urgently address these determinants of social exclusion, and they must be built on 'high-quality, timely and reliable data disaggregated by income, gender, age, race, ethnicity, migratory status, disability, geographic location and other characteristics relevant in national contexts', and data collection and management systems compliant with human rights standards and guarantees.

During my 2018 country visit to Mozambique, a member of the LGBT community noted that '[t]he whole system is designed to exclude lesbian, gay, bisexual and trans people. There is no widespread violence against [them], but [we] are subjected to exclusion, poverty and psychological violence ... The wounds of the soul do not heal, and they have a negative lifelong impact'.[118] All around the world, the price that has been paid by generations of LGBT and gender diverse persons is that of the full exploration of their potential and a condemnation to poverty. The achievements of the LGBT movement in the last 50 years have demonstrated that social change is possible, with significant results in relatively short time; it is now only a question of ensuring its continued momentum.

---

[118]   HRC (n 68) para 44.

12. Assessing racialized poverty: the case of Romani people in the European Union

Margareta Matache and Simona Barbu

"Widespread deprivation is destroying Roma lives [in the EU]. Families are living excluded from society in shocking conditions, while children with little education face bleak prospects for the future," concludes a 2016 report by the European Union Agency for Fundamental Rights (FRA).[1]

Poverty is racialized in the European Union (EU). The Gross Domestic Product (GDP) of the European Union is the second largest in the world.[2] Yet, an average 80 percent of the Roma[3] people interviewed in an FRA study live below the at-risk-of-poverty threshold, compared to an average 17 percent of the dominant majority populations in each respective country.[4] This indicator signals not only income poverty, but more so, injustice and inequality.

With an estimated population of 10–12 million in Europe, of which around six million live in the EU, Roma are the largest minority of the European continent.[5]

International and national institutions operate with somewhat rigid but easily assessible frameworks, such as a multidimensional poverty index or an absolute poverty measurement, which enable these institutions to measure poverty comparatively. In this chapter, we discuss the extent of Romani poverty by using basic approaches to multidimensional poverty, including economic well-being, capabilities, and social inclusion. However, we see the need for more nuanced approaches that can capture additional determinants and dimensions of Romani poverty. We argue that poverty policy and research agendas must include justice and human-rights approaches if we are to adequately understand and address anti-Roma racism as well as the denial of social and economic rights. This is true not only at the individual level, but also for neighborhoods and communities.

---

[1] "80% of Roma are at Risk of Poverty, New Survey Finds" (*European Union Agency for Fundamental Rights (FRA)*, 26 November 2016) <https://fra.europa.eu/en/press-release/2016/80-roma -are-risk-poverty-new-survey-finds> accessed 10 June 2020.

[2] Abby Budiman and Dorothy Manevich, "Few See EU as World's Top Economic Power Despite its Relative Might" (*Pew Research Center: FactTank*, 9 August 2019) <www.pewresearch.org/fact-tank/ 2017/08/09/few-see-eu-as-worlds-top-economic-power-despite-its-relative-might/> accessed 10 June 2020; 'GDP (current US$) – European Union, United States, China' (*The World Bank*). <https://data .worldbank.org/indicator/NY.GDP.MKTP.CD?locations=EU-US-CN> accessed 10 June 2020.

[3] The term "Roma" used at the Council of Europe refers to Roma, Sinti, Kale, and related groups in Europe, including Travellers and the Eastern groups (Dom and Lom). It covers the wide diversity of the groups concerned, including persons who identify themselves as Gypsies.

[4] "80% of Roma are at Risk of Poverty" (n 1).

[5] European Union Agency for Fundamental Rights, "The situation of Roma in 11 EU Member States – Survey results at a glance" *(Publications Office of the European Union, 2012)* <https://fra .europa.eu/en/publication/2012/situation-roma-11-eu-member-states-survey-results-glance> accessed 19 June 2020.

As researchers have already shown, income poverty provides a necessary but insufficient picture of poverty,[6] especially, in the case of historically oppressed and racialized peoples. Moreover, even a broad concept of economic well-being does not encompass the complex dimensions of racialized poverty and structural inequalities that the vast majority of Roma living in the EU face. Furthermore, anti-Roma racism, tied with the legacy of gadjo[7] economic, political, and cultural power, undermines Roma justice and their prospect to access fundamental rights and freedoms. These factors affect the job opportunities, incomes, dignity, and well-being of Romani people. Racism influences the way Roma respond and adapt, socially and collectively, to poverty or injustice.

To address the limitations of the traditional meaning of poverty, scholars have suggested a multidimensional approach to poverty as a more ample framework. This builds on the United Nations' Multidimensional Poverty Index, which encompasses three dimensions: standard of living, health, and education.[8] However, even such multiplex frameworks cannot encompass the legacy of oppression and the collective nature of racialized poverty and its determinants in racially segregated Romani neighborhoods and not only. Nor can they account for the overt and covert social and economic constraints facing individuals born in racialized neighborhoods: namely inadequate common resources, environmental injustice, and social isolation, among others. Moreover, the multidimensional approach fails to address wealth inequality[9] at either the family or group level, which is another phenomenon generated and perpetuated by the history of structural racism and economic exploitation from one generation to another in some countries of the EU. An example is the radical inequality[10] and economic and cultural exploitation that occurred in the cases of the Roma enslavement in Romania.

Therefore in this chapter we discuss poverty through the connected lens of human rights-based approaches, structural injustice and racism, the wealth gap, and poor neighborhoods, which together contribute to the racialized poverty of Romani families. We call for a focus on various axes of racism (e.g., ideological, institutional, interpersonal) and injustice, intergenerational wealth, and racially segregated neighborhoods as fundamental elements in the research and policy agendas focusing on racialized poverty in the case of the Roma.

---

[6] Dorata Weziak-Bialowolska and Lewis Dijkstra, *Monitoring Mulidimensional Poverty in the Regions of the European Union* (Publications Office of the European Union 2014) <https://publications .jrc.ec.europa.eu/repository/bitstream/JRC89430/mpi_report_online.pdf> accessed 10 June 2020.

[7] This term means "non-Roma" in Romani. Unlike Roma/Sinti/Kale, the term does not denote a people. This is the name which Roma apply to those outside their community, according to "Council of Europe Descriptive Glossary of Terms Relating to Roma Issues" (*Council of Europe*, 2012) <http://a .cs.coe.int/team20/cahrom/documents/Glossary%20Roma%20EN%20version%2018%20May%202012 .pdf> accessed 10 June 2020.

[8] "What is the Multidimensional Poverty Index" (*UNDP*) <http://hdr.undp.org/en/content/what -multidimensional-poverty-index> accessed 10 June 2020.

[9] Defined as "accumulated assets owned by households" and "ensures that privilege and advantage are passed down from generation to generation." "Falling Through the Cracks: Exposing Inequalities in the EU and Beyond" (*SDG Watch Europe, Make Europe Sustainable for All, and Faces of Inequality*, July 2019) <www.sdgwatcheurope.org/wp-content/uploads/2019/06/FALLING-THROUGH-THE -CRACKS-JUNE-2019.pdf> accessed 10 June 2020.

[10] Thomas Pogge, "Poverty and Human Rights" (*OHCHR*) <www2.ohchr.org/english/issues/ poverty/expert/docs/Thomas_Pogge_Summary.pdf> accessed 10 June 2020.

I.   MEASURING POVERTY

Rather than grasping the full implications of wealth or poverty, the at-risk-of-poverty rate merely measures low income.[11] While a wide range of critiques have pointed out its limitations,[12] income remains an important indicator of poverty, as households living under the at-risk-of-poverty threshold lack, at least momentarily, the material means for a minimal level of well-being, access to education, or access to healthcare. Income poverty also stands as a critical indicator in measuring income inequality. It can help us to tackle wage gaps and advance economic justice.

Among Roma in the EU, the at-risk-of-poverty rate remains very high; in 2016 the Fundamental Rights Agency (FRA) measured it at 80 percent, a decrease of only 6 percent from 2011.[13] However, this decrease was only observed in a few countries (the Czech Republic, Hungary, and Romania). In contrast, in most of the countries that the FRA surveyed in 2016, the percentage of Roma considered to be at risk of poverty had increased compared to 2011. In some countries, the percentage came close to 100 percent. In Spain it was 98 percent, up from 90 percent in 2011 (general population 22 percent). In Greece it was 96 percent, up from 83 percent (general population 21 percent). And in Croatia it was 93 percent, up from 92 percent (general population 20 percent). Such consistent and dramatic differences between the Romani and non-Romani populations point to racial inequality and injustice: the at-risk-of-poverty rate for the general population in the EU is still somewhere between 10 percent (2011) and 25 percent (2016).

Still, income poverty varies in intensity, incidence, and severity.[14] For instances, there are differences between those living below that threshold for one year and those who have been living in poverty for a longer period. Aiming to address the extent of poverty, the persistent at-risk-of-poverty rate measures one factor: the equivalized disposable income during the current and the previous three years.[15] Here we encounter a difficulty: there is no disaggregated data on ethnicity, as the European Union Statistics on Income and Living Conditions (EU-SILC) pointed out: "there is no information on ethnic status of respondents. So ethnic minorities, including the Roma, cannot be identified in EU-SILC."[16] Nevertheless, we know that the persistent at-risk-of-poverty rate is "the share of people who are currently poor and had also been poor for two out of three years prior to the survey."[17] We also know that, according

---

[11]   "Glossary: At-risk-of-poverty Rate" (*European Council: Eurostat*) <https://ec.europa.eu/eurostat/statistics-explained/index.php/Glossary: At-risk-of-poverty_rate> accessed 10 June 2020.

[12]   Starting with Amartya Sen in 1976. Amartya Sen, "Poverty: An Ordinal Approach to Measurement" (1976) 44 Econometrica 219.

[13]   European Union Agency for Fundamental Rights (FRA), Second European Union Minorities and Discrimination Survey: Roma – Selected Findings (FRA, 2016) <https://fra.europa.eu/sites/default/files/fra_uploads/fra-2016-eu-minorities-survey-roma-selected-findings_en.pdf> accessed 10 June 2020.

[14]   Nanak Kakwani and Jacques Silber (eds), *The Many Dimensions of Poverty* (Palgrave Macmillan 2013).

[15]   "Glossary: At-risk-of-poverty Rate" (n 11).

[16]   "EU Statistics on Income and Living Conditions (EU-SILC) Methodology – Definition of Dimensions" (*European Council: Eurostat*) <https://ec.europa.eu/eurostat/statistics-explained/index.php/EU_statistics_on_income_and_living_conditions_(EU-SILC)_methodology_-_definition_of_dimensions> accessed 10 June 2020.

[17]   Eurostat, *Smarter, Greener, More Inclusive? Indicators to Support the Europe 2020 Strategy* (European Union 2016) <https://ec.europa.eu/eurostat/documents/3217494/7566774/KS-EZ-16-001-EN-N.pdf > accessed 19 June 2020.

to the FRA, 80 percent of the EU Roma participating in their study were living at that level from 2011 to 2016. Thus, we can speculate that many of the Romani individuals and families who were poor in 2011 remained poor five years later and have been consistently living at risk of poverty.

Seasonal poverty, or the temporary lack of a minimal income, due for instance to a factory closure, has different consequences—and requires different solutions—than having been born into or living much longer in poverty. This is what David Hulme and Andy McKay call chronic poverty. It is clearly explained by a woman from Entropole, Bulgaria in a World Bank study: "[i]f we knew that there would be an end to this crisis, we would endure it somehow. Be it for one year, or even for 10 years. But now all we can do is sit and wait for the end to come."[18]

Whatever the factors that drive chronic poverty, some dutybearers in charge of welfare— like those in the larger society—tend to see two separate categories: the "deserving" and "undeserving" poor. Somehow, often, those who belong to an oppressed group and are also born into poverty or living in poverty for a longer time are seen and portrayed as "lazy" and "guilty" of their inability to overcome their destitution.

Consider on the other hand those who live momentarily under that income poverty threshold, but have accumulated intergenerational wealth, such as land and other assets, are politically or civically engaged, and benefit from indiscriminate access to good schools and quality health services for their families. Those people may employ and require different responses and solutions than those who are deprived simultaneously of intergenerational wealth and of most of their basic rights for an extended period due to their skin colour, Romani backgrounds, or other factors. Taking the example of Romania, the Romani people were stripped of any prospect of accumulated intergenerational wealth by a history of 500 years of economic exploitation through enslavement of the Roma, which lasted until 1856. Such a history of oppression leads not only to the oppressed being deprived of their rights but, as Thomas Pogge points out, also to a "huge inherited advantage in power" for the descendants of the oppressors.[19] Such inherited power continues to have an impact economically, socially, culturally, and ideologically, including in the form of white/gadjo normativity. The narratives, the policies, and the so-called "moral" justifications for the deprivation of minority groups, such as the Roma, are created and imposed ideologically, legally, and practically by the oppressors themselves or their descendants. At the same time, disempowerment forces members of the oppressed groups to identify individual and "collective strategies"[20] as well as social and "cultural adaptations"[21] to respond to racism and the white/gadjo norms.

Unjust wages are another important aspect to consider in looking at income poverty. When those in some job categories, such as teachers or custodial staff, have to work additional jobs to survive, it is not just a matter of low income, but also a matter of unjust pay. They may not

---

[18]   Deepa Narayan and others, *Voices of the Poor: Crying Out for Change* (OUP and The World Bank 2000) 46 <http://documents.worldbank.org/curated/en/501121468325204794/pdf/multi0page .pdf> accessed 11 June 2020.

[19]   Pogge (n 10).

[20]   Edna A Viruell-Fuentes, Patricia Y Miranda, and Sawsan Abdulrahim, "More than Culture: Structural Racism, Intersectionality Theory, and Immigrant Health" (2012) 75 Social Science & Medicine 2099.

[21]   William Julius Wilson, "Toward a Framework for Understanding Forces That Contribute to or Reinforce Racial Inequality" (2009) 1 Race and Social Problems 3.

be counted as poor based on their monthly income but they can only increase their income by submitting themselves to exhaustion, and thus to poor health and well-being outcomes.

Finally, those who lack identity documents face an even more dreadful situation as they are not even counted. For example, in 2012, in Timisoara, Romania, up to 20,000 people, predominantly Roma, lacked identity papers. In the Kuncz neighborhood alone, 250 people did not legally exist and consequently could not obtain child benefits, health care, or welfare support. According to mass media reports, "they don't have money even for bread, so from where would they have money to start the necessary processes for establishing and 'recovering' their identities?"[22] Nevertheless, in 2019 the Romanian Parliament initiated discussions regarding legislation that would for a minimum provide health care and access to education for children regardless of their documentation status.[23,24] The legislative acts made access to health and education non-dependent on the existence of an official registration of children, removing, at least on paper, one of the challenges that Roma face.

These examples prove once again that poverty is not just about income, and more importantly, the solutions are not just about jobs. As Alicia Ely Yamin and Paul Farmer put it, "the traditional view of poverty did not consider context or ability to convert income into access to food, education, housing, and health care."[25]

In the past few decades, researchers have shifted more toward exploring and measuring the multidimensionality of poverty, an encouraging direction but one that involves several challenges. Even experts from similar disciplines do not agree on the dimensions and the indicators to be measured.[26] Despite discussions about the multidimensionality of poverty, an interdisciplinary approach to measuring and addressing poverty has not become a broad reality. As Amartya Sen argues, it is hard

> to have an adequate understanding of the turmoil in the suburbs of Paris and other French cities in the autumn of 2005 only in terms of poverty and deprivation, without bringing in race and immigration. It would be similarly unsatisfactory to try to base a causal explanation only on race and immigration, without bringing in inequality and economic disparity.[27]

Moreover, the more dimensions we measure, the less comparative data (using similar methodologies or cross-national indicators) we can collect. Additionally, to measure capabilities and social inclusion, qualitative indicators and data are also necessary, and that presents a chal-

---

[22]   "They Live, but Do Not Exist! We Have Almost 20,000 People Without Identity in Timisoara" (*OpiniaTimisoarei*, 3 August 2012) <www.opiniatimisoarei.ro/traiesc-dar-nu-exista-avem-aproape-20 -000-de-oameni-fara-identitate-in-timisoara/03/08/2012> accessed 11 June 2020. The original text in Romanian: "nu au bani nici de paine, daramite pentru deschiderea proceselor de stabilire si 'recuperare' a identitatilor."

[23]   "Free Access to Medical Services for Children Without CNP" (*Formare Medicala*, 19 September 2020) <www.formaremedicala.ro/acces-gratuit-la-servicii-medicale-pentru-copiii-fara-cnp/> accessed 11 June 2020.

[24]   The initiative regarding access to health care was approved by issuing Law no. 186 for amending and supplementing Law no. 95/2006 regarding the reform in the field of health and for the completion of the Law of patient rights no. 46/2003, while access to education was ensured through Decree no. 833/2019 of the President of Romania.

[25]   Alicia Ely Yamin, *Power, Suffering, and the Struggle for Dignity: Human Rights Frameworks for Health and Why They Matter* (University of Pennsylvania Press 2017) 68.

[26]   Kakwani and Silber (n 14).

[27]   Amartya Sen, "Violence, Identity and Poverty" (2008) 45 JPR 5, 15.

lenge to consistency, comparisons, and data collection. "People, for example, may have either access to electricity or no access or they may be in a good health condition or not. How much better health condition is needed to undo the lack of access to electricity and vice versa?" asks Udaya R. Wagle, who analyzed qualitative indicators of multidimensional poverty.[28] Also, in the case of racialized poverty measures, legal challenges arise, as some countries' laws do not allow the collection of disaggregated ethnic data. Moreover, measuring racialized poverty requires an exploration of past and current structural racial injustices; it also requires a focus on the enablers of injustices, an intersectional approach, and a critical view of the norms and structures they have imposed based on their own realities, experiences, norms, standards, and interests.

II.   ROMA MULTIDIMENSIONAL POVERTY: DATA

Multidimensional poverty has proved to be a more powerful framework than income poverty. For instance, when poverty is conceptualized through economic well-being, it adds the concepts of consumption and welfare to income: "consumption of food, clothing, shelter and other basic necessities—such as being able to afford adequate healthcare and being in good health."[29] The United Nations Multidimensional Poverty Index looks at poverty in education, health, and living standards as critical dimensions in measuring multidimensional poverty.

What we notice is that when we move beyond income and extend our analysis to other indicators and dimensions, the nature of poverty and inequalities between Roma and non-Roma become even more evident, thus the reference to the racialization of poverty.

A.   Racialization of Poverty and the Multidimensional Approach

In the case of the Romani people in the EU, the FRA found that 30 percent of Romani children live in houses where someone went to bed hungry at least once during the month before the survey was conducted.[30] Also, 17 percent of the Roma in Croatia, 13 percent of those in Greece, and 11 percent of those in Hungary reported that they went to bed hungry. Moreover, according to a study of the European Commission across the Member States, 38 percent of the interviewed Roma were malnourished, compared to 5 percent among non-Roma.[31] At the same time, the food Roma consume is not the healthiest, as they eat fewer vegetables and less nutritious, higher fat foods. This leads to obesity and health problems.[32] A study published in 2018 by the European Commission, based on data collected in Romania between 2004 and

---

[28]   Udaya R Wagle, "The Counting-Based Measurement of Multidimensional Poverty: The Focus on Economic Resources, Inner Capabilities, and Relational Resources in the United States" (2014) 115 Soc Indic Res 223, 227.

[29]   Weziak-Bialowolska and Dijkstra (n 6) (citing Wagle and Boulanger et al.).

[30]   FRA (n 13).

[31]   Matrix, *Roma Health Report: Health Status of the Roma Population: Data Collection in the Member States of the European Union* (European Commission 2014) <https://publications.europa.eu/en/publication-detail/-/publication/61505667-ec87-4a71-ba4f-845a4a510e11/language-en/format-PDF/source-105528596> accessed 25 September 2019.

[32]   ibid.

2011, shows that "Roma have inferior diet diversity compared to the non-Roma."[33] The main factors limiting food consumption options are socio-economic factors and the discrimination Roma face in the labor market. The marginalization and segregation that Romani communities experience influence their access to diverse, sufficient, and good quality food.

Clothing is also an issue for the Roma, especially when they are preparing their children for school; teachers often ask for specific clothes or equipment, which can be expensive. This situation has been observed among Romani families in the UK,[34] as well as in Romania.[35]

The FRA EU Midis II study of 2016 also shows that 30 percent of the Roma in the EU countries surveyed live in households with no tap water and 46 percent have no indoor toilet, shower, or bathroom.[36] In all of the countries surveyed, the FRA researchers also noticed insufficient personal space at home. The average number of rooms per person in a Romani household is half that for the majority population.[37] Twice as many Romani families compared to the majority population have to squeeze into fewer heated rooms during the winter.[38]

In the nine countries the FRA surveyed, the Romani people interviewed are connected in general to electricity, but their living standards are still lower than those of the general population. In Romania, 68 percent of Roma live in households without tap water inside their dwelling; for the general population the percentage is 38 percent. In Hungary, the percentage is 33 percent for Roma, while the entire general population is connected to the water network.[39]

The percentages are even higher for Roma who do not have a toilet or a bathroom inside the house: 41 percent in Croatia, 44 percent in Bulgaria, and 79 percent in Romania.[40] For the general population, this percentage is highest in Romania (31 percent) and Bulgaria (12 percent); it is below 4 percent for the other countries.

Looking at the quality of housing, many Roma live in houses where the roof leaks, or where the floor, walls, or foundation are damp or have rot in them; the percentages range from 21 percent in Spain, to 44 percent in Hungary, and 66 percent in Portugal.[41] Of the Roma in Bulgaria, 29 percent did not have a cooking stove in their house, and only 13 percent had access to the internet.[42] Moreover, some 15,000 Roma in France live in the slums and shacks

---

[33]   Pavel Ciaian and others, "Food Consumption and Diet Quality Choices of Roma in Romania: A Counterfactual Analysis" (2018) 10 Food Security 437.

[34]   Brian Foster and Peter Norton, "Educational Equality for Gypsy, Roma and Traveller Children and Young People in the UK" (2012) 8 The Equal Rights Review 85.

[35]   Laura Surdu, Enikö Vincze, and Marius Wamsiedel, *Participation, School, Absenteeism and the Experience of Discrimination in the Case of Roma in Romania* (Unicef and Romani Criss 2011) <www.romanicriss.org/PDF/RC%202011%20-%20Participare,%20absenteism%20scolar%20si%20experienta%20discriminarii%20%28ro%29.pdf> accessed 11 June 2020.

[36]   FRA (n 13).

[37]   ibid 32, figure 16.

[38]   ibid 33, figure 17.

[39]   ibid.

[40]   ibid.

[41]   ibid 35, table 4.

[42]   Andrew Ivanov, Sheena Keller, and Ursula Till-Tentschert, "Roma Poverty and Deprivation: The Need for Multidimensional Anti-Poverty Measures" (2015) Oxford Poverty & Human Development Initiative (OPHI) Working Paper No 96 <https://ophi.org.uk/roma-poverty-and-deprivation-the-need-for-multidimensional-anti-poverty-measures/> accessed 11 June 2020.

on the outskirts of cities;[43] that figure includes an estimated 9,000 children and youth.[44] Other poor Romani families live in overcrowded households, shacks, and on the streets when pursuing better opportunities in EU countries.[45]

Across member states of the EU, some progress has recently been reported in the area of compulsory education for Romani children. Still, Romani children and youth are pushed out of school: seven out of ten Roma aged 18–24 years left school early.[46] At the preschool level, the gap between Roma and non-Roma was still very significant in 2016: 70 percent to 97 percent of non-Romani children aged 6–15 have attended preschool, as opposed to only 20 percent of the Romani children in Greece, and less than 50 percent of those in the Czech Republic, Portugal, Slovakia, and Spain.[47]

Across Europe, Romani people live for up to 20 years less than the general population.[48] In Belgium, the life expectancy of Roma is 55 while the life expectancy of the total population is 81.5[49]; in Romania it is 52.5 years for Roma compared to 68.8 for the majority population.[50]

The situation of the residentially segregated and excluded Roma is much worse; numbers from Slovakia show that mortality is two or three times higher for Roma living in these situations compared to those who are "integrated" living in mixed Romani and non-Romani neighbourhoods.[51] The child mortality rate is also higher for Roma compared to the majority. In Bulgaria, Roma infant mortality is twice as high as that for the general population; in Spain, it is three times that for other groups.[52]

The review of the poverty and inequalities along these multidimensional indicators help to reveal the racial element to poverty.

---

[43]   Myriam Allory, "Roma Children in France: Poor Children in a Rich Country" (Ann Green (trs), *Humanium*, 3 October 2016) <www.humanium.org/en/roma-children-in-france/#content> accessed 11 June 2020.

[44]   Colectif National Droits de l'Homme RomEurope, « Ados en bidonville et en squats: l'école impossible ? – Etude sur la scolarisation des jeunes âgés de 12 à 18 ans » (*RomEurope, 2016*) <http :// romeurope.org/wp-content/uploads/2016/09/etude_cdere_ados_bidonville_ecole_impossible.pdf> accessed 11 June 2020.

[45]   FRA, *A Persisting Concern: Anti-Gypsyism as a Barrier to Roma Inclusion* (Publications Office of the European Union 2018) < https://fra.europa.eu/sites/default/files/fra_uploads/fra-2018-anti-gypsyism -barrier-roma-inclusion_en.pdf> accessed 11 June 2020.

[46]   FRA, *Fundamental Rights Report 2018* (Publications Office of the European Union 2018) <https://fra.europa.eu/sites/default/files/fra_uploads/fra-2018-fundamental-rights-report-2018_en.pdf> accessed 11 June 2020.

[47]   FRA, *Roma survey – Data in Focus: Education: The Situation of Roma in 11 EU Member States* (Publications Office of the European Union 2014) <https://fra.europa.eu/sites/default/files/fra-2014 _roma-survey_education_tk0113748enc.pdf> accessed 11 June 2020.

[48]   Matrix (n 31).

[49]   "Life Expectancy" (*For a Healthy Belgium*, 2018) <www.healthybelgium.be/en/health-status/life -expectancy-and-quality-of-life/life-expectancy> accessed 11 June 2020.

[50]   "Closing the Life Expectancy Gap of Roma in Europe: Roma Health and Early Childhood Development" (*European Public Health Alliance (EPHA)*, December 2018) <https://epha.org/wp -content/uploads/2019/02/closing-the-life-expectancy-gap-of-roma-in-europe-study.pdf> accessed 25 September 2019.

[51]   ibid.

[52]   ibid.

B.   Participation and Political Exclusion

While still recognizing the importance of resources, Amartya Sen argues that it takes more to capture poverty. He conceptualized poverty through the lens of human capabilities to function, focusing on freedom and well-being, and in later studies he included opportunities. These factors essentially set out the human development approach and policy agenda.[53] And some of the poor agree with him. The *Voices* report of the World Bank, which involves people living in poverty in various parts of the world, confirms that the poor seek not only food but also freedom, dignity, voice, and choice.[54] But reports such as *Voices* also raise questions about who should participate in policy and research discussions regarding what poverty is, feels like, and means. All too often, the voices of the poor are utterly ignored.

In measuring Roma poverty specifically, Ivanov and Kagin endorse a human development approach: "[t]he multidimensional nature of Roma poverty calls for a 'human development' approach ... [that can] integrate the reduction of material deprivation with increasing *agency* and the achievement of fundamental civil rights."[55] And indeed, over the past two decades the United Nations Development Program (UNDP) has collected Roma-related data using such an approach. In 2002, the UNDP published the groundbreaking report, *Avoiding the Dependency Trap: The Roma in Central and Eastern Europe*,[56] which showed that Roma were socially, economically, and politically excluded in the five countries they surveyed.

On education, the most severe problem that UNDP found was segregation: on average, 19 percent of the households surveyed reported educational segregation, ranging from 12 percent in the Czech Republic to 27 percent in Bulgaria. Inclusive education, improving access to preschool education, and eliminating extra educational costs to parents (e.g., paying for school textbooks) were identified as mandatory to improve the access of the Roma to education.

The UNDP has also found that informal work was the option available to many Roma in ensuring family income. Overall they found the unemployment rate was 40 percent, less than what was generally estimated. In some countries though, the rate was very high: for example, 64 percent in Slovakia. Roma participating in the study said the main reasons they were not employed were discrimination based on their ethnic background, the general economic depression in the country, and their lack of education.

The survey showed that the health of Roma was deteriorating, with high infant mortality and negative situations for women's health, such as inadequate nutrition or reproductive health. On household income, the report concluded that Roma "often fall into a vicious circle of marginalization."[57] High poverty and low levels of education and employment keep Roma in this

---

[53]   Amartya Sen, *Development as Freedom* (Anchor Books 1999).

[54]   Narayan and others, *Voices of the Poor: Crying Out for Change* (n 18); Deepa Narayan, *Voices of the Poor: Can Anyone Hear Us?* (OUP and the World Bank 2002); Deepa Narayan and Patti Petesch, *Voices of the Poor: From Many Lands* (OUP and the World Bank 2002).

[55]   Andrey Ivanov and Justin Kagin, *Roma Poverty from a Human Development Perspective* (UNDP 2014) 4 (emphasis added) <www.eurasia.undp.org/content/rbec/en/home/library/roma/roma-poverty-human-development-perspective.html> accessed 11 June 2020.

[56]   UNDP, *Avoiding the Dependency Trap: The Roma in Central and Eastern Europe* (United Nations 2002) <http://hdr.undp.org/sites/default/files/avoiding_the_dependency_trap_en.pdf> accessed 11 June 2020.

[57]   ibid.

circle where more than half of their income is directed at obtaining food (e.g., 69 percent for Bulgaria); it also noted the high number of undernourished Romani children.

The UNDP also found that social interaction between Romani and non-Romani communities was usually determined by survival needs but also by children when they played together (the lowest registered percentage for playing together is 51 percent in Hungary). On political participation, it noted the need to involve more Romani representatives at the level of public services. People wished for more contact and more responsibility on the part of those in governmental structures, while they mostly trusted the local structures for help.

Thus, while the report looks at education, employment, health, and household income, it also includes political participation, which Wagle places into a specific dimension of social inclusion. Wagle argues that something "is missing from this operational push." He calls social inclusion, "the relational resource that also has both constitutive and instrumental values in securing well-being."[58] Having the choice to form fair, meaningful, dignified, and unbiased relationships with others can indeed increase social capital and networks; consequently, it opens doors to better jobs, education, and health as well as information, credit, support, and power.[59]

In the case of the Roma, relational resources, in the sense of social interactions and commitments with the majority groups, are often very poor. Despite sporadic improvements in some countries regarding Roma participation in elections, the overall situation remains dire, especially Roma representation on ballots. Mainstream political parties show reluctance to include Romani members on their lists.[60] Romani women are particularly under-represented in political life. Looking at the percentage of Roma among political candidates, we must conclude that the minority is insufficiently represented across Europe: in Spain's municipal elections in 2015, only ten Romani candidates were elected as councilors.[61] However more successfully, in Spain's 2019 Parliamentary election, four Roma were elected, including two women.[62] Latvia had only two Romani candidates in its 2014 parliamentary elections; none took part in the local elections in 2017.[63] The involvement of some Roma in consultative and advisory organizations has become a focus point for the member states in the EU, under the umbrella of the EU Framework for Roma. However, OSCE notes in its Third Status Report, "again, the varied outcomes serve as a reminder that the mere existence of formal consultation mechanisms does not guarantee effective public participation of Roma and Sinti."[64]

---

[58] Wagle (n 28) 228.

[59] ibid.

[60] Alexander Nitzsche (ed), *Annual Report 2013* (OSCE 2013) 51. <www.osce.org/files/f/documents/7/4/116947.pdf> accessed 11 June 2020.

[61] ERTF, "Fact Sheet on the Situation of Roma in Spain", (Strasbourg, January 2016) <www.presenciagitana.org/The_situation_of_Roma_in_Spain_06012016.pdf> accessed 20 June 2020.

[62] Gwendolyn Albert (trs), 'Spain: Two Romani Men and Two Romani Women Elected to National Legislature, an Historic Success' (*Romea*, 4 May 2019) <www.romea.cz/en/news/world/spain-two-romani-men-and-two-romani-women-elected-to-national-legislature-an-historic-success> accessed 11 June 2020.

[63] *Third Status Report: Implementation of the Action Plan on Improving the Situation of Roma and Sinti Within the OSCE Area* (OSCE Office for Democratic Institutions and Human Rights (ODIHR) 2018) <www.osce.org/files/f/documents/6/8/406127.pdf> accessed 11 June 2020.

[64] ibid.

C.   Toward a Roma Multidimensional Index

Finally, to measure Roma poverty specifically, Ivanov, Keller, and Till-Tentschert suggest a Roma Multidimensional Index, which looks at human capabilities (basic rights plus specific dimensions on education and health) and material well-being (housing, standard of living, employment) through twelve indicators. This framework is much more comprehensive and targeted to measuring Roma poverty than the at-risk-of-poverty threshold or the UN Multidimensional Poverty Index.

As these authors show, by using the 12-indicator approach it is possible to differentiate between "multidimensionally poor" and "severe multidimensionally poor."[65] While researchers found some improvement in the share of Romani families across the EU who live in poverty, the "severe poverty" share has only dropped significantly in a non-EU country: Bosnia and Herzegovina.[66]

The "basic rights" dimension developed by Ivanov et al. includes only one indicator of discrimination. The criterion of deprivation and the threshold of this indicator is that the "HH [household] member lives in a HH where a member has been discriminated against while looking for a job."[67] Yet, Ivanov and others also underline that "[u]nemployment, social exclusion, and marginalization are linked with (and mutually reinforcing) discrimination, anti-Gypsyism [anti-Roma racism], limited access to justice, and segregation."[68] And indeed, the inclusion of one single indicator on discrimination, namely discrimination on the job market, is simply not enough.

Non-discrimination in education also constitutes a necessary condition for knowledge and "the realization of other fundamental rights."[69] In 2016, the FRA showed that the percentage of educational segregation for Romani children has increased worryingly from 10 percent in 2011 to 15 percent in 2016 in the countries surveyed.[70] A segregated educational facility for the Roma is usually an institution that focuses on combating illiteracy, not on enhancing children's attainments.

Discrimination in access to health also needs to be measured, for instance, as it affects the chances that Romani women will seek treatment during pregnancy, which lowers life expectancy rates at birth for Romani people. An analysis from 2017 that included Bulgaria and England shows that pregnant Romani women are often denied or given poor treatment at medical facilities; some reported segregation within the hospital, racial slurs, and verbal abuse.[71]

Regardless of how we measure their situation, from economic well-being to human capabilities and relational resources, we cannot avoid finding that the income poverty, as well as the multidimensional poverty of individual Romani people and their households, is much worse than those for the dominant majorities in the EU. Moreover, Roma face a worse situation than their non-Romani peers in terms of access to basic rights such as education, employment,

---

[65]   Ivanov, Keller and Till-Tentschert (n 42).

[66]   ibid.

[67]   ibid.

[68]   Ivanov and Kagin (n 55).

[69]   Ivanov, Keller and Till-Tentschert (n 42) 27.

[70]   FRA, *A Persisting Concern* (n 45).

[71]   Helen L Watson and Soo Downe, "Discrimination Against Childbearing Romani Women in Maternity Care in Europe: A Mixed-Methods Systematic Review" (2017) 14 Reproductive Health 1.

health, and housing. This suggests that discrimination and, more so, structural racism on top of poverty and a worse socio-economic situation compound the problem, resulting in racialized poverty.

Thus, racial inequality persists. And the discrimination against Romani people in the access to fundamental rights intersects tremendously with what we today call poverty. Moreover, as Amartya Sen argues:

> [p]urely economic measures of inequality, such as the Gini coefficient or the ratio of incomes of top and bottom groups, do not bring out the social dimensions of the disparity involved. For example, when the people in the bottom income groups also have different non-economic characteristics, in terms of race (such as being black rather than white), or in immigration status (such as being recent arrivals rather than older residents), then the significance of the economic inequality is substantially magnified by its "coupling" with other divisions, linked to non-economic identity groups.[72]

Most would agree that education, health, employment, and food are all dimensions of poverty, and that access to them constitutes a fundamental human right. If so, then poverty should be indeed accepted as "a denial of human rights and human dignity."[73] As the Office of the United Nations High Commissioner for Human Rights (OHCHR) underlines, "[i]n a fundamental way, therefore, the denial of human rights forms part of the very definition of what it is to be poor."[74]

To illustrate this point, take the case of a Romani family from Romania we met while working with destitute migrants. The parents were born into poverty and have lived all their lives in a small hut with one window and no electricity in an impoverished and residentially segregated neighborhood with their five children. The parents could not obtain jobs at home, so they migrated abroad to make a living collecting scrap and recycling plastic bottles. While they were abroad, they became homeless, as they could barely earn enough to send money home to their children for food. Once a year when school starts, they make an effort to buy their children clothes and school supplies. Yet, the children continue to experience the same poverty from an early age, and they also end up missing out on school and on the chance to form strong networks with their peers. The family has lived their entire life separated from gadje, including at school, where most children are poor Roma – similar to the neighborhood where they live, the school is also segregated. This cycle of poverty, injustices, and discrimination has led to their further exclusion, including in terms of housing. These experiences would not allow them to escape the cycle of poverty. It is in this sense that failing to ensure human rights and to combat discrimination (e.g., in the labor market and schools) leads to maintaining poverty for those who are part of marginalized communities, in our case the Roma.

Another example of poverty as a denial of human rights is the Romani families in the village of Jarovnice, Slovakia. More than 5,600 Roma live in a slum there, in very poor and unhealthy conditions. While 97 percent of the population there is unemployed, even the few

---

[72]   Sen, 'Violence, Identity and Poverty' (n 27) 15.

[73]   See among others, Linda Jansen van Rensburg, "A Human Rights-Based Approach to Poverty: The South African Experience" in Nanak Kakwani and Jacques Silber (eds), *The Many Dimensions of Poverty* (Palgrave Macmillan 2013); Yamin (n 25).

[74]   OHCHR, "Principles and Guidelines for a Human Rights Approach to Poverty Reduction Strategies" (2017) UN Doc HR/PUB/06/12 <www.ohchr.org/Documents/Publications/PovertyStrategiesen.pdf> accessed 11 June 2020.

who have a formal job cannot imagine saving enough money to move out of the slum. One assistant teacher explained how he and his wife and children live in the same house with his wife's parents, and how difficult it is to afford moving out. In Slovakia, the Roma minority has a history of rights violations in all areas of life. As the European Roma Rights Centre (ERRC) noted, Roma "endure racism in the job market, housing and education fields and are often subjected to forced evictions, vigilante intimidation, disproportionate levels of police brutality and more subtle forms of discrimination."[75]

The authorities have not yet addressed the injustices that the Romani communities have suffered over the years; this contributes to maintaining the Romani people in a situation of extreme poverty, where they cannot access jobs or education. The Jarovnice community is just one such example. Abandoned by authorities and rejected by society where they face discrimination in all aspects of public life, Romani people in Jarovnice have been robbed of their human dignity and condemned to a life of poverty. This affront to their dignity has led some of them to give up the will to fight. As the director of the local school in Jarovnice explains, he no longer feels able to create change, because he does not believe anything can be changed.

As the examples show, the poverty that affects Romani communities, with the complex history of oppression and racism, should not be measured only in terms of disposable income. Taking an approach based on human rights, we must use new tools and innovative dimensions and indicators to measure access to fundamental rights, particularly within the Roma multidimensional poverty framework suggested by Ivanov and others. To start, a Roma Multidimensional Poverty Index should add at least discrimination in education and health as an indicator, intergenerational poverty, and wealth gap.

Romani people in the EU have far less opportunities to realize their social and economic rights compared to those in the dominant population. What obstructs those rights is structural racism, every-day discrimination, and an unaddressed legacy of oppression. That the EU has the second-largest GDP in the world should inform the measurement of the "progressive realization" of Roma social and economic rights. That principle is rooted in the rationale of available resources, which are not scarce in the EU. Romani people in the EU must be guaranteed access to their fundamental rights now.

III.   CANONS AND MEASUREMENTS OF RACIALIZED POVERTY

The in-power groups in the EU or dominant majorities have established most of the canons on poverty in the EU. Based on their experiences and realities, issues related to income and to individual violations of rights indeed constitute significant problems. But the experiences of racialized groups present additional challenges; if all those in the EU were to truly understand and address their oppression and histories, Roma would become equal partners with non-Roma in revisiting, challenging, and reimagining those canons. All too often policymakers, advocates, and academics discuss "Roma communities" as "integration" or social inclusion, alluding to biased notions of what they understand as affecting Roma. But that is

---

[75]   Patrick Strickland, "Life in Slovakia's Roma Slums: Poverty and Segregation" (*Aljazeera*, 10 May 2017)   <www.aljazeera.com/indepth/features/2017/04/life-slovakia-roma-slums-poverty-segregation -170425090756677.html> accessed 11 June 2020.

a trap that narrowly puts the focus on the oppressed, rather than recognizing and addressing the collective features of racialized Roma poverty. There is a clear nexus between racialized poor and segregated neighborhoods, wealth gap, and an unaddressed collective history of oppression and exploitation.

Efforts to measure Roma poverty solely through indicators related either to social and economic dimensions or to individual human rights cannot possibly encompass the collective and intergenerational facets of racialized poverty. Given the length and severity of their shared experience of destitution based on ethnic grounds, realizing the social and economic rights of the Roma will require more than evaluating only income poverty or individual human rights; it will require recognizing and implementing social justice, racial justice, reparatory justice, economic justice, and environmental justice.

Addressing Roma poverty is a matter of social and racial justice. While the multidimensional poverty and human-rights approaches focus merely on households and individual rights, Romani people have historically been, and continue to be, targeted by collective structural violence, which generates collective dimensions of racialized poverty. One example of such racial discrimination is the segregation of a large portion of Romani children in special schools based on a false and racialized diagnosis of mental disability, which has stripped them, along with other children, of educational and job opportunities and transformed them into unskilled and poor workers. The opportunities taken away from these children and their plight cannot be measured, justified, and addressed solely through the poverty lens. Roma and pro-Roma national and international organisations have advocated and used litigation as a mean of raising awareness on the issue of segregation of children in special schools. After years of work, the European Commission responded by starting infringement proceedings against the Czech Republic,[76] Slovakia,[77] and Hungary.[78] This was a consequence of the fact that those states have failed to implement the European frameworks and anti-discrimination legislation.

Living in racially segregated Romani neighborhoods is likely to result in poverty. In unpacking the influence of neighborhoods on education, David Harding et al. examine their subjects' geographical location, physical proximity, spatial mismatch, neighborhood resources, social isolation, social organization, and local incentives.[79] In this paradigm, which examines the poverty in individual neighborhoods, the researchers found that Romani students are even more underprivileged than their non-Romani peers. For instance, residential segregation, which often also involves a lack of political will and investment from the local authorities, affects 38 percent of the Roma surveyed across 11 EU member states, and 20 percent sur-

---

[76] "ERRC Hopes that EU's Proceedings against the Czech Republic Sends a Strong Signal to All Member States that Discrimination Will Not Be Tolerated" (*ERRC*, 24 September 2014) <www.errc .org/press-releases/errc-hopes-that-eus-proceedings-against-the-czech-republic-sends-a-strong-signal-to -all-member-states-that-discrimination-will-not-be-tolerated>, accessed 20 June 2020.

[77] "European Commission Targets Slovakia over Roma School Discrimination" (*Open Society Foundations*, 29 April 2015) <www.opensocietyfoundations.org/press-releases/european-commission -targets-slovakia-over-roma-school-discrimination> accessed 11 June 2020.

[78] "European Commission Launches Another Infringement Proceeding" (*The Budapest Beacon*, 26 May 2016) <https://budapestbeacon.com/European-commission-launches-another-infringement -proceeding/> accessed 11 June 2020.

[79] David Harding and others, "Unpacking Neighborhood Influences on Education Outcomes: Setting the Stage for Future Research" in Greg J Duncan and Richard J Murnane (eds), *Whither Opportunity? Rising Inequality, Schools, and Children's Life Chances* (Russell Sage Foundation Press 2011).

veyed live in slums or ruined houses.[80] The only educational facilities for the Roma are poorly equipped and lack laboratories or libraries. Many even have toilets outside of the school in small cement buildings that might also be used by other people; this is the case in Bulgaria.[81]

The quality of education in Roma-only educational facilities is far lower than that for the overall population.[82] Some Romani communities have no kindergartens, especially those in rural areas. This is the case for the Roma in Pata Rat, Cluj (Romania) who have been forcibly moved by local authorities to an area near the local landfill and where they have no access to kindergarten for their children.[83] Given this situation, what are the choices for a Romani child living in an impoverished racially segregated neighborhood? What can they do to maximize their chances to well-being to meet the chances of a non-Romani child who grew up in a privileged community, with access to adequate housing and quality pre-schooling?

In some cases, politicians purposefully segregate Romani neighborhoods. Sometimes, walls separate the neighborhoods from those of the majority population. Examples in Romania include Baia Mare, Tarlungeni, Brasov, Sfantu Gheorghe, Covasna, and Mehedinti. In Slovakia, Košice and Ostrovany have two of the 14 such walls around the country.[84] One in the Czech Republic is Ústí nad Labem.[85] Along with the fact that these are severe violations of human rights, the walls create many other negatives: the Romani children "behind the wall" continue to be discriminated against and dehumanized before their non-Romani peers, and their interactions are dramatically reduced. Thus, when we measure poverty through the lens of social and racial justice, other issues—residential segregation, segregated education, and institutional racism—become relevant.

The poverty of the Roma is also a matter of environmental justice. Environmental justice has been defined as "the fair treatment and meaningful involvement of all people regardless of race, colour, national origin, or income, with respect to the development, implementation, and enforcement of environmental laws, regulations, and policies."[86] Environmental justice can be achieved when everyone is equally protected from environmental and health hazards and when everyone is equally involved in the decision-making process to have a healthy environment in which to live, learn, and work.[87] Environmental injustices disproportionately affect people

---

[80]   FRA, *Roma survey* (n 47).

[81]   Jennifer Tanaka, "Parallel Worlds: Romani and Non-Romani Schools in Bulgaria" (*European Roma Rights Centre (ERRC)*, 03 October 2000) <www.errc.org/roma-rights-journal/parallel-worlds -romani-and-non-romani-schools-in-bulgaria> accessed 11 June 2020.

[82]   FRA, *Roma survey* (n 47).

[83]   Fotis Filippou, "Solidarity with the Roma from Miercurea Ciuc Seeking Justice Seven Years on" (*Amnesty International*, 3 August 2011) <www.amnesty.org/en/latest/campaigns/2011/08/solidarity -with-the-roma-from-miercurea-ciuc-seeking-justice-seven-years-on/> accessed 11 June 2020.

[84]   Dan Bilefsky, "Walls, Real and Imagined, Surround the Roma" (*The New York Times*, 2 April 2010) <www.nytimes.com/2010/04/03/world/europe/03roma.html> accessed 11 June 2020; "Slovakia: Activists Demolish Part of Segregation Wall, Ignoring Local Romani Opinion" (*Romea*, 16 September 2014)   <www.romea.cz/en/news/slovakia-activists-demolish-part-of-segregation-wall-ignoring-local -romani-opinion> accessed 11 June 2020.

[85]   Adam LeBor, "Czech Cities Wall off Gypsy Ghetto" (The Independent, 27 May 1998) <www .independent.co.uk/news/czech-cities-wall-off-gypsy-ghetto-1157495.html> accessed 11 June 2020.

[86]   "Environmental Justice" (*United States Environmental Protection Agency (EPA)*) <www.epa.gov/ environmentaljustice> accessed 30 September 2019.

[87]   ibid.

of minority ethnic or racial backgrounds and marginalized communities.[88] Therefore, environmental injustice (such as the one related to mining, waste dumping, and pollution) becomes a matter of social inclusion, participation in decision-making, and recognition.

One case of environmental injustice involves the Romani community in Pata Rat (Cluj-Napoca) in Romania; in 2010 the authorities forcefully evicted and then relocated 250 Romani people. To this day, they live 800 meters from a landfill and 200 meters from a former dump of pharmaceutical waste. They have no access to hot water, and connections to cold water are shared between four homes. Some dwellings have no sanitation or cooking facilities. Some households hold up to 12 people. Because transportation to the city is inadequate, people have lost jobs and children have no access to education. Meanwhile they live surrounded by health risks: exposure to toxic substances, leaks from the landfill, and constant smoke from burning waste.

A similar case of environmental injustice can be seen in Romani neighborhoods in Bulgaria, where people feel they are "treated like dogs" because they are left to live in polluted areas, without garbage collection or other communal services.[89] The Roma quarter Fakulteta in Sofia has not seen waste collection, potable water, or sanitation in 70 years.[90] However, authorities plan to build a wall[91] to separate the community from the railway and have no intention of remediating the situation of the estimated 30,000 people living in Fakulteta, most of them Roma.

Local municipalities often pair forced evictions with the relocation of Roma into toxic areas. Families, including children, are not provided with adequate shelter but are knowingly placed in inadequate conditions. This is the case in areas near landfills as in the Pata Rat case above, or in toxic areas, such as in Miercurea Ciuc, Romania.[92] In the latter, in the summer of 2004, around 100 Romani persons were forcibly evicted from the already poor buildings they were living in into containers next to the city garbage dump.[93] For almost 15 years,[94] adults and children lived in very unsanitary conditions. This was described and analyzed in many reports by Romani CRISS and Amnesty International. Authorities have continued to neglect this community and people are still living in an area where signs read "toxic danger."[95]

In another more recent example from early 2019, the mayor of Voyvodinovo village in Bulgaria came to the Romani community to announce that almost all of them had to leave

[88]   "Falling Through the Cracks" (n 9).
[89]   World Bank, Consultations with the Poor, National Synthesis Report Bulgaria (May 1999) <www
.participatorymethods.org/sites/participatorymethods.org/files/Bulgaria-National%20Report.pdf>
accessed 11 June 2020.
[90]   'In Roma Quarter Fakulteta Waste Collection Denied. Separation Wall Proposed, Sofia, Bulgaria'
(*Environmental Justice Atlas*, last updated 29 August 2019) <https://ejatlas.org/conflict/in-roma-quarter
-fakulteta-waste-collection-denied-separation-wall-proposed-sofia-bulgaria> accessed 11 June 2020.
[91]   ibid.
[92]   Marius Wamsiedel, "Roma Access to Housing" (*Romani CRISS*, 2016) <http://drepturile-omului
.info/wp-content/uploads/2015/06/Accesul-romilor-la-locuire-Romani-CRISS-2016.pdf> accessed 11
June 2020.
[93]   ibid.
[94]   From consultations with the organization Romani CRISS from Romania, at the time of 2018 the
people were still living in the same containers.
[95]   "Romania: Dumped by a Sewage Plant" (*Amnesty International*) <www.amnesty.org/download/
Documents/40000/eur390032010en.pdf> accessed 11 June 2020.

their small houses that same evening.[96] The town provided no eviction notice and offered no alternative housing; people simply had no options in the sub-zero temperatures. Soon, the town began to demolish their houses. In Bulgaria, a member of the EU since 2007, 399 out of 444 housing demolitions between 2012 and 2016 involved Romani families.[97]

Thus, when measuring Roma poverty it is important to adopt the lens of environmental justice and consider the nexus between Roma housing, evictions, and pollution, toxic areas, and dump waste.

Finally, Roma poverty is also a matter of reparatory and economic justice. As Thomas Pogge emphasizes, a "morally deeply tarnished history should not be allowed to result in radical inequality."[98] In the case of Romanian Roma for example, the social and economic power of the majority population over the Roma has been established for centuries, beginning with the 500 years of exploitation of enslaved Roma[99] and continuing with continuous racism and representation of Roma as inferior in policies, arts, culture, and attitudes. Upon abolition, 250,000 Romani people gained freedom, but that freedom was not backed up by reparations for the formerly enslaved.

Instead ironically, as in other countries, compensation went to the enslavers. As a result, many generations of Romani children have been born in poverty, lacking wealth, land, assets, and rights.[100] But the Romanian Orthodox church, along with the state and the descendants of the enslavers, inherited huge wealth from the legacy of enslavement. Part of the wealth gap in Romania stems from this history of economic exploitation. Given the wealth gap between Roma and non-Roma, we argue that states must envisage monetary redress and wealth redistribution to minimize the gap, and in this way, address poverty.

Present-day state-sponsored injustices also deepen Roma poverty. In former Czechoslovakia the placement of Romani children in special schools since 1927 has also left Roma behind. In the late 1920s, hard measures were adopted against the Romani population, culminating in 1927 with the Parliament approving Law No 117, "*O potulných cikánech a jiných podobných tulácich*" ("On the fight against G*psies, vagabonds, and those unwilling to work").[101] This law established the practice of identifying Roma in the country by fingerprinting them and requiring them to fill out a special form of registration. Such measures opened the way for the continuous monitoring of Roma, with frequent arrests that often included confiscating their properties.

Paragraph 12 of Law 117/1927 made it very easy to separate Romani children from their families. Since they could not be placed with foster families and the regular institutions refused to accept them, the only solution imposed by the government was to create special institutions for the Romani children. The practice of placing Romani children in segregated

---

[96]   "Forced Evictions, Discrimination Continue to Afflict Bulgaria's Roma" (*VOA*, 13 February 2019)   <www.voanews.com/europe/forced-evictions-discrimination-continue-afflict-bulgarias-roma> accessed 11 June 2020.

[97]   ibid.

[98]   Thomas Pogge, *World Poverty and Human Rights* (2nd edn, Polity 2008) 209.

[99]   Viorel Achim, *The Roma in Romanian History* (CEU Press 2004).

[100]   Margareta Matache and Jacqueline Bhabha, "Roma Slavery: The Case for Reparations" (*Foreign Policy in Focus*, 22 April 2016) <https://fpif.org/roma-slavery-case-reparations/> accessed 11 June 2020.

[101]   Victoria Schmidt, "Eugenics and Special Education in the Czech Lands During the Interwar Period: The Beginning of Segregation against Disabled and Roma" (2016) 14 *Social Work & Society* 1.

special schools/institutions has taken place ever since 1927; Law 117 was the beginning of this phenomenon. Since then, generation after generation of children have not benefited from equal opportunities in education and chances for higher education. Today, in the Czech Republic and Slovakia a very high proportion of young Roma between ages 16 and 24 are categorized as NEET (Not in Employment, Education, or Training). The figures for 2016 are, respectively, 51 percent, compared to seven percent for the general population, and 65 percent and 12 percent.[102]

Thus, this Law secured the privilege and wealth of the majority population. To address this wrongdoing, which also takes the form of racialized poverty, will require reparations, including compensation, but also acknowledgment, truth telling, accountability of the offenders, apologies, and guarantees of non-repetition. To address the wealth gap between Roma and non-Roma, which we can measure, requires monetary redress.

And thus, to address poverty through the lens of justice, we see that systematic economic inequality and injustice require reparations. Conceptualizing poverty in a justice framework requires reckoning, redress, and repair, much more than simply welfare. It also requires a shift in the canons we use to understand, measure, and address poverty, inequality, and the history of oppression and racist policy measures.

IV.   CONCLUSION

Genuine democracies are based on values, laws, and practices encompassing human rights and justice. Yet in most EU countries, in spite of existing policies and measures to overcome the inequality of income, wealth, or status, Romani people continue to have unjustly limited access to social and economic rights. Many factors—including structural racism, every-day discrimination, the accumulated social and economic power and privilege of the non-Roma, and the unrepaired historical oppression of the Roma—have generated, deepened, and maintained the huge structural inequalities between the European Union's Romani and non-Romani populations.

Poverty—or rather structural inequalities and injustice in access to education, labor market, health care, environment, housing, wealth, wages, and income—is deepened by the social and economic contexts in which Roma live today, including poor, racially segregated neighborhoods, and environmentally toxic areas.

Public discourse and policymaking must be built on the concept of justice if they are to work towards dismantling racialized poverty. Many policy actions have failed and the solutions have been drawn through the eye and the norms of the gadje. We need to have the courage to imagine justice focused solutions with the Roma. Universal basic income, just wages and economic justice, healthy environments and environmental justice, racial and reparatory justice, and reparations to address the wealth gap and economic and cultural exploitation—may better address poverty, racial injustice, and structural inequalities.

Academics and policymakers need new, interdisciplinary, courageous ways to think and act on poverty. The various axes of power and racism (ideological, institutional, or interpersonal) as well as racialized poverty, intergenerational wealth, and impoverished neighborhoods, con-

---

[102]   FRA, *Fundamental Rights Report 2018* (n 46).

stitute fundamental elements in the research and policy poverty agendas that affect the Roma. Thus, what is most needed is a focus on developing a vocabulary, concepts, measurement, and a practice of justice for the Roma. That practice must include social justice, racial justice, reparatory and redistributive justice, economic justice, and environmental justice.

13. Rights, racism and poverty: failures of the global commitment to leave no one behind

Gay McDougall

Poverty research using horizontal inequality comparisons (which examine measurements of political, social, economic, and income inequalities along identity lines) and social exclusion perspectives finds that inequalities between ethnic, religious, or linguistic social groups are common.[1] Further, there is ample evidence that when the element of longstanding discrimination is added, in every region of the world – developed and developing countries – racial, ethnic, caste minorities, and Indigenous Peoples who have been targets of racial discrimination also wind up being the poorest of the poor. As compared to the general population, they experience higher levels of poverty; have less access to education, health care, and basic services; and are denied most well-paid employment opportunities.[2]

The correlation between discrimination and poverty is undeniable. Economic exclusion is one of the most devastating consequences of long-term discrimination. Racial groups that face widespread discrimination or marginalization are much more likely than other groups to be impoverished. The poorest communities in almost every region of the world tend to be racialized minority communities that have been targets of longstanding discrimination, violence, and social exclusion. They are most often communities of color that are vilified, scapegoated, and lacking voice, representation, or agency. They are often the subjects of a complex system of human-rights denials that may have impacts that are inter-generational, stretching over decades, based largely on their visible identity.

These groups experience poverty that is disproportionate to that experienced in the larger society and seemingly intractable to most poverty-alleviation strategies. They are discriminated against in labor markets, denied equal servicing in the capital and financial markets, and live in relative isolation from the more privileged society, segregated into extremely inferior housing, schools, health facilities, and all 'public goods.'[3] They are frequently the targets of hate speech and hate crimes. Over generations, a sense of hopelessness becomes pervasive throughout their community.

---

[1]   Frances Stewart, Graham Brown and Luca Mancini, 'Why Horizontal Inequalities Matter: Some Implications for Measurement' (2005) CRISE Working Paper No. 19 <https://assets.publishing.service.gov.uk/media/57a08c95e5274a31e00012e4/wp19.pdf > accessed 8 June 2020.

[2]   Lais Abramo, Simone Cecchini and Beatriz Morales, *Social Programmes, Poverty Eradication and Labour Inclusion: Lessons From Latin America and the Caribbean* (ECLAC Books, 2019) 100–07; see also Gay McDougall, 'Minorities, Poverty, and the Millennium Development Goals: Assessing Global Issues' (2007) IJGR 333, 334.

[3]   Robert Rycroft (ed), *The Economics of Inequality, Poverty, and Discrimination in the 21st Century* (ABC-CLIO, 2013) 1–4 and 182; Merlin Schaeffer, 'Ethnic Diversity, Public Goods Provision and Social Cohesion: Lessons from an Inconclusive Literature' (2013) WZB Discussion Paper No. SP VI 2013-103, [11] <www.econstor.eu/bitstream/10419/86148/1/770694160.pdf> accessed 8 June 2020.

The poverty that these communities experience is a manifestation of the racism in the larger society, which is far more debilitating than simple bias. It becomes institutionalized and it sprouts tentacles that reach deep into the structures on which the larger society is built. It becomes the foundation which supports the privileged position of other groups.[4]

In the most serious situations, the disparities can be traced to a historical period in which acts of grave and massive abuse of rights occurred consisting of crimes against humanity, the maintenance of which may have required demonization of persons of the oppressed group. Examples of such massive injustices include conquest, slavery, colonialism, ethnic cleansing, and genocide. Today's disparities are, in large part, legacies of those historical abuses.[5] But the extant situation of many racialized communities is of an ongoing dynamic interaction; the privileges of the larger society are fed off the vulnerabilities of the other. These racialized communities are subjects of daily acts of active impoverishment. Acts of racial discrimination are repeatedly committed against communities disabled by historical injustices. Present day violations compound the legacies of the historical injustices. There are contemporary actors who are duty-bearers and rights-holders, all part of a vicious cycle of race-based impoverishment. These are not just wrongs of the past.

To date, efforts to address the problems faced by racialized communities imprisoned by inter-generational poverty, powerlessness, and despair have been unsuccessful as they have been largely undertaken within institutional silos: the silo of the UN human-rights machinery or the silo of the international development community (UN, NGOs, national professionals). While there have been efforts to merge the two through special initiatives such as the Millennium Development Goals (MDGs)[6] and the Agenda 2030 Sustainable Development Goals (SDGs),[7] the distance between the two remains un-bridged. Neither silo is equipped to achieve shifts in power dynamics. And neither has unlocked the essential formula to successfully gain the meaningful participation of the oppressed groups in developing the solutions.

This chapter seeks to raise questions for further inquiry and research into where and why the gaps remain, and why a coherent approach to securing the full rights of racialized communities to live in dignity remains elusive.

In order to highlight the stark disparities, data set out in Section I has been pulled only from countries in one region: the American Hemisphere, where the vast majority of the African diaspora live. Isolating the analysis to this one region simplifies the landscape and brings into sharper focus the disparities between social/racial groups in these countries. Countries in the American Hemisphere share a common history of conquest, colonialism, and slavery.[8] The region allows a comparison of both developed and developing economies. Language differences are limited (English, Spanish, Portuguese, and French, along with many Indigenous languages). The neo-colonial influences have been similar throughout the hemisphere. And

---

[4] Deborah Kenn, 'Institutionalized Legal Racism: Housing Segregation and Beyond' (2001) 11 B.U. Pub. Int. L.J. 35, 37 and 41–43; Dorothy E Roberts, 'The Most Shocking and Inhuman Inequality: Thinking Structurally About Poverty, Racism, and Health Inequities' (2018) 49 U. Mem. L. Rev. 167, 175.

[5] Tamar R Birkhead, 'The New Peonage' (2015) 72 Wash. & Lee L. Rev. 1595, 1609–26.

[6] UNGA 'United Nations Millennium Declaration' (18 September 2000) UN Doc A/RES/55/2.

[7] UNGA 'Transforming Our World: The 2030 Agenda for Sustainable Development' (21 October 2015) UN Doc A/Res70/1.

[8] Robert J Cottrol, *Long, Lingering Shadow: Slavery, Race, and Law in the American Hemisphere* (University of Georgia Press 2013) 296.

data can focus on three principal group identities: the African Descendants, the Indigenous Peoples and those that identify as of European descent.

In Section II, this Chapter considers some of the unique challenges to addressing the poverty faced by racialized groups. The potential of the SDGs to tackle those challenges is discussed briefly in Section III, followed by a look in Section IV at the work of the Committee on the Elimination of All Forms of Racial Discrimination (CERD) to implement provisions of the International Convention on the Elimination of All Forms of Racial Discrimination (ICERD or 'the Convention'), which could impact poverty in the region. This leads, in Section V, to a number of research questions that may chart the way forward.

I.   AFRICAN DESCENDANTS IN THE AMERICAS

The inextricable link between slavery and Black poverty, mirrored by the link between slavery and white wealth accumulation, has been the topic of documentation and analysis in the context of the growing public discourse in the Americas about reparations. The arguments for reparations for slavery have been built on the data of unjust enrichment as presented by writers like Ta-Nehisi Coates; the policy manifesto of the Movement for Black Lives; scholars like Michele Alexander, Eric Foner, and Katherine Franke; legislators such as Representative John Conyers and Representative Barbara Lee; and UN expert Tendayi Achiume.

Further, the story of the continuing subjugation of descendants of enslaved people, which has resulted in compounding white wealth since the end of slavery, has been well-documented by experts and scholars in many other parts of the Americas. According to the Economic Commission on Latin America and the Caribbean (ECLAC), '[e]thnic and racial origin and migrant status are component axes of the social inequality matrix in Latin America; racist and xenophobic practices contribute to … determining the levels of inclusion or exclusion … with respect to … rights, status and general well-being.'[9]

Myrian Sepúlveda dos Santos writes that in spite of the reality that African Brazilians form a majority of the population in Brazil, they have inherited a subordinate social status that continues to rob them of political power, and subjects them to pervasive discrimination and poorer economic conditions.[10]

In Colombia, poverty most affects the minority Afro-Colombian and Indigenous populations. The map of extreme poverty locations and the map of high-density Afro-Colombian and Indigenous populations coincide.[11] Some communities face a daily struggle for survival, lacking basic needs, including adequate food, water, electricity, health care, and access to education for their children. They are additionally subjected to violent attacks aimed to displace them from their traditional lands, which in recent years have been discovered to be the most mineral rich, bio-diverse territories of Colombia.

---

[9]   United Nations CEPAL, *Social Panorama of Latin America* (United Nations Publications 2019) 207.
[10]   Myrian Sepúlveda dos Santos, 'The Legacy of Slavery in Contemporary Brazil' in Ana Lucia Araujo (ed), *African Heritage and Memories of Slavery in Brazil and the South Atlantic World* (Cambria Press 2015).
[11]   'The Gap Matters: Poverty and Well-Being of Afro-Colombians and Indigenous Peoples' (*The World Bank*, 2005) 24–28 <http://documents.worldbank.org/curated/en/337791468242365622/pdf/330140CO.pdf> accessed 8 June 2020.

Afro-Colombian settlements in rural areas and urban ghettos are among the very poorest in the country, with extreme poverty rates of over 60 percent and a lack of access to social services and programs.[12] Government sources reveal disturbing statistics. The basic needs of 80 percent of the Afro-Colombian population are not met. A study of Afro descendants in Latin America conducted by the World Bank in 2018 found that 41 percent of Afro descendants suffered from poverty in Colombia, as compared to 27 percent of non-Afro descendants suffering from poverty.[13]

A national population and housing census was also conducted in 2018. However, in its 2019 review of Colombia, CERD noted that the results of the census do not adequately represent the Afro-Colombian population.[14] CERD further noted this exclusion was evident given that, according to census data, those belonging to ethnic minority groups had declined by almost 31 percent since the last census.[15] Given Afro-Colombians were not adequately reflected in the most recent census, the previous census, conducted in 2005, must instead be relied upon. The 2005 census revealed that nearly 15 percent of Afro-Colombians had insufficient food to avoid hunger one or more days in a week. This was over double the national average. Nearly a quarter of Afro-Colombians lacked sufficient income to ensure a basic nutritional diet. Access to clean water, sanitation, and electricity was at markedly lower levels for Afro-Colombians. Chocó, the department of the country with the highest percentage of Afro-Colombian population, has the lowest per capita level of social investment and is ranked last in education, health, and infrastructure. Life expectancy for Afro-Colombian women (66.7 years) is nearly 11 years less than the national average, while for men (64.6 years) it is nearly six years less. In Chocó, the child mortality rate is 54 per 1000, compared with Medellin where it is eight per 1000. The infant mortality rate of the Afro-Descendant population is 43.9, while the national average is 21.0. The maternal mortality national average is 73 deaths for every 100,000 live births, while in Chocó the rate is 250. Access to healthcare services is extremely poor for many, particularly rural communities.[16]

In a 2005 study, Ethnicity and the Millennium Development Goals (ECLAC), the Inter-American Development Bank, the United Nations Development Program, and the World Bank measured the poverty levels of people of African descent and Indigenous Peoples in 15 Latin American and Caribbean countries. In many countries, differences in per capita expenditure levels between ethnic groups was partly a reflection of differences in geographic locations, with minorities more likely to be found in less productive areas with difficult physical terrain, poor infrastructure, and lower accessibility to market opportunities and off-farm work. But while location in disadvantaged areas is a clear impediment for all groups, the effect is significantly more pronounced for ethnic minorities within the same location.[17]

---

[12]   ibid at 27.

[13]   World Bank Group, 'Afro-descendants in Latin America: Toward a Framework of Inclusion' (*The World Bank*, 2018) 22 <www.worldbank.org/en/region/lac/brief/afro-descendants-in-latin-america> accessed 8 June 2020.

[14]   CERD, 'Concluding Observations on the Combined Seventeenth to Nineteenth Periodic Reports of Colombia' (22 January 2020) UN Doc CERD/C/COL/CO/17-19.

[15]   ibid.

[16]   UN HRC, 'Report of the Independent Expert on Minority Issues, Gay McDougall' (25 January 2011) UN Doc A/HRC/16/45/Add.1, paras 22–23.

[17]   Economic Commission for Latin America and the Caribbean, Inter-American Development Bank, United Nations Development Program, and World Bank, *Ethnicity and the Millennium Development Goals* (UNDP, 2005) 52–66.

They found that, 'indigenous and afro-descendant people tend to be poorer and have worse living conditions than White individuals. These facts are robust in the sense that they do not depend on which index, poverty line or definition of income we use to compute poverty. Also, these differences are, in general, statistically significant.'[18]

Indigenous and Afro-descendant females, in contrast to males from their population groups, tend to have a lower rate of participation in the labor market and higher unemployment rates than their White counterparts.[19]

These disparities can also be seen in Brazil, Ecuador, Peru, and Uruguay. A report prepared by ECLAC in 2018 demonstrates the continued trend of African descendants being exposed to poverty at far greater rates than non-Afro-descendants. The report noted 25.5 percent of Afro-descendants in Brazil suffer from poverty, compared with 11.5 percent of people within the State who were neither Indigenous nor Afro descendant.[20] A report prepared by the World Bank also acknowledged this divergence in 2015 through a comparison of two households with similar socioeconomic conditions.[21] The findings of this report noted the probability of being poor was increased by seven percent if the head of household is Afro-descendant (whether male or female), and 16 percent if the household was located in rural areas.[22]

ECLAC conducted similar analyses of Ecuador, Peru and Uruguay, in which it found similar results. It found that 35.3 percent of Afro-descendants in Ecuador suffered from poverty, compared to 20.5 percent of people who were neither Indigenous nor Afro descendant.[23] In Peru, 19.6 percent of Afro-descendants suffered from poverty, compared to 9.9 percent of people who were neither Indigenous nor Afro-descendant.[24] Finally, findings in Uruguay demonstrated that 7.5 percent of Afro-descendants suffered from poverty, compared to 2.7 percent of people who were neither Indigenous nor Afro-descendant.[25] The World Bank also assessed Uruguay, in 2015, and found that Afro descendant children are 14 percent less likely than non-Afro descendant children to complete primary education, and 24 percent less likely to complete secondary education.[26]

This trend does not only exist within Latin America; it is consistent with findings in North America as well. A report of the UN Working Group of Experts on People of African Descent, published in 2017, indicated that 11 percent of African Canadian women were unemployed, compared with 7 percent for the 'general' Canadian population.[27] It reported that African-Canadian women earn 37 percent less than White men, and 15 percent less than White women.[28] Unsurprisingly, given the significant gaps between pay and employment, this has

---

[18]   Economic Commission for Latin America and the Caribbean, Inter-American Development Bank, United Nations Development Program, and World Bank, *Ethnicity and the Millennium Development Goals* (UNDP, 2005) 94.

[19]   ibid at 52.

[20]   United Nations CEPAL (n 9) 19.

[21]   World Bank Group (n 13) 21.

[22]   ibid at 22.

[23]   United Nations CEPAL (n 9) 19.

[24]   ibid.

[25]   ibid.

[26]   World Bank Group (n 13) 23.

[27]   UN HRC, 'Report of Working Group of Experts on People of African Descent on its Mission to Canada' (16 August 2017), UN Doc A/HRC/36/60/Add.1.

[28]   ibid.

resulted in 25 percent of African Canadian women living below the poverty line, compared with six percent of White Canadian women.[29]

The Organization for Economic Co-Operation and Development (OECD) works in partnership with governments, policy makers, and citizens to establish international standards pertaining to various social, economic, and environmental challenges. It consists of 37 Member countries across North and South America, Europe, and Asia-Pacific. The OECD reported that the United States had the highest poverty rate of all OECD countries in 2016, and noted in 2018 that 20.8 percent of Black people living in the United States were living below the poverty line, compared to 8.1 percent of White people.[30] A Report of the Economic Policy Institute produced in 2018 further broke down the areas in which clear discrimination was faced by African Americans, leading to the high rate of poverty in that population. According to the report, in the area of education, 22.8 percent of African Americans aged between 25 and 29 have a college diploma, and 42.1 percent of White Americans in the same age group have received one.[31] In 2017, 7.5 percent of African Americans were unemployed, but only 3.8 percent of White Americans were unemployed.[32] In terms of wages and income, there was significant disparity between earnings of African Descendants and White Americans. The report noted that a 'typical' Black household only received 61.6 percent of the annual income received by a 'typical' White household.[33]

The shocking outcome of these kinds of disparities, neglected over centuries, is laid bare by a global pandemic. The pattern that has emerged as of the date this chapter is being written reflects the deep inequalities in access to health care that runs along the fault-lines of race and class in America. Death rates due to COVID-19 of African Americans have been wildly disproportionate. In Michigan, of 2,900 deaths in May 2020, African Americans have been 40 percent, while only 14 percent of the population. In St. Louis 64 percent of deaths have been in the Black community, but they are only 45 percent of the population. There are similar racial disparities in Chicago, New York, and New Orleans.[34]

The impact of centuries of unaddressed health conditions as a consequence of inadequate access to health care, poor services, discriminatory housing, a lack of environmental protections, and food insecurity have left the Black community with a prevalence of the pre-existing conditions most likely to be a death sentence with the coronavirus: diabetes, asthma, hypertension, heart disease, and a well-founded lack of trust in the medical establishment.

The possibilities to take preventative measures are also split by race and class. The employment patterns show that those essential low-wage workers who cannot work from home are

---

[29]   ibid.

[30]   Eric Duffin, 'Poverty Rate in the United States by Ethnic Group 2018' (*Statista*, 2019). <www.statista.com/statistics/200476/us-poverty-rate-by-ethnic-group/> accessed 31 May 2020.

[31]   Janelle Jones, John Schmitt and Valerie Wilson, '50 years after the Kerner Commission' (*Economic Policy Institute*, 2018) 3 <https://files.epi.org/pdf/142084.pdf> accessed 8 June 2020.

[32]   ibid.

[33]   ibid.

[34]   Oliver Laughland and Lauren Zanolli, 'Why is Coronavirus Taking Such a Deadly Toll on Black Americans?' (*The Guardian*, 25 April 2020) <www.theguardian.com/world/2020/apr/25/coronavirus-racial-disparities-african-americans> accessed 31 May 2020.

largely Black and Latino.[35] Few of them have received protective coverings from employers and the early reports document racial bias in distribution of tests for the virus.[36]

II.   DISCRIMINATION IS A UNIQUE IMPEDIMENT TO POVERTY ELIMINATION

Efforts to reduce poverty are essential to larger efforts to promote the full range of civil, political, social, and economic rights for poor racialized communities. Equally, ensuring the enjoyment of all human rights is essential to poverty eradication. Those efforts must be shaped by an understanding of the multi-faceted nature of poverty in this context and the intricate interplay between poverty and discrimination.

To tackle these obstacles, appropriately targeted mechanisms are needed in both the public and private spheres. Racial discrimination results in poverty, which is often more pervasive, more deeply entrenched, and more persistent in comparison to poverty faced by others. Mainstreamed social-inclusion policies alone cannot tackle these issues. Confronting this kind of poverty requires acknowledgement that it is uniquely fueled by discrimination and often a deliberate intention to exclude certain groups.

Groups and communities trapped in poverty based on their visible identity lack more than income; their daily struggle is for more than basic sustenance. For generations they have been denied access to participate in political decision-making or to engage mechanisms of justice when their rights are violated. For generations they have suffered from extreme inequality in access to quality education, health care, significant employment opportunities, capital, and power. For generations, when members of their communities have tried to gain access to their rights, they have been rebuffed, humiliated, cheated, and subjected to physical attacks, even lynchings.

Over decades, the lessons they have learned have been that such attempts are at best futile, or at worst, fatal. So, ending poverty for most of these racialized groups will take more than better schools and healthcare, more than better affordable housing and the opportunity to start a successful business. Though all of that would be a good start, there is much more required to address the underlying structural and social forces that keep racialized groups excluded.

They must get justice: justice that is restorative of dignity and the human spirit. That process begins with respect for their full participation in decision-making about matters that affect them (most particularly the formulation of poverty-reduction strategies) and full inclusion in the public life of the entire society.

Ensuring the active, free, and meaningful participation by affected groups is an essential precondition of a human rights-based approach. It has been the stumbling point for many, if not most, development projects. But if managed well, it is the point in the process at which generations of distrust can be transformed into empowerment. Capacity-building of all stake-holders in the process – not just of the capacities of the racialized groups but also of the State actors – will be required, along with a deep and comprehensive understanding of the forces of

---

[35]   Audrey Kearney and Cailey Muñana, 'Taking Stock of Essential Workers' (*KFF*, 1 May 2020) <www.kff.org/coronavirus-policy-watch/taking-stock-of-essential-workers/> accessed 31 May 2020.
   [36]   ibid.

social exclusion experienced by racial groups and the complex array of defensive mechanisms developed over time by marginalized groups.

In general, poverty-reduction strategies have focused on national policies of economic growth rather than the development of differentiated programs targeted to the situation of excluded sub-groups of the population. The fundamental belief has been that 'a rising tide lifts all boats.' To the extent that subgroups – women, Indigenous Peoples – have become a focus of policy formulation, it has been because of continuous and effective advocacy on their parts. To date, African descendants have not yet achieved that.[37]

One consequence is a critical lack of data and statistics, which makes it difficult to identify the extent of the marginalization of people of African descent and how it differs from State to State.[38] It is necessary to look at how identities, social norms, and structural factors intersect to create distinct patterns of experience for many people of African descent. Two excellent sources of data, however, are the EU Agency for Fundamental Rights and the Economic Commission on Latin America.[39]

Further, poverty-reduction strategies must recognize and consider issues of indirect discrimination. It is rare that national non-discrimination legislation addresses the reality of institutional or systemic discrimination which is in many societies a major blockage to fully inclusive development. Truly tackling the roadblocks created by structures of indirect discrimination requires a thorough reassessment of all the core values of the society, such as the idea of a meritocracy, which are made manifest through the operation of those structures. Social norms and attitudes are made manifest through the structures and pathways of indirect discrimination. That may be 'a bridge too far' for many policymakers.

In many societies, inequality – economic, social, and political – is such that addressing the poverty of most racialized communities will demand dismantling, to a significant extent, the societal hierarchies that are inhibiting further equality. This will require tackling the hostile and engrained attitudes of many in the larger, more privileged society who have generated fictitious narratives of equality being a zero-sum game in which their diminishing status is directly, causally connected to the rising aspirations of racialized communities. The power and push-back of supremacist theories are generally under-appreciated by most anti-racism advocates.

These are all fundamental challenges which stand in the way of sustainable development for people of African descent.

---

[37]   UN Commission on Human Rights, 'Prevention of Discrimination and Protection of Minorities' (2 June 2004) UN Doc E/CN.4/Sub.2/2004/29/Add.1.

[38]   'HRC36 – WG People of African Descent: MRG's statement on the challenges of poverty, exclusion and development' (*Minority Rights Group International*, 27 September 2017) <https://minorityrights .org/advocacy-statements/mrg-welcomes-work-key-issue-poverty-exclusion-development-people -african-descent/> accessed 8 July 2020. The mainstream discourse in Europe ranges from 'colour blindness,' where social issues and inequality are presented largely as matters of class or citizenship, to varying degrees of commitment to multi-culturalism.

[39]   See 'Second European Union Minorities and Discrimination Survey: Being Black in the EU,' European Union Agency for Fundamental Rights, 2018.

III.   THE PROMISE TO LEAVE NO ONE BEHIND

While the 15-year experiment under the MDGs made impressive gains in some respects, the outcomes were greatly disappointing for racialized groups. One learning was that real and sustained progress can take place at a country level without any change in the situation of its most excluded minorities and Indigenous communities. In many cases national development plans, which may have generated considerable economic revenues for other sections of the population, left minorities and Indigenous Peoples actively worse off by violating their fundamental rights.[40]

The hope was that the 17 Goals of the SDGs would transform the world as we know it. Significantly, SDG Goal 10 focuses attention on 'inequality within and among countries.' This provision targets the bottom 40 percent of the population for special measures to accelerate their income growth faster than the norm. The political inclusion of marginalized groups is highlighted with the requirement that by 2030 countries should 'empower and promote the social, economic and political inclusion of all irrespective of … race, ethnicity, origin, religion … or other status.' In addition, it notes the need to 'ensure equal opportunity and reduce inequalities of outcome, including by eliminating discriminatory laws, policies and practices.' Wage and social protection issues are also addressed, while other SDGs deal with social disparities in areas such as health, malnutrition, and education.

According to the Center on Economic and Social Rights (CESR), which has closely followed these issues, there are some critical deficiencies that will likely hamper the transformative promise of Goal 10 with regards to tackling poverty, especially for groups excluded based on race. With respect to the framework supporting implementation of the SDGs, Goal 10 is vulnerable to 'strategic neglect.' Governments resisted its inclusion during the negotiations, financial commitments lag behind, and no dedicated thematic institution exists to continuously drive the focus on it, unlike, for example, the way that UN Women guarantees that Goal 5 on gender equity is constantly given the political and financial backing needed for its success. Given this void, the World Bank along with the corporate sector will most likely take the lead. Both have interests that are antithetical to the types of poverty-reduction policies best suited to address the special needs of poor communities struggling to escape poverty.[41]

If inequality and discrimination toward racialized communities are entrenched, then standardized approaches to development and poverty reduction may prove ineffective in benefitting those most marginalized. There must be carefully conceived policies targeted to their needs.

---

[40]   Gay McDougall, 'Foreword: Why Minorities and Indigenous Peoples must not be Sidelined in the Post-2015 Framework' in *Minorities, Indigenous People and the Post-2015 Framework* (*Minority Rights Group International*, 2015) <https://minorityrights.org/wp-content/uploads/2015/09/SDG-briefing _FINAL.pdf> accessed 31 May 2020.

The environmental impacts of mineral and extractive industries, such as oil spillages and other forms of pollution, have destroyed the well-being, livelihoods and ancestral lands of countless communities world-wide. Yet even measures that at one level appear to protect local environments – for example, bans on the use of forest goods and resources – can have negative effects if they fail to accommodate the traditional rights and sustainable practices of indigenous communities.

[41]   Kate Donald, 'Tackling Inequality: The Potential of the Sustainable Development Goals' (*Open Global Rights*, 2017) <www.openglobalrights.org/tackling-inequality-potential-of-sustainable -development-goals/> accessed 31 May 2020.

Finally, the SDGs in general have been established without a strong mechanism to guarantee accountability. The reporting process is voluntary, disaggregated data that reveals horizontal inequalities across different population groups is encouraged but not required, and while there are general references to human rights, there is no institutional oversight body identified in the framework with the expertise to evaluate proposed national policies against existing human rights guarantees to ensure that they truly offer the protections that are promised. The High Level Political Forum (HLPF), which has been tasked with the responsibility to monitor the 2030 Agenda and progress towards the SDGs, is ill-equipped to make rigorous judgements about the quality of the performance of countries.[42]

IV.   THE INTERNATIONAL CONVENTION ON THE ELIMINATION OF ALL FORMS OF RACIAL DISCRIMINATION

The prohibition against racial discrimination is fundamental and deeply entrenched in international law. It has been recognized as having the exceptional character of *jus cogens* which creates obligations *erga omnes*,[43] an obligation that every state has toward the international community as a whole from which no derogation is acceptable.

This central principle of customary law has been enshrined in the Universal Declaration of Human Rights. It is codified in the International Covenants on Civil and Political Rights and on Economic, Social and Cultural Rights and is restated in each of the core human rights treaties. The International Convention on the Elimination of All Forms of Racial Discrimination (the Convention) is the centerpiece of the international regime for the protection and enforcement of the right against racial discrimination.[44] All actors (state and non-state) have a responsibility to ensure universal respect for the *erga omnes* rights codified in the Convention.[45]

While the Convention was drafted in the 1960s and came into force in 1969, it remains the principal international human rights instrument defining and prohibiting racial discrimination in all sectors of private and public life. The Convention defines racial discrimination as:

> any distinction, exclusion, restriction or preference based on race, colour, descent, or national or ethnic origin which has the purpose or effect of nullifying or impairing the recognition, enjoyment or exercise, on an equal footing, of human rights and fundamental freedoms in the political, economic, social, cultural or any other field of public life.[46]

---

[42]   ibid.

[43]   Maurizio Ragazzi, *The Concept of International Obligations* Erga Omnes (Clarendon Press 2000) 118; Christian J. Tams, *Enforcing Obligations* Erga Omnes *in International Law* (CUP 2005) 257; Maurizio Gleider Hernández, *The International Court of Justice and the Judicial Function* (OUP 2014) 227.

[44]   UNGA, Contemporary Forms of Racism, Racial Discrimination, Xenophobia and Related Intolerance (19 August 2013) UN Doc A/68/333; Report of the World Conference against Racism, Racial Discrimination, Xenophobia and Related Intolerance (2001) UN Doc A/Conf.189/12.

[45]   *Case Concerning the Barcelona Traction, Light and Power Company, Limited* (*Belgium v Spain*) ICJ Rep 1970, paras 33–34.

[46]   ICERD (adopted 7 March 1966, entered into force 4 January 1969) 660 UNTS 195, sec 1.

While the words 'poverty' or 'extreme poverty' do not appear in the text of the Convention, Article 5 of the Convention lists the rights that must not be subjected to racial discrimination, including civil and political rights such as the right to political participation, freedom of speech, freedom of movement, and an elaboration of economic, social, and cultural rights, such as rights relating to work, housing, health care, and education. Included are the spectrum of rights deprivations that are identified with poverty.

This list is not exhaustive. The chapeau of Article 5 states that States Parties must guarantee 'equality before the law, notably in the enjoyment of the following rights.' Since the Convention seeks to 'eliminate racial discrimination in all areas of life,' presumably appropriate additions to the list could be identified, such as 'poverty' or 'extreme poverty.'

The States Parties ratifying the Convention undertake to eliminate racial discrimination through all appropriate means, including legislation, whether the discrimination was caused by the State itself or by any person, group, or organization. The Convention explicitly extends the prohibition against racial discrimination to cover actions that are intentionally discriminatory and those that may lack deliberateness but have a negative disparate impact on those groups protected by the Convention. This explicit extension of protections to indirect discrimination is important when considering state responsibility to take corrective actions affecting communities that have experienced poverty over generations. No evil actor or perpetrator needs to be identified.

The States Parties to the Convention elect independent experts to CERD, who are mandated to review implementation of the treaty and make recommendations. CERD reviews detailed periodic reports from State Parties, as well as alternative reports provided from other sources such as civil society, national human rights institutions, and UN partners. CERD has a six-hour dialogue with the State, on the basis of which it sets out a series of concluding observations and recommendations to help the States improve implementation.

Through this and other functions under its mandate, CERD accumulates data and develops an analysis of national, regional, and global trends and dynamics useful to an understanding of racial discrimination as a factor in generating economic marginalization or conversely, poverty eradication. The following is a consideration of the relationship between racial discrimination, poverty, and poverty alleviation based on the data and insights gathered by CERD in its review of States Parties over the past ten years (2010–19) limited, as discussed previously, to countries in the American Hemisphere.

CERD consistently acknowledged the relationship between eradicating poverty and achieving gender equality. The two are inextricably linked; poverty eradication depends on the extent to which discrimination based on gender is also eliminated. CERD made this point in reference to the situation of Afro-Peruvian women domestic workers suffering multiple forms of discrimination that impact their rights to education, health, access to justice and to be protected from gender-based violence.[47]

The Committee highlighted the additional discrimination African Colombian women faced in their access to education, employment, justice, health care, and sexual and reproductive health services.[48] With regards to women in the Dominican Republic, the Committee noted

---

[47]   CERD, 'Concluding Observations on the Combined Twenty-second and Twenty-third Periodic Reports of Peru' (23 May 2018) UN Doc CERD/C/PER/CO/22-23.

[48]   CERD, 'Concluding Observations on the Combined Fifteenth and Sixteenth Periodic Reports of Colombia' (25 September 2015) UN Doc CERD/C/COL/CO/15-16.

the requirement for a 'buena presencia,' or 'a good appearance,' as a proxy often used to deny appointments to skilled jobs, giving rise to discriminatory practices.[49] Specifically, the Committee noted the difficulties this practice poses to women of African descent in being able to secure jobs in skilled employment.[50] Access to housing was cited as an obstacle faced by women of African descent in Uruguay.[51] Domestic violence against women was highlighted as a particular concern of the Committee in its assessment of the United States, in which it concentrated on how women of African descent were disproportionately affected by such violence.[52] These concerns were mirrored in the Committee's reviews of Honduras,[53] Mexico,[54] Argentina,[55] Paraguay,[56] and El Salvador.[57]

CERD was explicit in linking the following situations to the existence or exacerbation of poverty: inadequate and sub-standard access to basic services (Belize);[58] to housing, water, electricity, and health care (El Salvador);[59] and to poor access to health care, employment and housing of undocumented migrants in Curaçao and Aruba (The Netherlands). CERD highlighted the importance of tackling poverty and racial discrimination in combination with actions taken to end hunger, improve health outcomes, reduce the inequality gap, and increase access to quality education (Argentina[60]), safe drinking water, and decent work opportunities.

Noting the persistent levels of poverty faced by Afro-Ecuadorians, CERD specifically highlighted the discrimination faced in access to basic services, education, employment, and public office and the inability for Afro-Ecuadorians to own property.[61] To combat these concerns, the Committee recommended the State implement socially inclusive poverty-reduction policies.[62] In its assessment of the United States, the Committee noted the impact historical patterns of segregation had on African American communities, specifically highlighting the connection between these patterns and the sub-standard conditions and services, such as poor housing

---

[49] CERD, 'Concluding Observations on the Thirteenth and Fourteenth Periodic Reports of the Dominican Republic' (19 April 2013) UN Doc CERD/C/DOM/CO/13-14.

[50] ibid.

[51] CERD, 'Consideration of Reports Submitted by States Parties under Article 9 of the Convention' (8 April 2011) UN Doc CERD/C/URY/CO/16-20.

[52] CERD, 'Concluding Observations on the Combined Seventh to Ninth Periodic Reports of United States of America' (25 September 2014) UN Doc CERD/C/USA/CO/7-9.

[53] CERD, 'Concluding Observations on the Combined Sixth to Eighth Periodic Reports of Honduras' (14 January 2019) UN Doc CERD/C/HND/CO/6-8.

[54] CERD, 'Concluding Observations on the Combined Eighteenth to Twenty-first Periodic Reports of Mexico' (19 September 2019) UN Doc CERD/C/MEX/CO/18-21.

[55] CERD, 'Concluding Observations on the Combined Twenty-first to Twenty-third Periodic Reports of Argentina' (11 January 2017) UN Doc CERD/C/ARG/CO/21-23.

[56] CERD, 'Concluding Observations on the Combined Fourth to Sixth Periodic Reports of Paraguay' (4 October 2016) UN Doc CERD/C/PRY/CO/4-6.

[57] CERD, 'Concluding Observations on the Combined Sixteenth and Seventeenth Periodic Reports of El Salvador' (25 September 2014) UN Doc CERD/C/SLV/CO/16-17.

[58] CERD, 'Consideration of Reports Submitted by States Parties Under Article 9 of the Convention: Concluding Observations of the Committee on the Elimination of Racial Discrimination Adopted Under the Review Procedure' (29 August 2012) UN Doc CERD/C/BLZ/CO/1.

[59] CERD (n 57).

[60] CERD (n 55).

[61] CERD, 'Concluding Observations on the Combined 20th to 22nd Periodic Reports of Ecuador' (24 October 2012) UN Doc CERD/C/ECU/CO/20-22.

[62] ibid.

conditions, limited employment opportunities, inadequate access to healthcare facilities, under-resourced schools, and higher exposure to crime and violence.[63]

In some cases, CERD identified that racial discrimination had become structural, making it more difficult to overcome and requiring more concerted measures that reach across society in response. For example, CERD identified structural barriers with respect to Afro-descendants in Costa Rica who have similar levels of access to education to the rest of the population yet suffer disparities in relation to employment, access to social security, and representation in the executive and judicial branches of Government. Another example cited chronic malnutrition among the Indigenous population in Guatemala, where the national 'zero target' hunger strategy failed to address the structural causes of hunger. Likewise, CERD concluded that structural discrimination in Peru, El Salvador,[64] and Uruguay was leading to poverty and social exclusion of Afro-descendants in those countries. Also, the Committee expressed its concerns for children whose mother tongue was not Spanish, making a connection between the absence of multi-lingual education and the high levels of illiteracy amongst Afro-Peruvian communities.[65]

The Committee has consistently focused on disparities in the criminal-justice systems in countries. In Canada, the Committee noted that the structural nature of discrimination against African-Canadians resulted in racial profiling, high rates of incarceration, lack of appropriate community services, over policing of certain populations, drug policies, and racially biased sentencing.[66] The Committee noted the over-representation of African-Canadians in the penal system is interconnected with poverty, stating it must be addressed through 'eliminating poverty, providing better social services, re-examining drug policies, and preventing racially biased sentencing through training of judges.'[67] These concerns were further highlighted in the Committee's assessment of the United States, as the Committee specifically noted the existence of laws and policies making homelessness a crime and the disproportionate impact on African Americans.[68] The Committee also noted the structural aspects of discrimination in Paraguay,[69] Honduras,[70] Dominican Republic,[71] and Mexico.[72]

CERD has recommended urgent actions be taken in the following areas to combat racial discrimination in the context of eradicating poverty.

---

[63] CERD (n 52).

[64] CERD, 'Concluding Observations on the Combined Eighteenth and Nineteenth Periodic Reports of El Salvador' (13 September 2019) UN Doc CERD/C/SLV/CO/18-19.

[65] CERD, 'Concluding Observations on the Eighteenth to Twenty-first Periodic Reports of Peru' (25 September 2014) UN Doc CERD/C/PER/CO/18-21.

[66] CERD, 'Concluding Observations on the Combined Twenty-first to Twenty-third Periodic Reports of Canada' (13 September 2017) UN Doc CERD/C/CAN/CO/21-23.

[67] ibid.

[68] CERD (n 52).

[69] CERD (n 56).

[70] CERD, 'Combined Observations on the Combined Initial and Second to Fifth Periodic Reports of Honduras' (13 March 2014) UN Doc CERD/C/HND/CO/1-5.

[71] CERD (n 49).

[72] CERD, 'Consideration of Reports Submitted by States Parties Under Article 9 of the Convention: Concluding Observations of the Committee on the Elimination of Racial Discrimination: Mexico' (4 April 2012) UN Doc CERD/C/MEX/CO/16-17.

A.   States Must Have a Rights-based Legal Framework

An important first step in prohibiting racial discrimination in the context of eradicating poverty is the adoption of rights-based laws and policies. For example, CERD proposed that Peru adopt a national policy on racism and racial discrimination that deals with the problem of structural discrimination, high levels of poverty, and social exclusion confronting Indigenous populations and Afro-Peruvians.

In addition to adopting a freestanding, comprehensive general law that declares racial discrimination to be unlawful, States should also mainstream policies to combat discrimination across other laws and policies. Examples of this can be seen in the Committee's assessments of Guatemala and Panama. With regard to Guatemala, the Committee recommended it combat the pervasive poverty and social exclusion faced by the Afro-descendant population through the incorporation of human-rights principles into the existing poverty-related policies and to provide the funding and staff needed to implement such policies.[73]

In a later report the Committee added to this, recommending the adoption of a national policy that aims to promote social inclusion and reduce high rates of poverty through the enjoyment of rights to food, health, and education by Afro-descendants.[74] To Panama, the Committee stressed the need to increase the resources allocated for policy implementation within the State for employment, housing, education, and basic services, such as water supply, electricity, sanitation, education, public housing programs, and microcredit.[75] The Committee made further recommendations that States adopt comprehensive national policies to combat racial discrimination and/or social exclusion, in order to end high levels of inequality and poverty existing among populations of African descent in its assessments of Honduras,[76] Peru,[77] Ecuador,[78] Argentina,[79] Paraguay,[80] El Salvador,[81] Venezuela,[82] and Mexico.[83]

In the process of formulating laws and policies, CERD emphasized that States must ensure the participation of representatives of relevant national, ethnic, and other groups. In relation to El Salvador, CERD encouraged participation of Afro-descendant communities in the development of intercultural health and education programs. CERD recommended Guatemala adopt a policy on mid-wives with participation of Indigenous communities.

---

[73]   CERD, 'Concluding Observations on the Combined Fourteenth and Fifteenth Periodic Reports of Guatemala' (12 June 2015) UN Doc CERD/C/GTM/CO/14-15.

[74]   CERD, 'Concluding Observations on the Combined Sixteenth and Seventeenth Periodic Reports of Guatemala' (27 May 2019) UN Doc CERD/C/GTM/CO/16-17.

[75]   CERD, 'Consideration of reports submitted by States parties under article 9 of the Convention: Concluding Observations of the Committee on the Elimination of Racial Discrimination: Panama' (19 May 2010) UN Doc CERD/C/PAN/CO/15-20.

[76]   CERD (n 70).

[77]   CERD (n 65); CERD (n 47).

[78]   CERD (n 61); CERD, 'Concluding Observations on the Combined Twenty-third and Twenty-fourth Periodic Reports of Ecuador' (15 September 2017) UN Doc CERD/C/ECU/CO/23-24.

[79]   CERD (n 55).

[80]   CERD (n 56).

[81]   CERD (n 57).

[82]   CERD, 'Concluding Observations on the Nineteenth to Twenty-first Periodic Reports of the Bolivarian Republic of Venezuela' (23 September 2013) UN Doc CERD/C/VEN/CO/19-21.

[83]   CERD (n 54).

CERD also always emphasized the importance of robust implementation of laws and policies to eradicate deeply rooted structural discrimination.

B.   States Must Guarantee Access to Justice

The importance of effective access-to-justice mechanisms cannot be over-stated, to enable those claiming violations of rights to seek a remedy and to help deter future violations.[84] An effective and equal justice system is essential to ensure respect for the Convention and avoid future breaches. For example, in the review of Uruguay, CERD recommended the State continually review racial equality in the judicial system and collect information as to the impact of the ethno-racial factor in access to justice.[85] In reviewing Peru, the Committee highlighted the gender-based violence Afro-Peruvian women are subjected to and urged the State to adopt an intercultural focus in improving access to justice, health, and education for women who are victims of discrimination and violence.[86] With respect to the disproportionately high rate of incarceration in Canada of members of minorities who suffer from mental or intellectual impairments or are subjected to racially based sentencing, the Committee recommended the State provide better social services, prevent racially biased sentencing through training programs aimed at judges, and provide better alternatives to incarceration for certain offences.[87]

C.   States Must Design Robust Special Measures (Affirmative Action) to Redress the Disadvantages of Racial Inequalities

The Convention requires that in certain situations, States must adopt special measures/affirmative action programs to rectify the unjustified disparities created by past discrimination and break the link between poverty and racism, particularly where discrimination is entrenched and structural. In other words, laws, policies, and practices to prohibit future discriminatory practices at times need supplementing by the adoption of temporary measures to 'level the playing field' and secure equal enjoyment of rights for all persons in society. Such measures might be executive, administrative, budgetary, or regulatory. Policies, programs, or preferential regimes could be designed which would seek to reset disparities that have plagued disadvantaged groups.[88] The temporary nature of such measures is crucial; the measures must be discontinued as soon as the objectives have been attained.

CERD recommended that Costa Rica adopt special measures in employment, health, housing, and social security, as well as representation in decision-making bodies. For Uruguay, CERD recommended the State to step up its implementation of its affirmative action plan with respect to Afro-descendants in the public and private sphere by including a detailed implementation plan and targets with specific time frames with a view to eradicating poverty and social exclusion.

---

[84]   International Convention on the Elimination of All Forms of Racial Discrimination, Art 6.
[85]   CERD (n 51).
[86]   CERD (n 47).
[87]   CERD (n 66).
[88]   CERD, 'General Recommendation No. 32: The Meaning and Scope of Special Measures in the International Convention on the Elimination of All Forms of Racial Discrimination' (24 September 2009) UN Doc CERD/C/GC/32, para 13.

The Committee urged Mexico to add people of African descent to its list of officially 'recognized' ethnic groups, and to adopt programs with the aim to promote the rights of Afro-descendants.[89] The Committee urged Honduras to implement social inclusion and identity-based development programs to reduce inequality and historical poverty in the State.[90] In achieving this, the Committee highlighted that it was essential to break the link between poverty and racism through the implementation of special measures and affirmative action by the State.[91]

The Committee also expressed its concern that for children in Aruba and Curaçao mandatory education extends only until the end of primary school. CERD recommended special measures be implemented to increase the level of educational achievement of children, give adequate recognition to mother tongues, and introduce bilingual education in Aruba and Curaçao.[92]

D.   Informed Policy Decisions Require Disaggregated Data

CERD repeatedly calls for States to report data that is disaggregated by race, national and ethnic origin, and other relevant grounds, including sex. Disaggregated data provides a fuller understanding of inequalities. It provides a baseline for the development of appropriate and targeted affirmative programs to redress those disparities. It also creates a framework for periodic evaluation of the effectiveness of the programs.[93]

The reality is that few States comply with CERD's request for population data that enables a comparative view of inequalities by racial and ethnic groups. For some, to merely acknowledge, even for the purposes of data collecting, the existence of racial or ethnic classifications challenges national conventions of equal status among citizens. In some countries, it recalls memories of racial persecutions from the past that are best forgotten. CERD is sensitive to these concerns.

It is important to emphasize that CERD recommends that data disaggregation be done in a manner that guarantees anonymity of all individuals and permits self-identification. CERD also notes that many countries need capacity-building to assist in the collection of high-quality disaggregated data and CERD encourages States to seek technical cooperation, including from UN agencies, to assist with the collection and disaggregation of data. CERD also encourages public access to the data through online databases when this is consistent with human rights principles and individual confidentiality.[94]

---

[89]   CERD (n 54).
[90]   CERD (n 53).
[91]   ibid.
[92]   CERD, 'Concluding Observations on the Combined Nineteenth to Twenty-first Periodic Reports of the Netherlands' (24 September 2015) UN Doc CERD/C/NLD/CO/19-21.
[93]   CERD (n 74); CERD (n 53); CERD (n 54); CERD (n 47); CERD (n 56).
[94]   OHCHR, 'A human rights-based approach to data: leaving no one behind in the 2030 Development Agenda' (*United Nations*, 2018) <www.ohchr.org/Documents/Issues/HRIndicators/GuidanceNoteonApproachtoData.pdf> accessed 8 June 2020.

V.   LOOKING FORWARD

As 2019 ended, CERD concluded its 100th session of interactions with States to evaluate and encourage their full implementation of the Convention. Particularly over recent years, CERD focused increased attention on economic and social rights violations, both historical and contemporary, as the root cause to the continuing extreme poverty faced by African descendant communities in the American Hemisphere. CERD's Concluding Recommendations have also become increasingly specific in describing the measures that should be taken to prohibit, remedy, and redress discriminatory actions. But progress in the region has been slow and CERD has limited follow-up procedures to evaluate the value-added of its pressure on State parties.

At an earlier point in its history, some scholars raised doubts about the commitment of CERD to ending poverty based on the mild language it used when urging States to take steps to eradicate the indices of inequality identified with poverty.[95] Later, a renowned expert and long-time member of CERD, Patrick Thornberry, responded in his exhaustive study of CERD practice that the fault must be placed on the lack of political will of the State Parties of the Convention.[96] The analysis of CERD practice above makes clear that CERD takes economic rights, including poverty, seriously and has, at least in recent years, pressed State Parties consistently on issues of apparent inequalities and discrimination.

Meanwhile, the 2030 Agenda and Sustainable Development Goals have taken center stage and with a vortex like force is pulling other mechanisms into its arena. Given the factors that may limit the success of the SDG project, summarized in Section II above, there could be useful synergies in a collaboration of some sort between the SDG process and CERD. In fact, it may be that only that kind of dynamic collaboration has a potential to significantly enhance country performance under Goal 10. CERD could clarify the human rights standards that must be fulfilled by policies aimed at meeting the indicators under Goal 10, and also guarantee genuine accountability.

To date, however, CERD has declined to take an active role in any aspect of standard-setting or monitoring State performance under the SDGs. Even if the Committee were enthusiastic about somehow offering its expertise to the HLPF, the modalities for this would have to be carefully considered alongside the time commitment required of members and staff. At a time when CERD feels under an existential threat from extreme budget shortfalls, pressures to merge some functions with other treaty bodies, and calendar constraints, it is highly unlikely that there would be agreement to play even a minor role in the SDG process.

Given that the Convention remains the centerpiece of the international community's mechanisms to combat racial discrimination with 50 years of concerted efforts to encourage compliance, it is well worth continued examination of CERD's limited success at achieving implementation by States.

A useful research agenda might tackle the following questions and explore more deeply some of the following issues.

---

[95]   William F Felice, 'The UN Committee on the Elimination of All Forms of Racial Discrimination: Race, and Economic and Social Human Rights' (2002) 24 Hum.Rts.Q. 205.

[96]   Patrick Thornberry, *The International Convention on the Elimination of All Forms of Racial Discrimination: A Commentary* (OUP 2016) 390–91.

What is the right to racial equality with respect to poverty? Is there a minimum core content with respect to the right? How far beyond 'non-discrimination' does the guarantee go? While Article 1 of the Convention defines prohibited discrimination as any distinctions having 'the purpose or effect' of impairing the full enjoyment of rights on an equal footing. Is the standard equality of opportunity or equality of outcome? Is the analysis different with respect to impact on individuals or identity groups?

More analysis is needed of special measures/affirmative action. Based on the responses of States over the years, there is widespread confusion about what is required and why. That seems to be the case even after CERD adopted General Recommendation 32 on the meaning and scope of special measures. Why have so few attempts been made? Why have good practices apparently failed? Is a lack of political will the answer here? Would an offer of technical assistance from the OHCHR move the needle on this?

The milestone of 100 sessions of CERD would appropriately occasion a research project on the track-record of CERD's accomplishments, particularly on the issue of making a difference with respect to the mitigation/elimination of poverty in communities of color.

A robust proactive role by CERD would require a reconsideration of most aspects of how CERD functions and the resources available to it. Within current constraints, in what ways might there be fashioned a closer working relationship with the ILO and CESCR. To date, there has been practically no engagement between CERD and the SDGs and Agenda 2030. Why not?

Consider the limitations of the methods of work of CERD, including the 'inter-active dialogue,' follow-up procedure, and inability to conduct in situ consultations.

B.   Poverty and Human Rights, Intersecting with Geography and Place

14. Immigration, poverty and human rights

Tally Kritzman-Amir

Can migration be instrumental in decreasing poverty? This is a question of great importance in a world where migration is such a prevalent feature on the one hand, and its desirability is so contested on the other hand. Arguably, the whole structure of exclusionary nation states is not conducive to the eradication of poverty. Limitations on exit, entry and stay, which are closely associated with the borders and immigration regimes of nation states, are constraints and distortions on the labor market that decrease the global welfare and cause sub-optimality.[1] This is especially true in light of the fact that migration occurs in a world influenced by colonialism and neo-colonialism and where states have equal formal powers but differ substantively in their actual power and independence, both broadly and more specifically in terms of the ability to include and exclude.[2]

Both emigration and immigration have economic implications. Emigration is sometimes feared to result in a 'brain drain',[3] or loss of human capital, but research also suggests the positive returns of emigration. Remittances are one of the dominant forms of positive returns,[4] but there is also return migration, skill transfer, initial incentives for education and the dynamic investment effects of citizens living abroad.[5] Economic benefits of migration extend also to the receiving First-World countries, where most research indicates positive economic outcomes from migration and does not support the fear of general wage depression or rise in unemploy-

---

[1] Michael J Trebilcock and Matthew Sudak, 'The Political Economy of Emigration and Immigration' (2006) 81 NYU L Rev 234–35.

[2] Tendayi Achiume, 'Migration as Decolonization' (2019) 71 Stan L Rev 1509.

[3] For the contradicting economic literature on the effect of brain drain, see, for example Andrew Mountford, 'Can a Brain Drain be Good for Growth in the Source Economy?' (1997) 53 J Development Eco 287; Michel Beine, Frédéric Docquier and Hillel Rapoport, 'Brain Drain and Economic Growth: Theory and Evidence' (2001) 64 J Development Eco 275; Frédéric Docquier and Hillel Rapoport, 'Globalization, Brain Drain, and Development' (2012) 50 J of Eco Lit 681.

[4] Remittances have well documented positive effects on poverty reduction: 'in some countries they generate more revenue than foreign aid and foreign investment'. Susan Eckstein, 'Immigration, Remittances and Transnational Social Capital Formation: A Cuban Case Study' (2010) 33 Ethnic & Racial Stu 1648. They have a mixed effect on development, however. Pia M Orrenius and others, 'Do Remittances Boost Economic Development?: Evidence from Mexican States' (2010) 16 LBRA 803. Remittances are perceived as an important anti-poverty tool, cutting down extreme poverty as well as 'ordinary' poverty, as they are mostly spent on basic needs such as food, medicine and shelter, and thus the regulation of which should not be excessive. Ezra Rosser, 'Immigrant Remittances' (2008) 41 Conn L Rev 1. However, there is some literature suggesting that the negative effects of remittance-driven migration are consistently downplayed, neglecting various costs and harms to sending countries, migrants and their families. Adam Feibelman, 'The Very Uneasy Case Against Remittances: An Ex Ante Perspective' (2010) 88 NC L Rev 1771. Also, there is growing politicization of remittances, both historically and in the Trump era, rendering it less effective in the effort to decrease poverty in sending countries. Stephen Wilks, 'A Complicated Alchemy: Theorizing Identity Politics and the Politicization of Migrant Remittances Under Donald Trump's Presidency' (2017) 50 Cornell Intl LJ 285.

[5] Trebilcock and Sudak (n 1).

ment levels.[6] Negative effects arguably include the impact of migrants on the employment of low-skilled native employees[7] but this could nevertheless be addressed or rectified through distributing means.

This chapter seeks to contribute to the literature on migration, human rights and poverty by distinguishing and fleshing out two connections between poverty and migration and exploring the role of human rights in both of those connections: (1) protection from poverty in countries of origin (or third countries) and (2) protection from poverty in destination countries. First, there is the issue of protecting migrants from being returned to a country in which they will experience poverty. Poverty can be a form of persecution in such countries, or a reason for persecution. I will highlight the partially unfulfilled potential of international human rights to grant such protection in Section I of this chapter and explain why international human rights has yet to offer sufficient protections. Second, international human rights plays a role in protecting migrants from poverty in receiving countries. Section II will demonstrate that not only are receiving countries not fulfilling their obligations under international human rights law to protect migrants in their territories from poverty, they are also, in some cases, actively contributing to the impoverishment of migrants for the sake of promoting their immigration policies. Section III offers some concluding thoughts in connection to both Section I and Section II.

I.   PROTECTING MIGRANTS FROM EXPOSURE TO POVERTY IN COUNTRY OF ORIGIN OR THIRD COUNTRIES

One of the most fundamental distinctions of immigration law is the binary of 'economic migrant' versus 'refugee'. As Rebecca Hamlin observes, '[t]his migrant/refugee binary is so ubiquitous and so unquestioned that many people seem to believe that it reflects reality'.[8] Refugees are deemed as the 'special kind of morally righteous border crosser, deserving of at least some protection as others are turned away'[9] as their immigration is not perceived to be a result of economic choice. This categorization was reiterated by the United Nations High Commissioner for Refugees (UNHCR), which throughout the years, despite the de facto expansion of its mandate to deal with persons in refugee-like situations, insisted on segregating refugees from migrants for the sake of advancing advocacy efforts.[10] Academics have

---

[6]   On the costs and benefits of migration for sending and receiving countries, and on ways to minimize adverse effects on either of them, see Anu Bradford, 'Sharing the Risks and Rewards of Economic Migration' (2013) 80 U Chi L Rev 29.

[7]   The issue of whether immigration actually effects low skilled migrants, unemployment or wages is contested. See, for example George J Borjas, 'The Labor Demand Curve is Downward Sloping: Reexamining the Impact of Immigration on the Labor Market' (2003) 118 QJ Econ 1335 (suggesting wage drops and unemployment in native low skilled workers due to immigration). But see also David Card, 'Is the New Immigration Really so Bad?' (2005) 115 Economic Journal 300 (suggesting that there is hardly any evidence that immigration impacts low-skilled native workers).

[8]   Rebecca Hamlin, *The Migrant/Refugee Binary and State Responses to Asylum Seekers* (2018) 1 (unpublished manuscript, on file with author).

[9]   ibid.

[10]   ibid 6.

also upheld the categorization; the minority of scholars that suggested challenging the binary[11] were met with significant resistance.[12]

The question of whether state A is responsible for a person if that person is located in state B and faces poverty there is not an easy question of international law. The answer may depend on whether the person is classified as a refugee. This is essentially a question of the extraterritorial obligations of states to honor the socio-economic rights of non-nationals.[13] Despite international efforts to create human rights instruments that suggest that states indeed have such an extraterritorial obligation in some cases,[14] as a matter of law, such obligations are somewhat limited at the moment. I would argue that the binary of refugee/economic migrant impedes the ability of migrants to escape poverty, making it difficult – though not always impossible – to receive protection from being returned to the country of origin and the poverty conditions there. Below I survey the current available forms of protection: protection through a broad interpretation of the definition of refugee, protection from refoulement to a place where a person may face poverty, and complementary protection outside the refugee convention.

A.   Protection through a Broad Interpretation of the Definition of Refugee

The current definition of refugee in the Convention Relating to the Status of Refugees (the Refugee Convention) defines a refugee as someone who

> owing to well-founded fear of being persecuted for reasons of race, religion, nationality, membership of a particular social group or political opinion, is outside the country of his nationality and is unable or, owing to such fear, is unwilling to avail himself of the protection of that country; or who, not having a nationality and being outside the country of his former habitual residence as a result of such events, is unable or, owing to such fear, is unwilling to return to it.[15]

States owe various duties to those who meet the requirement of the definition of refugees, including protecting them from refoulement – being returned to a place where their lives or liberty would be in danger. This principle, recognized by some as *jus cogens*, is found in Article 33 of the Refugee Convention:

> Prohibition of Expulsion or Return ('refoulement')

---

[11]   ibid 6–7; Roger Zetter, 'More Labels, Fewer Refugees: Remaking the Refugee Label in an Era of Globalization' (2007) 20 J Refugee Stud. 172; Tally Kritzman-Amir, 'Socio-Economic Refugees' (Ph.D. dissertation, Tel-Aviv University 2009); Heaven Crawley and Dimitris Skleparis, 'Refugees, Migrants, Neither, Both: Categorical Fetishism and the Politics of Bounding in Europe's "Migration Crisis"' (2018) 44 J Ethnic & Migration Stud 48.

[12]   Hamlin (n 8) 7; Alexander Betts and Paul Collier, *Refuge: Rethinking Refugee Policy in a Changing World* (OUP 2017) 101; James Hathaway, 'Forced Migration Studies: Could We Agree Just to "Date"?' (2007) 20 JRS 349.

[13]   Malcolm Langford, Katharine G Young and Ralph G Wilde, *Extra-Territorial Obligations and Economic and Social Rights* (forthcoming 2020).

[14]   Ralph G Wilde, 'Socioeconomic Rights, Extraterritorially' in Eyal Benvenisti and Georg Nolte (eds), *Community Interests Across International Law* (OUP 2018) 381.

[15]   Convention Relating to the Status of Refugees (adopted 28 July 1951, entered into force 22 April 1954) 189 UNTS 137 (Refugee Convention).

No Contracting State shall expel or return ('refouler') a refugee in any manner whatsoever to the frontiers of territories where his life or freedom would be threatened on account of his race, religion, nationality, membership of a particular social group or political opinion.

The benefit of the present provision may not, however, be claimed by a refugee when there are reasonable grounds for regarding as a danger to the security of the country in which he is, or who, having been convicted by a final judgment of a particularly serious crime, constitutes a danger to the community of that country.[16]

Some persons who are persecuted because they are poor or belonging to a low-ranked social class may, on some occasions, qualify under the definition of 'refugee'.[17] Persons whose persecution takes the form of socio-economic deprivation leading them to life in poverty, may also be considered refugees. Poverty thus can be a reason for persecution or a means of persecution. Through a broad interpretation of the category of refugee, it is sometimes possible to grant people both types of socio-economic migrants protection from poverty, as long as it is induced by their state of nationality or residence, in connection with one or more of the convention grounds. Social class could be, and sometimes is, considered as qualifying under the 'particular social group' convention ground.[18] Persecution through pushing a person into poverty is also sometimes recognized as meeting the requirements of the Refugee Convention. Goodwin-Gill finds that in some circumstances, the 'imposition of serious economic disadvantage, denial of access to employment, to the professions or to education' may constitute persecution.[19] This position was accepted in the United States since the enactment of the 1980 Refugee Act.[20] Case law acknowledges that persecution could take, for example, the form of denial of ability to work and support one's self or family,[21] or that of substantial economic

---

[16]   Refugee Convention, art. 33. In different contexts, this principle is also expressed in Article 3 of the UN Convention against Torture ('No State Party shall expel, return ("refouler") or extradite a person to another State where there are substantial grounds for believing that he would be in danger of being subjected to torture …'); Article 45 of the Geneva Convention Relative to the Protection of Civilian Persons in Time of War ('Protected persons shall not be transferred to a Power which is not a party to the Convention … In no circumstances shall a protected person be transferred to a country where he or she may have reason to fear persecution for his or her political opinions or religious beliefs.'). Similar arrangements can be found in regional treaties. This principle has also been reinforced in declarations and resolutions of international and regional organizations, including the UNHCR and the practices of states, and thus is viewed by many as a principle of customary international law. See Guy S Goodwin-Gill, *The Refugee in International Law* (2nd edn, OUP 1996) 124–37.
[17]   See for example Immigration and Refugee Board of Canada, 'Membership in a Particular Social Group as a Basis for a Well-Founded Fear of Persecution – Framework of Analysis' (*refworld*, December 1991) <www.refworld.org/docid/3ae6b32510.html> accessed 16 December 2019 ('"Particular social groups" have been defined by: kinship ties, colour, gender and clan or caste; *past economic, social or professional status* – e.g. the bourgeoisie, the peasant landowning class, civil servants.') (emphasis added).
[18]   ibid.
[19]   Guy S Goodwin-Gill, 'Entry and Exclusion of Refugees: The Obligations of States and the Protection Function of the Office of the United Nations High Commissioner for Refugees' [1982] Michigan Yearbook Intl L Studies 291, 298–99.
[20]   HR Rep No 95-549, at 5 (1978) reprinted in 1978 USCCAN 4700, at 4704. This legislation adheres to the principle set in *Kovac v INS*, 407 F.2d 102, 105–06 (9th Cir. 1969). See also, e.g.: *Chen v Holder*, 604 F.3d 324, 334 (7th Cir., 2010).
[21]   See, e.g., *Baballah v Ashcroft*, 335 F. 3d 981, 990-91 (9th Cir. 2003); Michelle Foster, *International Refugee Law and Socio-Economic Rights: Refuge from Deprivation* (CUP 2007) 101.

deprivation.[22] Some domestic courts have considered the inability of a child to receive education[23] or discrimination in access to medical care[24] as in themselves constituting a form of persecution. In a few extreme cases, confiscation of property has been viewed as persecution.[25] Additionally, the accumulation of different forms of socio-economic discriminatory steps or the combination of socio-economic discrimination with other forms of persecution may be sufficient grounds.[26]

However, most commonly, persons who flee poverty have difficulty establishing that their poverty is a result of a denial of their socio-economic rights which amounts to persecution, and struggle to establish a nexus between their alleged persecution and a convention ground.[27] Those who are compelled to leave their country due to a generalized lack of resources in their country may not be able to form a refugee claim and will be classified as economic migrants, and as such may not be eligible for protection from deportation.[28] Thus, many individuals who are driven to immigrate by socio-economic constraint are excluded from the definition of refugee and related protections.[29] This protection gap exists despite the fact that, morally speaking, there is little difference between those compelled to leave their country due to poverty and those compelled to leave due to a fear of being persecuted. It is therefore important to challenge the binary distinction between refugee and economic migrant and consider replacing the categorization with ones that have a more robust moral ground.[30] Regional instruments suggest that broadening the scope of protection is indeed due and also include in the definition of 'refugee' people fleeing generalized situations of disasters, which often correlate with poverty.[31]

---

[22] *Borca v INS*, 77 F.3d 210, 215–17 (7th Cir. 1996). Economic deprivation was considered persecution, even when one still had economic opportunities, so long as she was subjected to substantial deprivation. On the other hand, U.S. courts have refrained from treating incidents of job loss (*Medhin v Ashcroft*, 350 F.3d 685, 689 (7th Cir. 2003)), employment discrimination (*Barreto-Claro v US Attorney General*, 275 F.3d 1334, 1340 (11th Cir. 2001)), and economic hardship (*Capric v Ashcroft*, 355 F.3d 1075, 1092-95 (7th Cir. 2004)) as persecution. In Canada, however, loss of employment has sometimes been sufficient to fulfill the requirements of persecution. *Shao Mei He v Canada (Minister of Employment and Immigration)* [1994] F.C.J. No. 1243; *Xie v Canada* (Minister of Employment and Immigration) [1994] F.C.J. No. 286. To some extent, this was also the position of some American scholars, namely James Hathaway, and a similar position was also taken by the US courts. See Foster (n 21) 99 ff. These cases do affirm that asylum may be granted based on the deliberate imposition of substantial economic disadvantage, but it was still required to show nexus to one of the convention grounds.
[23] This is mostly the case in Canada and Denmark. See Foster (n 21) 103–04.
[24] ibid 104.
[25] ibid 109–10.
[26] ibid 105–07.
[27] Kritzman-Amir (n 11).
[28] ibid.
[29] ibid.
[30] Tally Kritzman-Amir, 'Looking Behind the "Protection Gap": The Moral Obligation of the State to Necessitous Immigrants' (2009) 13 U Pa JL & Soc Change 47.
[31] Organization of African Unity (OAU), Convention Governing the Specific Aspects of Refugee Problems in Africa (adopted 10 September 1969, entered into force 20 June 1974) 1001 UNTS 45, art 1.2 (OAU Convention) ('The term "refugee" shall also apply to every person who, owing to external aggression, occupation, foreign domination or events seriously disturbing public order in either part or the whole of his country of origin or nationality, is compelled to leave his place of habitual residence in order to seek refuge in another place outside his country of origin or nationality.') See also, 'Cartagena Declaration on Refugees, Colloquium on the International Protection of Refugees in Central America,

B.   Protection from Refoulement to a Place Where a Person is Likely to Experience Poverty

In addition, international human rights can protect a person from deportation if she is likely to experience poverty in the country to which she is supposed to be removed. As described below, on a number of occasions, the European Court of Human Rights (ECtHR) and the European Court of Justice (ECJ) ruled that persons cannot be deported to places where they will experience extreme poverty, as such deportation would be a violation of international human rights law.

In *MSS*,[32] an Afghan asylum seeker brought a case against Belgium,[33] which had returned him to Greece, the country through which he had entered Europe and where, pursuant to the Dublin Regulations,[34] he should have completed his asylum application. In Greece, MSS was subjected to, among other things, homelessness and extreme poverty. The ECtHR determined that though states are not required to provide migrants with 'financial assistance to enable them to maintain a certain standard of living', 'a situation of extreme material poverty [can] raise an issue'.[35] With respect to the impoverished living conditions in Greece, the Court also found that 'such living conditions, combined with the prolonged uncertainty in which he has remained and the total lack of any prospects of his situation improving' were severe enough to be incompatible with Article 3 of the European Convention on Human Rights (prohibition on torture or to inhuman or degrading treatment or punishment).[36] Likewise, in the *Jawo* case an asylum seeker sought protection from being returned from Germany to Italy – where he had

---

Mexico and Panama' (*Organization of American States*, 22 November 1984) <www.oas.org/dil/1984 _cartagena_declaration_on_refugees.pdf> accessed 25 June 2020. ('Hence the definition or concept of a refugee to be recommended for use in the region is one which, in addition to containing the elements of the 1951 Convention and the 1967 Protocol, includes among refugees persons who have fled their country because their lives, safety or freedom have been threatened by generalized violence, foreign aggression, internal conflicts, massive violation of human rights or other circumstances which have seriously disturbed public order.').

[32]   *MSS v Belgium and Greece* App no 30696/09 (ECtHR, 21 January 2011). In this case, removal was prohibited by the ECtHR, as it would have been a violation of Article 3 of the European Convention for the Protection of Human Rights and Fundamental Freedoms, which prohibits torture and inhuman or degrading treatment of punishment.

[33]   Council Regulation 604/2013 of the European Parliament and of the Council of 26 June 2013 establishing the criteria and mechanisms for determining the Member State responsible for examining an application for international protection lodged in one of the Member States by a third-country national or a stateless person [2013] OJ L 180/31. At the time of the *MSS* decision, the valid regulation was Council Regulation 343/2003 of 18 February 2003 establishing the criteria and mechanisms for determining the Member State responsible for examining an asylum application lodged in one of the Member States by a third-country national [2003] OJ L 50/1.

[34]   Council Regulation 604/2013 of the European Parliament and of the Council of 26 June 2013 establishing the criteria and mechanisms for determining the Member State responsible for examining an application for international protection lodged in one of the Member States by a third-country national or a stateless person [2013] OJ L 180/31. At the time of the *MSS* decision, the valid regulation was Council Regulation 343/2003 of 18 February 2003 establishing the criteria and mechanisms for determining the Member State responsible for examining an asylum application lodged in one of the Member States by a third-country national [2003] OJ L 50/1.

[35]   *MSS* (n 32) paras 252–53.

[36]   European Convention for the Protection of Human Rights and Fundamental Freedoms, as amended by Protocols Nos. 11 and 14. ETS No 5 [1950].

filed an asylum application – due to the harsh conditions in reception centers there. Though the ECJ found that that case did not meet the required level of severity, it set a standard of extreme material poverty as a protection from being returned to a country pursuant to the Dublin Regulations.[37] In later cases, the ECtHR distinguished between poor socio-economic conditions in the country to which removal was planned that are a result of intentional acts or omissions of the government versus a general lack of resources.[38] A more robust protection from removal was offered to persons who would be subjected to intentional deprivation, whereas persons whose claim was related to the general shortage of resources in their country had to prove the existence of compelling humanitarian circumstances.[39]

C.   Complementary and Subsidiary Protection: Temporary Protection and other forms of Protection

Many countries offer protection to persons outside the Refugee Convention on the basis of various temporary and subsidiary protection arrangements. Temporary Protection Status (TPS) was developed as such a category of inclusion in the United States and several other countries.[40] The United States created the mechanism of TPS in 1990,[41] as one form of protection[42] extended to nationals of designated countries[43] who met a set of criteria. Typical situations that result in TPS designation of a country include an ongoing armed conflict,[44] an environmental disaster[45] or other 'extraordinary and temporary conditions', all of which cor-

---

[37]   Case C-163/17 *Abubacarr Jawo v Bundesrepublik Deutschland* [2019] OJ C 318, 25.9.2017, paras 93–94. See also Case C 297/17 *Bashar Ibrahim v Bundesrepublik Deutschland* [2019] OJ C 309, 18.9.2017.

[38]   Marlies Hesselman, 'Sharing International Responsibility for Poor Migrants?: An Analysis of Extra-Territorial Socio-Economic Human Rights Law' (2013) 15 EJSS 187, 200–03.

[39]   ibid.

[40]   Joan Fitzpatrick, 'Temporary Protection of Refugees: Elements of a Formalized Regime' (2000) 94 Am J Int'l L 279, 282, 297–99. For Temporary Protection in Europe see Khalid Koser and Richard Black, 'Limits to Harmonization: The "Temporary Protection" of Refugees in the European Union' (1999) 37 Int'l Migration 521; Kim Rygiel, Feyzi Baban and Suzan Ilcan, 'The Syrian Refugee Crisis: The EU-Turkey "Deal" and Temporary Protection' (2016) 16 Global Soc Pol'y 315.

[41]   Susan Martin, Andy Schoenholtz and Deborah Waller Meyers, 'Temporary Protection: Towards a New Regional and Domestic Framework' (1998) 12 Geo. Immigr. L.J. 543, 544.

[42]   A similar mechanism activated even before TPS was created is Deferred Enforced Departure (DED), which allows for the designation of a country by the President. Bill Frelick and Barbara Kohnen, 'Filling the Gap: Temporary Protected Status' (1995) 8 JRS 339; *Adjudicator's Field Manual* (*U.S. Citizenship and Immigration Services*) para 38.2 <www.uscis.gov/sites/default/files/policymanual/afm/afm38-external.pdf> accessed 25 June 2020. Currently Liberia is the only designated country.

[43]   Ten countries are currently designated under TPS: El Salvador, Haiti, Honduras, Nepal, Nicaragua, Somalia, South Sudan, Sudan, Syria and Yemen. The US Government announced an intention to terminate the TPS but was prevented from doing so by the Court. For more about the termination of the TPS designation see Tally Kritzman-Amir, *The Shifting Categorization of Migrants* (2020) 58 Columbia Journal of Transnational Law 279–331.

[44]   For example, Syria was designated due to the ongoing armed conflict in its territory. Designation of Syrian Arab Republic for Temporary Protected Status, 77 Fed. Reg. 19026 (Mar. 29, 2012).

[45]   For example, El Salvador was designated after a series of earthquakes. Designation of El Salvador Under Temporary Protected Status, 66 Fed. Reg. 14214 (Mar. 9, 2001).

relate with poverty.[46] It is a form of group-based protection offered to those who fall outside the scope of the Refugee Convention and is legally grounded in international human rights obligations, including non-refoulement.[47] This category groups a pattern of migration from a certain country of origin, rather than migrants who share any substantive common denominator. In the absence of individual claims of rights, the protection afforded to beneficiaries is rather minimal, focusing on their short-term and immediate physical safety and their ability to support themselves until they are able to return to their country of nationality,[48] yet it renders the protected persons' lives liminal and offers no protection from poverty.[49] Similar subsidiary protection is granted in Europe to persons who present humanitarian reasons, which include systematic violations of economic rights or a range of situations of insecurity that correlate with poverty.[50]

To conclude this section, the ability to protect people in their countries of origin or third countries is compromised by the lack of commitment to the protection of persons whose social and economic human rights are violated in their countries and by the adherence to the refugee/economic migrant binary. Thus, escaping poverty in itself is only rarely a cause for imposing an obligation on a country to grant someone protection. For the most part, people escaping poverty in their countries of origin rely on the discretion of their destination states to allow them to stay as migrant workers. In addition, to address this protection gap, states have developed complementary means of protection, which grant a thinner form of protection to people who do not qualify as refugees and would otherwise be deported to situations which raise acute humanitarian concerns. These forms of protection fall short of the fuller protection afforded to refugees, giving more people less rights. While courts have sometimes prevented the removal of persons to extreme destitution, the protection gap still exists.

II.   PROTECTING MIGRANTS FROM POVERTY IN RECEIVING STATES

Poverty is quite often a part of the migration experience in the receiving country. Poverty rates among migrant populations are often higher than the native born population.[51] This is especially common among vulnerable migrants such as women, children, elderly persons and people with disabilities or health conditions.[52] High poverty rates are often, though not

---

[46]   Immigration and Nationality Act, 8 U.S.C. § 1254a(b)(1)(A),(B),(C). Haiti, for example was designated due to 'extraordinary and temporary conditions' from the earthquake that occurred in the country. See Designation of Haiti for Temporary Protected Status, 75 Fed. Reg. 3476 (Jan. 21, 2010).

[47]   Susan Martin, Andy Schoenholtz and Deborah Waller Meyers, 'Temporary Protection: Towards a New Regional and Domestic Framework' (1998) 12 Geo Immigr LJ 543, 544–45.

[48]   Joan Fitzpatrick, 'Temporary Protection of Refugees: Elements of a Formalized Regime' (2000) 94 AJIL 279, 282, 297–99.

[49]   Miranda Cady Hallett, 'Temporary Protection, Enduring Contradiction: The Contested and Contradictory Meanings of Temporary Immigration Status' (2014) 39 L & Soc Inquiry 621, 623.

[50]   Jane McAdam, *Complementary Protection in International Refugee Law* (OUP 2007) 53 ff.

[51]   OECD, 'Income of Immigrant Households' in *Indicators of Immigrant Integration 2015: Settling In* (OECD Publishing 2015) 159, 164-65 <https://doi.org/10.1787/9789264234024-11-en> accessed 26 June 2020.

[52]   Uma Kothari, 'Migration and Chronic Poverty' (2002) University of Manchester Working Paper No 16 <https://pdfs.semanticscholar.org/ad72/8e863a6a432dc5bca124558232f6de4b53b1.pdf> accessed 26 June 2020.

always, connected with other difficulties, such as food insecurity,[53] homelessness[54] or housing problems,[55] poor access to health services[56] and poor access to welfare services and benefits.[57] Research in the United States indicates that recently-arriving migrants display the highest poverty rates, as among them unemployment rates or low-skilled employment are more widespread. Poverty rates decline pretty steadily as migrants integrate into the receiving country's labor market, acquire language skills and develop social networks, which are a crucial source of information and socialization.[58]

A.   Migration, Poverty and Human Rights Instruments

It is possible to argue that receiving countries have legal duties to assist migrants, guarantee their access to social and economic rights and alleviate poverty among migrant populations. Employment-related rights, education, healthcare, housing assistance and access to welfare services are key components to decrease poverty rates. International human rights conven-

---

[53]   Mariana Chilton and others, 'Food Insecurity and Risk of Poor Health Among US-Born Children of Immigrants' (2009) 99 Am J Pub Health 556; Mustafa Koc and Jennifer Welsh, 'Food, Foodways and Immigrant Experience' (*Centre for Studies in Food Security*, 2002) 4 <www.researchgate.net/profile/Mustafa_Koc2/publication/253449347_Food_Foodways_and_Immigrant_Experience/links/0a85e52fe76e2cff51000000/Food-Foodways-and-Immigrant-Experience.pdf> accessed 26 June 2020; Tally Kritzman-Amir and Anda Barak-Bianco, 'Food as a Biopower Means of Control: The Use of Food in Asylum Regimes' (2019) 45 Am. J. L. and Med. 57.

[54]   See, for example Daniel Hiebert Silvia D'Addario and Kathy Sherrell, 'The Profile of Absolute and Relative Homelessness Among Immigrants, Refugees, and Refugee Claimants in the GVRD' (MOSAIC,   2005)   <www.mosaicbc.org/wp-content/uploads/2017/01/The-Profile-of-Absolute-and-Relative-Homelessness.pdf> accessed 26 June 2020; Gerald Daly, *Homeless: Policies, Strategies and Lives on the Streets* (Routledge 1996) 89–108.

[55]   Some of those housing problems include over-crowded, unaffordable, substandard, 'dirty', unpleasant, and poorly maintained accommodations. Other problems may include neighborhood safety issues, proximity to environmental hazards, etc. See, for example Michael Schill, Samantha Friedman and Emily Rosenbaum, 'The Housing Conditions of Immigrants in New York City' (1998) 9 J Housing Research 201; Parveen Mattu, 'A Survey on the Extent of Substandard Housing Problems Faced by Immigrants and Refugees in the Lower Mainland of British Columbia' (*MOSAIC*, 2002) <www.mosaicbc.org/wp-content/uploads/2017/01/SCPI-Summary-Report_0.pdf> accessed 4 December 2020; David Robinson, Kesia Reeve and Rionach Casey, *The Housing Pathways of New Immigrants* (Sheffield Hallam   University   2007)   <www4.shu.ac.uk/research/cresr/sites/shu.ac.uk/files/housing-pathways-new-immigrants.pdf> accessed 26 June 2020; Matthew Hall and Emily Greenman, 'Housing and Neighborhood Quality Among Undocumented Mexican and Central American Immigrants' (2013) 42 Social Science Research 1712.

[56]   Leighton Ku and Sheetal Matani, 'Left Out: Immigrants' Access to Health Care and Insurance' (2001) 20 Health Affairs 247; Román Romero-Ortuño, 'Access to Health Care for Illegal Immigrants in the EU: Should we be Concerned?' (2004) 11 EJHL 245; Kathryn Pitkin Derose and others, 'Review: Immigrants and Health Care Access, Quality, and Cost' (2009) 66 Medical Care Research and Review 355.

[57]   Diane Sainsbury, 'Immigrants' Social Rights in Comparative Perspective: Welfare Regimes, Forms in Immigration and Immigration Policy Regimes' (2006) 16 J European Soc Pol 229.

[58]   Steven A Camarota, 'Immigrants in the United States, 2010: A Profile of America's Foreign-Born Population: Poverty, Welfare, and the Uninsured' (*Center for Immigration Studies*, 8 August 2012) <https://cis.org/Immigrants-United-States-Profile-Americas-ForeignBorn-Population> accessed 26 June 2020; Steven Raphael and Eugene Smolensky, 'Immigration and Poverty in the United States' (2009) 26 Focus 27.

tions such as the International Covenant on Civil and Political Rights and the International Covenant on Social, Economic and Cultural Rights are applicable to migrants and refugees, as they apply to 'all individuals within [a State's] territory and subject to its jurisdiction',[59] or to 'everyone'.[60] Their applicability is not limited to citizens or lawfully staying persons, and they apply not just within a state's territory but also along its borders and in other areas where states exercise their jurisdiction or apply coercive force.[61] Though states may provide more expansive rights and protections to their nationals, the obligation to protect at least the most basic rights of non-nationals exists. Some of the later General Comments to the Covenants specifically recognize a duty to protect the rights of refugees and migrants.[62]

B.   Migration, Poverty and Migrants' Rights Instruments

Alongside the general human rights norms, there are also specific protections of migrants and refugees' rights, including their social and economic rights. Migrants' human rights are protected in several international instruments that are specific to categories of migrants, such as migrant workers.[63] However, these instruments offer limited protection to migrants for several reasons. First, these instruments were ratified primarily by origin countries, and receiving countries have displayed a reluctance to join them. Second, some of these instruments focus on migrants' labor rights, rather than the broader range of rights that are necessary to prevent poverty. Third, these instruments emphasize state sovereignty and prioritize it over the rights of migrants.[64] Because of the poor ratification rate of receiving countries, those instruments are unlikely to be of use to migrants.[65]

---

[59]   International Covenant on Civil and Political Rights (adopted 16 December 1966, entered into force 23 March 1976) 999 UNTS 171 (ICCPR) art. 2(1).

[60]   International Covenant on Economic, Social and Cultural Rights (adopted 16 December 1966, entered into force 3 January 1976) 993 UNTS 3 (ICESCR) preamble.

[61]   Tally Kritzman-Amir and Thomas Spijkerboer, 'On the Morality and Legality of Borders: Border Policies and Asylum Seekers' (2013) 26 Harv Hum Rts J 1, 10–28. See also the position of the HRC in *Lopez Burgos v Uruguay*, Communication No. 52/1979. UN Human Rights Committee, 'Selected Decisions under the Optional Protocol' (1985) UN Doc CCPR/C/OP/1, 91, para 12.2 (stating that the duties under the ICCPR refer not just 'to the place where the violation occurred, but rather to the relationship between the individual and the State in relation to a violation of any of the rights set forth in the Covenant; wherever they occurred'.).

[62]   See, e.g., UN Committee on Economic, Social and Cultural Rights (CESCR), 'General Comment No. 14: The Right to the Highest Attainable Standard of Health' (11 August 2000) UN Doc. E/C.12/2000/4, para 34; U.N. Committee on the Elimination of Discrimination Against Women (CEDAW), 'General Recommendation No. 32 on the Gender-Related Dimensions of Refugee Status, Asylum, Nationality and Statelessness of Women' (14 November 2014) UN Doc CEDAW/C/GC/32, paras 3, 11.

[63]   UNGA, 'International Convention on the Protection of the Rights of All Migrant Workers and Members of their Families' (18 December 1990) UN Doc A/RES/45/158; International Labour Organization (ILO), 'Migration for Employment Convention (Revised)' (1 July 1949, entered into force 22 January 1952) C97 <www.refworld.org/docid/3ddb64057.html> accessed 23 July 2019; ILO, 'Migrant Workers (Supplementary Provisions) Convention' (adopted 24 June 1975, entered into force 9 December 1978) C143 <www.refworld.org/docid/3ddb6ba64.html> accessed 23 July 2019.

[64]   Linda Bosniak, 'Human Rights, State Sovereignty and the Protection of Undocumented Migrants under the International Migrant Workers Convention' (1991) 5 Int'l Migration Rev 737.

[65]   For a more comprehensive analysis of the *International Convention on the Protection of the Rights of All Migrant Workers and Members of their Families* see Ryszard Cholewinski and others (eds), *Migration and Human Rights: The United Nations Convention on Migrant Workers' Rights* (CUP 2009).

Similarly, the Refugee Convention[66] grants different rights, including social and economic rights, in a selective manner to refugees based on their level of attachment to their country of asylum using legal categories such as 'subject to the state's jurisdiction',[67] 'lawfully present'[68] and 'lawfully staying'.[69] If the goal of international human rights law is to assert that there are universal human rights that should apply to all humans, the Refugee Convention carves out a swath of especially vulnerable human beings (refugees and asylum seekers) and offers them more limited protection.

C.   From Failing to Protect to Inducing Poverty

Despite the existence of general and particular norms on the eligibility of migrants to social and economic rights, migrants typically experience poor access to those rights, rendering them susceptible to poverty.

International human rights are often applied differently to citizens than to different categories of migrants, despite the explicit language of international human rights instruments.[70] While it might be permissible under international law for states to give some preferences to their nationals, the core and basic level of human rights, including economic rights, of migrants should nevertheless be protected under international human rights instruments by virtue of their being universal. For example, historically immigrants have been deemed undeserving of the same protection of the law[71] and public benefits, irrespective of their personal circumstances.[72] In many parts of the world, they do not enjoy the safety net of the welfare state.[73] An unwillingness to protect the welfare rights of immigrants and ensure their access to public benefits is symptomatic of the 'democratic deficit' – the lack of political voice and representation of migrants, which leads to a lack of accountability of the bureaucracy to the migrant population.[74] In some cases, international human rights arguments are utilized to impose obligations on states to protect the socio-economic rights of migrants and prevent poor living conditions. For example, several cases in Europe held that allowing migrants to remain

---

[66]   Refugee Convention (n 15).

[67]   See, for example, ibid art 20 (rationing).

[68]   See, for example, ibid art 18 (self-employment).

[69]   See ibid art 17 (wage earning employment), art 21 (housing), art 23 (public relief), art 24 (social security). Other forms of attachment include being subject to a state's jurisdiction, being physically present and obtaining durable residency.

[70]   In other words, states violate international human rights conventions by failing to protect the rights of migrants, even when they uphold the rights of their nationals. Jane McAdam, 'Research Paper No. 125: The Refugee Convention as a Rights Blueprint for Persons in Need of International Protection' (*UNHCR*, 2006) ('strong on principle but weak on delivery') <www.unhcr.org/en-us/44b7b7162.pdf> accessed 29 June 2020.

[71]   Kevin R Johnson, 'Hurricane Katrina: Lessons About Immigrants in the Administrative State' (2008) 45 Hous LR 11, 32.

[72]   ibid 16–17.

[73]   ibid; Assaf, 'Women Asylum Seekers in Israel: Vulnerable, Exploited and Lacking Authorities' Support' (March 2016), available online at: <https://tbinternet.ohchr.org/Treaties/CEDAW/Shared%20Documents/ISR/INT_CEDAW_NGO_ISR_24218_E.pdf> accessed 30 June 2020.

[74]   Johnson (n 71) 17–21, 43–44.

in poor living conditions amounts to inhumane treatment violating Article 3 of the European Convention on Human Rights.[75]

Given the absence of enforcement mechanisms for migrants' rights norms,[76] the rather weak language of the Refugee Convention[77] and the general 'compassion fatigue' towards migrants and refugees,[78] states are not inclined to offer broad protection of socio-economic rights to refugees and migrants, thus failing to protect them from abject poverty. For example, in many countries asylum laws include limitations on asylum seekers' ability to find gainful employment, such as a waiting period before an asylum seeker can apply to obtain employment authorization. This is despite protection of that right in the Refugee Convention. In the United States, '[a]n applicant for asylum is not entitled to employment authorization … An applicant who is not otherwise eligible for employment authorization shall not be granted such authorization prior to 180 days after the date of filing of the application for asylum'.[79] In the United Kingdom, asylum seekers may apply for an employment authorization if their asylum application was not decided within twelve months, and only for employment in certain occupations.[80] Israel refrains from authorizing the employment of most asylum seekers, though it refrains from enforcing the prohibition on their employment.[81]

Failing to protect social and economic rights of migrants is sometimes justified by state sovereignty. The argument suggests that since migration policy is perceived, by and large, as a matter that states may, and should, determine on the basis of their national interests, identity and morality, it should also entail the ability of a sovereign to determine the treatment and access to rights of the migrants in their territory. However, this argument is flawed. First, even if, legally speaking, migration policy is a sovereign matter, states' sovereign power is restricted by international and domestic law, including, but not limited to, the international and

---

[75]   McAdam (n 50) 206–08 (mentioning for example *Pančenko v Latvia* (1999) App No 40772/98 and *BB v France* (1998) App No 30930/96). See also *N.H. and Others v France* (2020) (application nos. 28820/13, 75547/13 and 13114/15).

[76]   Guy S Goodwin-Gill, 'The International Law of Refugee Protection' in Elena Fiddian-Qasmiyeh and others (eds), *The Oxford Handbook of Refugee and Forced Migration Studies* (OUP 2014) 36, 44.

[77]   The Refugee Convention requires states to fulfill a relative standard such as 'the most favourable treatment possible' or to apply a standard of non-discrimination (either in relation to the treatment of other non-nationals or, in some contexts, to the treatment of nationals), but does not require any specific threshold of implementation.

[78]   Maryellen Fullerton, 'The International and National Protection of Refugees' in Hurst Hanum (ed), *Guide to International Human Rights Practice* (4th edn, Transnational Pub Inc 2004) 245, 247.

[79]   8 USC § 1158 (b) (2) (A) and (d)(2) (2012). It should be noted that the United States has signed but not ratified the Refugee Convention. This, however, is not a policy measure unique to countries which are not members to the Refugee Convention. Finally, this policy is also going to be reformed. See: USCIS, 'USCIS Rule Strengthens Employment Eligibility Requirements for Asylum Seekers' (June 22, 2020), available at: <www.uscis.gov/news/news-releases/uscis-rule-strengthens-employment-eligibility -requirements-for-asylum-seekers> accessed 4 December 2020 (suggesting that the period might be extending the wait period for an employment authorization document to a year).

[80]   The UK is a party to the Refugee Convention. For comparison to the United Kingdom see: Home Office, 'Permission to Work and Volunteering for Asylum Seekers' (*UK Home Office*, 2019). <https:// assets.publishing.service.gov.uk/government/uploads/system/uploads/attachment_data/file/803596/ permission-to-work-v8.0-ext.pdf> accessed 26 June 2020.

[81]   Israel is a party to the refugee convention. See 'Employment' (*ASSAF*) <http://assaf.org.il/en/ node/139> [https://perma.cc/WP7R-ZY9Z] accessed 6 March 2019.

domestic law obligations towards refugees and the principle of non-refoulement.[82] Second, some scholars suggest that there are reasons to doubt this narrative of the sovereign power to exclude, and suggest that states should assume responsibility towards migrants, in light of the messy and complicated connections between colonialism, neocolonialism, and international migration.[83] Under this analysis, migrants are not political outsiders, since in many ways, due to colonialism, they already have a deep and meaningful relationship with the receiving political community. Therefore, the presumption that they can be excluded at the whim of the sovereign state is wrong, because they are already a part of the national community in this way. Third, once an immigrant is within a state's territory, the state has obligations towards the immigrant under international human rights law.[84] Even if a state could have legally (and perhaps even morally) excluded a person, once that person has entered its territory legal obligations exist. It would be wrong to deduce that there are no responsibilities and obligations towards migrants from the mere power to exclude them. Despite this, state sovereignty arguments have justified, with or without cause, blanket exclusions of migrants in times of economic crises, including most recently the restrictions on the entry of migrant workers following the Coronavirus outbreak in April 2020.[85]

Interestingly, this general lack of adherence to international human rights law when it comes to the protection of migrants' socio-economic rights, is complemented by national citizenship laws in some jurisdictions. Some countries require that persons who apply to naturalize not be recipients of welfare benefits.[86] Receipt of such benefits is viewed as an undesired risk that the naturalized individual would become a burden on the receiving society.

In the United States, several domestic acts bar migrants from enjoying access to socio-economic rights. The 1996 Personal Responsibility and Work Opportunity Reconciliation Act (PRWORA) barred various categories of immigrants from accessing certain forms of federal welfare assistance, including healthcare related benefits such as Medicare and Medicaid.[87] Amendments to the Illegal Immigration Reform and Immigrant Responsibility Act of 1996 strengthened the 'public charge' ground of inadmissibility, allowing the immigration authorities to exclude and deport persons on the basis of poverty if there is a fear that they

---

[82]   See mainly the Refugee Convention (n 15).

[83]   See, for example Tendayi Achiume, 'Migration as Decolonization' (2019) 71 Stan L Rev 1509.

[84]   See Linda Bosniak, 'Being Here: Ethical Territoriality and the Rights of Immigrants' (2007) 8 Theo Inq L 389, 390.

[85]   Donald J Trump, 'Proclamation Suspending Entry of Immigrants Who Present Risk to the U.S. Labor Market During the Economic Recovery Following the COVID-19 Outbreak' (*White House*, 22 April 2020) <www.whitehouse.gov/presidential-actions/proclamation-suspending-entry-immigrants -present-risk-u-s-labor-market-economic-recovery-following-covid-19-outbreak/> accessed 26 June 2020; Donald J Trump, 'Proclamation Suspending Entry of Aliens Who Present a Risk to the U.S. Labor Market Following the Coronavirus Outbreak' (*White House*, 22 June 2020) <www.whitehouse.gov/ presidential-actions/proclamation-suspending-entry-aliens-present-risk-u-s-labor-market-following -coronavirus-outbreak/> accessed 30 June 2020.

[86]   See, e.g. 'Becoming a Citizen' (*Swiss Info*, 3 January 2018) <www.swissinfo.ch/eng/becoming-a -citizen/29288376> accessed 26 June 2020. Germany requires candidates for naturalization to demonstrate their ability to support themselves without recourse to social assistance or unemployment benefits. See, for example 'Becoming a German Citizen by Naturalization' (*Federal Ministry of the Interior, Building and Community*) <www.bmi.bund.de/SharedDocs/faqs/EN/topics/migration/staatsang/Erwerb _der_deutschen_Staatsbuergerschaft_durch_Eingbuergerung_en.html > accessed 26 June 2020.

[87]   Polly J Price, 'Immigration Policy and Public Health' (2019) 16 Indiana Health L Rev 235, 240.

might become a 'public charge' and rely on government services or support.[88] While initially the federal government left the 'public charge' test open to interpretation, it quickly assured non-citizens that they need not fear obtaining various basic services such as food assistance or medical treatment.[89] On August 12, 2019 the Department of Homeland Security published an amendment to the regulations on 'public charge', defining the category rather broadly and depriving people of the ability to adjust their status, renew visas or from admissibility (there were exception for certain categories of migrants, such as asylum seekers and refugees).[90] Analysis of this rule when it was initially proposed found that it would disproportionately affect vulnerable groups of migrants, such as women, children and the elderly.[91] The likely result of this policy is that immigration law becomes a background norm, discouraging migrants from requesting welfare benefits, even when they are legally eligible to receive them, due to the immigration consequences they might carry. This results in turning away immigrants more susceptible to poverty and renders the welfare safety net irrelevant for them.[92] Not only does this conflict with international human rights obligations, but it also means that the United States is indirectly contributing to poverty in immigration populations, in an effort to portray migrants as a burden and subsequently exclude them. The harmful potential of the 'public charge rule' became evident amidst the outbreak of the Coronavirus pandemic in the spring of 2020 and the following economic crisis from physical distancing and closures enforced in various countries. Those measures had devastating impact on immigrants. Many immigrants were excluded from the stimulus plans[93] and were forced to continue to work in dangerous conditions in order to evade poverty, among other things, because they had no welfare safety net to fall back onto. In a global pandemic, this reality creates public health risks for everyone.

---

[88]   ibid 243.

[89]   ibid 243–244.

[90]   'Inadmissibility on Public Charge Grounds' 84 Fed. Reg. 41,292 (Aug. 14, 2019). The regulations were suspended in a nation-wide injunction, which was later stayed by the U.S. Supreme Court. Application for Stay, *Department of Homeland Security v New York*, No. 19A785, 589 U. S. ____ (2020) <www.supremecourt.gov/opinions/19pdf/19a785_j4ek.pdf> accessed 29 June 2020; Application for Stay, *Wolf v Cook County*, Illinois, No. 19A905, 589 U. S. ____ (2020) <www.supremecourt.gov/opinions/19pdf/19a905_7m48.pdf> accessed 29 June 2020.

[91]   Randy Capps and others, 'Gauging the Impact of DHS' Proposed Public-Charge Rule on U.S. Immigration' (*Migration Policy Institute*, November 2018) <www.migrationpolicy.org/research/impact-dhs-public-charge-rule-immigration> accessed 26 June 2020.

[92]   Michael D Shear and Eileen Sullivan, 'Trump Policy Favors Wealthier Immigrants for Green Cards'(*The New York Times*, 12 August 2019) <www.nytimes.com/2019/08/12/us/politics/trump-immigration-policy.html?smid=nytcore-ios-share&fbclid=IwAR1uwN271e956bYbyCMOFUa2jyH74iNq_iBCCUX81-OMejMh-Dwpo8Hup5Y> accessed 26 June 2020.

[93]   On the partial exclusion of migrants from the stimulus offered in the United States see Caroline Tang and Michael K Mahoney 'CARES Act: Foreign National and Immigrant Eligibility for Paid Leave, Unemployment Benefits, and Stimulus Rebates' (*The National Law Review*, 3 April 2020) <www.natlawreview.com/article/cares-act-foreign-national-and-immigrant-eligibility-paid-leave-unemployment> accessed 26 June 2020. Compare with Madeline Holcombe and Catherine E Shoichet, 'Why California is Giving its Own Stimulus Checks to Undocumented Immigrants' (*CNN*, 16 April 2020) <www.cnn.com/2020/04/16/us/california-stimulus-undocumented-immigrants/index.html> accessed 26 June 2020.

Interestingly, this was the case though many immigrants were defined as essential workers and contributed to the host societies in a very tangible manner.[94]

In other cases, it is possible to argue that receiving countries actively and directly contribute to poverty among migrants. One example is the Israeli 'Deposit Law'.[95] The law requires employers of undocumented entrants into Israel, typically asylum seekers, to 'deposit' one-fifth of their monthly salaries into a special account,[96] and these funds are available only upon their departure from the country. Since asylum seekers were already susceptible to precarious employment, with low wages and little job security, associated with their temporary status, this law resulted in abject poverty. For vulnerable asylum seekers, such as women and children, this was compounded with the structural forms of discrimination they endured in the labor market and society.[97] Documented effects include increased homelessness and home over-crowdedness, pushing people – especially women – to prostitution and exacerbated vulnerability to trafficking,[98] forcing people to opt out of their health insurance, increasing food insecurity, etc.[99] The vulnerability has peaked during the outbreak of the Coronavirus, as many asylum seekers became unemployed. Amidst discussions on allowing asylum seekers some access to their deposited earnings during the crisis, the Israeli High Court of Justice struck down parts of the 'deposit law' finding it to be an unconstitutional violation of the right to property.[100]

Some receiving states view their responsibility to protect migrants from poverty – and the dependence of migrants on the receiving states – as an opportunity to send a strong signal. Unable to fully control their borders, states make sure they signal to migrants that they are unwelcome unless they are self-sufficient; that they would not be fully included if they are dependent; that their membership is conditional. Failing to protect migrants from poverty has become a tool in the exclusionary efforts of First World states to prevent Third World migration, in the sense that migrants are left unprotected not only to prevent them from becoming an 'imposition', but also to deter others from coming. Economic exclusion complements the physical exclusion at the border. This tendency of receiving states is not merely problematic

---

[94]   'Immigrants Comprise 31 Percent of Workers in New York State Essential Businesses and 70 Percent of the State's Undocumented Labor Force Works in Essential Businesses' (*Center for Migration Studies of New York (CMS)*, April 2020) <https://cmsny.org/wp-content/uploads/2020/05/Printable-New-York-Essential-Workers-Report.pdf> accessed 26 June 2020.

[95]   Tali Heruti-Sover, 'Law Requiring Asylum Seekers to Deposit 20 Percent of Salary Not Being Enforced' (*Haaretz*, 30 April 2018) <www.haaretz.com/israel-news/.premium-law-forcing-asylum-seekers-to-deposit-fifth-of-salary-not-enforced-1.6045748> accessed 26 June 2020.

[96]   Employers were also required to deposit 16 percent of the salary out of their own pockets.

[97]   Amicus Brief submitted by The Women's Network and others in HCJ 2293/17 *Esther Tsegey Geresghar v The Israeli Knesset* (24 July 2017) <https://1pyiuo2cyzn53c8ors1kwg5l-wpengine.netdna-ssl.com/wp-content/uploads/2018/12/%D7%90%D7%A8%D7%92%D7%95%D7%A0%D7%99-%D7%A0%D7%A9%D7%99%D7%9D2.pdf> accessed 26 June 2020 (in Hebrew).

[98]   '2019 Trafficking in Persons Report: Israel' (*U.S. Department of State*, June 2019) <www.state.gov/reports/2019-trafficking-in-persons-report-2/israel/> accessed 24 July 2019.

[99]   Anat Guthmann and Noa Kaufmann, 'In Broad Daylight: The Deposit Law: Implementation and Impact' (*Kav LaOved* and *Hotline for Refugees and Migrants*, May 2019) <https://hotline.org.il/wp-content/uploads/2019/05/Eng-Deposit-Law-Report-HRM-KLO-2019-Web-2.pdf> accessed 29 June 2020.

[100]   HCJ 2293/17 *Esther Tsegey Geresghar v The Israeli Knesset* (2020) <https://supremedecisions.court.gov.il/Home/Download?path=HebrewVerdicts\17\930\022\v53&fileName=17022930.V53&type=4> accessed 29 June 2020 (in Hebrew).

because it violates international human rights law, but also for several other reasons. First, it ignores the broader context of international migration: colonialism and neo-colonialism, global power gaps and the structural exploitation of the global labor market. Second, it refers to migrants as means, rather than as ends. Third, it disregards the vulnerability of certain migrants, such as children, women, the elderly and people with disabilities.

D.   Immigration, Poverty and Responsibility Sharing

Finally, another reason for the increased vulnerability of migrants to poverty has to do with the uneven distribution of responsibility to migrants between the different countries in the world. While most press coverage of migration deals with the Third World to First World flows, a major portion of forced migration occurs between Third World countries. As Daniel Steinbock has noted:

> First, refugees do not move evenly around the globe, both because refugee-producing events are concentrated in particular countries or regions, and because most refugees cannot seek sanctuary far from their countries of origin. Second, despite the benefits individual refugees might ultimately bring, refugee-receiving countries regard refugees as an unwanted burden in just about every way imaginable. Third, countries vary widely in their ability to cope with refugees in their territory.[101]

The States from which refugees and other forced migrants originate, and other States that make it difficult for refugees and other forced migrants to enter and stay in them, are essentially creating an externality borne by the States that allow immigrants to enter their borders.[102]

Most forced migrants move from one poor and unstable country to another, imposing an additional burden on their politics and economies, which is in some cases devastating. The least politically and economically capable countries are forced to provide for the neediest immigrants and to bear the greatest part of the responsibility in caring for them.[103] Perhaps one of the most striking examples is the immigration of hundreds of thousands of people from Rwanda to Tanzania, which has caused political instability, additional poverty and security concerns in Tanzania.[104]

The Refugee Convention acknowledges the importance of responsibility sharing, both in its preamble and in the principle of non-refoulement, which prevents countries from dumping refugees onto one another.[105] The failure to develop adequate responsibility sharing mechanisms to date, despite the massive efforts to do so, the various models proposed[106] and the rather

---

[101]   Daniel J Steinbock, 'The Qualities of Mercy: Maximizing the Impact of U.S. Refugee Resettlement' (2003) 36 U Mich JL Reform 951, 985.

[102]   Tally Kritzman-Amir, 'Not in My Backyard: On the Morality of Responsibility Sharing in Refugee Law' (2009) 34 Brooklyn J Int'l L. 355, 359.

[103]   Benjamin Cook, 'Methods in Its Madness: The Endowment Effect in an Analysis of Refugee Burden-Sharing and Proposed Refugee Market' (2004) 19 Geo Immigr L.J. 333, 344.

[104]   James Milner, 'Sharing the Security Burden: Towards the Convergence of Refugee Protection and State Security' (2000) Refugee Studies Center Working Paper No 4 <www.rsc.ox.ac.uk/files/files-1/wp4 -sharing-the-security-burden-2000.pdf> accessed 29 June 2020 (detailing the burdens that Tanzania has assumed as a result of the forced migration of hundreds of thousands of Rwandans fleeing genocide).

[105]   Kritzman-Amir (n 102) 377.

[106]   ibid 378–88; Rebecca Dowd and Jane McAdam, 'International Cooperation and Responsibility-Sharing to Protect Refugees: What, Why and How?' (2017) 66 ICLQ 863; Patrick

obvious morality of it,[107] destine refugees to poverty in receiving countries while deteriorating the situation of receiving countries in mass influx situations. Not only have first-world countries failed to promote a fair regime of responsibility sharing, some of them have also engaged in third-country agreements that shift the responsibility of the protection of forced migrants onto countries which are far worse off economically, taking advantage of their political weakness and economic instability.[108]

III.   CONCLUSION

The continuous, tireless devolution of migrants' rights[109] and compassion fatigue[110] render migrants vulnerable to poverty. They are vulnerable in their countries of origin, as countries pose limitations on their ability to migrate in a documented manner and remain reluctant to interpret the definition of refugee in a broad enough manner in order to encompass most people who are fleeing their countries due to poverty, despite some willingness to refrain from deporting some people to extreme poverty. They are also vulnerable to poverty in the receiving states. In many of these countries migrants are less likely to enjoy the protection of the socio-economic rights that international human rights instruments guarantee them and might experience not only a lack of protection from poverty but also be subjected to policies which increase their vulnerability to poverty. This vulnerability stands in sharp contrast to the research suggesting the immigration is by and large economically beneficial to both sending and receiving countries. It seems that this vulnerability derives from the politicization of migration. Nationalist inclinations lead to the desire to limit migration, and failing to protect people from poverty is a means in this effort.

Wall, 'A New Link in the Chain: Could a Framework Convention for Refugee Responsibility Sharing Fulfil the Promise of the 1967 Protocol?' (2017) 29 IJRL 201; UN General Assembly, New York Declaration for Refugees and Migrants: resolution adopted by the General Assembly, 3 October 2016, A/RES/71/1, available at: https://www.refworld.org/docid/57ceb74a4.html [accessed 4 January 2021].

[107]   Kritzman-Amir (n 102) 363–72; Agnès Hurwitz, *The Collective Responsibility of States to Protect Refugees* (OUP 2009) (mostly pages 127–70).

[108]   Such is the US Third Country Agreement with Guatemala, Elizabeth Oglesby, 'Forcing Guatemala into a "Safe Third Country" Agreement is Jaw-Droppingly Insane' (*The Hill*, 29 July 2019). <https://thehill.com/opinion/immigration/455096-forcing-guatemala-into-a-safe-third-country-agreement-is-jaw-droppingly> accessed 29 June 2020, and the agreement between Israel and Rwanda and Uganda, Shani Bar-Tuvia, 'Australian and Israeli Agreements for the Permanent Transfer of Refugees: Stretching Further the (Il)legality and (Im)morality of Western Externalization Policies' (2018) 30 IJRL 474, 475, 476, 486-88. In both cases, countries with strong economies transferred migrants to countries with weaker economies, instead of shouldering the responsibility for them.

[109]   Deborah M Weissman and others, 'The Politics of Immigrant Rights: Between Political Geography and Transnational Interventions' [2018] Mich St L Rev 117.

[110]   Fullerton (n 78) and accompanying text.

15. Human rights and a-legality: destitution of persons seeking asylum in the EU

Eleni Karageorgiou

The main contemporary articulation of human rights, the Universal Declaration of Human Rights (UDHR),[1] claims and prescribes universality.[2] However, living in a world dominated by nation-states, human rights are to be ensured by national governments, primarily *vis-à-vis* their citizens. Non-citizens are entitled to fundamental human rights, yet practice reveals that aliens are oftentimes understood as outside the realm of entitlements explicitly guaranteed for citizens.[3] Refugees, i.e. persons who have crossed borders to seek protection, are non-citizens of the countries where they seek refuge. The particular elements of their cross-border movement – forced displacement, unauthorized entry in asylum or intermediary countries, and lack of a particular rights-conferring status until their claim is examined on the merits, inter alia – make them particularly vulnerable and prone to accept precarious living and working conditions that favor discrimination and exploitation.[4] In fact, international refugee law is designed to address this condition and as such, owes its existence to a rigid distinction between sub-groups of non-citizens: it protects refugees, defined through a set of criteria stipulated in the 1951 Refugee Convention,[5] a status to which a set of rights are attached, but does not protect migrants (regularized or not), who do not meet these criteria but rather move to another country in search of better prospects of living.[6]

---

[1]   Universal Declaration of Human Rights (adopted 10 December 1948) UNGA Res 217 A (III) (UDHR).

[2]   See Louis Henkin, 'The Universality of the Concept of Human Rights' (1989) 506 The Annals of the American Academy of Political and Social Science 10, 11. For an overview of critical approaches to human rights and their nature as universal see Marie-Bénédicte Dembour, 'Critiques' in Daniel Moeckli, Sangeeta Shah and Sandesh Sivakumaran (eds), *International Human Rights Law* (3rd edn, OUP 2018).

[3]   Article 1 of the UN Declaration on the Human Rights of Individuals who are not Nationals of the Country in which They Live (1985) defines alien as 'any individual who is not a national of the state in which he or she is present'.

[4]   On the concept of vulnerability in relation to individuals seeking protection and the distinction between 'situational' and 'individual' vulnerability see United Nations High Commissioner for Refugees (UNHCR), '"Migrants in Vulnerable Situations" UNHCR's Perspective' (*Refworld*, June 2017) <www .refworld.org/docid/596787174.html> accessed 14 July 2020.

[5]   UN Convention Relating to the Status of Refugees (adopted 28 July 1951) 189 UNTS 137 (XXI) (CSR); UN Protocol Relating to the Status of Refugees (adopted 31 January 1967, entered into force 4 October 1967) 606 UNTS 267 (The Refugee Convention).

[6]   Refugeehood presupposes that the bond with the country of origin is severed while an 'economic' migrant is considered to still be enjoying the protection of the country of origin and of the host country's national laws in line with regional and international migration-specific human rights treaties. See Andrew E Shacknove, 'Who Is a Refugee?' (1985) 95 Ethics, 274. This distinction permeates the process of the UNGA, 'New York Declaration for Refugees and Migrants' (3 October 2016) UN Doc A/RES/71/1, which called for the adoption of two separate instruments, namely the UNHCR, 'Global

The distinction between 'economic' migrants and refugees has been questioned both descriptively and normatively for not capturing the reality of the migration experience (mixed movements, overlap of displacement root causes) and for demonizing the movement for reasons linked to socio-economic deprivation.[7] What has not been adequately addressed is the peculiar legal condition that results from a further distinction, namely that between a refugee and an asylum-seeker.[8] Although the term 'asylum-seeker' does not appear in the Refugee Convention, it has been used for reasons of 'administrative convenience', specifically in countries with individualized refugee determination procedures, to denote a claim for international protection that has not been finally decided.[9] Asylum-seekers cannot be considered irregular, as international law recognizes the possibility of people using irregular means to access asylum in other countries,[10] but they do not possess a status which guarantees them certain rights. Even when they have been received into a country's asylum procedure, their status is still contested. Trapped in this temporariness until their claim is lodged or decided, their human rights become a matter of controversy.

This chapter aims at contributing to the debate about the intersection between legal status and destitution drawing on the law and policy for asylum-seekers at the international and regional level. Although the analysis zooms into the European policy on asylum to illustrate the precarious legal condition of asylum-seekers, the problem is global in scope and, therefore, its main finding can be applied by analogy in other regional contexts where similar practices on asylum are employed. The chapter starts by identifying the gaps of asylum-seekers' protection in international refugee and international human rights law. It then moves to a critical

---

Compact on Refugees' (2 August 2018) UN Doc A/73/12(Part II) and the UNGA, 'Global Compact for Safe, Orderly and Regular Migration' (adopted 19 December 2018) UN Doc A/RES/73/195.

[7]   Foster has questioned this oversimplified dichotomy as unhelpful in refugee determination processes. See Michelle Foster, 'Economic Migrant or Person in Need of Protection? Socio-Economic Rights and Persecution in International Refugee Law' in Bruce Burson and David James Cantor (eds), *Human Rights and the Refugee Definition: Comparative Legal Practice and Theory* (Martinus Nijhoff Publishers 2016); Michelle Foster, *International Refugee Law and Socio-Economic Rights: Refuge from Deprivation* (CUP 2007). Achiume also challenges this dichotomy from an international law perspective contending that '[t]he term "economic migrant" has become a moniker for a category of international migrant that national populations across the world view generally with suspicion, occasionally with pity, and increasingly with hostility'. She continues, '[u]nlike the refugee, whose international flight is by definition a last resort, the term "economic migrant" is typically reserved for groups or individuals whose movement is popularly and legally understood to be a matter of preference, defined by a fair degree of political agency, and motivated primarily by the desire for a better life'. Tendayi Achiume, 'Migration as Decolonization' (2019) 71 Stan L Rev 1509, 1512–13. On the blurriness between choice and coercion in the context of displacement see Anthony H Richmond, 'Reactive Migration: Sociological Perspectives on Refugee Movements' (1993) 6 Journal of Refugee Studies 7.

[8]   In this chapter an expansive definition of the term 'asylum seeker' is adopted, encompassing persons who have crossed borders to seek protection but have not formally lodged an asylum application, those who have lodged an asylum application which has not been examined on the merits, and those whose application has been considered inadmissible due to the fact that they should have sought protection elsewhere.

[9]   UNHCR, Status Determination and Protection Information Section, 'UNHCR Master Glossary of Terms Rev. 1' (*Refworld*, June 2006) 4 <www.refworld.org.es/cgi-bin/texis/vtx/rwmain/opendocpdf.pdf?reldoc=y&docid=5d82b8fa4> accessed 14 July 2020. It is noteworthy that the 'New York Declaration for Refugees and Migrants' (n 6) para 4 makes a brief reference to asylum-seekers as a sub-category of forcibly displaced people without addressing their particular situation.

[10]   CSR art 31.

examination of the so-called Common European Asylum System (CEAS)[11] and the way it treats asylum-seekers, and it concludes with some reflections on how the challenges at the international and regional level are exposed and exacerbated in times of 'crisis'. The main argument is that international and European refugee law are premised on an impossible conundrum of prohibiting return of refugees yet not imposing admission to territory. This constructs a contested legality for people seeking asylum, exposing them to increased risk of extreme poverty and destitution.

I.   THE UN REFUGEE CONVENTION: LAYERED RIGHTS, LAYERED LEGALITY

Refugee rights are set out in the Refugee Convention (CSR) and are supplemented by international human rights law. Although described as a human rights instrument in the legal doctrine, it has been suggested that the CSR is framed in the mode of interstate duties rather than of individual rights.[12] The CSR is considered as primarily addressing common standards of state conduct, of which the refugee is the beneficiary rather than the subject of regulation in her own right.[13] In particular, the content of the primary state obligation to provide refugee status under the CSR has been interpreted as applying *vis-à-vis* a group of beneficiaries with distinction.[14] The first tier of Convention entitlements refers to the term 'refugee' without any further qualification. This includes basic guarantees, such as the prohibition of discrimination (Article 3), free access to domestic courts (Article 16(1)), and protection against *refoulement* (Article 33(1)), applicable to 'refugees' under the jurisdiction of the State in question. The second tier, which covers mere physical presence within the territory, triggers guarantees such as the benefit of freedom of religion (Article 4), the delivery of identity papers (Article 27) and the prohibition of penalties on account of illegal entry (Article 31(1)). Third, lawful presence is required for self-employment (Article 18), for freedom of movement within the host country (Article 26) and for protection against expulsion (Article 32). Fourth, lawful stay in the territory of the asylum State is required for, inter alia the right of association (Article 15), access

---

[11]   This notion of the CEAS was introduced in 1999 by the European Council in its Tampere Conclusions. European Council, 'Presidency Conclusions, Tampere European Council' (15–16 October 1999) para 13.

[12]   Vincent Chetail, 'Are Refugee Rights Human Rights? An Unorthodox Questioning of the Relations between Refugee Law and Human Rights Law' in Ruth Rubio-Marin (ed), *Human Rights and Immigration* (OUP 2014) 39; see also Guy S Goodwin-Gill, 'The International Law of Refugee Protection' in Elena Fiddian-Qasmiyeh and others (eds), *The Oxford Handbook of Refugee and Forced Migration Studies* (OUP 2014) 44.

[13]   Chetail (12) 40. Chetail contends that the language of 'rights' found in other human rights treaties is not to be found in the CSR, except in a couple of provisions such as Article 12 and 26. The majority of provisions, he notes, are worded in a manner that emphasizes States' treatment towards refugees: 'The Contracting States shall accord to refugees …'. Along the same lines, Goodwin-Gill notes that '[t]he formal scheme of the Convention, however, remains one of obligations between states. The refugee is a beneficiary, beholden to the state, with a status to which certain standards of treatment and certain guarantees attach.' Guy S Goodwin-Gill, 'Refugees and their Human Rights' (2004) RSC Working Paper No 17, 7 <www.rsc.ox.ac.uk/files/files-1/wp17-refugees-and-their-human-rights-2004.pdf> accessed 14 July 2020.

[14]   Chetail (n 12) 41.

to wage-earning employment (Article 17), housing (Article 21), social security (Article 24) and issuance of travel documents (Article 28). Finally, further rights, such as access to legal assistance (Article 16(2)), accrue once habitual residence is secured.

In light of the above, the CSR provides for an incremental acquisition of rights that depends on the level of attachment of a refugee to her state of asylum.[15] The nature and level of this attachment is arguably a matter of domestic regulation. As a result, although the CSR does not distinguish between asylum-seekers and recognized refugees, the Contracting States are allowed to save the full set of rights enshrined in the Convention only for the latter or for a broader group of beneficiaries on the basis of criteria such as the lawfulness of their presence and residence, determined by national legislation.

It has been argued that mainly due to the declaratory nature of refugee status,[16] asylum-seekers do enjoy a degree of 'presumptive protection'.[17] The freedom from *refoulement* aside, the way asylum seekers are to be treated in the interim stage between the lodging of their claim and a final decision on the merits, remains elusive.[18] Chetail argues that asylum-seekers 'are entitled at a minimum to the core benefits applicable to refugees without further qualification' and, depending on the circumstances, to those accrued with physical and lawful presence within the state territory.[19] Even in the case that Contracting States favor this proposition, problems arise when lawfulness of presence is to be determined: does it suffice if individuals submit an application and are registered in the national system? Or should further administrative arrangements be fulfilled, such as the possession of a certificate or pre-registration form, which certifies that they have applied for asylum or registered as asylum seekers by the UNCHR?[20] This boils down to each State's procedural arrangements and policy.

In other words, the fact that recognition of refugee status is conceived as declaratory rather than constitutive does not alter much in practice. In order for a refugee to be granted the whole range of rights enshrined in the CSR, there has to be a State's official recognition that the person fulfills the inclusion and exclusion requirements under the Convention, through a decision taken by a competent authority. Until then, in the eyes of the law, they remain

---

[15] James C Hathaway, *The Rights of Refugees Under International Law* (CUP 2005) 154, 154–55; Chetail (n 12) 41.

[16] UNHCR, 'Note on Determination of Refugee Status Under the International Instruments' (24 August 1977) UN Doc EC/SCP/5, para 5. As acknowledged by the UNHCR Handbook, '[a] person is a refugee within the meaning of the 1951 Convention as soon as he fulfils the criteria contained in the definition. This would necessarily occur prior to the time at which his refugee status is formally determined. Recognition of his refugee status does not therefore make him a refugee but declares him to be one. He does not become a refugee because of recognition, but is recognized because he is a refugee'. UNHCR, 'Handbook on Procedures and Criteria for Determining Refugee Status Under the 1951 Convention and the 1967 Protocol Relating to the Status of Refugees' (1979) UN Doc HCR/IP/4/Eng/ Rev.1, para 28.

[17] Goodwin-Gill, 'Refugees and their Human Rights' (n 13) 7.

[18] The principle of *non-refoulement* prescribes that people should not be deported to where they may be subject to persecution or grave human rights violations. It is grounded on treaty law and is also considered to have acquired the status of a customary international law norm.

[19] Chetail (n 12) 43. See also UNHCR, 'Reception of Asylum-Seekers, Including Standards of Treatment, in the Context of Individual Asylum Systems' (2001) UN Doc EC/ GC/17, para 3.

[20] For a detailed analysis on what constitutes lawful stay, residence, etc. based on state practice and court decisions, see Hathaway (n 15) 156–92.

'asylum-seekers' entitled to a limited set of benefits based on the assumption that their presence is bound to be temporary for the sole purpose of examining their claims.

In particular, persons who have entered a State but have not yet lodged an asylum claim or have a pending claim are perceived to enjoy a borderline status of 'semi-compliance' with the State's migration and asylum legislation on the margins between regularity and irregularity.[21] Although in the case of refugees, entry or presence ought to be permitted for overriding legal reasons, unauthorized entry or residence signifies an action that has not been given official approval and is therefore *prima facie* unlawful. Costello argues that 'it would seem right and sensible to regard asylum seekers whose claims of international protection are being processed as temporarily being regular migrants (irrespective of their means of entry)'.[22] However, she continues, that position is contested. While EU law, for example, attaches a range of rights to individuals who have lodged an asylum application in an EU country,[23] governments and the European Court of Human Rights accept that applicants may be regarded as 'unauthorized entrants' and in some cases detained on that basis.[24] This does not resolve the situation where individuals, for administrative or other reasons, have not yet lodged an asylum application. The question of whether an individual is lawfully within the territory of a state is ultimately a national matter.[25]

Despite interpretations to the contrary, asylum-seekers – like all other 'unauthorized migrants' – are treated as having arrived unlawfully, and their presence either remains unlawful or is legally qualified after they have lodged a protection application. Migration control as a manifestation of state sovereignty in conjunction with the absence of an individual right to be granted asylum allows national governments to treat entries to a territory without previous authorization, even for seeking asylum, as irregular border crossings. The CSR makes no reference to a right to asylum. This reflects States' unwillingness to assume an international obligation to grant asylum. Although Article 14 of the UDHR stipulates 'the right to seek and enjoy in other countries asylum from persecution', the drafters maintained that granting asylum is the right of the sovereign State, not of the individual seeking it.[26] It has been argued that the right to asylum necessitates a right to a procedure of some sort in order to be meaningful,[27] yet the predominant view is that the CSR does not create a right of admission to the

---

[21] Shift in status or statuses may occur due to various factors relating, for instance, to legislative changes at domestic or regional level, ad-hoc executive practices such as regularization, judicial orders, and other procedural arrangements depending on the circumstances.

[22] Cathryn Costello, *The Human Rights of Migrants and Refugees in European Law* (OUP 2016) 65.

[23] Directive 2013/32/EU of the European Parliament and of the Council on Common Procedures for Granting and Withdrawing International Protection (Recast) [2013] OJ L180/60, art 9.

[24] *Saadi v United Kingdom* (2008) 47 EHRR 17; see also European Commission, 'Preparing the Next Steps in Border Management in the European Union' (13 February 2008) COM(2008) 69; European Commission, 'Communication on Migration' (4 May 2011) COM(2011) 248, 10 (includes the EU's illegal population, illegal entrants and overstayers).

[25] OHCHR, 'The Rights of Non-Citizens' (2006) UN Doc HR/PUB/06/11, 17; Human Rights Committee (HRC), 'General Comment 27: Freedom of Movement (Article 12)' (1 November 1999) UN Doc CCPR/C/21/Rev.1/Add.9, para 4; OHCHR, 'CCPR General Comment No. 15: The Position of Aliens Under the Covenant' (11 April 1986) paras 5, 6, 9.

[26] See H Lauterpacht, 'The Universal Declaration of Human Rights' (1948) 25 Brit YB Int'l L 354, 373–74.

[27] Thomas Gammeltoft-Hansen and Hans Gammeltoft-Hansen, 'The Right to Seek – Revisited. On the UN Human Rights Declaration Article 14 and Access to Asylum Procedures in the EU' (2008) 10(4) EJML 439.

territory *per se*. In the words of Goodwin-Gill and McAdam: 'States were not prepared to include in the Convention any article of admission of refugees; *non-refoulement* in the sense of even a limited obligation to allow entry may well have been seen as coming too close to the unwished-for duty to grant asylum'.[28]

Following the ratification of the CSR, the refugee definition is the criterion for granting asylum.[29] Nonetheless, the international legal obligation to grant asylum and the scope and content of the right to asylum remains unclear.

II.   INTERNATIONAL HUMAN RIGHTS LAW: MORE THAN FREEDOM FROM *REFOULEMENT*?

The development of international human rights law has significantly informed the refugee definition and the content of refugee protection without challenging the normative foundations of refugee law. The principle of *non-refoulement* is explicitly or implicitly recognized in a number of international and regional instruments, thus reinforcing and consolidating the cornerstone of refugee law as a common ground of protection.[30]

While international law does not afford refugees a right to protection in a particular state, or as discussed above a right to enter any particular state to seek asylum, the *non-refoulement* principle entails an obligation for states not to turn away those seeking protection.[31] Although *non-refoulement* is considered as primarily a negative obligation of result, admission to territory is the only practical means to ensure respect for Article 33 CSR. As has been suggested, due respect for the principle of *non-refoulement* implicitly requires 'a de facto duty to admit the refugee'.[32] Indeed, how can a State assess that the life or liberty of an individual is threatened upon return without beforehand granting temporary admission to territory and access to a procedure? Even in the context of ad-hoc interstate arrangements, such as readmission agreements, States are not exempted from the obligation to admit an asylum-seeker to its territory for the duration of deciding on her further removal to a safe country. Removal in this

---

[28]   Guy S Goodwin-Gill and Jane McAdam, *The Refugee in International Law* (3rd edn, OUP 2007) 206–07.

[29]   ibid 415.

[30]   See 1984 UN Convention Against Torture (Article 3), 2006 UN International Convention for the Protection of All Persons from Enforced Disappearance (Article 16), 1969 AU Convention, African Charter, 1969 American Convention on Human Rights (Article 22(8)), 1985 Inter-American Convention to Prevent and Punish Torture (Article 13(4)), 1950 European Convention of Human Rights (Article 3), 2000 Charter of Fundamental Rights of the European Union (Article 19(2)), and 2004 Arab Charter on Human Rights (Article 28). *Non-refoulement* provisions have been the basis for complementary protection being granted to persons who do not qualify as refugees under the CSR. See Jane McAdam, *Complementary Protection in International Refugee Law* (OUP 2007).

[31]   On the procedural consequences of the *non-refoulement* principle in the context of push-backs on the high seas see *Hirsi Jamaa and Others v Italy* App no 27765/09 (ECtHR, 23 February 2012); see also, Mariagiulia Giuffré, 'Access to Asylum at Sea? Non-refoulement and a Comprehensive Approach to Extraterritorial Human Rights Obligations' in Violeta Moreno-Lax and Efthymios Papastavridis (eds), *'Boat Refugees' and Migrants at Sea: A Comprehensive Approach: Integrating Maritime Security with Human Rights* (Brill | Nijhoff, 2016) 256.

[32]   Chetail (n 12) 32; see also Hathaway (n 15) 301; Goodwin-Gill and McAdam (n 28) 384; Costello (n 22) 231.

case is conditioned by the third country's consent to accept that person.[33] Also, the prohibition of collective expulsion has been acknowledged in all regional human rights treaties as an absolute prohibition without any possible exceptions.[34]

With regard to asylum-seekers who have been excluded from most of the provisions of the CSR through restrictive national interpretations, the added value of human rights law is profound and has been analyzed in detail in the literature. Such an analysis will not be repeated here. It suffices to mention the inclusive approach of, for example, the ICCPR[35] referring to 'all individuals', 'every human being', 'everyone' and 'all persons',[36] filling the gaps primarily pertaining to procedural guarantees afforded to refugees.[37] In particular, the Office of the UN High Commissioner for Human Rights (OHCHR) has stated that:

> Asylum-seekers should not be left in a destitute condition while awaiting examination of their asylum claims, since such poor conditions could reinforce prejudice, stereotypes and hostility towards asylum applicants. The procedure for determining eligibility for asylum should not be slow and States should ensure that applicants are given access to sufficient legal assistance. States should be encouraged to provide free legal advice to applicants. Time limits for registration to lodge asylum claims should not be so short as to deprive persons of the protection to which they are entitled under international law. International human rights law is also relevant in the context of defining adequate reception standards for asylum-seekers. Asylum-seekers should be granted the right to work.[38]

The failure however of human rights law to guarantee an individual right to asylum is rather telling of the dialectic[39] around which both international human rights law and international refugee law revolve; on the one hand, the fundamental state obligation of *non-refoulement* and, on the other hand, the sovereign right of controlling admission to territory. In fact, considerable limitations, in particular to the freedom of movement, have been the basis on which practices undermining protection for asylum seekers have been based.

First, as suggested earlier, international refugee law is premised on the likelihood that refugees will use irregular means to seek protection. This is why States undertake not to penalize them for doing so under Article 31 CSR. Nevertheless, non-penalization is conditioned on the fact that refugees should be coming directly from countries where they fear persecution, and

---

[33] See HRC, 'General Comment No. 15' (n 25) para 9, where it is stated that '[n]ormally an alien who is expelled must be allowed to leave for any country that agrees to take him.'

[34] Implicit in art 13 ICCPR; art 22(9) American Convention; art 12(5) African Charter; art 4 Protocol No. 4 of ECHR; art 26(b) Arab Charter; art 19(1) Charter of Fundamental Rights of the EU.

[35] International Covenant on Civil and Political Rights (adopted 16 December 1966, entered into force 23 March 1976) 999 UNTS 171 (ICCPR).

[36] See HRC, General Comment No. 31: The Nature of the General Legal Obligation Imposed on States Parties to the Covenant (26 May 2004) UN Doc CCPR/C/21/Rev.1/Add.13.

[37] See Santhosh Persaud, 'Protecting Refugees and Asylum Seekers Under the International Covenant on Civil and Political Rights' (2006) UNHCR New Issues in Refugee Research Paper No. 132 <www .unhcr.org/en-us/research/working/4552f0d82/protecting-refugees-asylum-seekers-under-international -covenant-civil-political.html> accessed 14 July 2020; OHCHR 'The Rights of Non-Citizens' (n 25) 29.

[38] OHCHR, 'The Rights of Non-Citizens' (n 25) 29. The study draws on country reports by the Council of Europe's European Commission against Racism and Intolerance, on the work of HRC, e.g., HRC, 'A v. Australia, Communication no 560/1993' (30 April 1997) UN Doc CCPR/C/59/D/560/1993 and on UNHCR views, e.g., Executive Committee of the UNHCR, 'Safeguarding Asylum No. 82 (XLVIII)' (17 October 1997) UN Doc 12A (A/52/12/Add.1).

[39] This term, along with 'existential dilemma', is used by Chetail (n 12) 34.

'necessary' restrictions to their movement may be imposed until their status is regularized.[40] This condition has two consequences in practice. First, an asylum-seeker's entry or presence in a State that is party to the Convention may be unlawful and entail criminal punishment pursuant to domestic law. Second, an asylum-seeker's movement may be restricted until her status is regularized. The latter has allowed for the emergence of safe third country practices,[41] namely the right of a State to deny protection on the basis that the person could have sought protection elsewhere.[42] Safe country practices have long been critiqued for rendering the principle of *refoulement* illusory, for downgrading protection standards for refugees in the intermediary countries and for shifting the burden to countries neighboring the regions in distress.[43]

Second, the ICCPR recognizes the right to leave any country (Article 13 (2)). Yet, the containment (*non-entrée*) policies of states around the globe have significantly curtailed this right, to the extent that even discussion of such a right 'probably sounds dated'.[44] Consistent with the concept of state sovereignty, the ICCPR does not recognize the right to enter or reside in the territory of a country of which a person is not citizen, although protection in relation to entry or residence may arise for example on the basis of prohibition of inhuman treatment and respect for family life considerations.[45] Costello refers to the 'static assumption' to connote precisely the notion of states' sovereign right to exclude aliens from territory and lawful

---

[40]   CSR art 31 para 2. It is noteworthy that the ICCPR recognizes a right to liberty of movement, but restricts this right to individuals 'lawfully within the territory of a State' (art 12 (1)). It can be deduced from this provision that a person who unlawfully enters or resides within a State may face some limitation on his or her freedom of movement. This restriction has been restated in several regional human rights instruments, such as Article 22 of the American Convention on Human Rights (ACHR), Protocol No. 4 to the European Convention on Human Rights (ECHR) and Declaration on the Rights of Non-Nationals Article 5(3).

[41]   See, eg the Migrant Protection Protocol (MPP) between the US and Mexico, known colloquially as 'Remain in Mexico' and the Australian policy of transferring asylum-seekers to Nauru, Manus Island and Papua New Guinea, known as the 'Pacific Solution'. For an academic account see Luisa Feline Freier, Eleni Karageorgiou, Kate Ogg, 'The Evolution of Safe Third Country Law and Practice' in Cathryn Costello, Michelle Foster and Jane McAdam (eds), *The Oxford Handbook of International Refugee Law* (OUP forthcoming 2021).

[42]   On safe third country rules see, eg, Morten Kjaerum, 'The Concept of Country of First Asylum' (1992) 4 IJRL 514; Sandra Lavenex, *Safe Third Countries: Extending the EU Asylum and Immigration Policies to Central and Eastern Europe* (Central European University Press 1999); Stephen Legomsky, 'Secondary Refugee Movements and the Return of Asylum Seekers to Third Countries: The Meaning of Effective Protection' (2003) 15 IJRL 567; J. Hathaway, 'The Michigan Guidelines on Protection Elsewhere: Adopted January 3, 2007' (2007) 28 Mich J Intl L 207; Violeta Moreno-Lax, 'The Legality of the "Safe Third Country" Notion Contested: Insights from the Law of Treaties' in Guy S Goodwin-Gill and Philippe Weckel (eds), *Migration & Refugee Protection in the 21st Century: International Legal Aspects* (Martinus Nijhoff 2015).

[43]   See Savitri Taylor, 'Protection Elsewhere/Nowhere' (2006) 18 IJRL 283; Madeline Garlick, 'The Dublin System, Solidarity and Individual Rights' in Vincent Chetail, Philippe De Bruycker and Francesco Maiani (eds), *Reforming the Common European Asylum System: The New European Refugee Law* (Brill 2016); '"We Can't Help You Here": US Returns of Asylum Seekers to Mexico' (*Human Rights Watch*, 2 July 2019) <www.hrw.org/report/2019/07/02/we-cant-help-you-here/us-returns-asylum-seekers-mexico> accessed 15 July 2020.

[44]   Guy Goodwin-Gill, 'The Right to Seek Asylum: Interception at Sea and the Principle of Non-Refoulement' (2011) 23 IJRL 443, 443.

[45]   HRC, General Comment No. 15 (n 25) para 5.

presence without justification.[46] This assumption manifests itself, according to Costello, in many human rights instruments, including the UDHR and ICCPR, where the right to leave a country is not followed by a right to enter another.[47] Along the same lines, Benhabib argues that 'a series of international contradictions between universal human rights and territorial sovereignty are built into the logic of the most comprehensive international law documents in our world'.[48] In fact, Benhabib highlights the paradox in the current human rights regime,[49] where absence of a legal obligation on states to admit leads to a clash between sovereign rights and human rights.

Third, human rights law strengthens protection from arbitrary detention by clarifying the grounds of detention and emphasizing on the role of remedial mechanisms.[50] While considering that the detention of asylum-seekers may be permissible under certain circumstances, the Human Rights Committee (HRC) observed that it must be duly justified on the basis of the 'particular reasons specific to the individual', assessing factors such as the likelihood of absconding and lack of cooperation.[51] The Committee also noted that '[i]ndividuals must not be detained indefinitely on immigration control grounds if the State party is unable to carry out their expulsion'.[52] Arguably, though, these factors have been interpreted broadly by states to justify detention *en masse*. And, although a person is entitled to complain against arbitrary detention or argue that the detention conditions constitute 'cruel, inhumane or degrading treatment', in practice, obstacles such as lack of access to legal assistance and effective legal remedies render their rights illusory.[53]

III.   A HYBRID LEGAL STATUS

In light of the analysis above, it is arguable that international refugee law and human rights instruments invite us to imagine individuals seeking asylum, like all aliens, pre-constructed with a status (legal or illegal), with only the lawfully residents entitled to a full set of rights.

Table 15.1 serves to summarize the rights of asylum-seekers as discussed in the previous sections.

---

[46]   Costello (n 22) 10; see also Helen O'Nions, *Asylum – A Right Denied: A Critical Analysis of European Asylum Policy* (Ashgate 2014) 92.

[47]   Costello (n 22) 10–11.

[48]   Seyla Benhabib, *The Rights of Others: Aliens, Residents, and Citizens* (CUP 2004) 11.

[49]   Seyla Benhabib, *The Claims of Culture: Equality and Diversity in the Global Era* (Princeton University Press 2002).

[50]   OHCHR, 'The Rights of Non-Citizens' (n 25) 29; HRC, 'A v. Australia' (n 38) para 9.2–9.6. But see *Saadi* (n 24) para 45.

[51]   HRC, 'Communication No. 2049/2011' (28 October 2013) CCPR/C/108/D/2094/2011, para 9.3 (views on *F.K.A.G. et al v Australia*).

[52]   ibid.

[53]   See *AEA v Greece* App no 39034/12 (ECtHR, 15 March 2018); *OSA and others v Greece* App no 39065/16 (ECtHR, 21 March 2019). But see *JR and Others v Greece* App no 22696/16 (ECtHR, 25 January 2018); *Ilias and Ahmed v Hungary* App no 47287/15 (ECtHR, 21 November 2019).

Table 15.1   Typology of asylum-seekers rights

Asylum Seeker	Transit Country	Destination Country	Country of Origin
Right to leave any country, opposable to all countries	Obligation to respect the exercise of the right to leave the country of origin	Obligation to respect the exercise of the right to leave the country of origin;	Obligation to readmit, owed to the citizen (asylum-seeker), to the destination country, and to the transit country
Right to unlawful entry or presence opposable to the transit country	Obligation to provide the minimum core, owed to the asylum-seeker	Obligation to provide the minimum core, owed to the asylum-seeker	
Right to a minimum set of rights opposable to all countries	Obligation to readmit owed to the destination country	Right to expel opposable to the country of origin, the transit country, and to the asylum-seeker	

Source: Table inspired by Gregor Noll, 'Why Refugees Still Matter: A Response to James Hathaway' (2007) 8 Melbourne Journal of International Law 536, 542.

This binary frame has been questioned both as an analytical construct and as a legal designation[54] primarily for rendering people rightless[55] and for leading to 'legal black holes'.[56] Both the aforementioned multi-level applicability of refugee rights, which results in 'layered' protection and the temporal shifts in status, reveal the complexity of the legal condition of asylum-seekers and confirm the existence of a grey zone of semi-legality.

The main proposition here is not that asylum-seekers are 'forced outside the pale of the law'[57] to a condition of 'extra-legality'[58] attributed to lack of protection. Rather, it is argued that the architecture of international law generates diverse normativities for groups of refugees depending on the stage of asylum procedure they are in. In relation to asylum-seekers, the notion of a-legality[59] may be helpful for shedding light to such normativity. Beyond the traditional binary legal structure, Lindahl's a-legality 'denotes behavior that calls into question the distinction itself between legality and illegality as drawn by a legal order in a given situation'.[60] In particular, a-legality reflects the tension between two peremptory norms of international law: an obligation to respect the *non-refoulement* principle against a right to withhold asylum for CSR refugees.[61] If taken to their extremes, these norms lead to the paradoxical position where a refugee is neither returned to a place where she fears persecution nor is offered admis-

---

54   See Costello (n 22) 63.

55   On rightlessness and migration see Gregor Noll, 'Why Human Rights Fail to Protect Undocumented Migrants' (2010) 12 EJML 241; Emma Larking, *Refugees and the Myth of Human Rights: Life Outside the Pale of the Law* (Ashgate 2014); Ayten Gündoğdu, *Rightlessness in an Age of Rights: Hannah Arendt and the Contemporary Struggles of Migrants* (OUP 2015).

56   For an elucidation of the problem in relation to human rights see Ralf Wilde, 'Legal "Black Hole"? Extraterritorial State Action and International Treaty Law on Civil and Political Rights' (2005) 26 Mich J Intl L 739; Itamar Mann, 'Maritime Legal Black Holes: Migration and Rightlessness in International Law' (2018) 29 EJIL 347.

57   Hannah Arendt, *The Origins of Totalitarianism* (Houghton Mifflin Harcourt 1973) 286.

58   Fleur Johns, *Non-Legality in International Law: Unruly Law* (CUP 2013).

59   Hans Lindahl, 'Border Crossings by Immigrants: Legality, Illegality, and Alegality' (2008) 14 Res Publica 117.

60   Hans Lindahl, *Fault Lines of Globalization: Legal Order and the Politics of A-Legality* (OUP 2013) 30–31.

61   Patricia Tuitt, 'A-Legality and the Death of the Refugee' (2016) 27 Law Critique 5, 6.

sion to territory and access to procedures.[62] Drawing on Lindahl's work, asylum-seekers can be said to intimate a possible legality of layered rights and hybrid compliance.

In what follows, I draw on European practice on asylum to problematize the way in which regional law and policy reproduce this hybrid and precarious legal status and how this leads to substandard treatment of people seeking asylum in the region.

IV. THE EUROPEAN ASYLUM SYSTEM AND THE INSTITUTIONALIZATION OF 'ASYLUM-SEEKERS' AS A MATTER OF BUREAUCRATIC CONVENIENCE

A. European Integration vs. Refugee Rights

European Union (EU) Member States are all parties to the 1951 Refugee Convention and have committed themselves to assisting displaced persons and not returning them back to where they may fear for their lives (principle of *non-refoulement*). Engagement with refugee protection in Europe is characterized by a sophisticated cooperation between EU countries since the early 1990s for the development of a body of harmonized rules on asylum, known as the Common European Asylum System (CEAS) in accordance with international human rights standards based on solidarity.[63] Such cooperation is grounded on the principle of mutual trust, namely the conviction that all EU countries observe fundamental rights and their international law obligations *vis-à-vis* refugees.[64]

The CEAS was established based on the assumption that the abolition of EU internal borders required measures such as the intensification of external border management and increased cooperation in the field of asylum and immigration to compensate for the supposed lack of control.[65] As suggested in the literature, the rationale behind the CEAS had two conflicting objectives: on the one hand, to enhance refugee protection in accordance with international law, and on the other hand, to combat 'asylum shopping' through secondary movements by containing refugees to specific EU states.[66] It was precisely to distinguish between recognized refugees and those whose claims are pending before the authorities that the need emerged for the institutionalization of an intermediary category of asylum-seeker.[67] This, in turn, led to a differentiation between the treatment of asylum-seekers compared to that of recognized

---

[62] In between these two extremes various possibilities lie, including the contested acts of letting asylum-seekers drown in the sea or containing them to first countries of asylum.

[63] Consolidated Version of the Treaty on the Functioning of the European Union [2012] OJ C326/47 (TFEU) arts 77–80 (Chapter 2, Policies on Border Checks, Asylum and Immigration).

[64] See, eg, Case C-120/78 *Rewe-Zentrale AG v Bundesmonopolverwaltung für Branntwein* [1979] ECR 649; Opinion 2/13 of the Court (Full Court) (ECJ, 18 December 2014) (Accession by the Union to the European Convention for the Protection of Human Rights and Fundamental Freedoms).

[65] Violeta Moreno-Lax, 'Life After Lisbon: EU Asylum Policy as a Factor of Migration Control' in Diego Acosta Arcarazo and Cian C Murphy (eds), *EU Security and Justice Law: After Lisbon and Stockholm* (Hart Publishing 2014) 146–67.

[66] Elspeth Guild, 'The Europeanisation of Europe's Asylum Policy' (2006) 18 IJRL 630, 640–41.

[67] For a historical overview see Ingrid Boccardi, *Europe and Refugees: Towards an EU Asylum Policy* (Kluwer Law International 2002).

refugees.[68] Thus, an inherent conflict between human rights protection, fairness and justice on the one hand and economic, efficiency/management and securitization goals on the other, has been part of the system since its inception.[69]

This conflict is reflected in the architecture of the CEAS and more specifically in its 'cornerstone', namely the Dublin Regulation 604/2013 (Dublin III),[70] which addresses the question of the allocation of asylum responsibilities amongst the EU Member States. The Dublin system is heavily based on safe country rules obliging States to reject an asylum claim as inadmissible on the ground that the asylum-seeker has or should have sought protection in another European country. This system was not intended to distribute hosting responsibilities in a fair manner as required by the CSR,[71] or to pay due regard to individual circumstances and integration prospects; rather, in line with the objectives of the internal market, it was meant to be a formal administrative responsibility assignment scheme in which the State that played the most significant role in the applicant's entry or residence in the EU would be responsible for examining her application, subject to exceptions designed to protect family unity. As Mitsilegas puts it, the Dublin system establishes a form of 'interstate cooperation based on automaticity and trust' that assumes that the treatment of asylum-seekers in all Member States complies with the requirements of the Charter of Fundamental Rights of the European Union, the CSR and the ECHR.[72] It thus provides rules that assign responsibility as a way of 'punishing' those EU Member States who deflect.[73] This is problematic for two reasons: first, because there are huge divergences in national asylum systems, which have been repeatedly reported by civil society organizations,[74] and, second, because it does not take into account agency on the part of the refugee.

---

[68]   The first EC Directive on reception conditions specifically targets asylum-seekers: Council Directive 2003/9/EC of 27 January 2003 laying down minimum standards for the reception of asylum seekers [2003] OJ L31/18. Considering the backlog of asylum applications and the delays in asylum procedures in many European countries in the 1990s and, more recently, in peripheral EU countries, such as Greece, it became administratively convenient and politically preferable to grant non-recognized – and likely to be rejected – asylum-seekers less rights compared to refugees.

[69]   Samantha Velluti, *Reforming the Common European Asylum System – Legislative Developments and Judicial Activism of the European Courts* (Springer 2014) 5.

[70]   Regulation (EU) No 604/2013 of the European Parliament and of the Council of 26 June 2013 establishing the criteria and mechanisms for determining the Member State responsible for examining an application for international protection lodged in one of the Member States by a third-country national or a stateless person (recast) [2013] OJL 180/31 (Dublin III Regulation).

[71]   Refugee Convention (n 5) preamble recital 4.

[72]   Valsamis Mitsilegas, 'Solidarity and Trust in the Common European Asylum System' (2014) 2 Comparative Migration Studies 181, 191.

[73]   On this, see Gregor Noll, *Negotiating Asylum: The EU Acquis, Extraterritorial Protection, and the Common Market of Deflection* (Martinus Nijhoff 2000).

[74]   See, e.g., 'Response to the European Commission's Green Paper on the Future Common European Asylum System' (*UNHCR*, September 2007) 38 <www.refworld.org/pdfid/46e159f82.pdf> accessed 15 July 2020; Minos Mouzourakis and Amanda Taylor, 'Wrong Counts and Closing Doors: The Reception of Refugees and Asylum Seekers in Europe' (*European Council of Refugees and Exiles*, March 2016) 31 <www.asylumineurope.org/sites/default/files/shadow-reports/aida_wrong_counts_and_closing_doors .pdf> accessed 15 July 2020.

In light of the above, the emphasis in European policy on asylum since its intergovernmental beginnings has been on control instead of protection.[75] Although the contribution of the European asylum system to refugee protection should not be overlooked, it has been suggested that obsession with borders and containment has undermined the benefits.[76] The emergence of the new category of an 'asylum-seeker' in conjunction with the fundamental inequality at the core of the Dublin rules gave Member States located at the EU external borders recourse to substandard protection, poverty and human rights violations to frustrate the system.

B.   The Dublin Regulation: Incentivizing Substandard Protection as a way to Avoid Responsibility

The Dublin system has evolved against the background of a European area without internal borders, which has progressively developed since the Schengen Agreement of 1985. In this context, the Dublin Regulation and the Schengen Code, which regulates border control, form the basis of a common EU asylum and immigration policy. The European Court of Human Rights (ECtHR) and the Court of Justice of the EU (CJEU) have challenged this form of cooperation based on human rights considerations. The ECtHR in *M.S.S. v. Belgium and Greece* determined that extreme poverty and homelessness in the receiving country, in combination with procedural shortcomings such as the lack of information and access to legal aid and long delays in delivering a decision, amount to inhuman or degrading treatment.[77] In light of this a State is prohibited from undertaking a Dublin transfer where there is real risk of the asylum-seeker being subject to such a condition that meets the threshold of cruel, inhuman or degrading treatment.[78] In the joint cases *N.S. and M.E.*, the CJEU declared the presumption that other EU States are safe for asylum-seekers and that their claims will be properly processed is rebuttable.[79] Despite challenging the automatic nature of Dublin transfers, the ruling has been criticized for imposing the high threshold of 'systemic deficiencies' for suspension, which excludes cases where the reception and asylum procedures conditions in the receiving State may suffer from operational flaws.[80]

The Grand Chamber of the CJEU decided on the living conditions of an individual after the grant of international protection in the responsible Member State. The Court stated that deficiencies in the social system do not, in and of themselves, amount to risk of inhuman and

---

[75]   See Marten Den Heijer, Jorrit Rijpma and Thomas Spijkerboer, 'Coercion, Prohibition, and Great Expectations: The Continuing Failure of the Common European Asylum System' (2016) 53 CML Rev 607; see also Gregor Noll, 'Why the EU Gets in the Way of Refugee Solidarity' (*OpenDemocracy*, 22 September 2015) <www.opendemocracy.net/en/can-europe-make-it/why-eu-gets-in-way-of-refugee -solidarity/> accessed 5 May 2020 (highlighting the problem of insufficient EU funding for protection, instead of border management).

[76]   Cathryn Costello, 'Overcoming Refugee Containment and Crisis' (2020) 21 German Law Journal 17.

[77]   *M.S.S. v Belgium and Greece* App no 30696/09 (ECtHR 21 January 2011) paras 230–34, 263–64, 300–22.

[78]   Joined Cases *N.S. v Secretary of State for the Home Department* (C-411/10) and *M.E. and Others v Refugee Applications Commissioner and Minister for Justice, Equality and Law Reform* (C-493/10) (ECJ, 21 December 2011) para 94.

[79]   ibid para 81.

[80]   See, e.g., Cathryn Costello, 'Courting Access to Asylum in Europe: Recent Supranational Jurisprudence Explored' (2012) 12 HRL Rev 287.

degrading treatment. Rather 'a situation of extreme material poverty that does not allow [the individual] to meet his most basic needs' is required.[81] According to the Court, a situation of extreme material poverty is one that 'does not allow [the applicant] to meet his most basic needs, such as, inter alia, food, personal hygiene and a place to live, and that undermines his physical or mental health or puts him in a state of degradation incompatible with human dignity'.[82] In sum, the Dublin system's construction and its underlying assumptions of norm sharing and safety have been challenged by the European courts from a human rights perspective. Nevertheless, its proper function continues to be the utmost priority in the EU policy on asylum. This is exemplified by the fact that the system remained intact during the 2015 'crisis' with the exception of the emergency relocation mechanism intended to offer short-term relief to Member States at the EU's external borders.[83] The Council of the EU adopted two relocation decisions, on 14 and 22 September 2015,[84] temporarily suspending the Dublin rules regarding persons in clear need of international protection, and relocating them to other EU Member States on the basis of a distribution key.[85] Such an arrangement, though, has led to mass containment of asylum-seekers in overcrowded facilities on the Greek islands, called 'hotspots', further analysed below.[86]

C.   'Hotspots' and the EU-Turkey Statement: Destitution in the Periphery of the EU and in Third Countries

One of the main EU policies adopted to address the 2015/2016 crisis was to build on existing cooperation with third countries, including the EU-Turkey cooperation framework. Through a joint statement on 18 March 2016,[87] Turkey committed to readmit migrants who have not applied for asylum in Greece or whose application has been found 'inadmissible' or unfounded under the EU's Asylum Procedure Directive (APD).[88] The EU accepted that, for every Syrian being returned to Turkey from the Greek islands, a Syrian will be resettled from Turkey to the EU. The EU also committed to accelerate visa liberalization for Turkish citizens and to 'speed up' the disbursement of 3 billion euros allocated under the Facility for Refugees

---

[81]   Case no C-163/17 *Abubacarr Jawo v Bundesrepublik Deutschland* (ECJ, 19 March 2019) paras 91–93.

[82]   ibid para 92. The Court referred to that effect to *M.S.S. v. Belgium and Greece* (n 77) paras 252–63.

[83]   European Commission Communication, 'A European Agenda on Migration' (13 May 2015) COM(2015) 240.

[84]   Council Decision (EU) 2015/1523 of 14 September 2015 establishing provisional measures in the area of international protection for the benefit of Italy and of Greece [2015] OJ L 239/146; Council Decision (EU) 2015/1601 of 22 September 2015 establishing provisional measures in the area of international protection for the benefit of Italy and Greece [2015] OJ L 248/80.

[85]   'Informal Meeting of EU Heads of State or Government on Migration, 23 September 2015 – Statement' (*European Council*, 23 September 2015) <www.consilium.europa.eu/en/press/press-releases/2015/09/23-statement-informal-meeting/> accessed 5 May 2020.

[86]   On the consequences of the hotspot approach See Nikolas Feith Tan, 'Fundamental Rights and the EU Hotspot Approach' (*Danish Refugee Council*, October 2017) <https://drc.ngo/media/4051855/fundamental-rights_web.pdf> accessed 15 July 2020.

[87]   'EU-Turkey Statement' (*European Council*, 18 March 2016) <www.consilium.europa.eu/en/press/press-releases/2016/03/18-eu-turkey-statement/> accessed 5 May 2020.

[88]   Council Directive 2005/85/EC of 1 December 2005 on minimum standards on procedures in Member States for granting and withdrawing refugee status [2005] OJ L326/13, art 27(1); Directive 2013/32/EU (n 23) art 38(1).

in Turkey, a fund constituted by the EU and its Member States, providing for humanitarian aid to refugees in Turkey.

It is noteworthy that Turkey has ratified the 1967 Protocol to the Refugee Convention but maintained the geographical limitation, meaning it is only obliged to consider as refugees those individuals who have fled from events taking place in Europe. This effectively excludes the majority of those currently seeking refuge in Turkey from protection in accordance with the Refugee Convention and whose legal status is contested.[89] Despite providing for the possibility of resettling Syrian refugees from Turkey to EU Member States and offering considerable financial assistance for refugee reception it is highly questionable that these measures address human rights violations in practice or tackle the precariousness of their legal status.[90] Arguably, this type of cooperation has legitimized the confinement of refugees to first countries of asylum and weakened protection in a manner that makes extreme material poverty likely.[91] NGO reports have shown how the establishment of 'hotspots' in Italy and Greece as a way to assist national authorities with the identification, registration and fingerprinting of incoming migrants has been a major component of the implementation of the EU-Turkey agreement.[92] In particular, Greek islands were considered as Europe's 'Nauru', filtering through the 'deserving few' and removing the undesirables. Essentially what started as a gesture of solidarity towards peripheral EU states, developed into a contested mechanism for managing mobility through prolonged detention and destitution, putting basic human rights in jeopardy. It is striking that these legal and policy arrangements have allowed for a situation in which the reception conditions for the asylum-seekers are arguably comparable to those found unacceptable by the ECtHR in the *MSS* judgment.

V.   HUMAN RIGHTS LIMITATIONS IN TIMES OF 'CRISIS' AND A-LEGALITY

What the analysis of the European asylum system has shown is that there is an *in-built* reliance on coercion and migration control, which exacerbates in times of 'crisis'. Despite the rights stipulated in the international and regional instruments discussed in Sections I and II, the vulnerability of asylum-seekers grows in times of crisis. Sophisticated border regimes are premised on preventing asylum-seekers, along with other unauthorized immigrants, from

---

[89]   Eleni Karageorgiou, 'The Distribution of Asylum Responsibilities in the EU: Dublin, Partnerships with Third Countries and the Question of Solidarity' (2019) 88(3) Nord J Intl L 315, 356.

[90]   See European Parliament, Briefing: Implementation of the EU Trust Funds and the Facility for Refugees in Turkey, Overview' (March 2020) PE 649.337, 10.

[91]   See, e.g., Amnesty International, 'No Safe Refuge: Asylum Seekers and Refugees Denied Protection in Turkey', March 2016. It is worth noting that the EU-Turkey agreement and its compatibility with human rights standards have not been assessed by the CJEU, as the General Court held it has no jurisdiction to decide the case and declared the applicants' appeals inadmissible. See Orders of the General Court in Cases T-192/16, T-193/16 and T-257/16 *NF, NG and NM v European Council* (GC, 28 February 2017); Order of the General Court in Joined Cases C-208/17 P to C-210/17 P *NF and others v European Council* (GC, 12 September 2018).

[92]   See 'Explanatory Note on the "Hotspot" Approach' (*State Watch*) <www.statewatch.org/news/2015/jul/eu-com-hotsposts.pdf> accessed 5 May 2020.

accessing State territory.[93] Goodwin-Gill and McAdam note that 'states retain considerable discretion to construct sophisticated interception and non-arrival policies within the letter, if not the spirit, of the law'.[94]

In the post-2015 European asylum policy, externalizing asylum and border management to third countries has become the norm. This means that, in theory, there is a right to seek asylum enshrined in EU law, but in practice there is deterrence; in theory, there is a system of protection, but in practice refugees need to break the law and take life threatening measures to access it; in theory, a number of rights are attached to refugee status so as to allow refugees to lead a decent and independent life, but in practice persons who arrive in EU countries without prior authorization, including asylum-seekers, are routinely denied access to basic substantive as well as procedural rights such as judicial review of their treatment by state authorities; in theory EU policy aims at combating 'illegal' migration, but in practice, it creates conditions that lie in between legality and illegality.

The term asylum-seeker has been used to imply a hybrid legality, often associated with the condition of outlaw. At the same time, people seeking asylum in the EU seem to intimate a possible legality of their illegality, contesting European legal order and its very architecture.[95] This is the point where a-legality comes into the fore to contest practices of containment and destitution.

VI.   CONCLUSION

Despite the fact that international human rights law has come a long way to develop and refine the CSR's normative frame, failure of both regimes to address questions of admission and reception condition standards of refugees has made instances of substandard protection and extreme poverty possible, especially in times of increased refugee movements framed as 'migration crises'. Migration management through containment shapes national and regional responses to human mobility based on the distinction between refugees and asylum-seekers. As suggested in this chapter, the case of asylum-seekers confirms the existence of situations of a-legality in human rights law. Thus, rethinking the notion of refugee protection in a way that reflects the nuanced reality of displacement and covers such situations seems to be the way forward. Asylum-seekers, unlike recognized refugees, form a particularly vulnerable group of individuals due to their 'semi-regular' status, being on the margins between refugeehood and irregular migration. Given that in order for refugee status to be granted there has to be a state's official decision through an asylum procedure, an administrative requirement was created at national and regional levels that necessitated an intermediary status, namely that

---

[93]   See, e.g., Thomas Gammeltoft-Hansen, *Access to Asylum: International Refugee Law and the Globalisation of Migration Control* (CUP 2011); James Hathaway and Thomas Gammeltoft-Hansen, 'Non-Refoulement in a World of Cooperative Deterrence' (2014) University of Michigan Law and Economics Working Paper No. 14-016 <https://papers.ssrn.com/sol3/papers.cfm?abstract_id=2479511> accessed 15 July 2020.

[94]   Goodwin-Gill and McAdam (n 28) 360.

[95]   In Lindahl's words, the 'a' of a-legality means that situations exist that disrupt a legal order 'by revealing *another legality*, other possibilities of drawing the distinction between legality and illegality in the legal order they contest. More precisely, a-legal acts contest a legal order by intimating a possible *legality of illegality*, and a possible *illegality of legality*'. Lindahl (n 59) 125.

of an 'asylum seeker'. Post-2015 state practice reveals that the very architecture of the CEAS – in the absence of a coherent global migration law – has created spaces in which people on the move become *de-jure* or *de-facto* rightless. International and regional obligations are circumvented, creating situations of 'legal black holes'. Examples of such spaces are the EU external borders such as the Greek-Turkish land border where refugees and asylum-seekers have been violently ping-ponged, the hotspots in Greece and Italy where they are kept in indefinite detention mainly for the purpose of being deported, the high seas where they lose their lives trying to cross the Mediterranean, and third countries such as Turkey, Nauru and Mexico. These countries are called to take on the responsibility of people in need of protection transiting their territories, implementing contested policies that have led to a normalization of deterrence, protection denial and prolonged containment and destitution.

16. Seeing human rights *like* a city: the prospects and perils of the 'urban turn'

Natalia Ángel-Cabo and Luisa Sotomayor

Between September and December of 2019 thousands of people in different Latin American cities took to the streets to protest against their governments. The famous Chilean song of the 1990s, '*El Baile de los que Sobran*' (The Dance of the Left Out), resonated loudly from Santiago to Bogotá. The movements behind the urban protests based their demands in the language of rights, mainly of social and economic rights: the rights to work, to health, to social security and to education. Protesters spoke about rights to illustrate how, despite the economic growth of the region, thousands of people were still in poverty and many of those who recently overcame it, at least in monetary terms, were close to being poor again.

In the previous decade, housing activists in Toronto, Canada invoked a human rights perspective to challenge zoning bylaw restrictions on the placement of group homes. Group homes are a type of housing arrangement where a small number of unrelated people in need of support or supervision reside, such as people with disabilities or mental health issues. The placement bylaw was seen by activists as a form of 'people zoning' because it reproduced urban disadvantages for vulnerable groups by singling them out and reducing their housing choices. Significantly, in 2014 a successful legal challenge by the 'Dream Team', a group of individuals with lived experiences of supportive housing, led the City of Toronto to change their land-use policy for group homes, applying a human rights test to former placement restrictions, distances and parking requirements.[1]

Far from extraordinary, these two examples illustrate important points long identified by commentators: that human rights are a key framework for social movements to formulate their demands and an important resource to reveal the inequities and complexities of the urban context. Furthermore, these cases speak to the vibrancy and highly contested political arena that cities have come to represent around issues of human rights, democracy, citizenship and identity.[2] They bring attention to the city both as an important site for the reclamation of rights and as a scale of government that, in its proximity to the citizen, might be better suited for the implementation of rights.

This chapter reflects on the potential of human rights approaches to poverty reduction from the perspective of the city. We ask what seeing *like* and *from* the city[3] may add to the long-standing debate about the promise of rights to produce social change. Contrary to the fierce

---

[1] See Sandeep Agrawal, 'Balancing Municipal Planning with Human Rights: A Case Study' (2015) 23 Canadian Journal of Urban Research 1; Carmen McCracken, 'Strategic Litigation and Advancing the Right to Housing in Canada' (Master's thesis York University 2019).

[2] Andrew EG Jonas and Sami Moisio, 'City Regionalism as Geopolitical Processes: A New Framework for Analysis' (2018) 42 Progress in Human Geography 350.

[3] See Warren Magnusson, *Politics of Urbanism: Seeing like a City* (Routledge 2011); Mariana Valverde, 'Seeing Like a City: The Dialectic of Modern and Premodern Ways of Seeing in Urban Governance' (2011) 45 L & Soc'y Rev 277.

critiques that dismiss altogether the relevance of human rights to confronting the world's pressing problems, we recognize some of its contributions and identify how a view from the city might abet the global human rights project by politicizing it from the vantage point of urbanization. We also stress several limits on human rights' ability to confront pervasive poverty and rising inequality, particularly given the way neoliberal agendas currently operate *in* and *through* cities.

In the last five decades, cities across the world have emerged as primary sites of innovation, economic growth and political power in a re-scaled capitalist world order characterized by inter-city competition.[4] From Delhi to London to Cape Town to Rio, central districts increasingly become the preferred location for professional and residential elites, while local politicians engage in urban boosterism tactics to attract human capital and investment.[5] But not everyone benefits from such an approach to urban policy. Cities are equal catalysts of privilege and poverty under capitalism.[6] Since the 1970s, national and urban inequality has been on the rise in many countries.[7] The 'urban age' has been shaped by metropolitan fragmentation, precarious jobs for youth and unskilled labor, socio-spatial marginality, gentrification and displacement[8] that all threaten the fulfillment of human rights for the urban poor.

In this chapter, 'seeing like a city' implies a view of a wide range of experiences of the urban. We argue that it is not enough to turn to the city-scale and the local authorities to fulfill the promises of human rights that, as Moyn[9] critically indicates, national governments and international agreements have failed to deliver over decades. In the era of worldwide urbanization, any engagement with the urban will require attention to the fuzzy, fragmented, sprawling and reterritorialized reality of contemporary urban regions; the formal and informal ways of mediating access to resources and power in the city; the struggles over the unequal production of capitalist urban development and the socio-spatial distribution of urban benefits; and the struggles for participation, recognition and inclusion of different voices in democratic processes. Finally, we argue that in order for the global human rights project to produce significant social change, it needs to regain relevance and legitimacy among both citizens and state institutions.

The chapter is organized as follows: The first section describes the rescaling of human rights to the city and brings attention to the multiple challenges of the urban. We address the increasing socio-spatial inequalities and the deepening of poverty that have arisen as a consequence of the dramatic changes of cities in the last decades. We focus on current trends that have deepened conditions of poverty and inequality. In the second section we discuss the potential

---

[4] Saskia Sassen, 'Global Cities and Global City-Regions: A Comparison' in Allen J Scott (ed), *Global City-Regions: Trends, Theory, Policy* (OUP 2001); Jonathan Friedman, 'Globalization and Localization' in Jonathan Xavier Inda and Renato Rosaldo (eds), *The Anthropology of Globalization* (Blackwell 2002); Roger Keil, 'The Urban Politics of Roll-with-it Neoliberalization' (2009) 13 City 230.

[5] Jamie Peck and Adam Tickell, 'Neoliberalizing Space' (2002) 34 Antipode 380.

[6] Thomas Piketty, 'Putting Distribution Back at the Center of Economics: Reflections on Capital in the Twenty-First Century' (2015) 29 Journal of Economic Perspectives 67.

[7] Joseph Eugene Stiglitz, 'Macroeconomic Fluctuations, Inequality, and Human Development' (2012) 13 Journal of Human Development and Capabilities 31; Anthony B Atkinson, *Inequality: What can be Done?* (Harvard University Press 2015).

[8] R Alan Walks, 'The Social Ecology of the Post-Fordist/Global City? Economic Restructuring and Socio-Spatial Polarisation in the Toronto Urban Region' (2001) 38 Urban Studies 407.

[9] Samuel Moyn, *Not Enough: Human Rights in an Unequal World* (Harvard University Press 2018).

of localized rights to confront such challenges. By localized rights we mean the attempt to foster the fulfillment of human rights at the local level. We discuss some of the positive contributions of the human rights framework and illustrate how the city may contribute to further them. Yet, by acknowledging the complexities of the urban, we also stress numerous limits of human rights approaches to transform the everyday lives of the urban poor. The final section concludes with an invitation for the global rights project to remain experimental and with a research agenda to better understand the prospects and challenges of localized rights to confront urban poverty.

I.   THE 'URBAN TURN' IN HUMAN RIGHTS AGENDAS AND THE CITY

In the last few decades, cities have become central to global development initiatives and international human rights agendas. The shift since the late 1980s towards decentralization gave cities in many countries increased responsibility for a number of new tasks that were previously within the realm of the national governments.[10] Currently, many of the activities of local governments relate in one way or another to the implementation of human rights, such as the provision of water, sanitation, public health, housing or education.[11] Precisely because of the prominence of cities, some proponents of human rights perspectives increasingly devise cities at the center, and local governments as key players, in the promotion and protection of human rights.

The persuasive discourse of the 'urban age' complements these trends and has further brought attention to cities and the problems associated with urbanization as a human rights concern.[12] It is argued that we are approaching a distinctive urban era, as for the first time in history cities are home to much of the world's population. The argument also recognizes that the largest share of future urban growth is expected to occur in low-income regions of the world, where cities lack institutional capacity or the resources to support a growing population. Trends indicate that while a minimum standard of living has been achieved in much of the Global North and in well-off urban areas of the Global South, wealth and access to urban benefits in thriving regions is increasingly mediated by growing income inequalities.[13] In response, international development agendas increasingly promote human rights approaches to urban poverty reduction.

Together, the 're-scaling' of traditional state functions to the city, the urban-age discourse, and the rise of global income inequality have reinvigorated debates about the bearing of the global human rights project on poverty reduction and human development. In discussion over implementation and applicability, proponents of the 'urban turn' have looked at cities with

---

[10]   Mario Polèse, 'Cities and National Economic Growth: A Reappraisal' (2005) 42 Urban Studies 1429; Luis Eslava, *Local Space, Global Life: The Everyday Operation of International Law and Development* (CUP 2016).

[11]   Martha F Davis, 'Scoping the New Urban Human Rights Agenda' (2019) 51 The Journal of Legal Pluralism and Unofficial Law 260.

[12]   Clive Barnett and Susan Parnell, 'Ideas, Implementation and Indicators: Epistemologies of the Post-2015 Urban Agenda' (2016) 28 Environment and Urbanization 87.

[13]   Vanessa Watson, 'Seeing from the South: Refocusing Urban Planning on the Globe's Central Urban Issues' (2009) 46 Urban Studies 2259.

the hopes of overcoming some of the recurrent critiques of human rights, including claims of irrelevance and concerns over their legitimacy, lack of material effectiveness and poor record of promoting distributive equality.[14]

The growing faith in the city as a privileged space for the realization of rights can be seen through a number of initiatives that have emerged in the past decades. One example is the human right cities movement, which encourages local or regional governments to explicitly commit to the respect for human rights.[15] At the moment, more than forty cities have declared themselves as a human rights city, although doubts persist on the implementation of their commitments. The 2030 Sustainable Development Goals (SDGs) and the recent New Urban Agenda are also good examples. The SDGs, including SDG 11 to '[m]ake cities and human settlements inclusive, safe, resilient and sustainable',[16] are explicitly grounded in the Universal Declaration of Human Rights and other international human rights treaties.[17] The New Urban Agenda,[18] a political declaration signed by all UN member states and which aimed to provide a vision and a road map for municipalities and cities in the years to come, sets a human rights-based approach to policy-making and service delivery towards an inclusive urban development[19] and explicitly acknowledges local authorities as responsible for the protection, respect and fulfillment of human rights of residents.

Given the amount of 'urban buzz' in international development and human rights communities, the lack of literature seriously connecting scholarship on urban studies, poverty and human rights is surprising. For example, while human geographers have long engaged with the spatial dimensions of injustice,[20] they have largely ignored debates on international human rights discourse and practice.[21] The same applies for urban practitioners, planners, politicians and policymakers who rarely engage with human rights talk on the field.[22]

Conversely, the human rights literature has yet to engage more deeply with urban theory and urban research. Initiatives such as the New Urban Agenda or the Human Rights Cities move-

---

[14]   Malcolm Langford, 'Critiques of Human Rights' (2018) 14 Annual Review of Law and Social Science 69.

[15]   See, for example, Martha F Davis, Thomas Gammeltoft Hansen and Emily Hanna (eds), *Human Rights Cities and Regions: Swedish and International Perspectives* (Raoul Wallenberg Institute 2017); Paul Gready and Liz Lockey, 'Rethinking Human Rights in York as a Human Rights City' (2019) 90 Pol Q 383; Barbara Oomen and Moritz Baumgärtel, 'Human Rights Cities' in Anja Mihr and Mark Gibney (eds), *The SAGE Handbook of Human Rights* (SAGE 2014).

[16]   UNGA, Transforming our World: the 2030 Agenda for Sustainable Development (18 September 2015) UN Doc A/70/L.1, 22.

[17]   ibid para 10.

[18]   United Nations Conference on Housing and Sustainable Urban Development, New Urban Agenda (20 October 2016) UN Doc A/Res/71/256.

[19]   Karina Gomes Da Silva, 'The New Urban Agenda and Human Rights Cities: Interconnections between the Global and the Local' (2018) 36 NQHR 290.

[20]   See, for example, David Harvey, *Spaces of Hope* (University of California Press 2000); Edward W Soja, *Seeking Spatial Justice* (University of Minnesota Press 2013).

[21]   Nicole Laliberté, 'Geographies of Human Rights: Mapping Responsibility' (2015) 9 Geography Compass 57; Jean C Carmalt, 'For Critical Geographies of Human Rights' (2018) 42 Progress in Human Geography 847.

[22]   Thijs van Lindert and Doutje Lettinga, 'Introduction.' in Thijs van Lindert and Doutje Lettinga (eds), *The Future of Human Rights in an Urban World* (Amnesty International Netherlands 2014); Carolyn Whitzman, 'Rights Talk, Needs Talk and Money Talk in Affordable Housing Partnerships' (2018) Journal of Planning Education and Research 1.

ment have certainly put a spotlight on cities, but only insofar as the city is understood as a legal jurisdiction, capable of channeling state action to observe and enact human rights within formal city boundaries. While useful to identify state institutions and conceptualize the role of the state in relation to human rights claims, such an approach follows either a municipalist or regionalist perspective to conceptualize the city as a 'territorial fix', without accounting for the worldwide territorial reconfiguration of the urban fabric that has taken place in the past four decades. Such a limited perspective may fail to capture those informal, spontaneous or radical forms of political practice that enable groups of people and movements to organize themselves around human rights and self-identify as collective political actors in the city.[23] More than a discrete geographical category or a type of settlement, as proponents of the planetary urbanization thesis suggest, '[t]oday, the urban represents an increasingly worldwide condition in which political-economic relations are enmeshed'.[24]

In the lines to follow, we aim to enrich the conversation about the potential of localized rights by illuminating urban processes and challenges that go beyond the limited understanding of the city as a local jurisdiction. This description will help us contextualize our later discussions about the potential of rights to transform the everyday lives of the poor. We examine urban development trends and discuss how current urbanization dynamics create challenges for poor households and people to enjoy a dignified quality of life, participate in decision-making affecting their lives, and access all the benefits and opportunities that the city has to offer. With the emergence of a worldwide urbanized society, and a growing share of the world's poverty now located within urban areas,[25] a view to city structures and the social dynamics of exclusion that generate and sustain poverty in cities may further reveal the potential contributions and limits of a human rights approach to poverty reduction.

A.   Cities, Poverty and Urban Disadvantage

Cities have been historically central to wealth generation and economic growth, as they provide infrastructures, qualified labour, markets, services and innovation systems that enable people and businesses to thrive. In terms of quality of life, cities have been associated with intergenerational social mobility by providing, for instance, better access to health, education and jobs. The hope for greater individual and collective prosperity has driven much of the world's urbanization[26] and, more recently, global suburbanization.[27] At the same time, it is unfortunately in cities where poverty, racial discrimination and segregation, homelessness, health inequities, unemployment, state abandonment and insecurity become most visible. This

---

[23]   Magnusson (n 3); Allan Cochrane, 'In and beyond Local Government: Making up New Spaces of Governance' [2019] Local Government Studies 1; James Holston, 'Metropolitan Rebellions and the Politics of Commoning the City' (2019) 19 Anthropological Theory 120.

[24]   Neil Brenner and Christian Schmid, 'Planetary Urbanisation' in Matthew Gandy (ed), *Urban Constellations* (Jovis 2012).

[25]   David Satterthwaite and Diana Mitlin, *Urban Poverty in the Global South: Scale and Nature* (Routledge 2013).

[26]   Oriol Nel-lo, 'Introduction: The Irresistible Rise of Urbanization' in Oriol Nel-lo and Renata Mele (eds), *Cities in the 21st Century* (Routledge 2016); Julio D Dávila, 'Cities as Innovation: Towards a New Understanding of Population Growth, Social Inequality and Urban Sustainability' in Oriol Nel-lo and Renata Mele (eds), *Cities in the 21st Century* (Routledge 2016).

[27]   Keil (n 4).

urban dilemma puts cities under constant scrutiny, with an ongoing need for 'fixing' through policy, planning and service provision, in the hopes that they continue enabling economic growth.[28]

Critical scholars argue that poverty and urban disadvantage are rooted in structural processes of political economy and the cultural systems and social relations that sustain them, with the state and urban policy often reinforcing these trends.[29] The causes of poverty and inequality are inevitably linked to the global system of production, and the social, political, institutional and cultural scaffolding that supports and legitimizes it. In turn, 'different representations and beliefs systems about social inequality … shape institutions and public policies affecting inequality dynamics',[30] such as policies in education (determining who has access to skills and higher education) or taxation (whose capital is to be exempted).

Systemic intersectional discrimination (based on race, class, ethnicity, ability, gender or sexuality) similarly limits the access of certain groups or identities to scarce resources. Even when there is access to them, a disenfranchised group may face obstacles to utilize them or may lack a level of collective appropriation to act upon these resources and improve their social mobility.[31] The political recognition and participation of marginalized groups can also be suppressed, directly or indirectly, through societal codes, norms or institutions, enabling elites to capture investments and urban benefits through the political system.[32] These economic, political and social dynamics find grounding in the situated practices that take place in the everyday life of the urban.

The spatiality of the city creates conditions for entrenched poverty and inequality, given that 'the spatial distribution of goods, information and people forms dynamic interdependencies with social structures'.[33] In their logic of density and agglomeration, cities crystallize and intensify forms of inequality, which may originate in wider societal relations and spheres of decision-making but come together and find articulation in the concrete spatiality of the city.[34] Considering that we live in a profoundly urbanized society, interrogating (in)justice from a spatial perspective means interrogating the city.[35]

Crucially then, while the causes of poverty are structural and multidimensional, social inequalities are mediated by the built environment: they are produced and experienced in place.[36] Thus, the spatial patterns of a city can seriously block or restrict access to dignified housing, transport networks and public facilities necessary to realize human rights and enjoy a digni-

---

[28]   Faranak Miraftab, David Wilson and Salo, K (eds), *Cities and Inequalities in a Global and Neoliberal World* (Routledge 2015).

[29]   Pierre Bourdieu and Alain Accardo (eds), *The Weight of the World: Social Suffering in Contemporary Society* (Polity Press 1999); Mustafa Dikeç, *Badlands of the Republic: Space, Politics and Urban Policy* (Blackwell Pub 2007); Loïc Wacquant, *Urban Outcasts: A Comparative Sociology of Advanced Marginality* (Reprinted, Polity Press 2010).

[30]   Piketty (n 6) 73.

[31]   Vincent Kaufmann, Manfred Max Bergman and Dominique Joye, 'Motility: Mobility as Capital' (2004) 28 International Journal of Urban and Regional Research 745; Peter Brand and Julio D Dávila, 'Mobility Innovation at the Urban Margins: Medellín's *Metrocables*' (2011) 15 City 647.

[32]   Nick Devas, 'Metropolitan Governance and Urban Poverty' (2005) 25 Public Administration and Development 351.

[33]   Kaufmann, Bergman and Joye (n 31) 745.

[34]   Dikeç (n 29).

[35]   Soja (n 20) 32.

[36]   Peter Marcuse, 'From Critical Urban Theory to the Right to the City' (2009) 13 City 185.

fied life. Land-uses, development patterns, infrastructure networks and associated settlement arrangements can similarly create unequal access to locational benefits, urban services and resources for excluded groups.[37] Lack of urban connectivity and neighborhood seclusion, for instance, can prevent the urban poor from physically reaching healthcare, education services, and jobs. Transit injustices may confine the urban poor to the periphery away from opportunities or leave them to rely on financially unsustainable forms of transportation that consume their valuable time and resources. Racialized and low-income communities can be unfairly burdened with locational externalities, with toxic dumps or highly polluting industries located in close proximity to their neighbourhood.[38] The spatiality of cities is therefore implicated in creating new forms of poverty and racial discrimination through the unequal disposition of urban space.

B.   Current Trends in Urban Development, Policy and Governance

Since the late 1970s cities have become a conduit for the expansion of financial markets and mobile capital under globalization, whereas the financialization of the economy, urban assets and built environments are increasingly central to capitalism.[39] With the rise of neoliberalism across the globe, an 'entrepreneurial turn' in urban governance has replaced redistributive territorial goals. In a number of cities, the trend has been for dismantling programs and services that either existed in previous decades or that the urban poor are still demanding in much of the urbanized world, such as public housing, social services, public spaces and infrastructure provision.[40] Current urban policy strategies aim to attract new investment, tourism, highly-skilled professionals and residential elites through strategies such as place marketing, beautification, free trade zones, redevelopment districts, public-private partnerships, privately operated public spaces or large-scale development projects.[41]

Both in the Global North and South, neoliberal urban governance has fragmented city regions and enabled the privatization of communal spaces, fulfilling the desire of middle- and upper-class elites to self-segregate through physical barriers and disconnected infrastructures. Gated communities, shopping centers, golf courses, condominium lifestyles and privatized highways, which characterize affluent North American suburbs, are now common in residential areas and suburbs of African, Asian and Latin American cities.[42] Gated communities often

---

[37]   Soja (n 20).

[38]   Isabelle Anguelovski, 'From Toxic Sites to Parks as (Green) LULUs? New Challenges of Inequity, Privilege, Gentrification, and Exclusion for Urban Environmental Justice' (2016) 31 Journal of Planning Literature 23.

[39]   Neil Brenner and Nik Theodore, 'Cities and the Geographies of "Actually Existing Neoliberalism"' (2002) 34 Antipode 349; Keil (n 4).

[40]   Peck and Tickell (n 5); Erik Swyngedouw, 'Governance Innovation and the Citizen: The Janus Face of Governance-beyond-the-State' (2005) 42 Urban Studies 1991.

[41]   Brenner and Theodore (n 39); Peck and Tickell (n 5).

[42]   Teresa Pires do Rio Caldeira, *City of Walls: Crime, Segregation, and Citizenship in São Paulo* (University of California Press 2000); Stephen Graham and Simon Marvin, *Splintering Urbanism: Networked Infrastructures, Technological Mobilities and the Urban Condition* (1st edn, Routledge 2002); Michael A Cohen, 'From Habitat II to Pachamama: A Growing Agenda and Diminishing Expectations for Habitat III' (2016) 28 Environment and Urbanization 35.

have their own sources of water, are designed exclusively for private automobile circulation, and devastate natural resources not always available to other groups.[43]

The outcome of uneven development is splintering urban morphologies, with gentrification and overinvestment in well-off areas and poverty, informality, precarious infrastructure, containment and coercion at the margins of the city. Discourses of privacy, safety and the portrayal of the urban poor as criminals are increasingly common in elites' justification of these spatial exclusions.[44] Local planning policies are equally complicit in exclusionary zoning through projects of gentrification – often under the guise of urban renewal – to keep marginalized communities contained or at a distance.[45]

The repercussions of uneven development are profound. As the majority of urban growth will continue to take place in low-income regions where local economies, institutions and infrastructure are precarious, future growth will likely be characterized by disconnected landscapes and expanding informality.[46] In previous decades, urban informality was often referred to as an exception and as a coping mechanism of the poor in the outskirts of sprawling cities of Latin America, Asia or Africa. Today, informality is seemingly the norm in the majority of the urbanized world.[47] It constitutes a fundamental way of relating to the state and negotiating life in the city, particularly to access income, housing and other resources.[48]

Violence and insecurity are yet another prevalent challenge for cities, predominantly in the so-called ghettos, favelas, projects or banlieues, where poverty, race, state disinvestment, recent immigration, and unemployment or underemployment converge. Often, former working-class neighborhoods – many of which in previous decades were successful examples of social housing projects or informal, self-constructed communities – have turned into derelict urban spaces. In these spaces, gang violence is common, and residents – particularly young men of colour or immigrant status – are stigmatized based on their race and place of residence. Residents often experience violence, including police brutality, or feel insecure in their daily lives.[49] It is in these 'grey zones' of urban exclusion where economic and political changes tend to have the biggest impact.[50]

Currently the right to an adequate standard of living, and the right to housing in particular, seems ever harder to fulfill.[51] In low-income countries, this right has been for decades called 'utopian' given the local scarcity of resources and the limited institutional capacity to implement it. But this limitation is also rising in countries of the Global North, where the right

---

[43]   Dávila (n 26).

[44]   Caldeira (n 42).

[45]   Ananya Roy, 'Why India Cannot Plan Its Cities: Informality, Insurgence and the Idiom of Urbanization' (2009) 8 Planning Theory 76.

[46]   Watson (n 13).

[47]   Ananya Roy, 'Urban Informality: Toward an Epistemology of Planning' (2005) 71 Journal of the American Planning Association 147.

[48]   Watson (n 13).

[49]   Wacquant (n 29); Dikeç (n 29); Luisa Sotomayor, 'Dealing with Dangerous Spaces: The Construction of Urban Policy in Medellín' (2017) 44 Latin American Perspectives 71; Luisa Sotomayor 'Medellín, Colombia: Social Urbanism to Build Human Security' in Sébastien Darchen and Glen Searle (eds), *Global Planning Innovations for Urban Sustainability* (Earthscan-Routledge 2019).

[50]   Dirk Kruijt and Kees Koonings, 'The Rise of Megacities and the Urbanization of Informality, Exclusion and Violence' in Kees Koonings and Dirk Kruijt (eds), *Mega-Cities: The Politics of Urban Exclusion and Violence in the Global South* (Zed Books 2009).

[51]   Samuel Stein, *Capital City: Gentrification and the Real Estate State* (Verso 2019).

to housing and an adequate standard of living are becoming unrealistic.[52] Under the current belief in housing as a means of wealth creation, 'the logic of capital accumulation increasingly trumps the right to housing, with the "exchange" value of housing as a financialized commodity and as a generator of wealth valued above the "use" value of housing as shelter'.[53] As the rise of real estate markets and the speculation of land are now a global phenomenon, low-income – and often racially segregated – communities that previously enjoyed secure housing are losing socio-economic rights through evictions and gentrification.[54]

City-governments often decide to suppress and contain the fall-out of market-driven development and austerity policies through a set of strategies equally detrimental to human rights goals, such as the increased surveillance of public spaces, over-policing of marginalized neighbourhoods and the penalization of the poor through the judiciary system.[55] The overarching goal of such initiatives is to employ urban space 'as an arena both for market-oriented economic growth and for elite consumption practices, while at the same time securing order and control amongst marginalized populations'.[56] Meanwhile, in the cities of the 'majority' world, poor households continue to settle informally at the sprawling margins of the city, where land is typically unserviced and unregulated, and where most of the current urban growth in the world is taking place.[57]

In sum, there are myriad challenges to poverty reduction in the 'urban age', particularly in relation to uneven territorial development, neoliberal austerity, the commoditization of housing, and socio-spatial and political exclusion. Undoubtedly, all people should be able to participate in the construction of the cities in which they live, access their benefits, including public services, and enjoy public spaces, housing, health and education. Given that socio-economic rights are increasingly hard to realize under neoliberalism, the assumption that cities will be able to enact human rights and reduce poverty without a deeper commitment to systemic change seems remote. We strongly agree that cities can and should promote the implementation of human rights, particularly in relation to poverty reduction. We also acknowledge the importance of recognizing the advances of human rights perspectives in the city, and as we elaborate in the following section, we conceive of extended urbanization as a field of possibilities for the advancement of rights. However, we are sceptical about cities being both the problem and the solution to socio-economic exclusions. Instead, we pay attention to the opportunities for political agency that the urban affords: how residents – whether national citizens, undocumented contributors to the city or social movements – may play out their politics and use the urban fora strategically in their struggle to reclaim rights. In looking at the local state, it may be fruitful to examine how municipal and regional authorities, as well

---

[52]   David J Madden and Peter Marcuse, *In Defense of Housing: The Politics of Crisis* (Verso 2016).

[53]   Whitzman (n 22) 1.

[54]   Jason Hackworth, 'Postrecession Gentrification in New York City' (2002) 37 Urban Affairs Review 815; Neil Smith, 'New Globalism, New Urbanism: Gentrification as Global Urban Strategy' (2002) 34 Antipode 427; David Harvey, 'The Right to the City' (2003) 27 International Journal of Urban and Regional Research 939; Sharon Zukin and others, 'New Retail Capital and Neighborhood Change: Boutiques and Gentrification in New York City' (2009) 8 City & Community 47.

[55]   Löic Wacquant, *Punishing the Poor: The Neoliberal Government of Social Insecurity* (Duke University Press 2009).

[56]   Jamie Peck, Nik Theodore and Neil Brenner, 'Neoliberal Urbanism: Models, Moments, Mutations' (2009) 29 SAIS Review of International Affairs 49, 58.

[57]   Watson (n 13); Cohen (n 42).

as other agencies and institutions, can improve their responses and efforts to fulfill localized rights; but we caution against glorifying their efforts or capacities to do so. With these caveats in mind, in the next section we examine the opportunities and limitations of seeing the rights debate with an urban framing.

II.   SEEING THE HUMAN RIGHTS DEBATE *LIKE (*AND *FROM)* THE CITY

This handbook invites reflection on the potential of human rights for poverty reduction. In this section we engage with this invitation from the perspective of the city, questioning the relevance of human rights approaches to confront the urban problems that we have just described. We ask to what extent seeing *like* and *from* the city may enrich the long-standing debate about the potential of human rights to produce social change. Certainly, numerous critiques of human rights have emerged with full force in recent years, with authors claiming their irrelevance and demise.[58] It is argued that 'human rights do more harm than good, as it provides an "ideological alibi to a global system whose governance structures sustain persistent unfairness and blatant injustice"'.[59] Furthermore, the relevance of human rights is questioned for not having fulfilled its core promise: the guarantee of equality for all human beings.[60]

It is easy to agree with some of the critical views that have appeared in the past decade, especially with those that stress the unfulfilled promises of human rights for the poor and the marginalized. But contrary to the fierce contenders, we side with those who believe that (although limited) human rights are far from irrelevant and that by looking at rights from the perspective of the city, one can devise some benefits that serve as counter-critiques to the various pessimistic views. Starting with the promises, the fact that around the world human rights are constantly being deployed by social movements and communities to advance their causes is not a minor contribution. The connection between human rights and social movements has been historically stressed, both by authors rooted in liberal traditions and by scholars with more critical views.[61] Upendra Baxi, for example, argues 'that over the last 60 years the oppressed of the world – mobilised in and through social movements – have been the hidden authors of contemporary developments in human rights'.[62]

To a great extent, such social movement mobilization occurs in cities. The city provides for the poor both formal and informal forms of participation. It contributes spaces for the emergence of an 'insurgent citizenship' that strongly claims 'a right to the city and a right to rights'.[63] Cities allow the flourishing of emerging citizen practices seeking to expand the public sphere and 'to generate "new sources of laws, and new participation in decisions that

---

[58]   Langford (n 14).

[59]   ibid 70 (citing Hopgood, 2014).

[60]   Moyn (n 9).

[61]   Neil Stammers, *Human Rights and Social Movements* (Palgrave Macmillan 2009); see, as examples, Henry J Steiner and Philip Alston, *International Human Rights in Context: Law, Politics, Morals: Text and Materials* (Clarendon Press and OUP 1996); Sally Engle Merry, *Human Rights and Gender Violence: Translating International Law into Local Justice* (University of Chicago Press 2006).

[62]   Stammers (n 61) 2 (citing Baxi, 2002).

[63]   James Holston, 'Insurgent Citizenship in an Era of Global Urban Peripheries: Insurgent Citizenship in an Era of Global Urban Peripheries' (2009) 21 City & Society 245, 245.

bind"'.[64] In short, the reclamation of socio-economic and other human rights is often grounded on urban conditions, which cast cities as the fundamental terrain of social movements and disenfranchised populations in their ongoing fight for social justice.[65]

Besides the deployment of rights by urban social movements, another positive effect of human rights approaches is to displace charity as the way in which the urban poor, especially in low-income countries, access services and resources such as water and sanitation, housing or education. The recognition of human rights brings with it the acceptance that all humans are rights holders and that, upon ratification of human rights instruments, states have binding obligations to respect, promote and fulfill them. In practice, human rights serve to set minimum standards and add value to public policy by legitimizing the interests of the most marginalized in society.[66] Human rights can generate a commitment that substantiates local interventions aimed to improve urban equity and protect the interests of vulnerable residents, in particular when political agendas are not emphatic in their defense or when, as the case of Toronto illustrates, urban planning, zoning bylaws or policy decisions are part of the problem. By endorsing a right to housing, for instance, it is expected that cities will commit to try to solve the underpinning causes of homelessness and protect other rights for which housing is required instead of criminalizing the experience of being homeless that further pushes people into poverty.[67] But as we mentioned before, in the era of extended (sub)urbanization, any engagement with the urban will require attention to the blurry, fragmented and fusing realities of urban regions and the patterns of daily life, which have, in practice, diluted dichotomous assumptions about urban/countryside or city/suburb[68] and which question exclusionary claims to citizenship.[69] It is within this complexity that human rights approaches also prove limited.

One challenge relates to the formal nature of human rights. Rights-based approaches 'may be insufficiently sensitive to the local context as it brings a focus on an established package of rights that are difficult to realise fully'.[70] The formal character of rights and the fact that they reinforce the role of formal systems and processes of urban development not only leaves little possibility for negotiation at the local level but also becomes a constraint for the urban poor that do not fit easily into formality.[71] As Satterthwaite and Mitlin articulate, in a country like South Africa, the right to water may assist the homeowner but offers little to the informal tenant. In this way, these authors conclude, rights approaches, 'are not necessarily pro-poor and may be used to exclude as well as include'.[72]

Also due to their formal nature, attempts to implement human rights are often reduced to a specific geography and a defined set of state actors or international development institutions,

---

[64]   Faranak Miraftab and Shana Wills, 'Insurgency and Spaces of Active Citizenship: The Story of Western Cape Anti-Eviction Campaign in South Africa' (2005) 25 Journal of Planning Education and Research 200, 208 (citing Holston and Appadurai 1999).

[65]   Marcuse (n 36); Holston (n 23).

[66]   Caroline Moser and Andrew Norton, *To Claim Our Rights: Livelihood Security, Human Rights and Sustainable Development* (Overseas Development Institute 2001).

[67]   Don Mitchell, 'The Annihilation of Space by Law: The Roots and Implications of Anti-Homeless Laws in the United States' (1997) 29 Antipode 303.

[68]   Brenner and Schmid (n 24).

[69]   Holston (n 23).

[70]   Satterthwaite and Mitlin (n 25) 42.

[71]   ibid.

[72]   ibid.

which ultimately makes the approach inadequate to tackle the diversity of urban experiences and the increasingly globalizing characteristics of urban poverty and inequality. Magnusson describes this phenomenon in terms of the difficulty of exercising sovereignty, as an issue of 'often claimed' but 'infinitely deferred' authority that does not match people's political expectations.[73] The disparate and fragmented landscape of entities that constitute the state similarly obscures responsibilities over the local implementation of human rights claims.

Next to this challenge is the question of institutional capacity. Cities and local governments may have firm commitments to the eradication of poverty and inequality and to the promotion of rights and yet be unable to fulfill them due to institutional capacity problems. As Parnell notes: 'Bizarrely, many cities appear to have made political commitments to distributive justice without ensuring that the requisite institutional arrangements are in place.'[74] Moreover, cities are profoundly diverse and unequally equipped to address the socio-economic challenges that often originate beyond their sphere of influence, in national policies or global processes of production. It would be unfair to expect cities to fix national governments' failures and entrenched legacies, given their very limited capacity. Adding new responsibilities to cities, particularly poor cities of middle and low-income countries, may be unrealistic given how little fiscal and policymaking capacity some of them have.

Given the extent of global urbanization, mainly during the last half of the twentieth century, many cities in the world have grown through peripheral urbanization, predominantly but not only in the Global South. In much of the Global North, generalized gentrification processes have similarly displaced recent immigrants, refugees and racialized residents of historic working-class centralities to low-income suburbs or banlieues. In both cases, the peripheries have emerged as both areas of socio-economic exclusion and promising sites of political action.

In examining how politics play out in the periphery of Sao Paulo, Holston proposes the recognition of a 'contributors right' articulated to Lefebvre's concept of right to the city – a right that recognizes that those residents who make and build the city in their work and in their daily lives have a claim to it, regardless of whether or not they are national citizens, the legality of their residence, or whether they contribute to formal or informal economies.[75] The claim to such a right today is expressed in the Sanctuary City movement, or municipal identity cards, as in some areas of California, which aim to protect broadly the human rights of undocumented residents. In the current right-wing, anti-immigrant populist moment, the realization of such a right seems remote in many places but would be required as part of a serious response to current urban mobilizations happening in a multitude of cities.

Beyond these salient tensions, a number of debates and challenges must be addressed for localized human rights to increase their efficacy in urban poverty reduction efforts. First, in many cities with high levels of urban poverty, the knowledge of rights is limited. The 'illiteracy' of human rights often leads to their violation or denial. Although several attempts have been made to promote knowledge of human rights at the local level, these initiatives are still limited.

---

[73]   Magnusson (n 3).
[74]   Susan Parnell, 'Building Developmental Local Government to Fight Poverty: Institutional Change in the City of Johannesburg' (2004) 26 International Development Planning Review 377, 378.
[75]   Holston (n 23).

Second, while it is true that the expansion of the rights catalogue to include social and economic rights influenced the discussion of rights in urban policies,[76] it is also true that a challenge for human rights approaches to respond to urban poverty is the claim that such rights are not enforceable. While this assertion is subject to debate, some governmental officials still assume that civil and political rights must be prioritized, while social and economic rights will depend exclusively on the level of development that a country has achieved. Certainly, civil and political rights are essential but without the fulfillment of social and economic rights it will be difficult (if not impossible) to eradicate urban poverty and inequality.

This leads to a third challenge: in globalized times, cities are under pressure to compete for investment and resources. The ubiquity and worlding aspects of neoliberal urban agendas and the discourses that sustain them as an economic imperative or 'common sense' have recast market-driven urban development as if it were the only alternative for cities to compete globally, and as such, a matter of political consensus inviting little debate. Some even see in this 'post-political' condition the roots for the current re-emergence of right-wing populism[77] and the biggest barrier to realization of socio-economic rights.

Finally, a recurrent critique of human rights discourse and practice has to do with the universality of human rights, which has tended to be interpreted in Eurocentric terms. For decades, social justice movements in the Global South have challenged this prevailing Eurocentric understanding embedded in human rights discourse, interpretation and practice. From an urban theory perspective, the persistence of a narrow understanding of rights often obscures the wide diversity of the urban contexts, experiences and relations to global economic processes, and the specificity of state policies that shape cities and connect them to one another in both the Global North and South.[78] If such narrow understanding could be overcome, a democratized and locally meaningful human rights approach could potentially help to solve the current critique of cities being differently theorized along a first world/third world divide, where poverty is ascribed to a reality of 'third world' or 'developing' countries and studied through an international development framework, while poverty in cities of the rich world is conceived in relation to social policies and the welfare state.

III.   CONCLUSION

Cities are fundamental arenas for social and democratic contestations against social injustices. As such, we have seen the growth of popular, professional and academic discourses that exalt cities as the solution to many of the world's intricate problems, from environmental sustainability to global poverty and racial injustice.[79] Such views often miss the point that urban

---

[76]   Oomen and Baumgärtel (n 15).

[77]   Erik Swyngedouw, 'Interrogating Post-Democratization: Reclaiming Egalitarian Political Spaces' (2011) 30 Political Geography 370; Mustafa Dikeç and Erik Swyngedouw, 'Theorizing the Politicizing City' (2017) 41 International Journal of Urban and Regional Research 1; Juan Rivero and others, 'Democratic Public or Populist Rabble: Repositioning the City Amidst Social Fracture' (2020) International Journal of Urban and Regional Research (Online First).

[78]   Jennifer Robinson, *Ordinary Cities: Between Modernity and Development* (Routledge 2006).

[79]   Hilary Angelo and David Wachsmuth, 'Why Does Everyone Think Cities Can Save the Planet?' in Jens Hoff, Quentin Gausset and Simon Lex (eds), *The Role of Non-State Actors in the Green Transition: Building a Sustainable Future* (Routledge 2019).

issues are enmeshed in the very same logic that produce and sustain contemporary cities. Current human rights and development discourses have glorified the city as a suitable scale of intervention for the implementation of poverty reduction initiatives based on a rights perspective. Our intention in this chapter is to offer a more sober view that avoids romanticizing either the city or the localized rights approach while recognizing the gains and opportunities that the local scale can provide to the global human rights project. We warn against throwing the baby out with the bathwater and recognize that it is the legacy and strength of the human rights project that has often provided social movements with a common language, a toolkit and a set of tactics to leverage their cause. However, we also insist that attention be paid to the challenges that remain for the localized rights discourse to hold real purchase globally.

There is still much to say in the matter. Building on the key points of this discussion, we want to propose some lines of inquiry for future research that could aid in better understanding the connection between human rights, cities and urban poverty. One first call is to deepen the scope of interdisciplinary research. Insights from geography, sociology, critical race studies, and urban planning could enrich the view and work of human rights scholars and practitioners who have not necessarily focused their attention on the complexities of the city. The next step in this interdisciplinary effort could be aimed at understanding up close the spatial dimension of rights, considering key questions, such as: (1) How are contemporary geographies of inequality, poverty and social justice restricting human rights in diverse urban contexts?; (2) How can the space of the city be transformed into an environment for the gradual realization of human rights?; and (3) How to integrate human rights to urban innovations and aspirations of globality so that they do not perpetuate inequality and segregation in cities?

Another key line of research to address human rights, poverty and the urban should build on studies of metropolization, immigration and global cities, particularly as distinctions between urban, suburban and regional no longer hold neatly. We believe it is essential to inquire about how to promote collaboration, redistribution and collective capacity among neighbouring jurisdictions so that all residents of a city-region, including those undocumented or at the margins, are not affected by jurisdictional policies or required to stay in one locality in order to overcome poverty and secure rights.

Attention to the New Urban Agenda is also important. So far, we know little about its implementation across countries. Who are the responsible actors? What kind of interventions are being deployed domestically? What practices seem effective? How is progress being measured? Since the Urban Agenda is intended to guide the efforts of nations, cities, regional leaders, and international development agencies towards the achievement of sustainable urban development within a 20-year span, such questions deserve a close and critical look.

In terms of the theoretical grounding, we find hope in returning first, to Lefebvre's radical proposition of the 'right to the city' as an immanent right of marginalized groups to demand the reconstitution of power relations underpinning the production of urban space.[80] The concept of the 'right to the city' signals a way to reimagine a struggle for rights in the city away from capital and state interests towards those who inhabit the city. This entails a double right to participation and appropriation[81] and a right to difference for which minority and marginalized groups must struggle against homogenizing and essentializing policies aimed to manage the

---

[80]   Henry Lefebvre, *The Urban Revolution* (University of Minnesota Press 2003).
[81]   Mark Purcell, 'Excavating Lefebvre: The Right to the City and Its Urban Politics of the Inhabitant' (2002) 58 GeoJournal 99.

poor and the different. Although in practice the concept of the 'right to the city' does not evoke the same implications for all its proponents,[82] it does generate a common discussion, with which further engagement is required, about urban citizenship, rights and their extension, and the possibilities that can be generated in a city so that people can enjoy a more just and democratic society.

An innovative angle through which the urban poverty-human rights nexus should be further explored includes Holston's proposal of recognizing a 'contributor's right'.[83] The struggle for the contributor's right is a definitive fight against a prevalent global form of exclusion from human rights at a time of war and generalized economic violence. Improving cities' capacity to engage with rights requires that all residents and marginalized groups gain the ability and the opportunity to, on the one hand, participate actively and directly in urban, economic and social processes of planning and change in the city and on the other hand, benefit directly from all of the physical, economic, cultural development and growth that is produced by it.

Finally, our invitation is for the global rights project to remain experimental and imaginative beyond the limits of liberal democracies. The challenges for the urban poor in contemporary cities are acute, but we must not only continue to learn from their efforts and innovative solutions to secure equal opportunities, but also, together, we should aim to rethink the meaning of the city for the advancement of rights of all dwellers – an invitation to collectively reimagine more just possible futures.

---

[82]   ibid; Kafui A Attoh, 'What *Kind* of Right is the Right to the City?' (2011) 35 Progress in Human Geography 669.

[83]   Holston (n 23).

17. Local authorities, poverty and the implementation of human rights norms

Moritz Baumgärtel

Cities, towns and their local authorities are often on the frontline when it comes to the fight against poverty. Their pivotal role becomes especially visible in crisis situations, as demonstrated by the recent outbreak of the coronavirus (COVID-19). When national governments had to take urgent measures to contain the spread of the pandemic and to keep economies afloat, many municipal authorities stepped in to ensure that socio-economically disadvantaged persons could survive the crisis. The German City of Düsseldorf, for instance, provided additional food packages and shelter for homeless persons.[1] The City of London booked 300 hotel rooms to make sure that homeless persons would be able to self-isolate.[2] In Spain's capital, Madrid, the City Council arranged continuous food delivery for 500 children from vulnerable families.[3] Finally, in what is probably one of the starkest cases of local action at a massive scale, the municipal government of New Delhi provided food to over 10,000 people per day in 234 shelter homes across the city.[4] There are many examples of localities, large and small, responding to the health-care and economic challenges that the outbreak of the virus posed to the poorest in society. Often helped by local civil-society organisations, municipal authorities immediately—and seemingly out of what has been described as 'a sense of direct responsibility'[5]—recognized that it was important for them to step in and mitigate the often desperate situations that their residents faced.

Admittedly, not all local authorities were exemplary actors, such as hotel-rich Las Vegas, which faced widespread criticism for 'sheltering' homeless persons in parking lots.[6] Yet,

---

[1]   Michael Buch (ed), 'Hilfen für wohnungslose Menschen in der Corona-Krise' (*Landeshauptsadt Düsseldorf*, 20 March 2020) <www.duesseldorf.de/index.php?id=700021325&tx_pld_frontpage %5Bnews%5D=32092> accessed 26 March 2020.

[2]   Anton Stoyanov, 'London Provides the Homeless with Hotel Rooms for Self-Isolation' (*The Mayor*, 22 March 2020) <www.themayor.eu/el/london-provides-the-homeless-with-hotel-rooms-for -self-isolation> accessed 26 March 2020.

[3]   'El Ayuntamiento Ofrecerá un Servicio de Comida Saludable a Domicilio para 500 Niños de Escuelas Infantiles de Cero a Tres Años' (*Ayuntamiento de Madrid*, 24 March 2020) <diario.madrid.es/ blog/notas-de-prensa/el-ayuntamiento-ofrecera-un-servicio-de-comida-saludable-a-domicilio-para-500 -ninos-de-escuelas-infantiles-de-cero-a-tres-anos> accessed 26 March 2020.

[4]   Barkha Mathur, 'Coronavirus Outbreak: Delhi Providing Food To Over 15,000 Homeless People Through Its Shelters Amid Lockdown' (*Benga Swasth India*, 15 April 2020) <swachhindia.ndtv.com/ coronavirus-outbreak-delhi-providing-food-to-over-15000-homeless-people-through-its-shelters-amid -lockdown-42757> accessed 15 June 2020.

[5]   Janne E Nijman, 'Renaissance of the City as Global Actor: The Role of Foreign Policy and International Law Practices in the Construction of Cities as Global Actors' in Andreas Fahrmeir, Gunther Hellmann and Miloš Vec (eds), *The Transformation of Foreign Policy: Drawing and Managing Boundaries from Antiquity to the Present* (OUP 2016) 221.

[6]   Alicia Lee, 'Las Vegas Homeless People are Sleeping in a Parking Lot – Six Feet Apart' (*CNN*, 31 March 2020) <edition.cnn.com/2020/03/30/us/coronavirus-las-vegas-homeless-cashman-center-trnd/ index.html> accessed 17 April 2020.

local governments' generally prominent, and in many cases forceful, involvement during the coronavirus crisis is no coincidence. Over the last two decades, cities have been on the rise as actors concerned with, as well as capable of addressing, global challenges.[7] This clout extends to the domain of international law, where localities emerged first as objects to be governed but have gradually transformed into enforcers and increasingly embrace a role as duty bearers.[8] Especially in the area of human rights law, the actions of cities and towns are seen to offer promising solutions to the perceived lack of effectiveness and legitimacy of the existing legal framework.[9] This proposition is based at least partly on an observed rise of 'human rights cities', where local authorities adopt the norms and language of human rights to inform and shape their own municipal policies.[10]

Building on these insights, this chapter discusses what role local administrations (can) play when it comes to implementing, and possibly even influencing, human rights norms that address questions of poverty. Consideration is also given to the related question: to what extent does human rights, as law and discourse, provide necessary or even useful frameworks for municipalities active in this domain? The focused attention in this contribution on local authorities as the lowest tier of government in no way intends to capture the full picture of what poverty alleviation entails; local decision-making is often 'fuzzy, fragmented, sprawling and reterritorialized'.[11] The point is rather that local governments deserve separate consideration due to the public and frontline qualities of their authority, which make them particularly relevant from the point of human rights law.[12]

This chapter is divided into four parts. The first section presents a brief overview of the responsibilities that local authorities generally hold in terms of international human rights law. Even in the absence of formal duties, important questions arise concerning their indirect responsibilities and accountability under emerging transnational standards. The second section moves to questions of poverty reduction and presents some of the most prominent examples of international organisations harnessing the capacities of local authorities to achieve this goal. However, as already mentioned, cities and their local authorities are also increasingly acting as subjects autonomous from national governments, both by taking individual measures and by teaming up through city networks. Seeking to offer a nuanced account of these developments, this chapter contrasts approaches that differ in their reliance on international human rights law and discourse. The third section discusses three specific examples of municipal efforts that do not have an explicit connection to human rights. The focus shifts then to human rights cities as entities whose approach to poverty reduction is specifically guided by human rights considera-

---

[7]   Michele Acuto, *Global Cities, Governance and Diplomacy: The Urban Link* (Routledge 2013); Benjamin R Barber, *If Mayors Ruled the World: Dysfunctional Nations, Rising Cities* (Yale UP 2013).

[8]   Yishai Blank, 'Localism in the New Global Legal Order' (2006) 47 Harvard Intl LJ 263.

[9]   Barbara Oomen and Moritz Baumgärtel, 'Frontier Cities: The Rise of Local Authorities as an Opportunity for International Human Rights Law' (2018) 29 EJIL 607.

[10]   Barbara Oomen, Martha F Davis and Michele Grigolo (eds), *Global Urban Justice: The Rise of Human Rights Cities* (CUP 2016).

[11]   Natalia Ángel-Cabo and Louisa Sotomayor in this volume. The same can be said for human rights as argued in Jonathan Darling, 'Defying the Demand to "Go Home": From Human Rights Cities to the Urbanisation of Human Rights' in Barbara Oomen, Martha F Davis and Michele Grigolo (eds), *Global Urban Justice: The Rise of Human Rights Cities* (CUP 2016).

[12]   Michael Goodhart, 'Human Rights Cities: Making the Global Local' in Alison Brysk and Michael Stohl (eds), *Contesting Human Rights: Norms, Institutions and Practice* (Edward Elgar 2019).

tions. The concluding section highlights questions for future research, ranging from addressing the significant gaps in our empirical understanding of when and how local authorities become involved to their relevance for processes of international norm creation.

I.   THE HUMAN RIGHTS RESPONSIBILITIES OF LOCAL AUTHORITIES

The rise of cities, and especially 'global cities'[13] such as New York and London, can no longer be described as a new phenomenon. The many reasons, which have been linked to the transformation of global political and economic orders,[14] are beyond the scope of this chapter. Importantly, however, the increased international visibility and clout of cities has brought up questions also for international lawyers.[15] One important aspect is whether and when local authorities hold responsibility under international law generally and human rights law specifically. Straightforward only at first glance, scholarship has recently shown that there is more to this question than has long been presumed. This section serves as a short introduction to this burgeoning literature, which will also help contextualize the subsequent parts of this chapter.

Historically, international law has dealt with the legal aspects arising from the interactions between nation states. One corollary of the core principles of state consent and *pacta sunt servanda* is that states, as the primary legal subjects, have a prerogative for holding rights and responsibilities under international law. Two additional points derive from this orthodox and formalist approach to international law,[16] which is reflected, amongst others, in the 2001 Articles on the Responsibility of States for Internationally Wrongful Acts.[17] First, states are considered to be unitary legal subjects. Second, they may not invoke provisions of their internal law to justify a failure to perform an international obligation.[18] The consequence is that, as for other subnational authorities, the responsibility of local administrations is subsumed under their state. According to Frug and Barron, 'under international law, virtually all the actions of cities will be treated as if they are the actions of the state'.[19]

A strictly positivist inquiry into the human rights responsibilities of local authorities ends here. However, there is much more to the story. First, questions concerning the legal responsibility of local authorities do not actually disappear but are reframed in terms of an 'indirect responsibility' where their actions are attributed to the state.[20] Though unproblematic from a formalist standpoint, such a conception has significant practical implications in many areas of international law and particularly for human rights law, where the implementation of

---

[13]   Saskia Sassen, *The Global City: New York, London, Tokyo* (2nd edn, Princeton UP 2001).

[14]   Simon Curtis, *Global Cities and Global Order* (OUP 2017).

[15]   Helmut Aust, 'Shining Cities on the Hill? The Global City, Climate Change, and International Law' (2015) 26 EJIL 255.

[16]   Katja Creutz, 'Responsibility' in Helmut Aust, Janne Nijman and Miha Marcenko (eds), *Research Handbook on International Law and Cities* (Edward Elgar forthcoming).

[17]   UNGA 'Responsibility of States for Internationally Wrongful Acts' (8 January 2008) UN Doc A/Res/62/61.

[18]   ibid arts 4 and 32.

[19]   Gerald E Frug and David J Barron, 'International Local Government Law' (2006) 38 Urb L 1, 19.

[20]   Creutz (n 16).

norms has always been a key concern.[21] One may consider, for example, that certain human rights treaties such as the Convention on the Rights of the Child explicitly confirm that legal obligations (in this case the consideration of the best interest of the child) are applicable to 'all actions … undertaken by public or private social welfare institutions, courts of law, administrative authorities or legislative bodies',[22] and hence also to the actions of local authorities. Such provisions, which are found also in other conventions,[23] can have important implications. They can, for example, encourage central governments to curb the competencies of sub-state actors to avoid international legal responsibility.[24] At the same time, they may lead to unintended but attributable breaches where cities and towns are unable to perform, or perhaps even unaware of, their 'indirect duties'.

The growing influence of local authorities is a concern not only for national governments but also for international organisations. This is reflected most prominently in the ambitious urban agendas of the European Union (EU), which was established with the Pact of Amsterdam in May 2016, and of UN Habitat III, which was adopted in Quito a few months later. The outlook of these organisations is largely optimistic as the growing involvement of cities and processes of urbanisation are presented as 'an engine of sustained and inclusive economic growth, social and cultural development, and environmental protection'.[25] The emergence of frameworks of 'good urban governance' brings about standards that probably do not yet qualify as binding international norms but that could, over time and with the persistent involvement of international bodies, develop into 'international local government law'.[26] In the context of human rights, the role of local authorities has recently been addressed in a separate report by the UN High Commissioner for Human Rights.[27] Treaty bodies such as the Committee on Economic, Social and Cultural Rights have also dealt with the implications of devolution, for example, in drawing attention to the 'limited awareness of local authorities as to their obligations in regard to the realization of Covenant rights' in their review of the country report of Sweden.[28] The rise to prominence of cities and towns has arguably been accelerated by the formation of transnational city networks: the climate network C40, for example, works in tandem with the World Bank to create requirements that cities need to meet to be eligible for funding.[29] The

[21] UNGA 'Role of Local Government in the Promotion and Protection of Human Rights – Final Report of the Human Rights Council Advisory Committee' (7 August 2015) UN Doc A/HRC/30/49 [26].

[22] Convention on the Rights of the Child (adopted 20 November 1989, entered into force 2 September 1990), 1577 UNTS 3, art 3.

[23] For example, International Covenant on Civil and Political Rights (adopted 16 December 1966, entered into force 23 March 1976) 999 UNTS 171 (ICCPR) art 10; International Covenant on Economic, Social and Cultural Rights (adopted 16 December 1966, entered into force 3 January 1976), 993 UNTS 3 (ICESCR) art. 28; International Convention on the Elimination of All Forms of Racial Discrimination (adopted 7 March 1966, entered into force 4 January 1969), 660 UNTS 195, art 2.

[24] Frug and Barron (n 19) 20.

[25] UNGA 'New Urban Agenda: Quito Declaration on Sustainable Cities and Human Settlements for All' (adopted 23 December 2016) UN Doc A/Res/71/256 4.

[26] Frug and Barron (n 19). See also Helmut Aust and Anél du Plessis (eds), *The Globalisation of Urban Governance* (Routledge 2018).

[27] UNGA 'Local Government and Human Rights: Report of the United Nations High Commissioner for Human Rights' (1 July 2019) UN Doc A/HRC/42/22.

[28] UN Economic and Social Council 'Committee on Economic, Social and Cultural Rights: Concluding Observations on the Sixth Periodic Report of Sweden' (14 July 2016) UN Doc E/C.12/SWE/CO/6 [7–8].

[29] Aust (n 15) 263.

normative impact of these transnational standards is often as high (and sometimes higher) as the impact of 'hard' rules of international law, underscoring the importance of adopting a broad conception of the responsibility of local authorities that also considers informal duties. Such considerations apply also to the domain of human rights.

Lastly, the growing influence and activities of cities, which themselves may exert a discernible 'normative pull',[30] challenges the state-centrism that underlies international law both as a profession and an academic discipline.[31] In the area of human rights, this tension is reflected in a visible schism within the regime where local authorities regularly adopt human rights as a discourse and a praxis of government—dimensions not defined by a strong state-centrism— even as they do not hold any formal responsibilities under international law.[32] In some cases, cities have even passed local ordinances based on human rights treaties, which inevitably brings to the fore questions of 'local accountability'.[33] It is therefore plausible to suggest that the engagement of local authorities with human rights will over time come to 'infiltrate' the instruments of positive law in a way that formalist approaches fail to appreciate.[34] Human rights cities (as discussed in the penultimate section of this chapter) play a particularly important role in this context, though one should keep in mind that the 'urbanisation' of human rights often involves grassroots practices of campaigning, activism and pragmatic negotiations that are discursive rather than formal in nature.[35]

In short, unless these are construed narrowly and formalistically, the question of the human rights responsibilities of local administrations has many facets. The fact that there are indirect responsibilities under the classical framework of international law, as well as novel local and transnational standards of normative significance has elevated local authorities to a place of visibility when it comes to the protection of human rights. This position is one that they have arguably enjoyed for an even longer time in international relations and the global economy.

II.   THE ROLE OF LOCAL AUTHORITIES IN POVERTY REDUCTION FROM AN INTERNATIONAL PERSPECTIVE

As is well-known, more people live in cities than rural areas, with projections indicating that this figure could increase to more than two-thirds of individuals living in cities by 2050.[36] Questions of poverty and inequality have likewise become more 'urban', with both economic ordering and its political contestation taking place in cities.[37] International and regional organi-

---

[30]   ibid 276.

[31]   Nijman (n 5).

[32]   Oomen and Baumgärtel (n 9).

[33]   Martha F Davis, 'Cities, Human Rights and Accountability: The United States Experience' in Barbara Oomen, Martha F Davis and Michele Grigolo (eds), *Global Urban Justice: The Rise of Human Rights Cities* (CUP 2016).

[34]   Elif Durmus, 'A Typology of Local Governments' Engagement with Human Rights: Legal Pluralist Contributions to International Law and Human Rights' (2020) 38 Netherlands Q Human Rights 30.

[35]   Darling (n 11).

[36]   '68% of the World Population Projected to Live in Urban Areas by 2050, says UN' (*United Nations*, 16 May 2018) <www.un.org/development/desa/en/news/population/2018-revision-of-world -urbanization-prospects.html> accessed 22 March 2020.

[37]   See chapter by Natalia Ángel-Cabo and Louisa Sotomayor in this volume.

sations have consequently been paying closer attention to urban poverty and the possible ways of addressing it, usually seeking to collaborate with local authorities. Some of their initiatives, which draw to a varying extent on the human rights framework, will be outlined in this section.

Perhaps the most visible expression of an 'emerging international consensus that good urban governance has become a matter of global concern'[38] is Sustainable Development Goal (SDG) 11, a part of the UN's 2030 Agenda for Sustainable Development, which aims to 'make cities and human settlements inclusive, safe, resilient and sustainable'.[39] It is 'closely linked'[40] to other SDGs, and most notably SDG 1, which expresses the ambition to end poverty in all its forms. SDG 11 is further sub-divided into ten specific targets, some of which are clearly informed by the international human rights framework, such as the need to ensure access for all to adequate, safe and affordable housing (target 1).[41] Both the SDGs in general and SDG 11 specifically are a clear reflection of a belief among members of the UN Sustainable Development Group that '[m]uch of the 2030 Agenda will be "fought and won" in urban centres'.[42] Initial progress assessments have consequently paid considerable attention to the tasks and capacities of local authorities.[43] However, the question of whether human rights are being integrated into the practical realisation of the SDGs is still a relatively open one.[44] In formulating policies, local authorities seem at times to get caught up in the long-standing (though arguably false) choice between prioritising sustainable development or human rights.[45]

Closely related to the question of sustainable development is the New Urban Agenda,[46] which was adopted by UN Habitat III in Quito in 2016. The Agenda recognizes local authorities as important stakeholders in tackling the questions of urban poverty, as it seeks to 'readdress[] the way cities and human settlements are planned, designed, financed, developed, governed and managed'.[47] The New Urban Agenda references both international human rights treaties and the 'right to the city' to highlight a commitment to equal access and participation.[48] It also alludes to human rights in setting out how 'sustainable urban development' aims to

---

[38]   Helmut Aust and Anél du Plessis, 'The Globalisation of Urban Governance – Legal Perspectives on Sustainable Development Goal 11' in Helmut Philipp Aust and Anél Du Plessis (eds), *The Globalisation of Urban Governance* (Routledge 2018).

[39]   UNGA, 'Transforming Our World: The 2030 Agenda for Sustainable Development' (21 October 2015) UN Doc A/Res/70/1.

[40]   UN Habitat, *Tracking Progress Towards Inclusive, Safe, Resilient and Sustainable Cities and Human Settlements: SDG 11 Synthesis Report* (2018) 10-11 <http://uis.unesco.org/sites/default/files/documents/sdg11-synthesis-report-2018-en.pdf> accessed 26 February 2020.

[41]   ibid 38.

[42]   'Cities are Engines for Achieving the Sustainable Development Goals' (*UN Habitat*, 17 July 2018) <unhabitat.org/cities-are-engines-for-achieving-the-sustainable-development-goals> accessed 26 February 2020.

[43]   UN Habitat (n 40).

[44]   Karina Gomes Da Silva, 'The New Urban Agenda and Human Rights Cities: Interconnections between the Global and the Local' (2018) 36 Netherlands Q Human Rights 290.

[45]   Morten Kjaerum and others, 'Human Rights and the SDGs' (*Raoul Wallenberg Institute* 2018) <portal.research.lu.se/portal/files/53375782/HR_Cities_and_SDGs_print_updated.pdf>.

[46]   See UN Habitat (n 40) 109. See also Sandra C Valencia and others, 'Adapting the Sustainable Development Goals and the New Urban Agenda to the City Level: Initial Reflections from a Comparative Research Project' (2019) 11 Intl J Urban Sustainable Development 4; Da Silva (n 44).

[47]   New Urban Agenda (n 25) 4.

[48]   ibid 11–13, 155.

'eradicate[] poverty in all its forms and dimensions, including extreme poverty'.[49] And while the Agenda likewise acknowledges the need to install 'multilevel consultation mechanisms' to promote cooperation between national, subnational and local administrations, which would include a follow-up mechanism,[50] there was scepticism early on whether local authorities would be implicated sufficiently given that states had already failed to involve them during the preparatory process.[51] At the time of writing, it still is too soon to tell whether the overall level of involvement of local authorities has substantially increased, not least because the New Urban Agenda lacks a formal implementation mechanism.[52]

Looking at past experience, and more specifically at negotiations regarding security of tenure, an important component of the international right to housing, one can be cautiously optimistic. In these negotiations, UN Habitat facilitated complex and highly interactive processes of norm negotiation where central state and local authorities, alongside other actors including civil society organisations, academics and international organisations, succeeded in modifying the meaning to be more responsive to local socio-political conditions.[53] However, the implementation of such norms remains an issue, with local authorities often facing constraints in terms of their competencies and capacities.[54]

At the regional level, the EU's 2016 Urban Agenda defines 'urban poverty' as one of its priority themes.[55] While the Urban Agenda does not create any specific competence for the EU regarding urban policy, it has been influential in facilitating the sharing of knowledge and coordinated action across Member States whilst also channelling EU funding to local authorities to achieve these goals.[56] Encompassing many aspects related to sustainable urban development, the issue of poverty reduction is taken up by the Urban Poverty Partnership (UPP), whose stated ambition is to 'reduce poverty and improve the inclusion of people in poverty or at risk of poverty in deprived neighbourhoods'.[57] The Partnership, coordinated by the French and Belgian governments and consisting of several Member States, cities, regions, NGOs and the EU Commission,[58] addresses questions of child poverty, urban deprived areas

---

[49]   ibid 25–26.

[50]   ibid 87, 169.

[51]   Ulrich Graute, 'Local Authorities Acting Globally for Sustainable Development' (2016) 50 Reg Studies 1931, 1940.

[52]   Valencia and others (n 46).

[53]   Miha Marcenko, 'International Assemblage of the Security of Tenure and the Interaction of City Politics with the International Normative Discourse' (2019) 51 J L Pluralism 151.

[54]   Ivan Turok and Andreas Scheba, '"Right to the City" and the New Urban Agenda: Learning from the Right to Housing' (2019) 7 Territory, Politics, Governance 494; Da Silva (n 44).

[55]   'Urban Agenda for the EU: Pact of Amsterdam' (*European Commission*, 30 May 2016) 10 <ec .europa.eu/regional_policy/sources/policy/themes/urban-development/agenda/pact-of-amsterdam.pdf> accessed 22 February 2020.

[56]   Interview with Martin Grisel, Director, European Urban Knowledge Network, The Hague, 24 February 2020.

[57]   Urban Poverty Partnership, 'Final Action Plan 2018' (*European Commission*, 2 February 2018) <ec.europa.eu/futurium/en/urban-poverty/final-action-plan-urban-poverty-partnership> accessed 25 February 2020.

[58]   The specific members include Belgium, France, Germany, Greece and Spain as states; Birmingham (UK), Daugavpils (LV), Kortrijk (BE), Keratsini-Drapetsona (EL), Lille (FR), Łódź (PL) and Timişoara (RO) as cities; the Brussels Capital Region and Ile de France Region; DG for Regional and Urban Policy and DG Employment, Social Affairs and Inclusion from the EU Commission; as well as EAPN, Eurochild, FEANTSA, UN Habitat, Eurocities, EUKN and URBACT as non-governmental stakeholders.

and neighbourhoods, homelessness and the vulnerability of Roma people in an approach seeking to 'strengthen human rights'.[59] The development of data to identify, measure, monitor and evaluate urban poverty is another stated objective. In opting for an inclusive and coordinative approach that seeks to integrate the efforts of a variety of stakeholders across levels, the UPP is a good example of a 'joined-up governance' approach that the EU has also taken in the past.[60] Importantly, whilst not creating any direct responsibilities, the conditionality of funding creates genuine incentives for local authorities to align themselves with the standards that are proposed.

Finally, in a context more specifically focused on human rights protection, the crucial role of local authorities has been pointed out repeatedly by the former UN Special Rapporteur on Extreme Poverty and Human Rights, Philip Alston. One recurrent thread in his reports is the lack of financial support given by central governments, even as competencies continue to devolve. Thus, reflecting on the situation in Romania in 2015, he emphasised that local authorities, which had been given 'considerable responsibilit[ies]' in terms of the provision of social services and benefits, were 'often not equipped with adequate financial and human resources to perform the job in a satisfactory manner'.[61] This impacted various issues, including the training and employment of social workers, with further adverse effects for the welfare of children and disabled persons. In the case of the UK, the Special Rapporteur charged that local governments had been one of the primary targets of recent national austerity measures. In a separate section dedicated to 'shrinking local government funding', his report described how an overall funding cut of 49 per cent forced from 2010–11 to 2017–18 has resulted in the deterioration of basic services such as child protection, emergency welfare funds and public facilities such as public libraries, which are often particularly salient for people living in poverty.[62] Finally, looking at the United States, Alston is critical of states denying cities and counties autonomy for action, which has detrimental consequences for policy innovation.[63] This conclusion resonates with the findings of the UN Human Rights Committee, which (in their earlier concluding observations on the periodic report of the US) highlighted the central role of local authorities in addressing homelessness through decriminalization and the implementation of effective solutions.[64] The UN Special Rapporteur on Adequate Housing

---

[59]   Urban Poverty Partnership (n 57) 13.

[60]   Barbara Oomen and Moritz Baumgärtel, 'Human Rights Cities' in Mark Gibney and Anja Mihr (eds), *The SAGE Handbook of Human Rights* (Sage Publishing 2014) 719.

[61]   'End-of-mission Statement on Romania, by Professor Philip Alston, United Nations Human Rights Council Special Rapporteur on Extreme Poverty and Human Rights' (*Office of the United Nations High Commissioner for Human Rights*, 11 November 2015) <www.ohchr.org/EN/NewsEvents/Pages/DisplayNews.aspx?NewsID=16737&LangID=E> accessed 3 March 2020.

[62]   UN Human Rights Council 'Visit to the United Kingdom of Great Britain and Northern Ireland: Report of the Special Rapporteur on Extreme Poverty and Human Rights' (23 April 2019) UN Doc A/HRC/41/39/Add.1, [39–43].

[63]   'Statement on Visit to the USA, by Professor Philip Alston, United Nations Special Rapporteur on Extreme Poverty and Human Rights' (Office of the United Nations High Commissioner for Human Rights, 15 December 2017) <www.ohchr.org/EN/NewsEvents/Pages/DisplayNews.aspx?NewsID=22533> accessed 3 March 2020.

[64]   UN Human Rights Committee, 'Concluding Observations on the Fourth Periodic Report of the United States of America' (23 April 2014) UN Doc CCPR/C/USA/CO/4, [19].

has likewise raised this point in a report dedicated specifically to the role of local and other subnational governments.[65]

Other examples exist of international organisations referring to local governments in their strategies to reduce poverty.[66] While it is beyond the scope of this section to provide a full overview, one can safely conclude that the involvement of local administration is perceived as critical in many different areas ranging from securing adequate housing to the revitalisation of deprived neighbourhoods and the alleviation of child poverty. They also play a crucial role when it comes to setting up and maintaining data collection and monitoring mechanisms.[67] At the same time, serious concerns exist as to whether there are always sufficient local capacities to address these challenges, both in terms of competencies and resources. Linkages to human rights, finally, are frequent but also unsystematic, which has led some authors to conclude that cities and towns themselves must take a lead in bridging the gap to bring human rights home.[68]

III.   LOCAL AUTHORITIES FIGHTING URBAN POVERTY WITHOUT USING HUMAN RIGHTS

While international organisations create comprehensive frameworks to address questions of poverty, solutions are also found in concrete local actions. Whether or not these rely on human rights as law and discourse merits being treated as an open empirical question that does not assume the relevance of the framework from the outset. In contrast to the next section dealing with human rights cities, the following paragraphs provide a general overview of the kinds of approaches and actions that local authorities take when considerations regarding human rights are subordinate or altogether absent. The three instances discussed here offer only snapshots of such practices that exist around the world, which each arise and are grounded in very different legal, political and economic contexts.[69] A crucial distinction is between rural and urban communities, which translates into specific challenges and contexts of vulnerability.[70] Against this background, the goal of this section is to discuss some examples that can be found in reports and other grey literature on the topic, whilst reflecting on their connection to human rights, even if it is not explicit.

A much-acclaimed example of a local government combatting poverty is Colombia's second largest city, Medellín. Routinely mentioned as a 'model of urban transformation',[71] the city began efforts to improve the conditions in slums and other poverty- and violence-stricken

---

[65]   UNGA, 'Report of the Special Rapporteur on Adequate Housing as a Component of the Right to an Adequate Standard of Living, and on the Right to Non-Discrimination in this Context, Leilani Farha' (2014) UN Doc A/HRC/28/62, [24].

[66]   See World Bank, *Systems of Cities: Harnessing Urbanization for Growth and Poverty Alleviation* (The World Bank 2009).

[67]   UN Habitat (n 40) 111.

[68]   Da Silva (n 44) 292.

[69]   Diana Mitlin and David Satterthwaite, *Urban Poverty in the Global South: Scale and Nature* (Routledge 2013) 149.

[70]   David Satterthwaite and Cecilia Tacoli, 'Seeking an Understanding of Poverty that Recognizes Rural–Urban Differences and Rural–Urban Linkages' in Tony Lloyd-Jones and Carole Rakodi (eds), *Urban Livelihoods: A People-Centred Approach to Reducing Poverty* (Earthscan Publications 2002).

[71]   Ede Ijjasz-Vasquez and Pamela Sofia Duran Vinueza, 'How is Medellin a Model of Urban Transformation and Social Resilience?' (*World Bank Blogs*, 2 June 2017) <blogs.worldbank.org/

areas in the early 1990s and then systematised the efforts into 'Integrated Urban Projects' (*Proyectos Urbanos Integrales*) in the early 2000s.[72] The approach was finally upgraded to a comprehensive strategy based on the realization of large-scale urban-development projects, which Medellín's former Mayor Sergio Fajardo dubbed 'social urbanism'.[73] The flagship policy, though described as mostly symbolic by some, is *Metrocables*, a public aerial cable-car system connecting the poorer parts of the city.[74] The overall results of the efforts seem impressive, with the percentage of people living in poverty falling from over 36 per cent in 2002 to about 14 per cent in 2015.[75] Significant challenges remain,[76] however, with one major point of critique being that the local authorities do not respect the 'right to the city', as they do not sufficiently involve local residents in the planning and realization of their large-scale projects.[77] Interestingly, this shortcoming has not prevented Medellín from being highly integrated and even taking a leadership role in the international scene, for example, by hosting the World Urban Forum of UN-Habitat in 2014. The resulting Medellín Declaration refers to 'multidimensional poverty' and stresses the importance of equity as a foundation of sustainable urban development.[78] In 2017, Medellín organized a living laboratory where 35 cities, the World Bank and the 100 Resilient Cities network (funded by the Rockefeller Foundation) shared methodologies and experiences on the topics of security, coexistence and resilience.[79]

One of the most important human rights relating to poverty alleviation, and also to SDG 11 (and specifically target 1), is the right to housing, as guaranteed in various human rights instruments such as Article 25 of the Universal Declaration of Human Rights.[80] Practice shows that the implementation of the right and the target is often not straightforward but requires several systematic steps, including mapping and data collection. The Know Your City (KYC) campaign operating in 30 countries in the global South provides a good example of such efforts. KYC, by its own description, 'unites organized slum dwellers and local governments in partnerships anchored by community-led slum profiling, enumeration, and mapping'.[81]

---

sustainablecities/how-medellin-model-urban-transformation-and-social-resilience> accessed 4 April 2020.

[72]   Jason Corburn and others, 'The Transformation of Medellin into a "City for Life": Insights for Healthy Cities' (2020) 4 Cities & Health 13.

[73]   Luisa Sotomayor, 'Equitable Planning Through Territories of Exception: The Contours of Medellín's Urban Development Projects' (2015) 37 Intl Development Planning R. 373.

[74]   Caren Levy and Julio D Dávila, 'Planning for Mobility and Socio-Environmental Justice: The Case of Medellín, Colombia' in Adriana Allen, Liza Griffin and Cassidy Johnson (eds), *Environmental Justice and Urban Resilience in the Global South* (Palgrave 2017).

[75]   Corburn and others (n 72).

[76]   See Sotomayor (n 73) as well as Levy and Dávila (n 74).

[77]   Colleen Hammelman and Alexis Saenz-Montoya, 'Territorializing the Urban-Rural Border in Medellín, Colombia: Socio-Ecological Assemblages and Disruptions' (2020) 19 J Latin American Geography 36. On the right to the city, see Eva García Chueca, 'Human Rights in the City and the Right to the City' in Barbara Oomen, Martha F Davis and Michele Grigolo (eds), *Global Urban Justice: The Rise of Human Rights Cities* (CUP 2016).

[78]   '7th World Urban Forum Medellin Declaration: Equity as a Foundation of Sustainable Urban Development' (*UN Habitat*) <unhabitat.org/7th-world-urban-forum-medellin-declaration> accessed 3 April 2020.

[79]   See n 71.

[80]   UN Habitat (n 40) 38. See also ICESCR, art 11.

[81]   Janet Byrne (ed), 'Know Your City: Slum Dwellers Count' (*Slum Dwellers International*, 2018) 4 < http://knowyourcity.info/wp-content/uploads/2018/02/SDI_StateofSlums_LOW_FINAL.pdf>.

The pilot, and first successful instance of creating such a profile, came from Zambia's capital Lusaka, where the City Council provided resources for the project and engaged with local communities to map and enumerate the households that exist in informal settlement.[82] After its successful completion, local authorities extended their commitment to city-wide slum upgrading, amongst others, by providing land for further development to the Zambian Slum Dwellers Federation.[83] KYC has now been enlarged to many other localities in Africa, Asia and Latin America with the support of United Cities and Local Governments, and local authorities are considered the key stakeholders together with the organised informal settlement communities.[84] The fact that KYC managed to profile as many as 7,712 slums in 224 cities by 2018 has been highlighted as a best practice with regard to SDG 11.[85]

In Europe, one of the most ambitious local programmes fighting poverty can be found in Kortrijk, a city of about 75,000 inhabitants in the Flemish region of Belgium. In 2013, local government presented a detailed and comprehensive poverty plan that included 185 local initiatives related, amongst others, to housing, health care and literacy.[86] One of many concrete outcomes is the opening of a people's restaurant (*volksrestaurant*) in 2018, which provides affordable and subsidised meals as well as courses aimed at fostering employment in the hospitality sector.[87] The city's poverty plan was assessed and revised in 2019, with the local authorities deciding to start rolling out local social benefits on the basis of income and specific questionnaires and to create as many as 750 social housings units.[88] In addition, a supplementary income was introduced for people whose wage does not provide for a decent living.[89] It is interesting to note the complete absence of any considerations of human rights law as well as the rare allusion to international and European initiatives.[90] To be sure, Kortrijk has been a member of the EU Urban Poverty Partnership, where it has been eager to share its experience and provide recommendations to its partners.[91] Nonetheless, its example demonstrates above all the autonomy of local authorities, which can develop ambitious programmes based on local motivations and needs, deciding in this case to address the stark contradiction of a prosperous city being the home to a relatively large number of persons living in poverty.[92]

Medellín, Lusaka and Kortrijk provide very different examples of local authorities strongly committed to fight poverty. Common to all three efforts is the fact that human rights do not

---

[82]   'Lusaka 2030 – A City Without Slums' (*Metropolis Urban Sustainability Exchange*) <use .metropolis.org/case-studies/know-your-city-a-city-2030-city-without-slums> accessed 29 March 2020.

[83]   'Annual Report 2016' (*Slum Dwellers International*, 2016) 36 <https://knowyourcity.info/wp -content/uploads/2016/11/Annual-Report_WEB_300916_singles.pdf> accessed 1 April 2020.

[84]   Byrne (n 81) 10–11.

[85]   UN Habitat (n 40) 43.

[86]   'Een Nieuw Plan voor Sociale Vooruitgang en Tegen Armoede' (*Stad Kortrijk*) 4 <www.kortrijk .be/sites/kortrijk/files/2019-10/Armoedeplan-2019_1.pdf> accessed 2 April 2020.

[87]   ibid 15.

[88]   Alexander Haezebrouck, 'Nieuw Plan Tegen Armoede: Kortrijk Bouwt 750 Nieuwe Sociale Woningen' (*Het Laatste Nieuws*, 16 October 2019) <www.hln.be/in-de-buurt/kortrijk/nieuw-plan-tegen -armoede-kortrijk-bouwt-750-nieuwe-sociale-woningen~a98c44aa/> accessed 2 April 2020.

[89]   ibid.

[90]   See n 86.

[91]   'Urban Agenda Partnership on Urban Poverty: Report of the Seminar on 27 September 2016 in Athens, Greece' (*European Urban Knowledge Network* December 2016) 5-6 <www.eukn.eu/fileadmin/ Files/Policy_Labs/2016_September_27/Policy_Lab_Report__EUKN.pdf>.

[92]   ibid 5.

play a central role, which is an important observation given that human rights cities have recently received much attention in scholarship, quite possibly to the detriment of cities and towns such as the ones discussed here. However, it should be kept in mind that the issue of poverty has been identified as an international and local priority also in other governance frameworks. Municipal action can bring about significant improvements in the enjoyment of human rights even where the latter is not a driving factor. We now turn to localities that, by contrast, consciously opt for a human rights-based approach, some of which have even taken on the label of human rights city.

IV.   HUMAN RIGHTS CITIES ADDRESSING CHALLENGES RELATED TO POVERTY

This final section focuses on the practices of human rights cities, which can be defined as 'an urban entity or local government that explicitly bases its policies, or some of them, on human rights as laid down in international treaties, thus distinguishing itself from other local authorities'.[93] Much has been written in recent years about their rise,[94] which suggests that the phenomenon continues to grow. Originally launched by the People's Movement for Human Rights Learning in 1993, local authorities around the world have declared their localities to be human rights cities, in some cases even adopting international treaties into their municipal law.[95] As could be expected, some human rights cities tackle the question of poverty reduction with a specific reference to the international legal framework. The following paragraphs provide a few examples to represent some of the typical observations that can be made in these contexts, again in the awareness that 'local human rights praxis' finds very different expressions in various urban, suburban and rural settings.[96] While all cases mentioned here hail from Europe, this does not imply any sort of regional monopoly. In fact, Rosario, Argentina was the world's first human rights city.[97]

One example of a human rights city taking on questions of poverty can be found in Utrecht, the Netherlands. Many typical features characterise this case, which therefore merits closer examination. In Utrecht, the human rights approach was introduced by an initial report published by the local authorities in 2011 to self-assess their human rights performance.[98] Poverty reduction was addressed explicitly, with the local government highlighting its municipal U-Pass as a measure to stimulate the participation of low-income households and individuals by enabling them to take part in courses, sports and recreation activities.[99] Particular attention was paid to children and whether they were able to participate in activities such as school

---

[93]   Oomen and Baumgärtel (n 60) 710.
[94]   See most notably Oomen and Baumgärtel (n 9); Oomen, Davis and Grigolo (n 10); Martha F Davis, 'Design Challenges for Human Rights Cities' (2017) 49 Columbia Human Rights L Rev 27; Michele Grigolo, *The Human Rights City: New York, San Francisco, Barcelona* (Routledge 2019).
[95]   Davis (n 94).
[96]   Goodhart (n 12) 154.
[97]   Oomen and Baumgärtel (n 60) 714.
[98]   Gemeente Utrecht, 'Human Rights in Utrecht: How Does Utrecht Give Effect to International Human Rights Treaties?' (*Municipality of Utrecht* 2011) <www.utrecht.nl/fileadmin/uploads/documenten/bestuur-en-organisatie/internationale-zaken/2015-10-Human-Rights-Utrecht.pdf>.
[99]   ibid 13. I thank Sara Miellet for drawing my attention to this example.

trips.[100] While the policy arguably pre-dates the city's turn to human rights, the report reflects a human rights perspective in that the municipality actively reaches out to schools, community centres, elderly homes and events to ensure that information about the U-Pass reaches its target audience.[101] Participation and equal access seem to be their key concerns. While the initiative is still in place, the range of activities has widened through time and under the guidance of a human rights partnership consisting of both the local authorities and civil-society organisations, including the Poverty Coalition (*Armoedecoalitie*), which was founded in 2009.[102]

The incorporation of a full range of local actors plays a key role not only in Utrecht but also in other human rights cities.[103] The example of Utrecht underlines the potential interconnection between a commitment to human rights and other international strategies aimed at poverty reduction: Utrecht is now not only a human rights city but has also highlighted its strong association with the SDGs by declaring itself a 'Global Goals City'.[104]

Another feature of human rights cities is that they can use human rights law and discourse to challenge policies adopted at the state or national levels.[105] Such defiance arises concerning issues relating to poverty, with one example pointing (perhaps surprisingly) to the relevance of civil and political rights. In 2001, the same year that the City of Graz in Austria declared itself a human rights city, it began rallying local civil society organisations and academics against a law that established a general ban on begging in the State of Styria.[106] This struggle transformed into domestic litigation, which, actively supported by Graz,[107] reached the Austrian Constitutional Court in 2012. The Court held in its ruling that the undifferentiated ban was unconstitutional because 'silent begging' is an expression of poverty protected by free speech.[108] However, the decision did not end discussions in Graz. Instead, the Mayor followed the advice of the local human rights advisory council to form an inter-institutional expert group charged with finding a generally acceptable policy solution to begging.[109] The group recommended the establishment of a service centre that would serve as a meeting and information point for both the beggars and other local residents.[110] In a national context where discussions flare up regularly, Graz is now cited as a best practice by opponents of bans on

---

[100] ibid 14.

[101] ibid.

[102] 'Over Ons' (*Armoedecoalitie Utrecht*) <www.armoedecoalitie-utrecht.nl/over-ons> accessed 3 April 2020.

[103] Barbara Oomen, 'Human Rights Cities: The Politics of Bringing Human Rights Home to the Local Level' in Jeff Handmaker and Karin Arts (eds), *Mobilising International Law for 'Global Justice'* (CUP 2018) 231.

[104] Deppy Keranidou and others, 'Utrecht: A Global Goals City – Utrecht's Approach to Localising the UN Sustainable Development Goals' (*City of Utrecht*, 2018) <www.local2030.org/library/447/Localising-the-SDGs-in-Utrecht-.pdf>.

[105] Oomen (n 103) 230.

[106] Da Silva (n 44) 302.

[107] Oomen (n 103) 216.

[108] Klaus Starl, 'Human Rights and the City: Obligations, Commitments and Opportunities' in Barbara Oomen, Martha F Davis and Michele Grigolo (eds), *Global Urban Justice: The Rise of Human Rights Cities* (CUP 2016) 212.

[109] 'Annual Report 2015' (*European Training and Research Centre for Human Rights and Democracy*, 2016) <www.etc-graz.at/typo3/fileadmin/user_upload/ETC-Hauptseite/publikationen/Jahresbericht/ETC-AnnualReport15-web.pdf> accessed 18 March 2020.

[110] Wolfgang Benedek, 'Sozialarbeit als Menschenrechtsprofession' (*soziales_kapital*, 2016) 16 <soziales-kapital.at/index.php/sozialeskapital/article/view/467/859> accessed 1 April 2020.

begging whereas other localities such as Salzburg, notably itself a human rights city, continue to struggle to formulate viable policy solutions.[111]

Declaring the status of a human rights city does not guarantee success in the fight against poverty, but it is usually the starting point for more meaningful action. The City of York, which officially declared itself the first human rights city in the UK in 2017,[112] is an example. Following the report by the UN Special Rapporteur on Extreme Poverty and Human Rights, the York Human Rights City Network dedicated its 2019 report to the issue of poverty, using the international human rights obligations concerning an adequate standard of living as a benchmark for its appraisal.[113] The report highlighted that child poverty was increasing, with almost a quarter of children living in poverty.[114] It also became clear that food security was an issue.[115] In its conclusion, the report recommended that the 'City of York Council and statutory agencies should review all relevant policies and interventions … to place the alleviation of poverty and the right to a decent standard of living at their core' in an effort to avoid York's commitment to human rights becoming a tale of two cities.[116] Time will tell whether the city has the determination and the resources to improve the difficult conditions confronting its poor. It is clear, however, that improvement will be difficult given the budgetary hit that local authorities in the UK have taken in times of austerity.[117]

Finally, an interesting initiative related to the creation of norms relevant to poverty reduction—although only 'soft' transnational laws for the time being—is the Homeless Bill of Rights that targets local governments specifically. On the website of one of its initiating organisations, FEANTSA, the Bill is described as 'a compilation of basic rights drawn from European and international human rights instruments specific to the situation of homeless people'.[118] It includes a range of rights including a right to decent emergency accommodation, equal treatment by municipal staff and services, the right to emergency services, the right to vote, and the right to privacy and data protection, as well as specific innovative rights such as a right to exit homelessness and a right to carry out practices necessary to survival.[119] Further, the Homeless Bill of Rights calls upon local authorities to 'to maximize their contribution to improving the living conditions of people who are homeless, and to lessen the negative effects of homelessness'.[120] Launched in 2017 at the EU Cities Forum and relaunched in 2019, the Bill

---

[111]   Stefanie Ruep, 'Verfassungsgericht: Salzburger Bettelverbot Gesetzeswidrig' (*Der Standard*, 4 July 2017) <www.derstandard.at/story/2000060746233/salzburger-bettelverbot-laut-verfassungsg erichtshof-gesetzeswidrig> accessed 1 April 2020.

[112]   Kjaerum and others (n 45) 13.

[113]   'York Human Rights Indicator Report – Human Rights: Reclaiming the Positive' (*York: Human Rights City*, 2019) 18–19 <www.yorkhumanrights.org/wp-content/uploads/2020/03/48546_Applied -Human-Rights-Booklet_v3.pdf> accessed 2 April 2020.

[114]   ibid 20.

[115]   ibid 24–25.

[116]   ibid 27.

[117]   See n 62.

[118]   'Homeless Bill of Rights' (*FEANTSA*, 17 November 2017) <www.feantsa.org/en/campaign/ 2017/11/21/homeless-bill-of-rights?bcParent=419> accessed 26 March 2020. The NGO Housing Rights Watch is the other initiator.

[119]   'Homeless Bill of Rights' (*Housing Rights Watch*) <www.housingrightswatch.org/sites/default/ files/Template%20Homeless%20Bill%20of%20Rights%20EN_0.pdf> accessed 26 March 2020.

[120]   ibid.

currently counts eight European cities as signatories,[121] including Barcelona, one of Europe's most proactive human rights cities.[122] At the beginning of 2020, a French version of the Bill was initiated by the Abbé Pierre Foundation with the support of a large number of other French NGOs.[123] If the initiative garners further support, it could come to influence the international human rights framework, for example in (and through) the reports of UN treaty bodies or the work of UN special rapporteurs.[124]

V.   CONCLUSION AND RECOMMENDATIONS FOR FUTURE RESEARCH

This chapter offered a general analysis into the question of whether and how local authorities are involved in combatting poverty and what role international human rights guarantees may play in this context. Looking at both the strategic frameworks formulated by international organisations and examples from specific cities, we can safely conclude that municipal governments are significant stakeholders in tackling the challenges that confront individuals living in poverty. In fact, it is striking that they are directly involved in the whole range of issues, including housing, facilitating mobility for socio-economically disadvantaged people, ensuring availability of nutritious foods, protecting the homeless and beggars from discrimination, and mapping and gathering information on informal settlements. Each of those aspects has been mentioned in at least one of the examples discussed in this chapter.

Looking at future research, one can point to several questions and challenges that will need to be addressed. First and foremost, more empirical research is needed since our understanding of the strategies taken by local authorities remains partial at best. For example, this chapter is the first to put the academic spotlight on the ambitious poverty plan of the Belgian city of Kortrijk, which has been in place for more than seven years and has received significant attention in the national media. This is perhaps not surprising considering that 'so much of the innovation in places where there are functioning local democracies is never documented because it is seen as the normal functioning of an effective local government'.[125] However, knowing more about when and how municipal authorities become active in this domain is a prerequisite for theorizing how human rights law and discourse feature in their efforts. Without further research, all that can be said is that some cities rely on human rights while others do not—somewhat of a truism.

A related empirical question that single-case and comparative empirical studies will have to tackle is how human rights fare in terms of their usefulness when compared to other international frameworks such as sustainable development. The approaches are not contradictory and perhaps even complementary, but they do come with their own international institutional arrangements, which different local authorities may find more or less attractive. Localities

---

[121]   The other cities are Móstoles and Santiago de Compostela in Spain, Villeurbanne in France, Thessaloniki in Greece, and Murska Sobota, Slovenj Gradec and Kranj in Slovenia.

[122]   See Grigolo (n 94).

[123]   'La Déclaration Réaffirme les Droits Fondamentaux des Personnes Sans Abri' (*Fondation Abbé Pierre*, 13 January 2020) <www.fondation-abbe-pierre.fr/droitsdespersonnessansabri> accessed 26 March 2020.

[124]   See text accompanying n 65.

[125]   David Satterthwaite, 'A New Urban Agenda?' (2016) 28 Environment & Urbanization 3, 9.

such as Medellín, Lusaka and Kortrijk that do not rely on human rights law and discourse to any significant extent, but are nonetheless active in the fight against poverty, deserve more scholarly attention in this regard. Moreover, the example of Utrecht shows that the different frameworks may also come to co-exist and interact, possibly setting in motion yet another set of institutional and discursive dynamics within a city.

One specific hypothesis that merits further investigation is that the actions of local governments are often driven by local civil society. Indeed, it may be one of the determining factors not only for the degree to which cities are engaged in the fight against poverty but also for the presence or absence of a human rights approach to questions of poverty reduction.[126] The empirical puzzle arising from this proposition has a normative counterpart in the advocacy of a 'right to the city', which suggest that the urban questions should be approached in a participatory, bottom-up manner as has often been the case in the global South.[127] Looking at the example of Medellín, we can see how such a perspective has the potential of revealing the blind spots of even the most ambitious anti-poverty policies taken by city authorities. In short, the question of the participation of local stakeholders, particularly from civil society, is a crucial one for both legal empiricists and critical scholars alike.

In addition, it will be important to understand whether the growing involvement of cities and towns, in their totality, influences the creation of human rights norms. Much like the question of their legal responsibilities, the contributions of local authorities have so far been relegated to the area of informality. However, a look at SDG 11 and the New Urban Agenda of UN-Habitat proves the extent to which their agency is by now recognized internationally. Rather than waiting until the 'precise tipping point' when the authority of local governments will become formal, legal scholars should keep a watchful eye on the gradual evolution of norms.[128] One interesting example is the Homeless Bill of Rights, which may well come to shape international policies in the future.

Lastly, we should be mindful of—but also appropriately sceptical towards—the emergence of human rights cities. While they can certainly contribute to popularising a rights-based approach to poverty reduction that is cognisant of the importance of participation and the multidimensionality of poverty, local authorities (such as York in this chapter) have not done their homework simply by declaring themselves a human rights city. Future research would be well-advised to adopt long-term perspectives that can offer empirical insights into whether any commitments made have been followed up in practice.

---

[126]   Cf Darling (n 11).
[127]   Chueca (n 77).
[128]   Aust (n 15) 273.

18. Addressing poverty at its base: the housing and land rights approach

Miloon Kothari

People who live in poverty exist in a space and place identified by its location: street, neighbourhood, region, locality and area. The most vulnerable of the poor, for example the homeless and landless, live on the streets, under flyovers, on benches, in parks, in fields or fallow land or other open spaces. Those who have a place to live but are living in poverty can be found in informal settlements in urban and rural areas, high density housing and inadequate and insecure shelters.

Studies on poverty have largely focused on the economic dimensions of poverty or on estimating income disparity and inequality as a measure of poverty. The housing, health, food, environmental, security and livelihood reality faced by the poor are almost never a focus of attention. These factors that should be obvious if the indivisibility of all human rights was the basis of analysis, are also contingent on where and in what conditions people live. Where people live often determines what services they have access to and whether they are recognized as legitimate citizens or residents of a state.

Studies on income disparity and inequality, similarly, have rarely focused on where the poor live and whether the disparity of income is also a reflection of disparity of location. A morphological approach to the study of poverty, e.g., why apartheid cities are being created across the world, would lend a different but critical dimension to studies on poverty. An area-based approach would also assist in knowing what policy support is necessary in what location. Tackling poverty would then also include the need for housing and land development strategies based on a human rights approach, a non-discriminatory approach to how urban and rural areas are developed that also derails the policies that lead to social exclusion and marginalisation of people and communities. The added dimension of the 'morphology approach' revolves around greater specificity and context that assists in better targeted interventions in the spaces and places where the marginalized live.

If the morphological approach is adopted, it would also require an inter-disciplinary approach drawing on the disciplines of geography, planning, environment, sociology and political science. Underpinning these fields of research and analysis, the human rights paradigm – with its requirement of meeting the needs of the most vulnerable first – offers the most promising direction.

The global housing and land rights emergency is marked by multiple crisis points centred on segregation and discrimination, affordability and the severe lack of housing and land. Each of these phenomena can be tackled by adopting, as a distinct part of the human rights paradigm, the morphological approach. This chapter seeks to outline the many dimensions of the 'morphological', 'human geography', 'spatial justice' approach, both to understand the gravity of housing and land poverty and to serve as a basis for seeking solutions. The chapter also explores the reality of 'place' and 'space' that are essential locational constructs through which we can understand housing vulnerability. Illustrations of academic studies and national legislations will demonstrate the value of aligning the human rights approach with the morphological approach. The chapter also calls for a combined human rights and morphology approach that would enable a comprehensive perspective to tackling poverty. The chapter also draws on the author's experience of conducting field studies using the morphological approach to visually depict the evolution of 'apartheid' cities across the world – an understudied dimension of work on poverty.

I.   WHY THE 'MORPHOLOGICAL' PERSPECTIVE?

The critical importance of 'space' and 'place' as locations that determine the nature of interventions necessary to overcome poverty needs to be highlighted as a criterion in the development of legal, policy and administrative measures to address poverty.

A number of professions that may not necessarily be associated with the adoption of human rights methodologies in their work, are critical to the practical application of the 'visual', 'morphological' 'spatial justice' approach. These include architects, planners, geographers, surveyors and others who rely on mapping settlements, and who understand urban or rural built form using geospatial technology (satellite imagery; global positioning systems (GPS), digital open source investigations (OSINT), and related applications and software).

If a comprehensive inter-disciplinary approach is applied, these professionals must be enlisted both to analyse where poverty exists and to propose solutions that can lead to more inclusive cities, towns and villages. A goal of this approach is that people can live in mixed neighbourhoods, i.e., areas where there is no segregation based on religion, class, income and other forms of distinction recognized across human rights standards.

A strictly legal approach without the 'visual' and 'location specific' dimension remains abstract and cannot truly capture the experience of people and communities who have to live a ghettoized, segregated existence that leads to numerous human rights violations.

Socio-economic and legal interventions across the world have invisibilized 'informal' settlements. It is critical, as this chapter argues, for a combined 'morphological' and 'human rights' approach to expose the reality of poor people's lives.

Academics working in the field of 'urban morphology', for example, have argued for greater attention to the characteristics of informal settlements, noting that:

> Within informal settlements, the blurring of boundaries between questionable property ownership and right of use, access to infrastructure and hazardous site, function and form, and public and private spaces, introduces a set of dynamics that existing methods of morphological study do not sufficiently address.[1]

The same authors succinctly explain the link between the attainment of human rights and morphology as a valid method to study poverty, asserting that a process of evaluating poor community's priorities 'would encourage analysis of the structures of these communities

---

[1]   Shelagh McCartney and Sukanya Krishnamurthy, 'Neglected? Strengthening the Morphological Study of Informal Settlements' (2018) 8 SAGE Open 1 <https://doi.org/10.1177/2158244018760375> accessed 13 July 2020.

and processes of formation and transformation, building conditions, and the blurring of lines between what is considered de jure and de facto public and private areas'.[2]

II.   THE HOUSING AND LAND RIGHTS APPROACH TO TACKLING POVERTY

The work on the development of the right to adequate housing and the emerging right to land from UN bodies, such as the UN Committee on Economic, Social and Cultural Rights (CESCR), three UN Special Rapporteurs and the work of the UN Human Rights Council, has yielded a detailed conceptual and substantive understanding of these rights. A review of the content of the normative standards that have been selected for an overview in this chapter reveal a clear pattern of a combined legal and morphological approach.[3] A diligent application of these standards at the national and local levels can have a strong bearing on actualising the goal to reduce poverty.

The importance of 'place' as a prerequisite for physical, social and cultural security, that becomes the location from which you gain and sustain your growth as an individual and foster community, is evident in the definition of the right to adequate housing (RAH) proposed by the first UN Special Rapporteur on Adequate Housing: 'The right to adequate housing is the right of every woman, man, youth and child *to gain and sustain a secure and safe home and community in which to live in peace and dignity*'.[4]

Relevant interpretive instruments for the right include General Comments 4[5] and 7[6] from the CESCR. General Comment 4 outlined the essential elements of the RAH, including several relating to place: (a) Legal security of tenure; (b) Availability of services, materials, facilities and infrastructure; (c) Affordability; (d) Habitability; (e) Accessibility; (f) *Location* and (g) Cultural adequacy. There have been further additions to the list of essential elements by the first UN Special Rapporteur on Adequate Housing to include: (h) Public goods and services; (i) *Environmental goods and services (including land and water);* (j) *Freedom from disposses-sion*; (k) Information, capacity and capacity-building; (l) Participation in decision-making; (m) *Resettlement*; (n) *Safe environment* and (o) Security (physical) and privacy.

The Committee on the Elimination of All Forms of Racial Discrimination (CERD) has also elaborated on the human rights impacts of types of residential patterns that exist in cities, towns and villages across the world:

---

[2]   ibid 5.
[3]   Words and phrases italicized in this section indicate the parts of these instruments that place importance to the morphological approach.
[4]   See United Nations (UN) Human Rights Committee (HRC), 'Report of the Special Rapporteur on Adequate Housing as a Component of the Right to an Adequate Standard of Living, and on the Right to Non-Discrimination in this context, Miloon Kothari' (13 February 2008) UN Doc A/HRC/7/16, para 4.
[5]   UN Committee on Economic, Social and Cultural Rights (CESCR), 'General Comment No. 4: The Right to Adequate Housing (Art. 11 (1) of the Covenant)' (13 December 1991) UN Doc E/1992/23 < https://bit.ly/32pTieo> accessed 16 July 2020.
[6]   CESCR, 'General Comment No. 7: The Right to Adequate Housing (Art. 11 (1) of the Covenant): Forced Evictions' (20 May 1997) UN Doc E/1998/22 <https://bit.ly/3evsb41> accessed 16 July 2020.

In many cities *residential patterns* are influenced by group differences in income, which are sometimes combined with differences of race, colour, descent and national or ethnic origin, so that inhabitants can be stigmatized and individuals suffer a form of discrimination in which *racial grounds are
mixed with other grounds*.[7]

The combined human rights and morphological approach, and its benefit in identifying violations and the realization of the right to adequate housing, is likewise evident in the analysis
contained in numerous annual reports from the Special Rapporteurs. The Special Rapporteurs
have also developed global standards to assist governments at all levels in alleviating the
conditions that create and perpetuate poverty. These instruments offer a step by step guide to
governments and third parties on how to safeguard people's RAH and related human rights.
These include: (1) Guidelines on Segregation and Discrimination;[8] (2) Basic Principles and
Guidelines on Development-based Evictions and Displacement[9] and (3) the Guiding Principles
on Security of Tenure.[10] These standards developed by the UN treaty bodies and the Special
Rapporteurs are of relevance to the broad range of issues this chapter seeks to address, that is,
reduction of spatial inequality and poverty in communities within the context of human rights
and sustainable urbanisation. These standards offer practical tools for city and regional level
practitioners to implement a combined human rights and morphological approach to tackle
poverty on the ground. While space constraints do not allow for a detailed explanation of the
salient features of all human rights standards developed by the UN human rights programme,
three standards described below are most pertinent to the topic at hand.

A.   UN Guidelines on Discrimination, Segregation and the Right to Adequate Housing

In his annual report to the Commission on Human Rights on 1 March 2002, the first UN
Special Rapporteur on adequate housing recommended guidelines on discrimination, segregation and the right to adequate housing.[11] These guidelines were developed in the context of

---

[7]   UN Committee on the Eradication of Racial Discrimination (CERD), 'General recommendation
XIX on Article 3 of the Convention' (1995) UN Doc A/50/18 <https://bit.ly/30fEqNb> accessed 16 July
2020.

[8]   UN Commission on Human Rights, 'Report of the Special Rapporteur on Adequate Housing as
a Component of the Right to an Adequate Standard of Living, Mr. Miloon Kothari' (1 March 2002) UN
Doc E/CN.4/2002/59, paras 37 et seq, 101(b) <https://bit.ly/2OxrvRi> accessed 16 July 2020.

[9]   See United Nations Office of the High Commissioner (OHCHR), 'Forced Evictions' <www.ohchr
.org/en/Issues/Housing/Pages/ForcedEvictions.aspx> accessed 11 June 2020. Also see the recommendation for State implementation of these guidelines in Preparatory Committee for the United Nations
Conference on Housing and Sustainable Urban Development (Habitat III), 'Policy Paper 1: Right
to the City and Cities for All' (6 June 2016) UN Doc A/Conf.226/PC.3/14 <https://bit.ly/30iYPkw>
accessed 16 July 2020; 'Issue Paper 22: Informal Settlements' (*Habitat III*, 31 May 2015) <https://bit.ly/
2WqQwlj> accessed 16 July 2020; Habitat III, 'Pretoria Declaration of the Habitat III Thematic Meeting
on Informal Settlements' (3 June 2016) UN Doc A/COONF.226/PC.3/12 <https://bit.ly/2OvMHaf >
accessed 16 July 2020.

[10]   See 'Guiding Principles on Security of Tenure' (*OHCHR*) <www.ohchr.org/EN/Issues/Housing/
Pages/StudyOnSecurityOfTenure.aspx> accessed 12 June 2020.

[11]   Commission on Human Rights (n 8).

follow-up to the World Conference against Racism, Racial Discrimination, Xenophobia and Related Intolerance held in Durban in September 2001.[12]

The guidelines place special emphasis on various factors leading to discrimination and segregation in the fulfilment of the right to adequate housing, citing grounds based on race, class or gender, poverty and economic marginalization.[13] Further, the guidelines urge States to reaffirm their corresponding obligations to take actions to ensure that the right to adequate housing can be gained and retained in an atmosphere free from racial and other forms of discrimination.[14] The focus on the removal of barriers that create discrimination and segregation, based on a spatial justice approach, as advocated by these guidelines, can assist in isolating and then removing poverty that exists for marginalized communities that reside in these areas.

B.   Guiding Principles on Security of Tenure

The second Special Rapporteur on Adequate Housing proposed in her annual report in 2014, the 'Guiding Principles on Security of Tenure'. These Guiding Principles provide useful guidance for local authorities to establish a process to tackle tenure insecurity in their jurisdictions. These principles also demonstrate a combined human rights and morphological approach.

The Special Rapporteur, in her 2013 annual report, had already outlined various contexts which undermine tenure security.[15] Tenure insecurity crisis is manifested in forced evictions, displacement resulting from development, natural disasters and conflicts and land grabbing. The compelling challenges are also evident in the conditions of millions of urban dwellers living under insecure tenure arrangements worldwide. In the Guiding Principles, the Special Rapporteur examined the wide range of existing tenure arrangements and existing guidance under international human rights law and asked the states to ensure security of tenure to all,

---

[12]   See UNGA, 'Report of the World Conference against Racism, Racial Discrimination, Xenophobia and Related Intolerance' (2001) A/CONF.189/12. The Declaration and the Programme of Action adopted at Durban World Conference on Racism is worth revisiting in the context of this EGM as it recognized the existence of discrimination in access to housing, along with other economic, social and cultural rights (para 33) and States were urged to recognize the effect of discrimination and to take appropriate measures to prevent racial discrimination against persons belonging to minorities in respect of employment, housing, social services and education and, in this context, forms of multiple discrimination should be taken into account (paras 48 and 49).

[13]   Commission on Human Rights (n 8) para 43.

[14]   Also of note in these guidelines are the recommendations for States to institutionalize ethical housing, land-use, and planning practices, including the preparation of city and regional master plans, such that segregated residential patterns and discrimination in facilities do not form based on group identity of race, colour, descent, national and ethnic origin, and religion. Moreover, it is essential that in the formulation and implementation of these plans, residents enjoy the right to participation, including through participatory budgetary processes, on a basis of non-discrimination and equality.

[15]   HRC, 'Report of the Special Rapporteur on Adequate Housing as a Component of the Right to an Adequate Standard of Living, and on the Right to Non-Discrimination in this Context, Raquel Rolnik' (24 December 2012) A/HRC/22/46, para 69 <https://bit.ly/2WqlU3n> accessed 16 July 2020.

irrespective of tenure type.[16] The principles also underscore the need for more specific and comprehensive human rights and operational guidance on security of tenure.[17]

The guiding principles urge harmonization of the range (continuum) of tenure within a state's integrated system of law, institutions, policies and practices. They incorporate the following principles: *prioritizing in situ solutions, promoting the social function of property, combating discrimination on the basis of tenure, promoting women's security of tenure*, empowering the urban poor, holding states accountable and ensuring access to justice. Ensuring security of tenure can lead to the provision of civic services and the protection against forced evictions, both of which are critical elements in removing poverty and ensuring that people and communities do not fall into situations of poverty.

C.   The UN Guidelines on Development-based Evictions and Displacement

The UN Guidelines on Development-based Evictions and Displacement[18] (UN Evictions Guidelines) provide operational guidance on protecting people and communities' human rights in the processes before, during and after evictions, displacement and resettlement. In this brief review of the contents of the guidelines the sections that recognize the importance on 'security of tenure' – the critical importance of 'space', 'place', 'land' and 'dwelling' are italicised.

In particular, the UN Evictions Guidelines define the practice of forced evictions (paras 4–8) and lay down stringent criteria under which displacement can occur in 'exceptional circumstances', with 'full justification' and procedural guarantees (para 21).

Further, they enumerate detailed steps to be taken by States to protect human rights prior to, during, and after evictions (paras 37, 58). Prior to displacement, they call for comprehensive 'eviction-impact assessments' (paras 32, 33, 42). After displacement, they call for provision of compensation, restitution and adequate rehabilitation consistent with human rights standards (paras 42, 60–63, 69, 70).

Across displacement scenarios, they provide useful guidance on other phenomena that lead to displacement such as disasters and climate change-induced displacement (paras 52, 55) and establish a 'right to resettle' consistent with the right to adequate housing for displaced com-

---

[16]   Consistent with standing obligations of States, the Special Rapporteur urged that 'All relevant laws, policies and programmes should be developed on the basis of human rights impact assessments [that] identify and prioritize the tenure arrangements of the most vulnerable and marginalized', promoting, strengthening and protecting, as appropriate, in the given context: possession rights, use rights, rental, freehold tenure and collective arrangements. HRC, 'Report of the Special Rapporteur on Adequate Housing as a Component of the Right to an Adequate Standard of Living, and on the Right to Non-Discrimination in this Context, Raquel Rolnik' (30 December 2013) UN Doc A/HRC/25/54, sec II, para 5(1) <https://undocs.org/A/HRC/25/54> accessed 13 July 2020.

[17]   ibid. The Guiding Principles urge harmonization of the range (continuum) of tenure within a state's integrated system of law, institutions, policies and practices. They also incorporate the foregoing principles of: Prioritizing in situ solutions; Promoting the social function of property; combating discrimination on the basis of tenure; promoting women's security of tenure; respecting security of tenure in business activities; strengthening security of tenure in development cooperation; empowering the urban poor and holding states accountable; and ensuring access to justice.

[18]   Contained in 'Human Rights Council: Report of the Special Rapporteur on Adequate Housing as a Component of the Right to an Adequate Standard of Living, Miloon Kothari' (5 February 2007) UN Doc A/HRC/4/18 <https://bit.ly/3j91aXK> accessed 16 July 2020.

munities living in adverse conditions (paras 16, 52–56). *They also call on States, in pursuance of an 'immediate obligation' to guarantee security of tenure to all those currently lacking titles to home and land (paras 23, 25).*[19]

There are a number of other human rights that intersect, with varying levels of dependency, with the right to adequate housing. The Guidelines enumerate a handful of the most proximate, including the human right to work/livelihood (paras 43, 52, 63), *the human right to land (paras 16, 22, 25, 26, 30, 43, 56, 60, 61, 63, 71)*, the human right to food (paras 52, 57), the human right to health (paras 16, 54–57, 63, 68); and the human right to education (paras 16, 52, 57, 60, 63).

The Guidelines also detail States' responsibilities vis-à-vis all of the actors involved in the protection of human rights, including the State itself. They call for the protection of the rights of human rights defenders (para 22). They also stress the obligation of non-State actors (paras 11, 71–73) and *call on States to take intervening measures to ensure that market forces do not increase the vulnerability of low income and marginalized groups to forced eviction (paras 8, 30)*.

Many sections of the UN Evictions Guidelines capture the morphological dimensions of evictions and their consequences. The Guidelines are organized according to the following categories: (1) Scope and Nature of the UN Guidelines; (2) Implementation of State Obligations; (3) Preventative strategies, policies and programmes; (4) Safeguards Prior to Evictions; (5) Safeguards During Evictions; (6) Safeguards After an Eviction and (7) Remedies for Forced Evictions, including Compensation. At the outset, the definition of forced evictions emphasizes morphological considerations, noting that forced evictions have the effect of *'eliminating or limiting the ability of an individual, group or community to reside or work in a particular dwelling, residence or location, without the provision of, and access to, appropriate forms of legal or other protection'.*[20] *The Guidelines further require consideration of legislative reform, remedies for forced eviction, and preventative measures recognizing basic needs and the importance of place to individuals' ability to fulfil those needs.*[21]

The Guidelines have been conceptualized as an 'operational' instrument. Such a practical approach when combined with the legal and morphological perspective infused in the Guidelines, is the reason that the UN Evictions Guidelines have found resonance across the disciplines, including from planners, surveyors, and geographers, among others. The approach, beyond just the legal, has allowed for these human rights standards to transcend their applicability in the required cross-disciplinary realm – without which the right to housing and land cannot be realized.

---

[19] HRC, 'Report of the Special Rapporteur on Adequate Housing as a Component of the Right to an Adequate Standard of Living, Miloon Kothari' (5 February 2007) UN Doc A/HRC/4/18/Annex I <https://bit.ly/3j91aXK> accessed 16 July 2020. There are also a number of provisions dealing directly with particular populations that are often at-risk across geographies. To this end, they provide a strong gender perspective, including protection and entitlements to women (paras 7, 15, 26, 29, 33, 34, 38, 39, 47, 50, 53, 54, 57 and 58). They also protect children's right to adequate housing (paras 21, 31, 33, 47, 50, 52, 54 and 56). Building on specific provisions for women and children, they emphasize the differential nature of impacts of evictions on marginalized groups and communities, including Indigenous Peoples, minorities, historically discriminated groups, persons with disabilities and older persons, and call for the protection of their human rights (paras 21, 29, 31, 33, 38, 39, 54 and 57).

[20] ibid para 4.

[21] ibid sec D.

The International Federation of Surveyors in 2010 adopted a Declaration on land acquisition in developing economies that cites the UN Evictions Guidelines.[22] Academic writing by Land and Property Surveyors and related professionals routinely cite the UN Evictions Guidelines.[23] The Guidelines are also contained in reference documents prepared for surveyors.[24]

Cultural geographers have also, in academic articles, cited the Guidelines as a framework for their work on social impact assessments in the context of large development projects.[25] Geographers have also used the Guidelines as one basis to determine whether in-kind compensation option can promote a spatially just and inclusive urban (re)development.[26] Additional examples from the work of planners, including planning departments at universities are cited in section III below.

In addition to the human rights standards outlined above, the UN human rights system has also elaborated other standards that exhibit a combined human rights and morphological approach. Of particular importance is the recently-adopted UN Declaration on the Rights of Peasants and other working in rural areas.[27] This declaration draws attention to the *neglected sector of landless and homeless peasants* which comprise, in many countries a significant part of people living in poverty. By recognising these groups and the places they live in, the Declaration seeks to contribute to uplifting these communities out of poverty. Another instrument deserving recognition is the General Recommendation No 34[28] from the UN Committee on the Elimination of All Forms of Discrimination against Women (CEDAW). *This interpretive instrument calls attention to the plight of women living in rural areas and the particular obstacles they face in claiming their human rights as a result of where they live.*

III.   WHAT DOES MORPHOLOGY BRING TO THE HUMAN RIGHTS APPROACH?

The discussion above has highlighted the relevance of human rights instruments in tackling poverty using the housing and land rights[29] approach. These instruments include a robust

---

[22]   Kauko Viitanen and others, 'Fig Publication No. 51: Hanoi Declaration: Land Acquisition in Emerging Economies' (International Federation of Surveyors (FIG), February 2010) <https://fig.net/resources/publications/figpub/pub51/figpub51.asp> accessed 1 May 2020; see also Jude Wallace, 'Land Acquisition in Developing Economies' (FIG, February 2010) FIG 1 <https://bit.ly/2Ot9iEo> accessed 16 July 2020.

[23]   Paul van der Molen, 'Property, Human Rights Law and Land Surveyors' (2016) 48 Survey Review 51.

[24]   Paul van der Molen, 'An Inventory of Human Rights Law Relevant for Surveyors' (FIG, 2015) <https://bit.ly/2Zx1Caq> accessed 16 July 2020.

[25]   Frank Vanclay, 'Project-Induced Displacement and Resettlement: From Impoverishment Risks to an Opportunity for Development?' (2017) 35 Impact Assessment and Project Appraisal 3.

[26]   Ernest Uwayezu and Walter de Vries, 'Can In-Kind Compensation for Expropriated Real Property Promote Spatial Justice? A Case Study Analysis of Resettlement in Kigali City, Rwanda' (2020) 12 Sustainability 3753.

[27]   Adopted by the UN General Assembly on 17 December 2018, UN Doc A/RES/73/165.

[28]   See Convention on the Elimination of Discrimination Against Women (CEDAW), 'General Recommendation No. 34 on the Rights of Rural Women' (7 March 2016) UN Doc CEDAW/C/GC/34.

[29]   For a discussion on how the emerging human right to land enlarges our understanding of the importance of place and space see Miloon Kothari, 'The Human Right to Adequate Housing and the New Human Right to Land: Congruent Entitlements' in Andreas von Arnauld, Kerstin von der Decken and

analysis of what causes poverty, including through the denial of basic human rights to housing, water, land and health. These instruments, in an attempt to provide a step-by-step guidance to overcome the obstacles to realising basic human rights, also offer prescriptions on how to overcome the obstacles to the removal of poverty. In addition to the foundational precepts of human rights – non-discrimination, gender equality, access to justice and so forth – a critical lesson drawn from human rights imperatives is that the human rights of the most vulnerable and the most marginalized need to be met first. This central precept of human rights is well captured by the Talisman we have been bestowed with by Mahatma Gandhi:

> I will give you a talisman. Whenever you are in doubt, or when the self becomes too much with you, apply the following test. Recall the face of the poorest and the weakest man whom you may have seen, and ask yourself, if the step you contemplate is going to be of any use to him. Will he gain anything by it? Will it restore him to a control over his own life and destiny? In other words, will it lead to swaraj [freedom] for the hungry and spiritually starving millions? Then you will find your doubts and yourself melt away.[30]

The spirit of upholding the human rights of the most marginalised and ensuring that all personal practices, institutional laws, policies and administrative actions must meet this precept, is also expressed in the Sustainable Development Goals (SDGs): 'Leave no one behind'.[31]

The morphological approach is increasingly being used by planners, architects and social science professionals to challenge　historical patterns, planning policies and prioritisation of speculative real estate policies that cause discrimination and segregation of communities in different cities across the world. The words that are dreaded by housing and land rights activists in cities capture the different phenomenon these groups have attempted to map: segregation, ghettoization, gated communities, and gentrification. Some examples of the role that the morphological approach plays in visually analysing the colossal damage of these phenomenon, but also in providing solutions, are given below.

A.　Forced Evictions, Displacement and Resettlement

The MIT Displacement Research Action Network (DRAN)[32] has developed analytical tools in Delhi, India and Boston, USA, that have assisted local human rights organisations conducting advocacy to highlight violations of housing rights in these cities. In Delhi, the team from DRAN, based on field research and consultations with local NGOs and experts, produced a historical mapping demonstrating how decades of planning and development interventions had resulted in the city becoming segregated on income and class lines. The DRAN team also

---

Mart Susi (eds), *The Cambridge Handbook of New Human Rights: Recognition, Novelty, Rhetoric* (CUP 2020).

[30]　'Gandhi's Talisman' <www.mkgandhi.org/gquots1.htm> accessed 7 May 2020 (quoting Pyarelal, *Mahatma Gandhi – The Last Phase* (vol II, Navajivan Publishing House (1958) 65)).

[31]　The overarching aim of this slogan from the SDGs is a somewhat diluted form of Mahatma Gandhi's Talisman as it can be easily used to justify the 'safety net', 'trickle down' and charitable approach that does not capture in full the human rights paradigm.

[32]　The MIT Displacement Action Network's website is available at: <http://mitdisplacement.org/> accessed 18 July 2020.

produced a visual plan on how the displacement that had caused this segregation could be halted using area-based planning strategies.[33]

In Boston, USA, DRAN worked with an NGO, the Chinese Progressive Association (CPA), to highlight how Boston's real estate-led urbanisation had resulted in 'gentrification' of Boston's once thriving Chinatown, resulting in the displacement of Chinese residents and the physical transformation of the area. The DRAN team produced a series of studies[34] that were then used by the CPA to aid their advocacy efforts with the City of Boston to bring about a change in the planning processes that had led to the dispossession of Chinese residents.

B.   Gentrification

Civil society groups have also used the morphological approach to showcase the colossal negative impact of the phenomenon of 'gentrification' that has spread across the world – spurred by speculative real estate practices based on the financialization of housing. An excellent example of this approach is the Anti-Evictions Mapping Project based in San Francisco. This project is self-described as

> a data-visualization, data analysis, and storytelling collective documenting the dispossession and resistance upon gentrifying landscapes … we are all volunteers producing digital maps, oral history work, film, murals, and community events. Working with a number of community partners and in solidarity with numerous housing movements, we study and visualize new entanglements of global capital, real estate, techno capitalism, and political economy. Our narrative oral history and video work centres the displacement of people and complex social worlds, but also modes of resistance. Maintaining antiracist and feminist analyses as well as decolonial methodology, the project creates tools and disseminates data contributing to collective resistance and movement building.[35]

The project has collaborated with housing justice movements and influenced a range of remarkable analytical reports that map the colossal 'gentrification' crisis in San Francisco but also the resistance from the ground.[36]

---

[33]   For more details on the project see 'The Geography of Post-eviction Resettlement in Delhi, India' *(Displacement Research & Action Network (DRAN)*, 12 December 2014) <http://mitdisplacement.org/delhi> accessed 14 June 2020. Also see the following videos demonstrating the use of the 'morphological' approach, MIT DRAN, 'The Geography of JJ Cluster Relocation in Delhi 1990-2010' (*Youtube*, 28 October 2014) <https://bit.ly/3j9A4zD> accessed 16 July 2020; MIT DRAN, 'Delhi Evictions 1990–2013' (*Youtube*, 28 October 2014) <https://bit.ly/2DQlzRh> accessed 16 July 2020.

[34]   For these studies, in the form of dynamic visual material, see 'Chinatown Displacement Mapping Project' (*DRAN*) <http://mitdisplacement.org/mapping-2#/2015-mapping-project/> accessed on 16 July 2020.

[35]   The Anti-Eviction's website is available at: <www.antievictionmap.com> accessed 18 July 2020.

[36]   See, e.g., 'City of Change: Fighting for San Francisco's Vanishing Communities' (*Eviction Defense Collaborative*, 2016) <https://bit.ly/30fKHZ7> accessed 16 July 2020. Another remarkable example of visualization of the dispossession of black communities in San Francisco is Anti-Eviction Mapping Project, '(Dis)location Black Exodus' (*Internet Archive*, 3 August 2019) <https://archive.org/details/dislocationblackexodus/page/n15/mode/2up> accessed 14 June 2020.

C.   Gated Communities/Apartheid Cities

The morphological approach has also been shown to bring a clear analysis to the spatial and ethnic dislocations that 'gated' communities have wrought around the world. An excellent example of this is an essay that demonstrates a hybrid approach combining legal and geographical disciplines. In this study the author demonstrates that the impact of Jewish 'gated' communities, in Occupied Palestine, and the use of these spaces, is a form of exclusion of Palestinians.[37] In another study on the impact of gated communities in Canada and Israel the authors quote Blakely and Snyder's well-known analysis, stating that: 'the meaning of the built environment is not fixed: "The setting of boundaries is always a political act. Boundaries determine membership: someone must be inside and someone outside. Boundaries also create and delineate space to facilitate the activities and purposes of political, economic and social life"'.[38] The authors then point to the fact that

> Critics describe these enclaves as manifestations of a discriminatory land regime that promotes ethnic exclusion and colonialism. In some places, government agencies manipulate planning and development procedures to favour Jewish middleclass groups while excluding, neglecting and alienating Arab Palestinian populations. Such discriminatory policies foster highly uneven development patterns and exacerbate socio-spatial disparities.[39]

D.   Segregation and Ghettoization

A study carried out in Jogeshwari East, Mumbai, India analyses the changes in neighbourhood patterns as a result of changes in housing and planning policies and laws. The study illustrates the changes using maps to demonstrate the systematic segregation, through ethnic riots, result in the ghettoization of the area's Muslim community.[40]

E.   Inadequate Housing and Living Conditions

A case study based in Dublin, Ireland uses the human rights based approach (HRBA).

The study illustrates how the HRBA has been applied by local authority tenants in partnership with community development organizations and supported by human rights expertise to campaign for improvements to substandard housing conditions and deprivation within a Dublin inner city social housing estate. It appraises the adoption of the HRBA as a response to inadequate housing conditions and delayed regeneration programmes. The impact of poor housing on the health of tenants was an integral element of the arguments used. The outcomes of using the HRBA for the rights holders (the tenants) are assessed. Overall, this campaign led

---

[37]   Manal Totry-Jubran, 'Beyond Walls and Fences: Exploring the Legal Geography of Gated Communities in Mixed Spaces' (2018) 26 J L.& Pol'y 123 <https://brooklynworks.brooklaw.edu/jlp/vol26/iss1/3> accessed 14 June 2020.

[38]   Gillad Rosen and Jill Grant, 'Reproducing Difference: Gated Communities in Canada and Israel' (2010) 35 Intl J of Urban and Regional Research 778, <https://doi.org/10.1111/j.1468-2427.2010.00981> (quoting EJ Blakely and MG Snyder (1997) *Fortress America: Gated Communities in the United States* (Brookings)).

[39]   ibid 783.

[40]   Miloon Kothari and Nasreen Contractor, *Planned Segregation: Riots, Evictions and Dispossession in Jogeshwari East, Mumbai/Bombay, India* (Youth for Unity and Voluntary Action 1996).

to significant improvements in conditions. The factors underlying the success centred on the way in which the HRBA framework, with its focus on measurable indicators of human rights violations, enabled community development organizations to create a human rights-based public campaign that exerted considerable political pressure through the empowerment of tenants, leveraging of human rights experts, and considerable media publicity. As stated by the authors this 'approach transcended many established NGO and state approaches to addressing poverty'.[41]

F.   National Legislations that Embrace the Combined 'Morphological' and 'Human Rights' Approach

Across the world we are also witnessing the growth of national legislations that embrace the combined human rights and morphological approach as they seek social and spatial justice for their most vulnerable people and communities.

In Brazil the Brazil City Statute[42] is revolutionary in that it redefines the concept of land ownership and promotes the social dimension of the right to urban property. The statute also promotes democratic participation in urban management, and provides for legal instruments to regularize informal settlements and to tax vacant under-used land. Particularly valuable from a human rights perspective is the provision in the statute that makes it mandatory for all municipalities in Brazil to designate 'special zones of social interest' and thereby protect the 'right to the city' for the cities' marginalized people and areas.

Legislative advances in India, since 2013, reinforce this link between the human rights and the morphological approaches. The Right to Homestead Act is of critical importance as it recognizes entitlements to both the right to housing and to land. Several states in India have adopted 'Homestead Acts' that recognize the RAH and the right to land of landless and marginalized communities.[43] This Act has been adopted in the Indian States of Madhya Pradesh and Bihar. In 2013, an attempt was also made to adopt a 'National Right to Homestead Act'. Following a campaign in 2018 by Ekta Parishad, the Indian National Movement for Land Rights, the Government of India has announced that it will reopen the issue of a national act. Adopting such a national act has become an even more urgent task given the severe dislocations that have resulted from the Covid-19 crisis.[44]

In the state of Odisha, India, the Legislative Assembly enacted the Odisha Land Rights to Slum Dwellers Act, 2017.[45] The landmark legislation aims at empowering slum dwellers in

---

[41]   Rory Hearne and Padraic Kenna, 'Using the Human Rights Based Approach to Tackle Housing Deprivation in an Irish Urban Housing Estate' (2014) 6 J Human Rights Practice 1 <https://bit.ly/30o86YG> accessed 16 July 2020.

[42]   Instituto Pólis, 'The Statute of the City: New Tools for Assuring the Right to the City in Brazil' (*WIEGO*, 2001 39–75 (text of Brazil City Statute, Law No 10.257 of July 10, 2001) <https://bit.ly/30f65Ol> accessed 16 July 2020.

[43]   For regular updates on homestead acts see 'Ekta Parishad' <www.ektaparishadindia.org/> accessed 16 July 2020.

[44]   Miloon Kothari and Ramesh Sharma, 'The Call of Home: It is Time the Centre Legislates on the Right to Homestead' *Indian Express* (15 June 2020) *Indian Express* <https://bit.ly/39051BV> accessed 16 July 2020.

[45]   'The Odisha Land Rights to Slum Dwellers Act' (2017) <http://govtpress.odisha.gov.in/pdf/2017/1652.pdf> accessed 18 July 2020.

the state with security of land tenure and accessibility to a liveable habitat. The Act aims to assign land rights to eligible slum dwellers for redevelopment, rehabilitation and up-gradation of slums in the Notified Area Councils (NAC) and municipalities. The Act has two interlinked objectives: first, to improve the living conditions of slum dwellers, and second, to provide security against the threats of demolition and eviction. The Act provides for *in situ* rehabilitation in general, and offsite rehabilitation in case of land important for the public interest, land unfit for human habitation, ecologically sensitive land, or heritage land.

The programme is likely to benefit one million people residing in 2,500 slums across the state over the next few years. Technical support was provided by numerous actors, including drone surveys and slum mapping, for around 100,000 households in ten districts of the state. Project planning involved large scale mapping of each individual slum tenement without any human error/subjectivity and linking of household data is done through aerial photographs which are processed through Photogrammetry and embedded in GIS.

Another example from India, announced in April 2020, is a national programme, the Swamitva Yojana (Survey of Villages and Mapping with Improvised Technology in Village Areas).[46] The Yojana plans to map the location of landless families across India. If implemented, such a programme in concert with a national homestead act has the potential to bring about a remarkable change in the lives of lower income people in rural India.

The Swamitva Yojana intends to use the latest surveying technology, including drones, for measuring the inhabited land in villages and rural areas. The drones will draw the digital map of every property falling in the geographical limit of each Indian village and its contiguous areas where there is human habitation. The scheme will create records of land ownership in villages and is intended to assist in settling disputes over property. Once the survey is complete the beneficiaries will be given rights to the land.

IV.   CONCLUSION: THE WAY FORWARD

The discussion in the chapter attempts to promote concepts and practice of human rights and morphology that combine to narrate a city, town or village's memory of people and their affinity to space and place. The critical importance of the 'place to live', 'to dwell' and 'to belong' needs to be recognized in both the human rights and morphology discourse as central to the survival and growth of people and communities.

This chapter has attempted to demonstrate the significant value of the morphological approach in tackling poverty. Initiatives taken in the global COVID-19 crisis further attest to the immense validity of the spatial justice approach. The entire attempt at arresting the spread of the virus is based on tracking, isolating in containment zones and then curing those affected by the virus. Numerous examples show that using the morphological approach is assisting in identifying not only where the poor live but what types of interventions are necessary. A remarkable example of this is the work of the Mathare-Special Planning Area Research Collective (M-SPARC) in Nairobi, Kenya. Utilising a combination of mapping and survey methodologies the M-SPARC was able to identify the specific needs of the affected community in which they found that 89 per cent of the residents did not have funds for food, rent or

---

[46]   Swamitva Yojana (Survey of Villages and Mapping with Improvised Technology in Village Areas) at: https://bit.ly/2DDyaao.

regular running water – all necessities for the prevention measures against COVID. Through this morphological exercise, M-SPARC has now been able to make concrete recommendations to the municipality of Nairobi.[47]

The post-COVID world will witness increasing poverty[48] and calls for much more robust attempts to tackle poverty and its structural causes. The value of the combination of human rights and the morphological approach needs to be scaled up. The evidence presented in this chapter provides pointers towards more research in this nascent field.

Two points of departure are clear for additional research avenues. First, the conceptual basis of the research and the methodologies on which the primary and secondary research will be based must result from inter-disciplinary collaborations. As the case studies presented in the chapter demonstrate, it is only when professionals across the disciplines come together that a combined human rights and morphology approach becomes feasible. Second, the research has to be participatory and must either begin in the community (as the Mathare example demonstrates) or include the voices of the people whose lives are being studied.

Based on these two starting points some suggestions can be given on the way forward. Spatial (in)justice, as evident in informal settlements all over the world, make it an enormous challenge to implement human rights obligations, such as the right to adequate housing, the right to health and so forth. Research is necessary to highlight good practices that demonstrate that reorganising informal settlements with minimum displacement is possible. A related, but second area, for further research is to show that cities can grow without replicating the 'high density' models where informal settlements (in marginal areas) are allowed to grow to service the better off urban population. Inclusive cities that are planned with spatially just distribution of social housing and civic services are required. Can international human rights instruments, some of which have been discussed in this chapter, assist in meeting this imperative?

Another necessary interface the emerging research must address is between 'politics' and 'space'. Can the governance systems that often depend, in the developing countries, on vote banks of dense informal settlements be sensitized to work towards spatially just cities with full participation of the poor and the municipalities? Any research work, to be successful, needs to disaggregate the human rights impacts and the solutions. Can the morphological approach that assists in identifying different population groups be useful for research that seeks to find solutions to decrease the inequality in income and space that is evident in cities across the world, and that is deepening with speculation of land and property, including through gentrification and ghettoization?

These research initiatives must contribute to increasing the credibility of a combined morphological and human rights approach such that space and place are made democratic and that the human rights of the people and communities that inhabit them are upheld. This chapter has argued for a 'spatial' approach over a particularly 'legal' approach. People inherently understand the concept and reality of 'being' of 'belonging', of 'dwelling' in a space. It is up to decision makers to display the same sensitivity and enable the world's cities, towns and villages to thrive based on the recognition of 'a place to live in security and dignity'.

---

[47]   For more details of the project: The Mathare-Special Planning Area Research Collective, 'Urgent Recommendations for a People-Centered Covid-19 Government Response in Mathare' (*Mathare Social Justice Centre*, 12 May 2020) <https://bit.ly/3eCW5n7> accessed 16 July 2020.

[48]   For some estimates see report by UNDESA at: https://www.un.org/development/desa/dpad/publication/un-desa-policy-brief-86-the-long-term-impact-of-covid-19-on-poverty/.

19. The land rights-poverty nexus

Alfred Lahai Gbabai Brownell Sr.

BACKGROUND

Securing land rights is an essential element in addressing, remedying and alleviating global poverty, especially for vulnerable West African populations, such as the poor rural and urban communities, indigenous peoples, women, minorities and migrants. There is little doubt that West Africa is endowed with abundant natural resources. The land of the region is home to some of the best and largest deposits of gold, bauxite, rutile, diamond, timber, oil and gas, iron ore, uranium, and coal. It is the site of the Upper Guinea Forest, the lungs of West and North Africa – a massive green fortress protecting the region from being captured by the Sahara Desert – and one of the largest carbon sinks in the region. The region is also blessed with abundant marine resources: lobster, shrimp, crab and fish in its oceans and some of the most scenic beaches, a tourist paradise.

Ironically, countries in the region are some of the world's poorest, plagued with a phenomenon referred to as the 'natural resource curse,' a conflict-governance-poverty dynamic where countries rich in natural wealth remain poor. I have conducted a study on the rights to land tenure security and natural resources governance in five of the countries in West Africa (Liberia, Sierra Leone, Guinea, Ivory Coast and Mali), which documented several factors characteristic of the 'natural resources curse.'[1] This information is systematized in an unpublished report based on interviews with key stakeholders and desk research. The remainder of material in this chapter, where not otherwise cited, comes from this study and report.

This study showed that citizens, especially local communities and Indigenous Peoples, lack the rights to their land and natural resources, health, sanitation and a safe environment including work, food, housing, security and freedoms as well as the rights not to be the subject of forced evictions. These factors were linked to the insecurity of land tenure and drove poverty in the affected communities.

The examination of the land rights situation in these five countries showcased the land rights-poverty nexus: how unsecured land rights undermine the local economy, obliterate the social, economic and political infrastructures and directly contribute to the poverty index of the affected local communities in the five countries that were the subject of the study. The study also showed how unsecured land rights negatively impact the social equilibrium necessary to cement community relationships and build strong and effective national institutions with major impact on the human development index. In sum, the study showed that a failure to make human rights a central consideration in the exploitation and management of the regions' natural resources exacerbated the lack of protection of communities' land rights, thereby undermining poverty reduction efforts.

---

[1]   Alfred Brownell, 'Natural Resources Rights and Governance Profile of Five West African Countries (Liberia, Sierra Leone, Guinea, Ivory Coast and Mali)' (September 2016) Green Advocates International, Monrovia, Liberia (on file with the author).

I.   NATURALLY ENDOWED YET POOR

Of the countries reviewed, the Ivory Coast occupies the 165th rank in the human development index. Guinea is ranked 174th and Liberia, 176th. Sierra Leone and Mali are ranked at 181st and 184th, respectively, placing these two countries in the ten poorest countries in the world.[2]

The factors leading to this poverty in the midst of abundance are clear. In Sierra Leone, the mining sector contributed to a systematic pattern of injustice. Further, poor local governance promoted by elite local leaders ensured that the benefits generated by natural resources did not constitute a value-added to the daily lives of the local communities in mining sites.

In Liberia, insecure tenure and elite greed, as well as control and authority over land and natural resources served as a catalyst underpinning most of the corruption and conflict. The result was massive poverty and the political and economic collapse of the country in the 1990s displacing millions of peoples as internal and external refugees.

In Mali, communities suffered from the toxic effect of the exploitation of gold mines without any substantial impact on their local economy or national development. This compromised the survival activities of communities totally dependent on their land for farming, gathering, hunting, and fishing and spiritual worship.

In all five countries, local communities and Indigenous Peoples living near these investments continued to suffer grinding poverty, marginalization, forceful displacement, deprivation, and environmental abuses, including destruction of their sacred and religious sites and the exploitation and denial of their livelihoods.

The blames reside fully with the region's governments that have failed to protect their citizens against abuse by both governmental and non-state actors associated with the management of their lands and natural resources. The history of the extractive sector in the region has enabled a legacy replete with examples of how the exploitation of land and natural resources fuels conflict and poverty, exacerbating problems of weak governance and corruption while imposing a heavy toll on livelihoods. That legacy also undermines faith in public administration and community-driven entrepreneurship, forging a direct nexus between rights to land and poverty.

II.   UNSECURED LAND RIGHTS: THE NATURAL RESOURCE CURSE FACTORS AND THE MISSING LINKS IN POVERTY CAUSE AND EFFECT ANALYSIS

To many people, including people from West Africa, land is life, wealth, an asset and collateral. It sometimes represents their culture, tradition, customs, history and religion. The land is thus everything to them. When the land is grabbed, those linkages are extinguished. The poorest of the poor are attacked[3] and farmlands are destroyed, leading to starvation.[4] In short,

---

[2]   United Nations Development Programme, '2019 Human Development Index Ranking' (n.d.) <http://hdr.undp.org/en/content/2019-human-development-index-ranking> accessed 7 June 2020.

[3]   Tomasz Johnson, 'The Global Land Grab' (2013) <www.ibanet.org/Article/NewDetail.aspx ?ArticleUid=03CFDC86-767F-4BA1-B95B-4DAAB95A4D3C> accessed 6 June 2020.

[4]   Jenna DiPaolo and Coimbra Sirica, Coimbra, 'Warning of Unrest, New Study Shows Millions Risk Losing Lands in Africa' (Rights and Resources Initiative, 2012) <www.eurekalert.org/pub _releases/2012-02/bc-nss013012.php> accessed 6 June 2020.

unsecured land rights is a 'natural resource curse factor,' often the missing link in the poverty cause and effect analysis, and thus a masked driver of poverty in West Africa.

In Mali, the establishment of mining operations resulted in the expropriation of agrarian communities' farming lands. The loss of lands was the main factor undermining the property rights and livelihood of the local inhabitants. It resulted in forced displacement to new lands, most often unfertile for agricultural purposes and very far from individuals' original homes. Hundreds of thousands of hectares of fertile agricultural land were out of reach of communities for agricultural, farming and pastoral activities due to expropriation for foreign direct invest-ment and industrial commercial activities. This materially changed the status of community members who were landowners thriving in their former communities and are now landless and squatting on farm lands in the neighboring villages.

The insecurity of tenure also contributed to the unfair compensation for the land, crops and natural resources grabbed as the result of the expropriation. International best practices, including the Food and Agriculture Organization guidelines on fair compensation due to forced displacement, provide that compensation should be calculated by taking into account prior losses, duly estimated inconveniences and loss of income.

This did not occur in Mali. Instead, the nation's mining laws confer a priority to the holders of the mining licenses on the use of lands (article 60 of the mining code). The landowners are practically obliged to give up their lands for a proportional compensation of the so-called 'value' of their land following false promises of jobs and revenue for national development. As a result, communities give up their lands on conditions totally below their value.

In Sierra Leone, the mining companies negotiated with the government for the land as con-cessions but failed to identify the affected community beneficiaries for compensation for their land and plantations. For example, during the study, there were many landowners belonging to a single landowning family. The compensation was given only to the head of the family and hundreds of farming community members were displaced and completely ignored even though their farms and crops were affected.

The compensation scheme was also not calculated based on the economic and market value of the crops and farm lands. For instance, in the Sierra Rutile Mining area, the company gives a compensation of US $12.60 for an acre of land, increased by 3 percent annually. In the local currency, this was estimated to about Le 60,000 (sixty thousand Leones).[5] However, farmers can yield millions of Leones from that same plot of land annually, which can sustain their families. This situation created conflict and friction between local traditional leaders, who are regarded as custodians of the land, and the individual land-owning families who were not compensated for the land. Compensation was not commensurate with the destruction caused to the environment, natural resources, farmlands and crops of the local communities.

In Liberia, mining operations resulted in the reduction of the rights of customary users, undermining ownership entitlements and thus opening the property to sale or alienation at the government's discretion. The government's proprietary right over minerals trumps all formal private property rights as well as informal customary rights. For formal property rights, the exercise of eminent domain is subject to due process requirements. However, this does not extend to customary property. Thus, a mining license is superior title and can extinguish prior rights that local communities hold over their farmlands and crops.

---

[5]   ibid.

The laws in these countries also do not protect surface users adequately. Free prior informed consent is not mandated and surface lease rights to customary land are not available. In addition, due process protective measures against arbitrary deprivation of property such as consultation or compensation are not mandated or guaranteed to customary land users.

As communal property rights are not formally recognized, local communities do not have means to assert due process rights against arbitrary deprivation, which could be a constitutional infringement at least in Liberia. The arbitrary deprivation of property used for subsistence can be interpreted as an infringement on the right to life. The displacement of indigenous communities further infringes on Indigenous Peoples' cultural rights and freedoms.

During the study, health, sanitation and environmental degradation strongly emerged as a natural resource curse factor in several local communities and among Indigenous Peoples.[6] For example, mining activities in Sierra Leone expose local communities to a wide range of diseases including diarrheal diseases as a result of interacting with water sources contaminated by mine wastes. Mining activities also caused heavy siltation in river beds and creeks affecting drinking water sources and devastated the land by clearing and digging up vegetated areas leaving the land exposed, degraded and unsuitable for farming. In Bo and Baomahum, Sierra Leone, the companies not only removed vegetation and economically valuable trees, but their activities also diverted surface drainage contributing to health hazards, potentially increasing the incidence of malaria and other water borne diseases.

At old Ferengbeya, Sierra Leone, the company provided a 5000 liter water tank for the community of over one thousand members. The community perceives the project as a replacement for streams that have been polluted by the company. The women once fetched water from the stream for their domestic chores. Now the entire village queues to fetch water from one tank that is hardly enough for the entire village.[7]

In Liberia, successive governments have disregarded environmental protection laws – especially in the agriculture plantation sector – and potentially dangerous agricultural waste products have been discharged into local communities' rivers and streams. In Owengrove, Liberia a community situated near a large American tire company, locals complained that industrial waste discharged into their river by the company polluted their ground waters and killed fish the locals relied on for livelihood and protein sources.[8] One community member remarked, 'we are fishermen without a river.'[9]

In Guinea, mining operations have negative impacts on the health and sanitation of mining communities as well as on the environment, including massive soil erosion, deforestation and habitat fragmentation causing acute food insecurity, diseases and poor sanitation.

---

[6]   ibid.

[7]   ibid.

[8]   Uwagbale Edward-Ekpu, 'The world's largest rubber company is being blamed again for pollution in a Liberian river' (2020) <https://qz.com/africa/1807681/bridgestone-tires-firestone-liberia-blamed -for-river-pollution/> accessed 6 June 2020.

[9]   Brownell (n 1).

III.   LAND RIGHTS ENABLE SUSTAINABILITY AND RESILIENCE OF LIVELIHOODS

The ability to access land for shelter, food production and other activities is arguably the most important single factor in the sustainability and resilience of livelihoods for billions of peoples around the globe, especially in rural and urban poor communities in West Africa. Labor is thus tied directly to the security of tenure and poverty reduction. Jobs are a primary incentive that governments and the private sector offer in exchange for the disenfranchisement of customary land rights of local communities and Indigenous Peoples. When the customary lands and property rights of local communities and Indigenous Peoples are extinguished to make way for oil, gas, mining, logging and agricultural operations, the inhabitants are left with little choice but to serve as slave laborers to the very companies removing them from their lands.

Former landowners, some of them local chiefs, now become workers subject to the caprices and arbitrary will of their employers. In some cases in Liberia and Sierra Leone, corporate activities attract workers from different regions and other countries and are a source of migration, mainly from rural to company operational areas creating a brain drain and a leadership deficit by attracting the best brains and talents. This is a great value for multinationals seeking to hire workers on low salaries and in slave-like conditions while exploiting the relationship between host local communities and migrants seeking jobs. Sometimes this results in clashes between host local communities and migrant workers, and more often between local communities, companies and state security.

These tensions are exploited despite legislation to the contrary in some of the focus countries. For example, the Sierra Leonean mining act accords a national preference to its citizens 'in all phases of operations under a mineral right, and in accordance with the national labor laws.'[10] This is also the situation in Mali which requires expatriate staff to be progressively replaced by skilled Malians.[11] Guinea officially prioritizes employment of local communities[12] while Liberia prohibits the hiring of non-Liberian citizens as unskilled workers.[13]

While the international legal framework does not recognize a right to land, the UN General Assembly has established that there is a 'right to safe and clean drinking water' subject to 'progressive realization' by states.[14] Interestingly, however, in a number of case study countries, such as Liberia, water rights are premised or dependent on land and natural resources (forest) rights.

In Sierra Leone, the water sources of local communities from Lunsar and Ferengbeya were contaminated by the use of chemicals and dynamite but alternative potable water sources were far below the needs of the people. In Guinea communities suffered cyanide contamination.

In Liberia, rivers, streams and creeks continued to be polluted by industrial operations resulting in fish kill and natural resources damage.[15] In one community industrial waste totally

---

[10]   The Mines and Minerals Act 2009 s 164, Employment and Training of Sierra Leone Citizens.

[11]   Mali Code minier 2012 s 126.

[12]   Code Minier de la République de Guinée 2011 s 108.

[13]   An Act Adopting a New Minerals and Mining Law 2000 s 1 (20.2).

[14]   Brian Palmer, 'Is Water a Human Right?' (2016) <www.nrdc.org/onearth/water-human-right> accessed 6 June 2020.

[15]   Uwagbale Edward-Ekpu, 'The World's Largest Rubber Company is Being Blamed Again for Pollution in a Liberian river' (2020) <https://qz.com/africa/1807681/bridgestone-tires-firestone-liberia -blamed-for-river-pollution/> accessed 6 June 2020.

compromised the ecological integrity of the river, killing fish and forcing some community members, who were mainly fishermen, to take up other occupations such as charcoal production and farming.[16]

These conditions were only possible because prior land rights of the local communities were extinguished in favor of leasehold rights granted by the government to a transnational corporation without the free prior informed consent of the communities, compounded by a flagrant violation of Liberia's environmental and health laws, which prohibit the dumping of wastes into the waters of the Republic of Liberia.

During the study local communities asserted that the swamps and wetlands were a source of food, including fishes, crabs and crayfish and a fertile ground for growing vegetables to complement culturally appropriate indigenous food. Local communities from Butaw, in Sinoe County, Liberia complained of lack of access to fuel wood to cook meals, lamenting that the cost for locally produced food had prohibitively increased, and community members had to travel far to procure these items.

The displacement of local populations from their original homelands resulted in the loss of sources of revenue and livelihood. This affected their right to food since they no longer had access to their land where they were growing crops. This situation was further aggravated by the fact that that compensation from land loss and crops was grossly inadequate to cover their needs and cost of food.

Furthermore, in areas where some community members were resettled, host communities did not recognize their right to acquire land, creating uncertainty and landlessness. The land was also not as fertile as the land at their original home, resulting in serious food insecurity.

Secured land tenure is critical to achieving the right to adequate housing and many of the other economic social and cultural rights. Under the International Covenant on Economic, Social and Cultural Rights (ICESCR) states must refrain from forced evictions and must take actions to stop third parties (non-state actors) from carrying out forced evictions.[17] This is further established under the International Covenant on Civil and Political Rights (ICCPR) which requires 'adequate protection,'[18] 'adequate compensation'[19] and 'effective remedy'[20] for those subject to forced evictions.

Consistently throughout the five countries, communities and Indigenous Peoples complained of persistent forceful evictions and displacement without adequate protection, lack of adequate compensation and no effective remedial system. Secured land rights and prohibition against forced eviction are integrally linked to the right to adequate housing.

In Liberia, Sierra Leone and Guinea resettlement provided by agricultural, logging and mining companies offered new housing, but local communities complained that the new houses built for them are not adapted to their rural way of life and are therefore inadequate.

The ability for land to thus provide shelter, food and water as has been documented above is under increasing pressure from the endless drive for economic growth, export-led develop-

---

[16]   Brownell (n 1).
[17]   International Covenant on Economic, Social and Cultural Rights 1976 Art 11 (1).
[18]   International Covenant on Civil and Political Rights (adopted 16 December 1966, entered into force 23 March 1976) 999 UNTS 171 (ICCPR) Art 26.
[19]   ibid Art 14 (6).
[20]   ibid Art 2 (3) (a).

ment and deregulated global economies,[21] demonstrated by continued expansion of agribusiness, large-scale resource extraction and conservation.[22]

Despite the evidence to the contrary, more often than not securing the rights to land, especially in West Africa, is treated as an incidental issue rather than a primary cause of poverty across the sub-region. The diagnosis offered by practitioners often refers to conflicts, violence, corruption, lack of resources and environmental degradations but the role of unsecured land rights is often not adequately evaluated. Thus, the linkages between rights to land and poverty reduction, in contrast to other issues such as unfair compensation, the right to work, the right to food, the right to adequate housing as well as the rights not to be the subject of forced evictions, have received insufficient treatment in the literature addressing poverty reduction across the world and particularly in West Africa.

IV. A MASKED POVERTY DRIVER: HOW UNSECURED LAND RIGHTS FURTHERS THE RURAL TO URBAN BRAIN DRAIN

Globally, and specifically in West Africa, the exploitation of unsecured land rights, sometimes referred to as land grabbing, is a masked poverty driver that triggers an initial uncoordinated small movement of individuals. These individuals, mainly youth in rural to urban migration drifts, create a deficit in leadership, demography and labor.[23]

In the five countries studied, the rural to urban migration drifts are often linked to forced evictions. In those instances, indigenous populations uprooted from their ancestral lands to accommodate concessions outside their free prior informed consent have been largely ignored and, in some places, ruthlessly crushed.

For example, in early 2005 the Liberia Agriculture Company (LAC) with the support of the Government of Liberia, decided to expand its rubber plantation covering tens of thousands of acres. In the process, LAC used its private security forces to enforce the eviction of several local communities to make way for the planting of additional trees displacing community members to nearby towns and the municipality of Buchanan city.

The eviction methods included burning down villages and the clear cutting and destruction of cash crops without the free prior informed consent and compensation. At the same time the company poisoned drinking water and destroyed forests crucial to customary and traditional practices, climatic stability and the protection of water catchments areas in violation of Liberia's environmental laws and international conventions to which Liberia is a contracting party.

---

[21] *The global need for food, fibre and fuel* (Åke Barklund, General Secretary and Managing Director, KSLA, Stockholm, Sweden).

[22] Market Research Blog, 'What Drives Demand for Natural Resources?' (2016) <https://blog.euromonitor.com/what-drives-demand-natural-resources/> accessed 6 June 2020.

[23] Nicholas Van Hear, Oliver Bakewell and Katy Long, 'Drivers of Migration' (2012) Oxford Research Programme Consortium <https://assets.publishing.service.gov.uk/media/57a08a7fed915d6 22c000787/WP1_Drivers_of_Migration.pdf> accessed 30 June 2020.

In Mali, the government award of gold mining licenses resulted into forced evictions and relocation of poor agrarian communities into remote non-arable areas far away from their original homelands.

A different forceful eviction strategy was employed in the case of Sierra Leone. The government and elite local community leaders were used as fronts in the theft of land resulting in the forceful evictions of hundreds of farming community members being displaced without any due process requirements. Sometimes, the evictions are carried out by the national security and private security forces of the companies. This poses a risk, limits free movements, shrinks civic spaces and undermines the safety and security of communities.

The security of local communities and Indigenous Peoples constitutes an acute issue. There are many abuses from national security agencies such as the police, gendarmerie or the national guards and in some cases, the private security agencies hired by companies to secure their investment areas. The criminalization of legitimate grievances and suppression of protest actions organized by communities to stop land grabbing, claim employment, prevent forced evictions, unfair compensations or the risks to health challenges the protection of fundamental liberties and tests the state duty to protect, respect and fulfill rights.

For example, the Government of Liberia has included in every key concession signed the rights to private security to protect infrastructure and ensure the rule of law. While the intent may be good, some private security forces have been linked to human rights violations including illegal search, arrest and detention of persons. They have often illegally detained people in their own facilities after making temporary arrests and some of the private security personnel are former rebel fighters who are alleged to have committed war crimes.

In a community called Freeman Reserve, located in Margibi County, inhabitants are engaged in community driven entrepreneurship such as charcoal and fuel wood production. There, ex-fighters hired as security personnel restricted access to the abandoned woods in the fields. Additionally, they intimidated the population, extorted money to access abandoned woods, confiscated charcoal bags and then illegally arrested and detained community members.

In some areas of Sierra Leone there is no presence of law enforcement or security operations. In other investment areas, the only mechanism put in place to address crime and security matters is the Community-Police Partnership (CPP) which handles all security and crime (civil offences) in the first instance and then refers the matter to a higher level. Despite these measures, there were detentions of youth in Ferengbeya and Kono for expressing their grievances against the operation of multinational mining companies without any charges or court hearing.

In Guinea the national defense and security forces raided the Zoghota village where the local community made claims for employment and protested the forceful grabbing of their lands. This reprisal resulted in arrest, detention and the deaths of community members.

Like Guinea and many other countries in the region, this is one of many drivers that triggers that rural to urban exodus contributing to the establishment and in most cases the expansion of slums and squatter communities, exacerbating vulnerabilities while escalating the poverty dynamics of the inhabitants and their communities.

V. A ZERO-SUM GAME: POVERTY CORRIDORS, END TO END POVERTY ENCRYPTION AND A FRAGILE POVERTY FAULT LINE

The rural to urban exodus and brain drain leaves communities poorer, more gender imbalanced and weaker with their strong, talented, youthful and experienced leaders pursuing safety and economic opportunities[24] in urban areas, which results in the often unnoticed and overlooked poverty corridors. This is despite the fact that local communities are important stakeholders in the land and natural resources sector. Yet they are the actors that are afforded the fewest benefits generated by their land and natural resources extracted under their feet.

Local communities are not only excluded from natural resource management and the distribution of wealth generated by the exploitation of natural resources, but they are also deeply affected by the actual and adverse impact of industrial commercial operations on the environment and their livelihood and health.

This is enabled by a diverse range of social, environmental and economic impacts along migration routes and within the host communities across the region. It also aggravates prior over-stretched and existing poverty circumstances erecting pressures on already scarce resources and services sometime leading to conflicts, crimes and xenophobic reactions.[25]

The end result is what I have observed to be an 'end to end poverty encryption,' where unsecured land rights enabled a range of rights violations creating insecurity for local communities that are forced to settle in new areas, which are also insecure with limited or no land rights. This cascading range of rights violations serves as poverty accelerators.

While more than a billion people globally have risen out of extreme poverty since 1990, global poverty reduction seems to be on a slippery slope, with almost a billion more either remaining or sliding back.[26] A dollar and ninety cents ($1.90) per day is the difference between striding out of and sliding back into extreme poverty. I called this the fragile global Poverty Fault Line. But the statistics demonstrate more than just a fault line. In ascending order, the regional comparative dynamics of people living in extreme poverty are alarming, ranging from as much as seven million to as high as half a billion people in regions such as Europe, Asia, the Middle East, Latin America but more troublingly in Sub-Saharan Africa.[27]

---

[24] Sarah Opitz Stapleton and others, 'Climate Change, Migration and Displacement: The Need for a Risk-Informed and Coherent Approach' (Overseas Development Institute and United Nations Development Programme 2017) <www.odi.org/sites/odi.org.uk/files/resource-documents/11874.pdf> accessed 6 June 2020.

[25] Jonathan Crush and Sujata Ramachandran, 'Xenophobia, International Migration and Development' (2010) HDCA 209.

[26] Action Against Hunger, 'Global Poverty and Hunger' (n.d.) <www.actionagainsthunger.org/global-poverty-hunger-facts> accessed 7 June 2020. There are currently about 780 million people globally who are living in extreme poverty, 17 millions of which are children suffering from severe acute malnutrition while 1,000 more per day die from water borne diseases and poor sanitation.

[27] Nirav Patel, 'Figure of the week: Understanding Poverty in Africa' (2018) <www.brookings.edu/blog/africa-in-focus/2018/11/21/figure-of-the-week-understanding-poverty-in-africa/> accessed 7 June 2020. The statistics on poverty in Africa, specifically sub-Saharan Africa are even more damning. Africa is undeniably the poorest region of the world, the home to the second largest population of hungry people not having access to basic human necessities food, clean water, and housing. While worldwide poverty is declining, in Africa the progress has been much slower. Of the world's 28 poorest countries, 27 are in sub-Saharan Africa all with a poverty rate above 30 percent.

VI.   A COMPARATIVE CONSTITUTIONAL AND LEGAL REVIEW OF LAND AND NATURAL RESOURCES RIGHTS IN FIVE WEST AFRICAN COUNTRIES

Liberia, Guinea, Sierra Leone, Ivory Coast and Mali are all state parties to different human rights instruments and have incorporated a number of human rights provisions in their constitutions and laws specific to land and natural resources rights.

The Liberian Constitution adopts a rights-based approach to natural resources governance recognizing that the people are vested with all powers, have the right to know (Article 15(c)) and must participate at the 'maximum feasible level' in decisions related to the management of their natural resources with exceptions only for mineral resources.[28] The Sierra Leonean Constitution mandates the state to 'manage and control the national economy in such a manner as to secure the maximum welfare and freedom of every citizen.'[29]

The Constitution of Guinea does not have specific dispositions on natural resources. However, Art. 19 reaffirms the state's supreme rights to its resources, which should benefit all citizens without discrimination, and ensures protection of its resources and environment. It also offers guarantees of fundamental rights to its citizens.[30]

Like that of Guinea, the Constitution of Mali does not have a specific disposition on natural resources but enshrines fundamental rights. It reaffirms the sacredness and inviolability of the right to life, liberty and security of the person (Art. 1), the principle of nondiscrimination (Art. 2), the protection against torture (Art. 3) and the right to fair trial and access to justice (Art. 9–11). The right to property is also a constitutional entitlement. Under Art. 13, this right can be restricted for public goods.

From the preceding section, one can notice that the issue of land and natural resources rights has been specifically addressed in the constitutions of Liberia (Art. 7 and 22(b)) and Sierra Leone (Art. 7(1-a); Art. 18 (3-a); Art. 21 (2-i); Art. 118 (6)). While the constitutions of Guinea and Mali do not emphasize natural resources, they recognize the basic principle of governance.[31]

Besides the constitutions, new laws and codes have also been adopted. This compensates for the lack of resource rights provision in the constitutions of Guinea and Mali. The laws address

---

[28]   Liberia Constitution, Art. 22(b) ('Private property rights, however, shall not extend to any mineral resources on or beneath any land or to any lands under the seas and waterways of the Republic').

[29]   Sierra Leone's Constitution of 1991, Reinstated in 1996, with Amendments through 2008 Art. 21(1)(c)(i-ii).

[30]   Guinea's Constitution of 2010 includes the right to dignity (Art. 5); the right to life and protection against torture (Art. 6); the right to liberty and security of the person (Art. 9); and the right to free expression and association (Art.10). The right to property is also a constitutional guaranty (Art. 13). In the case of expropriation for public good, citizens are entitled to fair compensation. This is important in the context of mining operations where populations are exposed to forced eviction or farming land expropriation without fair compensation. Displacement of populations in mining sites causes also the profanation of traditional belief worship places and can cause violations of Art. 14.

[31]   Guinea's Constitution of 2010; The Constitution of the Republic of Mali. These offer protection of citizens against abusive use of force against the population, be it by state security agents operating in mining areas or private security working on behalf of mining companies; guarantee the right to property or fair and prompt compensation in case of deprivation for public good; the right to safe and healthy environment; and the right to equal access to public service, employment and enjoyment of all social and economic rights.

dispositions specific to natural resources management, while reinforcing the Sierra Leone and Liberian national legal framework for mining and management of natural resources.

All five case study countries have promulgated new mining codes. The Minerals and Mining Act defines ownership of minerals in Liberia.[32] The Act makes provision for local communities' right to access to the benefits[33] and to prevention and restoration related to environmental hazards.[34]

The Sierra Leonean New Mines and Minerals Act, 2009 requires holders of mining licenses to realize an assessment of the environmental and potential impact of mining activities on the ecosystem and the life of communities living around mining sites.[35]

The Guinean Mining Code No L / 2011 /006/CNT aims at encouraging transparency in the management of mining resources, guaranteeing economic and social benefit to the people of Guinea in a fruitful partnership with investors. It covers different aspects related to the protection of the rights of communities living in mining sites requiring compensation for occupiers of land attributed to license holders in addition to plots of land necessary for their activities and compensation for the prevention of use due to expropriation (Article 124).[36]

The new mining Act of Mali was designed to address the plights of communities living in mining areas and to take into account the protection of rights to property, health and safe environment, and the enjoyment of social and economic rights.[37]

---

[32]   An Act Adopting a New Minerals and Mining Law 2000 s 1 (20.2) declares that: 'Property rights in minerals on the surface of the ground or in the soil or subsoil, rivers, streams, watercourses, territorial waters and continental shelf of Liberia are the property of the Republic and anything pertaining to their exploration, development, mining and export shall be governed by this law.' This does not exclude the protection of property rights of citizens and entitles communities or individuals to compensation when deprived of such rights for public good, although not specifically mentioned in the mining act. In addition, the Mines Act does not address the issues of community rights, save section 16.10 which prohibits the employment of children under the age sixteen. The protection offered under section 20.5 concerns fundamental rights of Liberian citizens as a whole not necessarily affected by the mining activities' adverse impact.

[33]   ibid. Concerning the local communities' right to access to the benefits generated by mining operation in their sites, the Act does not provide a development fund, but rather provides a mineral development fund (s 6.6 and 18) designated for mine workers and operators and their security.

[34]   ibid. In terms of environmental hazards caused by mining operations and chemicals used by mining companies or license holders, s 8.1 stipulates: 'Each holder of a mineral right shall take reasonable preventive corrective and restoratives measures to limit pollution or contamination of, or damage to streams, water bodies, dry land surface and the atmosphere as a result of exploration or mining.'

[35]   Supplement to the Sierra Leone Gazette Vol. CXLI, No. 3: The Mines and Minerals Act 2009.

[36]   Code Minier de la République de Guinée 2011. In terms of benefits generated by mining operations, Art. 130 requires that mining license holders agree with local communities residing in or alongside the mining sites on a convention of development. This makes transparent the contribution to these communities such as vocational training for the implementation of their development projects and funding of social programs, as well as the preservation of the environment through the mobilization of a local development funding that should be 0.5 percent to 1 percent of the revenue generated. In the case of closure of mining activities, mining companies are required under Art. 131 to eliminate risks to health and security of people living in the mining areas. During the lifetime of the mining exploitation, mining companies are prohibited under Art. 143 to use dangerous chemical products without minimal caution and health support; pollute the water, air and soil, and degrade the ecosystem and the biodiversity. At the end of the mining exploitation, mining companies are required to rehabilitate the site. Art.144 requires that funds for rehabilitation be secured prior to the effective mining operation.

[37]   Mali Code minier 2012. Under Art. 60(2), mining activities can start only after due compensation for landowners in the case of deprivation for public goods. Besides this guarantee, the Mining Act does

VII.   REALIZING LAND AND NATURAL RESOURCES RIGHTS TO ALLEVIATE POVERTY: INTERNATIONAL OBLIGATIONS AND CORPORATE ACCOUNTABILITY

The UN system elaborates important norms and responsibilities that impose upon corporations and states a duty to respect, protect and fulfill rights.[38] These norms govern states' duty to protect, the corporate responsibility to respect human rights, and the right to access to remedy. They are the principles guiding the legal framework set at different levels but also initiatives to brand human rights values and standards on states and transnational or multinational business operations.

Within the African region there are judicial and quasi-judicial mechanisms that can be used as recourse for remedy related to land and natural resources rights. For example, the African Commission for Human and Peoples' Rights has been reinforced by the African Court for Human and Peoples' Rights.

In the natural resource sector, the African Union (AU) has established the African Mining Vision (AMV)[39] – a common vision in the mining sector – and the African Peer Review Mechanism (APRM),[40] following the example of UN Human Rights Council review mechanisms. However, the core legal instrument within the African region remains the African Charter for Human and Peoples' Rights (ACHPR).[41] At the sub-regional level the Economic

---

not contain provisions requiring mining companies to contribute to the welfare of communities living in mining sites. However, it requires the construction of school and sanitary units for families of persons working for the mining companies (Art 125(b)). It emphasizes the protection of the environment by requiring mining companies to take measures to secure funds for the rehabilitation of the mining through a deposit in an internationally recognized bank (Art. 119(b)).

[38]   These norms are enshrined in the UN treaties including, but not limited to the ICCPR; see also ICESCR; UN General Assembly, Convention on the Rights of the Child, 20 November 1989, United Nations, Treaty Series, vol. 1577, p. 3; UN General Assembly, Declaration on the Right to Development: resolution / adopted by the General Assembly, 4 December 1986; UNTC, International Convention on Civil Liability for Oil Pollution Damage, 29 November 1969; UNTC, Convention on Biological Diversity, 5 June 1992.

[39]   'African Mining Vision' (Policy Framework 2009) <www.africaminingvision.org/amv_resources/ AMV/Africa_Mining_Vision_English.pdf> accessed 7 June 2020. The AMV offers a comprehensive strategic document with an insistence on natural resource governance and corporate responsibility guidelines and seeks to advocate for and promote 'mutually beneficial partnerships between the state, the private sector, civil society, local communities and other stakeholders.' It calls for a 'sustainable and well-governed mining sector that effectively garners and deploys resource rents and that is safe, healthy, gender & ethnically inclusive, environmentally friendly, socially responsible and appreciated by surrounding communities.'

[40]   'African Peer Review Mechanism' (2003) <www.aprm-au.org/> accessed 7 June 2020. The APRM sets an ambit of four main areas including corporate governance with the objectives to provide an enabling environment and effective regulatory framework for economic activities and ensure that corporations act as good corporate citizens with regard to human rights, social responsibility and environmental sustainability.

[41]   ACHPR's relevant provisions relate to land, natural resource rights and corporate responsibility, namely Art. 21 which provides: 'All peoples shall freely dispose of their wealth and natural resources. This right shall be exercised in the exclusive interest of the people. In no case shall a people be deprived of it.'

Commission of West African States directives (ECOWAS directives) promote good governance, democracy and transparency in natural resource management in the sub-region.[42]

VIII.   CONCLUSION

Although acknowledged in a number of global principles and best practices, there are no explicit provisions in the core human rights instruments recognizing rights to land. The nexus is often with respect to other economic social and cultural rights – such as the rights to adequate food, water, work, housing and the right not be the subject of forced evictions. This is despite the fact that insecurity of land unquestionably contributes to many of our most pressing global challenges that drive poverty – food insecurity, deforestation, land degradation, the climate crisis,[43] conflicts and mass migration.[44]

Possibly aware of this nexus, global stakeholders designing milestones for the implementation and monitoring of the Sustainable Development Goals (SDGs) included eight land rights targets and twelve indicators in five of the 17 goals covering: No Poverty (Goal 1), Zero Hunger (Goal 2), Gender Equality (Goal 5), Sustainable Cities and Communities (Goal 11) and Life on Land (Goal 15), evidencing the global importance of land rights and their connection to sustainable development.[45] This recognizes that securing land rights has very high potential to translate into poverty reduction.[46]

There is empirical evidence that securing rights to land, especially for women, poor rural and urban communities including Indigenous Peoples is a game changer for reducing poverty, removing poverty corridors and eliminating the end-to-end poverty encryptions created when insecure land rights results in rural to urban migration exacerbating pressure on already stressed resources in host communities and along the migration routes.

Securing land rights will be critical to building and sustaining the resilience of peoples and meeting the SDGs 2030 agenda especially as communities and organizations respond, mitigate

---

[42]   The ECOWAS directives C/DIR/05/09 offer important guidelines for transparency and corporate governance for states members and multinationals operating on their soils.

[43]   Christina Ospina, 'Reducing Carbon Emissions through Indigenous Land Titles' (2018) <http://climate.org/reducing-carbon-emissions-through-indigenous-land-titles/> accessed 7 June 2020.

[44]   OHCHR, 'Land and Human Rights' (n.d.) <www.ohchr.org/EN/Issues/LandAndHR/Pages/LandandHumanRightsIndex.aspx> accessed 7 June 2020 (noting that '[d]eliberate destruction and unlawful acquisition of land, land-related resources [and] land records are often results and drivers of today's armed conflicts'); see also J Bruce, 'Land and Conflict' (2013) <www.land-links.org/issue-brief/land-disputes-and-land-conflict/> accessed 7 June 2020.

[45]   For example, to achieve the goal of 'no poverty,' the target explicitly states that it is essential to ensure that 'all men and women, in particular the poor and the vulnerable, have … ownership and control over land.' See UN Member States, 'Sustainable Development Goals' (2015) <www.undp.org/content/undp/en/home/sustainable-development-goals.html> accessed 7 June 2020; 'Land and the Sustainable Development Goals' (n.d.) <https://landportal.org/book/sdgs> accessed 7 June 2020.

[46]   Rights + Resources Initiative, 'Securing Community Land Rights' [2017] RRI <https://rightsandresources.org/wp-content/uploads/2017/09/Stockholm-Prorities-and-Opportunities-Brief.pdf> accessed 6 June 2020.

and adapt to natural disasters, the climate crisis and destructive social conflicts in many parts of the globe.[47]

If rights to land are not secured, achieving the SDGs and poverty reduction will become unlikely and human rights may not be protected, respected and fulfilled.[48] It is therefore important that future research assess how current and future human rights-based advocacy and litigation campaigns have contributed to reform and improve the land and resource rights situations in these five countries and as a consequence of that, contributed to a reduction in poverty. Additionally, future research should rank and score improvements or declines on each of the 'natural resource curse factors' identified in this chapter as contributing elements to the insecurity of land tenure and poverty in affected communities in the five countries.

---

[47]   RRI and Tebtebba, 'Securing Indigenous and Community Lands as Key to Solving Global Problems of Human Rights, Climate Change, and Conflicts. Rights and Resources Initiative' (2015) <http://rightsandresources.org/wp-content/uploads/Policy-Brief-Securing-Indigenous-and-Community-Lands-as-Key-to-Solving-Global-Problems.pdf> accessed 6 June 2020.

[48]   Rhoda Howard-Hassmann, 'Reconsidering the Right to Own Property' (2013) J Hum Rights 12:180.

20. Indigenous Peoples' land rights: a culturally sensitive strategy for poverty eradication and sustainable development

Alejandro Fuentes[1]

Indigenous Peoples' struggle for the legal recognition and protection of their right to collective property over traditionally possessed, occupied or otherwise used lands has been ongoing for decades if not centuries.[2] In most parts of the world, Indigenous Peoples face disadvantageous social and economic conditions vis-á-vis the majority of the population.[3]

However, recent legal developments, such as the adoption of the UN Declaration on the Rights of Indigenous Peoples (UNDRIP) in 2007 and the appearance of an innovative jurisprudence developed by the Inter-American Court of Human Rights (IACrtHR), have introduced landmark steps toward the recognition of Indigenous Peoples' land rights.[4] This chapter critically analyses the culturally sensitive contribution of the regional tribunal on the interpretation of the rights recognized within the American Convention on Human Rights (ACHR),[5] in a manner that includes the protection of Indigenous Peoples' traditional land tenure systems and cultural identity.

As will be discussed below, the cultural identity of Indigenous Peoples is intimately connected with the special relationship that they have with their traditional lands and territories.[6] When they are prevented from having access to their traditional lands and territories, their

---

[1]   In the preparation of this chapter, I would like to express my gratitude to the assistance provided by Nuvola Galliani, in particular for her great effort devoted to assisting with sources, editing footnotes and proofreading the final version.

[2]   Regarding Indigenous Peoples' land struggles, see the initial and influential work of the UN Special Rapporteur J.R. Martínez Cobo, in particular: UN Special Rapporteur of the Sub-commission on Prevention of Discrimination and Protection of Minorities, 'Study of the Problem of Discrimination Against Indigenous Populations – Volume V: Conclusions, Proposals and Recommendations' (1987) UN Doc E/cn.4/Sub.2/1986/7/Add.4, para 215 *et seq.*

[3]   UN HRC, 'Report of the Special Rapporteur on the Rights of Indigenous Peoples, Victoria Tauli Corpuz' (11 August 2014) UN Doc A/HRC/27/52, para 42 *et seq.*

[4]   For more in depth analysis of the innovative jurisprudence of the IACrtHR, see my previous work, in particular Alejandro Fuentes, 'Judicial Interpretation and Indigenous Peoples' Right to Lands, Participation and Consultation. The Inter-American Court of Human Rights' Approach' (2016) 23 Int'l J on Minority & Group Rts 39.

[5]   American Convention on Human Rights (Pact of San Jose) (adopted 22 November 1969, entered into force 18 July 1978) 1144 UNTS 17955.

[6]   The UN Special Rapporteur Mrs. Daes stated 'it is difficult to separate the concept of indigenous peoples' relationship with their lands, territories and resources from that of their cultural differences and values. The relationship with the land and all living things is at the core of indigenous societies'. Commission on Human Rights, 'Prevention of Discrimination and Protection of Indigenous Peoples and Minorities: Indigenous Peoples and Their Relationship to Land: Final Working Paper Prepared by the Special Rapporteur Mrs. Erica-Irene A. Daes' (11 June 2001) UN Doc E/CN.4/Sub.2/2001/21, para 13 *et seq.*

right to collective property and cultural identity will be affected.[7] As their culture and cultural identity is affected, their right to have access to dignified conditions of life will suffer too.

According to the regional tribunal, Indigenous Peoples' rights to culture and cultural identity are intrinsically connected with their right to life, as recognized under Article 4 ACHR.[8] Hence, State authorities have an obligation to generate the necessary societal conditions to facilitate Indigenous Peoples' access to a decent life.[9] The most adequate strategy leading to the effective protection of Indigenous People, including eradication or – at least – mitigation of poverty, is to take into consideration the fact that their cultural distinctiveness is indivisible from their traditional land tenure and their special situation of structural vulnerability.[10]

This chapter highlights the need for developing normative frameworks and policies giving priority to Indigenous Peoples' own ethno-cultural development, based on their own cultural understandings, land tenure and environmental management systems.[11] The Indigenous Peoples' sustainable development demands respect for their own cultural understandings of not being poor, which is not being landless.[12]

I.   INDIGENOUS PEOPLES' RIGHTS TO COMMUNAL LANDS AND TERRITORIES

Indigenous Peoples' right to communal property over traditional land and territories is recognized and protected under Article 21 of the ACHR.[13] Since the adoption of the landmark judgment in the case of *The Mayagna (Sumo) Awas Tingni Community v Nicaragua* in 2001 (hereinafter *Awas Tingni* case),[14] the scope of protection of Article 21 ACHR not only guarantees the protection of the special relationship that indigenous communities have with their

---

[7]   See Antônio Augusto Cançado Trindade, 'The Right to Cultural Identity in the Evolving Jurisprudential Construction of the Inter-American Court of Human Rights', in Sienho Yee and Jacques-Yvan Morin (eds), *Multiculturalism and International Law: Essays in Honour of Edward McWhinney* (Martinus Nijhoff Publishers 2009) 477–99.

[8]   For the interconnection between land rights and the right to have a life with dignity, see Alejandro Fuentes, 'Protection of Indigenous Peoples' Traditional Lands and Exploitation of Natural Resources: The Inter-American Court of Human Rights' Safeguards' (2017) 24 Int'l J on Minority & Group Rts 229.

[9]   See *Sawhoyamaxa Indigenous Community v Paraguay* Judgement (Merits, Reparations and Costs) Inter-American Court of Human Rights Series C No 146 (29 March 2006) para 153.

[10]   See *Yakye Axa Indigenous Community v Paraguay* Judgement (Merits, Reparations and Costs) Inter-American Court of Human Rights Series C No 125 (17 June 2005) para 63.

[11]   See Luis Felipe Duchicela and others, 'Indigenous Peoples Development in World Bank Financed Projects: Our People, Our Resources: Striving for a Peaceful and Plentiful Planet: Case Studies Report' (*World Bank Group*, April 2015) XII <http://pubdocs.worldbank.org/en/707481444854126688/WB-IP-Report-Sept-28-2015-final-version.pdf> accessed 15 March 2020.

[12]   cf 'Input from Major Group: Indigenous Peoples: Eradicating Poverty and Promoting Prosperity in a Changing World' (*Sustainable Development Goals Knowledge Platform*, 2017) 2. <https://sustainabledevelopment.un.org/index.php?page=view&type=30022&nr=750&menu=3170> accessed 15 March 2020.

[13]   Article 21(1) ACHR states that '[e]veryone has the right to the use and enjoyment of his property. The law may subordinate such use and enjoyment to the interest of society'.

[14]   *Mayagna (Sumo) Awas Tingni Community v Nicaragua* Judgment (Merits, Reparations and Costs) Inter-American Court of Human Rights Series C No 79 (31 August 2001).

traditionally possessed or otherwise used ancestral lands and territories, but also their social, cultural and economic survival.[15]

These jurisprudential developments acknowledge the existence of a communitarian tradition related to the form of collective land tenure among Indigenous communities.[16] As stressed in the *Awas Tingni* case,[17] without the enjoyment of their traditional lands, Indigenous Peoples 'would be deprived of practicing, conserving and revitalizing their cultural habits, which give a meaning to their own existence, both individual and communitarian'.[18] In other words, 'just as the land they occupy belongs to them, they in turn belong to their land'.[19]

The ACHR acknowledges that the protection of Indigenous Peoples' collective property does not necessarily conform to the classic understanding of property.[20] As mentioned by the regional tribunal,

> [d]isregard for specific versions of use and enjoyment of property, springing from the culture, uses, customs, and beliefs of each people, would be tantamount to holding that there is only one way of using and disposing of property, which, in turn, would render protection under Article 21 of the Convention illusory for millions of persons.[21]

Therefore, traditional occupation and possession of their lands by Indigenous Peoples 'has equivalent effects to those of a state-granted full property title'.[22] This recognition of the right to collective property not only extends over the traditional lands but also over those natural resources found on and within their territories that have been traditionally used and are necessary for 'the very survival, development and continuation of such people's way of life'.[23] In other words, without their protection, 'the very physical and cultural survival of such peoples is at stake'.[24]

This right to collective property as recognized under Article 21 ACHR is not absolute.[25] Lands and territories not traditionally possessed, occupied or otherwise not traditionally used are excluded from the protection under this provision. The same applies to those natural

---

[15] See *Kichwa Indigenous People of Sarayaku v Ecuador* Judgment (Merits and Reparations) Inter-American Court of Human Rights Series C No 245 (27 June 2012) paras 145–46, 171.

[16] See ibid para 145.

[17] For further reading in connection with this case, see S James Anaya and Claudio Grossman, 'The Case of Awas Tingni v. Nicaragua: A New Step in the International Law of Indigenous Peoples' (2002) 19 Arizona Journal of International & Comparative Law 1; SJ Anaya, 'Divergent Discourses about International Law, Indigenous Peoples, and Rights Over Lands and Natural Resources: Toward a Realist Trend' (2005) 16 Colo J Int'l Envtl L & Pol'y 237.

[18] *Mayagna (Sumo) Awas Tingni Community* (n 14), Joint Separate Opinion of Judges A A Cançado Trindade, M Pacheco Gómez and A Abreu Burelli, paras 8–9. See also Cançado Trindade, 'The Right to Cultural Identity' (n 7) 477–99.

[19] *Mayagna (Sumo) Awas Tingni Community* (n 14), Joint Separate Opinion of Judges A A Cançado Trindade, M Pacheco Gómez and A Abreu Burelli, para 8. See also Fuentes, 'Judicial Interpretation and Indigenous Peoples' Rights to Lands, Participation and Consultation' (n 4) 38–45.

[20] See *Kichwa Indigenous People of Sarayaku* (n 15) para 145.

[21] *Sawhoyamaxa Indigenous Community* (n 9) para 120.

[22] ibid para 128.

[23] *Case of the Saramaka People v Suriname* Judgement (Preliminary Objections, Merits, Reparations, and Costs) Inter-American Court of Human Rights Series C No 172 (28 November 2007) para 122.

[24] ibid para 121.

[25] See ibid para 127.

resources that have not been traditionally used by indigenous communities, even when they are found on and within their traditional lands and territories. In this sense, the IACrtHR has stated, 'Article 21 of the Convention should not be interpreted in a way that prevents the State from granting any type of concession for the exploration and extraction of natural resources'.[26]

However, because concessions could affect the enjoyment of Indigenous Peoples' rights over the traditional lands and territories necessary for their survival,[27] they are subjected to the fulfilment of specific legal requirements in order to be justified. That is: 'a) they must be established by law; b) they must be necessary; c) they must be proportional, and d) their purpose must be to attain a legitimate goal in a democratic society'.[28]

In order to determine whether or not interference is needed for the achievement of a legitimate aim in a pluralist and democratic society,[29] another crucial factor to consider is 'whether the restriction amounts to a denial of their traditions and customs in a way that endangers the very survival of the group and of its members'.[30] In other words, a restriction to the enjoyment of Indigenous Peoples' land rights will be admissible only 'when it does not deny their survival as a tribal [or indigenous] people'.[31]

The protection of Indigenous Peoples' right to collective property under Article 21 ACHR is intimately connected with the protection of their culture and traditions and is a precondition for guaranteeing their survival as different peoples.[32] Conversely, the failure to guarantee this protection will not only infringe on their right to collective property but also affect their right to cultural identity.[33]

---

[26]   ibid para 126.
[27]   ibid. In a similar direction, the IACHR has emphasized that 'since the requirement to ensure their "survival" has the purpose of guaranteeing the special relationship between these peoples with their ancestral territories, reasonable deference should be given to the understanding that the indigenous and tribal peoples themselves have in regards to the scope of this relationship, as authorized interpreters of their cultures.' Inter-American Commission on Human Rights (IACHR), 'Indigenous Peoples, Afro-Descendent Communities, and Natural Resources: Human Rights Protection in the Context of Extraction, Exploitation, and Development Activities' (31 December 2015) OAS Doc 47/15 OEA/Ser.L/V/II, 13, para 83.
[28]   *Yakye Axa Indigenous Community* (n 10) para 144 *et seq.*
[29]   For the Inter-American Commission the 'recognition and protection as culturally different peoples requires wide political and institutional structures that allow them to participate in public life, and protect their cultural, social, economic and politic institutions in the decision-making process'. IACHR 'Indigenous Peoples, Afro-Descendent Communities, and Natural Resources' (n 27) para 150.
[30]   *Saramaka People* (n 23) para 128.
[31]   ibid. On the same line of thought, see UNHRC, 'Communication No. 511/1992: *Länsman et al. v Finland*' (8 November 1994) UN Doc CCPR/C/52/D/511/1992, para 9.4 (allowing States to pursue development activities that limit the rights of a minority culture as long as the activity does not fully extinguish the Indigenous Peoples' way of life).
[32]   See *Yakye Axa Indigenous Community* (n 10) paras 135–37.
[33]   The Expert Mechanism on the Rights of Indigenous Peoples stated that the '[l]ack of recognition of indigenous peoples' land rights and their relationships with their territories negatively affects their right to enjoy, access and promote their cultural heritage'. UNHRC, 'Promotion and Protection of the Rights of Indigenous Peoples with Respect to their Cultural Heritage: Study by the Expert Mechanism on the Rights of Indigenous Peoples' (19 August 2015) UN Doc A/HRC/30/53, 14.

II.   TRADITIONAL LANDS AND TERRITORIES AS AN ESSENTIAL ELEMENT OF INDIGENOUS PEOPLES' CULTURAL IDENTITY AND DIGNIFIED LIFE

The centrality of land rights and their interconnection with cultural rights is well established within the jurisprudence of the Inter-American human rights system.[34] The Inter-American Commission on Human Rights (IACHR) has stressed that 'the guarantee of the right to territorial property is a fundamental basis for the development of indigenous communities' culture, spiritual life, integrity and economic survival'.[35] Their access to traditionally occupied or possessed lands and territories not only provides access to material resources through agriculture, fishing and hunting practices, but also facilitates the development of their cultural practices, such as cultural festivals or rituals.[36] In other words, the comprehensive cultural relevance of the special relationship that Indigenous Peoples have with their traditional lands and territories is at the very core of their cultural identity.[37]

The UN Expert Mechanism on the Right of Indigenous Peoples (EMRIP) has also highlighted the interrelation between traditional lands, cultural heritage and identity.[38] In the views of this advisory body, Indigenous Peoples' cultural heritage includes 'tangible and intangible manifestations of their ways of life, world views, achievements and creativity, and should be considered an expression of their self-determination and their spiritual and physical relationships with their lands, territories and resources'.[39]

In the same line, the Inter-American Court has stressed the importance of preserving traditional lands and territories for the protection and safeguard of Indigenous Peoples' cultural identity.[40] In the *Saramaka* case, the Court stated that there is a 'need to protect the lands and resources [Indigenous Peoples] have traditionally used to prevent their extinction as a people'.[41] The aim and purpose of this jurisprudence is 'to guarantee that [Indigenous Peoples] may continue living their traditional way of life, and that their distinct cultural identity, social structure, economic system, customs, beliefs and traditions are respected, guaranteed and protected by States'.[42] Moreover, in the *Sawhoyamaxa* case, the Court mentioned that,

---

[34]   See Jérémie Gilbert, 'Land Rights as Human Rights: The Case for a Specific Right to Land' (2013) 18 SUR 115, 119 <https://sur.conectas.org/en/land-rights-human-rights/> accessed 8 March 2020.

[35]   IACHR, 'Indigenous and Tribal Peoples' Rights Over Their Ancestral Lands and Natural Resources: Norms and Jurisprudence of the Inter-American Human Rights System' (30 December 2009) OAS Doc no 56/09, 1.

[36]   See OHCHR, 'Land and Human Rights: Standards and Applications' (2015) UN Doc HR/PUB/15/5/Add.1, 60.

[37]   See Fuentes 'Protection of Indigenous Peoples' Traditional Lands and Exploitation of Natural Resources' (n 8) 233.

[38]   To know more about the UN Expert Mechanism on the Right of Indigenous Peoples (EMRIP) see the OHCHR's page on the mechanism: <www.ohchr.org/EN/Issues/IPeoples/EMRIP/Pages/EMRIPIndex.aspx>, accessed 10 March 2020.

[39]   UNHRC, 'Promotion and Protection of the Rights of Indigenous Peoples with Respect to their Cultural Heritage' (n 33) 4. In the views of the EMRIP, the notion of heritage also 'encompasses traditional practices in a broad sense, including language, art, music, dance, song, stories, sports and traditional games, sacred sites, and ancestral human remains'. ibid.

[40]   See *Saramaka People* (n 23) para 82.

[41]   ibid para 121.

[42]   ibid.

[t]he culture of the members of indigenous communities reflects a particular way of life, of being, seeing and acting in the world, the starting point of which is their close relation with their traditional lands and natural resources, not only because they are their main means of survival, but also because the [sic] form part of their worldview, of their religiousness, and consequently, of their cultural identity.[43]

This case law clearly indicates that the protection of Indigenous Peoples' right to collective property goes beyond the protection of their cultural identity and expands it to the protection of a dignified life – that is, a life in accordance with their own traditions, understandings and cultural beliefs.[44] As Judges Cançado Trindade and Ventura Robles stressed, 'if cultural identity suffers, the very right to life of the members of said indigenous community also inevitable [sic] suffers'.[45]

The right to life is guaranteed under Article 4 ACHR, which protects 'not only the right of every human being not to be deprived of his life arbitrarily', but also 'the right that he will not be prevented from having access to the conditions that guarantee a dignified existence'.[46] This means that public authorities not only have a negative obligation to prevent and restrain arbitrary violations of Indigenous Peoples' right to life but also the positive obligation to guarantee the necessary socio-cultural, economic and legal conditions that could allow them to live a dignified life or a life in dignity.[47]

It follows that the recognition of the collective right to property over Indigenous Peoples' traditional lands and territories could also be seen as essential not only for the protection of their right to cultural identity but also for guaranteeing their right to life.[48] The lack of protection of the right of Indigenous Peoples to enjoy and have access to their traditional lands and territories has 'a negative effect on the right of the members of the Community to a decent life'.[49] In fact, depriving Indigenous Peoples of access to their traditional territories means depriving them 'of the possibility of access to their traditional means of subsistence',[50] which could negatively affect the generation of living conditions capable to facilitate the realiza-

---

[43]   *Sawhoyamaxa Indigenous Community* (n 9) para 118; see also *Yakye Axa Indigenous Community* (n 10) para 135.

[44]   Judges Cançado Trindade and Ventura Robles emphasized in the *Yakye Axa* case that even if 'the right to life is a non-derogable right under the American Convention, while the right to property is not … the latter is especially significant because it is directly related to full enjoyment of the right to life including conditions for a decent life'. *Yakye Axa Indigenous Community v Paraguay* (n 10), Separate Dissenting Opinion of Judges AA Cançado Trindade and ME Ventura Robles, para 20.

[45]   ibid para 18.

[46]   *Case of the "Street Children" (Villagrán Morales et al.) v Guatemala* Judgment (Merits) Inter-American Court of Human Rights Series C No 63 (19 November 1999) para 144.

[47]   As mentioned by Judges Cançado Trindade and Ventura Robles, '[i]nterpretation of the right to life in a way that encompasses positive measures of protection for the indigenous peoples to enjoy the right to a decent life is based on international jurisprudence and doctrine, and it entails new steps forward in International Human Rights Law'. *Yakye Axa Indigenous Community* (n 10), Separate Dissenting Opinion of Judges AA Cançado Trindade and ME Ventura Robles, para 27.

[48]   See *Sawhoyamaxa Indigenous Community* (n 9), Separate Opinion by Judge AA Cançado Trindade, para 7.

[49]   *Yakye Axa Indigenous Community* (n 10) para 168.

[50]   ibid.

tion of their own project of life,[51] based in their own traditions, cultural understandings and worldviews.[52]

III.　CAUSAL RELATIONSHIP BETWEEN DESTITUTE LIVING CONDITIONS AND LACK OF ACCESS TO TRADITIONAL LANDS AND TERRITORIES

The enjoyment of Indigenous Peoples' right to communal property, as guaranteed by Article 21 ACHR, generates in State authorities a positive obligation to adopt special measures that guarantee the full enjoyment and equal exercise of that right.[53] Because of the inherited connection between their traditional lands and territories with their cultural identity, and therefore with their right to life, such special measures should include the creation of conditions able to guarantee a dignified existence.[54]

However, it is clear that state authorities 'cannot be responsible for all situations in which the right to life is at risk'.[55] Under the provisions of the American Convention, States are responsible for adopting any measure that may be necessary 'to protect the right of not being prevented from access to conditions that may guarantee a decent life'.[56] In creating such conditions, state authorities should also take into account the potential existence of 'particular needs of protection', 'personal conditions' or 'the specific situation [individuals] have to face, such as extreme poverty, exclusion or childhood'.[57]

In fact, the effective protection of the rights enshrined in the ACHR requires interpreting its provisions 'in such a way that the system for the protection of human rights has all its appropriate effects (*effet utile*)'.[58] This interpretation needs to take into account 'all circumstances and contextual factors of the specific case under analysis', including socio-economic, cultural and legal transformations that affect our societies.[59] In short, human rights provisions need to

---

[51]　In connection with the understanding of the Court regarding the concept of 'project of life', see *"Street Children"* (n 46) para 144.

[52]　In the case of the members of the Yakye Axa community, the Court established that the lack of recognition of the right to communal property 'has had a negative effect on the right of the members of the community to a decent life, because it has deprived them of the possibility of access to their traditional means of subsistence, as well as to use and enjoyment of the natural resources necessary to obtain clean water and to practice traditional medicine to prevent and cure illnesses'. *Yakye Axa Indigenous Community* (n 10) para 168.

[53]　See *Saramaka People* (n 23) para 91.

[54]　See *"Street Children"* (n 46) para 144.

[55]　*Sawhoyamaxa Indigenous Community* (n 9) para 155.

[56]　ibid para 153. See also *Yakye Axa Indigenous Community* (n 10) para 161; *"Street Children"* (n 46) para 144; *Case of the "Juvenile Reeducation Institute" v Paraguay* Judgment (Preliminary Objections, Merits, Reparations and Costs) Inter-American Court of Human Rights Series C No 112 (2 September 2004) para 156.

[57]　*Sawhoyamaxa Indigenous Community* (n 9) para 154.

[58]　*The Right to Information on Consular Assistance in the Framework of Guarantees for Due Legal Process*, Advisory Opinion OC-16/991, Inter-American Court of Human Rights Series A No 16 (1 October 1999) para 58.

[59]　Alejandro Fuentes and Marina Vannelli, 'Human Rights of Children in the Context of Migration Processes. Innovative Efforts for Integrating Regional Human Rights Standards in the Americas' (2019) 8 Laws 1, 4 *et seq.*

be interpreted in a contextual, historical and evolutive manner, always keeping in mind that 'human rights treaties are living instruments whose interpretation must consider the changes over time and present-day conditions'.[60]

The application of these interpretative principles to Article 4 ACHR assigns state authorities a responsibility for introducing specific positive measures leading to the creation of living conditions conducive to the effective realization of Indigenous Peoples' life projects. Moreover, because Indigenous Peoples' worldviews are often different from those prevailing in the Western culture,[61] the creation of societal conditions facilitating access to a dignified life need to take into account and preserve the 'integrity and identity' of their culture.[62] In this sense, the Court has expressed:

> As regards indigenous peoples, it is essential for the States to grant effective protection that takes into account their specificities, their economic and social characteristics, as well as their situation of special vulnerability, their customary law, values, and customs.[63]

Positive measures addressing the creation of conditions that could facilitate Indigenous Peoples' life projects should be able to guarantee their possibility to 'continue their traditional way of living, and that their distinctive cultural identity, social structure, economic system, customs, beliefs and traditions are respected, guaranteed and protected by the States'.[64] That is why, when adopting these appropriate measures, States should pay close attention to 'the especially vulnerable situation in which they were placed, given their different manner of life … and their life aspirations, both individual and collective'.[65]

In short, positive measures should take into account socio-economic and cultural living conditions in order to deliver effective justice to individuals affected by structural marginalization.[66] This means that positive actions have to be determined 'according to the particular needs of protection of the legal persons, whether due to their personal conditions or because of the specific situation they have to face, such as extreme poverty'.[67]

---

[60]   *The Right to Information on Consular Assistance* (n 58) para 114. See also *"Street Children"* (n 46) para 192 *et seq*; *Case of the Gómez Paquiyauri Brothers v Peru* Judgment (Merits, Reparations and Costs) Inter-American Court of Human Rights Series C No 110 (8 July 2004) para 165.

[61]   See *Yakye Axa Indigenous Community* (n 10) para 163.

[62]   See *Moiwana Community v Suriname* Judgment (Interpretation of the Judgment of Merits, Reparations, and Costs) Inter-American Court of Human Rights Series C No 145 (8 February 2006) para 17.

[63]   *Yakye Axa Indigenous Community* (n 10) para 63.

[64]   *Kichwa Indigenous People of Sarayaku* (n 15) para 146.

[65]   *Yakye Axa Indigenous Community* (n 10) para 163.

[66]   See Alejandro Fuentes, 'Expanding the Boundaries of International Human Rights Law. The Systemic Approach of the Inter-American Court of Human Rights' (2018) European Society of International Law (ESIL) 2017 Annual Conference Paper No 13/2017, 37 <https://ssrn.com/abstract= 3163088> accessed 3 April 2020.

[67]   *Sawhoyamaxa Indigenous Community* (n 9) para 154.

IV.   PROTECTION OF THE ACCESS TO TRADITIONAL LANDS AND TERRITORIES AS A STRATEGY FOR POVERTY ERADICATION AND SUSTAINABLE DEVELOPMENT

In the case of Indigenous Peoples, positive actions oriented toward the mitigation or eradication of extreme poverty need to take into consideration and be respectful of Indigenous Peoples' cultural distinctiveness. This is vital, especially if we consider that Indigenous Peoples are overrepresented among the world's poorest population groups. Approximately six percent of the global population are Indigenous Peoples, but they account for about 15 percent of the extreme poor.[68]

Indigenous Peoples' poor living conditions are clearly linked to their lack of access to their traditional lands, territories and natural resources. As affirmed by the Inter-American Commission,

> [t]he lack of access to land and natural resources can produce conditions of extreme poverty for the affected indigenous communities, given that the lack of possession of, and access to, their territories prevents them from using and enjoying the natural resources that they need to obtain the goods necessary for their subsistence, develop their traditional cultivation, hunting, fishing or gathering activities, access traditional health systems, and other key socio-cultural functions.[69]

The lack of protection of the right to collective property over their traditional lands and territories 'has had a negative effect on the right of the members of the Community to a decent life'.[70] For indigenous communities, access to their lands and territories is 'directly related, even a pre-requisite, to enjoyment of the rights to an existence under conditions of dignity'.[71] The deprivation of land and territories has been qualified as 'severe deprivation' and 'extreme poverty', amounting to a 'denial of economic, social, and cultural rights, including the rights to adequate nutrition, to health, to food, and to work'.[72]

The effective recognition of their right to collective property is paramount in guaranteeing decent living conditions to Indigenous Peoples as well as to address their destitute socio-economic and cultural situations. For instance, in the *Sawhoyamaxa* case, the IACrtHR determined that the State of Paraguay had not adopted the necessary measures for the members of the community to 'abandon the inadequate conditions that endangered, and continue endangering, their right to life'.[73] Adequate measures for preventing their material and spiritual suffering would have included the need to 'relocate them within their ancestral lands, where

---

[68]   'Indigenous Peoples' (*The World Bank*) <www.worldbank.org/en/topic/indigenouspeoples> accessed 07 June 2020.

[69]   IACHR, 'Indigenous and Tribal Peoples' Rights over their Ancestral Lands and Natural Resources' (n 35) 22.

[70]   *Yakye Axa Indigenous Community* (n 10) para 168.

[71]   IACHR, 'Indigenous and Tribal Peoples' Rights over their Ancestral Lands and Natural Resources' (n 35) 1.

[72]   *Yakye Axa Indigenous Community* (n 10), Partly Concurring and Partly Dissenting Opinion of Judge Ramon Fogel, para 28.

[73]   *Sawhoyamaxa Indigenous Community* (n 9) para 166. The extreme living conditions affecting the members of this indigenous community were described by the Court by saying, 'together with the lack of lands, the life of the members of the Sawhoyamaxa Community is characterized by unemployment, illiteracy, morbidity rates caused by evitable illnesses, malnutrition, precarious conditions in their dwell-

they could have used and enjoyed their natural resources, which resources are directly related to their survival capacity and the preservation of their ways of life'.[74] In this sense, the Court expressly mentioned that,

> the special significance of the land for indigenous peoples ... entails that any denial of the enjoyment or exercise of their territorial rights is detrimental to values that are very representative for the members of said peoples, who are at risk of losing or suffering irreparable damage to their cultural identity and life and to the cultural heritage to be passed on to future generations.[75]

The lack of effective guarantee of Indigenous Peoples' access to decent life conditions in their traditional lands and territories 'may imply subjecting them to situations of extreme unprotectedness, which entail violations of their rights to life, to personal integrity, to a dignified existence, to food, to water, to health, to education and children's rights, among others'.[76] Hence, state authorities have a responsibility to address the 'grave living conditions to which they have been subjected as a consequence of the State's delay in making their territorial rights effective'.[77] In other words, fighting poverty in the case of Indigenous Peoples means access to their traditional lands, territories and natural resources.

The UN Permanent Forum on Indigenous Issues (PFII) has ratified the direction indicated by the Inter-American Court by stressing that '[t]he root causes of the severe poverty and food insecurity that many Indigenous Peoples face lie in their lack of secure land rights'.[78] According to PFII, Indigenous Peoples define 'happiness' as intimately connected with 'the state of nature and their environment'.[79] Their well-being 'necessarily encompasses their access, management and control over lands, territories and resources under customary use and management, all of which are critical for their own sustainable development'.[80]

It is the loss of their traditional territories, access to land and natural resources, together with other factors such as climate-change induced vulnerabilities or lack of access to basic

---

ing places and environment, limitations to access and use health services and drinking water, as well as marginalization due to economic, geographic and cultural causes'. ibid para 168.

[74]   ibid para 164.

[75]   *Yakye Axa Indigenous Community* (n 10) para 203.

[76]   IACHR, 'Indigenous and Tribal Peoples' Rights over their Ancestral Lands and Natural Resources' (n 35) 22.

[77]   *Yakye Axa Indigenous Community* (n 10) para 202. The Inter-American Commission came to the same conclusion when it stated '[t]he failure of the State to guarantee indigenous communities' right to ancestral territory can imply a failure to comply with the duty to secure the life of their members; such was the case of the Yakye Axa community ... The State violates article 4.1 of the American Convention in relation to article 1.1, when it does not adopt "the necessary positive measures within its powers, which could reasonably be expected to prevent or avoid risking the right to life of the members of [an indigenous community]"'. IACHR, 'Indigenous and Tribal Peoples' Rights over their Ancestral Lands and Natural Resources' (n 35) para 154.

[78]   'Permanent Forum on Indigenous Issues (PFII): Suggestions for the High Level Political Forum's Consideration to Ensure That Indigenous Peoples Are Not Left Behind in the 2030 Agenda' (*Sustainable Development Goals Knowledge Platform*) <https://sustainabledevelopment.un.org/index.php?page=view&type=30022&nr=198&menu=3170> accessed 20 March 2020.

[79]   UN Department of Economic and Social Affairs (DESA), 'State of the World's Indigenous Peoples' (2009) UN Doc ST/ESA/328, 30.

[80]   ibid.

social services[81] that causes food insecurity and poverty among indigenous communities.[82] In fact, one of the biggest challenges faced by indigenous communities in relation to sustainable development is 'to ensure territorial security, legal recognition of ownership and control over customary land and resources, and the sustainable utilization of lands and other renewable resources for the cultural, economic and physical health and well-being of indigenous peoples'.[83]

The special relationship that Indigenous Peoples have with their traditional lands and territories is also relevant for the implementation of the UN 2030 Agenda in a manner that will make certain that Indigenous Peoples are not left behind.[84] The implementation of the Sustainable Development Goals (SDGs) needs to be in line with the protection of the right of Indigenous Peoples to their traditional lands and territories in order to guarantee their sustainable development as distinctive peoples. For instance, states' policies addressing the implementation of SDGs need to ensure that the 'promotion of resilient and sustainable agricultural practices and maintenance of seed diversity are consistent with efforts to promote for food security and poverty eradication amongst indigenous peoples'.[85] As stressed by the PFII,

> [a]n historical perspective and understanding of indigenous peoples' vital contribution to sustainable development is very important so that policies and actions can be taken at the international, regional, national and local levels in order to ensure the continued well-being of indigenous peoples. The future of indigenous peoples is closely linked with solutions to the crises in biodiversity and climate change, which must incorporate respect, protection and promotion of indigenous peoples' rights as an essential component of a global strategy.[86]

The Inter-American Court has also addressed the potentially negative effects that development projects or climate change could generate in the enjoyment of Indigenous Peoples' rights.[87] According to the regional tribunal, the issue of any concession for exploration or exploitation of natural resources, or the realization of any infrastructure development project, including the creation of biodiversity protected areas, within the Indigenous Peoples' ancestral lands and territories are subjected to the introduction of specific safeguards.[88]

First, indigenous communities need to be consulted before the issue or implementation of any concession over natural resources within their traditional lands or territories, or the introduction of development projects, which may interfere in the enjoyment of their rights.

---

[81]   As highlighted by the Major Group Indigenous Peoples, '[p]overty, caused largely by the expropriation of their lands, is a key factor of food insecurity, and the levels of hunger and malnutrition among indigenous populations are disproportionately high'. 'Input From Major Group: Indigenous Peoples' (n 12) 4.

[82]   Rishabh Kumar Dhir, 'Sustainable Development Goals: Indigenous Peoples in Focus' (*ILO*, 26 July 2016) 3 *et seq* <www.ilo.org/global/topics/indigenous-tribal/publications/WCMS_503715/lang--en/index.htm> accessed 21 March 2020.

[83]   DESA, 'State of the World's Indigenous Peoples' (n 79) 43.

[84]   See 'Permanent Forum on Indigenous Issues (PFII)' (n 78) 2.

[85]   'Briefing Note: Indigenous Peoples' Rights and the 2030 Agenda' (OHCHR, September 2017) 4   <www.un.org/development/desa/indigenouspeoples/wp-content/uploads/sites/19/2016/10/Briefing-Paper-on-Indigenous-Peoples-Rights-and-the-2030-Agenda.pdf> accessed 21 March 2020.

[86]   DESA, 'State of the World's Indigenous Peoples' (n 79) 43.

[87]   See Fuentes, 'Protection of Indigenous Peoples' Traditional Lands and Exploitation of Natural Resources' (n 8) 229–53.

[88]   See *Saramaka People* (n 23) para 129 *et seq*.

State authorities have the obligation to 'actively consult with said community according to their customs and traditions', and 'at the early stages of a development or investment plan, not only when the need arises to obtain approval from the community'.[89] Consultations need to be meaningful and effective, 'through culturally appropriate procedures and with the objective of reaching an agreement'. [90]

Second, affected indigenous communities need to be compensated for the interferences in the enjoyment of their rights. The right to obtain compensation under Article 21(2) ACHR 'extends not only to the total deprivation of property title by way of expropriation by the State ... but also to the deprivation of the regular use and enjoyment of such property'.[91] This safeguard is essential for guaranteeing the physical and cultural survival of indigenous communities. By receiving a 'reasonable equitable compensation', Indigenous Peoples could devote those resources to the sustainable development of their own management systems and practices.[92]

Third, in order to prevent socio-environmental consequences capable of affecting or even disrupting Indigenous Peoples' socio-ecological biodiversity and sustainable management systems,[93] public authorities should conduct a prior and independent environmental and social impact assessment (ESIA).[94] ESIA contributes to risk awareness, 'including environmental and health risks, in order that the proposed development or investment plan is accepted knowingly and voluntarily' by affected communities.[95] In addition, ESIA should include not only environmental considerations but also all potential socio-economic impacts generated by development projects, together with their cumulative impacts over the enjoyment of Indigenous Peoples' human rights.[96] Finally, ESIA should be able to indicate whether the level of impact of a development project could potentially 'deny the ability of the members of the [affected communities] to survive as a tribal [or indigenous] people'.[97]

Therefore, the preservation of indigenous physical and cultural survival emerges as a guiding interpretative principle that state authorities should consider when deciding upon concessions or development projects that could interfere with the enjoyment of Indigenous Peoples' rights. This is why, in the case of large-scale development or investment projects that could have a major or profound impact on the territory of Indigenous Peoples to the point of affecting their cultural and physical survival, public authorities have the additional duty 'to obtain their free, prior, and informed consent, according to their customs and traditions'. [98]

---

[89]   ibid para 133.

[90]   ibid.

[91]   ibid para 139.

[92]   ibid para 140.

[93]   See 'Permanent Forum on Indigenous Issues (PFII)' (n 78) 2.

[94]   See, e.g., Fuentes 'Protection of Indigenous Peoples' Traditional Lands and Exploitation of Natural Resources' (n 8) 242 *et seq.*

[95]   *Saramaka People v Suriname* Interpretation of the Judgment (Preliminary Objections, Merits, Reparations and Costs) Inter-American Court of Human Rights Series C No 185 (12 August 2008) para 40.

[96]   See *The Environment and Human Rights,* Advisory Opinion OC-23/17, Inter-American Court of Human Rights Series A No 23 (15 November 2017) paras 164 and 174.

[97]   *Saramaka People* (Interpretation) (n 95) para 42.

[98]   *Saramaka People* (n 23) para 134. Regarding whether or not the obligation to obtain indigenous peoples' free, prior and informed consent (FPIC) amounts to a potential 'veto power' in their hands, see, e.g., UNHRC, 'Promotion and Protection of All Human Rights, Civil, Political, Economic, Social and

The safeguards developed by IACrtHR not only protect Indigenous Peoples' right to land but also the effective enjoyment of their right to life, in accordance with their own traditions, cultural understandings and worldviews. These safeguards are instrumental for guaranteeing that concessions or development projects will not take place if their socio-environmental impacts amount to a denial of their material and cultural survival.[99]

V.   CONCLUSION

Indigenous Peoples' traditional lands and territories are essential for the maintenance and further development of their culture, identity and way of life. The close relationship that Indigenous Peoples have with their lands has also benefited the development of socio-ecological land tenure systems. Since immemorial times, Indigenous Peoples have acted as 'guardians of these natural environments and play a key role, through their traditions, in respectfully maintaining them for future generations'.[100]

When Indigenous Peoples' access to traditional lands is prevented, their physical and cultural survival is affected together with the preservation of their natural environment. Hence, in order to prevent the loss of bio-cultural diversity, public policies should focus on 'nurturing traditional ecological practices and knowledge, or utilizing cultural frameworks to address socio-economic problems'.[101]

Indigenous Peoples' traditional knowledge has much to contribute to the sustainable management of natural environments and efficient utilization of natural resources. Indigenous Peoples' traditional environmental management systems are important tools in the attainment of SDGs too. On one hand, it will support the realization of their 'own vision of shared prosperity and poverty reduction'.[102] On the other hand, Indigenous Peoples' bio-cultural management systems could also contribute to the promotion of sustainable and resilient agricultural practices, promotion of food security and poverty eradication, as stressed by the UN Agenda 2030.[103]

Disregarding Indigenous Peoples' own understandings of development will harm their ability to control their future and to develop in accordance with their own traditions and cultural understandings.[104] By contrast, the incorporation of Indigenous Peoples' develop-

---

Cultural Rights, Including the Right to Development: Report of the Special Rapporteur on the Situation of Human Rights and Fundamental Freedoms of Indigenous People, James Anaya' (15 July 2009) UN Doc A/HRC/12/34, para 46; Fuentes, 'Judicial Interpretation and Indigenous Peoples' Rights to Lands, Participation and Consultation' (n 4) 74–75.

[99]   *Saramaka People* (n 23) para 138.

[100]   UN Development Group, 'Guidelines on Indigenous Peoples' Issues' (2009) UN Doc HR/P/PT/16, 18.

[101]   Indigenous Peoples Major Group for Sustainable Development, 'Global Report on the Situation of Lands, Territories and Resources of Indigenous Peoples' (*IWGIA*, 2019) 51 <www.iwgia.org/en/resources/publications/3335-global-report-on-the-situation-of-lands-territories-and-resources-of-indigenous-peoples> accessed 05 April 2020.

[102]   Duchicela and others, 'Indigenous Peoples Development in World Bank Financed Projects' (n 11) IX.

[103]   'Briefing Note: Indigenous Peoples' Rights and the 2030 Agenda' (n 85) 4.

[104]   As stressed by DESA, '[a]ny measures of indigenous peoples' social and economic development must necessarily start from indigenous peoples' own definitions and indicators of poverty and well-being'. DESA 'State of the World's Indigenous Peoples' (n 79) 15.

ment perspectives could also contribute to new emerging conceptual frameworks, 'such as ethno-development and development with identity, which stress the importance of finding socially and culturally appropriate development alternatives for indigenous communities that allow them to be in control of their own development'.[105]

Inclusion of Indigenous Peoples in development strategies means not to exclusively base them on 'modern economic criteria, such as individual income or consumption';[106] it means to take into consideration the bio-cultural connection that Indigenous Peoples have with their traditional lands and territories.[107] Poverty and prosperity are intimately interconnected with Indigenous Peoples' access and enjoyment of their traditional lands and territories; for them, 'being "poor" is being landless, and "prosperity" means having the security to manage and utilize their land and resources to meet their needs'.[108] As stated by the Indigenous Peoples Major Group,

> [t]he historical subjugation, assimilation and systematic expropriation of indigenous peoples' lands, territories and resources; the non-recognition of their distinct identities; the denial of access to basic social services, and; the lack of participation in decision-making are the compounding factors for the widespread poverty amongst indigenous peoples.[109]

To conclude, in order to mitigate or eradicate poverty in the case of Indigenous Peoples, states need to guarantee the legal recognition and full enjoyment of their right to collective property over possessed or otherwise used traditional lands and territories. The interconnection between the protection of Indigenous Peoples' lands and territories and the elaboration of sustainable development agendas that take into account their own cultural understandings and traditions need to be further explored by additional scholarly contributions.

Research agendas could contribute to the further elaboration of culturally sensitive development approaches that take into account Indigenous Peoples' traditions and cultural understandings of development. In other words, research could contribute 'to resolve, in the twenty-first century, the problems inherited from preceding centuries'.[110]

---

[105] Duchicela and others, 'Indigenous Peoples Development in World Bank Financed Projects' (n 11) XII.

[106] ibid 6.

[107] According to the World Bank, this approach 'often includes culture-based activities, such as handicrafts, cultural tourism, and ethno-biological products, but it can also include larger productive activities, such as sustainable forest management, sustainable agriculture, and fisheries of native species'. ibid.

[108] 'Input from Major Group: Indigenous Peoples' (n 12) 2.

[109] ibid.

[110] *Yatama v Nicaragua* Judgment (Preliminary Objections, Merits, Reparations, Costs) Inter-American Court of Human Rights Series C No 127 (23 June 2005) Concurring Opinion of Judge Sergio Garcia-Ramirez, para 33.

C.   Poverty, Human Rights and Participation

21. Human rights, poverty and mobilizations
Domingo A. Lovera-Parmo[1]

Since 18 October 2019, after a fare hike was announced for the public transit, hundreds of thousands of people took to the streets of cities across Chile to pose critical social claims. Although the protests started with high school students evading subway fares, claims included challenges to the politico-constitutional structure in the areas of social security, access to health, education, minimum wages, labor rights and, more generally, inequality.[2] The government first responded to these claims with indolence, which drove people to the streets to show their dissatisfaction. There they were faced with fierce police repression, which resulted in more than twenty people killed and a shameful record of eye injuries that the press has aptly termed an 'epidemic'. Many Chileans believe that, as their basic needs are not met—and it is extremely difficult to make ends meet living paycheck to paycheck—they have, indeed, nothing to lose.[3] This explains why—despite police brutality—they stayed on the streets.

This chapter traces the relations between poverty and mobilizations from an international human rights perspective. In line with the aim that drives the entire volume, this chapter embraces an ample definition of poverty beyond strict financial calculations; it does not restrict its analysis only to the situation of those who lack basic income, but expands it to include those who, besides income poverty, experience 'human development poverty and social exclusion'.[4] Therefore, in terms of rights enjoyment, poverty includes the impairment of both civil and political rights[5] as well as social rights.[6] From there it examines international human rights law and asks whether rights may contribute to legally shielding poor people's mobilizations to pose their political demands. Has international human rights law been sensitive to poor people's movements resorting to protest as a critical means to participate in democratic life?

Section I argues that social protests are a protected form of participating in political affairs, specifically claiming protests themselves are a form of exercising rights. As will be argued below, the right to protest is composed of a cluster of human rights, most notably, although not exclusively, freedom of expression and freedom of assembly. This section illustrates how

---

[1]   For excellent research assistance, I am grateful to Sofia Andrade.

[2]   These massive waves of protests were not in vain and resulted in a constituent moment that will begin with Chileans being asked whether they want a new constitution or not in October 2020.

[3]   Jonathan Franklin, 'Chile protesters: "We are subjugated by the rich. It's time for that to end"' *The Guardian* (30 October 2019).

[4]   United Nations General Assembly (UNGA) 'Promotion and Protection of all Human Rights, Civil, Political, Economic, Social and Cultural Rights, Including the Right to Development' (28 February 2008) 7th Session UN Doc A/HRC/7/15 (13).

[5]   UNGA 'Extreme Poverty and Human Rights' (4 October 2017) UN Doc A/72/502. As shown below, there is a dramatic vicious circle if we consider that the violation of civil and political rights not only has a disproportionate impact on people living in poverty [6], but it also normally redounds in access to social rights, as the report duly notices [31 ff.].

[6]   UNGA 'Report of the Special Rapporteur on Extreme Poverty and Human Rights' (28 April 2016) UN Doc A/HRC/32/31 13 (showing that lack of access to social rights normally affects the enjoyment of civil and political rights).

international human rights standards deem protests as a protected means of political partici-pation. Section II analyses human rights sources, emphasizing that almost every human rights decision, comment and report touching on protests and mobilizations highlights the fact that those who usually resort to protests are those worst off socially.

Bearing that in mind, Section III explores current gaps that merit future research. First, it stresses the importance of bringing a more robust version of the equality principle into the analysis of protests regulation. In fact, international human rights law has welcomed current regulations of protests under the form of time, place and manner (TPM) restrictions, holding that these regulations per se do not violate human rights instruments. Therefore, human rights law is normally content with having general and content-neutral regulations imposed on protests rights. However, these standards usually do not pay sufficient attention to the social profile of those who resort to protests—or the different social conditions of those upon whom these regulations are placed. Drawing on the argument developed in Section II: if international human rights standards recognize that those who are most likely to resort to protests are those worst off because they lack access to other alternative means of political influence, it seems odd not to continue the attention on the social profile of those who protest when it comes the time to assess the acceptability of TPM regulations.

Finally this Section calls on the need to not 'proceduralize' protests rights. Despite the inner value protests have as forms of political participation, international human rights law should place its emphasis not so much on highlighting the best practices of negotiating approaches to protests regulations, but rather on the urgency of the substantive demands that protesters pose. Excessive attention on protests rights—as important as it may be—may reduce the claims protesters are bringing to the public agenda to secondary consideration.

I.   THE RIGHT TO PROTEST: THE PILLARS

In general terms, the right to protest is comprised of a cluster of rights, including freedom of expression and of assembly.[7] Whereas freedom of expression provides protection to the mes-sages that those mobilizing advance, sometimes including the very acts of mobilization as a form of communication, freedom of assembly provides protection for the organizational aspects of a mobilization—regardless of the communicative goals (if any) that a protest may have.

A.   Freedom of Expression

Several provisions in different human right treaties address the freedom of expression. The Universal Declaration of Human Rights (UDHR) recognizes the right to hold opinions without interference,[8] and the International Covenant on Civil and Political Rights (ICCPR) resorts to the same language.[9] At the regional level the European Convention on Human Rights (ECHR)

---

[7]   Other rights, such as the right to privacy and the right to freedom of movement, may also be included.

[8]   Universal Declaration of Human Rights (UDHR) (adopted 10 December 1948) UNGA Res 217 A(III) art 19.

[9]   International Covenant on Civil and Political Rights (ICCPR) (adopted 16 December 1966, entered into force 23 March 1976) 999 UNTS 171 art 19.1.

recognizes, in similar terms, the right to hold opinions and impart information.[10] The Banjul Charter (The African Charter on Human Rights and Peoples' Rights) does the same.[11] Last but not least, the American Convention on Human Rights (ACHR) also recognizes the freedom to seek, receive and impart information, adding—like the ICCPR—a specific protection of means: the freedom is to be exercised 'either orally, in writing, in print, in the form of art, or through any other medium of one's choice'.[12]

Whereas the ACHR and the ICCPR stand alone in explicitly recognizing that the means or mediums to disseminate expressions and opinions are ample, the interpretation of the different treaty clauses enshrining freedom of expression has proven wide enough to accommodate the protection of mobilizations and protests (although not of every non-verbal expression)[13] as a legitimate exercise of communication rights.[14] For instance the Human Rights Committee held in its landmark decision *Kivenmaa v. Finland*—a petition questioning the sanction of protesters who gathered in front of a governmental building and started distributing leaflets—that '[t]he right for an individual to express his political opinions ... forms part of the freedom of expression guaranteed by article 19 of the Covenant. In this particular case, the author of the communication exercised this right by raising a banner'.[15] This protection includes protests and other forms of 'non-verbal expressions'.[16] In the context of the ECHR, the European Court of Human Rights reiterated in *Tarenko v. Russia* that 'Article 10 protects not only the substance of the ideas and information expressed, but also the form in which they are conveyed'.[17] Accordingly, in *Murat Vural v. Turkey* it considered that pouring paint over a statue constituted protected political speech.[18]

B.   Freedom of Assembly

Freedom of assembly is the second pillar of the right to protest. It also finds recognition in the instruments. All treaty provisions begin by recognizing the freedom to assemble; whereas some of them include a mode of exercise—specifying the requirement that gatherings be peaceful or establishing specific grounds for limitation. Article 20.1 of the UDHR offers the most concise recognition, while the ICCPR offers one of the clauses with specific grounds for

---

[10]   Convention for the Protection of Human Rights and Fundamental Freedoms (European Convention on Human Rights, as amended) (ECHR) art 10.1.

[11]   African Charter on Human and Peoples' Rights (adopted 27 June 1981, entered into force 21 October 1986) (1982) 21 ILM 58 art 9.2.

[12]   Organization of American States (OAS), American Convention on Human Rights 'Pact of San Jose, Costa Rica' (B-32), 22 January 1969 art 13.1.

[13]   Michael O'Flaherty, 'Freedom of Expression: Article 19 of the International Covenant on Civil and Political Rights and the Human Rights Committee's General Comment No 34' (2012) 12 Human Rights L Rev 627, 637–38.

[14]   Eric Barendt, *Freedom of Speech* (OUP 2005) 289. On the relevance of understanding communication rights in a broad fashion, see Sharynne McLeod, 'Communication Rights: Fundamental Human Rights for All' (2018) 20 Int'l J Speech-Language Pathology 3.

[15]   *Kivenmaa v. Finland* (1994) No. 412/1990, UN Doc CCPR/C/50/D/412/1990.

[16]   Emily Howie, 'Protecting the Human Right to Freedom of Expression in International Law' (2018) 20 Int'l J Speech-Language Pathology 12, 13; Helen Fenwick and Gavin Phillipson, 'Public Protest, the Human Rights Act and Judicial Responses to Political Expression' (2009) Pub L 628.

[17]   *Tarenko v. Russia* (2014) App no 19554/05 (ECHR, 13 October 2014) 64.

[18]   *Murat Vural v. Turkey* (2012) App no 9540/07 (ECHR, 21 October 2012) 44.

limitation.[19] Regional instruments follow the ICCPR model by including specific conditions regulating public assemblies, as can be seen in Article 11 of the ECHR, Article 11 of the Banjul Charter, and Article 15 of the ACHR. In the case of the ACHR, it is specifically established that freedom of assembly is to be exercised 'without arms'.[20]

Whereas freedom of expression shields the messages conveyed by those who protest, freedom of assembly protects the organizational aspects of demonstrations.[21] Although this aspect of freedom of assembly is not always highlighted,[22] this view affords greater protection to mobilizations and configures freedom of assembly as an autonomous liberty.[23] For example, these organizational aspects were considered in the joint report of the United Nations (UN) Special Rapporteur on the rights to freedom of peaceful assembly and of association and the Special Rapporteur on extrajudicial, summary or arbitrary executions: 'The right to freedom of peaceful assembly includes the right to plan, organize, promote and advertise an assembly in any lawful manner'.[24] Likewise the Revised Draft of the General Comment No. 37 on Article 21 (Right of Peaceful Assembly) of the ICCPR[25] which is currently under elaboration, highlights that the general aim of human rights law standards is to have States obliged to facilitate and enable an 'environment for the exercise of assembly rights'.[26]

At the level of case law the Human Rights Committee has held that freedom of assembly 'entails the possibility of organizing and participating in a peaceful assembly, including the

---

[19]   ICCPR (n 9) art.21 ('No restrictions may be placed on the exercise of this right other than those imposed in conformity with the law and which are necessary in a democratic society in the interests of national security or public safety, public order (ordre public), the protection of public health or morals or the protection of the rights and freedoms of others'.).

[20]   While outside the scope of this discussion, it is not surprising that both internationally and domestically, freedom of assembly is the only freedom which is required to be exercised peacefully or 'without arms'. Is there any right, freedom or equality that may actually be exercised (regularly, as opposed to exceptionally like property rights) violently or with arms? As Sálat writes, these clauses represent an actual testament of its animadversion towards assemblies. Orsolya Sálat, *The Right to Freedom of Assembly. A Comparative Study* (Hart Publishing 2015) 3. The problem of this approach is two-fold: symbolically it configures freedom of assembly as a second-class liberty (one always under suspicion) and from a legal viewpoint it opens a vast field for possible limitations.

[21]   Barendt (n 14) 271–72 (showing that this means that to claim legal protection demonstrators do not need to justify that a protest has a message to convey (an expressive content)).

[22]   In fact, the HRC usually considers these organizational aspects to be secondary when compared to the right to manifest one's opinion. Thus, at times, once the HRC accepts violations of freedom of expression it rarely advances to examine whether freedom of assembly is also compromised. *Komarovsky v. Belarus*, No 1939/2008, UN Doc CCPR/C/109/D/1839/2008 (2008) [9.5]. Other times the secondary position freedom of assembly seems to have is expressly stated. Thus, in *Alekseev v. Russian Federation*, the HRC held that 'the right of peaceful assembly, as guaranteed under article 21 of the Covenant, is essential for the public expression of a person's views and opinions, and indispensable in a democratic society'. *Alekseev v. Russian Federation,* No 1873/2009, UN Doc CCPR/C/109/D/1873/2009 (2013) 9.3.

[23]   Tabatha Abu El-Haj, 'The Neglected Right of Assembly' (2009) 56 UCLA L Rev 543, 547.

[24]   UNGA 'Joint Report of the Special Rapporteur on the rights to freedom of peaceful assembly and of association and the Special Rapporteur on extrajudicial, summary or arbitrary executions on the proper management of assemblies', A/HRC/31/66, 4 February 2016 19.

[25]   UN Human Rights Committee (HRC) 'Revised Draft of the General Comment No. 37 on Article 21 (Right of Peaceful Assembly)' <www.ohchr.org/Documents/HRBodies/CCPR/GC37/ENGLISH _GC37.docx> accessed 22 June 2020.

[26]   ibid.

right to a stationary assembly (such as a picket) in a public location'.[27] Furthermore, it has specified that when restrictions are imposed on public assemblies in order to safeguard other interests that the very same Article 21 mentions, it is the State's duty 'to demonstrate that the restrictions imposed on the author were necessary'.[28] The Committee has also expressed that the ICCPR standards are met only when those restrictions on freedom of assembly are imposed by a law and when the State is able to show that there is a rational connection between the restriction and the goals the State claims to pursue.[29] The regulations 'should be guided by the aim of facilitating the right, rather than seeking unnecessary or disproportionate limitations to it'.[30] The European Court of Human Rights has developed similar criteria regarding freedom of assembly and, highlighting its organizational aspects, understood freedom of assembly to encompass the right to both organize and to take part in public meetings.[31] In the same vein, it has reasoned that 'one of the aims of freedom of assembly is to secure a forum for public debate and the open expression of protest'.[32] Although the Inter-American Court of Human Rights has not decided a single case specifically dealing with freedom of assembly, it has included its democratic relevance within the umbrella of what it has termed 'general political rights', as enshrined in Article 23 of the ACHR. In *Castañeda Gutman v. Mexico*, the Court stated political rights are tightly linked to other rights, such as freedom of assembly, in making the democratic interplay possible.[33]

II.   POVERTY AND MOBILIZATIONS

Is there any relation between protests and poverty? From a sociological perspective some voices claimed the success of poor people's movements depended on their disruptive character, dismissing the need of having organizations behind the movement. If organizations have done anything for poor people's movements, the argument went, it has been to placate and deprive challengers from their transformative force.[34] Others, however, warned that this critique has a specific form of organization in mind which leads them to 'ignore completely the contribution and courage of organizers in these movements'.[35]

---

[27]   *Turchenyak et al. v. Belarus*, No. 1948/2010, UN Doc CCPR/C/101/D/1948/2010 (2013) (7.4). In a similar vein, it has clarified that a single individual protesting does not amount to an assembly, *Levinov v. Belarus*, No. 2082/2011 UN Doc CCPR/C/117/D/2081/2011 (2012) (7.7, 8.2).

[28]   *Zalesskaya v. Belarus*, Communication No. 1604/2007, UN Doc CCPR/C/101/D/1604/2007 (2011) 10.6.

[29]   *Kovalenko v. Belarus*, Communication No. 1808/2008, UN Doc CCPR/C/108/D/1808/2008 (2013) 8.7, 8.8.

[30]   *Sekerko v. Belarus*, No. 1851/2008, UN Doc CCPR/C/109/D/1851/2008 (2013) 9.6.

[31]   *Christians Against Racism and Fascism* (1980) App. no 8440/78 (ECHR, 16 July 1980).

[32]   *Evá Molnár v. Hungary* (2008) App no 10346/05 (ECHR, 7 October 2008) 42.

[33]   *Caso Castañeda Gutman v. México,* Judgment, Inter-American Court of Human Rights (IACtHR) Series C No 184 (6 August 2008) 140. A similar approach was followed in *Caso Escaleras Mejía y Otros v. Honduras*, Judgment, IACHR Series C No 361 (26 September 2018) 61.

[34]   Frances Fox Piven and Richard Cloward, *Poor People's Movements: Why They Succeed, How They Fail* (Vintage 1978).

[35]   William A. Gamson and Emilie Schmeidler, 'Organizing the Poor' (1984) 13 Theory and Society 567, 583.

This chapter takes another look, although a parallel can be drawn. It looks at the standards of international human rights law and asks whether rights may contribute to legally shielding poor people's mobilizations in posing their political demands. To begin with, has international human rights law been sensitive to poor people's movements resorting to protest as a critical means to participate in democratic life? This is an important starting point considering scholarship has tended to remark that one of the most democratically pressing justifications for the right to protest stems from the fact that it gives voice to those usually disempowered.[36]

Furthermore, some domestic jurisdictions have specifically remarked that the social conditions of those worst off should be considered when assessing the constitutional protection afforded to the innovative repertoires of political participation they are pushed to deploy, protests included. The Constitutional Court of South Africa, for example, recently held that: 'The right to freedom of assembly is central to our constitutional democracy. It exists primarily to give a voice to the powerless. This includes groups that do not have political or economic power, and other vulnerable persons. It provides an outlet for their frustrations'.[37] Years ago, and in a similar vein, the German Constitutional Court reasoned that in current times '[l]arge associations, wealthy donors and the mass media can exercise considerable influence [on public opinion], whilst the citizen feels himself to be powerless by comparison'.[38] What is the alternative?

> In a society in which direct access to the media and the chance of expressing oneself through them is limited to a few, there only remains to the individual, besides organised co-operation in parties and associations in general, collective exertion of influence by using the freedom of assembly for demonstrations.[39]

Has this emphasis been followed in international human rights law? Despite some limitations that will be explained below, the answer is affirmative. In sum: international human rights standards assume that those who are more likely to resort to protest are those who lack access to other alternative (allegedly more conventional) means of political influence, such as sending letters or publishing an op-ed in a nationwide newspaper.

A.   Poverty and Political Participation

Consider first the delineation that the human right to political participation places on the structural conditions of poverty. Article 25 of the ICCPR states: 'Every citizen shall have the right and the opportunity, without any of the distinctions mentioned in article 2 and without unreasonable restrictions: (a) To take part in the conduct of public affairs, directly or through freely chosen representatives'. Article 2 prohibits discrimination in the enjoyment of rights. Though it may seem that Article 25 places special attention on the formal means of political participation, such as the right to vote, General Comment 25 has made it clear that it also protects the right of citizens to 'take part in the conduct of public affairs by exerting influence through public debate and dialogue with their representatives or through their capacity

---

[36] Helen Fenwick, 'The Right to Protest' (1999) 62 Modern L Rev 491, 493.
[37] *Mlungwana and Others v. S and Another* (2018) ZACC 45, 61.
[38] *BVerfGE 69, 315 - Brokdorf Decision of the First Senate 1 BvR 233, 341/81 f* (1985).
[39] ibid.

to organize themselves. This participation is supported by ensuring freedom of expression, assembly and association'.[40]

Human rights documents dealing in particular with poverty also provide important considerations to bear in mind. The 2010 report on the question of human rights and extreme poverty, submitted by then Independent Expert Magdalena Sepúlveda Carmona, emphasizes the State's obligation to secure citizen participation. It underscores the need to also open avenues to allow bottom-up flows of information, particularly when this participation involves 'vulnerable and disempowered groups'.[41] The Final Draft of the Guiding Principles on Extreme Poverty and Human Rights reiterates States are under the duty to secure the meaningful participation of people living in poverty in the decisions and policies that affect them—although when specific rights are detailed, freedom of assembly scored no mention.[42] Former Special Rapporteur on extreme poverty and human rights, Philip Alston, also claims that people living in poverty 'are disproportionately and differentially affected by practical and legal obstacles to the exercise of their right to political participation', reminding States of the duty to take special measures to address their special needs.[43]

B.   Protests as Political Participation

It is precisely before this panorama of rights that protests may be resorted to as a tool to overcome structural marginalization. The revised draft of General Comment No. 37 on Article 21 (Right of Peaceful Assembly) underscores that, '[t]he right of peaceful assembly is, moreover, a valuable tool that can and has been used for the realisation of a wide range of other human rights, including socio-economic rights. It can be of particular importance to marginalised and disenfranchised members of society'.[44] The UN Special Rapporteur on the rights to freedom of peaceful assembly and of association, Clément Nyaletsossi Voule, has also offered illustrative standards. His 2018 report traces a direct link between Article 25 of the ICCPR and protests as means of effective participation for those living in poverty. Thus, the Rapporteur insists on providing an ample conceptualization of the right to participate, explicitly indicating that it encompasses a wide range of interventions, 'including protests and demonstrations'.[45] Moreover, '[t]he [legally protected] possibility to organize or join peaceful assemblies and to form or join associations is crucial to empower and mobilize people around an issue, to formulate grievances and aspirations, and to influence public policy decisions. In other words, those rights are crucial for effective public participation'.[46] By conceptualizing the right to political participation broadly enough to include protests and demonstrations, 'the key actors

---

[40]   HRC, 'CCPR General Comment No. 25: Article 25 (Participation in Public Affairs and the Right to Vote), The Right to Participate in Public Affairs, Voting Rights and the Right of Equal Access to Public Service' (12 July 1996) UN Doc CCPR/C/21/Rev.1/Add.7.

[41]   UNGA, 'Report on the Question of Human Rights and Extreme Poverty' (9 August 2010) UN Doc A/65/259 88–92.

[42]   HRC, 'Final Draft of the Guiding Principles on Extreme Poverty and Human Rights' (18 July 2012) UN Doc A/HRC/21/39 38.

[43]   UNGA (n 5) 26.

[44]   HRC (n 25).

[45]   UNGA, 'Report of the Special Rapporteur on the Rights to Freedom of Peaceful Assembly and of Association' (7 August 2018) UN Doc A/73/279 28.

[46]   ibid 26.

in the 2030 Agenda are allowed greater participation and inclusiveness, including through the empowerment of the most marginalized, underrepresented and vulnerable individuals, groups and populations'.[47]

Generally, the same criteria have governed the Special Rapporteur's report on his different country visits. For instance, in the report of his visit to Rwanda, the Rapporteur noted that when avenues to express dissent and air grievances are limited, the State should facilitate disadvantaged groups' freedom to hold public assemblies.[48] In the report of his visit to Chile, the Rapporteur addressed the specific situation of the *Mapuche* people.[49] Noticing that *Mapuche* demonstrations are regularly conducted according to law, the report criticized the massive police presence in these protests. In his words, that approach, 'seen as a form of intimidation—hinders participation'.[50] In his visit to the United States (US), the report notes the hostility toward the Black Lives Matter movement. Most importantly, after highlighting the movement's aims toward more inclusion for a 'historically and continuously targeted community',[51] the report went on to criticize the 'free market fundamentalist approach'[52] as an obstacle to social development. The report also expressed concern with the different police treatment received by different communities based on 'racial, ethnic, cultural and class-based bias',[53] thus questioning the disparity with which restrictive measures were imposed on disadvantaged communities. In his most recent visit to Tunisia, the Special Rapporteur specifically addressed the protests that have followed the movements of the 2011 'Arab Spring'.[54] While noticing that the socio-economic situation remains unstable, the report stressed that this instability has become the main grievance that Tunisians raise through protests.[55] The report reiterated that

---

[47]   ibid 32.

[48]   UNGA, 'Report of the Special Rapporteur on the Rights to Freedom of Peaceful Assembly and of Association' (14 April 2014) UN Doc A/HRC/26/29/Add.2, 24–26.

[49]   It is worth noticing the situation of the *Mapuche* people in Chile has long been in the eye of human rights organizations; UNGA. 'Report of the Special Rapporteur on the Situation of Human Rights and Fundamental Freedoms of Indigenous People' 17 November 2003 (submitted in accordance with Commission resolution 2003/56) UN Doc E/CN.4/2004/80/Add.3, 17 (recommending the Chilean State to 'avoid criminalizing legitimate protest activities or social demands').

[50]   HRC, 'Report of the Special Rapporteur on the Rights to Freedom of Peaceful Assembly and of Association on his Mission to Chile' (24 October 2016) UN Doc A/HRC/32/36/Add.1, 65.

[51]   HRC, 'Report of the Special Rapporteur on the Rights to Freedom of Peaceful Assembly and of Association on his Follow-up Mission to the United States of America' (12 June 2017) UN Doc A/HRC/35/28/Add.2, 20.

[52]   ibid 21.

[53]   ibid 38.

[54]   This context is of special interest once we recall that one of the main issues behind the demands of those joining the 'Arab Spring' was, specifically, poverty and access to economic opportunities. Ufiem Maurice Ogbonnaya, 'Arab Spring in Tunisia, Egypt and Libya: A Comparative Analysis of Causes and Determinants' (2013) Alternatives: TJIR 12(3) <https://dergipark.org.tr/en/pub/alternatives/issue/1691/20875> accessed 10 April 2020 (explaining that it was not just (although it certainly also was) a matter of confronting an autocratic regime, extended corruption and human rights violations, but also one of social justice and long-held 'social struggle against exclusion and marginalization.'); Amor Boubakri, 'Interpreting the Tunisian Revolution: Beyond Bou'azizi' in Larbi Sadiki (ed), *Routledge Handbook of the Arab Spring: Rethinking Democratization* (Routledge 2015) 71–73.

[55]   HRC, 'Report of the Special Rapporteur on the Rights to Freedom of Peaceful Assembly and of Association' (25 June 2019) A/HRC/41/41/Add.3, 25, 16–17.

protests related to socio-economic rights are a legitimate means of expression,[56] which the State must welcome and include in a democratic dialogue.[57]

What has happened at regional level? In the Inter-American system, the Court has highlighted that the socio-economic profile of the *Mapuche* people in Chile 'was below the national average and also below that of Chile's non-indigenous population, with a poverty level that was also revealed by difficulties in access to services such as education and health care'.[58] With this in mind, the Court termed the different forms of mobilization the *Mapuche* were conducting as 'social protest', thus defined as the means through which the indigenous peoples were trying to call the attention of authorities about their claims.[59] Since his 2005 report, the Special Rapporteur for Freedom of Expression (the Rapporteurship) for the Inter-American system has argued that the right to protest, being a fundamental right for democracy, is a form of participation to which the most impoverished sectors of our region resort. The Rapporteurship has noted that groups that lack access to traditional channels of participation often find in protests an effective means to bring their demands to the public forum. For them, protests may well be the only means of participation at hand.[60]

Whereas the standards of the Rapporteurship are not always crystallized in the Inter-American Court decisions, they may impact the work of other bodies. For example, the Inter-American Commission on Human Rights published a press release concerning the wave of protests in Chile in late 2019 to address state violence. It condemned the excessive and disproportionate use of force by the Chilean State against those taking part in the social protests.[61] Later, and after concluding an *in loco* visit, the Commission stressed that the demands the Chilean people were posing were related to 'wage and income inequality, access to education, health, social security, water as well as other social rights', and called on the Chilean State to respect the participation of all sectors of society, especially when claims involve social rights of different disadvantaged groups affected by structural inequality.[62]

This link has also been made at the European level, although in a more contained fashion. In *Bączkowski* the Court held the State has both negative and positive duties regarding freedom of assembly. Whereas negative duties demand that the State refrain from interfering with

---

[56]   ibid 25.

[57]   ibid 32–34, 106.

[58]   *Case of Norín Catrimán et al. v. Chile,* Judgment, IACHR Series C No 279 (2014) 76.

[59]   ibid 79.

[60]   Organization of American States (OAS), 'Protest and Human Rights' (OEA/Ser.L./V/II 2019) <www.oas.org/en/iachr/expression/publications/Protesta/ProtestHumanRights.pdf> accessed 23 June 2020.

[61]   OAS, 'IACHR Condemns the Excessive Use of Force during Social Protests in Chile, Expresses Its Grave Concern at the High Number of Reported Human Rights Violations, and Rejects All Forms of Violence' (6 December 2019) <www.oas.org/en/iachr/media_center/PReleases/2019/317.asp> accessed 23 June 2020.

[62]   OAS, 'IACHR Issues Preliminary Observations and Recommendations Following On-Site Visit to Chile' (31 January 2020) <www.oas.org/en/iachr/media_center/PReleases/2020/018.asp> accessed 23 June 2020. A similar emphasis was made by the Office of the UN High Commissioner for Human Rights, which visited Chile during the development of the protests. In its report, the OHCHR called attention to the structural inequality that was behind the demands of the people mobilizing and also to the disparate impact that repression has had on certain disadvantaged groups who also experience higher levels of poverty. The Office of the UN High Commissioner for Human Rights, 'Report of the Mission to Chile: 30 October–22 November 2019' (13 December 2019) <www.ohchr.org/Documents/Countries/CL/Report_Chile_2019_EN.pdf> accessed 23 June 2020 [8–11, 103–120].

protests, positive duties compel States to 'secure the effective enjoyment of these freedoms', particularly when groups protesting belong to a minority.[63] In a more straightforward fashion, the Venice Commission has stated that freedom of assembly protects the public gatherings of 'individuals and groups with different backgrounds and beliefs'. In that understanding, it can 'help give voice to minority opinions and bring visibility to marginalized or underrepresented groups'.[64]

As stressed in the introduction of this handbook, the relation between human rights and poverty has frequently brought attention to the relative or absolute impairment that poor people experience in the enjoyment of their social rights. Here I have highlighted another, although connected, aspect: how the restriction of participatory rights—specifically the right to protest and voice economic, social and cultural rights (ESCR) violations—may deprive people of one of the only means they have at hand to pose their discontent. The UN Special Rapporteur on the rights of peaceful assembly and association has recently built upon this preoccupation:

> The Special Rapporteur believes that having enough material resources and access to basic services is critical to lifting many out of poverty, but it is not all that matters. Indeed, while much of the attention has been given to the fulfilment of social and economic rights as a means to address poverty and economic exclusion, the importance of civil and political rights, including the rights to freedom of peaceful assembly and of association, cannot be overstated.[65]

This is, on its own merit, a reason to call States to interpret restrictively and keep limitations to a minimum. However, when we consider the compelling conditions poor people face, and note the right to protest might be the only means they have at hand to present their grievances, that scrutiny should be even stricter.

III.   LOOKING AHEAD

Section II showed there is a contingent relation between protests and poverty. Despite the fact that this relation has been emphasized by the very standards of human rights law, it has been somewhat obscured when it comes time to assess domestic regulations on the right to protest. This section marks this shortcoming and proposes the need for future research and development in two specific areas. First, it stresses the importance of bringing the equality principle into the analysis of protests regulations, therefore considering de facto discriminations that neutral regulations may pose. Second, it warns against 'proceduralizing' protest rights at the cost of the substantive claims of those mobilizing.

A.   Neutral Regulations?

Today it is commonplace in human rights law to accept that the regulations that States place on protests are compatible with international treaties. These are regulations related to the time,

---

[63]   *Bączkowski and others v. Poland* (2007) App. no 1543/06 (ECHR, 3 May 2007) 64.
[64]   Venice Commission, 'European Commission for Democracy Through Law' (Guidelines) CDL-AD (2019) 017.
[65]   UNGA, 'Report of the Special Rapporteur on the Rights to Freedom of Peaceful Assembly and of Association' (11 September 2019) UN Doc. A/74/349, 8.

place and manners of the protest (TPM). Whereas the Human Rights Committee has held that these regulations are admissible as long as they are proportionate and have the aim of 'facilitating the right [of freedom of assembly], rather than seeking unnecessary or disproportionate limitations to it',[66] the admittedly more restrictive jurisprudence of the European Court of Human Rights has held TPM regulations to be legitimate restrictions, as long as they have legal basis and are formulated with sufficient precision.[67]

These regulations should be assessed with heightened scrutiny, because those resorting to social protest aim to take part in shaping collective public decisions from a condition of marginalization. Therefore, whereas it is true that social displays of power have often been met with facially neutral regulations, it is also true that these very same regulations have an uneven impact on different groups. As Reva Siegel has shown, law has a non-combustible capacity to accommodate status enforcement through what appear to be neutral regulations.[68] In the fields of race and gender—as in probably any other—'the state may enforce "facially neutral" policies and practices with a disparate impact on minorities or women so long as such policies or practices are not enacted for discriminatory purposes', a standard too difficult, if even possible, to satisfy.[69]

The analysis of TPM regulations seldom pays attention to the specific impact these regulations may have on marginalized groups, let alone people living in poverty. For example, the Revised Draft of the General Comment No. 37 on Article 21 accepts TPM regulations as not being *per se* contrary to human rights law, but (for now) says little on the exacerbated impact these regulations may have on marginalized groups, including people living in poverty.[70] This is why the 2017 statement of the Special Rapporteur on extreme poverty and human rights does very well in recriminating this lack of attention to poor people's specific needs in terms of civil and political rights enjoyment.[71] There, the Rapporteur rightly claims 'poor people experience violations both disproportionately and differently from others'.[72] However, something that should be a cause of concern as well, when it comes time to address the particular topic of rights to participation, the report ends up limiting itself to warn against possible limitations of formal instances of participation, namely the right to vote. The Rapporteur's report of his visit to Chile followed a similar trend: after linking the lack of social rights enjoyment with a low ability 'to influence the shape of the society in which they live political participation',[73] the report stressed that this distortion could be appreciated when noting 'the higher the socio-

---

[66]   *Pavel Kozlov et al. v Belarus* (2015) CCPR/C/113/D/1849/2010 (2014) 7.4.

[67]   *Djavit v. Turkey* (2003) App no 20652/92 (ECHR, 20 February 2003) 65 ('A rule cannot be regarded as "law" unless it is formulated with sufficient precision to enable the citizen to regulate his conduct: he must be able—if need be with appropriate advice—to foresee, to a degree that is reasonable in the circumstances, the consequences which a given action may entail.').

[68]   Reva Siegel, 'Why Equal Protection No Longer Protects: The Evolving Forms of Status-Enforcing State Actions' (1996) 49 Stanford L Rev. 1111.

[69]   ibid 1130–42.

[70]   UDHR (n 8).

[71]   UNGA (n 5).

[72]   ibid [4].

[73]   UNGA (n 6) 24.

economic status of students, the higher their expected electoral participation'.[74] Accordingly, recommendations remained focused on formal instances of participation.[75]

B.   Taking Unequal Participation Seriously

If one of the reasons that justify why the right to protest should be particularly protected before possible encroachments is the fact some groups can only voice their demands effectively by resorting to mobilizations, then that very reason should also be used to assess different *de facto* restrictions of the right. In other words, the disproportionate impact of state policies should also be assessed considering these other, more informal avenues of political participation that marginalized groups sensibly prefer. This is something that the Principles and Guidelines for a Human Rights Approach to Poverty Reduction Strategies state very well. If, as the Principles note, '[t]raditionally, people living in poverty are left out'[76] from the participatory stages that precede resources allocation, States have the duty to develop new practices that go beyond 'the practice of electoral democracy'.[77] Of course, this means not only devising new formal and institutional avenues—which of course are welcome—but also securing the right to freely and meaningfully participate in the conduct of public affairs by resorting to other rights such as freedom of assembly.[78] As Guideline 8 holds, people living in poverty enjoy, and should be protected in, their 'right to collectively express their opinions by organizing demonstrations and similar types of public meetings in order to attract the attention of the Government, the media and the public at large'.[79] A still developing concern can also be seen in the UN's conceptual framework on Human Rights and Poverty Reduction, where States are called to develop a particular 'pre-occupation with individuals and groups, who are vulnerable, marginal, disadvantaged or socially excluded'.[80]

Therefore, neutral, vague and general legislation, public policies and frameworks may well run against the special needs and considerations that these groups demand and deserve. In the same framework, States are called to assess the disparate impact that general policies may have on people living in poverty. As discrimination may take many forms, and not only straightforward exclusions, States should pay particular attention to 'policies that are blind to the needs of particular people'.[81] In fact:

> The human rights experience also confirms the importance of looking at effects, not intentions. For example, if the effect of a policy regime is to impoverish disproportionately women, indigenous peoples or any other group that is protected by one of the internationally prohibited grounds of discrimination, it is prima facie discriminatory, even if the policy-makers had no intention of discriminating against the group in question.[82]

---

[74]   ibid 33 ('Belonging to a public school in both years implied lower expectations of formal involvement in the political system').

[75]   ibid 34.

[76]   OHCHR, *Principles and Guidelines for a Human Rights Approach to Poverty Reduction Strategies* (UN 2004) 67.

[77]   ibid 72.

[78]   ibid 74.

[79]   ibid 218.

[80]   OHCHR, *Human Rights and Poverty Reduction. A Conceptual Framework* (UN 2004) 17.

[81]   ibid 18.

[82]   ibid 18.

This explains why, when that same report turns to participatory rights—tellingly a paragraph below equality and non-discrimination—it calls on States to pay attention to the other rights that are involved. These are rights such as the 'free[dom] to organize without restriction (right of association), to meet without impediment (right of assembly), and to say what they want without intimidation (freedom of expression)'.[83]

C.   A Reason for Specific Assessment, Not to Drop Regulations

This concern toward the disparate impact that regulations have on people living in poverty has been more recently developed by the Special Rapporteur on the rights to freedom of peaceful assembly and of association. His 2019 annual report recalls that while limitations and restrictions on freedom of peaceful assembly have a negative impact upon all citizens who want to engage in public affairs, 'certain groups are at particular risk owing to their marginalization. In the context of development, the Special Rapporteur has noted the impact of these restrictions not only on civil society organizations at large, but also on those most disadvantaged in society, those left behind and those hardest to reach'.[84]

Specifically addressing TPM regulations, the Rapporteur has noted that:

> The need for prior authorization in order to hold peaceful protests—contrary to international law—and burdensome notification proceedings may present particular difficulties to the people living in poverty and organizations working with them in staging peaceful assemblies, as a result of their lack of resources and other poverty-specific limitations, including the inability to gain access to information regarding authorization or notification procedures, access to user-friendly formats to request permits, burdensome information and time requirements, as well as costs involved in the processing of a request.[85]

The critique of vague and general regulations on freedom of assembly are not to be read as a critique of human rights regulations *per se*, let alone of the TPM regulations that States have a legitimate interest in pursuing. In fact, although restrictions must be implemented following a well-settled doctrine in international human rights law,[86] States have found little trouble in delineating (when not suffocating) its exercise.[87] However, what this critique suggests is that these regulations ought to be assessed in stricter terms, particularly in the face of a global trend toward restricting the right to protest.[88] That trend, coupled with neutral regulations, falls harder upon the poor's shoulders, thus perpetuating a cycle of exclusion from the public sphere

---

[83]   ibid 19.

[84]   UNGA (n 65) 3, 23 ('A restrictive space for civic engagement exacerbates the exclusion of those living in poverty, including marginalized groups, and perpetuates the privileges of those in power').

[85]   ibid 38.

[86]   *Poliakov v. Belarus* (2014) UN Doc CCPR/C/111/D/2030/2011 (holding that 'under article 21 of the Covenant, any restriction on the right of peaceful assembly must be imposed in conformity with the law and must be necessary in a democratic society for one of the public purposes specified in the Covenant ...').

[87]   A summary and articulation of these standards, together with the cases that have contributed to delineating them, is found in Nihal Jayawickrama, *The Judicial Application of Human Rights Law. National, Regional and International Jurisprudence* (CUP 2002) 725–34.

[88]   Emily Howie, 'Protecting the Human Right to Freedom of Expression in International Law' (2018) 20(1) Int'l J Speech-Language Pathology 12, 13–14.

that begins with economic inequality.[89] What I am suggesting here is that international human rights law already offers some basic standards that are only waiting to be read in light of the specific experiences of those who are literally pushed to protests.

The 2017 annual report of the Special Rapporteur on extreme poverty and human rights offers a clear path. Instead of assuming that the differential impact of legal regulations and policies is inevitable, States should fulfil their positive duties by 'taking additional and tailored measures to address that added vulnerability'.[90] Recall the country visit report to Tunisia of the Special Rapporteur on the rights to freedom of peaceful assembly. Despite noting that mobilizations there have been used to challenge the unfulfillment of ESCR, the report only calls on the State to open avenues for frank and permanent dialogue with groups mobilizing.[91] Again, there is nothing wrong with formal and institutional avenues for democratic dialogue. But that recommendation may run counter to the interests and means that people living in poverty conditions find more suitable to deliver their demands.[92]

Although it would be difficult to devise in advance which measures States should take, States are under the duty to consider the 'specific needs and challenges' these groups face when exercising their freedom of assembly.[93] Though all persons are entitled to protest, States should provide—as the Inter-American Rapporteurship has recalled—'special attention' when the sectors that resort to mobilizations are the most marginalized.[94] For instance, people living in poverty could be relieved of the general obligation to file a notification before authorities so that negotiations on TPM may start. In the case of people living in poverty, particularly considering the highly bureaucratic path these regulations have followed, no notification should be required at all.[95] This proposal I am making here, as an example, is different from (though related to) the admission of spontaneous protests protected by human rights law.[96] In fact, in *Evá Molnár* for example, the European Court seems to be relying on the particular social and political circumstances surrounding a specific issue that citizens may want to immediately address (for instance to voice their discontent) by means of a protest. Thus, the European Court held that the dispersal of a demonstration may be a disproportionate restriction if there are 'special circumstances when an immediate response might be justified, for example in relation to a political event'.[97] Therefore, it is important to examine not only the circumstances, but the socio-economic conditions of those resorting to protests.

[89]   Martha F. Davis, 'Occupy Wall Street and International Human Rights Law' (2012) 39 Fordham Urban L J 931, 952–55.

[90]   UNGA (n 5) 16.

[91]   HRC (n 55) 106.

[92]   UNGA (n 65) 26, 61(d) (explaining that States not only have a general duty to facilitate empowerment and review their legislation, but also their practices in order to determine whether they are acting according to human rights law or not).

[93]   Venice Commission (n 64) 84.

[94]   OAS (n 60) 16.

[95]   ibid 58–62.

[96]   *Molnár* (n 32) 36.

[97]   ibid. The same trend has been followed in other cases. David Mead, *The New Law of Peaceful Protest: Rights and Regulation in the Human Rights Era* (Hart Publishing 2010) 81–83.

D.   'Obscured by Clouds': Against Venerating Protests Too Much

Last but not least, despite this chapter's emphasis on calling attention to the need to respect and protect the right to protest, it must also warn about not succumbing to the temptation of focusing all the efforts solely on shielding protests without paying attention to the substantive claims citizens advance by means of mobilizations. Before structural and dramatic inequality, we need to take precautions not to protect protests for the sake of protests. I take this cautious note from the similar debate regarding indigenous consultation rights. According to César Rodríguez-Garavito, 'the predominance of procedural rationality and the power relations among (supposedly) equal parties'[98] has had the effect of displacing substantive matters (in indigenous rights and their right to control over land and natural resources) by ways of underscoring the procedural aspects of consultation rights. Thus, in Rodríguez-Garavito's words, the debates on 'procedural intricacies'—such as the ones I have noted above regarding TPM regulations—take precedence over ESCR violations, thus displacing, replacing or postponing 'the more substantive conflicts'.[99]

Therefore, despite the emphasis of this chapter on the right to protest as a meaningful way in which people living in poverty may take part in public affairs, we should not overlook the fact—the very substantive fact—that behind that public appearance, there are people with unsatisfied basic needs such as housing, access to health and social protection.[100] Put differently, most of the cases related to protests show people posing 'claims [that] have to do mainly with equality, rather than with freedom of expression. In other words, social protesters do not usually engage in actions of protests because they feel that their expressive rights are curtailed'.[101]

Two final remarks will be offered regarding this concern. First, protests and mobilizations are themselves means that help secure socio-economic rights satisfaction. In this regard, mobilizations work not just as a proxy to identify an unfulfilled social need but as a device that will help to advance a more sustainable development.[102] This is because of the inevitable sense of disrespect involved in a public policy imposed in a top-down fashion. After all, as the Rapporteur informs underscoring the intrinsic value of freedom of assembly,[103] 'being the passive recipients of aid and having no voice in the decisions and events that shape their own lives is part of what it means to be poor'.[104] Also, participating in delineating social policies is a matter of rights exercise.[105] The Rapporteur on the right to freedom of peaceful assembly

---

[98]   César Rodríguez-Garavito, 'Ethnicity.gov: Global Governance, Indigenous Peoples, and the Right to Prior Consultation in Social Minefields' (2010) 18 Indiana J Global L Studies, 1, 29.

[99]   ibid 30.

[100]   Roberto Gargarella, 'El Derecho Frente a la Protesta Social' (2008) 58 Revista Facultad Derecho México 183.

[101]   Roberto Gargarella, 'Law and Social Protests' (2012) 6 Criminal L & Philosophy 131, 142–43.

[102]   OHCHR (n 80) 19 ('Although free and fair elections are a crucial component of the right to participate, they are not enough to ensure that those living in poverty enjoy the right to participate in key decisions affecting their lives').

[103]   UNGA (n 65) 11 (holding that '[f]or those living in poverty and marginalization, the ability to exercise the rights to freedom of peaceful assembly and association is constitutive of their sense of agency and self-determination and is a crucial element of empowerment and participation').

[104]   ibid 9.

[105]   The interlink between participatory rights and socio-economic developments inevitably echoes Louis Henkin's words that 'just as there cannot be any freedom or dignity without development, there

and association explains that: 'as poverty becomes more entrenched and harder to root out and extreme inequalities continue to rise globally—in direct contradiction with the Sustainable Development Goals—a key concern is whether development policies and efforts can be sustainable without the active participation of individuals and civil society actors'.[106]

Second, if protests themselves are means to take part in public affairs, an innovative way to have a voice in shaping the social policies that will impact the poorest lives, they should also work as a proxy on which authorities should rely when determining people's needs. Instead of criminalizing protests, States should respect and guarantee the right to mobilize (as the standards reviewed above hold), but also take a closer look at the substantive and material claims of those mobilizing. The 2019 annual report of the UN Special Rapporteur on the rights to freedom of peaceful assembly and of association has set an important agenda that needs to be furthered. It rightly called attention to the fragile basis of socio-economic advances reached without citizen intervention.[107] Thus, it recommended States open civic spaces where people living in poverty could participate—either through formal or informal means—in the discussion, design, implementation, oversight and evaluation of socio-economic policies.[108] Genuine and solid social and economic development will only be possible by bringing citizens into the room; not just for the sake of bringing them to the picture, but in order to allow them to present their different narratives and discourse—in a bottom-up fashion—as to what is needed in terms of social and economic policies.

---

could not, equally, be any authentic development without freedom'. As quoted in Arun Thiruvengadam and Gedion Hessebon, 'Constitutionalism and Impoverishment: A Complex Dynamic' in Michel Rosenfeld and András Sajó (eds), *The Oxford Handbook of Comparative Constitutional Law* (OUP 2012) 160.

[106]   UNGA (n 65) 3.
[107]   ibid 35.
[108]   ibid 13.

22. Advancing human rights through legal empowerment of the disadvantaged

Lisa Hilbink and Valentina Salas[1]

Around the world, laws and policies are increasingly formulated using the language of human rights, with access to public protections, goods and services promised to all citizens, or all persons, on an equal basis. A commitment to such universal rights-informed policies has been at the center of rule of law reform initiatives promoted by international organizations for several decades.[2] Yet, in developed and developing countries alike, for those at the social margins, human rights norms, national or international, often remain no more than 'empty parchment promises'.[3] Because in many places public justice systems are woefully underfunded, dysfunctional and/or corrupt,[4] international rule of law programming has often focused on addressing institutional weaknesses, with varying success.[5] In so doing, however, reformers have tended to adopt a top-down, technical approach that has focused too heavily on what goes on with various actors in or around the courtroom and has typically excluded and left behind the disadvantaged.[6]

In this chapter, we argue that advancing human rights requires going beyond institutional reforms, adopting an approach anchored in legal empowerment. Legal empowerment is 'a process of systemic change through which the poor and excluded become able to use the law, the legal system, and legal services to protect and advance their rights and interests as citizens and economic actors'.[7] The legal empowerment concept, first articulated by Stephen Golub and Kim McQuay,[8] is based on Amartya Sen's theory 'that poverty is a deprivation of

---

[1] We thank Bianet Castellanos and Christina Ewig for their helpful feedback during the preparation of this chapter.

[2] Tom Bingham, *The Rule of Law* (Penguin 2010); Rachel Kleinfeld, *Advancing the Rule of Law Abroad: Next Generation Reform* (Carnegie Endowment for International Peace 2012).

[3] Gary Haugen and Victor Boutros, 'And Justice for all: Enforcing Human Rights for the World's Poor' (2010) 89 Foreign Affairs 51, 56.

[4] ibid.

[5] Linn Hammergren, *Envisioning Reform: Conceptual and Practical Obstacles to Improving Judicial Performance in Latin America* (Pennsylvania State Press 2007); Michael Zurn, Andre Nollkaemper and Randy Peerenboom (eds), *Rule of Law Dynamics: in an Era of International and Transnational Governance* (Cambridge University Press 2012).

[6] Stephen Golub, 'Focusing on Legal Empowerment: The UNDP LEAD Project in Indonesia' in Ayesha Kadwani Dias and Gita Honwana Welch (eds), *Justice for the Poor: Perspectives on Accelerating Access* (Oxford University Press 2011) 373–412; Task Force on Justice, 'Justice for All – The Report of the Task Force on Justice: Conference Version' (New York: Center on International Cooperation 2019) <https://cic.nyu.edu/publications/justice-for-all> accessed 7 July 2020.

[7] Commission on Legal Empowerment of the Poor and United Nations Development Programme, 'Making the Law Work for Everyone' (2008) 3 <www.un.org/ruleoflaw/files/Making_the_Law_Work_for_Everyone.pdf> accessed 7 July 2020.

[8] Asian Development Bank, *Law and Policy Reform at the Asian Development Bank* (2001) <www.adb.org/sites/default/files/publication/29683/lpr-adb.pdf> accessed 7 July 2020.

capabilities and opportunities, with external constraints inhibiting an individual's ability to shape and exercise his or her basic rights'.[9] Legal empowerment works to undo the marginalization and deprivation inherent in poverty by strengthening people's capacity to advocate for themselves and their communities (process) and by enhancing their chances of correcting the injustices they face and improving the conditions in which they live (outcomes).

Legal empowerment bridges two international agendas: development and poverty alleviation, on the one hand, and human rights protection, on the other, building on 'the assumption that … poverty is man-made and can be abolished by making the law work for all citizens'.[10] As the 'Legal Empowerment of the Poor and Eradication of Poverty' Report of the U.N. Secretary-General in 2009 states:

> A characteristic of virtually all communities living in poverty is that they do not have access, on an equal footing, to government institutions and services that protect and promote human rights – where such institutions exist in the first place. Often, they are also unable to adequately voice their needs, to seek redress against injustice, participate in public life, and influence policies that ultimately will shape their lives.[11]

Sepúlveda and Donald put it starkly: 'Globally, persons living in poverty are often prevented from challenging crimes, abuses, or human rights violations committed against them, therefore exacerbating their poverty and social exclusion in a vicious circle of impunity, poverty, powerlessness and injustice'.[12] Legal empowerment seeks to break this cycle by strengthening the direct capacity of marginalized populations to use the law to find solutions to their justice problems, to exercise their rights and to increase the control they exercise over their lives.[13]

A legal empowerment approach to advancing human rights thus has a different focus than the conventional institutional approach, in terms of whom it targets and how. The conventional approach linked to the so-called 'rule of law orthodoxy' emphasizes reform of 'institutions and processes in which lawyers play central roles'[14] and, thereby, works from the top down. A legal empowerment approach puts ordinary people, especially the disadvantaged, at the center of the endeavor and proceeds from the bottom up. It does not view individuals as 'victims requiring a technical service' but rather as rights-bearers and (potential) legal agents who should be empowered 'to understand and use the law themselves', when and as desired.[15]

---

9   Sukti Dhital, 'Reimagining Justice: Human Rights Through Legal Empowerment' (2018) Open Global Rights <www.openglobalrights.org/Reimagining-justice-human-rights-through-legal-empowerment/?lang=English> accessed 7 July 2020.

10   Mona Elisabeth Brøther, 'The Political Economy of Legal Empowerment of the Poor' in Dan Banik (ed), *Rights and Legal Empowerment in Eradicating Poverty* (Ashgate 2008) 47.

11   United Nations General Assembly (UNGA) 'Legal Empowerment of the Poor and Eradication of Poverty' (13 July 2009) UN Doc A/64/133 para 8.

12   Magdalena Sepúlveda Carmona and Kate Donald, 'Beyond Legal Empowerment: Improving Access to Justice from the Human Rights Perspective' (2015) 19/3 International Journal of Human Rights 242, 243.

13   Dhital (n 9); Laura Goodwin and Vivek Maru, 'What do we Know About Legal Empowerment? Mapping the Evidence' (2017) 9 Hague Journal on the Rule of Law 157; Vivek Maru, 'Access to Justice and Legal Empowerment: A Review of World Bank Practice' (2009) Justice and Development Working Paper Series.

14   Golub (n 6) 378.

15   Vivek Maru and Varun Gauri (eds), *Community Paralegals and the Pursuit of Justice* (Cambridge University Press 2018) 3, 5.

To make the case for a legal empowerment approach as a means of advancing human rights and fighting poverty and marginalization, this chapter first reviews the theories underpinning the legal empowerment approach and key strategies of legal empowerment in practice. It discusses programs in both developed and developing countries designed to enhance the legal knowledge and capacities of the disadvantaged in different stages in the process of accessing justice and exercising rights. In addition, it reflects on the impact that such initiatives have in strengthening people's legal agency. It then provides a brief summary and discussion of the authors' current research on Chile, a country whose conventional institutional reform-based approach has been successful in improving the performance of the judiciary, but whose population has very negative opinions of the justice system. Our focus group data reveal that disadvantaged groups perceive the improved justice institutions to be exclusionary and socially distant and display a lack of knowledge about their legal rights and about where and how to seek remedies for potential rights violations. The Chilean case illustrates that improving the quality of judicial institutions is not enough to advance the human rights of disadvantaged people; equally important is attending to legal empowerment, making 'equality in law possible through ... mechanisms that compensate for *de facto* inequalities'.[16]

I.   LEGAL EMPOWERMENT IN THEORY AND PRACTICE

A.   The Theory of Legal Empowerment

International human rights instruments obligate states to guarantee citizens equal access to justice and legal remedies for rights violations.[17] Access to justice is thus both a foundational human rights concern in and of itself and a pre-condition for advancing all other fundamental human rights.[18] Without such access people will find it difficult to protect their person and property, challenge discrimination or claim their rights to education and health care. In practice, however, enormous swaths of the global population, especially poor people and/or members of vulnerable groups,[19] cannot or do not claim rights or seek legal redress when faced with harms and abuses perpetrated by private or public actors.[20] Many people thus resign themselves to living with injustice or take matters into their own hands, with negative repercussions for their economic and social well-being.[21]

---

[16]   Silvina Ramírez, Leire Otamendi and Alejandro Álvarez, 'Access to Justice in Latin America: Approach and Experience' in Ayesha Kadwani Dias and Gita Honwana Welch (eds), *Justice for the Poor. Perspectives on Accelerating Access* (Oxford University Press 2009) 557.

[17]   The principle of access to justice and legal remedy as a human right is clearly established in both the Universal Declaration of Human Rights (UDHR) and the International Covenant on Civil and Political Rights (ICCPR). Both documents also enshrine equal protection of the law. UDHR (adopted 10 December 1948) UNGA Res 217 A(III) art 7,8; ICCPR (adopted 16 December 1966, entered into force 23 March 1976) 999 UNTS 171 art 2 and 26, s 3a and 3b.

[18]   Francesco Francioni (ed), *Access to Justice as a Human Right* (Oxford University Press 2007).

[19]   See chapters by Byrnes; Vandenhole; Campbell; Madrigal-Borloz; Matache and Barbu; McDougall; and Quinn in this volume.

[20]   Task Force on Justice (n 6).

[21]   ibid. The 2019 Task Force on Justice notes that those with unresolved justice problems 'lose an average of one month's wages', and often suffer damage to their physical and mental health.

In the past, access to justice has been conceived principally in material or physical terms, with policies focused on the geographic expansion of institutional infrastructure and the reduction of costs for low income people, in what might be called a focus on the 'supply side'. Although 'supply' elements continue to be important, recent years have seen an increasing emphasis on the 'demand side', that is, on the 'facilitation of the use of courts ... and of other mechanisms of claims making by the people'.[22] To promote equal access to justice, civil society, governmental agencies and international organizations now focus on strategies that promote the 'legal empowerment' of the disadvantaged by 'placing the power of law in the hands of ordinary people'.[23]

Empowerment refers to 'a process of change in the power relationships whereby marginalised and disadvantaged populations make their own life decisions'.[24] An empowered actor 'is able to envisage options and make a choice' within a given opportunity structure.[25] Legal empowerment 'recognizes law as a source of economic, social, and political power'.[26] It thus involves strengthening the direct capacity of the disadvantaged to exercise their agency as citizens by implementing strategies that enable them to be 'aware of their rights, ... able to assert them and also hold the state accountable for their adequate enforcement'.[27] Legal empowerment's ultimate goal is to reduce poverty and foster development by increasing disadvantaged populations' access to justice and protection under the rule of law, so all individuals can 'make effective and proactive use of law ... in the pursuit of all legitimate life objectives'[28] and 'to increase the control that [they] exercise over their lives'.[29] In other words, as Stephen Golub argues:

> legal empowerment is both a *process and a goal*. As a matter of process, legal empowerment includes legal reforms and services that improve the bargaining positions of: [for example] farmers seeking secure land tenure, [and] women battling domestic violence ... As a goal, it strengthens such populations in terms of their income, assets, health, physical security and/or, most generally, freedom. The essentially bottom-up nature of legal empowerment means that it aims to build such populations' capacities to act on their own.[30]

---

[22] Yash Ghai and Jill Cottrell, *Marginalized Communities and Access to Justice* (Routledge 2010) 5.

[23] Maru and Gauri (n 15) 3.

[24] Sahar Maranlou, *Access to Justice in Iran: Women, Perceptions, and Reality* (Cambridge University Press 2014) 142.

[25] Ruth Alsop, Mette Bertelsen and Jeremy Holland, *Empowerment in Practice: From Analysis to Implementation* (The World Bank 2006) 6.

[26] Robin Nielsen, 'Sustaining the Process of Legal Empowerment' in Open Society Justice Initiative, *Justice Initiatives* (2013) 112 <www.justiceinitiative.org/uploads/112318e4-a2b5-48e4-a14d -742bb3b8bcfb/justice-initiatives-legal-empowerment-20140102.pdf> accessed 7 July 2020.

[27] World Bank, *Legal Empowerment of the Poor: an Action Agenda for the World Bank (English)* (Washington, DC, World Bank 2006) 21 <http://documents.worldbank.org/curated/en/ 991871468331228461/Legal-empowerment-of-the-poor-an-action-agenda-for-the-World-Bank> accessed 7 July 2020.

[28] Daniel Brinks, *From Legal Poverty to Legal Agency: Establishing the Rule of Law in Latin America* (Report prepared for D. Caputo, Agenda-Informe Para La Democracia de Bienestar en América Latina, Washington, Organization of American States 2009) 22 <https://repositories.lib.utexas.edu/ handle/2152/22487> accessed 7 July 2020.

[29] Asian Development Bank (n 8).

[30] Stephen Golub, 'What is Legal Empowerment? An Introduction' in Stephen Golub and Thomas McInerney (eds), *Legal Empowerment: Practitioners' Perspectives* (International Development Law Organization 2010) 13 (our italics).

Legal empowerment thus addresses poverty not only through strategies that correct material deprivations but also that mitigate the experience of being marginalized and deprived from development itself. It does so by building people's agency so that they can use the law and participate in law-related processes to solve their problems.

This new 'people-centered approach' to access to justice specifically targets the disadvantaged, which includes 'the poor, but also women, minorities, certain castes, indigent criminal defendants, victims of human rights abuses and other populations afflicted by discrimination or other injustices'.[31] In addition, it promotes the use of law not only in relation to 'legislation or court rulings, but the many regulations, ordinances, processes, agreements and traditional justice systems that constitute the law for the disadvantaged'.[32] Legal empowerment strategies thus strengthen the capacities of marginalized people to 'engage a wide range of institutions, including customary tribunals and administrative agencies, marking a sharp distinction to the narrow focus on the judiciary in much of the rule of law sector'.[33]

B.   Legal Empowerment in Practice

Given its focus on reducing poverty, strategies around legal empowerment initially 'focused on formalising property rights as a tool for people to economically develop in a globalised economy'.[34] However, '[i]t has now developed into a broader conceptual and political framework where property rights bundled with other rights, and a balanced framework of protection and rights in combination, aims to promote overall socio-economic development in poor countries of the world'.[35]

Nowadays government and civil society initiatives for legal empowerment encompass diverse strategies that focus on different stages in the process of accessing justice and exercising rights. Legal empowerment in practice begins with the foundational element of securing legal registration and identity for all people. Beyond that basic step, the legal empowerment agenda also involves initiatives to promote legal literacy and rights claiming, the training of community paralegals and the development of programs to monitor laws and policies that affect disadvantaged communities. The overall objective can be summarized in the concept of 'legal competence', understood in the following terms:

> The competent subject will be aware of the relation between the realization of [their] interests and the machinery of law making and administration. [They] will know how to use this machinery and when to use it. Moreover, [they] will see assertion of [their] interests through legal channels as desirable and appropriate. The legally competent person has a sense of [themselves] as a possessor of rights and [they] see the legal system as a resource for validation of those rights. [They] know when and how to seek validation.[36]

---

[31]   ibid 13.
[32]   ibid.
[33]   Goodwin and Maru (n 13) 158.
[34]   Brøther (n 10) 47.
[35]   ibid.
[36]   Jerome Carlin, Jan Howard and Sheldon Messinger, *Civil Justice and the Poor* (New York: Russell Sage Foundation, 1967) cited in Austin Sarat, 'Studying American Legal Culture: An Assessment of Survey Evidence' (1977) Law and Society Review 427, at 449.

A common aspect of any of these legal empowerment strategies is their proactivity in public outreach, that is, active practices in the community to bring the justice system to the citizenry rather than the citizenry to the justice system.[37] While most legal empowerment programs generally combine more than one of the above-mentioned strategies,[38] for analytical purposes, in what follows we review these different types of legal empowerment initiatives separately and discuss some notable examples.

1. Securing legal identity

Legal identity is 'a life-long passport for the recognition of rights' and is thus indispensable to the ability to 'vote, marry or secure formal employment',[39] as well as to access financial services (for example, open bank accounts and take out loans) and to secure property rights. In addition, it allows people to be 'taken into account when policymakers use national and subnational statistics to inform the design and implementation of government projects and pro-grams'.[40] According to the Task Force on Justice in 2019, over one billion people worldwide lack legal identity,[41] and in many countries women are less likely than men to possess legal identification. This makes laws against child marriage, for example, more difficult to enforce, and means 'women cannot take advantage of economic opportunities and exercise their rights as citizens'.[42]

Recognizing that securing legal identity for marginalized populations is essential to the realization of other legal empowerment strategies, the legal empowerment approach includes programs 'to make birth registration free, simple and available at the local level' and 'to reach out to those who have previously been left out of the system'.[43] Successful examples include one conducted through mobile courts in Côte d' Ivoire, which benefited some 900,000 persons in the wake of the 2007 peace agreement,[44] and a UNICEF program in Bangladesh that 'combined birth registration with primary health and education services', equipping 'health workers and teachers [to] register children who came in for immunizations or primary school enrollment', thereby increasing the percentage of legally registered children under the age of 5 from less than 10 percent in 2006 to 53.6 percent in 2009.[45]

2. Legal literacy and rights claiming campaigns

Legal empowerment interventions often center on legal literacy and rights claiming cam-paigns.[46] Programs to enhance people's legal knowledge and skills have been created at the

---

[37] Brinks (n 28) 22.

[38] Goodwin and Maru (n 13) 170.

[39] UNGA, 'Birth Registration and the Right of Everyone to Recognition Everywhere as a Person Before the Law' (17 June 2014) UN Doc A/HRC/27/22 6.

[40] Megan O'Donnell, *Why Registration and ID Are Gender Equality Issues* (Center for Global Development 2016) <www.cgdev.org/blog/why-registration-and-id-are-gender-equality-issues> accessed 7 July 2020.

[41] Task Force on Justice (n 6).

[42] Mayra Buvinic and Megan O'Donnell, 'Identification and Gender Equality: A Two-Way Street' (Center for Global Development 2016) <www.cgdev.org/blog/identification-gender-equality-two-way -street> accessed 7 July 2020.

[43] Sepúlveda and Donald (n 12) 247.

[44] ibid.

[45] Goodwin and Maru (n 13) 172.

[46] ibid 169.

municipal, state and/or national level, in developing and developed countries alike. These programs build people's rights consciousness and their understanding of when, where and how to claim those rights, to seek legal remedies and solutions to their legal problems and/or to navigate judicial processes. In developing countries, technology has facilitated outreach to communities to provide otherwise excluded or marginalized people with 'access know-how'.

In Sierra Leone, for example, BBC Media Action worked with local partners from 2014 to 2016 to broadcast a radio drama and discussion programme, *Leh Wi Know* (Let Us Know), to provide women in target regions with information on human rights and gender violence.[47] Episodes were created by local journalists and delivered in local languages, and, facilitated by mobile technology, 'reached 15% of adults (40% of whom were women)'.[48] In Uganda, the nonprofit organization BarefootLaw has been carrying out a project ('LEWUTI') that, through a combination of technological and traditional means, equips women with knowledge and skills regarding their property rights, both in rural and urban areas of the country. Notable among the activities they have implemented is the development of 'an information technology platform through which women and members of the general public can get responses to a range of legal questions and concerns'.[49]

In developed countries, civil society and state programs have also been designed to support people to effectively claim their rights and pursue legal recourse. The Welfare Rights Advisors in the United Kingdom, for example, provide direct expert advice on social rights and welfare benefits to which people are entitled and on how to claim them. Their goal is to enable potential beneficiaries to make claims for welfare benefits, bridging 'the gap between people's lack of specialist knowledge and [their] wariness of a complex tax and benefit system, and the potential gains in financial and social well being that can derive from successful social security claims'.[50]

In the United States, the Housing Court Navigator Program in New York City employs volunteers to help unrepresented litigants in obtaining information and filling out court forms, finding resources to assist in resolving their cases, providing moral support and responding to factual questions on the case addressed by a judge or court attorney.[51] In the Bay Area, the organization Legal Link partners with community-based organizations that serve low-income and housing-insecure families to train their staff with knowledge of the legal system. They can then help their clients in need of legal services to 'identify and triage [their] most common legal issues', the resources available to them and how to navigate legal system institutions.[52]

---

[47]   Radio for women's rights, BBC, <https://www.bbc.co.uk/mediaaction/where-we-work/africa/sierra-leone/womens-rights-radio-show> accessed 6 January 2021.

[48]   Kanwal Ahluwalia and Elanor Jackson, How can media and communication address violence against women and girls? (30 November 2017) <https://www.bbc.co.uk/blogs/mediaactioninsight/entries/8ac5922b-360f-4f7f-91f8-7b1148d4fd83> accessed 6 January 2021

[49]   BarefootLaw, 'Our Mode' <https://barefootlaw.org/lewuti/> accessed 7 July 2020.

[50]   Jay Wiggan and Colin Talbot, 'The Benefits of Welfare Rights Advice: a Review of the Literature' (National Association of Welfare Rights Advisors 2006) 13 <https://nawra.org.uk/Documents/Benefits ofwelfarerightsadvicelitreview.pdf> accessed 7 July 2020.

[51]   Rebecca Sandefur and Thomas Clarke, 'Designing the Competition: A Future of Roles beyond Lawyers: The Case of the USA' (2015) 67 Hastings Law Journal 1467, 1471.

[52]   Legal Link, 'Our Mission + Model' <legallink.org/our-mission-model/> accessed 7 July 2020.

3.   The community paralegal strategy

A common strategy in the legal empowerment approach is the training of and subsequent out-reach by paralegals from and in the community. Community paralegals are grassroots actors who 'use knowledge of law and government and tools like mediation, organizing, education, and advocacy to [help people] seek concrete solutions to instances of injustice'.[53] Community paralegals work directly with and actively approach community members to monitor for possible rights violations and to provide them with knowledge about laws that affect them, legal remedies available to them and the steps to navigate the legal system.

Beyond campaigns on legal education, paralegals help communities to find the best course of action to resolve the injustices they experience. Using their knowledge about the law and government, and their connections to lawyers and formal and informal justice institutions, paralegals work as intermediaries between the law and its related institutions and citizens, de-monopolizing law from lawyers and justice institutions.[54] In other words, they 'try to demystify law – to transform it from something abstract and intimidating into something that people can understand, use, and shape'.[55]

In 2011, the first international movement of community paralegals, Namati, was founded 'to grow a robust, evidence-based, global field around community paralegals, legal empowerment, and primary justice services'.[56] Namati has convened the first global 'Legal Empowerment Network,' bringing together over 2000 organizations and 8000 individuals that carry out legal empowerment strategies in over 160 countries.[57] Through this network, practitioners meet, learn from each other's initiatives and produce publications based on the experiences of network members.

Some Latin American members of Namati's network offer notable examples of successful community paralegal programs that train and promote women leaders, in particular. Brazil's Popular Legal Promotors program has been training local female leaders on gender issues, legal instruments and justice system institutions since 1990, with the goal of strengthening their 'knowledge about the law, and [their] access to justice mechanisms and institutions'.[58] In Guatemala, the Women's Justice Initiative has developed a 'Women's Rights Education Program' which 'educates women on asserting and protecting their rights [in areas such as] domestic violence, sexual and reproductive rights, and property and inheritance'.[59] From this

---

[53]   'Kampala Declaration on Community Paralegals' (26 July 2012) <https://namati.org/wp-content/uploads/2015/02/Kampala_Declaration_on_Community_Paralegals.pdf> accessed 7 July 2020.

[54]   Pablo Vitale, María Natalia Echegoyemberry, Felipe Mesel and Mariano Valentini, 'Prácticas de Empoderamiento Jurídico y Abogacía Comunitaria en América Latina: Asentamientos y Pobreza Urbana' in Natalia Echegoyemberry, Sebastián Pilo, Luciana Bercovich and Marta Almela (eds), *Empoderamiento Jurídico y Abogacía Comunitaria en Latinoamérica: Experiencias de Acceso a la Justicia desde la Comunidad* (2019) 41 <https://namati.org/resources/emp-juridico-abog-comunitaria-latam/> accessed 7 July 2020.

[55]   Maru and Gauri (n 15) 10.

[56]   Namati, 'Our Story' <https://namati.org/who-we-are/> accessed 7 July 2020.

[57]   Namati, 'Legal Empowerment Network' <https://namati.org/network/> accessed 22 June 2020.

[58]   Denise Dora, 'Los Derechos de las Mujeres son Derechos Humanos: Género y Empoderamiento Legal en América Latina' in Echegoyemberry, Pilo, Bercovich and Almela (n 54) 192.

[59]   Women's Justice Initiative, 'Women's Rights Education Program' <http://womens-justice.org/our-work/our-programs/> accessed 7 July 2020.

program, the organization selects and trains graduates 'to serve in leadership positions ... as women's rights educators, and mentors to their peers'.[60]

Finally, in 2017–18 the Argentine 'Civil Association for Equality and Justice' (ACIJ) implemented a training program for 30 women in the shantytown 'Villa Inflamable' on their legal rights, how those relate to the material conditions of their everyday lives, 'the mechanisms and procedures for the defense of their rights,' and the 'identification of the organizations and agencies responsible for unmet legal needs'.[61] The impact of such programs is significant. For example, according to its organizers, the ACIJ training program 'allowed its participants to replicate what they learned in their communities'. Armed with an understanding of rights as actionable, the trained 'promotors' were able 'to manage claims and information requests from the responsible institutions and bodies on their own [and] to carry out basic rights promotion and diffusion activities'.[62]

Such results are not limited to this particular program. Reviewing 'all available evidence' on 199 civil society-led legal empowerment efforts worldwide, Goodwin and Maru find that 68 percent of these reports measured increases in the willingness to act or actual action among people in the targeted community, with most reporting both outcomes.[63] Seventy-three studies (37 percent) reported that interventions led to the successful acquisition of remedies, entitlements or information for those reached by the program under evaluation. In a 2018 book, Vivek Maru and Varun Gauri provide a first-of-its-kind comparative analysis of community paralegals in six developing countries: Indonesia, Kenya, Liberia, Philippines, Sierra Leone and South Africa. They offer quantitative and qualitative evidence to show that community paralegal services 'increased people's understanding of law and government, increased their confidence to take action, and allowed them to achieve at least a partial solution to an injustice they would have otherwise had to bear'.[64] Moreover, they find that paralegals have some of their greatest impact when dealing with disputes between people and the state and disputes between people and private firms, which shows the potential of this type of legal empowerment strategy in shifting power dynamics and improving the bargaining position of disadvantaged populations in legal processes.[65] Future studies can and should be designed to further assess the effectiveness of different legal empowerment strategies in bolstering people's legal knowledge and legal agency.

4.   Community monitoring initiatives

Finally, legal empowerment also covers strategies that strengthen the capacities of the disadvantaged 'to monitor the extent to which local service delivery institutions like health clinics and schools comply with the laws or policies that govern them'.[66] These community monitoring initiatives provide 'people opportunities to assert their rights through enforcing gov-

---

[60]   ibid.

[61]   María Natalia Echegoyemberry, Pablo Vitale and Felipe Mesel, 'Empoderamiento legal Comunitario: Fortaleciendo las capacidades comunitarias en contextos de segregación sociourbana. Estudio de caso' in Mauro Cristeche and Marina Lanfranco (eds), *Investigaciones Sociojurídicas Contemporáneas* (Malisia 2019) 156.

[62]   ibid 156–57.

[63]   Goodwin and Maru (n 13) 173.

[64]   Maru and Gauri (n 15) 14.

[65]   ibid 17–18.

[66]   Goodwin and Maru (n 13) 160.

ernment obligations (such as in service delivery) and/or to make decisions related to budgets, resource use, or other governance issues'.[67] That is, they enable disadvantaged populations to participate in and have their voices heard in advocacy processes to shape policies and laws that affect them at the local and national level.[68]

An example of this type of legal empowerment programs is the work that Namati has been leading in Mozambique. Since 2013 they have been equipping 'community members to hold the health care system accountable for its service provision quality'.[69] These grassroots health advocates (or *defensores de saúde*) hold public fora with community members and health care providers to identify and address system failures, raise awareness of rights and health policy, and work with community members to seek redress for their health-related grievances and complaints. These activities 'have resulted in improvements to access, infrastructure, and provider performance',[70] addressing the gap between policy and implementation.

Another example is the Association for Emancipation, Solidarity and Equality of Women (ESE) program in Macedonia, which seeks to improve access to health services and their quality for the Roma population in the country. In an alliance with Roma civic organizations, since 2011 they have led a community program that monitors the implementation of preventive health services in four municipalities.[71] This program strengthens the capacities of the Roma population through 'community empowerment, education and awareness raising, conducting community information gathering, community-led advocacy, and presentation of community score cards, both at the local and national levels'.[72]

These different strategies for legal empowerment in developed and developing countries have contributed to advancing human rights by making the power of the law available to disadvantaged people. A legal empowerment approach places the agency of these populations at the center of its interventions. It recognizes the importance of involving marginalized communities, as rights bearers, in the process of seeking remedies and solutions for their problems. In so doing, this bottom-up approach to access to justice complements institutional reforms in the promotion of human rights and the rule of law.

---

[67]   ibid 170–71.

[68]   Vitale, Echegoyemberry, Mesel and Valentini (n 54).

[69]   Namati, 'Coupling Social Accountability with Legal Empowerment in Mozambique' 1 <https://namati.org/resources/coupling-social-accountability-with-legal-empowerment-in-mozambique/> accessed 7 July 2020.

[70]   Ellie Feinglass, Nadja Gomes and Vivek Maru, 'Transforming Policy into Justice: The Role of Health Advocates in Mozambique' (2016) 18/2 Health and Human Rights 233 <https://namati.org/resources/transforming-policy-into-justice-health-advocates-mozambique/> accessed 7 July 2020.

[71]   Association for Emancipation, Solidarity and Equality of Women - ESE, 'Roma Health' <www.esem.org.mk/en/index.php/component/content/article/13-what-we-do/88-roma-health.html> accessed 7 July 2020.

[72]   Anuradha Joshi, 'Legal Empowerment and Social Accountability: Complementary Strategies Toward Rights-based Development in Health?' (2017) 99 World Development 160, 165.

II.   ON THE IMPORTANCE OF LEGAL EMPOWERMENT FOR ADVANCING HUMAN RIGHTS: INSIGHTS FROM CHILE

Chile offers an example of the importance of a legal empowerment approach to fully advance the human rights of the disadvantaged, beyond top-down institutional reforms. In 1990, when Chile returned to democracy after seventeen years of dictatorship and massive human rights violations, the judiciary was 'in crisis'.[73] Critics argued that the administration of justice was antiquated and inefficient, that corrupt practices had emerged at the highest levels of the judiciary, and that judges had failed to defend and protect human rights and rule of law principles during the dictatorship.[74] In the years since, policy makers have implemented a number of important reforms to the justice system, including modifications to judicial training and appointment processes that have brought about 'deep changes in the organic structure and culture of the institution'.[75] These have been reinforced by an increase in the number of courts across the territory, reforms to procedural codes in criminal, family and labor jurisdictions, and the creation of independent Public Prosecution, Public Defender and Human Rights institutions. In addition, the Ministry of Justice has expanded the availability of free legal advice through the *Corporación de Asistencia Judicial* for individuals who cannot afford legal services and representation.

According to a variety of assessments, these reforms have been quite successful.[76] Indeed, by international standards of judicial independence, corruption control and other rule of law elements, Chile has improved significantly, maintaining very respectable scores since the early 2000s.[77] In the area of transitional justice, as of 2019 Chilean courts have issued final rulings in 426 authoritarian-era human rights cases, providing legal resolution to cases involving a total of 968 victims.[78] In contemporary cases, judges have proven themselves to be more assertive in the defense of rights.[79] Despite these improvements in performance, however, public confi-

---

[73]   Jorge Correa Sutil, 'Cenicienta se queda en la fiesta: El poder judicial chileno en la década de los 90' in Paul Drake and Iván Jaksic (eds), *El modelo chileno: Democracia y desarrollo en los noventa* (LOM 1999), 293.

[74]   Eugenia Valenzuela Somarriva, 'Informe Final sobre Reformas al Sistema Judicial Chileno' (1991), 41 Estudios Públicos 171; Correa (n 73); Lisa Hilbink, *Judges beyond Politics in Democracy and Dictatorship: Lessons from Chile* (Cambridge University Press 2007).

[75]   Jorge Correa Sutil, "Hitos y Lecciones de la experiencia chilena de justicia transicional," (2009) 11.

[76]   Correa (n 73); Rafael Blanco, Richard Hutt and Hugo Rojas, 'Reform to the Criminal Justice System in Chile: Evaluation and Challenges' (2004) 2/2 Loyola University Chicago International Law Review 253; Lisa Bhansali and Christina Biebesheimer, 'Measuring the Impact of Criminal Justice Reform in Latin America' in Thomas Carothers (ed), *Promoting the Rule of Law Abroad: In Search of Knowledge* (Carnegie Endowment for International Peace 2006).

[77]   Drew Linzer and Jeffrey Staton, 'A Global Measure of Judicial Independence, 1948–2012' (2015), 3/2 Journal of Law and Courts 223; Transparency International, 'Corruption Perception Index' <www .transparency.org/en/cpi/2019/results/chl> accessed 8 July 2020; World Justice Project, 'Rule of Law Index' (2019) <https://worldjusticeproject.org/our-work/research-and-data/wjp-rule-law-index-2019> accessed 8 July 2020.

[78]   Centro de Derechos Humanos UDP, 'Informe Anual Sobre Derechos Humanos en Chile 2019' (2019), 71 <http://derechoshumanos.udp.cl/derechoshumanos/index.php/observatorio/publicaciones/ func-startdown/526/> accessed 8 July 2020.

[79]   Javier Couso and Lisa Hilbink, 'Informe de Situación Estados de Emergencia de Chile, Octubre de 2019' in Gretchen Helmke and Julio Rios-Figueroa (eds)*, Courts in Latin America* (Cambridge

dence in the justice system in Chile has declined and stagnated at very low levels.[80] Indeed, in surveys in Latin America, Chile repeatedly ranks among the countries with the lowest levels of such confidence, together with Honduras and Paraguay – countries whose levels of institutional capacity and stability are much lower than those of Chile.[81]

In 2017, under the auspices of the Human Rights Initiative at the University of Minnesota, we conducted focus groups in Santiago, Chile to explore where these negative citizen perceptions of the justice system come from and how these perceptions affect people's willingness and ability to access justice and claim rights.[82] Close to 40 percent of Chile's population lives in Santiago,[83] a city heavily segregated along socio-economic lines and one of the five most unequal cities in Latin America.[84] For example, in La Pintana, a municipality in the south of Santiago, 42.4 percent of the population lives in a situation of multidimensional poverty. In contrast, in Vitacura, a municipality in the northeast area of Santiago, only 2.8 percent live in such a situation.[85] The focus group method allowed us to probe beyond survey responses to explore in depth the perceptions, experiences and expectations around the justice system of people sharing common demographic characteristics (social class, gender and age).[86] In each focus group we asked participants what they could and would do (and why) in hypothetical scenarios involving different harms/rights violations, after which we posed questions that prompted participants to unpack and consider the origins of their opinions about the justice system in Chile.

Based on this study, we found that, even as they recognize improvements in some aspects of judicial performance,[87] low-income Chileans display an alienation from the justice system

University Press 2011); Asociación Nacional de Magistrados de Chile, 'Status of Emergency Report of Chile, October 2019'.

[80]   For examples, see Lisa Hilbink, 'Judges, Citizens, and a Democratic Rule of Law: Building Institutional Trustworthiness to Recover Public Trust' (2019) 5 *Latin American Legal Studies* 165.

[81]   UNDP, 'Auditoría a la Democracia. Más y mejor democracia para un Chile inclusivo' IV Encuesta Nacional 09 Septiembre 2016 (2016) <www.cl.undp.org/content/chile/es/home/presscenter/ pressreleases/2016/09/09/pnud-presenta-iv-encuesta-auditor-a-a-la-democracia.html> accessed 8 July 2020; Latinobarómetro, 'Analysis Online' <http://www.latinobarometro.org/latOnline.jsp> accessed 8 July 2020.

[82]   These focus groups were part of a broader comparative project, entitled 'Equal Rights & Unequal Remedies: Understanding Citizen Perceptions of and Engagement with the Judicial System,' exploring these questions in Medellín, Colombia and Santiago, Chile. This project was made possible by funding from the Human Rights Initiative of the University of Minnesota (IRB STUDY00000744) and the Initiative for Multi-Disciplinary Research Teams at Rutgers University-Newark (IRB 18-026M). Our academic collaborators are Janice Gallagher (Rutgers University, Newark), and Juliana Restrepo-Sanín (University of Florida, Gainesville).

[83]   INE, 'Síntesis de Resultados Censo 2017' (2018) <www.censo2017.cl/descargas/home/sintesis-de -resultados-censo2017.pdf> accessed 8 July 2020.

[84]   U.N. Habitat, 'State of the World's Cities 2010/2011. Bridging the Urban Divide' (2010) <https:// sustainabledevelopment.un.org/content/documents/11143016_alt.pdf> accessed 8 July 2020.

[85]   Ministerio de Desarrollo Social, 'Informe de estimaciones comunales de pobreza, con datos de Casen 2015' (2018), 21 <http://observatorio.ministeriodesarrollosocial.gob.cl/documentos/INFORME _estimaciones_pobreza_comunal_2015.pdf> accessed 8 July 2020.

[86]   We conducted eight focus groups in Santiago, each of which grouped participants that shared social class (higher or lower income), gender (male or female), and age (25–35 years old or 40–60 years old).

[87]   For example, across all groups participants showed a basic knowledge of the new criminal procedure and expressed a belief that if someone were falsely accused, when they were brought for arraignment, the judge would order them released from detention.

at two different levels: first, Chileans from low-income strata express a general sense of exclusion from the justice system, which they describe as socially detached and aloof from their lived experiences and not as institutions that effectively serve the justice needs of people like them. Second, when they experience harms and affronts to their dignity, disadvantaged people tend not to understand these in terms of legal rights nor do they know where to turn or what to do to seek remedies.

The sense of exclusion and social distance from the justice system was evident in both the general assessments and specific experiences shared by low-income focus group participants in Chile. Many noted that the justice system works differently for people with money, power and/or family and social networks, compared to how it works for people like them: 'Justice is not for everyone'; 'The law is made for the rich', and 'only protects some people'. Participants expressed that 'Social status influences greatly what happens to you' and that 'if you live in a poorer place, they aren't going to concern themselves with helping you, or they'll be less concerned'. Thus, 'If you are poor, better hope nothing happens to you, because you are sunk!' Moreover, many low-income participants indicated that justice institutions do not pay attention to the social contexts in which people like them live or their specific needs in the judicial process. They expressed that those who work in the judiciary 'lack humanity' or that they are 'removed from reality', resulting in perceived injustices. One young woman criticized the fact that the system punishes someone who sells pirated CDs at the market to earn a living the same way it does someone who kills or sells drugs: 'it's not the same [but] they have them all alike [there]'. Another woman from the same group commented that when she filed charges against her ex-partner for psychological abuse, 'none of [the options that they offer you] are useful when you have other needs'; for example 'if he is in prison during the day, it won't help you to get the income you need for your children, when what you need is for him to work or that he gets some kind of psychological treatment'.

On top of this sense of exclusion from the justice system, we found that low-income participants in Chile display a lack of knowledge about what their rights are and what to do when they experience or face hypothetical rights violations or justiciable problems. Chilean focus group participants mentioned the word 'right' or 'rights' on very few occasions.[88] Indeed, the time an exchange focused on rights took place was in the focus group with young men from low strata, when one of them shared his experience of being unfairly arrested by the police. Because of his previous but unfinished formal legal training, this young man said he 'knew his rights by the book', and this knowledge helped him to avoid being further abused by the police. When he shared with the other participants that, upon being detained, he had refused to take off his clothes for a strip search because that action 'violates his rights', the rest of the participants reacted surprised, saying they didn't know that the police should not request that. He responded, 'No guys, they cannot ask you to do that. And that is the law: if you do not want to take your clothes off, they cannot force you, you know what I mean? ... If I did not

---

[88]   An important finding of our comparative research is that low rights consciousness and lack of legal literacy are not structurally determined but vary across democratic contexts. In Medellín, Colombia, even disadvantaged participants in our focus groups displayed knowledge of their rights and were familiar with the institutional remedies for rights claiming and legal mechanisms for conflict resolution (Lisa Hilbink, Janice K. Gallagher, Juliana Restrepo-Sanin and Valentina Salas. 'Engaging Justice Amidst Inequality in Latin America' Open Global Rights, April 4, 2019, available at: https://www.openglobalrights.org/engaging-justice-amidst-inequality-in-latin-america/).

have the education I had, the policeman probably would've hit me, he wouldn't care … they violate your rights'. In addition to this general lack of awareness of legal rights, Chileans from low-income groups reported low levels of knowledge on how to navigate the justice system, evident in statements such as, 'I told my son we should report [police abuse] but I did not know how, I did not know where to go'. This was emblematic of a more broadly perceived 'lack of information … about what procedures should be followed' in cases of rights violations in Chile. As one older man put it,

> we're in a bad situation because … I had no idea, for example, that if they arrest you, they have to take you for a physical examination … we are not informed about that kind of thing … and it's good that we are talking about it, because we are realizing that, in reality, we don't know what to do in a specific situation.

Our focus group data indicate that the current judicial system in Chile, with all its institutional improvements, fails to enable disadvantaged people to use law and justice institutions when needed and as desired. The Chilean case thus offers a clear illustration of the limitations of an institutionally-focused approach to rule of law reform, one that, conceived and designed from the top-down, 'define[s] the legal system's problems and cures narrowly, in terms of courts, prosecutors, contracts, law reform, and other institutions and processes in which lawyers play central roles'.[89] Even in a context where these reforms have been quite successful, vast swaths of the population, disadvantaged in various, often intersecting ways, do not see themselves reflected in or served by the justice system. In other words, institutional improvements are not 'trickl[ing] down to the lives of individuals'.[90] The Chilean case strongly suggests that in order to advance human rights, a legal empowerment approach is needed to strengthen the capacity of the disadvantaged to understand and assert themselves as legal agents.

III.   CONCLUSION

Strong justice systems are crucial to overcoming poverty and marginalization because they serve as mechanisms 'to prevent those in power from taking away or blocking access to … goods and services'.[91] But advancing the human rights of the disadvantaged requires more than institutional reforms; it demands 'a comprehensive set of measures that go beyond specific interventions in the delivery of justice services and legal information to address some of the more structural, systemic causes of obstructed access to justice'.[92] The legal empowerment approach seeks to contribute to this effort by building people's identity as rights bearers and enhancing their ability to use law and justice institutions so they can increase control over their lives.

   In this chapter, we reviewed the legal empowerment approach in theory and practice, outlining key strategies and their impact on advancing human rights. Legal identity initiatives, rights awareness and claiming campaigns, and community paralegals and monitoring programs have

[89]   Golub (n 14) 377.
[90]   Aylin Aydın Çakır and Eser Şekercioğlu, 'Public confidence in the Judiciary: the Interaction Between Political Awareness and Level of Democracy' (2016) 23/4 Democratization 634, 645.
[91]   Haugen and Boutros (n 3) 56.
[92]   Sepúlveda and Donald (n 12) 246.

emerged in developed and developing countries to strengthen the capacities of the disadvantaged to 'voice their needs, to seek redress against injustice, participate in public life, and influence policies that ultimately will shape their lives'.[93] As our research in Chile demonstrates, even where public justice institutions have improved their performance, mechanisms of legal empowerment remain essential in order to shift power dynamics and bolster human agency of marginalized populations.

The discussion in this chapter suggests that future policy initiatives on advancing human rights, whether state- or society-led, need to include a legal empowerment approach that places the needs and capacities of disadvantaged communities at its center. As the U.N.-backed Task Force on Justice has recently recommended: 'Justice for all depends on close relationships between justice providers and the communities in which they work and live [and] a new culture of collaboration, of openness, and of responsiveness to people and their needs'.[94] This people-centered approach to justice should thus inform policy makers globally in designing human rights programs so these initiatives can 'be shaped by perspectives of the people who are intended to benefit'.[95]

In addition, while legal empowerment strategies need to be attentive to the particular situations of target communities, more research is needed to systematically evaluate the impact of these initiatives. Future studies need to assess the impact, through common indicators, that distinct legal empowerment initiatives have on the process of empowering individuals and communities in using the law and justice institutions, on the one hand, and on the outcomes of reducing poverty and marginalization, on the other. Such evaluations will allow policy makers and practitioners to learn from other experiences and to improve their initiatives so as to achieve their full potential in advancing human rights for all.

---

[93]   UNGA (n 11) para 8.
[94]   Task Force on Justice (n 6) 113.
[95]   Ayesha Kadwani Dias and Gita Honwana Welch, 'Epilogue. Future Directions for Access to Justice within the UN' in Ayesha Kadwani Dias and Gita Honwana Welch (eds), *Justice for the Poor. Perspectives on Accelerating Access* (Oxford University Press 2009), 631.

PART III

MECHANISMS AND POLICIES

23. A human rights critique of contemporary social policy paradigms: new behaviourism, social investment and new universalism

Volkan Yilmaz[1]

Social policy, both as a discipline and a practice, is distinctive in its focus on identifying the root causes of social problems and in its firm belief in the ability of both social action and policy to change the world for the better. These characteristics make social policy an intrinsically value-laden intellectual enterprise, opening it to normative cleavages and laying the ground for the emergence of different social policy paradigms. The intricacy of the relationship between social policy paradigms and social problems partly results from its dialogical character. Different social policy paradigms put forward distinct formulations of social problems, which invite different social policy responses. Together these formulations of problems and responses form a more or less coherent way of thinking and talking about different social problems and their solutions, as well as a way of enacting social policies.

These coherent frameworks are policy paradigms, which Hall defines as frameworks of 'ideas and standards that specif[y] not only the goals of policy and the kind of instruments that can be used to attain them, but also the very nature of the problems they are meant to be addressing'.[2] Despite the value-laden character of social policy, the relationship between social policy paradigms and the formulation of the problem is intricate and hardly lends itself to being easily conveyed, especially when these paradigms are elevated to the realm of scientific or political certainty.

In recent years, new behaviourism, social investment and new universalism have been lauded in the scientific and policy communities. New behaviourism was established as one of the dominant paradigms in social policy after Thaler received the 2017 Nobel Prize for Economics, and the US and the UK governments embraced the paradigm. Social investment, which is mostly associated with Hemerijck, became another dominant paradigm when the European Union (EU) adopted the Lisbon Strategy in 2000 – a policy emphasis that was strengthened with the adoption of the Social Investment Package in 2013. New universalism has also been elevated to the status of a dominant paradigm with the adoption of the 2000 United Nations (UN) Millennium Declaration that put forth the Millennium Development Goals (MDGs) and endorsed the Sustainable Development Goals (SDGs) in 2015.

This chapter offers a critical analysis of select paradigms in contemporary social policy literature: new behaviourism, social investment and new universalism. Relying on a comprehensive review of the recent literature on these social policy paradigms, it uses human rights

[1] The author would like to thank to Cemre Canbazer, researcher with the Social Policy Forum Research Centre, Bogazici University, for her invaluable help in carrying out the literature survey.
[2] Peter A Hall, 'Policy Paradigms, Social Learning, and the State: The Case of Economic Policymaking in Britain' (1993) 25 Comp. Pol. 275, 296.

as a perspective to explore and discuss how the select paradigms either implicitly or explicitly approach and respond to poverty and conceive of the state's obligation to alleviate poverty.

Given the scientific and political significance of these paradigms and their potential real-world impacts, examining the blind spots in their ways of conceiving of social problems from a human rights perspective is a crucial intellectual endeavour. This endeavour is of special importance as social policy paradigms produce concrete effects not only by informing policy action but also by shaping public and intellectual perceptions.[3] This chapter offers a critical reading of these paradigms' understanding of the contemporary world and their theories of poverty alleviation.

This chapter is structured as follows. First, the chapter discusses the ways in which a human rights perspective can be used as a lens for examining social policy paradigms. Second, it presents the socio-economic context within which the paradigms operate; then, the following three sections offer a critical analysis of each paradigm. The conclusion examines the differences and some similarities between the human rights implications and responses to poverty of the select paradigms; lastly, it offers an agenda for future research.

I.   BRIDGING THE RIGHTS-BASED APPROACH TO SOCIAL POLICY AND THE SOCIAL PROVISION APPROACH TO HUMAN RIGHTS

The 'rights-based approach' is a widely used term in the social policy literature. Nevertheless, the systematic application of the human rights perspective to the analysis of social policies and their paradigms is still uncommon.[4] Despite the central position of the rights-based approach in the social policy scholarship, its core elements have rarely been articulated clearly, and an intellectual consensus on its definition has often been assumed but arguably has not yet been attained. Two elements stand out as points of consensus. First, a rights-based approach is often contrasted with a needs-based approach.[5] By constructing this duality, social policy scholars emphasize broadly the importance of the rule of law and democracy for social policies to serve the progressive realization of human rights.[6] Second, scholars argue that the rights-based approach to social policy should be transformative rather than affirmative.[7] Fraser defines transformative remedies as those 'aimed at correcting inequitable outcomes precisely by restructuring the underlying generative framework'.[8] With reference to social protection, for example, the UN Research Institute for Social Development suggests that the rights-based approach to social policy is one that 'fosters solidarity, social cohesion and coalition building

---

[3]   Daniel Béland and Robert Henry Cox, 'Introduction: Ideas and Politics' in Daniel Béland and Robert Henry Cox (eds), *Ideas and Politics in Social Science Research* (OUP 2010).

[4]   Shirley Gatenio Gabel, *A Rights-Based Approach to Social Policy Analysis* (Springer 2016) 6.

[5]   ibid 4–6.

[6]   See International Covenant on Economic, Social and Cultural Rights (adopted 16 December 1966, entered into force 3 January 1976) 999 UNTS 3 (ICESCR) art 11.

[7]   For example, Tim Stainton, 'Empowerment and the Architecture of Rights Based Social Policy' (2005) 9 Journal of Intellectual Disabilities 289, 291–2.

[8]   Nancy Fraser, 'From Redistribution to Recognition? Dilemmas of Justice in a "Post-Socialist" Age' (1995) 212 New Left Review 68, 82.

among classes, groups and generations' by building comprehensive social protection systems rather than relying merely on targeted social assistance schemes.[9]

The disconnect between the literature on human rights and social policy is stark. This chapter, however, posits that three characteristics of the human rights perspective make it a suitable tool for a critical examination of social policy paradigms. First, as Thelle succinctly puts it, social policy and human rights share a common focus on the state's obligation to tackle social problems and examine the relationship between rights holders and duty bearers.[10] Second, Donnelly's call for an alternative use of human rights 'in terms of systems of social allocation and provision'[11] offers an entry point to an analysis of social policy paradigms by paving the way to a more comprehensive interpretation of positive state obligations.[12] This particular stance on human rights differs from the aversion of human rights scholars to engaging with discussions of policy solutions. Such aversion is understandable from an international law perspective, as social policies fall within the state's margin of appreciation. This stance, however, often leads human rights scholars to take the legalistic line, adopt the violations approach, mostly disregard policy questions and embrace an emphasis on minimum core obligations.[13] Third, while most human rights principles, such as indivisibility, interdependence and interrelatedness, often do not stand the test of empirical analysis,[14] they provide useful conceptual tools for researchers to investigate how policy paradigms manage, consciously or otherwise, the trade-offs between different human rights. In this regard, the human rights perspective is suitable to analysing social policy paradigms because of its ability to offer a broad enough framework based on its guiding principles.[15]

This chapter suggests that the key elements of the rights-based approach to social policy and Donnelly's conception of human rights as social provisions are compatible enough to offer a coherent referential framework to analyse the strengths and weaknesses of the social policy paradigms. While the economic and social rights framework is also beneficial in offering an international legal basis to analyse positive state obligations in poverty alleviation, the framework proposed in this chapter aims to go beyond the unsettling distinction between civil-political and economic-social rights.

Three human rights principles – universality, indivisibility and non-discrimination – can ground this framework. The universality principle refers to the categorical and egalitarian

---

[9]   United Nations Research Institute for Social Development (UNRISD), Combating Poverty and Inequality: Structural Change, Social Policy and Politics (UNRISD 2010) 17, 157. <www.unrisd .org/80256B3C005BCCF9/(httpAuxPages)/92B1D5057F43149CC125779600434441/$file/PovRep %20(small).pdf> accessed 17 June 2020. A similar point has been made before in Walter Korpi and Joakim Palme, 'The Paradox of Redistribution and Strategies of Equality: Welfare State Institutions, Inequality, and Poverty in the Western Countries' (1998) 63 American Sociological Review 5, 661–87.

[10]   Hatla Thelle, *Better to Rely on Ourselves: Changing Social Rights in Urban China since 1979* (Nordic Institute of Asian Studies Press 2004) 7.

[11]   Jack Donnelly, 'Human Rights and Social Provision' (2008) 7 Journal of Human Rights 123.

[12]   ibid.

[13]   ibid 129.

[14]   Ida Elisabeth Koch, *Human Rights as Indivisible Rights: The Protection of Socio-Economic Demands under the European Convention on Human Rights* (Martinus Nijhoff Publishers 2009).

[15]   Markus Kaltenborn, 'The Human Rights-Based Approach to Social Protection' in Katja Bender, Markus Kaltenborn and Christian Pfleiderer (eds), *Social Protection in Developing Countries: Reforming Systems* (Routledge 2013).

nature of human rights as they apply to every individual.[16] Indivisibility is understood here as the principle that stresses the importance of treating civil-political and economic-social rights as equal, regardless of arguments that the latter belongs to 'a different logical category from the traditional human rights'.[17] Third, non-discrimination is the foundational principle for the rule of law and contains an equal treatment obligation. While most scholars focus on horizontal inequalities (inequalities between different identity groups at risk of discrimination) in relation to non-discrimination,[18] this chapter adopts an unconventional yet emergent approach that incorporates vertical inequalities (wealth, income or social outcome inequalities) in its scope.[19]

II. PLACING CONTEMPORARY SOCIAL POLICY PARADIGMS IN CONTEXT

Social policy paradigms are historical products. They are significantly influenced by the broader social and economic context within which they emerge and are used. However, they are also political products. The historicity of these paradigms does not imply that they are mere reflections of the social and economic environment to which they belong. The political nature of these paradigms are evidenced by the diverse ways in which they understand their context and their preferred set of actions.

Titmuss provided the first account of social policy paradigms in their social and economic context. His tripartite typology of social policy paradigms in the post-Second World War context includes the residual welfare model, the industrial achievement-performance model and the institutional redistributive model. These paradigms differ in whether they see poverty as a social ill to be addressed and in how they approach and tackle, either implicitly or explicitly, the question of poverty. In the residual welfare model, social policies refer to temporary relief measures that compensate for family and market failures.[20] This model assumes that poverty is always a minority and a temporary social position that emerges because of otherwise well-functioning markets and families. The industrial achievement-performance model uses social policies to award merit, work performance and productivity and therefore promote economic growth.[21] This model does not explicitly aim to alleviate poverty, as its main objective is to facilitate economic growth through social policies, including education, which will end poverty at a societal level. The institutional redistributive model treats social policies as an

---

[16] Peter Kirchschläger, 'Universality of Human Rights' in The European Wergeland Centre (eds), *The EWC Statement Series: First Issue* (The European Wergeland Centre 2011) 22. <https://theewc.org/content/uploads/2020/02/EWC-Statement-Series-2011.pdf> accessed 17 June 2020.

[17] Maurice Cranston, *What are Human Rights?* (Basic Books 1962) 54.

[18] Gaby Oré Aguilar and Ignacio Saiz, 'Introducing the Debate on Economic Inequality: Can Human Rights Make a Difference?' (*Open Democracy*, 27 October 2015) <www.opendemocracy.net/en/openglobalrights-openpage/introducing-debate-on-economic-inequality-can-human-ri/> accessed 9 September 2019.

[19] David Barrett, 'Tackling Economic Inequality with the Right to Non-Discrimination' (*Open Democracy*, 25 October 2016) <www.opendemocracy.net/en/openglobalrights-openpage/tackling-economic-inequality-with-right-to-non-discrimination/> accessed 20 March 2020; 'Report of the Special Rapporteur on Extreme Poverty and Human Rights' (4 August 2015) UN Doc A/70/274.

[20] Richard M Titmuss, 'What is Social Policy?' in Brian Abel-Smith and Kay Titmuss (eds), *Social Policy: An Introduction* (Pantheon Books 1974) 30.

[21] ibid 31.

integral yet separate part of the social organization that serves the common needs of citizens through public funding and non-market provisions.[22] Differing from the former two models, the institutional redistributive model works with an implicit understanding of being 'at risk of poverty' as a common threat to all or most members of the society, which may actualize if markets are left to their own devices.

Much has changed in the global social and economic context since Titmuss developed his typology. The evaluation of what has actually changed since the 1980s depends on which definition of poverty one uses from a wide array of options ranging from monetary poverty to capability poverty.[23] The decrease in absolute income poverty in the period following the 1980s has not been accompanied by progress in tackling social exclusion[24] and reducing capability poverty.[25] In the period between the 1980s and mid-2010s, income inequality between countries has decreased, mostly due to the high rates of economic growth in China and India, but it has increased within countries.[26] A similar negative trend is also observed since the 2000s with respect to wealth inequality.[27] While the share of the world's population that is employed has declined since the mid-1990s,[28] the global share of total income paid to workers (labour income share) has also decreased in the period between 2004 and 2017.[29] Accompanying these troubling socio-economic changes, social protection schemes still cover less than half of the world's population[30] and, for instance, the share of world's population that spends more than a quarter of their household budget on healthcare rose considerably between 2000 and 2015.[31]

In this context, a new set of social policy paradigms, including new behaviourism, social investment and new universalism, have emerged, especially since the 1990s, amending and,

---

[22]   ibid 31, 32.

[23]   Caterina Ruggeri Laderchi, Ruhi Saith and Frances Stewart, 'Does it Matter that We do not Agree on the Definition of Poverty? A Comparison of Four Approaches' (2003) 31 Oxford Development Studies 243.

[24]   United Nations Department of Economic and Social Affairs, Leaving No One Behind: The Imperative of Inclusive Development (2016) UN Doc ST/ESA/362.

[25]   United Nations Development Programme (UNDP), *Human Development Report 2019: Beyond Income, Beyond Averages, Beyond Today: Inequalities in Human Development in the 21st Century* (UNDP 2019) <http://hdr.undp.org/sites/default/files/hdr2019.pdf> accessed 17 June 2020.

[26]   Facundo Alvaredo and others, 'World Inequality Report 2018' (*World Inequality Lab*, 2017) 11 <https://wir2018.wid.world/files/download/wir2018-full-report-english.pdf> accessed 17 June 2020.

[27]   Anthony Shorrocks, Jim Davies and Rodrigo Lluberas, 'Global Wealth Report 2019' (*Credit Suisse Research Institute*, October 2019) 2 <www.credit-suisse.com/about-us/en/reports-research/global-wealth-report.html> accessed 17 June 2020.

[28]   International Labour Organization (ILO), *World Employment and Social Outlook Trends 2020* (ILO 2020) 24 <www.ilo.org/wcmsp5/groups/public/---dgreports/---dcomm/---publ/documents/publication/wcms_734455.pdf> accessed 17 June 2020.

[29]   Data Production and Analysis Unit, ILO Department of Statistics, 'The Global Labour Income Share and Distribution' (ILO July 2019) <www.ilo.org/wcmsp5/groups/public/---dgreports/---stat/documents/publication/wcms_712232.pdf> accessed 17 June 2020.

[30]   ILO, *World Social Protection Report 2017–2019: Universal Social Protection to Achieve the Sustainable Development Goals* (International Labour Office 2017) xxix <www.ilo.org/wcmsp5/groups/public/---dgreports/---dcomm/---publ/documents/publication/wcms_604882.pdf> accessed 17 June 2020.

[31]   World Health Organization (WHO) and The World Bank, *Global Monitoring Report on Financial Protection in Health 2019* (WHO and the International Bank for Reconstruction and Development/The World Bank 2020) 14 <https://apps.who.int/iris/bitstream/handle/10665/331748/9789240003958-eng.pdf?ua=1> accessed 18 June 2020.

at times, replacing Titmuss's classical paradigms. This chapter may fail to do justice to the nuances of each paradigm, as it treats them as more or less coherent to enable a general analysis. The literature on each paradigm, however, is dynamic and includes valuable ongoing debates.

III.   NEW BEHAVIOURISM

Behaviourism has long been a part of the social policy frameworks – since the early Industrial Era.[32] A revised version of this paradigm has gained prominence in the last three decades. The reappearance of this social policy paradigm dates back to the emergence of welfare-to-work programmes and 'active' social programmes (as opposed to 'passive' social programmes) in the 1990s.[33] The scope of the paradigm has advanced to an increased emphasis on conditional cash transfers in the 2000s.[34] The marriage of cognitive psychology and microeconomics later provided a stronger intellectual basis to this paradigm,[35] which started to inform a new set of policies in the 2010s, mostly in the form of state regulation of market choices available to individuals.[36]

New behaviourism underlines the fallibility of individuals, which hampers their capacity to make good decisions[37] that would lift them out of poverty. The fallibility of individuals originates both from their cognitive limitations and their immediate context, which accentuates these limitations. This immediate context also includes social programmes that fail to activate the inner qualities that would help them improve their situation.

---

[32]   Felix Driver, *Power and Pauperism: The Workhouse System, 1834–1884* (CUP 2004).

[33]   For example, World Bank, *World Development Report 1990: Poverty* (OUP 1990) <http://documents.worldbank.org/curated/en/424631468163162670/pdf/PUB85070REPLACEMENT0WDR01990.pdf> accessed 18 June 2020; Judith M Gueron and Edward Pauly, *From Welfare to Work* (Russell Sage Foundation 1991); Eithne McLaughlin, 'Towards Active Labour Market Policies: An Overview' in Eithne McLaughlin (ed), *Understanding Unemployment: New Perspectives On Active Labour Market Policies* (Routledge 1992); Lars Caimfors, 'Active Labour Market Policy and Unemployment: A Framework for the Analysis of Crucial Design Features' (1994) 22 OECD Economic Studies 7(41).

[34]   For example, Ariel Fiszbein and others, *Conditional Cash Transfers: Reducing Present and Future Poverty* (World Bank 2009) <http://documents.worldbank.org/curated/en/914561468314712643/pdf/476030PUB0Cond101Official0Use0Only1.pdf> accessed 18 June 2020.

[35]   For example, Richard H Thaler and Cass R Sunstein, *Nudge: Improving Decisions about Health, Wealth, and Happiness* (Yale University Press 2008); Sendhil Mullainathan and Eldar Shafir, *Scarcity: Why Having Too Little Means So Much* (Times Books 2013); Adam Oliver, *The Origins of Behavioural Public Policy* (CUP 2017); Peter John, *How Far to Nudge? Assessing Behavioural Public Policy* (Edward Elgar Publications 2018).

[36]   For example, World Bank Group, *World Development Report 2015: Mind, Society, and Behavior* (International Bank for Reconstruction and Development/The World Bank 2015) <http://documents.worldbank.org/curated/en/645741468339541646/pdf/928630WDR0978100Box385358B00PUBLIC0.pdf> accessed 18 June 2020; OECD, *Behavioural Insights and Public Policy: Lessons from Around the World* (OECD Publishing 2017) <https://people.kth.se/~gryne/papers/OECD_2017.pdf> accessed 18 June 2020.

[37]   Thaler and Sunstein (n 35); Mullainathan and Shafir (n 35); World Bank, *World Development Report 2015* (n 36); John (n 35).

New behaviourism portrays poverty as a changeable cognitive state.[38] Scholars of new behaviourism, for example, define poverty as a 'mind-set',[39] 'cognitive burden'[40] or 'epigenetic inheritance'.[41] The following quote from Shafir offers a good example of how this paradigm frames the problem of poverty and its response:

> The wealthy have a 'big suitcase' which allows them to pack modest items casually. The poor have a 'small suitcase' which must be packed intently and with great care. The packer of a small suitcase must carefully consider the size of each new item, and what can be removed each time they want to put something in.[42]

In response to poverty, new behaviourism prescribes different forms of state intervention that range from market regulation to targeted and conditional social programmes for the poor. States, in this paradigm, are designers of individuals' choice architectures in a functioning competitive market economy. While there is a consensus in the literature on the need for an effective role of states,[43] scholars disagree about the level, intensity and specific forms of state interventions.[44] By setting the improvement of individual decision-making as its main objective, one strand of this paradigm carefully distances itself from classic paternalism of the earlier versions of behaviourism, which gave too much power to the state. However, in some welfare-to-work programmes, beneficiaries still face benefit cuts unless they continue meeting the conditions.[45] Nudge programmes, on the contrary, as the policy solutions of 'libertarian paternalists', rely on non-punitive forms of individual choice regulation, which respect the autonomy of individuals to make their own decisions.[46]

New behaviourism may fail to offer human rights-based solutions to poverty due to two features. First, the paradigm does not address the contemporary unequal distribution of material resources including wealth and income or the worsening conditions of the labour market. Its exclusive focus on individual decision-making makes poverty and escaping from poverty primarily an endogenous affair for those suffering from it.[47] Its presentation of all choices as market choices further limits its compatibility with the human rights perspective. Given that the ability to make choices in the marketplace depends to a great extent on individuals'

---

[38]   Mullainathan and Shafir (n 35); Eldar Shafir, 'Poverty and Civil Rights: A Behavioral Economics Perspective' [2014] U. Ill. L. Rev. 205 ; World Bank, *World Development Report 2015* (n 36).

[39]   Mullainathan and Shafir (n 35); World Bank, *World Development Report 2015* (n 36).

[40]   World Bank, *World Development Report 2015* (n 36); John (n 35).

[41]   John (n 35).

[42]   Shafir, 'Poverty and Civil Rights' (n 38).

[43]   For example, Thaler and Sunstein (n 35); Oliver (n 35); John (n 35).

[44]   For instance, while Adam Oliver argues for the role of behavioural economics only to be informing against harms in *The Origins of Behavioural Public Policy* (n 35), Richard Thaler and Cass Sunstein suggest more extensive use of nudging in *Nudge: Improving Decisions about Health, Wealth and Happiness* (n 35).

[45]   For instance, in the Work Programme which was implemented between 2011 and 2017 in the UK, financial sanctions were applicable in the case of non-compliance. 'House of Commons Work and Pensions Committee: Welfare-to-work: Second Report of Session 2015–16' (*House of Commons*, 14 October 2015) <https://publications.parliament.uk/pa/cm201516/cmselect/cmworpen/363/363.pdf> accessed 20 February 2019.

[46]   See Thaler and Sunstein (n 35).

[47]   Also discussed in Paul Crawshaw, 'Public Health Policy and the Behavioural Turn: The Case of Social Marketing' (2013) 33 Critical Social Policy 616.

incomes in the context of stark inequality and the paradigm's disregard of the existing level of inequality, the problem with presenting choice-making as a private cognitive activity becomes evident. New behaviourism's neglect of the impact of income inequality on the options available for individuals may provide an excuse for states' nonfulfillment of their positive obligations, such as securing an adequate standard of living for their citizens. Its exclusive focus on the behaviours of the poor clearly limits its transformative capacity.[48] Furthermore, despite the fact that the success of most conditional social programmes (such as cash transfers conditional upon vaccination or school attendance of children) depends heavily on the state's fulfilment of their positive obligations in healthcare and education,[49] this paradigm fails to acknowledge the importance of these supply-side measures in complementing its proposed policy actions.

Second, new behaviourism does not stipulate the existence of floor-level social security, below which any individual may fall in the case that they continue to make 'wrong' decisions or fail in complying with the behavioural conditions of social programmes. This deficiency of the paradigm overshadows the indivisibility principle,[50] as it may lead to people trading their civil rights for social support. Worse still, individuals making repeatedly 'wrong' choices may be subjected to discriminatory practices and, thus, this paradigm may conflict with the non-discrimination principle, unless it develops imaginative solutions to this issue or acknowledges the importance of floor-level social security for all.

IV.   SOCIAL INVESTMENT

The social investment paradigm signifies the rebirth of Titmuss's industrial achievement-performance model, albeit in a new socio-economic context. This paradigm was developed to promote economic growth while, at the same time, responding to the 'new social risks'.[51] These risks refer to a nebulously defined set of novel challenges: the proliferation of atypical employment, long-term unemployment and in-work poverty; changing family dynamics as a result of the gender revolution in the labour market and declining fertility rates; and increased pressure on the healthcare and pension public budgets due to ageing populations. The social investment paradigm has become the EU's official social policy framework since the adoption of the Lisbon Strategy in 2000.[52] While the paradigm has gained interna-

---

[48]   Also discussed in Sarah Cook, 'Rescuing Social Protection from the Poverty Trap: New Programmes and Historical Lessons' in Katja Bender, Markus Kaltenborn and Christian Pfleiderer (eds), *Social Protection in Developing Countries: Reforming Systems* (Routledge 2013) 17–18.

[49]   Paul Harvey and Sara Pavanello, 'Multi-Purpose Cash and Sectoral Outcomes: A Review of Evidence and Learning' (The UN Refugee Agency 2018) <www.unhcr.org/5b28c4157.pdf> accessed 18 June 2020.

[50]   Also discussed in Guy Standing, 'Conditionality and Human Rights' (*UNRISD: News & Views*, 19 May 2014) <www.unrisd.org/sp-hr-standing2014> accessed 13 May 2019.

[51]   Gøsta Esping-Andersen, 'Towards the Good Society, Once Again?' in Gøsta Esping-Andersen (ed), *Why We Need A New Welfare State* (OUP 2002) 20; Anton Hemerijck, 'Social Investment and Its Critics' in Anton Hemerijck (ed), *The Uses of Social Investment* (OUP 2017) 8.

[52]   European Parliament Directorate-General for Internal Policies, 'The Lisbon Strategy 2000–2010: An Analysis and Evaluation of the Methods Used and Results Achieved' (European Parliament 2010) <www.europarl.europa.eu/document/activities/cont/201107/20110718ATT24270/20110718ATT24270EN.pdf> accessed 5 August 2019.

tional relevance that transcends the boundaries of the EU,[53] the literature on it is concentrated on the European experiences and debates. In addition to the 'new social risks' listed above, the EU also sees intensified international competition as a significant risk to the sustainability of its economic success and considers the rise of the knowledge economy as an opportunity to reinstate its favourable international standing.[54]

Similar to Titmuss's characterization of the industrial achievement-performance model, the social investment paradigm does not directly engage with poverty as a social problem. The paradigm adopts a rather holistic approach to development and attributes key importance to the success of development in improving the living conditions in society. Different from the industrial achievement-performance model, however, this paradigm puts more emphasis on human capital development as a core component of its strategy to achieve and sustain high rates of economic growth.[55] Therefore, in this paradigm, poverty is not a social condition that a portion of society faces; rather, it is a symptom of the failure of economic and human capital development strategies.

To tackle the 'new social risks', the social investment paradigm offers a social policy strategy that is based on preventative[56] rather than compensatory social programmes[57] and capacitating[58] and active social services[59] rather than 'passive' social insurance programmes.[60] This strategy is developed in reference to the paradigm's criticisms of 'passive' social insurance programmes that dominated the classical welfare states in Europe after the Second World War.[61] Hemerijck describes the novelty of the paradigm as follows:

> Unlike traditional social security, based on compensation and mitigation through income support 'here and now' after social misfortune has struck, social investment policies aim at preparing rather than repairing, focusing on the roots of social problems and emphasizing prevention rather than cure, hence the focus on ex-ante service support for children and families and investment in human capital and capabilities throughout the life course.[62]

---

[53]   For example, Johan Sandberg and Moira Nelson, 'Social Investment in Latin America' in Anton Hemerijck (ed), *The Uses of Social Investment* (OUP 2017) 278–86. For an international early childhood education and care perspective, see also Hans-Peter Blossfeld and others (eds), *Childcare, Early Education and Social Inequality: An International Perspective* (Edward Elgar Publishing 2017). For the uses of social investment in South Korea, see also Timo Fleckenstein and Soohyun Christine Lee, 'A Social Investment Turn in East Asia? South Korea in Comparative Perspective' in Anton Hemerijck (ed), *The Uses of Social Investment* (OUP 2017) 266–77.

[54]   See Treaty of Lisbon [2007] OJ C 306/1, art 2 para 3 <https://eur-lex.europa.eu/legal-content/EN/TXT/?uri=celex:12007L/TXT> accessed 5 August 2019.

[55]   Esping-Andersen (n 51) 3; Duncan Gallie, 'The Quality of Working Life in Welfare Strategy' in Gøsta Esping-Andersen (ed), *Why We Need A New Welfare State* (OUP 2002) 126; Anton Hemerijck, *Changing Welfare States* (OUP 2013) 36; Hemerijck, 'Social Investment and Its Critics' (n 51) 21; David Stoesz, *The Investment State: Charting the Future of Social Policy* (OUP 2018) 157.

[56]   Esping-Andersen (n 51) 5; Gallie (n 55) 119; Hemerijck, 'Social Investment and Its Critics' (n 51) 19.

[57]   For example, Hemerijck, *Changing Welfare States* (n 55) 180.

[58]   For example, ibid 222; Hemerijck, 'Social Investment and Its Critics' (n 51) 7.

[59]   For example, Gallie (n 55) 119; Hemerijck, *Changing Welfare States* (n 55) 138; Hemerijck, 'Social Investment and Its Critics' (n 51) 21.

[60]   For example, Hemerijck, *Changing Welfare States* (n 55) 138, 180; Hemerijck, 'Social Investment and Its Critics' (n 51) 6, 8.

[61]   Esping-Andersen (n 51) 20; Hemerijck, *Changing Welfare States* (n 55) 138.

[62]   Anton Hemerijck, 'Social Investment and Its Critics' (n 51) 10.

This paradigm argues that the effectiveness of 'passive' social insurance programmes has to be questioned as they have dealt with social risks reactively rather than proactively.[63] The questioning of these programmes is seen as crucial because they offer monetary compensation for avoidable and undesired results rather than empowering individuals to take precautions against social risks and therefore prevent their suffering.[64] Consequently, the paradigm notes, these programmes have limited the human potential to act as partners of social and economic development and to self-improve. In other words, this paradigm hints at the tendency of 'traditional' social insurance programs to give rise to the problem of moral hazard. Moreover, the paradigm implies that reliance on these programmes has also resulted in increased public budgets.[65]

States have an ambitious role in social policy in the social investment paradigm,[66] which is described as that of future-maker and development agent. Two major roles of states are contributing to human capital investment – the 'stock' function[67] – and the facilitating of individuals' adaptation to the fast-changing economic environment and to any risks in life – the 'flow' function.[68] On the one hand, the role that this paradigm attributes to states bears a close resemblance to the new behaviourism because states are presented as agents that help individuals to help themselves. On the other hand, in this paradigm states are visionaries, and their policy responses can shift the broader socio-economic context. Unlike the perception of states in new behaviourism as altering the choice architecture of individuals as it applies to the marketplace only, social investment states aspire to change the socio-economic environment within which individuals are placed.

To perform the 'stock' function, states are expected to invest in early childhood education and care (ECEC) programmes[69] and active labour market programmes (ALMPs).[70] ECEC programmes have received special attention.[71] Drawing on the insights of developmental psychology, social investment scholars present ECEC programmes as a form of 'predistribution'[72] and a better alternative to redistributive programmes in adult life. When the paradigm is applied to the Global South, it is often simply reduced again to conditional cash transfers[73] – a lack of vision that this paradigm shares with new behaviourism.

[63]   Anton Hemerijck, *Changing Welfare States* (n 55) 138.

[64]   Hemerijck, 'Social Investment and Its Critics' (n 51) 10.

[65]   Hemerijck, *Changing Welfare States* (n 55) 206.

[66]   For example, Maurizio Ferrera, 'From the Welfare State to the Social Investment State' (2009) 117 Rivista Internazionale Di Scienze Sociali 513; Hemerijck, *Changing Welfare States* (n 55); Stoesz (n 55); Marius Busemeyer and others, 'The Future of the Social Investment State: Politics, Policies, and Outcomes' (2018) 25 J.E.P.P. 801.

[67]   Anton Hemerijck, 'Social Investment and Its Critics' (n 51) 20.

[68]   ibid.

[69]   For example, Gøsta Esping-Andersen, 'A Child-Centred Social Investment Strategy' in Gøsta Esping-Andersen (ed), *Why We Need A New Welfare State* (OUP 2002) 26–67; Hemerijck, 'Social Investment and Its Critics' (n 51) 3–41.

[70]   For example, Anton Hemerijck, 'The Uses of Affordable Social Investment' in Anton Hemerijck (ed), *The Uses of Social Investment* (OUP 2017) 386.

[71]   For example, Esping-Andersen, 'A Child-Centred Social Investment Strategy' (n 69) 26–67; Margarita León, 'Social Investment and Childcare Expansion: A Perfect Match?' in Anton Hemerijck (ed), *The Uses of Social Investment* (OUP 2017) 118–27; Susan Baines and others (eds), *Implementing Innovative Social Investment: Strategic Lessons from Europe* (Policy Press 2020).

[72]   James J Heckman, *Giving Kids a Fair Chance (A Strategy that Works)* (MIT Press 2013).

[73]   Jane Jenson, 'Developing and Spreading a Social Investment Perspective: The World Bank and OECD Compared' in Anton Hemerijck (ed), *The Uses of Social Investment* (OUP 2017) 207–16.

The social investment paradigm may fall short of delivering human rights-based solutions to poverty for two reasons. First, the strong focus on employability, as both a means to economic and human development and as evidence of such development, may fail to offer comprehensive protection from, and compensation for, poverty in the age of decreasing global employment and declining labour share. While the paradigm obviously makes a trade-off between job and employment security in the context of fast-changing production and strong competition in the global market, it fails to complement its employment-centred strategy with necessary safeguards to ensure access to work that pays a living wage. This deficiency of the paradigm undermines its promise for an improvement in living conditions for all. Furthermore, the paradigm makes no explicit commitment to the ideal of full employment. In this regard, its impact on those whose employability is (or has become) low or whose position in the labour market is vulnerable for reasons that are beyond their control should be carefully examined. How the social investment paradigm will articulate those individuals into its social policy is still an open question.

Second, the social investment paradigm may be overestimating the state's capacity for foresight and the ability of the preventive policies to avert all undesired outcomes. The paradigm, in its current version, has an unfounded expectation that individuals, empowered by preventive and capacitating programmes, will perfectly comply with its broader economic and human development objectives and all will succeed in the end. While social investment scholars mention the 'buffer'[74] function of social programmes, which refers to a form of guaranteed minimum, they nevertheless do not offer any clarification about the content and the scope of this function. The lack of a definition of the guaranteed minimum risks undermines the principle of universality, as it may lead to exclusion of the long-term unemployed and those whose employability is low from the benefits of the projected economic growth. Furthermore, the potential impact that scholars expect the social investment paradigm to have on existing welfare systems is unclear. This lack of clarification leaves the question open as to whether the social investment paradigm will decrease or complement the existing social protection programmes,[75] especially old-age pensions.

V.   NEW UNIVERSALISM

Universalism is another well-established paradigm in social policy and was discussed earlier, in Titmuss's writings, under the name of the institutional redistributive model. This paradigm played a key role in social policy-making in the heyday of the post-war classical welfare states and beyond[76] until the Washington Consensus in the late-1980s.[77] Despite losing ground for nearly two decades, a new version of universalism has once again become one of the influential social policy paradigms – especially with the adoption of the 2000 UN Millennium

---

[74]   Anton Hemerijck, 'Social Investment and Its Critics' (n 51) 21.

[75]   Also discussed in Jean-Claude Barbier, '"Social Investment": With or Against Social Protection?' in Anton Hemerijck (ed), *The Uses of Social Investment* (OUP 2017) 51.

[76]   The United Nations Children's Fund (UNICEF) and WHO, 'Declaration of Alma-Ata: International Conference on Primary Health Care, Alma Ata, USSR' (*WHO*, 6–12 September 1978) <www.who.int/publications/almaata_declaration_en.pdf> accessed 5 August 2019.

[77]   Bob Deacon, 'From "Safety Nets" Back to "Universal Social Provision": Is the Global Tide Turning?' (2005) 5 Global Social Policy 19, 21.

Declaration,[78] which put forth the MDGs.[79] Its position was further strengthened with the endorsement of the SDGs in 2015.[80]

Since its resurrection, however, the problem formulation in the universalism literature seems to have bifurcated: one problem formulation for the Global North[81] and one for the Global South.[82] While the former deals with the tension between diversity (especially immigration) and universalism, the latter deals with unmet needs for basic social services and coverage deficits in social protection systems. For example, Anttonen and Sipilä describe the main challenge to universalism in the Global North today as follows: 'Insofar as there are universal needs, there will still be some scope for universal measures. But sustaining procedural universalism in services that deal with context-specific needs or cultural preferences seems more difficult'.[83] However, as the International Labour Organization suggests, the major challenge in the Global South, for instance, is 'the extension of social protection coverage to those in the informal economy and facilitating their transition to the formal economy'.[84]

The inclusion of human diversity in social policy thinking and the questioning of citizenship-based rights have undoubtedly expanded the boundaries of the debate on universalism. The bifurcation of scholarly and policy debates on universalism, however, carries the risk of underestimating emerging unmet needs and coverage deficits in the Global North[85] and the challenge that diversity poses to the applicability of procedural universalism in the Global South. For the sake of coherence in the analysis of the paradigm's focus on poverty, the remaining part of this section focusses on the literature on universalism for the Global South.

Drawing on a theory of universal basic needs and capabilities,[86] this paradigm departs from a clear normative reference point – human rights. The new universalist paradigm, unlike the two paradigms discussed earlier, engages explicitly with the distributional dynamics and poverty-producing factors that are exogenous to individuals. Poverty, according to this paradigm, originates mainly from unjustified barriers that limit individual access to basic needs

---

[78]   UNGA, 'United Nations Millennium Declaration' (18 September 2000) UN Doc A/Res/55/2.

[79]   'Background' (*United Nations: Millennium Development Goals and Beyond 2015*) <www.un.org/millenniumgoals/bkgd.shtml> accessed 6 August 2019.

[80]   'Sustainable Development Goals' (*United Nations: Sustainable Development Goals*) <www.un.org/sustainabledevelopment/> accessed 6 August 2019.

[81]   For example, Simon Thompson and Paul Hoggett, 'Universalism, Selectivism and Particularism: Towards a Postmodern Social Policy' (1996) 16 Critical Social Policy 21; Anneli Anttonen and others, 'Universalism and the Challenge of Diversity' in Anneli Anttonen, Liisa Häikiö and Kolbeinn Stefánsson (eds), *Welfare State, Universalism and Diversity* (Edward Elgar 2012) 1–15.

[82]   For example, Simone Cecchini (eds), *Towards Universal Social Protection: Latin American Pathways and Policy Tools* (United Nations 2015) <https://repositorio.cepal.org/bitstream/handle/11362/39484/1/S1500752_en.pdf> accessed 18 June 2020; Juliana Martínez Franzoni and Diego Sánchez-Ancochea, 'Achieving Universalism in Developing Countries: 2016 UNDP Human Development Report Background Paper' (*UNDP*, 2016) <http://hdr.undp.org/sites/default/files/franzoni_sanchez_layout.pdf> accessed 6 August 2019.

[83]   Anneli Anttonen, Liisa Häikiö and Kolbeinn Stefánsson, 'The Future of Welfare State: Rethinking Universalism' in Anneli Anttonen, Liisa Häikiö and Kolbeinn Stefánsson (eds), *Welfare State, Universalism and Diversity* (Edward Elgar 2012) 191.

[84]   ILO, *World Social Protection Report 2017–19* (n 30) xxxiv.

[85]   Peter Taylor-Gooby, 'Ideology and Social Policy: New Developments in Theory and Practice' (1994) 30 The Australian and New Zealand Journal of Sociology 71.

[86]   Amartya Sen, *Development as Freedom* (Alfred A. Knopf 1999); Martha C Nussbaum, *Women and Human Development: The Capabilities Approach* (CUP 2000).

and services or from the unjust distribution of material resources such as income and lack of resources, or from both.[87] Furthermore, new universalism is the only paradigm of the three that incorporates social inequalities into its problem formulation. While this emphasis on social inequalities was lacking in the MDGs,[88] this has been partly compensated in the SDGs with the introduction of universal or zero-based targets in many areas and the inclusion of a standalone goal for reducing inequality (Goal 10).[89] The floor-level social security, below which no individual must fall, is relatively clear in the SDG indicators, especially when compared to the previous two paradigms. The policy responses that this paradigm puts forth include attempts to fill coverage gaps in countries where certain social programmes (e.g. old-age pensions and social healthcare insurance) already exist and to create such programmes where they do not exist. Policy responses that the literature on this paradigm mentions include universal basic income,[90] universal health coverage,[91] universal basic education,[92] social protection floors[93] and universal basic services.[94]

While human rights lie at the core of the new universalist paradigm, three concerns can be raised with respect to its ability to offer human rights-based solutions to poverty. First, targets and indicators chosen to monitor a country's performance with respect to Goal 10 have undermined the original promise of the SDGs to address extreme wealth and income inequalities.[95]

---

[87]   For example, ILO Advisory Group, *Social Protection Floor for a Fair and Inclusive Globalization* (ILO Publications 2011) <www.ilo.org/wcmsp5/groups/public/---dgreports/---dcomm/---publ/documents/publication/wcms_165750.pdf> accessed 18 June 2020.

[88]   Naila Kabeer, *Can the MDGs Provide a Pathway to Social Justice? The Challenge of Intersecting Inequalities* (UNDP 2010) 6 <www.mdgfund.org/sites/default/files/MDGs_and_Inequalities_Final_Report.pdf> accessed 18 June 2020.

[89]   Edward Anderson, 'Equality as a Global Goal' (2016) 30 Ethics & International Affairs 189; Gillian MacNaughton, 'Vertical Inequalities: Are the SDGs and Human Rights up to the Challenges?' (2017) 21 The International Journal of Human Rights 1050.

[90]   For example, Guy Standing, *Basic Income: A Guide for the Open-Minded* (Yale University Press 2017); Philippe Van Parijs and Yannick Vanderborght, *Basic Income: A Radical Proposal for a Free Society and a Sane Economy* (Harvard University Press 2017).

[91]   For example, Alan Derickson, *Health Security for All: Dreams of Universal Health Care in America* (Johns Hopkins University Press 2005); Daniel Cotlear and others, *Going Universal: How 24 Developing Countries are Implementing Universal Health Coverage Reforms from the Bottom up* (International Bank for Reconstruction and Development/The World Bank 2015) <http://documents.worldbank.org/curated/en/936881467992465464/Going-universal-how-24-developing-countries-are-implementing-universal-health-coverage-reforms-from-the-bottom-up> accessed 18 March 2019.

[92]   For example, Gene B Sperling, 'The Case for Universal Basic Education for the World's Poorest Boys and Girls' (2005) 87 Phi Delta Kappan Magazine 213; The United Nations Educational, Scientific and Cultural Organization (UNESCO), Global Education Monitoring Report Team, *EFA Global Monitoring Report 2015: Education for All 2000–2015: Achievements and Challenges* (UNESCO Publishing 2015) <https://unesdoc.unesco.org/ark:/48223/pf0000232205> accessed 18 June 2020.

[93]   For example, ILO Advisory Group (n 87); Markus Kaltenborn, 'Overcoming Extreme Poverty by Social Protection Floors – Approaches to Closing the Right to Social Security Gap' (2017) 10 Law and Development Review 237.

[94]   For example, Social Prosperity Network at the IGP and others, 'Social Prosperity for the Future: A Proposal for Universal Basic Services' (*Institute for Global Prosperity (IGP)*, 2017) <www.ucl.ac.uk/bartlett/igp/sites/bartlett/files/universal_basic_services_-_the_institute_for_global_prosperity_.pdf> accessed 6 August 2019; Ian Gough, 'Universal Basic Services: A Theoretical and Moral Framework' (2019) 90 The Political Quarterly 534.

[95]   MacNaughton (n 89) 1050–72; Joel E Oestreich, 'SDG 10: Reduce Inequality in and Among Countries' (2018) 37 Social Alternatives 34; Sakiko Fukuda-Parr, 'Keeping Out Extreme Inequality from the SDG Agenda–The Politics of Indicators' (2019) 10 Global Policy 61.

In fact, its reliance on 'income growth of the bottom 40 per cent' as an indicator for reduced inequalities is misleading, as it fails to account for the relational dynamics in income distribution. The only exception to this deficiency is the inclusion of labour share among the indicators for Goal 10 – albeit without a time limit.

Second, the new universalism does not necessarily promote comprehensive protection from social risks, equality in access to quality services and equality in outcomes.[96] Instead, this paradigm welcomes 'systemic universalism',[97] which implies bridging the gaps in coverage by introducing additional social programmes, the benefits and service coverage of which do not necessarily have to be equivalent to the original programmes or adequately comprehensive. While an unequal benefit structure in the case of old-age pensions might be considered compatible with universalism[98] provided that the lowest benefit allows for an adequate standard of living, this is not applicable to, for example, healthcare. The problem with the new universalism, therefore, lies in its indiscriminate welcoming of multi-tiered inegalitarian benefit or service provision structures if they together achieve universal coverage. In this regard, it fails to address whether inequalities in access to services and benefit structures can be tolerated and, if so, to what extent. The paradigm aims to compensate for this deficiency by introducing floor-level social security. However, the modesty of this floor-level social security significantly limits its universal appeal and relevance to all countries and imperils its commitment to the principle of progressive realization.

Third, this paradigm formulates the state's role in a manner that may water down its positive obligations. It presents the state as one of many stakeholders that can help achieve universal coverage. It embraces not only the private sector as another partner, but also public-private partnerships in social services and market means to achieve universal coverage.[99] Such a formulation may contradict the human rights perspective unless the paradigm reiterates the state's primary obligation to ensure the functioning of the private sector within the limits of public interest – a task that requires extensive regulatory capacity and functioning accountability mechanisms. In this regard, following Donnelly's critique,[100] its portrayal of the private sector as another partner of the new universalist project can be seen as evidence for its failure to address the profit-making and tax-averse motives of the private sector; it is also evidence of its failure to achieve a policy objective that often requires a curbing of those aims. Finally, the abovementioned strategy that new universalism adopts may also compromise human rights principles of universality and non-discrimination unless its potential to exacerbate inequalities in the scope and quality of services that different individuals and groups have access to is also addressed. The question of whether and to what extent inequalities in social protection

---

[96]   Goal 4, which aims at ensuring 'that all girls and boys complete free, equitable and quality primary and secondary education leading to relevant and effective learning outcomes', is an exception. UNGA, 'Transforming our World: The 2030 Agenda for Sustainable Development' (21 October 2015) UN Doc A/RES/70/1.

[97]   Lutz Leisering, *The Global Rise of Social Cash Transfers: How States and International Organizations Constructed a New Instrument for Combating Poverty* (OUP 2018) 358.

[98]   As discussed in Mikko Kautto, 'The Pension Puzzle: Pension Security for All without Universal Schemes?' in Anneli Anttonen, Liisa Häikiö and Kolbeinn Stefánsson (eds), *Welfare State, Universalism and Diversity* (Edward Elgar Publications 2012) 146–47.

[99]   For example, Mahmoud Mohieldin, 'SDGs and PPPs: What's the Connection?' (12 April 2018) <https://blogs.worldbank.org/ppps/sdgs-and-ppps-whats-connection> accessed 6 August 2019.

[100]   Jack Donnelly, 'Human Rights, Democracy and Development' (1999) 21 Hum Rts Q 608, 625.

and access to basic services, such as healthcare and education, can be tolerated remains to be answered.

VI.   CONCLUSION

How can a human rights perspective push the study of social policy ideas and paradigms towards a better understanding of their human rights implications for individuals and societies? The human rights perspective has thus far been used to examine procedures and outcomes. Alternatively, this chapter suggests that it also offers an integrated, stimulating and useful referential framework for researchers in their examination of ideas and frameworks in social policy.

How can the social policy discipline, with its theories, conceptual tools and methodologies, inform the human rights scholarship? One key idea that social policy can contribute to human rights scholarship is that non-judicial social institutions are necessary for the realization of human rights. From a social policy viewpoint, the exclusive focus of human rights scholarship on legal procedures and outcomes is insufficient in identifying and altering the conditions that facilitate or hamper the realization of human rights. While procedures are of critical importance in laying the ground for the protection of human rights, they often have to be complemented with non-judicial social institutions to attain desired outcomes, such as the alleviation of poverty. Bridging the rights-based approach to social policy and the social provision approach to human rights can create such analytical linkages.

Offering a human rights critique of three contemporary social policy paradigms, this chapter points to the significant mismatch between the high levels of inequality and poverty today and the widely shared disregard for such problems in the select paradigms, with the partial exception of new universalism. A similar tendency is also observed in their formulation of policy responses to poverty. It is striking that these policy frameworks largely ignore crucial questions related to the scope of positive state obligations towards its citizens; the mechanisms of financing social benefits, services and public goods provision; the determination of benefit levels, packages and their adequacy; and the setting of clear policy objectives to be attained in tackling inequality and poverty. The contemporary political and scientific saliency of these paradigms and their disconnect from the human rights framework require that human rights scholars be more involved in their examination and critique. Such intellectual exercise will generate a productive tension between the researchers' interpretations of human rights principles and trade-offs that are inherent in social policy paradigms. It will not only push researchers to develop more nuanced theoretical interpretations of human rights principles but also foster productive dialogue among them over the policy-oriented operationalization of the human rights perspective.

24. The human right to housing in the age of financialization

Leilani Farha and Kaitlin Schwan

As former United Nations Special Rapporteur on the right to adequate housing, author Leilani Farha has witnessed housing injustices in every corner of the world. Here, she recounts one such encounter:

> Many years ago, I met a woman in New Orleans named Naomi. I met Naomi outside of her home, which had been nearly destroyed by flooding during Hurricane Katrina. An African-American woman in her 60s, Naomi was disabled and used a wheelchair to navigate her world. Naomi graciously showed me her home. It was a small white bungalow structure, with steps leading up to the front door. I offered to help her get up the stairs but she refused, telling me she wanted me to see her daily reality. She hoisted herself out of her wheelchair and proceeded to drag herself up to the front porch, and then into the hallway. It was about 45 degrees in the house, and bugs swarmed around us. Her floorboards were torn up and I could see down to the foundation of the home. There was no working toilet, and there was no running water at all. She was using a dry toilet and then carting away the refuse when she could. It was – in my opinion – hell.
>
> After Naomi told me her story, I asked her how she felt living in these conditions in the richest country in the world. Naomi looked at me and without skipping a beat she said, 'abandoned.'[1]

It is this sense of abandonment that people experiencing homelessness describe. A profound sense of invisibility. People explain, over and over again, that to be poor and homeless is to be invisible. To be poor and homeless is to not count. To be poor and homeless is to be treated as sub-human.

Globally, we face levels of homelessness and housing need that stagger the imagination – both in relation to scale and with respect to causation. How did we get here? Why is it that at least 100 million people are living in the streets worldwide, facing daily threats to life and security? Why is it that there are 1.8 billion people globally who are living in informal settlements or encampments, lacking security and under constant threat of eviction?[2] Why is homelessness escalating in many of the wealthiest nations in the world, despite these governments having the funds, infrastructure, and expertise needed to end it?[3]

These outcomes are the direct result of a two-fold move by governments: (1) the adoption of legislation and policies that transform housing into advantageous investment opportunities, and (2) withdrawal from policies and legislation that recognize housing as a social good and

---

[1] Katy Reckdahl, 'United Nations group gets a look at post-Katrina housing woes' (*The Times-Picayune* 28 July 2009) <www.nola.com/news/article_4f74c21d-eb67-5266-8dfe-f605f4b533ca.html> accessed 23 June 2020.

[2] UNGA 'Report of the Special Rapporteur on adequate housing as a component of the right to an adequate standard of living, and on the right to non-discrimination in this context' (19 September 2018) A/73/310/Rev.1.

[3] OECD 'HC3.1 Homeless Population' (OECD Affordable Housing Database, 3 March 2020) <www.oecd.org/els/family/HC3-1-Homeless-population.pdf> accessed 16 June 2020.

human right. This new landscape is characterized by the 'financialization of housing' – the unprecedented expansion of financial actors' dominance in housing systems. In financialized housing markets, housing is no longer 'home' – a place to live in security and dignity – but instead is a tool for massive profit-generation for global investors, exceedingly out of reach for low and even middle class households.[4] In this context, it is no surprise that millions of people like Naomi feel abandoned. They have been. Financialized housing markets create, maintain, and exploit the degrading housing conditions suffered by Naomi and many like her. In fact, they depend upon it in order to generate wealth.

In this chapter, we explore the human right to housing in the context of the global financialization of housing. Utilizing a human rights lens, we highlight the ways in which financialized housing policies and practices drive homelessness, poverty, inequality, and human rights violations around the world. We explore governance in the age of financialization, underscoring the need for a seismic paradigmatic shift capable of reclaiming the human right to housing.

I.   THE HUMAN RIGHT TO HOUSING

The human right to adequate housing is codified in Article 11.1 of the International Covenant on Economic, Social and Cultural Rights (ICESCR), which recognizes 'the right of everyone to an adequate standard of living for himself and his family, including adequate food, clothing and housing, and to the continuous improvement of living conditions.'[5] In many ways, the right to adequate housing under international human rights law is not complicated. At its core, it is the right to live in dignity and security – a right enshrined in the Universal Declaration of Human Rights (UDHR).[6] The right to adequate housing has seven elements: legal security of tenure; affordability; habitability; availability of services, materials, facilities and infrastructure; location; and cultural adequacy.[7] We are far too familiar with violations of the right to housing experienced by individuals across the world, including mass homelessness, forced evictions of informal settlements, and the criminalization of sleeping rough.[8] These are all assaults on dignity and life, and challenge what it means to be human.

The right to adequate housing is indivisible from other human rights, and is recognized in a range of international human rights treaties, including the Convention on the Rights of Persons with Disabilities, the Convention on the Rights of the Child, and the Convention on

---

[4]   UNHRC 'Report of the Special Rapporteur on adequate housing as a component of the right to an adequate standard of living, and on the right to non-discrimination in this context' (10 January 2017) A/HRC/34/51.

[5]   International Covenant on Economic, Social and Cultural Rights (Adopted 16 December 1966, entered into force 3 January 1976) 993 UNTS 3 (UNGA).

[6]   Universal Declaration of Human Rights (adopted December 1948) UNGA Res 217 A(III) (UDHR) art 11.1. The Universal Declaration of Human Rights – the basis of all human rights – recognizes in its preamble that the inherent dignity and the equal rights of all members of the human family is the foundation of freedom, justice and peace in the world. Its first Article states, all human beings are born free and equal in dignity and rights.

[7]   CESCR 'General Comment No. 4: The Right to Adequate Housing (Art. 11 (1) of the Covenant)' (13 December 1991) E/1992/23.

[8]   UNHRC 'Report of the Special Rapporteur on adequate housing as a component of the right to an adequate standard of living, and on the right to non-discrimination in this context' (30 December 2015) A/HRC/31/54.

the Elimination of All Forms of Discrimination against Women.[9] In order to uphold the human right to housing, governments must: (a) refrain from actions that would violate the right to housing; (b) protect individuals, groups, and communities from violations of the right to housing by third parties (e.g., financial actors); and (c) seek to progressively realize the right to housing using the maximum available resources and through all appropriate means, including legislative measures.[10]

Some of the most egregious violations of the right to housing occur not as a result of state action, but due to governments' failures to take positive measures to address situations of homelessness, housing need, and other housing injustices.[11] The progressive realization of the right to housing requires that states take positive measures to 'fulfil the right to housing as swiftly and efficiently as possible,' utilizing the reasonableness standard developed by the Committee on Economic, Social and Cultural Rights.[12] The progressive realization of the right to housing must be established as a legal obligation under domestic law, and 'measures taken must be deliberate, concrete and targeted towards the fulfilment of the right to housing within a reasonable time frame.'[13] This requires that states implement and adopt strategies to realize the right to housing, in collaboration with relevant stakeholders and actors. Such strategies must 'clarify the responsibilities and roles of all levels of government, institutions and private actors, with goals, timelines, accountability mechanisms, appropriate budgetary allocations and measures to ensure access to justice.'[14] Further, if a State 'adopts a retrogressive measure, i.e., one that weakens the protection of the right to adequate housing, it will have to demonstrate that it carefully weighed all the options, considered the overall impact on all human rights of the measure and fully used all its available resources.'[15]

While progressive realization of the right to housing is the general obligation, there are circumstances that impose immediate obligations on States. For example, States are required to immediately develop and implement strategies to eliminate homelessness. Given that homelessness constitutes one of the most extreme violations of the right to housing, governments must respond to homelessness on an urgent and priority basis.[16] Under the ICESCR, any state that allows a significant number of people to experience homelessness is, *prima facie*,

---

[9]   For some of the additional human rights treaties that testify to the right to housing see: UNGA International Convention on the Elimination of All Forms of Racial Discrimination (adopted 21 December 1965, entry into force 4 January 1969) 660 UNTS 195; UNGA Convention Relating to the Status of Refugees (adopted 28 July 1951, entry into force 22 April 1954) 189 UNTS 137; UNGA International Covenant on Civil and Political Rights (adopted 16 December 1966, entry into force 23 March 1976) 999 UNTS 171; OHCHR Declaration of the Rights of Indigenous Peoples (adopted 29 June 2006, entry into force 13 September 2007).

[10]   OHCHR 'The Right to Adequate Housing' November 2009, Fact Sheet No. 21/Rev.1.

[11]   UNHRC 'Report of the Special Rapporteur on adequate housing as a component of the right to an adequate standard of living, and on the right to non-discrimination in this context' (2020) A/HRC/44/43, para. 17.

[12]   ibid, para 19.

[13]   ibid.

[14]   UNHRC 'Report of the Special Rapporteur on adequate housing as a component of the right to an adequate standard of living, and on the right to non-discrimination in this context' (18 January 2017) A/HRC/34/51.

[15]   OHCHR 'The Right to Adequate Housing' November 2009, Fact Sheet No. 21/Rev.1.

[16]   UNHRC 'Report of the Special Rapporteur on adequate housing as a component of the right to an adequate standard of living, and on the right to non-discrimination in this context' (26 February 2016) A/HRC/31/54.

failing to uphold its obligations under the Covenant.[17] As such, state parties 'are required to demonstrate that every effort has been made to use all resources that are at their disposition in an effort to satisfy, as a matter of priority, those minimum obligations.'[18] This obligation is linked to the fundamental indivisibility of the right to housing and other human rights, and the interconnectness between civil and social rights.[19]

Central to the right to housing is access to justice; human rights are illusory if they cannot be claimed. International human rights law emphasizes 'equality before the law and equal protection of the law without any discrimination,'[20] thereby prohibiting discrimination on the basis of housing status with respect to accessing justice. Given this, it is clear that

> Violations of the right to housing are as much failures in the administration of justice as they are failures of housing programmes. If those living in inadequate housing and in homelessness have no access to justice, they are deprived of agency to bring violations to light, to address root causes or ensure appropriate responses.[21]

The UN Special Rapporteur on the right to adequate housing outlines 16 key guidelines that should be followed in order for states to ensure access to justice for those whose right to housing has been violated, including the obligation to make available effective remedial mechanisms for individuals and groups.[22]

At its core, a rights-based approach to housing clarifies that all levels of government are accountable to people, particularly marginalized and vulnerable groups. It is in relation to these international human rights standards and obligations that we must assess government action in response to the financialization of housing.[23]

---

[17]   See CESCR 'General Comment No. 3: The Nature of States Parties' Obligations' (14 December 1990) E/1991/23, para. 10.

[18]   ibid.

[19]   UNHRC 'Report of the Special Rapporteur on adequate housing as a component of the right to an adequate standard of living, and on the right to non-discrimination in this context' (2020) A/HRC/43/43. For example, in the case law of the European Court of Human Rights, Article 8 (the right to respect for a person's 'private and family life, his home, and his correspondence') has been used to protect housing rights in concert with other human rights, thereby imposing immediate obligations on States. Alse see: *Chapman v. U.K.* App no 27238/95 (ECtHR, 18 January 2001).

[20]   See UNHRC 'CCPR General Comment No. 18: Non-discrimination' (10 November 1989) <http://ccprcentre.org/page/view/general_comments/27792> accessed 18 June 2020.

[21]   UNHRC 'Report of the Special Rapporteur on adequate housing as a component of the right to an adequate standard of living, and on the right to non-discrimination in this context' (1 March 2019) A/HRC/40/61, para 2.

[22]   UNHRC 'Report of the Special Rapporteur on adequate housing as a component of the right to an adequate standard of living, and on the right to non-discrimination in this context' (1 March 2019) A/HRC/40/61, para 2.

[23]   UNHRC 'Report of the Special Rapporteur on adequate housing as a component of the right to an adequate standard of living, and on the right to non-discrimination in this context' (26 February 2016) A/HRC/31/54.

II.   THE GLOBAL FINANCIALIZATION OF HOUSING: A THREAT TO HUMAN RIGHTS

A.   The Financialization of Housing

The financialization of housing involves the massive expansion and dominance of financial markets and corporations in the housing sector. While multiple definitions have been offered,[24] we use the term 'financialization of housing' to refer to 'structural changes in housing and financial markets and global investment whereby housing is treated as a commodity, a means of accumulating wealth and often as security for financial instruments that are traded and sold on global markets.'[25] Financialized housing markets treat housing as a financial instrument, rather than a home.

By its very nature, financialization demands that housing be divorced from its social value and function. In a financialized housing market, the value of housing is not its provision of safety or security, its link to health or wellbeing, its centrality to human dignity, its importance for human relationships, or its community-building function.[26] Instead, the central value and function of housing is profit generation. In so doing, financialized housing contributes to 'residential alienation,' characterized by 'the loss of the critical relationship to housing as a dwelling and the diverse set of social relationships that give it meaning.'[27]

The financialization of housing creates wealth, though rarely to the benefit of those experiencing poverty or housing need. The beneficiaries tend to be powerful financial actors, including banks, pension funds, private equity firms, real estate investment trusts (REITS), hedge funds, shareholders, and wealthy individuals. For these actors, the housing market provides a place to leverage extensive wealth and excess liquidity to turn profits, particularly on 'undervalued' properties. In countries around the globe, housing is increasingly the 'commodity of choice' for financial actors because of these high profits. This is reflected, for example, in data indicating that between mid-2013 and mid-2014, corporate purchases of large properties in the top 100 global cities increased from $600 billion to $1 trillion.[28]

Financial actors not only profit from inflated price of housing in so-called 'hedge cities' like Stockholm or Sydney, but also benefit from the housing crises that they had a hand in creating. This was powerfully exemplified in the 2007–08 global financial crisis, during which

---

[24]   See Manuel Aalbers, *The Financialization of Housing: A Political Economy Approach* (Routledge 2016); Radhika Balakrishnan and James Heintz and Diane Elson, *Rethinking Economic Policy for Social Justice: The Radical Potential of Human Rights* (Routledge 2016), p 85.

[25]   UNHRC 'Report of the Special Rapporteur on adequate housing as a component of the right to an adequate standard of living, and on the right to non-discrimination in this context' (18 January 2017) A/HRC/34/51, para 1.

[26]   See Manuel Aalbers, *The Financialization of Housing: A political economy approach* (Routledge 2016); UNHRC 'Report of the Special Rapporteur on adequate housing as a component of the right to an adequate standard of living, and on the right to non-discrimination in this context' (18 January 2017) A/HRC/34/51.

[27]   UNHRC 'Report of the Special Rapporteur on adequate housing as a component of the right to an adequate standard of living, and on the right to non-discrimination in this context' (18 January 2017) A/HRC/34/51 para 31 citing David Madden and Peter Marcuse, *In Defense of Housing: The Politics of Crisis* (Verso, 2016), chap 2.

[28]   Saskia Sassen, 'The global city: enabling economic intermediation and bearing its costs' 15 City & Community 97.

financial actors capitalized on historic opportunities to purchase distressed housing and real estate debt, 'package' these commodities, and sell them off at fire sale prices in countries like the UK, the US, Ireland, and Spain. The largest real estate private equity firm in the world, The Blackstone Group, spent $10 billion purchasing repossessed properties in the US during the financial crisis. As a result, Blackstone emerged as the largest landlord in America, and has purchased thousands of foreclosed homes in Spain and the UK.[29] Knowing that foreclosures create a huge population requiring housing, Blackstone rightly speculated that by converting these homes into rentals they could turn a profit for investors. In this new housing landscape, financial actors are incentivized to generate increased returns for investors, rather than prevent evictions or foreclosures, or maintain adequate housing conditions for tenants. The investor is the client, not the tenant.

Housing – as a commodity – has become a fixed feature of the global economic order. The scale of wealth generated through financialization is difficult to fathom. Globally, the value of real estate is approximately US $217 trillion, which constitutes nearly 60 percent of all global assets.[30] Of this, US $163 trillion is residential real estate. The financialization of housing is so lucrative that it now outpaces the 'productive economy' in wealth generation at the global scale.[31] This wealth generation transcends borders. In 2015, an American global real estate services firm – Cushman and Wakefield – calculated a record $443 billion generated in trans-border real estate investments, with residential properties comprising the largest single share.[32]

B.   The Effects of Financialization on Housing Systems

Housing systems around the world have been dramatically transformed by the financialization of housing. The influence of financial actors in housing markets has had a deleterious effect on affordability, with housing prices soaring to levels most residents cannot afford. In cities like Munich, Hong Kong, Toronto, and Buenos Aires, housing prices are no longer commensurate with household income levels, and staggering increases in rent mean that many poor and low-income people are priced out of the market and increasingly pushed to peri-urban areas that lack services, employment, and transportation.[33]

Corporate ownership and investor-driven housing markets transform neighborhoods in powerful ways. Where affordable residential properties still exist, particularly in so-called 'undervalued' neighborhoods, financial actors are particularly interested in upgrading and

---

[29]   J Beswick, G Alexandri, M Byrne and S Vives-Miro, 'Speculating on London's Housing Future: the Rise of Global Corporate Landlords in "Post-Crisis" Urban Landscapes' (2016) 20 City 323.

[30]   'What price the world?' (Savills UK, 28 January 2016) <www.savills.co.uk/research_articles/229130/198669-0> accessed 18 June 2020.

[31]   UNHRC 'Report of the Special Rapporteur on adequate housing as a component of the right to an adequate standard of living, and on the right to non-discrimination in this context' (18 January 2017) A/HRC/34/51.

[32]   Cushman and Wakefield, 'The Great Wall of Money' (2016) Cushman & Wakefield Capital Markets Research Publication 5 <https://cwrealkapital.no/wp-content/uploads/sites/2/2017/07/Great_Wall_of_Money_2016.pdf> (2016) accessed 22 June 2020.

[33]   UNHRC 'Report of the Special Rapporteur on adequate housing as a component of the right to an adequate standard of living, and on the right to non-discrimination in this context' (18 January 2017) A/HRC/34/51.

flipping these properties for profit. Corporations and wealthy individuals are also able to enter the housing market for profit through short-term rental platforms like Airbnb and Home Away, which result in increased luxury accommodation development and reductions in available housing stock that could be used for long-term affordable rentals. For example, a recent study on Airbnb in New York showed a loss of between 7,000 and 13,500 units of housing from its long-term rental market, in a city where 130,000 people are homeless throughout the year.[34] Such effects have been demonstrated at the national level as well. In countries like Portugal, the intrusion of short-term rental platforms has escalated housing prices and transformed neighborhoods.[35]

Importantly, many investor-owned properties remain empty. For example, in Melbourne approximately one fifth of investor-owned units are unoccupied.[36] Similarly, there was a 40 percent increase in investor-owned vacant units in the affluent boroughs of Chelsea and Kensington in London between 2013 and 2014.[37] In Vancouver there are more than 20,000 units that are under-utilized or empty.[38] The reality is that there are millions of vacant homes across the world, and yet at least 100 million people worldwide live in homelessness.

Corporate ownership of housing has also altered the experience of being a tenant. Amongst tenants of corporate-owned rental properties, common complaints include: poor maintenance, inadequate housing conditions, substandard and/or unnecessary renovations, dramatic increases in rent, illegal evictions, and hostile environments pressuring residents to move. Residents often report difficulty being able to communicate with corporate landlords or hold anyone accountable for their housing conditions.[39] These challenges are compounded for groups likely to experience discrimination in the housing market more broadly, including those receiving social assistance, people with disabilities, and Indigenous Peoples.[40]

Despite this new terrain, many politicians, governments, key stakeholders, and commentators continue to argue that the root of the housing crisis is a lack of supply that will be addressed

---

[34]   David Wachsmuth, David Chaney, Danielle Kerrigan, Andrea Shillolo and Robin Basalaev-Binder, 'The High Cost of Short-Term Rentals in New York City' (2018) Urban Planning and Governance research group 1 <https://mcgill.ca/newsroom/files/newsroom/channels/attach/airbnb-report.pdf> accessed 22 June 2020.

[35]   UNHRC 'Report of the Special Rapporteur on adequate housing as a component of the right to an adequate standard of living, and on the right to non-discrimination in this context' (18 January 2017) A/HRC/34/51.

[36]   Catherine Cashmore, 'Speculative Vacancies 8: The Empty Properties Ignored by Statistics' (2015) Prosper Australia 5 <www.prosper.org.au/wp-content/uploads/2015/12/11Final_Speculative-Vacancies-2015-1.pdf> accessed 22 June 2020.

[37]   For example, see MHCLG 'Vacant dwellings' (updated May 2020) London Datastore <https://data.london.gov.uk/dataset/vacant-dwellings/resource/c428a18b-9961-4b98-9cfe-b7f120114141> accessed 22 June 2020.

[38]   See City of Vancouver, 'Empty Homes Tax' (City of Vancouver, n.d.) <http://vancouver.ca/home-property-development/empty-homes-tax.aspx> accessed 22 June 2020.

[39]   UNHRC 'Report of the Special Rapporteur on adequate housing as a component of the right to an adequate standard of living, and on the right to non-discrimination in this context' (18 January 2017) A/HRC/34/51.

[40]   ibid; see also UN-Habitat, 'Indigenous Peoples' Right to Adequate Housing: A Global Overview' (2005) HS/734/05E; UNHRC 'Report of the Special Rapporteur on adequate housing as a component of the right to an adequate standard of living, and on the right to non-discrimination in this context' (7 December 2017) A/72/128.

by inviting investors in.[41] It is critical to understand, however, that the unprecedented investment of capital into housing has not resulted in the production of much-needed affordable housing. Nor is it meant to. Foreign investment in local housing markets and investor-owned mortgages largely transfer wealth out of communities, primarily concentrating it in the hands of wealthy corporate actors.[42] Increasing the supply of housing that is purpose-built to generate profit, rather than respond to housing need, is incapable of resolving the high levels of homelessness and housing stability we are seeing around the globe. More broadly, this logic fails to view the global housing crisis for what it is – a human rights crisis necessitating a human rights response.

C.   The Effects of Financialization on People and Neighborhoods: Homelessness, Poverty, and Inequality

In her travels as UN Special Rapporteur on the right to adequate housing, Leilani Farha recalls meeting Cassandra:

> I met Cassandra in California. An African American single mother in her 50s, until recently she had been working at a medical clinic. Her job was decent, above minimum wage, and she had been paying $1,200 for a one-bedroom apartment until her building was bought by a multi-national asset management firm. Her rent was increased by 30 percent almost overnight. Knowing she would not be able to afford it, she moved out and couch-surfed with a friend. When she felt she had outstayed her welcome, she wanted to move in with her sister. However, her sister had already taken in their mother, who was ill and had nowhere to live. With nowhere to go, I met this woman where she lives now: in a tent under a highway, where she struggles to find a place to take a shower and wash her clothes in order to keep her job. She explained that recently the tent encampment was threatened with eviction, and if that happened she had no idea where she would end up.[43]

Cassandra's experience is not an exception to the rule. The impacts of financialized housing are felt in every corner of the world. Key effects of financialization include increases in rent, foreclosures of homes, and decreases in affordable housing. Much private and corporate investment into housing preys on the misfortune of others, and increasingly forms the foundation of wealth inequality.[44] Surveys indicate that over half of ultra-high-net-worth individuals have increased their investments in residential properties between 2006 and 2016, largely with the intent of selling at a profit in the future.[45] Acquiring these properties requires the displacement and eviction of individuals, families, and whole communities – in some cases dispossessing households of a lifetime of savings.

---

[41]   See, e.g., 'The Horrible Housing Blunder: Why the Obsession with Home Ownership is So Harmful' (18–24 January 2020) *The Economist*.

[42]   UNHRC 'Report of the Special Rapporteur on adequate housing as a component of the right to an adequate standard of living, and on the right to non-discrimination in this context' (18 January 2017) A/HRC/34/51.

[43]   Leilani Farha, Keynote Address, *National Health Care for the Homeless Conference and Policy Symposium*, Washington, DC (24 May 2019).

[44]   See David Madden and Peter Marcuse, *In Defense of Housing: The Politics of Crisis* (Verso, 2016).

[45]   'The Wealth Report: the global perspective on prime property and investment' (2016) Knight Frank Research 1 <http://content.knightfrank.com/research/83/documents/en/wealth-report-2016-3579 .pdf> accessed 22 June 2020.

Research shows that in areas where investors move in, housing for people on low-incomes becomes more scarce, less secure, and more expensive.[46] Driven primarily by profit, institutional landlords are quick to threaten eviction when tenant payments are delayed, or when tenants request repairs or lodge complaints about housing conditions.[47] When tenants are evicted, they are generally replaced with those who can pay higher rents, or who are deemed more reliable with rent payments. Blackstone's business model, and other private equity firms like it, necessitates the charging of high rents in order to generate enough profits to satisfy investors.[48] In many cities and countries, this has resulted in unparalleled levels of eviction and foreclosure. In the United States, 13 million foreclosures resulted in the eviction of over 9 million households over the span of five years.[49] Spain, between 2008 and 2013, similarly witnessed more than half a million foreclosures that resulted in over 300,000 evictions.[50] In Hungary, there were almost one million foreclosures between 2009 and 2012.[51]

Amongst the most egregious effects of the financialization of housing is the escalation of homelessness globally, including within many of the wealthiest countries. While homelessness – particularly in the Global North – is commonly framed as the consequence of individual deficiency or pathology,[52] it is powerfully driven by the financialization of housing. Investor landlords show a particular interest in low-income housing – housing that often serves as home for individuals that are economically marginalized and live on the precipice of homelessness. Once purchased, investor landlords frequently use legal loopholes to significantly increase rent levels, leaving many tenants with no choice but to leave.[53] With few remaining affordable housing options in their area, former tenants may seek cheaper housing farther away from work, family, friends, and support networks, or may find themselves homeless.

The negative effects of financialization disproportionately accrue for groups and communities already experiencing oppression and marginalization, in many cases compounding exist-

---

[46]   UNHRC 'Report of the Special Rapporteur on adequate housing as a component of the right to an adequate standard of living, and on the right to non-discrimination in this context' (18 January 2017) A/HRC/34/51.

[47]   For example, researchers have documented that Invitation Homes (then a subsidiary of Blackstone) evicted 10 percent of its renters in 2013 in Charlotte, North Carolina – a much higher figure than other landlords in the same area. See Rebecca Burn, Michael Donley and Carmilla Manzanet, 'Game of Homes' (In These Times, 31 March 2014) <http://inthesetimes.com/article/16424/game_of_homes> accessed 22 June 2020.

[48]   UNHRC 'Report of the Special Rapporteur on adequate housing as a component of the right to an adequate standard of living, and on the right to non-discrimination in this context' (18 January 2017) A/HRC/34/51.

[49]   Saskia Sassen, 'Finance as Capability: Good, Bad, Dangerous' (2014) Arcade Stanford 1 <http://arcade.stanford.edu/occasion/finance-capability-good-bad-dangerous> accessed 22 June 2020.

[50]   'Housing Emergency in Spain: the crisis of foreclosures and evictions from a human rights perspective' (December 2013) OESC and Platform of Mortgage Victims <http://observatoridesc.org/sites/default/files/2013-housing-emergency-spain-observatory-desc.pdf> accessed 22 June 2020.

[51]   Saskia Sassen, 'Expulsions: Brutality and Complexity in the Global Economy' (2016) Harvard University Press 62. These trends are also linked to the expansion of debt and credit taken on by households who have been made vulnerable to predatory lending practices. See also David Madden and Peter Marcuse, *In Defense of Housing: The Politics of Crisis* (Verso, 2016).

[52]   Cameron Parsell and Mitch Parsell, 'Homelessness as a Choice' (2012) Housing, Theory, and Society 420.

[53]   See David Madden and Peter Marcuse, *In Defense of Housing: The Politics of Crisis* (Verso, 2016).

ing socio-economic and racial inequities that are visible as spatial segregation. For example, in South Africa, the urban core of cities has been dominated by private investment in ways that have sustained apartheid-era racial discrimination, with poorer black residents living on the outskirts of cities, and wealthy, largely white households residing closer to city centers. On the periphery of the city, Black South Africans have poorer access to the resources needed to improve their socio-economic wellbeing, including employment opportunities, transit, health, and social services, and education.[54] Similar trends have been observed in Chile[55] and the United States.[56]

Though financialization manifests differently in some places in the Global South, many of the effects have been similar, including widespread displacement and eviction, displacement, and reductions in affordable housing. If current trends continue, Africa will see an increase in both informal settlements and the wealth of ultra-high-net-worth individuals, whose wealth is forecasted to increase 50 percent in the next decade.[57] In some of the poorest countries in the Global South, like Lagos, Nigeria, for example, and Bangkok, Thailand, luxury commercial real estate and residential housing are increasingly replacing informal settlements, dislocating residents who often have limited options for recourse.[58]

Escalating climate change also has an enormous impact on the enjoyment of the right to housing within financialized housing markets, particularly for impoverished communities in the Global South. It is evident that some governments use the pretext of climate change to carry out gross violations of the right to housing in the interests of profit. Evictions of informal settlements have occurred in the Philippines, Indonesia, and Nigeria, all following a similar pattern: governments ostensibly evicting informal settlements in order to prevent harm caused by climate change, only to have these settlements replaced by luxury developments and other profit-driven housing.[59]

---

[54]   See 'Edged out: spatial mismatch and spatial justice in South Africa's main urban areas' (2016) SERI 1 <www.serisa.org/images/images/SERI_Edged_out_report_Final_high_res.pdf> accessed 22 June 2020.

[55]   Leilani Farha, 'Report of the Special Rapporteur on adequate housing as a component of the right to an adequate standard of living, and on the right to non-discrimination in this context, on her mission to Chile' (United Nations Human Rights Office of the High Commissioner, 2018) <www.ohchr.org/en/issues/housing/pages/leilanifarha.aspx> accessed 22 June 2020.

[56]   See Jacob Rugh and Douglas Massey, 'Racial Segregation and the American Foreclosure Crisis' (2010) Am Sociol Rev 629.

[57]   'The Wealth Report: the global perspective on prime property and investment' (2016) Knight Frank Research 1 <http://content.knightfrank.com/research/83/documents/en/wealth-report-2016-3579.pdf> accessed 22 June 2020.

[58]   UNHRC 'Report of the Special Rapporteur on adequate housing as a component of the right to an adequate standard of living, and on the right to non-discrimination in this context' (18 January 2017) A/HRC/34/51.

[59]   Julieta Perruca, 'Housing Rights and Climate Change' (25 December 2019) <www.youtube.com/watch?v=GwrciHD7Ls4> accessed 22 June 2020.

III.   THE HUMAN RIGHT TO HOUSING IN THE AGE OF FINANCIALIZATION

A.   Governments' Role in Enabling the Financialization of Housing, and its Human Rights Implications

The financialization of housing has not happened by accident, but has been facilitated by government policies and legislation. Many countries' adoption of neoliberal policy frameworks in the late 1970s through to the 1990s has enabled and encouraged investors and markets to operate according to their own laws and interests, irrespective of the effects on people. Further, domestic and international policy has created the conditions for governments' interests to become intertwined with the interests of central banks and international and regional financial institutions, who themselves are rarely held accountable to the human rights obligations of governments.[60] By enabling financial actors to enter and transform housing systems, many governments have fostered financialized housing markets. In doing so, governments have sub-contracted out the administration of a human right.

In many countries, governments are now closely aligned with the investment sector, as is clearly evidenced in taxation policy. Investments in residential properties are accompanied by tax advantages in many countries, providing tax immunities to offshore corporations who choose to invest in real estate. Such investments often require little transparency, and can be done in cash, enabling shell companies and financial actors to remain anonymous. For example, shell companies own more than 36,000 properties in London, many of whom are registered in offshore havens in places like Bermuda or the British Virgin Islands.[61] In effect, housing can function as a lucrative 'safety security box' for the rich – enabling advantages to access land at a speed and scale that rivals many governments.[62] In fact, some countries even provide citizenship and visas to foreign investors who buy property.

Many governments also provide tax advantages to homeowners, rather than renters. In Canada, for example, 93 percent of housing subsidies provided by the government went to homeowners during 2008/2009, and just seven percent went to renters.[63] In addition to providing preferential treatment to homeowners, many governments are simultaneously divesting from rental housing and social housing. Countless governments are selling off social and public housing stock, as well as land, as an asset and relying on the private market to meet the

---

[60]   UNHRC 'Report of the Special Rapporteur on adequate housing as a component of the right to an adequate standard of living, and on the right to non-discrimination in this context' (18 January 2017) A/HRC/34/51.

[61]   See Nick Maxwell, Matteo de Simone and Lloyd Barthrop, 'Corruption on your doorstep: how corrupt capital is used to buy property in the UK' (2015) TI UK <www.transparency.org.uk/publications/corruption-on-your-doorstep> accessed 22 June 2020.

[62]   See Rodrigo Fernandez, Annelore Hofman and Manuel Aalbers, 'London and New York as a safe deposit box for the transnational wealth elite' (2016) Environment and Planning 1.

[63]   Frank Clayton, 'Government Subsidies to Homeowners versus Renters in Ontario and Canada' (30 August 2010) <www.frpo.org/wp-content/uploads/2015/04/FRPO-Government-Subsidies-Report.pdf> accessed 22 June 2020.

housing needs of low- and middle-income households. Rental prices predictably rise as a result of these actions – often to the benefit of corporate landlords.[64]

The power of international and domestic financial institutions is particularly evident when governments face foreign debt crises. The International Monetary Fund and other creditors often impose strict accountability to global financial actors when countries experience a foreign debt crisis, with decisions driven by international financial institutions rather than households experiencing debt. For example, the 'Vienna Initiative' was established to address the debt crises in Central, Eastern, and South-Eastern Europe, bringing together a range of financial stakeholders to do so, including regional and international financial institutions, as well as Western European parent banks and national central banks. Decidedly absent were groups representing borrowing households and their interests.[65] In such circumstances, austerity measures imposed by creditors often result in cuts to housing programs and the sale of public housing or land to private equity firms, who benefit from these debt crises at the expense of indebted households.[66]

There are significant human rights implications to governments' role in enabling the financialization of housing. Importantly, the actions of international and domestic financial institutions are facilitated and sustained by governments that have human rights obligations. Under international human rights law, state governments are required to uphold the tripartite obligation to respect, protect, and fulfill the human right to housing.

Governments must 'manage the interaction between financial actors and housing systems in accordance with the right to adequate housing.'[67] This means that governments are required to intervene when the actions of markets and financial investors result in housing rights violations. In essence, international human rights law requires that financial actors be made accountable to governments' human rights obligations, and that governments must account to rights-holders.

Despite these human rights obligations, in many cases governments have replaced account-ability to rights-holders with accountability to markets and investors.

The interests of investors and other financial actors continue to powerfully influence gov-ernment policy and legislation on housing in many countries. Further, in many cases the obli-gation to uphold the human right to housing are interpreted too narrowly in policy and practice. Under international human rights law, governments must not merely prevent financial actors from actively violating human rights, but must act to ensure the fulfillment of the right to adequate housing by all appropriate means, including legislative measures. International human rights law requires that governments ensure financial institutions are accountable and responsive to the needs of communities and rights-holders, implement complaints procedures

---

[64]   UNHRC 'Report of the Special Rapporteur on adequate housing as a component of the right to an adequate standard of living, and on the right to non-discrimination in this context' (18 January 2017) A/HRC/34/51.

[65]   See Daniela Gabor, *Central Banking and Financialization: A Romanian Account of how Eastern Europe became Subprime* (Palgrave Macmillan 2011).

[66]   UNHRC 'Report of the Special Rapporteur on adequate housing as a component of the right to an adequate standard of living, and on the right to non-discrimination in this context' (18 January 2017) A/HRC/34/51.

[67]   ibid, para 12.

and access to effective remedies, and 'behave in a manner consistent with the full realization of the right to adequate housing.'[68]

B.   Government Efforts to Curb Financialization

Policy responses to the financialization of housing and its effects have primarily benefitted financial actors. However, there have been efforts by national and sub-national governments to restrain the role of corporate investors in the housing market, as well as to mitigate the effects of financialization. Tax measures have been critical tools to curbing the financialization of housing in some cities and countries, including taxes on luxury properties. Singapore, for example, has imposed an 18 percent property sales tax on wealthy property investors, with the revenues used to support homeownership for low-income households.[69] Restrictions on foreign buyers have also been introduced to mitigate the influence of international investors, including in Austria, China, the Philippines, New Zealand, Denmark, Thailand, and Vietnam.[70] In Canada, the province of British Columbia has also imposed a 15 percent tax on foreign homeowners.[71] Property speculation taxes have also been introduced in a number of countries, including, Malaysia, China, and Germany.[72]

In many places, cities are on the frontlines of efforts to deescalate financialization – including through legislation targeted to mitigate escalating rental prices and widespread vacancies. A growing number of cities struggling with rising rental prices have implemented rent freezes or rent caps, including Berlin, where rents were frozen for five years in 2020 in response to the doubling of rent over the previous ten years.[73] Vacancy taxes have also been employed in cities where speculative investment has resulted in largescale vacancies. In Vancouver, for example, a one percent tax on vacant homes was implemented to address the approximately 20,000 homes that remain vacant – the revenue of which is invested in affordable housing.[74] The expropriation of vacant homes has also been pursued in some jurisdictions.[75]

---

[68]   ibid.

[69]   See Sock-Yong Phang and Matthias Helbie, 'Housing policies in Singapore' (2016) ADBI Working Paper Series <www.adb.org/sites/default/files/publication/181599/adbi-wp559.pdf> accessed 23 June 2020.

[70]   UNHRC 'Report of the Special Rapporteur on adequate housing as a component of the right to an adequate standard of living, and on the right to non-discrimination in this context' (18 January 2017) A/HRC/34/51. In 2019, for example, Denmark began exploring legislation concerning rent control in response to rent hikes levied by Blackstone Group Inc. See Morten Butler, 'Denmark Is Reviewing Rent Control to Rein In Blackstone' (BNN Bloomberg, 25 October 2019) <www.bnnbloomberg.ca/denmark -is-reviewing-rent-control-to-rein-in-blackstone-1.1337589> accessed 23 June 2020.

[71]   'The Miscellaneous Statutes (Housing Priority Initiatives) Amendment Act' (5th Session) [Bill 28] 40th Parliament, British Columbia, 2016.

[72]   UNHRC 'Report of the Special Rapporteur on adequate housing as a component of the right to an adequate standard of living, and on the right to non-discrimination in this context' (18 January 2017) A/HRC/34/51.

[73]   Gurmeet Singh, 'Berlin's rent freeze shows the city is not simply a playground for the rich' (Fair Planet, 7 February 2020) <www.fairplanet.org/editors-pick/berlins-rent-freeze-shows-the-city-is-not -simply-a-playground-for-the-rich/> accessed 23 June 2020.

[74]   See City of Vancouver, 'Empty Homes Tax' (City of Vancouver, n.d.) <http://vancouver.ca/home -property-development/empty-homes-tax.aspx> accessed 22 June 2020.

[75]   See Manuel Aalbers, *The Financialization of Housing: A political economy approach* (Routledge 2016).

Governments have also sought to incentivize private investors to develop affordable housing units. For instance, the Algerian government finances rental housing development for households that earn less than 1.5 times the minimum wage, providing free government land for this housing.[76] In other cities and countries, including recently in Montreal, Quebec,[77] governments are requiring developers to include a proportion of affordable units in all new rental buildings (though definitions of 'affordable' frequently do not reflect the actual income levels of those in housing need).[78] Additional government strategies to improve access to affordable housing have included rent banks, access to credit for low-income households through micro-financing, strengthened eviction prevention legislation, and the expansion of social, public, or supportive housing.[79]

Amongst policy responses to the effects of financialization, responses to homelessness have been particularly inadequate. While many governments have established laws and policies that actively create and maintain widespread homelessness, most provide minimal resources to resolve this issue. Government responses largely employ a charitable model, addressing only the most basic and immediate needs. These efforts reveal little intent to dismantle the structures and systems that cause homelessness. At worst, governments actively de-humanize and criminalize those who are homeless. The laws and policies that facilitate this are extensive and include: move-along laws; no camping laws; laws that prohibit people from sleeping in cars; laws that fine individuals for urinating, defecating, sleeping, or resting on streets; laws that fine individuals or groups for providing food to people living on the streets; laws that enable the forced evictions of tent encampments; and policies that facilitate the destruction of the private property of people who are homeless.[80] Research consistently demonstrates that these laws and policies deepen poverty and homelessness, rather than ameliorate the issue.[81] Homelessness, particularly in affluent countries, should provoke outrage. Evidently, this outrage has been largely directed toward homeless people themselves.

On the whole, government efforts to curb the financialization of housing have been overwhelming piecemeal and sporadic. Most importantly, these policy responses have rarely employed a rights-based framework, or been implemented within a coherent housing strategy based in the human right to housing.

---

[76]   See 'Housing Finance in Africa Yearbook 2014' (2014) CAHF 1 <http://housingfinanceafrica.org/documents/housing-finance-in-africa-2014-yearbook/> accessed 23 June 2020.

[77]   Francois Goulet, '20-20-20: Montreal Sets New Goals for Inclusionary Zoning' (Planetizen 15 June 2019)   <www.planetizen.com/news/2019/06/104816-20-20-20-montreal-sets-new-goals-inclusionary-zoning> accessed 23 June 2020.

[78]   UNHRC 'Report of the Special Rapporteur on adequate housing as a component of the right to an adequate standard of living, and on the right to non-discrimination in this context' (18 January 2017) A/HRC/34/51.

[79]   See Manuel Aalbers, *The Financialization of Housing: A political economy approach* (Routledge 2016).

[80]   UNHRC 'Report of the Special Rapporteur on adequate housing as a component of the right to an adequate standard of living, and on the right to non-discrimination in this context' (18 January 2017) A/HRC/34/51.

[81]   See, e.g., Samara Jones, 'Mean Streets: A report on the criminalization of homelessness in Europe' (2013) FEANTSA.

IV.   MAKING THE SHIFT: A CALL TO REALIZE THE RIGHT TO HOUSING

Around the world, there are more than a billion people living in grossly inadequate housing, and millions more facing evictions, foreclosures, and displacements. The challenge we face is not just a global housing crisis, but a human rights crisis, underpinned by the global financialization of housing. Unfortunately, the financialization of housing has rarely been understood through the frame of human rights, and policies and legislation related to the financing of housing typically do not employ a human rights lens or reference human rights. As a result, the significant human rights implications of real estate sector behavior have largely gone unacknowledged and unregulated.[82]

To restore rights to people, we need a seismic shift that reclaims the value of housing as home, not as equity. This shift would affirm that deprivations of the right to adequate housing are not just program failures or policy challenges, but human rights violations of the highest order. These violations deprive those affected of the most basic human rights to dignity, security, and life itself – violations that people like Naomi and Cassandra endure every day. Given this, it is critical that housing no longer be understood as a commodity, an asset, or a place to grow wealth; it must be embraced as a social good necessary for the wellbeing of the individual and society alike. This requires that all actors engaged in housing – governments, non-profit housing providers, private financial actors, housing cooperatives – operate in ways that align with the right to housing.

Such a shift requires that governments reclaim their role in housing through the adoption of comprehensive human rights-based housing strategies. Given the scale and gravity of its effects, responses to financialization cannot take the form of policies targeted at only part of problem, only to be undercut by a policy-gap or conflict. Rent caps and tenant protections, for example, will not suffice when there are no available units because it is more profitable to leave them empty or list them on Airbnb or other short-term rental platforms. Rights-based strategies can facilitate a changed relationship between governments and the financial sector, and provide governments with a framework to ensure financial actors work in ways that are consistent with the realization of the human right to adequate housing.

Most importantly, rights-based housing strategies put people, as rights-holders, at the center of all housing policy and legislative decisions. This means that rights-based housing strategies not only change the relationship between governments and financial actors, they fundamentally transform the relationship between governments and people. Under a rights-based approach, governments have an obligation to prevent and end the insufferable and inhumane housing conditions experienced by people like Naomi and Cassandra. Governments must be held accountable to rights-holders for the policies, legislation, and practices that have facilitated the financialization of housing and its effects. Ultimately, the circumstances and dignity of rights-holders must be the standard by which we measure states' compliance with the right to housing.

Given the imperative to curb the financialization of housing, research is needed to better understand the efficacy of various policy, taxation, and legislative measures on the regulation

---

[82]   See, e.g., Samara Jones, 'Mean Streets: A report on the criminalization of homelessness in Europe' (2013) FEANTSA.

of financial actors in housing markets globally. Cross-national comparisons, with longitudinal data collection, would significantly improve knowledge in this area. Comparative accounts of the role of financialization in creating homelessness in the Global South and Global North respectively would also assist in illuminating the adaptive mechanisms that global financial actors use in varying economic and political contexts, and the consequences of these practices for diverse vulnerable populations. Further, given the centrality of climate change to housing futures around the globe, there is particular need to understand the intersection between climate change and the financialization of housing. Across all areas, the impact of COVID-19 on the practices of financial actors, and the adaptive responses of national and subnational governments, will be critical for imagining a world wherein the right to housing is realized.

In the face of escalating homelessness and housing affordability crises around the globe, combined with the consequences of a global pandemic, there is an urgent need for a changed approach. We can no longer tinker around the edges of an unsustainable model of economic development and expect it to deliver housing that meets peoples' needs. By implementing rights-based housing strategies, we can change the way that housing is currently conceived, valued, produced, and regulated. It is time to reclaim the right to housing.

25. The right to health for people living in poverty: a human rights perspective

Mette Hartlev

This chapter will look at the relation between poverty and health from a human rights-based perspective. It will explore how the human right to health relates to poverty and how poverty impacts on the right to health. By the end, it will also reflect upon how precision medicine (including precision public health) as an emerging health technology may influence the relation between health and poverty.

I.   THE HUMAN RIGHT TO HEALTH

The right to the highest attainable standard of health is a well-established socio-economic right recognized in several human rights instruments, such as the Universal Declaration of Human Rights (UDHR) and the International Covenant on Economic, Social and Cultural Rights (ICESCR). It is also considered as a basic patient's right.[1] According to article 12(1) of the ICESCR states parties to the Covenant must 'recognize the right of everyone to the enjoyment of the highest attainable standard of physical and mental health'. As will be clear, the right to health is a very ambitious right which encompasses both physical and mental health, and with a clear ambition to ensure the enjoyment of the highest standard of health.

The UN Committee on Economic, Social and Cultural Rights (CESCR) has provided a very comprehensive interpretation of the right to the highest attainable standard of health in its General Comment no. 14, which highlights the multiple dimensions of the right to health and the importance of the underlying determinants of health.[2] According to the General Comment, the full realization of the right to health requires not only access to health care services, but also a clear commitment from states parties to address the underlying determinants of health. It is stressed that the right to health is:

> an inclusive right extending not only to timely and appropriate health care but also to the underlying determinants of health, such as access to safe and potable water and adequate sanitation, an adequate supply of safe food, nutrition and housing, healthy occupational and environmental conditions, and access to health-related education and information, including on sexual and reproductive health.[3]

The wide scope of the right to health reflects the broad definition of health applied by the World Health Organization (WHO), where health is defined as a 'state of complete physical,

---

[1]   M Hartlev, 'Patients' Rights' in Brigit Toebes and others (eds), *Health and Human Rights in Europe* (Intersentia 2012) 111.

[2]   'General Comment No. 14, The Right to the Highest Attainable Standard of Health (Article 12)' (2000) UN Doc E/C12/2000/4.

[3]   ibid para 1.1.

mental and social wellbeing and not merely the absence of disease and infirmity'.[4] Audrey Chapman has critically discussed the use of the expression 'underlying determinants' in the human rights framework instead of 'social determinants', which is the term commonly applied by the WHO and in a public health context. She perceives 'underlying determinants' as a narrower and more partial expression than the more comprehensive understanding embedded in 'social determinants'. In contrast to 'underlying determinants', 'social determinants' pay more attention to e.g. social class as an important determinant of health, and to the interactive and cumulative effects various underlying determinants may have on individuals and communities life prospects and on structural injustices.[5] Although there might be differences between the human rights and public health communities in their approach to the conditions that shape our health, it nevertheless seems that both communities are promoting a comprehensive and non-reductionist approach to the link between health, inequities and poverty.

Apart from defining and clarifying the scope of the right to health, the General Comment also defines various aspects of the right to health which must be addressed by state parties. First of all, the right to health is closely related to other human rights, such as, e.g., the right to safe and adequate food and safe and potable water. Consequently, it is necessary to pay attention to a number of other human rights addressing basic human needs and capabilities to ensure the right to health. As to state obligations, the General Comment applies the distinctions in public health between health promotion, disease prevention and access to care.

From a public health perspective, health promotion is of special importance as it supports the population in keeping healthy. General Comment no. 14 specifically stresses that 'the right to health embraces a wide range of socio-economic factors that promote conditions in which people can lead a healthy life, and extends to the underlying determinants of health'.[6] Apart from access to food, housing, water and sanitation, underlying determinants also include safe and healthy working conditions, a healthy environment and access to health-related education. The importance of the participation of the population in health-related decision-making at the local/community, national and international levels is also stressed.[7] Health promotion falls under the obligations of the states parties and requires a broad focus on promoting life conditions for the population. At the same time the CESCR also recognizes that the state cannot be exclusively responsible, as some aspects of population health may be outside the control of state actors. Consequently the right to health should not be understood at a 'right to be healthy', and it is stressed that a state cannot itself ensure good health as, for example, genetic or environmental factors and the adoption of unhealthy or risky lifestyles may have an impact on an individual's health conditions.[8] The state must pursue and enable full realisation of the highest attainable standard of health, but there may be factors outside its control, and the individual may also have some responsibility in regards to health promotion.[9]

---

[4]   WHO, 'Preamble to the Constitution of the World Health Organization' (22 July 1946) Official Records of the World Health Organization No 2 para 100.

[5]   Audrey R. Chapman, 'The Social Determinants of Health, Health Equity and Human Rights' (2010) 12 (2) Health and Hum. Rts. J. 17.

[6]   General Comment (n 2).

[7]   ibid para 1.

[8]   ibid para 9.

[9]   Signild Vallgårda and others, 'Backward- and Forward-Looking Responsibility for Obesity: Policies from WHO, the EU and England' (2015) 25(5) Eur.J.Pub.Health 845.

While health promotion is focusing on general living conditions to enhance the health condition of the population (and the individual), disease prevention pays attention to more specific health risks such as occupational diseases, communicable diseases and environmental issues. ICESCR art. 12.2(b) refers both to the importance of improving all aspects of environmental and industrial hygiene and the prevention and reduction of the populations' exposure to harmful substances such as radiation and harmful chemicals or other detrimental environmental conditions that directly or indirectly impact human health.[10] Furthermore, art. 12.2(c) refers to the need for prevention, treatment and control of epidemic, endemic, occupational and other diseases. In regard to disease prevention, the obligations on the states parties are important, as these are typically health risks that are outside the control of the individual.

Access to health care services is obviously also an important component of the right to health. According to art. 12.2(d) of the ICESCR, the right to health implies a right to have access to health care facilities, goods and services, and it is specified in more details in General Comment no. 14 to include 'the provision of equal and timely access to basic preventative, curative, rehabilitative health services and health education; regular screening programmes; appropriate treatment of prevalent diseases, illnesses, injuries and disabilities, preferably at community level; the provision of essential drugs; and appropriate mental health treatment and care'.[11] The General Comment furthermore develops a set of guiding principles in access to health care services, the so-called AAAQ-standard. According to this standard, health care services must first of all be available to the entire population without discrimination. Secondly, health care services must be accessible, both in terms of physical and economic accessibility. They must also be informationally accessible, and accessible for all without discrimination. Thirdly, health care services must be acceptable in terms of being culturally appropriate and compliant with ethical standards, and finally of good quality.

Whereas the individual is the rights holder, the states parties to the ICESCR are the duty bearers. In general, states parties' obligations in regard to human rights are normally interpreted in terms of respect (non-interference), protect (protect individuals from incursions by third parties) and fulfil (to facilitate and provide). This typology, developed by scholars and adopted by the treaty bodies, reflects a set of legal obligations imposed primarily on states. All three obligations are relevant in regard to poverty and health.[12] The obligation to fulfil the right to health is clearly important to break the vicious cycle between poverty and health, and the obligation to protect of particular importance in regard to vulnerable groups. The obligation to respect requires States to refrain from, for example, adopting policies which will have damaging effects on people's health.

---

[10] General Comment (n 2) paras 15–16; See also Dainius Puras, UN General Assembly (UNGA) 'Report of the Special Rapporteur on the Right of Everyone to the Enjoyment of the Highest Attainable Standard of Physical and Mental Health' (5 August 2016) UN Doc A/71/304 para 20; UN Human Rights Council (UNHRC) 'Report of the Special Rapporteur on the Implications for Human Rights of the Environmentally Sound Management and Disposal of Hazardous Substances and Wastes' (20 July 2017) UN Doc A/HRC/36/41 paras 9–11, 112(a); UNGA 'Report of the Special Rapporteur on the Implications for Human Rights of the Environmentally Sound Management and Disposal of Hazardous Substances and Wastes' (7 October 2019) UN Doc A/74/480.

[11] General Comment (n 2) para 17.

[12] Magdalena Sepúlveda Carmona, UNHRC 'Final Draft of the Guiding Principles on Extreme Poverty and Human Rights Submitted by the Special Rapporteur on Extreme Poverty and Human Rights' (18 July 2012) UN Doc A/HRC/21/39 paras 81–82.

II.   THE RELATION BETWEEN THE HUMAN RIGHT TO HEALTH AND POVERTY

A.   Is there a Link Between Poverty and Health?

As established in the introduction to this book,[13] there are various definitions of poverty, ranging from more narrow perceptions of poverty as lack of income (either in absolute terms or relative to the rest of the population) to broader conceptions promoted by scholars such as Amartya Sen[14] and Martha Nussbaum,[15] who associate poverty with the deprivation of basic needs and freedoms and the failure of basic capabilities. The broader conception of poverty, which is commonly applied in a human rights context, will also be applied here.[16]

The link between human rights and poverty is generally acknowledged. Human rights scholar Asbjørn Eide has stressed that poverty would not exist if the internationally-recognized human rights in their entirety were fully implemented.[17] In the Office of the High Commissioner of Human Rights (OHCHR) report on poverty reduction, the link between human rights compliance and poverty is also stressed, while at the same time recognizing that not all human rights violations are related to poverty and that combatting poverty is not only a matter of compliance with human rights.[18]

As poverty is characterized by deprivation of basic social goods and capabilities, and health is determined by social conditions (see section I), it is obvious that poverty will have an impact on the health of individuals and populations. Indeed, the relation between poverty and health was a priority for Paul Hunt, the first UN Special Rapporteur on the right of everyone to the highest attainable standard of physical and mental health. In his first report to the Commission on Human Rights he stressed the important – but poorly elaborated – impact that the right to health has on poverty reduction.[19] Succeeding Special Rapporteurs have confirmed the importance of addressing the relation between health and poverty.[20]

---

[13]   See the Introduction to this volume.

[14]   Amartya Sen, *Inequality Reexamined* (Harvard University Press 1992); Amartya Sen, *Development as Freedom* (Oxford University Press 1999); Amartya Sen, 'Human Rights and Capabilities' (2005) 6(2) J. Hum. Dev. 151–66.

[15]   Martha Nussbaum, *Women and Human Development: The Capabilities Approach* (Cambridge University Press 2000); Martha Nussbaum, 'Women's Bodies: Violence, Security Capabilities' (2005) 6(2) J. Hum. Dev. 167–83; Martha Nussbaum, *Creating Capabilities. The Human Development Approach* (Harvard University Press 2011).

[16]   OHCHR 'Human Rights and Poverty Reduction: A Conceptual Framework' (2004); CESCR, 'Substantive Issues Arising in the Implementation of ICESCR: Poverty and ICESCR' (2001) UN Doc E/C.12/2001/10.

[17]   Asbjørn Eide, 'Human Rights and the Elimination of Poverty' in A Kjønstad and LH Veit Wilson (eds) *Law, Power and Poverty* (CROP Publishers 1997).

[18]   OHCHR 'Human Rights and Poverty Reduction: A Conceptual Framework' (2004) 5.

[19]   Report of the Special Rapporteur, 'The Right of Everyone to the Enjoyment of the Highest Attainable Standard of Physical and Mental Health' (13 February 2003) UN Doc E/CN.4/2003/58 paras 44–58.

[20]   UNHRC 'Report of the Special Rapporteur on the Right of Everyone to the Enjoyment of the Highest Attainable Standard of Physical and Mental Health' (31 March 2009) UN Doc A/HRC/11/12 paras 12–13; UNGA 'Report of the Special Rapporteur on the Right of Everyone to the Enjoyment of the Highest Attainable Standard of Physical and Mental Health' (16 March 2011) UN Doc A/HRC/17/43; UNHRC 'Report of the Special Rapporteur on the Right of Everyone to the Enjoyment of the Highest

Within public health it is well-documented that social determinants are responsible for health inequities and differences in health status both within a population and between countries.[21] The WHO defines social determinants as the 'conditions in which people are born, grow, live, work and age'.[22] These conditions include basic needs such as safe water, adequate housing, sufficient supply of food and nutrition, access to education, safe working conditions and the environment/climate. Since access to basic social needs is shaped by the distribution of money, power and resources at global, national and local levels, there is also clearly an economic dimension to health.[23]

At the same time health is also a determinant of poverty. People with poor health and disabilities experience greater deprivation in access to basic social needs than healthy individuals.[24] This constitutes a vicious circle, a poverty trap, which is challenging to defeat.[25] The UN Sustainable Development Goals (SDGs)[26] set out in Goal 1 to end poverty in all its forms and everywhere, and the SDG framework pays close attention to the link between basic social conditions and poverty. This interconnectedness is highlighted for example in target 1.3, which refers to the importance of nationally appropriate social protection systems to achieve substantial coverage of the poor and the vulnerable. Similarly, target 1.4 stresses the significance of equal rights for all men and women – and in particular the poor and the vulnerable – to economic resources, as well as 'access to basic services, ownership and control over land and other forms of property, inheritance, natural resources, appropriate new technology and financial services, including microfinance'. These provisions recognize that poverty, lack of access to basic social goods, and poor health are closely tied together.

B.   How Poverty Impacts the Right to Health and Vice Versa

Poverty intersects with each dimension of the right to health: health promotion, disease prevention and access to care (see section I). In regard to health promotion, states must provide conditions in which people can live a healthy life. This is challenging for many countries, due to the wide array of human rights and entitlements involved. In some situations, it is obvious

---

Attainable Standard of Physical and Mental Health' (12 April 2011) UN Doc A/HRC/17/25 paras 5–6, 11–13; UNHRC 'Report of the Special Rapporteur on the Right of Everyone to the Enjoyment of the Highest Attainable Standard of Physical and Mental Health' (2 April 2015) UN Doc A/HRC/29/33 para 55; UNGA 'Report of the Special Rapporteur on the Right of Everyone to the Enjoyment of the Highest Attainable Standard of Physical and Mental Health' (5 August 2016) UN Doc A/71/304 para 103(l).

[21]   WHO Commission on the Social Determinants of Health, 'Closing the Gap in a Generation. Health Equity Through Action on the Social Determinants of Health' (2008); M Marmot, 'Social Determinants of Health Inequalities' (2005) Lancet 1099.

[22]   WHO, 'About Social Determinants of Health' <www.who.int/social_determinants/sdh_definition/en/> accessed 13 June 2020.

[23]   OHCHR, 'Human Rights and Poverty Reduction: A Conceptual Framework' (OHCHR 2004).

[24]   WHO and the World Bank, 'Disability report' (2011); For the EU, see Eurostat, 'Disability Statistics – Poverty and Income Inequalities' (August 2015) <https://ec.europa.eu/eurostat/statistics-explained/pdfscache/34425.pdf > accessed 12 April 2020; Mónica Pinilla-Roncancio, 'Disability and Poverty. Two Related Conditions. A Literature Review' (2015) 63 Revista de la Facultad de Medicina 113.

[25]   Paula Braveman and Sofia Gruskin, 'Poverty, Equity, Human rights and Health' (2003) 81(7) Bulletin of the WHO: Int'l J. Pub. Health 539.

[26]   UNGA Res 70/1 (21 October 2015) A/RES/70/1.

that states parties to the ICESCR need to respond to for example a lack of access to potable water and sanitation and to safe and nutritious food. In other situations, basic conditions to live a healthy life may be in place in terms of food, water, shelter, education, access to health care services, health information and other factors. However, deprived individuals may still have difficulties in profiting from these conditions due to lack of capabilities, power and strength. People facing poverty are often exposed to a number of additional systemic burdens and obstacles of innumerable kinds, which cumulatively can make health goals such as quitting smoking, regularly exercising, making varied healthy home-cooked meals – goals that are often challenging for an average individual – virtually impossible to achieve for those living in poverty.[27] To adopt a healthy lifestyle and cook a healthy meal, take a run or quit smoking may be an overwhelming endeavour amidst all the other problems. This may be the reason why health inequalities seem to persist even in welfare states like the Nordic countries – a situation which is referred to as a paradox in the public health literature.[28]

When it comes to disease prevention, the most deprived will often be facing more difficulties than the more affluent part of the population. For example, vaccination and immunization are not widely available and accessible in all parts of the world or to all population groups within countries.[29] Risks of being exposed to environmental risks such as polluted water and health challenges provoked by climate change are also bigger for people living in poor areas.[30] Work environments for those with the lowest salary tend to involve bigger risk of health hazards than for employees with higher salaries. Low salaries may even be a health risk.[31] States parties clearly have a human rights obligation to respect and protect the right to health and to provide disease prevention without discrimination, but this is far from being reality, especially for the most deprived.

Finally, it is well known that access to health care services is not distributed equally among the population. In health care systems based on private insurance, it is obvious that the most affluent have better access to health care than the most deprived. But even in welfare societies with publicly financed health care provided free of charge, the most affluent parts of the population often have easier access to specialist care and to more advanced care than the more deprived parts of the population. Physical accessibility also differs as the most deprived part of the population tend to live either in remote, thinly inhabited areas or in limited space in bigger

---

[27]   UN HRC, 'Final Draft of the Guiding Principles on Extreme Poverty and Human Rights Submitted by the Special Rapporteur on Extreme Poverty and Human Rights' (18 July 2012) UN Doc A/HRC/21/39 paras 81–82; see also Z Strauss and D Horsten, 'A Human Rights-Based Approach to Poverty Reduction: The Role of the Right of Access to Medicine as an Element of the Right of Access to Health Care' (2013) 16(3) Potchefstroom E.L.J. 7.

[28]   J P Mackenbach, 'The Persistence of Inequalities in Modern Welfare States: The Explanation of a Paradox' (2012) 75 Soc. Sci. & Med. 761; J P Mackenbach, 'Review Article: Persistence of Social Inequalities in Modern Welfare States: The Explanation of a Paradox' (2017) 45 Scandinavian J. Pub. Health 113; M Marmot, 'The Health Gap: The Challenge of an Unequal World' (2015) 386 Lancet 2442.

[29]   María Clara Restrepo-Méndez and others, 'Inequalities in Full Immunization Coverage: Trends in Low- and Middle-Income Countries' (2016) 94 Bulletin of the WHO 794.

[30]   WHO, 'Quantitative Risk Assessment of the Effects of Climate Change on Selected Causes of Death, 2030s and 2050s' (2014); UNGA, 'Poverty and Climate Change. Report of the UN Special Rapporteur on Extreme Poverty and Human Rights' (17 July 2019) UN Doc A/HRC/41/39; See also chapter 31 by Sumudu Atapattu.

[31]   JP Leigh and R De Vogli, 'Low Wage as Environmental Health Hazards' (2016) 58(5) J.O.H. & Envtl. Med. 444.

cities where the number of general practitioners is lower than in middle- and upper-class neighbourhoods.[32] These are important examples of spatial poverty.

As mentioned above (section II A), poverty and health have a dual relation. Poverty is not only a contributor to poor health. Poor health may also lead to poverty – which subsequently will enforce ill-health, lead to more poverty, and thus create a vicious cycle.[33] Ill health can lead to loss of job and income, and medical treatment may be expensive and ruin a family economy. The impact may differ depending on the level of social security and availability of access to low cost treatment in the country. However, poor health conditions will normally always have an impact on access to basic social goods.[34] This is relevant for all health conditions,[35] but in case of longer periods of sickness or of disabilities the impact that poor health can have on access to basic social goods may be significant and could also be enforced by other – intersecting – factors such as disability, gender, age, ethnicity and migration status.[36] It is documented that persons with disabilities experience deprivation to a larger degree than others in regards to basic social goods.[37]

Seen from a poverty-eradication perspective, the human right to health provides a legal tool to fight poverty. Promotion of the right to health and its progressive realization could, consequently, help to reduce poverty.[38] However, to be successful it will be necessary not only to focus on the right to health but also to pay attention to the realization of other human rights on which the right to health depends, such as socio-economic rights to food, water and sanitation, shelter and education, and also civil and political rights, such as the right to life, right to privacy and freedom of speech. As stressed by Audrey Chapman, it is crucial to acknowledge the inter-connection and the 'interactive and cumulative effect' between these separate rights instead of focusing on them separately.[39] Furthermore, the capability to profit from basic social goods that may be available should also be at the centre of attention. This means that it is not sufficient that basic social goods are available. Individuals must also have the ability to profit from such opportunities. In this context applying a human rights-based approach could be helpful.

---

[32]   For rural areas see e.g. World Bank, *World Development Report* (2006) 29; AE Joseph and DR Phillips, *Accessibility and Utilization: Geographical Perspectives on Health Care Delivery* (Harper & Row 1984); OECD, 'Financial and Geographic Access to Health Care' in *Government at a Glance 2015* (OECD Publishing 2015). For urban spaces see e.g. Cookson R and others, 'Unequal Socioeconomic Distribution of the Primary Care Workforce: Whole-Population Small Area Longitudinal Study' (2016) BMJ Open 5; Rebecca Lee, 'How Poverty and Location Limit Access to Health Care' <https://blog.rendia.com/poverty-location-limit-access-health-care/> accessed 15 June 2020; UNHRC, 'Final Draft of the Guiding Principles on Extreme Poverty and Human Rights Submitted by the Special Rapporteur on Extreme Poverty and Human Rights' (18 July 2012) UN Doc. A/HRC/21/39 paras 81–82.
[33]   See n 24; J Braithwaite and D Mont, 'Disability as Poverty: A Survey of the World Bank Poverty Assessments and Implications' (2009) Eur. J. Disability Res. 219.
[34]   ibid.
[35]   A Wagstaff, 'Poverty and Health Sector Inequalities' (2002) 80(2) Bulletin of the WHO 97.
[36]   See chapter seven by Gerard Quinn on poverty and disability in this volume.
[37]   See n 33.
[38]   ibid.
[39]   See n 5.

III.   A HUMAN RIGHTS-BASED APPROACH TO HEALTH AND POVERTY

The concept of a human rights-based approach was originally introduced in the context of development with the aim of having a stronger focus on individuals' rights instead of exclusively addressing human needs. Since 1997 all UN agencies are expected to mainstream human rights into all their programmes and activities.[40] A common understanding of a human rights-based approach was developed in 2003 at an inter-agency workshop, where three constituting elements of a human rights-based approach to development was outlined.[41] First, all policies, programmes and actions should further the realization of human rights. Secondly, human rights standards and principles should guide all actions, cooperation and programming in all sectors and in all phases of the process.[42] Finally, all policies, programmes and actions should contribute to the development of capacities of the 'duty bearers' to meet their obligations and of the rights holders to claim their rights.

The WHO has specified the human rights-based approach in regards to health.[43] First, all health strategies and policies should aim at realizing the right to health and other health related rights. Consequently, a human rights-based approach to health also includes promotion of other rights, such as the right to nutritious food, access to water, shelter and education. The AAAQ standard (outlined in section I) also provides important directions for the full realization of the right to health. In addition, all health policy work and programmes should be 'guided by human rights standards and principles', such as participation, equality and non-discrimination and accountability.[44] Thus pursuing the right to health and other health related rights should be done with the inclusion and participation of those who are directly affected by decisions regarding health care plans and provision. Furthermore, equality and non-discrimination must be sought in all laws, policies and practices. Transparency regarding all decisions and decision-making processing serves to promote accountability, which is also promoted when states parties sign and ratify important human rights instruments promoting the right to health and other health related rights. Lastly, the final outcome should be to build capacity among duty bearers to fulfil their duties and to empower rights-holders to claim their rights to health and other health related rights.

The focus on empowerment of the rights holders is crucial from a poverty perspective. This serves to inform and create awareness among individuals regarding their rights and to empower them to claim them. Even in situations where the duty bearers – the governments – are committed to fulfil their obligations, empowerment is still important. The welfare state

---

[40]   UNGA, 'Renewing the United Nations: A Programme for Reform' (17 July 1997) UN Doc. A/51/950.

[41]   United Nations Sustainable Development Group (UNSDG), 'The Human Rights Based Approach to Development Cooperation – Towards a Common Understanding among the United Nations Agencies' (2003).

[42]   Human rights standards and principles includes universality and inalienability; indivisibility; inter-dependence and inter-relatedness; non-discrimination and equality; participation and inclusion; accountability and the rule of law.

[43]   WHO, 'A Human Rights-Based Approach to Health' <www.who.int/hhr/news/hrba_to_health2 .pdf> accessed 15 June 2020.

[44]   See n 41.

paradox mentioned in section II is a good example of the persistent nature of poverty even in states providing universal access to health care and other social goods.

The definition of poverty applied in this chapter stresses the importance of both basic social goods and capabilities. The welfare state paradox is an example of a situation where access to basic social goods is provided but where the capabilities are missing. Empowering individuals not only to claim their rights but also strengthening their capabilities to profit from the available social goods is crucial to fight poverty. In this context, it is not sufficient to provide opportunities to participate and be engaged. Deeply entrenched marginalization as well as the nearly insurmountable logistical barriers that are associated with living in poverty can often make opportunities to participate inaccessible in practice. This stresses the importance of actively reaching out to deprived individuals to ensure they have a voice in health-related decisions at both local, national and international levels.[45]

The Swedish hospital Angered in Gothenburg can serve as a promising example of how a human rights-based approach to health can work in a deprived neighbourhood. Angered hospital opened its doors in 2015. The intention was to establish a community-based hospital with a strong focus on public and community health and with a strong research component as well. From the beginning, Angered decided to adopt a human rights-based approach in its interaction with the local community.[46] The hospital applies a so-called 'comprehensive methodology',[47] which strives to shrink the social gap. Local community members and professionals collaborate on developing the priorities for how community health shall develop and decide which project to prioritize and how research should be done. Community health is understood in a broad sense. One of the projects focuses on teaching people not only to bike but also to repair and take care of their bikes. The strategy here is to reach out to the patients and to community members to engage them in developing and organizing health care services at the hospital as well as in community and home-care settings. Citizens are informed about their rights – and what a human rights-based approach implies – and empowered by the hospital's 'reach-out approach', where information about rights does not stand alone. Likewise, the professionals are similarly aware of and committed to their duties as duty bearers.

Angered hospital demonstrates the value of a human rights-based approach to fight poverty. Even though it will take time to reduce the health and social gap, it is important to take serious action. Preliminary results from some of the projects show that the reach-out initiatives together with the comprehensive methodology seem to move things in the right direction and both citizens and professionals are profiting from this new mindset.[48] More research is needed in this area to explore how a human rights-based approach can serve to strengthen the capabilities of the most deprived.

---

[45] The importance of the participation of the population in health-related decision-making at both local/community, national and international levels. General Comment (n 2) section 11.

[46] Information in English about Angered hospital is available here <www.angeredsnarsjukhus.se/om -angereds-narsjukhus/about-angered-hospital/> accessed 15 June 2020.

[47] In Swedish it is called 'helhetsmetodikken'.

[48] See e.g. results (in Swedish) from a project concerned with collaboration with families on timely analyses of small children with autism and other developmental disorders in the report 'dörren man öppnar och där finns allting' (you open the door, and then you find everything), <www.angeredsnarsjukhus.se/ om-angereds-narsjukhus/hjallbosamverkan/> accessed 12 April 2020.

IV.　NEW HEALTH TECHNOLOGIES: IMPACT ON HEALTH AND POVERTY?

As in many other areas of society, health care services are also committed to profit from new technologies and scientific advancements. The right to benefit from scientific progress is also a human right,[49] and new medical technologies have the potential to influence – positively or negatively – the realization of the right to health. It is therefore important to assess how new medical technologies may impact on health and poverty. Lack of access to medicine in general, and more specifically to pharmaceuticals and treatment for so-called neglected diseases, has been widely discussed in the public health and human rights literature.[50] This section will focus on a recent and less analysed issue: the impact new data-driven technologies could have on health and poverty.

Precision medicine is a new medical phenomenon that is prioritized in national health strategies across the globe.[51] This technology represents a new development in the way health care services provide health promotion, disease prevention, diagnostics and treatment to patients. The general idea behind precision medicine is to provide more tailored health care services to the individual patient (or to groups of similar patients) instead of treatment that works for the average patient but not necessarily for the individual patient. Precision medicine is a very information-intensive technology. It relies on new advances in gene technologies, such as comprehensive gene scans (Whole Genome Sequencing (WGS) and Genome Wide Association Studies (GWAS)), which provide comprehensive knowledge about the individual's genetic makeup. Such genetic information can be linked together with all sorts of other data from various sources – health data as well as socio-economic and environmental data – in a big data environment and create knowledge regarding risks, susceptibilities and the efficacy of pharmaceuticals and other treatments. Based on this knowledge it is possible to develop algorithms/AI-solutions which can assist the health care services and health professionals in stratifying patients to the right kind of health promotion, prevention and medical treatment.

Currently the development of precision medicine is first and foremost taking place in research settings. Its application in the clinic is still limited, and it is mostly used in regard to treatment of certain types of cancers. Its application as a public health tool is also in its infancy. However, many countries have adopted national strategies and provided funding to support research in this area with the clear intention to make it available as soon as possible.

---

[49]　UNGA 'Report of the Special Rapporteur in the Field of Cultural Rights Farida Shaheed, The Right to Enjoy the Benefits from Scientific Progress and its Applications' (12 May 2012) UN Doc A/HRC/20/26; A Chapman, 'Towards an Understanding of the Right to Enjoy the Benefits of Scientific Progress and its Applications' (2009) 8 J. Hum. Rts. 1.

[50]　See e.g. a number of articles in Health and Human Rights Journal 20(1) (2018) (neglected diseases); AE Yamin, 'Not Just a Tragedy: Access to Medications as a Right under International Law' (2003) 21 B.U.Int'l L.J. 325; J Lee and P Hunt, 'Human Rights Responsibilities of Pharmaceutical Companies in Relation to Access to Medicines' (2012) 40(2) J.L.M & E. 220; S Moon and others, 'Innovation and Access to Medicines for Neglected Populations: Could a Treaty Address a Broken Pharmaceutical R&D System?' (2012) 9(5) PLoSMed, e1001218; S Moon, 'Respecting the Right to Access to Medicines: Implications of the UN Guiding Principles on Business and Human Rights for the Pharmaceutical Industry' (2013) 15(1) Health & Hum. Rts. J. 32.

[51]　Precision medicine is also known as personalized medicine, individualized medicine, tailored medicine, individualized medicine and P4-medicine. There is no general agreement about the terminology.

The 100,000 Genomes Project in the UK[52] is an example, together with the Obama Precision Medicine Initiative.[53] Several other countries have also launched precision medicine initiatives, and the EU is supporting cross-Europe cooperation to integrate precision medicine into European Union's health care systems.[54]

Governments expect this new technology to be beneficial for both the individual and society. Individuals may gain from more tailored health promotion, prevention and treatment that will allow them to benefit from medical interventions without being subjected to medicine with poor effect and maybe even damaging side effects. It is also thought to be beneficial for society due to expected cost savings when prevention and treatment can be directed precisely to those who can actually benefit from it.[55]

Precision medicine initiatives have been criticized for focusing primarily on diagnostics and treatment and paying less attention to health promotion and prevention. It has also been argued that the importance of genetics is overemphasized, and the impact of social determinants almost ignored. The development of precision public health, where the same kind of data – genomic as well as other data (including socio-economic data) – are used to identify more suitable means of health promotion and prevention can be seen as the public health response to the clinical focus of many national precision medicine initiatives.[56] The World Health Assembly has adopted a resolution on digital health calling on the WHO to develop a strategy on digital health, and the WHO sent a draft strategy for public consultation in 2019.[57] This emphasizes the importance from the perspective of the public health community in making use of data and digital tools to promote public health.

As with any other technology there are of course also concerns, and both precision medicine and precision public health give rise to human rights concerns. Precision medicine raises issues about basic patients' rights, such as the right to information (and the right to not know), right to privacy and confidentiality, duties and rights in regard to relatives, and the risk of genetic discrimination. Due to possible biases in the available data sources and in the selection of data, the effect on equitable access to health care services – both nationally and globally – has also been questioned.[58] General Comment no. 14 stressed that health care services must be available to all – and in sufficient quantity. As precision medicine is expected to be an essential health care service, it must be available for all. Consequently, there are good reasons to

---

[52]   'The 100,000 Genomes Project' (*Genomics England*) <www.genomicsengland.co.uk/about-genomics-england/the-100000-genomes-project/> accessed 15 June 2020.

[53]   'Fact Sheet: President Obama's Precision Medicine Initiative' (*The White House*, 30 January 2015) <https://obamawhitehouse.archives.gov/the-press-office/2015/01/30/fact-sheet-president-obama-s-precision-medicine-initiative> accessed 15 June 2020.

[54]   Council Conclusions on Personalised Medicine for Patients (2015) OJ C/421/2.

[55]   It seems, however, that it is difficult to assess the economic effect of introducing precision medicine in the health care services. M Kasztura and others, 'Cost-Effectiveness of Precision Medicine – a Scoping Review' (2019) 109(6) Int J.Pub.Health.

[56]   See e.g. MJ Khoury and others, 'Precision Public Health for the Era of Precision Medicine' (2016) 109(6) Am J Prev Med 398.

[57]   WHO, 'Digital health' (26 May 2018) WHA71.7; 'WHO Releases First Guideline on Digital Health Interventions' (17 April 2019) <www.who.int/news-room/detail/17-04-2019-who-releases-first-guideline-on-digital-health-interventions> accessed 15 June 2020.

[58]   KA McClellan and others, 'Personalized Medicine and Access to Health Care: Potential for Inequitable Access' (2013) 21 Eur. J. Hum. Genetics 143; D Taylor-Robinson and F Kee, 'Precision Public Health – the Emperor's New Clothes' (2019) 48(1) Int. J Epidemiol, 1.

explore how the application of this new technology may affect poverty and the right to health. Precision public health provokes some of the same issues – especially the right to privacy, right to self-determination, transparency and risk of bias and discrimination.

To understand these potential human rights concerns, it is necessary to look closer at how precision medicine and precision public health will be developed and applied. As mentioned above, both precision medicine and precision public health rely on data generated through intensive data sourcing, where data – including genetic data – from a large part of the population is used to develop reference genomes or other models to stratify patients to the right kind of health prevention or treatment. Such models are suited to individuals who resemble the population group from whom data has been collected in terms of, for example, age, ethnicity and gender. They are less suited to serve as tools for individuals within another age group or with another ethnicity or gender. Some parts of the population produce less health data than others, either because they belong to a group with a limited number of individuals (e.g. a minority group), or because they are not using the health care services (or other services) to the same extent as others. As noted by the UN Special Rapporteur on Extreme Poverty, digital systems may not be satisfactory for vulnerable populations because they 'often operate on the law of average, in the interests of the majorities and the basis of predicted outcomes or likelihoods'.[59] In some countries with a private health care system, individuals with lower socio-economic status and/or without health insurance will visit health care services less often and thus leave less data behind. For example, being part of a minority ethnic group and under 40 has been shown to result in reduced accuracy of the precision medicine models used in regard to breast cancer,[60] and women are also often mentioned as underrepresented in medical trials.

If we apply the AAAQ standard (see section I) to precision medicine and precision public health, it may turn out that these digital technologies will not be available or beneficial for all population groups. If the data collection and selection is not organized in an inclusive manner, there is a risk that vulnerable and marginalized groups – those who are already left behind – will be deprived from profiting from this technology to the same extent as the average population.[61]

Some national strategies pay attention to the risk of bias and possible discriminatory effect of precision medicine. The U.S. precision medicine initiative is named the 'All of Us Research Program', and it is clearly stressed that the programme should reflect the diversity of the U.S. population and will enrol participants from diverse gender, social, racial/ethnic, ancestral, geographic and economic backgrounds as well as from all age groups and health statuses.[62] In contrast the Danish precision medicine policy stresses that Denmark is the perfect location for the development of precision medicine because the country is considered to be genetically homogeneous.[63] Compared to the U.S. programme, this sends a very different message to

---

[59]   UNGA, 'Digital Welfare States and Human Rights. Report of the UN Special Rapporteur on Extreme Poverty and Human Rights' (11 October 2019) UN Doc A/74/493 para 59.

[60]   See n 58.

[61]   E Vayena, A Blasimme, IG Cohen, 'Machine Learning in Medicine: Addressing Ethical Challenges' (6 November 2018) 15(11) PLoS Med; Z Obermeyer and others, 'Dissecting Racial Bias in an Algorithm Used to Manage the Health of Populations' (2019) 366 Science; Taylor-Robinson (n 58).

[62]   'All of Us Research Program' (*National Institutes of Health*) <www.researchallofus.org> accessed 15 June 2020.

[63]   'Analysis of Personal Medicine' (*DAMVAD*, 2 February 2016) <www.regioner.dk/media/3128/damvad-rapport-analyse-af-personlig-medicin.pdf> accessed 15 June 2020.

minority population groups in Denmark. They may not only feel excluded from profiting from this new health technology – they will actually be excluded and deprived of access to health care services which the majority of the population will profit from. This is indeed not compliant with the duty of states parties to make health care services available without discrimination.

If we look at the other criteria in the AAAQ standard, we can see that there may also be potential challenges. In terms of physical accessibility, precision medicine may reinforce existing barriers. As with all health care services, it would probably be easier to have access in bigger cities and in more affluent countries than in more remote areas and low income countries. Economic accessibility could be a special challenge – especially in countries with a private or insurance-based health care system. Even though a comprehensive gene scan has and will become cheaper, it will still not be economically accessible for many individuals – and a comprehensive genetic analysis is often necessary to benefit from precision medicine. In addition, the specialized counselling and treatment needed for each patient will also be a significant economic burden. As gene scans may reveal genetic predisposition to develop specific disorders, it may also create problems in having access to health insurance or sufficient insurance coverage. In countries with a tax-paid health care system, it may turn out that accessibility in practice is more limited for individuals in lower socio-economic strata, because the barriers for individuals in these groups are the same as with all other sorts of health care services (see above in section I). The algorithm could potentially also be used to stratify which patients would be provided with health prevention and treatment. For example, if data shows that people from lower socio-economic parts of the population are less likely to comply with public health guidelines on non-smoking, healthy eating and physical activity, it could potentially be used in algorithmic-based prioritization of treatments to patients or to determine whom should be approached by screening programmes. Finally, in regard to information accessibility, precision medicine may be difficult to understand and require comprehensive counselling and information in a treatment situation, which also may unevenly impact persons from lower socio-economic groups.

The acceptability criteria is concerned with the ethical and cultural aspects of the health care service provided. As already mentioned, precision medicine and precision public health give rise to a number of concerns in regard to respect for privacy, non-discrimination and stigmatization, and may thus turn out to be a health care service with low acceptability.

In regard to quality, precision medicine is anticipated to have the potential to provide better and more tailored care, and precision public health is thought to provide better targeted public health measures. The aim is treatment, health promotion or prevention that works for all individuals, instead of only for some, which is clearly a strength. However, experiences in using digital welfare services give rise to quality concerns, as data may be both biased and inaccurate.[64] The question is then whether precision medicine and precision public health will fulfil the high expectation and actually ensure good health promotion, prevention and healthcare for the entire population, or whether it will reinforce existing inequalities and divert needed resources from the healthcare system that could otherwise be used for more traditional types of health promotion.

---

[64] UNGA, 'Digital Welfare States and Human Rights. Report of the UN Special Rapporteur on Extreme Poverty and Human Rights' (11 October 2019) UN Doc A/74/493; Virginia Eubanks, *Automating Inequality: How High-Tech Tools Profile, Police, and Punish the Poor* (New York, St Martin's Press, 2018).

Another concern is how the 'predictive power' associated with the stratification of individuals based on genetic and other data will be approached and governed by societies. The information regarding the individual generated by comprehensive big data analyses will inevitably reveal vulnerabilities and susceptibilities which – seen from the perspective of society – could be used to stratify citizens toward various kinds of public services. One could imagine that it would not be considered economically sustainable to provide expensive university education or medical treatment to an individual whose genetic profile predict a poor life prospect. This and a number of other questions are still unanswered.

Precision medicine will be expensive and will likely benefit rich over poor. This could potentially result in an even larger divide between health in developed and developing countries and within countries. Application of precision public health will not be an economic burden to the citizens but could potentially turn out to benefit rich over poor and direct money from more low-tech and low-cost but highly efficient health promotion programmes. It could also be asked whether precision medicine and precision public health will alter the social contract between the state and the individual and serve as a means of shifting more responsibility from the state to the individual, especially in terms of avoiding non-communicable diseases such as those caused by poor diet and lack of physical activity.

Many questions are blowing in the wind and raise doubt as to whether this new medical technology will benefit all parts of the population equally, or whether it will follow the usual pattern of health inequities – and maybe even be used as a tool to stratify individuals into poverty. This is an area where more research is needed.

V.   THE POWER OF A HUMAN RIGHTS-BASED APPROACH TO POVERTY?

Looking at poverty and health through the lenses of human rights provides a tool to address the lack of access to basic goods and capabilities as an infringement of fundamental rights and not merely as a social problem.[65] Poverty has a profound and negative impact on the realization of the right to health, and ill-health may in itself be a determinant of and lead to poverty. There is a clear relation between poverty and health, and a comprehensive human rights-based approach may help to raise awareness of the responsibilities of governments in complying with their obligations to respect, protect and fulfil human rights. Therefore, more research is needed to develop a more comprehensive human rights-based approach that acknowledges the inter-connection between the right to health, other related socio-economic rights and civil and political rights.

The relation between the right to health and poverty exposes a kind of 'clash' between a human rights and public health approach. As critically discussed by Audrey Chapman (see section I), it seems that the human rights framework prefers to use the expression 'underlying determinants' of health, whereas the WHO and public health community in general favour the expression 'social determinants', which is perceived to pay more attention to root and structural causes of health disparities, such as social class and socio-economic conditions.

---

[65]   Z Strauss and D Horsten, 'A Human Rights-Based Approach to Poverty Reduction: The Role of the Right of Access to Medicine as an Element of the Right of Access to Health Care' (2013) 16(3) Potchefstroom Electronic Law Journal.

The intersection between a human rights and a public health approach to health and poverty is another important research avenue to explore.

As shown in this chapter, compliance with obligations to provide opportunities for people to live a healthy life is not enough to fight inequity in health and to enable people to move out of poverty. This means that availability of basic social services is not sufficient if individuals still do not have the capabilities needed to get out of the poverty trap. An important component of a human rights-based approach is to reach out to and truly engage individuals in all areas of life.[66] In regards to the right to health, General Comment no. 14 stresses the importance of the participation of the population in health-related decision-making at both local/community, national and international levels.[67] There are promising examples from Sweden of how outreach and engagement can serve to facilitate access to the health care services and to empower the most deprived part of the population. This is an area where more research would be welcomed.

Finally, the impact new health technologies may have on the right to health and poverty is also an important future research agenda, where a broad human rights approach encompassing both socio-economic rights (e.g., right to health, food, water, a decent standard of living) and civil and political rights (e.g., right to life, privacy, non-discrimination, freedom of speech) will be needed, together with insight in the design and dynamics of the technology itself.

All in all, innovative research is needed to promote the ambition of the UN Sustainable Development Goals of ending poverty and leaving no one behind. This requires research that moves beyond traditional disciplinary and sectoral boundaries and dichotomies.

---

[66] M Kjaeum, 'Go Local, Preserve the Global: Re-engage to Build Trust in Democracy and Human Rights' in P Hladschik and F. Steinert (eds), *Menschenrechten Gestald und Wirksamkeit verleihen. Making Human Rights Work. Festschrift für Manfred Nowak und Hannes Tretter* (Neuer Wissenschaftlicher Verlag / Wien-Graz, 2019) 153.

[67] General Comment (n 2) section 11.

26. Human rights and abortion access for people living in poverty: implications for the United States and globally

Risa E. Kaufman and Diana Kasdan

Reproductive rights are human rights. There is clear consensus by UN human rights treaty bodies and independent experts that human rights protections in areas including access to contraception, maternal health care, infertility care, and abortion are essential to achieving good health, gender equality, and empowering people[1] to determine their futures.

Less clear is how this wide recognition of reproductive rights as human rights might influence national jurisprudence to protect the reproductive rights of people in marginalized communities, including people living in poverty, as well as people of color, immigrants, people with disabilities, and other people experiencing multiple and intersecting forms of discrimination.

Abortion access in the United States offers an important point of inquiry for this analysis. In the United States, poverty disproportionately impacts marginalized communities. For people with marginalized identities, discrimination and poverty are often inter-related, threatening multiple human rights at once and leaving them more vulnerable to poor reproductive health outcomes and violations of their reproductive rights. UN human rights experts have issued numerous findings and recommendations with respect to reproductive rights violations in the United States and access to abortion for women living in poverty, in particular.[2] Crises, such as the COVID-19 pandemic, only heighten the inequities and challenges that people living in poverty face in accessing abortion in the United States.

Yet, U.S. constitutional law offers limited protection for people living in poverty to access abortion care. The U.S. Supreme Court has held that the government is not required to fund abortions under federal or state Medicaid programs. More generally, while the U.S. Supreme Court has repeatedly affirmed the constitutional right to abortion established in *Roe v. Wade*,[3] including more recently in *Whole Woman's Health v. Hellerstedt*,[4] it has not interpreted the U.S. Constitution to impose affirmative obligations on the government to protect economic and social rights, including reproductive health care access.

---

[1] Throughout, this chapter uses gender inclusive language to acknowledge that transgender men and some gender nonconforming people require access to contraception, maternal health care, infertility care, and safe abortion services. People of all gender identities experience reproductive rights violations.

[2] United Nations General Assembly 'Report of the Working Group on the issue of discrimination against women in law and practice on its mission to the United States of America' (7 June 2016) UN Doc A/HRC/32/44/Add.2 para 90, vii, x, xvi; UNGA 'Report of the Special Rapporteur Philip Alston on extreme poverty and human rights on his mission to the United States of America' (4 May 2018) UN Doc A/HRC/38/33/Add.1, para 56.

[3] 410 US 113 (1973).

[4] 136 S Ct 2292 (2016).

How might human rights make a difference in this jurisprudential approach? This chapter examines the potential impact of human rights on constitutional and other legal protections for reproductive rights. Using abortion access in the United States as a case study, this chapter seeks to identify opportunities for future research to evaluate where and how a human rights-based approach to litigation and supportive advocacy can advance a more holistic jurisprudential approach to reproductive rights, with particular implications for people living in poverty.

Section I provides an overview of the normative framework protecting reproductive rights as human rights, focusing on how human rights law engages an analysis of poverty in its protection of the right to abortion access. Section II explores the impact of human rights framing on jurisprudence to protect access to abortion for people who are living in poverty. Section III turns the focus to the United States. After setting the stage for how U.S. law and policy has failed to protect access to abortion care for people living in poverty, we survey the jurisprudential approaches (and potential approaches) to poverty and reproductive rights in the United States, as well as the potential impact of human rights in this area of U.S. jurisprudence. The concluding section discusses implications for future research.

I.   REPRODUCTIVE RIGHTS AS HUMAN RIGHTS

Reproductive rights are human rights, as formally recognized in the 1994 International Conference on Population and Development (ICPD) Programme of Action.[5] This consensus landmark document, signed by 179 states, spurred remarkable progress in international legal and human rights protections for women and girls' access to reproductive health care and their ability to make reproductive decisions.[6] It was confirmed and strengthened at the 1995 Fourth World Conference for Women in Beijing,[7] and subsequent review conferences.[8] Since then, human rights law has more fully explicated that reproductive rights are grounded in numerous fundamental human rights, including the rights to health, life, equality, information, educa-

---

[5]   'Programme of Action of the International Conference on Population and Development' (Cairo 5–13 Sept 1994) UN Doc A/CONF.171/13/Rev.1 paras 7.2–7.3.

[6]   See Katherine Mayall and Johanna B Fine, 'Briefing Paper: Abortion Worldwide: 20 Years of Reform' (Center for Reproductive Rights 2014) <www.reproductiverights.org/sites/crr.civicactions .net/files/documents/20Years_Reform_Report.pdf> accessed 7 June 2020; Laura Reichenbach and Mindy Jane Roseman (eds), *Reproductive Health and Human Rights: The Way Forward* (University of Pennsylvania Press 2009).

[7]   'Beijing Declaration and Platform for Action' The 1995 Fourth World Conference on Women: Action for Equality, Development and Peace (Beijing 4–15 Sept 1995) UN Doc A/CONF.177/20 para 94.

[8]   UNGA 'Key Actions for the Further Implementation of the Programme of Action' International Conference on Population and Development (New York 30 June–2 July 1999) 21st Special Session UN Doc A/S-21/5/Add.1 para 3, 40–41 [ICPD+5 Key Actions Document]; *Further actions and initiatives to implement the Beijing Declaration and the Platform for Action (Annex, Draft Resolution II)*, 'Report of the Ad Hoc Committee of the Whole of the Twenty-Third Special Session of the General Assembly' (New York, 5–9 June 2000) UN Doc A/S-23/10/Rev.1 para 72 (i)–(k) [Beijing+5 Review Document]; See Lucia Berro Pizzarossa, 'Here to Stay: The Evolution of Sexual and Reproductive Health and Rights in International Human Rights Law' (2018) 7 Laws 1, 10–11.

tion, privacy, freedom from discrimination and violence, and freedom from torture and cruel, inhuman, and degrading treatment.[9]

Human rights law recognizes and protects access to safe and legal abortion, in particular, noting its centrality to achieving autonomy and reproductive health. In recent years, UN human rights experts have expressed concern about the impact of severe legal restrictions, barriers, and stigma on abortion access. They have called on governments to amend legislation, lift barriers, remove criminal penalties, and prevent stigmatization of women and girls seeking abortion, so as to ensure effective access to safe, legal abortion services.[10]

UN human rights treaty-monitoring bodies have been particularly attentive to the barriers people living in poverty face in accessing abortion. They have established that when abortion is legal under domestic law, it must be available, accessible (including affordable), acceptable, and of good quality.[11] They have specified that states are obliged to abolish procedural barriers to abortion services, including third-party authorization requirements, mandatory delay periods, and biased counseling.[12] They have urged countries to provide financial support for those who cannot afford abortion services, guarantee the availability of skilled health care providers who can offer safe abortion services, and ensure that provider refusals on the grounds of religion or conscience do not interfere with access to services.[13]

And, importantly, the treaty bodies recognize that laws prohibiting abortion—thereby forcing people to choose between continuing a pregnancy and traveling to another country to access legal abortion services—can cause anguish and suffering, including financial, social, and health-related burdens and hardships.[14]

The Committee overseeing implementation of the Convention on the Elimination of All Forms of Discrimination Against Women (CEDAW) frames the right to abortion as an aspect of women's autonomy,[15] and emphasizes that a state's failure or refusal to provide reproductive health services constitutes gender discrimination.[16] In articulating the contours of states'

---

[9]   See 'Breaking Ground: Treaty Monitoring Bodies on Reproductive Rights' (Center for Reproductive Rights 2020) <www.reproductiverights.org/sites/crr.civicactions.net/files/documents/Breaking-Ground-2020.pdf> accessed 7 June 2020.
[10]   See 'Breaking Ground' (n 9). See also Charles G. Ngwena, 'Inscribing Abortion as a Human Right: Significance of the Protocol on the Rights of Women in Africa' (2010) 32 Hum.Rts.Q. 783, 787–94; Christina Zampas and Jaime M. Gher, 'Abortion as a Human Right—International and Regional Standards' (2008) 8 H.R.L.Rev. 249, 256–61; Lucia Berro Pizzarossa and Katrina Perehudoff, 'Global Survey of National Constitutions: Mapping Constitutional Commitments to Sexual and Reproductive Health and Rights' (2017) 19 Health & Hum.Rts.J. 279, 280–82.
[11]   See 'Breaking Ground' (n 9); Human Rights Committee 'General Comment 36 on article 6 of the International Covenant on Civil and Political Rights, on the right to life' (2018) UN Doc CCPR/C/GC/36 2018 para 8.
[12]   See 'Breaking Ground' (n 9).
[13]   ibid.
[14]   See *Siobhán Whelan v Ireland* (2017) Communication No. 2425/2014 UN Doc CCPR/C/119/D/2425/2014 para 7.5–7.7, 7.9, 7.11–7.12; *Amanda Jane Mellet v Ireland* (2016) Communication No. 2324/2013 UN Doc CCPR/C/116/D/2324/2013 paras 7.4–7.6, 7.8, 7.10–7.11.
[15]   See e.g. Convention on the Elimination of Discrimination against Women Committee 'Concluding Observations on New Zealand' (2012) UN Doc CEDAW/C/NZL/CO/7 para 35(a); CEDAW Committee 'Concluding Observations on Sierra Leone' (2014) UN Doc CEDAW/C/SLE/CO/6 para 32.
[16]   CEDAW Committee 'General Recommendation 24: Article 12 of the Convention (women and health)' (2008) UN Doc HRI/GEN/1/Rev.9 Vol. II para 11; see e.g., *L.C. v Peru* (2011) Communication No. 22/2009 UN Doc CEDAW/C/50/D/22/2009 para 8.17, 9, 12(iii).

obligations to realize the right to sexual and reproductive health, the Committee overseeing implementation of the International Covenant on Economic, Social and Cultural Rights (ICESCR) notes that equality is a cross-cutting objective requiring states to devote resources to traditionally neglected groups, including women living in poverty, in order to address systemic discrimination.[17]

In 2018, the UN Human Rights Committee made clear that the right to life includes the right to access safe and legal abortion.[18] The right to life requires states to provide safe, legal, and effective access to abortion, *inter alia*, where the life and health of the pregnant woman or girl is at risk or when carrying a pregnancy to term would cause the pregnant woman or girl substantial pain or suffering.[19] States may not introduce new barriers to abortion and should remove existing barriers that deny effective access by women and girls to safe and legal abortion.[20] States should likewise prevent the stigmatization of women and girls seeking abortion.[21]

The UN treaty bodies have also made clear that countries cannot roll back established rights. The Committee on Economic, Social and Cultural Rights (CESCR) has noted the particular importance of avoiding retrogressive measures in the area of sexual and reproductive health and rights, including the imposition of barriers to sexual and reproductive health information, goods, and services.[22]

UN human rights experts have reiterated concerns related to abortion access for people living in poverty. For example, in the context of efforts by some U.S. states to restrict abortion access during the COVID-19 pandemic, the UN Working Group on Discrimination Against Women and Girls noted that restrictions on access to abortion 'constitute human rights violations and can cause irreversible harm, in particular to low-income women and those belonging to racial minorities and immigrant communities.'[23]

Regional human rights systems likewise address access to abortion as a human rights concern. The Protocol to the African Charter on Human and Peoples' Rights on the Rights of Women in Africa (Maputo Protocol) requires states to ensure women's right to abortion, at a minimum, in instances of 'sexual assault, rape, incest, and where the continued pregnancy endangers the mental and physical health of the mother or the life of the mother or the foetus.'[24] The African Commission on Human and Peoples' Rights recognizes that inadequate access to safe abortion and post-abortion care can result in violations of the rights to privacy, confidentiality, and freedom from discrimination and cruel, inhuman, or degrading treatment.[25] The

---

[17] UNESCR Committee 'General Comment 22 on the right to sexual and reproductive health (article 12 of the International Covenant on Economic, Social and Cultural Rights)' (2016) UN Doc E/C.12/GC/22 ss 2, 23, 34, 40. See also Berro Pizzarossa and Perehudoff (n 10) 282.

[18] 'General Comment 36' (n 11) para 8.

[19] ibid.

[20] ibid.

[21] ibid.

[22] 'General Comment 22' (n 17) para 38.

[23] UN OHCHR 'United States: Authorities manipulating COVID-19 crisis to restrict access to abortion, say UN experts' (27 May 2020) <www.ohchr.org/EN/NewsEvents/Pages/DisplayNews.aspx?NewsID=25907&LangID=E> accessed 19 June 2020.

[24] Protocol to the African Charter on Human and Peoples' Rights on the Rights of Women in Africa, 2nd Ordinary Session Assembly of the Union (adopted 11 July 2003, entered into force 25 Nov 2005) CAB/LEG/66.6 (2000) art 14, para 2(c) [hereinafter Maputo Protocol].

[25] See African Commission on Human and Peoples' Rights, 'General Comment 2 on Article 14.1 (a), (b), (c) and (f) and Article 14.2 (a) and (c)' of the Protocol to the African Charter on Human and Peoples' Rights on the Rights of Women in Africa, 55th Ordinary Session (adopted 2014).

European Court of Human Rights is developing a robust body of jurisprudence on abortion,[26] and the Inter-American Commission on Human Rights has articulated important standards regarding access to safe and legal abortion.[27]

These human rights bodies recognize that safe and legal abortion services are essential for guaranteeing the full range of human rights.[28] Scholars suggest that, in doing so, they require states to affirmatively address the particular impact of abortion access barriers on people living in poverty.[29]

II.   IMPACT OF HUMAN RIGHTS ON JURISPRUDENCE REGARDING ABORTION ACCESS

Human rights principles do not automatically translate into change in people's lives. A wide body of literature explores the ways in which human rights law gets internalized and implemented domestically.[30] One mode of norm internalization is through national courts' integration of human rights principles.

National courts have drawn upon human rights law and normative principles in addressing reproductive rights concerns.[31] As Rachel Rebouché notes, courts rely on human rights 'to

---

[26]   Mayall and Fine, 'Briefing Paper: Abortion Worldwide' (n 6); Council of Europe Commissioner for Human Rights, 'Women's sexual and reproductive health and rights in Europe' (Issue Paper 2017); Johanna B Fine, Katherine Mayall, and Lilian Sepulveda, 'The Role of International Human Rights Norms in the Liberalization of Abortion Laws Globally' (2017) 19 Health & Hum.Rts. 69, 72; Johanna Westeson, 'Reproductive Health Information and Abortion Services: Standards Developed by the European Court of Human Rights' (2013) 122 Int'l J.Gynecology & Obstetrics 173; Federico Fabbrini, 'The European Court of Human Rights, The EU Charter of Fundamental Rights, And The Right To Abortion: Roe v. Wade on the Other Side of the Atlantic' (2011) 18 Colum.J.Eur.L. 1, 16–25.

[27]   Alma Beltran Y Puga, 'Paradigmatic Changes in Gender Justice: The Advancement of Reproductive Rights in International Human Rights Law' (2012) 3 Creighton Int'l & Comp.L.J. 158, 163–69; Ciara O'Connell, 'Litigating Reproductive Health Rights in the Inter American System: What Does Winning a Case Look Like?' (2014) 16 Health & Hum.Rts. 116, 121–22.

[28]   See 'Breaking Ground' (n 9); Zampas and Gher (n 10) 250–62, 268–84.

[29]   Martha F. Davis, 'Abortion Access in the Global Marketplace' (2010) 88 N.C.L.Rev. 1657, 1661, 1671; Barbara Stark, 'The Women's Convention, Reproductive Rights, and the Reproduction of Gender' (2011) 18 Duke J.Gender L. & Pol'y 261, 301; Lance Gable, 'Reproductive Health as a Human Right' (2010) 60 Case W.Res.L.Rev. 957, 986–87.

[30]   See e.g. Dinah Shelton (ed), *International Law and Domestic Legal Systems: Incorporation, Transformation, and Persuasion* (OUP 2011); Wayne Sandholtz, 'How Domestic Courts Use International Law' (2015) 38 Fordham Int'l L.J. 595, 603–05; Zachary Elkins, Tom Ginsburg, and Beth A Simmons, 'Getting to Rights: Treaty Ratification, Constitutional Convergence, and Human Rights Practice' (2013) 54 Harv.Int'l L.J. 61, 63; Cynthia Soohoo and Suzanne Stolz, 'Bringing Theories of Human Rights Change Home' (2008) 77 Fordham L.Rev. 459, 474–79; Sarah H Cleveland, 'Norm Internalization and U.S. Economic Sanctions' (2001) 26 Yale J.Int'l L. 1, 87–88; Harold Hongju Koh, 'The 1998 Frankel Lecture: Bringing International Law Home' (1998) 35 Hous.L.R. 623, 642.

[31]   Rebecca J Cook and Bernard M Dickens, 'Human Rights Dynamics of Abortion Law Reform' (2003) 25 Hum.Rts.Q. 1, 21–52; Fine, Mayall, and Sepulveda (n 26) 72–75; Reed Boland and Laura Katzive, 'Developments in Laws on Induced Abortion: 1998–2007' (2008) 34 Int'l Family Planning Perspectives 110, 117.

strengthen the legitimacy of their decisions and to align their opinions with universal, modern norms.'[32] This approach has potential to address access to abortion for people living in poverty.

A notable example is the *Lakshmi Dhikta* case, in which the Supreme Court of Nepal drew upon human rights to guarantee economic access to safe and legal abortion services for women living in poverty in Nepal.[33] Despite the decriminalization of abortion in Nepal in 2002, and the subsequent constitutional recognition of reproductive rights as fundamental rights, many people in Nepal remained unable to obtain abortions because of prohibitive fees, physically inaccessible facilities, and because they were unaware of the legal status of abortion.

Lakshmi Dhikta v. Nepal was filed in Nepal's Supreme Court on behalf of a pregnant woman with five children who was denied an abortion because she could not afford the fee. One central goal of the litigation was to ensure that abortion was available to all women, regardless of socioeconomic status and geographic location.[34] In 2009, the Supreme Court of Nepal issued a decision reiterating the inextricable link between the right to abortion and other rights, including the rights to self-determination, freedom, dignity and personal liberty, health, family planning, privacy, non-discrimination, and freedom from cruel, inhuman and degrading treatment. Stating that 'the right to abortion can be realized only if it is accessible and affordable,' the Court noted that 'it is the primary obligation of the state to prioritize the implementation of these rights.'[35] Based on these positive obligations, the Court directed the government to introduce a comprehensive abortion law and create a fund to cover the cost of services for low-income women or women without income.

Melissa Upreti examines the *Lakshmi Dhikta* decision through the lens of 'transformative equality,' and explores the ways in which the Court integrates human rights principles articulated by the CEDAW Committee to emphasize the government's positive obligation to address barriers, including economic, that women face in accessing safe abortion.[36] Others note the Court's reliance on the ICESCR in recognizing the need to ensure affordability, accessibility, and availability of abortion services.[37] The resulting decision by the Court obligates the government to address the multiple barriers women face in accessing abortion and ensure that all women, including those who face economic barriers, have access to safe abortion services.[38]

While this chapter focuses on jurisprudence, human rights are also core to law reform and other advocacy related to legalization of abortion and access for marginalized communities. For example, human rights influenced the legalization of abortion in democratic, post-Apartheid South Africa, and focused attention on social and economic conditions that impede meaningful access to safe abortion. Cathi Albertyn has noted the ways in which South African human rights advocates 'latched upon the spirit of the ICPD's Cairo Declaration' and its linking of reproductive rights and reproductive health to advance a legal right to abortion

---

[32]   Rachel Rebouché, 'Abortion Rights as Human Rights' (2016) 25 S. & L.S. 765, 766.
[33]   Supreme Court of Nepal, *Lakshmi Dhikta v Government of Nepal*, Writ petition no. WO-0757, 2067 (2009) <www.reproductiverights.org/sites/crr.civicactions.net/files/documents/Lakshmi%20Dhikta%20 -%20English%20translation.pdf> accessed 7 June 2020.
[34]   Melissa Upreti, 'Toward Transformative Equality in Nepal: The Lakshmi Decision' in Rebecca J Cook, Joanna N Erdman, and Bernard Dickens (eds), *Abortion Law in Transnational Perspective* (University of Pennsylvania Press 2014) 284.
[35]   Supreme Court of Nepal, *Lakshmi Dhikta v Government of Nepal* (n 33).
[36]   Upreti (n 34) 282.
[37]   Fine, Mayall, and Sepulveda (n 26) 69, 74.
[38]   Upreti (n 34) 279–300.

grounded in an understanding of substantive equality and the effects of race and class on the realities of access to abortion for Black women and rural women living in poverty.[39]

Despite this potential, there are substantial critiques of human rights as a basis for addressing needs of marginalized people, including through jurisprudential approaches. One scholar argues that a human rights approach may, in fact, 'distract from strategies that focus on economic inequalities.'[40] Indeed, it has been suggested that human rights lack both a normative basis for and ideological commitment to addressing issues of redistribution.[41] Others note that human rights lawyering, like other modes of social justice lawyering, has the potential to reify and essentialize the victimization of marginalized communities, including people living in poverty.[42] Importantly, scholars and advocates note that efforts to achieve the realization of reproductive rights as human rights will be successful only if connected to grassroots campaigns for economic justice and an end to poverty.[43] Such critiques significantly inform the concluding section of this chapter, on implications for further research.

III. CASE STUDY: THE VALUE-ADD OF HUMAN RIGHTS IN REPRODUCTIVE RIGHTS ADVOCACY FOR PEOPLE LIVING IN POVERTY IN THE UNITED STATES

Within the United States, led and inspired by decades of work by reproductive justice advocates,[44] a deep well of scholarship explores the ways in which Black and '[p]oor women's inadequate access to reproductive health services is bolstered by traditional [U.S.] constitutional jurisprudence.'[45] Instead of holding the government accountable for remedying

---

[39] Cathi Albertyn, 'Claiming and Defending Abortion Rights in South Africa' (2015) 22 Direito GV L.Rev. 429, 436–39; but see Lucia B Pizzarossa and Ebenezer Durojaye, 'International Human Rights Norms and the South African Choice on Termination of Pregnancy Act: And Argument for Vigilance and Modernisation' (2018) 35 SAJHR 50, 57–68.

[40] Rachel Rebouché, 'Reproducing Rights: The Intersection of Reproductive Justice and Human Rights' (2017) 7 U.C.Irvine L.Rev. 579, 598. See also Rebouché, 'Abortion Rights' (n 32) 776.

[41] Samuel Moyn, *Not Enough: Human Rights in an Unequal World* (The Belknap Press of Harvard University Press 2018).

[42] Caroline Bettinger-Lopez and others, 'Redefining Human Rights Lawyering Through the Lens of Critical Theory: Lessons for Pedagogy and Practice' (2011) 18 Geo.J.Poverty L.& Pol'y 337, 361–62.

[43] Rosalind P. Petchesky, 'Human Rights, Reproductive Health and Economic Justice: Why they are indivisible' (2000) 8 Reproductive Health Matters 12, 15–16; This is consistent with scholarship offering a critical lens on human rights lawyering more generally. See Caroline Bettinger-Lopez and others (n 42); Benjamin Hoffman and Marissa Vahlsing, 'Collaborative Lawyering in Transnational Human Rights Advocacy' (2014) 21 Clin.L.Rev. 255.

[44] Loretta J. Ross, 'Understanding Reproductive Justice' (SisterSong: Women of Color Reproductive Health Collective 2006) 2–5. <https://d3n8a8pro7vhmx.cloudfront.net/rrfp/pages/33/attachments/original/1456425809/Understanding_RJ_Sistersong.pdf?1456425809> accessed 7 June 2020; see also nn 90–93.

[45] Dorothy Roberts, *Killing the Black Body: Race, Reproduction, and the Meaning of Liberty* (20th Anniversary edn, Vintage Books 2017) 229. See also Melissa Murray, Katherine Shaw, and Reva B. Siegal (eds), *Reproductive Rights and Justice Stories* (Foundation Press 2019); Michele Goodwin and Erwin Chemerinsky, 'Pregnancy, Poverty, and the State' (Review of *Poverty of Privacy Rights* by Khiara M. Bridges) (2018) 127 Yale L.J. 1270, 1329; Jill E Adams and Melissa Mikesell, 'And Damned If They Don't: Prototype Theories To End Punitive Policies Against Pregnant People Living in Poverty' (2017)

reproductive oppression, U.S. court decisions have legitimized and reinforced laws, policies, institutions, and cultural norms that strip people living in poverty and women of color of their reproductive autonomy, thereby diminishing their economic and social well-being, political equality, and human dignity.[46]

While this problem extends beyond abortion rights,[47] the debate over the source and scope of the right to safe and legal abortion has shaped many of the government policies and court decisions impacting the health, lives, and rights of people living in poverty. Thus, consideration of how abortion and poverty intersect in U.S. law and constitutional doctrine can inform jurisprudential efforts to advance a transformative, human rights-based approach to reproductive rights and justice in the United States.

A.   Demographics of Abortion Access: Economic Barriers and Impacts

In the United States, nearly one in four women will have an abortion in their lifetime.[48] While abortion is a common component of comprehensive reproductive health care, there are notable disparities in rates of abortion across different populations.[49] The greatest demographic disparity is economic. Among all women obtaining abortions, a disproportionate share, 75 percent, are living in poverty or near poverty.[50] Government programs designed to subsidize medical costs for those with limited resources do not meet the need for abortion services, disproportionately impacting people living in poverty and women of color.[51]

For people living in poverty, denial of health-care coverage for abortion is rooted in numerous federal and state policies. This began with the Hyde Amendment, a law that—since 1977—has prohibited federal funding of abortion care in almost all circumstances. Under Hyde, Medicaid (the national program funding medical care for people living in poverty in the United States)[52] may cover abortion services only when pregnancy is the result of rape or incest or causes a 'physical condition' that would 'place the woman in danger of death

---

18 Geo.J.Gender & L. 283, 287–95; Khiara M. Bridges, 'Towards a Theory of State Visibility: Race, Poverty, and Equal Protection' (2010) 19 Colum.J.Gender & L. 965, 968, 1008.

[46] See nn 51–61 and accompanying text. See also nn 69–70 and accompanying text.

[47] Some examples outside the abortion context include lack of access to non-coercive and affordable contraception; systemic barriers to autonomous decision-making and non-biased maternal health care; and punitive treatment of women for their conduct during pregnancy or childbirth. See Adams and Mikesell (n 45).

[48] 'Abortion is a Common Experience for U.S. Women, Despite Dramatic Declines in Rates' (*Guttmacher Institute*, 19 October 2017) <www.guttmacher.org/news-release/2017/abortion-common -experience-us-women-despite-dramatic-declines-rates> accessed 7 June 2020.

[49] For details on disparities by race, see Rachel K Jones and Jenna Jerman, 'Population Group Abortion Rates and Lifetime Incidence of Abortion: United States, 2008–2014' (2017) 107 Am.J.Pub. Health <https://ajph.aphapublications.org/doi/10.2105/AJPH.2017.304042> accessed 7 June 2020.

[50] Jenna Jerman, Rachel K Jones, and Tsuyoshi Onda, 'Characteristics of U.S. Abortion Patients in 2014 and Changes Since 2008' (Guttmacher Institute 2016) <www.guttmacher.org/sites/default/files/ report_pdf/characteristics-us-abortion-patients-2014.pdf> accessed 18 December 2019.

[51] ibid 12; Megan K Donovan, 'In Real Life: Federal Restrictions on Abortion Coverage and the Women They Impact' (2017) 20 Guttmacher Pol'y Rev. 1, 2 <www.guttmacher.org/sites/default/files/ article_files/gpr2000116.pdf> accessed 7 June 2020.

[52] 'Medicaid's Role for Women' (Fact Sheet, *Henry J. Kaiser Family Foundation*, 28 March 2019) 1 <www.kff.org/womens-health-policy/fact-sheet/medicaids-role-for-women/> accessed 18 December 2019.

unless an abortion is performed.'[53] Enacted just three years after the *Roe v. Wade* decision constitutionalized the right to abortion, this funding ban has been in place every year since and expanded beyond Medicaid. For people living in poverty and others who rely on government programs, such as Indian Health Services, or people who are incarcerated in federal prisons and detention centers, similar restrictions block federal funding for almost all abortion care.[54]

While Hyde does not prohibit states from authorizing state funds and programs to cover abortion, most do not.[55] In addition to the lack of Medicaid coverage for poor and low-income residents in most states, half of the states also ban health insurance coverage for abortion in plans offered, or regulated, under the state Health Insurance Marketplace established under the Affordable Care Act.[56]

These policies, coupled with an ever-increasing web of state restrictions on abortion access,[57] disproportionately burden low-income people, women of color, and young women.[58]

For people already experiencing financial hardship, paying for abortion—and related travel costs—requires relying on family, friends, and private funding networks, while also diverting scarce personal funds needed for basics like food, housing, childcare, and transportation. That, in turn, can mean skipping or delaying payments for food, utilities, rent, childcare, and other essentials.[59] Often, by the time a person scrapes enough resources together, their pregnancy has advanced to a point when the abortion costs more or at which abortion services are not available or legal in the state.[60] Not all who need an abortion can overcome these obstacles. Research estimates indicate that about one-fourth of pregnant women who qualify for Medicaid give birth instead of having an abortion because Medicaid does not cover the costs.[61]

---

[53]   Hyde Amendment Codification Act 2013 (USA).

[54]   Terri-Ann Thompson and Brianna Keefe-Oates, 'Abortion coverage bans on public and private insurance: Access to abortion care limited for millions of women' (Ibis Reproductive Health 2017) 1–2 <https://ibisreproductivehealth.org/sites/default/files/files/publications/Impact%20of%20insurance%20bans%20formatted%208.17.pdf> accessed 7 June 2020 (citing sources).

[55]   'State Funding of Abortion Under Medicaid' (*Guttmacher Institute*, as of 1 June 2020) <www.guttmacher.org/state-policy/explore/state-funding-abortion-under-medicaid> accessed 7 June 2020.

[56]   Thompson and Keefe-Oates (n 54) 1.

[57]   For an overview of the types and numbers of abortion restrictions in each state, see 'An Overview of Abortion Laws' (*Guttmacher Institute*, as of 1 August 2019) <www.guttmacher.org/state-policy/explore/overview-abortion-laws> accessed 7 June 2020; 'Last Five Years Account for More Than One-quarter of All Abortion Restrictions Enacted Since Roe' (*Guttmacher Institute* 13 January 2016), at <www.guttmacher.org/article/2016/01/last-five-years-account-more-one-quarter-all-abortion-restrictions-enacted-roe> accessed 7 June 2020.

[58]   Thompson and Keefe-Oates (n 54) 2.

[59]   See Rachel K Jones, Ushma D Upadhyay, and Tracy A Weitz, 'At What Cost? Payment for Abortion Care by U.S. Women' (2013) 23 Women's Health Issues e173, e176–177 <www.whijournal.com/article/S1049-3867(13)00022-4/fulltext> accessed 7 June 2020.

[60]   ibid e174; Ushma D Upadhyay and others, 'Denial of Abortion Because of Provider Gestational Age Limits in the United States' (2014) 104 Am.J.Pub.Health 1687, 1689 <https://ajph.aphapublications.org/doi/pdf/10.2105/AJPH.2013.301378> accessed 7 June 2020.

[61]   Sara CM Roberts and others, 'Estimating the proportion of Medicaid-eligible pregnant women in Louisiana who do not get abortions when Medicaid does not cover abortion' (2019) 78 BMC Women's Health 1 <https://bmcwomenshealth.biomedcentral.com/articles/10.1186/s12905-019-0775-5> accessed 7 June 2020; Stanley K Henshaw and others, 'Restrictions on Medicaid Funding for Abortions: A Literature Review' (Guttmacher Institute 2009) <www.guttmacher.org/sites/default/files/report_pdf/medicaidlitreview.pdf> accessed 7 June 2020.

For these women, evidence suggests economic insecurity and hardship will increase over the longer-term.[62]

B.   Jurisprudential Landscape

In the United States, the legal right to abortion, particularly for people living in poverty, has been hollowed out by decades of restrictive state and federal laws and Supreme Court decisions affirming them. In particular, the U.S. Supreme Court has refused to recognize, under the U.S. Constitution, an affirmative state obligation to ensure all people, regardless of economic status, can effectively exercise their fundamental right to abortion.[63] Yet, strands of U.S. constitutional jurisprudence offer the potential for a more expansive judicial understanding of the impact of poverty on access to abortion, consistent with human rights.

Leading scholars have argued that the U.S. Constitution can and should provide heightened protection for people living in poverty.[64] Indeed, in the first half of the twentieth century, the Supreme Court was responsive to claims that the government was obligated, at least in certain contexts, to ensure individuals had resources necessary to exercise their fundamental rights. This approach is most evident in the Court's line of criminal due process 'access to justice' cases that peaked in the mid-1950s through 1960s.[65] Around this time, the Court took a similar approach in other contexts as well, including for poor people exercising their right to vote and to freely travel and establish residency in another state.[66]

However, the Court declined to adopt the view that laws that discriminate on the basis of poverty, or target the poor as a class, should be presumed 'suspect' and—on that basis alone—trigger a stricter level of constitutional scrutiny.[67] Instead, only where a liberty or other fundamental right was at stake did the Court invoke heightened protection for the indigent. Although the access to justice cases remain controlling law today, the Court declined to further expand rights for people living in poverty in a line of cases decided in the early 1970s.[68]

---

[62]   Diana Greene Foster and others, 'Socioeconomic Outcomes of Women Who Receive and Women Who Are Denied Wanted Abortions in the United States' (2018) 108 Am.J.Pub.Health <https://ajph .aphapublications.org/doi/10.2105/AJPH.2017.304247> accessed 7 June 2020.

[63]   Laurence H Tribe, 'The Abortion Funding Conundrum: Inalienable Rights, Affirmative Duties, and the Dilemma of Dependency' (1985) 99 Harv.L.Rev. 330, 336–37; Peter B Edelman, 'The Next Century of Our Constitution: Rethinking Our Duty to the Poor' (1987) 39 Hastings L.J. 1, 39–42.

[64]   See e.g. Frank I Michelman, 'Foreword: On Protecting The Poor Through the Fourteenth Amendment' (1969) 83 Harv.L.Rev. 7, 11–13; Edelman (n 63) 3–8; Erwin Chemerinsky, 'Making the Right Case for a Constitutional Right to Minimum Entitlements' (1993) 44 Mercer L.Rev. 525, 525–28; Martha C Nussbaum, 'Foreword: Constitutions and Capabilities: "Perception" Against Lofty Formalism' (2007) 121 Harv.L.Rev. 5, 7, 21–46; Julie A Nice, 'Whither the Canaries: On the Exclusion of Poor People from Equal Constitutional Protection' (2012) 60 Drake L.Rev. 1023, 1050–66.

[65]   These cases protect the rights of people who cannot afford legal counsel or court-related fees in criminal judicial proceedings. See *Douglas v California*, 372 US 353 (1963); *Gideon v Wainwright*, 372 US 335 (1963); *Griffin v Illinois*, 351 US 12 (1956).

[66]   See *Harper v Virginia State Bd of Elections*, 383 US 663 (1966); *Shapiro v Thompson*, 394 US 618 (1969); *Memorial Hosp v Maricopa Cty*, 415 US 250 (1974).

[67]   Mario L Barnes and Erwin Chemerinsky, 'The Disparate Treatment of Race and Class in Constitutional Jurisprudence' (2009) 72 LCP 109, 123–25.

[68]   In these cases, the Court refused to closely scrutinize laws that did not involve an established fundamental right, but did disproportionately burden people living in poverty as they sought adequate educational opportunities, public benefits, housing, and economic stability. See, e.g., *San Antonio Indep*

Those cases were quickly closing the courthouse door to poverty-based claims by the time the right to abortion was recognized in 1973, in *Roe v. Wade*. Then, in a series of abortion funding cases, the Court held that the government did not violate the Constitution when denying public funding or medical services to pregnant women living in poverty who sought to end, rather than continue, a pregnancy. In each of four cases, beginning with *Beal v. Doe* and *Maher v. Roe*, decided together in 1977, followed by its decisions in *Harris v. McRae* and *Williams v. Zbaraz*, both in 1980, the Court held that neither federal law nor the Constitution required state or federal Medicaid programs to fund abortion.[69] Notably, in *Harris*, plaintiffs had raised related equal protection and liberty rights claims together, to persuade the Court that even if there was no 'entitlement' to a system of welfare benefits in the first instance, these laws impermissibly discriminated against people living in poverty as they sought to exercise a fundamental right.[70] Relying on its earlier decision in *Maher*, the Court rejected the claims and upheld the Hyde Amendment's ban on federal funding for abortion in almost all circumstances.

Yet, even as the Court decisively shifted away from recognizing poverty as a suspect class, and despite the abortion funding decisions, the Court continued to consider financial disadvantage in a series of cases in which family-relationship rights were at stake for people living in poverty.[71] In so doing, it averted a roll-back of the access to justice doctrine and cemented its expanded protection of fundamental liberty rights.[72] And while not as apparent in the Court's opinions, a body of scholarship and historical writings document how concern for women living in poverty and lacking legal and political power drove successful reproductive rights litigation and informed the substantive due-process doctrine that protects liberty rights.[73] Cary Franklin, in particular, has examined how the class-based equality concerns driving the reproductive rights cases—the same concerns underlying the access to justice and family relationship cases—implicitly shaped the jurisprudence and continue to animate elements of modern abortion jurisprudence.[74]

The rationale underlying these cases is relevant in the context of protecting abortion access for marginalized communities, including people living in poverty. The threat of poverty to

---

Sch Dist v Rodriguez, 411 US 1, 28, 40 (1973); *Ortwein v Schwab*, 410 US 656, 660 (1973); *Dandridge v Williams*, 397 US 471, 475 (1970); *United States v Kras*, 409 US 434, 447–55 (1973); *Lindsey v Normet*, 405 US 56, 70–74 (1972).

[69]   See *Beal v Doe*, 432 US 438 (1977); *Maher v Roe*, 432 US 464 (1977); *Harris v McRae*, 448 US 297 (1980); *Williams v Zbaraz*, 448 US 358 (1980).

[70]   Rhonda Copelon and Sylvia A Law, '"Nearly Allied to Her Right to Be"—Medicaid Funding for Abortion: The Story of *Harris v. McRae*' in Elizabeth M Schneider and Stephanie M Wildman (eds), *Women & the Law: Stories* (Foundation Press 2011).

[71]   See *Boddie v Connecticut*, 401 US 371 (1971); *Little v Streater*, 452 US 1 (1981); *Lassiter v Dep't of Soc Servs of Durham*, 452 US 32 (1981); *MLB v SLJ*, 519 US 102 (1996).

[72]   See generally Kenneth Agran, 'When Government Must Pay: Compensating Rights and the Constitution' (2005) 22 Const. Comment. 97, 109. For analysis of the doctrinal intersection of the liberty rights of parenting, marriage, family formation, and procreation, see 'Roe and the Intersectional Liberty Doctrine' (Center for Reproductive Rights 2018) 4, 9 <https://reproductiverights.org/sites/default/files/documents/Liberty-Roe-Timeline-spread-for-web.pdf> accessed 7 June 2020.

[73]   Linda Greenhouse and Reva B Siegel, 'The Unfinished Story of *Roe v. Wade*' in Melissa Murray, Katherine Shaw, and Reva B Siegal (eds), *Reproductive Rights and Justice Stories* (Foundation Press 2019); Cary Franklin, 'The New Class Blindness' (2018) 128 Yale L.J. 1, 17–46; Reva B Siegel, '*Roe*'s Roots: The Women's Rights Claims that Engendered *Roe*' (2010) 90 B.U.L.Rev. 1875, 1879–94.

[74]   Franklin (n 73) 17–82.

family and personhood is harshly evident in the historical struggle of women to control and define their reproductive lives in the United States. In the early contraception and abortion cases of the 1960s and 1970s, advocates centered their evidence, arguments, and public narratives on the criminal risks and financial barriers preventing poor and low-income women from accessing contraception and abortion.[75] Ultimately, however, 'concerns about the lived experience of financially disadvantaged women seeking reproductive healthcare did not appear on the surface' of the Court's opinion in these cases.[76] Rather, the Court grounded reproductive rights in a right of privacy[77] and a broader liberty interest,[78] rather than equal protection.[79] Thus, coming on the heels of the Court's seminal decisions rejecting heightened scrutiny of laws preventing equitable access to non-fundamental rights,[80] *Roe v. Wade* secured heightened constitutional scrutiny for abortion in theory, though not always in fact.

Even as the abortion funding cases held that the Constitution does not generally require states to fund abortion, they did not foreclose constitutional consideration of how laws burden the rights of people who are financially disadvantaged. In the 1992 decision of *Casey v. Planned Parenthood*, the Court articulated the 'undue burden' standard for reviewing abortion restrictions.[81] Under this standard, if a law's requirements mean people living in poverty will face obstacles accessing abortion, then that is the relevant group for assessing the law's constitutionality. Problematically, the Court failed to adequately apply this test to the facts in *Casey* itself—despite extensive evidence in the lower court record.[82] Without rejecting the relevance of these facts, it concluded that even 'for those women who have the fewest financial resources,' a mandated waiting period of 24 hours between receiving informed consent and obtaining an abortion was not unconstitutional.[83] Nonetheless, as seen in subsequent decisions, *Casey* 'preserved the law's ability to respond to class-related deprivations of the fundamental right to abortion.'[84]

Nearly 25 years later, in *Whole Woman's Health v. Hellerstedt*, the Court reaffirmed *Casey*'s real-world context inquiry.[85] Under both *Casey* and *Whole Woman's Health*—and consistent with the class-equality concerns built into reproductive rights doctrine 'on a fundamental level'[86]—courts can, and often must, engage in exactly this analysis.

---

[75]   ibid 40–63.

[76]   ibid 56.

[77]   *Griswold v Connecticut*, 381 US 479, 484–87 (1965).

[78]   *Roe v Wade*, 410 US 113, 153 (1973).

[79]   Siegel, '*Roe*'s Roots' (n 73) 1900–03.

[80]   See n 68.

[81]   *Planned Parenthood of Se Pennsylvania v Casey*, 505 US 833, 894 (1992).

[82]   The district court struck down a mandatory waiting period on the grounds it was 'particularly burdensome to those women who have the least financial resources.' *Planned Parenthood of Se Pennsylvania v Casey*, 744 F Supp 1323, 1352 (ED Pa 1990).

[83]   *Casey* (n 81) 886.

[84]   Franklin (n 73) 69; see 'The Undue Burden Standard After *Whole Woman's Health v. Hellerstedt*' (Center for Reproductive Rights 2018) <www.reproductiverights.org/sites/crr.civicactions.net/files/documents/WWH-Undue-Burden-Report-07262018-Edit.pdf> accessed 7 June 2020.

[85]   *Whole Woman's Health* (n 4) 2308–10; *Casey* (n 81) 892–94.

[86]   Franklin (n 73) 46.

Much has been written on why the abortion funding decisions are analytically wrong, unsound, and morally indefensible.[87] And scholars continue to debate the utility of constitution-alizing abortion rights.[88] Moreover, with a newly cemented 6–3 majority of jurisprudentially conservative justices on the U.S. Supreme Court, there is deep concern that it will soon move to substantially weaken and undo longstanding protection for abortion rights.[89] Nevertheless, for theorists and practitioners who seek a constitutional jurisprudence that actively protects the reproductive rights of all people, including people living in poverty, interlocking due process, equal protection, and liberty doctrines continue to offer possibilities for a human rights-based approach, beyond the confines of the current jurisprudence. Indeed, more than ever, planting these jurisprudential seeds is necessary for achieving constitutional change over the long-term.

C.   Potential Impact of Human Rights on Litigation Efforts to Advance Access to Abortion for Marginalized Communities, including People Living in Poverty in the United States

Whether invoking equality, due process, liberty, or examining the 'real world context' of abortion restrictions on people's lived experiences, judges and litigators engaging in U.S. con-stitutional analysis can draw on human rights norms to harmonize these interests and realize a more positive-rights vision that ensures abortion access for marginalized communities, including people living in poverty in the United States.

Reproductive justice advocates in the United States have engaged a human rights analysis for decades. Developed in the 1990s by Black women who were inspired by the 1994 ICPD,[90] the reproductive justice framework draws on human rights to articulate the inherent dignity and humanity of all people and illuminate the ways in which structural and systemic discrim-

---

[87]   See Julie A Nice, 'No Scrutiny Whatsoever: Deconstitutionalization of Poverty Law, Dual Rules of Law, & Dialogic Default' (2008) 35 Fordham Urb.L.J. 629, 645–52; Edelman (n 63) 40, 42; Tribe (n 63) 336–38; Jill E Adams and Jessica Arons, 'A Travesty of Justice: Revisiting Harris v. McRae' (2014) 21 Wmj. & Mary J. Women & L. 5, 6–7, 12.

[88]   cf Robin West, 'From Choice to Reproductive Justice: De-Constitutionalizing Abortion Rights' (2009) 118 Yale L.J. 1394 *with* Franklin (n 73) 70–71; see generally Nice, 'No Scrutiny Whatsoever' (n 87) 633–65, 663–70.

[89]   In the last abortion case decided before a major shift in the Court's membership, *June Medical Services v. Russo,* a bare majority of justices adhered to controlling precedent to strike down a restric-tion. The Chief Justice joined, but also wrote a separate opinion expressing his alternative view of how the undue burden should be applied, one that would allow many more restrictions to stand. *June Medical Services LLC v Russo*, 140 S. Ct. 2103, 2112–33 (2020) (plurality opinion); ibid. at 2133–42 (Roberts, C.J., concurring in the judgement). Several months after that decision, Justice Ruth Bader Ginsburg – a staunch defender of gender equality and reproductive rights – died and her seat was filled by Justice Amy Coney Barrett, who adheres to a judicial philosophy that rejects constitutional protec-tion for abortion and other liberty rights. See generally Report of the Center for Reproductive Rights on the Nomination of Judge Amy Coney Barrett to be Associate Justice of the Supreme Court of the United States (Oct 2020) <https://reproductiverights.org/sites/default/files/documents/FINAL_Public%20Barrett%20Analysis%20%281%29.pdf> accessed 23 December 2020. This transformation of the Court means that, at the time of publication, there are currently enough votes not only to follow Chief Justice Robert's opinion, but even more drastically upend abortion jurisprudence.

[90]   'Reproductive Justice' (*SISTERSONG, Women of Color Reproductive Justice Collective*) <http://sistersong.net/reproductive justice/> accessed 7 June 2020.

ination lead to reproductive rights and justice violations for women of color.[91] This holistic framework recognizes that sexual and reproductive rights often depend upon the realization of other economic and social rights and embraces the concept of positive rights and the government's obligation to ensure their realization.[92] Importantly, the reproductive justice movement was founded, in part, because of the insufficiencies of the reproductive rights movement's 'singular focus' on abortion.[93] Human rights have been central in reproductive justice campaigns for access to reproductive health care in the United States.[94]

But there are specific challenges to advancing human rights frameworks in U.S. courts. Because of U.S. treaty ratification practice, international human rights treaty provisions are not directly enforceable in United States courts.[95] And there is a deep skepticism by some jurists of the relevance of international and foreign comparative law in U.S. courts, including in the context of abortion.[96] Nevertheless, international law and the reasoning of international and regional human rights bodies and experts can be invoked in and by federal and state courts as persuasive authority or to otherwise inform analysis when assessing constitutional questions

---

[91]   'A New Vision for Advancing our Movement for Reproductive Health, Reproductive Rights, and Reproductive Justice' (Asian Communities for Reproductive Justice 2005) < https://forwardtogether.org/wp-content/uploads/2017/12/ACRJ-A-New-Vision.pdf> accessed 7 June 2020; 'Reproductive Justice' (n 90). See also Loretta J Ross and Rickie Solinger, *Reproductive Justice: An Introduction* (University of California Press 2017) 10–17; Sarah London, 'Reproductive Justice: Developing a Lawyering Model' (2011) 13 Berkeley J.Afr.Am.L. & Pol'y 71, 76; 'What We Do: Reproductive Justice' (*National Latina Institute for Reproductive Health*) <www.latinainstitute.org/en/what-we-do/reproductive justice> accessed 7 June 2020; Courtney Chappell, 'Reclaiming Choice, Broadening the Movement: Sexual and Reproductive Justice and Asian Pacific American Women, A National Agenda for Action' (National Asian Pacific American Women's Forum 2005) <www.napawf.org/uploads/1/1/4/9/114909119/napawf _reclaiming_choice.pdf> accessed 7 June 2020; Marsha Jones, 'Executive Report, The State of Black Women In Texas: Maternal Mortality' (The Afiya Center 2019) 2 <https://static1.squarespace.com/static/5c6a3f48c46f6d34a488a0e9/t/5cdc9e64e4966b830c87eff4/1557962364157/State+of+Black+Women2019.pdf> accessed 7 June 2020; 'Our Work' (*Black Mamas Matter Alliance*) <https://blackmamasmatter.org/our-work/> accessed 7 June 2020.

[92]   Ross and Solinger (n 91) xxi. See also Soohoo and Stolz (n 30) 497–98.

[93]   ibid. See also West (n 88).

[94]   See e.g. 'Black Maternal Health Week' (*Black Mamas Matter Alliance*) <https://blackmamasmatter .org/bmhw/> accessed 7 June 2020; 'Learning from Nuestro Texas: A Community-Centered Human Rights Campaign for Reproductive Justice in the Rio Grande Valley' (Center for Reproductive Rights and National Latina Institute for Reproductive Health 2018) <www.reproductiverights.org/sites/crr .civicactions.net/files/documents/Learning-From-Nuestro-Texas.pdf> accessed 7 June 2020.

[95]   Louis Henkin, 'U.S. Ratification of Human Rights Conventions: The Ghost of Senator Bricker' (1955) 89 AJIL 341, 342–48.

[96]   See e.g. *Roper v Simmons*, 543 US 551 (2005) (Scalia, dissenting).

and dealing with novel legal issues. A wide body of scholarship explores this practice[97] and associated hesitance and critique.[98]

For example, as discussed previously, human rights norms can internalize and advance a more expansive understanding of substantive equality that recognizes the intersection of gender, race, and poverty. In contrast, U.S. constitutional jurisprudence has failed to extend heightened scrutiny to poverty-based claims.[99] Scholars note that rigorous application of CEDAW to the U.S. context would provide a framework for courts to articulate affirmative reproductive rights protections, in order to truly secure women's equality.[100] Such an analysis would, for example, lend support to a constitutional norm that recognizes a government duty to provide financial assistance for abortion care for people living in poverty.[101]

In addition to offering a more robust analysis and understanding of substantive equality, the human rights framework could strengthen courts' evaluation of liberty interests, especially in the context of determining whether abortion restrictions impose an 'undue burden' for people who experience financial disadvantage. Here, the right to life and the right to be free from inhuman, cruel, and degrading treatment can be instructive. The UN Human Rights Committee recently affirmed that the right to life requires governments to ensure access to essential goods and services such as food, water, shelter, and health care.[102] The right to life includes the right to reproductive health care and autonomy, including access to quality pre-natal health care and safe, legal, and effective access to abortion.[103] Consistent with the norm of non-retrogression, the right to life prohibits governments from introducing new barriers to abortion and also requires them to remove existing barriers that deny effective access to safe and legal abortion.[104] In addition, the Human Rights Committee recently affirmed that the denial of legal abortion services can amount to cruel, inhuman, and degrading treatment.[105] Abortion restrictions and bans recently imposed by U.S. states represent a significant rollback in the right to access safe and legal abortion. A human rights analysis drawing on the right to life, the right to freedom from cruel, inhuman, and degrading treatment, and the principle of non-retrogression would help to highlight how these restrictions, such as those requiring people to travel far distances to a clinic and either make a return trip or stay overnight, are

---

[97]   Sarah H Cleveland, 'Our International Constitution' (2006) 31 Yale J.Int'l L. 1, 11–88; Martha F Davis, 'The Spirit of Our Times: State Constitutions and International Human Rights' (2006) 30 N.Y.U.Rev.L. & Soc.Change 359, 368–89; Honorable Margaret H Marshall, '"Wise Parents Do Not Hesitate to Learn from their Children": Interpreting State Constitutions in an Age of Global Jurisprudence' (2004) 79 N.Y.U.L.Rev. 1633, 1639–43; Cathy Hollenberg Serrette, 'Invoking International Human Rights Law in Litigation: A Maryland Judge's Perspective' (2011) 45 Clearinghouse Rev. 238, 239–42; I India Thusi and Martha F Davis, 'Human Rights in State Courts' (Northeastern University School of Law, Program on Human Rights in the Global Economy and The Opportunity Agenda 2016) <www.northeastern.edu/law/pdfs/academics/phrge/state-courts-2016.pdf> accessed 7 June 2020.

[98]   See e.g. Frank I Michelman, 'Integrity-Anxiety?' in Michael Ignatieff (ed), *American Exceptionalism and Human Rights* (Princeton University Press 2009) 241; Roger P Alford, 'Misusing International Sources to Interpret the Constitution' (2004) 98 AJIL 57.

[99]   See n 67–68 and accompanying text.

[100]   Stark (n 29) 297–303.

[101]   ibid.

[102]   'General Comment 36' (n 11) para 26.

[103]   ibid para 8.

[104]   ibid.

[105]   *Whelan v Ireland* (n 14) paras 7.5–7.7, 8; *Mellet v Ireland* (n 14) paras 7.4–7.6, 8.

counter to government's affirmative obligations and also have direct and particular impact on access to abortion care for people in marginalized communities, including people living in poverty, as well as women of color, immigrants, people with disabilities, and other people experiencing multiple and intersecting forms of discrimination. Indeed, the Human Rights Committee recently acknowledged the human rights violations that stem from the financial, social, and health-related burdens and hardships that are placed on women forced to travel far from home in order to obtain abortion care.[106]

IV. CONCLUSION AND IMPLICATIONS FOR FUTURE RESEARCH

The human rights framework holds potential for shaping jurisprudence to ensure a more holistic approach to protecting access to abortion for all people. Within the United States, judges and advocates can integrate human rights principles into their constitutional analysis to develop an understanding of U.S. constitutional principles that recognizes the interlinkages between reproductive rights and other rights and more fully acknowledges and rectifies the impact of abortion restrictions and barriers on access to abortion for people living in poverty, in particular.[107] By embedding human rights in this way and over the long term, courts can build more robust legal guarantees to ensure reproductive autonomy and health for people living in poverty.

In order to more fully understand this potential, both in the United States and globally, future research will need to explore and test specific strategies for effective integration of human rights principles into litigation advocacy. This might include case studies investigating the synergies between contemporaneous reproductive justice advocacy and litigation campaigns within one jurisdiction.[108] Research should also explore strategies to ensure that policy wins are implemented and that rights are fully realized in practice.[109] And, importantly, future research should build on efforts exploring best practices to ensure that advocacy strategies seeking to advance reproductive rights as human rights both center and are led by the communities that are most impacted.[110]

---

[106] ibid.
[107] See e.g. Brief *Amici Curiae* of Organizations and Individuals Dedicated to the Fight for Reproductive Justice—Women With a Vision et al.—in Support of Petitioners *June Medical Services LLC v Russo* (2019) (Nos. 18-1323 and 18-1460) <https://reproductiverights.org/sites/default/files/documents/Reproductive%20Justice%20Advocates_1.pdf.> accessed 7 June 2020.
[108] See e.g. 'Learning from Nuestro Texas' (n 94) 18.
[109] Rachel Rebouché, 'Reproducing Rights' (n 40) 603.
[110] 'Lawyering for Reproductive Justice: Convening Report' (if/when/how 2016) <www.ifwhenhow.org/resources/lawyering-for-rj-convening-report/> accessed 7 June 2020; Gemma Donofrio, 'Exploring the Role of Lawyers in Supporting the Reproductive Justice Movement' (2018) 42 N.Y.U.Rev.L. & Soc. Change 221, 251–52.

27. What is wrong with the privatization of education as anti-poverty policy from a human rights perspective?

Antonio Barboza-Vergara and Esteban Hoyos-Ceballos

Education is the primary vehicle by which marginalized people can lift themselves out of poverty and obtain the means to participate fully in society. In 1948, education became a recognized international human right in the Universal Declaration of Human Rights. Following that recognition, many countries around the world adopted constitutional reforms that included the right to education as a basic social right. In the 1980s and 1990s, neoliberal economic policies based on the Washington Consensus[1] expanded throughout the world. While the inclusion of the right to education supposes a strong role of the State in providing, financing and regulating access to education, neoliberal economic doctrine recommends reducing the role of the State and public expenditure in education. According to this neoliberal approach, those who can afford it must access education through the market, limiting the States' social obligations to the poor. The tension between human rights discourses and neoliberal policies is evident.

In the case of the right to education, the neoliberal recipe conceives of different roles for private actors: they could either provide education only for people who can afford it or they can deliver education for the poor with State financing. Both roles may have potential negative effects according to the human rights framework. Both could lead to deep inequalities in the acceptability of education.[2] In the first case, one can find inequalities between private providers based on tuition fees or between private and public providers because of the availability of resources for each type of institution. In the case of private provision of education to the poor with public resources, the effects are disputed and still to be determined.[3] Here, the questions are whether private provision with public resources can provide high quality education and

---

[1] Narcis Serra, Shari Spiegel and Joseph Stiglitz, 'Introduction: From the Washington Consensus Towards a New Global Governance' in Narcis Serra and Joseph Stiglitz (eds), *The Washington Consensus reconsidered* (Oxford University Press 2008) 3.

[2] According to the former UN Special Rapporteur of the Right to Education Katarina Tomasevski, acceptability of education includes: 'parental choice of education for their children (with human rights correctives); enforcement of minimal standards (quality, safety, environmental health); language of instruction; freedom from censorship; and recognition of children as subjects of rights'. According to this, acceptability is a broader notion than quality of education and it is a concept used in the international human rights framework to assess the complexity of other social and economic rights. Katarina Tomaševski, 'Right to Education Primers No 3: Human Rights Obligations: Making Education Availabl e, Accessible, Acceptable and Adaptable' (*Right to Education*, 2001) <www.right-to-education.org/sites/ right-to-education.org/files/resource-attachments/Tomasevski_Primer%203.pdf> accessed 2 April 2020.

[3] Antoni Verger and Mauro Moschetti, 'Public-Private Partnerships in Education: Exploring Different Models and Policy Options' (Open Society Foundation, 2016) <https://ddd.uab.cat/record/ 174585> accessed 7 July 2020. Effects associated with the privatization of education are also explored in UN Human Rights Council (UNHRC), 'Report of the Special Rapporteur on the Right to Education, Kishore Singh: Protecting Education Against Commercialization' (10 June 2015) UN Doc A/HRC/29/30.

what factors contribute to this result. Additionally, it must be determined if this kind of provision does not deepen educational inequalities generating segregated systems.

According to a 2019 report of the UN Special Rapporteur on the Right to Education, the last twenty years have seen a significant increase in the provision of private education.[4] For instance, Kenya has seen an increase of 2,216 per cent of private schools between 1998 and 2013. In Morocco, the percentage of private enrolment at the primary level has tripled in less than 15 years. In the United States, the proportion of public schools that became charter schools increased from two to seven per cent in 15 years between 2000 and 2015.[5]

Private provision of education is diverse, and not all private provision follows a neoliberal privatization policy. Privatization is complex and involves a diverse range of stakeholders that must each be evaluated separately in order to determine the compatibility with human rights standards. For instance, not every privatization scheme implies the commercialization of education. This chapter aims to set out a future research agenda on this issue. We are interested in exploring further the question of the compatibility of the private provision of education with a human rights legal framework. Specifically, in this chapter we explore the question of whether the international human rights legal framework demands a specific model of organization in the delivery of education. We want to fully understand how privatization operates, how States deal with and organize the education system to fight poverty barriers and what type of systems are or not compatible with a human rights framework.

This chapter aims to delve into the nuances of these questions and to outline future lines of research on education, poverty and human rights. To achieve this goal, the structure of the chapter will be the following: First, we will present the different models of privatization of education and its relationship with neoliberal doctrine. Second, we will focus on the human rights standards in education that deal with private provision of education, and particularly State-funded private provision for people living in poverty. In the third section, we will critically review the question of the compatibility of the private provision of education with a human rights framework. Finally, we will conclude with a research agenda for the fields of human rights, private education and poverty.

I. PRIVATE PARTICIPATION IN THE EDUCATION SECTOR AS A POLICY AGAINST POVERTY

A. Neoliberalism, Privatization and Poverty

There is a consensus within international organizations about the great contribution that education can make to eradicate poverty. But to achieve this, it is not enough that children from poor households access classrooms without economic barriers and have well prepared teachers. It is also important that the curriculum focus on the acquisition of basic abilities for each and every child according to their learning needs. Besides that, benefits from schooling depend on

---

[4] UNGA, 'Report of the Special Rapporteur on the Right to Education' (26 August 2015) UN Doc A/70/342.

[5] UNHRC, 'Right to Education: The Implementation of the Right to Education and Sustainable Development Goal 4 in the Context of the Growth of Private Actors in Education: Report of the Special Rapporteur on the Right to Education' (10 April 2019) UN Doc A/HRC/41/37.

previous familiar contexts and childhood conditions. Therefore, it is important to question if and how public education, either directly provided by the state or a state funded private agent, can compensate for the particular obstacles faced by poor children.[6]

Neoliberals believe poverty is a problem from both moral and economic perspectives. Human existence below a minimum wellbeing threshold does not allow the kind of human agency promoted by neoliberalism. Competitive and free markets require rational, self-interested and autonomous agency. Therefore, neoliberals find some social public policies justified—such as education, health, food and housing policies targeted to eliminate poverty—but conditioned to their view about the limited role of the State's social and economic intervention.

The neoliberal motto is that free and competitive global and domestic markets are more efficient than States in producing and distributing wealth. Therefore, the proposal is to deregulate markets, sell loss-making and inefficient public enterprises and restrict the role of the State to facilitate market functioning, for instance, through the enforcement of property rights. Thus, neoliberalism sees poverty reduction basically as an indirect and inevitable consequence of economic growth in the long term. In the short term, it defends a residual State intervention only focused to assist the most vulnerable. According to the neoliberal recipe, for-profit private organizations should provide social services to the poor, and the role of the State should be limited to financing, regulating, setting quality service standards and supervising the private provision.

Neoliberalism identifies several problems with public education. Some of these problems are institutional or organizational and related to direction, provision, funding, regulation and management schemes. Neoliberals find public provision of education problematic because of the purported inefficiency due to the inflexibility of teachers and unions, poor administration of schools and low-quality teacher training. Other sets of problems have to do with curriculum and learning outcomes.[7] In particular, neoliberals are concerned because the market requires skills in areas such as math, science, engineering and literacy. For them, education has an instrumental value as a means to develop the human capital required for economic growth.[8] Curricular aspects are key, but this chapter focuses on the institutional dimensions of neoliberal critiques and proposals in education.

According to the neoliberal approach, market-based policies are more efficient ways to provide education to poor children. For instance, the World Bank Third Punjab Education Sector Project in Pakistan had as a goal to promote sustainable development and the reduction of poverty through improving access to school for the poorest. The means to achieve this goal was through '(a) providing vouchers to attend a low-cost private school; (b) expanding PPPs to enable students to attend low-cost private schools; and (c) providing stipends to attend secondary schools'.[9]

---

[6]   For a general analysis of how poverty and income inequalities influence learning outcomes, see respectively Abhijit Banerjee and Esther Duflo, *Poor Economics: A Radical Rethinking of the Way to Fight Global Poverty* (Public Affairs 2012) and Richard Wilkinson and Kate Pickett, *The Spirit Level: Why Greater Equality Makes Societies Stronger* (Bloomsbury Press 2011).

[7]   James Murphy, 'Neoliberalism and the Privatization of Social Rights in Education' in Gillian MacNaughton and Diane F Frey, *Economic and Social Rights in a Neoliberal World* (CUP 2018) 95.

[8]   ibid 94.

[9]   'Project Appraisal Document on a Proposed Loan in the Amount of US $300 Million to the Islamic Republic of Pakistan for a Third Punjab Education Sector Project' (*World Bank* 10 May 2016) <http://

B.   Models of Private Provision of Education

Even though neoliberalism encourages private actors' participation in the education sector, not all private provision of education is inspired by the neoliberal doctrine. Private institutions can take different forms. For example, they can be non-governmental organizations, religious bodies, interest groups, organized communities, foundations and for-profit businesses. Their commonality is that none are directly controlled or managed by State authorities.

In the delivery of education services, neoliberalism prefers for-profit private actors such as business organizations. These actors are motivated by commercial interests, believe education is a tradable good in the market and treat students as customers. This practice is labeled as the commercialization of education.[10] But the for-profit model is not the only one that can be found or recommended in the contemporary practice of global education reforms. In other words, not every privatization scheme implies the commercialization of education.

This section describes briefly some widespread and common practices of private provision of education and gives examples of these practices around the globe. This description is not exhaustive and aims only to illustrate a few paradigmatic cases.

1.   Voucher system[11]

The Chilean case represents one of the deepest applications of the neoliberal doctrine. In Chile, the privatization of education was part of a broader structural reform. The voucher system allows parents to freely choose the schools their children attend, either public or private, and the State transfers to the schools a fixed amount for each student enrolled. Schools may charge additional fees (top-up fees), making education a potentially lucrative sector and accentuating the segmentation of the educational system. Under this model, the results of a national test are often read as a measure of educational quality and play the role of a primary basis of information for families' school choices.[12]

Another example of universal voucher systems is the Netherlands' school-funding system. In this system, all primary and secondary school students are entitled to vouchers which can be used at all schools—public, private, religious and secular. The system has a special formula for low-income groups and minorities.[13] Unlike the Chilean system, in the Netherlands top-up fees are not allowed, there are extensive regulations for private schools and private schools cannot be for profit.

---

documents1.worldbank.org/curated/en/967701468198234577/pdf/PAD1641-PAD-P154524-R2016-0090-1-Box394887B-OUO-9.pdf> accessed 7 July 2020.

[10]   Rolla Moumné and Charlotte Saudemont, 'Overview of the Role of Private Providers in Education in Light of the Existing International Legal Framework' (2015) UNESCO Working Papers on Education Policy No 1, 14 <https://unesdoc.unesco.org/ark:/48223/pf0000243823> accessed 7 July 2020.

[11]   'A school voucher is a certificate or entitlement that parents can use to pay for the education of their children at a public or private school of their choice, rather than the public school that is closest to them or to which they have been assigned. Vouchers are paid from a public entity either directly to parents or to schools on the parents' behalf'. ibid 10.

[12]   Antoni Verger, Mauro Moschetti and Clara Fontdevila, 'La Privatización Educativa en América Latina: Una Cartografía de Políticas, Tendencias y Trayectorias' (*Education International*, April 2017) 28 <https://download.ei-ie.org/Docs/WebDepot/Privatizacion%201-Abril.pdf> accessed 7 July 2020.

[13]   Moumné and Saudemont (n 10) 10.

2.   Private management of public school

In this model, a private organization operates and manages a publicly owned and publicly funded school in exchange for payment. These schools do not charge tuition fees to students because they are publicly funded. Some examples of this practice are contract schools in the U.S., concession schools in Colombia (especially in Bogotá) and independent schools in Qatar.[14]

Beyond this general description, experiences vary according to the degree of flexibility and autonomy that is granted to the operator and the nature of the private provider (for profit or not). For example, in the cases of Colombia and Qatar, the operator must be a not-for-profit organization.[15] These programs can operate in poor districts, as in the Colombian case, as a form of policy targeted to enhance the quality of education for the poor.[16]

This model has clear neoliberal credentials especially when private operators are for-profit organizations. It arguably promotes efficiency through competition between private providers because they have to bid for the management contract in a competitive process. In addition, the continuity of the contract depends on the fulfillment of specific educative standards.

3.   Mandatory quotas in private schools for disadvantaged students

In India, the Right to Education Act establishes the duty of private providers of education to dedicate 25 per cent of school capacity to poor children for free. The State has to pay the private institution the same amount per capita as it would invest in the public school. The private school must subsidize the difference and provide equal access to education facilities.[17] This program is not neoliberal in its character, because the 'key purpose is to eliminate segregation and discrimination and foster diversity in schools'.[18]

4.   Low-cost for-profit private schools

Some developing countries, such as Kenya, Nigeria, Morocco, Peru, Dominican Republic and Jamaica have faced an exponential growth in commercial firms operating low-fee schools for profit in disadvantaged areas.[19] The existence of a market for low-fee for-profit private institutions can be actively promoted by the State, the result of the State passivity, or both.[20] In the first case, the State adopts and implements liberalization policies as to the activity of private educational providers. In the second scenario, known as 'de facto' or 'default' privatization, the absence of a robust public offer of education makes private education the only way for families and children to access education.[21] In addition, the low quality of the public offer of education puts pressure on the middle class to seek a better education in private schools.

---

[14]   ibid 9.

[15]   ibid 10.

[16]   Verger, Moschetti and Fontdevila (n 12) 35.

[17]   Sandra Fredman, 'State Funding of Private Education: The Role of Human Rights' in Frank Adamson and others (eds), *Realizing the Abidjan Principles: Human Rights, State Obligations, and the Role of Private Actors in Public Education* (Edward Elgar) (Forthcoming).

[18]   Sandra Fredman, *Comparative Human Rights Law* (OUP 2018) 380.

[19]   'Report of the Special Rapporteur on the Right to Education, Kishore Singh: Protecting Education Against Commercialization' (n 3).

[20]   Verger, Moschetti and Fontdevila (n 12) 35.

[21]   ibid 41. cf Moumné and Saudemont (n 10) 12.

5.   Private provision driven by particular historical causes

In some countries, a close cooperative relationship between the State and private agents, especially with religious organizations, existed prior to the emergence and expansion of neoliberal policies and discourses. This is the case in the Dominican Republic,[22] which has historically had precarious direct State investments in the public education system. Private Catholic schools provide education with public resources and some also charge access fees to families. Currently, the private Catholic schools have the alternative option to fully join the public system, but must eliminate tuition fees to do so.[23]

In the Argentinean case, where subsidies to private schools began in 1947, its initial objective was to help schools with low-income students to pay labor costs. The initially benefited schools were mainly Catholic, located in areas with only a scarce State presence. Although the initial scope of the policy was narrow, over time it was institutionalized and expanded because it was a cost-efficient way of expanding coverage in a context of budget constraints. The criteria for selecting the beneficiary schools and determining the amount of aid were the socioeconomic level of the served population and the proximity and availability of a similar State offer.[24] Although initially this policy did not have neoliberal credentials, its evolution shares some features with neoliberal educational policies against poverty, namely, it values efficiency, educational coverage and targeting the low-income population.

6.   Good quality private schools for the rich as an exercise of parents' freedoms

Finally, even in those countries where the public education system is strong, universal and of good quality, there are private schools for the rich as a result of the exercise of parents' freedom and capacity to educate children according to their customs and believes. Neoliberalism promotes the idea that education is an investment and students are seen as rational actors who should be encouraged to approach their education as self-investment in skills for the labor market.[25] Therefore, having quality private schools for the rich is in line with neoliberal ideas and policies. Regardless, the pursuit of private education can be motivated by religious reasons not related with economic neoliberal values.

In brief, this section showed that the practice of private provision of education is diverse and difficult to classify because policy implications have been adapted to local economic and political contexts. As we will see, this makes it difficult to evaluate the compatibility of these practices with human rights standards of education because similar schemes can produce different outcomes depending on the context. In the following section, we will present the human rights standards of education related to private provision of education.

---

[22]   In Europe, specifically in Spain, the Netherlands and Belgium, there have been many forms of historic public-private partnerships. Verger, Moschetti and Fontdevila (n 12) 44.

[23]   ibid 45.

[24]   ibid 46–49.

[25]   Murphy (n 7) 85.

II.   HUMAN RIGHTS STANDARDS RELATED TO PRIVATE PROVISION OF EDUCATION

Does the international human rights legal framework prioritize the public provision of education over publicly funded private provision?[26] The right to education has different dimensions: a social, a freedom and an equality dimension.[27] As to the social dimension, the right to education is the primary vehicle through which economically and socially marginalized adults and children can lift themselves out of poverty and obtain the means to participate fully in society. The freedom dimension of the right includes, among others, the liberty of parents to select the school for their children and the liberty of people and the private sector to found and direct these institutions. Finally, the equality dimension of the right protects individuals from discrimination within the education system and allows citizens to demand equal treatment with regards to education.[28]

These different dimensions of the right can conflict with each other. The freedom dimension of the right to education can enter into conflict with the equality dimension.[29] For instance, the decision to allow private provision of education can generate disparate outcomes, segregation and segmentation. International human rights instruments deal with these tensions. In this section, we will present human rights standards on the right to education that are relevant to the issue of privatization. We focus our analysis in the UN human rights system, particularly Article 13 of the International Covenant on Economic, Social and Cultural Rights (ICESCR), the Committee on Economic, Social and Cultural Rights' (CESCR) General Comment 13 on the Right to Education, the reports by the UN Special Rapporteur on the Right to Education and the UN Convention on the Rights of the Child (CRC). We also focus our analysis in the Abidjan Principles that specifically address the issue of privatization of education and the duties of States to regulate private involvement in education. This is not a definitive legal analysis. We acknowledge that these standards have different sources and varying degrees of legal authority.[30]

A.   Private Actors have the Liberty to Found and Direct Educational Institutions

International human rights law allows private individuals to establish and direct educational institutions. According to Article 13 of the ICESCR and Article 29 of the CRC, private actors in education must conform to minimum standards laid down by the State and to the general requirements of education under international law.[31] The liberty to establish and direct schools

---

[26]   Fredman, 'State Funding of Private Education' (n 17). The human right to education has not only legal dimensions but also ethical and cultural dimensions. It is also possible to criticize the neoliberal approach to the privatization of education from these perspectives. We focus only on the legal dimension of the right.

[27]   cf Sylvain Aubry and Delphine Dorsi, 'Towards a Human Rights Framework to Advance the Debate on the Role of Private Actors in Education' (2016) 42 Oxford Review of Education 612, 612.

[28]   Sandra Fredman, *Comparative Human Rights Law* (n 18) 358.

[29]   ibid 357; cf Aubry and Dorsi (n 27).

[30]   Fredman, 'State Funding of Private Education' (n 17).

[31]   Particularly, the goals of education are defined in paragraph 1 of article 13 of ICESCR:
    Education shall be directed to the full development of the human personality and the sense of its dignity, and shall strengthen the respect for human rights and fundamental freedoms. They further

is also associated with the State's obligation to respect the liberty of parents to select schools other than public institutions for their children.[32] The educational choice of parents ensures that families can select education that is in line with their own moral and religious convictions.

In any case, General Comment 13 of the CESCR notes that the State has an obligation to ensure that the liberty to establish and direct schools does not lead to extreme disparities of educational opportunity for some groups in society. There is an intrinsic tension in international human rights law between conceptions of freedom and equality related to education. On the one hand, there is an explicit recognition that education should not be exclusively public. On the other hand, there is the CESCR's affirmation, which results somewhat conflicting in practice, that the existence of private education cannot lead to the creation of disparities or the deepening those already existing in societies.

B.   Equality and Non-Discrimination in the Right to Education

States must respect, protect and fulfill the right to education of everyone within their jurisdiction in accordance with the rights to equality and non-discrimination. Article 2(2) of the ICESCR establishes that the States parties to the Covenant undertake to guarantee that the rights enunciated in the Covenant will be exercised without discrimination of any kind, including social origin. The right to education is no exception. According to CESCR General Comment 13, the prohibition of discrimination is an immediate obligation of the States. It applies fully and immediately to all aspects of education and encompasses all internationally prohibited grounds of discrimination. Finally, the CRC establishes that the State parties recognize the right of the child to education, with a view to achieving this right progressively and on the basis of equal opportunity.

C.   States Have the Primary Responsibility to Provide Education

Unlike Article 13 of the ICESCR, CESCR General Comment 13 is very clear in establishing that States have the primary responsibility to provide education directly in most circumstances. The Committee takes into account two sources to elaborate this standard. First, Article 13 of the ICESCR establishes the duties of the States to pursue and develop a system of schools at all levels. Second, the CESCR has said that the domestic law and practices of the different States parties to the Convention support this conclusion.

However, according to the General Comment, even though States parties have an enhanced obligation to fulfill the right to education, the extent of this obligation is not uniform for all levels of education. The wording is different for every level of education according to paragraph 2 of Article 13 of the ICESCR. While primary education shall be compulsory and free to all, secondary education shall be made generally available and accessible to all by every appropriate means, and in particular by the progressive introduction of free education. Higher education shall be made equally accessible to all, on the basis of capacity, by every appropriate means, and in particular by the progressive introduction of free education. There is an unfor-

---

agree that education shall enable all persons to participate effectively in a free society, promote understanding, tolerance and friendship among all nations and all racial, ethnic or religious groups, and further the activities of the United Nations for the maintenance of peace.

[32]   ibid.

tunate omission in international human rights law with regard to the obligations of the State in providing pre-school education.

D.   States Must Regulate and Monitor Private Provision of Education

As mentioned above, according to international human rights law, private education providers must meet minimum standards for the provision of education. This supposes a previous obligation of States to regulate and monitor the compliance of private providers with the minimum standards regarding the right to education. International law is not very specific on the content and scope of such regulation, particularly regarding the acceptability of education. A significant effort in this matter can be found in the recently approved Abidjan Principles on the human rights obligations of States on the right to education and to regulate private involvement in education.[33]

The Abidjan Principles acknowledge the reality of private education. They also reaffirm the freedom component of education. However, they state that private institutions must conform to standards established by the State in accordance with its obligation of regulation of education. The Principles say that private institutions can supplement public education in a way conducive to the realization of the right to education for all. According to the Principles, private education cannot lead to or maintain disparities of educational opportunity and outcomes for some groups. Moreover, private education must not affect or impair the capacity of the State to realize the right to free quality public education.

E.   No General Prohibition of Public Funding of Private Provision of Education

International law does not have a definitive position on whether States can meet their education obligations by providing funding to private providers. In any case, there is no absolute prohibition on State funding for private schools. According to Fredman, the CESCR suggests this is permissible when it asserts that if States decide to fund private education it should do it without discrimination.[34] In addition, CESCR General Comment 24 on State obligations in the context of business activities does not forbid privatization, but it calls attention to the fact that private education is not accessible to some society members. Therefore, for Fredman, the important question is under what conditions private education with public funds should be allowed.[35] As described above, States have duties to ensure that private providers conform to minimum educative standards and fulfill the main values attached to the right to education. These duties do not depend on the type of sources of funding. Therefore, according to Fredman, the specific question with regard to this standard is 'whether the State accrues extra obligations when it does provide public funding'.[36]

---

[33]   The Abidjan Principles were the result of a three-year process in which civil society in consultation with different education stakeholders and with the support of the academic community developed a guide of principles on the obligations of the States regarding education and particularly their duties of regulation and monitoring of the private provision of education.

[34]   Fredman, 'State Funding of Private Education' (n 17).

[35]   ibid.

[36]   ibid.

Based on the principle that the State remains responsible for the provision of education and the content of the States' duties to respect, protect and fulfill the right to education, Fredman deduced some specific human right standards for the case of private provision with public funding.[37] From the duty to respect, she extrapolates that 'public funding to private providers should not undermine or obstruct the right to education of every individual, whether in the State itself, or in a recipient of aid'.[38] A development of this standard states that 'the use of public funds for private education should not divert public funds away from public educa-tion'.[39] The duty to protect implies that the State must make such funding conditional to the observance of human rights standards. The duty to fulfill entails 'that the State should not discriminate in the provision of funding, nor allow funding to lead to further discrimination. This includes discrimination on grounds of socio-economic status'.[40] Public funding of private schools should not be done in a way which would worsen inequalities of education driven by poverty. This last standard is central to our analysis between poverty and privatization of education, because the most pervasive form of discrimination resulting from privatization of education is the one that is based on poverty.

Fredman does not find publicly financed for-profit private providers incompatible with the human rights framework. The incompatibility depends on how likely for-profit provision can meet the previous standards. Similarly, Moumné and Saudemont hold that the commercial-ization of education can be compatible with human rights standards if (1) for-profit private providers comply with State's regulations and monitoring, (2) the regulations are sufficient, (3) private providers contribute to the development of the educational system in general and (4) the arrangement does not create extreme educational disparities in society.[41]

The Abidjan Principles reiterate that the right to education does not entail an obligation for the State to fund private educational institutions. The provision of free quality public education is at the core of the Abidjan Principles. This means that the State should only fund private instructional educational institutions if they comply with human rights law and observe substantive, procedural and operational requirements. States must not fund institutions that charge fees in a way that substantially undermines access to education or more broadly, any institution that does not meet human rights legal standards. There seems to be a certain con-sensus with regards to these standards.

However, according to the Abidjan Principles, the private provision of education with public resources should be a time-bound measure which the State publicly demonstrates to be the only effective option to advance the realization of the right to education. Also, the private provision of education with public resources should not constitute or contribute to the commercialization of the education system. In addition, States must not fund any private insti-tution that is commercial or excessively pursues its own self-interests. This seems to be a more restrictive view of the (for-profit) private provision with public funding issue.

The Global Schools Forum, a community of education entrepreneurs who run and support schools in poor contexts, have contested this restrictive view and have argued against the

---

37 It is important to clarify that Fredman warns that she does not intend to do definitive legal analysis.
38 ibid.
39 ibid.
40 ibid.
41 Moumné and Saudemont (n 10) 14.

Abidjan Principles.[42] Particularly, they argue that the Principles go beyond international human rights law. According to their critique, governments should determine the best way to provide education—whether public, private or a combination of both—as long as this complies with human rights standards and principles and can be effectively monitored and regulated.[43] The Global Schools Forum also questions the legal basis of public funding to private education institutions as a time-bound measure only. This kind of critique shows the tensions and loopholes in international law regarding the content and scope of regulation and the margin of action of States to fulfill their obligation under international law.

III.   COMPATIBILITY BETWEEN PRIVATE PARTICIPATION IN EDUCATION AND HUMAN RIGHTS STANDARDS ON THE RIGHT TO EDUCATION

Some authors have proposed a three-fold categorization to characterize the models of privatization of education services.[44] These three forms of privatization are delegation, divestment and displacement (hereinafter the 3D Framework).

According to this categorization, delegation has to do with those circumstances in which the State delegates the production to the private sector but it is still responsible for the provision of the service. For instance, this is the case of the concession schools charter program, active in Bogota, Colombia since 1999. Divestment happens when governments transfer responsibilities, functions, enterprises or assets to private providers and avoid or neglect any responsibility in the provision of the service. Displacement occurs when, in a passive or indirect way, the State's provision of a service is substituted by the private sector. This is usually a consequence of deregulation. The clearest example of this mode of privatization is the phenomenon of low-cost, for-profit schools in certain African countries with no solid regulation.[45]

Fredman suggests, following this categorization, that funding through delegation may comply with human rights standards when the funding has specific conditions to adhere to those standards.[46] However, if conditions are ineffective or difficult to enforce, the State should cut the funding and desist of that scheme of funding.[47] Divestment is unlikely to comply with human rights standards unless there is a good local regulation framework with adequate enforcement. Finally, the most problematic system of funding is the one with a displacement effect. This is the case of certain countries that, as a result of deregulation, cede their main role as education providers.

We agree with Fredman that there is a wide range of practical examples of public funding of private education providers. But, for the same reason, we believe that the 3D framework

---

[42]   'The "Abidjan Principles" on Private Involvement in Education: A Useful Framework or a Step too Far?' (*UKFIET*, 2 July 2019) <www.ukfiet.org/2019/the-abidjan-principles-on-private-involvement-in-education-a-useful-framework-or-a-step-too-far/> accessed 7 July 2020.

[43]   ibid.

[44]   Fazal Rizvi, 'Privatization in Education: Trends and Consequences' (2016) UNESCO Education Research and Foresight Working Papers ED-2016/WP/2. cf Fredman, 'State Funding of Private Education' (n 17).

[45]   Rizvi (n 44) 5.

[46]   Fredman, 'State Funding of Private Education' (n 17).

[47]   ibid.

is insufficient to address the potential compliance of the different forms of privatization with human rights standards. The 3D framework does not fully comprehend the specific relevant details of every practice in localized contexts for the following reasons.

First, delegation includes different modes of privatization with different possible outcomes vis-à-vis a human rights framework. Some research has shown voucher programs and charter schools can create inequalities and both are forms of delegation, but this concept is insufficient to identify in every system what produces inequality. For example, in the case of Chile, inequality can be the result of admission requirements based on values and educative goals of particular private institutions. In charter schools, inequality problems can be caused by different factors. These include the nature of the private provider, an inadequate funding strategy, the contract regulation, the location of the school, the admission requirement standards and the quality of teaching staff. In Colombia, for example, the charter schools are located in poor neighborhoods, education is free, admission standards are the same as the public system and the provider cannot be for profit.[48]

Second, even within the same mode of privatization, there can be really different outcomes. The voucher system found in Chile and the Netherlands are both forms of delegation. As we mentioned before, the Netherlands' system is likely be more compatible with international human rights law. Unlike the Chilean system, in the Netherlands top-up fees are not allowed, there are extensive regulations for private schools, and private schools cannot be for profit. This last feature can make a big difference when evaluating the compatibility of these systems with human rights standards.

We believe that the 3D Framework does not clarify these nuances and does not bring to light what is wrong with privatization in each model. The key for policymakers is to understand which aspects of the specific scheme cause the incompatibility with the human rights legal framework. For instance, in the Chilean case, we want to know what features of the voucher system are causing the segregation that caught the attention of the United Nations Committee on the Rights of the Child.[49] The segregation, allegedly, violates the standard according to which public funding of private schools should not be done in a way which would worsen inequalities of education driven by poverty.

With respect to divestment, the first problem arises from the vagueness of the concept in terms of describing modes of privatization of education. This vagueness exists because the concept includes different grades of privatization, from selling companies or assets to transferring functions and responsibilities. Each represents a form of privatization with different implications from a human rights perspective.

Clearly, the most extreme form of divestment is full privatization, in which the State gives up all of its functions with regard to education services. There is a consensus that a fully private education system violates the State's primary responsibility to provide education.[50] This is the case even when the private provider is a not-for-profit actor. However, this hypothetical assumption is difficult to find in practice. In contrast, Fredman's example of divestment, the sale of property to a private corporation to build a school, could probably comply with human

[48] This Colombian example represents a very different scheme from the U.S. charter school system.

[49] Committee on the Rights of the Child, 'List of Issues in Relation to the Combined Fourth and Fifth Periodic Reports of Chile' (5 March 2015) UN Doc CRC/C/CHL/Q/4-5, para 14.

[50] Moumné and Saudemont (n 10) 12.

rights standards on education if there is proper regulation. In a full privatization scheme the condition of regulation is irrelevant.

Finally, the 3D framework does not capture the practice of good quality private schools for the wealthy in the exercise of parents' liberty. This is because the framework focuses on the transfers from the public to the private. The practice of private education for the wealthy is independent of that phenomenon. This is problematic because the parents' exercise of their liberty to educate their children may generate a dual education system – one for upper- and middle-class children enrolled in private institutions of alleged better quality and the other for poor children registered in public schools. Here, the problem is not one of a possibly low-quality or unacceptable education provided by the private school, but the low-quality of education provided by the public schools.[51] This inequality problem arises from both private provision and the lack of political will or resources to provide good quality public education. 3D forms of privatization are not the only source of inequalities.

IV.   CONCLUSION: THE RESEARCH AGENDA AHEAD

This chapter has addressed the issue of private provision in education and its compatibility with a human rights legal framework. We characterized different models of private provision of education, with particular attention on private provision with public funding. We also reviewed some human rights standards related to privatization of education and some specific and less clear standards related to private provision of education with State funding.

In the last section, with a critical perspective of the 3D framework of privatization, we showed the insufficiency of certain classifications to achieve conclusive judgments on the compatibility of certain models of privatization with human rights standards. More conclusive judgments on this issue of compatibility of education require a robust research agenda that should include, at least, the creation of more precise standards in terms of the quality of education that derives from the human rights framework. We also need more precise standards to measure disparities in education in order to establish compliance with the principle of equality of opportunity.

The research agenda should include a more detailed classification of the models of privatization in education to reach proper conclusions about the compatibility of private provision of education with human rights standards and how best to guarantee the full realization of the human right to education for children living in poverty. The fields of human rights, education and poverty need more empirical evidence of the effects of specific models of privatization in the full enjoyment of the human right to education. At the same time more research is needed on the precision of the international obligation of States according to the level of education when it is provided by the private sector. Also, the field can benefit from a deep study of how minimum standards are regulated at the domestic level to deal with the privatization phenomenon.

Finally, according to the best reading of international human rights law, we believe that a public policy of public financing of private education should not undermine the quality of

---

[51]   This dual system can be present in the context where public schools are excellent but well-off parents want a specialized (religious) education. But here the question is whether supporting the decision of parents is compatible with the human rights legal framework.

education already provided and it should ensure that private education financed with public resources is as good or better as public education. The challenge is to determine what the appropriate standards of good quality education are. Relevant questions include: what are the goals and quality standards fixed by human right legal framework and under what conditions, if any, can publicly funded private provision education meet these goals and standards, especially for people living in poverty?

28. Poverty, labour law and human rights: a necessary connection

Lee Swepston and Constance Thomas

There is an obvious connection between income generation and emergence from poverty. In order for income generating activities to offer viable pathways for emergence from poverty, basic human rights protection of workers must be assured along with employment promotion initiatives. Today, there are millions of men and women who find themselves among the 'working poor' or at high risk of falling into poverty. Whether poverty is described as an income below a minimum defined level or as social or rights deprivation, access to decent work is an indispensable component of preventing and remedying poverty. In the long term, it is not immediate measures of poverty relief that will make the difference but access to decent work with just incomes and protections. This approach involves addressing poverty and workers' rights from a perspective of social justice, inclusion, equality, non-discrimination, entitlements, capacities and duties.

There is also a distinction to be made between absolute poverty and relative poverty. Many of the labour-related rights discussed here, while relevant to both, are more apt to create and improve the quantity and quality of work rather than relieve the complete deprivation of absolute poverty. Absolute poverty is largely a matter for humanitarian intervention to implant basic levels of nutrition, housing, safety and related needs, but relative poverty can be addressed by helping to implant the capacity to generate income and establish livelihoods up to the average level of the particular society – in other words income-generating decent work. Not only does this have economic value, but it also addresses the human rights associated with work, such as equality of opportunity and treatment. And it is most often through the intervention of law and regulations and the capacity of national administrations that these matters are addressed most effectively.

At the international level, the rights related to work, and to the organization of economies as concerns work, are developed most fully in international labour standards adopted by the International Labour Organization (ILO). In many cases these rights were the basis for the related human rights provisions in other international human rights law. The ILO was established in 1919 with a fundamental concern of ending poverty. As the ILO Constitution states: 'Poverty anywhere constitutes a danger to prosperity everywhere'. It goes on, in Article I(d) of the 1944 Declaration of Philadelphia (incorporated into the ILO Constitution in 1946), to declare that:

> [T]he war against want requires to be carried on with unrelenting vigour within each nation, and by continuous and concerted international effort in which the representatives of workers and employers, enjoying equal status with those of governments, join with them in free discussion and democratic decision with a view to the promotion of the common welfare.

One of the ILO's basic goals is therefore the elimination of poverty, or 'the war against want'. The Universal Declaration of Human Rights, and the two international human rights

Covenants adopted in 1966, address these rights in a less detailed way, based on the foundation provided by the ILO, and firmly bring work-related rights into the broader human rights perspective. These questions are also addressed in other basic human rights instruments, such as those on racism, the rights of disabled persons, migrant workers, women's rights and many others adopted both by the UN and regional bodies.[1]

The adoption and application of labour law, and of laws relating to the workplace, was the first of the working methods of the ILO. Most ILO standards, which have been adopted to guide the creation of law and practice at the national level, are concerned with various means of overcoming poverty and enabling respect for the right to live and work with dignity. This chapter will set out the substantive human rights of workers and their linkage to overcoming poverty through decent work. It will provide examples of how international supervisory bodies have urged application of these rights to protect marginalized and exploited workers. The growing challenge with the informalization of working relationships, in both the developed and developing worlds, also is addressed as a matter of concern, in particular its undermining of labour relationships and the protections offered by labour law and its implementation.

Note that this aspect of the elimination of poverty is often neglected by the literature on rights and poverty, though the link has been recognized by those carrying out practical development work 'in the field'. Most textbooks on the international human rights regime give labour law minimal, if any, attention.[2] It has been suggested that this omission

> may result from the fact that some see labour law as governing work relationships and fail to consider the human rights dimensions of the employment or work arrangement. It may also result from the fact that those human rights scholars who focus on civil and political rights tend to see the State as the actor who violates the human rights of individuals. This is a very public law focus and most employment or work relations are the subject of private law.[3]

Whatever the reason, the United Nations Special Rapporteurs on Extreme Forms of Poverty, since the appointment of the first one in 1998, have made some references to work as a source of emergence from poverty, but have paid little attention to the human rights related to labour. The exception to this is a fairly comprehensive listing of social security and workers' compensation law, which deal with the transfer of resources rather than the facilitation and protection of employment and work. Provisions of the International Covenant on Economic, Social and Cultural Rights and other human rights treaties cited under 'International Standards' on the Special Rapporteur's site[4] mention many aspects of rights, but labour rights are omitted from these references.

Likewise the Millennium Development Goals adopted in 2000 entirely ignored questions relating to labour, including the law governing its use, as a means of achieving development and exiting from poverty. However in a radical reorientation the Sustainable Development

---

[1]   See, e.g., Lee Swepston, *The Development in International Law of Articles 23 and 24 of the Universal Declaration of Human Rights: The Labor Rights Articles* (Brill/Nijhoff 2014).

[2]   See, e.g., one of the most recent works on human rights, Olivier de Schutter, *International Human Rights Law: Cases, Materials, Commentary* (3rd edn, CUP 2019). It contains no more than passing references to workers' rights, or even economic, social and cultural rights in general.

[3]   Janice R Bellace and Beryl ter Haar (eds), *Research Handbook on Labour, Business and Human Rights Law* (Edward Elgar 2019) 2.

[4]   'International Standards' (*United Nations Human Rights Office of the High Commissioner*) <www.ohchr.org/EN/Issues/Poverty/Pages/IStandards.aspx> accessed 22 June 2020.

Goals adopted in 2015 have taken detailed account of decent work as a means of achieving sustainable development and eliminating poverty, especially in Goal 8 (Decent Work and Economic Growth). This has been a long-standing omission from human rights writing, in spite of a growing number of works taking fuller account of labour standards as an integral part of international human rights law.

It is increasingly recognized that labour law and the rights and duties that it establishes are essential to the construction of a functioning economy that assures sustainable development and the emergence of individuals and nations from poverty, and that recognizing the human rights component of economic governance is a crucial component of this. Beyond social insurance – which of course is vital – well drafted labour law having wide application provides basic building blocks. It serves to balance the interests of employers with that of less powerful individual workers in a just and fair manner and to provide protection to workers; and in some cases, it is intended to benefit society through restricting actions of particular actors. In addition to the labour rights deemed 'fundamental' by the ILO,[5] the legal instruments that establish and protect practical workers' rights, such as those on employment promotion, payment of wages, protection from illness and accidents at work, conditions of work, employment security and the enforcement of these rights, are essential to the proper functioning of national economies and to emerging from poverty. The international labour standards are not merely inspirational but also provide excellent guidance for drafting legislation and establishing necessary mechanisms that ensure that the human rights of workers are enforceable at the national level. A rights-based approach focusses not only on providing rights directly, to the extent that this is possible, but also on building capacity and mechanisms needed to claim and achieve these rights, such as legal literacy, labour administration and inspection, and judicial bodies.

I.   ILO AND POVERTY

The ILO's central message is social justice for all. It aims to achieve this largely through the adoption of international labour standards, a purpose for which it was created in 1919, supplemented by supervision of these standards, technical assistance and research. Unlike all other international organizations, the ILO is tripartite, meaning that organizations of employers and of workers have an equal say with governments in adopting standards and carrying forward the ILO's work. As soon as it was established, the ILO began adopting workers' protection standards, beginning with the protection of women and children, the regulation of hours of work and addressing high levels of unemployment. These had been the demands of the trade union movement as it began to look past the First World War and to the creation of a future society. During the early years, the ILO concentrated most of its work on the adoption and supervision of standards. When the ILO joined the UN system as the first of the specialized agencies, it added increased assistance to its member States, together with workers' and employers' organizations, to its continuing standard-setting mission, and began to intervene more directly in the establishment of laws and regulations, good governance, and workplace standards, as well as employment promotion and social protection.[6]

---

5   See Section III.A.

6   Extensive information on the origins of the ILO, its history and structures has been assembled for the 100th anniversary of the Organization in 2019, and may be found on the ILO's web site at: 'The ILO Centenary' (*International Labour Organization*) <www.ilo.org/100/en/> accessed 22 June 2020.

The ILO's work, along with that of others in the international system, has almost always been based on the developmental priority of poverty alleviation through employment promotion and the protection of workers through laws, regulations and collective bargaining, including reduction of informality. In 1969 the ILO launched the World Employment Programme (WEP), which focussed the ILO's work on poverty alleviation and developed the Basic Needs Approach; this concept gradually spilled over into the rest of the development community. Although the WEP did not take an explicit rights-based approach, it demonstrated the importance of linking the basic well-being of individuals (food, shelter and water) to any sustainable generation of income or employment. The WEP both relied on and stimulated the adoption of a number of ILO standards on employment and work, and thus had a legal as well as a developmental basis. By the time it came to an end in the early 1990s, the WEP's influence on the informal economy and the rights agenda throughout the UN system was profound.[7]

As was highlighted in the conclusions adopted by the International Labour Conference in 2002 on decent work and the informal economy:

> the promotion of decent work for all workers, women and men, irrespective of where they work, requires a broad strategy: realizing fundamental principles and rights at work; creating greater and better employment and income opportunities; extending social protection; and promoting social dialogue. These dimensions of decent work reinforce each other and comprise an integrated poverty reduction strategy.[8]

Today, the wider international community has begun to absorb the lesson that without decent work and the rights associated with it, there can be no sustainable development, and emergence from poverty will be nearly impossible.

II.   IMPORTANCE OF LAW IN COMBATTING POVERTY

Law – which refers here not only to legislation and regulatory instruments, but also to accompanying legal mechanisms established to promote, apply and enforce the law – is indispensable to the realization of rights, though not sufficient without additional measures of implementation. The establishment and application of international labour law is carried out by the ILO through the adoption of international Conventions and Recommendations, which provide the basis for national law and other regulatory instruments at the national level. The more than 8,000 ratifications of ILO Conventions by the end of 2019 have created a web of common obligations around the world and contribute to consistency among national laws on labour-related subjects. The ILO's active supervision of the implementation of the obligations undertaken by governments when they ratify these Conventions contributes to both the establishment and the maintenance of the legal and regulatory tools needed to accomplish this work.

---

[7]   For more information, see the documentation for the conference on the 50th Anniversary of the Launch of the World Employment Programme: 'The World Employment Programme: Past, Present and Future' (*International Labour Organization*) <www.ilo.org/employment/Whatwedo/Eventsandmeetings/WCMS_684554/lang--en/index.htm> accessed 22 June 2020.

[8]   International Labour Conference, 90th session, 'Report of the Committee on the Informal Economy' (ILO, 2002) 53, at: <www.ilo.org/public/english/standards/relm/ilc/ilc90/pdf/pr-25.pdf> accessed 22 June 2020.

And the close cooperation with organizations of employers and of workers, and their involvement in the ILO's work, helps to translate these rights into practical action.[9] Of course, even in countries with high levels of ratifications, and where basic labour and employment laws are in place, problems of the coverage and content of those laws and their implementation persist. To be effective, law needs to be clear, up to date, understood and used by workers and employers, wide in coverage and easily enforceable through functioning and accessible grievance procedures, complaint mechanisms and administrative and judicial bodies. These are points often raised by the ILO supervisory bodies and where political will is important in addressing them.

What is work? First of all, the terms 'work' and 'employment' are not synonymous. Employment is in fact a subset of the broader world of work, and only a minority of the world's population is actually in an employment relationship. For our purposes here, work is any economic activity resulting in the production of goods or services, and which normally generates income. Income itself can be broadly defined and does not include only wages or salaries but also includes remuneration in any form for work performed. It must be acknowledged that this concept of work, as it is generally used and regulated, excludes those household, caring and voluntary activities that are unrecognized, unpaid, undervalued and largely undertaken by women.

There is a great deal of economic activity that is outside the formal employment sector, and increasing attention is directed to the so-called informal economy.[10] The Special Rapporteurs and much of human rights writing, as it concerns work focusses on only some aspects of poverty alleviation related to work, and often those that most directly apply to the formal sector. Social security, for example, is in most cases the result of employment-based activity carried out within the national legal framework that either entitles people to payment or is the result of income-based schemes of insurance. Most of the world, however, has no access to social security or to any other form of social protection that depends on work, because they are outside the formal economic sector. This has occasioned some attempts by States to provide minimum social protection schemes, and in some cases basic income, to compensate for the lack of employment opportunity and security. However this is rare, and most income still depends on work.

The lack of formality in the world of work for large parts of the world's population has long been a concern of the international development community; estimates in some countries place the large majority of the population in the informal economy as a consequence of lack of

---

9   Space does not allow a detailed account of the ILO's structure and working methods in this chapter. For information, consult, e.g., ILO, *Rules of the Game: An Introduction to the Standards-Related Work of the International Labour Organization* (Centenary edn, ILO 2019) <www.ilo.org/global/standards/information-resources-and-publications/publications/WCMS_672549/lang--en/index.htm> accessed 22 June 2020.

10   As defined in Paragraph 2 of the ILO Recommendation 204 (Recommendation Concerning the Transition From the Informal to the Formal Economy) (104th Conference Session Geneva 12 June 2015),

'For the purposes of this Recommendation, the term "informal economy":

(a) refers to all economic activities by workers and economic units that are – in law or in practice – not covered or insufficiently covered by formal arrangements; and

(b) does not cover illicit activities, in particular the provision of services or the production, sale, possession or use of goods forbidden by law, including the illicit production and trafficking of drugs, the illicit manufacturing of and trafficking in firearms, trafficking in persons, and money laundering, as defined in the relevant international treaties.'

economic development. ILO estimates that at least 40 per cent of the world's population works in precarious employment.[11] But we are now experiencing the creation of new forms of informality, especially in some of the more developed countries, resulting from changes in employment structures and the creation of the so-called 'gig' economy. Employers have found ways of removing those who provide services from formal employment and re-contracting with them through various forms of remuneration, thus avoiding the cost of providing protections established over the last hundred years in employment and social security law. Absence from the formal economy creates rights deficits, because the laws that have been adopted to regulate workplaces are simply not applied to those working outside formal employment. This is both caused by and contributes to continuing poverty in these situations. In addition, there are some forms of work – for example slavery, bonded labour and other forms of extreme exploitation – that do not serve to alleviate poverty but may instead reinforce it. The increasing numbers of the 'working poor' continue to pose a challenge to labour market regulation. This makes it all the more important to focus on the quality of work, termed 'decent work' by the ILO, and the extension of rights protection through law, along with the mere fact of its availability.

In addition to and often overlapping with those in the informal economy are various categories of people who are in need of special attention for different reasons, including those already in the workforce and those trying to gain access. Both the ILO and the UN, as well as regional bodies, have adopted standards relating to marginalized groups vulnerable to poverty, including women, minorities, indigenous and tribal peoples, children, rural workers, migrants, refugees, LGBTQ+ persons, disabled persons, disaster-affected persons and displaced persons. There is not space in this chapter to examine in detail any one of them. All of them share the basic characteristic of needing protection in law and in policies, with the kind of attention needed varying with the group and the circumstances. These groups need to overcome rights deficits in order to gain a foothold in their national economies and get on the path towards emerging from or avoiding poverty. Some examples are included below in relation to how international supervision and the application of international labour rights and national labour law have been used to address poverty related exclusion and exploitation in the labour market.

III.   INTERNATIONAL LABOUR STANDARDS

For ease of examination, we can divide the international labour standards and the national laws that implement them into the categories of fundamental rights and other labour-related rights, as well as supporting policies. The rights and protections set out in the fundamental international labour standards, as well as many other standards, apply to all workers and not only those in formal employment.

In each of the following examples it should be noted that the adoption and implementation of laws and other legal instruments, are essential to making these rights effective. In each case the ILO's strong supervisory process pushes governments to take measures to comply with ILO Conventions, and the United Nations instruments have their own supervisory bodies that take the same approach. But international law and supervision rarely can take the entire credit

---

[11]   ILO, *World Employment and Social Outlook: Trends 2018* (ILO 2018) <www.ilo.org/wcmsp5/groups/public/---dgreports/---dcomm/---publ/documents/publication/wcms_615594.pdf> accessed 22 June 2020.

for making governments act; what they can do is stimulate action and help to shape the content of national measures. Indeed, the marked alignment of national labour law around the world is testament to this influence.

A.   Fundamental Rights

In its 1998 Declaration on Fundamental Principles and Rights at Work, the ILO designated four major subjects as fundamental rights: freedom of association and protection of the right to organize, and freedom from forced labour, child labour and discrimination. There are recent moves towards including health and safety at work in the list of fundamental rights. There is broad consensus that these rights form the minimum social floor that should apply to all workers regardless of their working status. None of these rights can be protected without the adoption of adequate legal frameworks that respect international standards and adapt to national situations. The protection of these rights by law and in practice is an essential tool to emerging from poverty.

1.   Freedom of association and protection of the right to organize

Freedom of association and the right to organize form the bedrock for establishing the human rights of workers at both the international and national level. This requires at least a minimum legal framework at the national level, which most often is based on the international standards adopted by the ILO. In addition, collective agreements produced by collective bargaining have the force of law and are essential to workplace regulation where they exist. The Freedom of Association and Protection of the Right to Organise Convention, 1948 (No. 87) and the Right to Organise and Collective Bargaining Convention, 1949 (No. 98) are the most important of the ILO's standards on the subject, and they are highly ratified. Both the International Covenant on Civil and Political Rights and the International Covenant on Economic, Social and Cultural Rights provide explicitly that Convention No. 87 is to be respected by all states that ratify the two Covenants.

The importance of freedom of association in the context of the elimination of poverty is that it provides workers with the right to combine to defend their interests and improve their conditions of work, including wages. Where trade unions or other workers' associations can organize and operate freely, there is a better chance of adopting protective legislation and collective agreements that remove their members from situations of poverty. The rights to freedom of association in the international labour standards are not limited to workers in the formal sector but extend to agricultural workers, migrant workers, home-based workers, domestic workers and other workers in the informal economy, though of course they are more difficult to implement in such situations.

Despite the transformative role that use of freedom of association rights can play, there are too many persons working who cannot or do not make use of such rights, often because of restrictions in national laws placed on such rights or failure of the laws to extend protection de jure or de facto. For example, many in the agricultural sector continue to be unorganized and thus unprotected, working in informal environments with low productivity, poor conditions of work and low incomes. And they often are not even covered by national legislation that would assure them of these rights.

The ILO supervisory bodies have been used to influence governments to ensure extension of freedom of association rights to excluded workers. The International Confederation of Free

Trade Unions (ICFTU) complained in an observation in 2003 on Convention No. 98 that in Niger the labour law applies to very few workers because 95 per cent of workers are in the informal economy where the Government does not enforce workers' rights. The Government replied that although most workers are in sustenance agriculture or other parts of the informal economy, all workers have the right to organize. So, in this instance it is not a matter of legal formulation but a matter of the application and use of the labour law.

The recent emergence of domestic workers' organizations and the growing extension of labour regulation to domestic work shows the strength of using labour rights. The right of migrant workers to form and join unions has consistently been reaffirmed by the ILO supervisory bodies and has assisted their struggles in a number of countries to address low pay and poor working conditions. Using these rights to form associations, agricultural workers have improved pay levels and reduced child labour. Informal entrepreneurs and venders have also used these rights to organize and negotiate agreements with public authorities that allow them to conduct their activities. Strangely enough, there has been a decline in the membership of trade unions, especially in some Western developed countries, but this is often because the unions have been instrumental in the past in ensuring workplace rights, and many workers no longer see the utility of belonging to them. These are exactly the situations in which those rights begin to be eroded anew.

2.   Forced labour

All forms of forced labour are violations of basic human rights, including rights at work. Forced labour both causes and reinforces poverty, so combating it is a direct contribution to the elimination of poverty. Slavery, an extreme form of forced labour, was the first human right to be dealt with by international agreement. While the ILO and the League of Nations began to adopt standards in 1919, the League only adopted one instrument that would later be included in the international human rights regime: The Slavery Convention in 1926. Four years later, the ILO adopted the Forced Labour Convention (No. 29) to complement the Slavery Convention. Neither Convention had a human rights orientation, both concentrating on the obligations of states to suppress these practices, but they were nevertheless the first human rights conventions adopted in the new international regime.

After World War II, the new UN system began to adopt a human rights approach in its standard setting. The UN adopted the Supplementary Convention on the Abolition of Slavery, the Slave Trade, and Institutions and Practices Similar to Slavery in 1956 and the ILO adopted the Abolition of Forced Labour Convention (No. 105) in 1957. These two instruments relied on their antecedents, adopted in 1926 and 1930 respectively, and pulled the abolition of forced labour strongly into the arena of international human rights. In addition, the 1948 Universal Declaration of Human Rights had already declared slavery to be a violation of human rights, and slavery and forced labour were prohibited in the international human rights Covenants adopted in 1966 and in multiple regional human rights instruments. There was a universal consensus that all forms of forced and compulsory labour should be prohibited.

Human trafficking has long been a feature of human rights violations, but its growth accelerated enormously with the lowering of borders, improved mobility and growing pressure for migration to richer countries. As people become desperate to obtain better lives for themselves and their families by moving, they risk becoming victims to trafficking and falling into situations of exploitation, impoverishment or even servitude. The Palermo Protocol against trafficking was adopted in 2000 to address this emerging problem, which is now the focus of a great deal of attention at the national and international levels. However, much of the focus has tended to be on the criminal law aspects of the problem rather than on its labour dimensions. This has sometimes resulted in even more intense hardship for those who have been trafficked. The international community and various countries, such as the UK with its Modern Slavery Act of 2015, have attempted to eliminate human trafficking and its abuses, but these efforts have been inconsistent and only partially successful.

Recently, the International Labour Conference in 2014 adopted a Protocol to the Forced Labour Convention (No. 29) and the Forced Labour (Supplementary Measures) Recommendation (No. 203), which laid out for the first time the practical measures that should be taken to eliminate forced labour and trafficking. These two instruments emphasized strongly the need to adopt, update and apply labour law, including labour law enforcement. They marked a real move into translating the more general prescriptions of international human rights law into practical measures. Article 2 of the Protocol provides, inter alia, that measures for the prevention of forced or compulsory labour shall ensure that the coverage and enforcement of legislation relevant to the prevention of forced or compulsory labour, including labour law as appropriate, apply to all workers and all sectors of the economy, and that labour inspection services and other services responsible for the implementation of this legislation should be strengthened.

This marks the first recognition in international treaty law that forced labour and trafficking must be dealt with not only as criminal law problems but that effective treatment of the problem must rely also on labour law. The importance of also having labour law as a tool is that in some cases it may afford better detection of trafficking, easier access to victims of trafficking and better remedies to their violations.

The ILO's 2016 *Global estimates of modern slavery: forced labour and forced marriage*[12] demonstrated that on any given day in 2016 some 25 million people in the world were in forced labour. International supervision has been important to draw attention to forced labour and to promote its elimination. There have been some successes. In its 2019 report,[13] the ILO's Committee of Experts was able to note that in two cases (Guinea and Vietnam), governments had taken measures under Convention No. 29 during the reporting period to comply with supervisory comments and reinforce their fight against forced labour; and in eight other cases governments had taken initiatives to improve compliance with the Convention during the same period. In 2017 the Committee expressed its satisfaction that Peru had adopted legislation to conform more closely to Convention No. 29, after the Committee had asked it to do so. For a number of years, the Committee had been examining the steps taken by the Government to combat the various forms of forced labour that exist in Peru (debt bondage inflicted on indigenous peoples in the logging sector, situations of forced labour in the small-scale mining sector, trafficking in persons and the exploitation of women in domestic service). It took note of the adoption on 5 February 2017 of legislation which strengthens action against femicide, family

---

[12]   ILO, *Global Estimates of Modern Slavery: Forced Labour and Forced Marriage* (ILO and Walk Free Foundation 2017) 5 <www.ilo.org/wcmsp5/groups/public/---dgreports/---dcomm/documents/publication/wcms_575479.pdf> accessed 22 June 2020.

[13]   International Labour Conference, 108th Session, Report III(A), 'Report of the Committee of Experts on the Application of Conventions and Recommendations' (ILO 2019) 25–28 <www.ilo.org/wcmsp5/groups/public/---ed_norm/---relconf/documents/meetingdocument/wcms_670146.pdf> accessed 22 June 2020.

violence and gender-related violence. The new law incorporated a number of provisions into the Penal Code that criminalize forced labour practices, including provisions that define what constitutes 'sexual exploitation' and 'slavery and other forms of exploitation' and establish penalties of imprisonment of ten to 15 years. The provisions also criminalize 'forced labour', defining it as subjecting or obliging a person, by whatever means or against his/her will, to perform work or service, whether paid or not, and providing for imprisonment of six to 12 years.

3.   Elimination of child labour

This form of work was long considered to be such an integral part of poverty that not much attention was paid to it as a human rights violation until the 1980s, although organizations such as UNICEF and various NGOs did deal with the extreme poverty and deprivation of many of the world's children. In 1973 the ILO Minimum Age Convention (No. 138) was adopted to stimulate progress in addressing child labour in all countries at different stages of development based largely on the understanding of the connection between child labour and the poverty cycle. By this time, most countries had adopted some form of child labour/minimum age laws, but they were ineffective and went largely unenforced. Child labour remained mostly invisible and was considered to be a natural response to help impoverished families. It was child rights groups and international and national labour movements that effectively brought the human rights dimension to the issue. In 1989 the UN adopted the Convention on the Rights of the Child, which refers in Article 32 to child economic exploitation, and the ILO followed in 1999 with the adoption of the Worst Forms of Child Labour Convention (No. 182).

The effort leading up to the adoption of Convention No. 182, the fact that it is the first human rights Convention to attain universal ratification and its significant impact on the reduction of child labour are largely the result of the technical cooperation and guidance of the ILO International Program for the Elimination of Child Labour (IPEC), the Worldwide Movement against Child Labour and significant international donor support. IPEC, a rights-based global programme, focussed on the multi-dimensional and complex nature of child labour, tackling its causes and consequences from the bottom up and the top down. Viewing child labour as, first and foremost, a human rights issue, but also as a poverty and development issue, it developed practical models in workplaces and communities to prevent, withdraw and rehabilitate child labourers. It recognized that child labour occurs in situations of poverty, and it occasions poverty. Therefore, to eliminate child labour, the economic situation of the family must be addressed, for example through improving employment opportunities and wage levels of parents, enhancing productivity of family farms and supporting trade union organizing.

There has been substantial progress in reducing the prevalence of child labour in the last two decades. From 2000 to 2016 the number of children in hazardous work fell by more than half, and there was a net reduction of 94 million children in child labour.[14] The pace and global scope of the progress in reducing child labour is unmatched in any other human rights area.

The role of law in this progress is fundamental. First, to identify and combat 'child labour', it is important to define it correctly in national legislation, on the basis of international law and the extensive research being done. It is not a simple equation, and everything from the ages at

---

[14]   'Global Estimates of Child Labour: Results and Trends, 2012–2016: Executive Summary' (*ILO*, 2017)   11   <www.ilo.org/wcmsp5/groups/public/@dgreports/@dcomm/documents/publication/wcms _575541.pdf> accessed 22 June 2020.

which particular activities may be undertaken, the conditions under which children work and the exact nature of hazardous activities prohibited for children must be defined. Laws and policies mandating compulsory education must be adopted, financed and implemented, because of the close links between education and child labour. National policy must be enunciated and implemented. Crucial linkages between law and policy and operational action at local levels in communities have produced these positive results.

Despite the success in the reduction of child labour many children, mostly in the agricultural sector and informal economy where labour law does not effectively reach, are still in situations of vulnerability and labour exploitation. The ILO supervisory bodies have had many occasions to call attention to the importance of implementing the Convention, especially by adopting national law and extending implementing national laws to child labour in the informal economy and in agriculture. In a 2005 observation to Mexico on Convention No. 182, the ILO Committee of Experts expressed concern over the large number of children involved in agriculture and informal activities, noted that such work can be hazardous work and recommended that the legislation of child labour should be enforced in such activities, the labour inspectorate strengthened and penalties imposed in cases of violation. The ILO Committee of Experts found in its 2019 report that after the Committee had urged more effective action, the Albanian Government adopted Law No. 18/2017 on the right and protection of children which provides, among others, for the right of every child to 'free and quality education' and the right to 'protection from economic exploitation'. Article 34 of this Law establishes 'various central and state institutional advisory and coordination mechanisms on the rights and protection of children'. Benin was noted in the same report for assuring the Committee that a new statistical system allowing child labour to be identified, tracked and eliminated would soon be up and running. Many other such instances are signalled each year by the Committee of Experts, of course alongside other cases in which governments have failed to take effective action. In many instances, the supervisory comments have been followed up by IPEC technical assistance and in-country cooperation projects to assist the countries in implementing the recommendations, including drafting of child labour laws and regulations and setting up child labour monitoring systems.

4.   Equality and non-discrimination

The right to equality and non-discrimination is fundamental to all human rights. There are more human rights conventions dedicated to these principles and rights than any other subject (for example, on racial discrimination, discrimination against women, persons with disabilities, and migrant workers). The ILO included in its Constitution the principle of equal remuneration between men and women for work of equal value – the first expression of a right to equality in international law and an acknowledgment that women are often underpaid compared to their male counterparts simply on the basis of sex.

In 1950 the ILO adopted the Equal Remuneration Convention (No. 100), concerning equal pay for work of equal value between men and women, and in 1958 it adopted the Discrimination (Employment and Occupation) Convention (No. 111). The latter covered all forms of discrimination related to work and all persons in relation to work and included a number of grounds upon which discrimination is to be prohibited including race, sex, national origin, social origin, colour and political opinion. The ILO supervisory bodies have noted that discriminatory attitudes and stereotypes based on prohibited grounds such as race and sex, result in men and women being excluded from employment and occupational opportunities, thus driving them into jobs in the informal economy. In its 2018 General Observation on Convention No. 111, the Committee of Experts noted that the deeply entrenched causes of discrimination and de facto inequalities resulting from entrenched discrimination and long-standing social exclusion cannot effectively be addressed without proactive measures.

The role of law is among the measures recognized as indispensable to improving equal opportunity and treatment and addressing both de jure and de facto discrimination. Among the means of action envisaged by Article 3 of Convention No. 111 to implement a policy of equality figure the following:

> to enact such legislation and to promote such educational programmes as may be calculated to secure the acceptance and observance of the policy;

> to repeal any statutory provisions and modify any administrative instructions or practices which are inconsistent with the policy.

The ILO's long experience in assisting member States to eliminate discrimination, and the work of its supervisory bodies, point to the importance of identifying and removing legal provisions and policies that directly or indirectly discriminate, as well as the importance of providing access to justice through the establishment of effective complaint mechanisms with adequate procedures and remedies. They also point to the importance of enacting legislation to prohibit discrimination on all grounds prohibited in the Convention. Hierarchies of protection against discrimination are inconsistent with the international law. Discrimination will always be present, but it is not until it is identified and prohibited in law that its elimination can begin. One example of the role of law in this area is the recognition of sexual harassment as a violation of the right to equality. It has taken time, but until the right to be free from sexual harassment is included in the national legal framework, its identification and elimination can hardly go forward.

International supervision on non-discrimination and equality has been particularly effective in signalling how discrimination figures in national law, and how it can be reduced or eliminated. One of the ways it does this is to point out shortcomings in content or scope of application of relevant laws and that some parts of national populations are much less protected than are other parts. Among the groups on which ILO focusses in this regard are minorities[15] and indigenous and tribal peoples, as well as occupational groups in which women, migrants and minorities, including particular ethnic communities, figure most heavily, such as agriculture and domestic work. It is striking that both the latter occupations have the highest rates of poverty in most countries and at the same time the national labour legislation in many countries simply does not apply to these two occupations.

Given the higher levels of poverty for women than for men, it is important to draw attention here to the situation of women and the role of international and national law to improve their position in the labour market. The jobs usually done by women are consistently undervalued and paid less than jobs usually done by men. In most countries the employment rate of women falls below that of men. They are often marginalized from formal employment and suffer

---

[15] See Committee of Experts on the Application of Conventions and Recommendations, *General Observation: Discrimination (Employment and Occupation) Convention, 1958 (No. 111)* (ILO, 2019) <www.ilo.org/wcmsp5/groups/public/---ed_norm/---normes/documents/publication/wcms_717510 .pdf> accessed 22 June 2020.

discrimination based on sex, pregnancy, maternity and family responsibilities, in regard to access to or retention of employment, remuneration, terms and conditions of work and promotional opportunities. As women have the reproductive role of giving birth and still bear the majority of family responsibilities, the burden of such discrimination falls mainly on them. In fact in many parts of the world, family responsibilities are considered the biggest obstacle to women achieving equality with men in the labour market.[16] The ILO Committee of Experts and the UN Special Rapporteur on Poverty consider that the gendered distribution of, and stereotypical assumptions about, family and caring responsibilities are at the root of much of the discrimination and limitations women experience in the labour market and thus are also associated with women's higher levels of poverty. To cope with all the care demands, a higher proportion of women work in part-time or 'marginal part-time work' jobs compared to men. Often out of necessity or constrained choice, women are also present in non-standard forms of employment and the informal economy where there is little or no labour law protection. These working arrangements often penalize women in terms of earnings and career development.

As stated above, Conventions Nos. 100 and 111 apply to all workers and Convention No. 111 applies to all occupations as well as all employment. The 2000 Maternity Protection Convention (No. 183) applies to all employment, including non-standard forms, and the 1981 Workers with Family Responsibilities Convention (No. 156) applies to all workers and all sectors and occupations. These instruments provide, inter alia, for paid maternity leave, prohibition of dismissal because of pregnancy, childbirth and family responsibilities, community childcare facilities and other protections. Without such measures, women may find themselves excluded from working life and highly vulnerable to poverty and exploitation. All these measures correspond to less-detailed requirements in general international human rights law, including for instance the Convention on the Elimination of all Forms of Discrimination against Women (CEDAW). Needless to say, well formatted and widely applied legislation that corresponds to the international law content is required to anchor these rights at local levels.

A clear example of the importance of taking a human rights-based approach through the adoption of laws to cover everyone, including all women and men in vulnerable situations, is found in the recently adopted 2019 Convention (No. 190) and Recommendation (No. 206) on the Elimination of Violence and Harassment in the World of Work. The Convention specifically takes into consideration the evolving nature of work and the existence of groups more vulnerable to and disproportionally affected by violence and harassment. It explicitly adopts an inclusive, integrated and gender-based approach to protect all persons in all sectors, including the informal economy and rural areas, and calls on ratifying States to do the same.

There has been a focus in the ILO on giving protection to the jobs that are dominated by women and are often unregulated. The prime recent example is the Domestic Workers Convention (No. 189) and its accompanying Recommendation (No. 201), adopted in 2011. These instruments are intended to extend the reach of labour law into the area of domestic work, which is simply excluded from any legal protection by most countries.

The ILO supervisory bodies have emphasized to States that these Conventions apply to all workers and so should national law. The ILO Committee of Experts has reminded States that the principle of equal remuneration applies everywhere including non-standard forms of employment, casual workers and part-time workers. Under Convention No. 111, the

---

[16]   See ILO, *Quantum Leap for Gender Equality* (ILO 2019) <www.ilo.org/wcmsp5/groups/public/---dgreports/---dcomm/---publ/documents/publication/wcms_674831.pdf> accessed 22 June 2020.

Committee has found exclusions from law for non-standard workers to be contrary to the Convention. Moreover, in one comment in 2016 the Committee has called on the Government of Korea, in consultation with social partners, to assess the effectiveness of the law reforms regarding non-regular workers to ensure that they do not in practice result in discrimination on the basis of sex or employment status.

Indigenous and tribal peoples are another category of the population most subject to discrimination, though an examination of their situation does not fall only under this subject. In every country in which they exist, informal research finds that these peoples are at the bottom of every social indicator – highest unemployment, lowest education, highest rate of incarceration and many others. The ILO has been examining the situation of indigenous and tribal peoples since its earliest days[17] and in 1957 adopted the Indigenous and Tribal Populations Convention (No. 107) in collaboration with the rest of the UN system. This Convention was revised and updated in 1989, again with others in the UN system, by the Indigenous and Tribal Peoples Convention (No. 169). These Conventions, which are the only international treaty law ever adopted specifically on this subject, are supplemented by the United Nations Declaration on the Rights of Indigenous Peoples, adopted in 2007. Article 20(1) of Convention No. 169 spells out the need for laws to protect these people in the workplace:

> Governments shall, within the framework of national laws and regulations, and in co-operation with the peoples concerned, adopt special measures to ensure the effective protection with regard to recruitment and conditions of employment of workers belonging to these peoples, to the extent that they are not effectively protected by laws applicable to workers in general.

B. Other Labour Law

The role of law in relieving poverty through the application of labour rights goes well beyond guaranteeing and implementing what are generally thought of as fundamental human rights. Establishing working economies that allow people to rise above poverty also requires the practical hard work of creating the conditions under which rights can flourish, and much of this work has to be done through legislation and regulation.

Into this category fall the standards adopted by the ILO and mostly translated into national law so long ago that we no longer even think of them as being rooted in international law. But we owe the general application of the eight-hour working day, holidays with pay, limitations on the use of hazardous materials such as asbestos or certain chemicals, maternity protection, and many of the other acquired rights that constitute decent work, to standards adopted by the ILO before World War II that have become an integral part of the fabric of everyday life. These points were reflected in the Universal Declaration of Human Rights in Article 24: 'Everyone has the right to rest and leisure, including reasonable limitation of working hours and periodic holidays with pay'. They were again taken up in 1966 in the International

---

[17] See generally Lee Swepston, *The Foundations of Modern International Law on Indigenous and Tribal Peoples: The Preparatory Documents of the Indigenous and Tribal Peoples Convention, and its Development Through Supervision, Volume 1: Basic Policy and Land Rights* (Brill/Nijhoff 2014); Lee Swepston, *The Foundations of Modern International Law on Indigenous and Tribal Peoples: The Preparatory Documents of the Indigenous and Tribal Peoples Convention, and its Development Through Supervision, Volume 2: Human Rights and Technical Subjects* (Brill/Nijhoff 2018). See also the dedicated pages on this subject on the ILO website at www.ilo.org.

Covenant on Economic, Social and Cultural Rights, and to a lesser extent in the International Covenant on Civil and Political Rights. The relevant provisions of the two Covenants are in many ways a brief summary of the standard-setting work of the ILO up to that time.

The standards on these subjects have been continually updated, new working processes covered, and hours of work adapted to new conditions, and these points all have had to be adopted into national law. All of the standards contribute to decent working conditions, and thus are indispensable to emerging from poverty. As pointed out above, it is precisely where the laws do not apply, where decent work is not guaranteed by law, that entire sectors of the population fall deeper into poverty and have a more difficult time emerging into prosperity. A few particular areas of international labour law should be highlighted.

1.   Safety and health at work[18]

There has been recent work on the incorporation of safety and health at work into the ILO's designated fundamental human rights instruments.[19] This vital subject is addressed in more than half of the ILO's standards, either as the focus of a Convention or Recommendation or as one element of the protection needed by workers and their families. There is also an extensive body of Codes of Conduct that are regularly used as the basis for national laws and regulations. It goes almost without saying that retaining the physical capacity to work is one of the chief elements in obtaining and retaining employment and that safety and health legislation and regulations are indispensable to workers' lives and livelihoods.

2.   Governance

The ILO has established a sub-category of standards that relates to the instruments of governance. These instruments demonstrate the law enforcement capacity of labour inspectors and the training necessary for them to be able to identify trafficked workers or hazardous conditions for child workers. This opens doors to the practical use of these governance instruments for the day-to-day implementation of human rights that can be so much more effective than simply announcing opposition to discrimination without working out practical ways of identifying and abolishing it. ILO standards on labour statistics, labour inspection and other instruments of labour administration form the basis for rights implementation and law enforcement in virtually every country in the world.

An aspect of this broader subject that has a particular resonance in implementing rights that relieve poverty is access to justice, which implies the ability to file complaints of violations without reprisals and with enforcement of the law. Until relatively recently much of the ILO's work on promoting these mechanisms lay in finding ways through technical assistance to help governments and organizations of employers and of workers achieve these rights in practice. More recently the right of access to justice has been incorporated into newer standards, such as the 2014 Protocol to the Forced Labour Convention and its accompanying Recommendation

---

[18]   Space does not allow reviewing in any detail the ILO extensive standard setting on this subject, but information can be obtained on the ILO's website, www.ilo.org.

[19]   See, e.g., the paper submitting a proposal to this effect to the ILO Governing Body: 'Follow-up to the resolution on the ILO Centenary Declaration for the Future of Work: Proposals for Including Safe and Healthy Working Conditions in the ILO's Framework of Fundamental Principles and Rights at Work' (337th session, ILO 7 October 2019) <www.ilo.org/wcmsp5/groups/public/---ed_norm/---relconf/documents/meetingdocument/wcms_723206.pdf> accessed 22 June 2020.

(No. 204), the 2017 Employment and Decent Work for Peace and Resilience Recommendation (No. 205), and the 2019 Violence and Harassment at Work Convention (No. 190). Convention No. 190, for instance, explicitly requires that 'each Member shall adopt laws and regulations to define and prohibit violence and harassment in the world of work, including gender-based violence and harassment' (Article 7), and that States enforce relevant laws and provide appropriate remedies (Article 10).

3.   Employment promotion

As indicated at the beginning of this chapter, insufficient attention has been paid to the need to promote employment and work as a pathway for emergence from poverty from a human rights perspective. This is not primarily a legal challenge but is rather a challenge to the priorities set by the international community and by nations, which of course must in many cases be implemented with the help of legislation. The basis for this area has been the 1964 Employment Policy Convention (No. 122), supplemented by Recommendations and a great deal of research and practical work.[20] As indicated earlier, the Sustainable Development Goals (SDGs) for 2030 filled a gap left open in the Millennium Development Goals. Goal 8 of the SDGs is to 'promote sustained, inclusive and sustainable economic growth, full and productive employment and decent work for all'. The importance here is that employment promotion, whether through active labour market policies or other measures, must be linked to labour rights protection and targeted at reducing poverty.

IV.   CONCLUDING REMARKS

This chapter – cursory as it had to be in some areas – may serve to illustrate for future research agendas that the human rights of workers are absolutely essential for achieving the right to be free from poverty. Nothing in this area can be achieved without incorporating the protections needed into well drafted and effective labour law and policies incorporating the rights set out in the international labour standards. To be more effective as a tool for poverty alleviation, national labour law and its application need to transpose the international standards more fully into labour rights protection for all workers. The international supervisory bodies could strengthen their call for wider and more effective application of labour law protection. Even where these laws are not seen as human rights measures, they can have the effect of promoting and implementing human rights and promoting decent work. Without sustainable decent work an end to poverty is entirely unobtainable.

---

[20]   See note 7 and accompanying text.

29. Minimum wage, poverty reduction and human rights in Cambodia: a case study

Sophal Chea

There have been many debates on the aspects of minimum wage related to poverty, from the economic dimensions to labour, human rights and institutional perspectives. It is not possible to raise minimum wage without encountering a significant negative employment effect. This chapter explains Cambodia's minimum wage development and its role in helping to reduce poverty in Cambodia. Then, it examines the human rights aspects of minimum wage such as the right to work and receive wages, the right to equal pay for work of equal value, and a fair wage. Cambodia applied an interesting model of statutory minimum wage exclusively for the garment and footwear sector.

The main purpose of minimum wage is to ensure that low-paid workers get a better standard of living; when there is an increase in minimum wage, workers who are covered under the statutory minimum wage or sectoral agreement earn more.[1] Most of the time, minimum wage in developing countries targets formal sector workers. Cambodia only applies the statutory minimum wage to the garment, footwear, travel goods and bag sectors. However, there have also been some discussions arguing the pros and cons of whether the increase of minimum wage could somehow reflect the success or failure of wage policy intervention. On the pro side is the idea that minimum wage provides help to lower income families depending on the distribution of wage gains. There is some indication that minimum wage increases could reduce poverty since low-paid workers – in particular women – benefit from minimum wage increases.[2] On the other side, the expectation of poverty reduction by minimum wage is small. If raising the minimum wage leads to job losses, for instance, employers could not continue their business due to high labour cost.[3] Scholars in this camp note that the minimum wage applies only to the working poor and in some cases, not all workers getting the minimum wage live in the families affected by the poverty.[4]

This chapter explains Cambodia's minimum wage policy development and its role in helping to reduce poverty in Cambodia. Then, it examines the human rights dimension of minimum wage. Cambodia experimented with minimum wage development only in the garment, textile and footwear industries when those industries took off in 1990s. The minimum wage was set through the Labour Advisory Committee at the rate of $40 USD in 1997[5] per month while the

---

[1]   Francois Eyraud and Catherine Saget, 'The Fundamentals of Minimum Wage Fixing' (2005) ILO 1.

[2]   Hansjorg Herr and Milka Kazandziska and Silke Mahnkopf-Praprotnik, 'The Theoretical Debate about Minimum Wage' (2009) GLU 1.

[3]   Arindrajit Dube, 'Minimum Wages and the Distribution of Family Incomes' (2019) American Economic Journal 268.

[4]   Thorsten Schulten, 'Statutory and Collective Agreed Minimum Wages in Europe – an International Overview' FES 1.

[5]   'Notice' (1997) No.06/97 S.K.Or MoSAVA.

poverty rate in Cambodia was 39 per cent in 1993/1994 and 36.1 per cent in 1997.[6] However, some countries allowed two approaches to minimum wage setting through statutory wage setting and collective bargaining agreement.

I.   MINIMUM WAGE POLICY AND POVERTY

A.   Minimum Wage and Addressing Poverty

If the minimum wage is set too low, there could be little effect protecting workers and their families from continuing as working poor. However, if the minimum wage is set too high, then it could be very hard for the employers to comply, and the minimum wage will have effects on employment. The poverty rate in Cambodia was 35 per cent in 2004 and the minimum wage set at time was $40 USD monthly from 1997 to 1999 and $45 USD per month from 2000 to 2005 for workers in the garment and textile sectors.[7] The establishment of a minimum wage in Cambodia took place through ministerial regulation setting up the first minimum wage of $30 USD per month for apprentices and $40 USD for regular and probationary workers in the garment and footwear industries in 1997.[8] The 1997 Cambodian Labour Law did not set the minimum wage but only stipulated that the wage should be at least equal to the minimum wage that would ensure the worker a decent standard of living with human dignity.[9]

The minimum wage determination did not go smoothly. According to the author's observation of various ministerial regulations and statements related to a minimum wage increase, there were 12 occasions of minimum wage adjustments over two decades from 1997 to 2019. There were two adjustments in 2013 increasing from $61 (2010)[10] to $80 (2013)[11] and $100 (2013)[12] due to an electoral year and unrest after the election. As usual, the amount of labour unrest (strikes) was high in the national election year compared to the prior and post years. There were 107 strikes taking place in 2003 with the loss of 130,284 person days compared to 84 strikes (107,000 person days lost) in 2004. The 2013 election witnessed 147 strikes (888,500 person days lost) compared to 108 strikes in 2014. However, the number of strikes was only nine (42,000 person days lost) in 2018. That year, there was no main opposition

---

[6]   'Poverty Profile Executive Summary: Kingdom of Cambodia' (2001) Japan Bank for International Cooperation 1.

[7]   Carlos Sobrado and others, 'Where Have All the Poor Gone? Cambodia Poverty Assessment 2013' (The World Bank, 26 May 2014) 1 <https://documents.worldbank.org/en/publication/documents-reports/documentdetail/824341468017405577/where-have-all-the-poor-gone-cambodia-poverty-assessment-2013> accessed 20 July 2020; International Labour Organization (ILO), 'How is Cambodia's Minimum Wage Adjusted?' (Cambodian Garment and Footwear Sector Bulletin, March 2016) 3 <www.ilo.org/wcmsp5/groups/public/---asia/---ro-bangkok/documents/publication/wcms_463849.pdf> accessed 20 July 2020.

[8]   ibid 1 (ILO).

[9]   Cambodia Labor Code (1997) art 104.

[10]   Ministry of Labour and Vocational Training, 'Kingdom of Cambodia: Nation Religion King' (2010) No. 049/10 K.B/S.C.N <www.ilo.org/dyn/natlex/docs/ELECTRONIC/89827/103282/F1122638522/KHM89827.pdf> accessed 23 June 2020.

[11]   Sobrado (n 7).

[12]   Ministry of Labour and Vocational Training, 'Prakas on Determination of Minimum Wage for Workers/Employees in the Textile, Garment and Footwear Industries' (2013) No. 317 KB/BrK.

among those who won parliamentarian seats in 2013. Key political parties, in particular, the opposition party Cambodia National Rescue Party (CNRP), pledged to raise the minimum wage to $150 USD per month if they won the election as one element of their seven-point political agenda during the electoral campaign prior to the July 2018 election. However, this party could not take part in the election due to its dissolution by the court in November 2017.[13]

By 2013, the garment and footwear sector employed nearly 500,000 workers in 497 factories. The total exports of the garment and footwear sector was $5.3 billion USD.[14] In late December 2013, after the July 2013 election, a massive number of garment workers walked out, demanding a minimum wage increase. After the Government declared a wage increase from $80 USD per month (decided in April 2013) to $100 USD (decided on 31 December 2013) the labour unrest continued until a violent strike ended with four people shot dead and 21 injured in early January 2014.[15]

There were no comparative indicators for why the minimum wage was set at that rate of $40 USD. There was no indication of consultation among worker representatives, such as between trade unions, to propose demands for minimum wage increases submitted by the workers' side for minimum wage negotiations, according to the 1997 Notice No. 6 dated 03 March 1997. The Notice outlined 15 points and stated that Ministry of Social Action and Veteran Affairs had continued discussions with the employers' association to determine the working conditions of workers in the garment factory and the wages for workers.[16] After the violent strike in January 2014, the Government and its social actors, such as the employers' association and trade unions, agreed on criteria to be taken into account in setting up the minimum wage in the future: (1) needs of workers and their families; (2) cost of living; (3) inflation; (4) productivity; (5) competitiveness; (6) labour market/employment and (7) profitability of the sector.[17]

The latest Law on the Minimum Wage defined the minimum wage as the lowest wage.[18] However, the Law on Minimum Wage does not specify what the lowest wage means, it only mentions that the lowest wage is set by Ministry in charge of Labour. Annually, Ministry in charge of Labour issues a ministerial regulation ('Prakas') which determines the minimum wage as the lowest wage to be complied by the employer. If the employers have topped up $1 USD or $5 USD on the minimum wage or lowest wage set by Ministry in charge of Labour, the employers could continue to do so. The UN Human Rights Office in Cambodia suggested the Government to take into consideration the minimum wage definition adopted by the ILO Committee of Experts on the Application of Conventions and Recommendations (CEACR). The definition states that the minimum wage is:

[13]   Alex Willemyns and Kuch Naren, 'For Reform Agenda, CPP Takes Cues from CNRP' (*The Cambodia Daily*, 12 January 2016) <https://english.cambodiadaily.com/editors-choice/for-reform-agenda-cpp-takes-cues-from-cnrp-105049/> accessed 24 June 2020.

[14]   ILO, 'Solid First Half of 2015 for Cambodia's Garment and Footwear Sector' (Cambodia Garment and Footwear Sector Bulletin, 2015) 1.

[15]   'Cambodia Garment Workers' Strike Turns Deadly' (*Al Jazeera*, 3 January 2014) <www.aljazeera.com/news/asia-pacific/2014/01/cambodia-garment-workers-strike-turns-deadly-2014134464180721.html> accessed 24 June 2020.

[16]   Sobrado and ILO (n 7).

[17]   ILO (n 7).

[18]   Cambodia New Law On Minimum Wage (6 July 2018) Royal Kram No. RS/RK/0718/015.

[T]he minimum sum payable to a worker for the work performed or services rendered, within a given period, whether calculated on the basis of time or output, which may not be reduced either by individual or collective agreement, which is guaranteed by law and which may be fixed in such a way as to cover the minimum needs of the worker and his or her family, in the light of national economic and social conditions.[19]

The elements to be taken into consideration for setting a minimum wage include (1) social criteria (family status, inflation and cost of living); and (2) economic criteria (productivity, competitiveness, labour market status and profitability of the sector).[20] In this case, the new Law on the Minimum Wage groups the seven points mentioned above into two main areas of social criteria and economic criteria. The determination of the minimum wage as per the new Law on the Minimum Wage outlines four principles, namely (1) the minimum wage discussion is convened by Labour Minister; (2) the minimum wage is changeable and predictable; (3) the minimum wage sticks to win-win principles; and (4) the official data from national institutions should be used and social and economic criteria should be considered as the basis for minimum wage discussion.[21]

The National Wage Council, which consists of at least 48 members from Government, employers, and workers, is a tripartite mechanism which has the task of studying and providing recommendations on the minimum wage and other benefits covered by the Labour Law.[22] The Council will coordinate relevant parties on studying and meeting to evaluate the minimum wage, disseminating awareness, and stimulating social dialogue on the minimum wage. It is too early to see how effectively this committee will function since its large membership is close to 50 people.[23] In its first meeting in August 2019, the Head of the National Wage Council announced the appointments of two deputies, one from employers' side and another from workers' side. The National Wage Council claimed that it was the first historic meeting on the minimum wage discussion among its members and determined to set the minimum wage every September for the following year.[24] There was no official study released on the minimum wage but the National Wage Council was cited as providing recommendations on a $5 USD increase of the minimum wage from $182 USD[25] to $187 USD (agreed by employers' and workers' representatives). With the final recommendation by the Cambodian Prime Minister, an additional $3 USD was added. Therefore, the minimum wage for 2020 is $190 USD per month for regular workers in the garment and footwear industries.[26] The minimum wage negotiation between trade union and employers in 2020 took place in the difficult context of the COVID-19 pandemic, including its impact on the industry and the cuts to Everything

---

[19] Office of the United Nations High Commissioner for Human Rights in Cambodia, 'A Human Rights Analysis of the Draft Law on Minimum Wage' (June 2018).

[20] Cambodia New Law on Minimum Wage (n 18) art 5.

[21] ibid art 10.

[22] ibid art 2.

[23] ibid art 17.

[24] Mom Kunthea, 'Minimum Wage Council Selects Vice Presidents' (*Khmer Times*, 30 August 2019) <www.khmertimeskh.com/638520/minimum-wage-council-selects-vice-presidents/> accessed 24 June 2020.

[25] 'Prakas on Determination of Minimum Wage for Workers/Employees in the Textile, Garment and Footwear Sector for 2019' (2019) No. 465 MoLVT.

[26] Ministry of Labour and Vocational Training, 'Prakas on Determination of Minimum Wage for Workers/Employees in the Textile, Garment and Footwear Sector' (2020) No. 389/19 KB/Br.K.Kh.L.

but Arms (EBA), a tariff scheme that affects 20 per cent of garment and footwear exports to the European Union. Employers proposed a $17 USD decrease of minimum wage while the unions wanted to have an increase of $12. The National Wage Council then decided that there was no increase for minimum wage. They approved a $190 minimum wage for 2021.[27] Since the minimum wage is a sensitive issue of the union asking for an increase and the employer asking for reduction, the Government then made a decision to add a $2 USD raise for the 2021 minimum wage taking effect from January 1, 2021.[28]

There are different perspectives on the pros and cons of raising the minimum wage. If raising the minimum wage in the formal sector causes only a small number of job losses, it is likely to reduce poverty. However, if higher wage increases would lead a significant number of workers to lose jobs in the sector, the minimum wage is not likely to reduce poverty.[29] The World Bank observed that the labour market in Cambodia is moving towards wage-based employment in the manufacturing and services sectors. The growth in textiles and apparel exports have contributed to drive poverty reduction.[30]

The policymakers often consider different approaches to ensure that poor people can work their way out of poverty by creating more employment opportunities, enhancing compliance with the minimum wage law,[31] and increasing access to those opportunities.[32] When Cambodia introduced a minimum wage of US $40 per month for regular workers in 2004, the poverty rate for Cambodia was 35 per cent.[33] Many young Cambodians lacked job opportunities. There were only around 15 per cent of Cambodians who were employed in wage employment in the formal sector in the 1990s.[34] In other developing countries, studies indicated that poverty could be reduced through the minimum wage by increasing earnings and not reducing jobs when the minimum wage is established by collective bargaining.[35] The Labour Law and Law on the Minimum Wage allows the minimum wage to be set by the Labour Ministry under the former Labour Advisory Committee and now the National Wage Council, which is chaired by the Labour Minister. Cambodia witnessed a dozen wage setting occurrences between 1997 to 2019. All of these wage settings applied to the textile, garment, footwear and travelling goods sectors.

---

[27]   Khuon Narim, 'Garment Industry Minimum Wage Raised by $2 for 2021' (September 11, 2020) <https://cambojanews.com/garment-industry-minimum-wage-raised-by-2-for-2021/> accessed 10 December 2020.

[28]   Mom Kunthea, 'Minimum Wage for Workers up to $192 for 2021' (September 10, 2020) <https://www.phnompenhpost.com/national/minimum-wage-workers-192-2021> accessed 10 December 2020.

[29]   T.H. Gindling, 'Does Increasing the Minimum Wage Reduce Poverty in Developing Countries?' (2014) IZA World of Labor 1 <https://wol.iza.org/uploads/articles/30/pdfs/does-increasing-the-minimum -wage-reduce-poverty-in-developing-countries.pdf> accessed 24 June 2020.

[30]   United States Agency for International Development (USAID), 'Resilience and Sustainable Poverty Escapes in Rural Cambodia' (November 2018) <www.agrilinks.org/sites/default/files/usaid-se -cambodia_case_study-final_508.pdf> accessed 20 July 2020.

[31]   ibid 9.

[32]   Chronic Poverty Advisory Network, 'Working out of Chronic Poverty: A Policy Guide' (Policy Guide 4, 2013) <www.odi.org/sites/odi.org.uk/files/odi-assets/publications-opinion-files/8515.pdf> accessed 20 July 2020.

[33]   'A Poverty Profile of Cambodia 2004' (National Institute of Statistics, 2006).

[34]   Royal Government of Cambodia, 'Interim Poverty Reduction Strategy Paper' (Phnom Penh, 2000).

[35]   Bard Andreassen, Stephen Marks and Arjun Sengupta, *Freedom from Poverty As a Human Right: Economic Perspectives* (United Nations Educational, 2011) 119.

It is hard to establish clearly that the minimum wage helped reduce poverty in Cambodia. However, the consolidated evidence and figures on employment growth and wage increases indicate that the introduction of the minimum wage into the textiles, apparel, footwear, travel goods and bags sectors have been pro-poor. The minimum wage has continued to increase gradually from $40 USD per month in 1997 to $45 USD in 2000, $50 USD in 2006, $61 USD in 2010, $80–$100 USD in 2013, $128 USD in 2014, $140 USD in 2015, $153 USD in 2017, $170 USD in 2018, $182 USD in 2019, and $190 USD in 2020. These wage changes have increased household income of those in poorly paid employment.[36] Further, the number of apparel and garment factories increased from 20 in 1995 to 197 in 2003 while the number of workers employed rose from 18,000 to 234,000.[37]

By 2018, there were over 600 garment and footwear factories, which employed over 660,000 workers.[38] This sector indirectly supports another two million Cambodians who provide associated services to workers such as food vendors, services providers and the banking sector. The minimum wage could have a direct impact on these workers and their families. Key institutions like the UN Development Programme (UNDP), the World Bank and the International Monetary Fund (IMF) observed tangible economic growth in Cambodia. The UN Human Development Index shows Cambodia on an upward path, and GDP per capita grew from $250 USD in 1993 to $1,500 USD in 2018.[39] The poverty headcount ratio at the national poverty line also dropped from 34 per cent in 2008 to 17.7 per cent in 2012.[40] The Asian Development Bank indicated 12.9 per cent of the population in Cambodia lived below the national poverty line in 2018.[41] The IMF found that 'strong macroeconomic policies have allowed Cambodia to achieve impressive growth and made inroads into poverty'.[42] The World Bank indicated that around 4.5 million Cambodians remain poor and they are vulnerable to falling back into poverty since the majority who have escaped poverty have done so by a small margin. With the impact of the COVID-19 pandemic, poverty in Cambodia could increase among households who have been working in key sectors such as tourism/hospitality, construction and manufacturing.[43] The Government is providing a wage subsidy of $40 USD a month for those unemployed because of the COVID-19 pandemic, especially in sectors such as tourism and the exports of garment, footwear and travel goods. This could partly help prevent them from falling back into poverty.[44]

---

[36]   USAID (n 30).
[37]   Omar Bargawi, 'Cambodia's Garment Industry – Origins and Future Prospects' (September 2005) Overseas Development Institute Working Paper 13 <www.odi.org/sites/odi.org.uk/files/odi-assets/publications-opinion-files/2513.pdf> accessed 20 July 2020.
[38]   Andrea Schill, 'The Footwear Sector – New Opportunities for Cambodia?' (ILO, 2019) 1.
[39]   The World Bank, 'GDP Per Capita (Current US$) – Cambodia' (31 May 2020) <https://data.worldbank.org/indicator/NY.GDP.PCAP.CD?locations=KH> accessed 20 July 2020.
[40]   ibid.
[41]   Asian Development Bank, 'Poverty Data: Cambodia' <www.adb.org/countries/cambodia/poverty> accessed 20 July 2020.
[42]   Peter Sutherland, 'Transforming Nations: How the WTO Boosts Economies and Open Societies' (Foreign Affairs, March/April 2008) 125 <www.foreignaffairs.com/articles/2008-03-02/transforming-nations> accessed 20 July 2020.
[43]   The World Bank, 'The World Bank in Cambodia: Overview' (14 October 2020) <https://www.worldbank.org/en/country/cambodia/overview> accessed 10 December 2020.
[44]   The World Bank, 'Cambodia Economic Update: Cambodia in the Time of Covid-19' (20 May 2020) 20 <http://documents1.worldbank.org/curated/en/165091590723843418/pdf/Cambodia

B.   Setting Minimum Wage and Labour Productivity

The law on minimum wage establishes that its purpose is improving living conditions, creating opportunities and increasing productivity.[45] The economic factors that could be taken into consideration in setting the minimum wage include the requirements for economic development, levels of productivity and maintaining employability in the sector.

Information on labour productivity is vital for setting minimum wage. It provides contextual information on the market value of what is produced by an average worker in a particular country by taking into consideration the existing levels of capital and technology. Labour productivity can also ensure workers receive a fair share of the economic progress. Article 5 of the Law on the Minimum Wage indicates productivity is one of economic criteria for setting minimum wage.[46]

The employers' association in Cambodia often claims that raising the minimum wage would make them lose competitive advantage. In principle, they say that there should be an increase in worker productivity as well if workers demand a very high minimum wage. From the government perspective, competitiveness is the result of the interaction of a number of factors such as market access, strengthening the domestic business environment, labour productivity and increasing value added.[47]

The government understands that total factor productivity and labour productivity are important elements for competiveness. This means that increases in productivity would allow for increased wages. In reality, the very first thing to do is to invest in productivity-related factors such as equipment that contains more advanced technology. The World Bank suggested a number of key areas that would help Cambodia strengthen growth, including boosting labour productivity to compensate for rising real wages by improving the quality of basic education, promoting vocational and technical skills and reducing energy costs.[48] Cambodia has had constant growth of its global market share in textiles. The export growth in textiles has been driven by its expanding global market share from 0.03 per cent in 1996 to 1.06 per cent in 2017.[49] The World Bank report also suggested improvement in the areas of public service delivery and public investment management, legal frameworks and implementation capacity in order for Cambodia to stay competitive.[50]

The minimum wage requirement extends to the footwear and travelling goods sector with their similar nature of work and production flow to the garment sector. One of the main

---

-Economic-Update-Cambodia-in-the-Time-of-COVID-19-Special-Focus-Teacher-Accountability-and -Student-Learning-Outcomes.pdf> accessed 10 December 2020.

[45]   Al Jazeera (n 15).

[46]   ibid.

[47]   Cambodia Trade Integration Strategy (CITS), 'Cambodian Trade Integration Strategy 2014–2018' (May 2013).

[48]   The World Bank, 'World Bank: Growth in Cambodia Remains Strong' (17 May 2017) <www.worldbank.org/en/news/press-release/2017/05/17/growth-in-cambodia-remains-strong-while -productivity-improvements-needed-going-forward> accessed 20 July 2020.

[49]   'Cambodia' (Atlas of Economic Complexity, n.d.) <https://atlas.cid.harvard.edu/countries/118> accessed 24 June 2020.

[50]   'Cambodia Economic Update: Staying Competitive through Improving Productivity' (The World Bank, April 2017) <www.worldbank.org/en/country/cambodia/publication/cambodia-economic-update -april-2017> accessed 25 June 2020.

productivity challenges is the low skilled workforce. Low skill and productivity limits the relocation of more complex stages of footwear and garment production to Cambodia.[51]

The latest minimum wage developments reveal that labour cost increases should correspond to productivity growth in order to ensure sustainability of the sector. The highest minimum wage jumped 31 per cent in 2013 and 28 per cent in 2014 when the Government increased the minimum wage from $61 USD to $80 USD in 2013 and from $100 USD to $128 USD in 2014. The Government increased minimum wage by 8 to 9 per cent from 2016 to 2020. The ILO report showed that during the 2013–2016 period, the real minimum wage growth in the Cambodian garment and footwear sector was averaging 20 per cent while the productivity rate fell by an average of 1 per cent per annum. However, the productivity growth picked up in 2016.[52]

One might revert that wages are low because productivity, what is created by a worker per hour, is low. However, this could be only one of the factors. The other factors could be related to social and economic development priorities. Cambodia expanded its formal export garment industry after its peace accord in 1993 and the installation of democratic institutions. To attract investment and create employment, Cambodia set the minimum wage of $40 USD per month for regular workers in 1997 due to the new employment workforce in the formal sector. Gradually, the minimum wage has been increased. The minimum wage for 2020 is $190 USD per month and $2 is added for the 2021 minimum wage, which took effect starting January 1, 2021.

II.   HUMAN RIGHTS DIMENSIONS OF MINIMUM WAGE

Workers and trade unions often claim that the minimum wage is not a living wage. On the other hand, employers argue that they are losing competitive advantage by increasing the minimum wage while the government wants to maintain both employment creation and increased investment. In this regard, a tripartite consultation on minimum wage and minimum wage adjustment takes place to reconcile these viewpoints. Both workers and employers have an opportunity to voice their concerns and demands through the consultation process.

One consideration on the table should be the labour rights and human rights involved. The Cambodia-US Trade Agreement from 1999 to 2005 linked increasing trade with improving workers' rights. The annual increase in quota was from 14 to 18 per cent if Cambodia substantially complied with Cambodian Labour Law and core labour standards.[53] The following sections examine the human rights aspects of the minimum wage, namely the right to work and receive wages, the right to equal pay for work of equal value, and the minimum wage as a living wage.

---

[51]   Al Jazeera (n 15).

[52]   ILO, 'What Explains Strong Export and Weak Employment Figures in the Cambodian Garment Sector?' (Cambodian Garment and Footwear Sector Bulletin, May 2017) issue 6; see Andrea Schill, 'The Footwear Sector – New Opportunities for Cambodia?' (ILO Better Factories Cambodia, 2019).

[53]   Office of the United States Trade Representative, 'U.S.-Cambodian Textile Agreement Links Increasing Trade with Improving Workers' Rights' (7 January 2002) <http://fordschool.umich.edu/rsie/acit/LaborStandards/LaborInUSCambodiaTextile.pdf> accessed 20 July 2020.

Cambodia has ratified a number of international human rights instruments, including the Convention on the Rights of the Child (CRC), the International Convention on Elimination of All Forms of Racial Discrimination (ICERD), and the International Covenant on Economic, Social and Cultural Rights (ICESCR). These are legally obligatory documents.

Article 32 of CRC recognizes 'the right of the child to be protected from economic exploitation and from performing any work that is like to be hazardous or be harmful to the child's health'. The Article requires member states to offer appropriate regulation of the hours and conditions of employment.[54]

A.   Right to Work and Receive Wages that Contribute to an Adequate Standard of Living

Cambodia ratified the ICESCR in 1992. The Covenant requires the state to recognize the right to work and the right to just and favourable conditions of work through ensuring fair wages and remuneration for work of equal value, a decent living for workers and their families, and safe and healthy working conditions.[55] Through his press statement, the UN Special Rapporteur on the situation of human rights in Cambodia stated that Cambodia has an obligation to guarantee the rights to employment for all people in Cambodia, including the obligation to ensure that the national minimum wage is set at a level sufficient to provide all workers and their families with a decent standard of living.[56] Cambodia's Labour Law also includes a similar requirement, stating that the wage must be at least equal to the guaranteed minimum wage and must ensure for every worker a decent standard of living compatible with human dignity.[57] The Labour Law does not define what decent standard of living means. The 2018 Law on the Minimum Wage also does not define the term 'decent living'; it indicates that certain elements should be taken into consideration in setting up the minimum wage such as economic conditions, cost of living and the actual situation of the country.[58] However, the Government regulates the minimum wage currently for only three sectors, namely textiles, garment/footwear and travelling goods. Beyond these statutes, Article 36 of the Constitution mentions that 'Khmer citizens of either sex shall enjoy the right to choose any employment according to their ability and to the needs of the society'.

The 1997 Cambodian Labour Law also provides that any person looking for employment can request to be registered with the Placement Office of the Ministry in Charge of Labour.[59] It took quite some time for Cambodia to work progressively toward ensuring the right to work in a place where standards of hygiene, health and safety are met and insurance against work-related accidents is provided. There are not sufficient health and safety regulations

---

[54]   Convention on the Rights of the Child (Adopted 20 November 1989, entered into force 2 September 1990) UN Doc Res 44/25 art 32.

[55]   International Covenant on Economic, Social and Cultural Rights (ICESCR) (Adopted 16 December 1966, entered into force 3 January 1976) UN Doc 993 UNTS 3 art 6 and 7.

[56]   United Nations Human Rights Office of the High Commissioner, 'Statement by the United Nations Special Rapporteur on the Situation of Human Rights in Cambodia, Professor Surya P. Subedi' (16 January 2014) <http://cambodia.ohchr.org/WebDOCs/DocStatements/2014/012014/SR_press_statement_16_January_2014_Eng.pdf> accessed 20 July 2020.

[57]   Cambodia Labor Code (1997) art 104.

[58]   Cambodia New Law On Minimum Wage (6 July 2018) Royal Kram No. RS/RK/0718/015 art 5.

[59]   Cambodia Labor Code (1997).

developed by Cambodia yet; a number of health and safety regulations appear as ministerial regulations. Also, Cambodia is currently working on a Safety Act. In general, Cambodia's Labour Law sets out general provisions indicating that employers need to maintain their work-places and ensure the health and safety of the workers.[60]

Insurance against work-related accidents is also fundamental for the right to work. The National Social Security Fund (NSSF) manages and administers the social security scheme for workers in the private sector. The scheme covers employment injury insurance for work-related accidents and health insurance.

B.   Rights to Equal Pay for Work of Equal Value

Minimum wage plays a key role in addressing unduly low pay and reducing wage inequality. Many countries introduce minimum wage systems to help reduce inequality; for example, an hourly minimum wage could facilitate equal treatment between full and part-time workers. The human rights aspects of these measures could include rights to equal pay for work of equal value, equality of opportunity in hiring and promotion and job security during and after pregnancy.

Cambodia has not ratified the ILO Convention No. 100 on Equal Remuneration, 1951 but its Constitution and Labour Law prohibit discrimination in employment and occupation. The Asian Development Bank report showed some requirements for Cambodia to move towards amending its law to properly enact the concept of 'equal remuneration for work of equal value'.[61] Those requirements include developing and implementing a minimum wage setting process by having transparent steps, applying objective criteria and integrating the involve-ment of social partners.[62] The Constitution of Cambodia provides that Cambodians of either sex shall receive equal pay for work of equal value.[63] Article 12 of Cambodian Labour Law ensures both men and women doing work of equal value receive same pay. Cambodian Labour Law also prohibits discrimination. Hiring, providing social benefits or termination of an employment contract may not be based on sex, race, colour, religion, political opinion, birth, social origin and membership of workers' union or the exercise of union activities.[64]

The Universal Declaration of Human Rights (UDHR), in Article 23(2), points out that equal pay for work of equal value is one of the basic human rights. The minimum wage law recog-nizes the contribution of the worker and is a key means of ensuring the principle of equal pay for work of equal value.

C.   A Living Wage

One of the main purposes of a minimum wage is to protect workers from being given unduly low pay and ensuring a minimum living wage to those who are employed. The minimum wage can also be a factor in policy development to address poverty.

---

[60]   ibid.
[61]   ILO, 'Gender Equality in the Labour Market in Cambodia' (2013) 1.
[62]   ibid.
[63]   The Constitution of the Kingdom of Cambodia, art 36.
[64]   Cambodia Labor Code (1997) Art 12.

The UDHR recognizes the right to a living wage. Articles 23(3) and 25(1) cover basic needs plus discretionary income. Both the UDHR and ICESCR provide a set of human rights and standards that require the Government to work progressively. Those rights are related to a living wage such as:

- '[T]he right to just and favourable remuneration ensuring for himself and his family an existence worthy of human dignity, and supplemented, if necessary, by other means of social protection';[65]
- The right of everyone 'to the enjoyment of just and favourable conditions of work which ensure remuneration providing to all workers as a minimum with (i) fair wages and equal remuneration for work of equal value, and (ii) a decent living for themselves and their families';[66]
- The right to earn a living and choose a job;[67] and
- The right to a standard of living adequate for the health and well-being of himself and of his family, including food, clothing, housing and medical care and necessary social services, and the right to security in the event of unemployment, sickness, disability, widowhood, old age or other lack of livelihood, in circumstances beyond his control.[68]

The minimum wage development in Cambodia took place in the early 1990s with $40 USD per month for workers in the garment and textile sector. It took quite some time for the relevant stakeholders to negotiate the increase of a minimum wage. There were different claims from different social actors. Trade unions often claimed the increase of minimum wage is inadequate and they demanded a living wage. The employers argued that increasing minimum wage will make them uncompetitive in terms of labour cost while the government wanted to balance the interests of both employers and trade unions, and at the same time they want to create employment in the sector.

The perspective from the trade unions is that a living wage should be significantly above the current wage. Normally, the demand for a living wage is higher than the minimum wage whenever there is wage increase negotiation. While the minimum wage has increased considerably, there remains a gap between the minimum wage (as of this writing) of $192 USD per month and a living wage.

III.   CONCLUSION

The development and direction of minimum wage policy play interacts with both poverty and human rights. The fixing of the minimum wage has been one of the critical factors in policy making for the country in that it helps create employment, maintain competitive advantages for employers, and protection of workers.

There have always been counter-arguments among social actors such as workers, employers and the government. The employers claim that raising the minimum wage could reduce their

---

[65]   Universal Declaration of Human Rights (adopted December 1948) UNGA Res 217 A(III) (UDHR).

[66]   ICESCR (n 55) arts 6, 7.

[67]   ibid art 6.

[68]   ibid art 11.

competiveness and investors could stop their investment in the country while the workers also argue that a low minimum wage cannot support a decent standard of living. In practice, the government at some point decides to intervene and balance the viewpoints of the social actors so that they can maintain job creation, and workers and employers can continue their minimum wage negotiations on a regular basis.

The decisions regarding minimum wage setting and adjustment should take into consideration the human rights aspects of minimum wage. The key human rights dimensions associated with minimum wage are the right to work and receive wages, the right to equal pay for work of equal value and the right to a fair wage. Further research and study are needed to conduct a more in-depth analysis of the minimum wage and its roles in eradicating the poverty in Cambodia, particularly since the Government of the Kingdom of Cambodia introduced the minimum wage only in certain sectors such as apparel and textiles, footwear and traveling goods. Thus, there are remaining sectors which are not covered by minimum wage, where workers might benefit from expanded attention to minimum wage policies as a means to address both poverty and human rights concerns.

30. Fair taxes to end poverty

Åsa Gunnarsson[1]

This chapter concerns economic rights as set out in the International Covenant on Economic, Social and Cultural Rights (ICESCR)[2] and relates to the recognition by the Special Rapporteur on Extreme Poverty and Human Rights that taxation policies are human rights policies.[3] It builds on the landmark contribution made by Philip Alston and Nikki Reisch in the book *Tax Inequality and Human Rights*, published in 2019, which expertly explores the links between human rights and tax norms, regarding both policies and regulations. Revenue, redistribution, regulation and representation all affect the realization of human rights and serve as a starting point for incorporating tax issues into the study of human rights and poverty.[4]

Conceiving of tax systems as the engine for resourcing human rights commitments to combat poverty feels like an overwhelming challenge when the world faces the most severe recession in nearly a century. However, in times of crisis, an opportunity for re-consideration opens. The fact that the world needs strong, well-targeted fiscal support to recover makes way for new policy directions.[5] A consolidated concept of fair and sustainable tax bases is a key issue in both a human rights-driven transformation of society to end poverty and in the process of economic recovery after the pandemic crisis. This is not a new argument, but, as will be explained in this chapter, the present neoliberal tax policy context that has dominated many national tax law reforms for decades, has created a magnitude of sustainability and inequality gaps that contradicts the aim of resourcing of human rights.

As also stated by Alston and Reisch, an important task is to show how human rights ought to frame tax policies and how human rights can make a bridge between tax policies and issues of social and economic justice, which demand multidisciplinary approaches.[6] In response to their view, I will link some of the key findings on fair and sustainable taxation that we made in the European Union's Horizon 2020 project, FairTax,[7] as a framework of how to advance tax reforms to mobilize resources and redistributive mechanisms as a human rights-based approach necessary in the fight against poverty. I will discuss what could be seen as structural

---

[1]   The research for this chapter is part of the FairTax EU project, which is funded by the European Union's Horizon 2020 research and innovation programme 2014–2018, grant agreement No. FairTax 649439.

[2]   International Covenant on Economic, Social and Cultural Rights (adopted 16 December 1966, entered into force 3 January 1976) 993 UNTS 3 (ICESCR).

[3]   Human Rights Council (HRC), 'Report of the Special Rapporteur on Extreme Poverty and Human Rights, Philip Alston' (27 May 2015) UN Doc A/HRC/29/31, 53.

[4]   Philip Alston and Nikki Reisch (eds), *Tax, Inequality, and Human Rights* (OUP 2019) 1–30.

[5]   'OECD Economic Outlook: The World Economy on a Tightrope' (*OECD*, June 2020) <www.oecd.org/economic-outlook/june-2020/> accessed 24 July 2020.

[6]   Alston and Reisch (n 4).

[7]   'Horizon 2020: Revisioning the "Fiscal EU": Fair, Sustainable, and Coordinated Tax and Social Policies' (*CORDIS*) <https://cordis.europa.eu/project/id/649439> accessed 24 July 2020 (project name is FairTax).

taxation problems that are counterproductive to the resource mobilization and redistribution necessary for the realization of human rights. Another ambition is to capture the ongoing change of the tax policy discourses as observed in material with varying status: academic works and debates, internationally recognized reports and policy documents, legal sources, news articles, websites, and blogs.

I.   TAXATION AS A PART OF ECONOMIC RIGHTS

Article 2 (1) of the ICESCR states that:

> Each State Party to the present Covenant undertakes to take steps, individually and through international assistance and co-operation, especially economic and technical, to the maximum of its available resources, with a view to achieving progressively the full realization of the rights recognized in the present Covenant by all appropriate means, including particularly the adoption of legislative measures.[8]

Tax laws are one field of such legislative measures. Olivier de Schutter has defined a normative framework consisting of four key norms that should guide the fulfilment of the ambition of the ICESCR to meet the needs of the poor. These are: widening the tax base, implementing progressive tax policies, combating tax evasion and illicit financial flows and strengthening tax administration.[9]

For legal scholarship, the challenge is to determine how the theoretical framework on the connection between taxation and human rights could be incorporated in tax laws and practice. This is an under-researched field. Normally, the frame of reference for tax law scholarship is the nation-state, under the rule of law-based perspective. Consequently, questions on how taxation could be connected to human rights and, as addressed in this book, become an active instrument in the mission of ending poverty, are outside the scope of traditional legal scholarship.[10] In section V of this chapter I will use social contract theory to show a possibility of broadening the theoretical perspective on the link between human rights and the justifications of tax laws.

II.   NEOLIBERAL TAX POLICY, FISCAL AUSTERITY AND STRUCTURAL ADJUSTMENT PROGRAMS

For several decades now the tax policy debate has been strongly influenced by a discourse that builds on what seems to be conflicting interests between taxing for growth and taxing for social justice. This conflict implies a trade-off between efficiency and equity. This dominant discourse has legitimized the worldwide implementation of a neoliberal economic rationale through a 'taxing for growth' paradigm focused on fiscal efficiency. Influenced by an optimal

---

[8]   ICESCR (n 2) art 2(1).

[9]   Olivier De Schutter 'Taxing for the Realization of Economic, Social, and Cultural Rights' in Alston and Reisch (n 4).

[10]   Åsa Gunnarsson, 'The Making of a Critical Tax Policy Framework' in Reza Banakar, Karl Dahlstrand and Lotti Ryberg Welander (eds), *Festskrift till Håkan Hydén* (Juristförlaget i Lund 2018).

tax theory, in which the idea of a trade-off between equity and efficiency is at the core, the discourse postulates that tax neutrality should be a guiding principle for the ultimate goal of taxing for growth. Neutral taxation aims to distort the economic efficiency of market processes as little as possible. Redistributive taxes and transfers are regarded as negatively affecting incentives to work and save.[11]

The international tax reform pattern, focused on introducing efficiency-oriented tax policies, has institutionalized on a global scale a one-path model for taxing for economic growth in tax law design.[12] Main features of tax reforms based on this concept can be summarized as follows:

- Broader labor income tax bases but low progressivity;
- Moderate taxation of capital and corporations;
- Uniform tax rates on the consumption of goods and services;
- Introduction of in-work tax subsidies;
- A shift from direct taxes to indirect taxes.[13]

Yet another element in this tax reform trend is detaxation. The concept aims to capture the systemic removal or reductions of tax rates and tax bases, leading to vaguely justified and non-transparent losses of revenue. The incentives for tax reforms are often passive as the policy-goals are non-specific and formulated in general terms such as enhancing growth or stimulating economic activity.[14] Even though many liberal parties in the OECD sphere have been open and explicit in introducing lower taxes during the past 20 years and more, the magnitude of tax cuts, particularly regarding capital income and corporate profit, is not coherent with organized politics. This development gives me reason to claim, that the concept of detaxation also contains a new elite-driven power order in the policy-making of the tax reform agenda, which has led to both intentional and unintentional increases of income inequalities. This form of under-the-radar tax politics is an example of how well-organized and skilled

---

[11]   James A. Mirrlees, 'An Exploration in the Theory of Optimum Income Taxation' (1971) 38 The Review of Economic Statistics 175; Peter Diamond and Emmanuel Saez, 'The Case for a Progressive Tax. From Basic Research to Policy Recommendations' (2011) 25 The Journal of Economic Perspectives 165.

[12]   Cedric Sandford, *Successful Tax Reform: Lessons from an Analysis of Tax Reform in Six Countries* (Fiscal Publications 1993); Sven Steinmo, 'The Evolution of Policy Ideas: Tax Policy in the 20th Century' (2003) 5 British Journal of Politics & International Relations 206; Matthias Schmelzer, *The Hegemony of Growth: The OECD and the Making of the Economic Growth Paradigm* (CUP 2016).

[13]   Ken Messere (ed), *The Tax System in Industrialized Countries* (OUP 1999); Peter Birch Sørensen, *Swedish Tax Policy: Recent Trends and Future Challenges* (Swedish Ministry of Finance 2010); Åsa Gunnarsson, Margit Schratzenstaller and Ulrike Spangenberg, 'Gender Equality and Taxation in the European Union' (*European Parliament*, 2017) (Research Paper for European Parliament's Committee on Women's Rights and Gender Equality and commissioned, overseen and published by the Policy Department for Citizen's Rights and Constitutional Affairs) <www.europarl.europa.eu/RegData/etudes/STUD/2017/583138/IPOL_STU(2017)583138_EN.pdf> accessed 24 July 2020.

[14]   Kathleen A Lahey, 'Uncovering Women in Taxation: The Gender Impact of Detaxation, Tax Expenditures, and Joint Tax/Benefit Units' (2015) 52 OHJL 427 <http://digitalcommons.osgoode.yorku.ca/ohlj/vol52/iss2/4> accessed 24 July 2020.

groups of stakeholders, through processes with little visibility, have managed to influence tax reforms from a perspective of self-interest.[15]

Fiscal austerity is also part of the policy. Austerity is a form of voluntary deflation of cutting public spending and introducing privatization to restore competitiveness and promote growth. Fiscal austerity promotes the increase of certain types of taxes but, most importantly, argues for not allowing taxes to be used for social investments in the reproductive part of the economy or in maintenance of the welfare state regimes.[16] Austerity policies are one important element in the structural adjustment programs traditionally imposed on developing nations by the International Monetary Fund (IMF) and the World Bank to ensure debt repayment and economic restructuring when lending money to poor economies in debt. These programs have been heavily criticized for resulting in poverty instead of reducing it.[17]

However, it is not only developing countries that have undergone these programs. In 1984 New Zealand was the first developed country to introduce what was already defined then as a pure neoliberal model of structural adjustment. The fiscal policy agenda shifted from tax fairness principles of ability to pay and redistributive profiles to efficiency and neoliberal norms. Jane Kelsey claims that this policy agenda of fiscal restraints on the state budget eroded the central governments' defense of the objectives of a comprehensive welfare base.[18] Fiscal austerity policies also got a renaissance in the aftermath of the global economic crisis in 2008 when governments raised taxes in the attempt to reduce structural deficits in the public budget. Structural adjustment policies have been implemented in the Eurozone in the wake of the financial crisis by the 'Troika', consisting of the IMF, the European Central Bank and the European Commission. The structural adjustment programs have been used as a policy instrument connected to those conditional bailout loans granted by the Troika to governments that cannot fund their budgets from domestic resources or international debt markets.[19] In the case of Greece, the EU institutions and European leaders imposed an austerity policy that created an unsustainable debt burden on the Greek state and its citizens, which led to a humanitarian crisis in terms of negative health effects, reversed growth, permanent high unemployment rates for young people and dismantling of the welfare state. The cost was borne solely by the Greek people, and contrary to an aversion to deficits recommended in the economic adjustment program, fiscal stimulus was needed.[20] The account of the Greek Minister of Finance,

---

[15]   Stefan Svallfors, 'Politics as Organised Combat – New Players and New Rules of the Game in Sweden' (2016) 21 *New Political Economy* 505.

[16]   Jane Kelsey, *The New Zealand experiment: A World Model for Structural Adjustment?* (Auckland University Press 1997); Mark Blyth, *Austerity: The History of a Dangerous Idea* (OUP 2013).

[17]   Scott L Greer, 'Structural Adjustment Comes to Europe: Lessons for the Eurozone from the Conditionality Debates' (2014) 14 Global Social Policy 51.

[18]   Kelsey (n 16).

[19]   Greer (n 17).

[20]   Directorate-General for Economic and Financial Affairs, *Occasional Papers No. 61: The Economic Adjustment Programme for Greece* (European Union 2010) <https://ec.europa.eu/economy_finance/publications/occasional_paper/2010/pdf/ocp61_en.pdf> accessed 24 July 2020; Alexander Kentikelenis and others, 'Health Effects of Financial Crisis: Omens of a Greek Tragedy' (2011) 378(9801) The Lancet 1457–58; Joseph E Stiglitz, *Rewriting the Rules of the European Economy* (Foundation for European Progressive Studies (FEPS) 2019) 15 <www.feps-europe.eu/attachments/publications/book_stiglitz-rewriting_rules.pdf> accessed 24 July 2020.

Yanis Varoufakis, confirms that Europe fights a battle on fiscal austerity policies and the actors in favor of the policy are very powerful.[21]

III.   TAX SUSTAINABILITY GAPS

The going for growth mantra and the ideology of fiscal taxation have received very powerful support from the European Commission, the Organization for Economic Co-operation and Development (OECD), the IMF and the World Bank. These institutions have guided an international trend in how to redesign national budgets and fiscal systems with a remarkable convergence of views by national governments.[22] A consequence is that the social justice dimension of tax law reforms has become a quite underdeveloped competence in both tax policy debate and research. This one-dimensional tax for growth policy paradigm neglects many general obligations of society for the human well-being and central indicators of welfare, which has created a magnitude of non-sustainable structural problems.[23] In the FairTax study of the European situation the following tax sustainability gaps were identified:

- A prevailing focus on market led economic growth tax policies;
- Unused potential to use taxation at the EU level to promote sustainable growth and development in Europe;
- An absence of tax measures that tackle inequalities in income and wealth;
- High and increasing weight of labor taxes;
- Decreasing importance of corrective – so-called Pigouvian taxes – particularly concerning environmental taxes;
- Intense tax competition;
- Tax compliance issues and tax fraud leading to revenue leakages;
- Decreasing progressivity of tax systems;
- Persisting intragenerational inequalities and a lack of coordinated life course approaches in tax and social policies;
- Persisting socio-economic inequalities between men and women and a lack of gender equality insights in national tax policies.[24]

A.   In Contexts of Regions and Economies

Regional and country-specific economic factors are important to consider when analyzing possible sustainability gaps in tax policies. Comparing the above list on tax sustainability gaps with the yearly OECD reports on tax policy developments among the member countries,

---

[21]   Yanis Varoufakis, *Adults in the Room: My Battle with Europe's Deep Establishment* (Vintage Digital 2017).

[22]   Sandford (n 12); Vito Tanzi, 'Government Role and the Efficiency of Policy Instruments' in Peter Birch Sørensen (ed), *Public Finance in a Changing World* (Palgrave Macmillan 1998); Steinmo (n 12).

[23]   Åsa Gunnarsson, 'The Good and the Bad: Taxing for Social Justice or Taxing for Growth?' in Dominic de Cogan and Peter Harris (eds), *Tax Justice and Tax Law: Understanding Unfairness in Tax Systems* (Hart Publishing 2020).

[24]   Ann Mumford and Åsa Gunnarsson, 'Sustainability in EU Tax Law' (2019) 54 Intereconomics 134; Gunnarsson, 'The Good and the Bad' (n 23).

with the addition of Argentina, Indonesia and South Africa, several similarities in tax trends can be detected. One example is that cuts in corporate income tax rates continues. It seems to be a reflection on how tax competition triggers a 'race to the bottom' as the decline has been constant since 2000, and countries with higher corporate tax rates have been responsible for the largest rate reductions.[25] For the oldest group of EU Member States (EU 15) this race is visualized by the reduction of the nominal corporate income tax rates from 38 percent to 25.9 percent between 1995 and 2016, and a 6 percent reduction of the average corporate tax rate between 1998 and 2015.[26]

For welfare state economies, the loss of fiscal capacity can undermine social security systems and risk the well-being of the most vulnerable group of citizens, which can lead to a humanitarian crisis, such as in the case of Greece. But the link between human rights approaches to eradicating poverty and the mobilizing of fiscal resources with redistributive objectives is especially relevant for low-income countries. For these economies, the first and overall tax sustainability objective is to raise sufficient domestic revenue. All sustainability gaps that are related to direct taxation are basically irrelevant, as a very low share of the total tax revenue derives from direct taxation of personal or corporate income.[27] Data on the fiscal situation in the over 50 states that make up the African continent is partial and gives only a fragmented picture of the fiscal situation. Some obvious characteristics are nevertheless clear. Africa has moved from the aid era to the tax era but states are still well below the revenue needed to reach the SDGs. Data indicates that more than half of the African countries have a tax quota lower than 15 percent of GDP. Africa is a rich continent but underdeveloped regarding tax collection.[28]

A study from Asia confirms that Asia-Pacific developing countries that are becoming middle-income and higher-middle income countries, such as China and India, have started to experience the negative impact of rising inequalities related to fast-growing economies. Fiscal redistribution is low. However, there are significant differences throughout the region. Malaysia, the Philippines and Thailand stand out for narrowing inequality, and fiscal reforms have partly contributed to the process.[29]

Two dimensions of inequality related to fiscal policy in the Latin America and Caribbean region are the distribution of income by household and social and economic disparities among territories. Despite progress in inequality reduction during recent years, the region is claimed to be the most unequal region in the world. Wealth, and extreme wealth, significates the economy, and the fact that the distribution of wealth between families is more unequal than the

---

[25] Tax Policy Reforms 2019: OECD and Selected Partner Economies (*OECD*, 5 September 2019) <www.oecd-ilibrary.org/taxation/tax-policy-reforms-2019_da56c295-en> accessed 24 July 2020.

[26] Gunnarsson, Schratzenstaller and Spangenberg (n 13).

[27] Alex Cobham, 'Tax Evasion, Tax Avoidance and Development Finance' (2005) QEH Working Paper no 29 <http://workingpapers.qeh.ox.ac.uk/RePEc/qeh/qehwps/qehwps129.pdf> accessed 24 July 2020.

[28] Mick Moore, Wilson Prichard and Odd-Helge Fjeldstad, *Taxing Africa: Coercion, Reform and Development* (Zed Books 2018); Attiya Waris, *Financing Africa* (Langaa Rpcig 2019); Frida Kvamme, 'Taxation and Tax Reform in Africa: Lessons from and for Tanzania' (*Norwegian Institute of International Affairs*, 26 April 2019) <www.nupi.no/nupi_eng/News/Taxation-and-tax-reform-in -Africa> accessed 24 July 2020.

[29] Sonali Jain-Chandra and others, 'Sharing the Growth Dividend: Analysis of Inequality in Asia' (2016) IMF Working Paper no 16/48 <www.imf.org/en/Publications/WP/Issues/2016/12/31/Sharing-the -Growth-Dividend-Analysis-of-Inequality-in-Asia-43767> accessed 24 July 2020.

distribution of income expresses the substance of the problem. Income tax revenues are low and wealth taxes are weak and do not exist regarding inheritance and property. Conclusively, the fiscal revenue in the region remains insufficient to finance the achievement of the SDGs.[30] Brazil can serve as an example. It is a country rich in natural resources, but the tax quota is not more than 33 percent of GDP. The tax system is complex and contributes to social inequality, as most taxes fall on consumption rather than income or wealth. Government tax subsidies for corporations have risen to almost 7 percent of GDP. High-income earners are lightly taxed. The revenue from income taxes are around 20 percent and almost 50 percent of revenue comes from indirect taxes on consumption. A long-postponed tax reform will likely be taken up in 2020, with the objective of creating a national value-added tax with uniform tax rates across all products. It would replace a patchwork of state-levied taxes as well as various federal taxes.[31]

B.   In the Context of Development Finance

Furthermore, the human rights consequences of some of these sustainability gaps needs to be discussed in the context of globalization. Internationalization of economies has increased mobility of capital and labor, incentivizing tax competition between jurisdictions, but also changing the behavior of taxpayers in their effort to reduce their tax liability. The international tax arena has opened up a vast field of tax minimization strategies, which have become a major global issue containing a multitude of complex problems. Aggressive tax planning, harmful tax practices, illicit financial flows, tax fraud, tax abuse, tax evasion and tax avoidance are practices that are used in this tax planning. Formally, most of these tax schemes are legal but seen as unethical and not obedient to the intention of the tax laws. Not all categories of practices are the result of an active tax competition between countries. Some practices exploit differences between two jurisdictions or use the most favorable tax treaties to the advantage of the tax payer.[32]

Yet another great threat to revenue raising and redistribution over the fiscal system, are the tax havens, today more correctly defined as secrecy jurisdictions to emphasize the legal characteristics of tax and financial schemes. An enormous amount of the world's wealth is hidden in tax havens, outside the scope of tax liability in any national state. Not until Gabriel Zucman presented his research on quantifying the hidden wealth was there a sense of the enormous sum of revenue lost.[33] The secrecy makes it impossible to see the whole picture, but more and more

---

[30]   UN CEPAL, *Fiscal Panorama of Latin America and the Caribbean 2019: Tax Policies for Resource Mobilization in the Framework of the 2030 Agenda for Sustainable Development* (United Nations 2019) <www.cepal.org/en/publications/44517-fiscal-panorama-latin-america-and-caribbean -2019-tax-policies-resource> accessed 24 July 2020.

[31]   Thomas J Trebat, 'Latin America's Growth Challenge: A New Way Forward for Brazil's Economy' (*Americas Quarterly*, 3 February 2020) <www.americasquarterly.org/article/a-new-way -forward-for-brazils-economy/> accessed 25 July 2020.

[32]   Martin Hearson, 'Tax-Motivated Illicit Financial Flows: A Guide for Development Practitioners' (*Anti-Corruption Resource Centre (U4)*, January 2014) <u4.no/publications/tax-motivated-illicit -financial-flows-a-guide-for-development-practitioners.pdf> accessed 24 July 2020.

[33]   Gabriel Zucman, *The Hidden Wealth of Nations: The Scourge of Tax Havens* (University of Chicago Press 2015).

figures are being presented, such as a figure from Latin America suggesting that tax evasion and avoidance added up to 6.3 percent of GDP in the region during 2017.[34]

After the financial crisis insights about the need to take more measures to limit the damaging effects of secrecy jurisdictions on domestic revenue mobilization in both developed and developing countries have emerged. Not surprisingly, developing countries have, before this crisis, been neglected in the multilateral institution driven policy research on tax havens.[35]

The history of neglect in not treating developing countries as equal partners and the lack of international collaboration necessary to take action against national revenue losses fuels the already destructive spiral of legitimacy problems in developing countries.[36] Post-colonial states in particular have a huge legitimacy deficit, originally related to the use of taxing power as the power to take. An analysis of the fiscal legitimacy situation in African countries, which is likely applicable to many other post-colonial states, reveals problems with layers of corruption; a lack of cultural, social and economic diversity; poor governance; incoherent and underdeveloped national tax laws; international interference through aid and loan programs; and, maybe most important, a very low degree of fiscal redistribution of revenue for the well-being of citizens.[37]

IV.   FAIR AND SUSTAINABLE TAX BASES

All of these structural problems are counterproductive to the resource mobilization and redistribution that are necessary for the realization of human rights. However, a new orientation in tax policy discussions has emerged based on lessons learnt from financial crises, economic recessions and increasing levels of income inequalities over the last decades in advanced economies. Both scholarly and political reconsiderations of the taxing for growth paradigm have evolved. After Thomas Piketty's book *Capital in the Twenty-First Century*,[38] a new wave of research with a stronger focus on the relations between inequalities, taxation and economic growth has emerged among economists. Concerns about the harmfulness of increasing income and wealth inequalities have been raised, which has framed a point of departure for critical analysis. One outcome is the literature on income inequality, which has revealed the rise of top incomes over time and explored options on how top earners can pay more taxes.[39]

An awareness of combining growth promoting tax reforms with analyses and policies on economic inequalities has also grown in institutions that earlier only promoted the one-way

[34]   UN CEPAL (n 30).
[35]   Alex Cobham, 'Tax Havens and Illicit Flows' in Peter Reuter (ed), *Draining Development?: Controlling Flows of Illicit Funds from Developing Countries* (The World Bank 2012) <https://openknowledge.worldbank.org/handle/10986/2242> accessed 25 July 2020.
[36]   SouthCentre GVA, 'Webinar - Tax Policy Options for Funding Post COVID19 Recovery' (*YouTube*, 23 July 2020) <www.youtube.com/watch?v=JTnqI4tOMoU> accessed 25 July 2020.
[37]   Waris (n 28).
[38]   Thomas Piketty, *Capital in the Twenty-First Century* (Belknap Press of Harvard University Press 2014).
[39]   Michael Förster, Ana Llena-Nozal, and Vahé Nafilyan, 'Trends in Top Incomes and their Taxation in OECD Countries' (2015) OECD Social, Employment and Migration Working Papers No 159 <https://doi.org/10.1787/1815199X> accessed 25 July 2020; Emmanuel Saez and Gabriel Zucman, *The Triumph of Injustice: How the Rich Dodge Taxes and How to Make Them Pay* (W.W. Norton & Company 2019).

message, such as the European Commission, the OECD and the IMF. As part of these developments, studies on the relation between redistribution, inequality and growth have been published.

The 2016 Survey on Tax Policies in the European Union published by the European Commission, starts out by stressing that the sheer level of the tax burden is not decisive for growth. It is rather the structure of a tax system that matters.[40] A study by IMF researchers took advantage of a cross-country dataset, enabling analysis of both the impacts of redistribution as well as market inequality. One finding is that economic growth is lower and periods of growth are shorter in countries that have high inequality. In the same paper, the researchers show that transfers (redistributions of income from upper to lower income individuals) do not harm economic growth – at least up to a point consistent with policies in other wealthy nations. This work thereby demonstrates that the combined direct and indirect effects of redistribution – including the growth effects of the resulting lower inequality – are on average pro-growth. Notably, this finding applies to both developed and developing countries.[41] OECD researcher Cingano arrived at a similar conclusion. He demonstrates that inequality has a negative impact on economic growth. Furthermore, it appears as if the extent of redistribution necessary to achieve a given level of net equality has no negative direct consequences on economic growth. Taken together, his results suggest that inequality in disposable incomes is bad for growth and that redistribution through taxes and transfers is, at worst, neutral to growth.[42] Another OECD study recognizes that if tax reforms are well designed, higher taxes and transfers to reduce inequality do not necessarily harm growth. Since taxes and transfers are so powerful in affecting both inequality and growth, the key challenge has become getting them right, rather than to focus on their distortive effects.[43]

A.   Inclusive Growth

The OECD new policy turn was documented in the initiative called New Approach to Economic Challenges, which recommends the adoption of longer-term perspectives in the institutional setting on how economies are shaped by history, social norms and political choices. The new policy is defined as 'tax design for inclusive growth' and launches four basic tax principles to support the policy:

- Broadening tax bases;
- Strengthening the overall progressivity of the fiscal system;
- Affecting pre-tax behaviors and opportunities;

---

[40]   Taxation and Customs Union, *Tax Policies in the European Union: 2016 Survey* (European Union 2016) <https://ec.europa.eu/taxation_customs/sites/taxation/files/tax_policies_survey_2016.pdf> accessed 25 July 2020.

[41]   Jonathan D Ostry, Andrew Berg and Charalambos G Tsangarides, 'Redistribution, Inequality and Growth' (*International Monetary Fund*, April 2014) <www.imf.org/external/pubs/ft/sdn/2014/sdn1402.pdf> accessed 25 July 2020.

[42]   Federico Cingano, 'Trends in Income Inequality and its Impact on Economic Growth' (2014) OECD Social, Employment and Migration Working Papers No 163 <http://dx.doi.org/10.1787/5jxrjncwxv6j-en> accessed 25 July 2020.

[43]   OECD, *In It Together: Why Less Inequality Benefits All* (OECD 2015) <https://read.oecd-ilibrary.org/employment/in-it-together-why-less-inequality-benefits-all_9789264235120-en#page1> accessed 25 July 2020.

- Enhancing tax policy and administration.[44]

The OECD researcher also makes a long list of additional work to develop the concept of inclusive growth. Those most relevant from a human right perspective are on the relation between taxation and gender and on taxes that can strengthen equality of opportunity.[45] The IMF came to a similar conclusion when arguing for a policy direction on tax measures to fulfill the 2030 Agenda. But inclusiveness does not give any direction for how low-income developing countries will be able to raise revenue to cover the additional spending that is necessary to fulfill the SDGs. An estimate from the IMF is that these countries need to raise, on average, an increase of revenue that represents 15 percent of their GDP.[46] Based on distributional equity objectives, the inclusive growth paradigm has been criticized for focusing entirely on market-led growth. A central concern is the alienation from the socio-economic realities of middle-income, poor and transition countries. One line of criticism is that inclusiveness has become a recognition of equality of opportunity, a formal access to possibilities, not part of a substantial, system-oriented view on distributional rights.[47]

In the wake of the pandemic crisis and the dramatic need for more and new sources of revenue, a much more confrontational, radical approach in the demand for new actions in tax policies can be observed. The Directorate for taxes and customs in the EU has delivered very strong opinions on tax evasion and avoidance and the huge sums lost in tax havens.[48] The untaxed sources of wealth is now in focus and IMF has proposed the introduction of 'solidarity surcharges' on wealth.[49]

B.   The Need for New Principles on Fair and Sustainable Taxation

Sustainability is not only about economic growth; it is also about a number of other different goals. The difficulty is that achieving one sustainable objective may threaten another. However, a basic principle for sustainability was given already in 1987 and serves well as a human rights perspective. In a report from the World Commission on the Environment and Development, a principle was formulated that future development of the planet would be considered sustainable if the present generation is able to satisfy its own needs, without

---

[44]   'Final NAEC Synthesis, New Approaches to Economic Challenges' (*OECD*, 2015) <www.oecd .org/naec/Final-NAEC-Synthesis-Report-CMIN2015-2.pdf> accessed 25 July 2020.

[45]   Bert Brys and others, 'Tax Design for Inclusive Economic Growth' (2016) OECD Taxation Working Papers No 26 <https://doi.org/10.1787/5jlv74ggk0g7-en> accessed 25 July 2020.

[46]   Vitor Gaspar and others, 'Fiscal Policy and Development: Human, Social, and Physical Investment for the SDGs' (January 2019) IMF Staff Discussion Note SDN/19/03 <www.imf.org/en/Publications/ Staff-Discussion-Notes/Issues/2019/01/18/Fiscal-Policy-and-Development-Human-Social-and-Physical -Investments-for-the-SDGs-46444> accessed 25 July 2020.

[47]   Alfredo Saad-Filho, 'Growth, Poverty and Inequality: From Washington Consensus to Inclusive Growth' (November 2010) DESA Working Paper no 100 <www.un.org/esa/desa/papers/2010/wp100 _2010.pdf> accessed 25 July 2020.

[48]   'The Fight Against Tax Fraud and Tax Evasion: A Huge Problem' (*European Commission*) <https://ec.europa.eu/taxation_customs/fight-against-tax-fraud-tax-evasion/a-huge-problem_en> accessed 25 July 2020.

[49]   'Special Series on Covid-19' (*IMF*, last updated 22 July 2020) <www.imf.org/en/Publications/ SPROLLs/covid19-special-notes> accessed 25 July 2020.

compromising the ability of future generations to do so as well.[50] To make tax law a part of the progress in ensuring a sustainable future for its citizens, the FairTax project has defined five dimensions of tax policies for sustainable tax systems that have to be considered: social, economic, environmental, institutional/cultural and equality.[51] An economic model for evaluating the sustainability of a national tax system on the basis of the five dimensions was also developed in the project.[52]

The social dimension of poverty and other economic inequalities ought to be indisputable, but under the taxing for growth paradigm it has been impossible to incorporate a recognition of the fact that fiscal systems have always been potentially decisive for redistributive policies and very often have been used as vehicles to promote social and equality policies. Politics of the welfare state draws on social justice to legitimize state intervention for the common good, and structures of revenue and social transfers are obviously intertwined in welfare state policies.[53] In FairTax we showed how intra-generational and gender equality aspects can be incorporated in tax principles and how human rights obligations regarding gender equality should guide tax policies and regulations.[54]

V.   SOCIAL CONTRACT APPROACH

One way of opening up the link between human rights and normative justifications of tax laws for broader theoretical considerations is to develop a critical tax policy framework based on a social contract concept to have a platform for an impartial perspective. This approach enables an argumentation of what constitutes a good tax system, the politics and principles of tax law, human rights views on equality and similar cross-cutting questions. It also makes room for a socio-legal recognition of how tax systems are shaped in competition or co-operation between political actors and organized interests with historical and comparative ambitions to study institutional contexts, deep layers of legal cultures and path-dependent large-scale processes that have accompanied changes in fiscal regimes.[55]

Through a critical, socio-legal lens, it is possible to go beyond many approaches in which tax fairness principles have been taken for granted. It makes way for interesting challenges. As Anthony Infanti has pointed out so well, irrespective of whether tax scholars advocate for vertical or horizontal tax equity principles, the concepts are traditionally solely occupied with economic factors, arguing for fair tax treatment in relation to income and wealth. A narrow economic perspective excludes the social context of the subordinated groups in relation to the dominant and powerful groups that own the tax policy agenda and can manipulate the agenda

---

[50] UNGA, 'Report of the World Commission on Environment and Development: Our Common Future' (4 August 1987) UN Doc A/42/427.

[51] Mumford and Gunnarsson (n 24).

[52] Danuše Nerudová, 'Tax System Sustainability Evaluation: A Model for EU Countries' (2019) 54 Intereconomics 138.

[53] Steinmo (n 12).

[54] Emer Mulligan, 'Pensions and the Challenges of Adequacy and Sustainability: Irish Citizens' Voices and Policy Implications' (2019) 54 Intereconomics 154; Åsa Gunnarsson and Ulrike Spangenberg, 'Gender Equality and Taxation Policies in the EU' (2019) 54 Intereconomics 141.

[55] Gunnarsson, 'The Making of a Critical Tax Policy Framework' (n 10).

to their own advantage. Without broader contexts, most perspectives of tax equality are left outside the scope of the tax policy debate.[56]

A.   Tax Justice From a Welfare State Perspective

Social contract theory has a long tradition that provides an idealistic, original idea on justice captured in a contract position.[57] The social contract model serves well to target the historical phases of large-scale, institutional processes that explain welfare state regulations on how to distribute resources and agency between capital and labor. In fact, the birth of the modern fiscal state, its underlying fiscal structure and the concept of citizenship emerged in the early 20th century and laid the foundation of the modern welfare state. Keynesian economic management of advanced capitalist economies and social justice principles controlled tax reforms.[58] Obviously, social justice is a basic political issue for every welfare state, which incorporates both democratic issues and the interest of social stability in welfare capitalism.[59] In theory, the recognition of citizens' social rights and the protection against social risks ought to correlate with the obligatory common responsibility to generate the public funding needed to pay for them. In that way, the obligation of the citizen is based on the legitimate demand that they support certain social needs. From this perspective social justice, on an aggregated collective level, is related to a fair and just connection between social burdens and benefits.[60]

However, in welfare state research not much attention has been paid to the financing of welfare states as a whole. Until the 1980s, social spending and taxation existed as 'two distinct realms of research' in welfare state scholarship.[61] As a consequence, questions concerning the nature of the tax system in relation to expenditure programs or central welfare state commitments have been quite neglected. The structures of revenue and social transfers are obviously intertwined in welfare state policies.[62] When the theoretical perspective does not encompass both the income and the expenditure side of the public budget, we end up with a fragmented picture of welfare state typologies of social contracts. Tax justice needs to be integrated with the recognition of how a welfare state depends on the underlying fiscal structure. Fiscal needs constitute fiscal citizenship characterized by styles of national governance, levels of tax compliance and differing concepts of the obligations of the welfare state. Public budgets are blueprints of governments' political priorities and also in a way constitute national states

---

[56]   Anthony C Infanti, 'Tax Equity' (2008) 55 Buffalo Law Review 1191.

[57]   David Hume, *A Treatise of Human Nature* (L.A. Selby-Bigge ed, Clarendon Press 1896); John Rawls, *A Theory of Justice: Revised Edition* (Harvard University Press 1971).

[58]   Steinmo (n 12).

[59]   Gøsta Esping-Andersen, *The Three Worlds of Welfare Capitalism* (Princeton University Press 1990).

[60]   John G Head, 'Tax-Fairness Principles: A Conceptual, Historical, and Practical Review' in Allan M Maslove (ed), *Fairness in Taxation: Exploring the Principles* (University of Toronto Press 1993); Nicola Lacey, *Unspeakable Subjects: Feminist Essays in Legal and Social Theory* (Hart Publishing 1998); Claire F L Young, 'Women, Tax and Social Programs: The Gendered Impact of Funding Social Programs Through the Tax System' (*Ottawa: Status of Women Canada*, 2000) <https://commons.allard.ubc.ca/cgi/viewcontent.cgi?article=1042&context=emeritus_pubs> accessed 25 July 2020.

[61]   Barbara Haskel, 'Paying for the Welfare State: Creating Political Durability' (1987) 59 Scandinavian Studies 221; Stephan Liebfried and Steffen Mau (eds), *Welfare States: Construction, Deconstruction, Reconstruction* (Edward Elgar Publishing 2008).

[62]   Ola Sjöberg, 'Paying for Social Rights' 28 Journal of Social Policy 275.

and identities.[63] Tax research that can target what human rights issues are relevant for welfare states, in times of increasing economic inequalities would be very useful for launching new directions in tax policies and tax law reforms.

B.   Tax Justice from a Global Perspective

One self-imposed limitation in ordinary contract theoretical thinking is the nation-state perspective, grown out of the need to identify and justify the duty-right relationship between the individual nation-state, the domestic market and citizens of that nation. In a globalized economy, this limitation should be questioned. As Allison Christians has argued, contractarian political philosophy provides a structure that also can be used to discuss nation-state duties in relation to a global social contract. The challenge is to justify what is a sovereign duty between nations. Even though it is easy to fall into sophisticated legal discussion on constitutional bases for sovereignty and how an international body of some sort can have tax sovereignty over the nation-state, we as tax scholars know that it already exists. I agree with Allision Christians that OECD's tax policy initiatives on harmful tax competition could be regarded as a global social contract with a common responsibility between states.[64] Base Erosion and Profit Shifting (BEPS) is a global project coordinated by OECD that indicates an acceptance that states have tax obligations between each other.[65] The issues of taxing rights between countries are also expressed in the OECD and UN Model Tax Conventions. The human rights dimensions of these Conventions need far more studies, particularly from the perspective that the UN Model provides more opportunities and justification for developing countries to impose their taxing rights.

Yet another aspect of global solidarity has been raised by Attiya Waris in her ambition to define a fiscal sociology approach adapted to legitimize a fiscal state model for post-colonial developing countries. Fiscal sociology provides a method for historical analysis on dominant drivers of institutional, economic, cultural, societal and legal change that have had an impact on the design of tax law and administrative regimes for tax collection. The analysis on the interplay between revenue and expenditures and how it is connected to the alleviation of poverty and the redistribution builds a frame for mapping typologies of fiscal states. She problematizes the social contract relationship between the state and society from a human rights perspective in order to find a neutral base for how fiscal policies could adjust to societal priorities for the well-being and social welfare of the citizens.[66]

From my experience, the use of a social contract model becomes particularly valuable to the effort of explaining what earlier in the text has been described as under-the-radar tax politics. Powerful stakeholders, such as national elites, non-elected supranational networks or consultative entities, and multinational corporates, influence tax policies in a way that gives rise to human rights claims in respect to taxing rights and obligations.[67] The history of economic

---

[63]   Margaret Levi, *Of Rule and Revenue* (University of California Press 1988).

[64]   Allison Christians, 'Sovereignty, Taxation and Social Contract' 18 Minnesota Journal of International Law 99.

[65]   Allison Christians, 'The Search for Human Rights in Tax' in Philip Alston and Nikki Reisch (eds), *Tax, Inequality, and Human Rights* (OUP 2019).

[66]   Attiya Waris, *Tax and Development: Solving Kenya's Fiscal Crisis through Human Rights* (LawAfrica Publishing 2013).

[67]   SouthCentre GVA (n 36).

and financial globalization and the actors controlling the policy discourse in the relationship between citizens, between citizens and states, and between states is an interesting field for further studies.

VI.   CONCLUDING REMARKS

The dominant tax policy discourse is not easy to change. If the political leaders of the world really want tax laws to become a progressive part in eradicating the extreme forms of poverty, human rights need to be an integrated part of tax policies. Political leaders should prepare themselves to ask the question of 'how to link tax laws and human rights?' This is a legal question that opens up for methods and theories in line with the fiscal sociology approaches, which will bring the knowledge that can build substantive capacity of fair tax reforms on the global, national and regional levels in order to create inclusive societies. Even though the taxing for growth discourse is powerful, it is still nothing more or less than a social construction. It is equally possible to create a human rights discourse around the problematic relation between human rights, poverty and tax fairness, in order to make way for future tax reforms in the mobilization and redistribution of resources that are necessary in the fight against poverty.

PART IV

STRUCTURAL BARRIERS

31. Climate change, human rights and poverty: intersections and challenges

Sumudu Atapattu

Floods, droughts, hurricanes, disasters, rising seas, increasing temperatures, water scarcity, impoverished lands, desertification, displacement and wildfires – all have unfortunately become part of our day-to-day vocabulary. Associated with climate change, these consequences have a disproportionate impact on the lives of the poor and marginalized.[1] Despite the multitude of poverty eradication programs since the UN was established, 1.3 billion people, half of whom are children, currently live in multidimensional poverty.[2] In her final report the former UN Special Rapporteur on Extreme Poverty and Human Rights, Magdalena Sepúlveda Carmona, called extreme poverty a moral outrage: 'In a world characterized by an unprecedented level of economic development, technological means and financial resources, that millions of persons are living in extreme poverty is a moral outrage'.[3] What is even more outrageous is the way wealth is concentrated in a handful of people: just 20 people, mostly men, control more wealth than half of the developing countries put together.[4] Poverty is not just an economic issue. It is a multidimensional issue and is closely related to being able to live a life of dignity.[5]

Climate change is projected to exacerbate poverty and other conditions of vulnerability.[6] The adverse consequences associated with climate change are wide and varied, ranging from sudden occurrences such as severe weather events to slow onset events such as sea level rise as well as many other localized effects. The Intergovernmental Panel on Climate Change (IPCC) predicts that the number of disasters and severe weather events will increase in both severity and intensity.[7] In addition, an increase in droughts, floods and desertification will add to water stress and food shortages. These consequences also have health impacts.

---

[1] See Human Rights Council, 'Report of the United Nations High Commissioner for Human Rights on the Relationship Between Climate Change and Human Rights' (15 January 2009) UN Doc A/HRC/10/61, para 42.

[2] United Nations Development Program (UNDP) and Oxford Poverty & Human Development Initiative (OPHI), 'The 2019 Global Multidimensional Poverty Index (MPI), Illuminating Inequalities' (*UNDP*, 2019) <http://hdr.undp.org/en/2019-MPI> accessed 8 June 2020.

[3] See Human Rights Council, 'Final Draft of the Guiding Principles on Extreme Poverty and Human Rights, Submitted by the Special Rapporteur on Extreme Poverty and Human Rights, Magdalena Sepúlveda Carmona' (18 July 2012) UN Doc A/HRC/21/39.

[4] Max Lawson and others, 'Public Good or Private Wealth?' (*Oxfam*, 2019) 12 <https://oxfamilibrary.openrepository.com/bitstream/handle/10546/620599/bp-public-good-or-private-wealth-210119-en.pdf> accessed 8 June 2020.

[5] UNDP and OPHI (n 2).

[6] See Human Rights Council, 'Climate Change and Poverty: Report of the Special Rapporteur on Extreme Poverty and Human Rights' (July 17, 2019) UN Doc A/HRC/41/39, [2].

[7] 'Climate Change 2014 Synthesis Report: Summary for Policymakers' (*IPCC*, 2014) <www.ipcc.ch/site/assets/uploads/2018/02/AR5_SYR_FINAL_SPM.pdf> accessed 8 June 2020.

The former UN Special Rapporteur on Extreme Poverty and Human Rights, Philip Alston, addressed climate change and poverty in 2019.[8] He pointed out that while climate change will have the greatest impact on those living in poverty, it also threatens democracy and human rights. Moreover, it could push 120 million more people into poverty by 2030.[9] Noting that it represents an emergency without precedent, the Special Rapporteur called on the human rights community to be bold and creative in their thinking and have a radically more robust, detailed and coordinated approach to climate change. He warned that 'as a full-blown crisis bears down on the world, "business as usual" is a response that invites disaster'.[10]

Bearing this warning in mind, this chapter examines the link between climate change, human rights and poverty, and how poverty will be exacerbated by the adverse impacts of climate change. It proceeds in five sections. Section I discusses the link between poverty and human rights and poverty as a human rights issue and the Sustainable Development Goals and poverty. Section II discusses the link between climate change and human rights and the impact of climate change on the enjoyment of rights. It identifies the groups that are particularly vulnerable to the consequences of climate change, including those who are living in poverty. Section III briefly examines the frameworks of intersectionality, dignity and justice. Section IV includes examples from around the world that exemplify the linkages between climate change, human rights and poverty and how climate change will undermine both the enjoyment of rights and the efforts to eradicate poverty. Section V offers concluding reflections on the intersections of climate change, human rights and poverty and how a human rights approach can lead to better results in relation to both climate change and poverty eradication, and suggests points for future research agendas.

I.   INTERNATIONAL RECOGNITION OF THE LINK AMONG POVERTY, ENVIRONMENT AND HUMAN RIGHTS

Poverty is very much a human rights issue as people living in poverty are at a greater risk of having their rights infringed.[11] Poverty was recognized as a human rights issue as far back as the Universal Declaration of Human Rights (UDHR)[12] and the link was further elaborated upon by the Committee on Economic, Social and Cultural Rights in 2001.[13] While poverty is not specifically mentioned in the International Covenant on Economic, Social and Cultural Rights (ICESCR), it is one of its central concerns. The Committee strongly believes that poverty constitutes a denial of human rights[14] and recognizes the need to help developing countries, noting that there are structural obstacles to eradicating poverty.[15] Many developing

---

[8]   Human Rights Council (n 6).
[9]   ibid.
[10]   ibid 2.
[11]   See Svitlana Kravchenko, 'The Myth of Public Participation in a World of Poverty' (2009) 23 Tul. Envtl. L.J. 33.
[12]   See Universal Declaration of Human Rights (adopted 10 December 1948) UNGA Res 217 A(III) (UDHR) preamble (referring to the freedom from want).
[13]   See Economic and Social Council, 'Statement Adopted by the Committee on Economic, Social and Cultural Rights on 4 May 2001' (10 May 2001) UN Doc E/C.12/2001/10.
[14]   ibid para 1.
[15]   ibid para 21.

countries, especially least developed countries, struggle to provide a decent standard of living for their people. Weather-related factors such as droughts and extreme weather events worsened by climate change exacerbate poverty.

Both human rights and environmental instruments address poverty. While poverty was not explicitly listed as a common challenge in the *Our Common Future* report, it recognized poverty as a major cause and effect of global environmental problems.[16] It noted that it is futile to attempt to deal with environmental problems without a broader perspective on the factors that underlie poverty and inequality.[17] The World Commission on Environment and Development (WCED) report was followed by the Rio Declaration on Environment and Development,[18] which recognized that eradicating poverty is an indispensable requirement for sustainable development.[19] The attention to poverty received a boost at the Copenhagen Summit on Social Development in 1996.[20] Chapter 2 of the Program of Action was devoted to poverty eradication, stating that over one billion people live under unacceptable conditions of poverty, mostly in developing countries. The Program of Action noted that poverty has various manifestations including lack of income, hunger and malnutrition; ill health; lack of access to education and other basic services; homelessness and inadequate housing; unhealthy environment; and social discrimination and exclusion.[21]

The latest attempt at addressing poverty and other inequalities is Agenda 2030 and the Sustainable Development Goals (SDGs): 'We recognize that eradicating poverty in all its forms and dimensions, including extreme poverty, is the greatest global challenge and an indispensable requirement for sustainable development'.[22] The SDGs are based on human rights and gender equality[23] and contain goals on both poverty and climate change. SDG 1 refers to the need to 'end poverty in all its forms everywhere'.[24] While the number of people living in extreme poverty has fallen in recent times, disasters are increasing and economic losses attributed to them are estimated at over USD $300 billion.[25] The UN affirms that '[t]his is among the highest losses in recent years, owing to three major hurricanes affecting the United States of America and several countries across the Caribbean'.[26] Scientists believe that climate change will give rise to more intense and frequent extreme weather events.[27]

---

[16] See World Commission on Environment and Development, *Our Common Future* (OUP 1987) (WCED report).

[17] ibid 3.

[18] 'Rio Declaration on Environment and Development 1992' (*United Nations*, 1992) <www.jus.uio.no/lm/environmental.development.rio.declaration.1992/portrait.a4.pdf> accessed 8 June 2020.

[19] ibid principle 5.

[20] UN World Summit for Social Development, 'Programme of Action for the World Summit for Social Development' (March 14, 1995) UN Doc A/CONF.166/9.

[21] ibid 10.

[22] See UNGA, 'Transforming Our World: The 2030 Agenda for Sustainable Development' (21 October 2015) UN Doc A/RES/70/1.

[23] ibid. See also 'Johannesburg Declaration on Sustainable Development' (*United Nations*, 4 September 2002) <https://www.un.org/esa/sustdev/documents/WSSD_POI_PD/English/POI_PD.htm> accessed 9 June 2020.

[24] UNGA (n 22) SDG 1.

[25] Progress of Goal 1 in 2018 (*UN Sustainable Development Goals Knowledge Platform*) <https://sustainabledevelopment.un.org/sdg1> accessed 9 June 2020.

[26] ibid.

[27] See 'Climate Change 2014 Synthesis Report' (n 7).

SDG 13 refers to the need to take urgent action to combat climate change and its impacts.[28] Moreover, poverty undermines the realization of other goals including Goal 2 (zero hunger), Goal 3 (health and well-being), Goal 4 (quality education), Goal 5 (gender equality), Goal 6 (clean water and sanitation), Goal 8 (decent work and economic growth) and Goal 10 (reduced inequalities).

The SDGs are the first international goals where all three dimensions of sustainable development are included in one global agenda. While a monumental task awaits the global community to achieve them, many positive strides have been taken to reduce global levels of poverty. Unfortunately, consequences of climate change could reverse these positive trends if poverty and climate change are not tackled together.[29] A report commissioned by the World Bank stressed that, while climate change is a threat to poverty eradication, climate-informed development can prevent most impacts on poverty.[30] The World Bank warns that if we continue down a business as usual path, it is unlikely that we will be able to halve the number of people in extreme poverty by 2030.[31]

II.   CLIMATE CHANGE, HUMAN RIGHTS AND VULNERABLE COMMUNITIES[32]

Writing over a decade ago, the United Nations Development Programme (UNDP) noted that 'millions of the world's poorest people are already being forced to cope with the impacts of climate change'.[33] It pointed out that climate change will undermine efforts to combat poverty and the achievement of Millennium Development Goals – the predecessor of SDGs. The report had a dire warning: the danger is that climate change will not stall, but *reverse* the progress that we have made over generations 'not just in cutting extreme poverty, but in health, nutrition, education and other areas'.[34]

It is the poor who bear the brunt of climate change; while rich countries are building climate fortifications and cities that can float on water, the poor are left to fend for themselves.[35] Moreover, climate change will exacerbate existing vulnerabilities and disparities. Adaptation measures must include the poor and the vulnerable and be accorded the same urgency and priority as mitigation measures. It was only at the 2010 United Nations Climate Change

---

[28]   UNGA (n 22) SDG 13.

[29]   ibid

[30]   World Bank Group, *Shock Waves: Managing the Impacts of Climate Change on Poverty* (The World Bank 2016), at: <https://openknowledge.worldbank.org/bitstream/handle/10986/22787/9781464806735.pdf?sequence=13&isAllowed=y> accessed 9 June 2020.

[31]   ibid.

[32]   This section is drawn from author's book Sumudu Atapattu, *Human Rights Approaches to Climate Change: Challenges and Opportunities* (2016 Routledge).

[33]   'Human Development Report 2007/08: Fighting Climate Change: Human Solidarity in a Divided World' (*UNDP*) 7, at: <http://hdr.undp.org/sites/default/files/hdr_20072008_summary_english.pdf> accessed 9 June 2020.

[34]   ibid.

[35]   ibid 9.

Conference (COP 16) in Cancun that adaptation was brought as a distinct pillar of climate action.[36]

Extreme weather events are already causing billions of dollars in damage to property, not to mention the human toll. For example, Hurricane Maria in Puerto Rico in 2017 caused over 4,000 deaths.[37] In addition, increases in droughts, floods and desertification will add to water stress and food shortages leading to both physical and mental health impacts. These events will have a detrimental impact on people, especially those who are already vulnerable and poor.

The link between climate change and human rights has received considerable attention in recent years.[38] Given the wide-ranging consequences associated with climate change, spanning from droughts to food and water scarcity and from conflicts to forced migration,[39] climate change will have a negative impact on the enjoyment of rights and exacerbate poverty.

In 2008 the UN Human Rights Council adopted its first resolution on climate change and human rights.[40] It expressed its concern that 'climate change poses an immediate and far-reaching threat to people and communities around the world and has implications for the full enjoyment of human rights'.[41] The resolution also recognized 'that the world's poor are especially vulnerable to the effects of climate change, in particular those concentrated in high-risk areas, and also tend to have more limited adaptation capacities'.[42] It requested the Office of the High Commissioner for Human Rights (OHCHR) to prepare an analytical report on the link between the two fields.

---

[36]   UN Framework Convention on Climate Change, 'Report of the Conference of the Parties on its Sixteenth Session, Held in Cancun from 29 November to 10 December 2010' (15 March 2011) UN Doc FCCC/CP/2010/7/Add.1.
[37]   The official count was only 64 deaths but a Harvard study has put this number at 4,600. See '2017 Hurricane Maria: Facts, FAQs, and How to Help' (*World Vision*) <www.worldvision.org/disaster-relief -news-stories/hurricane-maria-facts> accessed 9 June 2020.
[38]   See generally, Stephen Humphreys (ed), *Human Rights and Climate Change* (CUP 2010); Atapattu (n 32); John H Knox, 'Climate Change and Human Rights Law' (2009) 50 Va. J. Int'l L. 163; Pamela Stephens, 'Applying Human Rights Norms to Climate Change: The Elusive Remedy' (2010) 21 Colo. J. Int'l Envtl. L. & Pol'y 49; Amy Sinden 'Climate Change and Human Rights' (2007) 27 J. Land Resources Envtl. L 255; Simon Caney 'Cosmopolitan Justice, Rights and Global Climate Change' (2006) 19 CJLJ 255; Daniel Bodansky, 'Introduction: Climate Change and Human Rights: Unpacking the Issues' (2010) 38 Ga. J. Int'l. & Comp. L. 512; Deepa Badrinarayana, 'Global Warming: A Second Coming for International Law?' (2010) 85 Wash. L. Rev. 253; Sarah Nuffer 'Human Rights Violations and Climate Change: The Last Days of the Inuit People?' (2010) 37 Rutgers Law Record 182; Siobhán McInerney-Lankford, 'Climate Change and Human Rights: An Introduction to Legal Issues' (2009) 33 Harv. Envtl. L. Rev. 431; John H Knox, 'Linking Human Rights and Climate Change at the United Nations' (2009) 33 Harv. Envtl. L. Rev. 477; Siobhán McInerney-Lankford, Mac Darrow and Lavanya Rajamani, *Human Rights and Climate Change: A Review of the International Legal Dimensions* (The World Bank 2011) <http://documents.worldbank.org/curated/en/903741468339577637/pdf/61308 0PUB0Huma158344B09780821387207.pdf> accessed 9 June 2020; Timo Koivurova, Sébastien Duyck and Leena Heinämäki, 'Climate Change and Human Rights' in Erkki J Hollo, Kati Kulovesi and Michael Mehling (eds), *Climate Change and the Law* (Springer 2013); Sumudu Atapattu, 'Global Climate Change: Can Human Rights (and Human Beings) Survive this Onslaught?' (2008) 20 Colo. J. Int'l Envtl. L. & Pol'y 35.
[39]   Human Rights Council (n 1).
[40]   Human Rights and Climate Change (adopted 28 March 2008) HRC res 7/23 <https://ap.ohchr.org/ documents/E/HRC/resolutions/A_HRC_RES_7_23.pdf> accessed 9 June 2020.
[41]   ibid.
[42]   ibid.

In its report, OHCHR recognized that 'global warming will potentially have implications for the full range of human rights'[43] and identified the following as amongst the main consequences of climate change: contraction of snow-covered areas; sea level rise and higher thermal temperatures; increase in extreme weather events including droughts, heat waves and floods; and an increase in tropical cyclones.[44] In addition to these global impacts, the report noted that there will be more localized consequences, such as health effects; impacts on food and water availability and supply; changes in cultivation patterns; weather resistant crops; pests; and other issues that will have an impact on the day-to-day lives of millions of people.[45] While catastrophic events are more visible, we should not lose sight of these smaller, but longer lasting consequences of climate change that will also impact the enjoyment of human rights. The report recognized the unequal burden of climate change, with some states and communities being more impacted than others.[46]

The report also recognized that mitigation measures that states adopt may also have human rights implications.[47] Examples include agro-fuel production[48] and the UN-REDD program,[49] which have implications for food security and rights of Indigenous peoples. While noting that climate change has obvious implications for the enjoyment of human rights, the report stated that it is less obvious whether they can be qualified as human rights violations, especially because the causal link between the human right infringed and climate change is virtually impossible to establish.[50] This does not mean that human rights have no role to play vis-à-vis climate change. States are required to fulfil their human rights obligations in relation to climate action.

It took the international community almost two decades to include a provision on human rights in climate documents. The first time a reference was made to human rights was in 2010 at COP 16:[51] 'Parties should, in all climate change-related actions, fully respect human rights'.[52] Although a nonbinding document, it nonetheless signaled a turning point with regard to climate negotiations and paved the way for the parties to include a provision on human rights in the Paris Agreement.[53]

The enjoyment of almost all the substantive rights protected under human rights law, from the supreme right to life to the right to self-determination can be jeopardized by climate change. Climate change acts as a threat multiplier exacerbating existing vulnerabilities and further marginalizing those who are in subordinate positions. In the petition filed by the Inuit of Canada and the US against the US, the complainants invoked the violation of a range of

---

[43]   Human Rights Council (n 1) 8.
[44]   ibid.
[45]   ibid.
[46]   ibid.
[47]   ibid para 65.
[48]   ibid para 66.
[49]   ibid para 68.
[50]   ibid para 70.
[51]   UN Framework Convention on Climate Change (n 36).
[52]   ibid.
[53]   United Nations, 'Paris Agreement' (*UNFCCC* 2015) <http://unfccc.int/files/essential_background/convention/application/pdf/english_paris_agreement.pdf> accessed 9 June 2020.

rights including the right to life.[54] In addition, the rights to health,[55] food,[56] water, adequate housing, and sanitation are at risk. Scientists predict that consequences of climate change, such as sea level rise, increased salinity, severe weather events, wildfires and increased temperatures will lead to increased water and food scarcity, land degradation, and desertification. Despite the availability of an abundance of food, currently there are about 850 million malnourished people, and climate change will add about 650 million to this number.[57] Moreover, the rights relating to livelihood, self-determination, culture, property and freedom of movement with regard to the inhabitants of small island states and Indigenous peoples are some of the substantive rights that could be affected.

The procedural rights of right to information, right to participate in the decision-making process, and access to remedies could also be affected as a result of both climate change and poverty.[58] Poor and vulnerable people may not be consulted before they are relocated, adaptation plans may be drawn without their participation, relevant information may not be provided, and adequate remedies may not be available to victims or they not be able to afford them. These violations can become even more acute in the context of climate change, especially if there are multiple severe weather events.

In addition to these general impacts, vulnerable groups, particularly those who are dependent on climate-sensitive resources, such as farmers and fisherfolk, Indigenous groups, and women, are disproportionately affected as they are 'likely to be at the sharp end of the policy responses to climate change'.[59] These groups are often ignored when policy decisions are made on both mitigation and adaptation. The OHCHR report on human rights and climate change identified several groups of people who 'are already in vulnerable situations due to factors such as poverty, gender, age, minority status, and disability'.[60]

Women are especially vulnerable due to their role as caregivers. They also tend to be poorer than men. In many societies, they are responsible for collecting water and firewood and for providing food for the family. With increased food and water scarcity associated with climate change, women must walk longer distances in search of water and firewood. Women are often more vulnerable to severe weather events and face gender-based violence, harassment and exploitation during periods of displacement. Worldwide, women constitute the majority

---

[54]   'Petition to the Inter American Commission on Human Rights Seeking Relief from Violations Resulting from Global Warming Caused by Acts and Omissions of the United States' (Inuit Petition) (*Columbia Law*, 7 December 2005) <http://blogs2.law.columbia.edu/climate-change-litigation/wp-content/uploads/sites/16/non-us-case-documents/2005/20051208_na_petition.pdf> accessed 9 June 2020.

[55]   The link between the rights to health, water, and sanitation and adverse consequences of climate change was recognized by the Special Rapporteur on the Right to Health. He identified three main obstacles to realizing access to safe water and adequate sanitation: poverty, gender inequality, and global warming. See UNGA, 'Report of the Special Rapporteur on the Right of Everyone to the Enjoyment of the Highest Attainable Standard of Physical and Mental Health' (8 August 2007) UN Doc A/62/214.

[56]   See Human Rights Council, 'Report of the Special Rapporteur on Right to Food, Jean Ziegler' (10 January 2008) UN Doc A/HRC/7/5, para 5.

[57]   See UNDP and OPHI (n 2).

[58]   See Kravchenko (n 11).

[59]   See W Neil Adger, Jouni Paavola and Saleemul Huq, 'Toward Justice in Adaptation to Climate Change' in W Neil Adger and others (eds), *Fairness in Adaptation to Climate Change* (MIT Press 2006) 2. See the examples discussed in section IV.

[60]   Human Rights Council (n 1).

of small-scale farmers and are susceptible to climate-related disruptions. On the other hand, examples show that they tend to be more resilient and have better adaptive capacity. Their knowledge of the land and resources is crucial for adaptation programs.

Overall, children in developing countries are bearing the disease burden relating to climate change. Extreme weather events and increased water stress are already having an impact on malnutrition and infant and child mortality. Girls are disproportionately affected as they are responsible for collecting water and firewood. They also have a higher mortality rate due to severe weather events. The Convention on the Rights of the Child (CRC) requires states parties to take measures to ensure that the rights enshrined there are protected within their jurisdiction.[61] Children today are likely to experience worse consequences in the future. Moreover, half of all people living in poverty worldwide are children.[62]

Indigenous peoples are also disproportionately affected as they have a special relationship with their land and depend on forests for their daily subsistence. Many of them are also poor and impoverished. The petition filed by the Inuit peoples of US and Canada before the Inter-American Commission of Human Rights in 2005 highlighted how this Indigenous community is struggling to cope with the adverse consequences of climate change.[63] Another group that is especially vulnerable are 'climate refugees' who will be forced to move due to adverse consequences of climate change. By some estimates 150 million people could be displaced by 2050 due to climate change-related consequences, such as desertification, water scarcity, and severe weather events.[64] Such displacement will likely be primarily internal and will affect poorer regions of the world. It was only at the Paris Conference in 2015 that the international community decided to establish a taskforce to examine the issue. Currently people who cross an international border due to climate-related consequences are unprotected unless they can satisfy the criteria for a traditional refugee under the Geneva Convention.[65]

---

[61]   Convention on the Rights of the Child (adopted 20 November 1989, entered into force 2 September 1990) UNGA res 44/25 (CRC). The CRC enjoys near universal ratification with the US being the only country not to have ratified it. See Claire Fenton-Glynn (ed), *Children's Rights and Sustainable Development: Interpreting the UNCRC for Future Generations* (CUP, 2019).

[62]   'Half of World's Poor are Children' (*UNDP*, 20 September 2018) <www.undp.org/content/undp/en/home/news-centre/news/2018/half-of-world_s-poor-are-children.html> accessed 9 June 2020.

[63]   See 'Petition to the Inter American Commission' (n 54). The UN Declaration on the Rights of Indigenous Peoples (2007) seeks to protect their rights. United Nations Declaration on the Rights of Indigenous People (adopted 13 September 2007) UNGA res 61/295 <www.un.org/development/desa/indigenouspeoples/wp-content/uploads/sites/19/2018/11/UNDRIP_E_web.pdf> accessed 9 June 2020.

[64]   See ibid; Francesco Bassetti, 'Environmental Migrants: Up to 1 billion by 2050' (*Foresight*, 22 May 2019) <www.climateforesight.eu/migrations/environmental-migrants-up-to-1-billion-by-2050/> accessed 9 June 2020. The World Bank estimates that 143 million people will be internally displaced by 2050 if no action is taken. See 'Groundswell: Preparing for Internal Climate Migration' (*The World Bank*, 19 March 2018) <www.worldbank.org/en/news/infographic/2018/03/19/groundswell---preparing-for-internal-climate-migration> accessed 9 June 2020.

[65]   See Simon Behrman and Avidan Kent (eds), *'Climate Refugees': Beyond the Legal Impasse?* (Routledge 2018). Cf. decision by UN Human Rights Committee in *Teitiota v. New Zealand* (2020) that extended the principle of non-*refoulement* to consequences of climate change, Human Rights Committee, 'Views Adopted by the Committee Under Article 5(4) of the Option Protocol, Concerning Communication No. 2728/2016' (7 January 2020) UN Doc CCPR/C/127/D/2728/2016.

III. INTERSECTIONALITY, HUMAN DIGNITY AND CLIMATE JUSTICE[66]

Poverty exacerbates the vulnerabilities described above. There are, of course, other categories of people who are vulnerable and will be disproportionately affected by climate change: disabled people, older people, farmers, and peasants are some of them. Inhabitants of small island states are also disproportionately affected, many of whom are poor; they stand to lose everything they have, including their state.

The Framework Principles on Human Rights and the Environment, proposed by the former Special Rapporteur on Human Rights and Environment, John Knox, recognize that vulnerable peoples are at a greater risk of having their rights violated and their environment degraded.[67] Framework Principle 14 provides: 'States should take additional measures to protect the rights of those who are most vulnerable to, or at particular risk from, environmental harm, taking into account their needs, risks and capacities'.[68] Elaborating further, the Special Rapporteur notes that:

> Persons may be vulnerable because they are unusually susceptible to certain types of environmental harm, or because they are denied their human rights, or both. Vulnerability to environmental harm reflects the 'interface between exposure to the physical threats to human well-being and the capacity of people and communities to cope with those threats'.[69]

The Special Rapporteur identified several categories of vulnerable people including *persons living in poverty*,[70] who 'often lack adequate access to safe water and sanitation, and they are more likely to burn wood, coal and other solid fuels for heating and cooking, causing household air pollution'.[71]

However, poverty is not one-dimensional. It intersects with other social constructs and vulnerabilities. Intersectionality theory acknowledges that vulnerabilities can magnify when they intersect with one another. Thus, a poor minority (or Indigenous) woman may be more vulnerable than a poor white woman, while a poor, minority, disabled person may be more vulnerable than a poor white disabled person. Proposed originally by Kimberlé Crenshaw in relation to the intersection of race and gender,[72] intersectionality is an important lens to address vulnerability:

---

[66] The section on dignity and climate justice draws from author's article, Sumudu Atapattu, 'Climate Change and Displacement: Protecting "Climate Refugees" within a Framework of Justice and Human Rights' in Journal of Human Rights and the Environment, Vol 11, No 1 (March 2020), pp 86–113.

[67] See Human Rights Council, 'Report of the Special Rapporteur on the Issue of Human Rights Obligations Relating to the Enjoyment of a Safe, Clean, Healthy and Sustainable Environment' (24 January 2018) UN Doc A/HRC/37/59.

[68] ibid principle 14.

[69] ibid (footnotes omitted).

[70] ibid (emphasis added).

[71] ibid. Poor people are often blamed for environmentally 'harmful' practices such as burning wood and coal while the much more decadent lifestyle of affluent people including over-consumption of resources is overlooked.

[72] Kimberlé Crenshaw, 'Demarginalizing the Intersections of Race and Sex: A Black Feminist Critique of Antidiscrimination Doctrine, Feminist Theory and Antiracist Politics' [1989] University of Chicago Legal Forum 139.

If [we] began with addressing the needs and problems of those who are most disadvantaged and with restructuring and remaking the world where necessary, then others who are singularly disadvantaged would also benefit. In addition, it seems that placing those who are currently marginalized in the center is the most effective way to resist efforts to compartmentalize and undermine potential collective action.[73]

Compound injustice is closely related to the intersectionality theory.[74] Proposed by Henry Shue, 'compound injustice' occurs when an initial injustice paves the way for a second. An example is when colonial exploitation weakens the colonized nation to such an extent that the colonizer can impose unequal treaties upon it even after it gains independence.[75] The impact of climate change on poverty can be considered a form of compound injustice, as poverty that dates back to the colonial era of exploitation is exacerbated by adverse consequences of climate change.

Dignity is another framework that is useful in this context. If all rights are universal, inter-related and indivisible,[76] then all people(s) should be entitled to enjoy the basic rights recognized under international human rights law. Dignity rights, directly related to universality, form the basis of human rights.[77] Indeed, the very first sentence of the UDHR refers to human dignity[78] and Article 1 further elaborates on this.[79] The Stockholm Declaration on the Human Environment similarly referred to dignity in its near endorsement of a right to a healthy environment.[80] Thus, one can conclude that 'each of us, just by virtue of having been born human, is endowed with human dignity, and bestowed with equal worth'.[81] Dignity provides an important framework to protect the rights of poor people to ensure that they lead a life of dignity and well-being. Yet, despite dignity's inclusion in human rights instruments and in many national constitutions, it 'remains largely invisible in advancing environmental protection at international and domestic levels'.[82]

Based on the notions of equity and fairness and closely related to dignity, the justice framework recognizes the disproportionate distribution of burdens of polluting activities on low-income communities and racial minorities.[83] Although climate change is a global phenomenon, both the level of contribution and its impacts vary significantly across states and

---

[73] ibid 167.

[74] See Henry Shue, *Climate Justice: Vulnerability and Protection* (OUP 2016) 4.

[75] Antony Anghie, 'The Evolution of International Law: Colonial and Postcolonial Realities' (2006) 27 TWQ 739, 747.

[76] UNGA, 'Vienna Declaration and Programme of Action' (adopted 25 June 1993) UN Doc A/CONF.157/23.

[77] See Guiding Principles on Extreme Poverty and Human Rights (n 3).

[78] UDHR (n 12).

[79] ibid art 1.

[80] 'Report of the United Nations Conference on the Human Environment' (June 1972) UN Doc A/CONF.48/14/Rev.1 (emphasis added) Principle 1.

[81] Erin Daly, *Dignity Rights: Courts, Constitutions and the Worth of the Human Person* (University of Pennsylvania Press 2012); Erin Daly and James R May, 'Environmental Dignity Rights' in Sandrine Maljean-Dubois (ed), *The Effectiveness of Environmental Law*, vol 3 (Intersentia 2017).

[82] ibid.

[83] ibid.

communities. Similar to domestic environmental challenges, poor, vulnerable communities in both the Global North and South are disproportionately affected.[84]

Environmental problems often exacerbate already existing inequalities[85] and intensify economic and social disparities that might have their root causes elsewhere. Environmental justice coincides with the goal of achieving a more just society and is described as a 'marriage of the movement for social justice with environmentalism', integrating environmental concerns into a broader agenda that emphasizes social, racial and economic justice.[86] This intersectional complexity reveals that environmental justice cannot be separated from struggles for other forms of justice that often underlie the reasons for environmental problems, including the social structures and agents that are responsible.[87]

There are several, overlapping definitions of climate justice. The Mary Robinson Foundation, for example, provides that '[C]limate Justice links human rights and development to achieve a human-centered approach, safeguarding the rights of the most vulnerable and sharing the burdens and benefits of climate change and its resolution equitably and fairly'.[88] The International Bar Association, on the other hand, adopts a more rights-based approach with the right to a healthy environment as its core:

> To ensure that communities, individuals and governments have substantive legal and procedural rights to the enjoyment of a safe, clean, healthy and sustainable environment and the means to take or cause measures to be taken within their national legislative and judicial systems and, where necessary, at regional and international levels, to mitigate sources of climate change and provide for adaptation to its effects in a manner that respects human rights.[89]

Robert Kuehn advances a four-fold approach with distributive, procedural, corrective and social justice components,[90] while others rely on the capabilities and responsibility approaches.[91] These offer wide-ranging approaches to a justice-based response to climate change, and I argue that a justice and dignity framework would require states to address a range of responsibilities and obligations in relation to climate change and poverty, including: (1) acknowledging that the adverse consequences of climate change due to historic emissions have a disproportionate impact on certain communities and groups who are already in a vulnerable position; (2) giving teeth to the loss and damage mechanism[92] and providing compensation to

[84] See Carmen G Gonzalez, 'Environmental Justice, Human Rights, and the Global South', (2015) 13 Santa Clara J. Int'l L. 151.

[85] See Stephen Humphreys, 'Climate Justice: The Claim of the Past' (2014) 5 J. Hum. Rts. & Env't 134.

[86] See Robert R Kuehn, 'A Taxonomy of Environmental Justice' (2000) 30 Envtl. L. Rep. 10681.

[87] See Sheila Foster, 'Justice from the Ground Up: Distributive Inequities, Grassroots Resistance, and the Transformative Politics of the Environmental Justice Movement' (1998) 86 Calif. L. Rev. 775.

[88] 'Principles of Climate Justice' (*Mary Robinson Foundation Climate Justice*) <www.mrfcj.org/wp-content/uploads/2015/09/Principles-of-Climate-Justice.pdf> accessed 10 June 2020.

[89] See International Bar Association, *Achieving Justice and Human Rights in an Era of Climate Disruption: Climate Change Justice and Human Rights Task Force Report* (International Bar Association 2014) 35 (hereafter IBA report) <www.ibanet.org/Article/Detail.aspx?ArticleUid=96b93592-3761-4418-8a52-54a81b02c5f1> accessed 10 June 2020.

[90] Kuehn (n 86).

[91] For a discussion of these theories, see Atapattu (n 66).

[92] See Paris Agreement (n 53) art 8 and Maxine Burkett, 'Loss and Damage' (2014) 4 Climate Law 4 119–30.

those who are disproportionately affected, including the poor; (3) reducing their greenhouse gas emissions so that the temperature increase does not exceed 1.5 degrees Celsius;[93] (4) providing adaptation assistance especially with regard to extreme weather events and displacement; and (5) recognizing that poor, vulnerable communities are more likely than others to be trapped in dangerous situations due to lack of resources[94] and a human rights framing requires them to be afforded a minimum level of protection even if they are not citizens. More generally, states must ensure that climate change consequences are factored into poverty alleviation programs, disaster management, displacement and conflict situations.[95]

IV.   SOME EXAMPLES OF POVERTY AND CLIMATE CHANGE FROM AROUND THE WORLD

In this section I discuss some examples from around the world that highlight the relationship between climate change and poverty. They also illustrate that, while climate change is a global phenomenon, its effects are very much localized and that poor, vulnerable communities worldwide are already experiencing its negative consequences. Poor people tend to live in locales that are disaster prone and they tend to be engaged in livelihoods that are more susceptible to climatic changes such as agriculture or fisheries.

A.   Example 1 – Fishing Communities in Rural Sri Lanka

In Sri Lanka nearly 72 percent of the population depends on the agricultural sector for its livelihood.[96] While extreme poverty is rare in the country, many subsist just above the poverty line.[97] Being an island nation, people along the coast depend on fisheries.[98] Small-scale fisherwomen from four villages in Puttalam and Kalmunai districts in the Eastern part of the country were interviewed for this research who identified collecting drinking water as their biggest challenge: 'We have to walk three kilometers and need to carry pots on our heads. I know how

---

[93]   See ibid art 2.

[94]   See 'Foresight: Migration and Global Environmental Change' (*The Government Office for Science*, London, 2011) (referring to 'trapped populations') <https://assets.publishing.service.gov .uk/government/uploads/system/uploads/attachment_data/file/287717/11-1116-migration-and-global -environmental-change.pdf> accessed 10 June 2020.

[95]   Rights and Resources Initiative, *Seeing People Through the Trees: Scaling up Efforts to Advance Rights and Address Poverty, Conflict and Climate Change* (Rights and Resources Initiative 2008) <https://rightsandresources.org/wp-content/exported-pdf/seeingpeoplefinal.pdf> accessed 10 June 2020.

[96]   See MMGT De Silva and Akiyuki Kawasaki, 'Socioeconomic Vulnerability to Disaster Risk: A Case Study of Flood and Drought Impact in a Rural Sri Lankan Community' (2018) 152 Ecological Economics 131.

[97]   'The World Bank in Sri Lanka' (*The World Bank*, 12 April 2020) <www.worldbank.org/en/ country/srilanka/overview> accessed 10 June 2020. Sri Lanka reduced its poverty level from 22 percent in 2002 to 6.7 percent in 2015. 'Sri Lanka and ADB' (*Asian Development Bank*) <www.adb.org/ countries/sri-lanka/poverty> accessed 10 June 2020.

[98]   'Climate Justice Briefs: Rural Women's Adaptation Strategies: Sri Lanka' (*Asia Pacific Forum on Women, Law and Development (APWLD)*, 2011) <http://apwld.org/wp-content/uploads/2018/10/ Climate-Justice-Sri-Lanka.pdf> accessed 10 June 2020.

to ride a bicycle, but my husband and neighbors don't accept a woman riding a bicycle ... Five years ago, we had more than enough water, but now there is no more here'.[99]

Most women in these communities earn an income from processing fish, repairing nets and occasionally, by harvesting fish. Erratic weather patterns associated with climate change are having an impact on these women's income, increasing their social and economic vulnerability. Other adverse consequences include flooding of their homes, intense coastal storms, and sea level rise which has flooded the roads cutting off their villages from access to schools, healthcare facilities and markets. These women voiced concern about loss of income due to the lack of access to the market to sell their goods and the inability to access maternal healthcare. Moreover, existing barriers to girls' education worsened when the roads became impassable. Submergence of roads was identified as one of the biggest challenges in the community. Traditional gender roles and expectations have worsened their situation. Not only do they have to walk longer distances in search of water and firewood, they are also expected to wear traditional clothing even when floodwaters are high or in extreme heat.[100]

This example highlighted the intersectional nature of climate change, poverty and gender and how gender norms and perceived notions give rise to a vicious cycle of poverty and deprivation.[101] Not only do these women have to deal with the adverse impacts of climate change, they also have to tolerate gendered norms and inhibitions that exacerbate the impacts of both poverty and climate change. The intersectional nature of climate change, poverty and gender must be addressed together as well as the underlying discriminatory practices and gendered norms. Human rights, especially the Convention on the Elimination of All Forms of Discrimination against Women,[102] provides a useful lens to address these intersections and gender disparities. Gender mainstreaming is another tool that can be adopted.[103]

B.   Example 2 – Climate Change Challenges in Somalia

Another factor that exacerbates the consequences of climate change and poverty is conflict. Somalia illustrates this link as well as the relationship with governance structures:

> Somalia's three decades of conflict have been magnified by a series of increasingly severe droughts. The impacts of climate- and weather-related changes add pressure to the country's overburdened governance and judicial systems. This is a serious threat to Somalia's state-building process ...[104]

Approximately 94 percent of Somalia's nomadic population lives in poverty. Climate change has caused regular grazing routes to become unusable, forcing the nomadic population to

---

[99] ibid.

[100] ibid.

[101] See 'Human Development Report' (n 33).

[102] Convention on the Elimination of All Forms of Discrimination against Women (adopted 18 December 1979, entered into force 3 September 1981) UNGA Res 34/180 (CEDAW).

[103] According to the UN, gender mainstreaming involves ensuring that 'gender perspectives and attention to the goal of gender equality are central to all activities' from policy development to resource allocation and monitoring of programs and projects. 'Gender Mainstreaming' (*UN Women*) <www.un .org/womenwatch/osagi/gendermainstreaming.htm> accessed 10 June 2020.

[104] Stockholm International Peace Research Institute, 'Climate-related Security Risks and Peacebuilding in Somalia' (*reliefweb*, 23 October 2019) <https://reliefweb.int/report/somalia/climate -related-security-risks-and-peacebuilding-somalia-october-2019> accessed 10 June 2020.

move their livestock to areas that put them in conflict with farmers. Climate change has also increased the number of internally displaced people who are exposed to recruitment efforts by groups such as al-Shabab. Issues such as drought, strong winds, extreme flooding and high temperatures are associated with loss of livelihood, loss of livestock and increased poverty.[105] Moreover, people in conflict areas face food instability and 53,000 individuals have been displaced by drought.[106] While conflict situations are particularly challenging, states are required to abide by their human rights obligations even in such situations.

C.   Example 3 – Climate Change Challenges in Tuvalu

Small island states are at the forefront of climate change. Many of them are barely above the sea level and are disproportionately affected.[107] Tuvalu is one such island threatened by rising seas and severe weather. Thousands of people have already fled the island, 'which, because of their poverty and proximity to the sea, represent the "ground zero" of climate change'.[108]

Many of the families subsist on fish. It is their staple food and the only food item that Tuvalu does not import. Most families rely on traditional reef fishing in the lagoon. Because of increased temperatures, the coral is bleaching and dying. Moreover, sewage-water spills are increasingly causing algal blooms in the lagoon killing small fish and threatening larger fish populations that depend on them.[109] Subsistence fishers find it harder to get the daily fish for their families.[110] Poor waste and wastewater management has exacerbated the effects of coastal pollution and flooding. Saltwater intrusion is also having an impact on garden plants forcing people to turn to more expensive imported products. The islanders now import 80 percent of their food from Fiji, New Zealand and Australia. The Fisheries Department believes that decreasing fish stocks will have a huge impact on families who will be forced to buy food that they cannot easily afford.[111]

D.   Example 4 – Climate Change and Poverty in Rural Latin America[112]

Poverty levels are high among Indigenous people in the northern Argentine province of Salta, in the Chaco ecoregion, which is worsened by climate change. There are accounts of extreme

---

[105]   ibid.

[106]   ibid.

[107]   See M.B. Gerrard and G.E. Wannier (eds.), *Threatened Island Nations: Legal Implications of Rising Seas and a Changing Climate* (Cambridge: Cambridge University Press, 2013).

[108]   Tom Bawden, 'Global Warming: Thousands Flee Pacific Islands on Front Line of Climate Change' (*Independent*, 2 December 2015) <www.independent.co.uk/environment/climate-change/global-warming-thousands-flee-pacific-islands-on-front-line-of-climate-change-a6757796.html> accessed 10 June 2020.

[109]   Florent Baarsch and Lan Marie Berg, 'Warming Oceans and Human Waste Hit Tuvalu's Sustainable Way of Life' (*The Guardian*, 4 March 2011) <www.theguardian.com/global-development/poverty-matters/2011/mar/04/tuvalu-sustainable-way-of-life-disappears> accessed 10 June 2020.

[110]   ibid

[111]   ibid.

[112]   Daniel Gutman, 'Climate Change Drives up Rural Poverty in Latin America' (*Inter Press Service*, 24 November 2018) <www.ipsnews.net/2018/11/climate-change-drives-rural-poverty-latin-america/> accessed 10 June 2020.

drought followed by flash floods that destroy entire crops. Many agree that the decrease in agricultural yields and migration from the countryside are directly related to climate change.[113]

Across Latin America and the Caribbean there are 59 million poor people in rural areas of which 22.5 percent live in extreme poverty.[114] The Food and Agriculture Organization of the United Nations (FAO) noted that no country is safe from the impact of climate change: 'In the south, Argentina had the worst drought in 50 years this year, after crops had been lost to flooding the previous year. And in the Caribbean, Dominica's entire agricultural crop disappeared from the map in 2017 because of devastating hurricanes'.[115] Adapting to these consequences will take millions of dollars, money these poor countries can ill afford.

E.   Example 5 – Alaska, USA

While the above examples are from the Global South, it is important to note that climate change has an impact on poverty and human rights in the Global North as well. Alaska in the US is especially vulnerable to the impacts of climate change where many Indigenous communities have to be relocated to safer areas. Because they are to be relocated, no effort is being made to improve their living standards. Many live without indoor plumbing or running water. It is not clear who will pay for their relocation or even where they will move to. Newtok, Kivalina and Shishmarof are some of the communities that have to relocate.[116] Meanwhile, another community thousands of miles away, is currently making plans to relocate. An Indigenous group on Isle de Jean Charles off the coast of Louisiana received funding to relocate to the mainland. Many do not want to move but it is no longer safe for them to live on the island.[117] Two different communities, two different states but one shared fate – relocation.

F.   Applying a Combined Rights, Justice and Dignity Framework

In the previous section I discussed diverse examples that highlighted the link between climate change, human rights and poverty, as well as gender and conflict. Applying a human rights and justice framing to these examples would, at a minimum, require: (1) factoring in adverse consequences of climate change into poverty-eradication programs; (2) providing affected communities with relevant information; (3) ensuring that these communities participate in the decision-making process with regard to both mitigation and adaptation measures – this applies especially to women's groups and Indigenous communities; (4) ensuring that vulnerable

---

[113]   ibid.

[114]   See 'Panorama of Rural Poverty in Latin America and the Caribbean' (*Food and Agriculture Organization of the United Nations*), at: <www.fao.org/americas/publicaciones-audio-video/panoramaruralpoverty2018/en/> accessed 10 June 2020.

[115]   ibid.

[116]   Adaptation Advisory Group to the Alaska Climate Change Sub-Cabinet, 'Alaska's Climate Change Strategy: Addressing Impacts in Alaska' (*Alaska Department of Environmental Conservation*, 27 January 2010) <www.master-adaptation.fr/sites/master-adaptation.fr/files/Alaska_aag_all_rpt_27jan10.pdf> accessed 10 June 2020.

[117]   See Julie Dermansky, 'Isle de Jean Charles Tribe Turns Down Funds to Relocate First US "Climate Refugees" as Louisiana Buys Land Anyway' (*Desmog*, 11 January 2019) <www.desmogblog.com/2019/01/11/isle-de-jean-charles-tribe-turns-down-funds-relocate-climate-refugees-louisiana> accessed 10 June 2020.

groups are consulted; (5) ensuring free, prior and informed consent of Indigenous groups especially if they are to be relocated from their traditional lands; (6) ensuring a minimum standard
of living where basic necessities are met, even in situations where groups are to be eventually
relocated; and (7) providing compensation to the communities that must be permanently relocated and whose culture is being lost due to climate change, even though this aspect may be
politically unpalatable, especially for the Global North.

V.   CONCLUDING REFLECTIONS ON THE INTERSECTION OF CLIMATE CHANGE, HUMAN RIGHTS AND POVERTY

Climate change, human rights and poverty are intertwined in complex ways. Poverty is
a human rights issue. So is climate change. Both are global issues with local consequences.
Both can undermine people's ability to enjoy their rights. Moreover, climate change will exacerbate poverty and those in poverty will not have the capacity or the resources to adapt to the
adverse consequences of climate change.

Similarly, poverty exacerbates the adverse consequences of climate change. Poverty also
limits people's ability to adapt, including the possibility of migration. When discussing
poverty, we need to address both individual poverty and poverty at the macro level. Climate
change acts as a threat multiplier and the intersectional nature of climate change, poverty, and
other vulnerabilities must be addressed together.

The vast disparity in resources between rich and poor, evident in the gap between and
within countries (both North and South), is the deepest injustice of our age. This failure of
resource-fairness makes it impossible for billions of humans to lead decent lives. Climate
change both highlights and exacerbates this gulf in equality.[118] Thus, while developed countries have the resources to adapt to the climate change consequences, poor nations and communities do not have such luxuries.[119] A greater effort should be made to transfer technology,
assist with adaptation and promote international cooperation.

Climate change and poverty are two of the biggest global challenges facing the international
community today. They are intertwined; one challenge cannot be tackled without addressing
the other. Global efforts at poverty eradication will be severely threatened by adverse consequences of climate change. Policies and programs to address both issues should be informed
by a human rights approach.[120] Both challenges also require a critical examination of and
radical changes to the global economic system that has led to the systemic failures that led to
extreme poverty and climate change. As the Special Rapporteur on Extreme Poverty pointed
out, climate change is an unconscionable assault on the poor.[121]

On this basis, pressing topics for future research include:

- How does climate change undermine efforts to eradicate poverty in developing countries?

---

[118]   See 'Principles of Climate Justice' (n 88).
[119]   See IBA report (n 89).
[120]   See Human Rights Council (n 6) 14 (calling for a transformation of the international human rights
regime stating that 'an extraordinary challenge demands an extraordinary response').
[121]   ibid para 87.

- What is the impact of climate change and poverty on vulnerable populations? Does a rights and justice framework help?
- What does a human rights framework mean for impoverished communities who are facing disproportionate impacts of climate change?
- In a world experiencing adverse impacts of climate change, how can states achieve the SDGs, especially SDG 1 on poverty?

32. Corruption as a human rights violation

Khulekani Moyo

Corruption is one of the greatest evils in the fight to eradicate poverty and to ensure a dignified life for all people. Corruption impedes the fight against poverty as it increases the cost of service delivery through theft and misallocation of resources meant for the provision of public goods. It has been estimated that corruption costs more than five per cent of global GDP ($2.6 trillion USD) and that over $1 trillion USD is paid in bribes each year.[1] Corruption is also closely linked to severe loss of potential public revenue due to illicit financial flows. According to the High Level Panel on Illicit Financial Flows from Africa, the continent loses over 50 billion dollars USD annually due to illicit financial flows.[2] It is not surprising then that Sustainable Development Goal (SDG) 16 includes targets such as the reduction of corruption and bribery in all their forms.[3]

The realization of the SDGs is to a considerable extent predicated on transparency, participation and accountability[4] – values that are very important for an anti-corruption drive. There is little doubt that corruption is one of the biggest obstacles for an effective implementation of economic, social and cultural rights as well as civil and political rights.[5] Corruption is an impediment not only for the realization of human rights but also for development in general.[6] The diversion and siphoning off of public resources as a result of endemic corruption impacts heavily on the marginalized members of the community and denudes them of their dignity. Corruption is an impediment to the realization of the call in the 2030 Agenda that no one should be left behind. At the very least, corruption compromises a state's capacity to deliver public services, particularly socio-economic goods such as water, housing, sanitation, health care and education.

---

[1] International Chamber of Commerce, Transparency International, the United Nations Global Compact and the World Economic Forum Partnering Against Corruption Initiatives (PACI), Clean Business is Good Business; The Business Case Against Corruption (2008) <https://d306pr3pise04h .cloudfront.net/docs/issues_doc%2FAnti-Corruption%2Fclean_business_is_good_business.pdf> accessed 13 July 2020.

[2] AU/ECA Conference of Ministers of Finance, Planning and Economic Development, 'Illicit Financial Flow' <www.uneca.org/sites/default/files/PublicationFiles/iff_main_report_26feb_en.pdf> accessed 13 July 2020.

[3] The United Nations (UN) General Assembly, by resolution 70/1 (25 September 2015) formally adopted the 2030 Agenda for Sustainable Development on 25 September 2015 with a set of seventeen (17) goals and one hundred and sixty-nine (169) targets. See United Nations General Assembly (UNGA), 'Transforming our World: the 2030 Agenda for Sustainable Development' (21 October 2015) UN Doc A/RES/70/1 <www.refworld.org/docid/57b6e3e44.html> accessed 13 July 2020 (Goal 16.6: 'Develop effective, accountable and transparent institutions at all levels.').

[4] ibid.

[5] Raoul Wallenberg Institute, 'Anti-Corruption And Human Rights – How to Become Mutually Reinforcing?' (13–14 November 2017) <https://rwi.lu.se/app/uploads/2018/02/Anti-Corruption-and -Human-Rights-RWI.pdf> accessed 13 July 2020.

[6] ibid 3.

It is against this background that both practice and scholarship have increasingly courted a human rights-based approach in the fight against the scourge of corruption.[7] The Inter-American Commission on Human Rights summarized this approach as follows:

> [C]orruption is a complex phenomenon that affects human rights in their entirety – civil, political, economic, social, cultural and environmental –, as well as the right to development; weakens governance and democratic institutions, promotes impunity, undermines the rule of law and exacerbates inequality.[8]

This chapter examines how re-framing corruption as a rights violation has important normative and utilitarian implications and could improve enforcement at both national and international levels. This chapter seeks to address whether corruption can and should be conceptualized as a violation of human rights where individuals or groups living in poverty are denied access to public goods they are entitled to as a result of corrupt acts.

The remainder of this chapter is divided into three parts. Following this introductory section, Section I defines corruption, and Section II engages with the socio-economic impacts of corruption. Section III explores the relationship between corruption and human rights and attempts to answer the critical question on whether corruption is a human rights violation by providing a practical illustration.

I.   DEFINITION OF CORRUPTION

The most common definition of corruption is by Transparency International: 'corruption [is] the abuse of entrusted power for private gain.'[9] Corruption may happen on the level of day-to-day administration and public service (petty corruption) or at the high-level of political office (grand corruption).[10] Corrupt practices include bribery, nepotism, theft, and other abuses of public power for private benefit.[11] Corruption uses state resources and institutions to

---

[7]   Anne Peters, 'Corruption as a Violation of International Human Rights' (2018) 29 EJIL 1251, 1252; UNGA, 'Preventing and Combating Corrupt Practices and the Transfer of Proceeds of Corruption, Facilitating Asset Recovery and Returning Such Assets to Legitimate Owners, in Particular to Countries of Origin, in Accordance with the United Nations Convention against Corruption' (5 February 2015) UN Doc A/RES/69/199 <https://digitallibrary.un.org/record/860676?ln=en> accessed 13 July 2020; UNGA, 'Report of the Special Rapporteur on the Right of Everyone to the Enjoyment of the Highest Attainable Standard of Physical and Mental Health' (14 July 2017) UN Doc A 72/137 para 2 and summary < https://undocs.org/A/72/137> accessed 13 July 2020.

[8]   Inter-American Commission on Human Rights, 'Resolution 1/18 Corruption and Human Rights' (preamble) <www.oas.org/en/iachr/decisions/pdf/Resolution-1-18-en.pdf> accessed 13 July 2020.

[9]   Transparency International, 'What is Corruption?' <www.transparency.org/what-is-corruption> accessed 13 July 2020; IACHR (n 8) 8.

[10]   Peters (n 7) 1254–55. Shah and Schacter assert that corruption can take three broad forms: grand, petty and state capture. Anwar Shah and Mark Schacter 'Combating Corruption: Look Before you Leap' (December 2004) Finance and Development <www.imf.org/external/pubs/ft/fandd/2004/12/pdf/shah.pdf> accessed 13 July 2020.

[11]   Mustafa Ünver and Julide Yalçınkaya Koyuncu, 'The Impact of Poverty on Corruption' (2016) 3 Journal of Economics Library 633.

purloin, embezzle or enrich those in public office at the expense of the state's wealth and its citizens' welfare.[12]

The literature generally emphasizes corruption in the public sector, even though there is also private sector-driven corruption. The narrow notion of understanding corruption as the 'abuse of public office for private gain' should be challenged. Such an understanding of corruption neglects the corrupt tendencies that are rampant in the private sphere. It is imperative to understand the importance and implications of viewing corruption as a broader phenomenon where non-state actors share a significant responsibility for engaging and aiding corruption.[13]

Globalization, liberalization and privatization have resulted in the erosion of the state's primary role in the provision of public goods and services that are central to many social rights.[14] Multinational corporations are very active in important sectors of national economies such as extractive industries, health, agriculture and water services.[15] Corruption can and does occur between firms and individuals or between actors in the private sector and the public sector, for example through state capture, where private entities 'capture' state institutions for their own benefit.[16] The difficulties around the precise definition of corruption should not detract from the magnitude of the socio-economic devastation caused by corrupt practices. Corrupt acts and practices have enormous costs for developing countries, including the diversion of resources that could have been utilized for the welfare of the populace.[17] Focusing on corrupt practices rather than on a definition or measurement will allow policymakers to better understand the spectrum of actors and practices and thus better address the scourge.[18]

II.   SOCIO-ECONOMIC IMPACT OF CORRUPTION

The adverse impact of corruption on development is becoming increasingly evident. Empirical studies point to how corruption lowers investment, which in turn has a debilitating effect on overall economic performance.[19] Most significantly, corruption 'undermines social welfare by redistributing a nation's wealth in a manner that generates tensions or exacerbates existing ones'.[20] Corruption also creates obstacles to economic and political reform, and if it contin-

---

[12]   Angela Barkhouse, Hugo Hoyland and Marc Limon, 'Corruption: A Human Rights Impact Assessment' (2018) 2, at: <www.universal-rights.org/wp-content/uploads/2018/04/Policy_report _corruption_LR.pdf> accessed 13 July 2020.

[13]   United Nations Economic Commission for Africa (UNECA), 'Measuring Corruption in Africa: The International Dimension Matters. African Governance Report IV' (2016) viii <https://archives.au .int/handle/123456789/1411> accessed 13 July 2020.

[14]   D. Shelton, 'Protecting Human Rights in a Globalised World' (2002) 2 Boston Coll. Int'l & Comp.L.J.Rev. 273.

[15]   Khulekani Moyo and Sandra Liebenberg, 'The Privatization of Water Services: The Quest for Enhanced Human Rights Accountability' (2015) 37 Hum.Rts.Q. 691, 701.

[16]   UNECA (n 13) c20.

[17]   ibid c23.

[18]   ibid c18.

[19]   Matthew Murray and Andrew Spalding, 'Freedom from Corruption as a Human Right' (January 2015) Brookings Institution <www.brookings.edu/research/papers/2015/01/27-freedom-corruption -human-right-murray-spalding> accessed 13 July 2020.

[20]   R. Sinder and W. Kidane, 'Combating Corruption through International Law in Africa: A Comparative Analysis' (2007) 40 Cornell Int'l L.J. 691.

ues unabated, can lead to political and social turmoil. For instance, in 2010, and after being extorted for bribes by local police, a vegetable vendor named Mohamed Bouazizi immolated himself in front of the Governor's office in the Tunisian town of Sidi Bouzid. Bouazizi's sacrifice of his life to protest his lack of power to curb petty corruption sparked the Arab revolution whose devastating effects are still being felt today.[21]

A.   Corruption and Poverty

The economics literature provides empirical support that corruption is intimately linked to the diversion of public funds, especially away from the provision of public services.[22] The literature on corruption further reveals that corruption has an impact on the composition of government expenditure, especially where political decisions are made to procure military equipment instead of building a school or investing in health care infrastructure to service a remote rural area.[23] In developing countries, corruption is particularly widespread in the procurement and delivery of public goods and services.[24] Evidence from research studies indicates that the water, sanitation and sewage sectors are particularly vulnerable to corrupt practices.[25] Studies focusing on social sectors such as the provision of healthcare, electricity and education have reached similar conclusions.[26] The groups most affected by corruption are the economically disadvantaged and less privileged members of society such as women, children, persons with disabilities, the elderly and indigenous people.[27] Research shows that vulnerable members of society more often fall victim to corruption than other societal groups, either by having to pay bribes for basic services or being forced to procure services from dysfunctional public services providers due to corruption.[28]

Justesen and Bjørnskov have developed a model which suggests that poor people are more likely to be victims of corrupt behaviour by street-level government bureaucrats as poor people often rely heavily on services provided by government departments and are therefore more likely to be met by demands to pay bribes in return for obtaining those services.[29] The

---

[21]   Spalding and Murray (n 19).

[22]   Vito Tanzi, 'Corruption around the World: Causes, Consequences, Scope and Cures' (1998) 45 IMF Staff Papers 559; Sanjeev Gupta, Luiz de Mello and Raju Sharan, 'Corruption and Military Spending' (2001) 17 Europ.J.Pol.Econ. 749.

[23]   Tanzi, ibid, 118.

[24]   Janelle Plummer and Piers Cross, 'Tackling Corruption in the Water and Sanitation Sector in Africa: Starting the Dialogue' in Edgardo Campos and Sanjay Pradhan (eds) *The Many Faces of Corruption* (ch 7 World Bank 222–223 2007) <http://documents.worldbank.org/curated/en/571831468315566390/pdf/399850REPLACEM101OFFICIAL0USE0ONLY1.pdf> accessed 13 July 2020.

[25]   UNECA (n 13) 24.

[26]   ibid.

[27]   UN Human Rights Council, 'Resolution adopted by the Human Rights Council on 23 June 2017' (14 July 2017) UN Doc A/HRC/RES/35/25 (preamble) (emphasising that 'marginalized groups are at particular risk of suffering from the adverse impact of corruption on the enjoyment of human rights'.)

[28]   Raoul Wallenberg Institute (n 5) 5.

[29]   Mogens K. Justesen and Christian Bjørnskov, 'Exploiting the Poor: Bureaucratic Corruption and Poverty in Africa' (June 2014) 58 World Development <www.sciencedirect.com/science/article/abs/pii/S0305750X14000035> accessed 13 July 2020.

results from Justesen and Bjørnskov's study thus suggests that the people who are worst off materially are also more likely to be victims of corruption.[30]

What is clear from the literature is that there is an indisputable link between endemic corruption and poverty.[31] Corruption causes a decline in personal income, intensifies income inequality and poverty and lowers expenditures on socio-economic goods such as water, education and health care, thereby disproportionately affecting the less privileged.[32]

B.   International Law's Response to the Nexus between Corruption and Human Rights

The increasing international and national recognition of rights that protect interests closely related to poverty such as the rights to adequate health care, sufficient and safe water and sanitation, education, housing, and food has begun to change the landscape in the fight against corruption. Such rights are deeply important to the struggles of poor and marginalized groups in society as they speak directly to the material conditions of their lives.[33]

The 1990s saw the adoption of global and regional treaties aimed at addressing and curbing the scourge of corruption. This was a reaction to the globalization of corruption, an acknowledgement that corruption had acquired transboundary elements. The Organisation of American States' Inter-American Convention Against Corruption, adopted in March 1996,[34] was the first binding international instrument aimed at combating corruption. It marked the beginning of an international legal regime to combat corruption.

Another important international development relating to corruption was the adoption of the Organisation for Economic Cooperation and Development (OECD) Convention on Combating Bribery of Foreign Public Officials in International Business Transactions in November 1997.[35] The primary goal was to eliminate the unfair competitive advantages obtained by companies paying bribes in foreign markets. In 2003, the then-Organisation of African Unity, now the African Union (AU), adopted the Convention on Preventing and Combating Corruption.[36] Foremost among its objectives is promoting development by preventing, detecting and punishing acts of corruption on the African continent.[37]

---

[30]   ibid.

[31]   Mohammad Salahuddin and others, 'Globalisation, Poverty and Corruption: Retarding Progress in South Africa' (2019) Development Southern Africa 3.

[32]   ibid at 5.

[33]   Sandra Liebenberg, *Socio-Economic Rights: Adjudication under a Transformative Constitution* (Juta Academic 2010) 45.

[34]   The Inter-American Convention Against Corruption entered into force on March 6, 1997.

[35]   Organisation for Economic Co-operation and Development (OECD), 'Convention on Combating Bribery of Foreign Public Officials in International Business Transactions' (adopted 21 November 1997, entered into force 15 February 1999) art 1, 3 <www.oecd.org/daf/anti-bribery/ConvCombatBribery_ENG.pdf> accessed 14 July 2020.

[36]   African Union, 'African Union Convention on Preventing and Combating Corruption' (adopted 1 July 2003, entered into force 5 August 2006) <https://au.int/sites/default/files/treaties/36382-treaty-0028_-_african_union_convention_on_preventing_and_combating_corruption_e.pdf> accessed 14 July 2020.

[37]   ibid art 2 (articulating the objectives of the AU Convention).

The key global anti-corruption instrument, the United Nations Convention Against Corruption (UNCAC) adopted in 2003,[38] went beyond previous international agreements to require parties to criminalize not only basic forms of corruption such as bribery and embezzlement of public funds but also trading in influence and concealment and laundering of the proceeds of corruption. It is however noteworthy that the UNCAC avoids taking a concrete position on the relationship between corruption and human rights. Such a pattern is also observable in the OECD Corruption Convention.[39]

Certain regional anti-corruption instruments, however, do acknowledge corruption's impact on human rights.[40] They frame corruption as a means by which rights are negatively affected but not as a direct human rights violation. Examples include Europe's Group of States Against Corruption's Criminal Law Convention on Corruption, and its separate Civil Law Convention on Corruption which provides that 'corruption threatens the rule of law, democracy and human rights'.[41] The AU Corruption Convention also has a similar approach, stating in its preamble that it is '[c]oncerned about the negative effects of corruption and impunity on the political, economic, social and cultural stability of African States and its devastating effects on the economic and social development of the African peoples'.[42] The adoption of such international instruments is no doubt an acknowledgement of corruption's impact on human rights and the importance of a collective approach to address the scourge.

III. CLOSING THE GAP

Despite the limitations in the normative framework, a growing number of legal scholars and activists have pushed for a human rights approach to addressing corruption.[43] Some scholars have sought to base their arguments in existing international human rights instruments. Other scholars have advocated for a human right to a corruption-free society.[44] One proposal is that the fight against corruption could be advanced by framing it under a 'freedom from corruption' banner.[45] This would add a new and powerful dimension to the fight against corruption.[46] Some scholars have argued that corruption could qualify as a crime against humanity.[47]

---

[38] The UNCAC entered into force on December 14, 2005.

[39] Convention on Combating Bribery (n 35) art 1,3.

[40] The Inter-American Convention Against Corruption and the Asia Pacific Economic Co-operation Course of Action on Fighting Corruption and Ensuring Transparency make no reference to human rights.

[41] Council of Europe, 'The Fight Against Corruption: A Priority for the Council of Europe' <www.coe.int/en/web/greco/about-greco/priority-for-the-coe> accessed 14 July 2020.

[42] African Union (n 36) preamble.

[43] Cecily Rose 'The Limitations of a Human Rights Approach to Corruption' (2016) 65 ICLQ 405, 407.

[44] Martine Boersma, *Corruption: A Violation of Human Rights and a Crime under International Law?* (Intersentia 2012); Mary Dowell-Jones, *Contextualising the International Covenant on Economic, Social and Cultural Rights: Assessing the Economic Deficit* 81–95 (Martinus Nijhoff, 2004); C Raj Kumar, *Corruption and Human Rights in India: Comparative Perspectives on Transparency and Good Governance* (OUP 2011).

[45] Murray & Spalding (n 19) 4.

[46] Raoul Wallenberg Institute (n 5) 8.

[47] Boersma (n 44); Ndiva Kofele-Kale, 'The Right to a Corruption-Free Society as an Individual and Collective Human Right: Elevating Official Corruption to a Crime under International Law' (2000) 34 International Lawyer 149.

Individual states as well as intergovernmental organizations such as the African Union, the Southern African Development Community, the UN, the European Union, the Organization of American States and civil society have started to focus on the relationship between corruption and human rights.

As is discussed further below, the thrust of the argument to infuse human rights in the fight against corruption is that corruption has identifiable victims of human rights violations. The victim-oriented approach stemming from a human rights-based approach in the fight against corruption would complement the existing approaches to curb corruption. It is important to note that all human rights are endangered where corruption is endemic, and thus an approach predicated on human rights should be part of the arsenal in the fight against corruption.[48] Despite the recognition that corruption undermines human rights values and norms, efforts to combat corruption in many countries do not include a human rights perspective – even though many of them have constitutions that contain bills or declarations of rights.

A critical legal question when drawing a nexus between corruption and human rights is whether corrupt acts could and should be regarded as human rights violations. The traditional approach is to view corruption as impacting the realization of human rights but not as itself constituting a human rights violation.[49] Yet attention is quickly shifting to cast a spotlight on the groups and individuals whose lives are negatively affected by rampant corruption.[50]

The turn towards a human rights approach to corruption, which began in the late 1990s, appears to be motivated by a need to focus greater attention on the victims rather than solely on the perpetrators of such corrupt acts. The perpetrators of corruption are often the targets of international and regional treaties as well as domestic criminal laws that address corruption.[51] Some commentators see human rights law as empowering for victims, though they have not elaborated on exactly how.[52] Others consider a human rights approach to be imperative given the inadequacies of criminal law treaties in curbing corruption.[53] Some see that a human rights lens 'provides a valuable normative framework' to address corruption.[54] The added value of elevating an issue to the level of a human right is that it establishes a universal norm that becomes more difficult to disregard. This approach also emphasizes the duties of states, and in some cases non-state actors, as well as the rights of those negatively impacted by corruption.

---

[48]   Anita Ramasastry, 'Is There a Right to Be Free from Corruption?' (2015) 49 University of California Davis Law Review 703–39; Julio Bacio Terracino, 'Hard Law Connections Between Corruption and Human Rights' (2007) <www.ichrp.org/files/papers/130/131_-_Julio_Bacio_Terracino_-_2007.pdf> accesssed 14 July 2020; Khulekani Moyo, 'An Analysis of the Impact of Corruption on the Realisation of the Right to Development' (2017) 33 SAJHR 193.

[49]   Some scholars and policymakers have even suggested elevating grand corruption to the level of an international crime. See Ramasastry (n 48) 706.

[50]   ibid 705; International Council on Human Rights Policy (n 60) 84.

[51]   Rose (n 43) 409. The human rights-based approach to corruption exemplifies a general recent trend – namely, the infusion of various sub-fields of international law with human-rights considerations, which is sometimes called the 'righting' of a regime. See Peters (n 7) 1278.

[52]   Kenneth Asamoa Acheampong, 'Combating Grand Corruption: The Potential Impact of a United Nations Convention on the Prevention and Punishment of the Crime of Economic Genocide' (1998) 7 Review of the African Commission on Human and Peoples' Rights 38, 48–49.

[53]   John Hatchard, 'Adopting a Human Rights Approach Towards Combating Corruption' in Martine Boersma and Hans Nelen (eds), *Corruption and Human Rights: Interdisciplinary Perspectives* (Intersentia, 2010) 7, 14–16.

[54]   UNGA UN Doc. A 72/137 (n 7) para 4.

In that regard, the human rights framework helps to give a voice to those who otherwise are unable to assert their rights.

Acknowledging and deploying a human rights lens in the fight against corruption would significantly strengthen the impetus to adopt preventative actions aimed at eradicating the scourge of corruption.[55] The human rights approach can explicitly highlight the deleterious effects of corruption, for example the rights of persons denied access to safe drinking water, affordable housing and adequate health care due to misuse of public funds through corrupt activities.[56] A human rights approach is also likely to engage state duties in the fight against corruption and the possibility of engaging state responsibility for failing to protect the rights of those exposed to the damaging effects of corruption.

There is abundant literature describing corruption as a human rights violation, but others argue that the literature fails to show in a systematic manner the ways in which corrupt practices violate human rights.[57] It follows that there is no persuasive theoretical framework that has been advanced that seeks to logically explain how corruption could be regarded as a human rights violation. The next section attempts to establish the linkage.

A.   Is Corruption a Human Rights Violation?

A crucial legal question is whether corruption can and should be conceptualized as a violation of human rights where individuals or groups are thrust into poverty and denied access to public goods to which they are entitled as a result of corrupt acts. As noted by Peters, the link between corruption and human rights is often characterized by weaker vocabulary in the practice of the UN bodies.[58] Rather than using 'violations' terminology, the UN Human Rights Council often refer to corruption's 'negative impact' on the enjoyment of human rights.[59] The same approach

---

[55]   Peters (n 7) 1254–60.

[56]   ibid 1276.

[57]   A human rights approach to addressing corruption has been questioned for its alleged 'lack of conceptual clarity', see Rose (n 43) 417. There are dissenting voices questioning the efficacy of a human rights approach to the challenge of corruption. Morag Goodwin and Kate Rose-Sender have articulated the most forceful critique of the human rights approach to corruption, arguing in part that 'anti-corruptionism', as they call it, has ideological roots in a neo-liberal approach to economic development that diverts attention from other, more nuanced explanations of development failures. Morag Goodwin and Kate Rose-Sender, 'Linking Corruption and Human Rights: An Unwelcome Addition to the Development Discourse' in Martine Boersma and Hans Nelen (eds), *Corruption and Human Rights: Interdisciplinary Perspectives* (Intersentia 2010) 223–29. Goodwin and Rose-Sender have also argued that human rights law do little to help us understand the phenomenon of corruption and its role in development failures and social inequality. Further, many scholars, jurists and anti-corruption activists associate the corruption-and-rights discourse with a Western neoliberal ideology of international development that can lead multilateral institutions to impose conditionality on assistance to developing countries, see Spalding (n 19) 3.

[58]   Anne Peters, 'Corruption and Human Rights' (2015) Basel Institute of Governance Working Paper Series 20 <www.baselgovernance.org/publications/working-paper-20-corruption-and-human-rights> accessed 14 July 2020; UN Human Rights Council, 'The Negative Impact of Corruption on the Enjoyment of Human Rights' (14 July 2017) UN Doc A/HRC/RES/35/25 <https://undocs.org/A/HRC/RES/35/25> accessed 14 July 2020; Inter-American Commission on Human Rights Resolution 1/18 (n 8) para b.

[59]   UN Human Rights Council UN Doc A/HRC/RES/35/25 (n 58); UN Human Rights Council, 'Final Report of the Human Rights Council Advisory Committee on the Issue of the Negative Impact of

can be recognized in a report by the most prominent non-governmental organizations in the fight against corruption, Transparency International and the International Council on Human Rights Policy.[60] The two organizations explicitly acknowledge that 'the cycle of corruption facilitates, perpetuates and institutionalises human rights violations' but fail to acknowledge corruption as constituting a direct human-rights violation.[61] The two organizations assert that programs geared to fight corruption might incorporate 'human rights principles and methods',[62] but not that on its own corruption constitutes a rights violation.

In its report on the Philippines, for example, the UN Committee on Economic, Social and Cultural Rights (CESCR) noted 'with concern that, despite the efforts undertaken by the State party to curb corruption, including the establishment of a number of anti-corruption bodies such as the anti-corruption court, this phenomenon continues to be widespread'.[63] What is missing in the Committee's approach is an explicit characterization of corruption as a direct human rights violation and recommendations to states on appropriate measures to address corruption's harmful effects from a human rights perspective. Likewise, in its concluding observations on the Democratic Republic of Congo (DRC)'s state report, the CESCR noted 'with concern that corruption remains endemic', and it called on the DRC to 'recognize the urgency of eradicating corruption within all government agencies'.[64] However it did not use any violations language or reference any specific provisions of the Covenant.

Likewise, no other treaty body has gone so far as to treat corruption as a human rights violation. The UN Committee on the Rights of the Child has gone further and discusses corruption in the context of 'insufficient budget allocations to children' and 'the diversion of resources', but makes no reference to any specific provisions of the Convention that could have been violated by acts of corruption.[65] The Subcommittee on the Prevention of Torture has also observed that high levels of corruption within a state correlate to more instances of torture and ill-treatment, for example in cases where inmates bribe prison officials in order to access basic necessities.[66] Corruption in the context of customs and immigration has also prompted comment by the Committee on the Protection of the Rights of All Migrant Workers

---

Corruption on the Enjoyment of Human Rights' (5 January 2015) UN Doc A/ HRC/28/73 para 21 <www .refworld.org/docid/550fef884.html> accessed 14 July 2020.

[60]   International Council on Human Rights Policy and Transparency International, 'Corruption and Human Rights: Making the Connection' (2009) vi <www.ichrp.org/files/reports/40/131_web.pdf> accessed 14 July 2020.

[61]   ibid 3.

[62]   ibid.

[63]   UN Committee on Economic, Social, and Cultural Rights (CESCR), 'Concluding Observations: Philippines' (1 December 2008) UN Doc E/C.12/PHL/CO/4 para 14 <https://undocs.org/E/C.12/PHL/CO/4> accessed 14 July 2020.

[64]   CESCR, 'Concluding Observations: Democratic Republic of Congo' (22 May 2006) UN Doc E/C.12/COD/CO/4 para 11(a) < https://undocs.org/E/C.12/COD/CO/4> accessed 14 July 2020.

[65]   UN Committee on the Rights of the Child (CRC), 'Concluding Observations: Thailand' (17 February 2012) UN Doc CRC/C/THA/CO/3-4 para 21 <https://undocs.org/CRC/C/THA/CO/3-4> accessed 14 July 2020; CRC, 'Concluding Observations: Nigeria' (21 June 2010) UN Doc CRC/C/NGA/CO/3-4 para 16 <https://undocs.org/CRC/C/NGA/CO/3-4> accessed 14 July 2020.

[66]   Committee Against Torture, 'Seventh Annual Report of the Subcommittee on Prevention of Torture and Other Cruel, Inhuman or Degrading Treatment or Punishment' (20 March 2014) UN Doc CAT/C/52/2 paras 72–100 < https://undocs.org/CAT/C/52/2> accessed 14 July 2020.

and Members of Their Families.[67] The Committee expressed concern about allegations that migrant workers and their families often become victims of corruption when leaving or entering Tajikistan.[68] What is still missing in the approach of the UN treaty bodies cited above is the explicit embrace and deployment of the 'violations' terminology to describe the impact of corruption on the rights of those affected by this vice.

Similarly, where domestic courts have considered the consequences of corruption, they have tended to characterize corrupt acts as 'undermining' human rights rather than giving corruption the imprimatur of a human rights violation. In the case of *Glenister* v *President of the Republic of South Africa and others*, the South African Constitutional Court stated that 'corruption has deleterious effects … on the full enjoyment of fundamental rights and freedoms. It disenables the state from respecting, protecting, promoting and fulfilling them as required by section 7(2) of the Constitution'.[69] The court avoided characterizing corruption as a human rights violation.

There has been however some voices within the UN special mechanisms system who have made the case for corruption to be viewed as a human rights violation. In a 2004 report to the then-UN Sub-Commission on Human Rights, for example, the former UN Special Rapporteur on corruption, Christy Mbonu, argued that 'corruption, whether systemic, endemic or petty, violates citizens' enjoyment of all the rights contained in all the international instruments'.[70] Despite the above isolated call from Mbonu, UN human rights bodies have not articulated corruption as a human rights violation.

In terms of the question of identifiable victims, victims of corruption are not as far removed from the corrupt acts as may be imagined. As noted by Barkhouse, children may die of preventable diseases where the diversion of public funds for the immunization of children ends up in private pockets, thereby denying vulnerable children of their right to access basic healthcare.[71] Children may be deprived of their right to access education where money earmarked for constructing schools is purloined into private pockets as a result of corruption.[72] Within the context of the right to water, corrupt acts could directly lead to the failure to enforce laws meant to protect water sources from pollution, thereby leading to a violation of individuals and communities' right of access to adequate and safe water.[73] There are also numerous other examples in which corruption can be considered as a direct violation of human rights, such as those pertaining to workplace safety. Corrupt acts can lead to the violations of workers' rights to adequate working conditions. An example is the case of the 2013 Rana Plaza garment

---

[67]   UNGA, 'International Convention on the Protection of the Rights of All Migrant Workers and Members of their Families' (adopted 18 December 1990, entered into force 1 July 2003) UN Doc A/RES/45/158.

[68]   UN Committee on the Protection of the Rights of All Migrant Workers and Members of Their Families, 'Concluding Observations: Tajikistan' (16 May 2012) UN Doc CMW/C/TJK/CO/1 para 21 <https://undocs.org/en/CMW/C/TJK/CO/1> accessed 14 July 2020.

[69]   *Glenister v President of the Republic of South Africa and Others* (2011) 3 SA 347 (CC) para 83.

[70]   UN Commission on Human Rights, 'Corruption and its Impact on the Full Enjoyment of Human Rights, in Particular, Economic, Social and Cultural Rights' (7 July 2004) UN Doc E/CN.4/Sub.2/2004/23 para 57 <https://undocs.org/en/E/CN.4/Sub.2/2004/23> accessed 14 July 2020.

[71]   Barkhouse (n 12) 2.

[72]   ibid.

[73]   Matthew Jenkins, 'The Impact of Corruption on Access to Safe Water and Sanitation for People Living in Poverty' (2017) 3 <www.u4.no/publications/the-impact-of-corruption-on-access-to-safe-water-and-sanitation-for-people-living-in-poverty> accessed 14 July 2020.

factory collapse in Bangladesh, considered to be the deadliest structural failure accident in modern human history, in which the building owner was able to get away with building regulations violations largely due to his political connections.[74]

To consider whether an act of corruption constitutes a human rights violation, it becomes pertinent to first provide clarity on what a human rights violation is.[75] A human rights violation can take the form of a commission or omission. Due to the state-centric nature of the human rights system, the violation involves conduct or omission by an organ of the state. This is where an organ of the state falls short of what is required by its human rights obligations, either under its domestic or international law.[76] In order to ascertain whether a right has been violated, it is important to examine the nature of state obligations that are imposed by the human right in question.[77] Thus, the failure by a state to comply with its obligation to respect, protect, promote and fulfil the human rights of persons to whom it is responsible for results in a violation of the latter's rights.[78] It follows that the use of the violations terminology should only be deployed when a duty on the state's part and a right on the claimant's part are clearly identifiable.[79] The following section demonstrates how corruption can meet that threshold.

B.   An Illustration of How Corruption Can Violate Social and Economic Rights

Human rights as elaborated by the relevant treaty bodies give rise to three kinds of duties, namely the duties to respect, protect and fulfil the protected rights. According to the Maastricht Guidelines on Violations of Economic, Social and Cultural Rights, states may violate the rights guaranteed under the ICESCR through 'the reduction or diversion of specific public expenditure, when such reduction or diversion results in the non-enjoyment of such rights and is not accompanied by adequate measures to ensure minimum subsistence rights for everyone'.[80] Importantly, a state may be responsible for any violations of economic, social and cultural rights that result from their failure to exercise the necessary regulation and control of the behaviour of non-state actors.[81]

This section focuses on the rights protected under the ICESCR because most, if not all are commonly affected by all forms of corruption, be it petty or grand corruption. These include the right to work, trade union rights, right to social security, rights to food, water, housing, the right to health, and the right to education. Such socio-economic rights protect interests important to human dignity[82] and are aimed at addressing the underlying conditions of poverty.

---

[74]   Sushma Raman and Mathias Risse, 'Corruption and Human Rights: The Linkages, the Challenges and Paths for Progress' (30 May 2018) <https://carrcenter.hks.harvard.edu/publications/corruption-symposium-report> accessed 14 July 2020.

[75]   International Council on Human Rights Policy (n 60) 7; Moyo (n 48).

[76]   International Council on Human Rights Policy (n 60) 7.

[77]   Peters (n 58) 9.

[78]   International Council on Human Rights Policy (n 60) 77.

[79]   Scott Leckie, 'Another Step towards Indivisibility: Identifying the Key Features of Violations of Economic, Social and Cultural Rights' (1998) 20 HRQ 81, 91.

[80]   'The Maastricht Guidelines on Violations of Economic, Social and Cultural Rights' (1998) 20 HRQ 691 para 14(g).

[81]   ibid 698.

[82]   Malcolm Langford, 'The Justiciability of Social Rights: From Practice to Theory' in Malcolm Langford, *Social Rights Jurisprudence: Emerging Trends in International and Comparative Law* 33 (Cambridge, 2008).

Article 2(1) of the ICESCR obligates a state party to take steps to the maximum of its available resources to progressively achieve the full realization of the protected rights by all appropriate means, including the adoption of legislative measures. Although the ICESCR arguably establishes a low standard for compliance with its provisions, the presence of rampant corruption and the lack of appropriate or successful steps by the state to curtail it constitute a breach of the obligations imposed under Article 2(1).[83]

States are generally obliged to adopt legislative and non-legislative measures. The CESCR has further clarified that the steps taken by the state must be 'deliberate, concrete and targeted'.[84] Of particular significance is that the steps to be taken must include the eradication of obstacles that impede the realization of socio-economic rights. Because corruption constitutes such an obstacle to the realization of socio-economic rights, states have a duty under the ICESCR to adopt effective anti-corruption measures with a view to stemming acts of corruption.[85]

C.   Obligations to Respect, Protect and Fulfil Rights and the Impact of Corruption

Treaty bodies, courts and other tribunals have elaborated on the duties generated by socio-economic rights as the duties to respect, protect and fulfil human rights.[86] The duty to respect is essentially a negative obligation to refrain from infringements on the enjoyment of rights. The state is therefore required to refrain from obstructing or hindering the enjoyment of rights by adopting policies related to privatization, trade or commercialization that negatively interfere with the enjoyment of socio-economic rights.[87] The duty to protect refers to protection from rights infringements emanating from third parties. The duty to protect enjoins the state to act positively to regulate, prevent and remedy rights abuses by non-state actors.[88]

The duty to fulfil requires the state to adopt appropriate legislative and other measures to ensure the full realization of the right in question.[89] The positive duty to fulfil is key to the enjoyment of socio-economic rights. The CESCR has subdivided this duty into the three subcategories: facilitate, provide and promote rights. This duty thus requires the state to adopt appropriate measures to enable the enjoyment of rights by especially marginalized groups,

---

[83]   Rose (n 43) 414.

[84]   CESCR, 'General Comment No. 3 The Nature of States Parties' Obligations' (14 December 1990) UN Doc E/1991/23 paras 2–3.

[85]   Peters (n 58) 17.

[86]   The CESCR has adopted the quartet of state obligations in elucidating the obligations imposed by the various provisions of the Covenant though the obligation to promote tends to be encapsulated under the obligation to fulfil. See CESCR, 'General Comment No. 14: The Right to the Highest Attainable Standard of Health (Art. 12)' (11 August 2000) UN Doc E/C.12/2000/4 <www.refworld.org/pdfid/4538838d0.pdf> accessed 14 July 2020.

[87]   Khulekani Moyo, 'Extraterritorial Application of the Right to Water under the African System for the Protection of Human Rights' in L Chenwi and T Bulto, *Extraterritorial Human Rights Obligations from an African Perspective* (Intersentia 2018) 170.

[88]   See M Aeyal, 'The Right to Health in an Era of Privatisation and Globalisation: National and International Perspectives' in D Barak-Erez and AM Gross, *Exploring Social Rights: Between Theory and Practice* (2007) 303.

[89]   Olivier de Schutter, *International Human Rights: Cases, Materials, Commentary* (Cambridge University Press 2014) 461.

who, through their own means would not be able to afford the social goods. This duty is generally subject to the 'availability of resources' and 'progressive realization' qualifications.[90]

Peters has argued that because 'affordability' (such as the affordability of essential medicine) is a component of the human right to fulfil the right to health, the fact that bribery in procurement processes may make medicines more expensive could be seen as a human rights violation.[91] In such a case, there is a clear and direct nexus between corruption and the violation of the right to health. The breach of duty is when the state fails to put in place effective anti-corruption measures or fails to investigate, prosecute or punish those implicated in acts of corruption. A state taking seriously its duty to protect economic, social, and cultural rights would lead to the strengthening of legislative, regulatory and other measures aimed at curbing corruption.

Within the context of the state's duty to fulfil, the CESCR has identified misallocation of public resources as resulting in the non-enjoyment of the right to health by individuals and groups thereby impeding their enjoyment of that right.[92] Where financial resources budgeted for the provision of social services are misallocated resulting in the denial of health care services, the state could be found to be violating its duty to fulfil the right to adequate health care services.[93]

The determination of rights claims should always be a contextual inquiry.[94] Likewise, the extent to which any dimension of the state duties enunciated above is emphasized depends on the type of interest before the court or adjudicating authority.

D.   Corruption and the Progressive Realisation of Socio-economic Rights

The ICESCR requires state parties to take steps 'with a view to achieving progressively the full realization' of the rights guaranteed in that instrument.[95] The requirement to realize the protected socio-economic rights in a progressive fashion is a pragmatic acknowledgement of the resource-dependant nature of state duties, and particularly with regard to positive duties imposed by socio-economic rights.[96] As discussed above, progressive realization of human rights also encompasses the dismantling of obstacles such as corruption which impedes access to socio-economic rights protected under the ICESCR.[97] In the watershed case of *Grootboom*, the South African Constitutional Court explained that progressive realization means that 'accessibility should be progressively facilitated: legal, administrative, operational and financial hurdles should be examined and, where possible, lowered over time'.[98]

---

[90]   General Comment No. 3 (n 84) para 9.

[91]   Peters (n 7) 1254–55.

[92]   General Comment No. 14 (n 86) para 52.

[93]   International Council on Human Rights Policy (n 60) 44.

[94]   Sandra Liebenberg, 'Socio-Economic Rights under South Africa's Transformative Constitution' in Malcolm Langford (ed), *Social Rights Jurisprudence: Emerging Trends in International and Comparative Law* (Cambridge University Press 2008) 75, 78.

[95]   International Covenant on Economic, Social and Cultural Rights (adopted 16 December 1966, entered into force 3 January 1976) UNGA Res 2200A (XXI) (ICESCR) art 2(1).

[96]   General Comment No. 14 (n 86) para 9.

[97]   Eibe Riedel, 'Economic, Social and Cultural Rights' in Asborn Eide, Catarina Krause and Allan Rosas (eds), *Economic, Social and Cultural Rights* (Martinus Nijhoff Publishers 2001) 129.

[98]   *Government of the Republic of South Africa and Others v Grootboom and Others* 2001 (1) SA 46 (CC) para 45.

The embezzlement and theft of public funds violates the duty to utilize the maximum available resources to realize socio-economic rights, because the state by default allows it to take priority over the provision of socio-economic goods to rights-holders.[99] When a public office holder from a state party embezzles public finds for private use, such conduct arguably represents a violation of the rights set forth in Articles 5–16 of the ICESCR because the state is not utilizing maximum available resources to realize rights. The embezzlement completely eliminates the possibility that such public funds are contributing to the realization of the rights guaranteed under the ICESCR. Such corrupt conduct in the abuse of public funds constitutes a retrogressive rather than progressive measure as a state has a duty to deploy the maximum available resources to realize rights.[100] Retrogressive measures thereby create a rebuttable presumption that a state party has violated obligations under the ICESCR, particularly the stricture to progressively realize the guaranteed rights. Although the CESCR does not provide any examples of 'deliberately retrogressive measures', corruption arguably falls within the scope retrogressive measures as it impedes the capacity of the populace to progressively realize and enjoy its covenant rights.[101]

What are the state's obligations under the ICESCR where it is faced with a climate of rampant corruption? In such circumstances, a state has a duty to protect those within its jurisdiction against any deleterious human rights impacts engendered by acts of corruption. This entails a duty to adopt effective regulatory or other measures to prevent, investigate or mitigate the violations that occur, to prosecute the perpetrators as appropriate, and to provide appropriate redress to the victims of corrupt practices.[102]

This chapter has illustrated that corruption has a negative effect on the level of resources available for the implementation of the state's human rights obligations. In most African countries, systemic corruption imperils the country's ability to meet its obligation to deploy the maximum extent of available resources to fulfil its socio-economic rights duties. The abuse of public funds meant for the provision of socio-economic goods, and the absence of effective legislation, institutions and policies to curb such corrupt activities, it is argued, constitutes a violation of socio-economic rights when these two factors are linked to the deprivation or infringement of rights by an individual or group. In this case, the incidence of corruption and its diversion of resources meant for the provision of public goods and services constitute an obstacle to the realization of rights. The heavy burden of corruption is often felt the most by the poor and marginalized groups in society. Strengthening of the rights-based approach to corruption gives international and domestic laws greater normative weight, heightening their importance in public policy.[103] Rights violations are 'more resistant to trade-offs', or, as the prominent legal philosopher Ronald Dworkin famously said, rights are 'trumps'.[104]

---

[99]   Peters (n 58) 17.
[100]   Rose (n 43) 415.
[101]   ibid 414.
[102]   Office of the United Nations High Commissioner for Human Rights, 'The Negative Impact of Corruption on the Enjoyment of Human Rights' <www.ohchr.org/Documents/HRBodies/HRCouncil/AdvisoryCom/Corruption/OHCHR.pdf> accessed 14 July 2020.
[103]   Spalding (n 19) 5.
[104]   Ronald Dworkin, *Taking Rights Seriously* (Harvard University Press 1978).

IV.   CONCLUSION

Debate continues to rage on regarding the relationship between corruption and human rights. The national legal frameworks for combating corruption in many countries do not include a human rights perspective – even though many of them have constitutions that contain bills or declarations of rights. This chapter sought to address the question on whether corruption can and should be conceptualized as a violation of human rights where individuals or groups living in poverty are denied access to public goods they are entitled to as a result of corrupt acts.

In response to the phenomenon of corruption, individual states as well as intergovernmental organizations and civil society have started to focus on the relationship between corruption and human rights. A critical legal question that this chapter sought to address when drawing a nexus between corruption and human rights is whether corrupt acts could and must be regarded as human rights violations.

This chapter demonstrated that the thrust of the argument to infuse human rights in the fight against corruption is that corruption has identifiable victims. The victim-oriented approach stemming from a human rights-based approach in the fight against corruption could complement the existing approaches to curb corruption. Importantly, elevating any issue to the level of a human right establishes a universal norm that becomes more difficult to disregard, emphasizes the duties of states, and in some cases non-state actors as well as the rights of those negatively impacted by corruption. This chapter demonstrated that corruption is not only an impediment to the realization of human rights but a human rights violation in its own right. Acknowledging and deploying a human rights lens in the fight against corruption would significantly strengthen the impetus to adopt preventative actions aimed at eradicating the scourge of corruption. Significantly, a human rights approach is also likely to engage state duties in the fight against corruption, and the possibility of a state engaging state responsibility should it neglect to protect the rights of those exposed to the deleterious effects of corruption. Thus, reframing corruption as a rights violation has important normative and utilitarian implications, and could improve enforcement at both national and international levels.

33. Conflict, poverty and human rights violations

Zafer Kizilkaya

Poverty and conflict are closely interrelated, with poverty increasing the likelihood of the use of violence, and armed conflict causing deteriorating economic conditions and increased poverty.[1] The same holds true for the nexus between human rights and conflict, with violations of civil, political, economic, social and cultural rights precipitating violence, and conflict denying individuals the fundamental rights to life, liberty and security.[2] Conflict's relationship with poverty or human rights violations is not only reciprocal and causal but also circular. Terms like 'conflict trap', 'protracted and intractable conflicts' and 'fragility trap' all refer to the conditions where violence repeats itself, human rights violations persist and reducing poverty becomes unattainable.

In the literature on conflict studies, one of the main scholarly ambitions is to identify the causes of conflict. Statistical research or case studies on individual conflicts try to shed light on the relevance and significance of several potential determinants. Both poverty and human rights abuses have been subject to several studies with a focus on their tendency to trigger violence.[3] Considering conflict as a significant strategic barrier to reducing poverty and ensuring the non-violability of basic human rights, this chapter seeks to shed light on the other side of the coin, namely the impact of conflict on poverty and human rights violations. Linked to the challenges of collecting data in conflict zones and to the academic priority that has been devoted to the theories of violence, the role of conflict in exacerbating poverty and augmenting human rights infringements has remained rather under researched.[4] This will be explored in the first section of the chapter.

---

[1] Jonathan Goodhand, 'Violent Conflict, Poverty, and Chronic Poverty' (2001) Chronic Poverty Research Centre Working Paper No. 6 <https://papers.ssrn.com/sol3/papers.cfm?abstract_id=1754535> accessed 15 July 2020; Zoe Marks, 'Poverty and Conflict' (2016) Governance and Social Development Resource Centre (GSDRC) Professional Development Reading Pack No. 52 <https://gsdrc.org/professional-dev/poverty-and-conflict/> accessed 15 July 2020.

[2] Ram Manikkalingam, 'Is There a Tension Between Human Rights and Conflict Resolution? A Conflict Resolution Perspective' (2006) Armed Groups Project, Latin American Research Centre, University of Calgary Working Paper 7 <https://reliefweb.int/sites/reliefweb.int/files/resources/6B68B8DC96B4D FFDC12574A600328FFB-agp_Jun2006.pdf> accessed 15 July 2020.

[3] Markus Mayer and Hartmut Fünfgeld, 'Poverty and Conflict: an Analytical Framework' in Jayadeva Uyangoda (ed), *Conflict, Conflict Resolution and Peace Building: An Introduction to Theories and Practice* (GTZ Sri Lanka and University of Colombo) pp. 150–170; Brigitte Rohwerder, 'The Impact of Conflict on Poverty' (2014) GSDRC Helpdesk Research Report 1118 <https://assets.publishing.service.gov.uk/media/57a089a5ed915d3cfd000364/hdq1118.pdf> accessed 15 July 2020; Oskar N.T. Thoms and James Ron, 'Do Human Rights Violations Cause Internal Conflict?' (2007) 29 HRQ 674–705; Kjersti Skarstad and Havard Strand, 'Do Human Rights Violations Increase the Risk of Civil War?' (2016) 19(2) International Area Studies Review pp 107–130.

[4] Paul Corral and others, *Fragility and Conflict: On the Front Lines of the Fight against Poverty* (World Bank 2020); Jolle Demmers, *Theories of Violent Conflict: An Introduction* (Routledge 2012).

The second section will provide a discussion of conflict resolution attempts with a focus on poverty and human rights violations. How does or should conflict resolution involve poverty reduction and respect of human rights in preventing, containing or ending violence? What are the challenges when incorporating the issues of poverty and human rights violations in peace-building efforts? By reviewing primarily the strategic documents published by UN bodies and specialized agencies, this section will explain and criticize some of the current global initiatives to protect countries from conflict and fragility traps. The chapter will conclude by emphasizing the need to develop conflict resolution policies that are informed by human rights and poverty reduction agendas.

I.   CONFLICT'S IMPACT ON POVERTY AND HUMAN RIGHTS VIOLATIONS

A.   The Conflict–Poverty Nexus

There is a consensus of opinion that conflict affects poverty, but how the impact reveals itself at the micro (household) level is not extensively researched.[5] The available literature focuses on the macro (society or state) level. Here, when violent conflict erupts, human capital erodes rapidly; physical infrastructure gets damaged or destroyed; supply chains get disrupted; and malfunctioning of critical financial institutions leads economic conditions to deteriorate.[6] A three-year period of major violence slows poverty reduction by 2.7 per cent and on average, conflict-affected countries experience a poverty rate 21 per cent higher than those without violent conflict.[7] When a civil war erupts, GDP per capita is estimated to contract by nearly 18 per cent in four years and even six years after the end of it, GDP per capita is predicted to be 15 per cent lower than what it would be without the conflict.[8] The economic damage is higher in intense conflict situations as witnessed in Syria, which lost 19 to 36 per cent of its productive capacity, producing '20–38 billion USD less in value added each year'.[9] In such a setting, high investments in the rebuilding process may provide steady economic growth in the long-term but this is not easy to accomplish.[10]

At the macro-level, the real difficulty is experienced in 'fragile and conflict-affected situations (FCS)' where it becomes more challenging to exit extreme poverty.[11] According to World Bank figures, by the end of 2020, 'more than half of the world's poor will be living in FCS'.[12] Nevertheless, there is no reliable data on poverty rates in FCS. For some regions, there is no

---

5   Rohwerder (n 3).
6   Phil De Imus, Gaëlle Pierre and Björn Rother, 'The Cost of Conflict' (2017) 54 Finance & Development No. 4.
7   World Bank, 'World Development Report 2011: Conflict, Security, and Development' 4–5 < https://openknowledge.worldbank.org/handle/10986/4389> accessed 15 July 2020.
8   Hannes Mueller and Julia Tobias, 'The Cost of Violence: Estimating the Economic Effect of Conflict' (2016) International Growth Center (IGC) Brief 2.
9   ibid 3.
10   Patricia Justino, 'Poverty Dynamics, Violent Conflict, and Convergence in Rwanda' (2013) 59(1) Review of Income and Wealth 67.
11   Corral (n 4) 1.
12   ibid 5.

data at all; for some others, the data is outdated and additionally, there is only very limited data on the displaced people whose numbers have globally increased significantly in the last couple of years.[13] Security has been a key concern in collecting data in conflict-affected regions but with the advancement in mobile technology and social media, this is becoming safer.[14] Moreover, even in hot conflict zones, mobility may become feasible when fighting stops for humanitarian or other reasons. Based on the institutional, public and private developments in data collection, scholars need to devote more time to contribute to the World Bank's efforts to better comprehend poverty in FCS economies.

Scholarly research is more critical at the micro-level where we have limited knowledge about the impact of conflict on the economic conditions of individuals and households. For example, are the poor more vulnerable and do they get poorer when parties resort to arms? Likewise, more empirical research is needed to understand how people behave in the informal economies that emerge in war settings. Questions include, who benefits from the informal markets? And how do households sustain their lives where governance is provided by multiple actors?

War brings suffering to all layers of society but whether the negative economic, health and nutritional impacts are borne most by the poor is not obvious. For some, during times of conflict, chronically poor people are the most affected because violence destroys the social network they rely on to sustain their life.[15] The capacity of the state or the non-state actor that traditionally provides basic service to the poor is likely to decline in war, or in the best cases would be limited to some parts of the country. Furthermore, delivering humanitarian assistance might prove to be extremely difficult, requiring the full cooperation of all conflicting sides. In the post-conflict period, the needs of the poor can be ignored if a security-based approach prioritizes the demobilization and reintegration of ex-combatants, neglecting the most vulnerable, namely the children, women and the elderly.[16] The re-construction phase can also distinguish the loyals from the non-loyals, offer lucrative gains to a selected elite who undertake ostentatious mega-projects and give precedence to the consolidation of post-conflict power rather than addressing the demands of the poor people.[17]

There may also be cases where wealthier households suffer more from violence. If a certain geography is rich with natural resources or if it has a favorable geographic location which is coveted by the armed factions, the property of richer people can also be attacked.[18] In such circumstances, poorer households can even gain advantage depending on their connections with the militarily strong armed groups.[19] Here, 'the level of exposure to violence' is a critical determinant of the impact of conflict on welfare at the household level. The other significant

---

[13]   ibid 8.
[14]   Philip Verwimp, Patricia Justino and Tilman Brück, 'The Microeconomics of Violent Conflict' (2019) 141 Journal of Development Economics.
[15]   Tony Addison and others, 'Fragile States, Conflict and Chronic Poverty' (2010) Chronic Poverty Research Centre Policy Brief No. 24 3 <www.chronicpoverty.org/uploads/publication_files/PB%2024 .pdf> accessed 15 July 2020.
[16]   ibid 4.
[17]   International Crisis Group (ICG), 'Ways out of Europe's Syria Reconstruction Conundrum' (2019) Middle East Report N.209.
[18]   Patricia Justino, 'Poverty and Violent Conflict: A Micro-Level Perspective on the Causes and Duration of Warfare' (2009) 46 Journal of Peace Research pp. 315–333.
[19]   Justino (n 10).

factor is the adaptability to economic shocks which hinges on initial asset endowments, land holdings, incomes and the education level of the individuals inside the household.[20]

When violence erupts, free markets are under threat and those with arms can dominate the business and the trade. Warlordism and abuses of power are key drivers of poverty in long-running conflicts in countries like Somalia and Afghanistan.[21] Food aids and development benefits are distributed to people who have connections with those holding guns and the poor risk being neglected.[22] Despite these challenges, economic life continues in war settings but becomes increasingly informal. In such settings, households develop alternative strategies to thrive. They move to safer areas, they change economic activities and they collaborate with different actors who provide governance or collect taxes.[23] One recent example has been the civil war in Syria where most aspects of life have continued under the rule of different actors including the Syrian regime and various opposition groups.

Measuring the economic effects of conflict at the micro-level and exploring the informality in war zones is not painless. Nevertheless, as Verwimp, Justino and Brück contend, it is a myth to consider conflict zones 'out of reach for researchers' to carry out rigorous research.[24] In an exemplary study on this subject, Merciery, Ngenzebuke and Verwimp tracked households in Burundi that witnessed a civil war between 1993 to 2005.[25] They conducted nationwide surveys in 1998, 2007 and 2012 in order to understand the long-term impact of resorting to violence. Their findings reveal a correlation between exposure to violence and lower consumption at household level, with those in high-intensity conflict zones suffering more from deprivation even years after the conflict.[26] More empirical research is needed to shed better light on the household dynamics in different conflict zones which will prove crucial to facilitate post-conflict reconstruction and peacebuilding.

B.   The Conflict–Human Rights Nexus

Human rights and conflict are closely interrelated but scholarly studies investigating the nexus between them is rather limited and have mostly been on the role of human rights abuses in creating grievances and triggering violence.[27] One key reason is the divergent focus of political scientists and lawyers when dealing with the use of violence. The study of conflict and the mechanisms to transcend conflict are frequently analyzed by political scientists whereas human rights violations are more typically investigated and defended by lawyers and activists.[28] Likewise, in practice, despite sharing the same goals of ending violence and minimizing

---

[20]   ibid 87–88.
[21]   Marten Kimberly, 'Warlordism in Comparative Perspective' (2006) 31 (3) International Security 41–73; United Nations Office of the High Commissioner for Human Rights (OHCHR), 'Human Rights Dimension of Poverty in Afghanistan' (March 2010) <www.refworld.org/pdfid/4bbc313d2.pdf> accessed 16 July 2020.
[22]   ibid 5.
[23]   Verwimp (n 14) 2.
[24]   ibid.
[25]   Marion Merciery, Rama Lionel Ngenzebuke and Philip Verwimp, 'Violence Exposure and Deprivation: Evidence from the Burundi Civil War' (2017) Université Paris-Dauphine DIAL (Développement, Institutions et Mondialisation) Working Papers DT/2017/14.
[26]   ibid 35–37.
[27]   Skarstad and Strand (n 3).
[28]   Thoms and Ron (n 3).

the costs of armed conflict, human right activists and conflict resolution practitioners differ in their approach when responding to conflict. While the former group concentrates on collecting and verifying data on human rights violations, the latter group is more concerned with the conduct of mediation in order to reach a negotiated settlement.[29]

War brings out the worst in human behavior, and when tensions escalate into violent conflict, defenseless populations are denied their most fundamental 'right to life and physical safety'.[30] Among the most vulnerable are the women, children, internally displaced people (IDP), refugees and Indigenous People.[31] In several conflict zones today, women experience sexual violence and trafficking; children are exposed to the risks of abduction, sexual abuse or recruitment as child soldiers; and IDPs, refugees and Indigenous People are subject to grave human rights abuses such as forced displacement, denial of return, detention, torture, sexual assault and lack of access to food, water and health.[32]

To protect the rights of individuals and the most vulnerable once a conflict breaks out, there are two 'distinct but complementary bodies of law'.[33] The rules of International Humanitarian Law (IHL) aim at limiting the negative effects of armed conflict by restraining the means and methods used by the warring sides. It is only applicable during armed conflict, as distinguished from the International Human Rights Law (IHRL), which applies to both peace and war conditions.[34] IHL makes a distinction between the civilians and the combatants. It primarily seeks to protect civilians who do not directly take part in hostilities yet endure the worst atrocities. In contrast, the civilian/combatant distinction is unknown to IHRL, which looks at all individuals' rights.[35]

One key characteristic of modern warfare is the involvement of multiple non-state armed groups (NSAGs). This creates a particular challenge for the implementation of IHRL which lays down obligations for states to respect, protect and fulfill fundamental human rights.[36] Formally, non-state armed groups cannot become parties to international human rights treaties; however, if they have a de facto control over a territory, they are obligated to comply with IHRL and respect human rights norms.[37] Accordingly, in intra-state conflicts, the UN investigates and reports on the human rights violations of the state actors as well as on the abuses committed by the non-state ones.

---

[29]   Ellen Lutz, Eileen Babbitt and Hurst Hannum, 'Human Rights and Conflict Resolution from the Practitioners' Perspectives' (2011) 27 Fletcher Forum of World Affairs 173.

[30]   Michelle Maiese 'Human Rights Violations' (Beyond Intractability, July 2003).

[31]   Carmen Márquez Carrasco and others, 'Human Rights Violations in Conflict Settings' (2014) European Commission Large-Scale FP7 Collaborative Project Work Package No. 10 – Deliverable No. 1 <www.fp7-frame.eu/wp-content/uploads/2016/08/08-Deliverable-10.1.pdf> accessed 18 July 2020.

[32]   ibid.

[33]   International Committee of the Red Cross (ICRC), 'IHL and Human Rights Law' (29 November 2010)   <www.icrc.org/en/doc/war-and-law/ihl-other-legal-regmies/ihl-human-rights/overview-ihl-and-human-rights.htm> accessed 16 July 2020.

[34]   OHCHR, 'International Legal Protection of Human Rights in Armed Conflict' (2011) 5 <www.ohchr.org/Documents/Publications/HR_in_armed_conflict.pdf> accessed 16 July 2020.

[35]   ibid 21.

[36]   United Nations, 'The Foundation of International Human Rights Law' <www.un.org/en/sections/universal-declaration/foundation-international-human-rights-law/index.html> accessed 16 July 2020.

[37]   UN Human Rights Council, 'They have Erased the Dreams of my Children: Children's Rights in the Syrian Arab Republic' (16 January 2020) Conference Room Paper of the Independent International Commission of Inquiry on the Syrian Arab Republic.

Another contemporary challenge in ensuring the proper application of human rights is the increased use of digital technologies in war zones and the changing character of warfare. Advances in artificial intelligence, machine learning, cyber warfare, armed drones technology, genetic engineering and biological weapons create destruction that is quite different from the more direct and visible damage brought by the use of conventional weapons. In cyber space, it is trickier to measure the gradual and indirect adverse consequences for people's right to personal, social and economic security. More scholarly attention is necessary to explore the implications of the use of digital warfare on poverty and human rights violations.[38]

What can help research on the monitoring of human rights conditions in contemporary settings is the multitude of actors that investigate human rights abuses. In addition to official UN entities, and primarily the Office of the High Commissioner for Human Rights (OHCHR), government agencies, non-governmental organizations and networks established by opposition groups track and publish reports on human rights violations happening in different conflict regions. For instance, prominent international organizations, such as Human Rights Watch (HRW) and Amnesty International have worked and reported extensively on the Syrian civil war, one of the worst crises of our time.[39] On the same conflict, the Syrian Network for Human Rights (SNHR), a non-profit organization, was founded in June 2011 and has published several monthly and special reports.[40] Establishment of similar networks provides the benefit of access to real-time, detailed and valuable data on human rights violations. Nevertheless, their objectivity is often questionable, and they may be subject to criticism in terms of their failure to report on violations committed by certain actors. For example, SNHR is considered pro-opposition and is seen as giving less priority to non-regime abuses of human rights.[41]

A bad human rights record for a country can be a sign of future conflict if major inequalities lead to grievances – a key driver of conflict from a human rights perspective.[42] Nevertheless, as witnessed clearly in the Syrian conflict, things get significantly worse once violence erupts and weapons are involved. In this war-torn country, schools, medical facilities, residential areas, markets, agricultural facilities, mosques and churches have been intentionally attacked, denying the Syrian people their basic right to education, health, housing, an adequate standard of living, freedom of thought, belief and religion.[43] Around 13 million people were displaced: 6.7 million refugees (approximately 2.5 million children) and 6.2 million internally displaced (around 2.6 million children).[44] The failure in conflict prevention and containment, and the

---

[38]   For a recent attempt on addressing the application of IHRL in modern warfare, see Dapo Akande and others, *Human Rights and 21st Century Challenges: Poverty, Conflict, and the Environment* (OUP 2020).

[39]   Amnesty International, 'Syria: Country Overview', at: <www.amnesty.org/en/countries/middle-east-and-north-africa/syria/> accessed 16 July 2020; Human Rights Watch, 'Syria' (2020) <www.hrw.org/middle-east/n-africa/syria> accessed 16 July 2020.

[40]   Syria Network for Human Rights (SNHR) <http://sn4hr.org/> accessed 16 July 2020.

[41]   Max Blumenthal, 'Behind the Syrian Network for Human Rights: How an Opposition Front Group Became Western Media's Go-to monitor' (14 June 2019) Global Research <www.globalresearch.ca/behind-syrian-network-human-rights-how-opposition-front-group-became-western-medias-go-to-monitor/5681631> accessed 16 July 2020.

[42]   Jo Crichton and others, 'Human Rights: Topic Guide' (2015) <https://gsdrc.org/wp-content/uploads/2015/07/rights.pdf> accessed 16 July 2020.

[43]   UN Human Rights Council, 'Report of the Independent International Commission of Inquiry on the Syrian Arab Republic' (31 January 2019) UN Doc A/HRC/40/70.

[44]   They Have Erased the Dreams of my Children (n 37).

serious obstacles faced in the mediation efforts, have aggravated the dire economic and human-itarian situation in Syria, demonstrating the importance of working on the conflict-poverty and conflict-human rights nexuses in order to transcend incompatibilities and resolve conflicts.

II.   POVERTY, HUMAN RIGHTS VIOLATIONS AND CONFLICT RESOLUTION

The field of *Peace and Conflict Studies* deals primarily with two questions: 'Why do people fight?' and 'how can they be friends again?' (or at least end violence). The first question tries to understand what people fight over while the second one aims at developing mechanisms to dissolve the incompatibilities that ignite violence.[45] Theoretical explanations list discrimina-tion, needs, grievances and inequalities as some of the reasons behind the use of violent means to resolve conflicts. As mentioned in the first section, poverty and human rights conditions are adequately researched with their causal impacts on conflict formation. Concerning the second key question of conflict resolution, there has been an increased interest in the attempts to incor-porate poverty and human rights dynamics in developing mechanisms to transcend conflict. The UN and World Bank are leading the efforts on this while there is still room for scholarly research to address the gaps and contribute to the global efforts to end poverty, fragility, con-flict and violence which are all linked.[46]

In its World Development Report 2011, the World Bank underlined the fact that preventing or reducing violence can only be achieved by investing in: (1) development – creating jobs to alleviate poverty; (2) justice – promoting equity and inclusion, ensuring equitable access to state's resources and closing gender gaps; and (3) security – civilian oversight of the security forces, preventing and responding to gender-based violence (GBV) and increased commitment of military to accountability and human rights.[47] A particular challenge is to address the situa-tions of fragility across the world which are linked to 'poor governance and weak institutions' in certain countries.[48]

According to World Bank Group (WBG) forecasts, by 2030, two-thirds of world's poor population will be living in countries which are suffering from challenges associated with fra-gility, conflict and violence (FCV).[49] Ending extreme poverty and ensuring shared prosperity will not be possible unless required actions are taken to address FCV risks. In a joint report published in 2018, the UN and WBG emphasized the need to prevent and mitigate the risks of FCV across the full spectrum of violent conflict and fragility.[50] This involves preventing the outbreak of violence by strengthening resilience in fragile countries; being engaged in conflict situations to preserve institutional capacity; supporting countries in post-conflict

---

[45]   Peter Wallensteen, *Understanding Conflict Resolution* (Sage Fifth Edition 2019).
[46]   UN and the World Bank Group (WBG), 'Pathways for Peace: Inclusive Approaches to Preventing Violent Conflict' (2018) <https://openknowledge.worldbank.org/handle/10986/28337> accessed 16 July 2020; WBG, 'Strategy for Fragility, Conflict, and Violence 2020–2025' (26 February 2020) < www .worldbank.org/en/topic/fragilityconflictviolence/publication/world-bank-group-strategy-for-fragility -conflict-and-violence-2020-2025> accessed 16 July 2020.
[47]   Conflict, Security and Development (n 7) pp. 148–164.
[48]   Corral (n 4) 55.
[49]   ibid 18.
[50]   UN and WBG (n 46) 1–7.

reconstruction; and mitigating the negative spillover impacts of FCV such as forced migration, environmental degradation and food insecurity.[51]

'Resilience' is a popular term that has been used in several recent international documents. In 2015, the UN committed to 17 Sustainable Development Goals (SDGs) for 2030 and it specified eradicating poverty as the primary objective, which entails 'build[ing] the resilience of the poor and those in vulnerable situations and reduce their exposure and vulnerability to … shocks and disasters'.[52] Likewise, in its Global Strategy document of 2016, the EU identified investing in the 'resilience of states and societies' to its east and south as a primary policy objective.[53] Rather than an external and interventionist understanding of development aid, conflict prevention, peacemaking or peace building, resilience-driven approaches prioritize the empowerment of internal capacities and capabilities in fragile conditions.[54] This is definitely a good step considering the unpopularity of external interventions that aimed at regime change or democracy building. Nevertheless, caution is needed in determining the context of fragility and in identifying the societies or states whose resilience is at stake.

The indicators used for defining fragility differ from organization to organization. The World Bank's list of criteria that characterize fragility has also witnessed several changes.[55] There are some common indicators such as poor governance and weak institutions, but they are not easily explained by quantifiable variables. More research is needed to enhance shared learning on the markers of fragility. Moreover, it would be wrong to assume FCV to be an exclusive problem for low-income and lower-middle income countries (LICs and LMICs). According to World Bank, most of today's conflicts are taking place in middle-income countries (MICs) and key underlying reasons are political and economic inequalities, social injustices and more importantly, badness in governance.[56] When governance is not accountable, transparent and responsive to the needs of the citizens, it becomes difficult to provide sustainable human development and to build shared prosperity.

The pledge to eradicate poverty and to 'leave no one behind' as promised by 193 UN member states in the *2030 Agenda for Sustainable Development* and the ambitions to strengthen state and social resilience in fragile settings – such as the one mentioned by the EU in its *2016 Global Strategy*, taken together, require a human-rights based approach.[57] Citizens should be provided guarantees to enjoy their political and civil rights while having equal access to social, economic and cultural rights. Building state resilience without empowering individuals and overlooking human rights violations in the name of security or stability risks emboldening authoritarian regimes and would fail to help societies to exit fragility.[58] Addressing minority

---

[51]   Strategy for Fragility, Conflict, and Violence (n 46) 13.

[52]   UNGA, 'Transforming Our World: The 2030 Agenda For Sustainable Development' (21 October 2015) UN Doc A/Res/70/1.

[53]   European Union External Action, 'A Global Strategy for the European Union's Foreign And Security Policy' (15 December 2016) 9 <http://eeas.europa.eu/archives/docs/top_stories/pdf/eugs_review_web.pdf> accessed 16 July 2020.

[54]   David Chandler, 'Re-thinking the Conflict-Poverty Nexus: From Securitizing Intervention to Resilience' (2015) 4(1) Stability: International Journal of Security & Development 1–14.

[55]   Corral (n 4) 55.

[56]   Strategy for Fragility, Conflict, and Violence (n 46) 5–8.

[57]   Human Rights and Democracy Network (HRDN), 'Rights-based Approach to Resilience: HRDN's input to the EEAS and Commission Joint Communication on Resilience' (April 2017) <www.fidh.org/IMG/pdf/a-rights-based-approach-to-resilience.pdf> accessed 16 July 2020.

[58]   ibid.

rights or group grievances may still be relevant in establishing peace in conflict-affected regions. Nevertheless, frameworks for peace agreements should secure the rights of individuals as individuals rather than guaranteeing rights linked to certain group identities.

The identity dimension is particularly relevant for current conflicts which are primarily happening in the Middle East and Africa. Violence in this broad geography is linked to group grievances that are associated with ethnic, religious or sectarian identities of marginalized communities. When resolving conflicts in such settings, one objective has been to ensure governance by fair representation of various groups. For instance, following the Taif agreement of 1989, which ended the 15-year long civil war in Lebanon, critical posts in the Lebanese parliament and government were distributed among the main confessional communities in the country. The agreement defined 'abolishing political sectarianism' as a key national objective.[59] Nevertheless, more than thirty years after the end of the civil war, this has not been achieved. Confessionalism, the practice of distributing power among confessional groups, has ended the violence but did not accomplish restraining the political upheaval. The country could not end the sectarian politics and intercommunal tensions still persist.

Similar tensions exist in Iraq and Syria between the Kurds, Sunnis, Shias, Druzes and several other ethnic and sectarian groups. Disconnecting or separating the communitarian identity dimension in the analysis of conflict dynamics or in the resolution of conflicts is not a pragmatic step to take. Intercommunal strife has a long history in the region. Nevertheless, elevating the human rights dimension is necessary. People deserve fair and equal treatment as described in international human rights norms and legislation. They should perceive the fulfillment of their rights as a natural consequence of being a human being, rather than possessing a historically marginalized identity. Accordingly, the field of conflict resolution requires an increased involvement of human rights norms in building and sustaining peace.

A.   Connecting Conflict Resolution and Human-rights Norms: Peace, Justice and Amnesties

There are several benefits of integrating human rights into different aspects of conflict resolution. In peacemaking, human rights norms can establish certain standards for conflicting sides to agree on. This could be, for instance, on developing mechanisms to ensure minority rights that can be realized through power-sharing arrangements and anti-discrimination laws.[60] In negotiations, human rights advocates can counter the weight of spoilers and radicals by standing up for universal values, which can then empower the position of moderates who seek accommodation. The universality of human rights standards can also help mediators to advance neutral arguments when negotiations get stuck on certain interests. Additionally, in settling long-lasting conflicts, ensuring an effective protection of human rights will contribute to the establishment of justice and this will offer an opportunity to make peace more durable.[61]

---

[59]   The Taif Agreement (4 November 1989) <www.un.int/lebanon/sites/www.un.int/files/Lebanon/the_taif_agreement_english_version_.pdf> accessed 16 July 2020.
[60]   Manikkalingam (n 2) 2.
[61]   ibid 2–3.

On the justice-peace nexus, over time, there has been a global shift from 'peace or justice' towards a mentality that aims to achieve 'peace with justice'.[62] This corresponds to the move from policies that seek to establish negative peace – absence of violence, to positive peace – a constructive and sustainable peace that restores relations, alleviates grievances and creates better economic and social outcomes.[63] While there are still certain tensions between the human rights and conflict resolution practitioners, there is an increasing demand to balance the facilitative role of conflict resolution professionals with the advocacy role of human rights activists.[64] One big challenge is to decide on the timing and extent of amnesties.

Amnesties can help end civil wars. They may facilitate the efforts to reach a negotiated settlement as was the case in the peace agreement signed between the conflicting parties in Sierra Leone in 1999. The agreement granted amnesty for perpetrators of severe human rights abuses but had to be reworked due to strong criticism from the international community.[65] Amnesty International declared there was a 'peace agreement but no justice'.[66] There are other cases in which providing amnesties did not stop violence, such as the one granted to a fighting group – the National Congress for the Defence of the People (CNDP) – in the Democratic Republic of Congo in 1999.[67] Likewise, the 2012 amnesty provided to Yemen's President Ali Abdullah Saleh and his family enabled him to operate freely afterwards by fomenting unrest and organizing attacks against the running government.[68]

Analyzing the amnesties offered in intra-state conflicts after 1946, Geoff Dancy listed two main conditions for amnesties to be more effective: to be granted after conflict termination and to be embedded in peace agreements.[69] He also found that providing immunity for serious human rights violations has no observable positive impact on resolving incompatibilities and does not prevent conflict recurrence.[70] The UN position on this subject is clear: no amnesty provision in peace agreements for 'genocide, war crimes, crimes against humanity and gross violations of human rights'.[71] Blanket amnesties are ruled out and the establishment of the International Criminal Court (ICC) has added a global mechanism to prosecute grave violators of human rights. Nevertheless, without guaranteeing security to former leaders, officers and soldiers, peacemaking can also prove difficult. This requires innovative ways to handle human

---

[62]   Michelle Parlevliet, 'Rethinking Conflict Transformation from a Human Rights Perspective' (September 2009) Berghof Research Center for Constructive Conflict Management 4.

[63]   Institute for Economics and Peace, 'Positive Peace: The Lens to Achieve the Sustaining Peace Agenda' (2007) 54 <http://visionofhumanity.org/app/uploads/2017/10/Positive-Peace-Report-2017 .pdf> accessed 16 July 2020.

[64]   Parlevliet (n 62) 17.

[65]   Wallensteen (n 45) 144.

[66]   Amnesty International, 'Sierra Leone: A Peace Agreement But No Justice' (1999) AFR 51/007/1999.

[67]   Geoff Dancy, 'Deals with the Devil? Conflict Amnesties, Civil War, and Sustainable Peace' (2018) 72(02) International Organization 387–421.

[68]   Jamison Boley and others, 'A Conflict Overlooked: Yemen in Crisis' (2017) <https://reliefweb .int/sites/reliefweb.int/files/resources/1540_0.pdf> accessed 16 July 2020.

[69]   Dancy (n 67) 1.

[70]   ibid 31.

[71]   UN Security Council, 'The Rule of Law and Transitional Justice in Conflict and Post-conflict Societies' (23 August 2004) UN Doc S/2004/616, para 10.

rights abuses in order to achieve peace with justice. Truth and reconciliation commissions have been one of the mechanisms for dealing with past violations.[72]

The goal of a truth and reconciliation committee or a commission is to hold public hearings about past abuses of human rights where perpetrators and violators are given the floor to present their arguments and to defend their positions.[73] The objective is to give precedence to restorative justice rather than merely seeking retribution. A well-known implementation has been in South Africa which established its 'Truth and Reconciliation Commission' in 1995 to uncover the violations of human rights violations that happened during the 'apartheid' period in the country.[74] It provided a platform for the victims to tell their experiences and for the perpetrators to share their account of the past incidents and to request amnesty. Despite several challenges in the practice of holding hearings and implementing the decisions, the commission in South Africa granted around 1,500 amnesties for the perpetrators who cooperated and confessed to their past crimes. It became a platform to reconcile old grievances by disclosing the killings and tortures of the past so that they do not happen in the future.[75]

In addition to reconciliation, human rights issues also have an impact on the reconstruction of war-torn countries. A recent example has been the debate circulating around rebuilding Syria. With signs of the Syrian regime gaining control in large parts of the country, the international community and the European Union are discussing whether to contribute and fund the reconstruction efforts. The US and the EU imposed several sanctions on the Syrian government due to repression of civilians and the gross human violations committed by the regime and its affiliates.[76] The Western position to lift sanctions is tied to the condition of a 'genuine progress toward a political transition' and respect for fundamental human rights.[77] Nevertheless this does not appear to be realizable in the short to medium term. A more flexible and an incremental approach is necessary to alleviate human suffering. Funding small-scale rehabilitation projects can be an option if this is conditioned on the Syrian regime's willingness to stop certain human rights violations such as arbitrary arrest, torture and enforced military recruitment.[78]

---

[72] Wallensteen (n 45) 157.

[73] Bonny Ibhawoh, 'Do Truth and Reconciliation Commissions Heal Divided Nations?' (The Conversation 2019), at: <https://theconversation.com/do-truth-and-reconciliation-commissions-heal-divided-nations-109925> accessed 16 July 2020.

[74] Desmond Tutu, 'Truth and Reconciliation Commission, South Africa' (Encyclopædia Britannica 2019) <www.britannica.com/topic/Truth-and-Reconciliation-Commission-South-Africa/Challenges-and-limitations> accessed 16 July 2020.

[75] ibid.

[76] U.S. Department of the Treasury, 'Syria Sanctions' <www.treasury.gov/resource-center/sanctions/programs/pages/syria.aspx> accessed 16 July 2020; Council of the European Union, 'Syria: EU Renews Sanctions Against the Regime by One Year' (17 May 2019) <www.consilium.europa.eu/en/press/press-releases/2019/05/17/syria-eu-renews-sanctions-against-the-regime-by-one-year/> accessed 16 July 2020.

[77] International Crisis Group, 'Ways Out of Europe's Syria Reconstruction Conundrum' (25 November 2019) Middle East Report N.209. <https://d2071andvip0wj.cloudfront.net/209-syria-reconstruction_1.pdf> accessed 16 July 2020.

[78] ibid 28.

B.   Early Warning and Conflict Prevention

Human rights issues come into play at different stages of the conflict cycle and are associated with different forms of conflict resolution. The same holds true for poverty. Recent global emphasis, however, is placed on conflict prevention. In his first formal address to the UN Security Council as a Secretary General, António Guterres said prevention is 'not merely a priority, but the priority'.[79] In the joint report published with the World Bank Group in 2018 – *Pathways for Peace: Inclusive Approaches to Preventing Violent Conflict*, the UN stressed the need for prevention to permeate all activities of the organization.[80] Growth, poverty reduction, development of inclusive policies and prevention of human rights abuses are mentioned as crucial in sustaining peace. Effective conflict prevention requires detecting and responding to group grievances as early as possible. It demands creativity in developing systems and incentives that do not revert to violence when coping with disputes or potential threats to social harmony. Once weapons are used, it becomes more difficult to transcend incompatibilities in a conflict-affected society.[81]

Conflict prevention rests on the aspiration to generate 'contexts, structures and relations' between parties that reduce the likelihood of violence in the short-term while making it inconceivable in the long run.[82] It involves measures that not only seek to prevent the outbreak of violence but also aim to avoid a relapse into conflict. It is cost-effective in comparison to the money that needs to be spent in post-conflict reconstruction. Investing one dollar in prevention and confidence-building measures is estimated to be sixteen times cheaper than responding to the damage brought by the conflict afterwards.[83] Effective prevention demands the establishment of good early-warning systems in conflict-prone settings. It also calls for creativity to come up with non-violent solutions to lower tensions before things spiral out of control.

With advances in technology to collect, share and analyze large-scale data, early-warning tools have become quite sophisticated. They use different types of indicators to predict conflict – such as low per capita income, food crises, genocide, human rights abuses, high-levels of discrimination and violence in neighboring countries.[84] Nevertheless, contemporary security threats are becoming increasingly non-conventional exacerbated by environmental degradation, climate change, drought and water scarcity. Therefore, the effectiveness of modern early warning and global response capabilities in predicting and preventing violence is rather questionable.[85] More research is needed to shed light on the effectiveness of different tools used by different actors which can also help them to share best practices.

---

[79]   Faye Leone, 'Conflict Prevention is "The Priority," Says UN Secretary-General' (12 January 2017) SDG Knowledge Hub <http://sdg.iisd.org/news/conflict-prevention-is-the-priority-says-un-secretary-general/> accessed 16 July 2020.

[80]   UN and WBG (n 46) xi.

[81]   ibid xxi.

[82]   Oliver Ramsbotham, Tom Woodhouse and Hugh Miall, *Contemporary Conflict Resolution* (Polity Press 2016) 4th ed 14.

[83]   IEP, 'Measuring Peacebuilding Cost-Effectiveness' (2017) <http://visionofhumanity.org/app/uploads/2017/03/Measuring-Peacebuilding_WEB.pdf> accessed 16 July 2020.

[84]   Ramsbotham (n 82) 152.

[85]   OECD, 'Conflict and Fragility: Preventing Violence, War and State Collapse. The Future of Conflict Early Warning and Response' (2009) 85 <www.oecd.org/dac/conflict-fragility-resilience/docs/preventing%20violence%20war%20and%20state%20collapse.pdf> accessed 16 July 2020.

Based on early-warning data, conflict prevention may take two distinct forms. Direct or operational conflict prevention is concerned with the immediate causes of conflicts, and it involves preventive diplomacy, sanctions and other economic measures such as conditional offers of financial aid. Structural prevention aims to deal with the root causes of the conflict and tries to strengthen the resilience of the society by responding to political and economic grievances.[86] Poverty reduction strategies and corrective measures in the training and implementation of human rights norms are crucial components of structural conflict prevention. They manifest themselves in policies and practices to boost economic development, establish justice and promote democratic practices.[87] As the UN *2030 Agenda for Sustainable Development* mentions, 'There can be no sustainable development without peace and no peace without sustainable development.'[88] Likewise, without guaranteeing the protection of fundamental human rights, sustaining peace is not achievable. As a result, in the new security environment, a holistic approach is necessary to coordinate the efforts across the humanitarian-development-peace nexus.[89]

III.   CONCLUSION

With the decline in the number of inter-state wars and the increase in conflicts over government or territory within states, civilians are increasingly becoming the main victims of modern warfare. The majority of armed conflicts are taking place in situations of extreme poverty and in contexts of gross abuses of human rights. Resorting to violence and the use of armed means exacerbates the conditions of the poor while further undermining people's enjoyment of their fundamental political, civil, economic, social and cultural rights.[90]

This chapter tried to shed light on the conflict-poverty and conflict-human rights nexuses. The focus was on the impact of conflict on poverty and human rights violations, which has been relatively under researched in comparison to the studies that explore the causal role of poverty and human rights abuses in starting violent conflicts. More research is necessary particularly into the impact of conflict on poverty at the household level. The functioning of informal markets has the potential to redistribute wealth. In opposition controlled areas, the economy is governed by new and alternating actors. The new realities on the ground bring fortune for some while hitting others. These impacts have significant implications for the fight against poverty and deserve more scholarly attention. Fortunately, advances in social media and remote technologies facilitate data collection from conflict zones, creating opportunities for further research to quantify the adverse economic effects of conflict at both micro and macro levels.

The circular relationship between conflict on one side and poverty and human rights violations on the other requires conflict resolution efforts to intervene in every stages of conflict

---

[86]   Giovanni Faleg and Florence Gaub, 'Iceberg Ahead! Rethinking Conflict Prevention' European Union Institute for Security Studies (EUISS) 4.

[87]   Ramsbotham (n 82) 154–155.

[88]   The 2030 Agenda For Sustainable Development (n 52).

[89]   Strategy for Fragility, Conflict, and Violence (n 46) 25.

[90]   Wallensteen (n 45) 66–81; M. Brinton Lykes and Erzulie Coquillon, 'Psychosocial Trauma, Poverty, and Human Rights in Communities Emerging from War' in Dennis Fox, Isaac Prilleltensky and Stephanie Austin (eds), *Critical Psychology II, Edition: 2nd* (SAGE 2009) pp. 285–299.

cycle. This is particularly important in fragile settings where inequality, discrimination, deprivation and the resulting grievances lead to repeated episodes of violent confrontations. In such circumstances, conflict prevention becomes key in international efforts to combat poverty and to enable individuals to enjoy their inalienable rights. A human rights-based approach to conflict which frames social problems as 'unfulfilled rights' and makes 'the realization of all human rights the objective of social development' has a lot to offer for settling disputes and reducing tensions before people resort to violence.[91] Addressing group grievances in resolving conflicts is still very important. Nevertheless, there is a need to place the individual at the center in order to 'leave no one behind'.[92] Lifting more people out of poverty and protecting the rights of more people worldwide will remain key to achieving sustainable peace.

The rapid technological developments change the character of modern warfare. This is happening in a situation where humanity is faced with the threats coming from climate change, water scarcity, terrorism, radicalism and the more recent COVID-19 pandemic. In such a setting, further research is required in order to shed light on the role of poverty and human rights violations both as causes and outcomes of conflict. Finally, it is important to note that regional and international organizations are equipped with early-warning tools and mechanisms which also benefit from the advances in digital technologies. Whether they are effective in predicting humanitarian crises or violent conflicts is rather questionable. There is room for further research to elucidate this which will not only point to existing gaps but also create opportunities for shared learning.

---

[91]   Equitas International Centre for Human Rights Education and International Centre for Ethnic Studies, 'Conflict Mitigation Using a Human Rights-Based Approach' (2018) <https://equitas.org/wp-content/uploads/2019/04/Conflict-mitigation-using-a-human-rights-based-approach-A-guide-for-taking-action-to-mitigate-religious-and-ethnic-conflict.pdf> accessed 16 July 2020.

[92]   The 2030 Agenda For Sustainable Development (n 52).

34. Human rights, technology and poverty

Linnet Taylor and Hellen Mukiri-Smith

As digital technologies become increasingly common tools in the development sector, researchers are working to evaluate what the datafication – the shift towards digital data as a primary mode of knowing and acting – of development and poverty alleviation is achieving, and whether it has identifiable impacts on poverty and deprivation. In this chapter we explore the various shifts that occur when digital technologies are applied to measure and alleviate poverty, and the implications for rights. We interrogate the notion that only rights explicitly connected to digital communications, such as informational privacy and freedom of expression, are involved in these shifts, and we argue that instead we see a broad change in the way poverty is addressed by the development sector. This change has implications for a wide range of rights including economic, political, social and cultural, and implies that when using digital technologies development actors should not address these technologies as neutral tools. Instead they should be seen as ways of seeing, knowing and engaging with livelihoods and poverty that are not inherently benevolent and may be exploitative. In order to contribute to poverty alleviation, digital technologies and the global data economy to which they inevitably connect, must be used with attention to the power and information asymmetries they (re) produce.

We can distinguish two distinct perspectives on technology, development and human rights. The first is a traditional development perspective where we can see specific technological interventions shaping or exacerbating exclusionary dynamics in the economic and social spheres, which in turn emerge as poverty exacerbation and human rights violations. Second, we can also identify an epistemological perspective, facilitated by the arrival of technology firms and thinkers as new actors in the space of development. Importantly, these firms are taking on what have been the functions of the public sector and performing them either independently or with little state oversight, making it necessary to consider the private sector as a policy actor in development for the first time. This change is pervasive and will be explored throughout this chapter.[1] This shift involves new levels and types of intervention based on the already-familiar assumption that development is a technical problem that can be understood and addressed by technological intervention,[2] and we see these new types of intervention interacting with human rights in new ways.[3] This generates both new possibilities and directions for poverty

---

[1]   Linnet Taylor and Dennis Broeders, 'In the Name of Development: Power, Profit and the Datafication of the Global South' (2015) 64 Geoforum 229–37 <https://doi.org/10.1016/j.geoforum.2015.07.002> accessed 13 July 2020.
[2]   Linnet Taylor, 'The Ethics of Big Data as a Public Good: Which Public? Whose Good?' (2016) 374 Phil. Trans. R. Soc. < https://royalsocietypublishing.org/doi/10.1098/rsta.2016.0126> accessed 13 July 2020.
[3]   United Nations Data Revolution Group, 'A World That Counts' (2014) <www.undatarevolution.org/wp-content/uploads/2014/11/A-World-That-Counts.pdf> accessed 13 July 2020.

alleviation and rights violations on the level of political participation and the structuring of the economy, as well as new problems in terms of individual rights such as privacy and autonomy.

Both of these perspectives involve a tension between the traditional justice and rights-based vision of development and poverty alleviation and an emerging technological vision which is based on logics of creating economic opportunity through the insertion of new technologies and systems into national economies. This tension affects how we think about metrics, such as the United Nations' (UN) drive to make the Sustainable Development Goals (SDGs) more measurable than the Millennium Development Goals (MDGs) through the increased availability of big data. The UN claims that the SDGs will be measurable because of big data, but data will also affect how we weigh possibilities and objectives more broadly. In this chapter we begin from Amartya Sen's ground-breaking work on capabilities where he defined 'development as freedom' or 'development as a right',[4] demonstrating that there can be alternative norms and value judgments when defining development than those conventionally adopted by welfare economics.

Starting from an outline of the rights that are relevant to development and poverty alleviation, we explore the ways in which technology applied to the traditional fields of development appears to be supporting, or alternatively weakening, human rights, and we discuss the factors underpinning these dynamics and what measures are available to build, rather than weaken, justice and capabilities for the poor in relation to technology. We incorporate in our discussion the legal instruments developed to regulate the behaviour of the private sector in low-income countries, including the Ruggie principles and evolving data protection laws in many countries, and the notion of data justice,[5] which claims that people are entitled to autonomy and safety with regard to both their use of technology and the data they produce. We find that rights discussions in the technology and data sphere are not only concerned with infringements of civil rights such as the protection of freedoms of expression, privacy and data protection, but they also concern protection of development-related rights, economic, social and cultural rights.

I.   DEVELOPMENT AND HUMAN RIGHTS IN THE INFORMATION SOCIETY

Various international human rights instruments contain provisions that acknowledge that poverty is a human rights issue and which call for the promotion of the right to development. The Universal Declaration of Human Rights (UDHR) defines human rights as freedom from want while the 1993 Vienna Declaration affirms that poverty 'inhibits the full and effective enjoyment of human rights' (Article 14), which results in the violation of human dignity (Article 25). The Committee on Economic, Social and Cultural Rights (CESCR) in a 2001

---

   [4]   Amartya Sen, *Development as Freedom* (OUP 1999).

   [5]   Linnet Taylor, 'What Is Data Justice? The Case for Connecting Digital Rights and Freedoms Globally' (2017) 4 Big Data & Society <https://doi.org/10.1177/2053951717736335> accessed 13 July 2020.

statement recognized that poverty is the result of 'massive and systemic breaches' of international human rights laws.[6]

The Declaration on the Right to Development 1986 (DRD) attempts to offer a comprehensive legal expression of development-related rights, rights echoed by Amartya Sen's idea of 'capabilities' and 'functionings': the freedom to be and do what one values.[7] For the purposes of this chapter, development-related rights are rights aimed at, as provided in the DRD preamble and reflected in other human rights instruments, 'the constant improvement of the well-being of the entire population and of all individuals on the basis of their active, free and meaningful participation in development and in the fair distribution of benefits resulting'.[8] There have been debates on who rights holders are under the DRD, with the initial draft Declaration situating the right to development as a 'right of all states and people for peaceful, free and independent development'.[9] The final Declaration however makes people or individuals the rights holders, although the state can assert rights on their behalf internationally.[10] The DRD recognizes the interdependence and interrelated nature of civil and political rights (CPRs) and economic, social and cultural rights (ESCRs) in the realization of the right to development, echoing the provisions of other human rights instruments including the UDHR. Development is therefore seen as inclusive and participatory, 'an inalienable human right' by which 'every human person and all peoples are entitled to participate in, contribute to, and enjoy economic, social, cultural and political development'.[11] The DRD therefore calls for states to formulate national development policies whose aim is the 'constant improvement of the well-being of the entire population'.[12]

To realize development-related rights, states and other members of the international community such as private corporations, are increasingly defining inclusive and participatory development as dependent on use of technology and data.[13] Data is perceived as the 'lifeblood of decision-making' for governments and private corporations. Biometric databases, communication technologies such as mobile telephones and the internet, artificial intelligence, and block chain are seen as the answer to solving development challenges, promoting the right to development and the realization of the SDGs.[14] States see the realization of targets such

---

[6] United Nations Committee on Economic, Social and Cultural Rights, 'Substantive Issues Arising in the Implementation of the International Covenant on Economic, Social and Cultural Rights: Poverty and the International Covenant on Economic, Social and Cultural Rights' (10 May 2001) UN Doc E/C.12/2001/10.

[7] Sen (n 4) 74–75.

[8] United Nations General Assembly (UNGA), 'Declaration on the Right to Development' (4 December 1986) UN Doc A/RES/41/128 <www.refworld.org/docid/3b00f22544.html> accessed 13 July 2020.

[9] UN Commission on Human Rights (UNCHR), 'Report of the Working Group of Governmental Experts on the Right to Development' (9 December 1982) UN Doc E/CN.4/1983/11 <http://digitallibrary.un.org/record/42792> accessed 13 July 2020.

[10] M.E. Salomon and F. Marks, *Global Responsibility for Human Rights* (Vol 4 OUP 2007).

[11] Declaration on the Right to Development (n 8) art 1 para 1.

[12] ibid para 2.

[13] UN Economic and Social Council, 'Closing Digital Gap Vital to Attaining Sustainable Development, Speakers Stress, as Economic and Social Council Opens Forum on Science, Technology, Innovation' (14 May 2019) <www.un.org/press/en/2019/ecosoc6980.doc.htm> accessed 13 July 2020.

[14] World Bank, 'Enabling Digital Development: Digital Identity' (2016) <http://documents.worldbank.org/curated/en/896971468194972881/310436360_20160263021000/additional/102725-PUB-Replacement-PUBLIC.pdf> accessed 13 July 2020; International Finance Corporation (IFC),

as SDG 16.9 on peaceful and inclusive societies which aims to provide 'legal identity for all, including birth registration' as primarily possible through use of biometrics, and achievement of SDG1 on ending poverty as dependent on technologies such as mobile telephones in order to facilitate financial inclusion.[15]

II.   NEW SOURCES OF DATA ON POVERTY

New sources of data such as mobile phones, satellites, drones and digitized civil registration are taking the place of traditional studies of poverty conducted by either national statistical agencies or international development organizations. Since Jerven's observation[16] that the development sector had only 'poor numbers' on poverty, there has been a growing recognition that if the SDGs are to be more successful in tackling poverty than the MDGs, they will have to incorporate data sources and techniques that the MDGs lacked – more accurate baselines for poverty and other issues of focus, meaningful and comparable evaluation and monitoring, and the ability to merge and analyse those sources in more effective ways. Into this gap has stepped the language of 'big data for development',[17] which promotes universal visibility through data to create a situation where, in the words of the UN, 'never again should it be possible to say "we didn't know". No one should be invisible'.[18]

This brave new world of data analytics as a key tool for poverty alleviation and heightened visibility on the part of the poor is a shift from previous epistemologies connecting poverty alleviation to human rights. The traditional paradigm of the twentieth century incorporated calls for more and better data but was primarily based on a binary choice of approaches: either econometrics, which used official statistics to understand what states and multilaterals knew about poverty, or ethnographic and participatory research, which provided a critical micro-level perspective on 'who counts'[19] and what remains uncounted, and therefore unaddressed, in low-income communities. In contrast, the new big-data paradigm of the 2000s does not result in 'seeing like a state'[20] or alternatively like an anthropologist. Instead, data analytics experts see like corporations, through commercially produced big data,[21] using data mining, advanced statistical modelling and other epistemologies that are agnostic to traditional development and rights knowledge.

'Block Chain, Opportunities for Private Enterprises in Emerging Markets' (January 2019) <http://documents.worldbank.org/curated/en/260121548673898731/pdf/134063-WP-121278-2nd-edition-IFC-EMCompass-Blockchain-Report-PUBLIC.pdf> accessed 13 July 2020.

[15]   UN 'The Sustainable Development Goals Report' (2016) <https://unstats.un.org/sdgs/report/2016/> accessed 13 July 2020.

[16]   Morten Jerven, 'Poor Numbers and What to Do about Them' (2014) 383 The Lancet 594–95 <www.thelancet.com/pdfs/journals/lancet/PIIS0140-6736(14)60209-9.pdf> accessed 13 July 2020.

[17]   Vincent D. Blondel and others, 'Data for Development: The D4D Challenge on Mobile Phone Data' (29 September 2012) arXiv <http://arxiv.org/abs/1210.0137> accessed 13 July 2020.

[18]   United Nations Data Revolution Group (n 3).

[19]   Robert Chambers, 'Beyond "Whose Reality Counts?" New Methods We Now Need?' (1998) 4 Studies in Cultures, Organizations and Societies 279–301.

[20]   James C. Scott, *Seeing like a State: How Certain Schemes to Improve the Human Condition Have Failed* (Yale University Press 1998).

[21]   Taylor and Broeders (n 1).

Examples of the new ways of knowing poverty include the mobile network operator Orange making data from Cote d'Ivoire subscribers available to data analytics researchers from around the world, with no fieldwork involved, who produced nearly a hundred research projects estimating poverty, mobility and demographic divides in the country.[22] Accompanying formal challenges such as these are data on people's activities, movement and behaviour that are both produced and analysed by social media networks such as Facebook; data from gig economy firms such as Uber and Amazon Turk that explain how the poor are becoming part of new economic sectors and activities,[23] and new analytics groups such as UN Global Pulse, DataKind, and the epidemiological analysis group Flowminder, all of whom work with big data to understand poverty and its effects on health, labour markets and behaviour in general.

The most widely used of the new data sources on poverty and exclusion is mobile phone data. Due to the explosion in mobile phone penetration in low- and middle-income countries during the 2000s,[24] call detail records (CDRs) from operators serving poor populations has become a potentially powerful source of metrics for poverty. Analysts proxy for poverty with individual mobility levels[25] or add other sources such as night-time lights observed by satellite[26] to triangulate estimates of income. Development and humanitarian research using CDR data began with one-off, targeted collaborations between mobile operators and researchers in public health,[27] which then sparked a move to create larger-scale, more crowdsourced forms of data sharing for research. The demonstrated power of CDRs to supplement national statistics and generate new insights with regard to low- and middle-income countries has created a community of researchers, funders and intermediaries interested in using them. Central to this process has been the United Nations' call for a 'Data Revolution'[28] and the World Economic Forum's claim that big data should be considered a tool for development and humanitarian action.[29]

---

[22] Taylor (n 2).

[23] Mark Graham, *Towards a Fairer Gig Economy* (Meatspace Press 2017).

[24] International Telecommunication Union, 'Measuring Digital Development: Facts and Figures 2019' <www.itu.int/en/itu-d/statistics/pages/facts/default.aspx> accessed 13 July 2020.

[25] Thoralf Gutierrez, Gautier Krings, and Vincent D. Blondel, 'Evaluating Socio-Economic State of a Country Analyzing Airtime Credit and Mobile Phone Datasets' (17 September 2013) arXiv <http://arxiv.org/abs/1309.4496> accessed 13 July 2020.

[26] Neal Jean and others, 'Combining Satellite Imagery and Machine Learning to Predict Poverty' (August 19, 2016) 353 Science <https://doi.org/10.1126/science.aaf7894> accessed 13 July 2020.

[27] Linus Bengtsson and others, 'Using Mobile Phone Data to Predict the Spatial Spread of Cholera' (August 2015) 5 Scientific Reports 8923 <https://doi.org/10.1038/srep08923> accessed 13 July 2020; Deepa K Pindolia and others, 'Human Movement Data for Malaria Control and Elimination Strategic Planning' (December 2012) 11 *Malaria Journal* 205 <https://doi.org/10.1186/1475-2875-11-205> accessed 13 July 2020; A. Wesolowski and others, 'Quantifying the Impact of Human Mobility on Malaria' (12 October 2012) 338 *Science* 267–70 <https://doi.org/10.1126/science.1223467> accessed 13 July 2020.

[28] United Nations Data Revolution Group (n 3).

[29] World Economic Forum, 'Data-Driven Development Pathways for Progress' (January 2015).

III.   NEW OPPORTUNITIES, NEW VULNERABILITIES

Although the institutions with a history of working on poverty alleviation have welcomed the new data sources as an important contribution to their mission, there are signs that the new data sources merit caution with regard to human rights. Poverty data was previously collected by states as just another component of national statistics, or by development organizations as part of their state-approved mission. The new data sources – mobile phone customer call records, geolocation records from phones and other devices, social media data, financial transaction data and other digital traces – are not data that individuals are aware might be shared and reused. They reflect activities, behaviour and movement which together form a very intimate picture of people's lives, and which also potentially expose people to new forms of exploitation. The same analysis that can tell a multilateral such as the World Bank where young people are spending their welfare transfers could also help firms define the next mass youth market for cigarettes, and the same data that enables a foundation to contact individual farmers with agricultural information could also be sold to political parties to bolster their electoral chances. Cambridge Analytica has been found to have manipulated elections in 68 countries, most of them low- or middle-income,[30] using data sourced in similar ways to the new poverty data. These uses of data to identify groups who will behave one way or another under particular forms of manipulation and influence has given rise to the notion of 'group privacy',[31] an idea new to law but highly relevant to poverty studies – the notion that people may be identified by algorithms as collectives and manipulated as such, whether for electoral, policy or commercial motives, and that they deserve protection from aggregate influence and intervention as much as they do their individual right to privacy.

This is the new problem big data creates: when data analysts make 'poverty' visible, they are actually doing so by making the poor themselves visible, individually and collectively. This has implications for multiple human rights that have not previously been considered relevant to poverty alleviation. Privacy is clearly a concern, but also individual autonomy and community rights to self-determination (challenged, for example, when mobile network operators plan interventions as development policy, as occurred in the D4D challenge). Likewise, civil and political freedoms (challenged by election interference or other political manipulation) come into play. Those identified as poor are made visible in new ways, to new actors, not only those interested in alleviating poverty. Robert Kirkpatrick, director of the UN big data initiative Global Pulse and an early proponent of data for poverty alleviation, explicitly advocates ranking rights with regard to the new data sources when he says: 'Privacy is your right. So is access to food, water, humanitarian response. The challenge is that we see a lot of regulatory frameworks which don't have the right litmus test'.[32]

---

[30]   Martin Plaut, 'Cambridge Analytica and the Digital War in Africa' (New Statesman 20 March 2018) <www.newstatesman.com/world/2018/03/cambridge-analytica-facebook-elections-africa-kenya> accessed 13 July 2020; Matthew Rosenberg, 'Cambridge Analytica, Trump-Tied Political Firm, Offered to Entrap Politicians' (The New York Times 19 March 2018) <www.nytimes.com/2018/03/19/us/cambridge-analytica-alexander-nix.html> accessed 13 July 2020.

[31]   Linnet Taylor, Luciano Floridi, and Bart van der Sloot, *Group Privacy: New Challenges of Data Technologies* (Springer International Publishing 2017).

[32]   Interview with Robert Kirkpatrick, UN Global Pulse (18 August 2014).

The idea that there should be a new litmus test for regulators to determine whether they will allow data on the poor to be widely shared or not, is not a reassuring one. The reason is not only the power of the data to reveal and allow targeting on both the individual and group level. It is also that people may be inserted into markets before they gain access to their own rights and entitlements – that they may become forced to be consumers before they can exercise their rights as citizens.[33] Today's poor will constitute the next three billion users of the internet, and as such are already sought after as micro-workers by those who shape the gig economy[34] and as audiences for mass marketing by those who gather data on welfare recipients. Nandan Nilekani, the developer of India's Aadhaar population database, the world's largest biometric records system, already referred to the poor as 'customers' at the point where the database was primarily full of welfare recipients.[35] This is the same risk visible with financial technology platforms and services: the poor are a rich market for those who wish to exploit their few resources, and discrimination works in two directions: the poor are excluded from opportunity, but subject to 'predatory inclusion'.[36]

IV.   FINANCIAL TECHNOLOGIES: INCLUSION AND EXPLOITATION

Use of technologies for delivery of financial services is growing daily. Institutions such as the World Bank see new financial services technologies (Fintechs) such as mobile wallets or mobile payments and banking, 'online credit, peer to peer (p2p) lending and crowdfunding', as holding the promise for expanding financial inclusion, for the eradication of poverty.[37] This is particularly so in sub-Saharan Africa, Asia, Latin America and the Caribbean where there are large populations who lack credit histories or the collateral required to access traditional lending institutions. Within the European Union, there has also been a thrust towards the creation of a European market for retail financial services and an increase in the 'online alternative finance market' which includes also 'crowdfunding, peer-to-peer lending'.[38] The increase in alternative financial services has led to questions within the union about whether there are sufficient mechanisms to address data mining and sharing of data among creditors within Member States. For example, there have been questions raised by the European Commission about what is 'necessary' data for the purposes of credit assessments[39] under the Directive on mortgage credit (Article 18). Although Article 20 of the Directive provides that for the pur-

---

[33]   Taylor (n 5).

[34]   Graham (n 23).

[35]   Center for Global Development, 'Technology to Leapfrog Development:The Aadhaar Experience' (The Eighth Annual Richard H. Sabot Lecture 22 April 2013) <www.cgdev.org/sites/default/files/nandan-nilekani-sabot-lecture-transcript-technology-leapfrog-development.pdf> accessed 13 July 2020.

[36]   Louise Seamster and Raphaël Charron-Chénier, 'Predatory Inclusion and Education Debt: Rethinking the Racial Wealth Gap' (1 June 2017) 4 Social Currents 199–207.

[37]   World Bank, 'World Development Report 2019: The Changing Nature of Work' (2019) 31 <www.worldbank.org/en/publication/wdr2019> accessed 13 July 2020.

[38]   Bryan Zhang and others, 'Sustaining Momentum: The 2nd European Alternative Finance Industry Report' (7 September 2016) 120 Cambridge Centre for Alternative Finance 20.

[39]   European Commission, 'Green Paper on Retail Financial Services: Better Products, More Choice, and Greater Opportunities for Consumers and Businesses' (12 October 2015) 24; World Development Report 2019 (n 37).

poses of credit assessments, 'necessary' information on the creditors financial circumstances shall be obtained from 'internal and external sources', the Directive stops short at defining what is 'necessary' data.[40]

Although states still have a role and can influence development of overarching technology policies within their own jurisdictions, their role in the technology space is becoming increasingly limited. Private sector companies are usually the providers of Fintech services, services that rely on insights from big data also referred to as the 'holy grail of behavioral knowledge'.[41] This has meant that obligations for realization of development-related rights is increasingly in the hands of private sector companies and there is an emergence of new forms of exploitation as result of use of technologies. This raises questions about who then gets to do development and whether human rights mechanisms are sufficient to address or prevent data manipulations and exploitation. This is particularly because states are duty bearers of development-related rights in international human rights law.[42] Fintechs deliver financial solutions using artificial intelligence systems and big data,[43] practices that are often trade secrets and protected by intellectual property law,[44] making it difficult to understand their mining practices or to obtain a full picture of their exploitative practices. Companies collect data often without the knowledge of consumers, often from numerous, unrelated sources, mined from offline and online activities of consumers such as, consumers' internet browsing histories and social media.[45] This data, referred to as 'alternative data',[46] is fed into 'mathematical algorithms or statistical programs'.[47] The data helps companies profile and surveil consumers, to understand who we are, what we do, and why we do what we do, helping companies 'measure, manipulate and monetize online behaviour',[48] to offer products and services to customers or potential customers. These data mining activities are particularly detrimental for those living in poverty. Increased visibility through data opens up avenues for corporations to exploit poor individuals' financial and other socio-economic vulnerabilities. It allows corporations to market and lure them into taking out loans, which are almost always offered to them at high interest rates

---

[40]   Regulation (EU) 2016/679 of the European Parliament and of the Council of 27 April 2016 on the Protection of Natural Persons with Regard to the Processing of Personal Data and on the Free Movement of Such Data, and Repealing Directive 95/46/EC (General Data Protection Regulation) [2016] OJ L119/1 58.

[41]   Jose Van Dijck, 'Datafication, Dataism and Dataveillance: Big Data between Scientific Paradigm and Ideology' (9 May 2014) 12 Surveillance & Society 199 <https://doi.org/10.24908/ss.v12i2.4776> accessed 13 July 2020.

[42]   Morten Broberg and Hans-Otto Sano, 'Strengths and Weaknesses in a Human Rights-Based Approach to International Development – an Analysis of a Rights-Based Approach to Development Assistance Based on Practical Experiences' (28 May 2018) 22 IJHR 664–80 <https://doi.org/10.1080/13642987.2017.1408591> accessed 13 July 2020.

[43]   Federico Ferretti, 'Consumer Access to Capital in the Age of FinTech and Big Data: The Limits of EU Law' (1 August 2018) 25 Maastricht Journal of European and Comparative Law 484 <https://doi.org/10.1177/1023263X18794407> accessed 13 July 2020.

[44]   Julie E. Cohen, 'The Biopolitical Public Domain: The Legal Construction of the Surveillance Economy' (2017) 31 Philosophy & Technology 213–33 <https://doi.org/10.1007/s13347-017-0258-2> accessed 13 July 2020.

[45]   Ferretti (n 43) 486.

[46]   Rob Aitken, 'All Data Is Credit Data: Constituting the Unbanked' (August 2017) 21 Competition & Change 274–300 <https://doi.org/10.1177/1024529417712830> accessed 13 July 2020.

[47]   Ferretti (n 43) 485.

[48]   Van Dijck (n 41) 200.

and which they cannot pay back. This increases their poverty[49] by further excluding them from participating in economic and social activities as discussed below in the Kenya case study of the Branch lending app.

The existence of national and regional data protection frameworks, such as the European Union's General Data Protection Directive 2018 (GDPR) and the African Union Convention on Cyber Security and Personal Data Protection 2014, has not stopped unfair data mining practices of corporations. However, data protection frameworks have attempted to address data mining practices through for example, requirements that corporations undertake data impact assessments prior to processing data where processing is 'likely to result in a high risk to the rights and freedoms of natural persons'.[50] The hope is that data impact assessments can help corporations put in place safeguards and mechanisms to protect digital rights when processing data.

In Kenya, companies such as Safaricom, the largest telecommunications company in Kenya and several Silicon Valley-based companies, one of which is Branch, are offering Fintech services. Branch, a Californian based start-up company uses Safaricom's Mpesa payment services platform to disburse loans and receive payment for loans it offers through its app platform. The Branch app collects large amounts of data from various sources, by scraping through a user's mobile phone. People interested in taking out a Branch loan are required to download its app from Google Play Store on to their mobile phone and to then give Branch permissions on the app to access their 'call log, contacts, SMS messages, and precise location via GPS'.[51] Branch is therefore able to know, through your personal data, 'everything from where you spend your money to how you spend your time online … [to your] everyday movements and your darkest secrets'.[52] This information is exploited to make decisions on creditworthiness of individuals, often without the knowledge or proper consent of consumers and is unregulated because it is 'done outside (or above) laws, policy or ethical considerations'.[53]

In addition to exploiting user's data and their behaviour to offer loan products, there are additional layers of exploitation. Branch exploits users' labour without compensation, not only at the stage where users provide their data knowingly or otherwise, as a form of their labour, but by also requesting users who have used their platforms to refer their friends to their platform, creating additional sources of data or data points for Branch's business practices.[54] In addition to exploitation concerns, there are also worrying concerns that Fintechs are not promoting the right to development – that instead of promoting financial inclusion, they are excluding the poor from access to finances. There are reports that algorithmic predictions have led to wrong or poor lending decisions by companies, resulting in large populations using lending apps such as Branch in Kenya being blacklisted by credit bureaus, for as little as 100

---

[49]   Kevin Donovan and Emma Park, 'Perpetual Debt in the Silicon Savannah' (20 September 2019) Boston Review <https://bostonreview.net/class-inequality-global-justice/kevin-p-donovan-emma-park -perpetual-debt-silicon-savannah> accessed 13 July 2020.

[50]   Regulation (EU) 2016/679 (n 40).

[51]   Privacy International, 'Fintech: Privacy and Identity in the New Data-Intensive Financial Sector' (November 2017) 31 <www.privacyinternational.org/sites/default/files/2017-12/Fintech%20report.pdf> accessed 13 July 2020.

[52]   ibid 38.

[53]   ibid 39.

[54]   ibid 31.

Kenyan Shillings or 0.88 Euros.[55] The effect of blacklisting has meant that those targeted for financial inclusion are further excluded because they cannot access financial services for long periods, as long as five years while on the blacklist. As of July 2019, there were reports that 2.5 million out of the 7.5 million digital borrowers in Kenya had defaulted on their loans, with about 400,000 people having been blacklisted in credit bureaus.[56]

V.   NEW VULNERABILITIES CREATED BY TECHNOLOGY

Much of the language about rights in relation to technology revolves around privacy and protection, with the idea that people are inherently vulnerable to exploitation. When we think of poverty, however, it is clear that exploitative systems such as the fintech platforms and welfare systems, which are supposed to give the poor access to their entitlements, can actually create new vulnerabilities. The risk of this is highest when commercial systems are procured to take on public sector functions, effectively breaking the link between citizen and authorities. In the Indian Aadhaar biometric ID system, for example, which was initially a semi-private interface between welfare databases and the private sector and only later adopted into the public sector, it costs more for the poor to correct errors than the rich.[57] Eubanks has documented a similar level of unaccountability and impunity amongst the technology providers involved in US welfare systems.[58] The problem of effective redress for rights violations is only exacerbated when companies work across borders. Nancy Fraser in her work on 'abnormal justice' points out that 'in the wake of transnationalized production, globalized finance, and neoliberal trade and investment regimes, redistribution claims increasingly trespass the bounds of state-centered grammars and arenas of argument'.[59]

New vulnerabilities are created where the poor are expected to engage with authorities in unfamiliar ways using new digital systems, whose interfaces often use a language in which the poor are not comfortable, such as English in the case of many South African welfare recipients. In the South African case, the government contracted with the firm Cash Paymaster Services (CPS), owned by the technology firm Net1, to provide welfare payment distribution.[60] CPS became a monopoly provider due to the state's decision to establish technical capacity in electronic transfers and biometric verification as the basis for welfare grant distribution. The firm took advantage of this monopoly and grant recipients' poverty by using the data gathered through its services to create a private marketplace in which Net1's other subsidiary firms

---

[55]   Ngigi, George (2016), *Pain of Kenyans blacklisted for Amounts as Small as Sh100 in Mobile Loans, Bank Fees*, Daily Nation, accessed on 12 March 2020 at :<https://www.nation.co.ke/business/Pain-of-Kenyans-blacklisted-for-amounts-as-small-as-Sh100/996-3374952-k2dkdvz/index.html>.

[56]   Kamau, Macharia (2019), *Crisis as mobile lenders blacklist 2.5 million borrowers*, East African Standard, accessed on 13 March 2020 at: <https://www.standardmedia.co.ke/business/article/2001334661/crisis-as-mobile-lenders-blacklist-2-5-million-borrowers>.

[57]   Silvia Masiero and Soumyo Das, 'Datafying Anti-Poverty Programmes: Implications for Data Justice' (7 June 2019) 22 Information, Communication & Society 916–33 <https://doi.org/10.1080/1369118X.2019.1575448> accessed 13 July 2020.

[58]   Virginia Eubanks, *Automating Inequality: How High-Tech Tools Profile, Police, and Punish the Poor* (St. Martin's Press 2018).

[59]   Nancy Fraser, 'Abnormal Justice' (2008) 34 Critical Inquiry 393–422.

[60]   Robyn Foley and Mark Swilling, 'How One Word Can Change the Game: Case Study of State Capture and the South African Social Security Agency' (Stellenbosch, South Africa July 2018).

could sell products such as loans, prepaid electricity, insurance and airtime. This resulted in deductions directly from welfare recipients' welfare accounts, reducing some recipients' payments to zero. Recipients were surprised by this, because the unfamiliarity of e-commerce to those with extremely low incomes had meant they were not aware they were entering into a commercial contract when they clicked 'yes' to an offer within their SMS (text message) welfare payment notification.

These violations suggest, again, that regulation is of central importance in determining whether technology serves or exploits the poor. What can be an important advance in access to entitlements and services can turn into creation and exploitation of vulnerability where digital providers are given access to the poor as consumers, rather than positioning the right to development, service and welfare provision on the citizen-government axis. This raises questions about how best to regulate technology and data activities in order to protect consumers. As discussed, human rights instruments as they currently stand may not offer sufficient protections for technology users. A legally binding human rights instrument on business activities and human rights is not yet in place although the Working Group on transnational corporations has prepared a draft instrument.[61] Although human rights frameworks such as the UN Guiding Principles on Business and Human Rights place responsibilities on business enterprises to 'respect human rights',[62] issues of liability and enforcement when it comes to corporations remain substantially defined by states through national laws. States may not be in a position to adequately legislate on new technologies and business practices connected to new technologies because of the fast moving nature of technological advancements[63] and the business enclosure protections discussed earlier.

Additionally, the 'do no harm' responsibility placed on businesses under these principles may not adequately reflect the nuances of the types of rights that need protection as a result of exploitative data mining, profiling and surveillance. The legal force of the UN Guiding Principles is in question because, as specified in the Report of the Special Representative of the Secretary General on the issue of human rights and transnational corporations and other business enterprises, the intention of the principles was not 'the creation of new international law obligations' but to elaborate on 'the implications of existing standards and practices for States and businesses'.[64]

There may therefore be a need to consider developing sector specific frameworks that offer protections against new forms of exploitation which are becoming prevalent with the use of technology. There are examples of conventions that are tailored to specific sectors, for example by organizations such as the International Labour Organisation, outlining protections against

---

[61]   United Nations Human Rights Council, 'OHCHR – Fifth Session of the Open-Ended Intergovernmental Working Group on Transnational Corporations and Other Business Enterprises with Respect to Human Rights' (2020) <www.ohchr.org/EN/HRBodies/HRC/WGTransCorp/Session5/Pages/Session5.aspx> accessed 13 July 2020.

[62]   United Nations Human Rights Office of the High Commissioner, 'Guiding Principles on Business and Human Rights' (2011) <www.ohchr.org/documents/publications/guidingprinciplesbusinesshr_en.pdf> accessed 13 July 2020.

[63]   Mark Fenwick, Wulf A. Kaal, and Erik PM Vermeulen, 'Regulation Tomorrow: What Happens When Technology Is Faster than the Law' (2016) 6 Am. U. Bus. L. Rev. 581–82.

[64]   UN Human Rights Council, 'Guiding Principles on Business and Human Rights: Implementing the United Nations "Protect, Respect and Remedy" Framework' (21 March 2011) UN Doc A/HRC/17/31 5.

various forms of discrimination and exploitation such as Equal Remuneration Convention, 1951 (No. 100) on equal remuneration for men and women workers for work of equal value.

VI.   SHARING THE BENEFITS OF TECHNOLOGY

New digital technologies and the data they produce offer economic opportunity that can be shaped to alleviate poverty – but only if systems for sharing and using data are framed and designed actively with the poor in mind. Surveillance scholar David Lyon has said that surveillance operates on a spectrum between care and control.[65] The challenge is to shape the new data sources towards ends of care and opportunity rather than control and manipulation.

Mann has argued that if digitization is to have positive economic development effects for the poor, it matters who implements the systems that gather and handle data on low-income populations. 'The poor have been treated as beneficiaries, rather than as potential economic producers', she argues,[66] advocating for governments to develop industrial policies that enforce the transfer of reciprocal benefits to domestic firms from private foreign companies that currently control data and technologies in order to create more benefits for domestic companies and local people.[67] One major area where benefit sharing could happen is agricultural surveillance: agricultural technology firms collect data on their inputs to farming systems around the world, but that data is usually proprietary. Carbonell[68] argues that if firms can now aggregate data that used to belong to farmers, they gain a unique market position due to the insights they can draw on both micro and the macro-level practices and outcomes of farming – insights that could be used to capture market share at the expense of local firms and to influence government policy towards their interests. This creates a power asymmetry that needs rebalancing through the sharing of data and public-domain data analytics of agricultural data. If the problem is already significant in higher-income countries, we should expect the power (and resulting economic) asymmetry to be exponentially greater in lower-income ones where people will have less awareness of and legal traction over what happens to their data.

Without connectivity, there is little basis for sharing the benefits of technology. Gurumurthy et al. describe a 'democratic dividend' from data produced in lower-income environments where people can use information more effectively to claim their rights and to hold authorities to account, but warn that this 'necessitates a data capability at local levels that is sophisticated, which presupposes legal and institutional guarantees for citizens' right to connectivity'.[69] The idea of a right to connectivity was first put forward by the World Summit for the Information Society in 2003,[70] based on the rights of freedom of opinion and expression and to democracy

---

[65]   David Lyon, *Surveillance Studies: An Overview* (Polity 2007).

[66]   Laura Mann, 'Left to Other Peoples' Devices? A Political Economy Perspective on the Big Data Revolution in Development: A Political Economy of Big Data in Development' (4 October 2017) 49 Development and Change 7 <https://doi.org/10.1111/dech.12347> accessed 13 July 2020.

[67]   ibid 20.

[68]   Isabelle Carbonell, 'The Ethics of Big Data in Big Agriculture' (2016) 5 Internet Policy Review 5.

[69]   Anita Gurumurthy, Nandini Chami, and Deepti Bharthur, 'Democratic Accountability in the Digital Age' (2016) 2 <https://opendocs.ids.ac.uk/opendocs/handle/20.500.12413/13010> accessed 13 July 2020.

[70]   World Summit on the Information Society (WSIS), 'WSIS: Declaration of Principles' (12 December 2003) UN Doc WSIS-03/Geneva/Doc/4-E <www.itu.int/net/wsis/docs/geneva/official/dop.html> accessed 13 July 2020.

and development. The idea was further developed by the UN Special Rapporteur on the promotion and protection of the right to freedom of opinion and expression, Frank La Rue, in 2011,[71] when he argued that the internet by then underpinned various rights including freedom of expression, but also civil and political freedoms.

Interestingly, supporting Carbonell's argument that digitization will produce power asymmetries and injustice unless actively managed to reduce inequality, the rhetoric of the right to connectivity was substantially taken over during the 2010s by corporations with a financial interest in providing that connectivity. The leader in this field was Facebook, which used the language of a right to connectivity to promote its 'free basics' service in low-income countries around the world. This service allowed people to access a set of services via their mobile phones even if they could not afford a data plan. It was adopted in many countries, particularly in Sub-Saharan Africa, but met strong resistance in India as the country flexed its incipient superpower status. The Indian business community resisted on the basis that allowing Facebook to monopolize the provision of internet connectivity to the country's poorer citizens would halt the development of the domestic digital economy by forestalling the ability of local developers to find markets for their services and platforms.[72] Under pressure from the prime minister to allow Facebook in, and businesses to keep its role limited, the country's regulator rejected Facebook's plans. The episode illustrates how the way in which technology supports or undermines rights will be determined politically and structurally on the country level, and how regulation and policy play a central role in shaping how that happens.

There is a need to further explore how to position public law or rights frameworks to better protect the digital rights of technology users where the 'duty bearers are private sector' but in reality, especially in developing countries, the state remains the duty bearer even when they partner with private entities.[73] There is a case to be made that because states have delegated their development responsibilities to private actors, private actors are performing public functions in the development space and should therefore be liable in the same manner as states would be. There has been precedent on this in administrative law, in cases such as *R v Panel on Take-overs and Mergers, ex parte Datafin plc*[74] where courts have been prepared to allow judicial review proceedings on the actions of a private body excising a public function for accountability purposes. A starting point to help answer these questions can be more studies of the full impact of new technologies and use of big data in different contexts, the role of the private sector and the forms of exploitation that occur through technology. Amartya Sen's and Martha Nussbaum's capabilities approach that views development as promoting 'functionings people value'[75] may help us to better understand rights infringements when it comes to technology.

---

[71]   United Nations Human Rights Council, 'Report of the Special Rapporteur on the Promotion and Protection of the Right to Freedom of Opinion and Expression, Frank La Rue' (27 May 2011) UN Doc A/HRC/17/27/Add.1.

[72]   Rahul Bhatia, 'The Inside Story of Facebook's Biggest Setback' *The Guardian* (12 May 2016) <www.theguardian.com/technology/2016/may/12/facebook-free-basics-india-zuckerberg> accessed 13 July 2020.

[73]   Broberg and Sano (n 42) 667–68.

[74]   [1987] QB 815.

[75]   Sen (n 4) 75.

VII.   CONCLUSION: TAKING ACCOUNT OF TECHNOLOGY IN A JUSTICE AND RIGHTS-BASED DEVELOPMENT PARADIGM

The increased penetration of technology and use of big data globally means that digital rights of populations around the world are constantly in need of protecting, protecting from often unwarranted uses by states and private market players.[76] The case studies discussed highlight that while rights discussions in the technology and data sphere are concerned with infringements of civil rights such as the protection of freedoms of expression, privacy and data protection, use of technology and data impact on development-related rights, economic, social and cultural rights. Countries have enacted constitutional and legislative provisions on civil rights protections and there are now regional regulations on the protection of these rights such as the European Union's General Data Protection Directive 2018 and the African Union Convention on Cyber Security and Personal Data Protection 2014. There is however need to further study the impact of technology and data on economic, social and cultural rights in order to develop more comprehensive justice or rights-based frameworks that offer protection against new forms of exploitation which are becoming prevalent in the digital space.

As we consider the legal frameworks to help both understandings of and enforceability of rights to keep pace with technological advances, we must also question what principles of justice we wish to use to scaffold them and keep our attention on what is most important. We have argued[77] for a guiding vision based on both autonomy and support for those most exposed to technological intervention: according to principles of data justice, people should control their own digital visibility so that it benefits them rather than leading to exploitation; they should have autonomy with regard to new digital technologies so that they are not forced to adopt technologies that only benefit powerful interests, but also have access to new technologies that are beneficial for them. Finally, where poverty alleviation and commercial technologies intersect, it is the task of national and international authorities to make those technologies safe and non-discriminatory, rather than positioning the poor as consumers with choices about which technologies they use, and how exposed they are to unfairness and exploitation.

The risks and potential rewards of datafication for poverty alleviation we have explored here make a strong case for moving to a framework based on capabilities theory. Exploring how technology and data impacts on people's valued functionings,[78] can contribute to a better understanding of technology-related unfreedoms, and can help to inform definitions of justice, and consequently the content of rights-based frameworks in the technology and data sphere. We should also take account of Nancy Fraser's theory of abnormal justice, and particularly her insight that globalization (and, by connection, technology and digitization) have changed both the rights people need to claim, and the ways in which they claim them. It is no longer enough to ensure people are represented and exercise economic redistribution to support their needs.

---

[76]   Shoshana Zuboff, 'Big Other: Surveillance Capitalism and the Prospects of an Information Civilization' (2015) 30 Journal of Information Technology 75–89; Lyon (n 65).

[77]   Taylor (n 5).

[78]   Martha C. Nussbaum, 'Capabilities, Entitlements, Rights: Supplementation and Critique' (February 2011) 12 Journal of Human Development and Capabilities 23–37 <https://doi.org/10.1080/19452829.2011.541731> accessed 13 July 2020; Amartya Sen, 'Human Rights and Capabilities' (July 2005) 6 J. Hum. Dev. 151–66 <https://doi.org/10.1080/14649880500120491> accessed 13 July 2020.

Instead, justice has become more complex to define. Individual and group rights are both in play, and rights such as privacy that were claimed originally only by individuals may now be relevant to groups as well. Rights are formulated to be claimed against official authorities and on the national scale, yet technology's wide-ranging implementation and effects operate across borders and regions, and often begin from commercial actors rather than states. This means that rights claims are now often trans-jurisdictional, and the most relevant actors in violations may turn out to be commercial firms rather than governments. These shifts mean that there is a need for new ways of identifying and representing those whose interests are at stake, as well as for recognizing their claims and doing something about those claims.

If we can collectively make these shifts in recognizing and representing the subjects of technological intervention, and put in place the necessary principles and regulation to ensure rights can be enforced, we must also argue for a conceptualization of functionings and capabilities as a necessary framing for rights, in order to make positive engagement with technology possible for the poor.

35. Beyond the state: holding international institutions and private entities accountable for poverty alleviation

Lucy Williams

NGOs and grassroots groups frequently allege that projects funded by international and multilateral development banks either do not serve the purpose of reducing poverty or are complicit in increasing poverty and violating social and economic rights of poor people.[1] Likewise, grassroots activists frequently allege that subsidiaries of multinational corporations operating in 'less developed' countries destroy poor people's health, livelihood, living conditions and environment. A great challenge facing the human rights movement is to develop legal theories under which powerful non-state actors such as international/multilateral banks and multinational corporations may be held responsible for their actions and for their failure to take reasonable steps to alleviate poverty. This chapter explores recent cases that suggest avenues for imposing human rights liability on these entities both for their harmful actions and their omissions.

Over the past generation, poverty has come to be understood not only as a humanitarian issue but as a question of human rights. Poverty causes ill-health, malnutrition, unsustainable living conditions, failure of people to thrive, and death. Poverty is also inconsistent with democracy; humans cannot reach their potential for self-realization and political self-determination where

---

[1] For example, Petition by the Phalong Village Authority and the Center for Research and Advocacy, Manipur concerning the violations of Indigenous Peoples rights and destruction of their agriculture land and forest areas in Phalong Village and neighboring areas in Tamenglong District in interior Manipur due to the construction of the Kangchup - Tamenglong Road project financed by the Asian Development Bank. See 'Phalong farmers decry authority's avoidance' (*Centre for Research and Advocacy Manipur*, 16 May 2016) <https://cramanipur.wordpress.com/2018/05/17/phalong-farmers-decry-authoritys -avoidance/> accessed 11 March 2020. IFC Investments in Amalgamated Plantations Private Limited (APPL), India Project Numbers 25074 and 34562, January 23, 2019 Office of the Compliance Advisor Ombudsman (CAO), 23 January 2019, addressing complaint from three non-governmental organizations (NGOs) on behalf of workers from three APPL estates in Assam raising concerns about living and working conditions, specifically citing long working hours, inadequate compensation, economic displacement as a result of a fisheries program, restrictions on freedom of association, poor hygiene and health concerns, poor living conditions, and inadequate protection for workers using pesticides. See also 'Compliance Monitoring Report' (23 January 2019) CAC <www.cao-ombudsman.org/cases/ document-links/documents/CAOComplianceMonitoringReport_APPL2019.pdf> accessed 13 March 2020. Complaint regarding the harm to livelihoods caused by the Tanahu Hydropower Project in Tanahu, Nepal, 11 February 2020, on file with author, see IAP, 'Indigenous communities affected by the Tanahu Hydropower Project in Nepal file complaints with the Asian Development Bank and European Investment Bank' (*Medium*, 19 February 2020) <https://medium.com/@accountability/ indigenous-communities-affected-by-the-tanahu-hydropower-project-in-nepal-file-complaints-with-the -be02e0c021ce> accessed 13 March 2020.

poverty is entrenched.[2] The proposition is gradually acquiring consensus in human rights discourse that the existence of sustained and stubborn poverty is prima facie evidence of a rights violation when government does not reasonably take necessary and feasible steps to alleviate it.[3] In the past – and sadly still today in some quarters – poverty was considered either a background fact of life, like the weather,[4] or a product of individual personality defects (such as laziness) invidiously attributed to entire groups of people. Human rights discourse now squarely assigns responsibility for the durability of entrenched poverty to government policy and the conduct of certain private actors.

The chapters in this book discuss how leaders in the international human rights community have used core human rights treaties to challenge extreme economic inequalities and promote poverty alleviation. Although not judicially enforceable, UN Conventions and related instruments have been invoked to support rights to health, housing, the environment, government transparency, and many dimensions of equality, among other rights. In addition, a growing number of nations, many in the Global South, have entrenched justiciable social and economic rights in their constitutions. In this context, an exceedingly important development is the increasing recognition of obligations of government (and sometimes private actors) to enforce and fulfill social and economic rights and otherwise to affirmatively protect people from violence, hardship, and other threats to their well-being and dignity. Over the last several decades, human rights advocates have brought creative, cutting-edge litigation based on international instruments and economic and social human rights contained in constitutional provisions. Significant work has been done, with major impacts on the ground in some cases, to alleviate poverty and bring social and economic rights to fruition.

Much as I applaud this work,[5] I join the growing number of friendly critics within the human rights movement who point to a shortcoming of our approaches that limits their scope. Until recently, human rights advocacy for poverty alleviation has been almost entirely state centered. By this I mean that human rights work tends to see the solution to poverty as the adoption of good government policies, particularly spending policies to pump resources into poor communities.[6] A common mode of human rights advocacy, which some call 'human

---

[2]   See generally Karl Klare, 'Critical Perspectives on Social and Economic Rights, Democracy, and Separation of Powers,' in Helena Alviar García, Karl Klare and Lucy A Williams, *Social and Economic Rights in Theory and Practice: Critical Inquiries* (Routledge 2015).

[3]   See Karl Klare, 'Concluding Reflections: Legal Activism After Poverty Has Been Declared Unconstitutional' (2011) Stellenbosch Law Review 865.

[4]   To be sure, we are increasingly aware that extreme weather events can cause and/or exacerbate poverty. However, the human rights community has become acutely sensitive to the now-conclusive evidence that climate change, which is responsible for an increasing number of extreme weather events, is generated by human economic and social activity and by governmental failure to take appropriate, ameliorative measures.

[5]   Lucy Williams, 'Resource Questions in Social and Economic Rights Enforcement: a Preliminary View,' in Alviar, Klare and Williams (n 2); Lucy Williams, 'The Role of Courts in the Quantitative-Implementation of Social and Economic Rights: A Comparative Study' (2010) Constitutional Court Rev 141; Lucy Williams, 'Issues and Challenges in Addressing Poverty and Legal Rights: A Comparative United States/South African Analysis' (2005) South African J on Human Rights 436.

[6]   A notable exception is the 2011 United Nations Guiding Principles on Business and Human Rights that sets out both state duties to protect human rights and corporate responsibilities to respect human rights. See OHCHR 'Guiding Principles on Business and Human Rights' (2011) <www.ohchr.org/documents/publications/guidingprinciplesbusinesshr_en.pdf> accessed 2 April 2020. However, as Tara

rights fundamentalism,' is to invest enormous energy in correctly formulating social and economic rights and identifying in abstract terms the obligations these rights do or should impose on governments and hoping that appropriate outcomes will result.

A variation on this theme is to formulate poverty alleviation mandates in terms of equality rights, mandating government to assure access to social and economic benefits by historically excluded groups such as women, people of color, people living with disabilities, ethnic and sexual minorities. To be sure, equality mandates can be addressed to private parties, but the focus of much of our work is on the state as the default entity in charge of 'curing' poverty, as if only government were responsible for the perpetuation of poverty and as if the only solution is publicly funded social programs.

Of course, I wholeheartedly support expanded social spending programs. Activist legal work to achieve it is enormously valuable and has accomplished important, sometimes amazing successes. However, this chapter challenges human rights advocates to expand our efforts beyond appeals to and actions against nation-state governments and efforts to achieve correct interpretations of UN covenants. A state-centered focus is limited and problematical for several reasons. For one, private and mixed government-private actors bear significant responsibility for the maintenance of poverty, and we must strengthen the power of human rights law to hold them accountable. Some techniques for doing so have emerged in recent decades. The most notable is the concept of horizontal or direct application of constitutional and treaty obligations to private parties.[7]

A less obvious but ultimately just as, if not more important, limitation of state-centered rights-thinking is this. Poverty is caused and sustained not only by the failure of government to build houses, feed children, provide medical care, and distribute social security. Poverty is also caused and sustained by the background institutions, rules, and practices responsible for distributing wealth, income, and well-being in society. Poverty arises and endures, and consequently human rights are offended, when the background rules that structure economic entitlements and market behavior result in a distribution of resources and access to social goods that is unacceptable and inadequate from the standpoint of human rights law.[8] That is, poverty is perpetuated when the political community leaves in place private-law rules of property, contract, tort, inheritance, family law, and so on that build inequality and poverty into the economic and social status quo. Human rights advocacy must place increasing emphasis

---

Van Ho has noted, '[w]hile the need to secure remedies for victims is central to the Guiding Principles, … there remains a disconnect between the international expectations and the ability of victims to enforce those expectations through domestic legal systems.' Tara Van Ho, 'Vedanta Resources PLC and Another v. Lungowe and Others' (2019) AJIL Intl Decisions 110; Tara J Melish, 'Putting "Human Rights" Back into the UN Guiding Principles on Business and Human Rights: Shifting Frames and Embedding Participation Rights,' *Business and Human Rights: Beyond the End of the Beginning* (CUP 2017) 62.

[7]   A growing number of national constitutions and some transnational instruments impose obligations on private actors to observe constitutional norms and to fulfill constitutionally entrenched rights, including social and economic rights. In some cases this is by express terms. For example, see South African Constitution (1996) 8(2), stating: '[a] provision of the Bill of Rights binds a natural or a juristic person if, and to the extent that, it is applicable, taking into account the nature of the right and the nature of any duty imposed by the right.'

[8]   Gary Peller and Mark Tushnet, 'State Action and A New Birth of Freedom' (2004) Georgetown L J 779. As yet the concept of horizontal application has made limited inroads in the business and human rights area.

on developing conceptual and legal tools to interrogate and challenge the background rules of private law that perpetuate poverty.[9]

In the context of this short essay, I am unable to expand on these broad themes. Rather, I focus on two major decisions decided in 2019 that may open the field beyond state-centered human rights law. In February 2019, the United States Supreme Court held in *Budha Ismail Jam et al. v. International Finance Corporation* that the International Finance Corporation (IFC), the arm of the World Bank Group that finances projects by private corporations in poor and 'less developed' countries, does not enjoy absolute immunity from suit in the United States.[10] In April 2019, the Supreme Court of the United Kingdom held in *Vedanta Resources PLC and another v. Lungowe and other* that a claim brought by a group of Zambian villagers against UK-based Vedanta Resources PLC and its Zambian subsidiary, Konkola Copper Mines (KCM) could proceed in the UK.[11] Together these cases may open certain possibilities for human rights advocates to promote poverty alleviation by litigating against both international organizations that fund development projects and multinational corporations in their home states. In particular, they suggest intriguing possibilities for holding international institutions and private entities responsible for poverty alleviation. The cases also suggest new legal and conceptual challenges we must address.

In Section I, I briefly discuss the current human rights discourse that focuses on judicial enforcement of social and economic rights contained in national constitutions. As previously noted, other chapters extensively cover efforts to achieve poverty alleviation through UN instruments.

In Section II, I explore recent cases discussing the possibility of suing, respectively, international organizations that finance development projects and private businesses engaged in such projects, with particular emphasis on reaching the parent corporations in their home states. These cases may open new avenues for human rights advocates to obtain redress for desperately poor individuals and communities whose suffering and deprivation are deepened by 'development' projects.

In Section III, I address ways in which these two decisions are both significant, but also limited, raising areas requiring further research and monitoring.

I.   WORKING WITHIN THE FRAMEWORK OF THE STATE

As noted, in the last several decades a growing number of jurisdictions have adopted progressive constitutions that to varying degrees incorporate social and economic rights. Human rights advocates have utilized those provisions to bring about significant changes in poor people's living conditions. In Colombia, the Constitutional Court saved lives with decisions relating to social and economic rights of internally displaced persons during the protracted

---

[9]   On this point, see generally Lucy A Williams, 'Welfare Law and Legal Entitlements: The Social Roots of Poverty,' in D Kairys, *Politics of Law* (3rd edn Basic Books 1998). See also Dennis M Davis and Karl Klare, 'Transformative Constitutionalism and the Common and Customary Law' (2010) South African J on Human Rights 403.

[10]   *Jam v International Finance Corporation* [2019] 139 S Ct 759.

[11]   *Vedanta Resources PLC and another v Lungowe and others* [2019] Hilary Term UKSC 20 <www.supremecourt.uk/cases/docs/uksc-2017-0185-judgment.pdf> accessed 7 July 2020.

armed conflict.[12] It ordered the immediate delivery of basic rights such as food, health care, education and housing and set up a permanent monitoring chamber that held public hearings and established processes to hold government accountable for fulfilling its responsibilities under the court's orders. The same court utilized a similar model to redress huge inequities in health benefits by declaring health to be a fundamental right and thereafter unifying the two tiers of health benefit plans in Colombia.[13] In India, the *Right to Food* case mandated government provision of basic sustenance to millions of food-insecure people.[14] In South Africa, the Constitutional Court invoked the constitutional right to access to social security in finding that impoverished non-citizen, permanent residents were eligible for cash assistance old age, child-support and care-dependency state benefit schemes.[15] Scholars have persuasively argued that this litigation can both provide economic lifelines and facilitate democratic participation,[16] although others have provided important critical analyses.[17]

But one-sided reliance on state-led spending and delivery programs diverts attention from the importance of the distribution of property and entitlements and of market-based resource-allocation in sustaining inequality and poverty. The human rights community must make a priority of interrogating and struggling to revise the legal infrastructure of social and economic life.

Let me use the South African jurisprudence regarding evictions as an example.[18] The South African Constitution contains a generous provision on housing and evictions.[19] The Constitutional Court's residential eviction cases represent by far the most developed branch

---

[12]   Constitutional Court Ruling T-025/04, Judge Manuel José Cepeda Espinosa, [2004] <www .corteconstitucional.gov.co/relatoria/2004/t-025-04.htm> accessed 1 April 2020.

[13]   Constitutional Court Ruling T-760/08, Judge Manuel José Cepeda Espinosa, [2008] <www .corteconstitucional.gov.co/Relatoria/2008/T-760-08.htm> accessed 6 April 2020.

[14]   *People's Union for Civil Liberties v Union of India and others* (writ petition) [2001] Supreme Court of India.

[15]   *Khosa v Minister of Social Development*, [2004(6)] BCLR 569 (CC).

[16]   Natalia Angel-Cabo and Domingo Lovera Parmo, 'Latin American Social Constitutionalism: Courts and Popular Participation' in Alviar, Klare and Williams (n 2) 85; Lilian Chenwi, *Democratizing the Socio-Economic Rights-Enforcement Process* (Pulp 2007); Dennis M Davis, 'The Scope of the Judicial Role in the Enforcement of Social and Economic Rights: Limits and Possibilities Viewed From the South African Experience' in Alviar, Klare and Williams (n 2) 197; Roberto Gargarella, 'Deliberative Democracy, Dialogic Justice and the Promise of Social and Economic Rights' in Alviar, Klare and Williams (n 2) 105; Sandra Liebenberg and Katherine G. Young, 'Adjudicating Social and Economic Rights: Can Democratic Experimentalism Help?' in Alviar, Klare and Williams (n 2) 237.

[17]   Helena Alviar García, 'Distribution of Resources Led by Courts: A Few Words of Caution' in Alviar, Klare and Williams (n 2) 67; Octavio Luiz Motta Ferraz, 'Between Activism and Deference: Social Rights Adjudication in the Brazilian Supreme Federal Tribunal' in Alviar, Klare and Williams (n 2) 121.

[18]   See generally Lucy A Williams, 'The Right to Housing in South Africa: An Evolving Jurisprudence' (2014) Columbia Human Rights L Rev 816.

[19]   Section 26 of the Constitution provides:

(1) Everyone has the right to have access to adequate housing.

(2) The state must take reasonable legislative and other measures, within its available resources, to achieve the progressive realization of this right.

(3) No one may be evicted from their home, or have their home demolished, without an order of court made after considering all the relevant circumstances. No legislation may permit arbitrary evictions.

See Constitution of the Republic of South Africa, 1996 <www.gov.za/documents/constitution -republic-south-africa-1996> accessed 7 July 2020.

of social and economic jurisprudence, in significant part due to the profound trauma of racially-based expropriations and forced removals during the apartheid era.[20]

The constitutional guarantees are given effect, among other places, in the Unlawful Occupation of Land Act 19 of 1998 (PIE Act).[21] Under the PIE Act, courts asked to order an eviction must consider whether it would be 'just and equitable' to grant the eviction. In making this determination, the court must consider 'all the relevant circumstances, including the rights and needs of the elderly, children, disabled persons and households headed by women.'[22] Where unlawful occupiers have occupied land for more than six months, the Act requires the court to consider whether 'land has been made available or can reasonably be made available by a municipality or other organ of state or other land owner for the relocation of the unlawful occupier.'[23]

A leading case is the 2011 judgment of *City of Johannesburg Metro. Municipality v Blue Moonlight Properties*.[24] Blue Moonlight sought to evict 81 adults and five children who were occupants of an industrial building in the Johannesburg central business district in order to clear the way for development of the property.[25] One child was disabled, two adults were pensioners, and several households were headed by females.[26] All of them had lived in the warehouse for more than six months, one of them had lived there since 1976 and another since 1990.[27] Their occupation had previously been legal, they had paid rent until either 2004 or 2005, and Blue Moonlight Properties had purchased the building in 2004 knowing that it was occupied.[28]

The occupiers opposed the eviction on the ground that it would render them homeless, which in South Africa is a constitutionally problematic outcome.[29] The developers in turn claimed that their continued presence would amount to an 'arbitrary deprivation of property' in violation of Section 25(1) of the South African Constitution. The High Court ordered the eviction. When the case reached the Constitutional Court, the point of focus was whether, considering all the circumstances, the eviction was 'just and equitable' under the PIE Act read in light of the Constitution.[30] The Court stated that pertinent considerations to be addressed included: (1) the rights of the owner in a constitutional and PIE era; (2) the obligations of the City to provide accommodation; (3) the sufficiency of the City's resources; (4) the constitutionality of the City's emergency housing policy; and (5) an appropriate order to facilitate justice and equity in the light of the conclusions on the earlier issues.[31]

---

[20]   Michael Robertson, 'Dividing the Land: An Introduction to Apartheid Land Law' in Christina Murray and Catherine O'Regan, *No Place to Rest: Forced Removals and the Law in South Africa* (OUP 1990).

[21]   'Prevention of Illegal Eviction from and Unlawful Occupation of Land' (Act 19 of 1998) Republic of South Africa.

[22]   ibid sec 4(b)–(7).

[23]   ibid sec 4(7).

[24]   *City of Johannesburg Metro. Municipality v Blue Moonlight Properties* [2011] Constitutional Court of SA CCT 37/11.

[25]   ibid para 6.

[26]   ibid.

[27]   ibid para 7.

[28]   ibid paras 7–8, 39.

[29]   ibid para 11.

[30]   ibid para 30.

[31]   ibid para 33.

The Constitutional Court found that the developers were entitled to evict the occupiers, but that the eviction would not be 'just and equitable' under the PIE Act until the City provided the occupiers with temporary accommodation.[32] It ordered the City to provide the occupiers such accommodations within five months of the date of the judgment. In other words, in circumstances where an eviction of occupiers from private property would render the occupiers homeless, the rights of developers may have to yield to the occupiers' right to housing, albeit not indefinitely.[33]

Blue Moonlight, without doubt, was a victory for the poor residents. From a different perspective, however, the practical effect of the Court's order was to oblige the City to subsidize the private developer. Developers have strong incentivizes to buy up derelict properties, evict persons who have been staying on these properties in desperate circumstances for many years and then to reap handsome profits by way of gentrification. No party to the proceeding, nor the Court nor the progressive bar, addressed the distributive consequences of the decision, which were, in essence, that the City—that is, taxpayers—are forced to absorb the social-dislocation costs of economic development, with little or no contribution from the developers. Of course, it is better for the City to pay these costs than to visit them on the evicted tenants. As a long-term question, however, a coherent plan to supply housing for the poor requires assessment of at least some net social-dislocation costs to developers. Not to do so results in the taxpayer subsidizing the developer's profits while getting nothing in return that might be used to deliver social goods to the poor.

Two recent cases offer promising avenues for human rights advocates to move beyond a state-centered approach to poverty alleviation.

II.   THINKING BEYOND THE STATE

A.   Holding International Banking Institutions Accountable

In the period after World War II, new international organizations were founded including the United Nations, the World Bank, and the International Monetary Fund. Contemporaneously, the US Congress passed the International Organizations Immunities Act of 1945, 59 Stat. 669 (IOIA). The Act granted these international organizations the 'same immunity from suit and every form of judicial process as is enjoyed by foreign governments.'[34] From 1945–1952, the US Department of State held the view that foreign governments had absolute immunity. United States courts followed the Department of State view that because foreign governments had absolute immunity, so should the international organizations under the IOIA. However, after 1952, in light of an increase and broadening of commercial activities by nation states, the US State Department determined that it was necessary for people affected by such business to

---

[32]   The Court noted the length of time the occupiers had been on the property, the fact that the residency had once been lawful, the fact that the eviction would render the individuals homeless, and that there was no 'competing risk of homelessness on the part of Blue Moonlight.' ibid para 39.

[33]   In making this ruling, the Constitutional Court found that the protection against arbitrary deprivation of property must be balanced against the right to access to adequate housing and the right not to be arbitrarily evicted. ibid para 34.

[34]   'Privileges, exemptions, and immunities of internal organizations' 22 U.S.C. § 288a (b).

have access to the courts as arbiters of their rights. Accordingly, the State Department adopted a new 'restrictive' theory of sovereign immunity. Under this theory, foreign governments were entitled to immunity only for sovereign acts, but not for commercial activities. In 1976, in the Foreign Sovereign Immunities Act (FSIA), Congress codified the restrictive theory of foreign sovereign immunity. The FSIA provides that a foreign government may be subject to suit in US courts for commercial activity that has a sufficient nexus with the United States.[35]

The International Finance Corporation (IFC) was established in 1956 as the arm of the World Bank Group headquartered in Washington, D.C. to finance projects by private sector business interests in 'developing' countries around the world.[36] Since 1956, the IFC has leveraged $2.6 billion in capital to deliver more than $285 billion in financing for businesses in developing countries.[37]

The World Bank Group (which includes the IFC) has two overarching goals: 1) to end extreme poverty by reducing the share of the global population that lives in extreme poverty to 3 percent by 2030 and 2) to promote shared prosperity by increasing the incomes of the poorest 40 percent of people in every country.[38] According to the IFC's Articles of Agreement, the purpose of the IFC 'is to further economic development by encouraging the growth of productive private enterprise in member countries, particularly in the less developed areas.'[39] The IFC's 'mission is to fight poverty ...; to help people help themselves and their environment by providing resources, sharing knowledge, building capacity and forging partnerships in the public and private sectors. IFC believes that sound economic growth, grounded in sustainable private investment, is crucial to poverty reduction.'[40]

In 2008, the IFC loaned $450 million to the Indian company Coastal Gujarat Power Limited (CGPL) to finance the construction of the Tata Mundra Ultra Mega coal-fired power plant in the coastal state of Gujarat, India. The recipients of IFC loans are required to meet performance standards included in their loan agreements that are enforced by IFC internal review. In this case, CGPL had to comply with an environmental and social plan designed to protect areas surrounding the plant, the penalty for non-compliance being loan revocation. In October 2013, an IFC internal audit by the Compliance Advisor Ombudsman found that the company had not complied with the environmental and social plan, and that the IFC had not adequately supervised the project.

---

[35] 'General exceptions to the jurisdictional immunity of a foreign state' 28 U.S.C. § 1605(a)(2).
[36] Subsequently, multiple Multilateral Development Banks, such as the Asian Development Bank, European Investment Bank, Inter-American Development Bank and the African Development Bank have been established. See 'Multilateral Development Banks: Overview and Issues for Congress' (11 February 2020) Congressional Research Service <https://fas.org/sgp/crs/row/R41170.pdf> accessed 7 July 2020.
[37] 'Partner With Us' (*International Finance Corporation*, n.d.) <www.ifc.org/wps/wcm/connec t/corp_ext_content/ifc_external_corporate_site/home> accessed 1 April 2020.
[38] 'Who We Are' (*The World Bank*, n.d.) <www.worldbank.org/en/who-we-are> accessed 1 April 2020.
[39] 'Articles of Agreement' (*International Finance Corporation*, 16 April 2020) <www.ifc.org/wps/wcm/connect/d057dbd5-4b02-40f8-8065-9e6315c5a9aa/IFC_Articles_of_Agreement.pdf?MOD=AJPERES&CVID=jBfBkXT> accessed 1 April 2020.
[40] 'Policy on Environmental and Social Sustainability' (*IFC*, 1 January 2012) <www.ifc.org/wps/wcm/connect/7141585d-c6fa-490b-a812-2ba87245115b/SP_English_2012.pdf?MOD=AJPERES&CVID=kiIrw0g> accessed 1 April 2020.

Represented by EarthRights International, Budha Ismail Jam, a fisher and other deeply impoverished fishers and farmers, along with a fishers' organization and a village from the surrounding area, filed a suit in the US District Court for the District of Columbia against the IFC in 2015 for damages and injunctive relief on claims of negligence, negligent supervision, public nuisance, private nuisance, trespass, and breach of contract as third part beneficiaries. The plaintiffs alleged that the pollution from the power plant had threatened their health, property and livelihoods through depletion of fish stocks, because their wells were ruined by increased salinity of the groundwater, and because their farmland was damaged by the ash and dust from the plant. The meager amounts they were previously able to earn had been severely diminished while their costs had increased substantially.

In defense, the IFC claimed that it had an absolute immunity under the IOIA. Both the District Court and the federal Court of Appeals dismissed the plaintiffs' suit for lack of subject matter jurisdiction due to absolute immunity. Their decisions followed precedent in the D.C. Circuit that the IOIA granted international organizations the virtually absolute immunity that foreign governments enjoyed when the IOIA was enacted in 1945.[41]

However, in February 2019, in *Budha Ismail Jam et al. v. International Finance Corporation*, the US Supreme Court determined that the IFC did not have absolute immunity from suit in the United States.[42]

The Court held that Congress, in enacting the IOIA, had not granted a fixed or static type of immunity, but rather had adopted a law that was intended to develop parallel to and in tandem with the immunity of foreign states. Therefore, the immunity of the IFC should be the same as enjoyed by foreign governments, which is an 'external body of potentially evolving law.'[43] The Court noted that after the passage of the FSIA in 1976 in which Congress codified the restrictive theory of foreign sovereign immunity (discussed above), the State Department took the position that the immunity rules of the IOIA and the FSIA were now coterminous.[44]

The IFC objected that reducing the level of immunity would damage its mission by opening up one country's courts to challenge the decisions of its many member states, by exposing the organization to money damages, and by opening the floodgates to foreign plaintiff litigation because so much of its activity is commercial. The Court disagreed and stated that organizations can specify a different level of immunity in their charters under certain conditions.[45]

---

[41]   *Jam v IFC* [2016] 172 F Supp 3d 104; *Jam v IFC* [2017] 860 F3d 703 (citing *Atkinson v Inter-American Development Bank* [1998] CADC 156 F3d 1335).

[42]   *Jam* (n 10).

[43]   ibid 769.

[44]   ibid 771.

[45]   ibid 771–72. The discussion of which international organizations might be implicated by *Jam* and the sovereign immunity of each of those organizations, some of which have immunities contained in other statutes, treaties, or charters is beyond the scope of this chapter. However, this is the type of question that human rights activists will face in the decade ahead as they litigate the obligation of international organizations to provide social protections in financing development projects. Julian Arato, 'Equivalence and Translation: Further thoughts on IO Immunities in Jam v IFC' (*EJIL: Talk!* 11 March 2019) <www .ejiltalk.org/equivalence-and-translation-further-thoughts-on-io-immunities-in-jam-v-ifc/> accessed 10 April 2020. EarthRights argues that it is questionable whether the IFC can change its charter to contain an absolute immunity. Marco Simons, 'Jam v IFC: Some Questions and Answers After the Supreme Court's Ruling' (*EarthRights International Blog* 4 March 2019) <https://earthrights.org/blog/which -international-organizations-will-be-affected-most-by-the-supreme-courts-ruling/> accessed 12 April 2020.

However, the Court did not declare that the IFC's activity or the lending activity of other international development banks is definitely 'commercial' in nature or that the particular activity involved in the case, if commercial, bore a sufficient nexus to the US to permit the suit to go forward. The case was remanded to the District Court to address the questions whether the IFC's loan in this case was commercial in nature, and whether the harms alleged were sufficiently related to the US for the IFC to be held liable.

While not directly addressing the question of whether the activity was commercial in nature, the US District Court for the District of Columbia on 14 February 2020 dismissed the plaintiffs' complaint concluding that the commercial activity exception does not apply because the suit is not based on conduct carried on in the United States.[46] The court found that

> [T]he gravamen of the complaint is not that IFC's board of directors, in approving the loan, wrote CGPL a blank check without imposing any conditions to ensure protection of the environment and the local population. It is instead that IFC—after approving the loan—failed to enforce the conditions of the loan agreement designed to protect the environment and local population. These alleged failures of oversight by IFC are focused on conduct or inaction in India, not the United States.[47]

EarthRights International filed a motion for leave to amend their complaint and submitted extensive additional factual evidence to support their contention that virtually all of the IFC's actions and decisions relating to the power plant were made in the United States. Even if the district court again rules against the plaintiffs, EarthRights International will probably appeal that decision.[48]

B.   Holding Parent Companies Liable for Actions Taken by their Subsidiaries

Parent corporations in developed countries have enjoyed broad insulation from liability for human rights violations committed by their subsidiaries in less developed countries.[49] A recent case may be a welcome harbinger of change.

In April, 2019, the United Kingdom Supreme Court in *Vedanta Resources PLC and another v. Lungowe and other*,[50] upheld the jurisdiction of UK courts over a UK parent company for alleged actions of a Zambian subsidiary company that took place in Zambia. The decision potentially applies to UK parent companies with respect to their subsidiaries operating in other parts of the world. Such companies may now face liability in the UK for human rights violations committed by their foreign subsidiaries.

Suit was brought by 1,826 Zambian citizens from four different communities in the Chingola District who alleged serious injury to their health and ability to farm caused by the discharge of sulphuric acid and other toxins into their sole water source as a result of operations at the Nchanga Copper Mine. The mine, owned and operated by Konkola Copper Mines (KCM),

---

[46]   *Jam v IFC* [2020] DDC WL 759199.

[47]   ibid 8.

[48]   Marco Simons, 'Jam v. IFC: One year after the historic Supreme Court victory' (*EarthRights International*, 19 March 2020) <https://earthrights.org/blog/jam-v-ifc-one-year-after-the-historic-supreme-court-victory/> accessed 20 March 2020.

[49]   Note the limitation of utilizing the Alien Tort Statute in the US for similar cases: *Kiobel v. Royal Dutch Petroleum Co.* [2013] 133 S. Ct. 1659; *Jesner v. Arab Bank* [2018] 138 S. Ct. 1386.

[50]   *Vedanta Resources PLC* (n 11).

is one of the largest open cast mines in the world. KCM is Zambia's single largest employer and employs approximately 16,000 people.[51] Vedanta Resources plc (Vedanta), the ultimate UK parent company of KCM, is incorporated in the UK. The claims arise under common law negligence and breach of statutory duty, as against KCM because of its operation of the mine, and as against Vedanta because of its control and direction of KCM's compliance with health, safety, and environmental regulations.[52]

Both Vedanta and KCM challenged the jurisdiction of the UK courts over the case. To obtain jurisdiction over Vedanta, the claimants relied on article 4.1 of the Recast Brussels Regulation, which allows a claimant to sue a party that is domiciled in a member state where that party is domiciled, and over KCM as a necessary and proper party to the litigation under the English Procedural Code.[53] Both the High Court and the Court of Appeal dismissed the challenge to the courts' jurisdiction.

Before the UK Supreme Court, the defendants contended:

1. That the claimant's reliance on article 4.1 to establish jurisdiction over Vedanta as anchor defendant constituted an abuse of EU law because the claimants were using the claim against Vedanta merely as a vehicle to obtain jurisdiction over KCM;
2. That there was no real triable issue against Vedanta, primarily based on the question of whether under English law a parent company may owe a duty of care to persons harmed by the actions or omissions of its foreign subsidiary;
3. That Zambia, not England, was the proper place for the claim to be brought, and
4. That the lower court judge had erroneously found that there was a real risk that the claimants would be unable to obtain substantial justice in Zambia.[54]

The Court recognized that it would be an abuse of EU law to allow claimants to sue Vedanta solely to establish jurisdiction over KCM in the English courts, thus opening Vedanta to liability when they would otherwise not be sued. However, based on the facts of the case and the rulings of the lower courts, the Court determined that the claimants had a legitimate claim against Vedanta and a bona fide desire to obtain judgment against them, in part because of KCM's doubtful solvency.[55]

In deciding whether there was a real triable issue against Vedanta, the Court rejected the defendants' argument that establishing parent company liability raised a 'novel and controversial extension of the boundaries of the tort of negligence.'[56] What was before the Court was simply 'whether A owes a duty of care to C in respect of the harmful activities of B.'[57] The

---

[51]   Lee P McBride, Ben Stansfield and Nick Harding, 'Vedanta Resources PLC & Another v Lungowe & Others—Supreme Court Rules UK Correct Jurisdiction to Bring Claim Against Zambian Subsidiary' (*Gowling WLG*, 17 April 2019) <https://gowlingwlg.com/en/insights-resources/articles/2019/vedanta-resources-plc-another-v-lungowe-others/> accessed 4 March 2020.

[52]   This case did not rely on a theory of vicarious liability of a parent corporation for wrongs committed by its subsidiary. Vedanta was sued in its own right. For a discussion of UK law on vicarious liability for parent companies, see Philip Morgan, 'Vicarious Liability for Group Companies: the final frontier of vicarious liability' (2015) J of Professional Negligence 276.

[53]   Civil Procedure Rules, 'Practice Direction 6B – Service out of the Jurisdiction' para 3.1.

[54]   *Vedanta Resources PLC* (n 11) paras 20, 22.

[55]   ibid para 27.

[56]   ibid para 46.

[57]   ibid para 54.

claim against Vedanta arose not from its ownership of KCM, but from its direct control over and supervision of operations at the mine, its high level of intervention in KCM's activities, its knowledge of the dangers and likelihood of pollution, and published materials in which Vedanta itself asserted responsibility for establishing appropriate environmental control and sustainability standards, for implementing training consistent with these standards, and for monitoring and enforcement. This, the Court determined, was sufficient for Vedanta to incur a duty of care in tort to the claimants under UK common law.

The Court identified a number of ways in which group-wide policies, that is, policies covering all parts of a business group, might give rise to a duty of care over a subsidiary: 1) where the group-wide guidelines themselves contain systemic errors that cause harm to third parties, 2) where the 'group-wide policies do not of themselves give rise to such a duty of care to third parties ... [but the parent] takes active steps, by training, supervision and enforcement, to see that they are implemented by relevant subsidiaries', or 3) where the parent 'in published materials ... holds itself out as exercising that degree of supervision and control of its subsidiaries, even if it does not in fact do so.'[58] The Court found that this list is not exclusive and stated that 'there is no limit to the models of management and control which may be put in place within a multinational group of companies.'[59] The extent of Vedanta's actual managerial intervention was considered a pure question of fact. In upholding the lower court's finding that Vedanta arguably had a duty of care, the Court relied on a management services agreement and a report published by Vedanta entitled 'Embedding Sustainability' that emphasized how Vedanta's board had oversight over all of its subsidiaries.[60]

In setting out the numerous ways in which a duty of care can be established, the *Vedanta* Court significantly expanded the UK Court of Appeal's ruling in *Chandler v Cape plc*,[61] which had articulated a limited series of factors that established when a parent company owed a duty of care (in that case to the employees) of its subsidiary. *Vedanta* confirmed that the *Chandler* factors are only examples of such situations. Lord Briggs found that a parent company's duty could be established by reference to basic tort principles rather than 'by imposing a straitjacket derived from the *Chandler* case which, if anything, increased rather than reduced the claimants' burden in demonstrating a triable issue.'[62]

Next, the Court disagreed with the lower courts that England was the proper place for the litigation. Instead the Court determined that Zambia would ordinarily be the proper venue because of practical difficulties involved in getting the claimants to England; the locations of the evidence, relevant actions, and harm; a common language eliminating the need for translation; and because the case would be decided under Zambian law.[63]

---

[58] ibid paras 52–53.

[59] ibid para 51.

[60] ibid paras 55, 58; 'UK Supreme Court clarifies issues on parent company liability in Lungowe v. Vedanta' (*Norton Rose Fulbright Publication*, April 2019) <www.nortonrosefulbright.com/en-ca/knowledge/publications/70fc8211/uk-supreme-court-clarifies-issues-on-parent-company-liability-in-lungowe-v-vedanta> accessed 16 March 2020.

[61] *Chandler v Cape plc* [2012] 1 WLR 3111.

[62] *Vedanta Resources PLC* (n 11) paras 49–51, 60.

[63] Although all parties agreed that the applicable law was the law of Zambia, the UK Supreme Court found that the lower court had 'accepted that it was arguable that the Zambian courts would identify the relevant principles of Zambian common law in accordance with those established in England' and that '[i]t is now common ground that he was entitled on the evidence to do so.' ibid para 56.

Despite these considerations, the Court nevertheless concluded that in this case the claimants would probably be unable to obtain substantial justice in Zambia because (i) the claimants are living in poverty and are unable to fund legal representation (noting that conditional fee agreements are illegal in Zambia), and (ii) Zambia lacks legal teams with enough experience to handle litigation of this scale and complexity. In the UK, claimants were represented pro bono by the law firm Leigh Day that had been fighting for four years to have the case heard in the UK courts. These considerations outweighed the normal assumption that Zambia would be the proper place for the litigation. Accordingly, the Court dismissed the defendants' appeals and allowed the litigation to continue in the UK courts.

This ruling opened the way for the case to proceed to a full trial of the issues. According to the Supreme Court:

> In the absence of any admissions from the appellants which might serve to narrow the issues (and there are none), large aspects of the claimants' collective and individual claims will depend upon the presentation of expert evidence. They will include identifying the emissions which actually occurred, and their toxicity, establishing whether the system of operation of the Mine (both in its planning and implementation) fell short of that requisite to satisfy a duty of care, tracing the emissions through to watercourses in the vicinity of the claimants, proving (during a considerable period of time) that these emissions caused damage to particular claimants' land, business and health, and quantifying (save perhaps in relation to personal injuries) the diminution in the value of business and property thereby caused.[64]

The case is set for a 12-week trial in October 2021.[65]

III.   WHAT DO WE LEARN FROM THESE CASES? WHAT ARE NEXT STEPS?

The *Jam* and *Vedanta* judgments open exciting possibilities for imposing human rights liability on international funding institutions and multinational parent corporations, but they also raise challenging questions.

Jam opens the possibility that international financial institutions can be held liable for the social, economic and environmental harms caused by projects that they finance. Although the question of the IFC's liability for harms associated with this particular investment is now in the hands of the lower courts in the US, the *Jam* decision signals a weakening of the shield of immunity protecting international financial institutions. Going forward, litigation, much of it

---

[64]   *Vedanta Resources PLC* (n 11) para 94.
[65]   Email from Oliver Holland, Associate Solicitor, Leigh Day, London, on file with author. In the interim, the Zambian government, which owns 20 percent of KCM, has appointed a liquidator to operate KCM and is trying to seize KCM from Vedanta with an eye toward selling it. Holland says that the case will proceed against Vedanta regardless of the outcome of the litigation regarding the Zambian government's attempt to sell KCM.

See Tanisha Heiberg and Helen Reid, 'South African court blocks Zambian plan to sell Vedanta copper mine' (*Reuters*, 23 July 2019) <www.reuters.com/article/us-zambia-mining-vedanta/south-african-court-blocks-zambian-plan-to-sell-vedanta-copper-mine-idUSKCN1UI1Y6> accessed 4 April 2020; Chiponda Chimbelu, 'Lungowe v Vedanta: How to hold multinationals liable for harmful activities' (*DW Freedom*, 4 February 2020) <www.dw.com/en/lungowe-v-vedanta-how-to-hold-multinationals-liable-for-harmful-activities/a-52233779> accessed 4 April 2020.

highly fact-specific, can be expected on the questions of whether an organization's activities in a given case are 'commercial' in nature and whether these activities have a sufficient tie to the US. Though it is difficult to predict the future course of this litigation, *Jam* opened the door to substantial liability for international organizations that will have broad impact whatever the outcome in the particular case.

For example, the same organization that represents the plaintiffs in *Jam*, EarthRights International, has resumed litigation in a case against a palm oil plantation in Honduras, which had also received a loan from the IFC.[66] The plantation's private security forces allegedly attacked and killed community members. Similar to the situation in *Jam*, these events were documented in internal IFC reports by the Compliance Advisor Ombudsman. The district court stayed the case pending the Supreme Court's decision in *Jam*. The IFC may now be more inclined to settle because of its more limited immunity.[67] If not, subsequent cases will proceed in the courts perhaps filling in some of the doctrinal gaps left in *Jam*.

Academics, practitioners and activists have questioned what effects on the internal structures and deliberations of international financial institutions we might expect as a consequence of the *Jam* judgment. A salutary possibility is that the lower standard of immunity might dissuade the World Bank and other institutions from financing projects that are highly risky from a social and/or environmental standpoint. That is, if it is robust and effective, post-*Jam* litigation might force the international institutions to 'internalize' social and environmental dislocation costs and harms into their investment decisions. Even mainstream economic theory accepts that risks and harms are 'over-produced' when investment decisions ignore these 'externalities.' Other observers suggest that *Jam* might induce the international financial institutions to improve compliance by, e.g., improving compliance audit mechanisms and by conducting more proactive and aggressive monitoring and investigation of projects and contractors. Alongside these potential benefits we must be aware of potential negative consequences. Some observers worry that *Jam* and like decisions might have the perverse consequence of inducing the international banking institutions to dismantle or weaken their compliance and ombudsman mechanisms and their public commitments to affected communities, so as to avoid the risk of assuming duties of care.[68]

On March 9, 2020, the World Bank's Board of Executive Directors announced that it was enhancing its Inspection Panel toolkit and creating an expanded independent accountability mechanism.[69] However, Kristen Genovese, senior researcher from the Dutch Centre for Research on Multinational Corporations, has raised numerous concerns about transparency in

---

[66] *Juana Doe et al. v. IFC* [2019] D. Del. Civil Action No. 1:17-cv-1494-JFB-SRF.

[67] Indeed, on 18 February 2020, at the time this manuscript was submitted for publication, the parties filed a Stipulation and (Proposed) Order Staying Case to the US District Court agreeing that the litigation should be stayed for 90 days because productive settlement discussions had been ongoing over the past few months. ibid.

[68] Michael H Huneke and Ayoka Akinosi, 'U.S. Supreme Court Ruling in Jam v. IFC Increases Pressure on Multilateral Development Banks and Recipients of MDB-Financed Contracts to Detect and Prevent Corruption and Other Sanctionable Practices' (*Hughes Hubbard & Reed Client Advisories*, 17 May 2019) <www.hugheshubbard.com/news/u-s-supreme-court-ruling-in-jam-v-ifc-increases-pressure -on-multilateral-development-banks-and-recipients-of-mdb-financed-contracts-to-detect-and-prevent -corruption-and-other-sanctionable-practices> accessed 15 March 2020.

[69] www.worldbank.org/en/news/press-release/2020/03/09/world-bank-enhances-its-accountability, accessed 15 March 2020.

the development of the new mechanism and about its structure and effectiveness, specifically pointing to the fact that the Inspection Panel must obtain approval from the Board in order to monitor management's plans; the mechanism's one-year time limit for dispute resolution; and the fact that a complaint must fit within limited criteria in order to be eligible for dispute resolution.[70]

Turning from the liability of international organizations to that of parent companies, while the *Vedanta* ruling opens the door for transnational tort claims in the UK, expanding the scope of liability and raising the pressure for good corporate governance, subsequent events reveal some difficulties litigants will confront in securing jurisdiction in the English courts by suing a UK parent company. The cases are likely to be fact specific, and jurisdiction may not be achieved in all situations. In 2018, the Court of Appeal concluded in two similar cases, *Okpabi and others v Royal Dutch Shell Plc and another*[71] and *AAA and Others v Unilever PLC and Another*[72] that the UK courts did not have jurisdiction to hear claims brought by non-UK claimants against UK companies and their non-UK subsidiaries for acts occurring abroad.[73] While appeal to the Supreme Court was stayed in both cases pending the outcome in *Vedanta*, subsequently appeal has been granted in *Okpabi* (provisionally to be heard in the Supreme Court in June 2020), but denied in *Unilever*. In addition, the *Vedanta* decision may influence future cases in other large industrial states such as Germany and the Netherlands where courts follow principles of tort established in English law.[74]

Finally, in deciding whether Vedanta owed a duty of care to the communities harmed by the mining activities of its subsidiary, the UK Supreme Court relied in part on Vedanta's public disclosures made in its sustainability reports. Parent companies may be held accountable for their public commitments regarding their subsidiaries and their commitments to the communities they impact. Indeed, lawyers practicing in this area have taken steps to notify clients that

---

[70] Sophie Edwards, 'World Bank finally approves Inspection Panel reforms after 2-year standoff' (*Devex*, 11 March 2020) <www.devex.com/news/world-bank-finally-approves-inspection-panel-reforms -after-2-year-standoff-96730> accessed 4 April 2020; Kristen Genovese, 'Reviews of World Bank Group's accountability mechanisms too important to be done in secret' (*SOMO opinion*, 20 December 2019) <www.somo.nl/reviews-of-world-bank-groups-accountability-mechanisms-too-important-to-be -done-in-secret/> accessed 4 April 2020.

[71] *HRH Emere Godwin Bebe Okpabi and others v Royal Dutch Shell and Shell Petroleum Development Company of Nigeria Ltd* and *Lucky Alame and others v Royal Dutch Shell and Shell Petroleum Development Company of Nigeria Ltd* [2018] EWCA Civ 191 (concerning claims by victims of oil leaks from pipelines in the Niger delta).

[72] *AAA and others v Unilever PLC and Another* [2018] EWCA Civ 1532 (concerning appeal brought by employees and residents of a plantation owned by Unilever Tea Kenya for damage sustained during an outbreak of violence during the Kenyan 2007 national elections).

[73] 'UK Supreme Court ruling on parent company liability for act of its overseas subsidiaries' (*Norton Rose Fulbright Publication*, February 2020) <www.nortonrosefulbright.com/en/knowledge/ publications/721042ff/uk-supreme-court-ruling-on-parent-company-liability-for-acts-of-its-overseas -subsidiaries> accessed 4 April 2020.

[74] Erika Dailey, 'Case Watch: UK Supreme Court Provides Gateway for Zambian Farmers and Corporate Accountability' (*Open Society Justice Initiative*, 3 May 2019) <www.justiceinitiative .org/voices/case-watch-uk-supreme-court-provides-gateway-zambian-farmers-and-corporate -accountability> accessed 15 March 2020; Anil Yilmaz Vastardis, 'Vedanta v. Lungowe Symposium Potential Implications of the UKSC's Decision for Supply Chain Relationships' (*OpinioJuris*, 23 April 2019) <http://opiniojuris.org/2019/04/23/vedanta-v-lungowe-symposium-potential-implications-of-the -ukscs-decision-for-supply-chain-relationships> accessed 17 March 2020.

'this ruling could have wider implications for companies who make public commitments relating to their responsibilities to communities and the environment and then fail to put these into practice.'[75] Some parent companies might seek to limit their duty by divesting themselves of any responsibility for the operations of their subsidiaries, particularly through refraining from setting out policies in public documents. Conversely, the *Vedanta* judgment may provide an impetus for governments to enact statutes or promulgate regulations mandating transparency and due diligence for companies with regard to human rights consequences of their subsidiaries' actions. Activists should work toward that goal and more generally pressure governments to effectuate the existing obligations on states articulated in the 2011 United Nations Guiding Principles on Business and Human Rights.[76] The human rights community must pay careful attention to whether the *Vedanta* judgment contributes positively to the growing trend of states introducing or enacting mandatory human rights due diligence obligations.[77]

By whittling away at immunities and expanding duties of care, *Jam*, *Vedanta*, and related cases open a non-state-centered path for legal activists to tackle poverty and inequality. The human rights community should invest energy in monitoring further developments in this branch of the law and refining our strategies accordingly.

As promising as these new avenues are, however, it is important to note that they represent only one step in the direction of a comprehensive, non-state fixated approach to poverty alleviation. *Jam* and *Vedanta* remain largely rooted in the anachronistic mindset of 'negative' rights. These cases concern the important, but restricted question of whether non-state actors may be held liable for observable, direct harms visited upon vulnerable populations. As important as that is, the deeper question is whether human rights law can impose affirmative obligations on multinational corporations and international financial institutions (or developers as in the *Blue Moonlight* case) to address poverty alleviation proactively. The challenge ahead is to develop and eventually establish legal theories under which powerful non-state actors will be obliged to build poverty-alleviation strategies into their business and development plans and to devote resources to the goal of ending poverty.

---

[75] 'Supreme Court rules Zambian villagers' case against Vedanta to be heard in English courts' (*Leigh Day News and Events*, April 2019) <www.leighday.co.uk/News/2019/April-2019/Supreme-Court-rules-Zambian-villagers-case-against> accessed 13 March 2020.

[76] OHCHR (n 6).

[77] For example, France's duty of Vigilance Law, LOI n° 2017-399 du 27 mars 2017 relative au devoir de vigilance des sociétés mères et des entreprises donneuses d'ordre (1), the enforceability of which is currently being litigated, see Rebecca Rosman, 'French Judges tilt in favor of Total in landmark ruling' (*Aljazeera*, 30 January 2020) <www.aljazeera.com/ajimpact/french-judges-tilt-favour-total -landmark-ruling-200130223500626.html> accessed 14 April 2020; Germany's 2019 draft 'supply chain law' (Lieferkettengesetz) which would mandate human rights due diligence for German companies with regard to their contractors and subsidiaries abroad. See Business & Human Rights Resource Centre 'German Development Ministry drafts law on mandatory human rights due diligence for German companies' <www.business-humanrights.org/en/german-development-ministry-drafts-law-on -mandatory-human-rights-due-diligence-for-german-companies> accessed 4 April 2020; Tara Van Ho (n 6); Dr Irene Pietropaoli and Phil Bloomer, 'Governments Can Help Make Business More Diligent on Human Rights' (*Business and Human Rights Resource Centre*) <www.business-humanrights.org/en/ governments-can-help-make-business-more-diligent-on-human-rights> accessed 15 March 2020.

Index

Abidjan Principles 438, 440, 441–2
abnormal justice 544, 548
abortion 416–31
    jurisprudence
        impact of human rights on 420–22
        reproductive rights as human rights 417–20
        US case study 422–31
absolute poverty 90, 374, 446
accountability 4–5, 10, 15, 18, 19, 85, 146, 152,
    209, 408, 506, 544
    Guiding Principles on Extreme Poverty and
        Human Rights 85
    human rights and poverty reduction 89, 93,
        94, 95–6, 102
    international institutions and private entities
        320, 395, 396–7, 547, 550–65
    local authorities 283
    MDGs 85
    migrants 240
    military 527
    private body exercising public function 547
    SDGs 220, 227
    social-benefit schemes 156
adoption, international 153–4, 155
affirmative action 9, 118, 119, 225–6, 228
Afghanistan 524
Africa 270, 271, 289, 394, 442, 479, 481, 529
    corruption 506, 510, 511, 512, 519
    data protection 543
    older persons 126, 127
    sub-Saharan 56, 88–103, 126, 129, 142,
        289–90, 317, 541, 547
        affecting discourse on poverty 101–2, 103
        economic and livelihood empowerment
            98–9, 102
        Joseph Rowntree Foundation Report
            (2009) 94–5
        land rights-poverty nexus: West Africa
            309–22
        local experience of human rights-based
            efforts 96–8, 102
        non-monetary perspective 99–101, 103
        poverty, inequality and human rights
            linkages 92–6
        social mobility 101, 103
        state support 99, 102
        trends 90–92, 102, 103
    see also individual countries

African Charter on Human and Peoples' Rights
    (ACHPR) 137, 320, 340, 341, 419
African Commission on Human and Peoples'
    Rights 320, 419
African Court for Human and Peoples' Rights 320
African Union (AU) 320, 510, 511, 512, 543
age discrimination 6, 81, 134, 136–7, 139
agriculture 50, 311, 312, 313, 314–5, 316, 452,
    453, 456, 546
    climate change 494, 495, 496, 497, 501–3
    productivity 99
AIDS/HIV 29–30, 32, 34, 57, 177, 182
Albania 456
Albertyn, C 421–2
Algeria 398
Alston, P 55, 59, 60, 67, 69, 81, 86, 130, 286,
    344, 474, 490
American Convention on Human Rights (ACHR)
    323, 340, 341, 342
    art 4: right to life 324, 328–30
    art 21: communal property 324–6, 329, 334
amnesties 530–31
Anttonen, A 381
Anyidoho, NA 97
apartheid 79, 555
Arbour, L 53
Argentina 175, 182, 189, 222, 224, 290, 362, 437,
    479, 502–3
armed conflict *see* conflict
Aruba and Curaçao 222, 226
Asia 126, 270, 271, 289, 317, 479, 541
    South 129
    see also individual countries
Asian Development Bank 467, 471
assembly, freedom of 10, 75, 340–42, 343, 344–7,
    348, 349, 350, 351, 352
association, freedom of 10, 75, 79, 350, 452–3
asylum seekers 240, 243
    a-legality 256–7, 261–2
    admission to territory 251–2, 254–5,
        256–7, 261–2
    detention of 255, 261, 263
    in European Union 257–63
        CJEU 235–6, 259–60
    hybrid legal status 255–7, 262
    ICCPR 253, 254–5
    international human rights law 253–5, 261–2
    Israel 241, 244
    presumptive protection 250

Refugee Convention 247, 248, 249–52, 253, 257, 258, 261, 262
Atkinson, T 51
austerity 8, 27–8, 150, 272, 286, 292, 396, 477–8
Australia 126, 127–8, 134, 189, 391
Austria 291–2, 397
autonomy 23, 24, 26, 28, 33, 35, 36, 115, 540, 548
    abortion 418, 423, 430, 431
    children 153
    political rights 75
    relational 70–73, 86

Balakrishnan, R 59
Bangladesh 11, 24, 359, 515–6
bank loans 109, 159
Barkhouse, A 515
Barron, DJ 281
begging 173, 291–2
behaviourism, new 370–71, 374–7, 379, 384
Belgium 14, 199, 285, 289–90, 293
Belize 222
Benhabib, S 255
Benin 456
Bentham, J 71
Bjørnskov, C 509–10
Blakely, EJ 305
bodily integrity 184
Bolivia 11, 24, 186
Bosnia and Herzegovina 202
Botswana 186
Bourdieu, P 82
Brazil 56, 213, 215, 306, 361, 480
Brinks, DM 95
Brück, T 524
Bulgaria 198, 200, 201, 202, 206, 207–8
Burkina Faso 91
Burundi 524

Cambodia 462–73
    human rights dimensions of minimum wage 469–72
    minimum wage policy
        addressing poverty 463–7
        labour productivity 468–9
Cambridge Analytica 540
Canada 170, 176, 215, 223, 225, 264, 274, 305, 494–5, 496
    economic inequality 56
    housing 391, 395, 397, 398
    social condition discrimination 6
capabilities 200, 202, 354–5, 374, 381, 404, 406, 409, 499
    rights and social exclusion 37–52
        historical background 38–41

human rights perspective and policy 44–6
human rights, social rights and social exclusion 47–51
needs and rights 46–7
poverty as capability deprivation 41–3
poverty as violation of human rights 43–4
    and technology 536, 537, 547, 548, 549
capitalism 38, 39, 265, 270
Capuano, A 7
caravan dwellers 14
Carbonell, I 546, 547
care homes 13
Caribbean 28, 126, 214–5, 479–80, 491, 503, 541
Chambers, R 46
Chapman, A 402, 407, 414
Chetail, V 250
children 13, 14, 71, 135, 141–55, 180, 509, 523, 525, 526, 554
    Americas: Afro-descendant 215, 223, 226
    best interests of the child 26, 34, 143, 149, 152, 153, 154, 282
    budget allocation for child support 95
    challenges for children's rights approach 149–55
    child exploitation 154, 155
    child labour 148, 453, 455–6, 470
    child protection 143, 286
    climate change 496
    COVID-19 pandemic 279
    CRC *see* Convention on the Rights of the Child
    disability 32, 34, 65, 109, 112, 117, 122
    ECEC programmes 379
    economic inequality 57, 58, 65
    human rights cities 290–91, 292
    Indigenous Peoples 147, 332
    infant and child mortality 58, 199, 200, 214, 496, 515
    legal identity 359, 538
    LGBT 181
    local authorities 286
    migrants 234, 237, 243, 244, 245
    privacy 33
    rights-specific approach 143–9, 155
        children's rights-based approach 146, 152
        CRC Committee's approach 146–9, 155
        right to distributive equality 144–6
        right to protection against poverty 144
    Romani 197, 198, 199, 200–201, 203, 205–6, 207, 208–9
    school feeding program 30
    stigma 32, 34
    street 13, 32
    tax credit 28, 164, 168
    see also education; motherhood
Chile 172, 338, 345, 346, 348, 394, 435, 443

legal empowerment of disadvantaged
364–7, 368
Chimni, BS 82
China 56, 57, 172, 374, 397, 479
Christians, A 486
Cingano, F 482
cities 50, 52, 264–78, 295, 303, 308, 406–7,
413, 492
contributor's right 275, 278
COVID-19 pandemic 279–80
human rights agendas: 'urban turn' 266–73
cities, poverty and urban disadvantage
268–70
current trends in urban development,
policy and governance 270–73
human rights cities 267–8, 280–81, 283, 294
addressing poverty challenges 290–93
definition 290
human rights debate *like* and *from* the city
273–6
Know Your City 288–9
LGBT persons 173
local authorities 262, 265, 266, 271, 272–3,
275, 293–4
examples: human rights not used
287–90, 293–4
human rights cities 280–81, 283, 290–93
human rights responsibilities of 281–3
role in poverty reduction 283–7
New Urban Agenda 267–8, 277, 284–5, 294
right to the city 275, 277–8, 284, 288, 294, 306
sub-Saharan Africa 91, 92, 99, 102, 289–90
see also housing
civil rights 123, 137, 200, 276, 338, 373, 377,
407, 537
political rights: decoupling from 74
see also individual rights
civil society 94, 95, 120, 123, 163, 172, 188, 294,
304, 353
corruption 512, 520
legal empowerment 358, 360, 362
organizations 258, 279, 285, 291, 350
class 47, 72, 78–9, 216, 233, 296, 299, 305, 345,
386, 407, 414, 422
cities 270–71, 275, 303
education 436, 444
political rights of poor and class awareness
80–86, 87
relational approach 73
climate change 321, 332–3, 394, 406, 489–505, 532
combined rights, justice and dignity
framework 503–4
examples of poverty and 500–503
future research 400, 504–5

intersectionality, human dignity and climate
justice 497–500
poverty, environment and human rights
490–92
vulnerable communities 492–6
cognitive traps 15–16
Cold War 73
Colombia 213–4, 221, 287–8, 289–90, 294, 436,
442, 443, 553–4
colonialism 45, 212, 230, 242, 245, 498
Committee on Economic, Social and Cultural
Rights (CESCR) 53, 146, 228, 419, 490,
536–7
corruption 514, 517–8
definition of poverty 3, 21
disabilities 113
education 175, 438, 439, 440
fiscal consolidation policies 8
health 401–3, 411, 415
homelessness 179
housing 297, 387
local authorities 282
non-discrimination 5–7, 30–31
older persons 137, 138
participation 10
resource availability 150
same-sex unions 184–5
social security 138
Committee on the Elimination of Discrimination
against Women (CEDAW Committee)
302, 418, 421
Committee on the Elimination of Racial
Discrimination (CERD Committee) 214,
221–8, 297–8
Committee on the Rights of the Child (CRC
Committee) 145–6, 151, 152, 154, 443, 514
approach taken by 146–9, 155
austerity and impact assessments 150
best interests of the child 34
child poverty strategy 144
stigma 32
Committee on the Rights of Persons with
Disabilities (CRPD Committee) 116–7,
119, 122, 160
competition law 118
Comprehensive Africa Agriculture Development
Programme (CAADP) 99
conditional cash transfers programs (CCTs) 22,
28, 34, 375, 377, 379
conflict 92, 102, 236, 502, 521–34
conflict resolution 527–34
early warning and conflict prevention
532–3
and human-rights norms: peace, justice
and amnesties 529–31

conflict–human rights nexus 524–7
conflict–poverty nexus 522–4
disability 110–11, 120
future research 533, 534
housing 299
IDPs 502, 525, 526, 553–4
land and natural resources 310, 321
prevention 41, 532–3, 534
consent 168, 182, 427, 543
free, prior and informed 97, 184, 312, 314,
315, 334, 504
state 253, 281
consultation 201, 495, 503–4
children 147–8
Indigenous Peoples 333–4, 352
persons with disabilities 120–21
Convention Against Corruption (CAC) 511
Convention on the Elimination of All Forms of
Discrimination Against Women (CEDAW)
32, 386–7, 430, 458, 501
Convention on the Rights of the Child (CRC)
141, 143, 149, 151, 152, 153, 154–5, 282,
386, 496, 514
art 4: available resources 149–50
art 16: privacy 33
art 21: adoption 153, 154
art 29: education 438, 439
art 32: economic exploitation 455, 470
best interests of the child 34, 149, 154, 282
Convention on the Rights of Persons with
Disabilities (CRPD) 108, 115–21, 122–3,
124, 386
art 4.3: consultation 120
art 8: stereotypes and prejudices 32
art 12: autonomy and legal capacity 116
art 19: community living 116
art 24: education 117, 122, 139
art 27: employment 118–9, 122
art 28: standard of living and social
protection 117, 122
corruption 310, 354, 481, 506–20
closing the gap 511–9
human rights violation 513–6
progressive realisation 518–9
respect, protect and fulfil 517–8
social and economic rights 516–7, 518–9
definition of 507–8
socio-economic impact of 508–11
Costa Rica 175, 223, 225
Costello, C 251, 254–5
Côte d'Ivoire 309, 310, 314, 315, 318, 319, 359, 539
Council of Europe
European Committee for Social Rights 114–5
courts 5, 35, 77, 95, 225, 272, 343, 515
abortion 420–21, 422, 425–8, 430, 431

international banking institutions 553, 556–9,
562–3, 565
national constitutions 553–6
parent company liability for actions of
subsidiary 553, 559–63, 564–5
refugees 249
social-benefits scheme cases in UK 156–7,
162–70
see also individual courts; legal
empowerment of the disadvantaged
COVID-19 pandemic 130, 139, 142, 279–80, 306,
307–8, 400, 416
abortion 419
Cambodia 465, 467
gender-based curfews 174
migrant workers 242, 243–4
race 216–7
Crenshaw, K 497–8
crimes against humanity 212, 511, 530
criminal law/justice 172, 173–4, 178, 181, 185–6,
190, 223, 225, 316, 353, 386, 398, 418,
454, 455
corruption 512
migration 254
Croatia 194, 197, 198
Cuba 186
Czech Republic 194, 199, 200, 205, 206, 209
Czechoslovakia 208–9

DanChurchAid 98
Dancy, G 530
data collection 196–7, 226, 287, 400, 412, 413,
521, 522–3, 526
'missing poor' 13
participation 10–11, 19
quantitative and qualitative data 15–7, 18, 19
technology 523, 532, 533, 538–41
data protection 292, 536, 543
De Feyter, K 96
De Schutter, O 475
death penalty 173
deaths due to poverty-related causes 44
definitions of poverty xxv–xxvi, 128–9, 374
capability deprivation 42, 158, 404, 409
income- (or expenditure-) related 2, 11,
129, 157
international poverty line 90, 129–30, 317
methodologies of measurement 16–7, 23, 36
multidimensional 2–3, 11, 19, 21, 23–4,
32–3, 36, 52, 80, 82, 83, 90, 129,
157–8, 193
social exclusion 2–4, 11, 16, 19, 21, 49, 52,
129, 338
stigma and shame 23–4
subjective assessment 129

women 157–9
democracy 41, 45, 51, 58, 59, 72, 73, 75, 76, 77,
    78, 83, 83–4, 86, 87, 98, 209, 240, 321,
    349, 371, 490, 511, 546, 550–51, 554
Democratic Republic of Congo 96–7, 514, 530
Denmark 397, 412–3
deportation 235–6, 246, 263
Destrooper, T 96–7, 101
development assistance/international aid 51, 54,
    107, 120, 123, 481
development economics 39, 40
development, right to 84, 85, 537, 543, 545, 546–7
dignity 21–2, 23, 24, 25, 36, 89, 95, 130, 217,
    366, 489, 516
    abortion 421, 423, 428
    children 149
    disabilities 115, 116–7
    economic inequality 59, 60, 66
    from 'undeserving poor' to 'rights holders'
        34–5
    housing 386
    Indigenous Peoples 327–9, 332
    intersectionality, climate justice and 497–500
    migrants 260
    and rights at risk 24–5
        best interests of child 26, 34
        equality and non-discrimination 26,
            28, 30–33
        privacy and family life 26, 33
        social protection 25–30
    Roma 203, 204
    transformative equality 160
disability 29–30, 42, 48–9, 106–24, 173, 391,
    407, 431, 451, 495, 497, 509
    children 32, 34, 109, 112, 117, 122
        learning disabilities 65
    CRPD *see* Convention on the Rights of
        Persons with Disabilities
    discrimination 6, 32, 81, 113, 117, 118, 119
    human rights as part of problem 114–5
    legacy of invisibility and passive welfare
        110–11
    limited impact of human rights
        (1948–1990s) 111–4
    links between poverty and 108–10
    local authorities 286
    medicalization 112
    mental 32, 48–9, 111, 205
    migrants 237, 245
    older persons 126, 127, 132, 133, 135, 140
    re-purposing human rights 115–23
        SDGs 121–3, 124
        UN CRPD 116–21, 122–3, 124
    research agenda 123–4
discourse on poverty and human rights 101–2, 103

disempowerment 10, 11, 16, 19, 24, 30, 35, 36,
    83, 155, 343
domestic violence 100, 102, 103, 180, 222, 361
domestic workers 221, 452, 453, 457, 458
Dominica 503
Dominican Republic 221–2, 223, 436, 437
Donald, K 355
Donnelly, J 372, 383
Dorsey, E 97
drug/alcohol addiction 58
Dworkin, R 519

Economic Commission on Latin America and the
    Caribbean (ECLAC) 213, 214–5, 218
Economic Commission of West African States
    (ECOWAS) 320–21
economic growth and inequality 481–2
economic inequality 53–68, 83, 86, 170, 203, 351,
    422, 481–2
    equality rights beyond status-based
        nondiscrimination 59–62, 67
    middle-income countries 54
    negative societal impacts 54
    right to equal protection of economic and
        social rights 62–5
    social and 57
    social cohesion 58
    treaty interpretation 61–2, 64
    violation of human rights: social and 65–7
economics 123, 153
    development 39, 40
    human capital theory 40
Ecuador 186, 188, 215, 222, 224
education 130, 143, 145, 148, 149, 158, 269, 554
    Americas: African descendants 215, 216,
        217, 221, 222, 223, 224, 225, 226
    climate change 492, 501
    corruption 509, 510, 515, 516
    disabilities 106, 109, 110, 112, 117, 122
    ECEC programmes 379
    economic inequality 56, 57, 58, 59, 64
        equal funding 65
    health 402, 403, 405, 408
    Indigenous Peoples 332
    LGBT persons 173, 175–7, 186, 189
    migrants 234, 238
    privatization of *see separate entry*
    right to 64, 65, 264, 274, 417–8, 432–3, 439,
        456, 516, 526
    older persons 139
    Roma in EU 199, 200–201, 202–3, 204,
        205–6, 207, 208–9
    sub-Saharan Africa 90, 94, 99–101, 103, 433
    universal basic 382, 383–4
    women 159, 225

Eide, A 404
El Salvador 222, 223, 224
elderly *see* older persons
Elson, D 59
emic perspective 16
emigration *see* immigration
employment 48, 50, 289
    Americas: African descendants 215, 216–7,
        221–2, 223, 224, 225
    corruption 515–16
    decent work 66, 446, 448, 449, 451, 459,
        461, 492
    disabilities 106, 107, 109, 111, 118–20,
        122, 123
    fair wages 66, 146, 470, 472
    full 39, 49, 380
    gender pay gaps 138, 156, 160, 173, 178, 215
    income inequality 56–7, 66
    labour income share 374
    labour law *see separate entry*
    LGBT persons 174, 177–9, 186
    living wage 380, 469, 471–2
    migration 230–231, 238, 239, 241, 242,
        243–4, 245, 247, 249–50
    minimum wage *see* Cambodia
    older persons 128, 131, 133–4, 135, 136,
        138, 139, 140
    parents 148, 161
    precarious 49, 52, 83, 156, 158, 244, 247,
        265, 451
    right to work 136, 137, 221, 264, 301, 321, 516
    Roma in EU 200–201, 202–4, 205, 207, 209
    safety and health 405, 406, 407, 460,
        470–71, 515–16
    social investment paradigm 377, 379, 380
    unjust pay 195–6
    West Africa 313, 314
    women 138, 156, 158–60, 161–2, 165,
        167–9, 173, 178, 215, 221–2, 450,
        451, 454, 456–9, 462
        equal pay for work of equal value 61,
            66, 158–9, 160, 456, 458, 470,
            471, 472, 546
    work and 450
    see also informal economy
empowerment 3, 15, 17, 85, 306
    children 146, 152–3
    economic and livelihood self- 94
    health care 408–9
    legal empowerment of disadvantaged 354–68
    political 72
    poverty reduction and human rights 93, 94,
        95–6, 103
        economic and livelihood
            empowerment 98–9

    local experience 96, 98
    SDGs 123
entitlement 95
    relations 41
environment 319, 321, 402, 403, 405, 532
    climate change *see separate entry*
    justice 206–8, 499
    pollution 312, 313–4, 315, 317, 406, 502, 515
    right to healthy 498, 499
environmental and social impact assessments
    (ESIAs) 334
equality 5–9, 19, 48, 102, 140, 221, 228, 273,
    408, 552
    abortion 419, 421–2, 423, 426, 427, 428, 430
    children: distributive 144–6
    conditional cash transfers programs
        (CCTs) 28–9
    dignity 26, 28, 30–33
    disabilities 108, 112, 116–7, 121, 122, 123
    education 439
    fictitious narratives of zero-sum game 218
    horizontal and vertical inequalities 55, 67, 373
    housing 388
    labour law 456–9, 471
    LGBT persons 186, 190
    political rights 72–3
        egalitarian potential of 77–80
        of poor and class consciousness 80–86, 87
    relational autonomy 72
    reproductive rights 417
    rights beyond status-based nondiscrimination
        59–62, 67
    transformative 160–161, 162, 165–70, 421
    women 156–70, 456
        abortion 419, 421–2, 423, 426, 427,
            428, 430
        formal equality 159–60, 163–5
        substantive equality 160–161, 162,
            165–70, 421–2, 430
    see also inequality; non-discrimination
Ethiopia 91, 93, 100, 102
ethnic cleansing 212
ethnicity 34, 101, 173, 407
    discrimination *see under* race
    minorities 49, 54, 58, 132, 167–8, 412–13
etic perspective 16
Europe 126, 237, 317, 396
    corruption 511
    and economic inequality 56
    see also individual countries
European Convention on Human Rights 76, 258
    art 3: torture or inhuman or degrading
        treatment 235, 241, 259
    art 10: freedom of expression 339–40

art 11: freedom of assembly 341, 346–7, 348, 351
art 14: non-discrimination 81, 163
European Court of Human Rights (ECHR)
    abortion 420
    assembly, freedom of 342, 346–7, 348, 351
    children
        best interests of the child 34
        removal from family 152
    disabilities 112
    expression, freedom of 340
    margin of appreciation 31–2
    migrants/asylum seekers 235, 236, 240–41, 251, 259, 261
    non-discrimination 31–2
European Social Charter 113, 114–5, 137, 144
European Union 51, 466, 512, 528, 531
    asylum seekers 235–6, 257–63
    Charter of Fundamental Rights 137, 258
    Commission 39, 197–8, 205, 477, 478, 482, 541
    data protection 543
    financial services 541–2
    precision medicine 411
    Roma people of *see separate entry*
    social investment 370, 377–8
    of Supported Employment (EUSE) 119–20
    taxation 474, 477, 478, 479, 482, 483
    urban agendas 282, 285, 292–3
    Urban Poverty Partnership 285–6, 289
Eurozone 477
expression, freedom of 10, 75, 79, 83–4, 94, 176, 186, 221, 339–40, 344, 346, 350, 407, 535, 546, 547
    silent begging 291
extractive industries 97
    see also land rights-poverty nexus

fair taxes 474–87
    fair and sustainable tax bases 481–4
    neoliberalism 475–8
    social contract approach 484–7
    tax justice 485–7
    tax sustainability gaps 478–81
    taxation as part of economic rights 475
Fajardo, Sergio 288
Farha, Leilani 385, 392
Farmer, P 196
feminism 70, 72
feudalism 78
Fiji 186
financial technologies 541–4
financialization of housing 270, 272, 385–400
    beneficiaries of 389–90
    definition 389

effects of 390–94
    government efforts to curb 397–8
    governments' role in enabling 395–7
    profit generation 389
    right to housing 386–8
        call to realize 399–400
        government role 396–7, 398
    wealth generated through 390
fiscal consolidation 8
Fischer, AM 16
fishing communities 500–501, 502
food 41, 121, 137, 158, 279, 292, 301, 307–8
    Americas: African descendants 214, 216, 222, 224
    children 143, 148, 496
    climate change 492, 493, 494, 495, 502, 503
    conflict areas 502, 524, 525, 532
    corruption 510, 515
    disabilities 109
    health 402, 405, 406, 407, 408
    Indigenous Peoples 223, 314, 332–3
    land rights-poverty nexus 314, 321
    LGBT persons 190
    malnutrition 97, 100, 197, 223, 495, 496
    migrants 238, 243, 244, 260
    national courts 554
    people's restaurant 289
    Roma in EU 197–8, 200–201, 203
    sub-Saharan Africa 97, 99, 100
Food and Agriculture Organization 311, 503
forced labour 453–5, 460–61
France 10–11, 24, 57, 76, 78, 80, 175, 285
    Declaration of the Rights of Man (1789) 62, 79, 86
    Roma 198–9
Fraser, N 371, 544, 548
Fredman, S 160, 162, 170, 440–41, 442, 443
Frug, GE 281
Fukuda-Parr, S 60, 67
fundamentalism, human rights 551–2

Gandhi, Mahatma 303
gated communities 270–71, 303, 305
Gauri, V 95, 362
Gearty, C 110
gender 82, 158–9, 377, 405, 407, 412, 483, 527
    -based violence 221, 225, 360, 454–5, 461, 495, 527
    bias 71
    carers 106–7, 123, 132, 135, 138, 139, 152, 156, 159, 161, 165, 168–9, 495
    curfews 174
    discrimination *see* sex or gender discrimination
    education 99, 103

HIV, correct knowledge about 57
identity *see* sexual orientation and gender
    identity
life expectancy 126, 132
mainstreaming 501
norms 158, 173, 179, 189, 501
    change 98
older age 132, 134, 135, 138, 139, 140
pay gaps 138, 156, 160, 173, 178
quarantine laws 174
race and 132, 419, 422–3, 424, 428–9, 430,
    431, 497
relational approach 70, 71
relations 49, 159
SDG 5: equality 219, 321, 492
social protection 26–7, 29, 160–161
    social-benefits scheme cases in UK
        156–7, 162–70
sub-Saharan Africa 99, 101, 102, 103, 317
    stereotypes 100
genocide 212, 530, 532
Genovese, K 563–4
Georgia 186
Geremek, B 38
Germany 57, 98, 279, 343, 397, 564
Gewirth, A 43–4
Ghana 97, 101, 172
ghettoization 305
global financial crisis (2007–08) 389–90
global gag rule 182
global institutional order 45–6
global labor market 245
globalization 37, 49, 51–2, 270, 276, 480, 486–7,
    508, 544, 548
Golub, S 354, 357
Goodwin, L 362
Goodwin-Gill, GS 233, 252, 262
Gordon, D 48, 51
Gough, I 46–7
Greece 194, 197, 199, 260, 261, 263, 477–8, 479
Guatemala 223, 224, 361–2
Guiding Principles on Business and Human
    Rights 545, 565
Guiding Principles on Extreme Poverty and
    Human Rights 4, 8, 22, 143, 158
participation 10, 85, 344
Guinea 309, 310, 312, 313, 314, 315, 316, 318,
    319, 454
Gurumurthy, A 546
Guterres, António 532

Hafner-Burton, EM 96
Hall, PA 370
Hamlin, R 231
Harding, D 205

Haughton, J 93
health 83, 121, 130, 289, 305, 374, 477, 492
ageing population 377
Americas: African descendants 216, 217,
    221, 222, 223, 225
children 143, 145–6, 147, 149
community monitoring 363
conflict areas 525, 526
corruption 509, 510, 513, 516, 518
definition 401–2
economic inequality 54, 56, 57, 58, 59
    tiered health insurance 65–6
human rights-based approach to poverty
    and 408–9
power of 414–5
LGBT persons 177, 178, 181–5
medicines 145–6
migrants 237, 243, 244
older persons 126, 135, 137
right to 54, 59, 65–6, 181, 186, 264, 301,
    401–5, 417, 421, 495, 516, 518, 526,
    554
    how poverty impacts on health and vice
        versa 405–7
    Indigenous Peoples 332
    link: poverty and health 404–5
Roma in EU 196, 202, 203, 207
sexual and reproductive *see separate entry*
sub-Saharan Africa 90, 94, 95, 98, 99, 100,
    101, 312, 317
technologies, new health 410–14
universalism, new 382, 383–4
vaccination and immunization 28, 44,
    100–101, 359, 377, 406, 515
Heintz, J 59
Hemerijck, A 370, 378
Hidden Dimensions of Poverty research project
    10–11, 24
historical background of contemporary poverty
    debates 38–41
HIV/AIDS 29–30, 32, 34, 57, 177, 182
Holston, J 275, 278
homelessness 6, 13–14, 15, 203, 274, 286, 302,
    555–6
COVID-19 pandemic 279
financialization of housing 385–6, 387–8,
    391, 392, 393, 398, 400
Homeless Bill of Rights 292–3, 294
LGBT persons 173, 179–81, 189, 190
migrants 235, 238, 244, 259
United States 223, 279
Honduras 222, 223, 224, 226, 365, 563
housing 56, 95, 137, 158, 169, 402, 405, 408, 554
Americas: African descendants 216, 217,
    221, 222–3, 224, 225

children 143, 148, 515
cities 264, 269–70, 270–72, 288–9
corruption 510, 513, 515, 516
disability 117, 391
evictions 204, 207–8, 272, 299, 307, 314,
        315, 316, 321, 386, 391, 392, 393,
        394, 398, 554–6
    and displacement 300–302
gentrification 265, 271, 272, 275, 303, 304,
        308, 556
and land rights approach 295–308
    Guiding Principles on security of tenure
        299–300
    morphological perspective 296–7
    morphology and human rights
        approach 302–7
    UN Guidelines 298–9, 300–302
legal empowerment 360
LGBT persons 174, 179–81, 186
local authorities 286–7
migrants 235, 238, 244, 249, 259, 260
right to 64, 271–2, 274, 288–9, 297, 298–9,
        321, 386–8, 495, 516, 526
    financialization of housing *see*
        separate entry
Roma in EU 198–9, 203, 204, 205–6, 207–8
security of tenure 285, 299–300, 307, 314
UN Habitat 282, 284
    security of tenure 285
see also homelessness; land
housing and land rights approach 295–308
    Guidelines
        on Development-based Evictions and
            Displacement 300–302
        on Discrimination, Segregation and
            Right to Adequate Housing 298–9
    Guiding Principles on Security of Tenure
        299–300
    morphological perspective 296–7
    morphology 302–7
    way forward 307–8
Hulme, D 195
human capital theory 40
Human Development Index (HDI) 40, 41, 101, 467
human dignity *see* dignity
Human Opportunity Index (HOI) 100
Human Rights Committee 63, 64
    abortion 419, 430, 431
    assembly, freedom of 341–2, 344, 348
    detention of asylum seekers 255
    equality and non-discrimination 61
    LGBT persons 177
    local authorities 286
    older persons 137
    participation and right to vote 63, 343–4

protests 340
human trafficking 154, 155, 244, 453–4, 460, 525
Hungary 186, 194, 197, 198, 201, 205, 393

immigration 13, 14, 47, 187, 222, 230–46, 271,
        275, 277, 313
    abortion 419, 431
    corruption 514–5
    labour law 452, 453, 457
    new universalism 381
    protection from poverty in
        country of origin or third countries 231–7
        receiving States 237–46
    see also asylum seekers; refugees
immunization 28, 100, 101, 359, 406, 515
impact assessments
    data 543
    environmental and social 334
    human rights 8, 68, 150
India 56, 80, 95, 97, 170, 175, 189, 303–4, 374,
        557–9
    biometric records system 541, 544
    COVID-19 pandemic 279, 306
    education 436
    Facebook 547
    ghettoization 305
    mapping landless families 307
    Odisha: slum dwellers 306–7
    Right to Food case 554
    Right to Homestead Act 306
    taxation 479
indicators 35, 36, 40, 103, 148
    structural, process and outcome 5, 18
Indigenous Peoples 127, 173, 211, 212–3, 214–5,
        223, 224, 345, 391, 509
    advocacy 218
    children 147, 332
    climate change 494–5, 496, 502–3, 504
    conflict areas 525
    consultation 333–4, 352
    debt bondage 454
    economic inequality 58
    health 224, 332
    labour law 451, 454, 457, 459
    land rights 321, 323–36, 504
        -poverty nexus in West Africa 310, 312,
            313, 314, 315, 316
        access to traditional lands 331–5
        cultural identity and dignified life 327–9
        destitute living 329–30
    LGBT persons 189
    life expectancy 127–8
    malnutrition 223
    MDGs 219
    old age 135

women 215
Indonesia 175, 187, 362, 394, 479
inequality 47–8, 49, 50, 88–9, 136, 159, 168, 479,
    482, 527, 554
    Americas: African descendants 213, 217,
        218, 224, 226
    class relations 47
    CRC Committee 146
    economic *see separate entry*
    education 432–3, 441, 443, 444
    financialization of housing 392–4
    health 100–101, 406–7, 413
    horizontal and vertical 55, 67, 373
    income 56–7, 164–5, 194, 266, 374, 376–7,
        382–3, 476, 481, 510
    interaction of poverty reduction and trends of
        see poverty reduction in sub-Saharan
        Africa
    mobilizations: unequal participation 349–50
    Roma in EU 197–9, 208–9
    SDG 10: reduce 54, 58, 122, 190, 219, 227,
        382–3, 492
    urban 265, 266, 269, 275, 276
    wealth 57, 66, 78, 88, 193, 208–9, 283, 374,
        376, 382, 392, 394, 479–80, 481, 489
    see also equality; non-discrimination
Infanti, A 484
informal economy 132, 138, 178, 447, 449,
    450–51, 452, 453, 456–7, 458, 524
    older persons 128
    right to the city 275
    Roma in EU 200
    women 158, 159
informal settlements 289, 293, 295, 296–7, 306,
    308, 385, 386, 394
intellectual property rights 145–6, 542
Inter-American Commission on Human Rights
    327, 331, 346, 420, 496, 507
Inter-American Convention Against Corruption 510
Inter-American Court of Human Rights 32, 34,
    323, 342
    Indigenous Peoples 324–6, 327–8, 331–2,
        333–5, 346
interdisciplinary working/research 35, 36, 68,
    196, 209, 277, 295, 296, 308
intergenerational
    inherited power 195, 208–9
    social mobility: cities 268
    transmission of poverty 3, 11, 98–9, 100–101,
        106, 204, 205, 208–9, 211, 212
intergovernmental organizations 512, 520
internally displaced persons 496, 502, 525, 526,
    553–4
international aid *see* development assistance/
    international aid

international banking institutions 550, 556–9,
    562–3, 565
    regional development banks 92, 125, 467, 471
    World Bank Group *see separate entry*
International Convention on the Elimination
    of All Forms of Racial Discrimination
    (ICERD) 220–221, 228, 470
International Council on Human Rights Policy 514
International Covenant on Civil and Political
    Rights (ICCPR) 64–5, 73, 76, 177, 239,
    253, 254–5, 314, 446–7, 452, 453, 460
    Preamble 64
    art 2: non-discrimination 60, 61–2, 64, 137,
        220, 314, 439, 475
    art 5: destruction of rights 62, 63, 67
    art 9: liberty 113
    art 16: recognition before the law 113
    art 17: privacy 33
    art 19: freedom of expression 339, 340
    art 21: freedom of assembly 340–342, 348
    art 23(4): equal rights in marriage 61
    art 25: public affairs, vote, public service
        77, 343–4
    art 25(b): one-person-one-vote 63
    art 26: equality rights 61–2, 64, 67, 79, 81, 314
    disability 112, 113
International Covenant on Economic, Social and
    Cultural Rights (ICESCR) 39, 64–5, 67,
    76, 149, 239, 446–7, 452, 453, 459–60,
    470, 474, 490, 516, 518, 519
    art 2: non-discrimination 5–6, 7, 31, 60, 137,
        220, 517
    art 7(a)(i): fair wages and equal pay for equal
        work 61, 66, 470, 472
    arts 9 and 10: social protection 25, 64
    art 11: adequate standard of living 64, 314,
        386, 472
    art 12: health 401–3
    art 13: education 64, 65, 438–40
    abortion 421
    disability 112
    homelessness 387–8
International Finance Corporation (IFC) 553,
    557–9, 562–3
international financial institutions 50–51, 395,
    396, 562–4, 565
    IMF 51, 396, 467, 477, 478, 482, 483, 556
    international banking institutions *see*
        separate entry
    structural adjustment policies 136
international humanitarian law 525
International Labour Organization (ILO) 25–6,
    41, 49, 228, 446–7, 448–50, 451
    disabilities 117–8, 120
    fundamental rights 452–9, 471, 545–6

LGBT persons 175, 177
minimum wage 464–5
older persons 133, 134, 137–8, 139
other labour law 459–61
social protection 117–8, 137–8, 139, 381
International Monetary Fund (IMF) 51, 396, 467,
     477, 478, 482, 483, 556
international relations 40
internet 198, 537, 541, 542, 547
intersectionality 32, 82, 107, 116, 127, 139, 144,
     156, 167
     abortion 431
     cities 269
     health 407
     human dignity, climate justice and 497–500
     LGBT persons 172–3, 187
     single-parent households 163–4, 165
Iraq 529
Ireland 95, 188, 305–6, 390
Israel 118, 241, 244, 305
Italy 13–14, 261, 263
Ivanov, A 200, 202, 204
Ivory Coast 309, 310, 314, 315, 318, 319, 359, 539

Jamaica 176, 180, 436
Japan 57
Jones, S 16–7
jus cogens/peremptory norms 220, 232–3, 256–7
Justesen, MK 509–10
Justino, P 524

Kagin, J 200
Kazakhstan 176
Keller, S 202
Kelsey, J 477
Kenya 93, 98, 307–8, 362, 433, 436, 543–4
Khan, Irene 53
Khandker, SR 93
Kirkpatrick, Robert 540
Knox, John 497
Korea 108, 459
Kuehn, R 499

labour law 239, 446–61
     fundamental rights 452–9
     ILO and poverty 448–9
     importance of law in combatting poverty
          449–51
     international labour standards 451–61
     minimum wage *see* Cambodia
land
     housing and land rights approach 295–308
     India: mapping 307
     Indigenous Peoples 323–36, 504
     inherited 98, 102, 162

productivity and scarcity of 99
unsecured land rights: land rights-poverty
     nexus 309–22
women 159, 162
see also housing
land rights of Indigenous Peoples 323–36, 504
     communal lands and territories 324–6
          lack of access and destitute living
               conditions 329–30
          protection of access 331–5
     cultural identity and dignified life 327–9
     poverty eradication and sustainable
          development 331–5
land rights-poverty nexus 309–22
     background 309
     constitutional and legal review of rights 318–9
     naturally endowed yet poor 310
     realizing rights to alleviate poverty
          international obligations and corporate
               accountability 320–21
     sustainability and resilience of livelihoods
          313–5
     unsecured land rights 310–12
          rural to urban brain drain 315–6
     zero-sum game 317
Latin America 28, 126, 174, 213–5, 264, 270,
     271, 289, 317, 361, 365, 502–3, 541
     taxation 479–80, 481
     see also individual countries
Latvia 142, 201
Lebanon 529
legal aid/assistance 255, 259
legal empowerment of disadvantaged 354–68
     importance in advancing human rights: Chile
          364–7, 368
     in practice 358–63
     theory 356–8
LGBT and gender diverse persons *see* sexual
     orientation and gender identity
liberalism 71–2, 74, 78
Liberia 309, 310, 311–2, 313–14, 315, 316,
     318–9, 362
life expectancy 54, 58, 100, 101, 126–8, 132, 135,
     158, 199, 202, 214
life, right to 54, 149, 324, 328–30, 332, 407, 417,
     419, 430, 495
Lindahl, H 256, 257
Lithuania 142
living standard(s) 130, 266, 377, 491, 503, 504
     children 148–9, 152
     older persons 128, 131, 133, 134, 136, 137,
          139, 140, 383
     right to adequate 54, 117, 122, 136, 137–8,
          271–2, 292, 386, 472, 526
Roma in EU 198

sub-Saharan Africa 98, 99, 101
loan industry, exploitative 30
local authorities 207–8, 265, 266, 272–3, 275,
    279–94
    fighting urban poverty without using human
        rights 287–90
    funding 286
    future research 293–4
    human rights cities 267–8, 280–81, 283
        addressing poverty challenges 290–93
    human rights responsibilities of 281–3
    planning 271
    role in poverty reduction 283–7
localization 96
localized rights *see* cities
López Obrador, Andrés Manuel 27
Lyon, D 546

McAdam, J 252, 262
Macedonia 363
McKay, A 195
MacNaughton, G 145
McQuay, K 354
Magnusson, W 275
Malaysia 397, 479
Mali 100, 309, 310, 311, 313, 314, 315, 316,
    318, 319
Malta 186, 188, 189
Mann, L 546
Maputo Declaration (2003) 99
marriage 63, 102, 174, 184
Marshall, TH 39
Maru, V 362
Marx, K 76, 78–9
Mbonu, Christy 515
means testing 48, 135, 164
    proxy 29
measurement of poverty 9, 12, 18–20, 21–2, 36,
    129–30
    LGBT persons 171–3
    'missing poor' 13–14, 19
    non-take-up of rights 17–18, 19–20
    number and who are poor 12–3
    participation 10–12, 19
    quantitative and qualitative data 15–7, 18, 19
    Roma people of European Union *see*
        separate entry
    sub-Saharan Africa 90–92, 102, 103
media 27–8, 93, 188, 306, 343
    elite capture of 58
mental health/illness/disorder 13, 58, 113, 182,
    183, 225
Merciery, M 524
'Merging of Knowledge' methodology 11, 16–7
Merry, S Engle 96, 101

Mexico 27, 187, 222, 223, 224, 226, 456
micro-credit/-finance 109, 224, 398
Middle East 56, 317, 529
migration 407, 493
    IDPs 496, 502, 525, 526, 553–4
    international *see* immigration
    rural to urban 315, 316, 317, 321, 503
Mill, JS 78
Millennium Development Goals (MDGs) 53, 85,
    97, 103, 121, 136, 212, 219, 370, 380–1,
    382, 447, 461, 492
minimum wage
    Cambodia *see separate entry*
    housing subsidy and 398
Mitlin, D 274
Mitsilegas, V 258
mobile phones 537, 538, 539, 540, 541, 543, 547
mobilizations/protests 264, 273–4, 275, 316,
    338–53, 509
    assembly, freedom of 340–342, 343, 344–7,
        348, 349, 350, 351
    expression, freedom of 339–40, 344, 346, 350
    looking ahead 347–53
    political participation
        poverty and 343–4
        protests as 344–7
    right to protest 339–42
Moldova 172
Mongolia 172
monitoring of poverty reduction strategy 4–5, 19
Montenegro 175
moral hazard 379
Morocco 433, 436
Morsink, J 80
motherhood 33, 34, 58, 123, 202, 214
    caps on 162–70
        formal equality 163–5
        transformative equality model 165–70
    definition of women's poverty 157–9
    equality 159–62
        formal 159–60, 163–5
        non-discrimination 161–2
        substantive 160–61, 162, 165–70
Moumné, R 441
Moyn, S 47–8, 59, 60, 67, 69, 88, 265
Mozambique 16, 100, 190–91, 363
multi- or transnational corporations 50–51, 313,
    314, 316, 320, 486, 508, 545, 550, 553,
    559–62, 564–5
Multidimensional Poverty Index (MPI) 21–2, 23,
    40, 90, 101, 129, 193, 197, 202

Namati 361, 363
national human rights institutions 5, 12, 35
natural resource curse *see* land rights-poverty nexus

Nelson, PJ 97
neo-colonialism 154, 212, 230, 242, 245
neo-liberalism 49, 59, 60, 67, 156, 265, 270, 272, 276, 395, 544
    education 432–4, 435, 436, 437
    tax policy 474, 475–8
Nepal 421
Netherlands 189, 222, 226, 290, 294, 435, 443, 564
New International Economic Order (NIEO) 40, 51
New Zealand 126, 183, 188, 397, 477
Ngenzebuke, RL 524
Niger 453
Nigeria 95, 100, 122, 394, 436
Nilekani, Nandan 541
non-discrimination 5–9, 12, 19, 54, 59, 60, 137, 349
    behaviourism, new 377
    children 145, 146, 149, 152
    conditional cash transfers programs (CCTs) 28–9
    dignity 26, 28, 30–33
    disability 6, 32, 81, 113, 117, 118, 119
    education 439, 441
    equality and 79–80
    health care services 403, 406, 408, 411, 412–3
    horizontal and vertical inequalities 55, 67, 373
    housing 388
    poverty reduction and human rights 89, 94, 102, 103
        local experience 98
    race or ethnic origin *see under* race
    Refugee Convention 249
    reproductive rights/health 418, 419
        abortion 421, 425
    rights beyond status-based *see* economic inequality
    sex or gender discrimination *see separate entry*
    sexual orientation and gender identity *see separate entry*
    universalism, new 383
non-governmental organizations (NGOs) 35, 89, 95, 96, 98, 212, 261, 285, 293, 303, 304, 435, 455, 514, 526, 550
non-refoulement 232–3, 237, 242, 245, 249, 250, 252, 253, 254, 256–7
non-retrogression 430–31
non-state armed groups (NSAGs) 525
Nordic countries 406
    see also individual countries
North America
    see also individual countries
Norway 122
Nowak, M 62, 63
nudging 376
Nussbaum, M 44, 158, 404, 547
Nyaletsossi Voule, C 344

obesity 58, 197
Oceania 126
Oestreich, JE 97
older persons 13, 125–40, 189, 291, 497, 509, 523, 554
    category 127–8
    defining and measuring 128–30
    experience of poverty 130–35
        alleviating or avoiding 133–5
        patterns 131–3
    future: measures needed 139–40
    limited data 130, 134–5, 140
    migrants 237, 243, 245
    pension 106–7, 380, 382, 383
    population trends and ageing populations 126–7
    poverty and human rights of 135–9
Organisation for Economic Co-operation and Development (OECD) 129, 134, 142, 216, 478, 482–3, 486, 510, 511
Oxford Poverty and Human Development Initiative (OPHI) 90, 91, 99, 102

pacta sunt servanda 281
Pakistan 434
Palestine, Occupied 305
Panama 224
Paraguay 222, 223, 224, 365
paralegal strategy, community 361–2
parent company liable for actions of subsidiary *Vedanta Resources* 553, 559–62, 564–5
parliamentary committees 5, 35
Parnell, S 275
participation 46, 81, 89, 94, 96, 101, 102, 212, 308, 506, 554
    Americas: African descendants 217–18, 224
    children 143, 146, 152, 153
    cities 269, 273–4, 277–8, 284, 288–9, 294, 306, 308
    climate change 495, 503
    decision-making: mechanisms for 93
    definition and measurement of poverty 5, 8, 10–12, 15–16, 17, 19, 22, 23, 36
    disabilities 111, 117
    health 402, 408, 409
    human rights cities 290–291
    legal empowerment of disadvantaged *see separate entry*
    mobilizations/protests *see separate entry*
    older persons 137
    political 76–7, 78, 83–5, 86, 87, 201, 217, 221, 343–4
        cities 269
        economic inequality and 58, 59, 83
        LGBT persons 187–9

protests as 344–7
Roma in EU 200–201, 207
social assistance programs 35
women 169–70
paternalism 28, 35, 376
patriarchy 159, 179, 189
pensions 106–7, 110, 117, 127, 133, 134, 135,
   138–9, 140, 377, 380, 382, 383
   gender 132, 138
   LGBT persons 174, 177, 179, 187
Peru 215, 221, 223, 224, 225, 436, 454–5
Peters, A 513, 518
Philippines 187, 362, 394, 397, 479, 514
Pickett, K 58
Pogge, T 43, 44, 45–6, 51, 195, 208
Poland 122
political rights 69–87, 123, 137, 276, 338, 373,
   407, 537
   collective dimension of 75–7
   courts 77
   decoupling from civil rights 74
   egalitarian potential of 77–80
   first- and second-generation rights 73–4
   freedom of individual through sociality 76
   freedom as non-domination 78
   of poor and class awareness 80–86, 87
   relational autonomy 70–73, 86
   see also individual rights
populism 276
Portugal 142, 198, 199, 391
precarious 146
   employment 49, 52, 83, 156, 158, 244, 247,
      265, 451
   infrastructure 271
   legal condition of asylum seekers 248, 261
   living conditions 14, 247
   see also informal economy; informal
      settlements
Principles and Guidelines for a Human Rights
   Approach to Poverty Reduction Strategies
   (2006) 3, 12, 53, 349
privacy 63–4, 182, 184, 186, 292, 407, 411, 412,
   413, 418, 419, 421, 427, 535, 544
   and family life 26, 33
   group 540
   technology 540
private law 552–3
privatization of education 432–45
   human rights standards 438–42
      compatibility between private
         participation and 442–4
      equality and non-discrimination 439
      liberty of private actors 438–9
      no general prohibition of public funding
         440–42

primary responsibility: States 439–40
   States must regulate and monitor 440
   models 435–7
   neoliberalism, privatization and poverty 433–4
   research agenda ahead 433, 444–5
property, right to 244, 301, 495
protests *see* mobilizations/protests
public procurement 118, 509
public-private partnerships 270, 383, 434
Puerto Rico 493

Qatar 436
questionnaires 14

race 72, 82, 112, 132, 135, 167–8
   abortion 419, 422–3, 424, 428–9, 430, 431
   African descendants in Americas 213–7, 345
   cities 269, 270, 271, 272, 275, 297–8
   or ethnic origin discrimination 6, 211–28,
      269, 298–9, 305, 348, 394, 470
      CERD 214, 221–8, 297–8
      definition 220
      economic inequality 54
      future research 228
      indirect 218, 221
      labour law 456–7
      Roma 198, 200, 202–6, 209
      SDGs 219–20, 227, 228
      unique impediment to poverty
         elimination 217–8
   gender and 132, 419, 422–3, 424, 428–9,
      430, 431, 497
   LGBT persons 172–3, 187
   Roma people of European Union *see*
      separate entry
   SDGs 219–20
Ravallion, M 50
Rebouché, R 420–21
refugees 47, 231–2, 237, 240, 241–2, 243, 245,
   247, 256, 262–3, 451, 525, 526
   cities 275
   climate change 496
   Convention 232–3, 240, 241, 247, 248,
      249–52, 253–4, 257, 258, 261, 262, 496
   definition of 232, 233–4, 246, 247–8, 252
   European Union 257–9
   non-refoulement 232–3, 237, 242, 245, 249,
      250, 252, 253, 254, 256–7
   responsibility sharing 245–6
   in Turkey 260–61
   see also asylum seekers
regional development banks 92, 125
Reisch, N 474
relational autonomy 70–73, 86
relational dimensions of poverty 11, 16, 24

relative poverty 49, 50, 52, 90, 446
    income 131, 134, 141
religion 101, 153, 173, 174, 176, 208, 249, 296,
    310, 418, 435, 437, 526, 529
    ghettoization 305
reproductive rights 177, 361, 416–20
    abortion *see separate entry*
    justice 429
republicanism 74, 77
Robinson, Mary 89
    Foundation 499
Rodríguez-Garavito, C 352
Roma or Romani people 32, 363
    European Union 192–210, 286
Roma people of European Union 192–210, 286
    canons and measurements of racialized
        poverty 204–9
    measuring poverty 194–7
    multidimensional poverty: data 197–204
        participation and political exclusion
            200–201
        Roma Multidimensional Index 202–4
Romania 142, 193, 194, 195, 196, 198, 199, 203,
    206, 207, 286
Rosanvallon, P 75
rural poverty 132, 135, 140, 302, 307, 321
    abortion 422
    climate change 500–503
    LGBT persons 173
    Roma in EU 206
    sub-Saharan Africa 91, 92, 98–9, 101, 102
    see also land rights-poverty nexus
Russia 56
Rwanda 101, 245, 345

same-sex couples 174, 177, 180, 184–5, 187
Sanctuary City movement 275
sanitation 90, 94, 96–7, 98, 100, 121, 143, 148,
    158, 198, 206, 207, 214, 224, 274, 402,
    406, 407, 492, 495
    corruption 509, 510
Sano, H-O 97
Satterthwaite, D 274
Saudemont, C 441
Schultz, T 40, 50
Scotland 7–8
Sen, A 23, 40–2, 44–5, 69, 82, 83–4, 99, 101, 158,
    196, 200, 203, 354–5, 404, 536, 537, 547
Senegal 100
Sepúlveda Carmona, M 59–60, 344, 355, 489
Sepúlveda dos Santos, M 213
service statistics paradox 14
sex or gender discrimination 6, 32, 42, 54, 81,
    100, 132, 135, 138, 159
    CEDAW 32, 386–7, 430, 458, 501

Committee 302, 418, 421
    employment 221, 456–9
        equal pay for work of equal value 61,
            66, 158–9, 160, 456, 458, 470,
            471, 472, 546
    housing 299
    protest regulations 348
    reproductive rights 428–9
    sexual and reproductive health 418–9
    social-benefits cases in UK 156–7, 162–5,
        169–70
    structures and institutions 161–2, 165
sex work 173, 174, 178, 182, 244
sexual orientation and gender identity 32, 81, 101,
    171–91, 451
    dynamics of inclusion 185
        anti-discrimination legislation 186–7
        decriminalization 185–6
        political participation 187–9
        public policy 189–90
    law, policy and access to justice 173–4
    poverty: LGBT and gender diverse persons
        171–3
    systems of exclusion of LGBT persons 175
        education 175–7
        employment 177–9
        health 181–5
        housing 179–81
sexual and reproductive health 159, 177, 178,
    182, 184, 200, 221, 418–9, 421–2, 430
    justice 429
    see also reproductive rights
Shafir, E 376
shame 16, 158
    definition 23
    stigma and 22, 23–4, 30, 35, 36
Shklar, J 75
Shue, H 498
Siegel, R 348
Sierra Leone 309, 310, 311–2, 313, 314, 315, 316,
    318–9, 360, 362
Silver, H 48
Singapore 397
slavery 212, 213, 451, 453, 455
Slovakia 199, 200, 203–4, 205, 206, 209
Slovenia 180, 187, 190
Snyder, MG 305
social capital 24, 201
social citizenship 47
social cohesion 58
social contract 70–71
    approach to taxes 484–7
social exclusion 2–4, 11, 12–3, 16, 19, 21, 29, 32,
    35, 129, 338, 374
    capabilities, rights and 37–52

children 144, 147, 153
cities 275
disabilities 112, 114, 123
race 211, 223, 224, 225
sexual orientation and gender identity *see
    separate entry*
social inclusion 117–18, 122, 160, 169, 185–90,
    201, 207, 226
social insurance 26, 51, 132, 138, 378–9
social investment paradigm 370–371, 374–5,
    377–80, 384
social market 122
social media 523, 533, 539, 540, 542, 547
social movements 35, 67, 68, 74, 264, 272,
    273–4, 277
    see also mobilizations/protests
social origin or property, non-discrimination on
    grounds of 5–9, 80–81, 145
social policy paradigms 370–84
    context, socio-economic 373–5
    human rights perspective 371–3
    new behaviourism 370–71, 374–7, 379, 384
    new universalism 370–71, 374–5, 380–84
    social investment 370–71, 374–5, 377–80, 384
social protection 14, 48, 50, 56, 59, 72, 286, 374,
    377, 471, 544
    Americas: African descendants 223, 225
    capability perspective 42
    children 95, 142, 146, 148, 149, 150
        childcare costs 160
    courts
        South Africa 554
        United Kingdom 156–7, 162–70
    disabilities 107, 108, 109–11, 114, 115,
        117–8, 122, 123
    health 406, 407
    informal economy 381, 450, 451
    LGBT persons 180, 186, 187
    local authorities 289
    media 27–8
    migrants 238, 240, 242–3, 250, 259–60
    older persons 126, 127–8, 131, 134, 135,
        137–9, 140, 380, 382, 383, 554
        women 132, 138
    right to 25–30, 64, 264, 516
    rights-based approach 371–2
    Roma in EU 196
    SDGs 121, 122, 405
    social assistance programs 22, 25, 26–30, 391
        best interests of the child 34
        conditionalities 18, 22, 28–9, 33, 34,
            375, 376, 377, 379
        non-take-up 18, 24, 29
        participation 35
        privacy and family life 33

social investment paradigm 378–9, 380
support to make claims 360
technology 544–5
universal programs 34, 48, 51, 381, 382, 383–4
welfare state 9, 37, 39, 47, 49, 52, 240,
    378–9, 380, 477
    disabilities 110, 114
    international 50
    paradox 406, 408–9
    taxation 479, 485–6
women 26–7, 29, 160–61
    social-benefits scheme cases in UK
        156–7, 162–70
solidarity 11, 14, 16, 33, 48, 371–2, 486
    asylum seekers 257, 261
    poverty reduction in sub-Saharan Africa:
        HRBA work 98
    relational autonomy 72, 86
    surcharges on wealth 483
    UDHR 60
Somalia 501–2, 524
South Africa 95, 170, 175, 186, 274, 343, 362,
    394, 479, 554
    abortion 421–2
    apartheid 79, 555
    child support budget allocation 95
    corruption 515, 518
    evictions 554–6
    social protection 29, 544–5
    Truth and Reconciliation Commission 531
sovereignty 275, 486
    popular 77, 78
    state 239, 241–2, 251, 253, 254–5
Soviet Union 113
Spain 122, 194, 198, 199, 201, 279, 293, 390, 393
Sri Lanka 180, 500–501
state aid 118
state responsibility 281, 282, 513
Steinbock, D 245
stereotypes 6, 22, 24, 27, 29, 31, 32–3, 35, 100,
    116, 118, 135, 456
    LGBT persons 174, 179
    women 156, 158, 160, 161, 162, 165, 170,
        456–7
        controlling women's sexuality 167–8
        poverty: personal moral failing 166–7
Stewart, F 41, 46
stigma 3, 11, 18, 72, 116, 158, 160, 413
    abortion 418, 419
    cities 271
    discrimination 5, 31–3
    LGBT persons 172, 175, 176, 181, 183
    media 27–8
    shame and 22, 23–4, 30, 35, 36
    social assistance programs 22, 26–30, 34

types of 24–5
Streeten, P 46
structural adjustment programs 477
survival crime 33
survival sex 30
sustainable development
    2030 Agenda for 21, 36, 121, 125, 220, 227,
        321–2, 333, 338, 491, 533
    Goals (SDGs) 86, 97, 103, 108, 116, 121–3,
        124, 130, 136, 212, 219–20, 227, 228,
        267, 284, 291, 303, 335, 370, 381,
        382, 415, 447–8, 479, 480, 483, 491,
        506, 528, 536, 537–8
        (1) 21, 53, 58, 122, 136, 149, 190, 284,
            321, 405, 491, 538
        (2) 321, 492
        (3) 181, 492
        (4) 122, 492
        (5) 219, 321, 492
        (6) 492
        (8) 122, 190, 448, 461, 492
        (10) 54, 58, 122, 190, 219, 227,
            382–3, 492
        (11) 122, 190, 267, 284, 288–9, 294, 321
        (12) 122
        (13) 492
        (15) 321
        (16) 86, 122, 506, 538
Sweden 187, 282, 409, 415
Syria 522, 524, 526–7, 529, 531

Tajikistan 515
Tanzania 11, 24, 91, 245
taxation 28, 48, 142, 146, 269, 383
    economic inequality 54, 57, 60
    extreme poverty 54
    fair *see* fair taxes
    financial transaction tax 51
    housing 395, 397, 399–400
    tax havens 480–481, 483
    top earners 57
    US: surtax on compensation disparity 66
    vacant land/homes 306, 397
technology 535–49
    conflict zones 526, 534
        data collection 523, 532, 533
    development and human rights in
        information age 536–8
    financial services
        inclusion and exploitation 541–4
    justice and rights-based development
        paradigm 548–9
    new health technologies 410–414
    new opportunities, new vulnerabilities
        540–41

new sources of data on poverty 538–9
new vulnerabilities created by 544–6
sharing benefits of 546–7
Thailand 394, 397, 479
Thelle, H 372
Thornberry, P 227
Till-Tentschert, U 202
Titmuss, RM 373, 374, 375, 377, 378, 380
torture 182, 525, 531
    freedom from inhuman and degrading
        treatment and 184, 235, 254, 255,
        259–60, 418, 419, 421, 430, 514
totalitarianism 114, 115
Townsend, P 48, 50–51
trade unions 66, 118, 188, 448, 452–3, 464, 465,
    469, 472, 516
trans persons *see* sexual orientation and gender
    identity
transient and chronic poverty 13, 90–91, 195
transnational corporations *see* multi- or
    transnational corporations
transparency 42, 85, 319, 321, 408, 412, 506
    companies 395, 565
    World Bank 563–4
Transparency International 514
treaty interpretation 61–2, 64
Trump, Donald 27
truth and reconciliation commissions 531
Tunisia 345–6, 351, 509
Turkey 260–61, 263
Tuvalu 502
Tvedten, I 16–7

Uganda 101, 360
'undeserving poor' to 'rights holders' 34–5
unemployment 39, 47, 49, 52, 142, 200, 203, 377,
    380, 467, 477
    Americas: African descendants 215, 216
    cities 271
    migration 230–31, 244
    older persons 134
UNESCO 43, 53, 176, 177
UNICEF 141, 142, 359, 455
United Kingdom 10–11, 24, 80, 370, 390, 391,
    395, 454, 547
    asylum seekers 241
    definition of poverty 157
    disability 106
    economic inequality 57
    LGBT persons 182, 186, 188
    local government 286, 292
    neo-liberalism 156
    parent company in UK liable for subsidiary
        Vedanta Resources 553, 559–62, 564–5
    precision medicine 411

Roma 198, 202
Scotland 7–8
Wales 95
welfare benefits 27–8, 30, 286, 360
    benefit caps 163–70
    social-benefits scheme cases 156–7,
        162–70
United Nations 92, 97, 125, 212, 355, 371–2, 512,
    525, 527, 532, 556
    Charter 130
    corruption 515
    Declaration on the Rights of Peasants 302
    Development Program (UNDP) 21, 40, 109,
        128, 129, 200–201, 214, 467
    disability
        and development 107, 108–9
        Inclusion Strategy 120–21
    General Assembly 22, 64, 176, 313
    Guiding Principles on Business and Human
        Rights 545, 565
    Habitat 285, 288, 294
        III 282, 284
    Human Development Report 93
    Human Rights Council 43, 493, 513
        Guiding Principles on Extreme
            Poverty and Human Rights *see*
            separate entry
    Indigenous Peoples 323, 327, 332, 333, 459
    Office of High Commissioner for Human
        Rights 15, 85, 89, 173, 203, 253, 282,
        404, 493–4, 495, 526
    Special Rapporteurs 341, 450, 458, 470, 497
        extreme poverty and human rights 69,
            81, 82–3, 84, 86, 130, 158, 172,
            292, 348–9, 351, 412, 447, 474,
            489, 490, 504
        on freedom of assembly and of
            association 341, 344–6, 347, 350,
            351, 352–3
        on freedom of expression 176, 547
        right to adequate housing 6, 12, 15, 286–7,
            297, 298–302, 385, 388, 392
        on right to education 433, 438
        on right to health 183, 404
        rights of persons with disabilities 117
United States 10–11, 24, 76, 78, 216, 370, 531
    abortion *see separate entry*
    Cambodia 469
    children 142
    climate change 491, 494–5, 496, 503
    Constitution 64, 416, 425, 426, 427, 428,
        430, 431
        14th Amendment 62, 63–4, 67
    disabilities 108, 115–16, 119
    economic inequality 56, 57, 62, 63–4

        surtax on compensation disparity 66
    education 64, 433, 436
    homelessness 223, 279, 392
    housing 64, 304, 360, 390, 391, 392, 393, 394
    immunity: international organizations 553,
        556–9, 562–3, 565
    legal empowerment 360
    LGBT persons 182
    local authorities 286
    migration 238, 242–4
        asylum seekers 241, 243
        refugees 233–4, 243
        temporary protection status 236–7
    older persons 132
    precision medicine 411, 412
    race 216–7, 222–3, 345
        and gender 132, 412, 419, 422–3, 424,
            428–9, 430, 431
    sexual orientation and gender identity 172
    Supreme Court
        abortion 416, 425–8
        equal protection of the law 63–4, 67,
            426, 427, 428
        International Finance Corporation 553,
            557–9, 562
        right to vote 63
    welfare programs 27, 64, 242–3, 544
Universal Declaration of Human Rights (UDHR)
    25, 37, 38–9, 47, 69, 267, 386, 401, 432,
    453, 490, 498, 536
    assembly, freedom of (art 20.1) 340
    asylum (art 14) 251
    disability 111
    economic inequality 55, 60–61, 62, 65, 67
    equality rights (art 7) 60–61, 62, 65, 67, 79
    expression, freedom of 339
    housing (art 25) 288
    individuality realized through sociality 73
    migration 247, 251, 255
    non-discrimination 60, 62, 136–7, 471
        race 220
        social origin, property, birth or other
            status 80–81
    political rights and equality 77
    social security 136
    standard of living 136
    work 136, 446–7, 459, 471, 472
universalism, new 370–71, 374–5, 380–384
Upreti, M 421
urban turn *see* cities
Uruguay 187, 189, 215, 222, 223, 225

Van Bueren, G 143, 150
Vandenhole, W 102
Varoufakis, Y 478

Venezuela 224
Venice Commission 347
Verwimp, P 524
Vienna Convention on the Law of Treaties 62, 64
Vienna Declaration and Programme of Action
        (1993) 69, 84–5, 536
Vietnam 397, 454
violence 41, 83, 418, 458, 461, 464
    against children 34
    armed conflict *see* conflict
    child poverty 149
    cities 271
    domestic 100, 102, 103, 180, 222, 361
    gender-based 221, 225, 360, 454–5, 461,
        495, 527
    LGBT persons 171, 173, 175, 177, 178, 179,
        180, 182, 190
    racialized minorities 211, 223
    sub-Saharan Africa 96, 99, 100, 101, 102, 103
Vives, Juan Luis 38
vote, right to 10, 63, 65, 75, 77, 78, 83–4, 292,
        343, 348, 425
vulnerability 89, 94, 122, 212, 264, 286, 287, 303,
        316, 332, 349, 451
    big data 414
    children 147, 148, 152, 237, 243, 244, 245,
        451, 515
    communities and climate change 492–6,
        497–8, 499, 500, 503–4
    corruption 509, 515
    groups and health 403, 412
    income security 93
    LGBT persons 172, 174, 451
    migrants 237, 243, 244, 245, 246, 262, 451
    technology 540–541, 544–6
    see also intersectionality

Wagle, UR 197, 201
Wales 95
Walker, R 24–5
Waris, A 486
water 90, 94, 96–7, 98, 100, 121, 143, 148, 158,
        198, 207, 214, 222, 224, 274, 308, 321,
        332, 525, 532
    climate change 492, 493, 494, 495, 496,
        500–501, 503
    corruption 509, 510, 513, 515, 516
    gated communities 271
    health 402, 405, 406, 407, 408, 496
    mining/industrial operations/agribusiness
        312, 313, 315
    right to safe and clean drinking 313, 402,
        495, 515, 516
Weber, M 82
welfare state/programs *see* social protection

Wilkinson, R 58
women 49, 127, 219, 302, 405, 412, 451, 454,
        509, 523, 525
    Americas: Afro-descendant 215–16, 221–2,
        225
    capability approach 42
    carers 106–7, 123, 132, 135, 138, 139, 152,
        156, 159, 161, 165, 168–9, 450, 495
    climate change 495–6, 500–501, 503
    curfews 174
    definition of poverty 157–9
    disabilities 109, 132, 140
        carers 106–7, 123
    economic inequality 54, 58
        HIV, correct knowledge about 57
    formal equality 159–60, 163–5
    indigenous 215
    land rights 321
    legal empowerment 359, 360, 361–2, 363, 366
    life expectancy 126, 132, 214
    migrants 237, 243, 244, 245
    minimum wage 462
    older age 132, 134, 135, 138, 139, 140
    relational approach 70
    Romani 200, 201, 202
    sex or gender discrimination *see separate entry*
    social protection 26–7, 29, 160–61
        social-benefits scheme cases in UK
            156–7, 162–70
    stigma 32, 72, 418, 419
    sub-Saharan Africa 100, 102, 103
    substantive equality 160–161, 162, 165–70
    see also sexual orientation and gender
        identity
work/workers *see* employment
World Bank 40, 51, 57–8, 92, 125, 219, 282, 288,
        477, 556
    Africa report (2016) 99–100, 101
    Afro descendants in Latin America 214, 215
    Cambodia 467, 468
    children 141
    climate change 492
    education 434
    financial inclusion 541
    fragile and conflict-affected situations 522,
        527, 528
    Handbook on Poverty and Inequality 94
        anti-poverty activities 93
    Inspection Panel 563–4
    international poverty line (IPL) 90, 129–30
    non-monetary dimensions of poverty 99–100
    older persons 128
    societal poverty line (SPL) 90
    sub-Saharan Africa 91, 92, 99–100, 101
    taxation 478

Voices of the Poor 15, 69, 83, 84, 100, 200
    well-being 99, 101
World Bank Group 141, 527, 527–8, 532, 557
    International Finance Corporation (IFC) 553,
       557–9, 562–3
    World Bank *see separate entry*
World Health Organization (WHO) 65, 401–2,
    405, 408, 411, 414
World Summit for Social Development (1995) 2

Yamin, AE 196
Yemen 530

Young, KG 95
youth 58, 173, 180, 188, 189, 199, 209, 265,
    315, 316
    see also children

Zambia 109, 289–90
    UK court: parent company liable for action
      of subsidiary
        Vedanta Resources 553, 559–62, 564–5
Zimbabwe 109
Zucman, G 480

Printed and bound by CPI Group (UK) Ltd, Croydon, CR0 4YY

05/01/2023

03177609-0001